McGraw-Hill Higher Education

*A Division of The **McGraw-Hill** Companies*

ADVANCED ACCOUNTING

Material from the Uniform CPA Examination Questions and Unofficial Answers, Copyright © 11/90, 11/91, 5/92, 11/92, 11/93, 5/95 by the American Institute of Certified Public Accountants, Inc., is reprinted (or adapted) with permission.

1 2 3 4 5 6 7 8 9 0 VNH/VNH 0 9 8 7 6 5 4 3 2 1

ISBN 0072524081

Senior vice president/Editorial director: *Robin J. Zwettler*
Publisher: *K. Brent Gordon*
Executive editor: *Stewart Mattson*
Developmental editor: *Erin Cibula*
Marketing manager: *Richard Kolasa*
Project manager: *Jill Howell*
Production supervisor: *Rose Hepburn*
Senior designer: *Jennifer McQueen*
Supplement coordinator: *Matthew Perry*
Media technology producer: *Ed Przyzcki*
Cover designer: *JoAnne Schopler*
Cover image: *Copyright © 2000 PhotoDisc, Inc. All Rights Reserved*
Compositor: *GAC Indianapolis*
Typeface: *10/12 Times Roman*
Printer: *Von Hoffmann Press, Inc.*

Library of Congress Control Number: 2001096180

www.mhhe.com

UPDATED SIXTH EDITION

Advanced Accounting

JOE B. HOYLE

Associate Professor of Accounting
Robins School of Business
University of Richmond

THOMAS F. SCHAEFER

KPMG Professor of Accounting
Mendoza College of Business
University of Notre Dame

TIMOTHY S. DOUPNIK

Professor of Accounting
The Darla Moore School of Business
University of South Carolina

 McGraw-Hill Irwin

Boston   Burr Ridge, IL   Dubuque, IA   Madison, WI   New York   San Francisco   St. Louis
Bangkok   Bogotá   Caracas   Kuala Lumpur   Lisbon   London   Madrid   Mexico City
Milan   Montreal   New Delhi   Santiago   Seoul   Singapore   Sydney   Taipei   Toronto

To our families

The real purpose
of books is to trap
the mind into
doing its own
thinking.

Christopher Morley

Joe B. Hoyle is Associate Professor of Accounting at the Robins School of Business at the University of Richmond where he has been named a Distinguished Educator five times. He has been named Professor of the Year on two occasions. He serves as Chair of the Accounting Department and teaches Intermediate Accounting II and Advanced Accounting. He is also author of *Fast Track CPA Examination Review* and coauthor of *The Lakeside Company Case Studies in Auditing*. He is president of HoyleCPA Success which sells review materials worldwide.

Thomas F. Schaefer is the KPMG Professor of Accounting at the University of Notre Dame. Professor Schaefer has a Ph.D. in accounting from the University of Illinois and a CPA certificate. He has written a number of articles in scholarly journals such as *The Accounting Review, Journal of Accounting Research, Journal of Accounting & Economics, Accounting Horizons,* and others. His primary teaching and research interests are in financial accounting and reporting. Tom is active in the American Accounting Association and the Federation of Schools of Accounting.

Timothy S. Doupnik is Professor of Accounting at the University of South Carolina, where his primary teaching and research interest is in international accounting. He has published extensively in this area in journals such as *The International Journal of Accounting* and the *Journal of International Business Studies*. He has also written two research monographs on foreign currency translation published by the FASB. Tim is active in the American Accounting Association and recently completed a term as chair of the International Accounting Section.

On July 20, 2001, the Financial Accounting Standards Board issued two new standards: *No. 141*, "Business Combinations," and *No. 142*, "Goodwill and Other Intangible Assets." We have taken action and have revised the sixth edition of *Advanced Accounting* by Hoyle, Schaefer, and Doupnik to reflect these new standards. You and your students have access to the most up-to-date FASB information right now, right here in *Advanced Accounting,* **Updated** Sixth Edition.

Updated supplements are provided on the text Web site. Visit **www.mhhe.com/hoyle6e** for the most up-to-date learning tools.

In this fast-paced information age, how do you entice, engage, and challenge students without sacrificing quality and sophistication? This was our challenge when we wrote the Sixth Edition of *Advanced Accounting*. The Sixth Edition features many changes and advancements in content. Despite these changes, now more than ever the book fulfills Joe's vow of 1980 to create an accounting text that stimulates, challenges, and excites.

This edition incorporates many accounting standards that resulted from many FASB and GASB pronouncements. Fluid writing style, real-world examples, introduction to controversial topics, thorough discussion questions and techniques that were successfully developed in prior editions remain intact. Innovation is important, but in our innovation we have not sacrificed the elements that made *Advanced Accounting* the authority in its field.

UPDATING THIS EDITION

In general, we continue to provide relevant observations from business periodicals and numerous updated annual report examples to reflect current trends in financial reporting. We have incorporated all recent FASB and GASB Exposure Drafts and Standards. Listed below are specific changes that appear in the text:

In **Chapter 2,** we continue to present descriptions of three recent notable business combinations. In this edition, we focus on the combinations of Yahoo! and Broadcast.com, Pfizer's hostile takeover of Warner–Lambert, and the Exxon/Mobil merger. The underlying motivations and business strategies for the combination activity provide interesting background information for the subsequent development of accounting and financial reporting material.

Chapter 2 also addresses the major changes currently being considered in financial reporting for business combinations. These changes are documented in the FASB September 7, 1999, Exposure Draft, *Business Combinations and Intangible Assets*. One of the most important of these changes is the FASB recommendation that all business combinations should be accounted for using the purchase method, thus effectively eliminating the pooling of interests method. In this chapter, we first provide coverage of expansion through corporate takeovers and an overview of the consolidation process. Then we present the purchase method of accounting for business combinations with specific references to the Exposure Draft's recommended changes. Finally, coverage of pooling of interests is provided in a separate section. Although the FASB currently recommends the elimination of the pooling of interests method of accounting for business combinations, the recommendation is for prospective application only. Given the popularity of poolings in the last century, the financial statement effects of this method of accounting will likely be encountered for decades to come. Therefore, familiarity with the effects of poolings in consolidations subsequent to acquisition will continue to be an important part of understanding financial reporting for business combinations.

Finally, **Chapter 2** provides a new section on the topic of accounting for acquired in-process research and development costs and new categories of intangible assets recognized in purchase price allocations of newly acquired businesses.

Chapter 3 has been expanded to include coverage of the related amortizations for the new categories of purchased intangible assets, as suggested in FASB Exposure Draft, *Business Combinations and Intangible Assets*. **Chapter 3** also provides coverage of the recommended disclosures for goodwill as a separate line item in the balance sheet and a separate goodwill amortization line item in the income statement. The chapter also provides expanded coverage of SFAS No. 121, *Impairment of Long-Lived Assets Including Goodwill.* **Chapter 3** concludes with a revised computer project relating alternative investment procedures, amortization alternatives, and key financial performance ratios.

Chapter 4 continues its thorough coverage of accounting for the noncontrolling interest in a business combination. **Chapter 4** concludes with a revised computer project that requires a sensitivity analysis with respect to alternative concepts of financial reporting for the noncontrolling interest.

Chapter 5 includes two new exhibits. First, the relationship between the gross profit rate and markup on cost is explicitly addressed in Exhibit 5–1. Second, new worksheet examples are provided for intercompany inventory profits when the parent employs the equity method.

A modest departure from the previous editions in the adjusting and eliminating entries for intercompany profit in beginning inventories is also introduced in **Chapter 5** of the Sixth Edition. For downstream transfers where the parent employs the equity method, the Equity in Subsidiary Earnings account is now decreased for intercompany profits in beginning inventory, instead of increasing the Investment in Subsidiary account. This change provides better intuition regarding the worksheet adjustments relative to the accounting for the investment account when the equity method is employed by the parent. Finally, the coverage of intercompany depreciable asset transfers in **Chapter 5** has been increased by the inclusion of consolidation entries in the year of the transfer and subsequent periods.

Chapter 6 provides a new example of a consolidated Statement of Cash Flows. The example includes specific coverage of the SFAS No. 95, *Statement of Cash Flows*, requirement that changes in operating accounts be shown net of acquisition effects. The example also includes coverage of accounting for acquired in-process research and development costs in the cash flow statement. Chapter 6 also provides a new example of reporting consolidated earnings per share based on the separate recognition (net of tax) of goodwill amortization recommended by the 1999 FASB Exposure Draft.

Chapter 7 has been updated for changes in U.S. tax laws relating to loss carryforwards and carrybacks.

Chapter 8 from the previous edition, "Branch and Consignment Accounting," has been eliminated and Chapter 12 from the previous edition dealing with segment reporting has been moved to **Chapter 8** in the current edition. The new Chapter 8, "Segment and Interim Reporting," has been expanded to include a major section on interim reporting. In addition, Chapter 8 has been updated to include examples from annual reports of how companies are complying with SFAS No. 131, *Disclosures about Segments of an Enterprise and Related Information.* The chapter on segment and interim reporting more logically follows the consolidation chapters rather than the chapters related to international activities.

Chapter 9 has been updated to include the requirements in SFAS No. 133, *Accounting for Derivative Instruments and Hedging Activities,* related to foreign currency hedging. The Amerco Company examples used in the previous edition have been revised to reflect *SFAS 133* guidelines and an example of hedging a forecasted transaction has been added. Several new problems have been added to cover the concepts in *SFAS 133.*

In **Chapter 10,** the discussion surrounding translation methods has been streamlined, concentrating exclusively on the current rate and temporal methods. In discussing U.S. translation rules, much of the historical information related to *SFAS No. 8* has been eliminated. In addition, an electronic spreadsheet problem involving the consolidation of a foreign subsidiary has been added.

The section in **Chapter 11** on the International Accounting Standards Committee has been updated. It includes new sections on the IOSCO agreement, the restructuring of IASC, and the use of international accounting standards.

Coverage of the role and importance of the Securities and Exchange Commission (SEC) has been moved to **Chapter 12** from the very end of the book in the previous edition. More prominent placement of this material indicates the priority placed by the authors on helping students to understand the position of authority held by the SEC within the world of accounting. Students are introduced to the terminology as well as the functioning of the SEC in connection with registration statements and periodic reporting.

In **Chapter 13,** the authors cover one of the fastest growing areas within the accounting profession—working with bankrupt or financially troubled organizations. A large number of real-life examples are used to walk students through the steps and processes found in both a Chapter 7 and a Chapter 11 filing.

Partnership accounting is examined in **Chapters 14 and 15** from formation to liquidation. Alternative formats such as subchapter S corporations, limited liability partnerships, and limited liability companies are also described and discussed.

Some of the most important changes in this newest edition are covered in **Chapters 16 and 17** on accounting for state and local governments. The monumental Statement No. 34 of the Governmental Accounting Standards Board, "Basic Financial Statements—and Management's Discussion and Analysis—for State and Local Governments," provides the basis for an entirely new approach to reporting these government entities. These chapters describe the multitude of changes required by this new pronouncement. Chapter 17 also presents GASB Statement No. 35, "Basic Financial Statements—and Management's Discussion and Analysis—for Public Colleges and Universities," which provides a comprehensive structure for reporting these particular public institutions.

Chapter 18 covers the reporting that is now appropriate for private not-for-profit organizations, another rapidly growing segment of the accounting profession. Coverage includes Statement No. 136 of the FASB, "Transfers of Assets to a Not-for-Profit Organization or Charitable Trust That Raises or Holds Contributions for Others." The authors demonstrate the financial statements that are utilized by organizations such as Christian Children's Fund and Villanova University.

Chapter 19 concludes this book with a discussion of the accounting used by estates and trusts and the role typically played by accountants in estate planning.

EDUCATIONAL APPROACH

Many of the pedagogical elements of the five previous editions of *Advanced Accounting* have been retained, expanded, and refined. Each of these features is intended to get students involved in their own education and to encourage them to ask why a particular approach to reporting is considered appropriate rather than just how the numbers are calculated.

Introduction of Controversies   At many points throughout the book, the controversial side of accounting is introduced. The development of financial reporting is shown as a result of a history of considered debate that continues today and into the future. Dissents to official pronouncements are described as are comment letters to the FASB. Published articles are discussed, many of which criticize GAAP.

Writing Style   The writing style of the five previous editions was highly praised. We have made every effort to ensure that the writing style remains engaging, lively, and consistent.

Real-world Examples   As in earlier editions, we have incorporated information from actual situations so students better relate what they learn to what they will be encountering in the business world. Quotations and articles from *Forbes, The Wall Street Journal, Time,* and *Business Week* are incorporated throughout the text. Data have been pulled from business and government financial statements as well as official pronouncements.

Discussion Questions   Students and professors alike have praised the inclusion of discussion questions found in each chapter. Similar to mini-cases, these questions help explain the issues at hand in practical terms. Many times these cases are designed to demonstrate to students why a problem is a problem and worth considering. Often accounting rules are relatively easy to read and learn mechanically but are extremely difficult to apply in the business world. The Discussion Question feature facilitates student understanding of the underlying accounting principles at work in particular business events.

Library Assignments   Student research assignments and related suggested readings are listed at the end of each chapter. These assignments encourage students to take a proactive role in their education.

End-of-chapter Materials   As in previous editions, the homework material remains a strength of the text. Most of the material has been class tested by us in our own classes. Many of the questions from the fifth edition have been revised, rewritten, and updated to offer greater variety. Internet Assignments have been added in the Sixth Edition.

Web Site   The Fifth Edition Web site proved to be an extremely valuable resource for students and faculty. The site enabled the authors to respond quickly to FASB changes and provide a timely medium for faculty and students to get text updates. In addition, the text Web site also provides links to CPA and other accounting-related Web sites. Moreover, the Sixth Edition Web site will have online quizzes and other resources for students.

INSTRUCTOR SUPPLEMENTS

Instructor's Resource and Solutions Manual (ISBN: 0072321172): Includes the solutions to all discussion questions, end-of-chapter questions, and problems. In addition, chapter outlines are provided to assist instructors in preparing for class.

Solutions Transparencies (ISBN: 0072321199): To help clarify and reinforce the processes involved in solving the more complex problems in the text, the answers to selected problems are replicated on acetates that can be used in classroom presentations.

Test Bank (ISBN: 0072321210): The test bank contains a variety of questions ranging from multiple-choice questions to short answer questions to detailed problems.

Computerized Testing Software (ISBN: 0072437626): This is a computerized version of the printed test bank for more efficient use, available in a Windows version.

Check Figures (ISBN: 0072363118): A list of Check figures gives key amounts for the problems to assist students in working through homework problems. Check figures are available in bulk, free to adopters.

Instructor Spreadsheet Applications Template Software (SPATS) (ISBN: 0072360607): Spreadsheet Applications Template Software allows students to develop important spreadsheet skills by using Excel templates to solve selected assignments.

Web site: http://www.mhhe.com/business/accounting/hoyle6e

FOR THE STUDENT

Study Guide/Working Papers (ISBN: 0072321180): This combination study guide and working papers reinforces the key concepts of the book by providing students with chapter outlines, multiple-choice questions, and problems for each chapter in the text. In addition, this paperback contains all the forms necessary for completing the end-of-chapter material.

Spreadsheet Application Template Software (SPATS): This software package, developed by Doris deLespinasse is available on the text Web site. The software includes innovatively designed templates that may be used with Excel '97 to solve many complicated problems found in the book. These problems are identified by a logo in the margin such as the one shown on the previous page.

Web Site: http://www.mhhe.com/business/accounting/hoyle6e

ACKNOWLEDGMENTS

We could not produce a textbook of the quality and scope of *Advanced Accounting* without the help of a great number of people. We extend a special thank you to: Richard Rand at Tennessee Technological University for adding new material to the Study Guide, Test Bank, and PowerPoint®; Doris deLespinasse for creating Spreadsheet Applications Template Software for students to solve problems using Excel for selected end-of-chapter material; and James Emig at Villanova University for checking the text and supplements for accuracy.

We acknowledge that FASB Exposure Draft, *Business Combinations and Intangible Assets,* is copyrighted by the Financial Accounting Standards Board, 401 Merritt 7, P.O. Box 5116, Norwalk, Connecticut 06856-5116, U.S.A. Portions are reprinted with permission. Complete copies of this document are available from the FASB. GASB Statement No. 33, Accounting and Financial Reporting for Nonexchange Transactions, is copyrighted by the Governmental Accounting Standards Board, 401 Merritt 7, P.O. Box 5116, Norwalk, Connecticut 06856-5116, U.S.A. Portions are reprinted with permission. Complete copies of this document are available from the GASB.

We also want to thank the many people who participated in phone surveys, completed questionnaires, and reviewed the manuscript. Our sincerest thanks to them all:

Bruce C. Branson
North Carolina State University

Gary L. Bridges
University of Southern Colorado

Bruce P. Budge
University of Montana

Peter Budwitz
Central Connecticut State University

Ron Burrows
University of Dayton

Eric Carlsen
Kean University

Lynn H. Clements
Florida Southern College

Paul Copley
University of Georgia

Wagih Dafashy
College of William and Mary

John W. Dawson
Christopher Newport University

Charles Fazzi
Robert Morris College

Patrick Fort
University of Alaska–Anchorage

Donald Hicks
Christopher Newport University

David Jenkins
California State University–Stanislaus

Roger Luli
Baldwin-Wallace College

Robert J. Matthews
New Jersey City University

Mary D. Maury
St. John's University

Mark McCarthy
East Carolina University

Perry Glen Moore
David Lipscomb University

Gwen R. Pate
University of Southern Mississippi

Franklin J. Plewa
Idaho State University

Grace Pownall
Emory University

Richard S. Rand, Jr.
Tennessee Technological University

Reg Rezac
Texas Woman's University

Linda Schain
Hofstra University

Howard Turetsky
St. Mary's College of California

Abba Spero
Cleveland State University

David R. Vruwink
Kansas State University

Margaret M. Tanner
University of Northern Iowa

Hannah Wong
Rutgers University

Mark Trombley
University of Arizona

Roger A. Woods
Northwest Missouri State University

We also pass along a word of thanks to all the people at McGraw-Hill/Irwin who participated in the creation of the sixth and updated sixth editions. In particular, Kelly Delso and Jill Howell, Project Managers; Rose Hepburn, Production Supervisor; Jennifer McQueen, Designer; Jennifer Jackson and Erin Cibula, Developmental Editors; Stewart Mattson, Executive Editor; Ed Przyzycki, Media Technology Producer; Rich Kolasa, Marketing Manager; and Jeff Shelstad and Brent Gordon, Publishers, all contributed significantly to the project and we appreciate their efforts.

BRIEF CONTENTS

CONTENTS

Consolidated Financial Statements—Intercompany Asset Transactions, 217

Intercompany Debt, Consolidated Statement of Cash Flows, and Other Issues, 269

Translation of Foreign Currency Financial Statements, 469

Worldwide Accounting Diversity and International Standards, 523

CHAPTER 17

Accounting for State and Local Governments (Part Two), 767

Accounting and Reporting for Private Not-for-profit Organizations, 817

Accounting for Estates and Trusts, 857

1

The Equity Method of Accounting for Investments

QUESTIONS TO CONSIDER

- Why do corporations invest in ownership shares of other corporations?

- One corporation buys equity shares of another company. What methods are available to account for this investment and the income it generates? When is each method appropriate?

- What factors affect the way income is recognized (cash basis, accrual basis, or market value changes) from investments in other corporations? What factors affect how the investment asset account is reported (at cost, at equity, or at market value)?

- When significant influence over an investee company is achieved, should the owner recognize revenue at the time dividends are received or when income is earned by the investee?

- In recognizing income from investments on the accrual basis, how is the cost of the investment matched against the revenue from the investment?

- At what point should profits be recognized on inventory that is transferred between related parties?

The first seven chapters of this text present the accounting and reporting for investment activities of businesses. The focus is on investments where one firm possesses either significant influence or control over another through ownership of voting shares. When one firm owns enough voting shares to be able to affect the decisions of another, accounting for the investment becomes challenging and often complex. The source of such complexities typically stems from the fact that transactions among the firms affiliated through ownership cannot be considered independent, arm's-length transactions. As in all matters relating to financial reporting, we look to transactions with *outside parties* to provide a basis for accounting valuation. When firms are affiliated through a common set of owners, objectivity in accounting calls for measurements that recognize the relationships among the firms.

REPORTING INVESTMENTS IN CORPORATE EQUITY SECURITIES

In a recent annual report, the Walt Disney Company described the creation of the Go Network™ (www.go.com) through its 43 percent strategic investment in Infoseek Corporation. In its discussion, Disney stated "the Go Network seeks to be one of the leading portals on the Internet, serving as an interactive hub through which people can gain access to the Internet at large, as well as every form of information and entertainment that Disney offers." The investment in Infoseek will be accounted for under the equity method.

Such information is hardly unusual in the business world; corporate as well as individual investors frequently acquire ownership shares of both domestic and foreign businesses. These investments can range from the purchase of a few shares to the acquisition of 100 percent control. Although purchases of corporate equity securities (such as the one made by Disney) are not uncommon, they pose a considerable number of problems for the accountant because a close relationship has been established without the investor gaining actual control. These issues are currently addressed by the **equity method.** This chapter deals with the procedures utilized in accounting for stock investments that fall under the application of this method.

At present, accounting standards recognize three different approaches to the financial reporting of investments in corporate equity securities:

The fair-value method.

The equity method.

The consolidation of financial statements.

These three approaches are not interchangeable; a specific method is required by any given situation. The reporting of a particular investment depends on the degree of influence that the investor (stockholder) has over the investee, a factor best indicated by the relative size of ownership.

Fair-Value Method   In many instances, an investor possesses only a small percentage of an investee company's outstanding stock, perhaps only a few shares. Because of the limited level of ownership, the investor cannot expect to have a significant impact on the investee's operations or decision making. These shares are bought in anticipation of cash dividends or in appreciation of stock market values. Such investments are recorded at cost and periodically adjusted to fair value according to the Financial Accounting Standards Board (FASB) in its *Statement of Financial Accounting Standards No. 115 (SFAS 115),* "Accounting for Certain Investments in Debt and Equity Securities," May 1993.

Since a full coverage of *SFAS 115* is presented in intermediate accounting textbooks, only the following basic principles are noted here.

- Initial investments in equity securities are recorded at cost and subsequently adjusted to fair value if fair value is readily determinable, otherwise the investment remains at cost.
- Equity securities held for the purpose of selling them in the short term are classified as *trading securities* and reported at fair value, with unrealized gains and losses included in earnings.
- Equity securities not classified as trading securities are classified as *available-for-sale securities* and reported at fair value, with unrealized gains and losses excluded from earnings and reported in a separate component of shareholders' equity as part of *other comprehensive income.*
- Dividends received are recognized as income for both trading and available-for-sale securities.

These procedures are required for equity security investments when neither significant influence nor control is present. The recognition of unrealized gains and losses for *SFAS 115* investments represents a departure from past procedures that prevented the anticipation of income. As will be shown, the procedures for significant influence investments in equity securities, while somewhat complex, adhere more closely to traditional accrual accounting.

Consolidation of Financial Statements   Although many investments involve only a small percentage of stock, an investor can acquire enough shares to gain actual control over an investee's operation. In financial accounting, such control is recognized whenever a stockholder accumulates more than 50 percent of an organization's outstanding voting stock. At that point, rather than simply influencing the decisions of the investee, the investor clearly can direct the entire decision-making process. A review of the financial statements of America's largest organizations indicates that legal control of one or more subsidiary companies is an almost universal practice. PepsiCo, Inc., as just one example, holds a majority interest in the voting stock of literally hundreds of corporations.

A level of ownership large enough to enable an investor to control an investee presents an economic situation not adequately addressed by *SFAS 115*. Normally, when a majority of voting stock is held, the investor-investee relationship has become so closely connected that the two corporations are viewed as a single entity for reporting purposes. Hence, an entirely different set of accounting procedures is applicable. According to *Accounting Research Bulletin No. 51 (ARB No. 51),* "Consolidated Financial Statements," August 1959, control generally requires the consolidation of the accounting information produced by the individual companies. Thus, a single set of financial statements is created for external reporting purposes with all assets, liabilities, revenues, and expenses being brought together.[1] The various procedures applied within this consolidation process are examined in subsequent chapters of the textbook.

Equity Method   Finally, another investment relationship is appropriately accounted for using the equity method. Disney's ownership of 43 percent of the voting stock of Infoseek is less than enough to control the voting stock. Yet, despite the lack of voting control, Disney maintains a large interest in this investee company. Through its ownership, Disney can undoubtedly affect the decisions and operations of Infoseek.

Especially important is the investor's ability to influence the timing of dividend distributions. Because of this influence, the receipt of a dividend from an investee may not qualify as an objective basis for recording income to the investor firm. Because managerial compensation contracts often are based on net income, incentives exist for managers to use whatever discretion they have available in reporting net income. *Thus, to provide an objective basis for reporting investment income, the equity method requires that income be recognized by the investor as it is earned by the investee, not when dividends are received.*

In today's business world, many corporations such as Disney hold significant ownership interests in other companies without having actual control. Sears, Roebuck & Company alone holds between 20 and 50 percent ownership in dozens of separate corporations. Many other large investments are created through joint ventures whereby two or more companies form a new enterprise to carry out a specified operating purpose. For example, Microsoft and NBC formed a joint venture to operate MSNBC, a cable channel and online site to go with NBC's broadcast network. Each partner owns 50 percent of the joint venture.

For each of these investments, the investors do not possess absolute control because they hold less than a majority of the voting stock. Thus, the preparation of consolidated financial statements is inappropriate. However, the large percentage of ownership indicates that each investor possesses some ability to affect the decision-making process of the investee. To reflect this relationship, such investments are accounted for by the equity method as officially established by *Opinion 18,* "The Equity Method of Accounting for Investments in Common Stock," issued by the Accounting Principles Board (APB) in March of 1971, and as amended by *SFAS 142,* "Goodwill and Other Intangible Assets."

APPLYING THE EQUITY METHOD

An understanding of the equity method is best gained by initially examining the APB's treatment of two questions:

1.   What parameters identify the area of ownership where the equity method is applicable?
2.   How should the investor report this investment and the income generated by it to reflect the relationship between the two companies?

---

[1]As is discussed in the next chapter, owning a majority of the voting shares of an investee does not always lead to consolidated financial statements. The FASB is also considering whether control can be established without majority ownership.

Criteria for Utilizing the Equity Method

In sanctioning application of the equity method, the APB reasoned that an investor begins to gain the ability to influence the decision-making process of an investee as the level of ownership rises. According to *APB Opinion 18* (par. 17), achieving this "ability to exercise significant influence over operating and financial policies of an investee even though the investor holds 50 percent or less of the voting stock" is the sole criterion for requiring application of the equity method.

Clearly a term such as *the ability to exercise significant influence* is nebulous and subject to a variety of judgments and interpretations in practice. At what point does the acquisition of one additional share of stock give an owner the ability to exercise significant influence? This decision becomes even more difficult in that only the *ability* to exercise significant influence need be present: The pronouncement does not specify that any actual influence must have ever been applied.

APB Opinion 18 provides guidance to the accountant by listing several conditions that indicate the presence of this degree of influence:

- Investor representation on the board of directors of the investee.
- Investor participation in the policy-making process of the investee.
- Material intercompany transactions.
- Interchange of managerial personnel.
- Technological dependency.
- Extent of ownership by the investor in relation to the size and concentration of other ownership interests in the investee.

No single one of these guides should be used exclusively in assessing the applicability of the equity method. Instead, all are evaluated together to determine the presence or absence of the sole criterion: the ability to exercise significant influence over the investee.

These guidelines alone do not eliminate the leeway available to each investor when deciding whether use of the equity method is appropriate. To provide a degree of consistency in applying this standard, the APB established a general ownership test. *If an investor holds between 20 and 50 percent of the voting stock of the investee, significant influence is normally assumed and the equity method applied.*

> The Board recognizes that determining the ability of an investor to exercise such influence is not always clear and applying judgment is necessary to assess the status of each investment. In order to achieve a reasonable degree of uniformity in application, the Board concludes that an investment (direct or indirect) of 20 percent or more of the voting stock of an investee should lead to a presumption that in the absence of evidence to the contrary an investor has the ability to exercise significant influence over an investee. Conversely, an investment of less than 20 percent of the voting stock of an investee should lead to a presumption that an investor does not have the ability to exercise significant influence unless such ability can be demonstrated.[2]

At first, the 20 percent rule may appear to be an arbitrarily chosen boundary established merely to provide accountants with a consistent method of reporting all investments. However, the essential criterion is still the ability to significantly influence the investee, rather than 20 percent ownership.[3] If the absence of this ability is proven, the equity method should not be applied regardless of the percentage of shares held.

---

[2] *APB Opinion 18*, para. 17.

[3] Not everyone agrees with the wisdom of this rule. Two members of the APB, George R. Catlett and Charles T. Homgren, voted for *Opinion 18* but argued in an attached statement that "they do not agree with the arbitrary criterion of 20 percent combined with a variable test of 'significant influence' in paragraph 17, because such an approach is not convincing in concept and will be very difficult to apply in practice."

Conversely, whenever this ability can be demonstrated, the equity method is appropriate without concern for the degree of ownership.

As an example, in 1999 International Paper Company reported that it accounts for its investment in Scitex Corporation using the equity method despite holding only a 13 percent interest. In its annual report, International Paper cited its ability to exercise significant influence "because the Company is party to a shareowners' agreement with two other entities which together with the Company own just over 39% of Scitex."

Further guidance on the precise applicability of the equity method was provided in May 1981 when the FASB issued its *Interpretation 35,* "Criteria for Applying the Equity Method of Accounting for Investments in Common Stock." This pronouncement dealt specifically with using the equity method for investments in which the owner holds more than 20 percent of the outstanding shares. It is important because companies had tended to apply the equity method to all investments in the 20 to 50 percent range with little regard for the degree of influence actually present.

According to *Interpretation 35* (par. 3), above the 20 percent level of ownership, "the presumption that the investor has the ability to exercise significant influence over the investee's operating and financial policies stands until overcome by predominant evidence to the contrary." However, the pronouncement then went on to offer clarification by listing examples of occurrences that would provide evidence to nullify this presumption. *Interpretation 35* specifically states that the equity method is not appropriate for investments that demonstrate any of the following characteristics regardless of the investor's degree of ownership:

■ An agreement exists between investor and investee whereby the investor surrenders significant rights as a shareholder.

■ A concentration of ownership operates the investee without regard for the views of the investor.

■ The investor attempts but fails to obtain representation on the investee's board of directors.

To summarize, the following table indicates the method of accounting that is applicable to various stock investments:

Criterion	Normal Ownership Level	Applicable Accounting Method
Lack of ability to significantly influence	Less than 20%	Fair-value *(SFAS 115)* or cost
Presence of ability to significantly influence	20%–50%	Equity method *(APB Opinion 18* and *SFAS 142)*
Control	Over 50%	Consolidated financial statements* *(ARB No. 51,* and *SFAS 141* and *142)*

*As discussed in subsequent chapters, voting control over another company does not always lead to the consolidation of financial statements, for example, when such control may be only temporary.

Accounting for an Investment—The Equity Method

Now that the criteria leading to the application of the equity method have been identified, a review of its reporting procedures is appropriate. Knowledge of this accounting process is especially important to users of the investor's financial statements because the equity method affects both the timing of income recognition as well as the carrying value of the investment account.

In applying the equity method, the accounting objective is to report the investor's investment and investment income reflecting the close relationship between the companies. After recording the cost of the acquisition, two equity method entries periodically record the investment's impact:

■ The investor's investment account is *increased as the investee earns and reports income.* Also, investment income is recognized by the investor using the accrual method—that is, in the same time period as it is earned by the investee. If an investee reports income of $100,000, a 30 percent owner should immediately increase its own income by $30,000. This earnings accrual reflects the essence of the equity method by emphasizing the connection between the two companies; as the owners' equity of the investee increases through the earnings process, so the investment account also increases. Although the acquisition is initially recorded by the investor at cost, upward adjustments in the asset balance are recorded as soon as the investee makes a profit. A reduction is necessary if a loss is reported.

■ The investor's investment account is *decreased whenever a dividend is collected.* Since distribution of cash dividends reduces the book value of the investee company, the investor mirrors this change by recording the receipt as a decrease in the carrying value of the investment rather than as revenue. Once again, a parallel is established between the investment account and the underlying activities of the investee: the reduction in owners' equity of the investee creates a decrease in the investment. Furthermore, since income is recognized immediately by the investor when it is earned by the investee, double counting would occur if subsequent dividend collections also were recorded by the investor as revenue. Importantly, because of the investor's significant influence over the investee, the collection of a cash dividend is not an appropriate point for income recognition. Because the investor can influence the timing of investee dividend distributions, the receipt of a dividend is not an objective measure of the income generated from the investment.

Application of Equity Method

Investee Event	Investor Accounting
Income is earned.	Proportionate share of income is recognized.
Dividends are distributed.	Dividends received are recorded as a reduction in investment.

Application of the equity method causes the investment account on the investor's balance sheet to fluctuate in direct relation to changes occurring in the equity of the investee company. As an illustration, assume that an investor acquires a 40 percent interest in a business enterprise. If the investor has the ability to significantly influence the investee, the equity method must be utilized. If the investee subsequently reports net income of $50,000, the investor increases the investment account (and its own net income) by $20,000 in recognition of a 40 percent share of these earnings. Conversely, a $20,000 dividend collected from the investee necessitates a reduction of $8,000 in this same asset account (40 percent of the total payout).

In contrast, the fair-value method reports investments at market value if readily determinable. Also, income is only recognized on receipt of dividends. Consequently, financial reports can vary depending on whether the equity method or fair-value method is appropriate for reporting purposes.

To illustrate, assume that Big Company owns a 20 percent interest in Little Company purchased on January 1, 2001, for $200,000. Little then reports net income of $200,000, $300,000, and $400,000 in the next three years while paying dividends of $50,000, $100,000, and $200,000. The fair values of Little, as determined by market prices, were $235,000, $255,000, and $320,000 at the end of 2001, 2002, and 2003, respectively.

Exhibit 1–1 compares the accounting for Big's investment in Little across the two methods. The fair-value method carries the investment at its market values, presumed

Exhibit 1–1   Comparison of Equity Method and Fair-Value Method

Year	Income of Little Company	Dividends Paid by Little Company	Accounting by Big Company When Influence Is Not Significant (available-for-sale security)			Accounting by Big Company When Influence Is Significant (equity method)	
			Dividend Income	Carrying Value of Investment	Fair-Value Adjustment to Stockholders' Equity	Equity in Investee Income	Carrying Value of Investment
2002	$200,000	$ 50,000	$ 10,000	$235,000	$35,000	$ 40,000*	$230,000†
2003	300,000	100,000	20,000	255,000	55,000	60,000*	270,000†
2004	400,000	200,000	40,000	320,000	120,000	80,000*	310,000†
Total income recognized			$ 70,000			$180,000	

*Equity in investee income is 20 percent of the current year income reported by Little Company.

†The carrying value of an investment under the equity method is the original cost plus income recognized less dividends received. For 2002, as an example, the $230,000 reported balance is the $200,000 cost plus $40,000 equity income less $10,000 in dividends received.

to be readily available in this example. Because the investment is classified as an *available-for-sale security,* the excess of market value over cost is reported as a separate component of stockholders' equity.[4] Income is recognized as dividends are received.

In contrast, under the equity method, Big recognizes income as it is earned by Little. As shown in Exhibit 1–1, Big recognizes $180,000 in income over the three years and the carrying value of the investment is adjusted upward to $310,000. Dividends received are not considered an appropriate measure of income because of the assumed significant influence when the equity method is applied. Big's ability to influence the decisions of Little applies to the timing of dividend distributions. Therefore, dividends received do not represent an objective measure of Big's income from its investment in Little. However, as Little earns income, under the equity method Big recognizes its share (20%) of the income and increases the investment account. The equity method reflects the accrual model: Income is recognized as it is earned, not when cash (dividend) is received.

Exhibit 1–1 shows that the carrying value of the investment fluctuates each year under the equity method. This recording parallels the changes occurring in the net asset figures reported by the investee. If the owner's equity of the investee rises through income, an increase is made in the investment account; decreases such as losses and dividends cause reductions to be recorded. Thus, the equity method conveys information that describes the relationship created by the investor's ability to significantly influence the investee.

ACCOUNTING PROCEDURES USED IN APPLYING THE EQUITY METHOD

Once guidelines for the application of the equity method have been established, the mechanical process necessary for recording basic transactions is quite straightforward. The investor accrues its percentage of the earnings reported by the investee each period. Dividend declarations reduce the investment balance to reflect the decrease in the investee's book value.

Referring again to the information presented in Exhibit 1–1, Little Company reported a net income of $200,000 during 2002 and paid cash dividends of $50,000.

---

[4]Fluctuations in the market values of *trading securities* are recognized in income in the period in which they occur.

DISCUSSION QUESTION

Does the Equity Method Really Apply Here?

Abraham, Inc., a New Jersey corporation, operates 57 bakeries throughout the northeastern section of the United States. In the past, the company's outstanding common stock has been owned entirely by its founder, James Abraham. However, during the early part of this year, the corporation suffered a severe cash flow problem brought on by rapid expansion. To avoid bankruptcy, Abraham sought additional investment capital from a friend, Dennis Bostitch, who owned Highland Laboratories. Subsequently Highland paid $700,000 cash to Abraham, Inc., to acquire enough newly issued shares of common stock for a one-third ownership interest.

At the end of this year, the accountants for Highland Laboratories are discussing the proper method of reporting this investment. One argues for maintaining the asset at its original cost: "This purchase is no more than a loan to bail out the bakeries. Mr. Abraham will continue to run the organization with little or no attention paid to us. After all, what does anyone in our company know about baking bread? I would not be surprised if these shares are not reacquired by Abraham as soon as the bakery business is profitable again."

One of the other accountants disagrees, stating that the equity method is appropriate. "I realize that our company is not capable of running a bakery. However, the official rules state that we must have only the *ability* to exert significant influence. With one-third of the common stock in our possession, we certainly have that ability. Whether we use it or not, this ability means that we are required to apply the equity method."

How should Highland Laboratories account for its investment in Abraham, Inc.?

These figures indicate that Little's net assets have increased by $150,000 during the year. Therefore, in the financial records of Big Company, the following journal entries are made in applying the equity method:

Investment in Little Company	40,000	
Equity in Investee Income		40,000
To accrue earnings of a 20 percent owned investee ($200,000 × 20%).		
Cash	10,000	
Investment in Little Company		10,000
To record receipt of cash dividend from Little Company ($50,000 × 20%).		

In the first entry, Big accrues income based on the reported earnings of the investee even though this amount greatly exceeds the cash dividend. The second entry reflects the actual receipt of the dividend and the related reduction in Little's net assets. The $30,000 net increment recorded here in Big's investment account ($40,000 − $10,000) represents 20 percent of the $150,000 increase in Little's book value that occurred during the year.

Although these two entries illustrate the basic reporting process used in applying the equity method, several other issues must be explored for a full understanding of this approach. More specifically, special procedures are required in accounting for each of the following:

1. Reporting a change to the equity method.
2. Reporting investee income from sources other than continuing operations.
3. Reporting investee losses.
4. Reporting the sale of an equity investment.

Reporting a Change to the Equity Method

In many instances, an investor's ability to significantly influence an investee will not be gained through a single stock acquisition. The investor may possess only a minor ownership for some years before purchasing enough additional shares to require conversion to the equity method. Before the investor achieves significant influence, any investment should be reported by the fair-value method. After the investment reaches the point at which the equity method becomes applicable, a technical question arises about the appropriate means of changing from one method to the other.[5]

APB Opinion 18 (par. 19) answers this concern by stating that "the investment, results of operations (current and prior periods presented), and retained earnings of the investor should be adjusted retroactively." *Thus, all accounts are restated so that the investor's financial statements appear as if the equity method had been applied from the date of the first acquisition.* By mandating retroactive treatment, the APB is attempting to ensure comparability from year to year in the financial reporting of the investor company.[6]

To illustrate this restatement procedure, assume that Giant Company acquires a 10 percent ownership in Small Company on January 1, 2002. Officials of Giant do not believe that their company has gained the ability to exert significant influence over Small. The investment is properly recorded through the use of the fair-value method as an available-for-sale security. Subsequently, on January 1, 2004, Giant purchases an additional 30 percent of the outstanding voting stock of Small, thereby achieving the ability to significantly influence the investee's decision making. From 2002 through 2004, Small reports net income, pays cash dividends, and has fair values at January 1 of each year as follows:

Year	Net Income	Cash Dividends	Fair Value at at January 1
2002	$ 70,000	$20,000	$800,000
2003	110,000	40,000	840,000
2004	130,000	50,000	930,000

In Giant's 2002 and 2003 financial statements, as originally reported, dividend revenue of $2,000 and $4,000, respectively, would be recognized based on receiving 10 percent of these distributions. The investment account is maintained at fair value since it is readily determinable. Also, the change in the fair value of the investment results in a credit to an unrealized cumulative holding gain of $4,000 in 2002 and $13,000 in 2003 reported in Giant's stockholders' equity section. However, after changing to the equity method on January 1, 2004, Giant must restate these prior years to present the investment *as if the equity method had always been applied.* Subsequently, in comparative statements showing columns for previous periods, the 2002 statements should indicate equity income of $7,000 with $11,000 being disclosed for 2003 based on a 10 percent accrual of Small's income for each of these years.

The income restatement for these earlier years can be computed as follows:

Year	Equity in Investee Income (10%)	Income Reported from Dividends	Retroactive Adjustment
2002	$ 7,000	$2,000	$ 5,000
2003	11,000	4,000	7,000
Total adjustment to Retained Earnings			$12,000

Giant's reported earnings for 2002 will be increased by $5,000 with a $7,000 increment needed for 2003. To bring about this retroactive change to the equity method, Giant prepares the following journal entry on January 1, 2004:

---

[5]A switch to the equity method also may be required if the investee purchases a portion of its own shares as treasury stock. This transaction can increase the investor's percentage of outstanding stock.

[6]One member of the APB voted against issuance of *Opinion 18* based in part on this retroactive approach. In his dissent, Newman T. Halvorson contended that "at the time an investment qualifies for use of the equity method, a new reporting entity is created, and the accounts of the investor for periods prior to that time should not be adjusted retroactively to reflect an entity that did not exist."

Investment in Small Company............................	12,000	
Retained Earnings—Prior Period Adjustment—Equity in		
Investee Income		12,000

To adjust 2002 and 2003 records so that investment is accounted
for using the equity method in a consistent manner.

| Unrealized Holding Gain—Shareholders' Equity .... | 13,000 | |
| Fair Value Adjustment (Available-for-Sale)............. | | 13,000 |

To remove the investor's percentage of the increase in fair value
(10% × $130,000) from stockholders' equity and the
available-for-sale portfolio valuation account.

The $13,000 adjustment removes the accounts required by *SFAS No. 115* that pertain to the investment prior to the obtaining of significant influence. Because the investment is no longer part of the available-for-sale portfolio, it is carried under the equity method rather than at fair value. Accordingly, the fair value adjustment accounts are reduced as part of the reclassification.

Continuing with this example, Giant will make two other journal entries at the end of 2004, but they relate solely to the operations and distributions of that period.

| Investment in Small Company............................ | 52,000 | |
| Equity in Investee Income .... | | 52,000 |

To accrue 40 percent of the year 2004 income reported by the
Small Company ($130,000 × 40%).

| Cash .... | 20,000 | |
| Investment in Small Company...................... | | 20,000 |

To record receipt of year 2004 cash dividend from Small
Company ($50,000 × 40%).

Reporting Investee Income from Sources Other than Continuing Operations

Traditionally, certain elements of income are presented separately within a set of financial statements. Examples include extraordinary items (see *APB Opinion 30*, "Reporting the Results of Operations," June 1973) and prior period adjustments (see FASB *SFAS 16*, "Prior Period Adjustments," June 1977). A concern that arises in applying the equity method is whether items appearing separately in the investee's income statement require similar treatment by the investor.

To examine this issue, assume that Large Company owns 40 percent of the voting stock of Tiny Company and accounts for this investment by means of the equity method. In 2002, Tiny reports net income of $200,000, a figure composed of $250,000 in income from continuing operations and a $50,000 extraordinary loss. Large Company accrues earnings of $80,000 based on 40 percent of the $200,000 net figure. However, for proper disclosure, the extraordinary loss incurred by the investee must also be reported separately on the financial statements of the investor. This handling is intended, once again, to mirror the close relationship between the two companies.

Based on the level of ownership, Large recognizes $100,000 as a component of operating income (40 percent of Tiny Company's $250,000 income from continuing operations) along with a $20,000 extraordinary loss (40 percent of $50,000). The overall effect is still an $80,000 net increment in Large's earnings, but this amount has been appropriately allocated between income from continuing operations and extraordinary items.

The journal entry to record Large's equity interest in the income of Tiny would be as follows:

Investment in Tiny Company............................	80,000	
Extraordinary Loss of Investee........................	20,000	
Equity in Investee Income		100,000

To accrue operating income and extraordinary loss from
equity investment.

One additional aspect of this accounting should be noted. Even though this loss has already been judged as extraordinary by the investee, Large does not report its $20,000 share as a separate item unless that figure is considered to be material with respect to the investor's own operations.

Reporting Investee Losses

Although most of the previous illustrations are based on the recording of profits, accounting for losses incurred by the investee is handled in a similar manner. The investor recognizes the appropriate percentage of each loss and reduces the carrying value of the investment account. Even though these procedures are consistent with the concept of the equity method, they fail to take into account all possible loss situations.

Permanent Losses in Value   *APB Opinion 18* recognizes that investments may suffer permanent losses in market value that are not properly reflected through the equity method. Such declines can be caused by the loss of major customers, changes in economic conditions, loss of a significant patent or other legal right, damage to the company's reputation, and the like. Permanent reductions in market value resulting from such adverse events might not be reported immediately by the investor through the normal equity entries discussed previously. Thus, *APB Opinion 18* (par. 19) established the following guideline:

> A loss in value of an investment which is other than a temporary decline should be recognized the same as a loss in value of other long-term assets. Evidence of a loss in value might include, but would not necessarily be limited to, absence of an ability to recover the carrying amount of the investment or inability of the investee to sustain an earnings capacity which would justify the carrying amount of the investment.

Thus, when a permanent decline in an equity method investment's value occurs, the investor must reduce the asset to fair market value. However, *APB Opinion 18* stresses that this loss must be permanent before such recognition becomes necessary. Under the equity method, a temporary drop in the market value of an investment is simply ignored.

Investment Reduced to Zero   Through the recognition of reported losses as well as any permanent drops in market value, the investment account may eventually be reduced to a zero balance. This condition is most likely to occur if extreme losses have been suffered by the investee or if the original purchase was made at a low, bargain price. Regardless of the reason, the carrying value of the investment account could conceivably be eliminated in total.

At the point at which an investment account is reduced to zero, the investor should discontinue using the equity method, rather than establish a negative balance. The investment retains a zero balance until subsequent investee profits eliminate all unrealized losses. Once the original cost of the investment has been eliminated, no additional losses can accrue to the investor (since the entire cost has been written off) *unless* some further commitment has been made on behalf of the investee.

Noise Cancellation Technologies, Inc., for example, in recent financial statements explains the discontinued use of the equity method when the investment account has been reduced to zero:

> When the Company's share of cumulative losses equals its investment and the Company has no obligation or intention to fund such additional losses, the Company suspends applying the equity method. . . . The Company will not be able to record any equity in income with respect to an entity until its share of future profits is sufficient to recover any cumulative losses that have not previously been recorded.

Reporting the Sale of an Equity Investment

At any time, the investor may choose to sell part or all of its holdings in the investee company. If a sale occurs, the equity method continues to be applied until the transaction date, thus establishing an appropriate carrying value for the investment. The investor then reduces this balance by the percentage of shares being sold.

As an example, assume that Top Company owns 40 percent of the 100,000 outstanding shares of Bottom Company, an investment accounted for by the equity method. Although these 40,000 shares were acquired some years ago for $200,000, application of the equity method has increased the asset balance to $320,000 as of January 1, 2002. On July 1, 2002, Top elects to sell 10,000 of these shares (one-fourth of its investment) for $110,000 in cash, thereby reducing ownership in Bottom from 40 percent to 30 percent. Bottom Company reports income of $70,000 during the first six months of 2002 and distributes cash dividends of $30,000.

Top, as the investor, initially makes the following journal entries on July 1, 2002, to accrue the proper income and establish the correct investment balance:

Investment in Bottom Company.	28,000	
Equity in Investee Income		28,000
To accrue equity income for first six months of 2002 ($70,000 × 40%).		
Cash	12,000	
Investment in Bottom Company.		12,000
To record receipt of cash dividends from January through June 2002 ($30,000 × 40%).		

These two entries increase the carrying value of Top's investment by $16,000, creating a balance of $336,000 as of July 1, 2002. The sale of one-fourth of these shares can then be recorded as follows:

Cash	110,000	
Investment in Bottom Company.		84,000
Gain on Sale of Investment		26,000
To record sale of one-fourth of investment in Bottom Company (¼ × $336,000 = $84,000).		

After the sale has been consummated, Top continues to apply the equity method to this investment based on 30 percent ownership rather than 40 percent. However, if the sale had been of sufficient magnitude to cause Top to lose its ability to exercise significant influence over Bottom, the equity method ceases to be applicable. For example, if Top Company's holdings were reduced from 40 percent to 15 percent, the equity method might no longer be appropriate after the sale. The shares still being held are reported according to the fair-value method with the remaining book value becoming the new *cost* figure for the investment rather than the amount originally paid.

If an investor is required to change from the equity method to the fair-value method, no retroactive adjustment is made. Although, as previously demonstrated, a change to the equity method mandates a restatement of prior periods, the treatment is not the same when the investor's change is to the fair-value method.

EXCESS OF INVESTMENT COST OVER BOOK VALUE ACQUIRED

After the basic concepts and procedures of the equity method are mastered, more complex accounting issues can be introduced. Surely one of the most common problems encountered in applying the equity method concerns investment costs that exceed the proportionate book value of the investee company.[7]

---

[7]Although encountered less frequently, investments can be purchased at a cost that is less than the underlying book value of the investee. Accounting for this possibility is explored in later chapters.

Unless the investor acquires its ownership at the time of the investee's conception, paying an amount equal to book value is rare. Dell Computer Corporation, as just one example, reported a book value of approximately $.92 per share on January 29, 1999, but near that date, the company's common stock was routinely selling for over $40 per share on the NASDAQ Exchange. To obtain Dell Computer shares as well as the stock of many other businesses, payment of a significant premium is required.

A number of possible reasons exist for such a marked difference in the book value of a company and the price of its stock. A company's value at any time is based on a multitude of factors such as company profitability, the introduction of a new product, expected dividend payments, projected operating results, and general economic conditions. Furthermore, stock prices are based, at least partially, on the perceived worth of a company's net assets, amounts that often vary dramatically from underlying book values. Asset and liability accounts shown on a balance sheet tend to measure historical costs rather than current value. In addition, these reported figures are affected by the specific accounting methods adopted by a company. Inventory costing methods such as LIFO and FIFO, for example, obviously lead to different book values as do each of the acceptable depreciation methods.

If an investment is acquired at a price in excess of book value, logical reasons should explain the additional cost incurred by the investor. The source of the excess of cost over book value is important. Income recognition requires matching the income generated from the investment with its cost. Excess costs allocated to fixed assets will likely be expensed over longer periods than costs allocated to inventory. In applying the equity method, the cause of such an excess payment can be divided into two general categories:

1. Specific investee assets and liabilities may have market values that differ from their present book values. The excess payment can be identified directly with individual accounts such as inventory, equipment, franchise rights, etc.

2. The investor could be willing to pay an extra amount because future benefits are expected to accrue from the investment. Such benefits might be anticipated as the result of factors such as the estimated profitability of the investee or the relationship being established between the two companies. In this case, the additional payment is attributed to an intangible future value generally referred to as *goodwill* rather than to any specific investee asset or liability. For example, in a recent annual report, Ameritech Corporation disclosed that its long-term investment in Tele Danmark, accounted for under the equity method, includes goodwill of approximately $1.4 billion.

As an illustration, assume that Big Company is negotiating the acquisition of 30 percent of the outstanding shares of Little Company. Little's balance sheet reports assets of $500,000 and liabilities of $300,000 for a net book value of $200,000. After investigation, Big determines that Little's equipment is undervalued in the company's financial records by $60,000. One of its patents is also undervalued, but only by $40,000. By adding these valuation adjustments to Little's book value, Big arrives at an estimated worth for the company's net assets of $300,000. Based on this computation, Big offers $90,000 for a 30 percent share of the investee's outstanding stock.

Book value of Little Company (assets minus liabilities [or stockholders' equity])	$200,000
Undervaluation of equipment	60,000
Undervaluation of patent	40,000
Value of net assets	$300,000
Portion being acquired	30%
Acquisition price	$ 90,000

Although Big's purchase price is in excess of the proportionate share of Little's book value, this additional amount can be attributed to two specific accounts: Equipment and Patents. No part of the extra payment is traceable to any other projected future benefit. Thus, the cost of Big's investment is allocated as follows:

Payment by investor		$90,000
Percentage of book value acquired ($200,000 × 30%)		60,000
Payment in excess of book value		30,000
Excess payment identified with specific assets:		
Equipment ($60,000 undervaluation × 30%)................	$18,000	
Patent ($40,000 undervaluation × 30%)	12,000	30,000
Excess payment not identified with specific assets—goodwill		–0–

Of the $30,000 excess payment made by the investor, $18,000 is assigned to the equipment whereas $12,000 is traced to a patent and its undervaluation. No amount of the purchase price is allocated to goodwill.

To take this example one step further, assume that the owners of Little reject the $90,000 price proposed by Big. They believe that the value of the company as a going concern is greater than the market value of its net assets. Since the management of Big believes that valuable synergies will be created through this purchase, the bid price is raised to $125,000 and accepted. This new acquisition price is allocated as follows:

Payment by investor		$125,000
Percentage of book value acquired ($200,000 × 30%)		60,000
Payment in excess of book value		65,000
Excess payment identified with specific assets:		
Equipment ($60,000 undervaluation × 30%)................	18,000	
Patent ($40,000 undervaluation × 30%)	12,000	30,000
Excess payment not identified with specific assets—goodwill		$35,000

As can be seen from this example, *any extra payment that cannot be attributed to a specific asset or liability is assigned to the intangible asset goodwill.* Although the actual purchase price can be computed by a number of different techniques or simply result from negotiations, goodwill is always the excess amount not allocated to identifiable asset or liability accounts.

Under the equity method, the investor enters total cost in a single investment account, regardless of the allocation of any excess purchase price. If Big's bid of $125,000 is accepted by all parties, the acquisition is initially recorded at that amount despite the internal assignments made to equipment, patents, and goodwill. The entire $125,000 was paid to acquire this investment, and it is recorded as such.

The Amortization Process

The preceding extra payments were made in connection with specific assets (equipment, patents, and goodwill). Even though the actual dollar amounts are recorded within the Investment account, a definite historical cost can be attributed to these assets. With a cost to the investor as well as a specified life, the payment relating to each asset should be amortized over an appropriate time period.

Historically, goodwill implicit in equity method investments has been amortized over periods less than or equal to 40 years. However, in June 2001, the FASB approved a major and fundamental change in accounting for goodwill. *SFAS No. 142,* "Goodwill and Other Intangible Assets," states that for fiscal periods beginning December 15, 2001, and after, the useful life for goodwill is considered indefinite. Therefore, no goodwill amortization expense will be allowed in future periods. The change will be accounted for prospectively with no retroactive adjustments permitted. Firms will continue to amortize existing goodwill for the 2001 fiscal year (prior to the *SFAS 142* effective date) and then discontinue the practice. The unamortized portion of implicit goodwill will be carried forward without adjustment until the investment is sold or a permanent decline in value occurs.

In arriving at its decision, the FASB noted that goodwill seldom decreases in value and frequently increases over time. The notion of an indefinite life for goodwill recognizes the argument that amortization of goodwill over an arbitrary period fails to reflect economic reality and therefore may not provide useful information. A primary reason for the presumption of an indefinite life for goodwill relates to the accounting for business combinations (covered in Chapters 2 through 7). The FASB reasoned that goodwill associated with equity method investments should be accounted for in the same manner as goodwill arising from a business combination. One difference, however, is that goodwill arising from a business combination will be subject to annual impairment reviews, whereas goodwill implicit in equity investments will not. Equity method investments will continue to be tested for permanent declines in value as discussed later in this chapter.

Assume, for illustration purposes, that the equipment has a 10-year remaining life, the patent a 5-year life, and the goodwill an indefinite life. If the straight-line method is used with no salvage value, *the investor's cost* should be amortized initially as follows:[8]

Account	Cost Assigned	Useful Life	Annual Amortization
Equipment	$18,000	10 years	$1,800
Patent	12,000	5 years	2,400
Goodwill	35,000	Indefinite	–0–
Annual expense (for five years until patent cost is completely amortized)			$4,200

In recording this annual expense, Big is reducing a portion of the investment balance in the same way it would amortize the cost of any other asset that had a limited life. Therefore, at the end of the first year, the investor records the following journal entry under the equity method:

Equity in Investee Income	4,200	
Investment in Little Company		4,200
To record amortization of excess payment allocated to equipment and patent.		

Because this amortization relates to investee assets, the investor does not establish a specific expense account. Instead, as shown in the previous entry, the expense is recognized through a decrease in the equity income accruing from the investee company.

To illustrate this entire process, assume that Tall Company purchases 20 percent of Short Company for $200,000. Tall can exercise significant influence over the investee, thus, the equity method is appropriately applied. The acquisition is made on January 1, 2002, when Short holds net assets with a book value of $700,000. Tall believes that the investee's building (10-year life) is undervalued within the financial records by $80,000 and equipment with a 5-year life is undervalued by $120,000. Any goodwill established by this purchase is considered to have an indefinite life. During 2002, Short reports a net income of $150,000 and pays a cash dividend at year's end of $60,000.

Tall's three basic journal entries for 2002 pose little problem:

---

[8]Unless otherwise stated, all amortization computations are based on the straight-line method with no salvage value.

January 1, 2002

Investment in Short Company	200,000	
Cash		200,000

To record acquisition of 20 percent of the outstanding shares
of Short Company.

December 31, 2002

Investment in Short Company	30,000	
Equity in Investee Income		30,000

To accrue 20 percent of the 2002 reported earnings of investee
($150,000 × 20%).

Cash	12,000	
Investment in Short Company		12,000

To record receipt of 2002 cash dividend ($60,000 × 20%).

An allocation must be made of Tall's $200,000 purchase price to determine if an additional adjusting entry is necessary to recognize annual amortization associated with the extra payment:

Payment by investor		$200,000
Percentage of 1/1/02 book value ($700,000 × 20%)		140,000
Payment in excess of book value		60,000
Excess payment identified with specific assets:		
Building ($80,000 × 20%)	$16,000	
Equipment ($120,000 × 20%)	24,000	40,000
Excess payment not identified with specific assets—goodwill		$ 20,000

As can be seen, $16,000 of the purchase price is assigned to a building, $24,000 to equipment, with the remaining $20,000 attributed to goodwill. For each asset with a definite useful life, periodic amortization is required.

Asset	Attributed Cost	Useful Life	Annual Amortization
Building	$16,000	10 years	$1,600
Equipment	24,000	5 years	4,800
Goodwill	20,000	Indefinite	–0–
Total for 2002			$6,400

At the end of 2002, Tall must also record the following adjustment in connection with these cost allocations:

Equity in Investee Income	6,400	
Investment in Short Company		6,400

To record 2002 amortization of extra cost of building ($1,600)
and equipment ($4,800).

Although these entries are shown separately here for better explanation, Tall would probably net the income accrual for the year ($30,000) and the amortization ($6,400) to create a single entry increasing the investment and recognizing equity income of $23,600.

ELIMINATION OF UNREALIZED GAINS IN INVENTORY[9]

Many equity acquisitions establish ties between companies to facilitate the direct purchase and sale of inventory items. Such intercompany transactions may occur either on

---

[9]Unrealized gains may involve the sale of items other than inventory. The intercompany transfer of depreciable fixed assets and land are discussed in a later chapter.

E x h i b i t   1 – 2

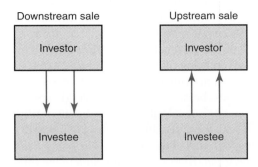

a regular basis or only sporadically. For example, the Coca-Cola Company recently disclosed that syrup and concentrate sales of $3.1 billion were made to its 40 percent-owned investee Coca-Cola Enterprises Inc.

Regardless of their frequency, inventory sales between investor and investee necessitate special accounting procedures to ensure proper timing of revenue recognition. An underlying principle of accounting is that "revenues are not recognized until earned . . . and revenues are considered to have been earned when the entity has substantially accomplished what it must do to be entitled to the benefits represented by the revenues."[10] In the sale of inventory to an unrelated party, recognition of revenue is normally not in question; substantial accomplishment is achieved when the exchange takes place unless special terms are included in the contract.

Unfortunately, the earning process is not so clearly delineated in sales made between related parties. *Because of the relationship between investor and investee, the seller of the goods is said to retain a partial stake in the inventory for as long as it is held by the buyer.* Thus, the earning process is not considered complete at the time of the original sale. For proper accounting, revenue recognition must be deferred until substantial accomplishment is proven. Consequently, when the investor applies the equity method, reporting of the related profit on intercompany transfers is delayed until the ultimate disposition of the goods by the buyer. When the inventory is eventually consumed within operations or resold to an unrelated party, the original sale is culminated and the gross profit is fully recognized.

In accounting, transactions between related companies are identified as either *downstream* or *upstream*. Downstream transfers refer to the sale of an item by the investor to the investee. Conversely, an upstream sale describes one made to the investor by the investee (see Exhibit 1–2). *Although this distinction is not significant for carrying out the procedures of the equity method, it has definite consequences in the consolidation of financial statements, as discussed in Chapter 5.* Therefore, these two types of intercompany sales are examined separately even at this introductory stage.

Downstream Sales of Inventory

Assume that Big Company owns a 40 percent share of Little Company and accounts for this investment through the equity method. In 2002, Big sells inventory to Little at a price of $50,000. This figure includes a markup of 30 percent, or $15,000. By the end of 2002, Little has sold $40,000 of these goods to outside parties while retaining $10,000 in inventory for sale during the subsequent year.

---

[10]FASB, *Statement of Financial Accounting Concepts No. 6,* "Recognition and Measurement in Financial Statements of Business Enterprises" (Stamford, Conn.: December 1984), para. 83.

Downstream sales have been made by the investor to the investee. In applying the equity method, recognition of the related profit must be delayed until these goods are disposed of by the buyer. Although total intercompany transfers amounted to $50,000 in 2002, $40,000 of this merchandise has already been resold to outsiders, thereby justifying the normal reporting of profits. For the $10,000 still in the investee's inventory, the earning process is not finished. In computing equity income, this portion of the intercompany gain must be deferred until the goods are disposed of by Little.

The markup on the original sale was 30 percent of the transfer price; therefore, Big's profit associated with these remaining items is $3,000 ($10,000 × 30%). *However, because only 40 percent of the investee's stock is held, just $1,200 ($3,000 × 40%) of this gain is unearned.* Big's ownership percentage reflects the intercompany portion of the gain. The total $3,000 gross profit within the ending inventory balance is not the amount deferred. Rather, 40 percent of that gain is viewed as the currently unrealized figure.

Remaining Ending Inventory	Gross Profit Percentage	Gain in Ending Inventory	Investor Ownership Percentage	Unrealized Intercompany Gain
$10,000	30%	$3,000	40%	$1,200

After calculating the appropriate deferral, the investor decreases current equity income by $1,200 to reflect the unearned portion of the intercompany gain. This procedure temporarily removes this portion of the profit from the books of the investor in 2002 until the inventory is disposed of by the investee in 2003. Big accomplishes the actual deferral through the following year-end journal entry:

Deferral of Unrealized Gain

Equity in Investee Income	1,200	
Investment in Little Company		1,200
To defer unrealized gain on sale of inventory to Little Company.		

In the subsequent year, when this inventory is eventually consumed by Little or sold to unrelated parties, the deferral is no longer needed. The earning process is complete and the $1,200 should be recognized by Big. By merely reversing the preceding deferral entry, the accountant succeeds in moving the investor's profit in the appropriate time period. Recognition is shifted from the year of transfer to the year in which the earning process is substantially accomplished.

Subsequent Realization of Intercompany Gain

Investment in Little Company	1,200	
Equity in Investee Income		1,200
To recognize income on intercompany sale that has now been earned through sales to outsiders.		

Upstream Sales of Inventory

Unlike consolidated financial statements (see Chapter 5), the equity method reports upstream sales of inventory in the same manner as downstream sales. Hence, unrealized gains remaining in ending inventory are deferred until the items are used or sold to unrelated parties. To illustrate, assume that Big Company once again owns 40 percent of Little Company. During the current year, Little sells merchandise costing $40,000 to Big for $60,000. At the end of the fiscal period, Big still retains $15,000 of these goods. Little reports net income of $120,000 for the year.

To reflect the basic accrual of the investee's earnings, Big records the following journal entry at the end of this year:

DISCUSSION QUESTION

Is This Really Only Significant Influence?

The Coca-Cola Company accounts for its ownership of Coca-Cola Enterprises (CCE) by use of the equity method as described here in Chapter 1. In 2000, Coca-Cola held approximately 40 percent of the outstanding stock of CCE. According to the financial statements of CCE, the products of The Coca-Cola Company account for approximately 90 percent of total CCE revenues. Moreover, four directors of CCE are executive officers or former executive officers of The Coca-Cola Company. CCE conducts its business primarily under agreements with The Coca-Cola Company. These agreements give the Company the exclusive right to market, distribute, and produce beverage products of The Coca-Cola Company in authorized containers in specified territories. These agreements provide The Coca-Cola Company with the ability, in its sole discretion, to establish prices, terms of payment, and other terms and conditions for the purchase of concentrates and syrups from The Coca-Cola Company.

If Coca-Cola acquires approximately 10 percent more of CCE, a majority of the stock will be held so that consolidation becomes a requirement. However, given the size of the present ownership and the dependence that CCE has on Coca-Cola for products and marketing, does Coca-Cola truly have no more than "the ability to exercise significant influence over the operating and financial policies" of CCE? Does the equity method fairly represent the relationship that exists? Or, does Coca-Cola actually control CCE despite the level of ownership, and should consolidation be required? Currently, the FASB is reexamining the boundary between the application of the equity method and consolidation. Should the rules be rewritten so that Coca-Cola must consolidate CCE rather than use the equity method? If so, at what level of ownership would the equity method no longer be appropriate?

Income Accrual

Investment in Little Company	48,000	
Equity in Investee Income		48,000

To accrue income from 40 percent owned investee ($120,000 × 40%).

The amount of the gain remaining unrealized at year-end is computed using the markup of 33 1/3 percent of the sales price ($20,000/$60,000):

Remaining Ending Inventory	Gross Profit Percentage	Gain in Ending Inventory	Investor Ownership Percentage	Unrealized Intercompany Gain
$15,000	33⅓%	$5,000	40%	$2,000

Based on this calculation, a second entry is required of the investor at year-end. Once again, a deferral of the unrealized gain created by the intercompany transfer is necessary for proper timing of income recognition. *Under the equity method, the direction of the sale has no influence on either the amount or the method of reporting.*

Deferral of Unrealized Gain

Equity in Investee Income	2,000	
Investment in Little Company		2,000

To defer recognition of intercompany unrealized gain until inventory is used or sold to unrelated parties.

After the adjustment, Big, the investor, reports earnings from this equity investment of $46,000 ($48,000 − $2,000). The income accrual is reduced because a portion of the intercompany gross profit is considered unrealized. When the $15,000 in merchandise is eventually consumed or sold by the investor, the preceding journal entry is reversed. In this way, the effects of the gain are reported in the proper accounting period when the gain is earned by sales to an outside party.

In an upstream sale, the investor's own Inventory account contains the unrealized gain. The previous entry, though, defers recognition of this profit by decreasing Big's investment account rather than the inventory balance. *APB Accounting Interpretation No. 1 of APB Opinion 18,* "Intercompany Profit Eliminations under Equity Method," November 1971, permits the direct reduction of the investor's inventory balance as a means of accounting for this gain. Although this alternative is acceptable, decreasing the investment remains the traditional approach for deferring unrealized gains, even for upstream sales.

As a final note, whether upstream or downstream, the investor's sales and purchases are still reported as if the transactions were carried out with outside parties. Only the unrealized gain is deferred and that amount is adjusted solely through the equity income account. Furthermore, since the companies are not consolidated, the investee's reported balances are not altered at all to reflect the nature of these sales/purchases. Obviously, readers of the financial statements need to be made aware of the inclusion of these amounts in the income statement. Thus, the FASB issued *Statement No. 57,* "Related Party Disclosures," in March 1982; it required reporting companies to disclose certain information about related party transactions. These disclosures include the nature of the relationship, a description of the transactions, the dollar amounts of the transactions, and amounts due to or from any related parties at year-end.

SUMMARY

1. The equity method of accounting for an investment reflects the close relationship that may exist between an investor and an investee. More specifically, this approach is applied whenever the owner achieves the ability to apply significant influence to the investee's operating and financial decisions. Significant influence is presumed to exist at the 20 to 50 percent ownership level. However, the accountant must evaluate each situation, regardless of the percentage of ownership, to determine whether this ability is actually present.

2. To mirror the relationship between the companies, the equity method requires the investor to accrue income when earned by the investee. In recording this profit or loss, the investor separately reports items such as extraordinary gains and losses as well as prior period adjustments to highlight their nonrecurring nature. Dividend payments decrease the owners' equity of the investee company; therefore, the investor reduces the investment account when collected.

3. When acquiring capital stock, an investor often pays an amount that exceeds the underlying book value of the investee company. For accounting purposes, such excess payments must be identified with either specific assets and liabilities (such as land or buildings) or allocated to an intangible asset referred to as goodwill. Each assigned cost (except for any amount attributed to land or goodwill after 2001) is then amortized by the investor over the expected useful lives of the assets and liabilities. This amortization reduces the amount of equity income being reported.

4. If the entire investment or any portion is sold, the equity method is applied consistently until the date of disposal. A gain or loss is computed based on the adjusted book value at that time. Remaining shares are accounted for by means of either the equity method or the fair-value method, depending on the investor's subsequent ability to significantly influence the investee.

5. Inventory (or other assets) may be transferred between investor and investee. Because of the relationship between the two companies, the equity income accrual should be reduced to defer the intercompany portion of any markup included on these transfers until the items are either sold to outsiders or consumed. Thus, the amount of intercompany gain in ending inventory decreases the amount of equity income being recognized in the current period although this effect is subsequently reversed.

COMPREHENSIVE ILLUSTRATION

Problem   *(Estimated Time: 30 to 50 Minutes)* Every chapter in this textbook concludes with an illustration designed to assist students in tying together the essential elements of the material presented.

After a careful reading of each chapter, attempt to work through the comprehensive problem. Then review the solution that follows the problem, noting the handling of each significant accounting issue.

Part A

On January 1, 2001, Big Company pays $70,000 for a 10 percent interest in Little Company. On that date, Little has a book value of $600,000, although equipment, which has a five-year life, is undervalued by $100,000 on its books. Little Company's stock is closely held by a few investors and is traded only infrequently. Because fair values are not readily available on a continuing basis, the investment account is appropriately maintained at cost.

On January 1, 2002, Big acquires an additional 30 percent of Little Company for $264,000. This second purchase provides Big with the ability to exert significant influence over Little. At the time of this transaction, Little's equipment with a four-year life was undervalued by only $80,000.

During these two years, Little reported the following operational results:

Year	Net Income	Cash Dividends Paid
2001	$210,000	$110,000
2002	250,000	$100,000

Additional Information:

- Cash dividends are always paid on July 1 of each year.
- Any goodwill is considered to have an indefinite life.

Required:

- *a.* What income did Big originally report for 2001 in connection with this investment?
- *b.* On comparative financial statements for 2001 and 2002, what figures should Big report in connection with this investment?

Part B (This problem is a continuation of Part A)

In 2003, Little Company reports $400,000 in income from continuing operations plus a $60,000 extraordinary gain. The company pays a $120,000 cash dividend. During this fiscal year, Big sells inventory costing $80,000 to Little for $100,000. Little continues to hold 30 percent of this merchandise at the end of 2003. Big maintains 40 percent ownership of Little throughout the period.

Required:

Prepare all necessary journal entries for Big for the year of 2003.

Solution

Part A

- *a.* Big Company accounts for its investment in Little Company at cost during 2001. Since only 10 percent of the outstanding shares were held, significant influence was apparently not present. Because the stock is not actively traded, fair values are not available and the investment remains at cost. Therefore, only the $11,000 ($110,000 × 10%) received as dividends is recorded by the investor as income in the original financial reporting for that year.
- *b.* To make comparative reports consistent, a change to the equity method is recorded retroactively. Therefore, when the ability to exert significant influence over the operations of Little is established on January 1, 2002, both Big's 2001 and 2002 financial statements must reflect the equity method.

Big first evaluates the initial purchase of Little's stock to determine if either goodwill or incremental asset values need be reflected within the equity method procedures.

Purchase of 10 Percent of Voting Stock on January 1, 2001

Payment by investor	$70,000
Percentage of book value acquired ($600,000 × 10%)	60,000
Payment in excess of book value	10,000
Excess payment identified with specific assets:	
Equipment ($100,000 × 10%)	10,000
Excess payment identified with specific assets—goodwill	–0–

As shown here, the $10,000 excess payment was made in recognition of the undervaluation of Little's equipment. This asset had a useful life at that time of five years; thus, the investor records amortization expense of $2,000 each year.

A similar calculation must be carried out for Big's second stock purchase:

Purchase of 30 Percent of Voting Stock on January 1, 2002

Payment by investor	$264,000
Percentage of book value* acquired ($700,000 × 30%)	210,000
Payment in excess of book value	54,000
Excess payment identified with specific assets:	
Equipment ($80,000 × 30%)	24,000
Excess payment not identified with specific assets—goodwill	$ 30,000

*Little's book value on January 1, 2002, is computed by adding the 2001 net income of $210,000 less dividends paid of $110,000 to the previous book value of $600,000.

In this second acquisition, $24,000 of the payment is attributable to the undervalued equipment with $30,000 assigned to goodwill. Since the equipment now has only a four-year remaining life, annual amortization of $6,000 is appropriate ($24,000/4).

After the additional shares are acquired on January 1, 2002, Big's financial records for 2001 must be retroactively restated as if the equity method had been applied from the date of the initial investment.

Financial Reporting—2001

Equity in Investee Income (Income Statement)	
Income reported by Little	$210,000
Big's ownership	10%
Accrual for 2001	$ 21,000
Less: Equipment amortization (first purchase)	(2,000)
Equity in investee income—2001	$ 19,000

Investment in Little (Balance Sheet)	
Cost of first acquisition	$ 70,000
2001 Equity in investee income (above)	19,000
Less: Dividends received ($110,000 × 10%)	(11,000)
Investment in Little—12/31/01	$ 78,000

Financial Reporting—2002

Equity in Investee Income (Income Statement)	
Income reported by Little	$250,000
Big's ownership	40%
Big's share of Little's reported income	$100,000
Less amortization expense:	
Equipment (first purchase)	(2,000)
Equipment (second purchase)	(6,000)
Equity in investee income—2002	$ 92,000

Investment in Little (Balance Sheet)	
Book value—12/31/01 (above)	$ 78,000
Cost of 2002 acquisition	264,000
Equity in investee income (above)	92,000
Less: Dividends received ($100,000 × 40%)	(40,000)
Investment in Little—12/31/02	$394,000

Part B

On July 1, 2003, Big receives a $48,000 cash dividend from Little (40% × $120,000). According to the equity method, receipt of this dividend reduces the carrying value of the investment account:

Cash	48,000	
Investment in Little Company		48,000

    To record receipt of 2003 dividend from investee.

Big records no other journal entries in connection with this investment until the end of 2003. At that time, the annual accrual of income is made as well as the adjustment to record amortization (see Part A for computation of expense). The investee's continuing income is reported separately from the extraordinary item.

Investment in Little Company	184,000	
Equity in Investee Income		160,000
Extraordinary Gain of Investee		24,000

    To recognize reported income of investee based on a
    40 percent ownership level of $400,000 operating income
    and $60,000 extraordinary gain.

Equity in Investee Income	8,000	
Investment in Little Company		8,000

    To record annual amortization on excess payment made in
    relation to equipment ($2,000 from first purchase and $6,000
    from second).

Big only needs to make one other equity entry during 2003. Intercompany sales have occurred and a portion of the inventory continues to be held by Little. Therefore, an unrealized gain exists that must be deferred. The markup on the sales price was 20 percent ($20,000/$100,000). Since $30,000 of this merchandise is still in the possession of the investee, the related gain is $6,000 ($30,000 × 20%). However, Big owns only 40 percent of the outstanding stock of Little; thus, the unrealized intercompany gain at year's end is $2,400 ($6,000 × 40%). That amount must be deferred until the inventory is consumed by Little or sold to unrelated parties in subsequent years.

Equity in Investee Company	2,400	
Investment in Little Company		2,400

    To defer unrealized gain on intercompany sale.

QUESTIONS

1. A company acquires a rather large investment in another corporation. What criteria determine whether the equity method of accounting should be applied by the investor to this investment?

2. What indicates an investor's ability to significantly influence the decision-making process of an investee?

3. Why does the equity method record dividends received from an investee as a reduction in the investment account and not as dividend income?

4. The Jones Company possesses a 25 percent interest in the outstanding voting shares of the Sandridge Company. Under what circumstances might Jones decide that the equity method would not be appropriate to account for this investment?

5. Smith, Inc., has maintained an ownership interest in Watts Corporation for a number of years. This investment has been accounted for by means of the equity method. What transactions or events create changes in the Investment in Watts Corporation account being recorded by Smith?

6. Although the equity method is a generally accepted accounting principle (GAAP), recognition of equity income has been criticized. What theoretical problems can be brought up by opponents of the equity method?

7. Because of the acquisition of additional investee shares, an investor may be forced to change from the fair-value method to the equity method. Which procedures are applied to effect this accounting change?

8. Riggins Company accounts for its investment in Bostic Company by means of the equity method. During the past fiscal year, Bostic reported an extraordinary gain on its income statement. How would this extraordinary item affect the financial records of the investor?

9. During the current year, the common stock of the Davis Company suffers a permanent drop in market value. In the past, Davis has made a significant portion of its sales to one customer. This buyer recently announced its decision to make no further purchases from the Davis Company, an action that led to the loss of market value. Hawkins, Inc., owns 35 percent of the outstanding shares of Davis, an investment that is recorded according to the equity method. How would the loss in value affect the financial reporting of this investor?

10. Wilson Company acquired 40 percent of Andrews Company at a bargain price because of losses expected to result from Andrews's failure in marketing several new products. The price paid by Wilson was only $100,000, although Andrews's corresponding book value was much higher. In the first year after acquisition, Andrews lost $300,000. In applying the equity method, how should Wilson account for this loss?

11. In a stock acquisition accounted for by the equity method, a portion of the purchase price often is attributed to goodwill or to specific assets or liabilities. How are these amounts determined at the time of acquisition? How are these amounts accounted for in subsequent periods?

12. Princeton Company holds a 40 percent interest in the outstanding voting stock of Yale Company. On June 19 of the current year, Princeton sells part of this investment. What accounting should Princeton make on June 19? What accounting will Princeton make for the remainder of the current year?

13. What is the difference between downstream and upstream sales? How does this difference impact application of the equity method?

14. How is the unrealized gain on intercompany sales calculated? What effect does an unrealized gain have on the recording of an investment if the equity method is applied?

15. How are intercompany transfers reported in the separate financial statements of an investee if the investor is using the equity method?

INTERNET ASSIGNMENT

Internet sites are time and date sensitive. It is the purpose of these exercises to have you explore the Internet. You may need to refer to the text's Web site at http://www.mhhe.com/hoyle6e to find the most up-to-date links for the Web sites listed in the Internet Assignments.

1. Retrieve the annual report for The Coca-Cola Company (www.thecocacolacompany.com), or any other firm with significant investments in equity securities. For these investments (both equity method and fair-value method), indicate the placement and amount of the respective balance sheet and income statement figures. What percentage of total assets do these investments constitute? Describe the information that is conveyed about these investments in the reporting company's notes to the financial statements.

LIBRARY ASSIGNMENTS

1. The September 1999 FASB Special Report, *Reporting Interests in Joint Ventures and Similar Arrangements,* seeks to develop an international consensus of the basic questions of accounting and disclosure of interests in joint ventures. Discuss the problems in defining a joint venture as discussed in the FASB Special Report. What specific alternatives does the Special Report consider and what is its final recommendation?

2. Read "Accounting for Non-Majority-Owned Intercorporate Investments: A Cash Flow Assessment of Alternative Methods," by Sharon McKinnon and Katherine Taylor Halvorsen in *Journal of Business Finance and Accounting,* January 1993. The article compares three methods of accounting for investments and examines their accuracy in

predicting future cash flows. Discuss its findings and whether or not this accuracy in prediction should be a primary determinant of the worth of investment accounting methods.

3. Read "The Influence of Accounting Principles on Management Investment Decisions: An Illustration" in the June 1988 issue of *Accounting Horizons*. The authors state that "The results of this survey indicate that the equity-accounting standard does impact investment decisions by influencing the size of the investment position taken." Should accounting principles affect a company's operating and financing decisions? How can accounting principles be written that would report only a company's activities and have no impact on operating and financing decisions?

PROBLEMS

1. When an investor uses the equity method to account for investments in common stock, cash dividends received by the investor from the investee should be recorded as:
   a. A deduction from the investor's share of the investee's profits.
   b. Dividend income.
   c. A deduction from the stockholders' equity account, dividends to stockholders.
   d. A deduction from the investment account.

   (AICPA adapted)

2. Which of the following is not an indication that an investor company has the ability to significantly influence an investee?
   a. Material intercompany transactions.
   b. The company owns 30 percent of the company but another owner holds the remaining 70 percent.
   c. Interchange of personnel.
   d. Technological dependency.

3. Sisk Company has owned 10 percent of Maust, Inc., for the past several years. This ownership did not allow Sisk to have significant influence over Maust. Recently, Sisk acquires an additional 30 percent of Maust and now does have this ability. How will this change be reported by the investor?
   a. A cumulative effect of an accounting change is shown in the current income statement.
   b. No change is recorded; the equity method is used from the date of the new acquisition.
   c. A retroactive adjustment is made to restate all prior years to the equity method.
   d. Sisk has the option of choosing the method to be used to show this change.

4. On January 1, Puckett Company paid $1.6 million for 50,000 shares of Harrison's voting common stock, which represents a 40 percent investment. No allocation to goodwill or other specific account was made. Significant influence over Harrison is achieved by this acquisition. Harrison distributed a dividend of $2 per share during the year and reported net income of $560,000. What is the balance in the Investment in Harrison account found in the financial records of Puckett as of December 31?
   a. $1,724,000.
   b. $1,784,000.
   c. $1,844,000.
   d. $1,884,000.

5. In January 2002, Wilkinson, Inc., acquired 20 percent of the outstanding common stock of Bremm, Inc., for $700,000. This investment gave Wilkinson the ability to exercise significant influence over Bremm. Bremm's assets on that date were recorded at $3,900,000 with liabilities of $900,000. Any excess of cost over book value of the investment was attributed to a patent having a remaining useful life of 10 years.

   In 2002, Bremm reported net income of $170,000. In 2003, Bremm reported net income of $210,000. Dividends of $70,000 were paid in each of these two years. What is the reported balance of Wilkinson's Investment in Bremm at December 31, 2003?
   a. $728,000.
   b. $748,000.
   c. $756,000.
   d. $776,000.

6. Ace purchases 40 percent of Baskett Company on January 1, for $500,000. Although not used, this acquisition did give Ace the ability to apply significant influence to the operating and financing policies of Baskett. Baskett reports assets on that date of $1,400,000 with liabilities of $500,000. One building with a seven-year life is undervalued on Baskett's books by $140,000. Also, Baskett's book value for equipment (10-year life) is undervalued by $210,000. During the year, Baskett reports net income of $90,000 while paying dividends of $30,000. What is the Investment in Baskett balance in Ace's financial records as of December 31?
   a. $504,000.
   b. $507,600.
   c. $513,900.
   d. $516,000.

7. Goldman Company reports net income of $140,000 each year and pays an annual cash dividend of $50,000. The company holds net assets of $1,200,000 on January 1, 2001. On that date, Wallace purchases 40 percent of the outstanding stock for $600,000, which gives Wallace the ability to significantly influence Goldman. At the purchase date, goodwill was assigned a useful life of 20 years. On December 31, 2003, what is the Investment in Goldman balance in Wallace's financial records?
   a. $600,000.
   b. $660,000.
   c. $690,000.
   d. $702,000.

8. Perez, Inc., owns 25 percent of Senior, Inc. During 2002, Perez sold goods with a 40 percent gross profit to Senior. Senior sold all of these goods in 2002. How should Perez report the effect of the intercompany sale on its 2002 income statement?
   a. Sales and cost of goods sold should be reduced by the intercompany sales.
   b. Sales and cost of goods sold should be reduced by 25 percent of the intercompany sales.
   c. Investment income should be reduced by 25 percent of the gross profit on intercompany sales.
   d. No adjustment is necessary.

9. Panner, Inc., owns 30 percent of Watkins and applies the equity method. During the current year, Panner buys inventory costing $54,000 and then sells it to Watkins for $90,000. At the end of the year, only $20,000 of merchandise is still being held by Watkins. What amount of unrealized gain must be deferred by Panner in reporting this investment on the equity method?
   a. $2,400.
   b. $4,800.
   c. $8,000.
   d. $10,800.

10. Camato, Inc., buys 40 percent of Swisher Company on January 1, 2002, for $530,000. The equity method of accounting is to be used. The net assets of Swisher on that date were $1.2 million. Any excess of cost over book value is attributable to a trade name with a 20-year remaining life. Swisher immediately begins supplying inventory to Camato as follows:

Year	Cost to Swisher	Transfer Price	Amount Held by Camato at Year-End (at Transfer Price)
2002	$70,000	$100,000	$25,000
2003	96,000	150,000	45,000

Inventory held at the end of one year by Camato is sold at the beginning of the next.
   Swisher reports net income of $80,000 in 2002 and $110,000 in 2003 while paying $30,000 in dividends each year. What is the equity income in Swisher to be reported by Camato in 2003?
   a. $34,050.
   b. $38,020.
   c. $46,230.
   d. $51,450.

11. On January 3, 2002, Haskins Corporation acquired 40 percent of the outstanding common stock of Clem Company for $990,000. This acquisition gave Haskins the ability to exercise significant influence over the investee. The book value of the acquired shares was $790,000. Any excess cost over the underlying book value was assigned to a patent that was undervalued on Clem's balance sheet. This patent has a remaining useful life of 10 years. For the year ended December 31, 2002, Clem reported net income of $260,000 and paid cash dividends of $80,000. At December 31, 2002, what should Haskins report as its Investment in Clem?

12. On January 1, 2002, Alison, Inc., paid $60,000 for a 40 percent interest in Holister Corporation. This investee had assets with a book value of $200,000 and liabilities of $75,000. A patent held by Holister having a $5,000 book value was actually worth $20,000. This patent had a six-year remaining life. Any goodwill associated with this acquisition will not be amortized. During 2002, Holister earned income of $30,000 and paid dividends of $10,000 while in 2003, income was $50,000 and dividends $15,000.

    Assuming that Alison has the ability to significantly influence the operations of Holister, what balance should appear in the Investment in Holister account as of December 31, 2003?

13. On January 1, 2002, Ruark Corporation acquired a 40 percent interest in Batson, Inc., for $210,000. On that date, Batson's balance sheet disclosed net assets of $360,000. During 2002, Batson reported net income of $80,000 and paid cash dividends of $25,000. Ruark sold inventory costing $30,000 to Batson during 2002 for $40,000. Batson used all of this merchandise in its operations during 2002. Make all of Ruark's journal entries for 2002 to apply the equity method to this investment.

14. Waters, Inc., acquires 10 percent of Denton Corporation on January 1, 2002, for $210,000 although the book value of Denton on that date was $1,700,000. Denton held land that was undervalued on its accounting records by $100,000. During 2002, Denton earned a net income of $240,000 while paying cash dividends of $90,000. On January 1, 2003, Waters purchased an additional 30 percent of Denton for $600,000. Denton's land is still undervalued on that date but now by $120,000. Any additional excess cost was attributable to a trademark with a 10-year life for the first purchase and a 9-year life for the second. The investment had been maintained at cost because fair values were not readily available. The equity method will now be applied. During 2003, Denton reported income of $300,000 and distributed dividends of $110,000. Prepare all of the 2003 journal entries for Waters.

15. McKeon Inc. sold $150,000 in inventory to Schilling Company during 2002 for $225,000. Schilling resold $105,000 of this merchandise in 2002 with the remainder to be disposed of during 2003. Assuming McKeon owns 25 percent of Schilling and applies the equity method, what journal entry is recorded at the end of 2003 to defer the unrealized gain?

16. Hager holds 30 percent of the outstanding shares of Jenkins and appropriately applies the equity method of accounting. Excess cost amortization (related to a patent) associated with this investment amounts to $9,000 per year. For 2002, Jenkins reports earnings of $80,000 and pays cash dividends of $30,000. During that year, Jenkins acquired inventory for $50,000, which was then sold to Hager for $80,000. At the end of 2002, Hager continues to hold merchandise with a transfer price of $40,000.
    a. What Equity in Investee Income should Hager report for 2002?
    b. How will the intercompany transfer affect Hager's reporting in 2003?
    c. If the inventory had been sold by Hager to Jenkins, how would the above answers have changed?

17. On January 1, 2001, Monroe, Inc., purchased 10,000 shares of Brown Company for $250,000, giving Monroe 10 percent ownership of Brown. On January 1, 2002, Monroe purchased an additional 20,000 shares (20 percent) for $590,000. This latest purchase gave Monroe the ability to apply significant influence over Brown. Assume that no goodwill is involved in either acquisition and the original 10 percent investment was categorized as an available-for-sale security.

    Brown reports net income and dividends as follows. These amounts are assumed to have occurred evenly throughout these years.

	Net Income	Cash Dividends (paid quarterly)
2001	$350,000	$100,000
2002	480,000	110,000
2003	500,000	120,000

On July 1, 2003, Monroe sells 2,000 shares of this investment for $46 per share, thus reducing its interest from 30 to 28 percent. However, the company retains the ability to significantly influence Brown. What amounts appear in Monroe's 2003 income statement?

18. Collins, Inc., purchases 10 percent of Merton Corporation on January 1, 2001, for $345,000. Collins acquires an additional 15 percent of Merton on January 1, 2002, for $580,000. The equity method of accounting has now become appropriate for this investment. No intercompany sales have occurred.
   a. How does Collins initially determine the income to be reported in 2001 in connection with its ownership of Merton?
   b. What factors should have influenced Collins in its decision to apply the equity method in 2002?
   c. What factors might have prevented Collins from adopting the equity method after this second purchase?
   d. What is the objective of the equity method of accounting?
   e. What criticisms have been leveled at the equity method?
   f. In comparative statements for 2001 and 2002, how would Collins determine the income to be reported in 2001 in connection with its ownership of Merton? Why is this accounting appropriate?
   g. How is the allocation of Collins's payments made?
   h. If Merton pays a cash dividend, what impact does it have on the financial records of Collins? Why is this accounting appropriate?
   i. On financial statements for 2002, what amounts are included in Collins's Investment in Merton account? What amounts are included in Collins's Equity in Income of Merton account?

19. Parrot Corporation holds a 42 percent ownership of Sunrise, Inc. The equity method is being applied. No goodwill or other allocation occurred in the purchase of this investment. During 2002, intercompany inventory transfers were made between the two companies. A portion of this merchandise was not resold until 2003. During 2003, additional transfers were made.
   a. What is the difference in upstream transfers and downstream transfers?
   b. How does the direction of an intercompany transfer (upstream versus downstream) affect the application of the equity method?
   c. How is the intercompany unrealized gain computed in applying the equity method?
   d. How should Parrot compute the amount of equity income to be recognized in 2002? What entry is made to record this income?
   e. How should Parrot compute the amount of equity income to be recognized in 2003?
   f. If none of the transferred inventory had remained at the end of 2002, how would application of the equity method have been affected by these transfers?
   g. How do these intercompany transfers affect the financial reporting of Sunrise?

20. Several years ago, Einstein, Inc., bought 40 percent of the outstanding voting stock of the Brooks Company. The equity method is appropriately applied. On August 1 of the current year, Einstein sold a portion of these shares.
   a. How does Einstein compute the book value of this investment on August 1 to determine its gain or loss on the sale?
   b. How should Einstein account for this investment after August 1?
   c. If Einstein retains only a 2 percent interest in Brooks so that virtually no influence is held, what figures appear in the investor's income statement for the current year?
   d. If Einstein retains only a 2 percent interest in Brooks so that virtually no influence is held, does the investor have to retroactively adjust any previously reported figures?

21. Russell owns 30 percent of the outstanding stock of Thacker and has the ability to significantly influence the investee's operations and decision making. On January 1, 2002, the balance in the Investment in Thacker account is $335,000. Amortization associated with this acquisition is $9,000 per year. In 2002, Thacker earns an income of $90,000 and pays cash dividends of $30,000. Previously, in 2001, Thacker had sold inventory costing $24,000 to Russell for $40,000. All but 25 percent of this merchandise was consumed by Russell during 2001. The remainder was used during the first few weeks of 2002. Additional sales were made to Russell in 2002; inventory costing $28,000 was transferred at a price of $50,000. Of this total, 40 percent was not consumed until 2003.

Required:

  a. What amount of income would Russell recognize in 2002 from its ownership interest in Thacker?
  b. What is the balance in the Investment in Thacker account at the end of 2002?

22. On January 1, 2001, Ace acquires 15 percent of Zip's outstanding common stock for $52,000 and categorizes the investment as an available-for-sale security. Zip earns a net income of $80,000 in 2001 and pays dividends totaling $30,000. On January 1, 2002, Ace buys an additional 10 percent of Zip for $43,800. This second purchase gives Ace the ability to significantly influence the decision making of Zip. During 2002, Zip earns $100,000 and pays $40,000 in dividends. In each purchase, Ace attributed any cost over book value to Zip's franchise agreements that had a remaining life of 10 years at January 1, 2001. As of December 31, 2002, Zip reports a net book value of $390,000.

  a. On Ace's December 31, 2002, balance sheet, what balance is reported for the Investment in Zip account?
  b. What amount of equity income should Ace report for 2002?

23. Anderson acquires 10 percent of the outstanding voting shares of Barringer on January 1, 2001, for $92,000 and categorizes the investment as an available-for-sale security. An additional 20 percent of the stock is purchased on January 1, 2002, for $210,000, which gives Anderson the ability to significantly influence Barringer. Barringer has a book value of $800,000 at January 1, 2001, and records net income of $180,000 for the following year. Dividends of $80,000 were paid by Barringer during 2001. The book values of Barringer's asset and liability accounts are considered as equal to fair market values, except for a copyright whose value accounted for Anderson's excess cost in each purchase. The copyright had a remaining life of 16 years at January 1, 2001.

  Barringer reports $210,000 in net income during 2002 and $230,000 in 2003. Dividends of $100,000 are paid in each of these years.

  a. On comparative income statements issued in 2003 by Anderson for 2001 and 2002, what amounts of income would be reported in connection with the company's investment in Barringer?
  b. If Anderson sells its entire investment in Barringer on January 1, 2004, for $400,000 cash, what is the impact on Anderson's income?
  c. Assume that Anderson sells inventory to Barringer during 2002 and 2003 as follows:

Year	Cost to Anderson	Price to Barringer	Year-End Balance (at Transfer Price)
2002	$35,000	$50,000	$20,000 (sold in following year)
2003	33,000	60,000	40,000 (sold in following year)

  What amount of equity income should be recognized by Anderson for the year 2003?

24. Smith purchases 5 percent of Barker's outstanding stock on October 1, 2001, for $7,475. An additional 10 percent of Barker is acquired for $14,900 on July 1, 2002. Both of these purchases were accounted for as available-for-sale investments. A final 20 percent is purchased on December 31, 2003, for $34,200. With this final acquisition, Smith achieves the ability to significantly influence the decision-making process of Barker.

  Barker has a book value of $100,000 as of January 1, 2001. Information follows concerning the operations of this company for the 2001–02 period. Assume all income and dividends occurred evenly throughout the years.

Year	Reported Income	Dividends
2001	$20,000	$ 8,000
2002	30,000	16,000
2003	24,000	9,000

On Barker's financial records, the book values of all assets and liabilities are the same as their fair market values. Any excess cost from either purchase relates to identifiable intangible assets. For each purchase, the excess cost is amortized over 15 years. Amortization for a portion of a year should be based on months.

Required:

    a.   On comparative income statements issued in 2004 for the years of 2001, 2002, and 2003, what would Smith report as its income derived from this Investment in Barker?

    b.   On a balance sheet as of December 31, 2003, what should Smith report as its Investment in Barker?

25. Hobson acquires 40 percent of the outstanding voting stock of the Stokes Company on January 1, 2002, for $210,000 in cash. The book value of Stokes's net assets on that date was $400,000, although one of the company's buildings, with a $60,000 carrying value, was actually worth $100,000. This building had a 10-year remaining life. A royalty agreement owned by Stokes with a 20-year remaining life was undervalued by $85,000.

    Stokes sells inventory to Hobson during 2002 with an original cost of $60,000. This merchandise was sold to Hobson at a price of $90,000. Hobson still holds $15,000 (transfer price) of this amount in inventory as of December 31, 2002. These goods are to be sold to outside parties during 2003.

    Stokes reports a loss of $60,000 for 2002, $40,000 from continuing operations and $20,000 from an extraordinary loss. The company still manages to pay a $10,000 cash dividend during the year.

    During 2003, Stokes reports a $40,000 net income and distributes a cash dividend of $12,000. Additional inventory sales of $80,000 are made to Hobson during the period. The original cost of the merchandise was $50,000. All but 30 percent of this inventory has been resold to outside parties by the end of the 2003 fiscal year.

    Prepare all journal entries for Hobson for 2002 and 2003 in connection with this investment. Assume that the equity method is applied.

26. Penston Company owns 40 percent (40,000 shares) of Scranton, Inc., which was purchased several years ago for $182,000. Since the date of acquisition, the equity method has been properly applied and the book value of the investment account as of January 1, 2002, is $248,000. Excess patent cost amortization of $12,000 is still being recognized each year. During 2002, Scranton reports net income of $200,000, $320,000 in operating income earned evenly throughout the year, and a $120,000 extraordinary loss incurred on October 1. No dividends were paid during the year. Penston sells 8,000 shares of Scranton on August 1, 2002, for $94,000 in cash. However, Penston does retain the ability to significantly influence the investee.

    During the last quarter of 2001, Penston sold $50,000 in inventory (which had originally cost Penston only $30,000) to Scranton. At the end of that fiscal year, Scranton's inventory retained $9,000 (at sales price) of this merchandise, which was subsequently sold in the first quarter of 2002.

    On Penston's financial statements for the year ended December 31, 2002, what income effects would be reported from its ownership in Scranton?

27. On July 1, 2001, the Abernethy Company acquires 65,000 of the outstanding shares of the Chapman Company for $13 per share. This acquisition gave Abernethy a 25 percent ownership of Chapman and allowed Abernethy to significantly influence the decisions of the investee.

    As of July 1, 2001, the investee had assets with a book value of $2 million and liabilities of $400,000. At the time, Chapman held equipment appraised at $120,000 above book value. Company land was valued at $160,000 above book value. The equipment was considered to have an eight-year life with no salvage value. Remaining excess cost is attributable to a copyright with a 15-year remaining life. Depreciation and amortization are computed using the straight-line method.

Chapman follows a policy of paying 50 cents per share as a cash dividend every April 1 and October 1. Chapman's income, earned evenly throughout each year, was 2001—$280,000; 2002—$360,000; and 2003—$380,000.

In addition, Abernethy sold inventory costing $90,000 to Chapman for $150,000 during 2002. Chapman resold $90,000 of this inventory during 2002 and the remaining $60,000 during 2003.

Required:

    a.   Prepare a schedule computing the equity income to be recognized by Abernethy during each of these years.

    b.   Compute Abernethy's investment balance as of December 31, 2003.

28. On January 1, 2001, Plano Company acquired 8 percent (16,000 shares) of the outstanding voting shares of the Sumter Company for $192,000, an amount equal to the underlying book value of Sumter. Sumter pays a cash dividend to its stockholders each year of $100,000 on September 15. Sumter reports net income of $300,000 in 2001, $360,000 in 2002, $400,000 in 2003, and $380,000 in 2004. Each income figure can be assumed to have been earned evenly throughout its respective year. In addition, the market value of these 16,000 shares was indeterminate and therefore the investment account remained at cost.

On January 1, 2003, Plano purchased an additional 32 percent (64,000 shares) of Sumter for $965,750 in cash. This price represented a $50,550 payment in excess of the book value of Sumter's underlying net assets. Plano was willing to make this extra payment because of a patent held by Sumter with a 15-year remaining life. All other assets were considered appropriately valued on Sumter's books.

On July 1, 2004, Plano sold 10 percent (20,000 shares) of the outstanding shares of Sumter for $425,000 in cash. Although this interest was sold, Plano maintained the ability to significantly influence the decision-making process of Sumter. Assume that a weighted average costing system is used by Plano.

Required:

Prepare the journal entries for Plano for the years of 2001 through 2004.

29. On January 1, 2002, Lake Company acquired 40 percent of the outstanding voting shares of Slide Company for $600,000. On that date, Slide reports assets and liabilities with book values of $1.8 million and $600,000, respectively. A building owned by Slide had an appraised value of $250,000, although it had a book value of only $100,000. This building had a 12-year remaining life and no salvage value. It was being depreciated on the straight-line method.

Slide generated net income of $250,000 in 2002 and a loss of $100,000 in 2003. In each of these two years, Slide paid a cash dividend of $60,000 to its stockholders.

During 2002, Slide sold inventory to Lake that had an original cost of $50,000. The merchandise was sold to Lake for $80,000. Of this balance, $60,000 was resold to outsiders during 2002 and the remainder was sold during 2003. In 2003, Slide sold inventory to Lake for $150,000. This inventory had cost only $90,000. Lake resold $100,000 of the inventory during 2003 and the rest during 2004.

Required:

For 2002 and then for 2003, compute the equity income to be reported by Lake for external reporting purposes.

2

Consolidation of Financial Information

QUESTIONS TO CONSIDER

- Why do firms engage in business combinations?

- When one company gains control over another company, how should the relationship between the two parties be presented for external reporting purposes?

- When the relationship between two companies is being assessed, how should control be determined?

- The assets and liabilities of some subsidiary organizations are added directly to the records of the parent company. In other cases, the parent chooses to let the new subsidiary remain in operation as a separate legal entity. How is the accounting process affected by this decision?

- Business combinations historically have been accounted for as either a purchase or a pooling of interests. Why were two methods available? How do they differ? Why did the FASB prohibit the pooling of interests method?

- Investment bankers and other financial advisors are paid millions of dollars for assisting one company in acquiring another. What accounting is made of these costs?

- How do firms account for the ongoing research and development activities of an acquired business? How do firms account for the wide range of intangible assets that frequently comprise a large proportion of the value in many business combinations?

- What are the recent changes in financial reporting for business combinations? Will these reporting changes affect the number of mergers and acquisitions?

Financial statements, published and distributed to owners, creditors, and other interested parties, appear to report the operations and financial position of a single company. In reality, these statements frequently represent a number of separate organizations tied together through common control (a *business combination*). Whenever financial statements represent more than one corporation, we refer to them as consolidated financial statements.

Consolidated financial statements are typical in today's business world. Most major organizations, and many smaller ones, hold control over an array of organizations. For example, between 1993 and 2001, Cisco Systems, Inc., reported over 40 business acquisitions that now are consolidated in its financial reports. PepsiCo, Inc., as another example, annually consolidates data from a multitude of companies into a single set of financial statements. By gaining control over these companies (often known as *subsidiaries*)—which include among others Pepsi-Cola Company, Tropicana Products, and Frito-Lay—a single business combination and single reporting entity is formed by PepsiCo (the *parent*).

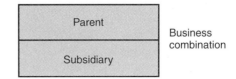

The consolidation of financial information as exemplified by Cisco Systems and PepsiCo is one of the most complex procedures in all of accounting. To comprehend this process completely, the theoretical logic that underlies the creation of a business combination must be understood.

33

Furthermore, a variety of procedural steps must be mastered to ensure that proper accounting is achieved for this single reporting entity. The following coverage introduces both of these aspects of the consolidation process.

Importantly, major changes have recently been introduced in financial reporting for business combinations. These changes are documented in the 2001 FASB pronouncements *SFAS 141*, "Business Combinations," and *SFAS 142*, "Goodwill and Other Intangible Assets." One of the most important of these changes is the FASB requirement that all business combinations should be accounted for using the purchase method, thus effectively eliminating the pooling of interests method.

In this chapter, we first provide coverage of expansion through corporate takeovers and an overview of the consolidation process. Then we present the purchase method of accounting for business combinations with specific references to *SFAS 141*. Finally, coverage of pooling of interests is provided in a separate section.

EXPANSION THROUGH CORPORATE TAKEOVERS

Why Do Firms Combine?

A common economic phenomenon is the combining of two or more businesses into a single entity under common management and owner control. During recent decades, the United States and the rest of the world have seen an enormous number of corporate mergers and takeovers, transactions in which one company gains control over another. According to *Mergerstat* (January 2001), the number of business combinations in 2000 totaled 9,602 with a total market value of $1.4 trillion, nearly tripling the 1996 value of $496 billion. As indicated by Exhibit 2–1, the magnitude of recent combinations continues to be large, although the average deal in 1999 was $425.5 million.

As with any other economic activity, business combinations can be part of an overall managerial strategy to maximize shareholder value. Shareholders—the owners of the firm—hire managers to direct resources so that the value of the firm grows over time. In this way, owners receive a return on their investment. Successful firms receive substantial benefits through enhanced share value. Importantly, the managers of successful firms also receive substantial benefits in salaries, especially if their compensation contracts are partly based on stock market performance of the firm's shares.

Exhibit 2–1
Recent Notable Business Combinations

Acquirer	Target	Cost (in billions)
America OnLine	Time Warner	$180.0
MCI Worldcom Inc.	Sprint Corp.	116.0
Pfizer, Inc.	Warner-Lambert, Inc.	80.0
Exxon Corp.	Mobil Corp.	80.0
Vodafone Group PLC	AirTouch Communications Inc.	62.8
AT&T Corp.	MediaOne Group Inc.	55.8
Qwest Communications Inc.	US West, Inc.	34.7
Viacom Inc.	CBS Corp.	34.5
BP Amoco PLC	Atlantic Richfield Inc.	26.6
Lucent Technologies Inc.	Ascend Communications Inc.	24.1
Yahoo! Inc.	Broadcast.com	4.3

If the goal of business activity is to maximize the value of the firm, in what ways do business combinations help achieve that goal? Clearly the business community is moving rapidly toward business combinations as a strategy for growth and competitiveness. Size and scale are obviously becoming critical as firms compete in today's markets. If larger firms can be more efficient in delivering goods and services, then they gain a competitive advantage and become more profitable for the owners. Increases in scale can produce larger profits from enhanced sales volume despite smaller (more competitive) profit margins. For example, if a combination can integrate successive stages of production and distribution of products, substantial savings can result in coordinating raw material purchases, manufacturing, and delivery. For example, when Ford Motor Co. acquired Hertz Rental (one of its largest customers), it not only enabled them to ensure demand for their cars, but also allowed them to closely coordinate production with the need for new rental cars. Other cost savings resulting from elimination of duplicate efforts, such as data processing and marketing, can make a single entity more profitable than the separate parent and subsidiary had been in the past.

Although no two business combinations are exactly alike, many share one or more of the following characteristics that potentially enhance profitability:

- Vertical integration of one firm's output and another firm's distribution or further processing.
- Cost savings through elimination of duplicate facilities and staff.
- Quick entry for new and existing products into domestic and foreign markets.
- Economies of scale allowing greater efficiency and negotiating power.
- The ability to access financing at more attractive rates. As firms grow in size, negotiating power with financial institutions can grow also.
- Diversification of business risk.

Business combinations also result because many firms seek the continuous expansion of their organizations, especially into diversified areas. Acquiring control over a vast network of different businesses has been a strategy utilized by a number of companies (sometimes known as conglomerates) for decades. Entry into new industries is immediately available to the parent without having to construct facilities, develop products, train management, or create market recognition. Many corporations have successfully utilized this strategy to produce huge, highly profitable organizations. Unfortunately, others have discovered that the task of managing a widely diverse group of businesses can prove to be a costly learning experience. Even combinations that purportedly take advantage of operating synergies and cost savings often fail if the integration is not managed carefully.[1]

Overall, the primary motivations for many business combinations can be traced to an increasingly competitive environment. Three recent examples of large business combinations provide interesting examples of some distinct motivations to combine: the Yahoo! acquisition of Broadcast.com, Pfizer's acquisition of Warner-Lambert, and Exxon's merger with Mobil Corporation. Each is discussed briefly in turn.

Yahoo! and Broadcast.com

On July 20, 1999, Yahoo! announced that it had completed its acquisition of Broadcast.com, a Web-based high-tech firm specializing in streaming audio and video. Yahoo! agreed to exchange 28,645,000 shares of its common stock for the remaining 37,096,000 shares of Broadcast.com that it did not already own. Yahoo!, Inc., is a global Internet media company (www.yahoo.com) that offers a branded network of comprehensive information, communication, and shopping services to users worldwide.

---

[1]Mark Sirower, "What Acquiring Minds Need to Know," *Wall Street Journal—Manager's Journal,* February 22, 1999.

Yahoo!'s revenues are derived principally from the sale of banner and sponsorship advertisements on or linked to its Web site. Broadcast.com provides a variety of programming over the Internet, including sports, music, news, and information. The company broadcasts from over 420 radio stations and 56 television stations and airs live concerts, sporting events, and music CDs.

As the Internet extends its reach into more and more markets, digital media and Web-based service firms such as Yahoo! are acquiring other fast-growth complementary service providers to expand both functionality and competitive market share. The acquisition of Broadcast.com represents the latest in a series of acquisitions that reflects a clear strategy of vertical integration and growth through combination. Since its incorporation in 1995, Yahoo! has also acquired Log-Me-On.com, a development stage enterprise involved in browser and toolbar technology; Viaweb, a provider of software and services for hosting online stores; WebCal, a privately held developer and marketer of Web-based scheduling products; HyperParallel, a company specializing in data analysis; Yoyodyne, a privately held, direct marketing services company; and GeoCities, an Internet online community aggregator. Other examples of this growth-by-acquisition strategy include Excite@Home's acquisition of the online E-greetings business of Blue Mountain Arts for $780 million, and @HomeNetwork's acquisition of Excite for $7.2 billion.

Pfizer and Warner-Lambert

On November 4, 1999, Pfizer, Inc., announced that it had made an offer to acquire all of the outstanding shares of Warner-Lambert Company by issuing stock valued at $80 billion. A Pfizer press release declared that the "merger of the two fastest-growing pharmaceutical companies will create the strongest, most dynamic pharmaceutical company in the world."

Pfizer's efforts to acquire Warner-Lambert represented the largest hostile takeover attempt to date.[2] At the time of Pfizer's bid, Warner-Lambert had already agreed to merge with American Home Products. Further complicating the merger was Pfizer's ongoing partnership with Warner-Lambert to produce and market Lipitor, a highly profitable cholesterol-reducing drug. The merger agreement between Warner-Lambert and American Home Products may have threatened the Lipitor alliance and thus prompted Pfizer to make its own merger bid for Warner-Lambert. The Pfizer and Warner-Lambert merger, however, may be attributable primarily to the need for economies of scale in the pharmaceutical industry.

Competition in the pharmaceutical industry increasingly rewards those firms that are able to quickly develop and market new drug therapies. In this environment, the ability to assemble and manage a large scientific infrastructure is essential for success and leads to a strategy of rapid growth. Because increases in research capacity can take years to develop, pharmaceutical firms such as Pfizer look to acquisition strategies as growth opportunities. Warner-Lambert, for example, has a modern lab in Ann Arbor, Michigan, and scientific staff that would significantly add to Pfizer's ability to develop new products. The combined research and development expenditures of the combined Pfizer–Warner-Lambert will approximate $4 billion annually, the largest in the pharmaceutical industry.

Exxon and Mobil

In December 1998 Exxon and Mobil announced the merger of the two companies into the Exxon Mobil Corporation. Under the terms of the agreement, each share of Mobil was converted into 1.32 shares of Exxon, leaving former Mobil shareholders with

---

[2]*Wall Street Journal,* "In Biggest Hostile Bid, Pfizer Offers $80 Billion for Warner-Lambert," November 5, 1999, p. 1.

30 percent of the combined firm and former Exxon shareholders with 70 percent. The combined firm was expected to have a 16.8 percent share of the U.S. gasoline market and follows other oil industry combinations such as BP-Amoco and the joint ventures of Texaco with Shell and Saudi Aramco.

As with many mergers, synergies were cited as a primary motivation for combining. Cost savings of $2.8 billion within two to three years were expected as the firms integrate operations and eliminate duplicate facilities such as pipelines and gas stations. In addition to cost savings, economies of scale likely played a role in the Exxon-Mobil merger. Searches for valuable oil reserves are increasingly taking place in remote or offshore areas that require extensive exploration efforts. Resulting oil field discoveries carry significant rewards when successful, but initially they require big upfront outlays and risks.[3] The combined firm carries greater resources, enabling more ambitious large-scale exploration and development activities.

THE CONSOLIDATION PROCESS

The consolidation of financial information into a single set of statements becomes necessary whenever a single economic entity is created by the business combination of two or more companies. As stated in *Accounting Research Bulletin No. 51* (abbreviated *ARB 51*), "Consolidated Financial Statements," August 1959 (par. 2): "There is a presumption that consolidated statements are more meaningful than separate statements and that they are usually necessary for a fair presentation when one of the companies in the group directly or indirectly has a controlling financial interest in the other companies."

This sentiment was reiterated nearly 30 years later in *Financial Accounting Standards Board Statement No. 94,* "Consolidation of All Majority-Owned Subsidiaries," October 1987 (par. 30): "Consolidated financial statements became common once it was recognized that boundaries between separate corporate entities must be ignored to report the business carried on by a group of affiliated corporations as the economic and financial whole that it actually is."

Thus, in producing financial statements for external distribution, the reporting entity transcends the boundaries of incorporation to encompass all companies where control is present. Even though the various companies may retain their legal identities as separate corporations, the resulting information is more meaningful to outside parties when consolidated into a single set of financial statements.

To explain the process of preparing consolidated financial statements for a business combination, we address three questions:

- How is a business combination formed?
- What constitutes a controlling financial interest?
- How is the consolidation process carried out?

Business Combinations—Creating a Single Economic Entity

A business combination refers to any set of conditions in which two or more organizations are joined together through common control. *SFAS 141* defines a business combination as follows:

A *business combination* occurs when an enterprise acquires net assets that constitute a business or equity interests of one or more other enterprises and obtains control over that enterprise or enterprises.

---

[3]Steven Mufson, "Deal Allowed Exxon to Expand Oil Reserve," *Washington Post*, December 2, 1998, p. 16A.

Business combinations are formed by a wide variety of transactions with various formats. For example, each of the following is identified as a business combination although differing widely in legal form. In every case, two or more enterprises are being united into a single economic entity so that consolidated financial statements are required.

1. One company obtains the assets, and often the liabilities, of another company in exchange for cash, other assets, liabilities, stock, or a combination of these. The second organization normally dissolves itself as a legal corporation. Thus, only the acquiring company remains in existence, having absorbed the acquired net assets directly into its own operations. Any business combination in which only one of the original companies continues to exist is referred to in legal terms as a *statutory merger.*

2. One company obtains the capital stock of another in exchange for cash, other assets, liabilities, stock, or a combination of these. After gaining control, the acquiring company may decide to transfer all assets and liabilities to its own financial records with the second company being dissolved as a separate corporation.[4] The business combination is, once again, a statutory merger because only one of the companies maintains legal existence. This statutory merger, however, is achieved by obtaining equity securities rather than by buying the target company's assets. Because stock is purchased, the acquiring company must gain 100 percent control of all shares before legally dissolving the subsidiary.

3. Two or more companies transfer either their assets or their capital stock to a newly formed corporation. The original companies both are dissolved, leaving only the new organization in existence. A business combination effected in this manner is a *statutory consolidation.* The use here of the term *consolidation* should not be confused with the accounting meaning of that same word. In accounting, consolidation refers to the mechanical process of bringing together the financial records of two or more organizations to form a single set of statements. A statutory consolidation denotes a specific type of business combination in which two or more existing companies are united under the ownership of a newly created company.

The business combination of NCNB Corporation and C&S/Sovran Corporation illustrates the formation of a statutory consolidation. The stockholders of these two organizations created a single entity by transferring their ownership interests to a newly established corporation known as NationsBank Corporation. Because only this new company remained in existence as a legal entity, the business combination is a statutory consolidation.

4. One company achieves legal control over another by the acquisition of a majority of voting stock. *Although control is present, no dissolution takes place; each company remains in existence as an incorporated operation.* The National Broadcasting Company (NBC), as an example, continued to retain its legal status as a corporation after being acquired by General Electric Company. Separate incorporation is frequently preferred to take full advantage of any intangible benefits accruing to the acquired company as a going concern. Better utilization of such factors as trade names, employee loyalty, and the company's reputation may be possible where the subsidiary maintains its own legal identity.

One important aspect of this final type of business combination should be noted. Because the asset and liability account balances are not physically combined as in statutory mergers and consolidations, each company continues to maintain an independent accounting system. To reflect the creation of the combination, the acquiring

---

[4]Although the acquired company has been legally dissolved, it frequently continues to operate as a separate division within the surviving company's organization.

Type of Combination	Action of Acquiring Company	Action of Acquired Company
Statutory merger through asset acquisition.	Acquires assets and often liabilities.	Dissolves and goes out of business.
Statutory merger through capital stock acquisition.	Acquires all stock and then transfers assets and liabilities to its own books.	Dissolves as a separate corporation, often remaining as a division of the acquiring company.
Statutory consolidation through capital stock or asset acquisition.	Newly created to receive assets or capital stock of original companies.	Original companies may dissolve while remaining as separate divisions of newly created company.
Acquisition of more than 50 percent of the voting stock.	Acquires stock that is recorded as an investment; controls decision making of acquired company.	Remains in existence as legal corporation, although now a subsidiary of the acquiring company.

company enters the financial impact of the takeover transaction into its own records by establishing a single investment asset account. However, the newly acquired subsidiary omits any recording of this event; the stock being obtained by the parent comes from the subsidiary's shareholders. Thus, the financial records of the subsidiary are not directly affected by a takeover.

As can be seen, business combinations are created in many distinct forms. Since the specific format is a critical factor in the subsequent consolidation of financial information, Exhibit 2–2 provides an overview of the various combinations.

Control—An Elusive Quality

ARB 51, as quoted previously, states that consolidated financial statements are usually necessary when one company has a controlling financial interest over another. However, nowhere in the official accounting pronouncements is a "controlling financial interest" actually defined. Traditionally, in the United States, control is considered to exist if one company holds more than 50 percent of another company's voting stock. Thus, control has been tied directly to ownership. However, in the decades since *ARB 51* was issued, the complexity of business combinations has grown significantly so that control is not always that easy to define.

The FASB has a comprehensive study underway of consolidation issues, including the question of control. Chances seem likely that consolidation will eventually be required for less-than-majority-owned subsidiaries if the parent has rights, risks, and benefits equivalent to those that result from majority ownership.

The types of situations that led the FASB to study the issue of control include the following cases. In none of these instances is a majority of the voting stock held. Thus, historically in the United States, consolidation would probably not occur.[5] However, one company certainly does have the potential to exercise a degree of authority over the other. In looking at such cases, two interrelated questions must be addressed: Does one company actually have a controlling financial interest over the other? Has a business combination been created that necessitates the production of consolidated financial statements?

---

[5]In contrast, Australia, Canada, New Zealand, the United Kingdom, and the European Community all have standards specifying control rather than ownership as the basis for consolidation.

- Company A owns 48 percent of Company B. At the stockholders' meeting each year, only about 90 percent of the outstanding shares are voted so that Company A always casts a majority of the shares on every ballot.
- Company C owns 40 percent of Company D. Ms. Z is president of Company D and owns 11 percent of its stock. Ms. Z is a former vice president and friend of Company C and has always voted her shares in the same manner as Company C.
- Company E owns none of Company F. However, Company E holds convertible bonds issued by Company F. Company E has the option at any time to convert these bonds into 51 percent of the outstanding voting shares of Company F.
- As described in Chapter 1, The Coca-Cola Company holds 40 percent of Coca-Cola Enterprises. Furthermore, the investee is heavily dependent on the investor for products and marketing.

In studying these issues, the FASB describes what is meant by control:

Control of an Entity: The ability of an entity to direct the policies and management that guide the ongoing activities of another entity so as to increase its benefits and limit its losses from that other entity's activities. For purposes of consolidated financial statements, control involves decision-making ability that is not shared with others.[6]

The FASB noted the following presumptions of control exist for those circumstances in which an entity:

- Has a majority voting interest in the election of a corporation's governing body or a right to appoint a majority of the members of its governing body.
- Has a large minority voting interest in the election of a corporation's governing body and no other party or organized group of parties has a significant voting interest.
- Has a unilateral ability to (1) obtain a majority voting interest in the election of a corporation's governing body or (2) obtain a right to appoint a majority of the corporation's governing body through the present ownership of convertible securities or other rights that are currently exercisable at the option of the holder and the expected benefit from converting those securities or exercising that right exceeds its expected cost.

Consolidation of Financial Information

Whenever one company gains control over another, a business combination is established. Financial data gathered from the individual companies is then brought together to form a single set of consolidated statements. Although this process can be complicated, the objectives of a consolidation are straightforward. The asset, liability, equity, revenue, and expense accounts of the companies simply are combined. As a part of this process, reciprocal accounts and intercompany transactions must be adjusted or eliminated to ensure that all reported balances truly represent the single entity.

Applicable consolidation procedures vary significantly depending on the legal format employed in creating a business combination. *For a statutory merger or a statutory consolidation, where the acquired company (or companies) is legally dissolved, only one accounting consolidation ever occurs.* On the date of the combination, the surviving company simply records the various account balances from each of the dissolving companies. Because all accounts are brought together permanently in this manner, no further consolidation procedures are necessary. After all of the balances are transferred to the survivor, the financial records of the acquired companies are closed out as part of the dissolution.

---

[6]Financial Accounting Standards Board Exposure Draft (Revised), *Consolidated Financial Statements: Purpose and Policy*, February 23, 1999.

Conversely, in a combination where all companies retain incorporation, a different set of consolidation procedures is appropriate. Because the companies preserve their legal identities, each continues to maintain its own independent accounting records. *Thus, no permanent consolidation of the account balances is ever made. Rather, the consolidation process must be carried out anew each time that the reporting entity prepares financial statements for external reporting purposes.*

Where separate record-keeping is maintained, the accountant faces a unique problem: The financial information must be brought together periodically without disturbing the accounting systems of the individual companies. Since these consolidations are produced outside the financial records, worksheets traditionally are used to expedite the process. Worksheets are neither part of either companies' accounting records nor the resulting financial statements. Instead, they are an efficient structure for organizing and adjusting the information used in the preparation of externally reported consolidated statements.

Consequently, the legal characteristics of a business combination have a significant impact on the approach taken to the consolidation process:

What is to be consolidated?

- If dissolution takes place, all account balances are physically consolidated in the financial records of the surviving company.
- If separate incorporation is maintained, only the financial statement information is consolidated and not the actual records.

When does the consolidation take place?

- If dissolution takes place, a permanent consolidation occurs at the date of the combination.
- If separate incorporation is maintained, the consolidation process is carried out at regular intervals whenever financial statements are to be prepared.

How are the accounting records affected?

- If dissolution takes place, the surviving company's accounts are adjusted to include all balances of the dissolved company. The dissolved company's records are closed out.
- If separate incorporation is maintained, each company continues to retain its own records. Using worksheets facilitates the periodic consolidation process without disturbing the individual accounting systems.

FINANCIAL REPORTING FOR BUSINESS COMBINATIONS—*SFAS 141*

The Purchase Method: Change in Ownership

The fundamental characteristic of any purchase—whether a single asset or a multibillion dollar corporation—is a change in ownership. In any exchange transaction, a basic accounting principle is the recording of the cost to the new owners. Thus, in a business combination accounted for as a purchase, the acquisition cost to the new owners provides the valuation basis for the net assets acquired. For example, as shown in Exhibit 2–3, AT&T recently purchased Tele-Communications, Inc. (TCI) for approximately $36 billion. This purchase price then served as the basis for valuing TCI's assets and liabilities in the preparation of AT&T's consolidated financial statements.

When a single asset is purchased, application of the cost principle is straightforward. In a business combination, however, the application of the cost principle is complicated because of the literally hundreds of assets and liabilities that often are acquired. *As a result, the purchase method not only establishes cost as the appropriate valuation basis for these items but also must allocate the total acquisition cost among the various assets and liabilities received in the bargained exchange.* The cost allocation procedure

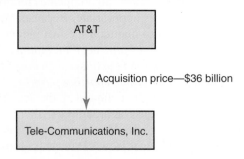

Exhibit 2-3
Business Combination—
Purchase

employed by the purchase method is based on the fair market values of the acquired assets and liabilities at the date of acquisition. Moreover, because income can only accrue to owners after the purchase of an asset (or an entire company), only revenues and expenses generated by these assets and liabilities after the acquisition date are attributed to the business combination.

PROCEDURES FOR CONSOLIDATING FINANCIAL INFORMATION

Legal as well as accounting distinctions divide business combinations into at least four separate categories. To facilitate the introduction of consolidation accounting, we present the various procedures utilized in this process according to the following sequence:

1. Purchase method where dissolution takes place.
2. Purchase method where separate incorporation is maintained.

As a basis for this coverage, assume that Smallport Company owns computers, telecommunications equipment, and software that allow its customers to implement billing and ordering systems through the Internet/World Wide Web. Although the computers and equipment have a book value of $400,000, they have a current value of $600,000. The software developed by Smallport has only a $100,000 value on its books—the costs of developing the software were primarily expensed as incurred. The observable fair market value of the software, however, is $1,600,000. Smallport also has a note payable of $200,000 incurred to help finance the software development. Because interest rates are currently low, this liability (incurred at a higher rate of interest) has a present value of $250,000.

BigNet Company owns Internet communications equipment and other business software applications that complement those of Smallport. BigNet wants to expand its operations and plans to acquire Smallport on December 31. The accounts reported by both BigNet and Smallport on that date are listed in Exhibit 2–4. In addition, the estimated fair market value of Smallport's assets and liabilities is included.

Smallport's net assets (assets less liabilities) have a book value of $600,000 but a fair market value of $2,250,000. Only the assets and liabilities have been appraised here; the capital stock, retained earnings, dividend, revenue, and expense accounts represent historical measurements rather than any type of future values. Although these equity and income accounts may give some indication of the overall worth of the organization, they are not property and thus not transferred in the combination.

Purchase Method Where Dissolution Takes Place

The purchase method employs the cost principle in recording a business combination— the total value assigned to the net assets received equals the total cost of the acquisition. The major accounting challenge, however, is the allocation of that cost among the various assets and liabilities obtained in the acquisition. These allocations depend on

Exhibit 2–4
Basic Consolidation
Information

	BigNet Company Book Value December 31	Smallport Company	
		Book Value December 31	Fair Market Value December 31
Current assets	$ 400,000	$ 300,000	$ 300,000
Computers and equipment (net)	2,000,000	400,000	600,000
Capitalized software (net)	500,000	100,000	1,600,000
Notes payable	(300,000)	(200,000)	(250,000)
Net assets	$2,600,000	$ 600,000	$2,250,000
Common stock—$5 par value	$1,600,000		
Common stock—$10 par value		$ 100,000	
Additional paid-in capital	40,000	20,000	
Retained earnings, 1/1	870,000	370,000	
Dividends paid	(110,000)	(10,000)	
Revenues	1,000,000	500,000	
Expenses	(800,000)	(380,000)	
Owners' equity 12/31	$2,600,000	$ 600,000	
Retained earnings, 12/31	960,000*	480,000*	

*Retained earnings balance after closing out revenues, expenses, and dividends paid.

the relation between total cost and the fair market values of the acquired firm's assets and liabilities. Therefore, we demonstrate the consolidation procedures in this initial section using four examples, each with a different price relative to fair market value.

Purchase Price Equals Fair Market Value   Assume that after negotiations with the owners of Smallport, BigNet agrees to pay $2,250,000 for all of Smallport's assets and liabilities: cash of $250,000 and 20,000 unissued shares of its $5 par value common stock that is currently selling for $100 per share. Smallport will then dissolve itself as a legal entity.

As with any acquisition, the price established here is based on the value of the consideration paid.

Cash	$ 250,000
Common stock issued (20,000 shares at a $100 per share fair market value)	2,000,000
Purchase price	$2,250,000

Therefore, BigNet's cost is exactly equal to the $2,250,000 fair market value of the individual assets and liabilities acquired.

The purchase method is appropriate for consolidating the financial information of these two companies—all of the essential characteristics are present. A bargained exchange occurred between BigNet, the acquiring company, and the owners of Smallport. This transaction indicates a $2,250,000 purchase price will form the basis for the consolidated figures in the financial statements of the resulting single economic entity.

At the date of acquisition, the purchase method consolidates all subsidiary asset and liability accounts based on their fair market values. The acquired assets and liabilities are recorded as if the parent had simply obtained them by paying market value. Because the negotiated price here equals this total value, the parent records each of these accounts as though purchased individually. As we subsequently demonstrate, variations from this rule exist if the parent pays less than market value.

Because Smallport Company will be dissolved, BigNet (the surviving company) directly records a consolidation entry in its financial records. As a purchase, BigNet consolidates Smallport's assets and liabilities at market value; original book values are ignored. Revenue, expense, dividend, and equity accounts cannot be transferred to a parent and are omitted in recording the business combination as a purchase.

Purchase Method—Parent Pays Market Value—Subsidiary Dissolved

BigNet Company's Financial Records—December 31

Current Assets.	300,000	
Computers and Equipment.	600,000	
Capitalized Software	1,600,000	
Notes Payable.		250,000
Cash (paid by BigNet)		250,000
Common Stock (20,000 shares issued by BigNet		
at $5 par value).		100,000
Additional Paid-In Capital (value of shares issued		
by BigNet in excess of par value).		1,900,000

To record purchase of net assets of Smallport Company for $2,250,000. Subsidiary accounts are recorded at market value which total (net) to the same $2,250,000.

BigNet's financial records now show $2,600,000 in the Computers and Equipment account ($2,000,000 former balance + $600,000 acquired), $2,100,000 in Capitalized Software ($500,000 + $1,600,000), and so forth. These items have been added into BigNet's balances (see Exhibit 2–4) at their fair market values. Conversely, BigNet's revenue balance continues to report the company's own $1,000,000 with expenses remaining at $800,000 and dividends of $110,000. *In a purchase, only the subsidiary's revenues, expenses, dividends, and equity transactions that occur subsequent to the takeover affect the business combination.*[7]

Purchase Price Exceeds Fair Market Value   The negotiated price in this second illustration is assumed to be $3,000,000 in exchange for all of Smallport's assets and liabilities. The mode of payment by BigNet will be $1,000,000 in cash plus 20,000 shares of common stock with a market value of $100 per share. The resulting purchase price is $750,000 more than the $2,250,000 fair market value of Smallport's net assets. In purchase combinations, such excess payments are not unusual. For example, when Amazon.com acquired Junglee, a provider of Web-based virtual database technology, substantially the entire $180 million purchase price was allocated to goodwill and other intangibles.

The $2,250,000 market value of Smallport's net assets certainly may influence any takeover offer. However, any number of other factors can affect BigNet's $3,000,000 acquisition offer, such as Smallport's history of profitability, the company's reputation, the quality of its personnel, or the economic condition of the industry in which it operates. If Smallport, for example, demonstrates the ability to generate especially high profits, BigNet may be willing to pay an extra amount for this company. One additional factor frequently affects an acquisition price—the presence of competitive buyers. If BigNet must outbid other companies to acquire Smallport, the purchase price may simply represent the bidding war.

Whenever the price paid in a purchase exceeds total fair market value, all of the subsidiary's assets and liabilities are consolidated at fair market value with the addi-

---

[7]Chapter 4 describes an alternative method of reporting a purchase that occurs within the current year. All of the subsidiary's revenues and expenses for the entire year are included in the consolidated totals with the income earned prior to the purchase then being subtracted on the income statement as a single Preacquisition Income figure. Thus, consolidated net income is not affected by subsidiary operations occurring before the purchase but the reported revenue and expense balances are more comparable with future periods.

tional payment allocated to the intangible asset goodwill. This excess amount may actually reflect the profitability often inherent in a going concern, the creative ability of a research group, market conditions that surrounded the acquisition, or myriad other possible factors. Because the conditions that can influence a purchase price are virtually unlimited, any amount paid in excess of the fair market value assigned to identifiable assets (both tangible and intangible) is simply assigned arbitrarily to goodwill.

Alternative account titles such as Unamortized Cost in Excess of Market Value or some variation have also been widely used in recent years to identify this general allocation of any excess purchase price. Unisys, for example, recently reported a $1.0 billion asset as a "cost in excess of net assets acquired" on its balance sheet. Traditionally, the term *goodwill* refers to a computationally derived excess payment based on the estimated future profits of a going concern. Because the extra amount paid in the purchase of another company may result from many factors, a more descriptive label such as the one reported by Unisys might be preferable. However, goodwill is specifically used in the FASB documents and professional literature and is, therefore, incorporated throughout this textbook.

Returning to BigNet's $3,000,000 purchase, $750,000 of this price was in excess of the fair market value of Smallport's net assets. Thus, goodwill of that amount is entered into BigNet's accounting system along with the fair market value of each individual account. The actual journal entry made by BigNet at the date of acquisition follows:

Purchase Method—Parent Pays More Than Market Value—Subsidiary Dissolved

BigNet Company's Financial Records—December 31

Current Assets.	300,000	
Computers and Equipment	600,000	
Capitalized Software	1,600,000	
Goodwill.	750,000	
Notes Payable		250,000
Cash (paid by BigNet)		1,000,000
Common Stock (20,000 shares issued by BigNet		
at $5 par value)		100,000
Additional Paid-In Capital (value of shares issued		
by BigNet in excess of par value).		1,900,000

To record purchase of net assets of Smallport Company for $3,000,000. Subsidiary accounts are recorded at market value with $750,000 excess payment attributed to goodwill.

Once again, BigNet's financial records show $2,600,000 in the Computers and Equipment account ($2,000,000 former balance + $600,000 acquired), $2,100,000 in Capitalized Software ($500,000 + $1,600,000), and so forth. As the only change, a Goodwill balance of $750,000 is established to account for the excess purchase price paid by BigNet.

Purchase Price Less Than Fair Market Value   For this third example, the price paid to the owners of Smallport is assumed to be $2,000,000. BigNet conveys no cash and issues 20,000 shares of common stock having a $100 per share fair market value. To add a new element to this illustration, BigNet elects to pay $30,000 in accountants' and lawyers' fees directly associated with the combination as well as $10,000 for registering and issuing the shares of common stock.

In this combination, the parent's cost comprises more than one component. According to current reporting standards, any direct costs of establishing a purchase combination is regarded as part of the total acquisition price. Expenditures such as payments to lawyers and accountants as well as finders' fees are necessary to carry out a purchase and are thus capitalized. Such combination costs can be significant. In describing the takeover battle for RJR Nabisco, *Time* magazine estimated that the "hundreds of lawyers and investment bankers involved in the bidding stand to earn a total of as much as $1 billion for their expertise."

The accountants' and lawyers' fees of $30,000 are thus included by BigNet in computing a purchase price of $2,030,000, the total cost of acquiring Smallport's assets and liabilities ($2,000,000 to the owners of Smallport and $30,000 for these direct costs). However, the remaining $10,000 was paid to register and issue the common stock. This amount is considered a cost associated with these securities rather than a cost of the purchase. As such, the $10,000 is assumed to be a reduction in the additional paid-in capital recorded for the newly issued shares.

BigNet's total purchase price of $2,030,000 is $220,000 less than the fair market value of Smallport's net assets. Allocation of full market values to each asset and liability is simply not possible; some reduction must be made. A cost of $2,030,000 cannot be assigned to accounts having a fair market value of $2,250,000 without an adjustment. To address this problem, the values otherwise assignable to noncurrent assets acquired should be reduced by a proportionate part of the excess to determine the assigned values.[8] *Therefore, when a purchase price is less than total fair market value of the net assets, noncurrent accounts, such as Computers and Equipment and Capitalized Software, are consolidated at reduced balances. All remaining assets and liabilities continue to be recorded at their fair market values.*

Because BigNet paid $220,000 less than fair market value ($2,250,000 − $2,030,000), the balances of any noncurrent assets being acquired (other than long-term investments in marketable securities) must be decreased by that amount. As indicated in Exhibit 2–4, the two applicable accounts in this example have a total fair market value of $2,200,000:

Noncurrent Asset Accounts	Fair Market Values	
Computers and Equipment	$ 600,000	27.27%
Capitalized Software	1,600,000	72.73
Total	$2,200,000	100%

Because of BigNet's payment, these two accounts must be reduced in consolidation by a total of $220,000 (from $2,200,000 to $1,980,000). The balance reported for Computers and Equipment is lowered by $60,000 ($220,000 × 27.27%). The remaining $160,000 ($220,000 × 72.73%) is assigned as a decrease to the Capitalized Software account. Therefore, for consolidation purposes, BigNet records Smallport's Computers and Equipment at $540,000 ($60,000 less than its $600,000 fair market value). The Capitalized Software account is entered at $1,440,000 ($1,600,000 − $160,000). All other assets and liabilities are consolidated at their fair market values.

Purchase Method—Parent Pays Less Than Market Value—Subsidiary Dissolved

BigNet Company's Financial Records—December 31

Current Assets.	300,000	
Computers and Equipment.	540,000	
Capitalized Software	1,440,000	
Notes Payable.		250,000
Common Stock (20,000 shares issued by BigNet at $5 par value).		100,000
Additional Paid-In Capital (value of shares issued by BigNet in excess of par value)		1,900,000
Cash (direct acquisition costs)		30,000

[8]Excluded from the proportionate reduction are financial assets other than equity method investments, assets to be disposed of by sale, deferred tax assets, and prepaid assets relating to pension or other postretirement benefit plans. According to *SFAS 141,* these assets should be recorded at assessed fair values.

Additional Paid-In Capital (stock costs)...................	10,000	
Cash		10,000

    To record purchase of net assets of Smallport. Payment includes
$30,000 direct acquisition costs and the $10,000 cost of registering
and issuing common stock. Total purchase price of $2,030,000
is $220,000 less than market value of the net assets, an amount
assigned to noncurrent assets.

Purchase Price Substantially Less Than Fair Market Value   In this final illustration, the exchange price for Smallport's net assets is assumed to be $40,000 with payment made entirely in cash. Obviously, expending this amount for net assets valued at $2,250,000 is an extreme case that indicates an unusual circumstance such as imminent bankruptcy, large contingent liabilities, or an urgent need by the present owners for immediate liquidation. A company, for example, that has its entire business centered on marketing one patent might see the price of its stock drop to nearly zero if the legality of that patent were seriously threatened.

    With a purchase price of only $40,000, Smallport's assets and liabilities must be consolidated at balances of $2,210,000—substantially less than their total fair market value of $2,250,000. As was indicated in the previous example, this decrease initially is made in recording the noncurrent assets. However, these two assets (Computers and Equipment and Capitalized Software) have a total worth of only $2,200,000. Even decreasing their balances to zero will not fully account for the $2,210,000 difference between the purchase price and total fair market value. A further reduction of $10,000 must be assigned within the consolidation process.

    Whenever a purchase price is less than fair market value so that the acquired applicable noncurrent asset balances are eliminated entirely, an additional reduction is needed. According to SFAS 141, the additional reduction is reported as an extraordinary gain.[9] All other assets and liabilities are still brought into the combination at fair market value. The extraordinary gain results from a bargain purchase, but only comes into existence after the applicable noncurrent assets are first decreased to zero. Thus, either the price has to be extremely low or the acquired noncurrent assets must be of a relatively small value.

    The FASB decision that an unallocated excess fair value over cost should be reported as an extraordinary gain was not without its critics. Some argued that to record a gain upon a purchase transaction is conceptually unsound. However, the FASB reasoned that the extraordinary gain treatment appropriately highlights the fact that an excess exists and that such occurrences are both infrequent and unusual in nature. The Board also observed that regardless of whether an extraordinary gain or a deferred credit results, income ultimately increases—either immediately or in future periods.

    Because the $40,000 price in this illustration is $2,210,000 less than fair market value, BigNet's journal entry to record its purchase of Smallport's assets and liabilities would:

1. Recognize no balances for the two noncurrent asset accounts.
2. Allocate the remaining $10,000 reduction to an extraordinary gain.
3. Report all remaining asset and liability accounts at fair market value.

---

[9]Prior to *SFAS 141,* such additional reductions were reported in a deferred credit account and systematically amortized to income.

Purchase Method—Parent Pays Substantially Less Than Market Value— Subsidiary Dissolved

BigNet Company's Financial Records—December 31

Current Assets....................................	300,000	
Computers and Equipment............................	–0–	
Capitalized Software	–0–	
Notes Payable....................................		250,000
Extraordinary Gain—Excess of Market Value over Cost of Acquisition..................................		10,000
Cash (paid by BigNet)		40,000

To record acquisition of Smallport's net assets for $40,000, an amount $2,210,000 below market value.

Summary of the Purchase Method   In a purchase, acquired assets and liabilities are normally consolidated at their fair market values. However, the relationship between purchase price and total market value can necessitate some alterations to this rule. An excess payment, for example, leads to the creation of a Goodwill account. A low purchase price forces a reduction in the recorded balance of applicable noncurrent assets and possibly the recognition of an extraordinary gain. Exhibit 2–5 summarizes the possible allocation scenarios.

Purchase Method Where Separate Incorporation Is Maintained

When each company retains separate incorporation in a purchase combination, many aspects of the consolidation process are identical to those demonstrated in the previous section. Fair market value, for example, remains as the basis for initially consolidating the subsidiary's asset and liability accounts.

Several significant differences exist in purchase combinations in which each company remains a legally incorporated entity. Most noticeably, the consolidation of the financial information is only simulated rather than having the acquiring company physically record the acquired assets and liabilities. Because dissolution does not occur, each company maintains independent record-keeping. To facilitate the preparation of consolidated financial statements, a worksheet and consolidation entries are employed using the data gathered from these separate companies.

A worksheet provides the structure for generating information to be reported by the single economic entity. An integral part of this process is the inclusion of consolidation worksheet entries. *These adjustments and eliminations are entered on the worksheet and represent alterations that would be required if the financial records were to be*

Exhibit 2–5
Consolidation Values—The Purchase Method

Purchase price equals the fair market value of net assets.	Acquired assets and liabilities are assigned their fair market values.
Purchase price is greater than the fair market value of the net assets.	Acquired assets and liabilities are assigned their fair market values. The excess payment is attributed to goodwill.
Purchase price is less than the fair market value of the net assets.	Current assets, liabilities, financial assets, deferred taxes, assets to be held for sale, and prepaid pension assets are assigned their fair market values. The values of other noncurrent assets are reduced proportionally. If necessary, an extraordinary gain is recognized.

physically united. Because no actual union occurs, consolidation entries are never formally recorded in the journals of either company. Instead, they are produced solely for use on the worksheet to assist in deriving consolidated account balances of the two separate companies. The resulting consolidated balances then form the basis for the financial reports of the consolidated entity.

To illustrate using the previous information, assume that BigNet acquires Smallport Company on December 31, by issuing 26,000 shares of $5 par value common stock valued at $100 per share (or $2,600,000 in total). Direct acquisition costs of $40,000 also are paid by BigNet, resulting in a total purchase price of $2,640,000.

For business reasons, BigNet decides to allow Smallport to continue as a separate corporation. Therefore, whenever financial statements for this combination are prepared, a worksheet is utilized in simulating the consolidation of these two companies. Although the assets and liabilities are not transferred, BigNet must still record the payment made to Smallport's owners. When the subsidiary remains separate, the parent establishes an Investment account that initially reflects the purchase price.

Purchase Method—Subsidiary Is Not Dissolved

BigNet Company's Financial Records—December 31

Investment in Smallport Company (purchase price)	2,640,000	
Cash (paid for direct acquisition costs)		40,000
Common Stock (26,000 shares issued by BigNet		
at $5 par value).		130,000
Additional Paid-In Capital (value of shares issued by		
BigNet in excess of par value)		2,470,000
To record purchase of Smallport Company, which will		
maintain its separate legal identity.		

As demonstrated in Exhibit 2–6, a worksheet can be prepared on the date of acquisition to arrive at consolidated totals for this combination. The entire process consists of seven steps:

Step 1   Whenever a worksheet is constructed, a formal allocation of the purchase price should be made as was done for the equity method in Chapter 1.[10] Thus, the following schedule is appropriate for BigNet's purchase of Smallport:

Purchase price paid by BigNet		$2,640,000
Book value of Smallport (see Exhibit 2–4)		600,000
Excess of cost over book value		$2,040,000
Allocations made to specific accounts based on difference		
in fair market values and book values:		
Computers and Equipment ($600,000 − $400,000)	$ 200,000	
Capitalized Software ($1,600,000 − $100,000)	1,500,000	
Notes Payable ($250,000 − $200,000)	(50,000)	1,650,000
Excess cost not identified with specific accounts—goodwill		$ 390,000

No part of the $2,040,000 excess payment is attributed to the current assets because the book value and market value are identical. The Notes Payable shows a negative allocation; because this debt's present value is more than book value, the company's net assets are actually worth *less.*

---

[10]This allocation procedure is helpful but not critical if dissolution occurs. Unless the purchase price is less than total market value, the asset and liability accounts are simply added directly into the parent's books at their assessed worth with any excess assigned to goodwill.

Exhibit 2–6   Purchase Method—Date of Acquisition

| | | | Consolidation Entries | | Consolidated |
Accounts	BigNet	Smallport	Debits	Credits	Totals
Income Statement					
Revenues	(1,000,000)				(1,000,000)
Expenses	800,000				800,000
Net income	(200,000)				(200,000)
Statement of Retained Earnings					
Retained earnings, 1/1	(870,000)				(870,000)
Net income (above)	(200,000)				(200,000)
Dividends paid	110,000				110,000
Retained earnings, 12/31	(960,000)				(960,000)
Balance Sheet					
Current assets	360,000 *	300,000			660,000
Investment in Smallport Company	2,640,000 *	–0–		(S) 600,000	–0–
				(A) 2,040,000	
Computers and equipment	2,000,000	400,000	(A) 200,000		2,600,000
Capitalized software	500,000	100,000	(A) 1,500,000		2,100,000
Goodwill	–0–	–0–	(A) 390,000		390,000
Total assets	5,500,000	800,000			5,750,000
Notes payable	(300,000)	(200,000)		(A) 50,000	(550,000)
Common stock	(1,730,000)*	(100,000)	(S) 100,000		(1,730,000)
Additional paid-in capital	(2,510,000)*	(20,000)	(S) 20,000		(2,510,000)
Retained earnings, 12/31 (above)	(960,000)	(480,000)	(S) 480,000		(960,000)
Total liabilities and equities	(5,500,000)	(800,000)			(5,750,000)

BIGNET COMPANY AND SMALLPORT COMPANY Consolidation Worksheet For Period Ending December 31

Note: Parentheses indicate a credit balance.
*Balances have been adjusted for issuance of stock and payment of consolidation costs.

Step 2 The financial figures from the separate companies as of the date of acquisition (see Exhibit 2–4) are shown in the first two columns of the worksheet (see Exhibit 2–6). BigNet's accounts have been adjusted for the investment entry recorded earlier. As another preliminary step, Smallport's revenue, expense, and dividend accounts have been closed into its retained earnings. In a purchase, the operations of the subsidiary prior to the December 31st takeover have no direct bearing on the business combination. These activities occurred before Smallport was acquired; thus, the resulting data should not be reported as income earned by the new owners in the consolidated statements.

Step 3 Smallport's stockholders' equity accounts are eliminated through consolidation Entry **S** (**S** is a reference to beginning subsidiary **S**tockholders' equity). These balances (Common Stock, Additional Paid-In Capital, and Retained Earnings) are historical measurements of subsidiary transactions that occurred prior to the combination. By removing these accounts, only Smallport's assets and liabilities remain to be combined with the parent company figures.

Step 4 Also in worksheet Entry **S,** the $600,000 component of the Investment in Smallport Company account that equates to the book value of the subsidiary's net assets is removed. For external reporting purposes, the combination should report each individual account rather than a single investment balance. In effect, this portion of the Investment in Smallport Company account is deleted and replaced by the specific assets and liabilities that it represents.

Step 5 In Entry **A,** the $2,040,000 excess payment in the Investment in Smallport Company is removed and assigned to the specific accounts indicated by the purchase price allocation. Consequently, Computers and Equipment is increased by $200,000 to agree with Smallport's market value; $1,500,000 is attributed to the Capitalized Software and $50,000 to the Notes Payable. The unexplained excess of $390,000 is recorded as goodwill. This entry is labeled entry **A** to indicate that it represents the **Al**locations made in connection with the parent's purchase price. It also completes the elimination of the entire Investment in Smallport account.

Step 6 All accounts are extended into the "Consolidated Totals" column. For accounts such as Current Assets, this process is no more than the addition of Smallport's book value to that of BigNet. However, where applicable, this extension also includes any allocations to establish the fair market value of Smallport's asset and liability accounts. Computers and Equipment, as an example, is increased by $200,000. By raising the subsidiary's book value to market value, the reported balances are the same as in the previous examples where dissolution occurred. The use of a worksheet does not alter the consolidated figures, only the method of deriving those numbers.

Step 7 Consolidated expenses are subtracted from revenues to arrive at a net income of $200,000. Note that because this is a date of acquisition worksheet, no amounts for Smallport's revenues and expenses are included in the Smallport Company column. BigNet has just purchased Smallport and therefore Smallport has not yet earned any income for the owners of BigNet. Consolidated revenues, expenses, and net income are identical to BigNet's balances. In years subsequent to acquisition, of course, Smallport's income accounts will be consolidated with BigNet's.

In general, totals (such as net income and ending retained earnings) are not directly consolidated on the worksheet. Rather, the components (such as revenues and expenses) are extended across and then combined to derive the appropriate figure. Net income is then carried down on the worksheet to the Statement of Retained Earnings and used (along with beginning retained earnings and dividends paid) to compute this December 31 equity balance. In the same manner, ending retained earnings of $960,000 is entered into the balance sheet to arrive at total liabilities and equities of $5,750,000, a number that reconciles with the total of consolidated assets.

The balances in the final column of Exhibit 2–6 are used to prepare consolidated financial statements for the business combination of BigNet Company and Smallport Company. The worksheet entries serve as a catalyst to bring together the two independent sets of financial information. Thus, the actual accounting records of both BigNet and Smallport remain unaltered by this consolidation process.

PURCHASE PRICE ALLOCATIONS—ADDITIONAL ISSUES—SFAS 141

Intangibles

An important accounting element of business combinations is the proper allocation of the purchase price to the underlying assets and liabilities acquired. In particular, the advent of the information age brings new challenges for a host of intangible assets that provide value in generating future cash flows. Often, intangible assets comprise the largest proportion of the purchase price of an acquired firm. For example, when Disney acquired Capital Cities/ABC, $18.9 billion of the purchase price was allocated to good-will. In addressing the importance of proper asset recognition, the FASB in *SFAS 141* observes that intangible assets include both current and noncurrent assets (not includ-ing financial instruments) that lack physical substance. Further, in determining whether to recognize an intangible asset in a business combination, *SFAS 141* relies on two es-sential attributes. First, does the intangible asset arise from contractual or other legal rights? Second, is the asset capable of being sold or otherwise separated from the ac-quired enterprise? As stated in *SFAS 141,*

> An intangible asset shall be recognized as an asset apart from goodwill if it arises from contractual or other legal rights (regardless of whether those rights are transferable or sep-arable from the acquired entity or from other rights and obligations). If an intangible asset does not arise from contractual or other legal rights, it shall be recognized as an asset apart from goodwill only if it is separable, that is, it is capable of being separated or divided from the acquired entity and sold, transferred, licensed, rented, or exchanged (regardless of whether there is an intent to do so). For purposes of this Statement, however, an intan-gible asset that cannot be sold, transferred, licensed, rented, or exchanged individually is considered separable if it can be sold, transferred, licensed, rented, or exchanged with a related contract, asset, or liability. For purposes of this statement, an assembled workforce shall not be recognized as an intangible asset apart from goodwill.

Exhibit 2–7 provides a listing of intangible assets with indications of whether they typ-ically meet the legal/contractual or separability criteria.

The FASB recognized the inherent difficulties in estimating the separate fair values of many intangibles and stated that

> Difficulties may arise in assigning the acquisition cost to individual intangible assets ac-quired in a basket purchase such as a business combination. Measuring some of those as-sets is less difficult than measuring other assets, particularly if they are exchangeable and traded regularly in the marketplace. . . . Nonetheless, even those assets that cannot be measured on that basis may have more cash flow streams directly or indirectly associated with them than can be used as the basis for measuring them. While the resulting measures may lack the precision of other measures, they provide information that is more repre-sentationally faithful than would be the case if those assets were simply subsumed into goodwill on the grounds of measurement difficulties. (FASB Exposure Draft, *Business Combinations and Intangible Assets*, para. 271)

Undoubtedly, as our knowledge economy continues its rapid growth, asset allocations to items such as those identified in Exhibit 2–7 are expected to be frequent.

Purchased In-Process Research and Development

As discussed in this chapter, the accounting for a purchase business combination be-gins with the identification of the tangible and intangible assets acquired and liabilities assumed by the acquirer. The fair values of the individual assets and liabilities then provide the basis for purchase price allocations and financial statement valuations.

Recently, many firms—especially those in high-tech industries—have allocated sig-nificant portions of the purchase cost of acquired businesses to in-process research and development (IPR&D). A unique characteristic of IPR&D assets is that they must be written off immediately unless those assets have an alternative future use. FASB Inter-pretation No. 4, *Applicability of FASB Statement No. 2 to Business Combinations Accounted for by the Purchase Method*, requires the identification and separation of as-sets resulting from research and development activities (for example, core technology) and assets to be used in research and development activities. The latter group of assets is considered to be "in-process research and development" and thus is expensed as part of the business combination. A common criterion employed in determining whether to expense or capitalize research and development costs is whether the resulting assets

Exhibit 2−7 Illustrative Examples of Intangible Assets That Meet the Criteria for Recognition Separately from Goodwill (*SFAS 141*)

The following are examples of intangible assets that meet the criteria for recognition as an asset apart from goodwill. The following illustrative list is not intended to be all-inclusive; thus, an acquired intangible asset might meet the recognition criteria of this Statement but not be included on that list. Assets designated by the symbol (c) are those that would generally be recognized separately from goodwill because they meet the contractual-legal criterion. Assets designated by the symbol (s) do not arise from contractual or other legal rights, but should nonetheless be recognized separately from goodwill because they meet the separability criterion. The determination of whether a specific acquired intangible asset meets the criteria in this Statement for recogniton apart from goodwill should be based on the facts and circumstances of each individual business combination.*

Marketing-related intangible assets:

1. Trademarks, tradenames.[c]
2. Service marks, collective marks, certification marks.[c]
3. Trade dress (unique color, shape, or package design).[c]
4. Newspaper mastheads.[c]
5. Internet domain names.[c]
6. Noncompetition agreements.[c]

Customer-related intangible assets:

1. Customer lists.[s]
2. Order or production backlog.[c]
3. Customer contracts and related customer relationships.[c]
4. Noncontractual customer relationships.[s]

Artistic-related intangible assets:

1. Plays, operas, and ballets.[c]
2. Books, magazines, newspapers, and other literary works.[c]
3. Musical works such as compositions, song lyrics, advertising jingles.[c]
4. Pictures and photographs.[c]
5. Video and audiovisual material, including motion pictures, music videos, and television programs.[c]

Contract-based intangible assets:

1. Licensing, royalty, standstill agreements.[c]
2. Advertising, construction, management, service, or supply contracts.[c]
3. Lease agreements.[c]
4. Construction permits.[c]
5. Franchise agreements.[c]
6. Operating and broadcast rights.[c]
7. Use rights such as landing, drilling, water, air, mineral, timber cutting, and route authorities.[c]
8. Servicing contracts such as mortgage servicing contracts.[c]
9. Employment contracts.[c]

Technology-based intangible assets:

1. Patented technology.[c]
2. Computer software and mask works.[c]
3. Unpatented technology.[s]
4. Databases, including title plants.[s]
5. Trade secrets, including secret formulas, processes, recipes.[c]

*The intangible assets designated by the symbol (c) also might meet the separability criterion. However, separability is not a necessary condition for an asset to meet the contractual-legal criterion.

have reached technological feasibility. If the decision is made to capitalize the costs, estimates of the fair value of the resulting assets must be made. Important in estimating the fair value of research and development costs are such factors as stage of completion, technological uncertainties, and projected costs to complete the project.

An example of an IPR&D expense is seen in the Yahoo! purchase of Log-Me-On.com. As noted in a recent Yahoo! 10-Q SEC filing, Log-Me-On's efforts were focused solely on developing an Internet browser technology that at the time was approximately 30 percent complete. This IPR&D was considered not to have reached technological feasibility and had no alternative future use as of the acquisition date. Of the $9.9 million purchase price for Log-Me-On.com, $9.8 million was allocated to IPR&D and immediately expensed. The remaining $100,000 was allocated to an intangible asset (work force in place) and was amortized over the related employment contract period.

The immediate expensing of IPR&D, although recently popular (see Exhibit 2–8), can be criticized as resulting in understated assets and distorted financial ratio results for many firms involved in purchase acquisitions. IPR&D in most cases clearly

Exhibit 2–8
Recent Notable In-Process
Research and Development
Write-Offs

Worldcom	$3,300 million
Compaq Computer	3,200 million
Dupont	1,441 million
Cadence Systems Design	339 million*

*Restated to $194 million in response to discussions with SEC.

possesses value—one party pays another for the right to future cash flows resulting from the ongoing activity. However, the relevant FASB pronouncements not only allow immediate expensing but require it when technological feasibility and alternative future uses are not present in a research and development activity. Moreover, many firms prefer the immediate expensing of IPR&D. Although a one-time reduction of reported earnings takes place in the period of an acquisition involving IPR&D, subsequent reported earnings are free from such expenses and result in enhanced measures of return on equity, return on assets, and earnings per share.

The current application of the rules for expensing IPR&D has generated a great deal of controversy drawing the attention of the SEC and the FASB. In 1998 and 1999, the SEC cited several firms for overstating the allocated portion of IPR&D in business combinations. In the September 9, 1998, letter to the AICPA, Lynn Turner, the chief accountant for the SEC, notes that

> Although there was no change in the relevant accounting literature, IPR&D write-offs increased significantly in the 1990s. More intense merger activity in the technology sector may explain some of the increases, but abuses in the valuation of IPR&D are also suspected. This trend of larger write-offs could undermine public confidence in financial statements and presents significant challenges for the accounting profession.

The SEC cited several problems in the way firms allocated acquisition costs to IPR&D. In some cases, acquired firms with significant IPR&D had no previously disclosed research and development expenditures in previous financial statements. In other cases, development work to update versions of existing products had been only partially completed at the time of acquisition. However, the vast majority of the purchase price was allocated to IPR&D, leaving little to support the value of the ongoing product. In several cases, firms were required to restate their IPR&D write-offs in response to SEC concerns. For example, in reporting on Digi International's fiscal third-quarter financial results on July 22, 1999, PR Newswire noted that

> In response to comments by the SEC regarding Digi's acquisition of ITK International, Inc., and Central Data Corporation, and the related purchase price allocation, the Company has elected to restate its previously issued financial statements to reduce the aggregate amount originally allocated to in-process research and development from $39.2 million to $16.1 million and, correspondingly, has increased the amount allocated to intangible assets and goodwill by $23.1 million.

The SEC has not been alone in struggling with the controversy surrounding purchased IPR&D. On February 24, 1999, the FASB voted unanimously to revise the accounting rules for IPR&D, calling for its capitalization and subsequent amortization to income. Nonetheless, the revision was short-lived as the FASB later reversed itself, allowing the continued immediate expensing of IPR&D. In *SFAS 141,* "Business Combinations," the FASB reaffirmed the continuation of present treatment of IPR&D until the matter is addressed comprehensively with consideration given to all research and development activities, not just those involving business combinations. Given the value placed on research ideas and process development in today's economy, the problem of how to report the uncertain benefits associated with IPR&D will likely receive continued attention from regulators.

UNCONSOLIDATED SUBSIDIARIES

Over the years, accountants have attempted to identify situations in which consolidation of financial information might not be appropriate for every subsidiary. The FASB addressed this issue in 1987 when it released *Statement No. 94.* This pronouncement required that all companies more than 50 percent owned must be consolidated with the exception of two cases:

1. An investment where control is only temporary. If the parent company anticipates surrendering control over a subsidiary in the near future through disposition of part or all of its ownership, consolidation would no longer be considered appropriate. As an illustration, a footnote to an annual report of Fuqua Industries, Inc., informed readers that a wholly owned subsidiary, Georgia Federal Bank, was omitted from consolidation because a contract had been signed to sell the operation. The temporary nature of the relationship nullifies any potential informational benefit derived from presenting consolidated financial statements.

2. An investment where control does not actually rest with the majority owners. Without control, the concept of a single economic entity is not applicable. In legal reorganizations and bankruptcies, for example, operational authority over the subsidiary is held by parties other than the parent company. Severe restrictions imposed by foreign governments also limit or remove the power held by the owners. For example, the financial statements of Unocal Corporation once reported "the consolidated financial statements of the company include the accounts of subsidiaries more than 50 percent owned, except for certain Brazilian subsidiaries which are accounted for by the cost method due to currency restrictions imposed by the Brazilian government."

Both of these exceptions to the consolidation principle are predicated on the tentative quality of the control held by the parent. The relationship does not indicate the existence of a single economic entity.

Prior to the issuance of *Statement 94,* another important exception to consolidation was allowed. At that time, business combinations were permitted to omit subsidiaries from consolidation because of nonhomogeneity. *ARB 51* had suggested that a subsidiary should remain unconsolidated if the nature of its operations differed so significantly from that of the parent that the combined companies could not be viewed as a single entity. Despite ownership of a majority of voting stock, these companies had to be reported by use of the equity method so that only an investment asset and an equity income balance appeared in the consolidated statements.

Because of the complex nature of the activities in most modern businesses, application of the nonhomogeneity rule was subject to individual judgment. Traditionally, companies gave a broad interpretation to the concept of a single economic entity, so that virtually all subsidiaries were consolidated despite apparent differences in the nature of their operations. However, one important exception to this general rule did exist. *ARB 51* stated, as an example, that "separate statements . . . may be preferable for a finance company where the parent and the other subsidiaries are engaged in manufacturing operations." Following the Board's suggestion, many business combinations segregated finance subsidiaries from their consolidated statements, reporting them on the equity basis. Thus, in 1987, for example, General Motors did not consolidate its finance subsidiary, General Motors Acceptance Corporation (GMAC).

The practice of omitting such subsidiaries from consolidation was criticized vigorously over the years as an excuse for removing large amounts of debt from the entity's balance sheet. Since the individual accounts of an unconsolidated subsidiary are not included in consolidated statements, finance operations could incur significant obligations that would not appear as liabilities of the business combination. One study found, for example, that the debt-to-equity ratio of Borg-Warner in 1985 was .70 without consolidation of a finance subsidiary but 3.06 with it included.[11]

---

[11]Joseph C. Rue and David E. Tosh, "Should We Consolidate Finance Subsidiaries?" *Management Accounting,* April 1987, p. 46.

THE POOLING OF INTERESTS METHOD OF ACCOUNTING FOR BUSINESS COMBINATIONS

In *SFAS 141,* "Business Combinations," the FASB states that "all business combinations should be accounted for using the purchase method," thereby eliminating the pooling method. However, the application of the purchase method will be applied prospectively, leaving intact long-lasting financial statement effects from past poolings. For example, the Yahoo!–Broadcast.com, Pfizer–Warner-Lambert, and Exxon–Mobil combinations highlighted at the beginning of this chapter are all accounted for as poolings. Moreover, because differences between the purchase and pooling methods relate to fundamental issues of asset valuation and income recognition, the financial ratios resulting from past poolings will be affected for years to come. Therefore, to appreciate fully the financial reporting for business combinations, a solid understanding of the pooling of interests accounting method remains necessary.

Continuity of Ownership

Historically, many transactions did not involve a clean break in ownership. Often, former owners of separate firms would agree to combine for their mutual benefit and continue as owners of a combined firm. In such cases, the distinction between acquiring company and acquired company was not always clear. The assets and liabilities of the former firms were never really bought or sold—former owners merely exchanged ownership shares to become joint owners of the combined firm.

The assertion also was made that no bargained transaction actually transpired between the companies when securities alone were exchanged. According to *Opinion 16* (par. 16), "an exchange of stock to effect a business combination is in substance a transaction between the combining stockholder groups and does not involve the corporate entities."

Combinations characterized by exchange of voting shares and continuation of previous ownership became known as pooling of interests. Rather than a purchase and sale transaction where one ownership group replaced another, a pooling of interests was characterized by a continuity of ownership interests before and after the business combination.

Because the basic characteristics of a purchase consolidation did not always appear in every business combination, the idea soon spread that two distinct types of combinations existed. Gradually, alternative consolidation procedures began to emerge based on pooling of interests concepts. Over the decades, this method was applied to a significant number of business combinations.

For example, the Goodyear Tire & Rubber Company exchanged nearly 25 million shares of its common stock for all of the outstanding common stock of Celeron Corporation to create a combination accounted for as a pooling of interests. As noted in Exhibit 2–9, Goodyear actually issued its stock in exchange for the shares held by the owners of Celeron. Consequently, the combined assets of these two companies were controlled by both the Goodyear shareholders and the previous Celeron owners (who now held Goodyear stock). Regardless of the number of shares exchanged, this same joint control has always been found in a pooling of interests.

E x h i b i t   2 – 9
Business Combination—
Pooling of Interests*

*This diagram is intended merely to represent the relationship created by a pooling of interests. The shares delivered by Celeron actually came from its owners who in turn received the 24.7 million shares of Goodyear Tire & Rubber directly from the company.

Thus, a pooling of interests was characterized as a continuation of ownership where neither a parent nor subsidiary could be easily identified. The combination was created by an exchange of voting stock and was not viewed as a bargained transaction with a precise acquisition price. To reflect these qualities, two important steps were required in accounting for a combination created as a pooling of interests:

1. The book values of the assets and liabilities of both companies became the book values reported by the combined entity. Because of the continuity of ownership, no new basis of accountability arose.

2. The revenue and expense accounts were combined retroactively as well as prospectively. Again, continuity of ownership allowed for the recognition of income accruing to the owners both before and after the combination.

Therefore, in a pooling, reported income is typically higher than under purchase accounting. Under pooling, not only do the firms retroactively combine incomes but the smaller asset bases also result in smaller depreciation and amortization expenses. Because net income reported in financial statements often is used in a variety of contracts, including managerial compensation, the pooling method was considered an attractive alternative to purchase accounting.

The APB, in *Opinion 16,* allowed both the purchase and pooling of interest methods to account for business combinations. However, the Board placed tight restrictions on the pooling method to prevent managers from engaging in purchase transactions and reporting them as poolings of interest. *Opinion 16* established 12 criteria that had to be present in a business combination to justify adoption of the pooling method. By setting strict guidelines, the Board hoped to ensure that only combinations clearly outside the essence of a purchase would fall under the pooling of interests classification. *Business combinations that failed to meet even 1 of these 12 criteria had to be accounted for by the purchase method.*

These criteria, which are presented in the appendix at the end of this chapter, had two overriding objectives: First, they defined a pooling of interests as a single transaction (or series of transactions occurring over a limited time) in which two independent companies are united solely through the exchange of voting common stock. To ensure the complete fusion of the two organizations, one company had to obtain substantially all (90 percent or more) of the voting stock of the other.

The second general objective of these criteria was to prevent purchase combinations from being disguised as poolings. Past experience had shown the APB that combination transactions were frequently manipulated so that they would qualify for pooling of interests treatment (usually to increase reported earnings). However, subsequent events, often involving cash being paid or received by the parties, revealed the true nature of the combination: One company was purchasing the other in a bargained exchange. The APB designed a number of the 12 criteria to stop this practice.

For example, to be considered a pooling of interests, no agreement could exist to reacquire any of the shares issued in creating the combination. This rule prevented the parties from eventually receiving cash or other assets as part of the transaction. For the same reason, significant assets of the combined companies could not be sold for two years unless duplication existed. These restrictions helped to ensure that only combinations meeting the essence of a pooling were given that treatment—a continuation of the companies and a continuation of the ownership.

A POOLING OF INTERESTS—RATIONALE FOR DIFFERENT ACCOUNTING

As stated previously, the pooling of interests method had evolved over the years as an alternative for reporting business combinations that demonstrated specific characteristics. In theory, a pooling involved the union of two companies so that a continuity of ownership was maintained. The underlying concept was that nothing had been changed by the combination except the composition of the reporting entity. *Thus, the*

Are Purchases and Poolings of Interests Truly Different?

James Atkinson is the sole owner of Acme Taxicab Company, a Smallport organization with 15 vehicles. He wants to expand his operation and approaches Roy Wilbury, owner of Wilbury's Cabs. Wilbury's company operates eight taxicabs in the same city.

Scenario One. Atkinson suggests to Wilbury that the two companies join together for their mutual benefit. "We can save money on advertisement, maintenance, and other overhead costs. Instead of two Smallport companies, we will be co-owners of a larger organization operating 23 taxicabs throughout the city. The resulting enterprise will simply be more profitable. I currently own all 1,000 shares of my company's common stock. I will issue another 600 shares to you in exchange for all of the outstanding shares of Wilbury's Cabs."

Scenario Two. Atkinson offers to buy Wilbury's Cabs to expand the Acme Taxicab Company. "I will pay you a fair value in cash for your entire company. I'll buy your assets or buy your stock. You could retire or you can even work for me but I want to have 23 taxicabs operating throughout the city."

What characteristics of a pooling of interests are seen in the first scenario? What characteristics of a purchase are found in the second? In both cases, the two companies would ultimately form a single economic entity with 23 vehicles. Are these transactions sufficiently different to warrant the application of two distinct accounting methods producing widely varying financial results?

book values of the two companies were simply brought together to form consolidated financial statements. This approach is in diametric contrast to a purchase where one company clearly acquires another and then utilizes the purchase price as a basis for valuing the subsidiary's assets and liabilities.

Accounting Research Study No. 5 (p. 15) explains that

> The "pooling-of-interests accounting" treatment is generally supported by reasoning that no new basis of accountability is required since the two (or more) companies are continuing operations as one company in a manner similar to that which existed in the past. The presumption is that in effect there has been no purchase or sale of assets, but merely a fusion, merging, or pooling of two formerly separate economic entities into one new economic entity.

Because a fusion of the companies rather than a takeover had occurred, no purchase price was computed in a pooling of interests. Without a cost figure, no basis existed for either revaluing acquired asset and liability accounts to fair market value or recognizing goodwill. Book values were simply retained. This absence of a purchase price created many of the significant reporting differences between the pooling of interests method and the purchase method.

The approach to consolidating revenues and expenses also was altered in a pooling of interests. Because a union had occurred, the operations of each company were said to continue in a manner unaffected by the combination. In theory, nothing had changed for either company except the composition of the reporting entity. Because the two companies had merged into one, the financial results of all past operations continued to be reported. *Consequently, in a pooling of interests, revenues and expenses were combined on a retroactive basis.* This treatment differed markedly from a purchase, where only the operations of the subsidiary after the date of acquisition are attributed to the consolidated entity.

The business combination of Cisco and GeoTel Communications serves as an illustration of this retroactive treatment. Although this pooling of interests did not occur until June 24, 1999, Cisco's consolidated income statement for 1999 (fiscal year-end July 31) included all revenues and expenses for both companies for the entire year. In this manner, the operations of the two companies were being reported as one entity. Furthermore, the same restatement procedure was applied to all prior years reported.

In contrast, if Cisco had acquired GeoTel Communications in 1999 through a purchase, the operations of the subsidiary prior to June 24 would have had no effect on the business combination. However, because the combination was a pooling, the past operating figures for the two companies were brought together. Although the companies were separate entities in 1998, the subsequently consolidated statements reflect the financial results of the business combination for that year. By restating the prior years, the operations of the component companies (Cisco and GeoTel Communications) are reported even though their combination had not yet been formed at that particular time.

Pooling of Interests Where Dissolution Takes Place

To demonstrate the formation of a pooling of interests, assume that BigNet Company and Smallport Company decide to join operations on December 31 (see Exhibit 2–4).[12] This combination is created when BigNet issues 23,000 new shares of its common stock, with a $5 par value and a $100 market value per share, to the owners of Smallport in exchange for all of the company's outstanding common shares. Smallport transfers its assets and liabilities to BigNet and dissolves itself as a separate corporation. Stock registration fees of $5,000 are paid by BigNet as well as $3,000 in other costs directly associated with the combination. In creating this business combination, the companies followed all 12 criteria established by *APB Opinion 16* for a pooling of interests (see the appendix at the end of the chapter).

As stated earlier, a pooling of interests consolidates all accounts at their historical book values. Therefore, the reported value of each of Smallport's accounts (assets, liabilities, revenues, expenses, and dividends paid) simply can be transferred into BigNet's financial records through a journal entry. To ensure that adequate disclosure is provided, *APB Opinion 16* does require that the details of the separate operations be presented in a note to the consolidated statements.

In contrast to the purchase method, no part of the $8,000 in combination costs is capitalized; the entire amount is recorded here as an expense. According to *APB Opinion 16* (par. 58), "The pooling of interests method records neither the acquiring of assets nor the obtaining of capital. Therefore, costs incurred to effect a combination accounted for by that method and to integrate the continuing operations are expenses of the combined corporation rather than additions to assets or direct reductions of stockholders' equity." To maintain book value, the cost of uniting the organizations is not viewed as a change in either asset or contributed capital accounts; thus, an expense is recorded by the combined entity.

Entering the book values of Smallport's assets, liabilities, revenues, expenses, and dividends into the records of BigNet poses little trouble.[13] Likewise, the $8,000 in direct combination costs is simply assigned directly to expense. However, the recording of the 23,000 shares of stock being issued by BigNet should be noted. According to Exhibit 2–4, Smallport is reporting contributed capital (the Common Stock and Additional Paid-In Capital accounts) of $120,000 and retained earnings of $370,000.[14] Because poolings retain book value, BigNet uses these same figures in recording the issuance of its own stock. In that way, Smallport's equity balances are included within the combined totals.

Regardless of the amounts reported by Smallport, BigNet's Common Stock account must be increased by $115,000 to reflect the $5 par value of these 23,000 shares. To arrive at the $120,000 figure that corresponds with Smallport's total contributed capital,

---

[12]We assume the initiation date for the combination occurs on or prior to June 30, 2001—the deadline for pooling accounting as stated in *SFAS 141*, "Business Combinations."

[13]As is discussed in Chapter 3, dividends paid between the related companies after a combination is created are intercompany transfers that have to be eliminated. In a pooling of interests, though, any amounts distributed to previous owners before the combination was created continue to be reported as Dividends Paid.

[14]Although the date of the pooling was December 31, Smallport's Retained Earnings balance as of the first day of the year is recorded by the combination with the company's current revenues, expenses, and dividends being reported separately.

BigNet also records $5,000 as additional paid-in capital. The entry is then completed with a $370,000 credit to retained earnings. Smallport's contributed capital total and retained earnings both have been added into the business combination at book value.

Pooling of Interests Method—Subsidiary Dissolved

BigNet Company's Financial Records—December 31

Current Assets.	300,000	
Computers and Equipment.	400,000	
Capitalized Software	100,000	
Dividends Paid.	10,000	
Expenses.	380,000	
Notes Payable.		200,000
Revenues.		500,000
Common Stock (23,000 shares issued by BigNet at $5 par value)		115,000
Additional Paid-In Capital (to equate contributed capital with $120,000 amount reported by Smallport).		5,000
Retained Earnings, 1/1 (to record amount equal to book value of Smallport).		370,000
Expenses (combination costs)	8,000	
Cash		8,000

To record book value of Smallport's account obtained through a pooling of interests. Direct combination costs are expensed.

After recording these accounts, BigNet's financial records show $692,000 in Current Assets ($400,000 + $300,000 − 8,000), $2,400,000 in Computers and Equipment ($2,000,000 + $400,000), and so on. The Revenues account now holds $1,500,000 ($1,000,000 + $500,000) while expenses are recorded at $1,188,000 ($800,000 + $380,000 + $8,000 in combination costs). *Because book values are retained, the various asset, liability, revenue, expense, and dividend balances are not affected by the number of shares issued by BigNet.* If 2,300 shares or 230,000 shares had been exchanged rather than 23,000, the same consolidated figures still would have been appropriate for these accounts.

By comparing this consolidation to previous illustrations, several areas of distinct contrast can be seen between the purchase method and the pooling of interests method:

	Consolidation	
	Purchase Method	**Pooling of Interests Method**
Assets and liabilities of subsidiary	Recorded at fair value.*	Recorded at book value.
Goodwill	Excess of purchase price over fair value of subsidiary net assets.	Not recognized.
Revenues and expenses of subsidiary	Accrued only after date of acquisition.	Recognized retroactively.
Shares issued to create business combination	Recorded at fair value if any shares are issued.	Based on book value of subsidiary's contributed capital and retained earnings at beginning of year.
Combination costs	Included as part of purchase price unless incurred in connection with issuance of stock, a cost which reduces paid-in capital.	Expensed immediately.

*If purchase price is less than fair market value, noncurrent assets (except for any long-term investments in marketable securities) are recorded at reduced amounts.

When reviewing the recording of a past pooling of interests, one potential variation to the previous entry may be encountered. Although poolings are based on retaining book values, the recording of contributed capital can cause a problem. Because issued shares are always credited for par value, BigNet's common stock had to be recorded as $115,000, although Smallport's balance for this same account was $100,000. As indicated, BigNet increased its additional paid-in capital by $5,000 so that total contributed capital equaled Smallport's $120,000 balance (see Exhibit 2–10).

If BigNet had originally issued only 18,000 shares, its Common Stock account would be credited for $90,000 with an accompanying $30,000 added to additional paid-in capital. Once again, the $120,000 total book value of Smallport's contributed capital is replicated by the entry. Conversely, as shown in Exhibit 2–10, if 26,000 shares with a par value of $130,000 were exchanged by BigNet to create this pooling, a $10,000 *reduction* to additional paid-in capital is necessary to arrive at the appropriate $120,000 total. In each case, the book value of Smallport's total contributed capital is retained by the combination.

A slightly different problem arises in recording total contributed capital for a pooling when the number of issued shares is relatively large. Assume, as an example, that 35,000 shares of common stock are exchanged by BigNet to establish this pooling of interests with Smallport. The $175,000 par value of the stock necessitates a $55,000 reduction in BigNet's additional paid-in capital to equal the $120,000 contributed capital reported by Smallport.

However, Exhibit 2–4 indicates that BigNet's Additional Paid-In Capital account only holds a $40,000 balance. Because a negative contributed capital balance is not possible, BigNet's additional paid-in capital is first dropped to zero with the remaining $15,000 decrease being made in retained earnings. Exhibit 2–10 shows that only $355,000 in retained earnings (rather than Smallport's $370,000 balance) is recorded by the business combination when 35,000 shares are issued. *Thus, if BigNet's issued shares have a total par value greater than Smallport's total contributed capital, a reduction must be made. BigNet initially decreases its own Additional Paid-In Capital account. However, if that amount proves to be insufficient, the Retained Earnings balance also must be reduced.*

Pooling of Interests Where Separate Incorporation Is Maintained

The combination of BigNet Company and Smallport Company is presented again to demonstrate a pooling of interests, one in which both companies retain their separate

---

Exhibit 2–10
Recording of Shares Issued in a Pooling of Interests

| (Exhibit 2–4) | Smallport's Book Values | BigNet Company Issues | | | |
		18,000 Shares	23,000 Shares	26,000 Shares	35,000 Shares
Common stock	$100,000	$ 90,000	$115,000	$130,000	$175,000
Additional paid-in capital	20,000	30,000	5,000	(10,000)	(40,000)*
Total contributed capital	120,000	120,000	120,000	120,000	135,000
Retained earnings, 1/1	370,000	370,000	370,000	370,000	355,000†

*BigNet's Additional Paid-In Capital account is reduced from $40,000 to zero.

†Because the contributed capital of issued shares is $55,000 greater than that reported by Smallport, BigNet's APIC is first reduced to zero ($40,000 reduction) and the amount recorded for retained earnings ($355,000) reflects the remaining $15,000 reduction.

DISCUSSION QUESTION

How Does a Purchase Differ from a Pooling of Interests?

On December 31, 2000, Acme Taxicab Company agrees to form a business combination with Wilbury's Cabs. Acme will exchange 600 shares of its previously unissued, $20 par value stock with Roy Wilbury for all of the outstanding shares of Wilbury's Cabs. Acme's common stock has a fair market value on that date of $100 per share.

The only assets owned by Wilbury's Cabs are eight used taxicabs having a fair market value of $5,000 each. Because of accelerated depreciation, the average book value of these assets is $2,000. Acme has 15 automobiles of its own with a total book value of $60,000 but a fair market value of $74,000.

During 2000, the two companies separately reported the following revenues and expenses:

	Acme	Wilbury
Revenues	$220,000	$95,000
Expenses	150,000	60,000

Based on the information presented here, no determination is possible as to whether a pooling of interests or a purchase has been created.

On a consolidated balance sheet as of December 31, 2000, how will the reported asset balances differ, depending on the type of method that is appropriate?

If a business combination is created as a purchase, one set of assets and liabilities is adjusted to fair market value whereas the other is left at book value. Why are both sets of assets and liabilities not revalued?

On a consolidated income statement for 2000, how will the balances differ, depending on the method considered appropriate?

Are external decision makers properly served by allowing such widely varying numbers to be reported depending on whether a purchase or a pooling of interests has taken place?

Based on the facts presented in the case, which set of financial statements best mirrors the economic reality of the business combination that has occurred?

legal identities. For this illustration, the same financial information is used as in the purchase consolidation shown in Exhibit 2–6. As in the purchase situation, BigNet issues 26,000 shares of common stock on December 31 for all of Smallport's outstanding shares. Also, direct combination costs of $40,000 are incurred. Smallport's accounts are not transferred to BigNet's financial records; both companies continue as separate corporations and maintain independent accounting systems. However, the assumption is made here that the combination has met all 12 requirements for a pooling of interests.

BigNet must first record the issuance of 26,000 shares of common stock to create this business combination. Because Smallport is not being dissolved, BigNet establishes an investment balance rather than recording Smallport's individual accounts. Because the combination is a pooling, this figure is based on Smallport's $490,000 book value as of the beginning of the year. Using the January 1 total allows the current revenues, expenses, and dividends to be included as separate items in recording the business combination.

The issued shares are recorded by BigNet at their par value of $130,000. BigNet's Additional Paid-In Capital account is reduced by $10,000 to arrive at total contributed capital of $120,000, the same book value as Smallport's contributed capital. Retained earnings at January 1 also are included in this entry because operating activities are retroactively consolidated in a pooling of interests. The direct combination costs are expensed immediately.

Pooling of Interests Method—Subsidiary Not Dissolved

BigNet's Financial Records—December 31

Investment in Smallport Company (1/1 book value)	490,000	
Additional Paid-In Capital (to align contributed capital with that of Smallport)	10,000	
Common Stock (26,000 shares at $5 par value).		130,000
Retained Earnings, 1/1 (to record balance equal to book value of Smallport).		370,000
Expenses (direct combination costs)	40,000	
Cash		40,000

To record issuance of 26,000 shares of stock in exchange for all of the outstanding shares of Smallport in a combination accounted for as a pooling of interests. Direct combination costs are properly expensed.

When the common stock shares are exchanged, the combination is formed, and consolidated financial statements can be prepared using the worksheet produced in Exhibit 2–11. This pooling of interests is carried out through the following series of steps:

Step 1 Prior to creating this worksheet, BigNet's balances are adjusted to show (1) the effect of its issuance of stock and (2) the direct combination costs. The updated accounts are then entered into the appropriate columns on the worksheet (see Exhibit 2–4 for original book values).

Step 2 The Investment in Smallport Company account is eliminated as part of the basic consolidation Entry S. In the same manner as the purchase method, the Investment account is not consolidated; rather, the specific accounts that it represents should be reported by the business combination. Therefore, the $490,000 investment is removed on the worksheet so that it can be replaced by the individual balances of Smallport Company.

Step 3 Smallport's stockholders' equity balances also are eliminated by this same Entry S. In a purchase, these figures are removed because only assets and liabilities can actually be transferred to the parent. Conversely, for a pooling where a fusion of ownership interests is said to occur, the equity figures for both companies must be included. However, Smallport's equity accounts have already been brought into the consolidated totals through the recording of BigNet's 26,000 shares of issued stock.

The initial investment entry has already added these equity balances to BigNet's records prior to consolidating the financial statements. Thus, Smallport's common stock, additional paid-in capital, and retained earnings must be eliminated on the worksheet to prevent their inclusion in the final figures a second time. The beginning-of-year balance for Smallport's retained earnings is being removed to allow the current year's revenues, expenses, and dividends to be reported by the business combination.

Step 4 For a pooling of interests, the consolidation process is carried out by adding together the book values of each account. For example, BigNet's revenue of $1,000,000 and Smallport's revenue of $500,000 are extended for a consolidated total of $1,500,000. Where a consolidation entry affects an account (such as the elimination of Smallport's equity accounts), the impact of that adjustment also must be reflected in this extension process. However, because a purchase price is not determined in a pooling, no goodwill is recognized and no valuation adjustments are made to any asset or liability.

Step 5 For each of the financial statements on the worksheet, a total is calculated. The income statement ends with a net income balance, the statement of retained

Exhibit 2–11   Pooling of Interests—Date of Acquisition

			Consolidation Entries		
Accounts	**BigNet Company**	**Smallport Company**	**Debits**	**Credits**	**Consolidated Totals**
Income Statement					
Revenues	(1,000,000)	(500,000)			(1,500,000)
Expenses	840,000	380,000			1,220,000
Net income	(160,000)	(120,000)			(280,000)
Statement of Retained Earnings					
Retained earnings, 1/1	(1,240,000)*	(370,000)	(S) 370,000		(1,240,000)
Net income (above)	(160,000)	(120,000)			(280,000)
Dividends paid	110,000	10,000			120,000
Retained earnings, 12/31	(1,290,000)	(480,000)			(1,400,000)
Balance Sheet					
Current assets	360,000 *	300,000			660,000
Investment in Smallport Company	490,000 *	–0–		(S) 490,000	–0–
Computers and equipment	2,000,000	400,000			2,400,000
Capitalized software	500,000	100,000			600,000
Total assets	3,350,000	800,000			3,660,000
Notes payable	(300,000)	(200,000)			(500,000)
Common stock	(1,730,000)*	(100,000)	(S) 100,000		(1,730,000)
Additional paid-in capital	(30,000)*	(20,000)	(S) 20,000		(30,000)
Retained earnings, 12/31 (above)	(1,290,000)	(480,000)			(1,400,000)
Total liabilities and equities	(3,350,000)	(800,000)			(3,660,000)

BIGNET COMPANY AND SMALLPORT COMPANY
Consolidation Worksheet
For Period Ending December 31

Note: Parentheses indicate a credit balance.

*Balances have been adjusted for issuance of stock and payment of consolidation costs.

earnings computes ending retained earnings, and the balance sheet arrives at total assets as well as total liabilities and equities. As discussed previously, these final figures are not derived by consolidating the respective balances of the separate companies. Instead, the components in each statement are extended and then used to compute the ending balance.

On the income statement demonstrated here, revenues and expenses are added to produce totals of $1,500,000 and $1,220,000, respectively, indicating consolidated net income of $280,000. This figure is moved to the corresponding line within the statement of retained earnings. Each of the other elements constituting this second statement are extended to produce ending retained earnings of $1,400,000. This total is then included within the stockholders' equity section of the consolidated balance sheet, enabling it to properly balance.

Step 6 After all accounts have been consolidated, the final balances on the worksheet are used to prepare financial statements for the business combination of BigNet Company and Smallport Company. Exhibit 2–12 provides a comparison of the figures developed for the purchase consolidation shown previously in Exhibit 2–6 and the

Exhibit 2–12

Comparison of Purchase Method and Pooling of Interests Method

General Information: 26,000 shares of BigNet Company (par value of $5 per share but a market value of $100 per share) issued for all outstanding shares of Smallport Company on December 31. Cash of $40,000 paid for direct consolidation costs.

	Purchase Method (Exhibit 2–6)	Pooling of Interests Method (Exhibit 2–11)
Revenues	$1,000,000	$ 1,500,000
Expenses	(800,000)	(1,220,000)
Net income	$ 200,000	$ 280,000
Beginning retained earnings	$ 870,000	$ 1,240,000
Net income (above)	200,000	280,000
Dividends paid	(110,000)	(120,000)
Ending retained earnings	$960,000	$ 1,400,000
Current assets	$ 660,000	$ 660,000
Computers and equipment	2,600,000	2,400,000
Capitalized software	2,100,000	600,000
Goodwill	390,000	–0–
Total assets	$5,750,000	$ 3,660,000
Notes payable	$ 550,000	$ 500,000
Common stock	1,730,000	1,730,000
Additional paid-in capital	2,510,000	30,000
Retained earnings (above)	960,000	140,000
Total liabilities and equities	$5,750,000	$ 3,660,000
Financial Performance Ratios		
Net Income/Total Assets	3.48%	7.65%
Net Income/Total Equity	3.85%	8.86%

pooling of interests in Exhibit 2–11. Note the more favorable portrayal of two popular financial performance ratios for pooling versus purchase despite the combination of identical firms.

POOLING OF INTERESTS—THE CONTROVERSY

Now that the basic characteristics of a pooling of interests have been presented, the long history of controversy that has surrounded this method can be better understood. Over the years, the legitimacy of the pooling of interests method has frequently been questioned. One major theoretical problem associated with the pooling method is that it ignores cost figures indicated by the transaction that created the combination. The number of shares exchanged has no impact on consolidated asset and liability balances. What is normally a significant event for both companies is simply omitted from any accounting consideration. *All book values are retained as if nothing has happened.* *APB Opinion 16* (par. 39) itself admits

> The most serious defect attributed to pooling of interests accounting by those who oppose it is that it does not accurately reflect the economic substance of the business combination transaction. They believe that the method ignores the bargaining which results in the combination by accounting only for the amounts previously shown in accounts of the combining companies.

As a further argument against pooling of interests, many accountants believe that only one accounting approach should be applicable for all business combinations.

They hold that all combinations are essentially the same. Even though a variety of formats do exist, critics contend that a parent and an acquisition price can be determined in virtually every case. In addition, conveying freely traded stock is held to be the same as conveying cash. According to this argument, the availability of two radically different accounting methods is simply not warranted. Interestingly, the pooling of interests method has been primarily found in the United States. "Of all the major industrialized countries, only Great Britain allows anything resembling pooling, and its rule makers are modifying the rules to prevent most poolings."[15]

The depth of controversy sparked by the pooling of interests method is clearly demonstrated in *Accounting Research Study No. 5 (ARS 5)* where Arthur Wyatt stated that "no basis exists in principle for a continuation of what is presently known as 'pooling-of-interests' accounting *if* the business combination involves an exchange of assets and/or equities between independent parties."[16]

Additionally, in a dissent to *APB Opinion 16,* Sidney Davidson, Charles Horngren, and J. S. Seidman asserted that

> The real abuse is pooling itself. On that, the only answer is to eliminate pooling. . . . Elimination of pooling will remove the confusion that comes from the coexistence of pooling and purchase accounting. Above all, the elimination of pooling would remove an aberration in historical cost accounting that permits an acquisition to be accounted for on the basis of the seller's cost rather than the buyer's cost of the assets obtained in a bargained exchange.

The acceptability of the pooling of interests method might, indeed, have been eliminated years ago except for its popularity in the business world. Preference for the pooling method has been based largely on the desirable impact that it usually produces on reported net income. The most obvious effect is the inclusion of the subsidiary's net income as if that company had always been part of the consolidated entity. This retroactive treatment can lead to immediate improvement in the profitability picture being reported. To the extent that managerial compensation contracts are based on accounting measures of profitability, a further motivation to employ the pooling of interests method to accounting for a business combination was provided.

Another income effect helped to further account for the popularity enjoyed by the pooling of interests method. In a purchase combination, the subsidiary's assets and liabilities are adjusted to fair market value with goodwill often recognized. Such allocations are viewed as cost figures of the business combination, costs that have only limited useful lives (except when relating to land). Thus, these amounts (which can be extremely large) required amortization over future accounting periods. The resulting expense, encountered only in the purchase method, served to reduce consolidated net income year after year.

Conversely, a pooling of interests consolidated all accounts at their book values so that no additional amortization expense was ever recognized. Therefore, in most past business combinations, the income reported for each succeeding year was higher using the pooling method than would have been the case if consolidated by the purchase method.[17]

Given these reporting advantages, the desire by businesses to create combinations that would qualify as poolings is not surprising. Historically, the accounting profession attempted to define the characteristics of a pooling of interests in such a way as to restrict its use to combinations that were clearly fusions of two independent companies.

---

[15]Michael Davis, "APB 16: Time to Reconsider," *Journal of Accountancy,* October 1991, p. 99.

[16]Arthur Wyatt, "A Critical Study of Accounting for Business Combinations," *Accounting Research Study No. 5* (New York: AICPA, 1963), p. 105.

[17]For example, see "Anatomy of a Pooling: The AT&T/NCR Merger," by Andrew Fioriti and Thomas Brady, *Ohio CPA Journal,* October 1994, p. 20.

Over the years, however, the identification of attributes considered to be essential to a pooling of interests proved to be a difficult task.

FASB Position

In an article supporting their unanimous decision to eliminate the pooling of interests method of accounting for business combinations, the FASB cited the following reasons for their action:

- The pooling method provides investors with less information—and less relevant information—than that provided by the purchase method.
- The pooling method ignores the values exchanged in a business combination, while the purchase method reflects them.
- Under the pooling method, financial statement readers cannot tell how much was invested in the transaction, nor can they track the subsequent performance of the investment.
- Having two methods of accounting makes it difficult for investors to compare companies when they have used different methods to account for their business combinations.
- Because future cash flows are the same whether the pooling or purchase method is used, the boost in earnings under the pooling method reflects artificial accounting differences rather than real economic differences.
- Business combinations are acquisitions and should be accounted for as such, based on the value of what is given up in exchange, regardless of whether it is cash, other assets, debt, or equity shares.[18]

The controversy over the elimination of pooling of interests was further exemplified by the letters received by the FASB in response to their request for comments from any interested parties. As noted in their January 25, 2000, *Summary of Comment Letters, FASB Exposure Draft Business Combinations and Intangible Assets*, most of the respondents commented on the decision to eliminate use of the pooling method. In the *Summary* the Board noted:

> The primary public policy points raised are summarized below.
>
> - Eliminating the pooling method would have far-reaching and detrimental effects on the entrepreneurial spirit in the technology community and the technological innovations that have fueled the economy in recent years. The pooling method is essential to the continued success of the venture capital industry and the emerging or high-growth sector.
> - The banking industry has experienced significant desirable consolidation in recent years and is likely to experience further consolidation following the repeal of the provisions of the Glass-Steagall Act. Because many of those transactions have been accounted for using the pooling method, the level of consolidation may be negatively impacted if that method is eliminated.

In contrast, others supported the Board's decision to eliminate pooling. For example, Aetna Corporation commented that

> We support the Board's decision to eliminate the pooling-of-interests method of accounting for business combinations. We believe the economics of a business combination are more appropriately reflected by the purchase method, which accounts for the business combination at fair value, rather than the pooling-of-interests, which accounts for the business combination at historical cost. We believe that the pooling-of-interests method

---

[18]"Why Eliminate the Pooling Method," August 31, *1999 Financial Accounting Series Status Report No. 316*, Financial Accounting Foundation/FASB.

distorts the fair value exchanged in a business combination and does not allow investors to readily compare investment returns associated with similar transactions that in substance are not economically different.

Further, we believe that history has shown that the existence of two vastly different accounting models (e.g., purchase or pooling-of-interests) has resulted in numerous accounting interpretations and diversity in practice.

We recognize that there are certain limited circumstances in which a true "merger of equals" exists. However, we believe that the benefits derived from applying the purchase method as the single method of accounting for business combinations significantly outweigh any economic issues that might arise from the very limited circumstances that might occur in a true "merger of equals." Therefore, we do not believe that modifying or narrowly applying the pooling criteria as a means to allow the pooling-of-interests method to be retained is an appropriate alternative to using the purchase method as the single method of accounting for business combinations.

Clearly, there existed a wide diversity of interest and opinion regarding the desirability of maintaining pooling of interest accounting. Despite the FASB decision to eliminate future poolings, because of the large volume of poolings over the past decade, accountants and those who rely on financial reports will continue to require a familiarity with the pooling of interests method.

SUMMARY

1. Consolidation of financial information is required for external reporting purposes whenever one organization gains control of another, thus forming a single economic entity. In many combinations, all but one of the companies is dissolved as a separate legal corporation. Therefore, the consolidation process is carried out only at the date of acquisition to bring together all accounts into a single set of financial records. In other combinations, the companies retain their identities as separate enterprises and continue to maintain their own individual accounting systems. For these cases, consolidation is a periodic process necessary whenever financial statements are to be produced. This periodic procedure is frequently accomplished through the use of a worksheet and consolidation entries.

2. A purchase occurs when one entity acquires control over another. The acquisition price is based on the exchange transaction and includes all direct consolidation costs unless expended in the issuance of stock. The assets and liabilities of the acquired company are consolidated based on their fair market values at the date of purchase. If the price paid exceeds the total fair market value of the net assets, the residual amount is recorded in the consolidated financial statements as goodwill, an intangible asset.

3. For a purchase, if the acquisition price is less than total fair market value, a reduction in the consolidated balances is necessary. The acquired company's assets and liabilities are recorded at fair market value, except for noncurrent assets (however, financial assets other than equity method investments, assets to be disposed of by sale, deferred tax assets, and prepaid pension assets still are recorded at fair market values). Because of the bargain purchase, these noncurrent assets are consolidated at amounts less than their fair values. The reduction is the difference between the parent's purchase price and the total fair market value of the subsidiary's assets and liabilities. This figure is prorated based on the fair market values of the various noncurrent assets. An extraordinary gain is reported if the reduction exceeds the total value of the applicable noncurrent assets.

4. Past policy allowed a business combination to be accounted for as either a purchase or a pooling of interests. To differentiate the applicable use of these methods, 12 criteria were established by the APB. If all 12 were satisfied, the combination was to be viewed as a pooling of interests. Otherwise, the purchase method was appropriate. The two methods were not interchangeable; a specific approach was required based on these criteria. However, the FASB has mandated elimination of the pooling method, thus requiring all combinations to be accounted for as purchases.

5. Past pooling of interests were formed by uniting the ownership of two companies through the exchange of securities. This method accounts for the new combination by

consolidating all accounts at book value. Neither goodwill nor any other account valuation adjustment is recognized because no acquisition price is established. Without a purchase price, direct consolidation costs cannot be capitalized; they must be expensed immediately. For a pooling of interests, all revenues, expenses, and other operational accounts are consolidated on a retroactive basis.

6. The pooling of interests method has been criticized often because it relies on book values only and, therefore, ignores the exchange transaction that formed the economic entity. Poolings also have been questioned because of the retroactive treatment of operating results. Consequently, companies were able to increase reported earnings by pooling with another company rather than by improving operating efficiency.

COMPREHENSIVE ILLUSTRATION

Problem

(Estimated Time: 45 to 65 Minutes) Following are the account balances of the Marston Company and the Richmond Company as of December 31, 2001. The appraised values of the Richmond Company assets and liabilities have also been included.

	Marston Company Book Value 12/31/01	Richmond Company Book Value 12/31/01	Richmond Company Appraised Valued 12/31/01
Cash	$ 600,000	$ 200,000	$ 200,000
Receivables	900,000	300,000	290,000
Inventory	1,100,000	600,000	720,000
Buildings (net)	3,000,000	800,000	1,000,000
Equipment (net)	6,000,000	500,000	600,000
Accounts payable	(400,000)	(200,000)	(200,000)
Notes payable	(3,400,000)	(1,100,000)	(1,100,000)
Totals	$ 7,800,000	$ 1,100,000	$ 1,510,000
Common stock—$20 par value	$(2,000,000)		
Common stock—$5 par value		$ (720,000)	
Additional paid-in capital	(900,000)	(100,000)	
Retained earnings, 1/1/01	(2,300,000)	(130,000)	
Revenues	(6,000,000)	(900,000)	
Expenses	3,400,000	750,000	

Note: Parentheses indicate a credit balance.

Additional Information (not recorded in the preceding figures):

- On December 31, 2001, Marston issues 50,000 shares of its $20 par value common stock for all of the outstanding shares of Richmond Company.
- In creating this combination, Marston pays $10,000 in stock issuance costs and $20,000 in other direct combination costs.

Required:

a. Assume that Marston's stock has a fair market value of $32.00 per share and that this combination is accounted for as a purchase. Prepare the necessary journal entries if Richmond is to dissolve itself as a separate legal entity.

b. Repeat requirement (a) but with the assumption that this transaction is accounted for as a pooling of interests.

c. Assume that Marston's stock has a fair market value of $28.52 per share and that this combination is accounted for as a purchase. Richmond will retain separate legal incorporation and maintain its own accounting systems. Prepare a worksheet to consolidate the accounts of the two companies.

d. Repeat requirement (*c*) but assume that this transaction is accounted for as a pooling of interests.

Solution

a. For a purchase, the accountant should first determine the parent company's acquisition price. Since Marston's stock is valued at $32.00 per share, the 50,000 issued shares are worth $1,600,000 in total. The $10,000 stock issuance cost is reported as a reduction to additional paid-in capital. The other $20,000 direct combination costs must be added to the value of the issued shares to arrive at a purchase price of $1,620,000. This total is compared to the $1,510,000 market value of Richmond's assets and liabilities. Since Marston has paid $110,000 over fair market value ($1,620,000 − $1,510,000), that figure would be recognized as goodwill.

　　Because dissolution is to occur, Richmond's asset and liability accounts are transferred to Marston and entered at fair market value with the excess recorded as goodwill. The payment of the stock issuance costs is journalized separately to avoid confusion.

Marston Company's Financial Records—December 31, 2001

Cash	200,000	
Receivables	290,000	
Inventory	720,000	
Buildings	1,000,000	
Equipment	600,000	
Goodwill	110,000	
Accounts Payable		200,000
Notes Payable		1,100,000
Common Stock (Marston) (par value)		1,000,000
Additional Paid-In Capital (market value in excess of par value)		600,000
Cash (paid for consolidation costs)		20,000

To record purchase of Richmond Company.

Additional Paid-In Capital	10,000	
Cash (stock issuance costs)		10,000

To record payment of stock issuance costs.

b. As a pooling of interests, Richmond's account balances (including revenues and expenses) are transferred at their book values. The biggest concern in this process is the recording of contributed capital. Richmond's accounts indicate total contributed capital of $820,000: common stock of $720,000 and additional paid-in capital of $100,000. However, the par value of the 50,000 shares issued by Marston is $1,000,000 (at $20 per share). To arrive at the same $820,000 figure reported by Richmond, Marston's Additional Paid-In Capital account must be reduced by $180,000 in recording these new shares.

　　Marston's recording of this combination follows. As this combination is a pooling of interests, all $30,000 of the consolidation costs are recorded as expenses.

Marston Company's Financial Records—December 31, 2001

Cash	200,000	
Receivables	300,000	
Inventory	600,000	
Buildings (net)	800,000	
Equipment (net)	500,000	
Expenses	750,000	
Additional Paid-In Capital (Marston) (to align contributed capital totals)	180,000	
Accounts Payable		200,000
Notes Payable		1,100,000
Common Stock (Marston) (par value)		1,000,000
Retained Earnings, 1/1/01		130,000
Revenues		900,000

To establish a pooling of interests with Richmond Company.

Expenses	30,000	
Cash		30,000

To record payment of combination costs.

c.   In this third illustration, a purchase combination is once again created. Since a different value is attributed to the issued shares, a new purchase price must be calculated:

50,000 shares of stock at $28.52 each	$1,426,000
Other direct combination costs	20,000
Purchase price	$1,446,000

As the subsidiary is maintaining separate incorporation, Marston has to establish an investment account to reflect the $1,446,000 purchase price:

Marston's Financial Records—December 31, 2001

Investment in Richmond Company	1,446,000	
Common Stock (Marston) (par value)		1,000,000
Additional Paid-In Capital (market value in excess		
of par value)		426,000
Cash (paid for combination costs)		20,000
To record purchase of Richmond Company.		
Additional Paid-In Capital	10,000	
Cash (paid for stock issuance costs)..................		10,000
To record payment of stock issuance costs.		

Separate incorporation is being maintained; thus, a worksheet must be developed for consolidation purposes. The parent needs to analyze the purchase price to determine the allocations required to the individual accounts:

Purchase price paid by Marston		$1,446,000
Book value of Richmond		1,100,000
Excess of cost over book value		$346,000
Allocations made to specific accounts based on difference in fair		
market values and book values:		
Receivables ($290,000 − $300,000)	$(10,000)	
Inventory ($720,000 − $600,000)	120,000	
Buildings ($1,000,000 − $800,000)	200,000	
Equipment ($600,000 − $500,000)	100,000	410,000
Bargain purchase		$ (64,000)

Marston's $1,446,000 purchase price is $64,000 less than the $1,510,000 fair market value of Richmond's individual accounts. This reduction must be assigned to the subsidiary's applicable noncurrent assets based on their fair market values:

	Fair Market Value	Percentage of Fair Market Value	Reduction	Percentage of Reduction
Buildings	$1,000,000	62.5%	$64,000	$40,000
Equipment	600,000	37.5	64,000	24,000
Totals	$1,600,000	100.0%		$64,000

Thus, within the consolidation worksheet, the subsidiary's buildings are assigned a reduced value of $960,000 ($1,000,000 − $40,000). The Equipment account is adjusted to $576,000 ($600,000 − $24,000).

Exhibit 2–13 can now be developed using the following steps to arrive at totals for the consolidated financial statements:

- Marston's balances have been updated on this worksheet to include the effect of both the newly issued shares of stock and the combination costs.
- Richmond's revenue and expense accounts have been closed out to retained earnings since this combination is a purchase.
- Entry S on the worksheet eliminates the $1,100,000 book value component of the Investment in Richmond Company account along with the subsidiary's stockholders' equity accounts.

Exhibit 2–13   Comprehensive Illustration—Solution—Purchase Method

MARSTON COMPANY AND RICHMOND COMPANY
Consolidation Worksheet
For Period Ending December 31, 2001

Accounts	Marston Company	Richmond Company	Consolidation Entries Debit	Consolidation Entries Credit	Consolidated Totals
Income Statement					
Revenues	(6,000,000)				(6,000,000)
Expenses	3,400,000				3,400,000
Net income	(2,600,000)				(2,600,000)
Statement of Retained Earnings					
Retained earnings, 1/1/01	(2,300,000)				(2,300,000)
Net income (above)	(2,600,000)				(2,600,000)
Retained earnings, 12/31/01	(4,900,000)				(4,900,000)
Balance Sheet					
Cash	570,000 *	200,000			770,000
Receivables	900,000	300,000		(A) 10,000	1,190,000
Inventory	1,100,000	600,000	(A) 120,000		1,820,000
Investment in Richmond Company	1,446,000 *	–0–		(S) 1,100,000	–0–
				(A) 346,000	
Buildings (net)	3,000,000	800,000	(A) 160,000		3,960,000
Equipment (net)	6,000,000	500,000	(A) 76,000		6,576,000
Total assets	13,016,000	2,400,000			14,316,000
Accounts payable	(400,000)	(200,000)			(600,000)
Notes payable	(3,400,000)	(1,100,000)			(4,500,000)
Common stock	(3,000,000)*	(720,000)	(S) 720,000		(3,000,000)
Additional paid-in capital	(1,316,000)*	(100,000)	(S) 100,000		(1,316,000)
Retained earnings, 12/31/01 (above)	(4,900,000)	(280,000)†	(S) 280,000		(4,900,000)
Total liabilities and equities	(13,016,000)	(2,400,000)			(14,316,000)

Note: Parentheses indicate a credit balance.

*Balances have been adjusted for issuance of stock and payment of combination costs.

†Beginning retained earnings plus revenues minus expenses.

■ Entry A adjusts all of Richmond's assets and liabilities to fair market value based on the allocations determined earlier. However, the values attributed to the Buildings account and the Equipment account have been reduced by a total of $64,000 to reflect the bargain purchase made.

d. This final example returns to the pooling of interests concept. As such, the change in value of Marston's common stock (to $28.52 per share) has no impact on consolidated totals; poolings are always based on book values.

Since separate accounting systems are maintained, Marston records the issuance of its 50,000 shares as an investment. As a pooling, the total is set equal to Richmond's $950,000 book value at January 1, 2001, a figure derived from the company's three stockholders' equity accounts. As in part (b), Marston must reduce its own additional paid-in capital so that total contributed capital of $820,000 is recorded, the same figure reported by the subsidiary. The par value of the shares issued by Giant ($1 million) less a reduction here of $180,000 gives this identical balance. Retained earnings as of January 1 of $130,000 also is recorded since poolings are reported on a retroactive basis.

Exhibit 2–14   Comprehensive Illustration—Solution—Pooling of Interests Method

MARSTON COMPANY AND RICHMOND COMPANY
Consolidation Worksheet
For Period Ending December 31, 2001

Accounts	Marston Company	Richmond Company	Consolidation Entries Debit	Consolidation Entries Credit	Consolidated Totals
Income Statement					
Revenues	(6,000,000)	(900,000)			(6,000,000)
Expenses	3,430,000 *	750,000			4,180,000
Net income	(2,570,000)	(150,000)			(2,720,000)
Statement of Retained Earnings					
Retained earnings, 1/1/01	(2,430,000)*	(130,000)	(S) 130,000		(2,430,000)
Net income (above)	(2,570,000)	(150,000)			(2,720,000)
Retained earnings, 12/31/01	(5,000,000)	(280,000)			(5,150,000)
Balance Sheet					
Cash	570,000 *	200,000			770,000
Receivables	900,000	300,000			1,200,000
Inventory	1,100,000	600,000			1,700,000
Investment in Richmond Company	950,000 *	–0–		(S) 950,000	–0–
Buildings (net)	3,000,000	800,000			3,800,000
Equipment (net)	6,000,000	500,000			6,500,000
Total assets	12,520,000	2,400,000			13,970,000
Accounts payable	(400,000)	(200,000)			(600,000)
Notes payable	(3,400,000)	(1,100,000)			(4,500,000)
Common stock	(3,000,000)*	(720,000)	(S) 720,000		(3,000,000)
Additional paid-in capital	(720,000)*	(100,000)	(S) 100,000		(720,000)
Retained earnings, 12/31/01 (above)	(5,000,000)	(280,000)			(5,150,000)
Total liabilities and equities	(12,520,000)	(2,400,000)			(13,970,000)

Note: Parentheses indicate a credit balance.

*Balances have been adjusted for combination transactions and payment of combination costs.

Marston's Financial Records—December 31, 2001

Investment in Richmond Company	950,000	
Additional Paid-In Capital (to align contributed capital totals)	180,000	
Common Stock (Marston) (par value)		1,000,000
Retained Earnings, 1/1/01		130,000

To record the issuance of 50,000 shares to create a pooling of interests with Richmond Company.

Expenses..	30,000	
Cash		30,000

To record payment of combination costs, which are viewed as expenses in a pooling of interests.

After Marston's entries have been recorded, the consolidation worksheet found in Exhibit 2–14 can be produced. The investment account is eliminated on this worksheet so that the book value of Richmond's individual accounts can be consolidated (assets, liabilities, revenues, and expenses). Richmond's stockholders' equity accounts also are removed on this worksheet since they have already been added to Marston's records through the first journal entry.

APPENDIX

1. Attributes of combining companies.
   a. Each of the combining companies is autonomous and has not been a subsidiary or division of another corporation within two years before the plan of combination is initiated.
   b. Each of the combining companies is independent of the other combining companies.
2. Characteristics of the combination.
   a. The combination is effected in a single transaction or is completed in accordance with a specific plan within one year after the plan is initiated.
   b. A corporation offers and issues only common stock with rights identical to those of the majority of its outstanding voting common stock in exchange for substantially all of the voting common stock interest of another company at the date the plan of combination is consummated. Substantially all of the voting common stock means 90 percent or more for this condition.
   c. None of the combining companies changes the equity interest of the voting common stock in contemplation of effecting the combination either within two years before the plan of combination is initiated or between the dates the combination is initiated and consummated; changes in contemplation of effecting the combination may include distributions to stockholders and additional issuances, exchanges, and retirements of securities.
   d. Each of the combining companies reacquires shares of voting common stock only for purposes other than business combinations, and no company reacquires more than a normal number of shares between the dates the plan of combination is initiated and consummated.
   e. The ratio of the interest of an individual common stockholder to those of other common stockholders in a combining company remains the same as a result of the exchange of stock to effect the combination.
   f. The voting rights to which the common stock ownership interests in the resulting combined corporation are entitled are exercisable by the stockholders; the stockholders are neither deprived of nor restricted in exercising those rights for a period.
   g. The combination is resolved at the date the plan is consummated and no provisions of the plan relating to the issue of securities or other consideration are pending.
3. Absence of planned transaction.
   a. The combined corporation does not agree directly or indirectly to retire or reacquire all or part of the common stock issued to effect the combination.
   b. The combined corporation does not enter into other financial arrangements for the benefit of the former stockholders of a combining company, such as a guaranty of loans secured by stock issued in the combination, which in effect negates the exchange of equity securities.
   c. The combined corporation does not intend or plan to dispose of a significant part of the assets of the combining companies within two years after the combination other than disposals in the ordinary course of business of the formerly separate companies and to eliminate duplicate facilities or excess capacity.

QUESTIONS

1. What is a business combination?
2. Describe the different types of legal arrangements that can take place to create a business combination.
3. What is meant by consolidated financial statements?
4. Within the consolidation process, what is the purpose of a worksheet?
5. What characteristics are associated with a business combination accounted for as a purchase? What characteristics are associated with a business combination accounted for as a pooling of interests?

6. Jones Company obtains all of the common stock of Hudson, Inc., by issuing 50,000 shares of its own stock. Under these circumstances, why might the determination of an acquisition price be difficult?

7. What is the accounting basis for consolidating assets and liabilities in a business combination recorded as a purchase? What is the accounting basis for consolidating assets and liabilities in a business combination recorded as a pooling of interests?

8. How are a subsidiary's revenues and expenses consolidated in a purchase? How are a subsidiary's revenues and expenses consolidated in a pooling of interests?

9. Morgan Company purchases all of the outstanding shares of Jennings, Inc., for cash. Morgan pays more than the fair market value of the company's net assets. How should the payment in excess of fair market value be accounted for in the consolidation process?

10. Catron Corporation is having liquidity problems, and as a result, all of its outstanding shares are sold to Lambert, Inc., for cash. Because of Catron's problems, Lambert is able to acquire this stock at less than the fair market value of the company's net assets. How is this reduction in price accounted for within the consolidation process?

11. Sloane, Inc., issues 25,000 shares of its own common stock in exchange for all of the outstanding shares of Benjamin Company. Benjamin will remain a separately incorporated operation. How does Sloane record the issuance of these shares in a purchase combination?

12. To obtain all of the stock of Molly, Inc., Harrison Corporation issued its own common stock. Harrison had to pay $98,000 to lawyers, accountants, and a stock brokerage firm in connection with services rendered during the creation of this business combination. In addition, Harrison paid $56,000 in costs associated with the stock issuance. In a purchase combination, how will these two costs be recorded?

13. Two companies that have been in business for a number of years have joined together to create a new business combination. If this arrangement has been appropriately recorded as a pooling of interests, how will the prior operations of the two companies be reported? If this arrangement has been appropriately recorded as a purchase, how will the prior operations of the two companies be reported?

INTERNET ASSIGNMENTS

Internet sites are time and date sensitive. It is the purpose of these exercises to have you explore the Internet. You may need to refer to the text's Web site at http://www.mhhe.com/hoyle6e to find the most up-to-date links for the Web sites listed in the Internet Assignments.

1. Access the most recent financial statement for one of the following firms:
   - Yahoo!
   - Cisco Systems
   - Cadence Designs
   - Pennzoil–Quaker State
   - Apple Computer
   - Amazon.com
   - America OnLine

   Write a brief report that describes the firm's merger and acquisition activity for the past several years. Be sure to identify the accounting methods employed, cost allocations for purchase acquisitions, and motivations cited for the merger activities.

2. Find the annual 10-K reports for any firms involved in recent merger and acquisition activity and identify several of their recent successful takeovers. Then determine the market value of the target firm two months prior to the takeover announcement. Write a brief report that
   - Compares the price paid in the acquisition with the previous market value.
   - Discusses possible motivations for any difference.
   - Identifies the Web sites used in your search.

3. Go to the FASB Web site and locate the most current information for the ongoing business combination projects. Write a report that describes the status of the projects, major recommendations for changes, and the timetable for implementation.

4. Search the Internet for financial reports containing references to purchased in-process research and development. Identify three firms that report purchased in-process research and development expenses in connection with merger and acquisition activities and
   - Discuss how they determined the proper amount for the write-off of the purchased in-process research and development.
   - Identify the percentage of the purchase price allocated to in-process research and development and other assets.

LIBRARY ASSIGNMENTS

1. Read "What Constitutes Control?" in the June 1999 issue of *Journal of Accountancy.* Write a short report discussing whether the FASB should set criteria for control (and consolidation) other than majority ownership.

2. Locate *The Wall Street Journal General Index* for the most recent year. Under the heading "Mergers and Acquisitions," find one or more articles describing a recent corporate takeover. After reading these stories, answer the following questions:
   - What was exchanged to create the combination?
   - Was the takeover hostile or negotiated? If hostile, did the company being acquired take any actions in hopes of preventing the takeover?
   - If this transaction was a purchase, does the article specify the amount, if any, of goodwill to be recognized?
   - Does the article speculate as to the impact of the acquisition on the acquiring company's future profits?

3. Read the following as well as any other published information concerning the pooling of interests method:
   > "The Financial Statement Effects of Eliminating the Pooling-of-Interests Method of Acquisition Accounting," *Accounting Horizons*, March 2000.
   > "Why Eliminate the Pooling Method," August 31, 1999, *Financial Accounting Series Status Report No. 316*, Financial Accounting Foundation/FASB.
   > "Special Report: The Battle Over Pooling of Interests," *Journal of Accountancy,* November 1999.
   > "FASB Plan Would Provide False Accounts," *Wall Street Journal,* January 31, 2000, Manager's Journal, page C1.
   > "Valuing the New Economy—How New Accounting Standards Will Inhibit Economically Sound Mergers and Hinder the Efficiency and Innovation of U.S. Business," *Merrill Lynch Forum White Paper*, June 1999.

   Write a report discussing whether you agree with the FASB decision to eliminate the pooling of interests method as a generally accepted accounting principle.

4. The June 3, 1996, issue of *The Nation* presents a series of articles concerning the effects of merger and acquisition activities on the media and entertainment industry. Discuss some of the political issues faced as a result of concentration in the media and entertainment industry.

5. Read the following materials on in-process research and development:
   > "Spoiled Rotten," *Electronic Business,* July 1999 (http://www.eg-mag.com/registrd/issues/9907/0799/spoiled.htm)
   > The remarks of Lynn Turner, chief accountant for the SEC, "Making Financial Statements Real: Recent Problems in the Accounting for Purchased In-Process Research and Development" (http://ftp.sec./govnews/speeches/spch251.htm)

   Write a short report that discusses the issues surrounding the current accounting treatment for in-process research and development costs. Provide three examples of footnote disclosure and discussion for IPR&D costs related to business combinations.

PROBLEMS

Note: Problems 1 through 24 relate to the purchase method of accounting for business combinations. Problems 25 through 42 relate to the pooling of interests method.

Purchase Method

1. Which of the following is the best theoretical justification for consolidated financial statements?
   a. In form the companies are one entity; in substance they are separate.
   b. In form the companies are separate; in substance they are one entity.
   c. In form and substance the companies are one entity.
   d. In form and substance the companies are separate.
   (AICPA)

2. What is a statutory merger?
   a. A merger approved by the Securities and Exchange Commission.
   b. An acquisition involving both the purchase of stock and assets.
   c. A takeover completed within one year of the initial tender offer.
   d. A business combination in which only one company continues to exist as a legal entity.

3. What is the appropriate accounting treatment for the value assigned to in-process research and development acquired in a business combination?
   a. Always expense upon acquisition.
   b. Always capitalize as an asset with future economic benefit.
   c. Expense if there is no alternative use for the assets used in the research and development and technological feasibility has yet to be reached.
   d. Expense until future economic benefits become certain and then capitalize as an asset.

4. Williams Company obtains all of the outstanding stock of Jaminson, Inc., in a purchase transaction. In a consolidation prepared immediately after the takeover, at what value will the inventory owned by Jaminson be consolidated?
   a. Jaminson's historical cost.
   b. A percentage of the acquisition cost paid by Williams.
   c. The inventory will be omitted in the consolidation.
   d. At the fair market value on the date of the purchase.

5. When is an extraordinary gain recognized in consolidating financial information?
   a. When any bargain purchase is created.
   b. In a combination created in the middle of a fiscal year.
   c. In a purchase, when the value of all assets and liabilities cannot be determined.
   d. When the amount of a bargain purchase exceeds the value of the applicable noncurrent assets (other than certain exceptions) held by the acquired company.

6. On June 1, 2002, Cline Co. paid $800,000 cash for all the issued and outstanding common stock of Renn Corp. The carrying values for Renn's assets and liabilities on June 1, 2002, follow:

Cash	$ 150,000
Accounts receivable	180,000
Capitalized software costs	320,000
Goodwill (net of accumulated amortization of $80,000)	100,000
Liabilities	(130,000)
Net assets	$ 620,000

On June 1, 2002, Renn's accounts receivable had a fair value of $140,000. Additionally, Renn's in-process research and development was estimated to have a fair value of $200,000. All other items were stated at their fair values. On Cline's June 1, 2002, consolidated balance sheet, how much is reported for goodwill?

a. $320,000
b. $120,000
c. $ 80,000
d. $ 20,000

7. Which of the following is not an appropriate reason for leaving a subsidiary unconsolidated?
   a. The subsidiary is in bankruptcy.
   b. The subsidiary is to be sold in the near future.
   c. A foreign government threatens to take over the assets of the subsidiary.
   d. The subsidiary is in an industry that is significantly different than that of the parent.

8. Prior to being united in a business combination, Atkins, Inc., and Waterson Corporation had the following stockholders' equity figures:

	Atkins	Waterson
Common stock ($1 par value)	$180,000	$45,000
Additional paid-in capital	90,000	20,000
Retained earnings	300,000	110,000

Atkins issues 51,000 new shares of its common stock valued at $3 per share for all of the outstanding stock of Waterson. Assume that Atkins acquired Waterson through a purchase. Immediately afterward, what are consolidated additional paid-in capital and retained earnings, respectively?
   a. $104,000 and $300,000.
   b. $110,000 and $410,000.
   c. $192,000 and $300,000.
   d. $212,000 and $410,000.

Problems 9 and 10 are based on the following information: Hampstead, Inc., has only three assets:

	Book Value	Fair Market Value
Inventory	$110,000	$150,000
Land	700,000	600,000
Buildings	700,000	900,000

Miller Corporation purchases Hampstead by issuing 100,000 shares of its $10 par value common stock.

9. If Miller's stock is worth $20 per share, at what value will the inventory, land, and buildings be consolidated, respectively?
   a. $110,000, $600,000, $900,000.
   b. $110,000, $700,000, $700,000.
   c. $150,000, $600,000, $900,000.
   d. $150,000, $700,000, $900,000.

10. If Miller's stock is worth $15 per share, at what value will the inventory, land, and buildings be consolidated, respectively?
   a. $110,000, $695,000, $695,000.
   b. $150,000, $525,000, $825,000.
   c. $150,000, $540,000, $810,000.
   d. $136,363, $545,455, $818,182.

Problems 11 through 14 are based on the following information: Allen, Inc., obtains control over Tucker, Inc., on July 1, 2002. The book value and fair market value of Tucker's accounts on that date (prior to creating the combination) follow, along with the book value of Allen's accounts:

	Allen Book Value	Tucker Book Value	Tucker Market Value
Revenues	$250,000	$130,000	
Expenses	170,000	80,000	
Retained earnings, 1/1/02	130,000	150,000	
Cash and receivables	140,000	60,000	$ 60,000
Inventory	190,000	145,000	175,000
Land	230,000	180,000	200,000
Buildings (net)	400,000	200,000	225,000
Equipment (net)	100,000	75,000	75,000
Liabilities	540,000	360,000	350,000
Common stock	300,000	70,000	
Additional paid-in capital	10,000	30,000	

11. Assume that Allen issues 10,000 shares of common stock with a $5 par value and a $40 fair market value to obtain all of Tucker's outstanding stock. How much goodwill should be recognized?
    a. –0–
    b. $15,000
    c. $35,000
    d. $100,000

12. For the fiscal year ending December 31, 2002, how will consolidated net income of this business combination be determined if Allen acquires all of Tucker's stock in a purchase?
    a. Allen's income for the past year plus Tucker's income for the past six months.
    b. Allen's income for the past year plus Tucker's income for the past year.
    c. Allen's income for the past six months plus Tucker's income for the past six months.
    d. Allen's income for the past six months plus Tucker's income for the past year.

13. Assume that Allen issues preferred stock with a par value of $200,000 and a fair market value of $335,000 for all shares of Tucker. What will be the balance in the consolidated Inventory, Land, and beginning Retained Earnings accounts?
    a. $365,000, $410,000, and $130,000.
    b. $365,000, $430,000, and $130,000.
    c. $352,500, $417,500, and $280,000.
    d. $335,000, $430,000, and $280,000.

14. Assume that Allen pays a total of $370,000 in cash for all of the shares of Tucker. In addition, Allen pays $30,000 to a group of attorneys for their work in arranging the acquisition. What will be the balance in consolidated goodwill and retained earnings?
    a. 0 and $90,000.
    b. 0 and $280,000.
    c. $15,000 and $280,000.
    d. $15,000 and $130,000.
    (AICPA adapted)

15. Bakel Corporation has the following account balances:

Receivables	$ 80,000
Inventory	200,000
Land	600,000
Building	500,000
Liabilities	400,000
Common stock	100,000
Additional paid-in capital	100,000
Retained earnings, 1/1/02	700,000
Revenues	300,000
Expenses	220,000

Several of Bakel's accounts have market values that differ from book value: land—$400,000; building—$600,000; inventory—$280,000; and liabilities—$330,000. Homewood, Inc., obtains all of the outstanding shares of Bakel by issuing 20,000 shares of common stock having a $5 par value but a $55 fair market value. Stock issuance costs amount to $10,000. The transaction is to be accounted for as a purchase.

  a. What is the purchase price in this combination?

  b. What is the book value of Bakel's net assets on the date of the takeover?

  c. How are the stock issuance costs handled?

  d. How does the issuance of these shares affect the stockholders' equity accounts of Homewood, the parent?

  e. What allocations are made of Homewood's purchase price to specific accounts and to goodwill?

  f. If Homewood had in-process research and development (with no alternative uses) valued at $60,000, how would the allocations in part (*e*) change? Where is acquired in-process research and development typically reported on consolidated financial statements?

  g. How do Bakel's revenues and expenses affect consolidated totals? Why?

  h. How do Bakel's common stock and additional paid-in capital balances affect consolidated totals?

  i. In financial statements prepared immediately following the takeover, what impact will this acquisition have on the various consolidated totals?

  j. If Homewood's stock had been worth only $40 per share rather than $55, how would the consolidation of Bakel's assets and liabilities have been affected?

16. Winston has the following account balances as of February 1, 2002.

Inventory	$ 600,000
Land	500,000
Buildings (net) (valued at $1,000,000)	900,000
Common stock ($10 par value)	800,000
Retained earnings (1/1/02)	1,100,000
Revenues	600,000
Expenses	500,000

Arlington pays $1.4 million cash and issues 10,000 shares of its $30 par value common stock (valued at $80 per share) for all of Winston's outstanding stock. Stock issuance costs amount to $30,000. Prior to recording these newly issued shares, Arlington reports a Common Stock account of $900,000 and Additional Paid-In Capital of $500,000.

Required:

For each of the following accounts, determine what balance would be included in a February 1, 2002, consolidation.

  a. Goodwill.

  b. Expenses.

  c. Retained Earnings, 1/1/02.

  d. Buildings.

17. Use the same information as presented in question (16) but assume that Arlington pays cash of $2.3 million. No stock is issued. An additional $40,000 is paid in direct combination costs.

Required:

For each of the following accounts, determine what balance would be included in a February 1, 2002, consolidation.

  a. Goodwill.

  b. Expenses.

  c. Retained Earnings, 1/1/02.

  d. Buildings.

18. Use the same information as presented in question (16) but assume that Arlington pays $2,020,000 in cash. An additional $20,000 is paid in direct combination costs.

Required:

For each of the following accounts, determine what balance will be included in a February 1, 2002, consolidation.

a. Inventory.
b. Goodwill.
c. Expenses.
d. Buildings.
e. Land.

19. On December 31, 2002, Bingham Company and Laredo Company have the following account balances:

	Bingham	Laredo
Revenues	$100,000	$ 80,000
Expenses	60,000	50,000
Net income	$ 40,000	$ 30,000
Retained earnings, 1/1/02	$210,000	$ 70,000
Net income	40,000	30,000
Dividends	30,000	–0–
Retained earnings, 12/31/02	$220,000	$100,000
Cash	$ 80,000	$ 20,000
Receivables	60,000	60,000
Inventory	100,000	70,000
Buildings and equipment (net)	200,000	100,000
Total assets	$440,000	$250,000
Current liabilities	$ 20,000	$ 10,000
Long-term liabilities	70,000	50,000
Common stock	110,000	90,000
Additional paid-in capital	20,000	–0–
Retained earnings, 12/31/02	220,000	100,000
Total liabilities and equities	$440,000	$250,000

After these figures were prepared, Bingham issued 10,000 shares of its $10 par value stock for all of the outstanding shares of Laredo. Bingham's stock had a $25 per share fair market value. Bingham also paid $10,000 in direct combination costs and $20,000 in stock issuance costs. Laredo holds a building that is worth $40,000 more than its current book value.

Required:

Determine consolidated balances for this combination as of December 31, 2002.

20. Following are the financial balances for the Parrot Company and the Sun Company as of December 31, 2002. Also included are fair market values for the Sun Company accounts.

	Parrot Company Book Value 12/31/02	Sun Company Book Value 12/31/02	Sun Company Market Value 12/31/02
Cash	$ 290,000	$ 120,000	$ 120,000
Receivables	220,000	300,000	300,000
Inventory	410,000	210,000	260,000
Land	600,000	130,000	110,000
Buildings (net)	600,000	270,000	330,000
Equipment (net)	220,000	190,000	220,000
Accounts payable	(190,000)	(120,000)	(120,000)
Accrued expenses	(90,000)	(30,000)	(30,000)
Long-term liabilities	(900,000)	(510,000)	(510,000)
Common stock—$20 par value ...	(660,000)		
Common stock—$5 par value		(210,000)	
Additional paid-in capital	(70,000)	(90,000)	
Retained earnings, 1/1/02	(390,000)	(240,000)	
Revenues	(960,000)	(330,000)	
Expenses	920,000	310,000	

Note: Parentheses indicate a credit balance.

Required:

In the following situations, determine the value that would be shown in consolidated financial statements for each of the accounts listed below. Each problem should be viewed as an independent occurrence. These transactions all take place on December 31, 2002.

Accounts	
Inventory	Revenues
Land	Additional Paid-In Capital
Buildings	Expenses
Goodwill	Retained Earnings, 1/1/02

a. Parrot acquires the outstanding stock of Sun by issuing $760,000 in long-term liabilities.

b. Parrot acquires the outstanding stock of Sun by paying $160,000 in cash and issuing 10,000 shares of its own common stock with a value of $40 per share. Direct combination costs of $20,000 are paid by Parrot as well as $5,000 in stock issuance costs.

21. The financial statements for Willeslye, Inc., and Barrett Company for the year ending December 31, 2003, follow:

	Willeslye	Barrett
Revenues	$ 900,000	$ 300,000
Expenses	660,000	200,000
Net income	$ 240,000	$ 100,000
Retained earnings, 1/1/03	$ 800,000	$ 200,000
Net income	240,000	100,000
Dividends paid	90,000	–0–
Retained earnings, 12/31/03	$ 950,000	$ 300,000
Cash	$ 80,000	$ 110,000
Receivables and inventory	400,000	170,000
Buildings (net)	900,000	300,000
Equipment (net)	700,000	600,000
Total assets	$2,080,000	$1,180,000
Liabilities	$ 500,000	$ 410,000
Common stock	360,000	200,000
Additional paid-in capital	270,000	270,000
Retained earnings	950,000	300,000
Total liabilities and equities	$2,080,000	$1,180,000

On December 31, 2003, Willeslye issues $300,000 in debt and 15,000 new shares of its $10 par value stock to the owners of Barrett to purchase all of the outstanding shares of that company. Willeslye shares had a fair market value of $40 per share.

Willeslye also paid $30,000 to a broker for arranging the transaction. In addition, Willeslye paid $40,000 in stock issuance costs. Barrett's equipment was actually worth $700,000 but its buildings were only valued at $280,000.

What are the consolidated balances for the following accounts?

- Net Income.
- Retained Earnings, 1/1/03.
- Equipment.
- Goodwill.
- Liabilities.
- Common Stock.
- Additional Paid-In Capital.

22. Merrill acquires 100 percent of the outstanding voting shares of Harriss Company on January 1, 2002. To obtain these shares, Merrill pays $200,000 in cash and issues 10,000 shares of its own $10 par value common stock. On this date, Merrill's stock has a fair market value of $18 per share. Merrill also pays $10,000 to a local investment company for arranging the acquisition. An additional $6,000 was paid by Merrill in stock issuance costs.

The book values for both Merrill and Harriss as of January 1, 2002, follow. The fair market value of each of Harriss's accounts is also included. In addition, Harriss holds a fully amortized patent that still retains a $30,000 value.

	Merrill, Inc. Book Value	Harriss Company Book Value	Harriss Company Fair Market Value
Cash	$300,000	$ 40,000	$ 40,000
Receivables	160,000	90,000	80,000
Inventory	220,000	130,000	130,000
Land	100,000	60,000	60,000
Buildings (net)	400,000	110,000	140,000
Equipment (net)	120,000	50,000	50,000
Accounts payable	160,000	30,000	30,000
Long-term liabilities	380,000	170,000	150,000
Common stock	400,000	40,000	
Retained earnings	360,000	240,000	

Required:

a.   Assume that this combination is a statutory merger so that Harriss's accounts are to be transferred to the records of Merrill with Harriss subsequently being dissolved as a legal corporation. Prepare the journal entries for Merrill that are required to record this merger.

b.   Assume that no dissolution is to take place in connection with this combination. Rather, both companies retain their separate legal identities. Prepare a worksheet to consolidate the two companies as of January 1, 2002.

23.   On January 1, 2002, the Lee Company purchased 100 percent of the outstanding common stock of Grant Company. To acquire these shares, Lee issued $200,000 in long-term liabilities and 20,000 shares of common stock having a par value of $1 per share but a fair market value of $10 per share. Lee paid $30,000 to accountants, lawyers, and brokers for assistance in bringing about this purchase. Another $12,000 was paid in connection with stock issuance costs.

Prior to these transactions, the balance sheets for the two companies were as follows:

	Lee Company Book Value	Grant Company Book Value
Cash	$ 60,000	$ 20,000
Receivables	270,000	90,000
Inventory	360,000	140,000
Land	200,000	180,000
Buildings (net)	420,000	220,000
Equipment (net)	160,000	50,000
Accounts payable	(150,000)	(40,000)
Long-term liabilities	(430,000)	(200,000)
Common stock—$1 par value	(110,000)	
Common stock—$20 par value		(120,000)
Additional paid-in capital	(360,000)	–0–
Retained earnings, 1/1/02	(420,000)	(340,000)

Note: Parentheses indicate a credit balance.

In Lee's appraisal of Grant, three accounts were deemed to be undervalued on the subsidiary's books: inventory by $5,000, land by $20,000, and buildings by $30,000.

Required:

a.   Determine the consolidated balance for each of these accounts.

b.   To verify the answers found in part (a), prepare a worksheet to consolidate the balance sheets of these two companies as of January 1, 2002.

24. The Landover Corporation purchased all of the outstanding shares of Smithers, Inc., on January 1, 2003, for $295,000 cash. Several of Smithers's accounts have market values that differ from their book values on this date:

	Book Value	Fair Market Value
Land	$20,000	$70,000
Buildings	60,000	80,000
Equipment	40,000	30,000
Notes payable	50,000	55,000

Prepare a consolidation worksheet at the date of acquisition based on the following information:

	Landover	Smithers
Cash	$ 36,000	$ 16,000
Receivables	116,000	52,000
Inventory	144,000	90,000
Investment in Smithers	295,000	–0–
Land	210,000	20,000
Buildings (net)	640,000	60,000
Equipment (net)	308,000	40,000
Total assets	$1,749,000	$278,000
Accounts payable	$ 88,000	$ 8,000
Notes payable	510,000	50,000
Common stock	380,000	80,000
Retained earnings	771,000	140,000
Total liabilities and equities	$1,749,000	$278,000

Pooling Method

25. Haynes, Inc., obtains all of the outstanding common stock of Tallent Company on October 1, 2000. Tallent earns net income of $10,000 per month. A consolidated income statement is to be prepared for the year ended December 31, 2000. What is the impact on net income of including Tallent in the consolidated statements?
   a. Increased by $120,000 in a purchase; increased by $120,000 in a pooling of interests.
   b. Increased by $120,000 in a purchase; increased by $30,000 in a pooling of interests.
   c. Increased by $30,000 in a purchase; increased by $120,000 in a pooling of interests.
   d. Increased by $30,000 in a purchase; increased by $30,000 in a pooling of interests.

26. A business combination was accounted for properly as a pooling of interests. Which of the following costs related to effecting the business combination should enter into the determination of the net income of a combined corporation for the period in which the expenses are incurred?

	Fees of Finders and Consultants	Registration Fees
a.	No	Yes
b.	No	No
c.	Yes	No
d.	Yes	Yes

(AICPA adapted)

27. How should equipment obtained in a business combination be shown under each of the following methods?

	Pooling of Interests	**Purchase**
a.	Recorded value	Recorded value
b.	Recorded value	Fair value
c.	Fair value	Fair value
d.	Fair value	Recorded value

(AICPA adapted)

28. Starten Company has common stock of $300,000 and retained earnings of $400,000. Premtick, Inc., has common stock of $600,000 and retained earnings of $800,000. On January 1, 2000, Premtick issues 31,000 shares of common stock with a $10 par value and a $30 fair market value for all of Starten's outstanding common stock. A pooling of interests has been created. Immediately after the combination is created, what is the balance in consolidated retained earnings?
   a. $800,000
   b. $1,200,000
   c. $1,190,000
   d. $1,420,000

29. Prior to being united in a business combination, Atkins, Inc., and Waterson Corporation had the following stockholders' equity figures:

	Atkins	**Waterson**
Common stock ($1 par value)	$180,000	$ 45,000
Additional paid-in capital	90,000	20,000
Retained earnings	300,000	110,000

Atkins issues 51,000 new shares of its common stock valued at $3 per share for all of the outstanding stock of Waterson. Assume that Atkins and Waterson were joined in a pooling of interests. Immediately afterward, what were consolidated additional paid-in capital and retained earnings, respectively?

   a. $104,000 and $300,000.
   b. $104,000 and $410,000.
   c. $110,000 and $300,000.
   d. $110,000 and $410,000.

Problems 30 through 33 are based on the following information: Allen, Inc., obtains control over Tucker, Inc., on July 1, 2000. The book value and fair market value of Tucker's accounts on that date (prior to creating the combination) follow, along with the book value of Allen's accounts:

	Allen	**Tucker**	
	Book Value	**Book Value**	**Market Value**
Revenues	$250,000	$130,000	
Expenses	170,000	80,000	
Retained earnings, 1/1/00	130,000	150,000	
Cash and receivables	140,000	60,000	$ 60,000
Inventory	190,000	145,000	175,000
Land	230,000	180,000	200,000
Buildings (net)	400,000	200,000	225,000
Equipment (net)	100,000	75,000	75,000
Liabilities	540,000	360,000	350,000
Common stock	300,000	70,000	
Additional paid-in capital	10,000	30,000	

30. Assume that Allen issued 10,000 shares of common stock with a $5 par value and a $40 fair market value for all of the outstanding stock of Tucker. What was the consolidated land balance if this transaction was a pooling of interests?
    a. $380,000
    b. $410,000
    c. $420,000
    d. $430,000

31. For the fiscal year ending December 31, 2000, how was consolidated net income of this business combination determined if Allen acquired all of Tucker's stock in a pooling of interests?
    a. Allen's income for the past year plus Tucker's income for the past six months.
    b. Allen's income for the past year plus Tucker's income for the past year.
    c. Allen's income for the past six months plus Tucker's income for the past six months.
    d. Allen's income for the past six months plus Tucker's income for the past year.

32. Assume that Allen issued 16,000 shares of common stock with a $5 per share par value and a $40 fair market value in exchange for all of the outstanding shares of Tucker. What was the consolidated Additional Paid-In Capital and Retained Earnings (January 1, 2000, balance) if this combination was recorded as a pooling of interests?
    a. $10,000 and $130,000.
    b. $30,000 and $280,000.
    c. $30,000 and $130,000.
    d. $40,000 and $280,000.

33. Assume that Allen issued 16,000 shares of common stock with a $10 per share par value and a $40 fair market value in exchange for all of the outstanding shares of Tucker. What was the consolidated Additional Paid-In Capital and Retained Earnings (January 1, 2000, balance) if this combination was recorded as a pooling of interests?
    a. $10,000 and $130,000.
    b. 0 and $230,000.
    c. 0 and $80,000.
    d. $40,000 and $280,000.

34. Flaherty Company entered into a business combination with Steeley Company during 2000. The combination was accounted for as a pooling of interests.

    Registration fees were incurred in issuing common stock in this combination. Other costs, such as legal and accounting fees, were also paid.

Required:

    a. In the business combination accounted for as a pooling of interests, how should the assets and liabilities of the two companies be included within consolidated statements? What is the rationale for accounting for a business combination as a pooling of interests?
    b. In the business combination accounted for as a pooling of interests, how should the registration fees and the other direct costs be recorded?
    c. In the business combination accounted for as a pooling of interests, how should the results of the operations for 2000 be reported?

(AICPA adapted)

35. Harcourt Company has the following account balances:

Receivables	$ 90,000
Inventory	500,000
Land	700,000
Buildings	200,000
Liabilities	800,000
Common stock	100,000
Additional paid-in capital	90,000
Retained earnings, 1/1/00	440,000
Revenues	400,000
Expenses	340,000

Several of Harcourt's accounts have market values that differ from book value: land—$900,000; building—$400,000; inventory—$470,000; and liabilities—$840,000. Lee Corporation obtains all of the outstanding shares of Harcourt by issuing 20,000 shares of common stock having a $10 par value but a $62 fair market value. Stock issuance costs amount to $10,000. The transaction is to be accounted for as a pooling of interests. Before recording the issuance of these new shares, Lee has a Common Stock account of $2 million and Additional Paid-In Capital of $1.3 million.

   a. What is the book value of Harcourt's net assets on the date of the takeover?
   b. How are the stock issuance costs handled?
   c. Assume that both companies will retain their identities as separate corporations. What journal entry would Lee record for the issuance of its stock?
   d. How would the answer to part (c) have changed if Lee's stock had a $1 per share par value rather than $10 per share?
   e. How would the answer to part (c) have changed if Lee's stock had a $10 per share par value but Lee issued 30,000 shares rather than 20,000?
   f. How do Harcourt's revenues and expenses affect consolidated totals? Why?
   g. In financial statements prepared immediately following the takeover, what impact would Harcourt's accounts have on the various consolidated totals?

36. Winston has the following account balances as of February 1, 2000:

Inventory	$ 600,000
Land	500,000
Buildings (net) (valued at $1,000,000)	900,000
Common stock ($10 par value)	800,000
Retained earnings, (1/1/00)	1,100,000
Revenues	600,000
Expenses	500,000

Assume that Arlington issues 30,000 shares of common stock ($30 par value but a fair market value of $80 per share) for all of Winston's outstanding stock in a transaction that has qualified as a pooling of interests. Stock issuance costs of $35,000 are paid along with $24,000 of other direct combination costs.

Required:
For each of the following accounts, determine what balance will be included in a February 1, 2000, consolidation.

   a. Buildings.
   b. Goodwill.
   c. Expenses.
   d. Retained Earnings, 1/1/00.

37. On December 31, 2000, Bingham Company and Laredo Company have the following account balances:

	Bingham	Laredo
Revenues	$100,000	$ 80,000
Expenses	60,000	50,000
Net income	$ 40,000	$ 30,000
Retained earnings, 1/1/00	$210,000	$ 70,000
Net income	40,000	30,000
Dividends	30,000	–0–
Retained earnings, 12/31/00	$220,000	$100,000
Cash	$ 80,000	$ 20,000
Receivables	60,000	60,000
Inventory	100,000	70,000
Buildings and equipment (net)	200,000	100,000
Total assets	$440,000	$250,000
Current liabilities	$ 20,000	$ 10,000
Long-term liabilities	70,000	50,000
Common stock	110,000	90,000
Additional paid-in capital	20,000	–0–
Retained earnings, 12/31/00	220,000	100,000
Total liabilities and equities	$440,000	$250,000

After these figures were prepared, Bingham issued 10,000 shares of its $10 par value stock for all of the outstanding shares of Laredo. Bingham's stock had a $25 per share fair market value. Bingham also paid $10,000 in direct combination costs and $20,000 in stock issuance costs. Laredo holds a building that is worth $40,000 more than its current book value.

Required:

Assume that this combination was a pooling of interests. Determine consolidated balances for this combination as of December 31, 2000.

38. Following are the financial balances for the Parrot Company and the Sun Company as of December 31, 2000. Also included are fair market values for the Sun Company accounts.

	Parrot Company Book Value 12/31/00	Sun Company	
		Book Value 12/31/00	Market Value 12/31/00
Cash	$ 290,000	$ 120,000	$ 120,000
Receivables	220,000	300,000	300,000
Inventory	410,000	210,000	260,000
Land	600,000	130,000	110,000
Buildings (net)	600,000	270,000	330,000
Equipment (net)	220,000	190,000	220,000
Accounts payable	(190,000)	(120,000)	(120,000)
Accrued expenses	(90,000)	(30,000)	(30,000)
Long-term liabilities	(900,000)	(510,000)	(510,000)
Common stock—$20 par value ...	(660,000)		
Common stock—$5 par value		(210,000)	
Additional paid-in capital	(70,000)	(90,000)	
Retained earnings, 1/1/00	(390,000)	(240,000)	
Revenues	(960,000)	(330,000)	
Expenses	920,000	310,000	

Note: Parentheses indicate a credit balance.

Required:

In the following situations, determine the value that would be shown in consolidated financial statements for each of the accounts listed below. Each problem should be viewed as an independent occurrence. These transactions all took place on December 31, 2000.

Accounts

Inventory	Revenues
Land	Additional Paid-In Capital
Buildings	Expenses
Goodwill	Retained Earnings, 1/1/00

a. Parrot obtains the outstanding stock of Sun by issuing 12,000 shares of common stock with a value of $40 per share. This transaction was accounted for as a pooling of interests.

b. Parrot obtains the outstanding stock of Sun by issuing 16,000 shares of common stock with a value of $40 per share. This transaction was accounted for as a pooling of interests. Stock issuance costs of $8,000 were paid.

c. Parrot obtains the outstanding stock of Sun by issuing 19,000 shares of its common stock with a value of $40 per share. This transaction was accounted for as a pooling of interests. Direct combination costs of $9,000 were paid by Parrot.

39. The financial statements for Hope, Inc., and Kaisley Corporation for the year ending December 31, 2000, follow. Kaisley's buildings are undervalued on its financial records by $50,000.

	Hope	Kaisley
Revenues	$ 400,000	$ 400,000
Expenses	240,000	240,000
Net income	$ 160,000	$ 160,000
Retained earnings, 1/1/00	$ 600,000	$ 400,000
Net income	160,000	160,000
Dividends paid	90,000	90,000
Retained earnings, 12/31/00	$ 670,000	$ 470,000
Cash	$ 130,000	$ 100,000
Receivables and inventory	200,000	200,000
Buildings (net)	600,000	300,000
Equipment (net)	600,000	500,000
Total assets	$1,530,000	$1,100,000
Liabilities	$ 200,000	$ 200,000
Common stock	630,000	360,000
Additional paid-in capital	30,000	70,000
Retained earnings	670,000	470,000
Total liabilities and equities	$1,530,000	$1,100,000

On December 31, 2000, Hope issued 45,000 new shares of its $10 par value stock to the owners of Kaisley in exchange for all of the outstanding shares of that company. Hope's shares had a fair market value on that date of $30 per share. Hope paid $30,000 to a bank for assisting in the arrangements. Hope also paid $20,000 in stock issuance costs. This combination was accounted for as a pooling of interests. What were the appropriate consolidated balances?

40. The following are preliminary financial statements for Green Company and Gold Company for the year ending December 31, 2000.

	Green Company	Gold Company
Sales	$ 300,000	$ 190,000
Expenses	(200,000)	(110,000)
Net income	$ 100,000	$ 80,000
Retained earnings, 1/1/00	$ 400,000	$ 210,000
Net income—above	100,000	80,000
Dividends paid	(30,000)	–0–
Retained earnings, 12/31/00	$ 470,000	$ 290,000
Current assets	$ 300,000	$ 100,000
Land	100,000	90,000
Buildings (net)	400,000	280,000
Total assets	$ 800,000	$ 470,000
Liabilities	$ 90,000	$ 110,000
Common stock	160,000	60,000
Additional paid-in capital	80,000	10,000
Retained earnings, 12/31/00	470,000	290,000
Total liabilities and equities	$ 800,000	$ 470,000

On December 31, 2000 (subsequent to the preceding statements), Green exchanged 8,000 shares of its $10 par value common stock for all of the outstanding shares of Gold. This transaction was accounted for as a pooling of interests. Green's stock on that date had a fair market value of $55 per share. Green was willing to issue 8,000 shares of stock because Gold's land was appraised at $170,000. Green also paid $12,000 to several attorneys and accountants who assisted in creating this combination.

Required:

    a. Assuming that these two companies retained their separate legal identities, prepare a consolidation worksheet as of December 31, 2000.

    b. Assuming that Gold's accounts were transferred to the records of Green, prepare the necessary journal entries within Green's accounting system as of December 31, 2000.

41.   The Lincoln Company obtains all of the outstanding shares of Swathmore, Inc., on
       December 31, 2000, in exchange for 7,000 shares of common stock. The combination
       was accounted for as a pooling of interests. Each of Lincoln's shares has a $10 par value
       and a $40 fair market value. Several of Swathmore's accounts have market values that
       differ from their book values on this date:

	Book Value	Fair Market Value
Inventory	$70,000	$100,000
Land	30,000	30,000
Equipment	50,000	60,000
Notes payable	50,000	45,000

Financial statements for 2000 for the two companies are as follows:

	Lincoln	Swathmore
Revenues	$ 990,000	$ 540,000
Expenses	(640,000)	(330,000)
Net income	$ 350,000	$ 210,000
Retained earnings, 1/1/00	$ 830,000	$ 110,000
Net income	350,000	210,000
Dividends paid	(220,000)	(130,000)
Retained earnings, 12/31/00	$ 960,000	$ 190,000
Cash	$ 60,000	$ 29,000
Receivables	150,000	65,000
Inventory	190,000	120,000
Land	310,000	30,000
Buildings (net)	840,000	60,000
Equipment (net)	320,000	50,000
Totals	$1,870,000	$ 354,000
Accounts payable	$ 110,000	$ 34,000
Notes payable	370,000	50,000
Common stock	400,000	50,000
Additional paid-in capital	30,000	30,000
Retained earnings	960,000	190,000
Totals	$1,870,000	$ 354,000

Required:

a.   Determine the consolidated balance for each of these accounts.
b.   To verify the answers found in part (a), prepare a worksheet to consolidate the
      financial statements of these two companies.

42. On December 31, 2000, the Sherman Company exchanged 17,000 shares of its common stock with a market value of $57 per share for 100 percent of the outstanding shares of the Atlanta Company. This transaction was accounted for as a pooling of interests. Prior to the exchange, the trial balances of both companies for the year 2000 are as follows:

	Sherman Company Book Value	Atlanta Company Book Value
Debits		
Cash	$110,000	$ 20,000
Receivables (net)	300,000	290,000
Inventory	440,000	260,000
Land	280,000	80,000
Buildings (net)	270,000	290,000
Equipment (net)	810,000	320,000
Expenses	540,000	210,000
Dividends	30,000	–0–
Credits		
Accounts payable	120,000	60,000
Long-term liabilities	960,000	330,000
Common stock—$20 par value	520,000	
Common stock—$25 par value		300,000
Additional paid-in capital	110,000	100,000
Retained earnings, 1/1/00	470,000	200,000
Revenues	600,000	480,000

Additional Information:

■ After the preparation of these trial balances, Sherman paid $20,000 in cash for costs incurred relating to this exchange. These expenditures covered the fees charged by lawyers and accountants involved with creating the business combination.

■ Atlanta possesses land that has greatly appreciated in value since it was acquired. The book value of this land is estimated to be $60,000 less than fair market value.

Required:

a. Prepare a worksheet to consolidate the financial information of these two companies for the year ending December 31, 2000.

b. Prepare a worksheet to consolidate the financial information of these two companies for the year ending December 31, 2000, assuming that this combination was actually a purchase.

Consolidations— Subsequent to the Date of Acquisition

QUESTIONS TO CONSIDER

- How does a parent company account for a subsidiary organization in the years that follow the creation of a business combination?

- What impact does the parent's method of accounting for a subsidiary have on each subsequent consolidation?

- Why do intercompany balances exist within the financial records of the separate companies? How are these reciprocals eliminated on a consolidation worksheet?

- Why did the FASB decide that goodwill amortization should not be allowed and that instead goodwill should be periodically tested for impairment? How do firms determine when and if goodwill is impaired? How are goodwill impairment losses recognized in consolidated financial statements?

- How is the amortization of other purchase price allocations recognized within consolidated financial statements?

- If the exact purchase price of a subsidiary is based on a future event, what effect does this contingency have on the consolidation process?

- Should a subsidiary company report on its own financial statements the purchase price allocations and subsequent amortization that can result from the purchase price paid by the parent?

In the mid-1980s, the General Electric Co. (GE) acquired the National Broadcasting Company (NBC) as part of its $6.4 billion cash purchase of RCA Corporation. Although this transaction involved well-known companies, it was not unique; mergers and acquisitions have long been common in the business world. In 1995, 3,510 mergers and acquisitions involved U.S. companies, a number that rose dramatically to 9,602 transactions in 2000 (with a monetary value of $1.4 trillion).[1]

The current financial statements of GE indicate that NBC is still a component of this economic entity. However, NBC continues to be a separately incorporated concern long after its purchase. As discussed in Chapter 2, a parent often chooses to let a subsidiary retain its identity as a legal corporation to better utilize the value inherent in a going concern.

For external reporting purposes, maintenance of incorporation creates an ongoing challenge for the accountant. In each subsequent period, consolidation must be simulated anew through the use of a worksheet and consolidation entries. Thus, for more than 15 years, the financial data for GE and NBC have been brought together periodically to provide figures for the financial statements that represent this business combination.

CONSOLIDATION—THE EFFECTS CREATED BY THE PASSAGE OF TIME

In the previous chapter, consolidation accounting is analyzed at the date that a combination is created. The present chapter carries this

---

[1]Mergerstat (www.mergerstat.com).

process one step further by examining the consolidation procedures that must be followed in subsequent periods whenever separate incorporation of the subsidiary is maintained.

Despite complexities created by the passage of time, the basic objective of all consolidations remains the same: to combine asset, liability, revenue, expense, and equity accounts of a parent and its subsidiaries. From a mechanical perspective, a worksheet and consolidation entries continue to provide structure for the production of a single set of financial statements for the combined business entity.

When a time factor is introduced into the consolidation process, additional complications are encountered. For internal record-keeping purposes, the parent must select and apply an accounting method to monitor the relationship between the two companies. The investment balance recorded by the parent varies over time as a result of the method chosen, as does the income subsequently recognized. These differences affect the periodic consolidation process but not the figures to be reported by the combined entity. Regardless of the amount, the parent's Investment account is eliminated on the worksheet so that the subsidiary's actual assets and liabilities can be consolidated. Likewise, the income figure accrued by the parent is removed each period so that the subsidiary's revenues and expenses can be included when creating an income statement for the combined business entity.

INVESTMENT ACCOUNTING BY THE ACQUIRING COMPANY

For external reporting, consolidation of a subsidiary becomes necessary whenever control exists. For internal record-keeping, though, the parent has the choice of three alternatives for monitoring the activities of its subsidiaries: the cost method, the equity method, or the partial equity method. *Because both the resulting investment balance as well as the related income is eliminated as part of every recurring consolidation, the selection of a particular method does not affect the totals ultimately reported for the combined companies.* Rather, this decision dictates the specific procedures subsequently utilized in consolidating the financial information of the separate organizations.

The actual choice of a method is often based on the internal reporting philosophy of the acquiring company. The *cost method* might be selected because it is easy to apply. The investment balance remains permanently on the parent's balance sheet at original cost. The cost method uses the cash basis for income recognition. Therefore only the dividends subsequently received from the subsidiary are recognized as income. No other adjustments are recorded. Thus, this method requires little effort while providing an accurate measure of the cash flows between the two companies.

In contrast, under the *equity method* the acquiring company accrues income when earned by the subsidiary. To match acquisition costs against income, amortization expense stemming from the original acquisition is recognized through periodic adjusting entries. Unrealized gains on intercompany transactions are deferred; dividends paid by the subsidiary serve to reduce the investment balance. As discussed in Chapter 1, the equity method is designed to create a parallel between the parent's investment accounts and the underlying operations of the acquired company.[2]

Under the equity method, the parent's accounts reflect the income of the entire combined business entity. Consequently, the equity method often is referred to in accounting as a single-line consolidation. The equity method is especially popular in companies where management wants to get a picture of overall profitability by looking at the periodic (such as monthly) figures developed by the parent.

---

[2]In Chapter 1, the equity method was introduced in connection with the external reporting of investments in which the owner held the ability to apply significant influence over the investee (usually by possessing 20 to 50 percent of the company's voting stock). Here, the equity method is utilized for the *internal* reporting of the parent for investments in which control is maintained. Although the accounting procedures are identical, the reason for using the equity method is different.

Exhibit 3-1   Internal Reporting of Investment Accounts by Acquiring Company

Method	Investment Account	Income Account	Advantages
Equity	Continually adjusted to reflect ownership of acquired company.	Income is accrued as earned; amortization and other adjustments are recognized.	Acquiring company totals give a true representation of consolidation figures.
Cost	Remains at initially recorded cost.	Cash received is recorded as Dividend Income.	Easy to apply; measures cash flows.
Partial equity	Adjusted only for accrued income and dividends received from acquired company.	Income is accrued as earned; no other adjustments are recognized.	Usually gives balances approximating consolidation figures, but is easier to apply than equity method.

A third method available to the acquiring company is a *partial application of the equity method.* Under this approach, income accruing from the subsidiary is recognized immediately by the parent. Dividends that are collected reduce the investment balance. However, no other equity adjustments (amortization or deferral of unrealized gains) are recorded. Thus, in many cases, earnings figures on the parent's books approximate consolidated totals but without the effort associated with a full application of the equity method.

Each acquiring company must decide for itself the appropriate approach in recording the operations of its subsidiaries. For example, Alliant Food Service, Inc., applies the equity method. According to Joe Tomczak, vice president and controller of Alliant Food Service, Inc., "we maintain the parent holding company books on an equity basis. This approach provides the best method of providing information for our operational decisions."[3]

In contrast, Reynolds Metals Corporation has chosen to utilize the partial equity method approach. Allen Earehart, director of corporate accounting for Reynolds, states "we do adjust the carrying value of our investments annually to reflect the earnings of each subsidiary. We want to be able to evaluate the parent company on a stand-alone basis and a regular equity accrual is, therefore, necessary. However, we do separate certain adjustments such as the elimination of intercompany gains and losses and record them solely within the development of consolidated financial statements."[4]

Exhibit 3–1 provides a summary of these three reporting techniques. The method adopted only affects the acquiring company's separate financial records. No changes are created in either the subsidiary's accounts or the consolidated totals.

Because specific worksheet procedures differ based on the investment method being utilized by the parent, the consolidation process subsequent to the date of combination will be introduced twice. Initially, consolidations in which the acquiring company uses the equity method are reviewed. All procedures are then redeveloped where the investment is recorded by one of the alternative methods.

SFAS 142—GOODWILL AND INTANGIBLE ASSETS

In *SFAS 142,* "Goodwill and Other Intangible Assets," July 2001, the FASB approved significant changes in the way income is determined for combined business entities. The most prominent of these changes relates to the treatment of goodwill in periods subsequent to acquisition. For fiscal periods beginning after December 15, 2001, goodwill will no longer be amortized systematically over time.[5] Instead, goodwill will be

---

[3]Telephone conversation with Joe Tomczak.

[4]Telephone conversation with Allen Earehart.

[5]Additionally, goodwill will not be amortized for new business combinations occurring subsequent to June 30, 2001.

subject to an annual test for impairment. This nonamortization approach will be applied to both previously recognized and newly acquired goodwill. Consequently, goodwill that arose from pre–*SFAS 142* combinations will simply be carried forward at unamortized cost as of the beginning of annual reporting periods in 2002.

For consolidations of parent and subsidiary companies, goodwill amortization expense will no longer appear on the combined income statement. The consolidated balance sheet will frequently carry acquisition-related goodwill at its original cost. Only upon the recognition of an impairment loss (or partial sale of a subsidiary) will goodwill decline from one period to the next. In the next several sections of this chapter, the relation of the parent's investment accounting to the adjustments required for consolidation will be presented along with specific procedures for amortizing the cost of a business combination and testing for impairment as appropriate.

SUBSEQUENT CONSOLIDATION—INVESTMENT RECORDED BY THE EQUITY METHOD

Acquisition Made during the Current Year

As a basis for this illustration, assume that Parrot Company obtains all of the outstanding common stock of Sun Company on January 1, 2002. Parrot acquires this stock for $760,000 in cash but pays an additional $40,000 in direct combination costs. Because cash is paid, the purchase method is applicable; a pooling of interests requires that the business combination be created only through the exchange of voting common stock.

The book values as well as the appraised values of Sun's accounts are as follows:

	Book Value 1/1/02	Fair Market Value 1/1/02	Difference
Current assets	$ 320,000	$ 320,000	–0–
Land	200,000	220,000	+ 20,000
Buildings (10-year life)	320,000	450,000	+130,000
Equipment (5-year life)	180,000	150,000	(30,000)
Liabilities	(420,000)	(420,000)	–0–
Net book value	$ 600,000	$ 720,000	$120,000
Common stock—$40 par value	$(200,000)		
Additional paid-in capital	(20,000)		
Retained earnings, 1/1/02	(380,000)		

For this combination, the assumption is being made that any amortization relating to purchase price allocations is calculated using the straight-line method with no estimated salvage value.[6]

With the inclusion of the $40,000 direct consolidation costs, a total of $800,000 has been paid by Parrot in this purchase of Sun Company. As shown in Exhibit 3–2, individual allocations are used to adjust Sun's accounts from their book values on January 1, 2002, to fair market values. Since the total value of these assets and liabilities was only $720,000, goodwill of $80,000 must be recognized for consolidation purposes.

Each of these allocated amounts (other than the $20,000 attributed to land and the $80,000 for goodwill) represents a cost incurred by Parrot that is associated with an account having a definite life. As discussed in Chapter 1, Parrot must amortize each of these cost figures over their expected lives. The expense recognition necessitated by this purchase price allocation is calculated in Exhibit 3–3.

---

[6]Unless otherwise stated, all amortization expense computations in this textbook are based on the straight-line method with no salvage value.

Exhibit 3-2

PARROT COMPANY
Allocation of Purchase Price
January 1, 2002

Purchase price by Parrot Company		$ 800,000
Book value of Sun Company		(600,000)
Excess of cost over book value		200,000
Allocation to specific accounts based on fair market values:		
Land	$ 20,000	
Buildings	130,000	
Equipment (overvalued)	(30,000)	120,000
Excess cost not identified with specific accounts—goodwill . . .		$ 80,000

Exhibit 3-3
Annual Excess Amortization

PARROT COMPANY
Excess Amortization Schedule—Allocation of Purchase Price

Account	Allocation	Useful Life	Annual Excess Amortizations
Land	$ 20,000	Indefinite	–0–
Buildings	130,000	10 years	$13,000
Equipment	(30,000)	5 years	(6,000)
Goodwill	80,000	Indefinite	–0–
			$ 7,000*

*Total excess amortizations will be $7,000 annually for five years until the equipment allocation is fully removed. At the end of each asset's life, future amortizations will change.

One aspect of this amortization schedule warrants explanation. The fair market value of Sun's Equipment account was $30,000 *less* than book value. Therefore, instead of attributing an additional cost to this asset, the $30,000 allocation actually reflects a cost reduction. As such, the amortization shown in Exhibit 3–3 relating to Equipment is not an additional expense but rather an expense reduction.

Having determined the allocation of the purchase price in the previous example as well as the associated amortization, the parent's separate record-keeping for 2002 can be constructed as shown on the next page. Assume that Sun earns income of $100,000 during the year and pays a $40,000 cash dividend on August 1, 2002.

In this initial illustration, Parrot has adopted the equity method. Apparently, this company believes that the information derived from using the equity method is useful in its evaluation of Sun.

Application of the Equity Method

Parrot's Financial Records

1/1/02	Investment in Sun Company.		800,000	
	Cash			800,000
	To record purchase of Sun Company including direct combination costs.			
8/1/02	Cash		40,000	
	Investment in Sun Company.			40,000
	To record receipt of cash dividend from subsidiary, an investment that is being accounted for by means of the equity method.			

| 12/31/02 | Investment in Sun Company................... | 100,000 | |
| | Equity in subsidiary earnings.............. | | 100,000 |

To accrue income earned by 100 percent owned
subsidiary.

| 12/31/02 | Equity in subsidiary earnings................... | 7,000 | |
| | Investment in Sun Company............... | | 7,000 |

To recognize amortizations on allocations made
in purchase of subsidiary (see Exhibit 3–3).

Parrot's application of the equity method, as shown in this series of entries, causes the Investment in Sun Company account balance to rise from $800,000 to $853,000 ($800,000 − $40,000 + $100,000 − $7,000). During the same period, a $93,000 equity income figure (the $100,000 earnings accrual less the $7,000 excess amortization expenses) is recognized by the parent.

The consolidation procedures for Parrot and Sun one year after the date of acquisition are illustrated next. For this purpose, Exhibit 3–4 presents the separate 2002 financial statements for these two companies. Both investment accounts (the $853,000 asset balance and the $93,000 income accrual) have been recorded by Parrot based on applying the equity method.

Determining Consolidated Totals

Before becoming immersed in the mechanical aspects of a consolidation, the objective of this process should be understood. As indicated in Chapter 2, the revenue, expense, asset, and liability accounts of the subsidiary are added to the parent company balances. Within this procedure, several important guidelines must be followed:

- Sun's assets and liabilities are adjusted to reflect any allocations originating from the purchase price.
- Because of the passage of time, the income effects (e.g., amortizations) of these allocations must also be recorded within the consolidation process.
- Any reciprocal or intercompany accounts have to be offset. If, for example, one of the companies owes money to the other, the receivable and the payable balances have no connection with an outside party. Both should be eliminated for external reporting purposes. When the companies are viewed as a single entity, the receivable and the payable are intercompany balances to be removed.

A consolidation of the two sets of financial information in Exhibit 3–4 is a relatively uncomplicated task and can even be carried out without the use of a worksheet. Understanding the origin of each reported figure is the first step in gaining a knowledge of this process.

- *Revenues* = $1,900,000. The revenues of the parent and the subsidiary are added together.
- *Cost of goods sold* = $950,000. The cost of goods sold of the parent and subsidiary are added together.
- *Depreciation expense* = $257,000. The depreciation expenses of the parent and subsidiary are added together along with the $13,000 additional building depreciation and the $6,000 reduction in equipment depreciation as indicated in Exhibit 3–3.
- *Equity in subsidiary earnings* = –0–. The investment income recorded by the parent is eliminated so that the subsidiary's revenues and expenses can be included in the consolidated totals.
- *Net income* = $693,000. Consolidated revenues less consolidated expenses.
- *Retained earnings, 1/1/02* = $840,000. The parent figure only because the subsidiary was not owned prior to that date.

Exhibit 3–4
Separate Records—Equity
Method Applied

PARROT COMPANY AND SUN COMPANY
Financial Statements
For Year Ending December 31, 2002

	Parrot Company	Sun Company
Income Statement		
Revenues	$(1,500,000)	$ (400,000)
Cost of goods sold	700,000	250,000
Depreciation expense	200,000	50,000
Equity in subsidiary earnings	(93,000)	–0–
Net income	$ (693,000)	$ (100,000)
Statement of Retained Earnings		
Retained earnings, 1/1/02	$ (840,000)	$ (380,000)
Net income (above)	(693,000)	(100,000)
Dividends paid	120,000	40,000
Retained earnings, 12/31/02	$(1,413,000)	$ (440,000)
Balance Sheet		
Current assets	$ 1,040,000	$ 400,000
Investment in Sun Company (at equity)	853,000	–0–
Land	600,000	200,000
Buildings (net)	370,000	288,000
Equipment (net)	250,000	220,000
Total assets	$ 3,113,000	$ 1,108,000
Liabilities	$ (980,000)	$ (448,000)
Common stock	(600,000)	(200,000)
Additional paid-in capital	(120,000)	(20,000)
Retained earnings, 12/31/02 (above)	(1,413,000)	(440,000)
Total liabilities and equities	$(3,113,000)	$(1,108,000)

Note: Parentheses indicate a credit balance.

- *Dividends paid* = $120,000. The parent company balance only because the subsidiary's dividends were paid intercompany to the parent and not to an outside party.
- *Retained earnings, 12/31/02* = $1,413,000. Consolidated retained earnings as of the beginning of the year plus consolidated net income less consolidated dividends paid.
- *Current assets* = $1,440,000. The parent's book value plus the subsidiary's book value.
- *Investment in Sun Company* = –0–. The asset recorded by the parent is eliminated so that the subsidiary's assets and liabilities can be included in the consolidated totals.
- *Land* = $820,000. The parent's book value plus the subsidiary's book value plus the $20,000 allocation within the purchase price.
- *Buildings* = $775,000. The parent's book value plus the subsidiary's book value plus the $130,000 allocation within the purchase price less 2002 amortization of $13,000.

- *Equipment* = $446,000. The parent's book value plus the subsidiary's book value less the $30,000 cost reduction allocation plus the 2002 expense reduction of $6,000.
- *Goodwill* = $80,000. The residual allocation shown in Exhibit 3–2. Note that goodwill is not amortized.
- *Total assets* = $3,561,000. Summation of consolidated assets.
- *Liabilities* = $1,428,000. The parent's book value plus the subsidiary's book value.
- *Common stock* = $600,000. The parent's book value since this combination was a purchase.
- *Additional paid-in capital* = $120,000. The parent's book value since this combination was a purchase.
- *Retained earnings, 12/31/02* = $1,413,000. Computed above.
- *Total liabilities and equities* = $3,561,000. Summation of consolidated liabilities and equities.

Consolidation Worksheet

Although the consolidated figures to be reported can be computed as just shown, accountants normally prefer to use a worksheet. A worksheet provides an organized structure for this process, a benefit that becomes especially important in consolidating complex combinations.

For Parrot and Sun, only five consolidation entries are needed to arrive at the same figures previously derived for this business combination. As discussed in Chapter *2, worksheet entries are the catalyst for developing totals to be reported by the entity but are not physically recorded in the individual account balances of either company.*

Consolidation Entry S

Common Stock (Sun Company)............................	200,000	
Additional Paid-In Capital (Sun Company).................	20,000	
Retained Earnings, 1/1/02 (Sun Company)	380,000	
Investment in Sun Company		600,000

As shown in Exhibit 3–2, Parrot's $800,000 purchase price reflects two components: (1) a $600,000 amount equal to Sun's book value and (2) a $200,000 figure attributed to the difference, at January 1, 2002, between the book value and market value of Sun's assets and liabilities (with a residual allocation made to goodwill). Entry S removes the $600,000 component of the Investment in Sun Company account so that the *book value* of each subsidiary asset and liability can be included in the consolidated figures. A second worksheet entry (Entry A) eliminates the remaining $200,000 portion of the purchase price, allowing the specific allocations to be recorded along with any goodwill.

Entry S also removes Sun's stockholders' equity accounts as of the beginning of the year. As a purchase, subsidiary equity balances generated prior to the acquisition are not relevant to the business combination and should be deleted. The elimination is made through this entry because the equity accounts and the $600,000 component of the Investment account represent reciprocal balances: Both provide a measure of Sun's book value as of January 1, 2002.

Before moving to the next consolidation entry, a clarification point should be made. In actual practice, worksheet entries are usually identified numerically. However as in the previous chapter, the label "Entry S" used in this example refers to the elimination of Sun's beginning **S**tockholders' equity. As a reminder of the purpose being served, all worksheet entries are identified in a similar fashion. Thus, throughout this textbook, "Entry S" always refers to the removal of the subsidiary's beginning stockholders' equity balances for the year against the book value portion of the Investment account.

Consolidation Entry A

Land	20,000	
Buildings.	130,000	
Goodwill.	80,000	
Equipment.		30,000
Investment in Sun Company		200,000

As indicated previously, the second worksheet entry removes the $200,000 component of the purchase price, replacing it with the specific allocations from the original purchase price (see Exhibit 3–2). In this manner, the individual assets and liabilities of the consolidated entity now reflect the cost incurred by Parrot in making this purchase. Sun's accounts are adjusted based on the $200,000 paid at the time of acquisition that was in excess of Sun's book value. No basis exists for continually revaluing the accounts to newly determined market values at the date of each subsequent consolidation.

    This entry is labeled "Entry A" to indicate that it represents the **A**llocations made in connection with the parent's purchase price.

Consolidation Entry I

Equity in subsidiary earnings	93,000	
Investment in Sun Company		93,000

"Entry I" (for **I**ncome) removes the subsidiary income recognized by Parrot during the year so that the underlying revenue and expense accounts of Sun (and the current amortization expense) can be brought into the consolidated totals. The $93,000 figure eliminated here represents the $100,000 income accrual recognized by Parrot, reduced by the $7,000 in excess amortizations. For consolidation purposes, the one-line amount appearing in the parent's records is not appropriate and is removed so that the individual balances can be included. The entry originally recorded by the parent is simply reversed on the worksheet to remove its impact.

Consolidation Entry D

Investment in Sun Company	40,000	
Dividends paid		40,000

The dividends distributed by the subsidiary during 2002 also must be eliminated from the consolidated totals. The entire $40,000 payment was made to the parent so that, from the viewpoint of the consolidated entity, it is simply an intercompany transfer of cash. The distribution did not affect any outside party. Therefore, "Entry D" (for **D**ividends) is designed to offset the impact of this transaction by removing the subsidiary's Dividends Paid account. Because the equity method has been applied, receipt of this money by Parrot was recorded originally as a decrease in the Investment in Sun Company account. To eliminate the impact of this reduction, the Investment account is increased here.

Consolidation Entry E

Depreciation expense	7,000	
Equipment.	6,000	
Buildings.		13,000

This final worksheet entry records the current year's excess amortization expenses relating to Parrot's purchase price. Because the equity method amortization was eliminated within Entry I, "Entry E" (for **E**xpense) now records the 2002 expense attributed to each of the specific account allocations (see Exhibit 3–3).

Thus, the worksheet entries necessary for consolidation when the parent has applied the equity method are as follows:

> *Entry S*—Eliminates the subsidiary's stockholders' equity accounts as of the beginning of the current year along with the equivalent book value component within the parent's purchase price in the Investment account.
>
> *Entry A*—Recognizes the unamortized allocations as of the beginning of the current year, costs that were associated with the original purchase price.
>
> *Entry I*—Eliminates the impact of intercompany income accrued by the parent.
>
> *Entry D*—Eliminates the impact of intercompany dividend payments made by the subsidiary.
>
> *Entry E*—Recognizes excess amortization expenses for the current period on the allocations within the original purchase price.

Exhibit 3–5 provides a complete presentation of the December 31, 2002, consolidation worksheet developed for Parrot Company and Sun Company. The series of entries just described successfully brings together the separate financial statements of these two organizations. Note that the consolidated totals are the same as those computed previously for this combination.

One aspect of this worksheet should be explained. Parrot is separately reporting net income of $693,000 as well as ending retained earnings of $1,413,000, figures that are identical to the totals generated for the consolidated entity. However, in a purchase combination, subsidiary income earned after the date of acquisition is to be *added* to that of the parent. Thus, a question arises in this example as to why the parent company figures alone equal the consolidated balances of both operations.

In reality, Sun's income for this period is contained in both Parrot's reported balances as well as in the consolidated totals. Through the application of the equity method, the 2002 earnings of the subsidiary have already been accrued by Parrot along with the appropriate amortization expense. *The parent's Equity in Subsidiary Earnings account is, therefore, an accurate representation of Sun's effect on consolidated net income.* If the equity method is employed properly, the worksheet process simply replaces this single $93,000 balance with the specific revenue and expense accounts that it represents. *Consequently, the parent's net income and retained earnings mirror consolidated totals.*

Consolidation Subsequent to Year of Acquisition—Equity Method

In many ways, every consolidation of Parrot and Sun prepared after the date of acquisition incorporates the same basic procedures outlined in the previous section. However, the continual financial evolution undergone by the companies prohibits an exact repetition of the consolidation entries demonstrated in Exhibit 3–5.

As a basis for analyzing the procedural changes necessitated by the passage of time, assume that Parrot Company continues to hold its ownership of Sun Company as of December 31, 2005. This date was selected at random; any date subsequent to 2002 would serve equally well to illustrate this process. As an additional factor, assume that Sun now has a $40,000 liability that is payable to Parrot.

For this consolidation, assume that the January 1, 2005, retained earnings balance of Sun Company has risen to $600,000. Since that account had a reported total of only $380,000 on January 1, 2002, Sun's book value apparently has increased by $220,000 during the 2002–2004 period. Although knowledge of individual operating figures in the past is not required, Sun's reported totals help to clarify the consolidation procedures.

Exhibit 3–5

			Consolidation Entries		

PARROT COMPANY AND SUN COMPANY
Consolidation: Purchase Method   **Consolidated Worksheet**
Investment: Equity Method   **For Year Ending December 31, 2002**

Accounts	Parrot Company	Sun Company	Debit	Credit	Consolidated Totals
Income Statement					
Revenues	(1,500,000)	(400,000)			(1,900,000)
Cost of goods sold	700,000	250,000			950,000
Depreciation expense	200,000	50,000	(E) 7,000		257,000
Equity in subsidiary earnings	(93,000)	–0–	(I) 93,000		–0–
Net income	(693,000)	(100,000)			(693,000)
Statement of Retained Earnings					
Retained earnings, 1/1/02	(840,000)	(380,000)	(S) 380,000		(840,000)
Net income (above)	(693,000)	(100,000)			(693,000)
Dividends paid	120,000	40,000		(D) 40,000	120,000
Retained earnings, 12/31/02	(1,413,000)	(440,000)			(1,413,000)
Balance Sheet					
Current assets	1,040,000	400,000			1,440,000
Investment in Sun Company	853,000	–0–	(D) 40,000	(S) 600,000	–0–
				(A) 200,000	
				(I) 93,000	
Land	600,000	200,000	(A) 20,000		820,000
Buildings (net)	370,000	288,000	(A) 130,000	(E) 13,000	775,000
Equipment (net)	250,000	220,000	(E) 6,000	(A) 30,000	446,000
Goodwill	–0–	–0–	(A) 80,000		80,000
Total assets	3,113,000	1,108,000			3,561,000
Liabilities	(980,000)	(448,000)			(1,428,000)
Common stock	(600,000)	(200,000)	(S) 200,000		(600,000)
Additional paid-in capital	(120,000)	(20,000)	(S) 20,000		(120,000)
Retained earnings, 12/31/02 (above)	(1,413,000)	(440,000)			(1,413,000)
Total liabilities and equities	(3,113,000)	(1,108,000)			(3,561,000)

Note: Parentheses indicate a credit balance.
Consolidation entries:
  (S) Elimination of Sun's stockholders' equity accounts as of January 1, 2002, and book value portion of purchase price.
  (A) Allocation of Parrot's cost in excess of Sun's book value.
  (I)   Elimination of intercompany equity income.
  (D) Elimination of intercompany dividends.
  (E) Recognition of excess amortization expenses on purchase price allocations.

Year	Sun Company Net Income	Dividends Paid	Increase in Book Value	Ending Retained Earnings
2002	$100,000	$ 40,000	$ 60,000	$440,000
2003	140,000	50,000	90,000	530,000
2004	90,000	20,000	70,000	600,000
	$330,000	$110,000	$220,000	

For 2005, the current year, the assumption will be made that Sun reports net income of $160,000 and pays cash dividends of $70,000. Because it applies the equity method, earnings of $160,000 are recognized by Parrot. Furthermore, as shown in Exhibit 3–3, amortization expense of $7,000 is applicable to 2005 and must also be recorded by the parent. Consequently, Parrot reports an Equity in Subsidiary Earnings balance for the year of $153,000 ($160,000 − $7,000).

Although this income figure can be reconstructed with little difficulty, the current balance in the Investment in Sun Company account is more complicated. Over the years, the initial $800,000 purchase price has been subjected to adjustments for:

1. The annual accrual of Sun's income.
2. The receipt of dividends from Sun.
3. The recognition of annual excess amortization expenses.

However, by analyzing these changes, Exhibit 3–6 can be developed to show the components of the balance in the Investment in Sun Company account as of December 31, 2005.

Following the construction of the Investment in Sun Company account, the consolidation worksheet developed in Exhibit 3–7 should be easier to understand. Current figures for both companies are presented in the first two columns. The parent's investment balance and equity income accrual as well as Sun's income and stockholders' equity accounts correspond to the information given previously. Worksheet entries (lettered to agree with the previous illustration) are then utilized to consolidate all balances.

Several steps are necessary to arrive at these reported totals. The subsidiary's assets, liabilities, revenues, and expenses are added to those same accounts of the parent. The unamortized portion of the original purchase price allocations are included along with current excess amortization expenses. The investment and equity income balances are both eliminated as is the subsidiary's stockholders' equity accounts. Intercompany

Exhibit 3–6

PARROT COMPANY		
Investment in Sun Company Account		
As of December 31, 2005		
Equity Method Applied		
Purchase price		$ 800,000
Entries recorded in prior years:		
Accrual of Sun Company's income		
2002	$100,000	
2003	140,000	
2004	90,000	330,000
Sun Company—Dividends paid		
2002	$ 40,000	
2003	50,000	
2004	20,000	(110,000)
Excess amortization expenses		
2002	$ 7,000	
2003	7,000	
2004	7,000	(21,000)
Entries recorded in current year—2005:		
Accrual of Sun Company's income	$160,000	
Sun Company—Dividends paid	(70,000)	
Excess amortization expenses	(7,000)	83,000
Investment in Sun Company, 12/31/05		$1,082,000

Exhibit 3-7

	PARROT COMPANY AND SUN COMPANY				
Consolidation: Purchase Method	Consolidated Worksheet				
Investment: Equity Method	For Year Ending December 31, 2005				

Accounts	Parrot Company	Sun Company	Consolidation Entries		Consolidated Totals
			Debit	Credit	
Income Statement					
Revenues	(2,100,000)	(600,000)			(2,700,000)
Cost of goods sold	1,000,000	380,000			1,380,000
Depreciation expense	300,000	60,000	(E) 7,000		367,000
Equity in subsidiary earnings	(153,000)	–0–	(I) 153,000		–0–
Net income	(953,000)	(160,000)			(953,000)
Statement of Retained Earnings					
Retained earnings, 1/1/05	(2,044,000)	(600,000)	(S) 600,000		(2,044,000)
Net income (above)	(953,000)	(160,000)			(953,000)
Dividends paid	420,000	70,000		(D) 70,000	420,000
Retained earnings, 12/31/05	(2,577,000)	(690,000)			(2,577,000)
Balance Sheet					
Current assets	1,705,000	500,000		(P) 40,000	2,165,000
Investment in Sun Company	1,082,000	–0–	(D) 70,000	(S) 820,000	–0–
				(A) 179,000	
				(I) 153,000	
Land	600,000	240,000	(A) 20,000		860,000
Buildings (net)	540,000	420,000	(A) 91,000	(E) 13,000	1,038,000
Equipment (net)	420,000	210,000	(E) 6,000	(A) 12,000	624,000
Goodwill	–0–	–0–	(A) 80,000		80,000
Total assets	4,347,000	1,370,000			4,767,000
Liabilities	(1,050,000)	(460,000)	(P) 40,000		(1,470,000)
Common stock	(600,000)	(200,000)	(S) 200,000		(600,000)
Additional paid-in capital	(120,000)	(20,000)	(S) 20,000		(120,000)
Retained earnings, 12/31/05 (above)	(2,577,000)	(690,000)			(2,577,000)
Total liabilities and equities	(4,347,000)	(1,370,000)			(4,767,000)

Note: Parentheses indicate a credit balance.

Consolidation entries:
  (S) Elimination of Sun's stockholders' equity accounts as of January 1, 2005, and book value portion of Investment account.
  (A) Allocation of Parrot's cost in excess of Sun's book value, unamortized values as of January 1, 2005.
  (I) Elimination of intercompany income.
  (D) Elimination of intercompany dividends.
  (E) Recognition of excess amortization expenses on purchase price allocations.
  (P) Elimination of intercompany receivable/payable balances.

dividends are removed with the same treatment required for the debt existing between the two companies.

Consolidation Entry S   Once again, this first consolidation entry offsets reciprocal amounts representing the subsidiary's book value as of the beginning of the current year. Sun's January 1, 2005, stockholders' equity accounts are eliminated against the book value portion of the parent's Investment account. Here, though, the amount eliminated is $920,000 rather than the $600,000 shown in Exhibit 3–5 for 2002. Both balances have changed during the 2002–2004 period. Sun's operations caused a $220,000 increase in retained earnings. Parrot's application of the equity method created a parallel effect on its Investment in Sun Company account (the income accrual of $330,000 less dividends collected of $110,000).

Although Sun's retained earnings balance is removed in this entry, the income earned by this company since the date of purchase is still included in the consolidated figures. Parrot accrues these profits annually through application of the equity method. Thus, elimination of the subsidiary's entire retained earnings is necessary; a portion was earned prior to the purchase and the remainder has already been recorded by the parent.

Entry S removes these balances as of the first day of 2005 rather than at the end of the year. The consolidation process is made a bit simpler by segregating the effect of preceding operations from the transactions of the current year. Thus, *all worksheet entries relate specifically to either the previous years (S and A) or the current period (I, D, E, and P).*

Consolidation Entry A   In the initial consolidation (2002), cost allocations amounting to $200,000 were recorded but these balances have now undergone three years of amortization. As computed in Exhibit 3–8, expenses for these prior years totaled $21,000, leaving a balance of $179,000. Allocation of this amount to the individual accounts is also determined in Exhibit 3–8 and reflected in worksheet Entry A. As with Entry S, these balances are calculated as of January 1, 2005, so that the current year expenses may be recorded separately (in Entry E).

Consolidation Entry I   As before, this entry eliminates the equity income recorded currently by Parrot ($153,000) in connection with its ownership of Sun. The subsidiary's revenue and expense accounts are left intact so they can be included in the consolidated figures.

Consolidation Entry D   This worksheet entry offsets the $70,000 intercompany dividend payment made by Sun to Parrot during the current period.

Consolidation Entry E   Excess amortization expenses relating to Parrot's purchase price are individually recorded for 2005.

Before progressing to the final worksheet entry, note the close similarity of these entries with the five incorporated in the 2002 consolidation (Exhibit 3–5). Except for the numerical changes created by the passage of time, the entries are identical.

Exhibit 3–8

Excess Amortizations Relating to Individual Accounts as of January 1, 2005

Accounts	Original Allocation	Annual Excess Amortizations			Balance 1/1/05
		2002	**2003**	**2004**	
Land	$ 20,000	–0–	–0–	–0–	$ 20,000
Buildings	130,000	$13,000	$13,000	$13,000	91,000
Equipment	(30,000)	(6,000)	(6,000)	(6,000)	(12,000)
Goodwill	80,000	–0–	–0–	–0–	80,000
	$200,000	$ 7,000	$ 7,000	$ 7,000	$179,000
			$21,000		

Consolidation Entry P   This last entry (labeled "Entry P" because it eliminates an intercompany **P**ayable) introduces a new element to the consolidation process. As noted earlier, intercompany debt transactions do not relate to outside parties. Therefore, Sun's $40,000 payable and Parrot's $40,000 receivable are reciprocals that must be removed on the worksheet because the companies are being reported as a single entity.

In reviewing Exhibit 3–7, note several aspects of the consolidation process:

- The stockholders' equity accounts of the subsidiary are removed.
- The Investment in Sun Company and the Equity in Subsidiary Earnings are both removed.
- The parent's retained earnings balance is not adjusted. Since the equity method has been applied, this account should be correct.
- The original allocations created by the purchase price are recognized but only after adjustment for annual excess amortization expenses.
- Intercompany transactions such as dividend payments and the receivable/payable are offset.

SUBSEQUENT CONSOLIDATIONS—INVESTMENT RECORDED ON OTHER THAN THE EQUITY METHOD

Acquisition Made during the Current Year

As discussed at the beginning of this chapter, the parent company may opt to use the cost method or the partial equity method for internal record-keeping rather than the equity method. Application of either alternative changes the balances recorded by the parent over time and, thus, the procedures followed in creating consolidations. However, *choosing one of these other approaches does not affect any of the final consolidated figures to be reported.*

Where the equity method is utilized, all reciprocal accounts are eliminated, unamortized cost allocations are assigned to specific accounts, and amortization expense is recorded for the current year. Application of either the cost method or the partial equity method has no effect on this basic process. For this reason, a number of the consolidation entries remain the same regardless of the accounting method being applied by the parent.

In reality, just three of the parent's accounts actually vary because of the method applied:

- The investment account.
- The income recognized from the subsidiary.
- The parent's retained earnings (in periods after the initial year of the combination).

Only the differences found in these balances affect the consolidation process when another method is applied. Thus, any time after the date of purchase, accounting for these three accounts is of special importance.

To illustrate the modifications required by the adoption of an alternative accounting method, the consolidation of Parrot and Sun as of December 31, 2002, is reconstructed. Only one differing factor is introduced: the method by which Parrot accounts for its investment. Exhibit 3–9 presents the 2002 consolidation based on Parrot's use of the cost method. Exhibit 3–10 demonstrates this same process assuming that the partial equity method was applied by the parent. Each entry on these worksheets is labeled to correspond with the 2002 consolidation in which the parent used the equity method (Exhibit 3–5). Furthermore, differences with the equity method (both on the parent company records and with the consolidation entries) are highlighted on each of the worksheets.

Exhibit 3-9

	PARROT COMPANY AND SUN COMPANY				
Consolidation: Purchase Method Investment: Cost Method	Consolidated Worksheet For Year Ending December 31, 2002				

Accounts	Parrot Company	Sun Company	Consolidation Entries		Consolidated Totals
			Debit	Credit	
Income Statement					
Revenues	(1,500,000)	(400,000)			(1,900,000)
Cost of goods sold	700,000	250,000			950,000
Depreciation expense	200,000	50,000	(E) 7,000		257,000
Dividend income	(40,000) *	–0–	(I) 40,000 *		–0–
Net income	(640,000)	(100,000)			(693,000)
Statement of Retained Earnings					
Retained earnings, 1/1/02	(840,000)	(380,000)	(S) 380,000		(840,000)
Net income (above)	(640,000)	(100,000)			(693,000)
Dividends paid	120,000	40,000		(I) 40,000 *	120,000
Retained earnings, 12/31/02	(1,360,000)	(440,000)			(1,413,000)
Balance Sheet					
Current assets	1,040,000	400,000			1,440,000
Investment in Sun Company	800,000 *	–0–		(S) 600,000 (A) 200,000	–0–
Land	600,000	200,000	(A) 20,000		820,000
Buildings (net)	370,000	288,000	(A) 130,000	(E) 13,000	775,000
Equipment (net)	250,000	220,000	(E) 6,000	(A) 30,000	446,000
Goodwill	–0–	–0–	(A) 80,000		80,000
Total assets	3,060,000	1,108,000			3,561,000
Liabilities	(980,000)	(448,000)			(1,428,000)
Common stock	(600,000)	(200,000)	(S) 200,000		(600,000)
Additional paid-in capital	(120,000)	(20,000)	(S) 20,000		(120,000)
Retained earnings, 12/31/02 (above)	(1,360,000)	(440,000)			(1,413,000)
Total liabilities and equities	(3,060,000)	(1,108,000)			(3,561,000)

Note: Parentheses indicate a credit balance.

*Boxed items highlight differences with consolidation in Exhibit 3–5.

Consolidation entries:

  (S)   Elimination of Sun's stockholders' equity accounts as of January 1, 2002, and book value portion of purchase price.

  (A)   Allocation of Parrot's cost in excess of Sun's book value.

  (I)   Elimination of intercompany dividends recognized by parent as income.

  (D)   Entry is not needed when cost method is applied because Entry I eliminates intercompany dividends.

  (E)   Recognition of excess amortization expenses on purchase price allocations.

Cost Method Applied—2002 Consolidation   Although the cost method theoretically stands in marked contrast to the equity method, just a narrow range of reporting differences actually result. In the year of acquisition, Parrot's income and investment accounts relating to the subsidiary are the only accounts altered.

    Under the cost method, income recognition in 2002 is limited to the $40,000 dividend received by the parent; no equity income accrual is made. At the same time, the

Exhibit 3–10

	PARROT COMPANY AND SUN COMPANY				
Consolidation: Purchase Method	Consolidated Worksheet				
Investment: Partial Equity Method	For Year Ending December 31, 2002				

Accounts	Parrot Company	Sun Company	Consolidation Entries		Consolidated Totals
			Debit	Credit	
Income Statement					
Revenues	(1,500,000)	(400,000)			(1,900,000)
Cost of goods sold	700,000	250,000			950,000
Depreciation expense	200,000	50,000	(E) 7,000		257,000
Equity in subsidiary earnings	(100,000) *	–0–	(I) 100,000 *		–0–
Net income	(700,000)	(100,000)			(693,000)
Statement of Retained Earnings					
Retained earnings, 1/1/02	(840,000)	(380,000)	(S) 380,000		(840,000)
Net income (above)	(700,000)	(100,000)			(693,000)
Dividends paid	120,000	40,000		(D) 40,000	120,000
Retained earnings, 12/31/02	(1,420,000)	(440,000)			(1,413,000)
Balance Sheet					
Current assets	1,040,000	400,000			1,440,000
Investment in Sun Company	860,000 *	–0–	(D) 40,000	(S) 600,000	–0–
				(A) 200,000	
				(I) 100,000 *	
Land	600,000	200,000	(A) 20,000		820,000
Buildings (net)	370,000	288,000	(A) 130,000	(E) 13,000	775,000
Equipment (net)	250,000	220,000	(E) 6,000	(A) 30,000	446,000
Goodwill	–0–	–0–	(A) 80,000		80,000
Total assets	3,120,000	1,108,000			3,561,000
Liabilities	(980,000)	(448,000)			(1,428,000)
Common stock	(600,000)	(200,000)	(S) 200,000		(600,000)
Additional paid-in capital	(120,000)	(20,000)	(S) 20,000		(120,000)
Retained earnings, 12/31/02 (above)	(1,420,000)	(440,000)			(1,413,000)
Total liabilities and equities	(3,120,000)	(1,108,000)			(3,561,000)

Note: Parentheses indicate a credit balance.

*Boxed items highlight differences with consolidation in Exhibit 3–5.

Consolidation entries:

 (S) Elimination of Sun's stockholders' equity accounts as of January 1, 2002, and book value portion of purchase price.

 (A) Allocation of Parrot's cost in excess of Sun's book value.

 (I) Elimination of parent's equity income accrual.

 (D) Elimination of intercompany dividend payment.

 (E) Recognition of excess amortization expenses on purchase price allocations.

Investment account retains its $800,000 cost. Unlike the equity method, no adjustments are recorded within this asset in connection with the current year operations, the dividends paid by the subsidiary, or amortization of any purchase price allocations.

After the composition of these two accounts has been established, worksheet entries can be used to produce the consolidated figures found in Exhibit 3–9 as of December 31, 2002.

Consolidation Entry S   As with the previous Entry S in Exhibit 3–5, the $600,000 component of the Investment account is eliminated against the beginning stockholders' equity of the subsidiary. Both are equivalent to Sun's net assets at January 1, 2002, and are, therefore, reciprocal balances that must be offset. This entry is not affected by the accounting method in use.

Consolidation Entry A   Parrot's $200,000 excess payment is allocated to Sun's assets and liabilities based on the fair market values at the date of acquisition. The $80,000 residual is attributed to goodwill. This procedure is also identical to the corresponding entry in Exhibit 3–5 where the equity method was applied.

Consolidation Entry I   Under the cost method, the parent records dividend collections as income. Entry I removes this Dividend Income account along with Sun's Dividends Paid. From a consolidated perspective, these two $40,000 balances represent an intercompany transfer of cash that had no financial impact outside of the entity. In contrast to the equity method, subsidiary income has not been accrued by Parrot nor has amortization been recorded; thus, no further income elimination is needed.

Dividend Income	40,000	
Dividend Paid		40,000
To eliminate intercompany income.		

Consolidation Entry D   When the cost method is applied, intercompany dividends are recorded by the parent as income. Because these distributions were already removed from the consolidated totals by Entry I, no separate Entry D is required.

Consolidation Entry E   Regardless of the parent's method of accounting, the reporting entity must recognize excess amortizations for the current year in connection with the original purchase price allocations. Thus, Entry E serves to bring the 2002 expenses into the consolidated financial statements.

Consequently, using the cost method rather than the equity method changes only Entries I and D in the year of acquisition. Despite the change in methods, reported figures are still derived by (1) eliminating all reciprocals, (2) allocating the excess portion of the purchase price, and (3) recording amortizations on these allocations. As indicated previously, the consolidated totals appearing in Exhibit 3–9 are identical to the figures produced previously in Exhibit 3–5. Although the income and the investment accounts on the parent company's separate statements vary, the consolidated balances are not affected.

One significant difference between the cost method and equity method does exist: The parent's separate statements do not reflect consolidated income totals when the cost method is used. Because equity adjustments (such as excess amortizations) are ignored, neither Parrot's reported net income of $640,000 nor its retained earnings of $1,360,000 provides an accurate portrayal of consolidated figures.

Partial Equity Method Applied—2002 Consolidation   Exhibit 3–10 presents a worksheet to consolidate these two companies for 2002 (the year of acquisition) based on the assumption that Parrot applied the partial equity method. Again, the only changes from previous examples are found in (1) the parent's separate records for this investment and its related income and (2) worksheet Entries I and D.

As discussed earlier, under the partial equity approach the parent's record-keeping is limited to two periodic journal entries: the annual accrual of subsidiary income and the receipt of dividends. Hence, within the parent's records, only a few differences exist when the partial equity method is applied rather than the cost method. The entries recorded by Parrot in connection with Sun's 2002 operations illustrate both of these approaches.

Parrot Company **Cost Method** **2002**			**Parrot Company** **Partial Equity Method** **2002**		
Cash	40,000		Cash	40,000	
Dividend Income . .		40,000	Investment in Sun		
Dividends collected			Company		40,000
from subsidiary.			Dividends collected		
			from subsidiary.		
			Investment in Sun		
			Company	100,000	
			Equity in Subsidiary		
			Earnings		100,000
			Accrual of subsidiary		
			income.		

Therefore, by applying the partial equity method, the Investment account on the parent's balance sheet rises to $860,000 by the end of 2002. This total is comprised of the original $800,000 purchase price adjusted for the $100,000 income recognition and the $40,000 cash dividend payment. The same $100,000 equity income figure appears within the parent's income statement. These two balances are appropriately found in Parrot's records in Exhibit 3–10.

Because of the handling of income recognition and dividend payments, Entries I and D again differ on the worksheet. For the partial equity method, the $100,000 equity income is eliminated (Entry 1) by reversing the parent's entry. Removing this accrual allows the individual revenue and expense accounts of the subsidiary to be reported without double-counting. The $40,000 intercompany dividend payment must also be removed (Entry D). The Dividend Paid account is simply deleted. However, elimination of the dividend from the Investment in Sun Company actually causes an increase because receipt was recorded by Parrot as a reduction in that account. All other consolidation entries (Entries S, A, and E) are the same for all three methods.

Consolidation Subsequent to Year of Acquisition—Other than the Equity Method

By again incorporating the December 31, 2005, financial data for Parrot and Sun (presented in Exhibit 3–7), consolidation procedures for the cost method and the partial equity method can be examined for years subsequent to the date of acquisition. *In both cases, establishment of an appropriate beginning retained earnings figure becomes a significant goal of the consolidation.*

This concern was not faced previously when the equity method was adopted. Under that approach, the parent's retained earnings balance mirrors the consolidated total so that no adjustment is necessary. In the earlier illustration, the $330,000 income accrual for the 2002–2004 period as well as the $21,000 amortization expense were recognized by the parent based on employment of the equity method (see Exhibit 3–6). Having been recorded in this manner, these two balances form a permanent part of Parrot's retained earnings and are included automatically in the consolidated total. Consequently, if the equity method is applied, the process is simplified; no worksheet entries are needed to adjust the parent's retained earnings to record subsidiary operations or amortization for past years.

Conversely, if a method other than the equity method is used, a worksheet change must be made to the parent's beginning retained earnings (in every subsequent year) to equate this balance with the consolidated total. To quantify this adjustment, the parent's recognized income for these past three years under each method is first determined

Exhibit 3–11

	Equity Method	**Cost Method**	**Partial Equity Method**
	PARROT COMPANY AND SUN COMPANY Previous Years—2002–2004		
Equity accrual	$330,000	–0–	$330,000
Dividend income	–0–	$110,000	–0–
Excess amortization expenses	(21,000)	–0–	–0–
Increase in parent's retained earnings	$309,000	$110,000	$330,000

(Exhibit 3–11). For consolidation purposes, beginning retained earnings must then be increased or decreased to create the same effect as the equity method.

Cost Method Applied—Subsequent Consolidation   As shown in Exhibit 3–11, if the cost method is applied by Parrot during the 2002–2004 period, $199,000 less income is recognized than under the equity method ($309,000 − $110,000). This difference has two causes. First, the $220,000 increase in the subsidiary's book value in the period prior to the current year has not been accrued by Parrot. Although the $110,000 in dividends were recorded as income, the remainder of the $330,000 earned by the subsidiary was never recognized by the parent.[7] Second, no accounting has been made of the $21,000 excess amortization expenses. Thus, the parent's beginning retained earnings are $199,000 ($220,000 − $21,000) below the appropriate consolidated total and must be adjusted.[8]

To simulate the equity method so that the parent's beginning retained earnings agree with that of the combination, this $199,000 increase is recorded through a worksheet entry. The cost method figures reported by the parent are effectively being converted into equity method balances.

Consolidation Entry *C

Investment in Sun Company.   199,000
      Retained Earnings, 1/1/05 (Parrot Company)   199,000
    To convert parent's beginning retained earnings from cost method to equity method.

This adjustment has been labeled Entry *C. The C refers to the conversion being made to equity method totals. The asterisk indicates that this equity simulation relates solely to transactions of prior periods. Thus, *Entry *C should be recorded before the other worksheet entries to align the beginning balances for the year.*

---

[7]Two different methods are indicated here for determining the $220,000 in nonrecorded income for prior years: (1) subsidiary income less dividends paid and (2) the change in the subsidiary's book value as of the first day of the current year. The second method works only if the subsidiary has had no other equity transactions such as the issuance of new stock or the purchase of treasury shares. Unless otherwise stated, the assumption is made that no such transactions have occurred.

[8]Since neither the income in excess of dividends nor excess amortization is recorded by the parent under the cost method, its beginning retained earnings are $199,000 less than the $2,044,000 reported under the equity method (Exhibit 3–7). Thus, a $1,845,000 balance is shown in Exhibit 3–12 ($2,044,000 − this $199,000). Conversely if the partial equity method had been applied, Parrot's failure to record amortization would cause retained earnings to be $21,000 higher than the figure derived by the equity method. For this reason, Exhibit 3–13 shows the parent with beginning retained earnings of $2,065,000 rather than $2,044,000.

Exhibit 3–12 provides a complete presentation of the consolidation of Parrot and Sun as of December 31, 2005, based on the parent's application of the cost method. After Entry *C has been recorded on the worksheet, the remainder of this consolidation follows the same pattern as previous examples. Sun's stockholders' equity accounts are eliminated (Entry S) while the allocations stemming from the $800,000 purchase price are recorded (Entry A) at their unamortized balances as of January 1, 2005 (see Exhibit 3–8). Intercompany dividend income is removed (Entry I) and current year excess amortization expenses are recognized (Entry E). To complete this process, the intercompany debt of $40,000 is offset (Entry P).

In retrospect, the only new element introduced here is the adjustment of the parent's beginning retained earnings. For a consolidation produced after the initial year of acquisition, an Entry *C is required if the equity method has not been applied by the parent.

Partial Equity Method Applied—Subsequent Consolidation   Exhibit 3–13 demonstrates the worksheet consolidation of Parrot and Sun as of December 31, 2005, where the investment accounts have been recorded by the parent using the partial equity method. This approach accrues subsidiary income each year but records no other equity adjustments. Therefore, as of December 31, 2005, Parrot's Investment in Sun Company account has a balance of $1,110,000:

Purchase price		$ 800,000
Sun Company's 2002–2004 increase in book value:		
Accrual of Sun Company's Income	$330,000	
Collection of Sun Company's Dividends	(110,000)	220,000
Sun Company's 2005 operations:		
Accrual of Sun Company's income	$160,000	
Collection of Sun Company's dividends.	(70,000)	90,000
Investment in Sun Company, 12/31/05 (Partial equity method) .		$1,110,000

As indicated here and in Exhibit 3–11, the yearly equity income accrual has been properly recognized by Parrot but amortization has not. Consequently, if the partial equity method is in use, the parent's beginning retained earnings must be adjusted to include this expense. The $21,000 amortization is recorded through Entry *C to simulate the equity method and, hence, consolidated totals.

Consolidation Entry *C

Retained Earnings, 1/1/05 (Parrot Company)	21,000	
Investment in Sun Company		21,000

To convert parent's beginning retained earnings from partial
equity method to equity method by including excess amortizations.

By recording Entry *C on the worksheet, all of the subsidiary's operational results for the 2002–2004 period are included in the consolidation. As shown in Exhibit 3–13, the remainder of the worksheet entries follow the same basic pattern as that illustrated previously for the year of acquisition (Exhibit 3–10).

Summary of Investment Methods   Having three investment methods available to the parent means that three sets of entries must be understood to arrive at reported figures appropriate for a business combination. The process may initially seem like a confusing overlap of procedures. However, at this point in the coverage, only three worksheet entries actually are affected by the choice of either the equity method, partial equity method, or cost method: Entries *C, I, and D. Furthermore, accountants should never get so involved with a worksheet and its entries that they lose sight of the

Exhibit 3–12

	PARROT COMPANY AND SUN COMPANY				
Consolidation: Purchase Method	Consolidated Worksheet				
Investment: Cost Method	For Year Ending December 31, 2005				

Accounts	Parrot Company	Sun Company	Consolidation Entries Debit	Consolidation Entries Credit	Consolidated Totals
Income Statement					
Revenues	(2,100,000)	(600,000)			(2,700,000)
Cost of goods sold	1,000,000	380,000			1,380,000
Depreciation expense	300,000	60,000	(E) 7,000		367,000
Dividend income	(70,000) *	–0–	(I) 70,000 *		–0–
Net income	(870,000)	(160,000)			(953,000)
Statement of Retained Earnings					
Retained earnings, 1/1/05:					
Parrot Company	(1,845,000)† *			(*C) 199,000 *	(2,044,000)
Sun Company		(600,000)	(S) 600,000		–0–
Net income (above)	(870,000)	(160,000)			(953,000)
Dividends paid	420,000	70,000		(I) 70,000 *	420,000
Retained earnings, 12/31/05	(2,295,000)	(690,000)			(2,577,000)
Balance Sheet					
Current assets	1,705,000	500,000		(P) 40,000	2,165,000
Investment in Sun Company	800,000 *	–0–	(*C) 199,000	(S) 820,000	–0–
				(A) 179,000	
Land	600,000	240,000	(A) 20,000		860,000
Buildings (net)	540,000	420,000	(A) 91,000	(E) 13,000	1,038,000
Equipment (net)	420,000	210,000	(E) 6,000	(A) 12,000	624,000
Goodwill	–0–	–0–	(A) 80,000		80,000
Total assets	4,065,000	1,370,000			4,767,000
Liabilities	(1,050,000)	(460,000)	(P) 40,000		(1,470,000)
Common stock	(600,000)	(200,000)	(S) 200,000		(600,000)
Additional paid-in capital	(120,000)	(20,000)	(S) 20,000		(120,000)
Retained earnings, 12/31/05 (above)	(2,295,000)	(690,000)			(2,577,000)
Total liabilities and equities	(4,065,000)	(1,370,000)			(4,767,000)

Note: Parentheses indicate a credit balance.

*Boxed items highlight differences with consolidation in Exhibit 3–7.

†See footnote 8.

Consolidation entries:

(*C)   To recognize additional earnings and amortization relating to ownership of subsidiary for years prior to 2005.

(S)   Elimination of Sun's stockholders' equity accounts as of January 1, 2005, and book value portion of Investment account.

(A)   Allocation of Parrot's cost in excess of Sun's book value, unamortized values as of January 1, 2005.

(I)   Elimination of intercompany dividends recognized by parent as income.

(D)   Entry is not needed when cost method is applied because Entry I eliminates intercompany dividend income.

(E)   Recognition of excess amortization expenses on purchase price allocations.

(P)   Elimination of intercompany receivable/payable balances.

Exhibit 3–13

	PARROT COMPANY AND SUN COMPANY				
Consolidation: Purchase Method *Investment: Partial Equity Method*	Consolidated Worksheet For Year Ending December 31, 2005				
Accounts	**Parrot Company**	**Sun Company**	**Consolidation Entries**		**Consolidated Totals**
			Debit	**Credit**	
Income Statement					
Revenues	(2,100,000)	(600,000)			(2,700,000)
Cost of goods sold	1,000,000	380,000			1,380,000
Depreciation expense	300,000	60,000	(E) 7,000		367,000
Equity in subsidiary earnings	(160,000) *	–0–	(I) 160,000 *		–0–
Net income	(960,000)	(160,000)			(953,000)
Statement of Retained Earnings					
Retained earnings, 1/1/05:					
Parrot Company	(2,065,000)† *		(*C) 21,000 *		(2,044,000)
Sun Company		(600,000)	(S) 600,000		–0–
Net income (above)	(960,000)	(160,000)			(953,000)
Dividends paid	420,000	70,000		(D) 70,000	420,000
Retained earnings, 12/31/05	(2,605,000)	(690,000)			(2,577,000)
Balance Sheet					
Current assets	1,705,000	500,000		(P) 40,000	2,165,000
Investment in Sun Company	1,110,000 *	–0–	(D) 70,000	(*C) 21,000 *	–0–
				(S) 820,000	
				(A) 179,000	
				(I) 160,000 *	
Land	600,000	240,000	(A) 20,000		860,000
Buildings (net)	540,000	420,000	(A) 91,000	(E) 13,000	1,038,000
Equipment (net)	420,000	210,000	(E) 6,000	(A) 12,000	624,000
Goodwill	–0–	–0–	(A) 80,000		80,000
Total assets	4,375,000	1,370,000			4,767,000
Liabilities	(1,050,000)	(460,000)	(P) 40,000		(1,470,000)
Common stock	(600,000)	(200,000)	(S) 200,000		(600,000)
Additional paid-in capital	(120,000)	(20,000)	(S) 20,000		(120,000)
Retained earnings, 12/31/05 (above)	(2,605,000)	(690,000)			(2,577,000)
Total liabilities and equities	(4,375,000)	(1,370,000)			(4,767,000)

Note: Parentheses indicate a credit balance.

*Boxed items highlight differences with consolidation in Exhibit 3–7.

†See footnote 8.

Consolidation entries:

(*C) To record amortization of acquisition price allocations for years prior to 2005.

(S) Elimination of Sun's stockholders' equity accounts as of January 1, 2005, and book value portion of Investment account.

(A) Allocation of Parrot's cost in excess of Sun's book value, unamortized values as of January 1, 2005.

(I) Elimination of parent's equity income accrual.

(D) Elimination of intercompany dividend payment.

(E) Recognition of excess amortization expenses on purchase price allocations.

(P) Elimination of intercompany receivable/payable balances.

DISCUSSION QUESTION

How Does a Company Really Decide Which Investment Method to Apply?

During the early stages of 2002, Pilgrim Products, Inc., buys a controlling interest in the common stock of Crestwood Corporation. Shortly after the acquisition, a meeting of Pilgrim's accounting department is convened to discuss the internal reporting procedures required by the ownership of this subsidiary. Each member of the staff has a definite opinion as to whether the equity method, cost method, or partial equity method should be adopted. To resolve this issue, Pilgrim's chief financial officer outlines several of her concerns about the decision.

"I already understand how each method works. I know the general advantages and disadvantages of all three. I realize, for example, that the equity method provides more detailed information whereas the cost method is much easier to apply. What I need to know are the factors specific to our situation that should be considered in deciding which method to adopt. I must make a recommendation to the president on this matter, and he will want firm reasons for my favoring a particular approach. I don't want us to select a method and then find out in six months that the information is not adequate for our needs or that the cost of adapting our system to monitor Crestwood outweighs the benefits derived from the data."

What are the factors that Pilgrim's officials should evaluate when making this decision?

balances that this process is designed to calculate. These figures are never impacted by the parent's choice of an accounting method.

Consolidated Totals Subsequent to Acquisition—Purchase Method*

Current revenues	Parent revenues are included.
	Subsidiary revenues are included but only for the period since the acquisition.
Current expenses	Parent expenses are included.
	Subsidiary expenses are included but only for the period since the acquisition.
	Excess amortization expenses on the purchase price allocations are included by recognition on the worksheet.
Investment (or dividend) income	Income recognized by parent is eliminated on the worksheet so that the balance is not included in consolidated figures.
Retained earnings, beginning balance	Parent balance is included.
	Subsidiary balance since the acquisition is included either as a regular accrual by the parent or through a worksheet entry to increase parent balance.
	Past excess amortization expenses on the purchase price allocations are included either as a part of parent balance or through a worksheet entry.
Assets and liabilities	Parent balances are included.
	Subsidiary balances are included.
	Remaining undepreciated purchase price allocations are included.
	Intercompany receivable/payable balances are eliminated.
Goodwill	Original purchase price allocation is included.
Investment in subsidiary	Asset account recorded by parent is eliminated on the worksheet so that the balance is not included in consolidated figures.
Capital stock and additional paid-in capital	Parent balances only are included although they will have been adjusted at date of purchase if stock was issued.

*The next few chapters discuss the necessity of altering some of these balances for consolidation purposes. Thus, this table is not definitive but only included to provide a basic overview of the consolidation process as it has been described to this point.

Exhibit 3–14   Consolidation Worksheet Entries—Purchase Method

	Equity Method Applied	**Cost Method Applied**	**Partial Equity Method Applied**
Any time during year of acquisition:			
Entry S	Beginning stockholders' equity of subsidiary is eliminated against book value portion of investment account.	Same as equity method.	Same as equity method.
Entry A	Excess purchase price is allocated to assets and liabilities based on difference in book values and fair market values; residual is assigned to goodwill.	Same as equity method.	Same as equity method.
Entry I	Equity income accrual (including amortization expense) is eliminated.	Dividend income is eliminated.	Equity income accrual is eliminated.
Entry D	Intercompany dividends paid by subsidiary are eliminated.	No entry—intercompany dividends are eliminated in Entry I.	Same as equity method.
Entry E	Current year excess amortization expenses of cost allocations are recorded.	Same as equity method.	Same as equity method.
Entry P	Intercompany payable/receivable balances are offset.	Same as equity method.	Same as equity method.
Any time following year of acquisition:			
Entry *C	No entry—equity income for prior years has already been recognized along with amortization expenses.	Increase in subsidiary's book value during prior years as well as excess amortization expenses are recognized (conversion is made to equity method).	Excess amortization expenses for prior years are recognized (conversion is made to equity method).
Entry S	Same as initial year.	Same as initial year.	Same as initial year.
Entry A	Unamortized cost at beginning of year is allocated to specific accounts and to goodwill.	Same as equity method.	Same as equity method.
Entry I	Same as initial year.	Same as initial year.	Same as initial year.
Entry D	Same as initial year.	Same as initial year.	Same as initial year.
Entry E	Same as initial year.	Same as initial year.	Same as initial year.
Entry P	Same as initial year.	Same as initial year.	Same as initial year.

Once the appropriate balance for each account is understood, worksheet entries assist the accountant in deriving these figures. To help clarify the consolidation process required under each of the three accounting methods, Exhibit 3–14 describes the purpose of each worksheet entry: first during the year of acquisition and second for any period following the year of acquisition.

INTANGIBLES ACQUIRED IN BUSINESS COMBINATIONS AND RELATED AMORTIZATIONS

As discussed in Chapter 2, *SFAS 141,* "Business Combinations," does not alter significantly the purchase price allocation procedures required in a business acquisition. *SFAS 141* does, however, suggest several categories of purchased intangible assets for possible recognition in a business combination. Examples include noncompetition agreements, customer lists, patents, subscriber databases, trademarks, lease agreements, and licenses.

If fair values can be measured reliably for the identified intangibles in a business combination, they are separately recognized and subsequently amortized if appropriate. If a separate fair value estimation is unavailable or unreliable for a particular intangible, then any remaining unallocated purchase price is simply recognized as goodwill.

SFAS 142, "Goodwill and Other Intangible Assets," recommends that all identified intangible assets should be amortized over their economic useful life, unless such life is considered *indefinite*. The term *indefinite life* is defined as a life that extends beyond the foreseeable future. A recognized intangible asset with an indefinite life should not be amortized unless and until its life is determined to be finite. Importantly, indefinite does not mean infinite. Also, the useful life on an intangible asset should not be considered indefinite because a precise finite life is not known.

For those intangible assets with finite lives, the method of amortization should reflect the pattern of decline in the economic usefulness of the asset. If no such pattern is apparent, the straight-line method of amortization should be used. The amount to be amortized should be the value assigned to the intangible asset less any residual value. In most cases the residual value is presumed to be zero. However, that presumption may be overcome if the acquiring enterprise has a commitment from a third party to purchase the intangible at the end of its useful life, or an observable market exists for the intangible asset that provides a basis for estimating a terminal value.

The length of the amortization period for identifiable intangibles (i.e., those not included in goodwill) depends primarily on the assumed economic life of the asset. Factors that should be considered in determining the useful life of an intangible asset include:

- Legal, regulatory, or contractual provisions.
- The effects of obsolescence, demand, competition, industry stability, rate of technological change, and expected changes in distribution channels.
- The expected use of the intangible asset by the enterprise.
- The level of maintenance expenditure required to obtain the asset's expected future benefits.

Any recognized intangible assets considered to possess indefinite lives are not amortized but instead are tested for impairment on an annual basis.[9] To test for impairment, the carrying amount of the intangible asset is compared to its fair value. If the fair value is less than the carrying amount, then the intangible asset is considered impaired and an impairment loss is recognized. The asset's carrying value is reduced accordingly.

SFAS 142—GOODWILL IMPAIRMENT

A major change in accounting for goodwill is the *SFAS 142* requirement of an annual test for impairment. The FASB reasoned that while goodwill may decrease over time, it does not do so in the "rational and systematic" manner that periodic amortization suggests.[10] Thus, amortization was not viewed as representationally faithful of the pattern of goodwill decline. Moreover, because *SFAS 141* provides greater guidelines for recognizing identifiable intangibles, it was argued that future amounts included in goodwill were more likely to be nonwasting. Ultimately, the FASB decided to record a decline in the value of goodwill only when

---

[9] Impairment tests should also be conducted on an interim basis if an event or circumstance occurs between annual tests indicating that an intangible asset may be impaired.

[10] L. Todd Johnson and Kimberly R. Petrone, *FASB Viewpoints*, "Why Did the Board Change Its Mind on Goodwill Amortization?" December 2000.

- It is apparent that goodwill becomes impaired—that is, when the carrying amount of goodwill exceeds its implied fair value, an impairment loss is recognized equal to that excess, or
- The operating unit where goodwill resides is partially or completely sold.

Goodwill impairment losses can be substantial. For example, as a possible precursor of future goodwill impairments, the high-tech fiber optic giant JDS Uniphase (www.jdsuniphase.com) announced in April 2001 that it would recognize a $40 billion writedown of goodwill out of a total $56.2 billion on its balance sheet. The amount of the writedown was equal to the extent that the market capitalization of the entire company was less than the carrying value of its net assets.

Testing Goodwill for Impairment

The notion that goodwill has an indefinite life allows firms to continue to report over time the original amount of goodwill acquired in a business combination at its assigned purchase value. However, such goodwill may, at some point in time, become impaired, requiring loss recognition and a reduction in the amount reported in the consolidated balance sheet. Unlike amortization, which periodically reduces goodwill, impairment must first be revealed before a writedown is justified. To detect when an impairment has occurred, a testing procedure is utilized.

Testing for goodwill impairment consists of two steps. In the first step, fair values of the consolidated entity's reporting units with allocated goodwill are compared to their carrying values. As long as an individual reporting unit maintains its total fair value, its goodwill is not considered impaired and remains at the amount assigned at the date of the business combination. In fact, once a detailed determination of the fair value of a reporting unit is made, that fair value may be used in subsequent periods if all of the following criteria have been met (*SFAS 142*):

- The assets and liabilities that comprise the reporting unit have not changed significantly since the most recent fair value determination. (A recent acquisition or a reorganization of an entity's segment reporting structure are examples of events that might significantly change the composition of a reporting unit.)
- The most recent fair value determination resulted in an amount that exceeded the carrying amount of the reporting unit by a substantial margin.
- Based on an analysis of events that have occurred and circumstances that have changed since the most recent fair value determination, it is remote that a current fair value determination would be less than the current carrying amount of the reporting unit.

However, if any of the above criteria are not met, an updated determination of the reporting unit's fair value is required.

If the fair value of a reporting unit falls below its carrying value, then the second step in testing is performed. The second test is designed to determine the fair value of the related goodwill. If goodwill's fair value has declined below its carrying value, an impairment loss is recognized. However, determining fair values for reporting units and goodwill can be complex, making implementation of the necessary comparisons costly. These complexities are described in terms of three key attributes that govern the process of testing goodwill for impairment:

1. The assignment of acquisition values to reporting units.
2. The periodic determination of the fair values of reporting units.
3. The determination of goodwill implied fair value.

Assigning Values to Reporting Units In deciding to forgo amortization in favor of impairment testing for goodwill, the FASB noted that goodwill is primarily associated with individual *reporting units* within the consolidated entity. Such goodwill is often considered "synergistic" because it arises from the interaction of the assets of the acquired company with those of the acquirer in specific ways. To better assess potential declines in value for goodwill (in place of amortization), the most specific business level at which goodwill is evident was chosen as the appropriate level for impairment testing. This specific business level is referred to as the reporting unit. The FASB also noted that, in practice, goodwill is often assigned to reporting units either at the level of a reporting segment—as described in *SFAS 131,* "Disclosures about Segments of an Enterprise and Related Information"—or at a lower level within a segment of a combined enterprise. Consequently, the reporting unit became the designated enterprise component for tests of goodwill impairment. Reporting units may thus include the following:

- A component of an operating segment at a level below the operating segment. Segment management should review and assess performance at this level. Also, the component should be a business in which discrete financial information is available and should differ economically from other components of the operating segment.
- The segments of an enterprise.
- The entire enterprise.

For example, Intel Corporation reports five product-line operating segments in its recent annual report: The Intel Architecture Group, the Wireless Communications and Computing Group, the Communications Products Group, the Network Communications Group, and the New Business Group. In its report, Intel disclosed the following allocation of acquired subsidiaries to its segments:

> The consolidated financial statements include the operating results of acquired businesses from the dates of acquisition. The operating results of Ambient, GIGA, Basis, Trillium Level One, Softcom and NetBoost have been included in the Network Communications Group operating segment. The operating results of Picazo, Ziatech, Shiva, Dialogic and IPivot have been included in the Communications Products Group operating segment. The operating results of DSP Communications have been included in the Wireless Communications and Computing Group operating segment. All of these groups are part of the "all other" category for segment reporting purposes. The operating results of Chips and Technologies have been included in the Intel Architecture Group operating segment.

Each of the above acquired businesses resulted in goodwill. Presumably, these acquired subsidiaries within Intel's operating segments will be primary candidates for designation as reporting units for goodwill impairment testing purposes.

In implementing impairment tests, it is essential to first identify the reporting units resulting from the acquisition. The assets and liabilities (including goodwill) acquired in a business combination are then assigned to these identified reporting units. The assignment should consider where the acquired assets and liabilities will be employed and whether they will be included in determining the reporting unit's fair value. The goodwill should be assigned to those reporting units that are expected to benefit from the synergies of the combination. Overall, the objective of the assignment of acquired assets and liabilities to reporting units is to facilitate the required fair value/carrying value comparisons for periodic impairment testing.

Periodic Determination of the Fair Values of Reporting Units   The necessary comparisons to determine if goodwill is impaired depend first on the fair value computation of the reporting unit and then, if necessary, the fair value computation for goodwill. But how are such values computed? How can fair values be known if the subsidiary is wholly owned and thus not traded publicly?

Several alternative methods exist for determining the fair values of the reporting units that comprise a consolidated entity. First, any quoted market prices that exist can provide a basis for assessing fair value—particularly for subsidiaries with actively traded noncontrolling interests. Second, comparable businesses may exist that can help indicate market values. Third, there are a variety of present value techniques for assessing the fair value of an identifiable set of future cash flow streams, or profit projections discounted for the riskiness of the future flows. Clearly, portions of consolidated entities are frequently bought and sold. In these transactions, parties do derive fair values. However, the required periodic assessment of fair value in 2002 and beyond will be a new valuation exercise for many firms. These annual determinations of fair values will likely be a costly impact from implementing the provisions of *SFAS 141* and *SFAS 142.*

Determination of Goodwill Implied Fair Value   If the fair value of a reporting unit, once determined, falls below its carrying value, a second test focuses in on the possibility that goodwill may be impaired. Just as in the initial test of the reporting unit, now the fair value of goodwill must be determined in order to make the relevant comparison to its carrying value. Because, by definition, goodwill is not separable from other assets, it is not possible to directly observe its market value. Therefore, an *implied* value for goodwill is calculated in a similar manner to the determination of goodwill in a business combination. The fair value of the reporting unit is treated as the "purchase price" as if the reporting unit were being acquired in a business combination. Then this "purchase price" is allocated to all the reporting unit's identifiable assets and liabilities with any remaining excess considered as the fair value of goodwill. This procedure is only used for assessing the fair value of goodwill. None of the other values allocated to assets and liabilities in the testing comparison are used to adjust their reported amounts.

Example—Accounting and Reporting for a Goodwill Impairment Loss
To illustrate the procedure for recognizing goodwill impairment, assume that on January 1, 2002, Newcall Corporation was formed to consolidate the telecommunications operations of DSM, Inc., Rocketel Company, and Visiontalk Company in a deal valued at $3 billion. Each of the three former firms is considered an operating segment and each will be maintained as a subsidiary of Newcall. Additionally, DSM is comprised of two divisions—DSM Wired and DSM Wireless—that along with Rocketel and Visiontalk are treated as independent reporting units for internal performance evaluation and management reviews. Following *SFAS 141,* "Business Combinations," Newcall allocated $220 million value to goodwill at the merger date to its reporting units. That information and each unit's purchase price were as follows:

Newcall's Reporting Units	Goodwill	Purchase Price January 1, 2002
DSM Wired	$ 22,000,000	$950,000,000
DSM Wireless	155,000,000	748,000,000
Rocketel	38,000,000	492,000,000
Visiontalk	6,000,000	710,000,000

In December 2002, Newcall tested each of its four reporting units for goodwill impairment. Accordingly, Newcall compared the fair market value of its reporting units to its carrying value. The comparisons revealed that the fair market value of each reporting unit exceeded its carrying value except for DSM Wireless, whose market value had fallen to $600 million, well below its current carrying value. The decline in value was attributed to a failure to realize expected cost-saving synergies with Rocketel.

As indicated by *SFAS 142,* Newcall then compared the implied fair value of the DSM Wireless goodwill to its carrying value. Newcall derived the implied fair value of goodwill through the following allocation of the fair value of DSM Wireless:

DSM Wireless Dec. 31, 2002, fair market value		$600,000,000
Fair values of DSM Wireless net assets at Dec. 31, 2002:		
Current assets	$ 50,000,000	
Property	125,000,000	
Equipment	265,000,000	
Subscriber list	140,000,000	
Patented technology	185,000,000	
Current liabilities	(44,000,000)	
Long-term debt	(125,000,000)	
Value assigned to identifiable net assets		596,000,000
Value assigned to goodwill		4,000,000
Carrying value before impairment		155,000,000
Impairment loss		$151,000,000

Thus, $151,000,000 is reported as a separate line item in the operating section of Newcall's consolidated income statement as a goodwill impairment loss. Additional disclosures are required describing (1) the facts and circumstances leading to the impairment, and (2) the method of determining the fair value of the associated reporting unit (e.g., market prices, comparable business, present value technique, etc.).

Although the amount reported for goodwill is changed, the amounts for the other assets and liabilities of DSM Wireless are not changed. The reported values for all of DSM Wireless's remaining assets and liabilities continue to be based on amounts assigned at the business combination date.

PURCHASE PRICE—CONTINGENT CONSIDERATION

In its annual financial report, Computer Horizons Corporation noted the following contingency:

> The company acquired the assets of Enterprise Solutions Group, LLC (ESG), a Cincinnati, Ohio–based technology organization that provides training and educational services as well as consulting services for Fortune 500 companies. The acquisition was accounted for as a purchase. The total purchase price was approximately $7,333,000 in cash and common stock. The purchase price may be adjusted based on the actual earnings of the company for the twelve months ended December 31, 1998, up to a maximum purchase price of $11,000,000. The remaining purchase price is to be paid out in three payments starting December 1998 and ending December 2000.

A business combination has been formed here but, as this footnote describes, a portion of the purchase price being paid by the parent will not be finalized until several years after the date of acquisition.

Where a subsequent payment, such as that described by Computer Horizon's statements, is based solely on future earnings, the contingency has no initial impact on the purchase price or the consolidated figures. The potential disbursement should be disclosed only in a note to the financial statements similar to the one just presented. When the contingency is ultimately resolved, any further payment made by the parent is simply added to the purchase price.

Thus, if goodwill was recognized at the date of acquisition, any later disbursement is assigned to this same intangible asset. Should another $100,000 be paid, for example, reported goodwill is increased by this amount. Conversely, if the original price was below fair market value so that the balances assigned to specific noncurrent assets were reduced, a subsequent payment serves to decrease the amount of these reductions. In either case, an increase in the initial purchase price resulting from a contingency of this type is not accounted for in a retroactive manner. Any resulting amortization expense is only recorded over the *remaining* life of the appropriate account.

DISCUSSION QUESTION

Is This Income?

Artilio Corporation pays $1 million for all of the outstanding stock of Zepthan, Inc. Because of an urgent need for cash, the owners of Zepthan are forced to accept this price although the company's net assets have a value of $1.6 million.

Based on the guidelines for a bargain purchase previously demonstrated in Chapter 2, the $600,000 reduction is assigned to the subsidiary's noncurrent assets (other than certain specific exceptions). Consequently, assume that the consolidated value of Zepthan's land is reduced by $50,000 with its buildings and equipment decreased by a total of $550,000. If the buildings and equipment have a life of 10 years, these negative allocations reduce depreciation expense by $55,000 per year and, hence, increase income by that amount. Consolidated net income for the combination is projected to be approximately $250,000 per year for the foreseeable future. Thus, 22 percent is attributable to the bargain purchase ($55,000/$250,000). Despite the positive impact on income, depreciation of bargain purchase figures is required.

Because of the annual decrease from depreciation, a bargain purchase creates a consolidated entity that reports more income than the sum of the two component companies. As in the case of Artilio and Zepthan, the amount can be very significant.

Should a business combination be allowed to increase reported earnings based on paying a bargain price to acquire a new subsidiary? Does this practice distort earnings? Does a reasonable alternative exist?

A contingency can also result from the acquisition of a subsidiary if the price is based on the future value of the stock issued. Such arrangements are designed to ensure that the previous owners receive compensation that retains a minimum value for a specified period. For example, in discussing an earlier acquisition, financial statements of Munsingwear, Inc., once stated that "the Company is obligated to issue additional shares of common stock . . . in the event of a decline in the market value of the common stock." From an accounting perspective, this second type of extra payment is not viewed as an increase in the parent's purchase price. Rather, the possible distribution is a guarantee of the value of the consideration conveyed in the original transaction. Thus, no change is made in goodwill or any other allocations.

If additional shares of the parent's stock must be issued because of a subsequent drop in price, the parent records the new shares at fair market value. At the same time, the total attributed to the shares originally issued at the date of purchase is reduced by a corresponding amount to reflect the decrease in value. The net effect is that the parent's stock account is increased by the par value of the new shares issued with additional paid-in capital reduced by the same amount. The purchase price does not change.

To illustrate, assume that Large issues 10,000 shares of its $10 par value stock to acquire Small. This stock had a value on that date of $25 per share ($250,000 in total). In recording this transaction, Large increases:

- Its Common Stock account by the $100,000 par value of these shares.
- Additional Paid-In Capital by $150,000 to reflect the value in excess of par ($25 − $10).

Subsequently, the market value of this stock drops to $20 per share. Assume that the purchase agreement specified that the market value of the shares issued could not be reduced for a given period. To maintain the total value at $250,000, 2,500 more shares are issued to Small's previous owners. At $20 per share, the new total of 12,500 shares has the appropriate value of $250,000. The new shares are recorded at par value ($25,000, or 2,500 shares at $10 per share) with an accompanying reduction in additional paid-in capital. Therefore, total contributed capital from this purchase remains at $250,000.

Large's Financial Records—Subsequent Issuance of Shares

Additional Paid-In Capital	25,000	
Common Stock (par value).		25,000

To record issuance of 2,500 new shares of stock in
connection with previous acquisition of Small. Additional
shares were required because of drop in market value
of shares originally issued.

PUSH-DOWN ACCOUNTING

External Reporting

In the analysis of business combinations to this point, discussion has focused on (1) the recording by the parent company and (2) required consolidation procedures. Unfortunately, official accounting pronouncements give virtually no guidance as to the impact of a purchase on the separate financial statements of the subsidiary.

This issue has become especially significant in recent years because of a rash of management-led buy-outs as well as corporate reorganizations. An organization, for example, might acquire a company and subsequently offer the shares back to the public in hopes of making a large profit. What should be reported in the subsidiary's financial statements being distributed with this offering? Such deals have reheated a long-standing debate over the merits of *push-down accounting,* the direct recording by a subsidiary of purchase price allocations and subsequent amortization.

For this reason, the FASB continues to explore various methods of reporting by a company that has been acquired or reorganized. To illustrate, assume that Yarrow Company owns one asset: a building with a book value of $200,000 but a fair market value of $900,000. Mannen Corporation pays exactly $900,000 in cash to acquire Yarrow. Consolidation offers no real problem here: The building will be reported by the business combination at $900,000.

However, if Yarrow continues to issue separate financial statements (for example, to its creditors or potential stockholders), should the building be reported at $200,000 or $900,000? If adjusted, should the $700,000 increase be reported as a gain by the subsidiary or as an addition to contributed capital? Should depreciation be based on $200,000 or $900,000? If the subsidiary is to be viewed as a new entity with a new basis for its assets and liabilities, should retained earnings be returned to zero? If the parent acquires only 51 percent of Yarrow, does that change the answers to the previous questions? These questions represent just a few of the difficult issues currently being explored.

Proponents of push-down accounting argue that a change in ownership creates a new basis for subsidiary assets and liabilities. An unadjusted balance ($200,000 in the preceding illustration) is a cost figure applicable to previous stockholders. That total is no longer relevant information. Rather, according to this argument, it is the historical cost *paid by the current owner* that is important, a figure that is best reflected by the expenditure made in acquiring the subsidiary. Balance sheet accounts should be reported at the cost incurred by the present stockholders ($900,000 in the illustration) rather than the cost incurred by the company.

Currently, primary guidance concerning push-down accounting for external reporting purposes is provided by the Securities and Exchange Commission (SEC). Through Staff Accounting Bulletin No. 54 *(Application of "Push Down" Basis of Accounting in Financial Statements of Subsidiaries Acquired by Purchase)* and Staff Accounting Bulletin No. 73 *("Push Down" Basis of Accounting for Parent Company Debt Related to Subsidiary Acquisitions),* the SEC has indicated that

> push down accounting should be used in the separate financial statements of a "substantially wholly owned" subsidiary. . . . That view is based on the notion that when the form of ownership is within the control of the parent company, the accounting basis should be

the same whether the entity continues to exist or is merged into the parent's operations. If a purchase of a "substantially wholly owned" subsidiary is financed by debt of the parent, that debt generally must be pushed down to the subsidiary. . . . As a general rule, the SEC requires push down accounting when the ownership change is greater than 95 percent and objects to push down accounting when the ownership change is less than 80 percent. However, if the acquired subsidiary has outstanding public debt or preferred stock, push down accounting is encouraged by the SEC but not required.[11]

Thus, the SEC requires the use of push-down accounting for the separate financial statements of any subsidiary where no substantial outside ownership exists of the company's common stock, preferred stock, and publicly held debt. Apparently, the SEC believes that a change in ownership of that degree justifies a new basis of reporting for the subsidiary's assets and liabilities. Until the FASB takes action, though, application is only required when the subsidiary desires to issue securities (stock or debt) to the public as regulated by the SEC.

Push-Down Accounting—Internal Reporting

Although the use of push-down accounting for external reporting is limited, this approach has gained significant popularity in recent years for internal reporting purposes.

> Subsidiaries owned by the Chesapeake Corporation are recorded using push-down accounting. Under this theory, the subsidiary adjusts its assets and liabilities to current value at the time of the acquisition while also recording the necessary goodwill. The subsidiary's net assets, as adjusted, would equal the amount recorded by the parent as the investment in subsidiary.[12]
>
> At the time of acquisition of each subsidiary, purchase method accounting is applied by James River Corporation on a push-down basis. The parent's investment equals the net book value of the subsidiary through an allocation of the purchase price to the net assets of the subsidiary on a fair market value basis.[13]

Push-down accounting has several advantages for internal reporting. For example, it simplifies the consolidation process. Because the allocations and amortization are already entered into the records of the subsidiary, worksheet Entries A (to recognize the allocations originating from the purchase price) and E (amortization expense) are not needed. Therefore, except for eliminating the effects of intercompany transactions, the assets, liabilities, revenues, and expenses of the subsidiary can be added directly to those of the parent to derive consolidated totals.

More importantly, push-down accounting provides better information for internal evaluation. Since the subsidiary's separate figures include amortization expense, the net income reported by the company is a good representation of the impact that the acquisition has on the earnings of the business combination. As an example, assume that Ace Corporation owns 100 percent of Waxworth, Inc. Waxworth uses push-down accounting and reports net income of $500,000: $600,000 from operations less $100,000 in amortization expense resulting from purchase price allocations. Thus, officials of Ace Corporation know that this acquisition has added $500,000 to the consolidated net income of the business combination. They can then evaluate whether these earnings provide a sufficient return for the parent's investment.

However, the recording of amortization expense by the subsidiary can lead to dissension. Members of the subsidiary's management may argue that they are being forced to record a large expense over which they have no control or responsibility. This

---

[11]FASB Discussion Memorandum, *An Analysis of Issues Related to New Basis Accounting,* December 18, 1991, p. 54.

[12]Letter from Timothy M. Harhan, senior corporate accountant with Chesapeake Corporation.

[13]Letter from Catherine M. Freeman, manager—financial projects with James River Corporation.

amortization comes directly from the purchase price paid by the parent and is not a re-sult of any action taken by the subsidiary. Chesapeake Corporation has considered this problem and resolved it in the following manner: "For internal reporting of income statement activity, earnings from operations are identified separately from amortization. This allows management to analyze the subsidiary's results without the effect of amortization."[14]

SUBSEQUENT CONSOLIDATIONS—POOLING OF INTERESTS

Although the FASB prohibits the pooling of interests method of accounting for busi-ness combinations initiated after June 30, 2001, this restriction is for prospective ap-plication only. Given the popularity of poolings in the last century, the financial statement effects of this method of accounting will likely be encountered for decades to come. Therefore, familiarity with the effects of poolings in consolidations subse-quent to acquisition will continue to be an important part of understanding financial re-porting for business combinations.

For consolidations prepared after the date of combination, the pooling of interests method requires a slightly less complex set of procedures than does the purchase method. By reflecting on the fundamental concepts of a pooling, the essential differ-ences between the subsequent consolidation entries employed by these two methods can be understood.

Pooling of interests combinations were assumed to be formed by a union of two companies. Because a takeover had not occurred, no acquisition price was ever calcu-lated for a pooling. All assets and liabilities were simply consolidated at their book values. No allocations based on fair market value were computed nor was any good-will recognized. Hence, amortization that may have been associated with such cost fac-tors was not encountered in a pooling of interests.

In mechanical terms, the absence of a purchase price means that worksheet en-tries relating to cost allocations (Entry A) and subsequent amortization expense (Entry E) are never found in a pooling. Obviously, as with push-down accounting, allevi-ating the necessity of working with these entries simplifies the entire consolidation process.

The company that issued its stock to consummate a pooling of interests recorded these shares along with the resulting investment. This company must then have adopted a method to account for this investment. One possibility is to apply the equity method to accrue income as it is earned by the other company and to adjust for inter-company transactions (as discussed in Chapter 5). The partial equity method also might be selected so that recording is limited to the periodic accrual of income.

Any reference to a cost method of interests would be a misnomer in a pooling, be-cause no acquisition cost is ever established. Thus, for internal reporting purposes, the cost method is replaced by a *book value method* that has the same essential character-istics: The investment account permanently retains its initial balance (the book value of the other company), with any dividends received being recognized as income.

To illustrate the consolidation techniques employed in a pooling of interests, assume that Brother Company obtains 100 percent of the outstanding voting shares of Sister Company on January 1, 2001. To create this combination, Brother issued 10,000 shares of its own common stock in an exchange that met all 12 requirements for a pooling of interests. On that date, Sister reported a total book value of $700,000 although market value was $950,000. For reporting purposes, the additional $250,000 is unimportant; only book value is relevant in accounting for a pooling of interests. Consequently, $700,000 is recorded by Brother as an investment. The book value method is applied by Brother; thus, this balance remains unchanged over the years.

---

[14]Letter from Timothy H. Harhan.

Exhibit 3-15

Consolidation: Pooling of Interests Method Investment: Book Value Method					
BROTHER COMPANY AND SISTER COMPANY **Consolidated Worksheet** **For Year Ending December 31, 2004**					

Accounts	Brother Company	Sister Company	Consolidation Entries		Consolidated Totals
			Debit	**Credit**	
Income Statement					
Revenues	(1,600,000)	(550,000)			(2,150,000)
Expenses	1,220,000	440,000			1,660,000
Dividend income	(40,000)	–0–	(I) 40,000		–0–
Net income	(420,000)	(110,000)			(490,000)
Statement of Retained Earnings					
Retained earnings, 1/1/04	(2,260,000)	(910,000)	(S) 910,000	(*C) 610,000	(2,870,000)
Net income (above)	(420,000)	(110,000)			(490,000)
Dividends paid	60,000	40,000		(I) 40,000	60,000
Retained earnings, 12/31/04	(2,620,000)	(980,000)			(3,300,000)
Balance Sheet					
Cash and receivables	590,000	140,000		(P) 90,000	640,000
Inventory	940,000	480,000			1,420,000
Investment in Sister Company	700,000	–0–	(*C) 610,000	(S) 1,310,000	–0–
Land	600,000	340,000			940,000
Buildings (net)	970,000	270,000			1,240,000
Equipment (net)	730,000	520,000			1,250,000
Total assets	4,530,000	1,750,000			5,490,000
Liabilities	(810,000)	(370,000)	(P) 90,000		(1,090,000)
Common stock	(800,000)	(300,000)	(S) 300,000		(800,000)
Additional paid-in capital	(300,000)	(100,000)	(S) 100,000		(300,000)
Retained earnings, 12/31/04 (above)	(2,620,000)	(980,000)			(3,300,000)
Total liabilities and equities	(4,530,000)	(1,750,000)			(5,490,000)

Note: Parentheses indicate a credit balance.

Consolidation entries:

(*C) To recognize increase in book value of affiliate company during years prior to 2004.

(S) Elimination of Sister's stockholders' equity accounts as of January 1, 2004, and book value portion of Investment account.

(I) Elimination of intercompany dividends recognized by Brother as income.

(P) Elimination of intercompany receivable/payable balances.

For this example, consolidated financial statements are prepared as of December 31, 2004. Sister's book value has risen by $610,000 to $1,310,000 as of the first day of 2004. Assume also that Sister owes $90,000 to Brother at the end of this year. Exhibit 3–15 presents the worksheet for the 2004 consolidation of these two companies under the pooling of interests concept. Once again, the entries have been labeled to parallel the earlier consolidation examples, although neither Entry A nor Entry E is applicable to a pooling.

Because Brother applies the book value method, no recognition has been made of the increase in Sister's book value since the date of combination. Consequently, Brother's retained earnings at January 1, 2004, do not reflect a consolidated total; the $610,000 increment is not included. An Entry *C must be recorded on the worksheet to accrue this income that has been earned by Sister in excess of dividends distributed (the increase in net book value). After Brother's beginning retained earnings have been properly adjusted in this manner, the remaining consolidation entries eliminate Sister's stockholders' equity (Entry S), the intercompany dividend income (Entry I), and the intercompany debt (Entry P).

SUMMARY

1. The procedures used to consolidate financial information generated by the separate companies in a business combination are affected by both the passage of time and the method applied by the parent in accounting for the subsidiary. Thus, no single consolidation process can be described that is applicable to all business combinations.

2. The parent might elect to utilize the equity method to account for a subsidiary. As discussed in Chapter 1, income is accrued by the parent when earned by the subsidiary and dividend receipts are recorded as reductions in the Investment account. The effects of excess amortizations or any intercompany transactions also are reflected within the parent's financial records. The equity method provides the parent with accurate information concerning the subsidiary's impact on consolidated totals; however, it is usually somewhat complicated to apply.

3. The cost method and the partial equity method are two alternatives to the equity method. The cost method recognizes only the subsidiary's dividends as income while the asset balance remains at cost. This approach is simple and provides a measure of cash flows between the two companies. Under the partial equity method, the parent accrues the subsidiary's income as earned but does not record adjustments that might be required by excess amortizations or intercompany transfers. The partial equity method is easier to apply than the equity method, but, in many cases, the parent's income is a reasonable approximation of the consolidated total.

4. For a consolidation in any subsequent period, all reciprocal balances have to be eliminated. Thus, the subsidiary's equity accounts, the parent's investment balance, and intercompany income, dividends, and liabilities are removed. In addition, the remaining unamortized portions of the purchase price allocations are recognized along with excess amortization expenses for the period. If the equity method has not been applied, the beginning retained earnings of the parent also must be adjusted for any previous income or excess amortizations that have not yet been recorded.

5. For each purchase of a subsidiary, the parent must assign the acquired assets and liabilities (including goodwill) to individual reporting units of its combined operations. The reporting units should be at the level of operating segment or lower and must provide the basis for future assessments of fair value. Any value assigned to goodwill is not amortized but instead is tested annually for impairment. This test consists of two steps. First, if the fair values of any of the consolidated entity's reporting units fall below their carrying values, then the implied value of the associated goodwill must be recomputed. Second, the recomputed implied value of goodwill is compared to its carrying value. An impairment loss must then be recognized if the carrying value of goodwill exceeds its implied value.

6. Push-down accounting is the adjustment of the subsidiary's account balances to recognize allocations and goodwill stemming from the parent's purchase price. Subsequent amortization of these cost figures also is recorded by the subsidiary as an expense. At this time, push-down accounting is required by the SEC for the separate statements of the subsidiary only when no substantial outside ownership exists. The FASB is currently studying push-down accounting and may issue more specific rules on its application. However, for internal reporting purposes, push-down accounting is gaining popularity because it aids company officials in evaluating the impact that the subsidiary has on the business combination.

7. The purchase price of a subsidiary can be based, at least in part, on future income levels or stock prices. If a subsequent payment is made because a specified amount of income is earned, consolidated goodwill is increased. However, if additional shares are issued because of a drop in the price of the parent's stock, the Common Stock and Additional Paid-In Capital accounts are realigned to agree with the new price.

COMPREHENSIVE ILLUSTRATION

Problem

(Estimated Time: 40 to 65 Minutes) On January 1, 2002, Top Company acquired all of the outstanding common stock of Bottom Company for $800,000 in cash. As of that date, one of Bottom's buildings with a five-year remaining life was undervalued on its financial records by $30,000. Equipment with a 10-year life was undervalued but only by $10,000. The book values of all of Bottom's other assets and liabilities were equal to their fair market values at that time, except for an unrecorded licensing agreement with an assessed value of $40,000 and a 20-year remaining useful life. Bottom's book value at January 1, 2002, was $720,000.

During 2002, Bottom reported net income of $100,000 and paid $30,000 in dividends. Earnings were $120,000 in 2003 with $20,000 in dividends distributed by the subsidiary. As of December 31, 2004, the companies reported the following selected balances:

	Top Company December 31, 2004		Bottom Company December 31, 2004	
	Debit	**Credit**	**Debit**	**Credit**
Buildings	$1,540,000		$460,000	
Cash and receivables	50,000		90,000	
Common stock		$ 900,000		$400,000
Dividends paid	70,000		10,000	
Equipment	280,000		200,000	
Cost of goods sold	500,000		120,000	
Depreciation expense	100,000		60,000	
Inventory	280,000		260,000	
Land	330,000		250,000	
Liabilities		480,000		260,000
Retained earnings, 1/1/04		1,360,000		490,000
Revenues		900,000		300,000

Required:

a. If the equity method is applied by Top, what are its investment account balances as of December 31, 2004?

b. If the cost method is applied by Top, what are its investment account balances as of December 31, 2004?

c. Regardless of the accounting method in use by Top, what are the consolidated totals as of December 31, 2004, for each of the following accounts:

Buildings	Revenues
Equipment	Net Income
Land	Investment in Bottom
Depreciation Expense	Dividends Paid
Amortization Expense	

d. If this combination had been initiated prior to June 30, 2001, and was recorded as a pooling of interests, what would be the consolidated totals as of December 31, 2004, for the accounts listed in requirement (c)?

e. Prepare the worksheet entries required on December 31, 2003, to consolidate the financial records of these two companies. Assume that Top applied the equity method to its investment accounts and that the combination is a purchase.

f. How would the worksheet entries in requirement (e) be altered if Top has used the cost method?

Solution

a. To determine the investment balances under the equity method, four items must be known: the original cost, the income accrual, dividend payments, and amortization of excess cost. Although the first three are indicated in the problem, amortizations must be calculated separately.

An allocation of Top's purchase prices as well as the related amortization expense follows.

Purchase price paid by Top Company . . . . $ 800,000
Book value of Bottom Company, 1/1/02 . . . .   (720,000)

Excess cost over book value   80,000

Excess cost allocated to specific accounts
 based on fair market values:

		Life (years)	Annual Amortization
Buildings	30,000	5	$6,000
Equipment	10,000	10	$1,000
Licensing agreement	–0–	20	$2,000
Total annual expense	$40,000		$9,000

Thus, if Top adopts the equity method to account for this subsidiary, the Investment in Bottom account holds a December 31, 2004, balance of $1,053,000, computed as follows:

Purchase price . . . . $ 800,000
Bottom Company's 2002–03 increase in book value
 (income less dividends)   170,000
Excess amortizations for 2002–2003 ($9,000 per year for
 two years) . . . .   (18,000)
Current year recognition (2004):
 Equity income accrual (Bottom's revenues
  less its expenses) . . . . $ 120,000
 Excess amortization expenses . . . .   (9,000)
 Dividend from Bottom . . . .   (10,000)   101,000

Investment in Bottom Company, 12/31/04 . . . . $1,053,000

The $120,000 income accrual for 2004 and the $9,000 excess amortization expenses indicate that an Equity in Subsidiary Earnings balance of $111,000 appears in Top's income statement for the current period.

b. If Top Company applies the cost method, the Investment in Bottom Company account permanently retains its original $800,000 balance and only the intercompany dividend of $10,000 is recognized by the parent as income in 2004.

c. ■ The consolidated Buildings account as of December 31, 2004, holds a balance of $2,012,000. Although the two book value figures total to only $2 million, a $30,000 purchase price allocation was made to this account based on fair market value at date of acquisition. Because this amount is being depreciated at the rate of $6,000 per year, the original allocation will have been reduced by $18,000 by the end of 2004, leaving only a $12,000 increase.

■ On December 31, 2004, the consolidated Equipment account amounts to $487,000. The book values found in the financial records of Top and Bottom provide a total of $480,000. Once again, the allocation ($10,000) established by the purchase price must be included in the consolidated balance after being adjusted for three years of depreciation ($1,000 × 3 years or $3,000).

■ Land has a consolidated total of $580,000. Since the book value and fair market value of Bottom's land were in agreement at the date of acquisition, no allocation of the purchase price was made to this account. Thus, the book values are simply added together to derive a consolidated figure.

■ Cost of goods sold = $620,000. The cost of goods sold of the parent and subsidiary are added together.

■ Depreciation expense = $167,000. The depreciation expenses of the parent and subsidiary are added together along with the $6,000 additional building depreciation and the $1,000 additional equipment depreciation as presented in the purchase price allocation schedule.

- Amortization expense = $2,000. An additional expense of $2,000 is recognized from the amortization of the licensing agreement acquired in the business combination.
- The Revenues account appears as $1.2 million in the consolidated income statement. None of the worksheet entries in this example affects the individual balances of either company. Consolidation results merely from the addition of the two book values.
- Net income for this business combination is $411,000: consolidated expenses of $789,000 subtracted from revenues of $1.2 million.
- The parent's Investment in Bottom account is removed entirely on the worksheet so that no balance is reported. For consolidation purposes, this account is always eliminated so that the individual assets and liabilities of the subsidiary can be included.
- Dividends paid by the combination should be reported as $70,000, the amount distributed by Top. Because Bottom's dividend payments are entirely intercompany, they are deleted in arriving at consolidated figures.

d. The consolidation of companies under the pooling of interests method is based primarily on the addition of book values. Therefore, consolidated totals for the first five accounts in this question can be determined merely by summing the separate balances:

- Buildings = $2,000,000 ($1,540,000 + $460,000)
- Equipment = $480,000 ($280,000 + $200,000)
- Land = $580,000 ($330,000 + $250,000)
- Cost of goods sold = $620,000 ($500,000 + $120,000)
- Depreciation expense = $160,000 ($100,000 + $60,000)
- Revenues = $1,200,000 ($900,000 + $300,000)
- Consolidated net income is calculated by subtracting the $780,000 in expenses (just computed) from revenues of $1.2 million for a reported total of $420,000.
- As in a purchase, the Investment in Bottom account is eliminated so that the subsidiary's individual balances can be included.
- Only the parent's dividend ($70,000) is reported in the consolidated statements since Bottom's payment is an intercompany cash transfer.

e. Consolidation Entries Assuming Equity Method Used by Parent

Entry S

Common Stock (Bottom Company)	400,000	
Retained Earnings, 1/1/04		
(Bottom Company)	490,000	
Investment in Bottom Company		890,000

Elimination of subsidiary's beginning stockholders' equity accounts against book value portion of investment account.

Entry A

Buildings	18,000	
Equipment	8,000	
Licensing Agreement	36,000	
Investment in Bottom Company		62,000

To recognize allocation of parent's unamortized cost in excess of subsidiary's book value. Balances represent original allocations less two years of amortization for the 2002–03 period.

Entry I

Equity in Subsidiary Earnings	111,000	
Investment in Bottom Company		111,000

To eliminate parent's equity income accrual, balance is computed in requirement (a).

Entry D

Investment in Bottom	10,000	
Dividends Paid		10,000

To eliminate intercompany dividend payment made by
subsidiary to the parent (and recorded as a reduction in the
investment account since the equity method is in use).

Entry E

Depreciation expense	7,000	
Amortization expense	2,000	
Equipment		1,000
Buildings		6,000
Licensing Agreement		2,000

To recognize excess cost depreciation and amortization
for 2004.

    f. If the cost method rather than the equity method is utilized by Top, three changes are
required in the development of consolidation entries:

    (1) An Entry *C is required to update the beginning retained earnings of the parent
as if the equity method had been applied. Both an income accrual as well as excess
amortizations for the prior two years must be recognized since these balances were
not recorded by the parent.

Entry *C

Investment in Bottom Company	152,000	
Retained Earnings, 1/1/04 (Top Company)		152,000

To convert cost figures to the equity method by accruing
the net effect of the subsidiary's operations (income less
dividends) for the prior two years ($170,000) along with
excess amortization expenses ($18,000) for this same period.

    (2) An alteration is needed in Entry I since, under the cost method, only dividend
payments are recorded by the parent as income.

Entry I

Dividend Income	10,000	
Dividends Paid		10,000

To eliminate intercompany dividend payments recorded by
parent as income.

    (3) Finally, because the intercompany dividends have been eliminated in Entry I, no
separate Entry D is needed.

QUESTIONS

    1. CCES Corporation acquires a controlling interest in Schmaling, Inc., in a purchase
transaction. CCES may utilize any one of three methods to account for this investment.
Describe each of these methods, indicating their advantages and disadvantages.

    2. Maguire Company obtains 100 percent control over Williams Company. Several years
after the takeover, consolidated financial statements are being produced. For each of the
following accounts, indicate the values that should be included in consolidated totals.
Assume that Maguire acquired Williams in a transaction that must be viewed as a
purchase.
       a. Equipment.
       b. Investment in Williams Company.
       c. Dividends paid.
       d. Goodwill.

    e. Revenues.

    f. Expenses.

    g. Common stock.

    h. Net income.

3. Using the information presented in question 2, determine each of the consolidated totals if the combination was accounted for as a pooling of interests.

4. When a parent company uses the equity method to account for an investment in a subsidiary, why do both the parent's net income and retained earnings balances agree with the consolidated totals?

5. When a parent company uses the equity method to account for a purchased investment, the amortization expense entry recorded during the year is eliminated on a consolidation worksheet as a component of Entry I. What is the necessity of removing this amortization?

6. When a parent company is applying the cost method or the partial equity method to an investment, an adjustment must be made to the parent's beginning retained earnings (Entry *C) in every period after the year of acquisition. What is the necessity for this entry? Why is no similar entry found when the equity method is utilized by the parent?

7. Several years ago, Jenkins Company acquired a controlling interest in Lambert Company. Lambert recently borrowed $100,000 from Jenkins. In consolidating the financial records of these two companies, how will this debt be handled?

8. Benns Company acquires Waters Company in a combination accounted for as a purchase. Benns adopts the equity method. At the end of six years, Benns reports an investment in Waters of $920,000. What figures constitute this balance?

9. One company is acquired by another in a purchase transaction in which $100,000 of the acquisition price is assigned to goodwill. Several years later a worksheet is being produced to consolidate these two companies. How is the reported value of the goodwill determined at this date?

10. Remo Company purchases Albane Corporation on January 1, 2003. As part of the purchase agreement, the parent states that an additional $100,000 payment to the former owners of Albane may be required in 2004, depending on the outcome of specified conditions. If this payment is subsequently made, how will Remo account for the extra cost?

11. When is the use of push-down accounting required and what is the rationale for its application?

12. How are the individual financial records of both the parent and the subsidiary affected in cases where push-down accounting is being applied?

13. Why has push-down accounting gained popularity for internal reporting purposes?

14. The consolidation process applicable to a pooling of interests often is viewed as easier than that used for a purchase. What creates this perception?

15. When should a parent consider recognizing an impairment loss for goodwill associated with a purchased subsidiary? How should the loss be reported in the financial statements?

INTERNET ASSIGNMENTS

Internet sites are time and date sensitive. It is the purpose of these exercises to have you explore the Internet. You may need to refer to the text's Web site at http://www.mhhe.com/hoyle6e to find the most up-to-date links for the Web sites listed in the Internet Assignments.

1. Go to the Kimberly-Clark Co. Web site (www.kimberly-clark.com) or search to find any firm with a recent goodwill impairment loss. Describe the disclosures regarding the write-down of goodwill with particular attention to the assumptions used in measuring goodwill impairment. Also describe the effect of the impairment loss on earnings per share.

2. In the Amazon.com Web site, find your way to the annual report. In the income statement find the merger and acquisition related costs and related footnote information. Discuss the treatment of these merger costs. What is the period used for goodwill amortization?

3. Use the Rutgers Accounting Web site (www.rutgers.edu/Accounting/) to access the FASB Web site. Search for current standard-setting activities and identify the primary issues relating to the recognition and amortization of intangible assets.

4. Use the Rutgers Accounting Web site (www.rutgers.edu/Accounting/) to access the FASB Web site. Search for current standard-setting activities and identify the primary issues relating to the use of push-down accounting for purchase price allocations.

LIBRARY ASSIGNMENTS

1. Read the following as well as any other published information concerning goodwill:

   "Why Did the Board Change Its Mind on Goodwill Amortization?" *FASB Viewpoints*, December 29, 2000.

   "Why Not Eliminate Goodwill?" FASB, *Financial Accounting Series: Status Report*, November 19, 1999.

   "The Goodwill Game," *Chartered Accountants Magazine*, March 1995.

   "Goodwill—An Eternal Controversy," *CPA Journal*, April 1993.

   "Accounting for Goodwill," *Accounting Horizons*, March 1988.

   Write a report to either justify the current treatment required for the recognition and testing for impairment of goodwill or recommend an alternative method of accounting.

2. Read the following as well as any other published information concerning push-down accounting:

   "Comment Letter to the FASB Discussion Memorandum 'New Basis of Accounting,'" *Accounting Horizons*, March 1994.

   "Understanding the FASB's New Basis Project," *Journal of Accountancy*, May 1992.

   "Push-Down Accounting: FASB 200?" *Management Accounting*, November 1988.

   "Business Combinations: Goodwill and Push-Down Accounting," *CPA Journal*, August 1988.

   "The Push-Down Accounting Controversy," *Management Accounting*, January 1987.

   "Push Down Accounting: A Descriptive Assessment," *Accounting Horizons*, September 1988.

   "Push-Down Accounting: Pros and Cons," *Journal of Accountancy*, June 1984.

   Write a report suggesting actions that the FASB should take in connection with the future application of push-down accounting.

PROBLEMS

1. A company acquires a subsidiary on January 1, 2002, and will prepare consolidated financial statements for the year ending December 31, 2002. For internal reporting purposes, the company has decided to apply the cost method. Why might the company have made this decision?
   a. It is a relatively easy method to apply.
   b. Operating results appearing on the parent's financial records reflect consolidated totals.
   c. The FASB now requires the use of this particular method for internal reporting purposes.
   d. Consolidation is not required when the cost method is used by the parent.

2. A company acquires a subsidiary on January 1, 2002, and will prepare consolidated financial statements for the year ending December 31, 2002. For internal reporting purposes, the company has decided to apply the equity method during 2002. Why might the company have made this decision?

    a.   It is a relatively easy method to apply.

    b.   Operating results appearing on the parent's financial records reflect consolidated totals.

    c.   The FASB now requires the use of this particular method for internal reporting purposes.

    d.   Consolidation is not required when the equity method is used by the parent.

3. When should a consolidated entity recognize a goodwill impairment loss?

    a.   If both the market value of a reporting unit and its associated implied goodwill fall below their respective carrying values.

    b.   Whenever the market value of the entity declines significantly.

    c.   If the market value of a reporting unit falls below its original acquisition price.

    d.   Annually on a systematic and rational basis.

4. Willkom Corporation buys 100 percent of Szabo, Inc., on January 1, 2002, at a price in excess of the subsidiary's fair market value. On that date, Willkom's equipment (10-year life) has a book value of $300,000 but a fair market value of $400,000. Szabo has equipment (10-year life) with a book value of $200,000 but a fair market value of $300,000. Willkom uses the partial equity method to record its investment in Szabo. On December 31, 2004, Willkom has equipment with a book value of $210,000 but a fair market value of $330,000. Szabo has equipment with a book value of $140,000 but a fair market value of $270,000. What is the consolidated balance for the Equipment account as of December 31, 2004?

    a. $600,000

    b. $490,000

    c. $480,000

    d. $420,000

5. How would the answer to problem 4 have been affected if the parent had applied the cost method rather than the partial equity method?

    a.   No effect: The method used by the parent is for internal reporting purposes only and has no impact on consolidated totals.

    b.   The consolidated Equipment account would have a higher reported balance.

    c.   The consolidated Equipment account would have a lower reported balance.

    d.   The balance in the consolidated Equipment account cannot be determined for the cost method using the information given.

6. Dosmann, Incorporated buys all of the outstanding shares of Lizzi Corporation on January 1, 2002, for $700,000 in cash. This price resulted in a $35,000 allocation to equipment and goodwill of $88,000. Because the subsidiary subsequently earned especially high profits, Dosmann was required to pay the previous owners of Lizzi an additional $110,000 on January 1, 2004. How should this extra amount be reported?

    a.   The additional $110,000 payment is a reduction in consolidated retained earnings.

    b.   A retroactive adjustment is made to record the $110,000 as an additional expense for the year ending December 31, 2002.

    c.   Consolidated goodwill as of January 1, 2004, is increased by $110,000.

    d.   The $110,000 is recorded as an expense in 2004.

7. Lauren Corporation purchases Sarah, Inc., on January 1, 2002, by issuing 13,000 shares of common stock with a $10 per share par value and a $23 fair market value. This transaction results in the recording of $62,000 of goodwill. Subsequently, on January 1, 2004, Lauren is required to issue an additional 3,000 shares of stock to Sarah's previous owners because of a drop in the market value of the initial 13,000 shares. How is this additional issuance of stock recorded?

    a.   The fair market value of the newly issued shares increases the Goodwill account balance.

    b.   The Investment balance is not affected but the parent's Additional Paid-In Capital is reduced by the par value of the newly issued shares.

    c.   All of the subsidiary's asset and liability accounts must be revalued for consolidation purposes based on their fair market values as of January 1, 2004.

    d.   The additional shares are assumed to have been issued on January 1, 2002, so that a retroactive adjustment is required.

8. What is push-down accounting?
   a. A requirement that a subsidiary must use the same accounting principles as a parent company.
   b. Inventory transfers made from a parent company to a subsidiary.
   c. Recording by a subsidiary of the market value allocations found within the purchase price paid by a parent as well as subsequent amortization.
   d. The adjustments required for consolidation when a parent has applied the cost method of accounting for internal reporting purposes.

9. Treadway Corporation purchases Hooker, Inc., on January 1, 2002. The parent pays more than the fair market value of the subsidiary's net assets. On that date, Treadway has equipment with a book value of $420,000 and a fair market value of $530,000. Hooker has equipment with a book value of $330,000 and a fair market value of $390,000. Hooker is going to use push-down accounting. Immediately after the acquisition, what Equipment account appears on Hooker's separate balance sheet and on the consolidated balance sheet?
   a. $330,000 and $750,000.
   b. $330,000 and $860,000.
   c. $390,000 and $810,000.
   d. $390,000 and $920,000.

Problems 10 through 12 are based on the following information:

Hans, Inc., purchases all of the outstanding stock of Sysk Corporation on January 1, 2002, for $310,000. Equipment with a 10-year life was undervalued on Sysk's financial records by $66,000. Goodwill resulting from this combination is $56,000 and will not be amortized.

Sysk earned a reported net income of $150,000 in 2002 and $180,000 in 2003. Dividends of $60,000 were paid in each of these two years.

Selected account balances as of December 31, 2004, for the two companies follow.

	Hans	Sysk
Revenues	$900,000	$700,000
Expenses	400,000	500,000
Investment income	not given	—
Retained earnings, 1/1/04	700,000	298,000
Dividends paid	110,000	60,000

10. If the partial equity method has been applied, what is the consolidated net income?
    a. $700,000
    b. $693,400
    c. $690,600
    d. $640,000

11. If the equity method has been applied, what is the Investment in Sysk account balance within the records of Hans at the end of 2004?
    a. $640,200
    b. $506,800
    c. $520,000
    d. $645,900

12. Assuming the cost method has been applied, what is the consolidated retained earnings balance as of January 1, 2004?
    a. $700,000
    b. $910,000
    c. $896,800
    d. $1,030,200

13. Herbert, Inc., buys all of the outstanding stock of Rambis Company on January 1, 2001, for $574,000. Annual excess amortization of $12,000 results from this purchase transaction. On the date of the takeover, Herbert reported retained earnings of $400,000 while Rambis reported a $200,000 balance. Herbert reported internal income of $40,000 in 2001 and $50,000 in 2002 and paid $10,000 in dividends each year. Rambis reported net income of $20,000 in 2001 and $30,000 in 2002 and paid $5,000 in dividends each year.

Required:

a. Assume that Herbert's internal income does not include any income derived from the subsidiary.

- If the parent uses the equity method, what are consolidated retained earnings on December 31, 2002?
- If the parent uses the partial equity method, what are consolidated retained earnings on December 31, 2002?
- If the parent uses the cost method, what are consolidated retained earnings on December 31, 2002?

b. Under each of the following situations, what is the Investment in Rambis account balance on Herbert's books on January 1, 2002?

- The parent uses the equity method.
- The parent uses the partial equity method.
- The parent uses the cost method.

c. Under each of the following situations, what is Entry *C on a 2002 consolidation worksheet?

- The parent uses the equity method.
- The parent uses the partial equity method.
- The parent uses the cost method.

14. Haynes, Inc., obtains 100 percent of Turner Company's common stock on January 1, 2002, by issuing 9,000 shares of $10 par value common stock. Haynes's shares had a $15 per share fair market value. On that date, Turner reported a net book value of $100,000. However, its equipment (with a five-year remaining life) was undervalued by $5,000 in the company's accounting records. Also, Turner had developed a customer list with an assessed value of $30,000, although no value had been recorded on Turner's books. The customer list had an estimated remaining useful life of 10 years.

The following figures come from the individual accounting records of these two companies as of December 31, 2002:

	Haynes	**Turner**
Revenues	$600,000	$230,000
Expenses	440,000	120,000
Investment income	not given	—
Dividends paid	80,000	50,000

The following figures come from the individual accounting records of these two companies as of December 31, 2003:

	Haynes	**Turner**
Revenues	$700,000	$280,000
Expenses	460,000	150,000
Investment income	not given	—
Dividends paid	90,000	40,000
Equipment	500,000	300,000

Required:

a. What balance does Haynes's Investment in Turner account show on December 31, 2003, when the equity method is applied?
b. What is the consolidated net income for the year ending December 31, 2003?
c. What is the consolidated equipment balance as of December 31, 2003? How would this answer be affected by the investment method applied by the parent?

   d. If Haynes has applied the cost method to account for its investment, what adjustment is needed to beginning retained earnings on a December 31, 2003, consolidation worksheet? How would this answer change if the partial equity method had been in use? How would this answer change if the equity method had been in use?

15. On January 1, 2001, Pure, Inc., issues 58 shares of previously unissued common stock for all of the outstanding shares of Simple Company. Pure's stock has a par value of $1 per share but a fair market value of $10 per share.

     Just prior to the creation of this combination, the following information is known about these two companies:

	Pure, Inc. Book Value	Simple Company Book Value	Simple Company Fair Market Value
Current assets	$150	$ 60	$ 60
Equipment (10-year life)	600	200	260
Buildings (20-year life)	900	300	340
Liabilities	450	160	160
Common stock	500	100	
Additional paid-in capital ...	100	50	
Retained earnings	600	250	

During 2001, Pure reported $100 in net income (excluding any investment or dividend income) and distributed $30 in dividends; Simple had $80 in net income and $20 in dividends. At the end of 2002, the following figures were reported by the two separate companies. Once again, Pure's figures do not include any investment or dividend income.

	Pure, Inc.	Simple Company
Revenues	$400	$250
Expenses	280	160
Dividends paid	40	30
Equipment	700	220
Buildings	800	280

Required:

   a. If this business combination was accounted for as a purchase, what would be the consolidated revenues, expenses, and net income for the year ending December 31, 2002?

   b. If this business combination was accounted for as a pooling of interests, what would be the consolidated revenues, expenses, and net income for the year ending December 31, 2002?

   c. If this business combination was accounted for as a purchase, what would be the consolidated balance of the Investment in Simple Company account and the Investment Income account as of December 31, 2002?

   d. If this business combination was accounted for as a purchase, what would be the consolidated balance of the Buildings account on December 31, 2002?

   e. If this business combination was accounted for as a pooling of interests, what would be the consolidated balance of the Buildings account on December 31, 2002?

   f. If this business combination was accounted for as a purchase, what would be the consolidated balance of retained earnings at December 31, 2002? What would be the consolidated retained earnings if this combination met all of the criteria for a pooling of interests?

16. Texas, Inc., obtains all of the outstanding stock of Chainsaw Corporation on January 1, 2002. At that date, Chainsaw owns only three assets and has no liabilities:

	Book Value	Fair Market Value
Inventory	$ 30,000	$ 40,000
Equipment (5-year life)	70,000	50,000
Building (10-year life)	100,000	150,000

Required:

a. If Texas pays $250,000 in cash for Chainsaw, what allocation should be assigned to the subsidiary's Building account and its Equipment account in a December 31, 2004, consolidation?

b. If Texas pays $220,000 in cash for Chainsaw, what allocation should be assigned to the subsidiary's Building account and its Equipment account in a December 31, 2004, consolidation?

c. If Texas pays $180,000 in cash for Chainsaw, what allocation should be assigned to the subsidiary's Building account and its Equipment account in a December 31, 2004, consolidation?

d. If Texas issued common stock valued at $180,000 (rather than paying cash) for Chainsaw in a pooling of interests, what allocation should be assigned to the subsidiary's Building account and its Equipment account in a December 31, 2004, consolidation?

Problems 17 through 21 are based on the following data:

Chapman Company obtains 100 percent of the stock of Abernethy Company on January 1, 2002. As of that date, Abernethy has the following trial balance:

	Debit	Credit
Accounts payable		$ 50,000
Accounts receivable	$ 40,000	
Additional paid-in capital		50,000
Buildings (net) (4-year life)	120,000	
Cash and short-term investments	60,000	
Common stock		250,000
Equipment (net) (5-year life)	200,000	
Inventory	90,000	
Land	80,000	
Long-term liabilities (mature 12/31/05)		150,000
Retained earnings, 1/1/02		100,000
Supplies	10,000	
Totals	$600,000	$600,000

During 2002, Abernethy reported income of $80,000 while paying dividends of $10,000. During 2003, Abernethy reported income of $110,000 while paying dividends of $30,000.

The following five problems should be viewed as independent situations.

17. Assume that Chapman Company acquired the common stock of Abernethy for $490,000 in cash. As of January 1, 2002, Abernethy's land had a fair market value of $90,000, its buildings were valued at $160,000, and its equipment was appraised at $180,000. Chapman uses the equity method for this investment. Prepare consolidation worksheet entries for December 31, 2002, and December 31, 2003.

18. Assume that Chapman Company acquired the common stock of Abernethy for $500,000 in cash. Assume that the equipment and long-term liabilities had fair market values of $220,000 and $120,000, respectively, on that date. Chapman uses the cost method to account for its investment. Prepare consolidation worksheet entries for December 31, 2002, and December 31, 2003.

19. Assume that Chapman Company acquired the common stock of Abernethy by issuing 10,000 shares of its $30 par value common stock. The stock had a fair market value of $42 per share on January 1, 2002. This transaction met all 12 requirements for a pooling of interests and was initiated prior to June 30, 2001. Assume that Abernethy's land on that date had a fair market value of $110,000, while the inventory was valued at $120,000. Chapman uses the book value method to account for this investment. Prepare consolidation worksheet entries for December 31, 2002, and December 31, 2003.

20. Assume that Chapman Company acquires the common stock of Abernethy by issuing 10,000 shares of its $30 par value common stock. The stock has a $42 per share fair market value on January 1, 2002. This transaction is accounted for as a purchase. On

January 1, 2002, Abernethy's inventory had a fair market value of $150,000. All of this inventory is assumed to have been sold during 2002. Chapman applies the equity method to account for this investment. Prepare the consolidation worksheet entries for December 31, 2002, and December 31, 2003.

21. Assume that Chapman Company acquired the common stock of Abernethy by paying $520,000 in cash. All accounts of Abernethy are estimated to have a value approximately equal to present book values. Chapman uses the partial equity method to account for its investment. Prepare the consolidation worksheet entries for December 31, 2002, and December 31, 2003.

22. Jefferson, Inc., purchases Hamilton Corporation on January 1, 2002. Immediately after the acquisition, the two companies have the following account balances. Hamilton's equipment (with a five-year life) is actually worth $450,000. Any goodwill is considered to have an indefinite life.

	Jefferson	Hamilton
Current assets	$300,000	$210,000
Investment in Hamilton	510,000	
Equipment	600,000	400,000
Liabilities	200,000	160,000
Common stock	350,000	150,000
Retained earnings	860,000	300,000

In 2002, Hamilton earns a net income of $55,000 and pays a $5,000 cash dividend. At the end of 2003, selected account balances for the two companies are as follows:

	Jefferson	Hamilton
Revenues	$400,000	$240,000
Expenses	290,000	180,000
Investment income	not given	
Retained earnings, 1/1/03	not given	350,000
Current assets	360,000	140,000
Investment in Hamilton	not given	
Equipment	520,000	420,000
Liabilities	170,000	190,000

Required:

a. What will be the December 31, 2003, balance in the Investment Income account and the Investment in Hamilton account under each of the three methods described in this chapter?

b. How is the consolidated Expense account affected by the accounting method used by the parent to record ownership of this subsidiary?

c. How is the consolidated Equipment account affected by the accounting method used by the parent to record ownership of this subsidiary?

d. What is Jefferson's Retained Earnings balance as of January 1, 2003, under each of the three methods described in this chapter?

e. What is Entry *C on a consolidation worksheet for 2003 under each of the three methods described in this chapter?

f. What is Entry S on a consolidation worksheet for 2003 under each of the three methods described in this chapter?

g. What is consolidated net income for 2003?

23. Following are selected account balances from the Profitt Company and Simon Corporation as of December 31, 2002:

	Profitt	**Simon**
Revenues	$700,000	$ 400,000
Cost of goods sold	250,000	100,000
Depreciation expense	150,000	200,000
Investment income	not given	
Dividends paid	80,000	60,000
Retained earnings, 1/1/02	600,000	200,000
Current assets	400,000	500,000
Buildings (net)	900,000	400,000
Equipment (net)	600,000	1,000,000
Investment in Simon	not given	
Liabilities	500,000	1,380,000
Common stock	600,000 ($20 par)	200,000 ($10 par)
Additional paid-in capital	150,000	80,000

On January 1, 2002, Profitt purchased all of the outstanding stock of Simon for $660,000 in cash and common stock. Profitt also pays $20,000 in lawyers' fees and other combination costs as well as $10,000 in stock issuance costs. At the date of acquisition, Simon's buildings (with a six-year remaining life) have a $440,000 book value but a fair market value of $560,000.

Required:

   a. As of December 31, 2002, what is the consolidated Buildings balance?

   b. As of December 31, 2002, what is the consolidated Retained Earnings balance?

   c. For the year ending December 31, 2002, what is consolidated net income?

   d. As of December 31, 2002, what is the consolidated balance to be reported for goodwill?

24. Foxx Corporation purchases all of the outstanding stock of Greenburg Company on January 1, 2002, for $600,000. Greenburg had net assets on that date of $470,000, although equipment with a 10-year life was undervalued on the records by $90,000. Any recognized goodwill is considered to have an indefinite life.

Greenburg reports net income in 2002 of $90,000 and $100,000 in 2003. Dividends of $20,000 are paid by the subsidiary in each of these two years.

Financial figures for the year ending December 31, 2004, follow:

	Foxx	**Greenburg**
Revenues	$ 800,000	$ 600,000
Cost of goods sold	(100,000)	(150,000)
Depreciation expense	300,000	350,000
Investment income	20,000	–0–
Net income	$ 420,000	$ 100,000
Retained earnings, 1/1/04	$1,100,000	$ 320,000
Net income	420,000	100,000
Dividends paid	(120,000)	(20,000)
Retained earnings, 12/31/04	$1,400,000	$ 400,000
Current assets	$ 300,000	$ 100,000
Investment in subsidiary	600,000	–0–
Equipment (net)	900,000	600,000
Buildings (net)	800,000	400,000
Land	600,000	100,000
Total assets	$3,200,000	$1,200,000
Liabilities	$ 900,000	$ 500,000
Common stock	900,000	300,000
Retained earnings	1,400,000	400,000
Total liabilities and equities	$3,200,000	$1,200,000

Required:

a. Determine the consolidated balance for each of the following accounts:

    Depreciation Expense   Buildings

    Dividends Paid   Goodwill

    Revenues   Common Stock

    Equipment

b. How does the parent's choice of an accounting method for its investment affect the balances computed in requirement (*a*)?

c. Which method of accounting for this subsidiary is the parent actually using for internal reporting purposes?

d. If a different method of accounting for this investment had been used by the parent company, how could that method have been identified?

e. What would be Foxx's balance for retained earnings as of January 1, 2004, if each of the following methods had been in use?

    Cost method

    Partial equity method

    Equity method

25. Big Corporation purchased Little Company on January 1, 2002, for $400,000 in cash. Little reported net assets at that time of $320,000. However, several of Little's accounts had fair market values that differed from book values:

	Book Value	Fair Market Value
Land	$ 60,000	$ 50,000
Buildings (10-year life)	100,000	120,000
Equipment (6-year life)	60,000	90,000

Any goodwill is considered to have an indefinite life.

Following are financial statements for these two companies for the year ending December 31, 2002. Credit balances are indicated by parentheses.

	Big	Little
Revenues	$ (600,000)	$(300,000)
Cost of goods sold	300,000	110,000
Depreciation expense	100,000	70,000
Income of Little	(113,000)	–0–
Net income	$ (313,000)	$(120,000)
Retained earnings, 1/1/02	$ (700,000)	$(220,000)
Net income (above)	(313,000)	(120,000)
Dividends paid	142,000	80,000
Retained earnings, 12/31/02	$ (871,000)	$(260,000)
Cash	$ 176,000	$ 80,000
Receivables	210,000	90,000
Inventory	190,000	130,000
Investment in Little	433,000	–0–
Land	350,000	60,000
Buildings (net)	343,000	90,000
Equipment (net)	190,000	50,000
Goodwill	–0–	–0–
Total assets	$ 1,892,000	$ 500,000
Liabilities	$ (621,000)	$(140,000)
Common stock	(400,000)	(100,000)
Retained earnings (above)	(871,000)	(260,000)
Total liabilities and equity	$(1,892,000)	$(500,000)

a. How was the $113,000 Income of Little balance computed?

b. Without preparing a worksheet or consolidation entries, determine the totals to be reported for this business combination for the year ending December 31, 2002.

c. Verify the totals determined in part (b) by producing a consolidation worksheet for Big and Little for the year ending December 31, 2002.

26. Following are separate financial statements for Mitchell Company and Andrews Company as of December 31, 2002. Mitchell acquired all of the outstanding stock of Andrews on January 1, 1998, by issuing 9,000 shares of its own common stock. This stock was valued at $50 per share while having a par value of $30 per share. In addition, Mitchell paid $20,000 to lawyers, accountants, and other parties for costs incurred in creating the combination. The combination is accounted for as a purchase.

	Mitchell Company 12/31/02	Andrews Company 12/31/02
Revenues	$ (610,000)	$ (370,000)
Cost of goods sold	270,000	140,000
Depreciation expense	115,000	80,000
Dividend income	(5,000)	–0–
Net income	$ (230,000)	$ (150,000)
Retained earnings, 1/1/02	$ (880,000)	$ (490,000)
Net income (above)	(230,000)	(150,000)
Dividends paid	90,000	5,000
Retained earnings, 12/31/02	$(1,020,000)	$ (635,000)
Cash	$ 110,000	$ 15,000
Receivables	380,000	220,000
Inventory	560,000	280,000
Investment in Andrews Company	470,000	–0–
Land	460,000	340,000
Buildings and equipment (net)	920,000	380,000
Total assets	$2,900,000	$1,235,000
Liabilities	$ (780,000)	$ (470,000)
Preferred stock	(300,000)	–0–
Common stock	(500,000)	(100,000)
Additional paid-in capital	(300,000)	(30,000)
Retained earnings, 12/31/02	(1,020,000)	(635,000)
Total liabilities and equities	$(2,900,000)	$(1,235,000)

On the date of purchase, Andrews reported retained earnings of $230,000 and a total book value of $360,000. At that time its buildings and equipment were undervalued by $60,000. This property was assumed to have a six-year life with no salvage value. Additionally, Andrews owned a trademark with a fair value of $50,000 and a 10-year remaining life that was not reflected on its books.

a. Using the preceding information, prepare a consolidation worksheet for these two companies as of December 31, 2002.

b. Assuming that Mitchell applied the equity method to this investment, what account balances would be altered on the parent's individual financial statements?

c. Assuming that Mitchell applied the equity method to this investment, what changes would be necessary in the consolidation entries found on a December 31, 2002, worksheet?

d. Assuming that Mitchell applied the equity method to this investment, what changes would be created in the consolidated figures to be reported by this combination?

27. Tucson Company has reported the following income and dividend figures during the past few years:

	Net Income	Dividends Paid
2001	$80,000	$30,000
2000	70,000	30,000
1999	40,000	20,000
1998	50,000	20,000

Account balances for Arizona, Inc., and Tucson Company as of December 31, 2002, follow. Some of Arizona's accounts have been omitted from this list.

	Arizona	Tucson
Revenues	$600,000	$400,000
Cost of goods sold	230,000	115,000
Depreciation expense	170,000	135,000
Investment income	not given	
Retained earnings, 1/1/02	900,000	800,000
Dividends paid	130,000	40,000
Current assets	200,000	690,000
Land	300,000	290,000
Buildings (net)	500,000	230,000
Equipment (net)	200,000	250,000
Liabilities	400,000	350,000
Common stock	300,000	40,000
Additional paid-in capital	50,000	160,000

On January 1, 1998, Arizona acquired all of Tucson's stock by paying $1 million cash. Tucson's equipment (10-year life) was overvalued at that time by $30,000 but its buildings were undervalued by $50,000. These buildings had a five-year life. A franchise agreement with a useful life of 20 years was undervalued on Tucson's books by $120,000. There was no goodwill associated with the purchase.

Required:

    a. Assuming that Arizona has applied the cost method, prepare consolidation entries as of December 31, 2002. What is the purpose of Entry *C?

    b. Determine the consolidated totals for the following accounts; assume that the parent applies the partial equity method:

        Net Income

        Equipment (net)

        Buildings (net)

    c. Determine the consolidated totals for the following accounts; assume that the parent applies the equity method:

        Net Income

        Equipment (net)

        Buildings (net)

28. Following are the trial balances for the High Company and the Low Company as of December 31, 2002:

	High Company Trial Balance 12/31/02		Low Company Trial Balance 12/31/02	
	Debit	Credit	Debit	Credit
Accounts payable		$ 170,000		$ 200,000
Accounts receivable	$ 440,000		$ 80,000	
Buildings (net)	1,510,000		660,000	
Cash	60,000		10,000	
Common stock		700,000		400,000
Dividends paid	100,000		20,000	
Cost of Goods sold	275,000		110,000	
Depreciation expense	165,000		85,000	
Inventory	640,000		610,000	
Investment in Low Company ...	1,260,000		–0–	
Investment income		50,000		–0–
Long-term liabilities		690,000		500,000
Machinery (net)	660,000		460,000	
Retained earnings, 1/1/02		2,630,000		690,000
Revenues		870,000		245,000
Totals	$5,110,000	$5,110,000	$2,035,000	$2,035,000

High Company acquired all of the outstanding common stock of Low Company on January 1, 1999, for $940,000 in cash. On that date, Low's buildings (20-year life) were undervalued in the company's records by $100,000 while its machinery (10-year life) was overvalued by $20,000. Low also owns a secret formula that High valued at $60,000 (20-year useful life). The secret formula is not reflected on Low's financial records. Low's book value on the date of acquisition was $800,000. High uses the partial equity method to account for this investment.

As of December 31, 2002, Low owes $20,000 to High.

Required:

Determine the consolidated figures that will be reported by the business combination of High Company and Low Company as of December 31, 2002.

29. Giant purchased all of the common stock of Small on January 1, 2002. Over the next few years, Giant applied the equity method to the recording of this investment. At the date of the original purchase, $90,000 of the price was attributed to undervalued land, while $50,000 was assigned to equipment having a 10-year life. The remaining $60,000 unallocated portion of the purchase price was viewed as goodwill.

Following are individual financial statements for the year ending December 31, 2006. On that date, Small owes Giant $10,000. Credits are indicated by parentheses.

	Giant	Small
Revenues	$(1,175,000)	$ (360,000)
Cost of goods sold	550,000	90,000
Depreciation expense	172,000	130,000
Equity in income of Small	(135,000)	–0–
Net income	$ (588,000)	$ (140,000)
Retained earnings, 1/1/06	$(1,417,000)	$ (620,000)
Net income (above)	(588,000)	(140,000)
Dividends paid	310,000	110,000
Retained earnings, 12/31/06	$(1,695,000)	$ (650,000)

(continued)

	Giant	Small
Current assets	$ 398,000	$ 318,000
Investment in Small	995,000	–0–
Land	440,000	165,000
Buildings (net)	304,000	419,000
Equipment (net)	648,000	286,000
Goodwill	–0–	–0–
Total assets	$ 2,785,000	$ 1,188,000
Liabilities	$ (840,000)	$ (368,000)
Common stock	(250,000)	(170,000)
Retained earnings (above)	(1,695,000)	(650,000)
Total liabilities and equity	$(2,785,000)	$(1,188,000)

a. How was the $135,000 Equity in Income of Small balance computed?

b. Without preparing a worksheet or consolidation entries, determine the totals to be reported by this business combination for the year ending December 31, 2006.

c. Verify the figures determined in part (*b*) by producing a consolidation worksheet for Giant and Small for the year ending December 31, 2006.

d. If Giant determined that the entire amount of goodwill from its investment in Small was impaired in 2006, how would the accounts of the parent reflect the impairment loss? How would the worksheet process change? What impact does an impairment loss have on consolidated financial statements?

30. Following are selected accounts for Mergaronite Company and Hill, Inc., as of December 31, 2002. Several of Mergaronite's accounts have been omitted.

	Mergaronite	Hill
Revenues	$600,000	$250,000
Cost of goods sold	280,000	100,000
Depreciation expense	120,000	50,000
Investment income	not given	
Retained earnings, 1/1/02	900,000	600,000
Dividends paid	130,000	40,000
Current assets	200,000	690,000
Land	300,000	90,000
Buildings (net)	500,000	140,000
Equipment (net)	200,000	250,000
Liabilities	400,000	310,000
Common stock	300,000	40,000
Additional paid-in capital	50,000	160,000

Assume that Mergaronite took over Hill on January 1, 1998, in a purchase by issuing 7,000 shares of common stock having a par value of $10 per share but a fair market value of $100 each. On January 1, 1998, Hill's land was undervalued by $20,000, its buildings were overvalued by $30,000, and equipment was undervalued by $60,000. The buildings had a 10-year life; the equipment had a 5-year life. A customer list with an appraised value of $100,000 was developed internally by Hill and was to be written off over a 20-year period.

Required:

a. What are the December 31, 2002, consolidated totals for the following accounts:

Revenues
Expenses
Buildings
Equipment
Customer List
Common Stock
Additional Paid-In Capital

b. In requirement (*a*), why can the consolidated totals be determined without knowing which method the parent has used to account for the subsidiary?

c. If the equity method is used by the parent, what consolidation entries would be used on a 2002 worksheet?

31. Alton Company acquired Zeidner, Inc., on January 1, 1997, in a business combination properly accounted for as a purchase. On that date, Zeidner held assets and liabilities with book values of $700,000 and $200,000, respectively. Alton paid a total of $670,000 to acquire all of the outstanding stock of Zeidner. At the date of this purchase, Zeidner possessed equipment (with a five-year life) that had a value $50,000 in excess of its book value. In addition, Zeidner had buildings worth $80,000 more than their book value. These buildings had a remaining life expectancy of 20 years. Any goodwill that resulted from the acquisition was initially amortized over a 20-year period.

Following are the individual financial statements for these two companies for the year ending December 31, 2006. Alton owes Zeidner $30,000 at this point in time. Without preparing consolidation entries or setting up a worksheet, determine the consolidated totals for Alton Company and Zeidner, Inc.

	Alton Company	Zeidner, Inc.
Income Statement		
Revenues	$ 600,000	$ 500,000
Cost of goods sold	(175,000)	(160,000)
Depreciation expense	(125,000)	(140,000)
Investment income from Zeidner Company	200,000	–0–
Net income	$ 500,000	$ 200,000
Statement of Retained Earnings		
Retained earnings, 1/1/06	$1,500,000	$ 650,000
Net income (above)	500,000	200,000
Dividends paid	(200,000)	(50,000)
Retained earnings, 12/31/06	$1,800,000	$ 800,000
Balance Sheet		
Current assets	$ 230,000	$ 300,000
Investment in Zeidner Company	1,270,000	–0–
Land	100,000	200,000
Buildings	300,000	400,000
Equipment	600,000	300,000
Goodwill	–0–	–0–
Total assets	$2,500,000	$1,200,000
Liabilities	$ 300,000	$ 100,000
Common stock	400,000	300,000
Retained earnings, 12/31/06	1,800,000	800,000
Total liabilities and equities	$2,500,000	$1,200,000

32. On January 1, 2002, Romeo, Incorporated, exchanged 10,000 shares of previously unissued common stock for all of the outstanding shares of Juliet Company. This was accounted for as a pooling of interests that was initiated prior to June 30, 2001. Romeo's common stock had a $20 par value but a fair market value of $48 per share. On the date of the exchange, Juliet reported $370,000 in stockholders' equity:

Common Stock	$200,000
Additional Paid-In Capital	50,000
Retained Earnings	120,000

Romeo originally offered only 8,000 shares for Juliet's stock but raised that bid based on favorable earnings projections. In addition, equipment held by the subsidiary (with a 10-year remaining life) was estimated to be undervalued on the accounting records by $70,000.

During 2002, Juliet reported net income of $80,000 and paid cash dividends of $60,000. In accounting for this investment, Romeo utilized the equity method.

Following are the December 31, 2003, trial balances for these two companies.

	Romeo, Incorporated	Juliet Company
Debits		
Accounts receivable	$ 140,000	$ 40,000
Buildings	620,000	260,000
Cash	60,000	10,000
Dividends paid	130,000	60,000
Equipment	490,000	330,000
Expenses	390,000	110,000
Inventory	190,000	110,000
Investment in Juliet Company	420,000	–0–
Land	300,000	200,000
Total debits	$2,740,000	$1,120,000
Credits		
Additional paid-in capital	$ 190,000	$ 50,000
Common stock	600,000	200,000
Investment income from Juliet Company	90,000	–0–
Liabilities	580,000	530,000
Retained earnings, 1/1/03	680,000	140,000
Revenues	600,000	200,000
Total credits	$2,740,000	$1,120,000

Required:

Determine the consolidated balances that would be reported by this combination.

33. Broome paid $430,000 cash for all of the outstanding common stock of Charlotte, Inc., on January 1, 2002. The subsidiary had a book value of $340,000 on that date (common stock of $200,000 and retained earnings of $140,000), although equipment recorded at $40,000 (with a five-year remaining life) was assessed as having an actual worth of $70,000.

During the subsequent three years, Charlotte reported the following balances:

	Net Income	Dividends Paid
2002	$65,000	$25,000
2003	75,000	35,000
2004	80,000	40,000

On January 1, 2004, Broome paid an additional $20,000 to the previous owners of Charlotte, an amount that was due because the subsidiary's earnings for the first two years had exceeded $120,000.

a. Prepare consolidation worksheet entries as of December 31, 2004, assuming that Broome has applied the cost method.

b. Prepare consolidation worksheet entries as of December 31, 2004, assuming that Broome has applied the partial equity method.

34. Palm Company acquired 100 percent of the voting stock of Storm Company on January 1, 1998, by issuing 10,000 shares of its $10 par value common stock (having a fair market value of $13 per share). Palm also paid $10,000 in consolidation costs to

lawyers and investment analysts. As of that date, Storm had stockholders' equity totaling $105,000. Land shown on Storm's accounting records was undervalued by $10,000. Equipment (with a five-year life) was undervalued by $5,000. A secret formula developed by Storm was appraised at $20,000 with an estimated life of 20 years.

Following are the separate financial statements for the two companies for the year ending December 31, 2002. The combination was accounted for as a purchase.

	Palm Company	Storm Company
Revenues	$ 485,000	$190,000
Cost of goods sold	(160,000)	(70,000)
Depreciation expense	(130,000)	(52,000)
Equity in subsidiary earnings	66,000	–0–
Net income	$ 261,000	$ 68,000
Retained earnings, 1/1/02	$ 659,000	$ 98,000
Net income (above)	261,000	68,000
Dividends paid	(175,500)	(40,000)
Retained earnings, 12/31/02	$ 744,500	$126,000
Current assets	$ 268,000	$ 75,000
Investment in Storm Company	216,000	–0–
Land	427,500	58,000
Buildings and equipment (net)	713,000	161,000
Total assets	$1,624,500	$294,000
Current liabilities	$ 110,000	$ 19,000
Long-term liabilities	80,000	84,000
Common stock	600,000	60,000
Additional paid-in capital	90,000	5,000
Retained earnings, 12/31/02	744,500	126,000
Total liabilities and equities	$1,624,500	$294,000

a. How was the $66,000 balance in the Equity in Subsidiary Earnings account derived?

b. Prepare a worksheet to consolidate the financial information for these two companies.

c. How would Storm's individual financial records differ if the push-down method of accounting had been applied?

35. The Tyler Company acquired all of the outstanding stock of Jasmine Company on January 1, 2002, for $206,000 in cash. Jasmine had a book value of only $140,000 on that date. However, equipment (having an eight-year life) was undervalued by $54,400 on Jasmine's financial records. A building with a 20-year life was overvalued by $10,000. Subsequent to the acquisition, Jasmine reported the following:

	Net Income	Dividends Paid
2002	$50,000	$10,000
2003	60,000	40,000
2004	30,000	20,000

In accounting for this investment, Tyler has used the equity method. Selected accounts taken from the financial records of these two companies as of December 31, 2004, are as follows:

	Tyler Company	Jasmine Company
Revenues—operating	$310,000	$104,000
Expenses	198,000	74,000
Equipment (net)	320,000	50,000
Buildings (net)	220,000	68,000
Common stock	290,000	50,000
Retained earnings, 12/31/04 balance	410,000	160,000

Required:

Determine the following account balances as of December 31, 2004:
> *a.* Investment in Jasmine Company (on Tyler's individual financial records).
> *b.* Equity in subsidiary earnings (on Tyler's individual financial records).
> *c.* Consolidated net income.
> *d.* Consolidated equipment (net).
> *e.* Consolidated buildings (net).
> *f.* Consolidated goodwill (net).
> *g.* Consolidated common stock.
> *h.* Consolidated retained earnings, 12/31/04.

36. During 2000, Abbott Corporation issued shares of its common stock for all of the outstanding stock of Drexel, Inc., in a transaction accounted for as a pooling of interests. Drexel's book value was only $120,000 at the time, but Abbott issued 10,000 shares valued at $18 per share. Abbott was willing to convey these shares because it felt that buildings (10-year life) were undervalued on Drexel's records by $40,000 while equipment (5-year life) was undervalued by $20,000.

   Following are the individual financial records for these two companies for the year ending December 31, 2003.

	Abbott	Drexel
Revenues	$ 310,000	$ 90,000
Operating expenses	(220,000)	(60,000)
Equity in subsidiary earnings	30,000	–0–
Net income	$ 120,000	$ 30,000
Retained earnings, 1/1/03	$ 640,000	$ 85,000
Net income	120,000	30,000
Less: Dividends paid	(70,000)	(20,000)
Retained earnings, 12/31/03	$ 690,000	$ 95,000
Current assets	$ 159,000	$ 57,000
Investment in Drexel	155,000	–0–
Buildings (net)	472,000	71,000
Equipment (net)	404,000	107,000
Total assets	$1,190,000	$235,000
Liabilities	$ 160,000	$ 80,000
Common stock	300,000	60,000
Additional paid-in capital	40,000	–0–
Retained earnings, 12/31/03 (above)	690,000	95,000
Total liabilities and equities	$1,190,000	$235,000

   a. Without making consolidation entries or setting up a worksheet, determine the consolidated totals for this business combination.
   b. Verify the balances determined in part (*a*) by preparing a worksheet as of December 31, 2003.

37. On January 1, 2002, Prine, Inc., purchased 100 percent of the common stock of Lydia Company for $120,000,000 in cash and stock. Lydia's assets and liabilities equaled their fair values except for its equipment, which was undervalued by $500,000 and had a 10-year remaining life.

   Prine specializes in media distribution and viewed its acquisition of Lydia as a strategic move into content ownership and creation. Prine expected both cost and revenue synergies from controlling Lydia's artistic content (a large library of classic movies) and its sports programming specialty video operation. Accordingly, Prine allocated Lydia's assets and liabilities (including $50,000,000 of goodwill) to a newly formed Creative Management operating segment appropriately designated as a reporting unit.

The market values of the Creative Management segment's identifiable assets and liabilities through the first year of operations were as follows.

	Fair Values	
Account	1/1/02	12/31/02
Cash	$ 215,000	$ 109,000
Receivables (net)	525,000	897,000
Movie library (25-year life)	40,000,000	60,000,000
Broadcast licenses (indefinite life)	15,000,000	20,000,000
Equipment (10-year life)	20,750,000	19,000,000
Current liabilities	(490,000)	(650,000)
Long-term debt	(6,000,000)	(6,250,000)

However, Lydia's assets have taken longer than anticipated to produce the expected synergies with Prine's operations. At year-end, Prine reduced its assessment of the Creative Management reporting unit's fair value to $110,000,000.

At December 31, 2002, Prine and Lydia submitted the following balances for consolidation:

	Prine, Inc.	Lydia Co.
Revenues	$ (18,000,000)	$(12,000,000)
Operating expenses	10,350,000	11,800,000
Equity in Lydia earnings	(150,000)	
Dividends paid	300,000	80,000
Retained earnings, 1/1/02	(52,000,000)	(2,000,000)
Cash	260,000	109,000
Receivables (net)	210,000	897,000
Investment in Lydia	120,070,000	
Broadcast licenses	350,000	14,014,000
Movie library	365,000	45,000,000
Equipment (net)	136,000,000	17,500,000
Current liabilities	(755,000)	(650,000)
Long-term debt	(22,000,000)	(7,250,000)
Common stock	(175,000,000)	(67,500,000)

Required:

a. What is the relevant initial test to determine whether Creative Management's goodwill may be impaired?

b. At what amount should Prine record an impairment loss for its Creative Management reporting unit for 2002?

c. What is consolidated net income for 2002?

d. What is the December 31, 2002, consolidated balance for goodwill?

e. What is the December 31, 2002, consoidated balance for broadcast licenses?

f. Prepare a consolidated worksheet for Prine and Lydia (Prine's trial balance should first be adjusted for any appropriate impairment loss).

COMPUTER PROJECT

Alternative Investment Methods, Goodwill Impairment, and Consolidated Financial Statements

In this project you are to provide an analysis of alternative accounting methods for controlling interest investments and subsequent effects on consolidated reporting. The project requires the use of a computer and a spreadsheet software package (Microsoft Excel, Lotus 123, etc.). The use of these tools allows assessment of the sensitivity of alternative accounting methods on consolidated financial reporting without the necessity of preparing several similar worksheets by hand. Also, by modeling a worksheet process, a better understanding of accounting for combined reporting entities may result.

Consolidated Worksheet Preparation   You will be creating and entering formulas to complete four worksheets. The first objective is to demonstrate the effect of different methods of accounting for the investments (equity, cost, and partial equity) on the parent company's trial balance and on the consolidated worksheet subsequent to acquisition. The second objective is to show the effect on consolidated balances and key financial ratios of recognizing a goodwill impairment loss.

The project requires preparation of the following four separate worksheets:

1. Consolidated Information Worksheet (provided below).
2. Equity Method Consolidation Worksheet.
3. Cost Method Consolidation Worksheet.
4. Partial Equity Method Consolidation Worksheet.

If your spreadsheet package has multiple worksheet capabilities (e.g., Excel) separate worksheets can be used; otherwise, each of the four worksheets can reside in a separate area of a single spreadsheet.

In formulating your solution, each worksheet should link directly to the first worksheet. Also, feel free to create supplemental schedules to enhance the capabilities of your worksheet.

Project Scenario   Palm Company acquired 100 percent of Sand's outstanding stock for $1,000,000 cash on January 1, 2002, when Sand Company had the following balance sheet:

Assets		Liabilities and Equity	
Cash	$ 50,000	Liabilities	$(280,000)
Receivables	40,000		
Inventory	135,000	Common stock	(100,000)
Land	60,000	Retained earnings	(110,000)
Equipment (net)	105,000		
Patents	100,000		
Total assets	$490,000	Total liabilities and equity	$(490,000)

At the purchase date, the fair market values of each identifiable asset and liability that differed from book value were as follows:

Land	$ 50,000	
Equipment	150,000	(5-year estimated useful life)
Patents	235,000	(15-year estimated useful life)
In-process R&D	300,000	(management does not expect any alternative uses for the in-process R&D assets)

The following additional information is available:

- Palm's policy is to not amortize goodwill, but it will reduce its Investment in Sand account for any goodwill impairment losses. Management is interested in the effect of a potential goodwill impairment total loss on its performance ratios.
- During 2002, Sand earns $60,000 and pays no dividends.
- Selected amounts from Palm and Sand's separate financial statements at December 31, 2003, are presented in the Consolidation Information worksheet. All consolidated worksheets are to be prepared as of December 31, 2003, two years subsequent to acquisition.
- Palm's 1/1/03 retained earnings—before any effect from Sand's 2002 income—are ($700,000) (credit balance).
- Palm has 200,000 common shares outstanding for EPS calculations and reported $2,300,000 of consolidated assets at the beginning of the year.

Following are the Consolidation Information worksheet and a template for each of the three subsequent worksheets.

	A	B	C
1	**December 31, 2003, trial balances**		
2			
3		**Palm**	**Sand**
4	Revenues	$ (885,000)	$ (295,000)
5	Operating expenses	$ 730,000	$ 180,000
6	Amortization—identifiable intangibles	$ 15,000	$ 5,000
7	Goodwill impairment loss	?	
8	Income of Sand	?	
9	Net income	?	$ (110,000)
10			
11	Retained earnings—Palm 1/1/03	?	
12	Retained earnings—Sand 1/1/03		$ (170,000)
13	Net income (above)	?	$ (110,000)
14	Dividends paid	$ 150,000	$ 20,000
15	Retained earnings 12/31/03	?	$ (260,000)
16			
17	Cash	$ 90,000	$ 70,000
18	Receivables	$ 220,000	$ 90,000
19	Inventory	$ 237,000	$ 210,000
20	Investment in Sand	?	
21			
22			
23			
24	Land	$ 495,000	$ 60,000
25	Equipment (net)	$ 190,000	$ 85,000
26	Patents		$ 95,000
27	Other intangibles	$ 145,000	
28	Goodwill	$ 0	$ 0
29	Total assets	?	$ 610,000
30			
31	Liabilities	$ (1,267,000)	$ (250,000)
32	Common stock	$ (400,000)	$ (100,000)
33	Retained earnings (above)	?	$ (260,000)
34	Total liabilities and equity	?	$ (610,000)
35			
36	**Cost Allocation Schedule**		
37	Price Paid	$ 1,000,000	
38	Book Value	$ (210,000)	
39	Excess Cost	$ 790,000	
40	to Land	$ (10,000)	
41	to Equipment	$ 45,000	
42	to Patents	$ 135,000	
43	to IPR&D	$ 300,000	
44	to Goodwill	$ 320,000	
45			
46	**Sand's RE Changes**	**Income**	**Dividends**
47	2002	$ 60,000	$ 0
48	2003	$ 110,000	$ 20,000

Consolidated Worksheet Template

Consolidated Worksheet—12-31-03			Consolidation Entries		Consolidated
	Palm	**Sand**	**Debit**	**Credit**	**Totals**
Revenues					
Operating expenses					
Amortization—identifiable intangibles					
Goodwill impairment loss					
Income of Sand					
Net income					
Retained earnings—Palm 1/1/03					
Retained earnings—Sand 1/1/03					
Net income (above)					
Dividends paid					
Retained earnings 12/31/03					
Cash					
Receivables					
Inventory					
Investment in Sand					
Land					
Equipment (net)					
Patents					
Other intangibles					
Goodwill					
Total assets					
Liabilities					
Common stock					
Retained earnings (above)					
Total liabilities and equity					

Project Requirements

■ Complete the four worksheets as follows:

1. Input the **Consolidated Information Worksheet** provided and complete the cost allocation schedule by computing the excess amortizations for 2002 and 2003.

2. Using separate worksheets, prepare Palm's trial balances for each of the indicated accounting methods (equity, cost, and partial equity). **Use only formulas for the Investment in Sand, the Income of Sand, and Retained Earnings accounts.**

3. **Using references to other cells only (either from the Consolidation Information Worksheet or from the separate method sheets)** prepare for each of the three consolidating worksheets:
   - Adjustments and eliminations
   - Consolidated balances

4. Calculate and present the effects of a 2003 total goodwill impairment loss on the following ratios for the consolidated entity:
   - Earnings-per-share
   - Return on assets
   - Return on equity
   - Debt-to-equity

Your worksheets should have the capability to adjust immediately for the possibility that all acquisition goodwill may be considered impaired in 2003.

Prepare a word-processed report that describes and discusses the following worksheet results:

1. The effects of alternative investment accounting methods on the parent's trial balances and the final consolidation figures.

2. The relation between consolidated retained earnings and the parent's retained earnings under each of the three (equity, cost, partial equity) investment accounting methods.

3. The effect on EPS, return on assets, return on equity, and debt-to-equity ratios of the recognition that all acquisition-related goodwill is considered impaired in 2003.

Consolidated Financial Statements and Outside Ownership

- Total ownership is not an absolute requirement for consolidation; a parent need only gain control of another company to create a business combination. If less than 100 percent of a subsidiary's voting stock is obtained, how is the presence of the other owners reflected in consolidated financial statements? What accounting is appropriate for this noncontrolling interest? How are these figures computed and where are they reported on the consolidated statements?

- If a parent holds less than complete ownership, are the subsidiary's assets and liabilities consolidated at 100 percent of their fair market values or should the reported figures be affected by the degree of the parent's ownership?

- If a parent acquires several blocks of a subsidiary's stock over a period of time prior to gaining control, how are the various purchases consolidated?

- How are a subsidiary's revenues and expenses reported on a consolidated income statement when the parent gains control within the current year?

- When a portion, or all, of a subsidiary's stock is sold, how is the resulting gain or loss calculated? By what accounting method are any shares that remain reported?

A note to recent financial statements of Merck & Co., Inc., contains the following information:

> The consolidated financial statements include the accounts of the Company and all of its subsidiaries in which a controlling interest is maintained. For those consolidated subsidiaries where Company ownership is less than 100%, the outside stockholders' interests are shown as Minority interests. Investments in affiliates over which the Company has significant influence but not a controlling interest are carried on the equity basis.

Merck includes *all of the financial figures* generated by both its wholly and majority-owned subsidiaries within consolidated financial statements. How does Merck account for the partial ownership interest of the non-controlling owners of its subsidiaries?

A number of reasons exist for one company to hold less than 100 percent ownership of a subsidiary. The parent may not have had sufficient resources available to obtain all of the outstanding stock. As a second possibility, a few stockholders of the subsidiary could have elected to retain their ownership, perhaps in hopes of getting a better price at a later date.

Lack of total ownership is frequently encountered with foreign subsidiaries. The laws of some countries prohibit outsiders from maintaining complete control of domestic business enterprises. In other areas of the world, a parent may seek to establish better relations with a subsidiary's employees, customers, and local government by maintaining some percentage of native ownership.

Regardless of the reason for owning less than 100 percent, the parent consolidates the financial data of every subsidiary where control is present. As discussed in Chapter 2, *complete ownership is not a prerequisite for consolidation.* A single economic entity is formed whenever one company is able to control the decision-making process of another.

Although most parent companies do possess 100 percent ownership of their subsidiaries, a significant number, such as Merck & Co., establish control with a lesser amount of stock. The remaining outside owners are collectively referred to as a *noncontrolling interest* or by the more traditional term *minority interest.* The presence of these other stockholders poses a number of reporting questions for the accountant. Whenever less than 100 percent of a subsidiary's voting stock is held, how should the subsidiary's accounts be valued within consolidated financial statements? How should the presence of these additional owners be acknowledged?

CONSOLIDATIONS INVOLVING A NONCONTROLLING INTEREST[1]

In any combination in which a noncontrolling interest remains, an intriguing theoretical controversy is created as to (1) the appropriate consolidation values that should be assigned to the subsidiary's accounts and (2) the method of disclosing the presence of the other owners. This debate involves more than a reporting problem; it ultimately concerns the fundamental objectives of consolidated financial statements.

When total ownership exists, the subsidiary's assets and liabilities are always consolidated based on their fair market values at the date of acquisition with any excess cost assigned to goodwill.[2] Since no other owners would exist, disclosure of a noncontrolling interest is not relevant. In contrast, whenever less than 100 percent of a subsidiary is acquired, several different theoretical methods exist to calculate the consolidated values of the acquired accounts. Each of these approaches uses a different technique for reporting the presence of the noncontrolling interest.

As a basis for examining these alternative valuation theories, assume that Small Company possesses net assets as follows:

Book value of net assets	$110,000
Fair market value of identifiable net assets	130,000

In the current year, Big Company purchases 70 percent of the outstanding voting stock of Small for $140,000. Big's willingness to pay this price can be viewed as an indication that Small, taken as a whole, has an implied value of $200,000 ($140,000/70 percent). *The accounting controversy centers on whether the parent's $140,000 cost or the $200,000 implied value of the subsidiary should serve as the valuation basis for subsequently consolidated figures.*[3]

---

[1] The term *minority interest* has been used almost universally over the decades to identify the presence of other outside owners. However, in the FASB's October 16, 1995, Exposure Draft, *Consolidated Financial Statements: Policy and Procedures,* the term *noncontrolling interest* was applied. Because this newer term is more descriptive, it is used throughout this textbook.

[2] To avoid unnecessary complexities in analyzing this issue, bargain purchases are not illustrated. In addition, this controversy does not relate to a pooling of interests where accounts are always consolidated at their book values.

[3] In a 100 percent purchase, the implied value of the subsidiary is the parent's purchase price. Thus, only one valuation basis is present and, at least from a mechanical perspective, no problem exists.

DISCUSSION QUESTION

How Do We Report This Other Owner?

The Hartstone Company was created 15 years ago and presently owns several large retail clothing stores in and around Lakeland, Minnesota. Hartstone's capital stock is held equally by its four founders: Scott Arnold, Janine Bostio, Garrison Cantleberry, and Ingrid Jorgesson.

Until recently, Thomas Warwick was the sole owner of a competing business in the nearby city of Kalshburg. Because Warwick was nearing retirement age, he opted to sell 90 percent of his company (which encompassed only one store) to Hartstone. Because the business had been in Warwick's family for several generations, he wanted to retain 10 percent ownership. Hartstone paid cash for this acquisition. Based on past profitability, the negotiated price for the shares was set to indicate a total value of $2 million, although the current book value of the store was only $1.4 million.

At the end of the current year, the owners of Hartstone must produce consolidated financial statements for the first time. Consequently, they are having a discussion with their accountant concerning the appropriate method of reporting Thomas Warwick's 10 percent interest in the Kalshburg store.

Scott Arnold: These statements are designed to represent the Hartstone Company and our assets, liabilities, revenues, and expenses. Warwick owns none of our stock. I see no reason to include any figure at all for him. Readers would naturally assume that he controls a portion of Hartstone; we would be misleading them. He has nothing to do with our company.

Janine Bostio: I think you are wrong. Warwick owns 10 percent of one of our stores. He is a partial owner of this asset, and since we are consolidating the entire Kalshburg store, we have to recognize that he has an equity interest. The price indicates a $2,000,000 value; so his ownership should be recognized at $200,000.

Garrison Cantleberry: I agree with Scott; the statements are designed to represent Hartstone Company, and Warwick is certainly not a stockholder of Hartstone. However, we do have a legal obligation to him. If we ever liquidate the Kalshburg store, he would be entitled to a portion of the residual. Even now, when the store pays a dividend, he must be paid 10 percent of each distribution. We have an obligation to him that can only be properly disclosed as a liability.

Ingrid Jorgesson: I have trouble with recording a liability. I understand that we eventually might have a debt to Warwick, but at this point in time we are under no obligation to him. To me, a possible future claim should not be recorded as an actual liability. However, Warwick has retained a $140,000 investment in one of our assets. That is his cost. Since this amount doesn't seem to be either debt or equity, why don't we record it separately between our liabilities and the stockholders' equity? Anyone reading the statements can add this figure to either balance if desired or simply ignore it entirely.

As the accountant, what recommendation would you make to your clients and why? Should Warwick's interest be recognized? If so, where should the figure be reported and what amount should be disclosed?

Incorporating the cost figure suggests that consolidated statements are primarily intended as a report of the parent company and the results of its $140,000 investment. Conversely, by utilizing the $200,000 implied value, the emphasis is focused on accounting for Big and Small as two individual components forming a single economic entity.

Unfortunately, virtually nothing in official accounting pronouncements has ever addressed the issue of valuation theory in combinations involving less than 100 percent ownership. Thus, the positions adopted at present are based on traditional approaches that have evolved over the years. However, this issue continues to be examined by the FASB.[4] This examination might possibly lead to the issuance of an official standard that requires one theory to be used. However, until that time, companies are free to apply any one of several approaches in reporting the accounts of a subsidiary. The following section presents three of the theories outlined by the FASB.[5]

---

[4]See FASB, *Business Combinations: Procedures and New Basis Accounting,* Project Summary, January 26, 2000.

[5]Variations do exist of each approach presented here. To avoid unnecessary complication, only three of the basic theories are described.

The Economic Unit Concept[6]

If the accounting emphasis in preparing consolidated statements is placed on the business combination being formed (rather than on the parent's investment), an approach referred to as the *economic unit concept* (also known as the *entity theory*) is generally endorsed. This concept is founded on the proposition that the subsidiary and especially the subsidiary's individual accounts cannot be divided along ownership lines. A controlled company must always be consolidated as a whole regardless of the parent's level of ownership.

Proponents argue that this concept provides the most consistent perspective of the consolidation process. It also gives the best view of the assets and liabilities that have come under the control of the parent company. If, in the previous illustration, Small owns land with a book value of $8,000 but a fair market value of $10,000, the economic unit concept requires the $10,000 figure to be reported within consolidated statements whether the parent acquires 70 percent, 100 percent, or any other level of control. The owners of Big control all of the resources of both Big and Small despite holding only 70 percent of the subsidiary's voting stock.

Therefore, in accounting for Big's acquisition of Small, the economic unit concept bases consolidated totals on the $200,000 implied value of the subsidiary taken as a whole. All of the subsidiary's assets and liabilities are included at their fair market values with any excess assigned to goodwill. Because the individual market values total only $130,000 but the implied value of the company as a whole equals $200,000, the excess $70,000 is assigned to goodwill.

Because the total value of every asset and liability is attributed to the consolidated entity, the partial ownership held by outside parties must also be acknowledged. *Including 100 percent of the value of a subsidiary's accounts when only 70 percent of the stock is owned creates an imbalance that requires the recognition of a 30 percent noncontrolling interest.* Hence, $60,000 (30 percent of the total implied value being included in the consolidation) is attributed to the other owners of Small.

Economic Unit Concept

Implied value of Small ($140,000/70%)	$200,000
Fair market value assigned to Small's accounts	130,000
Fair market value not assigned to identifiable accounts—goodwill	$ 70,000
Noncontrolling interest (30% of the $200,000 implied value included in consolidated totals)	$ 60,000

Although Small's outside owners do not possess an equity interest in the parent company, the $60,000 balance is presented within the consolidated stockholders' equity section when the economic unit concept is in use. This placement is based on the assertion that the two companies should be viewed together as a single entity. The outside parties own a component part of the resulting business combination; thus, their interest is viewed as an equity (or ownership) balance to be reported within the consolidated balance sheet.

After the balance sheet valuations are established for the economic unit concept, a logical extension can be made to the construction of a consolidated income statement. Once again this approach recognizes 100 percent of the subsidiary's balances. Its entire income is included. By consolidating every account in total, the fundamental objective of reporting the subsidiary as an indivisible unit within the consolidated entity is being fulfilled. Furthermore, this approach effectively reports the income that is generated by the net assets under the control of the parent company.

---

[6]In their June 1996 Working Draft revision of the *Consolidated Financial Statements: Policy and Procedures* Exposure Draft, the FASB recommends the adoption of the economic unit concept as discussed in this section. The issue continues to be considered as part of the FASB's *Business Combinations: Procedures and New Basis Accounting* Project.

Consequently, for Big's acquisition of Small, 100 percent of the subsidiary's revenues and expenses should be included in the consolidated figures. Because only 70 percent of Small is owned by the parent, a 30 percent claim to the subsidiary's earnings must be deducted separately in recognition of the noncontrolling interest. This portion of consolidated net income is viewed as an allocation to these other owners.

In computing the part of consolidated income to be assigned to the noncontrolling interest, a theoretical question arises concerning the impact of any excess amortization incurred in connection with the price paid by the parent. As shown in Chapter 3, expense recognition is necessitated by the allocations made to specific accounts as well as to goodwill. Within the business combination, are these expenses attributed to the parent or to the subsidiary?

A logical extension of the economic unit concept is that each purchase price allocation is perceived as a revaluation of a subsidiary asset or liability to fair market value. Subsequent amortization of these costs, therefore, relates to the subsidiary rather than the parent. Because the expense is viewed as an adjustment to the subsidiary's net income, it affects the computation of the noncontrolling interest's share of these earnings.

For example, what is the noncontrolling interest in the subsidiary's income in the following situation?

Portion of subsidiary owned by parent	90 percent
Subsidiary's reported net income	$300,000
Amortization expenses on purchase price allocations	$ 40,000

The economic unit concept presumes that excess amortizations relate to the subsidiary's assets. Thus, the allocation of consolidated income made to the noncontrolling interest is $26,000 (or 10 percent of earnings less excess amortization expenses).

Under the economic unit theory, all consolidated totals (except for noncontrolling interest figures) are identical regardless of the degree of parent ownership. The parent controls the entire decision-making process of the subsidiary whenever control exists. Therefore, the economic unit concept views the subsidiary as an indivisible unit within the business combination. As such, fair market value serves as the basis for consolidating each asset and liability, even though the parent's interest may be significantly below 100 percent control. Any contrived division of the subsidiary accounts is, thus, avoided.

The Proportionate Consolidation Concept

The *proportionate consolidation concept* presumes that the ultimate objective of consolidated financial statements is to serve as a report to the stockholders of the parent company. These owners are perceived as being primarily interested in an accounting of parent company resources. Returning to the previous illustration, the accounting emphasis is placed on Big's $140,000 investment to acquire a 70 percent interest in Small.

Under proportionate consolidation, the values utilized for consolidation reflect the parent's payment attributed to each asset and liability. Big is paying for these assets and not for the company. Because 70 percent ownership has been acquired, that percentage of every account's fair market value at the date of purchase forms the basis for consolidated figures. If, for example, Small owns land with a book value of $8,000 but a fair market value of $10,000, a $7,000 component of the price (70 percent of fair market value) is said to have been Big's cost incurred in connection with this asset.

Under proportionate consolidation, goodwill of $49,000 is recognized: the amount of the purchase price in excess of the appropriate portion of the net assets' fair market value.

Proportionate Consolidation Concept

Purchase price	$140,000
Fair market value assigned to Small's accounts ($130,000 × 70%)	91,000
Cost in excess of fair market value—goodwill	$ 49,000
Noncontrolling interest	–0–

Although goodwill is computed here as a residual cost element, a more consistent view of proportionate consolidation is that this figure represents 70 percent of the subsidiary's total goodwill. As shown in the previous section, a goodwill figure of $70,000 is appropriate for the subsidiary as a whole (the $200,000 implied value of the company less the $130,000 market value of its net assets). Thus, the portion of this goodwill that is applicable to Big's investment is $49,000 ($70,000 × 70%).

A unique feature of proportionate consolidation is the reporting of the noncontrolling interest; these outside owners are totally ignored in consolidated statements. Proponents of this theory hold that the presence of a noncontrolling interest is irrelevant to the stockholders of the parent company. An outside owner of a subsidiary has no capital invested in the parent company; furthermore, the parent has no legal obligation to this group. Thus, including any type of balance within consolidated financial statements to reflect a noncontrolling interest is viewed as serving no purpose.

Before leaving this discussion of proportionate consolidation, a quick extension of this concept can be made to income statement reporting. Not surprisingly, Big Company includes 70 percent of each of the subsidiary's revenue and expense accounts in the consolidated balances while showing no amount of the income total as associated with the noncontrolling interest. Within the framework of proportionate consolidation, this presentation is consistent. The parent's ownership entitles it to accrue only 70 percent of the subsidiary's income; the remaining 30 percent is applicable to outside owners. Any recording of this 30 percent share of Small's net income has no apparent relevance to the owners of Big Company.

In actual practice, little evidence exists to indicate significant usage of proportionate consolidation. Although omitting any mention of outside stockholders may be appealing, the division of each subsidiary account based on the ownership percentage is hard to justify. The parent has achieved control over all assets and liabilities, not just a 70 percent interest of each. However, this concept has recently gained some support for use in cases where control is present without majority ownership. As discussed in Chapter 2, a parent may effectively control a subsidiary although holding only 50 percent or even less of the outstanding voting stock. Proponents argue that proportionate consolidation would be a better reflection of the relationship between the two companies than the equity method that is currently required.

The Parent Company Concept

The *parent company concept* is sometimes viewed as a hybrid method because it incorporates a mixture of the assumptions found in the economic unit concept and proportionate consolidation. Two fundamental assertions underlie this approach to consolidation valuation:

1.   Holding control of a subsidiary provides the parent with an indivisible interest in that company. This statement is clearly derived from the economic unit concept.

2.   Consolidated financial statements are produced primarily for the benefit of parent company stockholders. This idea is, of course, the basic argument used to substantiate proportionate consolidation.

Both of the assertions attributed to the parent company concept appear to have merit. However, as shown in the previous sections, they lead to radically differing sets of consolidated financial statements: one based on the implied value of the entire subsidiary and the other on the cost incurred in a partial acquisition. The parent company approach combines both of these ideas in valuing the consolidated enterprise. The subsidiary's book value and the purchase price paid by the parent are viewed as separate elements that can be accounted for individually within the consolidation process.

The book value of each subsidiary asset and liability is presumed to be indivisible and, therefore, not subject to an artificial allocation because of the specific level of ownership. Conversely, differences between the market value and underlying book value of these same accounts are recognized only because of the purchase price paid by the parent. Thus, if the parent acquires less than 100 percent of the subsidiary's voting stock, allocations attributed to individual accounts at the date of purchase should be based on the resulting ownership percentage. *The subsidiary's book value is consolidated in total along the lines of the economic unit concept whereas any cost in excess of book value is assumed to be a parent company expenditure appropriately allocated as indicated by the proportionate consolidation.*

Returning to Big's acquisition of Small, the appropriate consolidation values to be assigned under the parent company concept are computed as follows:

Parent Company Concept

Purchase price		$140,000
Book value of Small (100%)	$110,000	
Less: Recognition of noncontrolling interest (30%)	(33,000)	(77,000)
Cost in excess of underlying book value		63,000
Allocation based on fair market value in excess of book value ($130,000 − $110,000) × 70%		(14,000)
Goodwill		$ 49,000

The parent company concept includes the entire book value of each of Small's accounts within the consolidated statements but only 70 percent of the difference between fair market value and book value. Proponents justify this approach by pointing out that the subsidiary's cost figures are not affected by the parent's purchase and, therefore, should be consolidated in total. In contrast, the various allocations result solely from the price paid by the parent in a transaction negotiated to acquire 70 percent ownership. Thus, the investment is assumed to reflect only 70 percent of the change in the value of individual accounts.

As a practical example, Small's land, with an $8,000 cost but a fair market value of $10,000, is consolidated at a $9,400 balance: the entire $8,000 book value plus 70 percent of the $2,000 increase in its worth ($10,000 − $8,000). The subsidiary originally expended $8,000 for this land and the parent has now paid an additional $1,400 within the purchase price as a reflection of this change in value. Thus, to the business combination, the land's cost totals $9,400.

In the valuation schedule presented earlier, a noncontrolling interest of $33,000 is computed on the basis of Small's $110,000 book value rather than on either the fair market value of the net assets or the implied worth of the company taken as a whole. Under the parent company concept, only the book value of the subsidiary's accounts is consolidated in total. Although Big holds just 70 percent ownership, 100 percent of each book value is brought into the consolidation. Consequently, the presence of a noncontrolling interest equivalent to 30 percent of that particular total must also be recognized. The payment made by Big in excess of book value, however, has no impact on the remaining outside owners and is not included in this calculation.

Some amount of disagreement exists among the users of the parent company concept as to the appropriate placement of the noncontrolling interest figure within the consolidated balance sheet. Arguments can be made for showing the balance as either a liability or an equity. However, proponents of this theory are most likely to isolate the noncontrolling interest between liabilities and stockholders' equity.

The parent company concept views the consolidated financial statements as those of the parent—with the assets, liabilities, revenues, and expenses of the subsidiary merely substituting for the parent's investment on the balance sheet. . . . From that perspective, the noncontrolling (minority) interest is not a liability because the parent does not have a present obligation to pay cash or other assets. Nor does it appear to be owners' equity from a parent company perspective because the noncontrolling investors in a subsidiary do not have an ownership interest in the subsidiary's parent. . . . Thus, the parent company concept generally reports noncontrolling interest below liabilities but above stockholders' equity in consolidated statements.[7]

Currently, in practice, the appropriate placement of a noncontrolling interest balance remains an unresolved question. *Statement of Financial Accounting Concepts No. 6 (SFAC 6),* "Elements of Financial Statements," issued by the FASB recommends inclusion within equity (par. 254):

Minority interests in net assets of consolidated subsidiaries do not represent present obligations of the enterprise to pay cash or distribute other assets to minority stockholders. *Rather, those stockholders have ownership or residual interests in components of a consolidated enterprise.* The definitions in this Statement do not, of course, preclude showing minority interests separately from majority interests or preclude emphasizing the interests of majority stockholders for whom consolidated statements are primarily provided. Stock purchase warrants are also sometimes called liabilities but entirely lack the characteristics of liabilities. They also are part of equity (emphasis added).

Consistent with the *SFAC 6* reasoning, in their 1995 Exposure Draft *Consolidated Financial Statements: Policy and Procedures,* the FASB recommends the following (par. 22):

The aggregate amount of the noncontrolling interest in subsidiaries that are not wholly owned by the parent shall be reported in consolidated financial statements as a separate component of equity. That amount shall be appropriately labeled, for example, as *noncontrolling interest in subsidiaries,* to distinguish it from the components of equity attributable to the controlling interest.

Interestingly, *International Accounting Standard No. 27,* "Consolidated Financial Statements and Accounting for Investments in Subsidiaries," 1989 (par. 33), addresses this same issue as follows: "Minority interests should be presented in the consolidated balance sheet separately from liabilities and parent shareholders' equity." In contrast to *SFAC 6,* this statement rejects the classification of a noncontrolling interest as an equity figure. Placement between the liability and equity sections is recommended in the same manner as used by the parent company concept.

Obviously, disagreement continues to exist as to the appropriate location of this balance sheet item. Today, the placement of a noncontrolling interest continues to vary with the reporting entity. Many companies disclose this figure as a single balance appearing directly after noncurrent liabilities. No accumulated total is provided for liabilities or equities, so that the reader is forced to decide whether the noncontrolling interest should be included in either classification or viewed as an item separate from both. Although this placement is often encountered in practice, no consensus currently exists as to the appropriate classification of this balance. However, if the FASB eventually takes action on consolidation policies and procedures, a specific location for the noncontrolling interest may well be required in the future.

In constructing a consolidated income statement, the parent company theory again demonstrates characteristics applicable to both the economic unit concept and proportionate consolidation. As with the economic unit concept, the book values of the various subsidiary accounts are included in the total. Since these revenues and expenses are consolidated at 100 percent of their recorded balances, a 30 percent share of the subsidiary's net income is identified with the noncontrolling interest.

---

[7]FASB Discussion Memorandum, *An Analysis of Issues Related to Consolidation Policy and Procedures,* September 10, 1991, paragraphs 69 and 70.

DISCUSSION QUESTION

What Decision Should the FASB Make?

Whenever the FASB is studying an accounting issue, the Board always seems to get plenty of advice. In response to its discussion memorandum, "An Analysis of Issues Related to Consolidation Policy and Procedures," the FASB received more than 70 letters. A sampling of these letters includes the following recommendations.

M. R. Schools, Jr., Virginia Power: Virginia Power believes that accounting information prepared under the proportionate consolidation approach provides the most relevant accounting information because it includes the interests of only the parent company shareholders.

David K. Owens, Edison Electric Institute: We generally support the "Parent Company Concept" because it emphasizes the interests of the parent shareholders and is most consistent with current practice.

Richard G. Rademacher, Sara Lee Corporation: By purchasing a controlling interest in an entity, management obtains the control of 100 percent of all assets and liabilities. It does not control only a proportionate share of each asset (i. e., 70% of a building) and the value of an asset recorded in consolidation does not vary dependent upon the percentage of ownership obtained. Therefore, we strongly oppose the parent company and proportionate share concepts of consolidation.

J. Michael Kelly, GTE Corporation: GTE has consistently responded in support of the parent company concept. The thrust of our support stems from this concept's emphasis on the interests of the parent's shareholders.

P. J. Lynch, Texaco Inc.: It is Texaco's view that neither the economic unit nor the parent company concept can be applied exclusively to all the issues raised in the DM. Accordingly any future promulgation concerning consolidation policy should be a hybrid of the two concepts.

Joseph J. Martin, IBM: While we take a parent's view of deciding when to consolidate, we generally favor an economic unit theory approach on the mechanics of consolidation and financial statement presentation.

John J. Mesloh, Pfizer Inc.: You may note that we favor the Parent Company view (which is consistent with our view of current written GAAP) of consolidation, as identified by the FASB. In short, we do not have too many issues with the current state of consolidation accounting.

What should the FASB decide to do?

However, similar to proportionate consolidation, excess amortization is associated solely with the parent's investment because the allocations that create the expense result from the original payment. Consequently, such amortizations do not affect the calculation of noncontrolling interest. The additional cost is presumed to be that of the parent company and, thus, the expense is not directly related to the subsidiary's operations. For reporting purposes, the subsidiary's income is simply multiplied times the outside ownership percentage.

Under the parent company concept, the resulting noncontrolling interest figure has traditionally appeared as a reduction in arriving at consolidated net income. For example, following is the bottom portion of a typical income statement as reported by Sears, Roebuck and Co.:

SEARS, ROEBUCK AND CO.
Year Ended December 31, 2000
(in millions)

Income before income taxes and minority interests	$2,223
Income taxes	831
Minority interests	49
Net income	$1,343

As mentioned earlier, the FASB is currently studying valuation theories with the possibility that one concept may be mandated. Until that time, companies are free to select any approach and are not even required to disclose their choice. Although evidence is not readily available, the parent company concept is generally considered to be most commonly used in current practice. Therefore, except where noted, that concept is used throughout the remainder of this textbook. Knowledge of the alternatives is important, though; companies do apply these other approaches and their use may be promoted or required by the FASB in the future.

Valuation Theories—Overview

To provide a complete illustration of these three concepts, assume that Anderson Company acquires 60 percent of the voting stock of Zebulon Company on January 1, 2002. Anderson purchases this interest for $360,000 in cash at a time when Zebulon's assets and liabilities have the following values:

	Book Value 1/1/02	Fair Market Value 1/1/02
Current assets less liabilities	$160,000	$160,000
Buildings and equipment (10-year life)	240,000	360,000
	$400,000	$520,000

Because Anderson's $360,000 payment was made to acquire 60 percent interest, Zebulon is apparently worth $600,000 when taken as a whole ($360,000/60 percent). In comparison to the $520,000 appraised value of the net assets, this implied value signifies *total* goodwill associated with Zebulon of $80,000.

Exhibit 4–1 presents alternative values that can be attributed to Zebulon's accounts on consolidated statements produced as of the date of acquisition. Quite obviously, differing figures are derived from each of the three valuation theories. The economic unit concept makes no division of any balance, whereas proportionate consolidation includes only 60 percent of subsidiary accounts because that portion represents the parent's ownership. The parent company concept adopts a compromise position: The book values of the subsidiary's assets and liabilities remain intact while all cost allocations (based on the difference in book values and fair market values) are computed using the parent's ownership percentage.

To carry this illustration to a natural conclusion, assume that Zebulon reports the following condensed income statement for the year of 2002:

Revenues	$400,000
Expenses	300,000
Net income	$100,000

These balances permit an examination of the totals to be included in the 2002 consolidated income statement. Exhibit 4–2 presents these figures, once again computed under each of the three theories described in this chapter. The economic unit concept consolidates all accounts and assumes that amortization expense relates to the subsidiary. Proportionate consolidation includes only 60 percent of each revenue and expense and discloses no balance for the noncontrolling interest. The parent company concept recognizes all of the subsidiary's income statement accounts but attributes amortization to the parent so that the noncontrolling interest is not affected.

CONSOLIDATIONS INVOLVING A NONCONTROLLING INTEREST—SUBSEQUENT TO ACQUISITION

Having reviewed the basic philosophies of each of these three theories, this textbook now concentrates on the mechanical aspects of the consolidation process when an outside ownership is present. More specifically, consolidations for time periods subsequent to the date of acquisition are examined to analyze the full range of accounting complexities created by a noncontrolling interest. As indicated previously, this discussion centers on the parent company concept because it appears to be the most prevalent method in practice.

Exhibit 4–1   Valuation Theories in Practice—Balance Sheet

ANDERSON COMPANY AND ZEBULON COMPANY
Subsidiary Consolidation Figures
Balance Sheet
January 1, 2002

	Economic Unit Concept	Proportionate Consolidation Concept	Parent Company Concept
Current assets and liabilities:			
Book value	$160,000 (100%)	$ 96,000 (60%)	$160,000 (100%)
Allocation based on fair market value	–0–	–0–	–0–
Consolidated value	$160,000	$ 96,000	$160,000
Buildings and equipment:			
Book value	$240,000 (100%)	$144,000 (60%)	$240,000 (100%)
Allocation based on fair market value	120,000 (100%)	72,000 (60%)	72,000 (60%)
Consolidated value	$360,000	$216,000	$312,000
Goodwill*	$ 80,000 (100%)	$ 48,000 (60%)	$ 48,000 (60%)
Noncontrolling interest, 1/1/02	$240,000 (40% of implied value)*	–0–	$160,000 (40% of book value)
Annual amortizations of allocations:			
Buildings and equipment (10-year life)	$ 12,000	$ 7,200	$ 7,200
Goodwill (indefinite life)	–0–	–0–	–0–
Annual expense	$ 12,000	$ 7,200	$ 7,200

*Implied value of company is $600,000 ($360,000/60%) with the value of net assets only $520,000. Total goodwill is $80,000 ($600,000 − $520,000).

Exhibit 4–2   Valuation Theories in Practice—Income Statement

ANDERSON COMPANY AND ZEBULON COMPANY
Subsidiary Consolidation Figures
Income Statement
For Year Ending December 31, 2002

	Economic Unit Concept	Proportionate Consolidation Concept	Parent Company Concept
Revenues	$400,000 (100%)	$240,000 (60%)	$400,000 (100%)
Expenses	300,000 (100%)	180,000 (60%)	300,000 (100%)
Excess amortization expenses (see Exhibit 4–1)	12,000	7,200	7,200
Noncontrolling interest in subsidiary's net income			40,000 (40% of subsidiary income, no amortization)
Net effect on consolidated income	$ 88,000	$ 52,800	$ 52,800
Allocation of income:			
To controlling interest (60%)	$ 52,800		
To noncontrolling interest (40%)	$ 33,600		

Computation of Noncontrolling Interest Balances

The presence of a noncontrolling interest does not dramatically alter the consolidation procedures demonstrated in Chapter 3. The unamortized balance of each purchase price allocation (as well as any goodwill or deferred credit) must still be computed and included within the consolidated totals. Excess amortization expenses are recognized each year on these allocations. Reciprocal balances are eliminated.

Beyond these basic steps, the valuation and recognition of four noncontrolling interest balances add a new dimension to the process of consolidating financial information. The accountant must determine and then enter each of these figures when constructing a worksheet:

■ Noncontrolling interest in the subsidiary as of the beginning of the current year.
■ Noncontrolling interest in the subsidiary's current year income.
■ Noncontrolling interest in the subsidiary's dividend payments.
■ Noncontrolling interest as of the end of the year (found by combining the three balances above).

To illustrate, assume that King Company acquires 80 percent of the outstanding stock of Pawn Company on January 1, 2002, for $960,000 in cash. The combination is to be accounted for as a purchase. King makes an additional $20,000 payment to lawyers, accountants, and appraisers to cover the direct costs associated with this acquisition. Exhibit 4–3 presents the book value of Pawn's accounts as well as the fair market value of each asset and liability on the date of purchase.

Including direct consolidation costs, King's payment totals $980,000. This purchase price is attributed to Pawn's accounts as shown in Exhibit 4–4. Annual amortization relating to these allocations also is included in this schedule. Although expense figures are computed for only the initial years, some amount of amortization is recognized in each of the 20 years following the acquisition (since that life is assumed for the buildings).

Assume that consolidated financial statements are to be produced for the year ending December 31, 2003. This date was chosen arbitrarily. Any time period subsequent to 2002 could have served to demonstrate the applicable consolidation procedures. Having already calculated the purchase price allocations and related amortization, the consolidation of these two companies can be constructed along the lines demonstrated in Chapter 3. Only the presence of the 20 percent noncontrolling interest alters the previously explained process.

To complete the information needed for this combination, assume that Pawn Company reports the following changes in book value since King's acquisition:

Exhibit 4–3
Subsidiary Accounts—Date of Acquisition

PAWN COMPANY Account Balances January 1, 2002			
	Book Value	Fair Market Value	Differences
Current assets	$ 440,000	$ 440,000	–0–
Land	260,000	320,000	+$ 60,000
Buildings (20-year life)	480,000	600,000	+ 120,000
Equipment (10-year life)	110,000	100,000	(10,000)
Long-term liabilities (8-year maturity)	(550,000)	(510,000)	+ 40,000
Net assets	$ 740,000	$ 950,000	+$210,000
Common stock	$(230,000)		
Retained earnings, 1/1/02	(510,000)		
Note: Parentheses indicate a credit balance.			

Exhibit 4–4

KING COMPANY AND PAWN COMPANY			
Purchase Price Allocation and Amortization			
January 1, 2002			
	Allocation	Estimated Life (years)	Annual Excess Amortizations
Purchase price paid by King Company	$980,000		
80% of subsidiary book value ($740,000) (King Company's ownership)*	592,000		
Cost in excess of book value	388,000		
Allocation to specific accounts based on difference between fair market value and book value:			
Land ($60,000 × 80%)	48,000		
Buildings ($120,000 × 80%)	96,000	20	4,800
Equipment ($10,000 × 80%)	(8,000)	10	(800)
Long-term liabilities ($40,000 × 80%) . . .	32,000	8	4,000
Goodwill	$220,000	Indefinite	–0–
Annual amortizations (initial years)			$8,000

*The parent company concept consolidates 100 percent of all asset and liability book values but also records an offsetting noncontrolling interest of 20 percent. The net effect is equal to 80 percent of the subsidiary's book value.

Current year (2003)

Net income . . . . $ 90,000
Less: Dividends paid . . . .   (50,000)

Increase in book value . . . . $ 40,000

Prior years (only 2002 in this illustration):
Increase in book value . . . . $ 70,000

Assuming that King Company has applied the equity method, the Investment in Pawn Company account as of December 31, 2003, can be constructed as shown in Exhibit 4–5.

Exhibit 4–6 presents the separate financial statements for these two companies as of December 31, 2003, and the year then ended based on the information provided.

Consolidated Totals   Although the inclusion of a 20 percent outside ownership complicates the consolidation process, the 2003 totals to be reported by this business combination can still be determined without the use of a worksheet:

- *Revenues* = $1,340,000. The revenues of the parent and the subsidiary are added together. Under the parent company concept, the subsidiary's book value is included in total although only 80 percent of the stock is owned by King.

- *Cost of goods sold* = $550,000. The cost of goods sold of the parent and subsidiary are added together.

- *Depreciation expense* = $259,000. The depreciation expenses of the parent and subsidiary are added together along with the $4,800 additional building depreciation and the $800 reduction in equipment depreciation as indicated in Exhibit 4–4.

- *Interest expense* = $119,000. The interest expenses of the parent and subsidiary are added along with an additional $4,000. As indicated in Exhibit 4–4, a reduction to market value of Pawn's long-term debt accounted for $32,000 of the excess purchase price. Because the maturity value remains constant, the $32,000

Exhibit 4–5

KING COMPANY
Investment in Pawn Company
Equity Method
December 31, 2003

Purchase price		$ 980,000
Prior year (2002):		
Increase in book value (80% × $70,000)	$ 56,000	
Excess amortization expenses (Exhibit 4–4)	(8,000)	48,000
Current year (2003):		
Income accrual (80% × $90,000)	72,000	
Excess amortization expense (Exhibit 4–4)	(8,000)	
Equity in subsidiary earnings	64,000*	
Dividends received (80% × $50,000)	(40,000)	24,000
Balance, 12/31/03		$1,052,000

*This figure appears in King's 2003 income statement.

Exhibit 4–6

KING COMPANY AND PAWN COMPANY
Separate Financial Statements
For December 31, 2003 and the Year Then Ended

	King	Pawn
Revenues	$ 910,000	$ 430,000
Cost of goods sold	(350,000)	(200,000)
Depreciation expense	(160,000)	(95,000)
Interest expense	(70,000)	(45,000)
Equity in subsidiary earnings (see Exhibit 4–5)	64,000	–0–
Net income	$ 394,000	$ 90,000
Retained earnings, 1/1/03	$ 881,600	$ 580,000
Net income (above)	394,000	90,000
Dividends paid	(60,000)	(50,000)
Retained earnings, 12/31/03	$1,215,600	$ 620,000
Current assets	$ 626,000	$ 445,000
Land	298,000	295,000
Buildings (net)	880,000	540,000
Equipment (net)	290,000	160,000
Investment in Pawn Company (see Exhibit 4–5)	1,052,000	–0–
Total assets	$3,146,000	$1,440,000
Long-term liabilities	$1,080,400	$ 590,000
Common stock	850,000	230,000
Retained earnings, 12/31/03	1,215,600	620,000
Total liabilities and equities	$3,146,000	$1,440,000

represents a discount that is amortized to interest expense over the remaining eight-year life of the debt.

- *Equity in subsidiary earnings* = –0–. The investment income recorded by the parent is eliminated so that the subsidiary's revenues and expenses can be included in the consolidated totals.

- *Noncontrolling interest in subsidiary's income* = $18,000. The outside owners are assigned 20 percent of Pawn's reported income of $90,000. According to the parent company concept, that amount is shown as a reduction within the consolidated income statement.

- *Net income* = $394,000. Both consolidated expenses and the amount allocated to the noncontrolling interest are subtracted from consolidated revenues.

- *Retained earnings, 1/1/03* = $881,600. The parent company figure equals the consolidated total since the equity method was applied. If the cost method or the partial equity method had been used, the parent's balance would require adjustment to include any omitted figures.

- *Dividends paid* = $60,000. Only the parent company balance is reported. Part of the subsidiary's payments (80 percent) were intercompany to the parent and are eliminated. The remaining distribution was made to the outside owners and serves to reduce the balance attributed to them.

- *Retained earnings, 12/31/03* = $1,215,600. Balance is found by adding consolidated net income to the beginning retained earnings balance and then subtracting the consolidated dividends paid. Because the equity method is utilized, the parent company figure reflects the total for the business combination.

- *Current assets* = $1,071,000. The parent's book value is added to the subsidiary's book value.

- *Land* = $641,000. The parent's book value is added to the subsidiary's book value plus the $48,000 allocation within the purchase price (see Exhibit 4–4).

- *Buildings* = $1,506,400. The parent's book value is added to the subsidiary's book value plus the $96,000 allocation within the purchase price less 2002 and 2003 excess amortization of $4,800 per year (see Exhibit 4–4).

- *Equipment* = $443,600. The parent's book value is added to the subsidiary's book value less the $8,000 cost reduction allocation plus the 2002 and 2003 expense reduction of $800 per year (see Exhibit 4–4).

- *Investment in Pawn Company* = –0–. The balance reported by the parent is eliminated so that the subsidiary's assets and liabilities can be included in the consolidated totals.

- *Goodwill* = $220,000. The original allocation shown in Exhibit 4–4 is reported.

- *Total assets* = $3,882,000. This balance is a summation of the consolidated assets.

- *Long-term liabilities* = $1,646,400. The parent's book value is added to the subsidiary's book value less the $32,000 allocation within the purchase price plus 2002 and 2003 amortization of $4,000 per year (see Exhibit 4–4).

- *Noncontrolling interest in subsidiary* = $170,000. The outside ownership is 20 percent of the subsidiary's year-end book value (common stock plus ending retained earnings) of $850,000. This $170,000 total can also be calculated as follows:

Noncontrolling interest at 1/1/03 (20 percent of $810,000 beginning book value—common stock plus 1/1/03 retained earnings)	$162,000
Noncontrolling interest in subsidiary's income (computed above)	18,000
Dividends paid to noncontrolling interest (20 percent of $50,000 total)	(10,000)
Noncontrolling interest at 12/31/03	$170,000

- *Common stock* = $850,000. Only the parent's book value is reported since this combination is a purchase.

- *Retained earnings, 12/31/03* = $1,215,600. Computed above.

- *Total liabilities and equities* = $3,882,000. This total is a summation of consolidated liabilities, noncontrolling interest, and equities.

Worksheet Process The consolidated totals for King and Pawn also can be determined by means of a worksheet as shown in Exhibit 4–7. A comparison of the

E x h i b i t   4 – 7   Noncontrolling Interest Illustrated

KING COMPANY AND PAWN COMPANY
Consolidation Worksheet
For Year Ending December 31, 2003

Consolidation: Purchase Method
Investment: Equity Method

Ownership: 80%

Accounts	King Company*	Pawn Company*	Consolidation Entries Debit	Consolidation Entries Credit	Noncontrolling Interest	Consolidated Totals
Income Statement						
Revenues	(910,000)	(430,000)				(1,340,000)
Cost of goods sold	350,000	200,000				550,000
Depreciation expense	160,000	95,000	(E) 4,000			259,000
Interest expense	70,000	45,000	(E) 4,000			119,000
Equity in subsidiary earnings	(64,000)	–0–	(I) 64,000			–0–
Noncontrolling interest in Pawn Company's income	–0–	–0–			(18,000)	18,000
Net income	(394,000)	(90,000)				(394,000)
Statement of Retained Earnings						
Retained earnings, 1/1/03:						
King Company	(881,600)					(881,600)
Pawn Company		(580,000)	(S) 580,000			–0–
Net income (above)	(394,000)	(90,000)				(394,000)
Dividends paid	60,000	50,000		(D) 40,000	10,000	60,000
Retained earnings, 12/31/03	(1,215,600)	(620,000)				(1,215,600)

Balance Sheet

			Consolidation Entries		Noncontrolling Interest	Consolidated Totals
Current assets	626,000	445,000				1,071,000
Land	298,000	295,000	(A) 48,000			641,000
Buildings (net)	880,000	540,000	(A) 91,200	(E) 4,800		1,506,400
Equipment (net)	290,000	160,000	(E) 800	(A) 7,200		443,600
Investment in Pawn Company	1,052,000	-0-	(D) 40,000	(S) 648,000 (A) 380,000 (I) 64,000		-0-
Goodwill	-0-	-0-	(A) 220,000			220,000
Total assets	3,146,000	1,440,000				3,882,000
Long-term liabilities	(1,080,400)	(590,000)	(A) 28,000	(E) 4,000		(1,646,400)
Noncontrolling interest in Pawn Company, 1/1/03	-0-	-0-		(S) 162,000	(162,000)	
Noncontrolling interest in Pawn Company, 12/31/03	-0-	-0-			(170,000)	(170,000)
Common stock	(850,000)	(230,000)	(S) 230,000			(850,000)
Retained earnings, 12/31/03 (above)	(1,215,600)	(620,000)				(1,215,600)
Total liabilities and equities	(3,146,000)	(1,440,000)				(3,882,000)

*See Exhibit 4–6.

Note: Parentheses indicate a credit balance.

Consolidation entries:

(S) Elimination of subsidiary's stockholders' equity accounts along with recognition of January 1, 2003, noncontrolling interest.

(A) Allocation of parent's cost in excess of subsidiary's book value, unamortized balances as of January 1, 2003.

(I) Elimination of intercompany income (equity accrual less amortization expenses).

(D) Elimination of intercompany dividend payments.

(E) Recognition of amortization expenses on purchase price allocations.

worksheet entries made in this example with the entries incorporated in Chapter 3 (Exhibit 3-7) indicates that the presence of a noncontrolling interest does not create a significant number of changes in the consolidation procedures.

The worksheet still includes elimination of the subsidiary's stockholders' equity accounts (Entry S) although, as explained next, this entry is expanded to record the beginning noncontrolling interest for the year. The second worksheet entry recognizes the purchase price allocations at January 1 after one year of amortization (Entry A). Intercompany income as well as dividend payments are removed also (Entries I and D), while current year excess amortization expenses are recognized (Entry E). The differences that can be cited with illustrations in the previous chapter relate exclusively to the recognition of four noncontrolling interest balances. In addition, *a separate Noncontrolling Interest column is added to the worksheet to accumulate the components that form the year-end figure to be reported on the consolidated balance sheet.*

Noncontrolling Interest—Beginning of Year   As discussed previously, Pawn's stockholders' equity accounts (common stock and beginning retained earnings) indicate a January 1, 2003, book value of $810,000. Thus, the 20 percent outside ownership is valued at $162,000 ($810,000 × 20 percent) as of the first day of the current year. This balance is recognized on the worksheet by means of Entry S:

Consolidation Entry S

Common Stock (Pawn).................................	230,000	
Retained Earnings, 1/1/03 (Pawn)	580,000	
Investment in Pawn Company (80%)..................		648,000
Noncontrolling Interest in Subsidiary, 1/1/03 (20%)		162,000
To eliminate beginning stockholders' equity accounts of		
subsidiary along with book value portion of investment (equal		
to 80 percent ownership). Noncontrolling interest of 20 percent		
is also recognized.		

The $162,000 balance assigned here to the outside owners at the beginning of the year is extended on the worksheet into the Noncontrolling Interest column (see Exhibit 4–7).

Noncontrolling Interest—Current Year Income   Exhibit 4–2 indicates that the parent company concept calculates the noncontrolling interest's share of current year earnings based on the subsidiary's income without regard for amortization. Thus, Pawn's 2003 earnings of $90,000 necessitate an assignment of $18,000 (20 percent) to the outside owners. This figure is shown as a reduction in arriving at consolidated net income. In effect, 100 percent of each subsidiary revenue and expense account is consolidated with an accompanying 20 percent decrease to reflect the presence of the noncontrolling interest. The 80 percent net effect corresponds to King's ownership.

Because this $18,000 portion of consolidated income is viewed as accruing to the noncontrolling interest, an increase is necessary in the $162,000 beginning balance assigned (in Entry S) to these outside owners. The amount attributed to the noncontrolling interest is raised because the subsidiary generated a profit during the period.

Although this allocation could be recorded on the worksheet through an additional entry, the $18,000 is usually shown, as in Exhibit 4–7, by means of a columnar adjustment. The current year accrual is simultaneously entered in the consolidated Income Statement column as a *reduction* and in the Noncontrolling Interest column as an *increase.* This procedure indicates that a portion of the earnings included in the consolidated figures must be assigned to the outside owners rather than to the business combination.

Noncontrolling Interest—Dividend Payments   The $40,000 dividend that went to the parent company is eliminated routinely through Entry D, but the remainder of Pawn's dividend was paid to noncontrolling interest. The impact of the dividend (20 percent of the subsidiary's total payment) distributed to the other owners must be acknowledged. As shown in Exhibit 4–7, this remaining $10,000 is extended directly into the Noncontrolling Interest column on the worksheet as a reduction. It represents the drop in the underlying book value of the outside ownership that resulted from the subsidiary's asset distribution.

Noncontrolling Interest—End of Year   The ending assignment for these other owners is calculated by a summation of:

1. The beginning balance for the year ($162,000).
2. Plus the appropriate share of the subsidiary's current income ($18,000).
3. Less the dividends paid to the outside owners ($10,000).

The Noncontrolling Interest column on the worksheet in Exhibit 4–7 accumulates these figures. The $170,000 total is then transferred to the balance sheet where it appears in the consolidated statements.

Consolidated Financial Statements   Having successfully consolidated the information for King and Pawn, the resulting financial statements for these two companies is produced in Exhibit 4–8. These figures can be computed directly or can be taken from the consolidation worksheet.

Effects Created by Alternative Investment Methods

One final aspect of the accounting for a noncontrolling interest needs to be explored. In the King and Pawn illustration, the equity method was utilized by the parent, with all worksheet entries based on that approach. As discussed in Chapter 3, had King incorporated either the cost method or the partial equity method, a few specific changes in the consolidation process would be required although the reported figures are not affected.

Cost Method   As in Chapter 3, two balances are omitted by the parent if the cost method is applied. First, dividend income is recognized rather than an equity income accrual. Thus, the parent fails to accrue the percentage of the subsidiary's income earned in past years in excess of dividends (the increase in book value). Second, amortization expense is not recorded under the cost method and must also be included in the consolidation process if proper totals are to be achieved. Because neither of these figures is recognized in applying the cost method, an Entry *C is added to the worksheet to convert the previously recorded balances to the equity method. The parent's beginning retained earnings is affected by this adjustment as well as the Investment in Subsidiary account. The exact amount is computed as follows.

*Conversion to Equity Method from Cost Method (Entry *C)*   Combine:

1. The increase (since acquisition) in the subsidiary's book value during past years (income less dividends) times the parent's ownership percentage.
2. Total amortization expense for these same past years.

Exhibit 4–8
Consolidated Statements
with Noncontrolling Interest

KING COMPANY AND CONSOLIDATED SUBSIDIARY
Income Statement
For Year Ending December 31, 2003

Revenues	$1,340,000
Cost of goods sold	(550,000)
Depreciation expense	(259,000)
Interest expense	(119,000)
Noncontrolling interest in subsidiary income	(18,000)
Consolidated net income	$ 394,000

KING COMPANY AND CONSOLIDATED SUBSIDIARY
Statement of Retained Earnings
For Year Ending December 31, 2003

Retained earnings, January 1, 2003	$ 881,600
Consolidated net income	394,000
Less: Dividends paid	(60,000)
Retained earnings, December 31, 2003	$1,215,600

KING COMPANY AND CONSOLIDATED SUBSIDIARY
Balance Sheet
December 31, 2003

Assets

Current assets	$1,071,000
Land	641,000
Buildings (net)	1,506,400
Equipment (net)	443,600
Goodwill	220,000
Total assets	$3,882,000

Liabilities and Equities

Long-term liabilities	$1,646,400
Noncontrolling interest in subsidiary	170,000
Common stock—King Company	850,000
Retained earnings (above)	1,215,600
Total liabilities and equities	$3,882,000

One other procedural change is required when the cost method is in use. Since no equity income accrual is recognized, only dividends received from the subsidiary are recorded by the parent as income. Entry I is used on the worksheet to remove this intercompany income. Because the dividends are eliminated in this manner, no Entry D is required.

Partial Equity Method Again, an Entry *C is needed to convert the parent's retained earnings as of January 1, 2003, to the equity method. In this case, however, only the amortization expense for the prior years must be included. Under the partial equity method, the income accrual is appropriately recognized each period by the parent company so that no further adjustment is necessary.

STEP ACQUISITIONS

Marriott International, Inc., reported in its 1999 annual financial statements that:

> we increased our ownership interest in The Ritz-Carlton Hotel Company LLC, a luxury hotel brand and management company, to 99 percent from 49 percent. We expect to acquire the remaining one percent of this company within the next several years.

In all previous consolidation illustrations, control over a subsidiary was assumed to have been achieved through a single transaction. Obviously, Marriott International's takeover of Ritz-Carlton Hotel Co. shows that a combination also may be the result of a series of stock purchases. These step acquisitions further complicate the consolidation process. The financial information of the separate companies must still be brought together, but no single purchase price exists. How do the initial acquisitions affect this process?

> If a parent-subsidiary relationship is established in a step acquisition, a problem arises that does not exist if the parent-subsidiary relationship is established in a single transaction. *That problem is how to include in consolidated financial statements the portion of the parent's interest in the subsidiary that was purchased prior to the date the parent-subsidiary relationship is established* (emphasis added).[8]

For example, in consolidating the accounts of Ritz-Carlton Hotel, the values to be reported could vary significantly depending on Marriott's handling of the 49 percent ownership that it held prior to gaining control.

Step Acquisitions—Parent Company Concept

Under the parent company concept, each investment is viewed as an individual purchase (sometimes referred to as a *layer*) with its own cost allocations and related amortization. To illustrate, assume that Art Company purchases 30 percent of Zip Company on January 1, 2001, for $164,000 in cash. As of the date of this acquisition, Zip is reporting a net book value of $400,000.

Assuming that Art has gained the ability to significantly influence the decision-making process of Zip, this investment, for external reporting purposes, is accounted for by means of the equity method as discussed in Chapter 1. Thus, Art must determine any allocations and amortization associated with its purchase price (see Exhibit 4–9). A customer base with a 20-year life represented the initial excess payment.

Exhibit 4–9
Allocation of First Purchase

ART COMPANY AND ZIP COMPANY Purchase Price Allocation and Amortization January 1, 2001	
Purchase price	$ 164,000
Book value equivalent of Art's ownership ($400,000 × 30%)	(120,000)
Customer base	$ 44,000
Assumed life	20 years
Annual amortization expense	$ 2,200

---

[8]FASB, *An Analysis of Issues Related to Consolidation Policy and Procedures,* paragraph 289.

Exhibit 4–10
Allocation of Second
Purchase

ART COMPANY AND ZIP COMPANY	
Purchase Price Allocation and Amortization	
January 1, 2003	
Purchase price	$ 350,000
Book value equivalent of Art's ownership ($500,000 × 50%)	(250,000)
Customer base	$ 100,000
Assumed life	20 years
Annual amortization expense	$ 5,000

As discussed previously, application of the equity method requires the immediate accrual of investee income by the parent while any dividends received are recorded as a decrease in the Investment account. Art must also reduce both the income and asset balances in recognition of the annual $2,200 amortization indicated in Exhibit 4–9. If, over the next two years, Zip reports a total of $140,000 in net income and pays dividends of $40,000, the subsidiary's book value rises from $400,000 to $500,000. At the same time, the parent's investment account grows to $189,600:

Purchase price—1/1/01	$164,000
Accrual of 2001–02 equity income ($140,000 × 30 percent) ..	42,000
Dividends received 2001–02 ($40,000 × 30%)	(12,000)
Amortization ($2,200 per year for 2 years)	(4,400)
Investment in Zip, 12/31/02	$189,600

On January 1, 2003, Art's ownership is raised to 80 percent by the purchase of another 50 percent of the outstanding common stock of Zip Company for $350,000. Although the equity method can still be utilized for internal reporting, this second purchase necessitates the preparation of consolidated financial statements beginning in 2003. Art now controls Zip; the two companies should be viewed as a single economic entity for external reporting purposes.

Before computing any consolidated balances, Art must make a separate cost allocation for this second purchase (Exhibit 4–10). In this purchase, the excess is attributable to Zip's substantially expanded customer base. This schedule does not supersede the allocation made in Exhibit 4–9 but merely supplements it for the price paid in acquiring the 50 percent block of Zip's stock.

Worksheet Consolidation for a Step Acquisition

To complete this example, assume that the subsidiary earns $100,000 in net income during 2003 and distributes $20,000 as a cash dividend. If the parent company continues applying the equity method to this investment, Art reports an Equity in Subsidiary Earnings balance of $72,800 for 2003 and an Investment in Zip Company of $596,400:

Investment in Zip, 12/31/02 (computed above)		$189,600
January 1, 2003—Second acquisition		350,000
Dividends received—2003 ($20,000 × 80%)		(16,000)
Equity income accrual—2003 ($100,000 × 80%)	$80,000	
2003 amortization: First purchase (Exhibit 4–9)	(2,200)	
Second purchase (Exhibit 4–10)	(5,000)	72,800
Investment in Zip, 12/31/03		$596,400

Once both investment balances have been determined, the worksheet shown in Exhibit 4–11 can be developed. Although this step acquisition might appear to be more complex than a single purchase, the actual consolidation process is the same as in previous examples.

■ No conversion to the equity method (Entry *C) is required since that method has been applied by the parent. If a different approach were used, amortization expense for prior years would have to be recognized along with, possibly, the proportionate increase in the subsidiary's book value for this same period.

■ The stockholders' equity accounts of Zip are removed through Entry S. This worksheet entry also establishes the $100,000 beginning balance for the 20 percent noncontrolling interest that still remains (20 percent multiplied by the $500,000 stockholders' equity as of January 1, 2003).

■ The unamortized purchase price allocations are brought into the consolidation through Entry A. The $44,000 balance resulting from the first transaction has already undergone two years of amortization. Thus, only a cost of $39,600 remains at the beginning of the current period. Since the second allocation ($100,000) was made on January 1 of the current year, no expense has been recorded in prior years.

■ Entry I on the worksheet eliminates the $72,800 equity income accrual calculated above.

■ Entry D removes the $16,000 intercompany dividend paid to the parent in 2000. The remaining 20 percent ($4,000) was paid to the outside owners. Thus, that amount is extended to the Noncontrolling Interest column on the worksheet as a reduction.

■ The final consolidation entry (Entry E) recognizes total excess amortizations for the current period.

■ The noncontrolling interest balances to be reported on the income statement and balance sheet must be computed before the worksheet can be completed. Since Art now holds 80 percent of Zip, the outside owner's share of the subsidiary's income is 20 percent of the $100,000 reported earnings (or $20,000). Once again, this assignment is recorded on the worksheet through a columnar entry: The Noncontrolling Interest column is increased by that amount with a parallel decrease to consolidated net income.

For the balance sheet, the ending amount applicable to these outside owners is determined within the Noncontrolling Interest column: Assigned income of $20,000 is added to the $100,000 beginning balance with dividends of $4,000 being subtracted. The $116,000 total then is reported on the balance sheet between the liabilities and stockholders' equity.

Retroactive Treatment Created by Step Acquisition

Because the initial 30 percent acquisition gave Art the ability to maintain significant influence over Zip, the investment balances in 2001 and 2002 were recorded using the equity method. For external reporting, the subsidiary's operations as well as related amortization were accounted for in those years in a manner that parallels the consolidation process. Thus, financial statements prepared and distributed by Art in 2001 and 2002 are considered comparable with the consolidated statements produced for 2003. Consequently, no retroactive adjustment of the earlier figures is required by Art's change in the method of reporting its investment in Zip.

Conversely, if Art had originally secured only a small percentage of Zip's shares (achieving less than significant influence), the market-value method would have been applied during 2001 and 2002. Under this approach, except for amounts received in the

Exhibit 4–11   Step Acquisition Illustrated

Consolidation: Purchase Method
Investment: Equity Method

ART COMPANY AND ZIP COMPANY
Consolidation Worksheet
For Year Ending December 31, 2003

Accounts	Art Company	ZIP Company	Consolidation Entries Debit	Consolidation Entries Credit	Noncontrolling Interest	Consolidated Totals
Income Statement						
Revenues	(600,000)	(260,000)				(860,000)
Expenses	425,000	160,000	(E) 7,200			592,200
Equity in subsidiary earnings	(72,800)	–0–	(I) 72,800			–0–
Noncontrolling interest in Zip Company's income	–0–	–0–			(20,000)	20,000
Net income	(247,800)	(100,000)				(247,800)
Statement of Retained Earnings						
Retained earnings, 1/1/03:						
Art Company	(757,800)					(757,800)
Zip Company		(230,000)	(S) 230,000			
Net income (above)	(247,800)	(100,000)				(247,800)
Dividends paid	126,400	20,000		(D) 16,000	4,000	126,400
Retained earnings, 12/31/03	(879,200)	(310,000)				(879,200)

Balance Sheet

Balance Sheet						
Current assets	505,800	280,000				785,800
Land	205,000	90,000				295,000
Buildings (net)	646,000	310,000				956,000
Investment in Zip Company	596,400	-0-	(D) 16,000	(A) 139,600 (S) 400,000 (I) 72,800		-0-
Customer base	-0-	-0-	(A) 39,600 (A) 100,000	(E) 2,200 (E) 5,000		132,400
Total assets	1,953,200	680,000				2,169,200
Liabilities	(459,000)	(100,000)				(559,000)
Noncontrolling interest in Zip Company, 1/1/03	-0-	-0-		(S) 100,000	(100,000)	(100,000)
Noncontrolling interest in Zip Company, 12/31/03					(116,000)	(116,000)
Common stock	(355,000)	(200,000)	(S) 200,000			(355,000)
Additional paid-in capital	(260,000)	(70,000)	(S) 70,000			(260,000)
Retained earnings, 12/31/03 (above)	(879,200)	(310,000)				(879,200)
Total liabilities and equities	(1,953,200)	(680,000)				(2,169,200)

Note: Parentheses indicate a credit balance.

Consolidation entries:

(S) Elimination of subsidiary's stockholders' equity accounts along with recognition of January 1, 2003, noncontrolling interest.

(A) Allocation of parent's cost in excess of subsidiary's book value for unamortized balances as of January 1, 2003. Two separate allocations are shown because two purchases were made.

(I) Elimination of intercompany income (equity accrual less amortization expense).

(D) Elimination of intercompany dividend payments.

(E) Recognition of amortization expense on customer base and franchise agreement resulting from purchase price.

form of dividends, subsidiary income is ignored by the owner as is the recording of any amortization. However, gaining control of Zip in 2003 necessitates a transformation to consolidated statements, a change that strains the comparability of the results reported in the earlier years. Thus, to establish a proper degree of consistency, both the investment and income accounts are restated by the parent as if the equity method had been utilized from the date of the first acquisition.

ARB 51 (par. 9) does allow one exception to this restatement policy by indicating that "if small purchases are made over a period of time and then a purchase is made which results in control, the date of the latest purchase, as a matter of convenience, may be considered as the date of acquisition." Therefore, retroactive adjustment is not required when initial acquisition levels are relatively small. The ARB apparently felt that the difficulties encountered in restating such minor amounts outweighed the benefits derived from establishing comparability.

Step Acquisitions—Economic Unit Concept

Although this textbook primarily uses the parent company concept for illustration purposes, comparison with the economic unit concept demonstrates significant differences. Because the FASB is studying the issue of consolidation policies, one method or the other might eventually be mandated or an entirely new approach could be required. The economic unit concept, in particular, has received much attention.

To illustrate a step acquisition using the economic unit concept, assume that on January 1, 2002, Amanda Co. purchases 70 percent of Zoe, Inc., for $350,000. Because Zoe's net assets have book values equal to their fair market values of $400,000, under the economic unit concept, goodwill of $100,000 (10-year life) is recognized as the difference between the implied value of $500,000 ($350,000 ÷ 70%) and net asset market value of $400,000. On January 1, 2003, when Zoe's book value has grown to $420,000, Amanda buys another 20 percent of Zoe for $95,000, bringing its total ownership up to 90 percent.

Under the economic unit concept, the valuation basis for Zoe's net assets was established on January 1, 2002, the date Amanda obtained control. Subsequent transactions in the subsidiary's stock (purchases or sales) are now viewed as transactions in the economic unit's own stock. Therefore, no gains or losses are recognized and differences between transaction prices and the underlying subsidiary book value are simply treated as adjustments to additional paid-in capital. The difference between the $95,000 price and the underlying consolidated book value is computed as follows:

1/1/03 Purchase price for 20 percent interest		$ 95,000
Noncontrolling interest acquired:		
Book value (20%) 1/1/03	$84,000	
Goodwill (20%)	20,000	
Noncontrolling interest book value 1/1/03		104,000
Additional paid-in capital from 20 percent NCI acquisition		$ 9,000

By purchasing 20 percent of Zoe for $95,000 the consolidated entity's owners have acquired a portion of their own firm at a price $9,000 less than consolidated book value. From a worksheet perspective, the recognition of the additional $104,000 in consolidated net assets from the 20 percent purchase is offset by the $95,000 purchase price and a $9,000 credit to additional paid-in capital. Importantly, the $95,000 purchase price for the 20 percent interest in Zoe's net assets does not affect consolidated asset valuation. From the economic unit perspective, the basis for the reported values in the consolidated financial statements was established on the date control was obtained.

PREACQUISITION INCOME

In virtually all of the previous examples in this textbook, the parent has gained control of the subsidiary on the first day of the fiscal year. How is the consolidation process affected if a purchase is made on April 1 or August 19 or some other day within the year?[9]

If control is gained at a different time, a few obvious changes occur. The subsidiary's book value as of that date has to be computed so that an appropriate comparison with the purchase price can be made to determine allocations and goodwill. Amortization expense as well as any equity accrual and dividend collections are recognized for a period shorter than a year. The real issue to be resolved, though, is in consolidating the subsidiary's revenues and expenses. Obviously, these balances can be included just for the months after the takeover. However, this approach gives totals that may not be comparable to the figures reported in the future when ownership is for a full year.

Paragraph 10 of *ARB 51* addresses this issue by stating:

> When a subsidiary is purchased during the year, there are alternative ways of dealing with the results of its operations in the consolidated income statement. One method, which usually is preferable, especially where there are several dates of acquisition of blocks of shares, is to include the subsidiary in the consolidation as though it had been acquired at the beginning of the year, and to deduct at the bottom of the consolidated income statement the preacquisition earnings applicable to each block of stock. This method presents results which are more indicative of the current status of the group, and facilitates future comparison with subsequent years.

Thus, when a purchase combination is created during the current year, this pronouncement recommends that the reporting emphasis be placed on promoting the statement user's ability to compare current and future periods. *To achieve this objective, the income statement accounts should be consolidated as if the parent had possessed its interest for the entire year.* Consequently, revenues and expenses are included in total within the consolidated figures. However, a single-line reduction (often referred to as *preacquisition income*) appears at the bottom of the income statement to remove the portion of these earnings that apply to the previous owners.

For example, Environmental Safeguards, Inc., reported the following in its recent financial reports regarding its December 17, 1997, acquisition of OnSite:

> This acquisition has been accounted for using the purchase method of accounting and the results of operations of OnSite have been consolidated with the Company's for the year ended December 31, 1997, with a deduction in the consolidated statement of operations for preacquisition earnings attributable to Parker's interest prior to December 17, 1997.

Inclusion of this balance is a means of accounting for the prior group of stockholders in a manner similar to that accorded to any noncontrolling interest that remains. The only difference is that these previous owners ceased during the current year to be associated with the subsidiary. Thus, although an income allocation is reported for the period of their ownership, no end-of-year balance is recognized. Any dividends paid to the previous owners are likewise omitted from consolidation consideration.

To illustrate, assume that Berkeley Company purchases 90 percent of Waltins Company on October 1, 2002. The 2002 operations of this new subsidiary would impact the consolidated income statement as follows:

---

[9]In a pooling of interests, operating results are consolidated retroactively as if the companies had always been together. Therefore, the specific date on which a pooling is formed has no impact on the resulting income statement.

Impact on Consolidated Income Statement—2002

Berkeley owns 90 percent of Waltins for last three months

Revenues	100% of subsidiary's revenues are included.
Expenses	100% of subsidiary's expenses are included plus amortization expense for three months.
Noncontrolling interest	Reduction is 10% of subsidiary's income for the entire year.
Preacquisition income	Reduction is 90% of subsidiary's income for the first nine months of the year.
Net impact on consolidated net income	Increased by 90% of subsidiary's income for the last three months of the year, reduced by any amortization expense for this same period.

The establishment of a Preacquisition Income account permits comparability between the figures reported for current and future years. The reader of the financial statements is able to measure the full impact of creating this combination through the inclusion of 100 percent of each subsidiary revenue and expense account. By reporting reductions for the noncontrolling interest (10 percent) and the previous owners (90 percent for nine months), consolidated net income successfully mirrors the parent's 90 percent ownership for the last three months of the year. Thus, the *ARB*'s suggested handling of this matter has no effect on the amount of consolidated net income. Rather, the pronouncement simply constructs the income statement in a manner that provides comparability with future periods.

Before leaving this illustration, one further comment should be made. The term *preacquisition income* has been incorporated here since it appears to be most prevalent in practice. As can be observed in much of accounting, financial statement terminology is not always particularly descriptive. This allocation could also be reported as: *current year income accruing to previous owners prior to the date subsidiary was acquired.* This title is significantly more wordy but less subject to misinterpretation by the users of the financial data. Most companies, however, elect to stay with traditional terms such as *preacquisition income* when preparing statements for external reporting purposes.

Closing the Subsidiary Books at Acquisition Date

Reporting a *preacquisition income* amount in the year of an acquisition is a useful technique to account for subsidiary income earned prior to the purchase date. By combining the preacquisition revenues and expenses into the single *preacquisition income* figure, the parent establishes a total income cutoff process without the cost of closing its new subsidiary's books. However, as internal information systems become more sophisticated, closing the income accounts on the subsidiary books at the date of acquisition becomes less costly. Moreover, such a closing effectively separates preacquisition and postacquisition revenues and expenses. The consolidation process then simply combines the end-of-period (postacquisition) remaining balances of each revenue and expense account. Thus, when an acquisition is accompanied by a closing of the revenue and expense accounts on the subsidiary books, no *preacquisition income* account is needed. Instead, the postacquisition revenue and expenses are individually combined with the parent's full-year amounts.

SALES OF SUBSIDIARY STOCK

Although this textbook has concentrated on the acquisition and ownership of large blocks of corporate securities, the eventual sale of these stocks is also encountered in the business world. For example, a note to the 1999 financial statements of CSX Corporation states:

On June 30, 1998, CSX conveyed its wholly owned barge subsidiary, American Commercial Lines LLC (ACL), to a venture formed with Vectura Group Inc. CSX has a 32% common ownership in the new venture. Due to the reduction in its ownership interest, CSX has accounted for its investment in the venture under the equity method for the fiscal years ended Dec. 25, 1998, and Dec. 31, 1999. For periods prior to fiscal year 1998, ACL was accounted for as a consolidated subsidiary.

Under the parent company concept, accounting for the disposition of such shares parallels the sale of any corporate asset: The investment is adjusted to the appropriate book value as of the date of sale and then removed from the records of the parent company.[10] Any difference in the recorded balance and the consideration being received is recognized as a gain or loss.

Establishment of Investment Book Value

Any needed adjustment to the investment account depends on the accounting method used by the parent for internal reporting purposes. If the equity method has been applied, little problem should exist in recording the transaction. The investment is correctly reported by the parent as of the beginning of the year so that only the normal equity method adjustments are needed to reflect operations and amortization for the current period.

However, if either the cost or the partial equity method has been utilized, the adjustment process is more complicated. As indicated previously, both of these alternatives offer a convenient means to monitor a subsidiary. Unfortunately, neither produces the accurate book value necessary for recording a sales transaction. Therefore, when either of these other methods has been applied, the parent's Investment in Subsidiary account must be updated as if the equity method had been applied since the date of acquisition.

To illustrate, assume that Giant Company owns 80 percent of Tiny Company. Initially, a 50 percent interest was acquired in 1998 for $600,000 with the additional 30 percent being purchased in 2000 for $440,000. If Giant elects to account for this subsidiary using the equity method, the Investment in Tiny account contains a $1,245,000 balance as of January 1, 2002, based on the following assumed figures:

	Cost	Income Accrual Since Acquisition	Dividends	Excess Amortization	Investment Balance 1/1/02
1998 purchase ...	$ 600,000	$200,000	$(15,000)	$(40,000)	$ 745,000
2000 purchase ...	440,000	100,000	(6,000)	(34,000)	500,000
Totals	$1,040,000	$300,000	$(21,000)	$(74,000)	$1,245,000

Sale Made at Beginning of Year Appropriate application of the equity method signifies that the $1,245,000 is a correctly recorded balance. Assuming that Giant sells this entire interest on January 1, 2002, for $1,400,000, the transaction is recorded as follows:[11]

---

[10]Unless control is surrendered, the economic unit concept views the sale of a subsidiary's stock as a treasury stock transaction so that no gain or loss is recognized.

[11]Under the guidelines of *APB Opinion 30,* Giant may have to report this sale as the disposal of a segment. Because this issue is covered in most intermediate accounting textbooks, it is not explored here.

Giant's Financial Records—January 1, 2002

Cash (or other assets)	1,400,000	
Investment in Tiny Company		1,245,000
Gain on Sale of Investment		155,000
To record January 1, 2002, sale of subsidiary.		

Because the sale is made on the first day of the year, no adjustment is required to recognize the 2002 operations of the subsidiary.

In contrast, if one of the alternative methods has been utilized by Giant, a preliminary entry is needed to establish the appropriate $1,245,000 balance.

Application of the cost method. The $1,040,000 total of the two original payments continues to be reported by the parent for this investment so that a $205,000 increase is necessary (income in excess of dividends and amortization).

Application of the partial equity method. A book value of $1,319,000 (income and dividends are recognized by the parent but not the $74,000 amortization) is found. An adjustment must be made to record the amortization.

Hence, depending on the method in use, one of the following entries is required of the parent prior to recording the sales transaction:

Giant's Financial Records—January 1, 2002
Cost Method Has Been Applied

Investment in Tiny Company	205,000	
Retained Earnings, 1/1/02 (Giant)		205,000
To establish correct equity balance by recognizing income accrual (in excess of dividends) for previous years as well as amortization.		

Partial Equity Method Has Been Applied

Retained Earnings, 1/1/02 (Giant)	74,000	
Investment in Tiny Company		74,000
To establish correct equity balance by recognizing amortization relating to previous years.		

These adjustments are equivalent to the Entry *C used in past consolidations to update the investment account when either the cost or partial equity method has been applied. However, for a sale, this entry must be recorded directly into the parent's books rather than as a part of the worksheet process. Following the adjustment to $1,245,000, the parent records the sales transaction using the same journal entry presented in connection with the equity method.

Sale Made during the Year   If this sale had transpired *within* the fiscal year, Giant still adjusts the investment to $1,245,000 (if necessary) but then extends application of the equity method over the period that the stock is held during 2002. The resulting book value must be correct as of the date of sale. The income accruing to Giant during this portion of the year is reported as a single-line item in the 2002 income statement. In this manner, subsidiary earnings continue to be recognized throughout the period of ownership even though consolidation is no longer applicable.

Cost-Flow Assumptions

If less than an entire investment is sold, the parent must select an appropriate cost-flow assumption whenever more than one purchase has been made. In the sale of securities, the use of specific identification based on serial numbers is acceptable, although averaging or FIFO assumptions often are applied. Use of the averaging method is especially appealing in that all shares are truly identical, creating little justification for identifying different cost figures with individual shares.

Returning to Giant's ownership of Tiny Company, assume that the parent sold only a 20 percent portion of the subsidiary on January 1, 2002 (thereby reducing its holdings from 80 to 60 percent). Averaging dictates the removal of $311,250 (20 percent/80 percent × $1,245,000) from the investment account. Conversely, adoption of FIFO requires that $298,000 be written off based on the currently reported value of the initial 1997 acquisition (20 percent/50 percent × $745,000).

Accounting for Shares That Remain

If only a portion of Giant's investment is sold, a determination also must be made as to the proper method of accounting for the shares that remain. Three possible scenarios can be envisioned:

1. Giant's interest may have been so drastically reduced that the parent no longer controls the subsidiary or even has the ability to significantly influence its decision making. For example, assume that Giant's ownership drops from 80 to 5 percent. In the current period prior to the sale, the 80 percent investment is reported by means of the equity method with the market-value method used for the 5 percent that remains thereafter. Consolidated financial statements are no longer applicable.

2. Giant may still be able to apply significant influence over the operations of Tiny, although control is no longer maintained. A drop in the level of ownership from 80 to 30 percent would normally meet this condition. In this case, the equity method is utilized by the parent for the entire year. Application is based on 80 percent until the time of sale and then on 30 percent for the remainder of the year. Again, consolidated statements cease to be appropriate because control has been lost.

3. The decrease in ownership may be relatively small so that the parent continues to maintain control over the subsidiary even after the sale. Giant's reduction of its ownership in Tiny from 80 to 60 percent is an example of this situation. After the disposal, consolidated financial statements are still required but the process is based on the *end-of-year ownership percentage*. As with step acquisitions, the accounting emphasis is placed here on maintaining comparability with future years. However, since only the retained shares (60 percent in this case) are consolidated, separate recognition must be made of any current year income accruing to the parent from its terminated interest. Thus, earnings on this portion of the investment (a 20 percent interest in Tiny for the time during the year that it is held) are shown in the consolidated income statement as a single-line item computed by means of the equity method.

SUMMARY

1. A parent company need not acquire 100 percent of a subsidiary's stock to form a business combination. Only control over the decision-making process is necessary, a level that has historically been achieved by obtaining a majority of the voting shares. Ownership of any subsidiary stock that is retained by outside, unrelated parties is collectively referred to as a noncontrolling interest.

2. A purchase consolidation takes on an added degree of complexity when a noncontrolling interest is present. A decision must be made as to the theoretical approach by which subsidiary assets and liabilities are to be valued within the financial statements of the business combination. One alternative, the economic unit concept, presumes that the combination is composed of two identifiable companies and should be accounted for as such. Allocations associated with the subsidiary's assets and liabilities are determined

using their total fair market value regardless of the degree of parent ownership. The calculation of any noncontrolling interest is based on this total and reported by the business combination as a component of stockholders' equity.

3. The proportionate consolidation concept focuses on the parent company by stressing the cost of buying a portion of the subsidiary. Under this approach, allocations are computed using the ownership percentage of each account's fair market value. No recognition of noncontrolling interest is reported in either the consolidated balance sheet or income statement.

4. In practice, the parent company concept appears to be most popular. According to this method, the book value of each subsidiary asset and liability is included in the total whereas the difference between fair market value and book value is consolidated based on the parent's ownership percentage. Any noncontrolling interest is measured using only the subsidiary's book value and reported between the liabilities and stockholders' equity.

5. Four noncontrolling interest figures actually appear in the annual consolidation process. Calculation of each is derived by multiplying the percentage of outside ownership by the subsidiary's book value. A balance as of the beginning of the year is brought into the worksheet first (through Entry S) followed by the noncontrolling interest's share of the subsidiary's income for the period (recorded by a columnar entry). A decrease is recognized because of any dividends paid to these unrelated owners (with the amount appearing on the worksheet as the subsidiary's dividends that were not eliminated as intercompany). The final balance for the year is found as a summation of the Noncontrolling Interest column and is presented on the consolidated balance sheet, usually between the Liability and Stockholders' Equity sections. The income figure appears as a reduction within the income statement.

6. A parent may obtain control of a subsidiary by means of several separate purchases occurring over time, a process often referred to as a *step acquisition.* In such cases, each purchase is viewed as an individual investment with separate allocations and amortization.

7. When a purchase is made within a year, operating figures should be reported that are comparable with those of future years. Thus, revenues and expenses can be consolidated as if the acquisition had taken place on the first day of the year. A *preacquisition income* figure is then subtracted within the consolidated income statement to remove the effects of the subsidiary's operations relating to the time prior to the takeover.

8. A parent company also may sell all, or a portion, of a subsidiary. The appropriate book value for the investment must be established within the parent's separate records so that the gain or loss can be computed accurately. If the equity method has not been applied, the parent's investment balance should be restated to recognize any income and amortization previously omitted. The resulting balance is then compared to the amount received for the stock to arrive at the gain or loss. Any shares still being held will subsequently be reported by either consolidation, the equity method, or the market-value method, depending on the influence retained by the parent.

COMPREHENSIVE ILLUSTRATION

Problem

(Estimated Time: 60 to 75 Minutes) On January 1, 1998, Father Company purchased an 80 percent interest in Sun Company for $410,000. As of that date, Sun reported total stockholders' equity of $400,000: $100,000 in common stock and $300,000 in retained earnings. In setting the acquisition price, Father had appraised four accounts as having values different from the balances reported within Sun's financial records.

Buildings (eight-year life)	Undervalued by $20,000
Land	Undervalued by $50,000
Equipment (five-year life)	Undervalued by $12,500
Royalty agreement (20-year life)	Not recorded, valued at $30,000

As of December 31, 2002, the trial balances of these two companies are as follows:

	Father Company	Sun Company
Debits		
Current assets	$ 620,000	$ 280,000
Investment in Sun Company	410,000	–0–
Land	200,000	300,000
Buildings (net)	640,000	290,000
Equipment (net)	380,000	160,000
Expenses	550,000	190,000
Dividends	90,000	20,000
Total debits	$2,890,000	$1,240,000
Credits		
Liabilities	$ 910,000	$ 300,000
Common stock	480,000	100,000
Retained earnings, 1/1/02	704,000	480,000
Revenues	780,000	360,000
Dividend income	16,000	–0–
Total credits	$2,890,000	$1,240,000

Within these figures, Sun has a $20,000 debt to the parent company.

Required:

a. Determine consolidated totals for Father Company and Sun Company for the year of 2002. Assume that the parent company concept is to be applied.

b. Prepare worksheet entries to consolidate the trial balances of Father Company and Sun Company for the year of 2002.

c. Assume that Father acquires an additional 5 percent of the outstanding shares of Sun Company on December 31, 2002. Discuss the effects of this transaction on the consolidated figures computed in requirement (a).

d. Assume that Father uses the economic unit concept rather than the parent company concept. Discuss the effects of this change on the consolidated figures computed in requirement (a).

Solution

a. The consolidation of Father Company and Sun Company should begin with the allocation of the purchase price as shown in Exhibit 4–12. This process is based on the parent company concept and the parent's $410,000 expenditure. Since this consolidation is taking place after several years, the unamortized balances for the various allocations at the start of the current year also should be determined (see Exhibit 4–13).

   Next, the parent's method of accounting for its subsidiary should be ascertained. The continuing presence in the investment account of the original $410,000 acquisition price indicates that Father is applying the cost method. This same determination can be made from the Dividend Income account that equals 80 percent of the subsidiary's dividends. Thus, the increase in Sun's book value as well as the excess amortization expenses for the prior periods of ownership have been ignored in Father's accounting records. These amounts have to be added to the parent's January 1, 2002, retained earnings to arrive at a properly consolidated balance.

   During the 1998–2001 period of ownership, Sun's Retained Earnings account rose by $180,000 ($480,000 − $300,000). Father's 80 percent interest necessitates an accrual of $144,000 ($180,000 × 80 percent) for these years. In addition, the purchase price allocations require the recognition of $20,800 in excess amortization expenses for this same period ($5,200 × 4 years). Thus, a net increase of $123,200 ($144,000 − $20,800) is needed to correct the parent's beginning retained earnings balance for the year.

   Once the adjustment from the cost method to the equity method has been determined, the consolidated figures for 2002 can be calculated:

   Current assets = $880,000. The parent's book value is added to the subsidiary's book value. The $20,000 intercompany balance is eliminated.

Exhibit 4-12

FATHER COMPANY AND SUN COMPANY
Purchase Price Allocation and Amortization
January 1, 1998

	Allocation	Estimated Life (years)	Annual Excess Amortization
Purchase price paid by Father Company	$ 410,000		
80% of subsidiary's $400,000 book value (Father Company's ownership)	(320,000)		
Cost in excess of book value	90,000		
Allocation to specific accounts based on fair market value:			
Buildings ($20,000 × 80%)	16,000	8	$ 2,000
Land ($50,000 × 80%)	40,000		
Equipment ($12,500 × 80%)	10,000	5	2,000
Royalty agreement ($30,000 × 80%) ..	24,000	20	1,200
	-0-		
Annual excess amortization and depreciation expense			$ 5,200
1998–2001 excess amortization and depreciation expense ($5,200 × 4)			$20,800

Exhibit 4-13

FATHER COMPANY AND SUN COMPANY
Unamortized Cost Allocation
January 1, 2002, Balances

Account	Excess Original Allocation	Unamortized Amortization 1998–2001	Balance 1/1/02
Buildings	$16,000	$8,000	$ 8,000
Land	40,000	-0-	40,000
Equipment	10,000	8,000	2,000
Royalty	24,000	4,800	19,200
Total			$69,200

Investment in Sun Company = –0–. The intercompany ownership is eliminated so that the subsidiary's specific assets and liabilities can be consolidated.

Land = $540,000. The parent's book value is added to the subsidiary's book value plus the purchase price allocation (see Exhibit 4–12).

Buildings (net) = $936,000. The parent's book value is added to the subsidiary's book value plus the related purchase price allocation (see Exhibit 4–13) after taking into account five years of amortization (1998 through 2002).

Equipment (net) = $540,000. The parent's book value is added to the subsidiary's book value. The purchase price allocation has been completely amortized after five years.

Expenses = $745,200. The parent's book value is added to the subsidiary's book value plus amortization expenses on the purchase price allocations for the year (see Exhibit 4–12).

Dividends Paid = $90,000. Only the parent company dividends are consolidated. The subsidiary's dividends that were paid to the parent are eliminated; the remainder serve as a reduction in the Noncontrolling Interest balance.

Royalty Agreement = $18,000. The original residual allocation from the purchase price is recognized after taking into account five years of amortization (see Exhibit 4–13).

Noncontrolling Interest in Subsidiary's Income = $34,000. The outside owners are assigned a 20 percent share of the subsidiary's income (revenues of $360,000 less expenses of $190,000 or $170,000).

Total of Consolidated Debit Balances = $3,782,800. This figure is a summation of the preceding balances.

Liabilities = $1,190,000. The parent's book value is added to the subsidiary's book value. The $20,000 intercompany balance is eliminated.

Common Stock = $480,000. The parent company balance only is reported.

Retained Earnings, 1/1/02 = $827,200. The parent company balance only is reported after a $123,200 increase is made as explained earlier to convert the parent's use of the cost method to the equity method.

Revenues = $1,140,000. The parent's book value is added to the subsidiary's book value.

Dividend Income = –0–. The intercompany dividend receipts are eliminated.

Noncontrolling Interest in Subsidiary, 12/31/02 = $146,000. The beginning balance is $116,000, 20 percent of the subsidiary's 1/1/02 book value ($580,000 as shown by the stockholders' equity accounts). This figure is increased by the noncontrolling interest's share of net income ($34,000 as computed above). The dividends paid to the outside owners (20 percent of $20,000, or $4,000) serve to decrease the balance. The consolidated total is then derived from these three balances.

Total of Consolidated Credit Balances = $3,782,800. This figure is a summation of the preceding balances.

b. Five worksheet entries are necessary to produce a consolidation worksheet for Father Company and Sun Company.

Entry *C

Investment in Sun Company	123,200	
Retained Earnings, 1/1/02 (parent)		123,200

As discussed earlier, this increment is required to adjust the parent's retained earnings from the cost method to the equity method. The amount is $144,000 (80 percent of the $180,000 increase in the subsidiary's book value during previous years) less $20,800 in excess amortization over this same four-year period ($5,200 × 4 years).

Entry S

Common Stock (subsidiary)	100,000	
Retained Earnings, 1/1/02 (subsidiary)	480,000	
Investment in Sun Company (80 percent)		464,000
Noncontrolling Interest in Sun Company (20 percent)		116,000

To eliminate beginning stockholders' equity accounts of the subsidiary and recognize the beginning balance attributed to the outside owners (20 percent).

Entry A

Buildings	8,000	
Land	40,000	
Equipment	2,000	
Royalty Agreement	19,200	
Investment in Sun Company		69,200

To recognize unamortized purchase price allocations as of the first day of the current year (see Exhibit 4–13).

Entry I

Dividend Income	16,000	
Dividends Paid		16,000

To eliminate intercompany dividend payments recorded by parent (using the cost method) as income.

Entry E

Depreciation Expense	1,200	
Amortization Expense	4,000	
Buildings		2,000
Equipment		2,000
Royalty Agreement		1,200

To record excess amortization expenses for the current year (see Exhibit 4–12).

c.   *This* question asks about the impact created by Father's purchase of an additional 5 percent of Sun on December 31, 2002. Three direct effects can be listed:

1.   All of the noncontrolling interest balances will be calculated as if only 15 percent of the subsidiary's shares had been held by outside parties during the entire year. This handling allows for production of financial statements that will be comparable with the results reported in future years.

2.   A Preacquisition Income account is established to reflect the portion of Sun's 2002 income (5 percent) accruing to the previous owners. This balance reduces consolidated net income for the current year. In addition, any dividends paid to former stockholders must be eliminated since this group no longer holds an equity interest in Sun.

3.   Any cost in excess of book value paid by Father in this latest purchase must be allocated to specific accounts and then recognized within the consolidated balance sheet. Because the acquisition occurs at the end of the fiscal year, no additional amortization expense is necessary for 2002.

d.   Recall that under the economic unit concept not only is an implied value for 100 percent of the subsidiary used in allocating market values to subsidiary assets but adjustments also are made for 100 percent of the differences in market and book values. The following cost allocation schedule reflects the economic unit concept for Father's purchase of Sun on January 1, 1998:

	Allocation	Estimated Life (years)	Annual Excess Amortization
Implied value ($410,000 ÷ 80%)	$512,500		
Sun book value (100%)	400,000		
Excess implied value	112,500		
Allocation to specific subsidiary accounts based on fair market value:			
Buildings	$ 20,000	8	$2,500
Land	50,000		
Equipment	12,500	5	2,500
Royalty agreement	$ 30,000	20	1,500
	–0–		
Annual excess amortization expenses (economic unit concept)			$6,500

Father's consolidated statements would therefore reflect the total market values of the subsidiary at acquisition date less the above amortizations. To offset the increased asset values, a larger noncontrolling interest also is recognized.

The noncontrolling interest would be reported in the December 31, 2002, stockholders' equity section of Father's consolidated balance sheet at $162,500, computed as follows:

NCI in Sun's 1/1/02 book value (20% × $580,000)	$116,000
NCI in unamortized excess allocations (20% × $86,500)	17,300
January 1, 2002, NCI in Sun implied value	$133,300
NCI in Sun's economic unit income 20% × ($360,000 − 196,500)	32,700
NCI dividend share 20% × $20,000	(4,000)
Total noncontrolling interest December 31, 2002	$162,000

Note that the $162,000 noncontrolling interest amount is the same as the $146,000 amount reported in part (a), plus 20 percent of the $80,000 unamortized excess allocations at December 31, 2002 ($112,500 − 5 years × $6,500).

The noncontrolling interest's share of the subsidiary's net income is not reported on the consolidated income statement but rather as a separate allocation. This amount is based on the subsidiary's net income after deducting amortization expense, which is attributed to the company's asset and liability accounts.

QUESTIONS

1. What is meant by the term *noncontrolling interest?*
2. Atwater Company acquires 80 percent of the outstanding voting stock of Belwood Company. On that date, Belwood possesses a building with a $160,000 book value but a fair market value of $220,000. Assuming that a bargain purchase has not been made, at what value would this building be consolidated under each of the following?
   a. Economic unit concept.
   b. Proportionate consolidation concept.
   c. Parent company concept.
3. Giant Company acquired 70 percent of Small Company at the beginning of 2002. Subsequently, Giant reports net income for 2002 of $60,000 (without regard for the investment in Small). For the same period, this subsidiary reports earnings of $30,000. In acquiring this interest, Giant paid a total of $224,000, although Small's book value was only $200,000 at the time. A building with a 10-year life was undervalued on Small's accounting records by $10,000. Any other excess amount was attributed to a copyright with a 20-year life. Under each of the following, what is the consolidated net income for 2002 after reduction is made for the noncontrolling interest's claims?
   a. Economic unit concept.
   b. Proportionate consolidation concept.
   c. Parent company theory.
4. How does the parent company concept merge the ideas put forth under the economic unit concept and proportionate consolidation?
5. Where should the noncontrolling interest's claims be reported in a consolidated set of financial statements?
6. How is the noncontrolling interest in a subsidiary company calculated as of the end of the current year?
7. Consolidated financial statements are being prepared by Sandridge Company and its consolidated subsidiary. Preacquisition income of $55,000 is presented within these statements. What does this Preacquisition Income account represent? How was the amount computed?
8. Tree, Inc., has held a 10 percent interest in the stock of Limb Company for several years. Because of the level of ownership, this investment has been accounted for by means of the market value method. At the beginning of the current year, Tree acquires an additional 70 percent interest which provides the company with control over Limb. In preparing consolidated financial statements for this business combination, how is the previous 10 percent ownership interest accounted for by Tree?
9. Duke Corporation owns a 70 percent equity interest in UNCCH, a subsidiary corporation. During the current year, a portion of this stock is sold to an outside party. Before recording this transaction, Duke adjusts the book value of its investment account. What is the purpose of this adjustment?

10. In question 9, how would the parent record the sales transaction?
11. In question 9, how would the parent record the sales transaction if the economic unit concept is being used and control is retained?
12. In question 9, how would Duke account for the remainder of its investment subsequent to the sale of this partial interest?

INTERNET ASSIGNMENTS

Internet sites are time and date sensitive. It is the purpose of these exercises to have you explore the Internet. You may need to refer to the text's Web site at http://www.mhhe.com/hoyle6e to find the most up-to-date links for the Web sites listed in the Internet Assignments.

1. At the Wal-Mart Web site (www.wal-mart.com), find the 1999 annual report. Locate the description of the July 31, 1999, controlling interest acquisition of ASDA Group LLC (third largest retailer in the United Kingdom with 230 stores). Determine how Wal-Mart accounts for the minority interest in ASDA and how it accounts for the income of ASDA earned prior to the purchase date of its controlling interest.

2. At the Yahoo! Web site (www.yahoo.com) find a recent annual report. Locate, identify, and discuss the references to minority interests throughout the financial statements and footnotes.

3. At the Eastman Kodak Web site (www.kodak.com) search the annual report for the term *minority interest* and discover the way the minority interest is reported in the firm's balance sheet.

LIBRARY ASSIGNMENTS

1. Read the following articles and any others that might be available discussing the method of accounting for a noncontrolling interest:

"Response to the FASB Exposure Draft: *Proposed Statement of Financial Accounting Standards—Consolidated Financial Statements: Policy and Procedures,*" *Accounting Horizons,* September 1996.

"FASB Proposes Significant Changes in Consolidation Policies and Procedures," *Ohio CPA Journal,* April 1996.

"FASB Presents View on Consolidated Statements," *Journal of Accountancy,* November 1994.

"Consolidated Financial Statements—Understanding Their Theories," *The Woman CPA,* April 1984.

"Proportionate Consolidation and Financial Analysis," *Accounting Horizons,* December 1992.

"Minority Interest: Opposing Views," *Journal of Accountancy,* March 1986.

Prepare a report to justify the selection of one particular concept of consolidated values where a noncontrolling interest is present as well as a preferred placement for the balances reported for the noncontrolling interest.

2. Obtain the latest financial statements for the Atlantic Richfield Corporation, Sara Lee Corporation, or any other company reporting a noncontrolling interest. Indicate the placement of both the balance sheet and the income statement figures. Describe the information conveyed about the noncontrolling interest within the reporting company's notes to its financial statements.

PROBLEMS

Note: Unless otherwise stated, assume that the parent company concept is being used.

1. Bailey, Inc., buys 60 percent of the outstanding stock of Luebs, Inc., in a purchase that resulted in the recognition of goodwill. Luebs owns a piece of land that cost $200,000 but was worth $500,000 at the date of purchase. For each of the three concepts described in this chapter, what value would be attributed to this land in a consolidated balance sheet at the date of takeover?

	Economic Unit Concept	Proportionate Consolidation	Parent Company Concept
a.	$500,000	$300,000	$500,000
b.	$200,000	$120,000	$500,000
c.	$200,000	$120,000	$380,000
d.	$500,000	$300,000	$380,000

2. Jordan, Inc., holds 75 percent of the outstanding stock of Paxson Corporation. Paxson currently owes Jordan $400,000 for inventory acquired over the past few months. In preparing consolidated financial statements, what amount of this debt should be eliminated?
   a. $0
   b. $100,000
   c. $300,000
   d. $400,000

3. On January 1, 2002, Brendan, Inc., reports net assets of $760,000 although equipment (with a four-year life) having a book value of $440,000 is worth $500,000 and an unrecorded patent is valued at $45,000. Hope Corporation pays $692,000 on that date for an 80 percent ownership in Brendan. If the patent is to be written off over a 10-year period, at what amount should the patent be reported on consolidated statements at December 31, 2003?
   a. $20,800
   b. $28,800
   c. $34,200
   d. $67,200

4. On January 1, 2001, Turner Inc., reports net assets of $480,000 although a building (with a 10-year life) having a book value of $260,000 is now worth $310,000. Plaster Corporation pays $400,000 on that date for a 70 percent ownership in Turner. On December 31, 2003, Turner reports a Building account of $245,000 while Plaster reports a Building account of $510,000. What is the consolidated balance of the Building account?
   a. $779,500
   b. $783,500
   c. $790,000
   d. $805,000

5. On January 1, 2002, Hygille, Inc., reports net assets of $880,000 although a building (with a 10-year life) having a book value of $330,000 is now worth $400,000. Nuyt Corporation pays $840,000 on that date for an 80 percent ownership in Hygille. On December 31, 2004, Hygille reports total expenses of $621,000 while Nuyt reports expenses of $714,000. What is the consolidated total expense balance?
   a. $1,335,000
   b. $1,339,000
   c. $1,345,300
   d. $1,340,600

6. On January 1, 2001, Chamberlain Corporation pays $388,000 for a 60 percent ownership in Neville. Annual excess amortization of $8,800 results from the purchase. On December 31, 2003, Neville reports revenues of $400,000 and expenses of $300,000 while Chamberlain reports revenues of $700,000 and expenses of $400,000. The parent figures contain no income from the subsidiary. What is consolidated net income?
   a. $349,600
   b. $351,200
   c. $360,000
   d. $391,200

7. What is a basic premise of the economic unit concept?
   a. Consolidated financial statements should be primarily for the benefit of the stockholders of the parent company.
   b. Consolidated financial statements should be produced only if both the parent and the subsidiary are in the same basic industry.
   c. A subsidiary is an indivisible part of a business combination and should be included in whole regardless of the degree of ownership.
   d. Consolidated financial statements should not report a noncontrolling interest balance since these outside owners do not hold stock in the parent company.

8. A preacquisition income account
   a. Is an adjustment to retained earnings when a pooling of interests is created.
   b. Is a reduction in consolidated net income that allows a subsidiary's revenues and expenses to be reported for the entire year even though acquisition took place during the current year.
   c. Is an income figure that requires the parent to pay an additional amount to create a business combination.
   d. Is the balance in a subsidiary's retained earnings account on the date that a business combination is created.

9. Ames, Inc., has a book value of $400,000 on January 1, 2002, and $550,000 on January 1, 2004. On both dates, the book value of the company's assets and liabilities were the same as fair market value. Hitchcock Corporation acquires 30 percent of Ames on January 1, 2002, for $160,000 in cash. Hitchcock purchases an additional 40 percent of Ames on January 1, 2004, for $240,000. On a consolidated balance sheet as of December 31, 2004, what amount of goodwill is reported?
   a. $60,000
   b. $54,000
   c. $53,000
   d. $52,000

10. A parent buys 32 percent of a subsidiary in 2000 and then buys an additional 40 percent in 2002. In a step acquisition of this type, how does the economic unit concept differ from the parent company concept?
    a. In using the economic unit concept, all subsequent purchases are valued based on the implied value at the time of the first acquisition.
    b. In using the economic unit concept, the two purchases are recorded as separate acquisitions with their own allocations and goodwill.
    c. In using the economic unit concept, the first purchase is adjusted to its implied value based on the acquisition price of the second transaction with a resulting gain or loss being recorded.
    d. The economic unit concept views each company as a whole and, thus, cannot be applied unless 100 percent of the subsidiary's stock is held.

11. On April 1, 2002, Guns, Inc., purchases 70 percent of the outstanding stock of Roses Corporation for $430,000. The subsidiary's book value on that date was $500,000. Any excess cost was attributable to goodwill. During 2002, Roses generates revenues of $600,000 and expenses of $360,000. Both figures occur evenly throughout the year. On a December 31, 2002 consolidated income statement, what should be reported as the noncontrolling interest in the subsidiary's net income and as preacquisition income?
    a. $72,000 and $42,000.
    b. $70,800 and $60,000.
    c. $70,800 and $41,000.
    d. $72,000 and $41,300.

Use the following information for Problems 12 through 14:

David Company acquired 60 percent of Mark Company for $300,000 when Mark's book value was $400,000. On that date, Mark had equipment (with a 10-year life) that was undervalued in the financial records by $60,000. Also, buildings (with a 20-year life) were undervalued by $40,000. Two years later, the following figures are reported by these two companies (stockholders' equity accounts have been omitted).

	David Company Book Value	Mark Company Book Value	Mark Company Fair Market Value
Current assets	$ 620,000	$ 300,000	$ 320,000
Equipment	260,000	200,000	280,000
Buildings	410,000	150,000	150,000
Liabilities	(390,000)	(120,000)	(120,000)
Revenues	(900,000)	(400,000)	
Expenses	500,000	300,000	
Investment income	not given		

12. What is consolidated net income prior to the reduction for the noncontrolling interest's share of the subsidiary's income?
    a. $455,200
    b. $494,000
    c. $497,000
    d. $495,200

13. What is the noncontrolling interest's share of the subsidiary's income and what is the ending balance of the noncontrolling interest in the subsidiary?
    a. $42,000 and $252,000.
    b. $40,000 and $212,000.
    c. $38,080 and $208,160.
    d. $35,200 and $207,200.

14. What is the consolidated balance of the Equipment account?
    a. $488,800
    b. $498,400
    c. $500,800
    d. $508,000

Use the following information for Problems 15 through 19:

On January 1, 2003, Polk Corporation and Strass Corporation had condensed balance sheets as follows:

	Polk	Strass
Current assets	$ 70,000	$20,000
Noncurrent assets	90,000	40,000
Total assets	$160,000	$60,000
Current liabilities	$ 30,000	$10,000
Long-term debt	50,000	—
Stockholders' equity	80,000	50,000
Total liabilities and equities	$160,000	$60,000

On January 2, 2003, Polk borrowed $60,000 and used the proceeds to purchase 90 percent of the outstanding common shares of Strass. This debt is payable in 10 equal annual principal payments, plus interest, beginning December 31, 2003. The excess cost of the investment over the underlying book value of the acquired net assets is allocated to inventory (60 percent) and to goodwill (40 percent). On a consolidated balance sheet as of January 2, 2003,

15. Current assets should be:
    a. $99,000
    b. $96,000
    c. $90,000
    d. $79,000

16. Noncurrent assets should be:
    a. $130,000
    b. $134,000
    c. $136,000
    d. $140,000

17. Current liabilities should be:
    a. $50,000
    b. $46,000
    c. $40,000
    d. $30,000

18. Noncurrent liabilities, including noncontrolling interest, should be:
    a. $115,000
    b. $109,000
    c. $104,000
    d. $55,000

19. Stockholders' equity should be:
    a. $80,000
    b. $85,000
    c. $90,000
    d. $130,000

    (AICPA adapted)

20. On January 1, 2002, Harrison, Inc., purchased 90 percent of Starr Company. Annual amortization of $8,000 resulted from this transaction. Starr Company reported a Common Stock account of $100,000 and Retained Earnings of $200,000 at that date. The subsidiary earned $70,000 in 2002 and $90,000 in 2003 with dividend payments of $30,000 each year. Without regard for this investment, Harrison had income of $220,000 in 2002 and $260,000 in 2003.
    a. What is consolidated net income in each of these two years?
    b. What is the ending noncontrolling interest balance as of December 31, 2003?

21. Pistol, Inc., purchases 70 percent of Bytvl Company for $406,000. On that date, Bytvl had the following accounts:

	Book Value	**Fair Market Value**
Current assets	$210,000	$210,000
Land	170,000	180,000
Buildings	300,000	330,000
Liabilities	280,000	280,000

The buildings have a 10-year life. In addition, Bytvl holds a patent worth $140,000 that has a five-year life but is not recorded on its financial records.
    a. Assume that the purchase took place on January 1, 2002. At the end of 2002, the two companies report the following balances:

	Pistol	**Bytvl**
Revenues	$900,000	$600,000
Expenses	600,000	400,000

What figures would appear in a consolidated income statement for this year?
    b. Assume that the purchase took place on April 1, 2002. At the end of 2002, the two companies report the following balances:

	Pistol	**Bytvl**
Revenues	$760,000	$590,000
Expenses	540,000	380,000

What figures would appear in a consolidated income statement for this year?

22. On January 1, 2002, Alva Company has one asset, an invention with a cost of $10,000. The asset has an estimated life of 10 years and a fair market value of $50,000. Menlo, Inc., buys 60 percent of the outstanding stock of Alva on that date for $42,000.

    During 2002, Alva generates revenues of $50,000 and expenses of $20,000.

Required:

For each of the following, determine the amounts included in the 2002 consolidated financial statements for Alva's revenues, expenses (plus amortization, if applicable), noncontrolling interest in the subsidiary's income, goodwill, and the invention:

   a. Economic unit concept.
   b. Proportionate consolidation.
   c. Parent company concept.

23. Mabry, Inc., purchases 60 percent of Thompson Corporation on August 1, 2001, and an additional 30 percent on October 1, 2002. Annual amortization of $6,000 relates to the first acquisition and $10,000 to the second. Thompson reports the following figures for 2002:

Revenues	$600,000
Expenses	420,000
Retained earnings, 1/1/02	540,000
Dividends paid	70,000
Common stock	310,000

    Without regard for this investment, Mabry earns $360,000 in net income during 2002.
    a. What is consolidated net income for 2002?
    b. What is the noncontrolling interest as of December 31, 2002?

24. Clark Corporation acquired 50 percent of Lamp, Inc., several years ago and an additional 30 percent on April 1 of the current year. An excess cost allocation to equipment of $60,000 was computed in connection with the first acquisition, and that amount is being amortized over a 20-year life. No excess amortizations resulted from the second acquisition. The following figures are reported by these two companies for the current year. Investment income is not included within the balances for Clark shown here. Income is assumed to have been earned evenly throughout the year, and no dividends were paid.

	Clark Corporation	Lamp, Inc.
Revenues	$600,000	$500,000
Expenses	380,000	300,000

    a. What is the noncontrolling interest's share of the subsidiary's net income?
    b. What is the amount of preacquisition income?
    c. What is the consolidated net income for these two companies?

25. Wilson Company acquired 7,000 of the 10,000 outstanding shares of Green Company on January 1, 1998, for $800,000. The subsidiary's book value on that date was $1,000,000. Any cost of this purchase in excess of Green's book value was assigned to a patent with a 10-year life. On January 1, 2002, Wilson reported a $1,085,000 balance in the Investment in Green Company account based on application of the partial equity method. On October 1, 2002, Wilson sells 1,000 shares of the investment for $191,000. During 2002, Green reported net income of $120,000 and paid dividends of $40,000. These amounts are assumed to have been incurred evenly throughout the year.
    a. How are the 1,000 shares reported for the period from January 1, 2002, until October 1, 2002?
    b. What is the effect on net income of this sale of 1,000 shares?
    c. What accounting is now made of the 6,000 shares that Wilson continues to hold?

26. Robert Palmer and Anita Blackwood are the sole owners of Quinn Corporation. Palmer holds 70 percent of the stock while Blackwood owns the remaining 30 percent. On January 1, 2002, Quinn reports $10,000 in common stock and $90,000 in retained earnings. During each month of 2002, the company earns $15,000 in net income. Dividends of $5,000 are paid every month. At the end of the year, Quinn's net income is

$180,000 (revenues of $400,000 less $220,000 in expenses), while $60,000 in dividends have been paid.

The book value of Quinn Corporation on December 1, 2002, is $210,000 ($100,000 beginning balance plus $10,000 growth for 11 months). On that date, Brown, Inc., buys all of Palmer's interest. Blackwood retains her 30 percent share of the company's stock. Brown pays exactly book value for these shares ($147,000, or 70 percent of $210,000). The individual fair market values of Quinn's assets and liabilities are equal to their book values.

Brown, Inc., is currently preparing consolidated financial statements for the year ending December 31, 2002.

a. What amount of Quinn's revenues would be included in the consolidated income statement?
b. What balance should be reported as the noncontrolling interest in Quinn's net income? Who is the noncontrolling interest?
c. For consolidation purposes, what happens to the $3,500 per month in dividends that Palmer received for the first 11 months of the year?
d. What amount of preacquisition income should be reported for consolidation purposes? Where is this figure disclosed? To whom does this income accrue?
e. Prepare the worksheet entry to eliminate the subsidiary's stockholders' equity. Assume Brown uses the cost method to account for its investment in Quinn.

27. Narcissus acquired 80 percent of the outstanding stock of Goldmund for $156,000. Just prior to this purchase, the following information is gathered from the two companies:

	Narcissus Book Value	Goldmund Book Value	Goldmund Fair Market Value
Current assets	$500,000	$150,000	$150,000
Land	100,000	30,000	40,000
Buildings and equipment (net)	600,000	160,000	180,000
Liabilities	300,000	200,000	200,000
Common stock	400,000	40,000	
Retained earnings	500,000	100,000	

The buildings and equipment have a 10-year remaining life; any goodwill is assumed to have an indefinite life.

Subsequently, on December 31, 2003, the two companies are reporting the following account balances. Fair market values are presented where applicable.

	Narcissus Book Value	Goldmund Book Value	Goldmund Fair Market Value
Current assets	$300,000	$90,000	$90,000
Investment in Goldmund	156,000	–0–	–0–
Land	150,000	60,000	74,000
Buildings and equipment (net)	570,000	180,000	216,000
Liabilities	246,000	185,000	185,000
Common stock	400,000	40,000	
Retained earnings, 1/1/03	470,000	95,000	
Revenues	300,000	100,000	
Expenses	200,000	90,000	
Dividends paid	40,000	–0–	

Required:

a. On consolidated financial statements as of the date of acquisition, what balances are reported for the Buildings and Equipment account and the Goodwill account?
b. Assume that the purchase was made on January 1, 1999. What would be the consolidated Buildings and Equipment balance on December 31, 2003?
c. Assume that the purchase was made during 2002. What is the consolidated net income for 2003 before subtracting the noncontrolling interest's share of the subsidiary's income?

    d. Assume that the purchase was made during 2001. What is the noncontrolling interest's share of the subsidiary's income for the year ending December 31, 2003?

    e. Assume that the purchase was made on July 1, 2003. Prepare a consolidated income statement for the year ending December 31, 2003.

    f. Assume that the purchase was made on January 1, 2002. On October 1, 2003, Narcissus sells one-fourth of these shares for $82,000 in cash. What income effects appear on the consolidated income statement for 2003?

28. On January 1, 2002, Thacker purchases 70 percent of Barker for $410,000 cash. The new subsidiary reported common stock on that date of $300,000, with retained earnings of $180,000. A building was undervalued in the company's financial records by $20,000. This building had a 10-year remaining life. Goodwill of $60,000 was recognized.

    Barker earns income and pays cash dividends as follows:

Year	Net Income	Dividends Paid
2002	$ 75,000	$39,000
2003	96,000	44,000
2004	110,000	60,000

On December 31, 2004, Thacker owes $22,000 to Barker.

    a. If the equity method has been applied by Thacker, what are the consolidation entries needed as of December 31, 2004?

    b. If the cost method has been applied by Thacker, what Entry *C is needed for a 2004 consolidation?

    c. If the partial equity method has been applied by Thacker, what Entry *C is needed for a 2004 consolidation?

    d. What noncontrolling interest balances will appear in consolidated financial statements for 2004?

29. The Hearts Company acquired an 80 percent interest in Dylan Company as of January 1, 2002. Hearts paid $620,000 to the owners of Dylan to purchase these shares. In addition, Hearts paid several lawyers and merger analysts $44,000 for assisting in the acquisition.

    On January 1, 2002, Dylan reported a book value of $600,000 (common stock—$300,000; additional paid-in capital—$90,000; retained earnings—$210,000). Several of Dylan's buildings were undervalued by a total of $80,000. These buildings had a remaining life of 20 years. Any goodwill resulting from the takeover was assumed to have an indefinite life.

    During the 2002–04 time period, Dylan reported the following figures:

Year	Net Income	Dividends Paid
2002	$ 70,000	$10,000
2003	90,000	15,000
2004	100,000	20,000

Required:

Determine the appropriate answers for each of the following questions:

    a. What amount of amortization expense would be recognized in the consolidated financial statements for the initial years following this purchase?

    b. If a consolidated balance sheet is prepared as of January 1, 2002, what amount of goodwill would be recognized?

    c. If a consolidation worksheet is prepared as of January 1, 2002, what Entry S should be included?

    d. On the separate financial records of the parent company, what amount of investment income would be reported for 2002 under each of the following accounting methods:

        (1) The equity method.

        (2) The partial equity method.

        (3) The cost method.

    e. On the separate financial records of the parent company, what would be the December 31, 2004, balance for the Investment in Dylan Company account under each of the following accounting methods:

(1) The equity method.

(2) The partial equity method.

(3) The cost method.

f. As of December 31, 2003, Hearts has a Buildings account on its separate records with a balance of $800,000 while Dylan has a similar account with a $300,000 balance. What would be the consolidated balance for the Buildings account? What would be the balance if the economic unit concept was used?

g. What would be the balance of consolidated goodwill as of December 31, 2004?

h. Assume that the parent company has been applying the equity method to this investment. On December 31, 2004, the separate financial statements for the two companies present the following information:

	Hearts Company	Dylan Company
Common stock	$500,000	$300,000
Additional paid-in capital	280,000	90,000
Retained earnings, 12/31/04	620,000	425,000

What will be the consolidated balance of each of these accounts?

30. Following are several of the account balances taken from the records of Bigston and Lytle as of December 31, 2002. A few asset accounts have been omitted here. All revenues, expenses, and dividends occurred evenly throughout the year. Any goodwill is assumed to have an indefinite life.

	Bigston	Lytle
Sales	$ 800,000	$500,000
Cost of goods sold	400,000	280,000
Expenses	200,000	100,000
Investment income	not given	–0–
Retained earnings, 1/1/02	1,400,000	700,000
Dividends	80,000	20,000
Land	600,000	200,000
Buildings (net)	700,000	300,000
Equipment (net)	400,000	400,000
Liabilities	500,000	200,000
Common stock ($10 par value)	400,000	100,000
Additional paid-in capital	500,000	600,000

On July 1, 2002, Bigston purchased 80 percent of Lytle for $1,300,000 in cash. In addition, Big paid $30,000 in direct consolidation costs. At that time, Lytle's buildings (with a 10-year life) were undervalued on its books by $100,000. On a consolidation prepared at the end of 2002, what balances would be reported for the following:

Preacquisition Income	Net Income
Sales	Retained Earnings, 1/1/02
Expenses	Buildings (Net)
Noncontrolling Interest in	Land
Subsidiary's Net Income	Goodwill

31. Monroe, Inc., acquires 60 percent of Sunrise Corporation for $414,000 cash on January 1, 2001. On that date, Sunrise had the following accounts:

	Book Value	Fair Market Value
Current assets	$150,000	$150,000
Land	200,000	200,000
Buildings (net) (6-year life)	300,000	360,000
Equipment (net) (4-year life)	300,000	280,000
Patent (10-year life)	–0–	100,000
Liabilities	400,000	400,000

The companies' financial statements for the year ending December 31, 2004, follow. Determine all consolidated balances.

	Monroe	Sunrise
Revenues	$ 600,000	$ 300,000
Operating expenses	410,000	210,000
Investment income	42,000	
Net income	$ 232,000	$ 90,000
Retained earnings, 1/1/04	$ 700,000	$ 300,000
Net income	232,000	90,000
Dividends paid	92,000	70,000
Retained earnings, 12/31/04	$ 840,000	$ 320,000
Current assets	$ 330,000	$ 100,000
Land	220,000	200,000
Buildings (net)	700,000	200,000
Equipment (net)	400,000	500,000
Investment in Sunrise	414,000	–0–
Total assets	$2,064,000	$1,000,000
Liabilities	$ 500,000	$ 200,000
Common stock	724,000	480,000
Retained earnings, 12/31/04	840,000	320,000
Total liabilities and equities	$2,064,000	$1,000,000

Answer the following questions:

a. How can the accountant determine that the cost method has been applied by the parent?

b. What is the annual excess amortization initially recognized in connection with this purchase?

c. If the partial equity method had been applied, what Investment Income would have been recorded by the parent in 2004? What if the equity method had been applied?

d. What is the consolidated balance for retained earnings as of January 1, 2004?

e. What is the noncontrolling interest in the subsidiary's 2004 income?

f. What is consolidated net income for 2004?

g. Within consolidated statements at January 1, 2001, what balance is included for the subsidiary's Buildings account?

h. What is the consolidated Buildings account as of December 31, 2004?

32. Father, Inc., buys 80 percent of the outstanding common stock of Sam Corporation on January 1, 2002, for $680,000 cash. Total book value of Sam on that date was only $600,000. However, Sam possessed several accounts that had fair market values differing from their book values:

	Book Value	Fair Market Value
Land	$ 60,000	$225,000
Buildings and equipment (10-year remaining life)	275,000	250,000
Copyright (20-year life)	100,000	200,000
Notes payable (due in 8 years)	130,000	120,000

For internal reporting purposes, Father, Inc., employs the equity method to account for this investment.

The following account balances are for the year ending December 31, 2002, for both companies. Determine consolidated balances for this business combination (either through individual computations or the use of a worksheet).

	Father	Sam
Revenues	$(1,360,000)	$(540,000)
Cost of goods sold	700,000	385,000
Depreciation expense	260,000	10,000
Amortization expense	–0–	5,000
Interest expense	44,000	5,000
Equity in income of Sam	(105,000)	–0–
Net income	$ (461,000)	$(135,000)
Retained earnings, 1/1/02	$(1,265,000)	$(440,000)
Net income (above)	(461,000)	(135,000)
Dividends paid	260,000	65,000
Retained earnings, 12/31/02	$(1,466,000)	$(510,000)
Current assets	$ 965,000	$ 528,000
Investment in Sam	733,000	–0–
Land	292,000	60,000
Buildings and equipment (net)	877,000	265,000
Copyright	–0–	95,000
Total assets	$ 2,867,000	$ 948,000
Accounts payable	$ (191,000)	$(148,000)
Notes payable	(460,000)	(130,000)
Common stock	(300,000)	(100,000)
Additional paid-in capital	(450,000)	(60,000)
Retained earnings (above)	(1,466,000)	(510,000)
Total liabilities and equities	$(2,867,000)	$(948,000)

Note: Credits are indicated by parentheses.

33. Answer problem 32 again, this time using the economic unit concept.

34. Burke Corporation purchased 90 percent of the outstanding voting shares of Drexel, Inc., on December 31, 2002. Burke paid a total of $602,000 in cash for these shares. As of that date, Drexel had the following account balances:

	Book Value	Fair Market Value
Current assets	$160,000	$160,000
Land	120,000	150,000
Buildings (10-year life)	220,000	200,000
Equipment (5-year life)	160,000	200,000
Patents (10-year life)	–0–	50,000
Liabilities (5-year life)	200,000	180,000
Common stock	180,000	
Retained earnings, 12/31/02	280,000	

December 31, 2004, adjusted trial balances for the two companies follow:

	Burke Corporation	Drexel, Inc.
Debits		
Current assets	$ 611,000	$ 250,000
Land	380,000	150,000
Buildings	490,000	250,000
Equipment	873,000	150,000
Investment in Drexel, Inc.	701,000	–0–
Cost of goods sold	500,000	100,000
Depreciation expense	100,000	55,000
Interest expense	20,000	5,000
Dividends paid	110,000	70,000
Total debits	$3,785,000	$1,030,000

(continued)

	Burke Corporation	Drexel, Inc.
Credits		
Liabilities	$ 860,000	$ 230,000
Common stock	510,000	180,000
Retained earnings, 1/1/04	1,367,000	340,000
Revenues	940,000	280,000
Investment income	108,000	–0–
Total credits	$3,785,000	$1,030,000

Required:

a. Without using a worksheet or consolidation entries, determine the balances to be reported as of December 31, 2004, for this business combination. Any goodwill is not amortized.

b. To verify the figures determined in requirement (a), prepare a consolidation worksheet for Burke Corporation and Drexel, Inc., as of December 31, 2004.

35. Using the information presented in problem 34, produce a worksheet to consolidate the financial statements of Burke and Drexel incorporating the economic unit concept rather than the parent company concept.

36. Following are the individual financial statements for Up and Down for the year ending December 31, 2002:

	Up	Down
Sales	$ 600,000	$ 300,000
Cost of goods sold	300,000	140,000
Operating expenses	174,000	60,000
Dividend income	24,000	–0–
Net income	$ 150,000	$ 100,000
Retained earnings, 1/1/02	$ 700,000	$ 400,000
Net income	150,000	100,000
Dividends paid	80,000	40,000
Retained earnings, 12/31/02	$ 770,000	$ 460,000
Cash and receivables	$ 250,000	$ 100,000
Inventory	500,000	190,000
Investment in Down	526,000	–0–
Buildings (net)	524,000	600,000
Equipment (net)	400,000	400,000
Total assets	$2,200,000	$1,290,000
Liabilities	800,000	490,000
Common stock	630,000	340,000
Retained earnings, 12/31/02	770,000	460,000
Totals liabilities and stockholders' equity	$2,200,000	$1,290,000

Up acquired 60 percent of Down on April 1, 2002, for $526,000. On that date, equipment (with a six-year life) was overvalued by $30,000. Goodwill is not amortized. Income is earned by Down evenly during the year but the dividend was paid entirely on November 1, 2002.

Required:

a. Prepare a consolidated income statement for the year ending December 31, 2002.

b. Determine the consolidated balance for each of the following accounts as of December 31, 2002:

Goodwill	Buildings (net)
Equipment (net)	Dividends Paid
Common Stock	

37. Bon Air, Inc., acquired 70 percent (2,800 shares) of the outstanding voting stock of Creedmoor Corporation on January 1, 2002, for $250,000 cash. Creedmoor's net assets on that date totaled $230,000, but this balance included three accounts having actual values that differed from their book values:

	Book Value	Fair Market Value
Land	$30,000	$40,000
Equipment (14-year life)	50,000	118,000
Liabilities (10-year life)	70,000	50,000

Any goodwill created by this combination will not be amortized.

As of December 31, 2005, the two companies report the following balances:

	Bon Air	Creedmoor
Revenues	$ 694,800	$250,000
Operating expenses	(630,000)	(180,000)
Investment income	44,200	–0–
Net income	$ 109,000	$ 70,000
Retained earnings, 1/1/05	$ 760,000	$260,000
Net income	109,000	70,000
Dividends paid	(68,000)	(10,000)
Retained earnings, 12/31/05	$ 801,000	$320,000
Current assets	$ 72,000	$120,000
Investment in Creedmoor Corp.	321,800	–0–
Land	241,000	50,000
Buildings (net)	289,000	200,000
Equipment (net)	165,200	40,000
Total assets	$1,089,000	$410,000
Liabilities	$ 180,000	$ 50,000
Common stock	50,000	40,000
Additional paid-in capital	58,000	–0–
Retained earnings, 12/31/05	801,000	320,000
Total liabilities and equities	$1,089,000	$410,000

Required:

(Each of the following are independent questions.)

a. Consolidated financial statements are being prepared on December 31, 2005. What balance should be reported for each of the following figures?

> Operating expenses
> Noncontrolling interest in Creedmoor's net income
> Revenues
> Retained earnings, 1/1/05
> Net income
> Dividends paid
> Land
> Equipment
> Liabilities
> Common stock
> Retained earnings, 12/31/05
> Noncontrolling interest in Creedmoor, 12/31/05

b. If Bon Air sells 400 shares of this stock on December 31, 2005, for $60,000 cash, what journal entry is recorded?

38. The Seals Corporation purchased 80 percent of the outstanding stock of Croft, Inc., for $384,000. An appraisal of Croft made on that date determined that all book values appropriately reflected the actual worth of the underlying accounts except that a building with a 10-year life was undervalued by $20,000 and a fully amortized trademark with an estimated 20-year remaining life had an $80,000 fair value.

Following are the separate financial statements for the year ending December 31, 2002. Croft's income is assumed to have been earned evenly throughout the year. In addition, the subsidiary's dividend payments have been made as four equal quarterly payments. Seals has inappropriately included the receipt of dividends in its Sales account rather than a separate Dividend Income account.

	Seals Corporation	Croft, Inc.
Sales	$ 600,000	$210,000
Cost of goods sold	(200,000)	(80,000)
Operating expenses	(246,000)	(70,000)
Dividend income	–0–	–0–
Net income	$ 154,000	$ 60,000
Retained earnings, 1/1/02	$ 700,000	$280,000
Net income (above)	154,000	60,000
Dividends paid	(70,000)	(20,000)
Retained earnings, 12/31/02	$ 784,000	$320,000
Current assets	$ 400,000	$220,000
Investment in Croft, Inc.	384,000	–0–
Buildings (net)	320,000	180,000
Equipment (net)	360,000	210,000
Total assets	$1,464,000	$610,000
Liabilities	$ 470,000	$190,000
Common stock	210,000	100,000
Retained earnings, 12/31/02 (above)	784,000	320,000
Total liabilities and equities	$1,464,000	$610,000

Required:

a. Prepare a worksheet to consolidate these two companies on the assumption that the purchase was made on January 1, 2002.

b. Without using a worksheet determine consolidated totals for these two companies on the assumption that the purchase was made on October 1, 2002, for $408,000.

39. Watson, Inc., acquires 60 percent of Houston, Inc., on January 1, 2002, for $400,000 in cash. On that date, assets and liabilities of the subsidiary had the following values:

	Book Value	Fair Market Value
Current assets	$320,000	$320,000
Equipment (net)(10-year life)	410,000	380,000
Buildings (net)(15-year life)	300,000	455,000
Current liabilities	190,000	190,000
Bonds payable (due in 10 years)	370,000	350,000

On December 31, 2005, these two companies report the following figures:

	Watson	Houston
Revenues	$ 640,000	$ 280,000
Operating expenses	(480,000)	(210,000)
Equity in subsidiary earnings	36,400	–0–
Net income	$ 196,400	$ 70,000
Retained earnings, 1/1/05	$ 683,400	$ 380,000
Net income	196,400	70,000
Dividends paid	(60,200)	(40,000)
Retained earnings, 12/31/05	$ 819,600	$ 410,000
Current assets	$ 215,000	$ 260,000
Investment in Houston	491,600	–0–
Equipment (net)	500,000	420,000
Buildings (net)	413,000	520,000
Total assets	$1,619,600	$1,200,000
Current liabilities	$ 390,000	$ 170,000
Bonds payable	100,000	370,000
Common stock	310,000	250,000
Retained earnings, 12/31/05	819,600	410,000
Total liabilities and equities	$1,619,600	$1,200,000

Answer each of the following questions:

a. The parent is recognizing a $36,400 balance as its "equity in subsidiary earnings." How was this balance calculated?

b. Is an adjustment needed to the parent's retained earnings as of January 1, 2005? Why or why not?

c. How much total amortization expense should be recognized for consolidation purposes in 2005?

d. What is the noncontrolling interest in the subsidiary's net income?

e. Prepare a consolidated income statement.

f. What allocations were made as a result of the purchase price? What amount of each allocation remains at the end of 2005?

g. What is the December 31, 2005, noncontrolling interest in the subsidiary? What three components make up this total?

h. Prepare a consolidated balance sheet.

40. Good Corporation acquired 80 percent of the outstanding stock of Morning, Inc., on January 1, 2002, for $1,400,000 in cash, debt, and stock. One of Morning's buildings, with a 10-year remaining life, was undervalued on the company's accounting records by $80,000. Also, Morning's newly developed unpatented technology, with an estimated 10-year life, was assessed to have a fair value of $550,000.

During subsequent years, Morning reports the following:

	Net Income	Dividends Paid
2002	$180,000	$100,000
2003	200,000	100,000
2004	300,000	100,000
2005	400,000	120,000

The following trial balances are for these two companies as of December 31, 2005. Morning owes Good $100,000 as of this date.

	Good	Morning
Debits		
Cash	$ 300,000	$ 200,000
Receivables	700,000	400,000
Inventory	400,000	500,000
Investment in Morning	1,400,000	–0–
Land	700,000	600,000
Buildings (net)	300,000	700,000
Operating expenses	400,000	100,000
Dividends paid	380,000	120,000
Total debits	$4,580,000	$2,620,000
Credits		
Liabilities	$ 200,000	$ 620,000
Common stock	1,000,000	460,000
Additional paid-in capital	600,000	40,000
Retained earnings, 1/1/05	1,800,000	1,000,000
Revenues	884,000	500,000
Dividend income	96,000	–0–
Total credits	$4,580,000	$2,620,000

Required:

Prepare consolidated financial statements for this business combination.

41. On January 1, 2002, Turner Company bought a 30 percent interest in Atlanta Company. The acquisition price was $257,000 and was negotiated under the assumption that all of Atlanta's accounts were fairly valued within the company's accounting records. Any remaining excess cost was assumed to be attributable to goodwill with an indefinite life.

   During 2002, Atlanta reported net income of $90,000 and paid cash dividends of $60,000. Turner felt that the ability to significantly influence the operations of Atlanta had been achieved and, therefore, accounted for this investment by means of the equity method.

   On April 1, 2003, Turner acquired an additional 30 percent interest in Atlanta for $309,000 in cash. As of this date, the parent believed that a patent developed by Atlanta was worth $100,000, even though it was not recorded within the financial records of the subsidiary. This patent is anticipated to have a remaining life of six years. Although the financial statements now have to be consolidated, Turner elects to continue applying the equity method to this investment for internal reporting purposes.

   The following financial information is for these two companies for 2003. In addition, all of the subsidiary's operations as well as dividend payments are considered to have occurred evenly throughout the year.

	Turner Company	Atlanta Company
Revenues	$ 660,000	$ 400,000
Operating expenses	(398,000)	(280,000)
Income of subsidiary	59,250	
Net income	$ 321,250	$ 120,000
Retained earnings, 1/1/03	$ 823,000	$ 500,000
Net income (above)	321,250	120,000
Cash dividends paid to stockholders	(148,000)	(80,000)
Retained earnings, ending balance	$ 996,250	$ 540,000
Current assets	$ 481,000	$ 410,000
Investment in subsidiary	592,250	
Land	388,000	200,000
Buildings	700,900	630,000
Total assets	$2,162,150	$1,240,000
Liabilities	$ 660,900	$ 380,000
Common stock	95,000	300,000
Additional paid-in capital	410,000	20,000
Retained earnings, 12/31/03	996,250	540,000
Total liabilities and equities	$2,162,150	$1,240,000

Answer the following questions:

a. What allocation would Turner have made of the initial $257,000 acquisition price?

b. What is the book value of the Investment in Atlanta account at the end of 2002?

c. What allocation would Turner have made of the second $309,000 acquisition price?

d. On Turner's separate income statement for 2003, the Income of Subsidiary account has a balance of $59,250. How was this amount derived?

e. On Turner's separate balance sheet as of December 31, 2003, the Investment in Subsidiary account reports a balance of $592,250. How was this balance derived?

f. What is the consolidated retained earnings balance as of January 1, 2003? How is this amount determined?

g. Prepare a worksheet to consolidate the financial statements of these two companies as of December 31, 2003.

42. On January 1, 2002, Ace, Incorporated, acquired 60 percent of the outstanding shares of Holt Company for $566,000 in cash. At the time of this purchase, Holt held a building (six-year remaining life) that was undervalued in the accounting records by $70,000. During 2002, Holt reported net income of $150,000 and paid cash dividends of $80,000. On May 1, 2003, Ace bought an additional 30 percent interest in Holt for $366,000. Ace reappraised Holt's assets and liabilities on this date and estimated that the company's buildings were currently undervalued by $260,000. At the time of this second purchase, these buildings had a five-year remaining life. Any goodwill was not to be amortized.

The following financial information is for these two companies for 2003. Holt issued no additional capital stock during either 2002 or 2003. Income and dividends can be assumed as having been earned and paid evenly throughout each of the years.

	Ace, Incorporated	Holt Company
Revenues	$ 400,000	$ 300,000
Operating expenses	(200,000)	(120,000)
Investment income (partial equity method)	144,000	
Net income	$ 344,000	$ 180,000
Retained earnings, 1/1/03	$ 800,000	$ 500,000
Net income (above)	344,000	180,000
Dividends paid	(144,000)	(60,000)
Retained earnings, 12/31/03	$1,000,000	$ 620,000
Current assets	$ 200,000	$ 190,000
Investment in Holt Company	1,070,000	
Land	100,000	600,000
Buildings (net)	210,000	300,000
Equipment (net)	380,000	110,000
Total assets	$1,960,000	$1,200,000
Liabilities	$ 500,000	$ 200,000
Common stock	400,000	300,000
Additional paid-in capital	60,000	80,000
Retained earnings, 12/31/03	1,000,000	620,000
Total liabilities and equities	$1,960,000	$1,200,000

Required:

Determine the appropriate balances for consolidated financial statements for Ace, Incorporated, and Holt Company for December 31, 2003, and the year then ended. Show supporting computations in good form.

43. On January 1, 1999, Wilbourne Company acquired 6,000 of the 10,000 outstanding shares of Hampton Corporation. The purchase price included an allocation of $120,000 for a customer base that was not reflected on Hampton's books. All other assets and liabilities of Hampton had fair market values equal to their book values. The customer base was to be amortized over a 20-year life.

On January 1, 2002, Wilbourne bought an additional 2,000 shares of Hampton, increasing ownership to an 80 percent interest. In making this second acquisition, Wilbourne assigned $40,000 of the purchase price to a patent (life of 10 years) held by Hampton. An additional $40,000 was attributed to Hampton's expanding customer base to be amortized at $2,000 per year.

In need of raising cash, Wilbourne sold 1,000 shares of its investment in Hampton on April 1, 2003, for $140,000 in cash. A problem arose in connection with the recording of this sale. Wilbourne's accountants could not agree on the appropriate gain or loss to be recognized so they simply debited cash for $140,000 and credited the Investment account for the same amount. Because of the confusion, Wilbourne prepared no other entries for the investment for the year of 2003, although the equity method had been properly applied prior to this time.

The following individual financial records are for these two companies for 2003. Prepare a consolidation worksheet and the resulting financial statements. Assume that an averaging system is used to determine the appropriate book value of the shares that were sold.

	Wilbourne Company	Hampton Corporation
Revenues	$ 920,000	$ 600,000
Expenses	(650,000)	(440,000)
Equity income of Hampton Corporation	–0–	–0–
Net income	$ 270,000	$ 160,000
Retained earnings, 1/1/03	$1,417,000	$ 750,000
Net income (above)	270,000	160,000
Dividends paid	(150,000)	–0–
Retained earnings, 12/31/03	$1,537,000	$ 910,000
Cash	$ 60,000	$ 98,000
Receivables	430,000	210,000
Inventories	677,000	620,000
Investment in Hampton Corporation	870,000	–0–
Buildings and equipment (net)	620,000	514,000
Patents (net)	40,000	90,000
Total assets	$2,697,000	$1,532,000
Liabilities	$ 690,000	$ 322,000
Common stock	470,000	300,000
Retained earnings, 12/31/03	1,537,000	910,000
Total liabilities and equities	$2,697,000	$1,532,000

COMPUTER PROJECT

A Comparison of Consolidated Financial Statements under the Economic Unit Concept and the Parent Company Concept

The purpose of this project is to assess the sensitivity of alternative concepts of non-controlling interest valuation on consolidated financial reporting. The project requires the use of a computer and a spreadsheet software package (Microsoft Excel, Lotus 123, etc.). The use of these tools allows assessment of the sensitivity of alternative accounting methods on consolidated financial reporting without the necessity of preparing several similar worksheets by hand. Also, by modeling a worksheet process, a better understanding of accounting for combined reporting entities may result.

The project involves preparing two consolidated worksheets for a parent and subsidiary. The first worksheet uses the economic unit concept for the consolidated entity. The second worksheet uses the parent company concept (most prevalent in current practice). Additional analysis is provided to assess the sensitivity of each approach to changes in the percentage of the subsidiary owned by the noncontrolling interest.

Project Scenario—On January 1, 2002, Pinter purchased a controlling interest in Strong, Inc., for $800,000. At that date Strong's book value was $600,000. Strong's assets and liabilities approximated their market values except for the following items:

	Market Value	Book Value
Land	$ 88,000	$100,000
Building (six-year remaining life)	170,000	140,000
Equipment (three-year remaining life) ...	370,000	325,000

Pinter accounts for its investment in Strong using the equity method. Strong declared a $25,000 dividend late in 2002. The dividend had not been paid as of December 31, 2002.

Pinter and Strong submit trial balances for consolidation as of December 31, 2002, as indicated in the accompanying worksheet template. Note that the trial balance for

Pinter reflects an 80 percent ownership of Strong. However, to provide insights regarding varying levels of outside ownership, the trial balance must be programmed so that this percentage can vary.

Instructions:

1. Input the information from the **worksheet template** into your spreadsheet as a starting point for two separate consolidation worksheets—one for the economic unit concept and one for the parent company concept. Use either separate worksheets available in Excel or Lotus, or use distinct areas of a single spreadsheet for each consolidation.

2. Designate a single cell as the percentage of Strong acquired by Pinter. Use this cell (e.g., B38 in the worksheet template) as a reference in other cell formulas. **Your worksheets should automatically change when different percentages are entered in this designated cell.**

3. On each worksheet, prepare separate cost allocation schedules using formulas to allow for alternative ownership percentages.

4. To accommodate alternative ownership percentages, the following accounts in Pinter's trial balances require formulas: Equity income of Strong, Dividend receivable, Investment in Strong, as well as the carrydown figures (income and retained earnings) and the totals. For example, in Excel, cell B17 in Pinter's trial balance can be entered as =C12*B38 so that it will change whenever cell B38 changes. No accounts in Strong's trial balances require formulas.

5. Complete the worksheet adjusting and eliminating entries, the noncontrolling interest amounts, and consolidated balances. Be sure to use formulas to enable the worksheets to automatically change when the percentage acquired is changed.

6. Prepare an accompanying written report that compares and explains the differences between the economic unit concept and parent company concept consolidated figures at 80 percent ownership. Describe the effects on the consolidated balances when 100 percent ownership exists. Indicate which concept you believe should be used in financial reporting and why.

Worksheet Template

	A	B	C	D	E	F	G
1	**December 31, 2002**					Noncontrolling	
2		**Pinter**	**Strong**	Adjustments & Eliminations		Interest	Consolidated
3	Revenues	$ (840,000)	$(740,000)				
4	Operating expenses	$ 690,000	$ 550,000				
5	Equity income of Strong	$ (136,000)					
6	Noncontrolling interest in Strong's income						
7	Net income	$ (286,000)	$(190,000)				
8							
9	Retained earnings—Pinter, 1/1/02	$ (775,000)					
10	Retained earnings—Strong, 1/1/02		$(350,000)				
11	Net income (above)	$ (286,000)	$(190,000)				
12	Dividends declared	$ 115,000	$ 25,000				
13	Retained earnings, 12/31/02	$ (946,000)	$(515,000)				
14							
15	Cash	$ 102,000	$ 32,000				
16	Accounts receivable	$ 96,000	$ 140,000				
17	Dividends receivable	$ 20,000					
18	Inventory	$ 225,000	$ 208,000				
19	Investment in Strong	$ 916,000					
20							
21							
22							
23	Land	$ 200,000	$ 100,000				
24	Buildings (net)	$ 550,000	$ 120,000				
25	Equipment (net)	$ 350,000	$ 310,000				
26	Goodwill						
27	Total assets	$ 2,459,000	$ 910,000				
28							
29	Dividends payable		$ (25,000)				
30	Liabilities	$ (513,000)	$(120,000)				
31	Common stock	$(1,000,000)	$(250,000)				
32	Noncontrolling interest						
33							
34							
35	Retained earnings (above)	$ (946,000)	$(515,000)				
36	Total liabilities and equity	$(2,459,000)	$(910,000)				
37							
38	**Percentage acquired**	**80%**					

Consolidated Financial Statements— Intercompany Asset Transactions

QUESTIONS TO CONSIDER

- How does the intercompany transfer of inventory or other assets between parent and subsidiary affect the consolidation process?

- Gains on intercompany transactions are considered unrealized until the assets are resold to outsiders or consumed. Prior to the realization of these gains, what adjustments are required in producing consolidated financial statements?

- How does the presence of intercompany transactions affect the balances reported for any noncontrolling interest? What impact does the direction of these transfers (upstream versus downstream) have on the reporting of a noncontrolling interest?

- The intercompany sale of land and depreciable assets also can occur between the members of a business combination. What impact does the specific type of property being conveyed have on the consolidation process?

- Why does the transfer of a depreciable asset frequently result in the recording of excess depreciation in subsequent years?

In Chapter 1, the deferral and subsequent recognition of gains created by inventory transfers between two affiliated companies is analyzed in connection with equity method accounting. The central theme of that discussion is that intercompany profits are not considered to be realized until the earning process is culminated by a sale to an unrelated party. This same accounting logic applies to transactions between companies within a business combination. Because a single economic entity is formed, such sales create neither profits nor losses. In reference to this issue, *ARB 51* (par. 7) states:

> As consolidated statements are based on the assumption that they represent the financial position and operating results of a single business enterprise, such statements should not include gain or loss on transactions among the companies in the group. Accordingly, any intercompany profit or loss on assets remaining within the group should be eliminated; the concept usually applied for this purpose is gross profit or loss.

The elimination of the accounting effects created by intercompany transactions is one of the most significant problems encountered in the consolidation process. The mere volume of transfers within most large enterprises can be staggering. The 1999 annual report for the Ford Motor Company shows the elimination of intersegment revenues amounting to over $22 billion!

Such transactions are especially common in companies that have been constructed as a vertically integrated chain of organizations. These entities reduce their costs by developing affiliations where one operation furnishes products to another. As observed by *Mergers & Acquisitions:*

Downstream acquisitions . . . are aimed at securing critical sources of materials and components, streamlining manufacturing and materials planning, gaining economies of scale, entering new markets, and enhancing overall competitiveness. Manufacturers that combine with suppliers are often able to assert total control over such critical areas as product quality and resource planning.[1]

Intercompany asset transactions take several forms. In particular, inventory transfers are especially prevalent. However, the sale of land as well as depreciable assets also can occur between the parties within a combination. This chapter examines the consolidation procedures necessitated by each of these different types of intercompany asset transfers.

INTERCOMPANY INVENTORY TRANSACTIONS

As discussed in previous chapters, companies that make up a business combination frequently retain their legal identities as separate operating centers and maintain their own record-keeping. Thus, any inventory sales between these companies trigger the independent accounting systems of both parties. Revenue is duly recorded by the seller, while the purchase is simultaneously entered into the accounts of the buyer. For internal reporting purposes, recording an inventory transfer as a sale/purchase provides vital data to help measure the operational efficiency of each enterprise.[2]

Despite the informational benefits of accounting for the transaction in this manner, from a consolidated perspective neither a sale nor a purchase has occurred. *An intercompany transfer is merely the internal movement of inventory, an event that creates no net change in the financial position of the business combination taken as a whole.* Thus, in producing consolidated financial statements, the recorded effects of these transfers are eliminated so that consolidated statements reflect only transactions with outside parties. Worksheet entries serve this purpose; they adapt the financial information reported by the separate companies to the perspective of the consolidated enterprise. The entire impact of the intercompany transactions must be identified and then removed. The deleting of the actual transfer is described here first.

The Sales and Purchases Accounts

To account for related companies as a single economic entity, all intercompany sales/purchases accounts are eliminated. For example, if Arlington Company makes an $80,000 inventory sale to Zirkin Company, an affiliated party within a business combination, both parties record the transfer as a normal sale/purchase. The following worksheet entry is then necessary to remove the resulting balances from the consolidated figures. Cost of Goods Sold is reduced here under the assumption that the Purchases account usually is closed out prior to the consolidation process.

Consolidation Entry TI

Sales	80,000	
Cost of Goods Sold (purchases component)		80,000
To eliminate effects of intercompany transfer of inventory.		
(Labeled "TI" in reference to the transferred inventory.)		

---

[1]"Acquiring along the Value Chain," *Mergers & Acquisitions,* June–July 1996, p. 8.

[2]For all intercompany transactions, the two parties involved view the events from different perspectives. Thus, the transfer is both a sale and a purchase, often creating both a receivable and a payable. To indicate the dual nature of such transactions, these accounts are indicated within this text as sales/purchases, receivables/payables, and so on.

In the preparation of consolidated financial statements, the preceding elimination must be made for all intercompany inventory transfers. The total recorded (intercompany) sales figure is deleted regardless of whether the transaction was downstream (from parent to subsidiary) or upstream (from subsidiary to parent).[3] Furthermore, the elimination is unaffected by any markup included in the transfer price. Because the entire amount of the transfer was between related parties, the total effect must be removed in preparing the consolidated statements.[4]

Unrealized Gains—Year of Transfer (Year One)

Removal of the sale/purchase is often just the first in a series of consolidation entries necessitated by inventory transfers. Despite the previous elimination, unrealized gains created by such sales may still exist in the accounting records at year's end. These gains initially result when the merchandise is priced at more than historical cost. Actual transfer prices are established in several ways, including the normal sales price of the inventory, sales price less a specified discount, or at a predetermined markup above cost. In a footnote to its recent financial statements, Ford Motor Company explains that

> Intercompany sales among geographic areas consist primarily of vehicles, parts, and components manufactured by the company and various subsidiaries and sold to different entities within the consolidated group; transfer prices for these transactions are established by agreement between the affected entities.

Regardless of the method used for this pricing decision, intercompany gains that remain unrealized at year-end must be removed in arriving at consolidated figures.

All Inventory Remains at Year-End   In the preceding illustration, assume that Arlington acquired or produced this inventory at a cost of $50,000 and then sold it to Zirkin, an affiliated party, at the indicated price of $80,000. From a consolidated perspective, the inventory still has a historical cost of only $50,000. However, it is now reported in Zirkin's records as an asset at the $80,000 transfer price. In addition, because of the markup, Arlington has recorded a $30,000 gross profit as a result of this intercompany sale. Because the transaction did not occur with an outside party, recognition of this profit is not appropriate for the combination as a whole.

Thus, although the sale/purchase figures are eliminated by consolidation entry TI shown earlier, the $30,000 inflation created by the transfer price still exists in two areas of the individual statements:

■ Ending inventory remains overstated by $30,000.
■ Gross profit is artificially overstated by this same amount.

Correction of the ending inventory only requires a reduction in the asset. However, before decreasing gross profit, the accounts affected by the unrealized gain must be identified. The ending inventory total serves as a negative component within the Cost of Goods Sold computation; it represents the portion of acquired inventory that was not sold. Thus, the $30,000 overstatement of the inventory that is still held incorrectly lowers this expense (the inventory that was sold). *Despite Entry TI, the inflated ending inventory figure causes cost of goods sold to be too low and, thus, profits to be too high*

---

[3]Downstream and upstream transactions were introduced in Chapter 1. Although the direction of the transfer did not influence the equity method of accounting (for external reporting), the distinction is significant in the preparation of consolidated statements.

[4]As is shown in the appendix to this chapter, alternative theoretical approaches to consolidation that advocate removing only the parent's portion of intercompany sales/purchases when a noncontrolling interest is present can be identified. In current practice, elimination of all intercompany sales/purchases (as shown here) appears to predominate.

by $30,000. For consolidation purposes, the expense must be raised by this amount, through a worksheet adjustment that properly removes the unrealized gain from consolidated net income.

Consequently, if all of the transferred inventory is retained by the business combination at the end of the year, the following worksheet entry also has to be included to eliminate the effects of the gain that remains unrealized within ending inventory.

Consolidation Entry G—Year of Transfer (Year One)
All Inventory Remains

Cost of Goods Sold (ending inventory component)...........	30,000	
Inventory (balance sheet account)		30,000
To remove unrealized gain created by intercompany sale.		

This entry (labeled G for gain) reduces the consolidated Inventory account to its original $50,000 historical cost. Furthermore, increasing cost of goods sold by $30,000 effectively removes the unrealized gain from gross profit. Thus, both reporting problems created by the transfer price markup are resolved by this worksheet entry.

Only a Portion of Inventory Remains   Obviously, a company does not buy inventory to hold it for an indefinite time. The acquired items are used within the company's operations or resold to unrelated, outside parties. Intercompany gains ultimately are realized by the subsequent consumption or reselling of these goods. Therefore, only the transferred inventory still held at year's end continues to be recorded in the separate statements at a value more than the historical cost. For this reason, *the elimination of unrealized gains (Entry G) is not based on total intercompany sales but only on the amount of transferred merchandise retained within the business at the end of the year.*

To illustrate, assume that Arlington transferred inventory costing $50,000 to Zirkin, a related company, for $80,000, thus recording a gross profit of $30,000. Assume further that by year's end Zirkin has resold $60,000 of these goods to unrelated parties but retains the other $20,000 (for resale in the following year). From the viewpoint of the consolidated company, the gain on the $60,000 portion of the intercompany sale has now been earned and no adjustment is required for consolidation purposes.

Conversely, any gain recorded in connection with the $20,000 in merchandise that remains is still a component within Zirkin's Inventory account. Because the markup was 37½ percent ($30,000 gross profit/$80,000 transfer price), this retained inventory is stated at a value $7,500 more than its original cost ($20,000 × 37½%). The required reduction (Entry G) is not the entire $30,000 shown previously but only the $7,500 unrealized gain that remains in ending inventory.

Consolidation Entry G—Year of Transfer (Year One)
40% of Inventory Remains (replaces previous entry)

Cost of Goods Sold (ending inventory component)...........	7,500	
Inventory.......................................		7,500
To remove portion of intercompany gain which is unrealized in year of transfer.		

Unrealized Gains—Year Following Transfer (Year Two)

Whenever an unrealized intercompany gain is present in ending Inventory, one further consolidation entry is eventually required. Although Entry G removes the gain from the *consolidated* inventory balances in the year of transfer, the $7,500 overstatement remains within the separate financial records of the buyer and seller. The effects of this gain are carried into their beginning balances in the subsequent year. Hence, another worksheet elimination is necessary in the period following the transfer. For consolidation purposes, the unrealized portion of the intercompany gain must be adjusted in two successive years (from ending inventory in the year of transfer and from beginning inventory of the next period).

Referring again to Arlington's sale of inventory to Zirkin, the $7,500 unrealized gain is still in Zirkin's Inventory account at the start of the subsequent year. Once again, the overstatement is removed within the consolidation process but this time from the beginning inventory balance (which appears in the financial statements only as a positive component of cost of goods sold). This elimination is termed *Entry *G.* The asterisk indicates that the intercompany gain was created by a transfer made in a previous year.

Consolidation Entry *G—Year Following Transfer (Year Two)

Retained Earnings (beginning balance of seller)	7,500	
Cost of Goods Sold (beginning inventory component)		7,500

To remove unrealized gain from beginning figures so that it can be recognized currently in the period in which the earning process is completed.

By reducing cost of goods sold (beginning inventory) through this worksheet entry, the gross profit reported for this second year is increased. For consolidation purposes, the gain on the transfer is recognized in the period in which the items are actually sold to outside parties. As shown in the following diagram, Entry G initially deferred the $7,500 gain because this amount was unrealized in the year of transfer. Entry *G now increases consolidated net income (by decreasing cost of goods sold) to reflect the earning process in the current year.

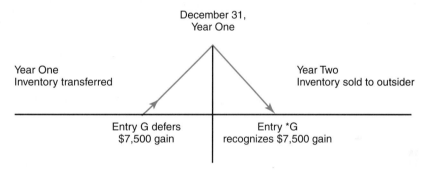

In Entry *G, removal of the $7,500 from beginning inventory (within cost of goods sold) appropriately increases current income and should not pose a significant conceptual problem. However, the rationale for decreasing the seller's beginning retained earnings deserves further explanation. This reduction removes the unrealized gain (recognized by the seller in the year of transfer) so that the profit is reported in the period when it is earned. Despite the consolidation entries in Year One, the $7,500 gain remained on this company's separate books and was closed to retained earnings at the end of the period. Recall that consolidation entries are never posted to the individual affiliate's books. Therefore, from a consolidated view, the buyer's inventory and the seller's retained earnings as of the beginning of Year Two contain the unrealized profit and must both be reduced in Entry *G.

Intercompany Beginning Inventory Gain Adjustment—Downstream Sales When Parent Uses Equity Method   The worksheet elimination of the sales/purchases balances (Entry TI) as well as the entry to remove the unrealized gain from ending inventory in Year One (Entry G) are both standard, regardless of the circumstances of the consolidation. Conversely, in one specific situation, the procedure used to eliminate the intercompany gain from Year Two's beginning accounts differs from the Entry *G just presented. If (1) the original transfer is downstream (made by the parent) and (2) the equity method has been applied for internal accounting purposes, the Equity in Subsidiary Earnings account replaces beginning retained earnings in Entry *G.

When using the equity method, the parent maintains appropriate income balances within its own individual financial records. Thus, the parent defers any unrealized gain at the end of Year One through an equity method adjustment that also decreases the Investment in Subsidiary account. With the gain deferred, the retained earnings of the parent/seller at the beginning of the following year is correctly stated. The parent's retained earnings does not contain the unrealized gain and needs no adjustment.[5]

At the end of Year Two, both the Equity in Subsidiary Earnings and the Investment account are increased in recognition of the previously deferred intercompany gain. The Investment account—having been decreased in Year One and increased in Year Two for the intercompany gain—thus no longer reflects any effects from the original deferral. For consolidation purposes, the income effect of the realized gain is simply transferred from the Equity in Subsidiary Earnings account to Cost of Goods Sold in Entry *G, appropriately increasing current consolidated income. The remaining balance in the Equity in Subsidiary Earnings account now reflects the same activity represented in the Investment account and is then eliminated against the Investment account.

Consolidation Entry *G—Year Following Transfer (Year Two)
(replaces previous Entry *G when transfers have been downstream
and the equity method is in use)

Equity in Subsidiary Earnings..............................	7,500	
Cost of Goods Sold (beginning inventory component).......		7,500

    To recognize the previously deferred unrealized downstream inventory gain as part of current year income. The Equity in Subsidiary Earnings account replaces the Retained Earnings account (used for upstream profit adjustments) when adjusting for downstream sales. The parent's retained earnings have already been corrected by application of the equity method.

Finally, various markup percentages are employed to determine the dollar values for intercompany profit deferrals. Exhibit 5–1 shows formulas for both the gross profit rate and markup on cost and the relation between the two.

Exhibit 5–1

Relationship between Gross Profit Rate and Markup on Cost

In determining appropriate amounts of intercompany profits for deferral and subsequent recognition in consolidated financial reports, two alternative—but mathematically related—profit percentages are often seen. Recalling that Gross Profit = Sales − Cost of Goods Sold, then

$$\textbf{Gross Profit Rate (GPR)} = \frac{\text{Gross Profit}}{\text{Sales}} = \frac{MC}{1 + MC}$$

$$\textbf{Markup on Cost (MC)} = \frac{\text{Gross Profit}}{\text{Cost of Goods Sold}} = \frac{GPR}{1 - GPR}$$

Example:	Sales (transfer price)	$1,000
	Cost of goods sold	800
	Gross profit	$ 200

Here the GPR = (200 ÷ 1,000) = 20% and the MC = (200 ÷ 800) = 25%. In most intercompany purchases and sales, the sales (transfer) price is known and therefore the GPR is the simplest percentage to use to determine the amount of intercompany profit.

Intercompany profit = Transfer price × GPR

Instead, if the markup on cost is available, it readily converts to a GPR by the above formula. In this case (.25 ÷ 1.25) = 20%.

---

[5]For upstream intercompany gains in beginning inventory, the subsidiary's retained earnings remain overstated and must be adjusted through Entry *G.

Unrealized Gains—Effect on Noncontrolling Interest Valuation

The effects of intercompany inventory transfers on business combinations are appropriately accounted for by the worksheet entries just described. However, one question remains: What impact do these procedures have on the valuation of a noncontrolling interest? In regard to this issue, paragraph 13 of *ARB 51* states:

> The amount of intercompany profit or loss to be eliminated in accordance with paragraph 7 is not affected by the existence of a minority interest. The complete elimination of the intercompany profit or loss is consistent with the underlying assumption that consolidated statements represent the financial position and operating results of a single business enterprise. The elimination of the intercompany profit or loss *may be allocated proportionately* between the majority and minority interests (emphasis added).

The last sentence indicates that alternative approaches are available in computing the noncontrolling interest's share of a subsidiary's net income. According to this pronouncement, recognition of outside ownership *may or may not be* affected by unrealized gains resulting from intercompany transfers. Because consolidated net income is reduced by the amount attributed to a noncontrolling interest, the handling of this issue can affect the reported profitability of a business combination.

To illustrate, assume that Large Company owns 70 percent of the voting stock of Small Company. To avoid extraneous complications assume that no amortization expense resulted from this purchase. Assume further that Large reports current net income (from separate operations) of $500,000, while Small earns $100,000. During the current period, intercompany transfers of $200,000 occur with a total markup of $90,000. At the end of the year, an unrealized intercompany gain of $40,000 remains within the inventory accounts.

Clearly, the consolidated net income prior to the reduction for the 30 percent noncontrolling interest is $560,000, the two income balances less the unrealized gain. The problem facing the accountant is the computation of the noncontrolling interest's share of Small's income. Because of the flexibility allowed by *ARB 51*, this figure may be reported as either $30,000 (30 percent of the $100,000 earnings of the subsidiary) or $18,000 (30 percent of reported income after that figure is reduced by the $40,000 unrealized gain).

To determine an appropriate valuation for this noncontrolling interest allocation, an analysis must be made of the relationship between an intercompany transaction and the outside owners. If a transfer is downstream (the parent sells inventory to the subsidiary), a logical view would seem to be that the unrealized gain is that of the parent company. The parent made the original sale, therefore, the gross profit is included in its financial records. Because the subsidiary's income is unaffected, little justification exists for adjusting the noncontrolling interest to reflect the deferral of the unrealized gain. Consequently, in the example of Large and Small, if the transfers were downstream, the 30 percent noncontrolling interest would be $30,000 based on Small's reported income of $100,000.

In contrast, if inventory is sold by the subsidiary to the parent (an upstream transfer), the gross profit would be recognized in the subsidiary's financial records, even though part of this income remains unrealized from a consolidation perspective. Because the outside owners possess their interest in the subsidiary, a reasonable conclusion would be that valuation of the noncontrolling interest is calculated on the income actually earned by this company. The 1995 FASB Exposure Draft, *Consolidated Financial Statements: Policy and Procedures,* supports allocating a proportionate amount of the intercompany profit adjustments (from upstream sales) to the noncontrolling interest:

> The effects on equity of eliminating intercompany profit and losses on assets that remain within the group shall be allocated between the controlling interest and the noncontrolling interest on the basis of their proportionate interest in the selling affiliate.

In this textbook, the noncontrolling interest's share of consolidated net income is computed based on *the reported income of the subsidiary after adjustment for any unrealized upstream gains.* Returning to Large Company and Small Company, if the $40,000 unrealized gain was the result of an upstream sale from subsidiary to parent, only $60,000 of Small's $100,000 reported income actually has been earned by the end of the year. The allocation to the noncontrolling interest is, therefore, reported as $18,000, or 30 percent of this realized income figure.

Alternative Concepts of a Noncontrolling Interest   Although the noncontrolling interest figure is based here on the subsidiary's reported income adjusted for the effects of upstream intercompany transfers, *ARB 51,* as quoted earlier, does not require this treatment. Giving effect to upstream transfers in this calculation but not to downstream transfers is no more than an attempt to select the most logical approach from among acceptable alternatives. Over the years a number of possible methods of consolidating the results of intercompany transfers have been considered. Several of these alternatives are in the appendix at the end of this chapter.

Intercompany Inventory Transfers Summarized

To assist in overcoming the complications created by intercompany transfers, the consolidation process is demonstrated in three different ways:

- Before proceeding to a numerical example, the impact of intercompany transfers on consolidated figures is reviewed. Ultimately, the accountant must understand how the balances to be reported by a business combination are derived when unrealized gains result from either upstream or downstream sales.
- Next, two different consolidation worksheets are produced: one for downstream transfers and the other for upstream. The various consolidation procedures used in these worksheets are explained and analyzed.
- Finally, several of the worksheet entries used in developing a consolidation worksheet are shown side by side so that the differences created by the direction of the transfers can be better understood.

The Development of Consolidated Totals   The following summary discusses only the accounts impacted by intercompany transactions:

Revenues. The parent's balance is added to the subsidiary's balance but all intercompany transfers are then removed.

Cost of Goods Sold. This expense is one of the most difficult figures computed within the consolidation process. The parent's balance is added to the subsidiary's balance but all intercompany transfers are removed. The resulting total is decreased by any beginning unrealized gain (thus, raising net income) and increased by any ending unrealized gain (to reduce net income).

Expenses. The parent's balance is added to the subsidiary's balance plus any amortization expense for the year recognized on the purchase price allocations.[6]

Noncontrolling Interest in Subsidiary's Net Income. The subsidiary's reported net income is adjusted for the effects of unrealized gains on upstream transfers (but not downstream transfers) and then multiplied by the percentage of outside ownership.

Retained Earnings at the Beginning of the Year. As in previous chapters, if the equity method has been applied, the parent's balance mirrors the consolidated total. When any other method is used, the parent's beginning retained earnings must be converted to the equity method by Entry *C. Accruals for this purpose

---

[6]As discussed later in this chapter, consolidated expenses also have to be reduced to remove excess depreciation recognized whenever a depreciable asset is transferred between the companies within a business combination at a price more than the book value.

are based on the income actually earned by the subsidiary in previous years (reported income adjusted for any unrealized upstream gains).

Inventory. The parent's balance is added to the subsidiary's balance. Any unrealized gain remaining at the end of the current year is removed to lower the reported balance to historical cost.

Land, Buildings, and Equipment. The parent's balance is added to the subsidiary's balance. This total is adjusted for any purchase price allocations and subsequent amortization.[7]

Noncontrolling Interest in Subsidiary at End of Year. The final total begins with the noncontrolling interest at the beginning of the year. This figure is based on the subsidiary's book value on that date after removing any unrealized gains on upstream sales. The beginning balance is updated by adding the portion of the subsidiary's income assigned to these outside owners (computed above) and subtracting the noncontrolling interest's share of the subsidiary's dividend payments.

Intercompany Inventory Transfers Illustrated

To examine the various consolidation procedures relative to intercompany inventory transfers, assume that Top Company purchases 80 percent of the voting stock of Bottom Company on January 1, 2001. The parent pays a total of $400,000, a price that includes all directly related consolidation costs. Allocation of $40,000 is made to a database, a figure amortized at the rate of $2,000 per year for 20 years.

The subsidiary reports net income of $30,000 in 2001 and $70,000 in 2002, the current year. Dividend payments are $20,000 in the first year and $50,000 in the second. Top applies the cost method so that dividend income of $16,000 ($20,000 × 80 percent) and $40,000 ($50,000 × 80 percent) is recorded by the parent during these two years. Using the cost method in this initial example avoids the problem of computing the parent's investment account balances. However, this illustration is extended to demonstrate the changes necessary if the parent applies the equity method.

After the takeover, intercompany inventory sales occurred between the two companies as shown in Exhibit 5–2. A $10,000 intercompany debt also exists as of December 31, 2002.

The 2002 consolidation of Top and Bottom is presented twice. First, the transfers are assumed to be downstream from parent to subsidiary. Second, consolidated figures are recomputed with the transfers being viewed as upstream. This distinction is only significant because of a noncontrolling interest.

Downstream Sales   In the first example, all inventory transfers are assumed to have been *downstream* from Top to Bottom. Based on that perspective, the worksheet to consolidate these two companies for the year ending December 31, 2002, is in Exhibit 5–3.

Exhibit 5–2
Intercompany Transfers

	2001	2002
Transfer prices	$80,000	$100,000
Historical cost	60,000	70,000
Gross profit	$20,000	$ 30,000
Inventory remaining at year's end (at transfer price)	$16,000	$ 20,000

[7]As discussed later in this chapter, if land, buildings, or equipment have been transferred between parent and subsidiary, the separately reported balances must be returned to historical cost figures in deriving consolidated totals.

Exhibit 5–3   Downstream Inventory Transfers

Consolidation: Purchase Method
Investment: Cost Method

TOP COMPANY AND BOTTOM COMPANY
Consolidation Worksheet
For Year Ending December 31, 2002

Ownership: 80%

Accounts	Top Company	Bottom Company	Consolidated Totals Debit	Consolidated Totals Credit	Noncontrolling Interest	Consolidated Totals
Income Statement						
Sales	(600,000)	(300,000)	(TI) 100,000			(800,000)
Cost of goods sold	320,000	180,000	(G) 6,000	(*G) 4,000		402,000
				(TI) 100,000		
Expenses	170,000	50,000	(E) 2,000			222,000
Dividend income	(40,000)	–0–	(I) 40,000			–0–
Noncontrolling interest in Bottom						
Company's income	–0–	–0–			(14,000)‡	14,000
Net income	(150,000)	(70,000)				(162,000)
Statement of Retained Earnings						
Retained earnings, 1/1/02:						
Top Company	(650,000)			(*C) 6,000		(652,000)
Bottom Company		(310,000)	(*G) 4,000			–0–
			(S) 310,000†			
Net income (above)	(150,000)	(70,000)				(162,000)
Dividends paid	70,000	50,000		(I) 40,000	10,000	70,000
Retained earnings, 12/31/02	(730,000)	(330,000)				(744,000)

Balance Sheet

			Consolidation Entries		
			Debit	Credit	Consolidated
Cash and receivables	280,000	120,000		(P) 10,000	390,000
Inventory	220,000	160,000		(G) 6,000	374,000
Investment in Bottom Company	400,000	—0—	(*C) 6,000	(S) 368,000 (A) 38,000	—0—
Land	410,000	200,000			610,000
Plant assets (net)	190,000	170,000			360,000
Database	—0—	—0—	(A) 38,000	(E) 2,000	36,000
Total assets	1,500,000	650,000			1,770,000
Liabilities	(340,000)	(170,000)	(P) 10,000		(500,000)
Noncontrolling interest in Bottom Company, 1/1/02	—0—	—0—		(S) 92,000	
Noncontrolling interest in Bottom Company, 12/31/02				(96,000)	(96,000)
Common stock	(430,000)	(150,000)	(S) 150,000		(430,000)
Retained earnings, 12/31/02 (above)	(730,000)	(330,000)			(744,000)
Total liabilities and equities	(1,500,000)	(650,000)			(1,770,000)

Note: Parentheses indicate a credit balance.

†Boxed items highlight differences with upstream transfers examined in Exhibit 5–4.

‡Because intercompany sales are made downstream (by the parent), the subsidiary's earned income is the $70,000 reported figure with the 20% noncontrolling interest being allocated ($14,000).

Consolidation entries:

(*G) Removal of unrealized gain from beginning figures so that it can be recognized in current period. Downstream sales attributed to parent.

(*C) Recognition of increase in book value and amortization relating to ownership of subsidiary for year prior to 2002.

(S) Elimination of subsidiary's stockholders' equity accounts along with recognition of January 1, 2002, noncontrolling interest.

(A) Allocation of parent's cost in excess of subsidiary's book value, unamortized balance as of January 1, 2002.

(I) Elimination of intercompany dividends recorded by parent as income.

(E) Recognition of amortization expense for current year on database.

(P) Elimination of intercompany receivable/payable balances.

(TI) Elimination of intercompany sales/purchases balances.

(G) Removal of unrealized gain from ending figures so that it can be recognized in subsequent period.

Most of the worksheet entries found in Exhibit 5–3 are described and analyzed in previous chapters of this textbook. Thus, only four of these entries are examined in detail along with the computation of the noncontrolling interests in the subsidiary's income.

*Entry *G*   Entry *G removes the unrealized gains carried over from the previous period. As $16,000 in transferred merchandise was retained by Bottom at the first of the current year, any related gain is unearned and must be deferred. The 2001 gross profit rate on these items was 25 percent ($20,000 gross profit/$80,000 transfer price), indicating an unrealized gain of $4,000 (25 percent of the remaining $16,000 in inventory). Thus, Entry *G reduces cost of goods sold (or the beginning inventory component of that expense) by that amount as well as the January 1, 2002, Retained Earnings of Top (the seller of the goods).

Two effects are created by Entry *G: First, last year's profits, as reflected by the seller's beginning retained earnings, are reduced because the $4,000 gain was not earned at that time. Second, through the reduction in cost of goods sold, an increase in current year income is created. From a consolidation perspective, the gain is being correctly recognized in 2002 when the inventory is sold to an outside party.

*Entry *C*   Entry *C is introduced in Chapter 3 as an initial consolidation adjustment required whenever the equity method is not applied by the parent company. Entry *C converts the parent's beginning retained earnings to a consolidated total. In the current illustration, Top did not accrue its portion of the 2001 increase in Bottom's book value [($30,000 income less $20,000 paid in dividends) × 80% or $8,000] or record the $2,000 amortization expense for this same period. Because neither number has been recognized within the parent's individual records, both must be brought into the consolidation process through a $6,000 adjustment (Entry *C). The intercompany transfers did not affect this entry because they were downstream; the gains had no impact on the income recognized in connection with the subsidiary.

Entry TI   The intercompany sales/purchases for 2002 are eliminated by Entry TI. The entire $100,000 transfer recorded by the two parties during the current period is removed to arrive at consolidated figures for the business combination.

Entry G   Entry G defers the unrealized gain remaining at the end of 2002. The $20,000 in transferred merchandise retained by Bottom has a markup of 30 percent ($30,000 gross profit/$100,000 transfer price); thus, the unrealized gain amounts to $6,000. On the worksheet, Entry G eliminates this overstatement in the Inventory asset balance as well as the ending inventory (negative) component of cost of goods sold. Because the gain remains unrealized, the increase in this expense account has the appropriate effect of lowering consolidated income.

Noncontrolling Interest's Share of the Subsidiary's Income   In this first illustration, the intercompany transfers are downstream. Thus, the unrealized gains are considered to relate solely to the parent company, creating no effect on the subsidiary or the outside ownership. For this reason, the noncontrolling interest's share of consolidated income is recorded as a columnar entry of $14,000, 20 percent of the $70,000 net income reported by Bottom.

By including these entries along with the other routine worksheet eliminations and adjustments, the accounting information generated by Top and Bottom can be brought together into a single set of consolidated financial statements. However, this process does more than simply delete intercompany transactions; reported income is affected. A $4,000 gain is being removed on the worksheet from 2001 figures so that it can be recognized in 2002 (Entry *G). A $6,000 gain is deferred in a similar fashion from 2002 (Entry G) and subsequently recognized in 2003. However, these changes do not affect the noncontrolling interest since the transfers were downstream.

Upstream Sales A different set of consolidation procedures is necessary if the intercompany transfers are upstream from Bottom to Top. As previously discussed, upstream gains are attributed to the subsidiary rather than to the parent company. Therefore, had these transfers been upstream, the $4,000 gain moved from 2001 into the current year (Entry *G) as well as the $6,000 unrealized gain deferred from 2002 into the future (Entry G) are both considered adjustments to Bottom's reported totals.

Tying upstream gains to Bottom's income may be a logical perspective, but such treatment complicates the consolidation process in several ways:

- Deferring the $4,000 gain from 2001 into 2002 dictates that the beginning retained earnings balance of the subsidiary (as the seller of the goods) should be adjusted to $306,000 rather than $310,000 found in the company's separate records on the worksheet.

- Because $4,000 of the income reported for 2001 was unearned at that time, Bottom's book value did not increase by $10,000 during the previous period (income less dividends as stated in the introduction) but only by an earned amount of $6,000.

- Bottom's earned income for the year of 2002 is $68,000 rather than the $70,000 found within the company's separate financial statements. This $68,000 figure is based on adjusting the timing of the reported income to reflect the deferral and recognition of the intercompany gains.

Earned Income of Subsidiary—Upstream Transfers

Income Reported by Bottom Company, 2002	Add: Gain from Previous Period Realized in 2002	Less: Gain Reported in 2002 to Be Realized in Later Period	2002 Income of Bottom Company from Consolidated Perspective
$70,000	$4,000	$(6,000)	$68,000

Determining Bottom's beginning retained earnings (realized) to be $306,000 and its 2002 income as $68,000 are preliminary calculations made in anticipation of the consolidation process. These newly computed totals are significant because they serve as the basis for several of the worksheet entries. However, the financial records of the subsidiary remain unaffected. In addition, because the cost method has been applied, no change is required in any of the parent's accounts on the worksheet.

To illustrate the effects of upstream inventory transfers, in Exhibit 5–4 we consolidate the financial statements of Top and Bottom once again. *The individual records of the two companies are unchanged from Exhibit 5–3: The only difference in this second worksheet is that the intercompany transfers are assumed to have been made upstream from Bottom to Top.* This single change creates several important differences between Exhibits 5–3 and 5–4:

1. Because the intercompany sales are made upstream, the $4,000 deferral of the beginning unrealized gain (Entry *G) is no longer a reduction in the retained earnings of the parent company. Bottom was the seller of the merchandise; thus, the elimination made in Exhibit 5–4 reduces that company's January 1, 2002, equity balance. Following this entry, Bottom's beginning retained earnings on the worksheet is $306,000 which is, as discussed earlier, the appropriate total from a consolidated perspective.

2. Because $4,000 of Bottom's 2001 income is being deferred into 2002, the increase in the subsidiary's book value in the previous year is only $6,000 rather than $10,000 as reported. Consequently, conversion to the equity method (Entry *C) requires an increase of just $2,800:

$6,000 earned increase in subsidiary's book value during 2001 × 80%	$ 4,800
2001 amortization expense	(2,000)
Increase in parent's beginning retained earnings (Entry *C)	$ 2,800

Exhibit 5–4 Upstream Inventory Transfers

Consolidation: Purchase Method
Investment: Cost Method

TOP COMPANY AND BOTTOM COMPANY
Consolidation Worksheet
For Year Ending December 31, 2002

Ownership: 80%

Accounts	Top Company	Bottom Company	Consolidation Entries Debit	Consolidation Entries Credit	Noncontrolling Interest	Consolidated Totals
Income Statement						
Sales	(600,000)	(300,000)	(TI) 100,000			(800,000)
Cost of goods sold	320,000	180,000	(G) 6,000	(*G) 4,000 (TI) 100,000		402,000
Expenses	170,000	50,000	(E) 2,000			222,000
Dividend income	(40,000)	-0-	(I) 40,000			-0-
Noncontrolling interest in Bottom Company's income	-0-	-0-			(13,600)‡	13,600
Net income	(150,000)	(70,000)			(13,600)	(162,400)
Statement of Retained Earnings						
Retained earnings, 1/1/02:						
Top Company	(650,000)		(*C) 4,000 (S) 306,000†			(652,800)
Bottom Company		(310,000)		(*C) 2,800		-0-
Net income (above)	(150,000)	(70,000)			(13,600)	(162,400)
Dividends paid	70,000	50,000		(I) 40,000	10,000	70,000
Retained earnings, 12/31/02	(730,000)	(330,000)				(745,200)

Balance Sheet

			Consolidation Entries		
			Debit	Credit	
Cash and receivables	280,000	120,000			390,000
Inventory	220,000	160,000			374,000
Investment in Bottom Company	400,000	-0-	(*C) 2,800	(P) 10,000 (G) 6,000 (S) 364,800 (A) 38,000	-0-
Land	410,000	200,000			610,000
Plant assets (net)	190,000	170,000			360,000
Database	-0-	-0-	(A) 38,000	(E) 2,000	36,000
Total assets	1,500,000	650,000			1,770,000
Liabilities	(340,000)	(170,000)	(P) 10,000		(500,000)
Noncontrolling interest in Bottom Company, 1/1/02	-0-	-0-		(S) 91,200	(91,200)
Noncontrolling interest in Bottom Company, 12/31/02				(94,800)	(94,800)
Common stock	(430,000)	(150,000)	(S) 150,000		(430,000)
Retained earnings, 12/31/02 (above)	(730,000)	(330,000)			(745,200)
Total liabilities and equities	(1,500,000)	(650,000)			(1,770,000)

Note: Parentheses indicate a credit balance.

†Boxed items highlight differences with downstream transfers examined in Exhibit 5–3.

‡Because intercompany sales are made upstream (by the subsidiary), the subsidiary's realized income is the $68,000 ($70,000 reported balance plus $4,000 gain deferred from previous year less $6,000 deferred into next year) with the 20% noncontrolling interest being allocated $13,600.

Consolidation entries:

(*G) Removal of unrealized gain from beginning figures so that it can be recognized in current period. Upstream sales attributed to subsidiary.

(*C) Recognition of earned increase in book value and amortization relating to ownership of subsidiary for year prior to 2002.

(S) Elimination of adjusted stockholders' equity accounts along with recognition of January 1, 2002, noncontrolling interest.

(A) Allocation of parent's cost in excess of subsidiary's book value, unamortized balance as of January 1, 2002.

(I) Elimination of intercompany dividends recorded by parent as income.

(E) Recognition of amortization expense for current year on cost allocated to value of database.

(P) Elimination of intercompany receivable/payable balances.

(TI) Elimination of intercompany sales/purchases balances.

(G) Removal of unrealized gain from ending figures so that it can be recognized in subsequent period.

3. Within Entry S, the valuation of the initial noncontrolling interest as well as the portion of the parent's investment account to be eliminated differ from the previous example. This worksheet entry removes the stockholders' equity accounts of the subsidiary as of the beginning of the current year. Thus, the $4,000 reduction made to Bottom's retained earnings to remove the 2001 unrealized gain must be taken into account in developing Entry S. After posting Entry *G, only $456,000 remains as the subsidiary's January 1, 2002, book value (the total of common stock and beginning retained earnings after adjustment for Entry *G). This figure forms the basis for the 20 percent noncontrolling interest ($91,200) and elimination of the 80 percent parent company investment ($364,800).

4. Finally, to complete the consolidation, the noncontrolling interest's share of the subsidiary's net income is recorded on the worksheet as $13,600. This balance represents a 20 percent allocation of the $68,000 earned income figure attributed to Bottom. Upstream transfers affect this computation although the downstream sales in the previous example did not. Thus, the noncontrolling interest balance reported previously in the income statement in Exhibit 5–3 differs from the allocation in Exhibit 5–4.

Consolidations—Downstream versus Upstream Transfers   To help clarify the effect of downstream and upstream transfers, the worksheet entries that differ can be examined in greater detail.

Downstream Transfers	**Upstream Transfers**
(Exhibit 5–3)	(Exhibit 5–4)

Entry *G

Retained earnings,
1/1/02—Top   4,000
    Cost of goods sold   4,000
To remove 2001 unrealized gain from beginning balances of the seller.

Entry *G

Retained earnings,
1/1/02—Bottom   4,000
    Cost of goods sold   4,000
To remove 2001 unrealized gain from beginning balances of the seller.

Entry *C

Investment in Bottom   6,000
    Retained earnings,
        1/1/02—Top   6,000
To convert 1/1/02 cost figures to the equity method. Income accrual is 80% of reported income of $10,000 less $2,000 amortization.

Entry *C

Investment in Bottom   2,800
    Retained earnings,
        1/1/02—Top   2,800
To convert 1/1/02 cost figures to the equity method. Income accrual is 80% of earned income of $6,000 (after removal of unrealized gain) less $2,000 amortization.

Entry S

Common
    stock—Bottom   150,000
Retained earnings,
    1/1/02—Bottom 310,000
        Investment in
        Bottom (80%) 368,000
        Noncontrolling
            interest—1/1/02
            (20%)   92,000
To remove subsidiary's stockholders' equity accounts and portion of investment balance. Book value at beginning of year is appropriate.

Entry S

Common
    stock—Bottom 150,000
Retained earnings,
    1/1/02—Bottom (as
    adjusted) 306,000
        Investment in
        Bottom (80%) 364,800
        Noncontrolling
            interest—1/1/02
            (20%)   91,200
To remove subsidiary's stockholders' equity accounts (as adjusted in Entry *G) and portion of investment balance. Adjusted book value at beginning of year is appropriate.

Noncontrolling Interest in Subsidiary's Income = $14,000. 20 percent of Bottom's reported income.

Noncontrolling Interest in Subsidiary's Income = $13,600. 20 percent of Bottom's earned income (reported income after adjustment for unrealized gains).

DISCUSSION QUESTION

What Price Should We Charge Ourselves?

Slagle Corporation is a large manufacturing organization. Over the past several years, Slagle has obtained an important component used in its production process exclusively from Harrison, Inc., a relatively small company in Topeka, Kansas. Harrison charges $90 per unit for this part:

Variable cost per unit	$40.00
Fixed cost assigned per unit	30.00
Markup	20.00
Total price	$90.00

In hopes of reducing manufacturing costs, Slagle purchases all of the outstanding common stock of Harrison. This new subsidiary continues to sell merchandise to a number of outside customers as well as to Slagle. Thus, for internal reporting purposes, Harrison is being viewed as a separate profit center.

A controversy has now arisen among company officials about the amount that Harrison should charge Slagle for each component. The administrator in charge of the subsidiary wants to continue with a price of $90.00 as in the past. He believes this figure best reflects the profitability of the division: "If we are to be judged by our profits, why should we be punished for selling to our own parent company? If that occurs, my figures will look better if I forget Slagle as a customer and try to market my goods solely to outsiders."

In contrast, the vice president in charge of Slagle's production wants the price set at variable cost, total cost, or some derivative of these numbers. "We bought Harrison to bring our costs down. It only makes sense to reduce the transfer price, otherwise the benefits of acquiring this subsidiary are not apparent. I pushed the company to buy Harrison; if our operating results are not improved, I will get the blame."

- Will the decision about the transfer price affect consolidated net income?
- Which method would be easiest for the company's accountant to administer?
- As the company's accountant, what advice would you give to these officials?

Effects on Consolidation of Alternative Investment Methods

In Exhibits 5–3 and 5–4, the cost method was utilized. However, when using either the equity method or the partial equity method, consolidation procedures normally continue to follow the same patterns analyzed in the previous chapters of this textbook. As described earlier, though, a variation in Entry *G is required when the equity method is applied and downstream transfers have occurred. The equity in subsidiary earnings account is decreased rather than recording a reduction in the beginning retained earnings of the parent/seller with the remaining amount in equity in subsidiary earnings eliminated in Entry I. Otherwise, the specific accounting method in use creates no unique impact on the consolidation process for intercompany transactions.

The major complication when the parent uses the equity method is not always related to a consolidation procedure. Frequently, the composition of the investment balances appearing on the parent's separate financial records proves to be the most complex element of the entire process. Under the equity method, the investment accounts are subjected to (1) income accrual, (2) amortization, (3) dividends, and (4) adjustments required by unrealized intercompany gains. Thus, if Top Company applies the equity method and the transfers are downstream, the Investment in Bottom Company account would grow from $400,000 to $414,000 by the end of 2002. For that year, the Equity Income—Bottom Company account registers a $52,000 balance. Both of these totals result from the accounting shown in Exhibit 5–5.

If transfers are upstream, the individual investment accounts reported by the parent can be determined in the same manner as in Exhibit 5–5. Because of the change in direction, the gains are now attributed to the subsidiary. Thus, both investment accounts hold balances that vary from the totals computed earlier. The Investment in Bottom

E x h i b i t   5 – 5
Investment Balances—
Equity Method—
downstream sales

Investment in Bottom Company Analysis, 1/1/01 to 12/31/02		
Cost 1/1/01		$400,000
Top's share of Bottom Co. reported income		
for 2001 (80%)	$ 24,000	
Database amortization	(2,000)	
Deferred profit from Top's 2001 unrealized gain	(4,000)	
Equity in earnings of Bottom Company, 2001		18,000
Top's share of Bottom Co. dividends, 2001 (80%)		(16,000)
Balance 12/31/01		$402,000
Top's share of Bottom Co. income for 2002 (80%)	$ 56,000	
Database amortization	(2,000)	
Recognized profit from Top's 2001 unrealized gain	4,000	
Deferred profit from Top's 2002 unrealized gain	(6,000)	
Equity in earnings of Bottom Company, 2002		$ 52,000
Top's share of Bottom Co. dividends, 2002 (80%)		(40,000)
Balance 12/31/02		$414,000

E x h i b i t   5 – 6
Investment Balances—
Equity Method—
upstream sales

Investment in Bottom Company Analysis, 1/1/01 to 12/31/02		
Cost 1/1/01		$400,000
Bottom Co. reported income for 2001	$ 30,000	
Deferred profit from Bottom's 2001 unrealized gain	(4,000)	
Bottom Company adjusted earnings	26,000	
Top Company ownership	80%	
Top's share of Bottom's 2001 earnings	$ 20,800	
Database amortization	(2,000)	
Equity in earnings of Bottom Company, 2001		18,800
Top's share of Bottom Co. dividends, 2001 (80%)		(16,000)
Balance 12/31/01		$402,800
Bottom Co. reported income for 2001	$ 70,000	
Recognized profit from Bottom's 2001		
unrealized gain	4,000	
Deferred profit from Bottom's 2002 unrealized gain	(6,000)	
Bottom Company adjusted earnings	68,000	
Top Company ownership	80%	
Top's share of Bottom's 2001 earnings	$ 54,400	
Database amortization	(2,000)	
Equity in earnings of Bottom Company, 2001		$ 52,400
Top's share of Bottom Co. dividends, 2001 (80%)		(40,000)
Balance 12/31/01		$415,200

Company balance becomes $415,200, whereas the Equity Income—Bottom Company account for the year is $52,400. The differences are the result of having upstream rather than downstream transactions. The components of these accounts are identified in Exhibit 5–6. Consolidated worksheets for downstream and upstream inventory transfers when Top uses the equity method are shown in Exhibit 5–7 and Exhibit 5–8.

INTERCOMPANY LAND TRANSFERS

Although not as prevalent as inventory transactions, intercompany sales of other assets occur occasionally. The final two sections of this chapter examine the worksheet procedures necessitated by noninventory transfers. Land transactions are analyzed followed by a discussion of the effects created by the intercompany sale of depreciable assets such as buildings and equipment.

Accounting for Land Transactions

The consolidation procedures necessitated by intercompany land transfers partially parallel those for intercompany inventory. As with inventory, the sale of land creates a series of effects on the individual records of the two companies. The worksheet process must then adjust the account balances to present all transactions from the perspective of a single economic entity.

By reviewing the sequence of events occurring in an intercompany land sale, the similarities to inventory transfers can be ascertained as well as the unique features of this transaction.

1. A gain (losses are rare in intercompany asset transfers) is reported by the original seller of the land, even though the transaction occurred between related parties. At the same time, the acquiring company capitalizes the inflated transfer price rather than the land's historical cost to the business combination.

2. The unrealized gain recorded by the seller is closed into retained earnings at the end of the year. From a consolidated perspective, this account has been artificially increased. Thus, both the Land account of the buyer and the Retained Earnings of the seller continue to contain the unrealized profit.

3. Only when the land is subsequently disposed of to an outside party is the gain on the original transfer actually earned. Therefore, appropriate consolidation techniques must be designed to eliminate the intercompany gain each period until the time of resale.

Clearly, two characteristics encountered in inventory transfers also are present in intercompany land transactions: inflated book values and unrealized gains subsequently culminated through sales to outside parties. Despite these similarities, significant differences exist. Because of the nature of the transaction, no sales/purchases balances are recorded by the individual companies when land is transferred. Instead, a separate gain account is established by the seller. Because this gain is unearned, the balance has to be eliminated when preparing consolidated statements.

In addition, the subsequent resale of land to an outside party does not always occur in the year immediately following the transfer. Although inventory is normally disposed of within a relatively short time, land is often held by the buyer for years if not permanently. Thus, the overvalued Land account can remain on the books of the acquiring company indefinitely. As long as the land is retained, elimination of the effects of the unrealized gain (the equivalent of Entry *G in inventory transfers) must be made for each subsequent consolidation. By repeating this worksheet entry every year, both the Land and the Retained Earnings accounts are properly stated in the consolidated financial statements.

Eliminating Unrealized Gains—Land Transfers

To illustrate these worksheet procedures, assume that Hastings Company and Patrick Company are related parties. On July 1, 2001, land that originally cost $60,000 is sold

Exhibit 5–7   Downstream Inventory Transfers

Consolidation: Purchase Method
Investment: Equity Method

TOP COMPANY AND BOTTOM COMPANY
Consolidation Worksheet
For Year Ending December 31, 2002

Accounts	Top	Bottom	Adjustments & Eliminations		NCI	Consolidated Totals
Income Statement						
Sales	(600,000)	(300,000)	(TI) 100,000	(TI) 100,000		(800,000)
Cost of goods sold	320,000	180,000	(G) 6,000	(*G) 4,000		402,000
Operating expenses	170,000	50,000	(E) 2,000			222,000
Noncontrolling interest in Bottom Company's income					(14,000) ‡	14,000
Equity earnings of Bottom	(52,000)		(I) 48,000 (*G) 4,000 †			-0-
Net income	(162,000)	(70,000)				(162,000)
Statement of Retained Earnings						
Retained earnings, 1/1/02						
Top Company	(652,000)					(652,000)
Bottom Company		(310,000)	(S) 310,000			
Net income	(162,000)	(70,000)				(162,000)
Dividends paid	70,000	50,000		(D) 40,000	10,000	70,000
Retained earnings, 12/31/02	(744,000)	(330,000)				(744,000)

Balance Sheet

Account	Parent	Subsidiary	Debit	Credit	Noncontrolling Interest	Consolidated Totals
Cash and receivables	280,000	120,000		(P) 10,000		390,000
Inventory	220,000	160,000		(G) 6,000		374,000
Investment in Bottom Company	414,000		(D) 40,000	(I) 48,000 (S) 368,000 (A) 38,000		–0–
Land	410,000	200,000				610,000
Plant assets (net)	190,000	170,000				360,000
Database			(A) 38,000	(E) 2,000		36,000
Total assets	1,514,000	650,000				1,770,000
Liabilities	(340,000)	(170,000)	(P) 10,000			(500,000)
Noncontrolling interest in Bottom Company, 1/1/02				(S) 92,000	(92,000)	
Noncontrolling interest in Bottom Company, 12/31/02					(96,000)	(96,000)
Common stock	(430,000)	(150,000)	(S) 150,000			(430,000)
Retained earnings, 12/31/02	(744,000)	(330,000)				(744,000)
Total liabilities and equities	(1,514,000)	(650,000)				(1,770,000)

Note: Parentheses indicate a credit balance.

†Boxed items highlight differences with upstream transfers examined in Exhibit 5–8.

‡Because intercompany sales are made downstream (by the parent), the subsidiary's earned income is the $70,000 reported figure with the 20% noncontrolling interest being allocated ($14,000).

Consolidation entries:

(*G) Removal of unrealized gain from beginning figures so that it can be recognized in current period. Downstream sales attributed to parent.

(S) Elimination of subsidiary's stockholders' equity accounts along with recognition of January 1, 2002, noncontrolling interest.

(A) Allocation of parent's cost in excess of subsidiary's book value, unamortized balance as of January 1, 2002.

(I) Elimination of intercompany income remaining after *G elimination.

(D) Elimination of intercompany dividend.

(E) Recognition of amortization expense for current year on cost allocated to database.

(P) Elimination of intercompany receivable/payable balances.

(TI) Elimination of intercompany sales/purchases balances.

(G) Removal of unrealized gain from ending figures so that it can be recognized in subsequent period.

Exhibit 5–8   Upstream Inventory Transfers

Consolidation: Purchase Method
Investment: Equity Method

TOP COMPANY AND BOTTOM COMPANY
Consolidation Worksheet
For Year Ending December 31, 2002

Accounts	Top	Bottom	Adjustments & Eliminations		Consolidated NCI	Totals
Income Statement						
Sales	(600,000)	(300,000)	(TI) 100,000	(TI) 100,000		(800,000)
Cost of goods sold	320,000	180,000	(G) 6,000	(G) 4,000		402,000
Operating expenses	170,000	50,000	(E) 2,000			222,000
Noncontrolling interest in Bottom Company's income					(13,600)‡	13,600
Equity earnings of Bottom	(52,400)		(I) 52,400 ‡			
Net income	(162,400)	(70,000)				(162,400)
Statement of Retained Earnings						
Retained earnings, 1/1/02						
Top Company	(652,800)		(*G) 4,000			(652,800)
Bottom Company		(310,000)	(S) 306,000			
Net income	(162,400)	(70,000)				(162,400)
Dividends paid	70,000	50,000		(D) 40,000	10,000	70,000
Retained earnings, 12/31/02	(745,200)	(330,000)				(745,200)

Balance Sheet

Account			Debit	Credit	Noncontrolling Interest	Consolidated Totals
Cash and receivables	280,000	120,000		(P) 10,000		390,000
Inventory	220,000	160,000		(G) 6,000		374,000
Investment in Bottom Company	415,200		(D) 40,000	(I) 52,400 / (S) 364,800 / (A) 38,000		-0-
Land	410,000	200,000				610,000
Plant assets (net)	190,000	170,000				360,000
Database			(A) 38,000	(E) 2,000		36,000
Total assets	1,515,200	650,000				1,770,000
Liabilities	(340,000)	(170,000)	(P) 10,000			(500,000)
Noncontrolling interest in Bottom Company, 1/1/02				(S) 91,200	(91,200)	
Noncontrolling interest in Bottom Company, 12/31/02					(94,800)	(94,800)
Common stock	(430,000)	(150,000)	(S) 150,000			(430,000)
Retained earnings, 12/31/02	(745,200)	(330,000)				(745,200)
Total liabilities and equities	(1,515,200)	(650,000)				(1,770,000)

Note: Parentheses indicate a credit balance.

†Boxed items highlight differences with downstream transfers examined in Exhibit 5–7.

‡Because intercompany sales are made upstream (by the subsidiary), the subsidiary's realized income is the $68,000 ($70,000 reported balance plus $4,000 gain deferred from previous year less $6,000 deferred into next year) with the 20% noncontrolling interest being allocated $13,600.

Consolidation entries:

(*G) Removal of unrealized gain from beginning figures so that it can be recognized in current period. Upstream sales attributed to subsidiary.

(S) Elimination of adjusted stockholders' equity accounts along with recognition of January 1, 2002, noncontrolling interest.

(A) Allocation of parent's cost in excess of subsidiary's book value, unamortized balance as of January 1, 2002.

(I) Elimination of intercompany income.

(D) Elimination of intercompany dividends.

(E) Recognition of amortization expense for current year on database.

(P) Elimination of intercompany receivable/payable balances.

(TI) Elimination of intercompany sales/purchases balances.

(G) Removal of unrealized gain from ending figures so that it can be recognized in subsequent period.

by Hastings to Patrick at a $100,000 transfer price. The seller reports a $40,000 gain; the buyer records the land at the $100,000 acquisition price. At the end of this fiscal period, the intercompany effect of this transaction must be eliminated for consolidation purposes:

Consolidation Entry TL (year of transfer)

Gain on Sale of Land 40,000
    Land 40,000
    To eliminate effects of intercompany transfer of land.
    (Labeled "TL" in reference to the transferred land.)

This worksheet entry eliminates the unrealized gain from the consolidated statements of 2001. However, as with the transfer of inventory, the effects created by the original transaction remain in the financial records of the individual companies for as long as the property is held. The gain recorded by Hastings carries through to retained earnings while Patrick's Land account retains the inflated transfer price. *Therefore, for every subsequent consolidation until the land is eventually sold, the elimination process must be repeated.* By including the following entry on each subsequent worksheet, the unrealized gain is removed from the asset and from the earnings reported by the combination.

Consolidation Entry *GL (every year following transfer)

Retained Earnings (beginning balance of seller) 40,000
    Land 40,000
    To eliminate effects of intercompany transfer of land made in a
    previous year. (Labeled as "*GL" in reference to the gain on a
    land transfer occurring in a prior year.)

Note that the reduction in retained earnings is changed to an increase in the Investment account whenever the original sale is downstream and the equity method has been applied by the parent. In that specific situation, equity method adjustments have already corrected the timing of the parent's unrealized gain. Removing the gain has created a reduction in the Investment account that is appropriately allocated to the subsidiary's land account on the worksheet. Conversely, if sales were upstream, the retained earnings of the seller (the subsidiary) continue to be overstated even if the parent applies the equity method.

One final consolidation concern exists in accounting for intercompany transfers of land. If the property is ever sold to an outside party, the company making the sale records a gain or loss based on its recorded book value. However, this cost figure is actually the internal transfer price. The gain or loss being recognized is incorrect for consolidation purposes; it has not been computed by comparison to the land's historical cost. Once again, the separate financial records fail to reflect the transaction from the perspective of the single economic entity.

Therefore, if the land is eventually sold, the gain deferred at the time of the original transfer must be recognized. This profit finally has been earned by the sale of the property to outsiders. On the worksheet, the gain is removed one last time from beginning retained earnings (or the Investment account, if applicable). In this instance, though, the entry is completed by reclassifying the amount as a realized gain. The timing of income recognition has been switched from the year of transfer into the fiscal period in which the land is sold to the unrelated party.

Returning to the previous illustration, land was acquired by Hastings for $60,000 and sold to Patrick, a related party, for $100,000. Consequently, the $40,000 unrealized gain was eliminated on the consolidation worksheet in the year of transfer as well as in each succeeding period. However, if this land is subsequently sold to an outside party for $115,000, Patrick would recognize only a $15,000 gain. From the viewpoint of the business combination, the land (having been bought for $60,000) was actually sold at a $55,000 gain. To correct the reporting, the following consolidation entry must be made in the year that the property is sold to the unrelated party. This adjustment increases the $15,000 gain recorded by Patrick to the consolidated balance of $55,000.

Consolidation Entry *GL (year of sale to outside party)

Retained Earnings (Hastings)............................	40,000	
Gain on Sale of Land		40,000

To remove intercompany gain from year of transfer so that total profit can be recognized in the current period when land is sold to an outside party.

As in the accounting for inventory transfers, the entire consolidation process demonstrated here accomplishes two major objectives:

1. Historical cost is reported for the transferred land for as long as it remains within the business combination.

2. Income recognition is deferred until the land is sold to outside parties.

Effect on Noncontrolling Interest Valuation—Land Transfers

The preceding discussion of intercompany land transfers has ignored the possible presence of a noncontrolling interest. In constructing financial statements for an economic entity that includes outside ownership, the guidelines already established for inventory transfers remain applicable.

If the original sale was a *downstream* transaction, neither the annual deferral nor the eventual recognition of the unrealized gain has any effect on the noncontrolling interest. The rationale for this treatment, as previously indicated, is that profits from downstream transfers relate solely to the parent company.

Conversely, if the transfer is made *upstream,* deferral and recognition of gains are attributed to the subsidiary and, hence, to the valuation of the noncontrolling interest. As with inventory, all noncontrolling interest balances are to be computed on the reported earnings of the subsidiary after adjustment for any upstream transfers.

To reiterate, the accounting consequences stemming from land transfers are:

1. In the year of transfer, any unrealized gain is deferred and the land account is reduced to historical cost. When the gain is created by an upstream sale, the amount also is excluded in calculating the noncontrolling interest's share of the subsidiary's net income for that year.

2. Each year thereafter, the unrealized gain will be removed from the beginning retained earnings of the seller. If the transfer was upstream, eliminating this earlier gain directly affects the balances recorded within both Entry *C (if conversion to the equity method is required) and Entry S. The additional equity accrual (Entry *C, if needed) as well as the elimination of beginning stockholders' equity (Entry S) must be based on the newly adjusted balance in the subsidiary's retained earnings. This deferral process also has an impact on the noncontrolling interest's share of the subsidiary's income but only in the year of transfer and the eventual year of sale.

3. In the event that the land is ever sold to an outside party, the original gain is earned and must be reported by the consolidated entity.

INTERCOMPANY TRANSFER OF DEPRECIABLE ASSETS

Just as land can be transferred between related parties, the intercompany sale of a host of other assets is possible. Equipment, patents, franchises, buildings, as well as other long-lived assets may be involved. Accounting for these transactions resembles that demonstrated for land sales. However, the subsequent calculation of depreciation or amortization provides an added challenge in the development of consolidated statements.[8]

The Deferral of Unrealized Gains

When faced with intercompany sales of depreciable assets, the accountant's basic objective remains unchanged: *the deferral of unrealized gains to establish both historical cost balances and appropriate income recognition within the consolidated statements.* More specifically, gains created by these transfers are deferred until such time as the subsequent use or resale of the asset consummates the original transaction. For inventory sales, the culminating disposal normally occurs currently or in the year following the transfer. In contrast, transferred land is quite often never resold, thus permanently deferring the recognition of the intercompany profit.

For depreciable asset transfers, the ultimate realization of the gain normally occurs in a different manner; the property's use within the buyer's operations is reflected through depreciation. Recognition of this expense reduces the asset's book value every year and, hence, the overvaluation within that balance.

The depreciation systematically eliminates the unrealized gain not only from the asset account but also from retained earnings. For the buyer, excess expense results each year because the computation is based on the inflated transfer cost. This depreciation is then closed annually into retained earnings. *From a consolidated perspective, the extra expense gradually offsets the unrealized gain within this equity account. In fact, over the life of the asset, the depreciation process eliminates all effects of the transfer from both the asset balance as well as the Retained Earnings account.*

Depreciable Asset Transfers Illustrated

To examine the consolidation procedures required by the intercompany transfer of a depreciable asset, assume that Able Company sells equipment to Baker Company at the current market value of $90,000. The equipment originally had been acquired by Able for $100,000 several years ago; since that time, $40,000 in accumulated depreciation has been recorded. The transfer is made on January 1, 2001, when the equipment has a 10-year remaining life.

Year of Transfer   The 2001 effects on the separate financial accounts of the two companies can be quickly enumerated:

1. Baker, as the buyer, enters the equipment into its records at the $90,000 transfer price. However, from a consolidated view, the $60,000 book value ($100,000 cost less $40,000 accumulated depreciation) is still appropriate.
2. Able, as the seller, reports a profit of $30,000, although nothing has yet been earned by the combination. This gain is then closed into the company's Retained Earnings account at the end of 2001.
3. Assuming application of the straight-line method of depreciation with no salvage value, Baker records expense of $9,000 at the end of 2001 ($90,000 transfer price/10 years). The buyer recognizes this amount rather than the $6,000 depreciation figure applicable to the consolidated entity ($60,000 book value/10 years).

To report these events as seen by the business combination, both the $30,000 unrealized gain and the $3,000 inflation in depreciation expense must be eliminated on the worksheet. For clarification purposes, two separate consolidation entries are shown here for 2001. However, they can be combined into a single adjustment.

---

[8]To avoid redundancy within this analysis, all further references are made to depreciation expense alone, although this discussion is equally applicable to the amortization of intangible assets or the depletion of wasting assets.

Consolidation Entry TA (year of transfer)

Gain on Sale of Equipment...............................	30,000	
Equipment..	10,000	
Accumulated Depreciation..........................		40,000

To remove unrealized gain and return equipment accounts to balances based on original historical cost. (Labeled "TA" in reference to transferred asset.)

Consolidation Entry ED (year of transfer)

Accumulated Depreciation..............................	3,000	
Depreciation Expense..............................		3,000

To eliminate overstatement of depreciation expense caused by inflated transfer price. (Labeled "ED" in reference to excess depreciation.)
Entry must be repeated for all 10 years of the equipment's life.

From the viewpoint of a single entity, these entries accomplish several objectives.

- The asset's historical cost of $100,000 is reinstated.
- By recording accumulated depreciation of $40,000, the January 1, 2001, book value is returned to the appropriate $60,000 figure.
- The $30,000 unrealized gain recorded by Able is eliminated so that this intercompany profit does not appear in the consolidated income statement.
- Depreciation for the year is reduced from $9,000 to $6,000, the appropriate expense based on historical cost.

In the year of the intercompany depreciable asset transfer, the above consolidation entries TA and ED are applicable regardless of whether the transfer was upstream or downstream. They are likewise applicable regardless of whether the parent applies the equity method, cost method, or partial equity method of accounting for its investment. As discussed below, however, in the years following the intercompany transfer, a slight modification must be made to the Consolidation Entry *TA when the equity method is applied and the transfer was downstream.

Years Following Transfer   Once again, the preceding worksheet entries do not actually remove the effects of the intercompany transfer from the individual records of these two organizations. Both the unrealized gain and the excess depreciation expense remain on the separate books and are closed into the retained earnings of the respective companies at year's end. Similarly, the Equipment account along with the related accumulated depreciation continue to hold balances based on the transfer price and not historical cost. *Thus, for every subsequent period, the separately reported figures must be adjusted on the worksheet to present the consolidated totals from the perspective of a single entity.*

To derive worksheet entries at any future point, the balances in the accounts of the individual companies must be ascertained and compared to the figures appropriate for the business combination. As an illustration, the separate records of Able and Baker two years after the transfer (December 31, 2002) follow. Consolidated totals are calculated based on the original historical cost of $100,000 and accumulated depreciation of $40,000.

Account	Individual Records	Consolidated Perspective	Worksheet Adjustments
Equipment 12/31/02	$ 90,000	$100,000	$ 10,000
Accumulated Depreciation 12/31/02	(18,000)	(52,000)*	(34,000)
Depreciation Expense 12/31/02	9,000	6,000	(3,000)
1/1/02 Retained Earnings effect	(21,000)†	6,000	27,000

*Accumulated depreciation before transfer $(40,000) plus 2 years × $(6,000).

†Intercompany transfer gain $(30,000) less one year's depreciation of $9,000.

Note: Parentheses indicate a credit.

Because effects of the transfer continue to exist in the separate financial records, the various accounts have to be corrected in each succeeding consolidation. However, the amounts involved must be updated every period because of the continual impact that depreciation has on these balances. As an example, to adjust the individual figures to the consolidated totals derived earlier, the 2002 worksheet must include the following entries:

Consolidation Entry *TA (year following transfer)

Equipment.	10,000	
Retained Earnings, 1/1/02 (Able).	27,000	
Accumulated Depreciation.		37,000

To return the equipment account to original historical cost and correct the 1/1/02 balances of retained earnings and accumulated depreciation.

Consolidation Entry ED (year following transfer)

Accumulated Depreciation	3,000	
Depreciation Expense.		3,000

To remove excess depreciation expense on the intercompany transfer price and adjust accumulated depreciation to its correct 12/31/02 balance.

Note that the $34,000 increase in 12/31/02 consolidated accumulated depreciation is accomplished by a $37,000 credit in Entry *TA and a $3,000 debit in Entry ED.

Although adjustments of the asset and depreciation expense remain constant, the change in beginning retained earnings and accumulated depreciation vary with each succeeding consolidation. At December 31, 2001, the individual companies closed out both the unrealized gain of $30,000 and the initial $3,000 overstatement of depreciation expense. Therefore, as reflected in Entry *TA, the beginning retained earnings account for 2002 is overvalued by a net amount of only $27,000 rather than $30,000. *Over the life of the asset, the unrealized gain in retained earnings will be systematically reduced to zero as excess depreciation expense ($3,000) is closed out each year.* Hence, on subsequent consolidation worksheets, the beginning retained earnings account is decreased by $27,000 in 2002, by $24,000 in 2003, and $21,000 in the following period. This reduction continues until the effect of the unrealized gain no longer exists at the end of 10 years.

If this equipment is ever resold to an outside party, the remaining portion of the gain would be consummated. As in the previous discussion of land, the intercompany profit that exists at that date must be recognized on the consolidated income statement to arrive at the appropriate amount of gain or loss on the sale.

Depreciable Intercompany Asset Transfers—Downstream Transfers When the Parent Uses the Equity Method

A slight modification to Consolidation Entry *TA is required when the intercompany depreciable asset transfer is downstream and the parent uses the equity method. In applying the equity method, the parent adjusts its book income for both the original transfer gain and periodic depreciation expense adjustments. Thus, in downstream intercompany transfers when the equity method is used, from a consolidated view the book value of the parent's retained earnings balance has been already reduced for the gain. Therefore, continuing with the previous example, the following worksheet consolidation entries would be made for a downstream sale assuming (1) Able is the parent and (2) Able has applied the equity method to account for its investment in Baker.

Consolidation Entry *TA (year following transfer)

Equipment.	10,000	
Investment in Baker	27,000	
Accumulated Depreciation.		37,000

Consolidation Entry ED (year following transfer)

Accumulated Depreciation	3,000	
Depreciation Expense............................		3,000

In Entry *TA, note that the Investment in Baker account replaces the parent's retained earnings. The debit to the Investment account effectively allocates the writedown necessitated by the intercompany transfer to the appropriate subsidiary equipment and accumulated depreciation accounts.

Effect on Noncontrolling Interest Valuation—Depreciable Asset Transfers

Because of the lack of official guidance, no easy answer exists about the assignment of any income effects created within the consolidation process. Consistent with the previous sections of this chapter, all income is assigned here to the original seller. In Entry *TA, for example, the beginning retained earnings account of Able (the seller) is reduced. Both the unrealized gain on the transfer and the excess depreciation expense subsequently recognized are assigned to that party.

Thus, once again, downstream sales are assumed to have no effect on any noncontrolling interest values. The parent made the sale rather than the subsidiary. Conversely, the impact on income created by upstream sales must be taken into account in computing the balances attributed to these outside owners. Currently, this approach is one of many acceptable alternatives. However, in its future deliberations on consolidation policies and procedures, the FASB may possibly mandate a specific allocation pattern.

SUMMARY

1. The transfer of assets, especially inventory, between the members of a business combination is a common practice. In producing consolidated financial statements, any effects on the separate accounting records created by such transfers must be removed because the transactions did not occur with an outside, unrelated party.

2. Inventory transfers are the most prevalent form of intercompany asset transaction. Despite being only a transfer, one company records a sale while the other reports a purchase. These balances are reciprocals that have to be offset on the worksheet in the process of producing consolidated figures.

3. Additional accounting problems result if inventory is transferred at a markup. Any portion of the merchandise still held at year-end would be valued at more than historical cost because of the inflation in price. Furthermore, the gross profit reported by the seller on these goods is unrealized from a consolidation perspective. Thus, this gain must be removed from ending inventory, a figure that appears as an asset on the balance sheet and as a negative component within cost of goods sold.

4. Unrealized inventory gains also create a consolidation problem in the year following the transfer. Within the separate accounting systems, the seller closes the gross profit to retained earnings. The buyer's ending inventory becomes the beginning balance (within cost of goods sold) of the next period. Therefore, the inflation must be removed again but this time in the subsequent year. Beginning retained earnings of the seller is decreased to eliminate the unrealized gain while cost of goods sold is reduced to remove the overstatement from the beginning inventory component. Through this process, the intercompany profit is deferred from the year of transfer so that recognition can be made at the point of disposal or consumption.

5. The deferral and subsequent realization of intercompany gains raises a question concerning the valuation of noncontrolling interest balances: Does the change in the period of recognition alter these calculations? Although the issue is currently under debate, no formal answer to this question is yet found in official accounting pronouncements. In this textbook, the deferral of gains from upstream transfers (from

subsidiary to parent) is assumed to affect the noncontrolling interest whereas downstream transactions (from parent to subsidiary) do not. When upstream transfers are involved, noncontrolling interest values are based on the earned figures remaining after adjustment for any unrealized gains.

6. Inventory is not the only asset that can be sold between the members of a business combination. For example, transfers of land sometimes occur. Once again, if the price exceeds original cost, the asset is stated on the buyer's records at an inflated value while an unrealized gain is recognized by the seller. As with inventory, the consolidation process must return the asset's recorded balance to cost while deferring the gain. Repetition of this procedure is necessary in every consolidation for as long as the land remains within the business combination.

7. The consolidation process required by the intercompany transfer of depreciable assets differs somewhat from that demonstrated for inventory and land. Unrealized gain created by the transaction must still be eliminated along with the overstatement of the asset. However, because of subsequent depreciation, these adjustments systematically change from period to period. Following the transfer, depreciation is computed by the buyer based on the new inflated transfer price. Thus, expense is recorded that reduces the carrying value of the asset at a rate in excess of appropriate depreciation; the book value moves closer to the historical cost figure each time that depreciation is recorded. Additionally, because the excess depreciation is closed annually to retained earnings, the overstatement of the equity account resulting from the unrealized gain is constantly reduced. To produce consolidated figures at any point in time, the remaining inflation in these figures (as well as in the current depreciation expense) must be determined and removed.

COMPREHENSIVE ILLUSTRATION

Problem

(Estimated Time: 45 to 65 Minutes) On January 1, 1996, Daisy Company purchased 80 percent of Rose Company for $594,000 in cash. The total book value of Rose on that date was $610,000. The newly acquired subsidiary possessed equipment (10-year remaining life) that was undervalued by $75,000 in the company's accounting records and land that was undervalued by $15,000. Any excess intangibles within the purchase will be amortized over 10 years.

Daisy decided to acquire Rose so that the subsidiary could furnish component parts for the parent's production process. During the ensuing years, Rose sold inventory to Daisy as follows:

Year	Cost to Rose Company	Transfer Price	Markup on Transfer Price	Transferred Inventory Being Held at End of Year (at transfer price)
1996	$ 60,000	$ 90,000	33.3%	$10,000
1997	80,000	100,000	20.0	15,000
1998	90,000	120,000	25.0	10,000
1999	100,000	140,000	28.6	20,000
2000	100,000	150,000	33.3	30,000
2001	96,000	160,000	40.0	40,000

Any transferred merchandise retained by Daisy at the end of a year was always put into production during the following period.

On January 1, 1999, Daisy sold several pieces of equipment to Rose. These assets had a 10-year remaining life and were being depreciated on the straight-line method with no salvage value. This equipment was transferred at an $80,000 price, although it had an original cost to Daisy of $100,000 and a book value at the date of exchange of $44,000.

On January 1, 2001, Daisy sold land to Rose for $60,000, the fair market value at that date. The original cost had been only $40,000. By the end of 2001, no payment had yet been made by Rose.

The following separate financial statements are for Daisy and Rose as of December 31, 2001. Daisy has applied the equity method to account for this investment.

	Daisy Company	Rose Company
Sales	$ 900,000	$ 500,000
Cost of goods sold	(600,000)	(300,000)
Operating expenses	(210,000)	(80,000)
Gain on sale of land	20,000	–0–
Income of Rose Company	65,400	–0–
Net income	$ 175,400	$ 120,000
Retained earnings, 1/1/01	$ 620,000	$ 430,000
Net income	175,400	120,000
Dividends paid	(55,400)	(50,000)
Retained earnings, 12/31/01	$ 740,000	$ 500,000
Cash and accounts receivable	$ 380,000	$ 410,000
Inventory	421,600	190,000
Investment in Rose Company	711,600	–0–
Land	452,800	280,000
Equipment	270,000	190,000
Accumulated depreciation	(180,000)	(50,000)
Total assets	$2,056,000	$1,020,000
Liabilities	716,000	120,000
Common stock	600,000	400,000
Retained earnings, 12/31/01	740,000	500,000
Total liabilities and equities	$2,056,000	$1,020,000

Required:

Answer the following questions:

a. By how much did Rose's book value increase during the period from January 1, 1996, through December 31, 2000?

b. During the initial years after the takeover, what annual amortization expense was recognized in connection with the parent's purchase price?

c. What amount of unrealized gain exists within the parent's inventory figures at the beginning and at the end of 2001?

d. Equipment has been transferred between the companies. What amount of excess depreciation is recognized in 2001 because of this transfer?

e. The parent reports Income of Rose Company for 2001 of $65,400. How was this figure calculated?

f. Without using a worksheet, determine consolidated totals.

g. Prepare the worksheet entries required at December 31, 2001, by the transfer of inventory, land, and equipment.

Solution

a. The subsidiary's book value on the date of purchase was given as $610,000. At the beginning of 2001, the company's common stock and retained earnings total to $830,000 ($400,000 and $430,000, respectively). In the previous years, Rose's book value has apparently grown by $220,000 ($830,000 − $610,000).

b. To determine amortization, an allocation of the purchase price must first be made. The following allocations to equipment ($60,000) and intangibles (residual $34,000) lead to additional annual expenses of $9,400 for the initial years of the combination. The $12,000 assigned to land is not subject to amortization.

Cost Allocation and Excess Amortization Schedule

Purchase price	$ 594,000
Book value of Rose Company ($610,000 × 80%)	(488,000)
Excess cost over book value	106,000

	Life (years)	Annual Excess Amortizations	Excess Amortizations 1996–2001	Unamortized Value, 12/31/01
Equipment undervaluation ($75,000 × 80%) ... 60,000	10	$6,000	$36,000	$24,000
Land undervaluation ($15,000 × 80%) ... 12,000				
Intangibles $34,000	10	3,400	20,400	13,600
		$9,400		

c. Of the inventory transferred to Daisy during 2000, $30,000 is still held at the beginning of 2001. This merchandise contains an unrealized gain of $10,000 ($30,000 × 33.3% [rounded] markup for that year). At year's end, $16,000 ($40,000 remaining inventory × 40% markup) is viewed as an unrealized gain.

d. Excess depreciation for 2001 is $3,600. Equipment with a book value of $44,000 was transferred at a price of $80,000. The addition of $36,000 to this asset's account balance would be written off over 10 years for an extra $3,600 per year.

e. According to the separate statements given, the subsidiary reports net income of $120,000. However, in determining the income allocation between the parent and the noncontrolling interest, this reported figure must be adjusted for the effects of any *upstream* transfers. Because the inventory was sold upstream from Rose to Daisy, the $10,000 gain deferred in requirement (c) from 2000 into the current period is attributed to the subsidiary (as the seller). Likewise, the $16,000 unrealized gain at year's end is viewed as a reduction in Rose's income.

    All other transfers are downstream and not considered to have an effect on the subsidiary. Therefore, the Income of Rose Company balance can be verified as follows:

Rose Company's reported income—2001	$120,000
Recognition of 2000 unrealized gain	+10,000
Deferral of 2001 unrealized gain	(16,000)
Earned income of subsidiary from consolidated perspective	114,000
Parent's ownership percentage	80%
Equity income accrual	$ 91,200
Adjustments attributed to parent's ownership:	
Excess amortization expense—2001 (see requirement b)	(9,400)
Deferral of unrealized gain—land	(20,000)
Removal of excess depreciation (see requirement d)	+3,600
Income of Rose Company—2001	$ 65,400

f. Each of the 2001 consolidated totals for this business combination can be determined as follows:

Sales = $1,240,000. The parent's balance is added to the subsidiary's balance less the $160,000 in intercompany transfers for the period.

Cost of Goods Sold = $746,000. The computation begins by adding the parent's balance to the subsidiary's balance less the $160,000 in intercompany transfers for the period. The $10,000 unrealized gain from the previous year is deducted to recognize this income currently. Next, the $16,000 ending unrealized gain is added to cost of goods sold to defer the income until a later year when the goods are sold to an outside party.

Operating Expenses = $295,800. The parent's balance is added to the subsidiary's balance. Annual amortization of $9,400 on the purchase price allocations (see requirement b) must also be included. Excess depreciation of $3,600 resulting from the transfer of equipment (see requirement e) is removed.

Gain on Sale of Land = –0–. This amount is eliminated for consolidation purposes because the transaction was intercompany.

Income of Rose Company = 0. The equity income figure is removed so that the actual revenues and expenses of the subsidiary can be included in the financial statements without double-counting.

Noncontrolling Interest in Subsidiary's Income = $22,800. In requirement (*d*), the earned income of the subsidiary was computed as $114,000 after adjustments were made for unrealized upstream gains. Because outsiders hold 20 percent of the subsidiary, an allocation of $22,800 ($114,000 × 20%) is necessary.

Net Income = $175,400. This total is derived from the previous consolidated balances. Because the equity method has been applied, consolidated net income is also equal to the balance reported by the parent.

Retained Earnings, 1/1/01 = $620,000. The equity method has been applied; therefore, the parent's balance is equal to the consolidated total.

Dividends Paid = $55,400. Only the amount the parent paid is shown in the consolidated statements. Distributions made by the subsidiary to the parent are eliminated as intercompany transfers. Any payment to the noncontrolling interest reduces the ending balance attributed to these outside owners.

Cash and Accounts Receivable = $730,000. The two balances are added after removal of the $60,000 intercompany receivable created by the transfer of land.

Inventory = $595,600. The two balances are added after removal of the $16,000 ending unrealized gain (see requirement *c*).

Investment in Rose Company = –0–. The investment balance is eliminated so that the actual assets and liabilities of the subsidiary can be included.

Land = $724,800. The two balances are added. The $20,000 unrealized gain created by the transfer is removed. The $12,000 allocation from the purchase price is added.

Equipment = $540,000. The two balances are added. Because of the intercompany transfer, $20,000 must also be included to adjust the $80,000 transfer price to the original $100,000 cost of the asset. A $60,000 allocation within the purchase price must also be recognized.

Accumulated Depreciation = $311,200. The balances are added together along with the $36,000 that has been written off in connection with the purchase price allocation to equipment ($6,000 per year for six years). The $56,000 in accumulated depreciation on the equipment (before its transfer) must also be reinstated. A reduction of $10,800 is made to remove the excess depreciation subsequently recorded on this same equipment ($3,600 per year for three years).

Intangibles = $13,600. The $34,000 allocation is recognized less six years of amortization ($20,400, or $3,400 per year for six years).

Total Assets = $2,292,800. This figure is a summation of the preceding consolidated assets.

Liabilities = $776,000. The two balances are added after removal of the $60,000 intercompany payable created by the transfer of land.

Noncontrolling Interest in Subsidiary, 12/31/01 = $176,800. This figure is composed of several different balances:

Book value of subsidiary, 1/1/01 (common stock and beginning retained earnings)	$830,000
Unrealized gain on upstream transfer as of beginning of year	(10,000)
Earned book value of subsidiary, 1/1/01	$820,000
Noncontrolling interest	20%
Noncontrolling interest, 1/1/01	$164,000
Noncontrolling interest in subsidiary's income (see above)	22,800
Less: Dividends paid to noncontrolling interest ($50,000 × 20%)	(10,000)
Noncontrolling interest, 12/31/01	$176,800

Common Stock = $600,000. The parent company balance only is reported within the consolidated statements.

Retained Earnings, 12/31/01 = $740,000. Retained earnings are found by adding consolidated net income to the beginning retained earnings balance and then subtracting the dividends paid. All of these figures have been computed previously.

Total Liabilities and Equities = $2,292,800. This figure is the summation of all consolidated liabilities and equities.

CONSOLIDATION WORKSHEET ENTRIES— INTERCOMPANY TRANSACTIONS
December 31, 2001

Inventory

Entry *G

Retained Earnings, 1/1/01—Subsidiary	10,000	
Cost of Goods Sold		10,000

To remove 2000 unrealized gain from beginning balances of the current year. Because transfers were upstream, retained earnings of the subsidiary (as the original seller) are being reduced. Balance is computed in requirement (*c*).

Entry TI

Sales	160,000	
Cost of Goods Sold		160,000

To eliminate current year intercompany transfer of inventory.

Entry G

Cost of Goods Sold	16,000	
Inventory		16,000

To remove 2001 unrealized gain from ending accounts of the current year. Balance is computed in requirement (*c*).

Land

Entry TL

Gain on Sale of Land	20,000	
Land		20,000

To eliminate gain created on first day of current year by an intercompany transfer of land.

Equipment

Entry *TA

Equipment	20,000	
Investment in Rose Company	28,800	
Accumulated Depreciation		48,800

To remove unrealized gain (as of January 1, 2001) created by intercompany transfer of equipment and to adjust equipment and accumulated depreciation to historical cost figures.

Equipment is increased from the $80,000 transfer price to $100,000 cost.

Accumulated depreciation of $56,000 was eliminated at time of transfer. Excess depreciation of $3,600 per year has been recorded for the two prior years ($7,200); thus, the accumulated depreciation is now only $48,800 less than cost-based figure.

The unrealized gain on the transfer was $36,000 ($80,000 less $44,000). That figure has now been reduced by two years of excess depreciation ($7,200). Because the parent used the equity method and this transfer was downstream, the adjustment here is to the investment account rather than the parent's beginning retained earnings.

Entry ED

Accumulated Depreciation	3,600	
Operating Expenses (depreciation)		3,600

To eliminate the current year overstatement of depreciation created by inflated transfer price.

APPENDIX

Transfers—Alternative Approaches

In this chapter, we use one method in consolidating the effects of intercompany transfers and unrealized gains when a noncontrolling interest is present. This approach was chosen because it is consistent with the guidelines put forth in *ARB 51*. Over the years, several other possibilities have been devised and considered. The FASB's discussion memorandum, *An Analysis of Issues Related to Consolidation Policy and Procedures,* describes eight methods of consolidating intercompany transactions (three for downstream transfers and five for upstream). The following table indicates the range of potential effects on consolidated totals by demonstrating six of these approaches (two for downstream and four for upstream). All methods except for proportionate consolidation have been included.

The figures used in this illustration are the same as in the Large Company and Small Company example in the first section of this chapter.

Large owns 70 percent of the outstanding stock of Small.

Intercompany inventory transfers during the year amount to $200,000.

The remaining unrealized gain at the end of the year is $40,000.

Subsidiary reported income is $100,000.

Downstream Transfers (from parent to subsidiary)

	*ARB 51** Economic Unit Concept One Variation of Parent Company Concept (method used in this textbook)	Another Variation of Parent Company Concept
Sales	Eliminate all $200,000 transfers	Eliminate $140,000 (70%) of the transfers
Purchases	Eliminate all $200,000 transfers	Eliminate $140,000 (70%) of the transfers
Unrealized gain	Eliminate all $40,000	Eliminate $28,000 (70%)
Income assigned to noncontrolling interests	30% of $100,000 reported income or $30,000	30% of $100,000 reported income or $30,000

Upstream Transfers (from subsidiary to parent)

	ARB 51 Economic Unit Concept (method used in this textbook)	One Variation of Parent Company Concept	Another Approach Based on *ARB 51*	Another Variation of Parent Company Concept
Sales	Eliminate all $200,000 transfers	Eliminate $140,000 (70%) of the transfers	Eliminate all $200,000 transfers	Eliminate all $200,000 transfers
Purchases	Eliminate all $200,000 transfers	Eliminate $140,000 (70%) of the transfers	Eliminate all $200,000 transfers	Eliminate all $200,000 transfers
Unrealized gain	Eliminate all $40,000	Eliminate $28,000 (70%)	Eliminate all $40,000	Eliminate $28,000 (70%)
Income assigned to noncontrolling interests	30% of $60,000 realized income after removing $40,000 unrealized gain or $18,000	30% of $100,000 reported income or $30,000	30% of $100,000 reported income or $30,000	30% of $100,000 reported income or $30,000

*Titles indicate authority for each approach.

QUESTIONS

1. Intercompany transfers between the component companies of a business combination are quite common. Why do these intercompany transactions occur so frequently?

2. Barker Company owns 80 percent of the outstanding voting stock of Walden Company. During the current year, intercompany sales amount to $100,000. These transactions

were made with a markup equal to 40 percent of the transfer price. In consolidating the two companies, what amount of these sales would be eliminated?

3. Padlock Corp. owns 90 percent of Safeco, Inc. During the year Padlock sold 3,000 locking mechanisms to Safeco for $900,000. By the end of the year Safeco had sold all but 500 of the locking mechanisms to outside parties. Padlock marks up the cost of its locking mechanisms by 60 percent in computing its sale price to affiliated and nonaffiliated customers. How much intercompany profit remains in Safeco's inventory at year-end?

4. How are unrealized inventory gains created, and what consolidation entries are necessitated by the presence of these gains?

5. James, Inc., sells inventory to Matthews Company, a related party. The inventory was sold at James's standard markup. At the end of the current fiscal year, some portion of this inventory is still being held by Matthews. If consolidated financial statements are to be prepared, why are worksheet entries required in two different fiscal periods?

6. When intercompany gains are present in any year, how are the noncontrolling interest calculations affected?

7. A worksheet is being developed to consolidate Williams, Incorporated, and Brown Company. Considerable intercompany transactions have been made between these two organizations. How would the consolidation process be affected if these transfers were downstream? How would the consolidation process be affected if these transfers were upstream?

8. King Company owns a 90 percent interest in the outstanding voting shares of Pawn Company. Pawn reports a net income of $110,000 for the current year. Intercompany sales are made at regular intervals between the two companies. Unrealized gains of $30,000 were present in the beginning inventory balances, whereas $60,000 in similar gains were recorded at the end of the year. What is the noncontrolling interest's share of the subsidiary's net income?

9. When a subsidiary sells inventory to a parent, the intercompany profit is removed from the subsidiary's income and reduces the income allocation to the noncontrolling interest. Is the profit permanently eliminated from the noncontrolling interest or is it merely shifted from one period to the next? Explain.

10. The consolidation process that is applicable when intercompany land transfers have occurred is somewhat different from that used for intercompany inventory sales. What differences should be noted?

11. A subsidiary sells land to the parent company at a significant gain. The parent holds the land for two years and then sells it to an outside party, also for a gain. How are these events accounted for by the business combination?

12. Why does an intercompany sale of a depreciable asset (such as equipment or a building) require subsequent adjustments to depreciation expense within the consolidation process?

13. If an intercompany sale of a depreciable asset has been made at a price above book value, the beginning retained earnings of the seller are reduced when preparing each subsequent consolidation. Why does the amount of the adjustment change from year to year?

INTERNET ASSIGNMENT

Internet sites are time and date sensitive. It is the purpose of these exercises to have you explore the Internet. You may need to refer to the text's Web site at http://www.mhhe.com/hoyle6e to find the most up-to-date links for the Web sites listed in the Internet Assignments.

1. Locate recent annual reports through the Web sites of Alltel (www.alltel.com), CSX Corporation (www.csx.com), Ford Motor Co. (www.ford.com), General Motors (www.gm.com), or any other consolidated entity with significant intercompany transactions. Prepare a brief report addressing the following:

   ■ What amount is disclosed as intercompany profits (often listed as intersegment revenue)?

- Is the method of pricing intercompany sales disclosed?
- Calculate the percentage of total segment revenues represented by intersegment activity.
- Discuss how intercompany sales contribute to the business strategies of consolidated organizations.

LIBRARY ASSIGNMENTS

1. As discussed in "Track Stars" (*Journal of Accountancy*, July 1999), a recent trend of issuing tracking stocks is evident in firms such as GM, USX, U.S. West, Pittston, Georgia-Pacific, Ralston-Purina, and DuPont. Read this article and report on the motivations behind the use of tracking stocks and the potential measurement issues that arise when the related entities sell inventory to one another.

2. Read the following as well as any other published materials that might be available concerning transfer pricing:

   "The Transfer Price Is Right," *Strategic Finance*, July 1999.

   "Transfer Pricing by Multinational Marketers: Risky Business," *Business Horizons,* January 1996.

   "Setting the Right Transfer Price," *Management Accounting,* December 1994.

   "Transfer Pricing in the 1990s," *Management Accounting,* February 1992.

   Write a report outlining several methods of setting transfer prices on intercompany transfers. Select one approach as preferable and justify its application.

3. Read Chapter 6, "Intercompany Transactions," of the FASB discussion memorandum, *An Analysis of Issues Related to Consolidation Policy and Procedures.* Select an approach that should be used in preparing consolidated financial statements where intercompany transfers occur and then justify its adoption.

PROBLEMS

1. What is the impact on consolidated financial statements of upstream and downstream transfers?
   - *a.* No difference exists in consolidated financial statements between upstream and downstream transfers.
   - *b.* Downstream transfers affect the computation of the noncontrolling interest's share of the subsidiary's income but upstream transfers do not.
   - *c.* Upstream transfers affect the computation of the noncontrolling interest's share of the subsidiary's income but downstream transfers do not.
   - *d.* Downstream transfers may be ignored since they are made by the parent company.

2. King Corporation owns 80 percent of Lee Corporation's common stock. During October 2001, Lee sold merchandise to King for $100,000. At December 31, 2001, 50 percent of this merchandise remains in King's inventory. For 2001, gross profit percentages were 30 percent for King and 40 percent for Lee. The amount of unrealized intercompany profit in ending inventory at December 31, 2001, that should be eliminated in the consolidation process is:
   - *a.* $40,000
   - *b.* $20,000
   - *c.* $16,000
   - *d.* $15,000

   (AICPA adapted)

3. When intercompany transfers occur, how is the noncontrolling interest's share of the subsidiary's income computed?
   - *a.* The subsidiary's reported income is adjusted for the impact of upstream transfers prior to computing the noncontrolling interest's allocation.
   - *b.* The subsidiary's reported income is adjusted for the impact of all transfers prior to computing the noncontrolling interest's allocation.

    c. The subsidiary's reported income is not adjusted for the impact of transfers prior to computing the noncontrolling interest's allocation.

    d. The subsidiary's reported income is adjusted for the impact of downstream transfers prior to computing the noncontrolling interest's allocation.

4. Bellgrade, Inc., acquired a 60 percent interest in the Hansen Company several years ago. During 2000, Hansen sold inventory costing $75,000 to Bellgrade for $100,000. A total of 16 percent of this inventory was not sold to outsiders until 2001. During 2001, Hansen sold inventory costing $96,000 to Bellgrade for $120,000. A total of 35 percent of this inventory was not sold to outsiders until 2002. In 2001, Bellgrade reported cost of goods sold of $380,000 while Hansen reported $210,000. What is consolidated cost of goods sold?

    a. $465,600

    b. $473,440

    c. $474,400

    d. $522,400

5. Top Company holds 90 percent of the common stock of Bottom Company. In 2001, Top reports sales of $800,000 and cost of goods sold of $600,000. For this same period, Bottom has sales of $300,000 and cost of goods sold of $180,000. During 2001, Top sold merchandise to Bottom for $100,000. The subsidiary still possesses 40 percent of this inventory at the end of 2001. Top had established the transfer price based on its normal markup. What are consolidated sales and cost of goods sold?

    a. $1,000,000 and $690,000.

    b. $1,000,000 and $705,000.

    c. $1,000,000 and $740,000.

    d. $970,000 and $696,000.

6. Use the same information as in problem 5 except assume that the transfers were from Bottom Company to Top Company. What are the consolidated sales and cost of goods sold for 2001?

    a. $1,000,000 and $720,000.

    b. $1,000,000 and $755,000.

    c. $1,000,000 and $696,000.

    d. $970,000 and $712,000.

7. Hardwood, Inc., holds a 90 percent interest in Pittstoni Company. During 2000, Pittstoni sold inventory costing $77,000 to Hardwood for $110,000. A total of $40,000 of this inventory was not sold to outsiders until 2001. During 2001, Pittstoni sold inventory costing $72,000 to Hardwood for $120,000. A total of $50,000 of this inventory was not sold to outsiders until 2002. In 2001, Hardwood reported net income of $150,000 while Pittstoni reported $90,000. What is the noncontrolling interest in the income of the subsidiary?

    a. $8,000

    b. $8,200

    c. $9,000

    d. $9,800

8. Dunn Corporation owns 100 percent of Grey Corporation's common stock. On January 2, 2001, Dunn sold to Grey, for $40,000, machinery with a carrying amount of $30,000. Grey is depreciating the acquired machinery over a five-year life by the straight-line method. The net adjustments to compute 2001 and 2002 consolidated net income would be an increase (decrease) of

	2001	2002
a.	$(8,000)	$2,000
b.	$(8,000)	–0–
c.	$(10,000)	$2,000
d.	$(10,000)	–0–

(AICPA adapted)

9. Wallton Corporation owns 70 percent of the outstanding stock of Hastings, Incorporated. On January 1, 1999, Wallton acquired a building with a 10-year life for $300,000. No salvage value was anticipated and the building was to be depreciated on

the straight-line method. On January 1, 2001, Wallton sold this building to Hastings for $280,000. At that time, the building had a remaining life of eight years but still no expected salvage value. In preparing financial statements for 2001, how does this transfer affect the computation of consolidated net income?

a. Income must be reduced by $32,000.
b. Income must be reduced by $35,000.
c. Income must be reduced by $36,000.
d. Income must be reduced by $40,000.

Use the following data for problems 10–15:

On January 1, 2001, Jarel bought 80 percent of the outstanding voting stock of Suarez for $260,000. Of this payment, $20,000 was allocated to equipment (with a five-year life) that had been undervalued on Suarez's books by $25,000. Any excess purchase price will be allocated to secret formulas and amortized over a 20-year life.

As of December 31, 2001, the financial statements appeared as follows:

	Jarel	Suarez
Revenues	$ 300,000	$200,000
Cost of goods sold	140,000	80,000
Expenses	20,000	10,000
Net income	$ 140,000	$110,000
Retained earnings, 1/1/01	$ 300,000	$150,000
Net income	140,000	110,000
Dividends paid	–0–	–0–
Retained earnings, 12/31/01	$ 440,000	$260,000
Cash and receivables	$ 210,000	$ 90,000
Inventory	150,000	110,000
Investment in Jarel	260,000	–0–
Equipment (net)	440,000	300,000
Total assets	$1,060,000	$500,000
Liabilities	$ 420,000	$140,000
Common stock	200,000	100,000
Retained earnings, 12/31/01	440,000	260,000
Total liabilities and equities	$1,060,000	$500,000

During 2001, Jarel bought inventory for $80,000 and sold it to Suarez for $100,000. Only half of this purchase has been paid for by Suarez by the end of the year. Sixty percent of these goods are still in the company's possession on December 31.

10. What is the total of consolidated revenues?
    a. $500,000
    b. $460,000
    c. $420,000
    d. $400,000

11. What is the total of consolidated expenses?
    a. $30,000
    b. $36,000
    c. $33,000
    d. $39,000

12. What is the total of consolidated cost of goods sold?
    a. $140,000
    b. $152,000
    c. $132,000
    d. $145,000

13. What is the consolidated total of noncontrolling interest appearing on the balance sheet?
    a. $72,000
    b. $69,600
    c. $67,000
    d. $70,600

14. What is the consolidated total for equipment (net) at December 31?
    a. $680,000
    b. $756,000
    c. $764,000
    d. $848,000

15. What is the consolidated total for inventory at December 31?
    a. $240,000
    b. $248,000
    c. $250,000
    d. $260,000

16. Following are several figures reported for Pop and Sam as of December 31, 2001:

	Pop	Sam
Inventory	$300,000	$100,000
Sales	700,000	500,000
Investment income	not given	
Cost of goods sold	300,000	200,000
Operating expenses	200,000	200,000

Pop acquired 80 percent of Sam on January 1, 1994. An excess $180,000 is allocated to an intangible asset and amortized over a 20-year life. During 2001, Sam sells inventory costing $100,000 to Pop for $150,000. Of this inventory, 10 percent remains at year's end. On a 2001 consolidation, determine the totals that would be reported for the following accounts:
    Inventory
    Sales
    Cost of Goods Sold
    Operating Expenses
    Noncontrolling Interest in the Subsidiary's Net Income

17. On January 1, 2001, Corrigan Company purchased 80 percent of the outstanding voting stock of Smashing, Inc., for $980,000 in cash and other consideration. At the purchase date Smashing had common stock of $700,000 and retained earnings of $250,000. Corrigan attributed the excess of cost over Smashing's book value to various covenants with a 20-year life. Corrigan uses the equity method to account for its investment in Smashing.
    During the next two years Smashing reported the following:

	Income	Dividends	Purchases from Corrigan
2001	$150,000	$35,000	$100,000
2002	130,000	45,000	120,000

Corrigan sells inventory to Smashing using a 60 percent markup on sales price. At the end of 2001 and 2002, 40 percent of the current year purchases remain in Smashing's inventory.

Required:

    a. Compute the equity method balance in Corrigan's Investment in Smashing, Inc., account as of 12/31/02.
    b. Prepare the worksheet adjustments for the 12/31/02 consolidation of Corrigan and Smashing.

18. Smith Corporation acquired 80 percent of the outstanding voting stock of Kane, Inc., on January 1, 1994, when Kane had a net book value of $400,000. Any unexplained excess purchase price is assigned to intangible assets and amortized at a rate of $5,000 per year.

Smith reported net income for 2001 of $300,000 while Kane reported $110,000. Smith distributed $100,000 in dividends during this period; Kane paid $40,000. At the end of the year, selected figures from the two companies' balance sheets were as follows:

	Smith Corporation	Kane, Inc.
Inventory	$140,000	$ 90,000
Land	600,000	200,000
Equipment (net)	400,000	300,000
Common stock	400,000	200,000
Retained earnings, 12/31/01	600,000	400,000

During 2000, intercompany sales of $90,000 (original cost of $54,000) were made. Only 20 percent of this inventory was still being held at the end of 2000. In 2001, $120,000 in intercompany sales were made with an original cost of $66,000. Of this merchandise, 30 percent had not been resold to outside parties by the end of the year.

Each of the following questions should be considered as an independent situation.

a. If the intercompany sales were upstream, what would be the noncontrolling interest's share of the subsidiary's 2001 net income?

b. What is the consolidated balance in the ending Inventory account?

c. If the intercompany sales were downstream, what would be the noncontrolling interest's share of the subsidiary's 2001 net income?

d. If the intercompany sales were downstream, what would be the consolidated net income prior to the reduction for the noncontrolling interest's share of the subsidiary's income? Assume that Smith uses the cost method to account for this investment.

e. If the intercompany sales were downstream, what would be the consolidated balance for retained earnings as of the end of 2001? Assume that Smith uses the partial equity method to account for this investment.

f. If the intercompany sales were upstream, what would be the consolidated balance for retained earnings as of the end of 2001? Assume that Smith uses the partial equity method to account for this investment.

g. Assume that no intercompany inventory sales occurred between Smith and Kane. Instead, in 1998, Kane sold land costing $30,000 to Smith for $50,000. On the 2001 consolidated balance sheet, what value should be reported for land?

h. Assume that no intercompany inventory or land sales occurred between Smith and Kane. Instead, on January 1, 2000, Kane sold equipment (that originally cost $100,000 but had a $60,000 book value on that date) to Smith for $80,000. At the time of sale, the equipment had a remaining useful life of five years. What worksheet entries are made for a December 31, 2001, consolidation of these two companies to eliminate the impact of the intercompany transfer? For 2001, what is the noncontrolling interest's share of Kane's net income?

19. Rockney owns 60 percent of the outstanding stock of Dabney. Dabney reports net income for 2001 of $120,000. Since being acquired, the subsidiary has regularly supplied inventory to Rockney at 20 percent more than cost. Sales to Rockney amounted to $252,000 in 2000 and $288,000 in 2001. Approximately one-tenth of the inventory purchased during any one year is not used until the following period.

Required:

a. What is the noncontrolling interest's share of Dabney's income in 2001?

b. Prepare the 2001 and 2002 consolidation entries that would be required by the preceding intercompany inventory transfers.

20. Several years ago Penguin, Inc., purchased an 80 percent interest in Snow Company. The book values of Snow's asset and liability accounts at that time were considered to be equal to their fair market values. Penguin paid an amount corresponding to the underlying book value of Snow so that no allocations or goodwill resulted from the purchase price.

The following selected account balances are from the individual financial records of these two companies as of December 31, 2001:

	Penguin	Snow
Sales	$640,000	$360,000
Cost of goods sold	290,000	197,000
Operating expenses	150,000	105,000
Retained earnings, 1/1/01	740,000	180,000
Inventory	346,000	110,000
Buildings (net)	358,000	157,000
Investment income	not given	

Each of the following problems is an independent situation.

a. Assume that Penguin sells inventory to Snow at a markup equal to 40 percent of cost. Intercompany transfers were $90,000 in 2000 and $110,000 in 2001. Of this inventory, $28,000 of the 2000 transfers were retained and then sold by Snow in 2001 while $42,000 of the 2001 transfers were held until 2002.

On consolidated financial statements for 2001, determine the balances that would appear for the following accounts:
   Cost of Goods Sold
   Inventory
   Noncontrolling Interest in Subsidiary's Net Income

b. Assume that Snow sells inventory to Penguin at a markup equal to 40 percent of cost. Intercompany transfers were $50,000 in 2000 and $80,000 in 2001. Of this inventory, $21,000 of the 2000 transfers were retained and then sold by Penguin in 2001, whereas $35,000 of the 2001 transfers were held until 2002.

On consolidated financial statements for 2001, determine the balances that would appear for the following accounts:
   Cost of Goods Sold
   Inventory
   Noncontrolling Interest in Subsidiary's Net Income

c. Penguin sells a building to Snow on January 1, 2000, for $80,000, although the book value of this asset was only $50,000 on this date. The building had a five-year remaining life and was to be depreciated using the straight-line method with no salvage value.

On consolidated financial statements for 2001, determine the balances that would appear for the following accounts:
   Buildings (net)
   Expenses
   Noncontrolling Interest in Subsidiary's Net Income

21. Allen, Inc., owns all of the outstanding stock of Bowen Corporation. Amortization expense of $9,000 per year resulted from the original purchase. For 2001, the companies had the following account balances:

	Allen	Bowen
Sales	$900,000	$500,000
Cost of goods sold	400,000	300,000
Operating expenses	300,000	120,000
Investment income	not given	–0–
Dividends paid	60,000	40,000

Intercompany sales of $200,000 occurred during 2000 and again in 2001. This merchandise cost $140,000 each year. Of the total transfers, $60,000 was still held on December 31, 2000, with $45,000 unsold on December 31, 2001.

Required:

a. For consolidation purposes, does the direction of the transfers (upstream or downstream) affect the balances to be reported here?

b. Prepare a consolidated income statement for the year ending December 31, 2001.

22. On January 1, 2001, PortFast Company purchased 90 percent of the outstanding voting stock of SpeedNet, Inc., for $1,400,000 in cash and stock options. At the purchase date SpeedNet had common stock of $900,000 and retained earnings of $300,000. PortFast attributed the excess of cost over SpeedNet's book value to a database with a five-year life. PortFast uses the equity method to account for its investment in SpeedNet.

    During the next two years SpeedNet reported the following:

	Income	Dividends
2001	$ 80,000	$5,000
2002	115,000	8,000

    On July 1, 2001, PortFast sold communication equipment to SpeedNet for $42,000. The equipment originally cost $48,000, had accumulated depreciation of $9,000, and an estimated remaining life of three years at the date of the intercompany transfer.

Required:

    a.   Compute the equity method balance in PortFast's Investment in SpeedNet, Inc., account as of 12/31/02.

    b.   Prepare the worksheet adjustments for the 12/31/02 consolidation of PortFast and SpeedNet.

23. Plimpton holds 100 percent of the outstanding shares of Stanger. On January 1, 1999, Plimpton transferred equipment to Stanger for $70,000. The equipment had cost $110,000 originally but had a $40,000 book value and five-year remaining life at the date of transfer. Depreciation expense is computed according to the straight-line method with no salvage value.

    Consolidated financial statements for 2001 currently are being prepared. What worksheet entries are needed in connection with the consolidation of this asset? Assume that the parent applies the partial equity method.

24. On January 1, 2001, Slaughter sold equipment to Bennett (a wholly owned subsidiary) for $120,000 in cash. The equipment had originally cost $100,000 but had a book value of only $70,000 when transferred. On that date, the equipment had a five-year remaining life. Depreciation expense is computed using the straight-line method.

    Slaughter earned $220,000 in net income in 2001 (not including any investment income) while Bennett reported $90,000.

Required:

    a.   What is the consolidated net income for 2001?

    b.   What is the consolidated net income for 2001 if Slaughter owns only 90 percent of Bennett?

    c.   What is the consolidated net income for 2001 if Slaughter owns only 90 percent of Bennett and the equipment transfer was upstream?

    d.   What is the consolidated net income for 2002 if Slaughter reports $240,000 (does not include investment income) and Bennett $100,000 in income? Assume that Bennett is a wholly owned subsidiary and the equipment transfer was downstream.

25. Anchovy purchased 90 percent of Yelton on January 1, 1999. Of the original price paid by the parent, $60,000 was allocated to undervalued equipment (with a 10-year life) and $80,000 was attributed to franchises (to be written off over a 20-year period).

    Since the takeover, Yelton has transferred inventory to its parent as follows:

Year	Cost	Transfer Price	Remaining at Year-End
1999	$20,000	$ 50,000	$20,000 (at transfer price)
2000	49,000	70,000	30,000 (at transfer price)
2001	50,000	100,000	40,000 (at transfer price)

    On January 1, 2000, Anchovy sold a building to Yelton for $50,000. The building had originally cost $70,000 but had a book value at the date of transfer of only $30,000. The building is estimated to have a five-year remaining life (straight-line depreciation is used with no salvage value).

    Selected figures from the December 31, 2001, trial balances of these two companies are as follows:

	Anchovy	Yelton
Sales	$600,000	$500,000
Cost of goods sold	400,000	260,000
Operating expenses	120,000	80,000
Investment income	not given	
Inventory	220,000	80,000
Equipment (net)	140,000	110,000
Buildings (net)	350,000	190,000

Determine consolidated totals for each of these account balances.

26. On January 1, 2001, Sledge has common stock of $120,000 and retained earnings of $260,000. During that year, Sledge reported sales of $130,000, cost of goods sold of $70,000, and operating expenses of $40,000.

On January 1, 1996, 80 percent of Sledge's outstanding voting stock was acquired by Percy, Inc. At that date, $60,000 of the purchase price was assigned to contracts (with a 20-year life) and $20,000 to an undervalued building (with a 10-year life).

In 2000, Sledge sold inventory costing $9,000 to Percy for $15,000. Of this merchandise, Percy continued to hold $5,000 at the end of that period. During 2001, inventory costing $11,000 was transferred to Percy for $20,000. Half of these items are still being held at year's end.

On January 1, 2000, Percy sold equipment to Sledge for $12,000. This asset originally cost $16,000 but had a January 1, 2000, book value of $9,000. At the time of transfer, the equipment's remaining life was estimated to be five years.

Percy has properly applied the equity method to the investment in Sledge.

Required:

a. Prepare worksheet entries to consolidate these two companies as of December 31, 2001.

b. Compute the noncontrolling interest in the subsidiary's income for 2001.

27. Big purchased 90 percent of the outstanding shares of Little on January 1, 1999, for $345,000 in cash. The subsidiary's stockholders' equity accounts totaled $330,000 on that day. However, a building held by Little (with a nine-year remaining life) was undervalued in the accounting records by $20,000. Any excess purchase price is assigned to technical expertise to be amortized over a 10-year period.

Little reported net income of $60,000 in 1999 and $80,000 in 2000. The company followed a policy of paying dividends each year equal to 30 percent of income.

Little sells inventory to Big as follows:

Year	Cost to Little	Transfer Price to Big	Inventory Remaining at Year's End (at transfer price)
1999	$69,000	$115,000	$25,000
2000	81,000	135,000	37,500
2001	92,800	160,000	50,000

At December 31, 2001, Big owes Little $16,000 for inventory acquired during the current period.

The following separate account balances are for these two companies for December 31, 2001, and the year then ended. Credits are indicated by parentheses.

	Big	Little
Sales revenues	$ (862,000)	$(366,000)
Cost of goods sold	515,000	209,000
Expenses	186,600	67,000
Investment income—Little	(70,600)	—
Net income	$ (231,000)	$ (90,000)

	Big	Little
Retained earnings, 1/1/01	$ (488,000)	$(278,000)
Net income (above)	(231,000)	(90,000)
Dividends paid	136,000	27,000
Retained earnings, 12/31/01	$ (583,000)	$(341,000)
Cash and receivables	$ 146,000	$ 98,000
Inventory	255,000	136,000
Investment in Little	456,000	—
Land, buildings, and equipment (net)	959,000	328,000
Total assets	$ 1,816,000	$ 562,000
Liabilities	$ (718,000)	$ (71,000)
Common stock	(515,000)	(150,000)
Retained earnings, 12/31/01	(583,000)	(341,000)
Total liabilities and equities	$(1,816,000)	$(562,000)

Answer each of the following questions:

a. How much did the book value of the subsidiary increase during the previous two years of ownership (1999 and 2000)?
b. What was the annual amortization resulting from the purchase price allocations?
c. Were the intercompany transfers upstream or downstream?
d. What unrealized gain existed as of January 1, 2001?
e. What was the subsidiary's realized retained earnings as of January 1, 2001?
f. What unrealized gain existed as of December 31, 2001?
g. What was the subsidiary's realized net income for 2001?
h. What amounts make up the $70,600 Investment Income—Little account balance for 2001?
i. What was the noncontrolling interest's share of the subsidiary's net income for 2001?
j. What amounts make up the $456,000 Investment in Little account balance as of December 31, 2001?
k. What Entry S is required in producing a 2001 consolidation worksheet?
l. Without preparing a worksheet or consolidation entries, determine the consolidation balances for these two companies.

28. Asphalt acquired 70 percent of Broadway on June 11, 1990. Based on the purchase price, an intangible of $300,000 was recognized which is being amortized at the rate of $10,000 per year. The 2001 financial statements are as follows:

	Asphalt	Broadway
Sales	$ 800,000	$ 600,000
Cost of goods sold	(535,000)	(400,000)
Operating expenses	(100,000)	(100,000)
Dividend income	35,000	–0–
Net income	$ 200,000	$ 100,000
Retained earnings, 1/1/01	$1,300,000	$ 850,000
Net income	200,000	100,000
Dividends paid	(100,000)	(50,000)
Retained earnings, 12/31/01	$1,400,000	$ 900,000

(continued)

	Asphalt	Broadway
Cash and receivables	$ 400,000	$ 300,000
Inventory	298,000	700,000
Investment in Broadway	902,000	–0–
Fixed assets	1,000,000	600,000
Accumulated depreciation	(300,000)	(200,000)
Totals	$2,300,000	$1,400,000
Liabilities	$ 600,000	$ 400,000
Common stock	300,000	100,000
Retained earnings	1,400,000	900,000
Totals	$2,300,000	$1,400,000

Asphalt sells inventory costing $72,000 to Broadway during 2000 for $120,000. At year's end, 30 percent is left. Asphalt sells inventory costing $200,000 to Broadway during 2001 for $250,000. At year's end, 20 percent is left. Under these circumstances, determine the consolidated balances for the following accounts:

Sales
Cost of Goods Sold
Operating Expenses
Dividend Income
Noncontrolling Interest in Consolidated Income
Inventory
Noncontrolling Interest in Subsidiary, 12/31/01

29. Compute the balances in problem 28 again assuming that the intercompany transfers were all made from Broadway to Asphalt.

30. Following are financial statements for Topper Company and Kirby Company for 2001:

	Topper	Kirby
Sales and other income	$ 800,000	$ 600,000
Cost of goods sold	500,000	400,000
Operating and interest expense	100,000	160,000
Net income	$ 200,000	$ 40,000
Retained earnings, 1/1/01	$ 990,000	$ 500,000
Net income	200,000	40,000
Dividends paid	130,000	–0–
Retained earnings, 12/31/01	$1,060,000	$ 540,000
Cash and receivables	$ 220,000	$ 170,000
Inventory	224,000	160,000
Investment in Kirby	654,000	–0–
Equipment (net)	600,000	400,000
Buildings	1,000,000	800,000
Accumulated depreciation—buildings ...	(100,000)	(200,000)
Other assets	200,000	100,000
Total assets	$2,798,000	$1,430,000
Liabilities	$1,138,000	$ 590,000
Common stock	600,000	300,000
Retained earnings, 12/31/01	1,060,000	540,000
Total liabilities and equity	$2,798,000	$1,430,000

■ Topper purchased 90 percent of Kirby on January 1, 1990, for $654,000 in cash. On the date of acquisition, Kirby held equipment (five-year life) that was undervalued on the financial records by $50,000 and liabilities (20-year life) that were overvalued by $30,000. Any excess price is assigned to brand names to be amortized over a 40-year life.

- Between January 1, 1990, and December 31, 2000, Kirby earned a net income of $600,000 and paid dividends of $340,000.
- Kirby sells inventory each year to Topper with a markup equal to 20 percent of the transfer price. Intercompany sales were $145,000 in 2000 and $160,000 in 2001. On January 1, 2001, 30 percent of the 2000 transfers were still on hand and, on December 31, 2001, 40 percent of the 2001 transfers remained in inventory. Topper still owes $20,000 on the final shipment.
- Topper sold a building to Kirby on January 1, 2000. It had cost Topper $100,000 but had $90,000 in accumulated depreciation at the time of this transfer. The price was $25,000 in cash. At that time, the building had a five-year remaining life.

Required:

Determine all consolidated balances either computationally or by the use of a worksheet.

31. Atkins, Inc., and Smith, Inc., formed a business combination on January 1, 1995, when Atkins acquired a 60 percent interest in the common stock of Smith for $372,000. The book value of Smith on that day was $350,000. Patents held by the subsidiary (with a 12-year remaining life) were undervalued within the company's accounting records by $120,000. Any excess purchase price is assigned to technical expertise to be amortized over 10 years.

    Intercompany inventory sales between the two companies have been made as follows:

Year	Cost to Atkins	Transfer Price to Smith	Ending Balance (at transfer price)
1995	$ 60,000	$ 72,000	$15,000
1996	70,000	84,000	25,000
1997	80,000	100,000	20,000
1998	100,000	125,000	40,000
1999	90,000	120,000	30,000
2000	120,000	150,000	50,000
2001	112,000	160,000	40,000

    Smith sold a building to Atkins on January 1, 1999, for $80,000. The building had a net book value of $30,000 on that date and a five-year life. No salvage value was expected for this asset, which was being depreciated by the straight-line method.

    The individual financial statements for these two companies as of December 31, 2001, and the year then ended follow:

	Atkins, Inc.	Smith, Inc.
Sales	$ 700,000	$ 300,000
Cost of goods sold	(460,000)	(205,000)
Operating expenses	(170,000)	(70,000)
Income of Smith	15,000	–0–
Net income	$ 85,000	$ 25,000
Retained earnings, 1/1/01	$ 690,000	$ 400,000
Net income (above)	85,000	25,000
Dividends paid	(45,000)	(5,000)
Retained earnings, 12/31/01	$ 730,000	$ 420,000
Cash and receivables	$ 185,000	$ 142,000
Inventory	233,000	229,000
Investment in Smith	474,000	–0–
Buildings (net)	308,000	202,000
Equipment (net)	220,000	86,000
Patents (net)	–0–	20,000
Total assets	$1,420,000	$ 679,000

(continued)

	Atkins, Inc.	Smith, Inc.
Liabilities	$390,000	$ 159,000
Common stock	300,000	100,000
Retained earnings, 12/31/01	730,000	420,000
Total liabilities and equities	$1,420,000	$ 679,000

For each of the following accounts, determine the 2001 consolidated balance:
a. Cost of Goods Sold
b. Operating Expenses
c. Net Income
d. Retained Earnings, 1/1/01
e. Inventory
f. Buildings (net)
g. Patents (net)
h. Common Stock
i. Noncontrolling Interest in Smith, 12/31/01

32. Tall Company purchased 60 percent of the outstanding stock of Short, Inc., on January 1, 1999. A $70,000 portion of the purchase price was allocated to equipment with a 10-year remaining life while $40,000 was attributed to a building having a 20-year life. A huge database was assigned $60,000 and has been amortized over a 30-year period.

Short sells inventory to Tall at a markup equal to 25 percent of the transfer price. Sales have been as follows:

Year	Transfer Price to Tall	Inventory Remaining at Year's End (at transfer price)
1999	$ 90,000	$30,000
2000	120,000	20,000
2001	140,000	40,000

Tall still owes $30,000 to Short for the last inventory shipment.

Following are the account balances at December 31, 2001, for both companies. Credit balances are indicated with parentheses.

	Tall	Short
Revenues	$ (984,000)	$(438,000)
Cost of goods sold	551,000	286,000
Operating expenses	198,000	112,000
Equity earnings of Short	(10,000)	–0–
Net income	$ (245,000)	$ (40,000)
Retained earnings, 1/1/01	$ (871,000)	$(350,000)
Net income (above)	(245,000)	(40,000)
Dividends paid	110,000	25,000
Retained earnings, 12/31/01	$(1,006,000)	$(365,000)
Cash and receivables	$ 239,000	$ 57,000
Inventory	454,000	95,000
Investment in Short	440,000	–0–
Land and buildings (net)	722,000	394,000
Equipment (net)	328,000	257,000
Total assets	$ 2,183,000	$ 803,000
Liabilities	$ (686,000)	$(288,000)
Common stock	(320,000)	(90,000)
Additional paid-in capital	(171,000)	(60,000)
Retained earnings	(1,006,000)	(365,000)
Total liabilities and stockholders' equity	$(2,183,000)	$(803,000)

Required:

    a.   The parent applies the equity method. How was the $10,000 balance in the Equity Earnings of Short account determined?

    b.   Construct a worksheet to arrive at consolidated figures to be used for external reporting purposes.

33.   On December 31, 1998, the Silvey Company acquired 70 percent of the outstanding common stock of the Young Company for $665,000. The stockholders' equity accounts reported by Young on that date were as follows:

Common stock—$10 par value	$300,000
Additional paid-in capital	90,000
Retained earnings	410,000

In establishing the purchase price, Silvey appraised the assets of Young and ascertained that a building (with a five-year life) was undervalued within the accounting records by $50,000. Any excess purchase price is allocated to covenants to be amortized over 10 years.

    During the subsequent years, Young sold inventory to Silvey at a 30 percent markup on the transfer price. Silvey consistently resold this merchandise in the year of acquisition or in the period immediately following. Transfers for the three years after this business combination was created amounted to:

Year	Transfer Price	Remaining Inventory— Year's End (at transfer price)
1999	$60,000	$10,000
2000	80,000	12,000
2001	90,000	18,000

In addition, Silvey sold several pieces of fully depreciated equipment to Young on January 1, 2000, for $20,000. The equipment had originally cost Silvey $50,000. Young plans to depreciate the cost of these assets over a five-year period.

    In 2001, Young earns a net income of $160,000 while distributing $50,000 in cash dividends. These figures increase the subsidiary's retained earnings to a $740,000 balance at the end of 2001. During this same year, Silvey reported dividend income of $35,000 and an investment account containing the original cost balance of $665,000.

Required:

Prepare the 2001 consolidation worksheet entries for Silvey and Young. In addition, compute the noncontrolling interest's share of the subsidiary's net income for 2001.

34.   Assume the same basic information as presented in problem 33 except that Silvey has employed the equity method of accounting. Hence, investment income is being reported for 2001 as $100,740 with an investment account balance of $838,220. Under these circumstances, prepare the worksheet entries required for the consolidation of Silvey Company and Young Company.

35.   The individual financial statements for Bumpus Company and Keller Company for the year ending December 31, 2001, follow. Bumpus acquired a 60 percent interest in Keller on January 1, 1996. Technical expertise was assigned $100,000 within the original purchase price. This intangible asset is being amortized over 20 years.

    Bumpus sold land with a book value of $60,000 to Keller on January 1, 1998, for $100,000. Keller still holds this land at the end of the current year.

    Keller annually transfers inventory to Bumpus. In 2000, inventory costing $100,000 was shipped to Bumpus at a price of $150,000. During 2001, intercompany shipments totaled $200,000, although the original cost to Keller was only $140,000. In each of these years, 20 percent of the merchandise was not resold to outside parties until the period following the transfer. Bumpus owes Keller $40,000 at the end of 2001.

	Bumpus Company	Keller Company
Sales	$ 800,000	$ 500,000
Cost of goods sold	(500,000)	(300,000)
Operating expenses	(100,000)	(60,000)
Income of Keller Company	84,000	–0–
Net income	$ 284,000	$ 140,000
Retained earnings, 1/1/01	$1,116,000	$ 620,000
Net income (above)	284,000	140,000
Dividends paid	(115,000)	(60,000)
Retained earnings, 12/31/01	$1,285,000	$ 700,000
Cash	$ 177,000	$ 90,000
Accounts receivable	316,000	410,000
Inventory	440,000	320,000
Investment in Keller Company	766,000	–0–
Land	180,000	390,000
Buildings and equipment (net)	496,000	300,000
Total assets	$2,375,000	$1,510,000
Liabilities	$ 480,000	$ 400,000
Common stock	610,000	320,000
Additional paid-in capital	–0–	90,000
Retained earnings, 12/31/01	1,285,000	700,000
Total liabilities and equities	$2,375,000	$1,510,000

Required:

  a. Prepare a worksheet to consolidate the separate 2001 financial statements produced by Bumpus and Keller.

  b. How would the consolidation entries in requirement (*a*) have differed if Bumpus had sold a building with a $60,000 book value (cost of $140,000) to Keller for $100,000 instead of land, as the problem reports? Assume that the building had a 10-year remaining life at the date of transfer.

36. Greene, Inc., obtained 100 percent of Meadow Corporation on January 1, 1997. Meadow reported total stockholders' equity on this date of $300,000 although the stock issued by Greene in the transaction had a $170,000 par value but a fair market value of $450,000. On January 1, 1997, Meadow held land that was undervalued in the company's accounting records by $30,000. Any excess purchase price is assigned to a franchise contract that is to be amortized over a 40-year life.

Inventory has been regularly transferred by Meadow to Greene. In 2000, merchandise costing $60,000 was sold to Greene for $100,000. Of this total, 30 percent was not resold to unrelated parties until the following year. In 2001, $75,000 in inventory was shipped to Greene for $150,000 with $20,000 (transfer price) still held at the end of the period.

On June 19, 2001, Greene sold land costing $12,000 to Meadow for $17,000. This money has not yet been paid.

The following account balances are for both companies as of December 31, 2001, and the year then ended. The parent has used the equity method to record this investment. Produce a worksheet to arrive at consolidated financial statements for this business combination. Credit balances are indicated by parentheses.

	Greene	Meadow
Revenues	$ (477,000)	$(358,000)
Cost of goods sold	289,000	195,000
General and administrative expenses	170,000	75,000
Gain on sale of land	(5,000)	–0–
Investment income	(82,000)	–0–
Net income	$ (105,000)	$ (88,000)
Retained earnings, 1/1/01	$ (365,000)	$(292,000)
Net income	(105,000)	(88,000)
Dividends distributed	70,000	20,000
Retained earnings, 12/31/01	$ (400,000)	$(360,000)
Cash and receivables	$169,000	$ 210,000
Inventory	281,000	232,000
Investment in Meadow	630,000	–0–
Land, buildings, and equipment (net)	487,000	284,000
Total assets	$ 1,567,000	$ 726,000
Liabilities	$ (466,000)	$(216,000)
Common stock	(410,000)	(120,000)
Additional paid-in capital	(291,000)	(30,000)
Retained earnings, 12/31/01	(400,000)	(360,000)
Total liabilities and stockholders' equity	$(1,567,000)	$(726,000)

C H A P T E R

6

Intercompany Debt, Consolidated Statement of Cash Flows, and Other Issues

QUESTIONS TO CONSIDER

- When an affiliate's debt instrument is bought from an outside party, the reciprocal balances (investment and debt, interest revenue and expense, etc.) usually do not agree. How is the consolidation process carried out in the year of acquisition as well as in each succeeding period?

- Some preferred stocks are viewed as equity interests but others, because of the rights conveyed, are considered to be equivalent to debts. How is this distinction drawn, and what impact does the nature of a subsidiary's preferred stock have on the consolidation process?

- What effect does the inclusion of a subsidiary have on the preparation of a consolidated statement of cash flows?

- If a subsidiary has debt or preferred stock or other items outstanding that can be exchanged for common stock, how are basic and diluted earnings per share computed for the business combination?

- Why would a subsidiary buy or sell more shares of its own stock after coming under the control of a parent company? What effect do such transactions have on consolidated financial statements?

The consolidation of financial information can be a highly complex process often encompassing a number of practical challenges. This chapter examines the procedures required by several additional issues:

- Intercompany debt.

- Subsidiary preferred stock.

- The consolidated statement of cash flows.

- Computation of consolidated earnings per share.

- Subsidiary stock transactions.

Each of these can create potential difficulties for an accountant attempting to produce fairly presented financial statements for a business combination.

INTERCOMPANY DEBT TRANSACTIONS

The previous chapter explored the consolidation procedures required by the intercompany transfer of inventory, land, and depreciable assets. In consolidating these transactions, all resulting gains were deferred until earned through either use of the asset or its resale to outside parties. Deferral was necessary because these gains, although legitimately recognized by the individual companies, were unearned from the perspective of the consolidated entity. The separate financial information of each company was adjusted on the worksheet to be consistent with the view that the related companies actually composed a single economic concern.

This same objective applies in consolidating all intercompany transactions: The financial statements must represent the business combination as one enterprise rather than as a group of independent organizations. Consequently, in designing consolidation procedures for intercompany transactions, the effects recorded by the individual companies first must be isolated. After the impact of each action is analyzed, the worksheet entries necessary to recast these events from the vantage point of the business combination are developed. Although this process involves a number of nuances and complexities, the desire for reporting financial information solely from the perspective of the consolidated entity remains constant.

The intercompany sales of inventory, land, and depreciable assets were introduced together (in Chapter 5) because these transfers result in similar consolidation procedures. In each case, one of the affiliated companies recognizes a gain prior to its actually being earned by the consolidated entity. The worksheet entries required by these transactions simply realign the separate financial information to agree with the viewpoint of the business combination. The gain is removed and the inflated asset value is reduced to historical cost.

The first section of this chapter examines the intercompany acquisition of bonds and notes. Although accounting for the related companies as a single economic entity continues to be the central goal, the consolidation procedures applied to intercompany debt transactions are in diametric contrast to the process utilized in Chapter 5 for asset transfers.

Before delving into this topic, note that *direct* loans used to transfer funds between affiliated companies create no unique consolidation problems. Regardless of whether such amounts are generated by bonds or notes, the resulting receivable/payable balances are necessarily identical. Because no money is owed to or from an outside party, these reciprocal accounts must be eliminated in each subsequent consolidation. A worksheet entry simply offsets the two corresponding balances. Furthermore, the interest revenue/expense accounts associated with direct loans also agree and are removed in the same fashion.

Acquisition of Affiliate's Debt from an Outside Party

The difficulties encountered in consolidating intercompany liabilities relate to a specific type of transaction: the purchase from an outside third party of an affiliate's debt instrument. A parent company, for example, might acquire a bond previously issued by a subsidiary on the open market. Despite the intercompany nature of this transaction, the debt remains an outstanding obligation of the original issuer while simultaneously being recorded as an investment by the acquiring company. Thereafter, even though related parties are involved, interest payments pass periodically between the two organizations.

Although the individual companies continue to report both the debt and the investment, from a consolidation viewpoint this liability is retired as of the date of acquisition. From that time forward, the debt is no longer owed to a party outside of the business combination. Subsequent interest payments are simply intercompany cash transfers. To create consolidated statements, worksheet entries must be developed that adjust the various balances to report the effective retirement of the debt.

Acquiring an affiliate's bond or note from an unrelated party poses no significant consolidation problems if the purchase price equals the corresponding book value of the liability. Reciprocal balances within the individual records would always be identical in value and easily offset in each subsequent consolidation.

Realistically though, such reciprocity is rare when a debt is purchased from a third party. A variety of economic factors typically produces a difference between the price paid for the investment and the carrying amount of the obligation. The debt is originally sold under market conditions at a particular time. Any premium or discount associated with this issuance is then amortized over the life of the bond, creating a continuous adjustment to book value. The acquisition of this instrument at a later date is made at a price influenced by current economic conditions, prevailing interest rates, and myriad other financial and market factors.

Therefore, the cost paid to purchase the debt might be either more or less than the book value of the liability currently found within the financial records of the issuing company. *To the business combination, this difference is a gain or loss because the acquisition effectively retires the bond; the debt is no longer owed to an outside party.* For external reporting purposes, this gain or loss must be recognized immediately by the consolidated entity as required by *APB Opinion 26,* "Early Extinguishment of Debt," October 1972.

Accounting for Intercompany Debt Transactions—Individual Financial Records

The accounting problems encountered in consolidating intercompany debt transactions are fourfold:

1. Both the investment and debt accounts have to be eliminated now and for each future consolidation despite containing differing balances.
2. Subsequent interest revenue/expense (as well as any interest receivable/payable accounts) must be removed although these balances also fail to agree in amount.
3. Changes in all of the preceding accounts occur constantly because of the amortization process.
4. The gain or loss on retirement of the debt must be recognized by the business combination, even though this balance does not appear within the financial records of either company.

To illustrate, assume that Alpha Company possesses an 80 percent interest in the outstanding voting stock of Omega Company. On January 1, 1999, Omega issues $1 million in 10-year term bonds paying cash interest annually of 9 percent. Because of market conditions prevailing on that date, the debt is sold for $938,555 to yield an effective interest rate of 10 percent per year. Shortly thereafter, the prime interest rate begins to fall, and by January 1, 2001, the decision is made to retire this debt prematurely and refinance it at the currently lower rates. To carry out this plan, Alpha purchases all of these bonds in the open market on January 1, 2001, for $1,057,466. This price was based on an effective yield of 8 percent, which is assumed to be in line with the interest rates at the time.

Many reasons could exist for having Alpha, rather than Omega, reacquire this debt. For example, company cash levels at that date might necessitate Alpha's role as the purchasing agent. Also, contractual limitations may prohibit Omega from repurchasing its own bonds.

In accounting for this business combination, an early extinguishment of the debt has occurred. Thus, the difference between the $1,057,466 payment and the January 1, 2001, book value of the liability must be recognized in the consolidated statements as a gain or loss. The exact account balance reported for the debt on that date depends on the amortization process. Although the issue was recorded initially at the $938,555 exchange price, after two years the carrying value has increased to $946,651, calculated as follows:[1]

Bonds Payable—Book Value—January 1, 2001

Year	Book Value	Effective Interest (10 percent rate)	Cash Interest	Amortization	Year-End Book Value
1999	$938,555	$93,855	$90,000	$3,855	$942,410
2000	942,410	94,241	90,000	4,241	946,651

---

[1]The effective rate method of amortization is demonstrated here because this approach is theoretically preferable. However, the straight-line method can be applied if the resulting balances are not materially different than the figures computed using the effective rate method.

Because Alpha paid $110,815 in excess of the recorded liability ($1,057,466 − $946,651), a loss of this amount must be recognized by the consolidated concern. If material, the $110,815 is highlighted as an extraordinary item. After the loss has been acknowledged, the bond is considered to be retired and no further reporting would be necessary by the *business combination* after January 1, 2001.

Despite the simplicity of this approach, neither company accounts for the event in this manner. Omega retains the $1 million debt balance within its separate financial records while amortizing the remaining discount each year. Annual cash interest payments of $90,000 (9 percent) continue to be made. At the same time, the investment is recorded by Alpha at the historical cost of $1,057,466, an amount that also requires periodic amortization. Furthermore, as the owner of these bonds, Alpha receives the $90,000 interest payments made by Omega.

To organize the accountant's approach to this consolidation, a complete analysis of the subsequent financial recording made by each of these companies should be produced. Only two journal entries would be recorded by Omega during 2001 if the assumption is made that interest is paid each December 31.

Omega Company's Financial Records

12/31/01	Interest Expense...............................	90,000	
	Cash....................................		90,000
	To record payment of annual cash interest on $1 million, 9 percent bonds payable.		
12/31/01	Interest Expense...............................	4,665	
	Bonds Payable (or Discount on Bonds Payable)		4,665
	To adjust interest expense to effective rate based on original yield rate of 10 percent ($946,651 book value for 2001 × 10% = $94,665). Book value increases to $951,316.		

Concurrently, Alpha journalizes entries to record its ownership of this investment:

Alpha Company's Financial Record

1/1/01	Investment in Omega Company Bonds...........	1,057,466	
	Cash....................................		1,057,466
	To record acquisition of $1,000,000 in Omega Company bonds paying 9 percent cash interest, acquired to yield an effective rate of 8 percent.		
12/31/01	Cash.......................................	90,000	
	Interest Income.........................		90,000
	To record receipt of cash interest from Omega Company bonds ($1,000,000 × 9%).		
12/31/01	Interest Income.............................	5,403	
	Investment in Omega Company Bonds.......		5,403
	To reduce $90,000 interest income to effective rate based on original yield rate of 8 percent ($1,057,466 book value for 2001 × 8% = $84,597). Book value decreases to $1,052,063.		

Even a brief review of these entries indicates that the reciprocal accounts to be eliminated within the consolidation process do not agree in amount. You can see the dollar amounts appearing in each set of financial records in Exhibit 6–1. Despite the presence of these recorded balances, none of the four intercompany accounts (the liability, investment, interest expense, and interest revenue) appear in the consolidated financial statements. *The only figure to be reported by the business combination is the $110,815 loss created by the extinguishment of this debt.*

Exhibit 6–1

ALPHA COMPANY AND OMEGA COMPANY
Effects of Intercompany Debt Transaction
2001

	Omega Company Reported Debt	Alpha Company Investment
2001 interest expense*	$ 94,665	$ –0–
2001 interest income†	–0–	84,597
Bonds payable*	(951,316)	–0–
Investment in bonds, 12/31/01†	–0–	1,052,063
Loss on retirement	–0–	–0–

Note: Parentheses indicate credit balances.

*Company total is adjusted for 2001 amortization of $4,665 (see journal entry).

†Adjusted for 2001 amortization of $5,403 (see journal entry).

Effects on Consolidation Process

As indicated in previous discussions, consolidation procedures serve to convert information generated by the individual accounting systems to the perspective of a single economic entity. A worksheet entry is, therefore, required on December 31, 2001, to eliminate the intercompany balances shown in Exhibit 6–1 and to recognize the loss resulting from the repurchase. Mechanically, the differences in the liability and investment balances as well as the interest expense and interest income accounts stem from the $110,815 deviation between the purchase price of the investment and the book value of the liability. Recognition of this loss, in effect, bridges the gap between the divergent figures.

Consolidation Entry B (December 31, 2001)

Bonds Payable	951,316	
Interest Income	84,597 ✓	
Extraordinary Loss on Retirement of Bond	110,815	
Investment in Omega Company Bonds		1,052,063
Interest Expense		94,665

To remove intercompany bonds and related interest accounts
and record loss on the early extinguishment of this debt.
(Labeled "B" in reference to bonds.)

The preceding entry successfully transforms the separate financial reporting of Alpha and Omega to that appropriate for the business combination. The objective of the consolidation process has been met: The statements present the bonds as having been retired on January 1, 2001. The debt as well as the corresponding investment is eliminated along with both interest accounts. Only the loss now appears on the worksheet to be reported within the consolidated financial statements.

Assignment of Retirement Gain or Loss

Perhaps the most intriguing issue to be addressed in accounting for intercompany debt transactions concerns the assignment of any gains and losses created by the retirement. Should the $110,815 loss just reported be attributed to Alpha or to Omega? From a practical perspective, this assignment is only important in the calculation and reporting of noncontrolling interest figures. However, at least four different possible allocations can be identified, each of which demonstrates theoretical merit.

Who Lost This $300,000?

Several years ago, the Penston Company purchased 90 percent of the outstanding shares of Swansan Corporation. The acquisition was made because Swansan produced a vital component used in Penston's manufacturing process. Penston wanted to ensure an adequate supply of this item at a reasonable price. The remaining 10 percent of Swansan's stock was retained by the former owner, James Swansan, who agreed to continue managing this organization. He was given responsibility over the subsidiary's daily manufacturing operations but not any of the financial decisions.

The takeover of Swansan has proven to be a successful undertaking for Penston. The subsidiary has managed to supply all of the parent's inventory needs as well as distribute a variety of items to outside customers.

At a recent meeting, the president of Penston and the company's chief financial officer began discussing Swansan's debt position. The subsidiary had a debt to equity ratio that seemed unreasonably high considering the significant amount of cash flows being generated by both companies. Payment of the interest expense, especially on the subsidiary's outstanding bonds, was a major cost, one that the corporate officials hoped to reduce. However, the bond indenture specified that Swansan could only retire this debt prior to maturity by paying 107 percent of face value.

This premium was considered prohibitive. Thus, to avoid contractual problems, Penston acquired a large portion of Swansan's liability on the open market for 101 percent of face value. Penston's purchase created an effective loss on the debt of $300,000: the excess of the price over the book value of the debt as reported on Swansan's books.

Company accountants currently are computing the noncontrolling interest's share of consolidated net income to be reported for the current year. They are unsure about the impact of this $300,000 loss. The subsidiary's debt was retired but the decision was made by officials of the parent company. Who lost this $300,000?

First, a strong argument can be made that the liability being extinguished is that of the issuing company and, thus, any resulting income relates solely to that party. This approach assumes that only the debtor is affected by the retirement of any obligation. Proponents of this position hold that the acquiring company is merely serving as a purchasing agent for the original issuer of the bonds. Accordingly, in the previous illustration, the benefits derived from paying off the liability should accrue to Omega because that company's interest rate has been reduced through refinancing. The loss was incurred solely to obtain these lower rates. Therefore, under this assumption, the entire $110,815 is assigned to Omega, the issuer of the debt. This assignment is usually considered to be consistent with the economic unit concept and was recommended in the 1995 FASB Exposure Draft, *Consolidated Financial Statements: Policy and Procedures.*

Second, other accountants argue that the loss should be assigned solely to the investor (Alpha). According to proponents of this approach, the income effect is created by the acquisition of the bonds and the price negotiated by the buyer.

A third hypothesis is that the resulting gain or loss should be split in some manner between the two companies. This approach is consistent with both the parent company concept and proportionate consolidation. Since both parties are involved with the debt, this proposition contends that assigning income to only one company is arbitrary and misleading. Normally, such a division is based on the original face value of the debt. Hence, $57,466 of the loss would be allocated to Alpha with the remaining $53,349 assigned to Omega:

	Alpha		Omega
Purchase price	$1,057,466	Book value	$ 946,651
Face value	1,000,000	Face value	1,000,000
Loss—Alpha	$ 57,466	Loss—Omega	$ 53,349

Exhibit 6-2

	ALPHA COMPANY AND OMEGA COMPANY Effects of Intercompany Debt Transactions 2002	
	Omega Company Reported Debt	**Alpha Company Investment**
2002 interest expense*	$ 95,132	–0–
2002 interest income†	–0–	$ (84,165)
Bonds payable*	(956,448)	–0–
Investment in bonds, 12/31/02†	–0–	1,046,228
Income effect within retained earnings, 1/1/99‡ ...	94,665	(84,597)

Note: Parentheses indicate credit balance.

*Company total is adjusted for 2002 amortization of $5,132 (see journal entry).

†Adjusted for 2002 amortization of $5,835 (see journal entry).

‡The balance shown for the Retained Earnings accounts of the individual companies represents the 2001 reported interest figures.

Allocating the loss in this manner is an enticing solution; the subsequent accounting process creates an identical division within the individual financial records. Because both Alpha's premium and Omega's discount must be amortized, the loss figures eventually affect the reported earnings of the respective companies. Over the life of the bond, the $57,466 is recorded by Alpha as an interest income reduction while Omega increases its own interest expense by $53,349 because of the amortization of the discount.

A fourth perspective takes a more practical view of intercompany debt transactions: All repurchases are ultimately orchestrated by the parent company. As the controlling party in a business combination, the ultimate responsibility for retiring any obligation lies with the parent. The gain or loss resulting from the decision should, thus, be assigned solely to the parent regardless of the specific identity of the debt issuer or the acquiring company. In the current example, Alpha maintains control over Omega. Therefore, according to this theory, the financial consequences of reacquiring these bonds rest with Alpha so that the entire $110,815 loss must be attributed to that party.

Each of these arguments does have conceptual merit, and if the FASB eventually sets an official standard, any one approach (or possibly a hybrid) might be required. Unless otherwise stated, however, all income effects in this textbook relating to intercompany debt transactions are assigned solely to the parent company, as discussed in the final approach. Consequently, the results of extinguishing debt always are attributed to the party most likely to have been responsible for the action.

Intercompany Debt Transactions—Subsequent to Year of Acquisition

Even though the preceding Entry B correctly eliminates Omega's bonds in the year of retirement, the debt remains within the financial accounts of both companies until maturity. Therefore, in each succeeding time period, all balances must again be consolidated so that the liability is always reported as having been extinguished on January 1, 2001. Unfortunately, a simple repetition of Entry B is not possible. Developing the appropriate worksheet entry is complicated by the amortization process that produces continual change in the various account balances. Thus, as a preliminary step in each subsequent consolidation, current book values, as reported by the two parties, must be identified.

To illustrate, the 2002 journal entries for Alpha and Omega follow. Exhibit 6–2 shows the resulting account balances as of the end of that year.

Omega Company's Financial Records—December 31, 2002

Interest Expense	90,000	
Cash		90,000

To record payment of annual cash interest on $1 million,
9 percent bonds payable.

Interest Expense	5,132	
Bonds Payable (or Discount on Bonds Payable)		5,132

To adjust interest expense to effective rate based on an original
yield rate of 10 percent ($951,316 book value for 2002 × 10%
= $95,132). Book value increases to $956,448.

Alpha Company's Financial Records—December 31, 2002

Cash	90,000	
Interest Income		90,000

To record receipt of cash interest from Omega Company bonds.

Interest Income	5,835	
Investment in Omega Company Bonds		5,835

To reduce $90,000 interest income to effective rate based on an
original yield rate of 8 percent ($1,052,063 book value for
2002 × 8% = $84,165). Book value decreases to $1,046,228.

After the information in Exhibit 6–2 has been assembled, the necessary consolidation entry as of December 31, 2002, can be produced. This entry removes the balances reported at that date for the intercompany bonds, along with both of the interest accounts, to reflect the extinguishment of the debt on January 1, 2001. Since retirement took place in a prior period, the adjustment on the worksheet must also create a $110,815 reduction in retained earnings to represent the original loss.

Consolidation Entry *B (December 31, 2002)

Bonds Payable	956,448	
Interest Income	84,165	
Retained Earnings, 1/1/02 (Alpha)	100,747	
Investment in Omega Company Bonds		1,046,228
Interest Expense		95,132

To eliminate intercompany bond and related interest accounts
and to adjust retained earnings from $10,068 (currently
recorded net balance) to $110,815. (Labeled as "*B" in
reference to prior year bond transaction.)

In analyzing this latest consolidation entry, several important factors should be emphasized:

1. The individual account balances change during the present fiscal period so that the current consolidation entry differs from Entry B. These alterations are a result of the amortization process. To ensure the accuracy of the worksheet entry, the adjusted balances are isolated in Exhibit 6–2.

2. As indicated previously, all income effects arising from intercompany debt transactions are assigned to the parent company. For this reason, the adjustment to beginning retained earnings in Entry *B is attributed to Alpha as is the $10,967 increase in current income ($95,132 interest expense elimination less the $84,165 interest revenue elimination).[2] Consequently, the noncontrolling interest balances are not altered by Entry *B.

---

[2]Had the effects of the retirement been attributed solely to the original issuer of the bonds, the $10,967 reduction in current income would have been assigned to Omega (the subsidiary), thus creating a change in the noncontrolling interest computations.

3. The 2002 reduction to beginning retained earnings in Entry *B ($100,747) does not agree with the original $110,815 retirement loss. A net deficit balance of $10,068 (the amount by which previous interest expense exceeds interest revenue) has already been recorded by the individual companies at the start of 2002. To achieve the proper consolidated total, an adjustment of only $100,747 is required ($110,815 − $10,068).

Retained earnings balance—consolidation perspective (loss on retirement of debt)		$110,815
Individual retained earnings balances, 1/1/02:		
Omega Company (interest expense—2001)	$ 94,665	
Alpha Company (interest income—2001)	(84,597)	10,068
Adjustment to consolidated retained earnings, 1/1/02		$100,747

Parentheses indicate a credit balance.

The periodic amortization of both the bond payable discount and the premium on the investment impacts the interest expense and revenue recorded by the two companies. As shown in this schedule, these two interest accounts do not offset exactly; a $10,068 net residual amount remains in retained earnings after the first year. Because this balance continues to grow each year, the subsequent consolidation adjustments to record the loss decrease to $100,747 in 2002 and constantly get smaller thereafter. *Over the life of the bond, the amortization process gradually brings the totals in the individual Retained Earnings accounts into agreement with the consolidated balance.*

4. Entry *B as shown is appropriate for consolidations in which the parent has applied either the cost or the partial equity method. However, a deviation is required if the parent uses the equity method for internal reporting purposes. As discussed in Chapter 5, proper application of the equity method ensures that the parent's income and, hence, its retained earnings are correctly stated prior to consolidation. Alpha would have already recognized the loss in accounting for this investment. Consequently, no adjustment to retained earnings would be needed. In this one case, the $100,747 debit in Entry *B is made to the Investment in Omega Company because the loss has become a component of that account.

SUBSIDIARY PREFERRED STOCK

When Kohlberg Kravis Roberts & Company purchased the outstanding common stock of Owens-Illinois, Inc., for $60.50 per share, they also acquired all of the preferred stock of Owens-Illinois for $363 per share or a total of $25.8 million. Although preferred shares are routinely issued by both small and large corporations, their presence within the equity structure of a subsidiary adds a new dimension to the consolidation process. What accounting should be made of a subsidiary's preferred stock and the parent's payments, such as this $25.8 million, that are made to acquire these shares?

The consolidation measures required to report the preferred stock of a subsidiary depend on the specific nature of the shares. Controversy has long existed as to whether such issues are more akin to equity or debt, a distinction that depends on the specified rights granted to the holders. The characteristics of many preferred shares resemble those attributed to long-term liabilities rather than to equity securities. For example, a stock with a call value and no rights except for a set, cumulative dividend is in substance almost identical to a bond payable. Conversely, preferred shares that offer voting and/or participation rights clearly demonstrate essential characteristics associated with an ownership interest.

However, not all preferred stocks lend themselves to easy classification: The legal rights given to shareholders often vary significantly from issue to issue. For example,

Ford Motor Company in a recent annual report shows both Series A and Series B preferred stock outstanding, each with specific rights as to dividends, convertibility to common stock, and redemption prices. Such attributes can make the distinction between debt and equity quite nebulous. Because of this identification problem, the FASB has plans to study the issue within its financial instruments project. However, until a guideline is established, as is utilized in earnings per share computations, determining the true nature of many types of preferred stock still requires considerable individual judgment.

In consolidating subsidiary preferred stock, the accountant must evaluate whether the shares are more similar to debt or to equity. If the stock resembles a debt, any shares acquired by the parent are recorded as if retired. Conversely, if a preferred stock is truly an equity instrument, the combination accounts for the purchased shares in the same manner as common stock: Allocations are made to specific assets and liabilities with any residual payment assigned to goodwill.

Preferred Stock Viewed as a Debt Instrument

If a subsidiary's preferred stock has characteristics that primarily resemble a liability, consolidation techniques should parallel the process previously demonstrated for intercompany debt. To illustrate, assume that on January 1, 2001, High Corporation acquires control over Low Company by purchasing 80 percent of its outstanding common stock as well as 60 percent of its nonvoting, cumulative, preferred stock. Low owns land that is undervalued in its records by $100,000.

The purchase price paid by High was $1 million for the common shares and $62,400 for the preferred. On the date of acquisition, Low reported the following stockholders' equity balances. Note that the 1,000 shares of preferred stock outstanding have a $100 par value but can be called (retired) by Low for $110 per share.

Common stock, $20 par value (20,000 shares outstanding)	$ 400,000
Preferred stock, 6% cumulative with a par value of $100 and a $110 call value (1,000 shares outstanding)	100,000
Additional paid-in capital	200,000
Retained earnings	516,400
Total stockholders' equity (book value)	$1,216,400

Low's preferred stock carries no rights other than its cumulative dividend; thus, this issue is considered a debt instrument in nature. The $62,400 price paid by High is handled in a manner consistent with that of an intercompany bond. The payment made for these shares has no influence on the valuation of specific subsidiary accounts (such as the undervalued land) or the recognition of goodwill. Instead, the preferred stock acquired by the parent is eliminated on each subsequent worksheet as if the shares had been retired.

Although this handling parallels that of a long-term liability, one important distinction must be drawn. Preferred stock is legally an equity; thus, its retirement cannot result in the reporting of a gain or loss to the consolidated entity. Instead, the difference between the stock's par value and the acquisition price paid by the parent must be recorded as an adjustment to Additional Paid-In Capital (or to Retained Earnings if a reduction is required and the Additional Paid-In Capital account is not of sufficient size).

The consolidation entry to account for this preferred stock acquisition follows. *Because the stock is viewed as the equivalent of debt, these shares (60 percent of the 1,000 outstanding) are simply eliminated as if retired.*

Preferred Stock (the 60% owned by High)	60,000	
Additional Paid-In Capital	2,400	
Investment in Low Company's Preferred Stock		62,400
To eliminate preferred stock of Low Company acquired by		
the parent company.		

This entry assumes that no part of the cumulative dividend is in arrears at the date of purchase. If a dividend had been owed on the preferred stock, a reduction in the subsidiary's retained earnings equal to that amount would have been included here rather than assigning the entire $2,400 difference to additional paid-in capital. This alteration presumes that a portion of the purchase price is paid to reimburse the former owners for the missed dividends.

Although the preceding worksheet entry removes the effects of High's acquisition, it ignores the residual 40 percent noncontrolling interest in the preferred stock. In recording an allocation to these outside owners, the appropriate amount to be recognized must be determined. When preferred stock is viewed as a debt, the call value (if present) is considered to be more relevant to the consolidated entity than par value. Thus, the outside owners are assigned a balance equal to the call value of the securities (plus any dividends in arrears). In the current illustration, the $110 figure reflects the cost required to retire each of the remaining 400 shares (40% of 1,000). Thus, the worksheet entry to recognize this noncontrolling interest is as follows:

Preferred Stock (40% owned by outsiders)	40,000	
Additional Paid-In Capital	4,000	
Noncontrolling Interest in Low Company (call value).		44,000
To recognize the outside ownership of 40 percent of Low Company's preferred stock.		

These entries have been presented separately to clarify the difference in consolidating parent-owned and outside-owned shares. In practice, these figures are combined to eliminate all of the subsidiary's preferred stock. Thus, a single consolidation entry actually should be incorporated in this illustration:

Consolidation Entry PS

Preferred Stock	100,000	
Additional Paid-In Capital	6,400	
Investment in Low Company's Preferred Stock.		62,400
Noncontrolling Interest in Low Company		44,000
To eliminate preferred stock of subsidiary (viewed as a debt) and record noncontrolling interest. (Labeled as "PS" in reference to preferred stock.)		

Having accounted for Low's preferred stock, now the elimination of the company's remaining stockholders' equity accounts can be made. As with any purchase combination, a preliminary allocation of the purchase price paid for the common stock is essential. Because of the amounts attributed to preferred stock, only $1,110,000 of Low's total book value is assigned to the common stock at the date of acquisition:

Total book value of Low Company, 1/1/01		$1,216,400
Allocated to preferred stock ownership:		
Acquisition price of High Company's interest	$62,400	
Call value of noncontrolling interest	44,000	(106,400)
Book value allocated to common stock		$1,110,000

Based on this book value, the $1 million paid by High for 80 percent of Low's common stock is allocated as shown in Exhibit 6–3. As indicated previously, land owned by Low is assumed here to be undervalued on the subsidiary's records by $100,000.

By utilizing the information from Exhibit 6–3, basic worksheet entries can be constructed as of January 1, 2001 (the date of purchase). After Entry PS removes the preferred shares and recognizes the noncontrolling interest in that stock, the remainder of Low's stockholders' equity accounts are eliminated by Entry S. In addition, a 20 percent noncontrolling interest in Low's common stock is established as $222,000 (20 percent of the $1,110,000 book value). The allocations made to the undervalued land

HIGH COMPANY AND LOW COMPANY Allocation of Common Stock Purchase Price January 1, 2001	
Purchase price paid for common stock	$1,000,000
Common stock book value equivalent to High's ownership 　($1,110,000 × 80%)	(888,000)
Cost in excess of book value　.	112,000
Allocation to specific accounts based on fair market value: 　Land ($100,000 × 80%)	80,000
Excess cost not identified with specific accounts—goodwill　.	$　　32,000

and to goodwill then are recognized in Entry A. No other consolidation entries are needed as no time has passed since the acquisition took place.

Consolidation Entry S

Common Stock (Low Company)	400,000	
Additional Paid-In Capital (Low Company)	193,600	
Retained Earnings (Low Company).	516,400	
Investment in Low Company's Common Stock (80%)		888,000
Noncontrolling Interest in Low Company (20%).		222,000

To eliminate remaining stockholders' equity accounts after removal of preferred stock and to recognize noncontrolling interest in common stock.

Consolidation Entry A

Land	80,000	
Goodwill.	32,000	
Investment in Low Company's Common Stock.		112,000

To allocate excess cost paid for Low's common stock to specific account based on fair market value and to goodwill (see Exhibit 6–3).

In working with this illustration, note the structure that is followed in consolidating a subsidiary's preferred stock. First, a determination is made of the nature of the stock. Identifying Low Company's issue as a debt-type instrument significantly influenced the development of the consolidation process. Second, the subsidiary's book value is divided between the preferred and common stock interests. Assigning $106,400 of Low's book value to the preferred stock (the price of the purchased shares plus the call value of remainder) and the residual $1,110,000 to common stock led directly to the valuations and eliminations incorporated in this consolidation. As is subsequently demonstrated, this allocation of book value can vary considerably depending on the specific rights granted to the preferred shareholders.

Allocation of Subsidiary Income　The final factor influencing a consolidation that includes subsidiary preferred shares is the allocation of the company's income between the two types of stock. A division must be made for every period subsequent to the takeover (1) to compute the noncontrolling interest's share and (2) for the parent's own recognition purposes. For a cumulative, nonparticipating preferred stock such as the one presently being examined, only the specified annual dividend is attributed to the preferred stock with all remaining income assigned to common stock. Consequently, if the assumption is made that Low reports earnings of $100,000 in 2001 while paying the annual $6,000 dividend on its preferred stock, income is allocated for consolidation purposes as follows:

	Income
Subsidiary total	$100,000
Preferred stock (6% dividend × $100,000 par value of the stock)	$ 6,000
Common stock (residual amount)	94,000

During 2001, High Company, as the parent, would be entitled to $3,600 in dividends from Low's preferred stock because of its 60 percent ownership. In addition, High holds 80 percent of Low's common stock so that another $75,200 of the income ($94,000 × 80 percent) is attributed to the parent. The noncontrolling interest in the subsidiary's income can be calculated in a similar fashion:

		Percent Outside Ownership	Noncontrolling Interest
Preferred stock dividend	$ 6,000	40%	$ 2,400
Income attributed to common stock	94,000	20	18,800
Noncontrolling interest in subsidiary's income			$21,200

Preferred Stock Viewed as an Equity Interest

Having established basic principles for a consolidation that includes subsidiary preferred stock that resembles debt, a second example can be utilized in which the stock is considered an equity. Continuing to employ High's acquisition of Low, assume now that the dividends of the subsidiary's preferred stock are fully participating as well as cumulative. Furthermore, the stock is not callable. Because the preferred shares convey additional rights, the relative values of the two classes of stock differ from that of the previous example. Therefore, High is assumed to have paid only $894,496 for an 80 percent interest in Low's common stock but $149,968 for 60 percent of the preferred.

The ability to participate in the earnings of Low Company provides the preferred shareholders with an ownership interest that is akin to that of common stock. Thus, altering the rights of this issue has changed its essential nature to that of an equity interest rather than a debt. When subsidiary preferred stock is viewed as an equity, the consolidation process differs significantly from that examined in the previous illustration. *The preferred stock is handled in the same manner as common stock: Any purchase price in excess of underlying book value is allocated to specific accounts as well as to goodwill. Income is accrued by the owners based on subsidiary earnings rather than on dividends.*

The cumulative participation rights entitle the holders of Low's preferred shares to a portion of the subsidiary's earnings each year. The specific division of income would be stipulated on the preferred stock certificate. That percentage is often based on the ratio of the total par values of the two classes of equity. Thus, 20 percent ($100,000 par value of the preferred stock divided by $500,000 total par value) of Low's annual income is assigned to the preferred shares. Additionally, because of the cumulative right, 20 percent of the subsidiary's retained earnings should also be attributed to the preferred stock (assuming that both classes of stock were originally issued on the same date). With these particular rights in force, allocation of the January 1, 2001, book value of Low Company is as follows:

Total book value of Low Company, 1/1/01		$1,216,400
Allocated to preferred stock ownership:		
Par value of preferred stock (no call value)	$100,000	
20% of total retained earnings ($516,400) based on cumulative, participation rights	103,280	(203,280)
Book value allocated to common stock (residual)		$1,013,120

Exhibit 6–4

HIGH COMPANY AND LOW COMPANY
Allocation of Preferred and Common Stock Purchase Prices
January 1, 2001

Preferred Stock

Purchase price paid for preferred stock	$ 149,968
Preferred stock book value equivalent to High's ownership ($203,280 × 60%)	(121,968)
Cost in excess of book value	$ 28,000
Allocation to specific accounts: Land ($20,000 × 60%)	12,000
Excess cost not identified with specific accounts—goodwill	$ 16,000

Common Stock

Purchase price paid for common stock	$ 894,496
Common stock book value equivalent to High's ownership ($1,013,120 × 80%)	(810,496)
Cost in excess of book value	$ 84,000
Allocation to specific accounts: Land ($80,000 × 80%)	64,000
Excess cost not identified with specific accounts—goodwill	$ 20,000

Once the division of the subsidiary's book value has been established, High must allocate each of the acquisition payments. In this manner, the preferred stock is being accounted for as a true equity interest. Exhibit 6–4 analyzes both purchases: The $149,968 price paid for the preferred stock is shown first followed by the $894,496 amount invested in common stock. To complete this allocation, one theoretical question must be addressed: How is the undervaluation of the subsidiary's land to be treated? Since both stocks are considered equity interests, the $100,000 undervaluation is assumed to be reflected in each purchase price. Because of the participation feature of the preferred shares, the logical approach is to divide this $100,000 unrealized gain between the two stocks according to the par value ratio (20:80) or $20,000 to preferred stock and $80,000 to common.

From the information produced in Exhibit 6–4, the following consolidation entries for January 1, 2001 (the date of purchase) can be developed. Note that Entry A has been split into "A1" and "A2" to identify the allocations resulting from the preferred stock and common stock, respectively. This segregation is made merely to clarify the process; these two worksheet entries could easily be combined.

Consolidation Entry PS

Preferred Stock (Low Company)	100,000	
Retained Earnings (Low Company) (20%)	103,280	
Investment in Low Company Preferred Stock (60% ownership)		121,968
Noncontrolling Interest in Low Company (40%)		81,312

To eliminate subsidiary's preferred stockholders' equity accounts ($203,280) and recognize noncontrolling interest in preferred stock. Retained earnings is based on par value assignment.

Consolidation Entry S

Common Stock (Low Company)	400,000	
Additional Paid-In Capital (Low Company)	200,000	
Retained Earnings (Low Company) (80%)	413,120	
Investment in Low Company Common Stock (80% ownership)		810,496
Noncontrolling Interest in Low Company (20%)		202,624

To eliminate subsidiary's remaining stockholders' equity accounts ($1,013,120) and recognize noncontrolling interest in common stock. Retained earnings reflects Entry PS.

Consolidation Entry A1

Land	12,000	
Goodwill.	16,000	
Investment in Low Company Preferred Stock		28,000

To allocate cost paid for preferred stock in excess of book value. (See Exhibit 6–4.)

Consolidation Entry A2

Land	64,000	
Goodwill.	20,000	
Investment in Low Company Common Stock		84,000

To allocate cost paid for common stock in excess of book value. (See Exhibit 6–4.)

Allocation of Subsidiary Income   The specific rights granted to the owners of the preferred stock also affect the subsequent allocation of the subsidiary's income each year. If the assumption is again made that Low reports net income for 2001 of $100,000, this amount must be divided between the two ownership interests based on the cumulative, participating rights of the preferred stock. These shares constitute 20 percent of the subsidiary's total par value with the remaining 80 percent coming from the holders of the common stock. Thus, net income is prorated according to this same ratio.

	Income
Subsidiary totals	$100,000
Preferred stock—possesses rights to 20% of total (based on relative par values)	$ 20,000
Common stock—residual 80% interest	80,000

Based on this allocation of the subsidiary's income for 2001, the noncontrolling interest's share of consolidated income can be determined:

		Percent Outside Ownership	Noncontrolling Interest
Income attributed to preferred stock	$20,000	40%	$ 8,000
Income attributed to common stock	80,000	20	16,000
Noncontrolling interest in subsidiary's income			$24,000

CONSOLIDATED STATEMENT OF CASH FLOWS

In November of 1987, the Financial Accounting Standards Board issued its *Statement No. 95,* "Statement of Cash Flows," mandating that companies include a statement of cash flows within a set of financial statements. Because of this pronouncement, details of an organization's cash flows must be reported for each period in which an income statement is presented.

Importantly, the consolidated statement of cash flows is not prepared from the individual cash flows of the separate companies. Instead, the income statements and balance sheets are first brought together on the worksheet. The cash flows statement is based then on the resulting consolidated figures. *Thus, this statement is not actually produced by consolidation but rather it is created from numbers generated by that process.*

However, preparing a statement of cash flows for a business combination does introduce several accounting issues. In preparing this statement, noncontrolling interest balances, amortization, and intercompany transactions must all be properly handled.

Noncontrolling Interest   On the consolidated income statement, the outside ownership of a noncontrolling interest is reflected as a decrease in net income. This reduction represents the earnings accrual assigned to these other owners. However, the only cash actually distributed to the noncontrolling interest is the portion of dividends paid to them by the subsidiary. Although the income statement presents the accrual rather than the dividend, the opposite is true of the cash flow statement: Only cash transactions are included. *Thus, for this statement, two adjustments are made. First, the noncontrolling interest's share of the subsidiary's net income must be eliminated; second, the dividends paid to the outside owners are included.*

The noncontrolling interest's income accrual can be removed from the statement of cash flows in either of two ways. If the business combination is using the direct approach to disclose cash generated by operations, the specific cash inflows and outflows are identified. For example, the cash collected from customers is disclosed along with the cash paid for inventory and expenses. Because the noncontrolling interest's share of consolidated income is a noncash item, this balance is simply omitted from the statement.

The business combination could also, instead, determine the cash from operations by applying the indirect approach. Under this alternative, noncash as well as nonoperational items are removed from net income, which leaves a residual figure representing the increase or decrease in cash resulting from operations. If the indirect approach is used, the noncontrolling interest's share of consolidated income must be eliminated from net income since this reduction in earnings is a noncash amount. The noncontrolling interest balance does not represent an actual cash payment or collection. Because the earnings assigned to these outside owners is a decrease (or negative) within consolidated income, the amount is eliminated by adding the number to net income.

Regardless of which approach is used, the noncontrolling interest income accrual is removed in computing the cash derived from operations. However, any dividend paid to the other owners during the period is an actual cash outflow incurred by the combination and must be included on the statement. Because this distribution is made to an owner, the amount is listed separately under the "Cash Flows from Financing Activities" section of the statement of cash flows.

Amortizations   The amortizations of allocations made to specific accounts are recorded in the consolidation process by means of a worksheet adjustment (Entry E). These expenses do not appear on either set of individual records but are reported in the income statement of the business combination. As a noncash decrease in income, this expense impacts the statement of cash flows in the same manner as the noncontrolling interest's share of consolidated income. If the direct approach is used by the business combination, the balance is omitted because this expense does not affect the amount of cash. In contrast, if the indirect approach is applied, the amortization expense is removed by adding the balance to net income.

Intercompany Transactions   As discussed previously in this text, a significant volume of transfers often occur between the related companies composing a business combination. The resulting effects of this intercompany activity must be eliminated on the worksheet so that the consolidated income statement and balance sheet reflect only transactions with outside parties. Likewise, the consolidated statement of cash flows should not include the impact of these transfers. Although the cash flows may be large, intercompany sales and purchases do not change the amount of cash being held by the business combination when viewed as a whole.

Because the statement of cash flows is derived from the consolidated balance sheet and income statement, the impact of all transfers has been removed prior to producing this last statement. Therefore, no special adjustments are needed to arrive at a proper presentation of cash flows. The elimination entries made on the worksheet have the added effect of providing correct data for the consolidated statement of cash flows.

Acquisition Year Cash Flow Adjustments   In the year of a business acquisition, several additional considerations arise that must be properly reflected in the consolidated cash flow statement. For many business combinations the following issues frequently are present:

- Cash purchases of businesses must be accounted for as an investing activity. Importantly, the *net cash outflow* (cash paid less subsidiary cash acquired) is reported as the amount paid in a business acquisition.

- For intraperiod purchase acquisitions, *SFAS No. 95* requires that any adjustments from changes in operating balance sheet accounts (accounts receivable, inventory, accounts payable, etc.) reflect the amounts acquired in the combination. Therefore, any changes in operating assets and liabilities are reported net of effects of acquired businesses in computing the necessary adjustments to convert consolidated net income to operating cash flows. Under the direct approach of presenting operating cash flows, the separate computations of cash collected from customers and cash paid for inventory are also reported net of effects of any acquired businesses.

- Any adjustments arising from the subsidiary's revenues or expenses (e.g., depreciation, amortization) must reflect only post-acquisition amounts. Closing the subsidiary's books at the date of acquisition facilitates the determination of the appropriate post-acquisition subsidiary effects on the consolidated entity's cash flows.

- Acquired in-process research and development may represent an allocation of the purchase price that is expensed in the consolidated income statement in the acquisition year. Such in-process research and development costs are considered cash outflows from investing activities.[3] Therefore, under the indirect method, the expense is added back to consolidated net income in determining cash flows from operating activities.

Consolidated Statement of Cash Flows Illustration   Assume that on July 1, 2001, Pinto Company purchases 90 percent of the outstanding stock of Salida Company for $775,000 in cash. At the date of acquisition Pinto prepares the following cost allocation schedule based on the fair market values of Salida's assets and liabilities:

Acquisition cost, July 1, 2001		$775,000
Cash	$ 35,000	
Accounts receivable	145,000	
Inventory	90,000	
Land	100,000	
Buildings	136,000	
Equipment	259,000	
Accounts payable	(15,000)	
Net book value	$750,000	
Percent acquired	× 90%	675,000
		100,000
Excess cost over book value allocation		
Equipment (four-year life)	$ 40,000	
In-process research and development	22,000	
Database (four-year life)	38,000	100,000
		–0–

---

[3]See Compaq's acquisition of Digital or several of DuPont's acquisitions in the late 1990s for examples of acquired in-process research and development classified as an investing activity.

At the end of 2001, the following comparative balance sheets and consolidated income statement are available.

PINTO COMPANY AND SUBSIDIARY SALIDA COMPANY
Comparative Balance Sheets

	Pinto Co. January 1, 2001	Consolidated December 31, 2001
Cash	$ 170,000	$ 449,500
Accounts receivable (net)	118,000	319,000
Inventory	310,000	395,000
Land	250,000	350,000
Buildings (net)	350,000	426,000
Equipment (net)	1,145,000	1,379,000
Database		33,250
Total assets	$2,343,000	$3,351,750
Accounts payable	$ 50,000	$ 45,000
Long-term liabilities	18,000	519,500
Common stock	1,500,000	1,500,000
Noncontrolling interest		87,500
Retained earnings	775,000	1,199,750
Total liabilities and equities	$2,343,000	$3,351,750

In preparing the consolidated statement of cash flows, note that each adjustment derives from the consolidated income statement or changes from Pinto's January 1, 2001, balance sheet to the consolidated balance sheet at December 31, 2001.

Depreciation and Amortization These expenses do not represent current operating cash outflows and thus are added back to convert accrual basis income to cash provided by operating activities.

Increase in Accounts Receivable, Inventory, and Accounts Payable (net of acquisition)
SFAS No. 95 requires that changes in balance sheet accounts affecting operating cash flows reflect amounts acquired in business acquisitions. In this case note that the changes in accounts receivable, inventory, and accounts payable are computed as follows:

	Accounts Receivable	Inventory	Accounts Payable
Pinto's balance 1/1/01	$118,000	$310,000	$50,000
Increase from Salida acquisition	145,000	90,000	15,000
Adjusted beginning balance	$263,000	$400,000	$65,000
Consolidated balance 12/31/01	319,000	395,000	45,000
Operating cash flow adjustment	$ 56,000	$ 5,000	$20,000

Acquired In-Process Research and Development The purchase price for Salida Company includes $22,000 for in-process research and development which is expensed by the combined entity immediately upon acquisition. The $22,000 is added back to net income and included as part of cash outflows from investing activities.

Noncontrolling Interest The noncontrolling interest's share of the combined entity's net income represents neither a distribution nor a collection of cash and therefore is added back to consolidated net income. Ownership divisions between the noncontrolling and controlling interests do not affect reporting for the entity's operating cash flows.

Purchase of Salida Company   The investing activities section of the cash flow statement shows increases and decreases in assets purchased or sold involving cash. The cash outflow from the purchase of Salida Company's assets is determined as follows:

Purchase price for 90 percent interest in Salida	$775,000
Cash acquired	(35,000)
Net cash paid for Salida investment	$740,000

Note here that although Pinto acquires only 90 percent of Salida, 100 percent of Salida's cash is offset against the purchase price in determining the investing cash outflow. Ownership divisions between the noncontrolling and controlling interests do not affect reporting for the entity's investing cash flows.

Issue of Long-Term Debt   Pinto Company's issuance of long-term debt represents a cash inflow from financing activities.

Dividends   The dividends paid to Pinto Company owners ($50,000) combined with the dividends paid to the noncontrolling interest ($2,500) represent cash outflows from financing activities.

PINTO COMPANY AND SUBSIDIARY SALIDA COMPANY
Consolidated Income Statement
For the Year Ended December 31, 2001

Revenues		$1,255,000
Cost of goods sold	$600,000	
Depreciation	125,000	
Database amortization	4,750	
In-process research and development	22,000	
Interest and other expenses	13,500	
Noncontrolling interest in Salida's income	15,000	780,250
Net income		$ 474,750

Additional Information

- At the date of acquisition, Salida Company closed its books. Consequently, the consolidated income statement totals include Salida's post-acquisition revenues and expenses.
- During 2001, Pinto paid $50,000 in dividends. On August 1, 2001, Salida paid a $25,000 dividend.
- During 2001, Pinto issued $501,500 in long-term debt at par value.
- No other asset purchases or dispositions occurred during 2001 other than the purchase of Salida.
- The acquired in-process research and development was judged to have no alternative future uses.

Based on the consolidated totals from the comparative balance sheets and the combined income statements, the following consolidated statement of cash flows is then prepared. Pinto chooses to use the indirect method of reporting cash flows from operating activities.

PINTO COMPANY AND SUBSIDIARY SALIDA COMPANY
Consolidated Statement of Cash Flows
For the Year Ended December 31, 2001

Consolidated net income		$ 474,750
Depreciation expense	$125,000	
Amortization expense	4,750	
Increase in accounts receivable (net of acquisition effects)	(56,000)	
Decrease in inventory (net of acquisition effects)	5,000	
Decrease in accounts payable (net of acquisition effects)	(20,000)	
Acquired in-process research and development	22,000	
Noncontrolling interest in income	15,000	95,750
Net cash provided by operations		$ 570,500
Purchase of Salida Company (net of cash acquired)		
Net cash used in investing activities		(740,000)
Issue long-term debt	$501,500	
Dividends	(52,500)	
Net cash provided by financing activities		449,000
Increase in Cash 1/1/01 to 12/31/01		**$ 279,500**

CONSOLIDATED EARNINGS PER SHARE

One other intermediate accounting topic, the computation of earnings per share (EPS), is affected by the consolidation process. As required by *Statement of Financial Accounting Standards No. 128* (March 1997), "Earnings per Share," publicly held companies must disclose EPS each period.

Such figures are calculated through the following steps:

■ Basic earnings per share is determined by dividing net income (after reduction for preferred stock dividends) by the weighted average number of common stock shares outstanding for the period. If the reporting entity has no dilutive options, warrants, or other convertible items, only basic EPS is presented on the face of the income statement. However, diluted earnings per share also must be presented if any dilutive convertibles are present.

■ Diluted earnings per share is computed by combining the effects of *any dilutive securities* with basic earnings per share. Stock options, stock warrants, convertible debt, and convertible preferred stock often qualify as dilutive securities.[4]

In most instances, the computation of earnings per share for a business combination follows the same general pattern. Consolidated net income along with the number of outstanding parent shares provides the basis for calculating basic EPS. Any convertibles, warrants, or options for the parent's stock that can possibly dilute the reported figure must be included as described earlier in determining diluted EPS.

However, a problem arises if warrants, options, or convertibles are outstanding that can dilute the subsidiary's earnings. Although the parent company is not directly affected, the potential impact of these items on consolidated net income must be given weight in computing diluted earnings per share for the business combination as a

---

[4]Complete coverage of the earnings per share computation can be found in virtually any intermediate accounting textbook. To achieve an adequate understanding of this process, a number of complex procedures must be mastered, including:

■ Calculation of the weighted average number of common shares outstanding.

■ Understanding the method of including stock rights, convertible debt, and convertible preferred stock within the computation of diluted earnings per share.

■ Determination of whether a convertible is antidilutive.

whole. Because of possible conversion, the subsidiary earnings figure included in consolidated net income is not necessarily applicable to the diluted earnings per share computation. *Thus, the accountant must make a separate determination of the amount of subsidiary income that should be used in deriving diluted earnings per share for the business combination.*

Earnings per Share Illustration   Assume that Big Corporation has 100,000 shares of its common stock outstanding during the current year. The company also has issued 20,000 shares of nonvoting preferred stock paying an annual cumulative dividend of $5 per share ($100,000 total). Each of these preferred shares is convertible into two shares of Big's common stock.

Assume further that Big owns 90 percent of Little's common stock and 60 percent of its preferred stock (which pays $12,000 in dividends per year). Annual amortization is $24,000 attributable solely to goodwill. EPS computations currently are being made for 2001. During the year, Big reported separate income of $600,000 while Little earned $100,000. A simplified consolidation of the figures for the year indicates net income for the business combination of $662,400:

Big's separate income for 2001		$600,000
Amortization expense resulting from original purchase price		(24,000)
Little's separate income for 2001	100,000	
Noncontrolling interest in Little—common stock (10% of income after $12,000 in preferred stock dividends)	(8,800)	
Noncontrolling interest in Little—preferred stock (40% of dividends)	(4,800)	86,400
Consolidated net income		$662,400

Little has 20,000 shares of common stock and 4,000 shares of preferred stock outstanding. The preferred shares pay a $3 per year dividend and each can be converted into two shares of common stock (or 8,000 shares in total). Since Big owns only 60 percent of Little's preferred stock, a $4,800 dividend is distributed each year to the outside owners (40 percent of $12,000 total payment).

Assume finally that the subsidiary also has $200,000 in convertible bonds outstanding that were originally issued at face value. This debt has a cash and an effective interest rate of 10 percent ($20,000 per year) and can be converted by the owners into 9,000 shares of Little's common stock. None of these bonds are owned by Big. The tax rate applicable to Little is 30 percent.

To better visualize these factors, the convertible items are scheduled as follows:

Company	Item	Interest or Dividend	Conversion	Big Owns
Big	Preferred stock	$100,000/year	40,000 shares	Not applicable
Little	Preferred stock	12,000/year	8,000 shares	60%
Little	Bonds	14,000/year*	9,000 shares	–0–

*Interest on the bonds is shown net of the 30 percent tax effect ($20,000 interest less $6,000 tax savings). No tax is computed for the preferred shares because distributed dividends do not create a tax impact.

Because the subsidiary has convertible items that may affect the company's outstanding shares and net income, Little's diluted earnings per share must be derived *before* consolidated diluted EPS can be determined. As shown in Exhibit 6–5, Little's diluted earnings per share are $3.08. Two aspects of this schedule should be noted:

■   The individual impact of the convertibles ($1.50 for the preferred stock and $1.56 for the bonds) did not raise the earnings per share figures. Thus, neither the preferred stock nor the bonds are antidilutive and both are properly included in these computations.

Exhibit 6–5
Subsidiary's Diluted
Earnings per Share

	Earnings	Shares	
LITTLE COMPANY			
Diluted Earnings per Common Share			
For Year Ending December 31, 2001			
As reported	$100,000	20,000	
Preferred stock dividends	(12,000)		
Effect of possible preferred stock conversion:			
Dividends saved	12,000 New shares	8,000	$1.50 Impact (12,000/8,000)
Effect of possible bond conversion:			
Interest saved (net of taxes) . . .	14,000	9,000	$1.56 Impact (14,000/9,000)
Diluted EPS	$114,000	37,000	$3.08 (rounded)

- Determining diluted earnings per share of the subsidiary is only necessary because of the possible dilutive impact. Without the subsidiary's convertible bonds and preferred stock, consolidated net income would form the basis for computing EPS for the business combination and only basic EPS would be reported.

According to Exhibit 6–5, Little's income is $114,000 for diluted EPS. The issue for the accountant is how much of this amount should be included in computing consolidated diluted earnings per share. This allocation is based on the percentage of shares controlled by the parent. Note that if the subsidiary preferred stock and bonds are converted into common shares, Big's ownership falls from 90 to 62 percent. For diluted EPS, 37,000 shares are appropriate. Big's 62 percent ownership (22,800/37,000) is the basis for allocating the subsidiary's $114,000 income to the parent.

Supporting Calculations for Diluted Earnings per Share

	Little Company Shares	Big's Percentage	Big's Ownership
Common stock	20,000	90%	18,000
Possible new shares—preferred stock	8,000	60	4,800
Possible new shares—bonds	9,000	–0–	–0–
Total	37,000		22,800

Big's ownership (diluted): 22,800/37,000 = 62% (rounded)
Income assigned to Big (diluted earnings per share computation):
   $114,000 × 62% = $70,680

Consolidated earnings per share now can be determined. Only $70,680 of subsidiary income is appropriate for the diluted EPS computation. Because two different income figures are utilized, basic and diluted calculations are made separately as shown in Exhibit 6–6. Consequently, as determined in these schedules, this business combination should report basic earnings per share of $5.62, with diluted earnings per share of $4.62.

SUBSIDIARY STOCK TRANSACTIONS

A footnote to the financial statements of the Gerber Products Company disclosed a transaction carried out by one of the organization's subsidiaries: "The Company's wholly owned Mexican subsidiary sold previously unissued shares of common stock to Grupo Coral, S.A., a Mexican food company, at a price in excess of the shares' net book value." The footnote went on to state that Gerber had increased consolidated additional paid-in capital by $432,000 as a result of this stock sale.

Exhibit 6-6

BIG COMPANY AND CONSOLIDATED SUBSIDIARY		
Consolidated Basic Earnings per Common Share		
For Year Ending December 31, 2001		
	Earnings	**Shares**
Consolidated net income	$ 662,400	
Big's shares outstanding		100,000
Preferred stock dividends (Big)	(100,000)	
Basic EPS	$ 562,400	100,000 $5.62

Consolidated Diluted Earnings per Common Share		
For Year Ending December 31, 2001		
	Earnings	**Shares**
Computed below	$ 646,680*	
Big's shares outstanding		100,000
Preferred stock dividends (Big)	(100,000)	
Effect of possible preferred stock (Big) conversion:		
Dividends saved	100,000	New shares 40,000 $2.50 impact (100,000/40,000)
Diluted EPS	$ 646,680	140,000 $4.62 (rounded)

*Net income computation:

Big's separate income for 2001 ..	$600,000	
Amortization expense resulting from original purchase price ..	(24,000)	
Portion of Little's income assigned to diluted earnings per share calculation	70,680	(computed previously)
Earnings of the business combination applicable to diluted earnings per share	$646,680	

As shown by this illustration, subsidiary stock transactions can alter the level of parent ownership. A subsidiary, for example, may decide to sell previously unissued stock to raise needed capital. Although the parent company may acquire a portion or even all of these new shares, such issues frequently are marketed entirely to outsiders. A subsidiary might also be legally forced to sell additional shares of its stock. As an example, companies holding control over foreign subsidiaries occasionally encounter this problem because of laws in the individual localities. Issuance of new shares may be mandated if regulations require a certain percentage of local ownership as a prerequisite for operating within a country. Of course, changes in the level of parent ownership do not result solely from stock sales: A subsidiary also can repurchase its own stock. The acquisition, and possible retirement, of such treasury shares serves as a means of reducing the percentage of outside ownership.

Changes in Subsidiary Book Value—Stock Transactions

When a subsidiary subsequently buys or sells its own stock, a nonoperational increase or decrease occurs in the company's book value. Because the transaction need not involve the parent, the effect of this change is not automatically reflected in the parent's investment account. *Thus, a separate adjustment must be recorded to maintain reciprocity between the subsidiary's stockholders' equity accounts and the parent's investment balance.* The accountant measures the impact that the stock transaction has on the parent to ensure that this effect is appropriately recorded within the consolidation process.

An example demonstrates the mechanics of this issue. Assume that on January 1, 2001, Small Company's book value is $700,000 as follows:

Common stock ($1.00 par value with 70,000 shares issued and outstanding)	$ 70,000
Retained earnings	630,000
Total stockholders' equity	$700,000

Based on the 70,000 outstanding shares, Small's book value at this time is $10 per common share ($700,000/70,000 shares).

On this same date, Giant Company acquired in the open market an 80 percent interest in Small Company (56,000 of the outstanding shares). To avoid unnecessary complications, the price of this stock is assumed to be $560,000, or $10 per share, exactly equivalent to the book value of the purchased shares. The assumption also is made that no goodwill or other revaluations are indicated by this acquisition.

Under these conditions, the consolidation process is uncomplicated. On the purchase date only a single worksheet entry is required. The investment account is eliminated and the 20 percent noncontrolling interest recognized through the following routine entry:

Consolidation Entry S (January 1, 2001)

Common Stock (Small Company)	70,000	
Retained Earnings (Small Company)	630,000	
Investment in Small Company (80%)		560,000
Noncontrolling Interest in Small Company (20%).		140,000
To eliminate subsidiary's stockholders' equity accounts and record noncontrolling interest balance on this date.		

A subsidiary stock transaction is now introduced to demonstrate the effect created on the consolidation process. Assume that on January 2, 2001, Small sells 10,000 previously unissued shares of its common stock to outside parties for $16 per share.[5] Because of this transaction, Giant no longer possesses an 80 percent interest in a subsidiary having a $700,000 net book value. Instead, the parent now holds 70 percent (56,000 shares out of a total of 80,000) of a company with a book value of $860,000 ($700,000 previous book value plus $160,000 capital generated by the sale of additional shares). *Independently of any action by the parent company, the book value equivalency of this investment has risen from $560,000 to $602,000 (70% of $860,000).* This increase has been created by Small's ability to sell shares of stock at $6.00 more than the book value.

Small's new stock issuance has increased the underlying book value component of Giant's investment by $42,000 ($602,000 − $560,000). Thus, even with the rise in outside ownership, the business combination has grown in size by this amount, a change that must be reflected within the consolidated financial figures. As indicated by the Gerber example, this adjustment is frequently recorded to additional paid-in capital. Because the subsidiary's stockholders' equity is eliminated on the worksheet, any equity increase accruing to the business combination must be recognized by the parent. Therefore, the $42,000 increment is entered into Giant's financial records as an

---

[5] This example has been created solely for demonstration purposes. Obviously, having the parent acquire stock at book value on one day with an outsider paying $6 per share more than book value on the following day is an unlikely situation. Normally, the prices would be similar or a greater length of time would transpire between the two acquisitions. In either case, the consolidation process is fundamentally unchanged.

adjustment in both the investment account (since the underlying book value of the subsidiary has increased) as well as additional paid-in capital.

Giant Company's Financial Records—January 2, 2001

Investment in Small Company........................	42,000	
Additional Paid-In Capital (Giant Company)...........		42,000

To recognize change in equity of business combination created by issuance of 10,000 additional shares of common stock by Small Company, the subsidiary, at above-book value.

Once the change in the parent's records has been made, the consolidation process can be carried out in a normal fashion. If, for example, the financial statements are brought together immediately following the sale of these additional shares, the following worksheet Entry S can be constructed. *Although the investment and subsidiary equity accounts are removed here, the change recorded earlier in Giant's additional paid-in capital remains within the consolidated figures.* Thus, the subsidiary's issuance of stock at more than the book value has increased the reported equity of the business combination.

Consolidation Entry S—January 2, 2001—After Subsidiary's Stock Issuance

Common Stock (Small Company)......................	80,000	
Additional Paid-In Capital (Small Company)..............	150,000	
Retained Earnings (Small Company).....................	630,000	
Investment in Small Company (70%).................		602,000
Noncontrolling Interest in Small Company (30%)........		258,000

To eliminate subsidiary's stockholders' equity accounts and record noncontrolling interest balance on this date. Small's capital accounts have been updated to reflect the issuance of 10,000 shares of $1 par value common stock at $16 per share. The investment balance has also been adjusted for the $42,000 increment recorded earlier by the parent.

In 1983, because of a lack of formal guidance, the staff of the SEC decided that an adjustment necessitated by subsidiary stock transactions could be made to either additional paid-in capital or to a gain or loss account. For example, Atlantic Richfield Company disclosed that a previously wholly owned subsidiary had "completed an initial public offering of 19,550,000 shares of its common stock, thereby decreasing ARCO's percentage ownership to 80.4 percent. The Company recognized an after-tax gain of $185 million from this transaction."

In its October 1995 Exposure Draft, *Consolidated Financial Statements: Policy and Procedures,* however, the FASB clearly supported the view that the effects on a parent of a subsidiary's transactions in its own stock should be reported as adjustments to additional paid-in capital, not as gains or losses. As stated in the Exposure Draft:

> Transactions in the stock of a subsidiary by any of the affiliates, whether purchases or sales by the parent or another subsidiary or reacquisitions or issuances of its own stock by the subsidiary, are transactions in the equity of the reporting entity comprising a parent and its subsidiaries. . . . Therefore, no gains or losses should be recognized on those transactions (paragraph 128).

The FASB thus recommended the following for reacquisition or issuance of additional shares by a subsidiary:

> The amount of the change in a parent's proportionate ownership interest in a subsidiary is reported as an increase or decrease in additional paid-in capital and as a corresponding decrease or increase in the noncontrolling interest (paragraph 29).

Consistent with the recommendation in the Exposure Draft, this textbook treats the effects from subsidiary stock transactions on the consolidated entity as adjustments to additional paid-in capital.

Subsidiary Stock Transactions—Illustrated

No single example can demonstrate the many possible variations that could be created by different types of subsidiary stock transactions. To provide a working knowledge of this process, several additional cases are analyzed briefly. The original balances presented for Small (the 80-percent-owned subsidiary) and Giant (the parent) as of January 1, 2001, serve as the basis for these illustrations:

Small Company (subsidiary):	
Shares outstanding	70,000
Book value of company	$700,000
Book value per share	$ 10.00
Giant Company (parent):	
Shares owned of Small Company	56,000
Book value of investment	$560,000 (80%)

Each of the following cases should be viewed as an independent situation. Also, all adjustments are made here to additional paid-in capital although, as discussed, recognition of a gain or loss remains a possible alternative.

Case 1   Assume that Small Company sells 10,000 shares of previously unissued common stock to outside parties for $8 per share.

Small is issuing its stock here at a price below the company's current book value of $10 per share. Selling shares to outsiders at a discount necessitates a drop in the recorded value of consolidated additional paid-in capital. The parent's ownership interest is being diluted, thus creating a decrease in the underlying book value of the parent's investment. This reduction can be measured as follows:

Adjusted book value of subsidiary ($700,000 + $80,000)	$780,000
Current parent ownership (56,000 shares/80,000 shares)	70%
Book value equivalency of ownership	546,000
Current book value of investment account	560,000
Required *reduction*	$ 14,000

In the original illustration, new shares were sold by the subsidiary at $6 more than book value, thus increasing consolidated equity. Here, the opposite transpires; the shares are issued at a price less than book value, creating a decrease.

Giant Company's Financial Records

Additional Paid-In Capital (or Retained Earnings)		
(Giant Company)	14,000	
Investment in Small Company		14,000
To recognize change in equity of business combination created by issuance of 10,000 additional shares of Small's common stock at less than book value.		

Case 2   Assume that Small issues 10,000 new shares of common stock for $16 per share. Of this total, Giant acquires 8,000 shares to maintain its 80 percent level of ownership. Giant pays a total of $128,000 (8,000 × $16) for this additional stock. The remaining shares are bought by outside parties.

Under these circumstances, both the parent's investment account and the book value of the subsidiary are altered by the stock transaction. Thus, both figures must be updated prior to determining the necessity of an equity revaluation:

Adjusted book value of subsidiary ($700,000 + $160,000)	$860,000
Current parent ownership (64,000 shares/80,000 shares)	80%
Book value equivalency of ownership	688,000
Current book value of investment (after including additional $128,000 acquisition)	688,000
Required change	$ –0–

No adjustment is required in this case because Giant's underlying interest remains properly aligned with the subsidiary's book value. Any time that new stock is sold to the parent in the same ratio as previous ownership, consolidated additional paid-in capital is unaffected. No proportionate increase or decrease is created by the transaction.

Case 3   Assume that Small issues 10,000 additional shares of common stock solely to Giant for $16 per share.

A different type of situation is faced here. As shown in the following computational schedule, this issuance causes the parent's investment account to again be in excess of the subsidiary's underlying book value (as in Case 1). However, in this latest example, the $10,500 difference is created by a parent company purchase rather than by the subsidiary's sale of common stock to outside parties. Thus, the reporting of this impact has to be altered to reflect Giant's acquisition of these new shares.

Adjusted book value of subsidiary ($700,000 + $160,000)	$860,000
Current parent ownership (66,000 shares/80,000 shares)	82.5%
Book value equivalency of ownership	709,500
Current book value of investment (after including additional $160,000 acquisition)	720,000
Differences in subsidiary book value and investment book value after second purchase	$ 10,500

The $14,000 reduction in Case 1 was caused by the subsidiary's sale of stock to outsiders at a price less than book value, a transaction that mathematically diluted the value of the parent's investment. Because this action realigned the ownership interests to the apparent detriment of the business combination, additional paid-in capital was reduced. This result was achieved for consolidation purposes through a decrease in the parent's equity account as well as in the Investment in Small Company.

Conversely, in Case 3, the $10,500 difference has been created solely by an expenditure made by the parent. Since the price paid was more than the corresponding book value of the subsidiary, the excess is attributed to goodwill (unless the amount can be traced to specific asset or liability accounts). As in any purchase combination, Giant records the entire $160,000 payment as an investment and then utilizes Entry A on the consolidation worksheet to report the allocation. Because the parent made the acquisition, the transaction is handled differently than a subsidiary's sale of stock to outsiders at less than book value.

Case 4   Assume that instead of issuing new stock, Small reacquires 10,000 shares from outside owners. The price paid for this treasury stock is $16 per share.

This illustration is designed to present another type of subsidiary stock transaction: the acquisition of treasury stock. Although the subsidiary's actions have changed, the basic accounting procedures are unaffected.

Adjusted book value of subsidiary ($700,000 − $160,000)	$540,000
Current parent ownership (56,000 shares/60,000 shares)	93⅓%
Book value equivalency of ownership	504,000
Current book value of investment	560,000
Required *reduction*	$ 56,000

The subsidiary paid an amount in excess of the treasury stock's $10 per share book value. Consequently, the parent's interest is once again being diluted. This effect is created by a transaction between the subsidiary and the noncontrolling interest; the reduction is not the result of a purchase made by the parent. As in Case 1, the change must be reported as an adjustment in the parent's additional paid-in capital accompanied by a corresponding decrease in the investment account (to $504,000 in this case). Again, for reporting purposes, this transaction results in lowering consolidated additional paid-in capital.

Giant Company's Financial Records

Additional Paid-In Capital (Giant Company)...............	56,000	
Investment in Small Company		56,000

To recognize change in equity of business combination created by acquisition of 10,000 treasury shares by Small at above-book value.

This fourth illustration represents a different subsidiary stock transaction, the purchase of treasury stock. Therefore, display of consolidation Entry S should also be presented. This entry demonstrates the worksheet elimination required when the subsidiary holds treasury shares.

Consolidation Entry S

Common Stock (Small Company)	70,000	
Retained Earnings (Small Company)......................	630,000	
Treasury Stock (Small Company) (at cost)		160,000
Investment in Small Company (93⅓%—subsequent to adjustment)...................................		504,000
Noncontrolling Interest (6⅔% of net book value)		36,000

To eliminate equity accounts of Small Company and recognize appropriate noncontrolling interest. Book value of Small is now $540,000.

Case 5   Assume that Small issues a 10 percent stock dividend (7,000 new shares) to its owners at a time when the fair market value of the stock is $16 per share.

This final case illustrates that not all subsidiary stock transactions produce discernible effects on the consolidation process. A stock dividend, whether large or small, serves to capitalize a portion of the issuing company's retained earnings and, thus, does not alter book value. Shareholders recognize the receipt of a stock dividend only as a change in the recorded cost of each share rather than as any type of adjustment in the investment balance. Because no net effect is perceived by either party, the consolidation process proceeds in a routine fashion. Therefore, a subsidiary stock dividend requires no special treatment prior to development of a worksheet.

Book value of subsidiary (no adjustment required)	$700,000
Current parent ownership (adjusted for 10% stock dividend— 61,600 shares/77,000 shares)	80%
Book value equivalency of ownership	560,000
Current book value of investment	560,000
Adjustment required by stock dividend	$ –0–

The consolidation Entry S that would be made just after the issuance of this stock dividend follows. The $560,000 component of the investment account continues to be offset against the stockholders' equity of the subsidiary. Although the parent's investment was not affected by the dividend, the equity accounts of the subsidiary have been realigned in recognition of the $112,000 stock dividend (7,000 shares of $1 par value stock valued at $16 per share).

Consolidation Entry S

Common Stock (Small Company)	77,000	
Additional Paid-In Capital (Small Company)	105,000	
Retained Earnings (Small Company)	518,000	
Investment in Small Company (80%)		560,000
Noncontrolling interest (20%)		140,000

To eliminate stockholders' equity accounts of subsidiary and recognize noncontrolling interest following issuance of stock dividend.

SUMMARY

1. If one member of a business combination acquires an affiliate's debt instrument (a bond or note, for example) from an outside party, the purchase price usually differs from the book value of the liability. Thus, a gain or loss has been incurred from the perspective of the business combination. However, both the debt and investment remain in the individual financial accounts of the two companies while the gain or loss goes unrecorded. In the consolidation process, all balances must be adjusted to reflect the effective retirement of the debt.

2. Following the acquisition of one company's debt by a related party, interest income and expense are recognized. Because these accounts result from intercompany transactions, they also must be removed in every subsequent consolidation along with the debt and investment figures. Retained earnings also require adjustment in each year after the purchase to record the impact of the gain or loss.

3. Amortization of intercompany debt/investment balances often is necessary because of discounts and/or premiums. Consequently, the interest income and interest expense figures reported by the two parties will not agree. The closing of these two accounts into retained earnings each year gradually reduces the consolidation adjustment that must be made to this equity account.

4. When acquired, many subsidiaries have preferred stock outstanding as well as common stock. The method of handling any subsidiary preferred shares within the consolidation process is dependent on the nature of the stock. Preferred issues that have a call value, no voting rights, and a set cumulative dividend are not easily distinguished from a debt. Conversely, preferred shares with a voting or participation right are clearly an ownership interest resembling common stock.

5. If a subsidiary's preferred stock is viewed as a debt-type instrument, any shares acquired by the parent are eliminated on the worksheet as if the stock had been retired. Because a gain or loss cannot be recognized in connection with a company's own stock transactions, the difference between par value and the parent's cost is adjusted through additional paid-in capital or retained earnings. Any shares still held by outside parties are reported as a noncontrolling interest, based on the call value of the stock.

6. A subsidiary preferred stock that is perceived as an equity interest is accounted for in the same manner as a common stock purchase. Any excess acquisition price paid for the preferred stock is assigned to specific accounts based on fair market value with any residual reported as goodwill. As a prerequisite to this process, the book value of the subsidiary must be divided between the two equity interests. This calculation is based on the rights specified for the preferred shareholders.

7. A statement of cash flows is required of every business combination. This statement is not created by consolidating the individual cash flows of the separate companies. Instead, both a consolidated income statement and balance sheet are produced and the cash flows statement is developed from these figures. Within this statement, the noncontrolling interest's share of the subsidiary's income is not included because no cash flows result. However, the dividends paid to these outside owners must be listed as a financing activity.

8. For most business combinations, the determination of consolidated earnings per share follows the normal pattern presented in intermediate accounting textbooks. However, if the subsidiary has potentially dilutive items outstanding (stock warrants, convertible

preferred stock, convertible bonds, etc.), a different process must be followed. The subsidiary's own diluted earnings per share are computed as a preliminary procedure. The earnings used in each of these calculations are then allocated between the parent and the outside owners based on the ownership levels of the subsidiary's shares and the dilutive items. The portion of income assigned to the parent is included in determining the diluted earnings per share figures to be reported for the business combination.

9. A subsidiary may enter into stock transactions after the combination is created such as the issuance of additional shares or the acquisition of treasury stock. Such actions normally create a proportional increase or decrease in the subsidiary's equity when compared with the parent's investment. The change is measured and then reflected in the consolidated statements through the Additional Paid-In Capital account. Recognition of a gain or loss is also a possibility. To achieve the appropriate accounting, the parent adjusts the Investment in Subsidiary account as well as its own additional paid-in capital. Since this equity balance is not eliminated on the worksheet, the required increase or decrease is created in the consolidated figures.

COMPREHENSIVE ILLUSTRATION

Because several topics have been covered in this chapter, two comprehensive illustrations are presented.

Problem One: Intercompany Bonds, Preferred Stock, and Stock Transactions

(Estimated Time: 50 to 65 Minutes) The individual financial statements for Big Company and Little Corporation for the year ending December 31, 2001, follow:

	Big Company	Little Corporation
Revenues	$ 900,000	$ 389,026
Expenses	(702,000)	(200,000)
Interest income	–0–	10,974
Dividend income—Little Corporation preferred stock	2,400	–0–
Income of subsidiary—Little Corporation common stock	116,400	–0–
Net income	$ 316,800	$ 200,000
Retained earnings, 1/1/01	$1,300,000	$ 700,000
Net income (above)	316,800	200,000
Dividends—preferred stock	–0–	(6,000)
Dividends—common stock	(136,800)	(24,000)
Retained earnings, 12/31/01	$1,480,000	$ 870,000
Current assets	$484,525	$ 850,000
Investment in Big Company bonds	–0–	108,711
Investment in Little Corporation preferred stock	26,800	–0–
Investment in Little Corporation common stock	958,000	–0–
Land, buildings, and equipment (net)	600,000	750,000
Total assets	$2,069,325	$1,708,711
Current liabilities	$ 202,000	$ 138,711
Bonds payable ($200,000 face value)	177,325	–0–
Preferred stock—$60 par value; 1,000 shares outstanding	–0–	60,000
Common stock—$4 par value; 50,000 shares outstanding	200,000	
Common stock—$10 par value; 24,000 shares outstanding		240,000
Additional paid-in capital	10,000	400,000
Retained earnings (above)	1,480,000	870,000
Total liabilities and equities	$2,069,325	$1,708,711

Note: Parentheses indicate a reduction.

Additional Information:

On January 1, 1996, Big Company purchased 14,400 shares of Little's common stock (80 percent of the 18,000 shares outstanding at that date). Big also bought 40 percent of the company's outstanding preferred stock (400 shares). A total of $530,800 was paid by Big for these two investments: $504,000 for the common stock and $26,800 for the preferred. At the date of acquisition, Big believed that no significant difference existed between the book value of Little's assets and liabilities and their fair market values. Little Corporation reported the following stockholders' equity accounts on January 1, 1996:

Preferred stock—$60 par value, 10% cumulative dividend, nonparticipating, nonvoting; call value of $72 per share; 1,000 shares outstanding	$ 60,000
Common stock—$10 par value; 18,000 shares outstanding	180,000
Additional paid-in capital	100,000
Retained earnings	260,000
Total stockholders' equity	$600,000

On January 1, 2000, Little acquired on the open market half of the $200,000 outstanding bonds payable of Big Company. The bonds pay 12 percent cash interest each December 31 but were originally issued at a price yielding an effective rate of 15 percent. On the date of Little's purchase, Big was reporting a total book value for this debt of $173,100. Because of a recent decline in the prime interest rate, Little had to pay $110,670 for these bonds. This price was calculated to produce a 10 percent yield. Each company uses the effective interest rate method of amortization.

To raise new capital for expansion, Little Corporation issued an additional 6,000 shares of common stock to outsiders on January 1, 2001. Because of the company's profitability, the stock was sold for $60 per share. Because none of these shares were acquired by Big, the parent did not record the transaction.

Big has applied the partial equity method to the investment in Little's common stock while using the cost method for preferred shares. From 1996 through 2000, Little's retained earnings went up $440,000. Since preferred stock dividends were paid in full each year, the entire increase was directly attributable to the common shares (80 percent owned by Big).

Because of Little's sale of additional shares at the beginning of 2001, Big now holds only 60 percent of the common stock (14,400/24,000). Thus, the parent recognized equity income of $116,400 in 2001 in connection with its ownership of the subsidiary's common stock, 60 percent of the $194,000 income applicable to common stock (the $200,000 reported total less the $6,000 preferred stock dividend). The year-end investment in the common stock balance is made up of the following components:

Purchase price—common stock	$504,000
Increase in book value during prior years ($440,000 × 80%)	352,000
Equity accrual for current year	116,400
Dividends paid on common stock during current year ($24,000 × 60%)	(14,400)
Investment in Little Corporation common stock—12/31/01	$958,000

Any excess amount within the purchase price is to be allocated to franchise contracts and amortized over 40 years.

Required:

Prepare consolidated balances for Big and Little for 2001 financial statements.

Solution (One)

Specifying a single definitive approach to consolidating a complex business combination is not realistically possible. Clearly, though, certain aspects of the process should be handled first. Allocation of the purchase price routinely has been an initial step in previous examples. In this illustration, the allocation is complicated by the presence of Little's preferred stock. The nature of these shares must be identified as a prerequisite for the valuation of the common stock acquisition.

Exhibit 6–7

BIG COMPANY AND LITTLE CORPORATION Common Stock Purchase Price Allocation January 1, 1996	
Purchase price of common stock	$ 504,000
Common stock book value equivalent to Big's ownership ($530,000 × 80%)	(424,000)
Cost in excess of book value—all allocated to franchises	$ 80,000
Life of franchises	40 years
Annual amortization	$ 2,000

As the preferred stock is listed as nonvoting and nonparticipating, it possesses the basic characteristics of a debt issue and is handled in a corresponding manner. Thus, the price paid for the preferred shares does not directly affect the calculation of the amount to be allocated to the franchises. Instead, 40 percent of the subsidiary's preferred stock is viewed as having been retired by Big's acquisition. Under this assumption, $70,000 of the January 1, 1996, book value is allocated to this stock.

Acquisition price paid by Big Company—400 shares of preferred stock (40% ownership)	$26,800
Call value of remaining 600 shares—$72 per share (noncontrolling interest)	43,200
Book value attributable to preferred stock	$70,000

Having allotted $70,000 to the preferred stock interest, the remaining $530,000 of Little's January 1, 1996, book value is applicable to the common shares. Based on this residual value, Exhibit 6–7 can be constructed to allocate the $504,000 purchase price paid by Big to acquire 80 percent ownership in Little's common stock. No similar schedule is necessary for the preferred shares because that stock is viewed, in this case, as a debt-type instrument.

A second concern to be addressed at the start of this consolidation revolves around the subsidiary stock transaction. Since Big (as stated in the problem) made no entry to reflect the change on the business combination, an adjustment must be recorded. Big originally acquired 80 percent of Little's outstanding common stock (14,400 shares out of a total of 18,000). However, the issuance of 6,000 new shares to outsiders reduces the parent's level of ownership to 60 percent (14,400/24,000 shares). Selling this stock for $60 per share also has increased Little's book value by $360,000. The impact of the subsidiary stock transaction can be measured as follows:

Little Corporation's 1/1/01 book value prior to stock sale
  ($600,000 book value at acquisition plus the $440,000
  increment for the 1996–2000 period) ....
	$1,040,000

Little Corporation's 1/1/01 book value subsequent to stock issuance ($1,040,000 + $360,000)	$1,400,000
Little Corporation's book value applicable to preferred stock (see above)	(70,000)
Residual book value applicable to common stock	1,330,000
Current ownership by Big	60%
Book value equivalency of Big's common stock ownership	798,000
Unadjusted book value of Big's common stock investment [($1,040,000 previous book value − $70,000) × 80%]	776,000
Required increase in investment account created by subsidiary stock issuance	$ 22,000

The issuance of these new shares has created a $22,000 increase in the underlying equity of Little Corporation that is held by the parent. This transaction creates a change in the additional paid-in capital reported by the business combination. Although the increase could have been recorded by the parent at the time of sale, no entry was made. Consequently, an adjustment of $22,000 must be made to Big's additional paid-in capital.

After accounting for the previous computations, an analysis should be made of the intercompany bond transaction. Little's payment of $110,670 to retire a liability with a book value on Big's records of only $86,550 (half of the $173,100 total) produced an immediate loss of $24,120 on January 1, 2000. However, since the companies are being accounted for as two separate entities, neither the retirement nor the loss were recognized by either party. Both the debtor and creditor continue to account for these bonds as if they were still outstanding. Interest payments are made periodically as required while each company amortizes the difference between the book value of the bonds and their face value.

The bond and interest accounts found in Big's December 31, 2001, accounting records have been calculated in the following schedule. This presentation determines these balances for only one-half of the bonds payable because only that amount currently is held within the business combination.

Big Company's Financial Records—Bonds Payable

Year	Beginning Book Value	Effective Interest (15 percent rate)	Cash Interest (12 percent rate)	Amortization	Year-End Book Value
2000	$86,550	$12,983	$12,000	$ 983	$87,533
2001	87,533	13,130	12,000	1,130	88,663

During this time, Little would have accounted for the investment in these same bonds as follows:

Little Corporation's Financial Records—Investment in Bonds

Year	Beginning Book Value	Effective Interest (10 percent rate)	Cash Interest (12 percent rate)	Amortization	Year-End Book Value
2000	$110,670	$11,067	$12,000	$ 933	$109,737
2001	109,737	10,974	12,000	1,026	108,711

After the financial figures relative to the intercompany bonds have been isolated, an appropriate elimination can be produced. Consolidated balances must report these bonds as having been retired on the date they were acquired by the subsidiary. Thus, the current $88,663 book value of the liability is removed as well as the $108,711 investment balance. At the same time, both the $13,130 interest expense reported by Big for the current period and the $10,974 interest income recognized by Little are eliminated.

To complete the handling of this bond, a $22,204 reduction is made to the parent's beginning retained earnings. Although the loss was actually $24,120, the previous $983 amortization of the bond payable discount in 2000 and the $933 amortization of the investment premium have already reduced the 2001 beginning retained earnings by a total of $1,916. A decrease of only $22,204 is needed to reflect the loss on retirement.

As the final step in establishing appropriate 2001 balances, Big's beginning retained earnings must be restated to be in conformity with application of the equity method for this investment. The $22,204 adjustment necessitated by the bond retirement was just explained. In addition, a $10,000 reduction is needed to recognize $2,000 of franchise amortization (as computed in Exhibit 6–7) for each of the five years from 1996 through 2000.

Having analyzed this information, consolidated balances for the business combination of Big and Little for December 31, 2001, and the year then ended can be developed:

Revenues = $1,289,026. Since no intercompany inventory transfers took place between Big and Little, the two account balances are simply added together.

Expenses = $890,870. Amortization expense of $2,000 must be added to the book values while $13,130 in interest expense on the intercompany bond is removed.

Interest income = –0–. The amount reported by Little is an intercompany figure produced by the investment in Big's bonds. For consolidation purposes, this figure is removed entirely.

Dividend income—Little preferred stock = –0–. This intercompany cash transfer is eliminated.

Equity income—Little common stock = –0–. The accrual recorded by the parent is eliminated so that the specific revenues and expenses of the subsidiary can be included in the consolidated figures.

Noncontrolling interest in income attributed to Little's preferred stock = $3,600. This figure is 60 percent of the amount of dividends paid since the parent owns only 40 percent.

Noncontrolling interest in income attributed to Little's common stock = $77,600. This figure is 40 percent of the income earned by the subsidiary after payment of the preferred stock dividend ($200,000 − $6,000, or $194,000). Although Big originally purchased 80 percent of Little, the subsequent issuance of additional shares has reduced the parent's ownership to 60 percent.

Net income = $316,956. Consolidated expenses and the amounts attributed to the outside owners are subtracted from consolidated revenues.

Retained earnings, 1/1/01 = $1,267,796. Because the parent is applying the partial equity method, the amortization expense for the five previous years must be recognized ($2,000 for five years, or $10,000) as well as the $22,204 reduction in connection with the loss on bond retirement (computation made above).

Dividends paid on preferred stock = –0–. The dividends paid by the subsidiary are eliminated as intercompany (40 percent) or attributed to the noncontrolling interest (60 percent).

Dividends paid on common stock = $136,800. This balance represents the amount distributed by the parent. The subsidiary's dividends are eliminated as intercompany or are attributed to the noncontrolling interest.

Retained earnings, 12/31/01 = $1,447,952. The consolidated beginning retained earnings balance plus net income for the year less the dividends paid.

Current assets = $1,334,525. The book values are added together.

Investment in Big Company bonds = –0–. The balance is eliminated as an intercompany account.

Investment in Little Corporation preferred stock = –0–. The balance is eliminated as an intercompany account.

Investment in Little Corporation common stock = –0–. The balance is eliminated so that the individual assets and liabilities of the subsidiary can be included in the consolidated figures.

Land, buildings, and equipment = $1,350,000. The two book values are added.

Franchises = $68,000. The original allocation to the franchises was $80,000, an amount which has now been reduced by six years of amortization at $2,000 per year.

Total assets = $2,752,525. This figure is a summation of the consolidated asset balances.

Current liabilities = $340,711. The book values are added.

Bonds payable = $88,662. Half of the reported bonds are eliminated as an intercompany investment.

Noncontrolling interest in Little's preferred stock = $43,200. This figure is the call value of the shares held by outsiders (600 shares at $72 per share).

Noncontrolling interest in Little's common stock = $600,000. This balance is computed as follows:

40% of subsidiary's common stock book value at 1/1/01 ($1,330,000—based on stockholders' equity accounts at beginning of year after subtracting $70,000 applicable to preferred shares)	$532,000
Noncontrolling interest in Little's net income—common stock (computed above)	77,600
Noncontrolling interest in Little's dividends—common stock ($24,000 × 40%)	(9,600)
Year-end balance	$600,000

Preferred stock = –0–. Only parent figure is reported for contributed capital and Big has no preferred stock.

Common stock = $200,000. Parent company balance only is presented.

Additional paid-in capital = $32,000. Parent company balance is reported after the $22,000 adjustment is made because of the subsidiary's sale of additional shares of stock.

Retained earnings, 12/31/01 = $1,447,952. Amount is computed above.

Total liabilities and stockholders' equity = $2,752,525. Summation of the consolidated liabilities and equity accounts.

Problem Two: Consolidated Statement of Cash Flows and Earnings per Share

(Estimated Time: 35 to 45 Minutes) Pop, Inc., acquires 90 percent of the 20,000 shares of Son Company's outstanding common stock on December 31, 2000. Of the purchase price, $80,000 was allocated to goodwill, a figure amortized at the rate of $2,000 per year. Immediately following the purchase, a consolidated balance sheet was constructed:

Cash	$ 130,000
Accounts receivable	220,000
Inventory	278,000
Land, buildings, and equipment (net)	1,120,000
Covenants	80,000
Total assets	$1,828,000
Accounts payable	$ 296,000
Long-term liabilities	550,000
Noncontrolling interest	34,000
Preferred stock (2,000 shares outstanding)	100,000
Common stock (26,000 shares outstanding)	520,000
Retained earnings, 12/31/00	328,000
Total liabilities and stockholders' equity	$1,828,000

During 2001, Pop transferred inventory costing $60,000 to Son for $100,000. By year's end, all but 10 percent of this merchandise had been sold to outside parties.

On January 17, 2001, Pop borrowed $100,000 from a local bank. Several months later, the parent acquired equipment for $60,000 cash. On November 10, 2001, Son sold a building with a $40,000 book value, receiving cash of $50,000. These transactions were all with outside parties.

Pop pays a $10,000 dividend each year to the holders of the company's preferred stock. Each share of this stock can be converted into three shares of common. Son's long-term debt also is convertible. Interest expense in 2001 (net of taxes) was $16,000. The debt can be exchanged for 10,000 shares of the subsidiary's common stock. Pop owns none of this debt.

Presented in Exhibit 6–8 is the 2001 consolidation worksheet for Pop and Son. Pop applies the equity method to account for the investment in Son. The $48,000 equity income figure reported by the parent is derived from the $54,000 annual accrual (90 percent of the $60,000 reported income of the subsidiary) less the $2,000 amortization and the $4,000 unrealized gain (10 percent of the original intercompany gross profit). The noncontrolling interest in Son's income is 10 percent of the subsidiary's reported income for 2001.

Required:

a. Prepare a consolidated statement of cash flows for Pop, Inc., and Son Company for the year ending December 31, 2001. Use the indirect approach for determining the amount of cash generated by normal operations.[6]

b. Compute basic earnings per share and diluted earnings per share for this business combination.

---

[6]Prior to attempting this problem, a review of an intermediate accounting textbook might be useful to obtain a complete overview of the production of a statement of cash flows.

E x h i b i t   6 – 8

Consolidation: Purchase Method
Investment: Equity Method

POP, INC., AND SON COMPANY
Consolidation Worksheet
For Year Ending December 31, 2001

	Pop, Inc.	Son Company	Consolidation Entries Debit	Consolidation Entries Credit	Noncontrolling Interest	Consolidated Totals
Revenues	600,000	300,000	(TI) 100,000	(TI) 100,000		800,000
Cost of goods sold	(400,000)	(180,000)	(G) 4,000			(484,000)
Depreciation and amortization	(20,000)	(30,000)	(E) 2,000			(52,000)
Other expenses	(56,000)	(40,000)				(96,000)
Gain on sale of building	–0–	10,000				10,000
Equity in Son's income	48,000	–0–	(I) 48,000			–0–
Noncontrolling interest in Son's income	–0–	–0–			6,000	(6,000)
Net income	172,000	60,000				172,000
Retained earnings, 1/1/01	328,000	140,000	(S) 140,000			328,000
Net income	172,000	60,000				172,000
Dividends paid	(50,000)	(20,000)		(D) 18,000	(2,000)	(50,000)
Retained earnings, 12/31/01	450,000	180,000				450,000
Cash	180,000	30,000				210,000
Accounts receivable	260,000	90,000		(G) 4,000		350,000
Inventory	254,000	70,000		(S) 306,000		320,000
Investment in Son	416,000	–0–	(D) 18,000	(A) 80,000		–0–
				(I) 48,000		

	Parent	Son	Debit	Credit	Noncontrolling Interest	Consolidated
Land, buildings, and equipment (net)	640,000	450,000				1,090,000
Covenants	-0-	-0-	(A) 80,000	(E) 2,000		78,000
Total assets	1,750,000	640,000				2,048,000
Accounts payable	210,000	80,000				290,000
Long-term liabilities	470,000	180,000				650,000
Noncontrolling interest in Son, 1/1/01	-0-	-0-		(S) 34,000	34,000	
Noncontrolling interest in Son, 12/31/01	-0-	-0-			38,000	38,000
Preferred stock	100,000	-0-				100,000
Common stock	520,000	200,000	(S) 200,000			520,000
Retained earnings (above)	450,000	180,000				450,000
Total liabilities and stockholders' equity	1,750,000	640,000				2,048,000

Note: Parentheses indicate a reduction.

Consolidation entries:

(S) Elimination of subsidiary's stockholders' equity accounts along with recognition of January 1, 2001, noncontrolling interest.

(A) Allocation of parent's cost in excess of subsidiary's book value.

(I) Elimination of intercompany income.

(D) Elimination of intercompany dividends.

(E) Recognition of amortization expense for 2001.

(TI) Elimination of intercompany sales/purchases balances.

(G) Deferral of unrealized gain so that it can be recognized in 2002.

Solution (Two)

a. *Consolidated Statement of Cash Flows*

The problem specifies that the indirect approach should be used in preparing the consolidated statement of cash flows. Therefore, all items that do not represent cash flows from operations must be removed from the $172,000 consolidated net income. For example, the depreciation and amortization both are eliminated (noncash items) as well as the gain on the sale of the building (a nonoperational item). As discussed in the chapter, the noncontrolling interest's share of Son's net income is another noncash reduction that also is removed. In addition, the changes in consolidated accounts receivable, inventory, and accounts payable each produce a noncash impact on net income. The increase in accounts receivable, for example, indicates that the sales figure for the period was larger than the amount of cash collected so that adjustment is required in producing this statement.

From the information given, only five nonoperational changes in cash can be determined: the bank loan, the acquisition of equipment, the sale of a building, the dividend paid by Son to the minority interest, and the dividend paid by the parent. These transactions are each included in the consolidated statement of cash flows shown in Exhibit 6–9, which explains the $80,000 increase in cash experienced by the entity during 2001.

b. *Consolidated Earnings per Share*

The subsidiary's convertible debt has a potentially dilutive effect on earnings per share. Therefore, diluted EPS cannot be determined for the business combination directly from consolidated net income. First, the diluted EPS figure must be calculated for the subsidiary. This information then is used in the computations made by the consolidated entity.

Diluted earnings per share of $2.53 for the subsidiary is determined as follows:

Exhibit 6–9

POP, INC., AND SON COMPANY
Consolidated Statement of Cash Flows
Year Ending December 31, 2001

Cash flows from operating activities		
Net income		$ 172,000
Adjustments to reconcile net income to net cash provided by operating activities:		
Depreciation and amortization	$ 52,000	
Gain on sale of building	(10,000)	
Noncontrolling interest in Son's income	6,000	
Increase in accounts receivable	(130,000)	
Increase in inventory	(42,000)	
Decrease in accounts payable	(6,000)	(130,000)
Net cash provided by operations		$ 42,000
Cash flows from investing activities		
Purchase of equipment	$ (60,000)	
Sale of building	50,000	
Net cash used in investing activities		(10,000)
Cash flows from financing activities		
Payment of cash dividend—Pop	$ (50,000)	
Payment of cash dividend to noncontrolling owners of Son	(2,000)	
Borrowed from bank	100,000	
Net cash provided by financing activities		48,000
Net increase in cash		$ 80,000
Cash, January 1, 2001		130,000
Cash, December 31, 2001		$ 210,000

Son Company—Diluted Earnings per Share

	Earnings		Shares	
As reported	$60,000		20,000	$3.00
Effect of possible debt conversion:				
Interest saved (net of taxes)	16,000	New shares	10,000	$1.60 impact
				(16,000/10,000)
Diluted EPS	$76,000		30,000	$2.53 (rounded)

The parent owns none of the convertible debt included in computing diluted earnings per share. Pop holds only 18,000 (90 percent of the outstanding common stock) of the 30,000 shares used in this EPS calculation. Consequently, in determining diluted EPS for the entire business combination, just $45,600 of the subsidiary's income is applicable:

$$\$76,000 \times 18,000/30,000 = \$45,600$$

Exhibit 6–10 reveals consolidated basic earnings per share of $6.62 and diluted EPS of $5.11. Because the subsidiary's earnings figure is included separately in the computation of diluted EPS, the individual income of the parent must be identified in the same manner. Thus, the effect of the equity income, intercompany (downstream) transactions, and amortization are taken into account in arriving at the parent's earnings alone.

Exhibit 6–10

POP, INC., AND SON COMPANY
Consolidated Earnings per Share
Year Ending December 31, 2001

	Earnings		Shares	
	Basic Earnings per Share			
Basic EPS	$172,000		26,000	$6.62 (rounded)
	Diluted Earnings per Share			
Pop's reported income	$172,000			
Remove equity income	(48,000)			
Remove unrealized gain	(4,000)			
Recognize amortization expense	(2,000)			
Preferred stock dividend	(10,000)			
Common shares outstanding (Pop, Inc.)				
Common stock income—Pop (for EPS computations)	$108,000		26,000	
Income of Son (above—for diluted EPS)	45,600			
	$153,600		26,000	$5.91 (rounded)
Effect of possible preferred stock conversion:				
Dividends saved.................................	10,000	New shares	6,000	$1.67 impact
				(10,000/6,000)
Diluted EPS	$163,600		32,000	$5.11

QUESTIONS

1. A parent company acquires from a third party bonds that had been issued originally by one of its subsidiaries. What accounting problems are created by this purchase?

2. In question 1, why is the consolidation process simpler if the bonds had been acquired directly from the subsidiary rather than from a third party?

3. When one company's debt instruments are acquired by an affiliated company from a third party, how is the gain or loss on extinguishment of the debt calculated? When should this balance be recognized?

4. Several years ago, Bennett, Inc., bought a portion of the outstanding bonds of Smith Corporation, a subsidiary organization. The acquisition was made from an outside party. In the current year, how should these intercompany bonds be accounted for within the consolidation process?

5. One company purchases the outstanding debt instruments of an affiliated company on the open market. This transaction creates a gain that is appropriately recognized in the consolidated financial statements of that year. Thereafter, a worksheet adjustment is required to correct the beginning balance of the consolidated retained earnings. Why is the amount of this adjustment reduced from year to year?

6. A parent acquires the outstanding bonds of a subsidiary company directly from an outside third party. For consolidation purposes, this transaction creates a gain of $45,000. Should this gain be allocated to the parent or the subsidiary? Why?

7. Some preferred stocks possess characteristics that resemble an equity or ownership interest. Others, however, demonstrate traits similar to a debt instrument. How is the distinction drawn as to whether the preferred stock is actually an equity or a debt?

8. Perkins Company acquires 90 percent of the outstanding common stock of the Butterfly Corporation as well as 55 percent of its preferred stock. Because of the rights being conveyed, the preferred stock is considered to be a debt-type instrument. How should these preferred shares be accounted for within the consolidation process? How should the book value of Butterfly be allocated between the common and the preferred stock?

9. Assume the same information as in question 8 except that the preferred stock is viewed as an equity interest. How is the preferred stock now accounted for within the consolidation process? How should the book value of Butterfly be allocated between the common and the preferred stock?

10. A consolidated statement of cash flows is not produced using a worksheet as are the income statement and the balance sheet. What process is followed in preparing a consolidated statement of cash flows?

11. How do noncontrolling interest balances affect the consolidated statement of cash flows?

12. In many cases, consolidated earnings per share is computed based on consolidated net income and parent company shares and convertibles. However, a different process must be used for some business combinations. When is this alternative approach required?

13. A subsidiary has (1) a convertible preferred stock and (2) a convertible bond. How are these items factored into the computation of earnings per share for the business combination?

14. Why might a subsidiary decide to issue new shares of common stock to parties outside of the business combination?

15. Washburn Company owns 75 percent of the outstanding common stock of Metcalf Company. During the current year, Metcalf issues additional shares to outside parties at a price more than book value. How does this transaction affect the business combination? How is this impact recorded within the consolidated statements?

16. Assume the same information as in question 15 except that the new shares are issued primarily to Washburn. How does this transaction affect the business combination?

17. Assume the same information as in question 15 except that Metcalf issues a 10 percent stock dividend instead of selling new shares of stock. How does this transaction affect the business combination?

18. If a parent must increase its investment because a subsidiary issues additional shares of stock, in what two ways can the adjustment be recorded?

INTERNET ASSIGNMENT

Internet sites are time and date sensitive. It is the purpose of these exercises to have you explore the Internet. You may need to refer to the text's Web site at http://www.mhhe.com/hoyle6e to find the most up-to-date links for the Web sites listed in the Internet Assignments.

1. Find a recent annual report for a firm with business acquisitions (e.g., Compaq, GE, etc.) accounted for under the purchase method. Locate the firm's consolidated statement of cash flows and answer the following:
    - Does the firm employ the direct or indirect method of accounting for operating cash flows?
    - How does the firm account for the balances in balance sheet operating accounts (e.g., accounts receivable, inventory, accounts payable) in determining operating cash flows?
    - Describe the accounting for cash paid for business acquisitions in the statement of cash flows.
    - Describe the accounting for any noncontrolling subsidiary interest, acquired in-process research and development costs, and any other business combination–related items in the consolidated statement of cash flows.

LIBRARY ASSIGNMENTS

1. Locate articles about FASB *Statement 141,* "Business Combinations," and FASB *Statement 142,* "Goodwill and Other Intangible Assets." Suggested sources include publications such as the *Journal of Accountancy, Fortune, Forbes,* and the *Wall Street Journal.* Write a report answering the following questions:
    a. What aspects of the new standards are most stressed in the articles?
    b. What is the perceived impact of these two new standards?
    c. What is the rationale given for these standards?
    d. Does the business community seem to be in favor of the changes being made?
    e. Does there appear to be adequate theoretical justification for making these changes?

2. Read the following as well as any other published materials concerning the characteristics of preferred stocks:

    "Innovative Forms of Preferred Stock: Debt or Equity?" *Commercial Lending Review,* Fall 1995.

    "New Instruments Create New Questions in Preferred Stock Investments," *Journal of Taxation Investments,* Autumn 1994.

    "Usefulness of Hybrid Security Classifications: Evidence from Redeemable Preferred Stock," *The Accounting Review,* January 1995.

    "Financial Instruments: A Report on the Liability-Equity Comment Letters and Public Hearings," (Status Report published by FASB), *Financial Accounting Series No. 103,* May 31, 1991.

    Write a report outlining an approach that can be taken to determine whether a preferred stock issue should be considered a debt instrument or an equity interest.

3. Read paragraphs 380–84 of the FASB's discussion memorandum, *An Analysis of Issues Related to Consolidation Policy and Procedures.* Write a short report justifying one method of allocating any gains and losses that result from an intercompany bond transaction.

PROBLEMS

1. A subsidiary has a debt outstanding that was originally issued at a discount. At the beginning of the current year, the debt was acquired at a slight premium from outside parties by the parent company. Which of the following statements is true?
   a. Whether the balances agree or not, both the subsequent interest income and interest expense should be reported in a consolidated income statement.
   b. The interest income and interest expense will agree in amount and should be offset for consolidation purposes.
   c. In computing any noncontrolling interest allocation, the interest income should be included but not the interest expense.
   d. Although subsequent interest income and interest expense will not agree in amount, both balances should be eliminated for consolidation purposes.

2. A subsidiary issues a bond directly to its parent at a discount. Which of the following statements is true?
   a. Elimination is not necessary for consolidation purposes since the bond was acquired directly from the subsidiary.
   b. Because of the discount, the various interest accounts on the two sets of financial records will not agree.
   c. Since the bond was issued by the subsidiary, the amount attributed to a noncontrolling interest is always affected.
   d. All interest balances exactly offset for consolidation purposes.

3. A bond that had been issued by a parent company at a discount was acquired several years ago by its subsidiary from an outside party at a premium. Which of the following statements is true?
   a. The bond has no impact on a current consolidation because the acquisition was made in the past.
   b. The original loss would be reported in the current year's consolidated income statement.
   c. For consolidation purposes, retained earnings must be reduced at the beginning of the current year but by an amount smaller than the original loss.
   d. The various interest balances exactly offset so that no adjustment to retained earnings or to income is necessary.

4. A parent company acquires all of a subsidiary's common stock but only 70 percent of its preferred shares. This preferred stock is callable and pays a 7 percent annual cumulative dividend. No dividends are in arrears at the current time. How is the noncontrolling interest's share of the subsidiary's income computed?
   a. As 30 percent of the subsidiary's preferred dividend.
   b. No allocation is made since the dividends have been paid.
   c. As 30 percent of the subsidiary's income after all dividends have been subtracted.
   d. Income is assigned to the preferred stock based on total par value and 30 percent of that amount is allocated to the noncontrolling interest.

5. Aceton Corporation owns 80 percent of the outstanding stock of Voctax, Inc. During the current year, Voctax made $140,000 in sales to Aceton. How does this transfer affect the consolidated statement of cash flows?
   a. The transaction should be included if payment has been made.
   b. Only 80 percent of the transfers should be included because the sales were made by the subsidiary.
   c. Because the transfers were from a subsidiary organization, the cash flows are reported as investing activities.
   d. Because of the intercompany nature of the transfers, the amount is not reported in the consolidated cash flow statement.

6. Warrenton, Inc., owns 80 percent of Aminable Corporation. On a consolidated income statement, the Noncontrolling Interest in the Subsidiary's Income is reported as $37,000. Aminable paid a total cash dividend of $100,000 for the year. How is the consolidated statement of cash flows impacted?
   a. The dividends paid to the outside owners are reported as a financing activity but the noncontrolling interest figure is not viewed as a cash flow.

    b. The noncontrolling interest figure is reported as an investing activity but the dividends paid to the outside owners is omitted entirely.

    c. Neither figure is reported on the statement of cash flows.

    d. Both dividends paid and the noncontrolling interest are viewed as financing activities.

7. Thuoy Corporation is computing consolidated earnings per share. One of its subsidiaries has stock warrants outstanding. How do these convertible items affect the consolidated earnings per share computation?

    a. No effect is created since the stock warrants were for the shares of the subsidiary company.

    b. The stock warrants are not included in the computation unless they are antidilutive.

    c. The effect of the stock warrants must be computed in deriving the amount of subsidiary income that is to be included in making the consolidated diluted earnings per share calculation.

    d. The stock warrants are only included in basic earnings per share but never in diluted earnings per share.

8. A parent company owns a controlling interest in a subsidiary whose stock has a book value of $31 per share. At the end of the current year, the subsidiary issues new shares entirely to outside parties at $45 per share. The parent still holds control over this subsidiary. Which of the following statements is true?

    a. Since the shares were all sold to outside parties, the parent's Investment account is not affected.

    b. Since the parent now owns a smaller percentage of the subsidiary, the parent's Investment account must be reduced.

    c. Since the shares were sold for more than book value, the parent's Investment account must be increased.

    d. Since the sale was made at the end of the year, the parent's Investment account is not affected.

9. Rodgers, Inc., owns Ferdinal Corporation. For 2001, Rodgers reports net income (without consideration of its investment in Ferdinal) of $200,000 while the subsidiary reports $80,000. The parent had a bond payable outstanding on January 1, 2001, with a book value of $212,000. The subsidiary acquired the bond on that date for $199,000. During 2001, Rodgers reported interest income of $22,000 while Ferdinal reported interest expense of $21,000. What is consolidated net income?

    a. $266,000

    b. $268,000

    c. $292,000

    d. $294,000

10. Thompkins, Inc., owns Pastimer Company. The subsidiary had a bond payable outstanding on January 1, 2000, with a book value of $189,000. The parent acquired the bond on that date for $206,000. Subsequently, Pastimer reported interest income of $18,000 in 2000 while Thompkins reported interest expense of $21,000. Consolidated financial statements are being prepared for 2001. What adjustment is needed for the retained earnings balance as of January 1, 2001?

    a. Reduction of $20,000.

    b. Reduction of $14,000.

    c. Reduction of $3,000.

    d. Reduction of $22,000.

11. Ace Company reports current earnings of $400,000 while paying $40,000 in cash dividends. Byrd Company earns $100,000 in net income and distributes $10,000 in dividends. Ace has held a 70 percent interest in Byrd for several years, an investment that it originally purchased at a price equal to the book value of the underlying net assets. Ace uses the cost method to account for these shares.

    On January 1 of the current year, Byrd acquired in the open market $50,000 of Ace's 8 percent bonds. The bonds had originally been issued several years ago for 92, reflecting a 10 percent effective interest rate. On the date of purchase, the book value of the bonds payable was $48,300. Byrd paid $46,600 based on a 12 percent effective interest rate over the remaining life of the bonds.

What is consolidated net income for this year prior to reduction for the noncontrolling interest's share of the subsidiary's net income?

a. $492,160
b. $493,938
c. $499,160
d. $500,258

12. Using the same information presented in problem 11, what is the noncontrolling interest's share of the subsidiary's net income?

a. $27,000
b. $28,290
c. $28,620
d. $30,000

13. Able Company possesses 80 percent of the outstanding voting stock of Baker Company. Able uses the partial equity method to account for this investment. On January 1, 1998, Able sold 9 percent bonds payable with a $10 million face value (maturing in 20 years) on the open market at a premium of $600,000. On January 1, 2001, Baker acquired 40 percent of these same bonds from an outside party at 96.6 of face value. Both companies use the straight-line method of amortization. For a 2000 consolidation, what adjustment should be made to Able's beginning retained earnings as a result of this bond acquisition?

a. $320,000 increase
b. $326,000 increase
c. $331,000 increase
d. $340,000 increase

14. A company has common stock with a total par value of $400,000 and preferred stock with a total par value of $100,000. The book value of the company is $890,000. The preferred stock pays an 8 percent annual dividend whereas the common stock normally distributes a dividend each year that is equal to 10 percent of its par value. If this company is acquired by another, what portion of the book value should be assigned to the preferred stock? The preferred stock is considered an equity. (Round to the nearest dollar.)

a. $100,000
b. $395,555
c. $148,333
d. $178,000

15. Top Company spent a total of $4,384,000 to acquire control over Bottom Company. This price was based on paying $424,000 for 20 percent of Bottom's preferred stock and $3,960,000 for 90 percent of its outstanding common stock. As of the date of purchase, Bottom's stockholders' equity accounts were as follows:

Preferred stock—9%, $100 par value, cumulative and participating; 10,000 shares outstanding	$1,000,000
Common stock—$50 par value; 40,000 shares outstanding	2,000,000
Retained earnings	3,000,000
Total stockholders' equity	$6,000,000

The owners of the preferred stock vote on any issues considered by the owners of the common stock.

Top believes that all of Bottom's accounts are correctly valued within the company's financial statements. What amount of consolidated goodwill should be recognized?

a. $300,000
b. $316,000
c. $364,000
d. $384,000

16. On January 1, 2001, Mitchell Company has a net book value of $1,500,000 as follows:

1,000 shares of preferred stock; par value $100 per share; cumulative, nonparticipating, nonvoting; call value $108 per share	$ 100,000
20,000 shares of common stock; par value $40 per share	800,000
Retained earnings	600,000
Total	$1,500,000

Andrews Company acquires all of the outstanding preferred shares for $106,000 and 60 percent of the common stock for $916,400. Andrews believed that one of Mitchell's buildings, with a 12-year life, was undervalued on the company's financial records by $50,000.

What amount of consolidated goodwill would be recognized from this purchase?
a. $50,000
b. $51,200
c. $52,400
d. $56,000

17. Aedion Company owns control over Breedlove, Inc. Aedion reports sales of $300,000 during 2001 while Breedlove reports $200,000. Inventory costing $20,000 was transferred from Breedlove to Aedion (upstream) during the year for $40,000. Of this amount, 25 percent is still in ending inventory at year's end. Total receivables on the consolidated balance sheet were $80,000 at the first of the year and $110,000 at year-end. No intercompany debt existed at the beginning or ending of the year. Using the direct approach, what is the consolidated amount of cash collected by the business combination from its customers?
a. $430,000
b. $460,000
c. $490,000
d. $510,000

18. Ames owns 100 percent of Nestlum, Inc. Although the Investment in Nestlum account has a balance of $596,000, the subsidiary's 12,000 shares have an underlying book value of only $40 per share. On January 1, 2001, Nestlum issues 3,000 new shares to the public for $50 per share. How does this transaction affect the Investment in Nestlum account?
a. It is not affected since the shares were sold to outside parties.
b. It should be increased by $24,000.
c. It should be decreased by $119,200.
d. It should be increased by $30,000.

Problems 19 through 21 are based on the following information:

Chapman Company purchases 80 percent of the common stock of Russell Company on January 1, 1995, when Russell has the following stockholders' equity accounts:

Common stock—40,000 shares outstanding	$100,000
Additional paid-in capital	75,000
Retained earnings	340,000
Total stockholders' equity	$515,000

To acquire this interest in Russell, Chapman pays a total of $487,000 with any excess cost being allocated to goodwill.

On January 1, 2001, Russell reports a net book value of $795,000. Chapman has accrued the increase in Russell's book value through application of the equity method.

The following problems should be viewed as independent situations.

19. On January 1, 2001, Russell issues 10,000 additional shares of common stock for $25 per share. Chapman acquires 8,000 of these shares. How will this transaction affect the additional paid-in capital of the parent company?
a. –0–.
b. Increase it by $20,500.

      c.   Increase it by $36,400.

      d.   Increase it by $82,300.

20.   On January 1, 2001, Russell issues 10,000 additional shares of common stock for $15 per share. Chapman does not acquire any of this newly issued stock. How would this transaction affect the additional paid-in capital of the parent company?

      a.   –0–.

      b.   Increase it by $16,600.

      c.   Decrease it by $31,200.

      d.   Decrease it by $48,750.

21.   On January 1, 1997, Russell reacquires 8,000 of the outstanding shares of its own common stock for $24 per share. None of these shares belonged to Chapman. How would this transaction affect the additional paid-in capital of the parent company?

      a.   –0–.

      b.   Decrease it by $22,000.

      c.   Decrease it by $30,500.

      d.   Decrease it by $33,000.

22.   Darges owns 51 percent of the voting stock of Walrus, Inc. The parent's interest was acquired several years ago on the date that the subsidiary was formed. Consequently, no goodwill or other allocation was recorded in connection with the purchase price.

      On January 1, 1999, Walrus sold $1,000,000 in 10-year bonds to the public for 105. The bonds had a cash interest rate of 9 percent payable every December 31. Darges acquired 40 percent of these bonds on January 1, 2001, for 96 percent of face value. Both companies utilize the straight-line method of amortization.

Required:

      a.   What consolidation entry would be recorded in connection with these intercompany bonds on December 31, 2001?

      b.   What consolidation entry would be recorded in connection with these intercompany bonds on December 31, 2002?

      c.   What consolidation entry would be recorded in connection with these intercompany bonds on December 31, 2003?

23.   Highlight, Inc., owns all of the outstanding stock of Kiort Corporation. The two companies report the following balances for the year ending December 31, 2001:

	Highlight	**Kiort**
Revenues and interest income	$ 670,000	$ 390,000
Operating and interest expense	(540,000)	(221,000)
Other gains and losses	120,000	32,000
Net income	$ 250,000	$ 201,000

      On January 1, 2001, Highlight acquired bonds on the open market for $108,000 originally issued by Kiort. This investment had an effective rate of 8 percent. The bonds had a face value of $100,000 and a cash interest rate of 9 percent. At the date of acquisition, these bonds were shown as liabilities by Kiort with a book value of $84,000 (based on an effective rate of 11 percent). Determine the balances that should appear on a consolidated income statement for 2001.

24.   Several years ago Absalom, Inc., sold $800,000 in bonds to the public. Annual cash interest of 8 percent ($64,000) was to be paid on this debt. The bonds were issued at a discount to yield 10 percent. At the beginning of 2001, McDowell Corporation (a wholly owned subsidiary of Absalom) purchased $100,000 of these bonds on the open market for $121,655, a price that was based on an effective interest rate of 6 percent. The bond liability had a book value on that date of $668,778.

Required:

      a.   What consolidation entry would be required for these bonds on December 31, 2001?

      b.   What consolidation entry would be required for these bonds on December 31, 2003?

25. Opus, Incorporated, owns 90 percent of Bloom Company. On December 31, 2001, Opus acquires half of Bloom's $500,000 in outstanding bonds. These bonds had been sold on the open market on January 1, 1999, at a 12 percent effective rate. The bonds pay a cash interest rate of 10 percent every December 31 and are scheduled to come due on December 31, 2009. Bloom issued this debt originally for $435,763. Opus paid $283,550 for this investment indicating an 8 percent effective yield.

Required:

   a. Assuming that both parties use the effective rate method, what gain or loss should be reported on the consolidated income statement for 2001 from the retirement of this debt?

   b. Assuming that both parties use the effective rate method, what balances should appear in the Investment in Bloom Bonds account on Opus's records and the Bonds Payable account of Bloom as of December 31, 2002?

   c. Assuming that both parties use the straight-line method, what consolidation entry would be required on December 31, 2002, because of these bonds? Assume that the parent is not applying the equity method.

26. Hapinst Corporation has the following stockholders' equity accounts:

Preferred stock (6% cumulative dividend)	$500,000
Common stock	750,000
Additional paid-in capital	300,000
Retained earnings	950,000

The preferred stock is participating and, therefore, is considered an equity instrument. Westyln Corporation buys 90 percent of this common stock for $1,600,000 and 70 percent of the preferred stock for $800,000. All of the subsidiary's assets and liabilities are viewed as having market values equal to their book values. What amount is attributed to goodwill on the date of acquisition?

27. Mace, Inc., acquires 90 percent of the outstanding common stock of Blade Company from the company's president for $2,520,000 and 40 percent of the preferred stock for $250,000. On the date of purchase, Blade had the following stockholders' equity accounts:

Common stock	$ 800,000
Preferred stock	200,000
Retained earnings	2,000,000
Total	$3,000,000

Required:

   a. Assume that the preferred stock is both cumulative and fully participating and is, therefore, considered an equity interest. What is the total amount of goodwill to be recognized within consolidated financial statements?

   b. Assume that the preferred stock is callable at 120 percent of par value and is, therefore, considered a debt instrument. What is the total amount of goodwill to be recognized within consolidated financial statements?

   c. Assume that the preferred stock is callable at 120 percent of par value and is, therefore, considered a debt instrument. What is the total value assigned to the noncontrolling interest on the date of acquisition?

28. Smith, Inc., has the following stockholders' equity accounts as of January 1, 2001:

Preferred stock—$100 par, nonvoting and nonparticipating, 8 percent cumulative dividend	$ 2,000,000
Common stock—$20 par value	4,000,000
Retained earnings	10,000,000

Haried Company purchases all of the common stock of Smith on January 1, 2001, for $14,040,000. The preferred stock (which is callable at 108) remains in the hands of outside parties. Any excess purchase price will be assigned to franchise contracts with a 40-year life.

During 2001, Smith reports earning $450,000 in net income and pays $360,000 in cash dividends. Haried applies the equity method to this investment.

Required:

    a.   What is the noncontrolling interest's share of consolidated net income for this period?

    b.   What is the balance in the Investment in Smith account as of December 31, 2001?

    c.   What consolidation entries would be needed for 2001?

29.   Through the payment of $10,468,000 in cash, Drexel Company acquires voting control over Young Company. This price was paid for 60 percent of the subsidiary's 100,000 outstanding common shares ($40 par value) as well as all 10,000 shares of 8 percent, cumulative, $100 par value preferred stock. Of the total payment, $3.1 million was attributed to the fully participating and fully voting preferred stock with the remainder paid for the common. This purchase is carried out on January 1, 2001, when Young reports retained earnings of $10 million and a total book value of $15 million. On this same date, a building owned by Young (with a five-year remaining life) is undervalued in the financial records by $200,000, while equipment with a 10-year life is overvalued by $100,000. Any excess payment is assigned to covenant contracts with a 20-year life.

    During 2001, Young reports net income of $900,000 while paying $400,000 in cash dividends. Drexel has used the cost method to account for both of these investments.

Required:

Prepare consolidation entries that would be appropriate for the year of 2001.

30.   The following information has been taken from the consolidation worksheet of Peak and its 90-percent-owned subsidiary, Valley:

- Peak reports a $12,000 gain on the sale of a building. The building had a book value of $32,000 but was sold for $44,000 cash.
- The noncontrolling interest in Valley's income is reported as $23,000.
- Intercompany inventory transfers of $129,000 occurred during the current period.
- A $30,000 dividend was paid by Valley during the year with $27,000 of this amount going to Peak.
- Amortization of an intangible asset recognized by Peak's purchase was $16,000 for the current period.
- Consolidated accounts payable decreased by $11,000 during the year.

Required:

Indicate how each of these events is reflected on a consolidated statement of cash flows.

31.   Ames Company and its 80-percent-owned subsidiary, Wallace, have the following income statements for 2001:

	Ames	**Wallace**
Revenues	$ 500,000	$ 230,000
Cost of goods sold	(300,000)	(140,000)
Depreciation and amortization	(40,000)	(10,000)
Other expenses	(20,000)	(20,000)
Gain on sale of equipment	30,000	–0–
Equity in earnings of Wallace	48,000	–0–
Net income	$ 218,000	$ 60,000

Additional Information

- Intercompany transfers during 2001 amounted to $90,000 and were downstream from Ames to Wallace.
- Unrealized inventory gains at January 1, 2001, were $6,000, but at December 31, 2001, unrealized gains are $9,000.
- Annual amortization expense resulting from the purchase price is $11,000.
- Wallace paid dividends totaling $20,000.

- The noncontrolling interest's share of the subsidiary's income is $12,000.
- During 2001, consolidated inventory rose by $11,000 while accounts receivable and accounts payable declined by $8,000 and $6,000, respectively.

Required:

Using either the direct or the indirect approach, determine the amount of cash generated from operations during the period by this business combination.

32. Parent Corporation owns all 30,000 shares of the common stock of Subsid, Inc. Parent has 60,000 shares of its own common stock outstanding. In 2001, Parent earns income (without any consideration of its investment in Subsid) of $150,000 while Subsid reports $130,000. Annual amortization of $10,000 is recognized each year on the consolidation worksheet based on allocations within the original purchase price. Both companies have convertible bonds outstanding. During 2001, interest expense (net of taxes) is $32,000 for Parent and $24,000 for Subsid. Parent's bonds can be converted into 10,000 shares of common stock; Subsid's bonds can be converted into 12,000 shares. Parent owns 20 percent of Subsid's bonds. For consolidation purposes, what are basic and diluted earnings per share for this business combination?

33. Primus, Inc., owns all of the outstanding stock of Sonston, Inc. For 2001, Primus reports income (exclusive of any investment income) of $600,000. Primus has 100,000 shares of common stock outstanding. Sonston reports net income of $200,000 for the period with 40,000 shares of common stock outstanding. Sonston also has 10,000 stock warrants outstanding that allow the holder to acquire shares at $10 per share. The value of this stock was $20 per share throughout the year. Primus owns 2,000 of these warrants. What is the consolidated diluted earnings per share?

34. Garfun, Inc., owns all of the stock of Simon, Inc. For 2001, Garfun reports income (exclusive of any investment income) of $480,000. Garfun has 80,000 shares of common stock outstanding. Garfun also has 5,000 shares of preferred stock outstanding that pay a dividend of $15,000 per year. Simon reports net income of $290,000 for the period with 80,000 shares of common stock outstanding. Simon also has a liability for 10,000 $100 bonds that pay annual interest of $8 per bond. Each of these bonds can be converted into three shares of common stock. Garfun owns none of these bonds. Assume a tax rate of 30 percent. What is the consolidated diluted earnings per share?

35. The following separate income statements are for Mason and its 80-percent-owned subsidiary, Dixon:

	Mason	Dixon
Revenues	$ 400,000	$ 300,000
Expenses	(290,000)	(225,000)
Gain on sale of equipment	–0–	15,000
Equity earnings of subsidiary	72,000	–0–
Net income	$ 182,000	$ 90,000
Outstanding common shares	50,000	30,000

Additional Information

- Amortization expense resulting from the purchase price paid by Mason is $20,000 per year.
- Mason has convertible preferred stock outstanding. Each of these 5,000 shares is paid a dividend of $4.00 per year. Each share can be converted into four shares of common stock.
- Stock warrants to buy 10,000 shares of Dixon are also outstanding. For $20, each warrant can be converted into a share of Dixon's common stock. The fair market value of this stock is $25 throughout the year. Mason owns none of these warrants.
- Dixon has convertible bonds payable that paid interest of $30,000 (after taxes) during the year. These bonds can be exchanged for 20,000 shares of common stock. Mason holds 15 percent of these bonds.

Required:

Compute basic and diluted earnings per share for this business combination.

36. Alice, Inc., owns 100 percent of Rughty, Inc. On Alice's books, the Investment in Rughty account currently is shown as $731,000 although the subsidiary's 40,000 shares have an underlying book value of only $12 per share.

Rughty issues 10,000 new shares to the public for $15.75 per share. How does this transaction affect the Investment in Rughty account that appears on Alice's financial records?

37. Davis, Incorporated, acquired 16,000 shares of Maxwell Company several years ago. At the present time, Maxwell is reporting $800,000 as total stockholders' equity, which is broken down as follows:

Common stock ($10 par value)	$200,000
Additional paid-in capital	230,000
Retained earnings	370,000
Total	$800,000

The following cases should be viewed as independent situations:

a. Maxwell issues 5,000 shares of previously unissued common stock to the public for $50 per share. None of this stock is purchased by Davis. What journal entry should Davis make to recognize the impact of this stock transaction?

b. Maxwell issues 4,000 shares of previously unissued common stock to the public for $25 per share. None of this stock is purchased by Davis. What journal entry should Davis make to recognize the impact of this stock transaction?

c. Maxwell issues 5,000 shares of previously unissued common stock for $42 per share. All of these shares are purchased by Davis. How would this transaction affect a consolidation prepared immediately thereafter?

38. On January 1, 1999, Abraham Company purchased 90 percent of the outstanding shares of Sparks Company. Sparks had a net book value on that date of $480,000: common stock ($10 par value) of $200,000 and retained earnings of $280,000. Sparks also possessed a tract of land that was undervalued by $80,000 on its financial statements.

Abraham paid $584,000 for this investment. Any excess payment is assigned to copyrights which are to be amortized over a 20-year period. Subsequent to the purchase, Abraham applied the cost method to its investment accounts.

In the 1999–2000 period, the subsidiary's book value rose by $100,000. During 2001, Sparks earned income of $80,000 while paying $20,000 in dividends. Also, at the beginning of the year, Sparks issued 4,000 new shares of common stock for $36 per share to finance the expansion of its corporate facilities. None of these additional shares were sold to Abraham and, hence, no entry was recorded by the parent company.

Required:

a. Prepare the consolidation entries that would be appropriate for these two companies for the year of 2001.

b. Assume that Sparks actually issued 5,000 new shares of stock (rather than 4,000 shares) at the beginning of 2001 for $25 per share. Abraham purchased 4,500 of these shares and recorded the acquisition at cost. Under these altered circumstances, prepare consolidation entries for 2001.

39. Giant purchases all of the outstanding shares of Little on January 1, 1998, for $460,000 in cash. Of this price, $30,000 was attributed to equipment with a 10-year remaining life and $40,000 was assigned to trademarks that will be expensed over a 20-year period. Giant applies the partial equity method so that income is accrued each period based solely on the earnings reported by the subsidiary.

On January 1, 2001, Giant reports $200,000 in bonds outstanding with a book value of $188,000. Little purchases half of these bonds on the open market for $97,000.

During 2001, Giant begins to sell merchandise to Little. During that year, inventory costing $80,000 was transferred at a price of $100,000. All but $10,000 (at sales price) of these goods were resold to outside parties by year's end. Little still owes $36,000 for inventory shipped from Giant during December.

The following financial figures are for the two companies for the year ending December 31, 2001. Prepare a worksheet to produce consolidated balances. (Credits are indicated by parentheses.)

	Giant	Little
Revenues	$ (639,000)	$(466,000)
Cost of goods sold	345,000	198,000
Expenses	134,000	161,000
Interest expense—bonds	24,000	–0–
Interest income—bond investment	–0–	(118,000)
Equity in income of Little	(118,000)	–0–
Net income	$ (254,000)	$(118,000)
Retained earnings, 1/1/01	$ (345,000)	
Retained earnings, 1/1/01		$(361,000)
Net income (above)	(254,000)	(118,000)
Dividends paid	155,000	61,000
Retained earnings, 12/31/01	$ (444,000)	$(418,000)
Cash and receivables	$ 133,000	$78,000
Inventory	171,000	87,000
Investment in Little	608,000	–0–
Investment in Giant bonds	–0–	98,000
Land, buildings, and equipment (net)	249,000	541,000
Total assets	$ 1,161,000	$ 804,000
Accounts payable	$ (225,000)	$(166,000)
Bonds payable	(200,000)	(100,000)
Discount on bonds	8,000	–0–
Common stock	(300,000)	(120,000)
Retained earnings (above)	(444,000)	(418,000)
Total liabilities and stockholders' equity	$(1,161,000)	$(804,000)

40. Fred, Inc., and Bub Corporation formed a business combination on January 1, 1997, when Fred purchased a 60 percent interest in the common stock of Bub for $310,000 in cash. The book value of Bub's assets and liabilities on that day totaled $300,000. Patents being held by Bub (with a 12-year remaining life) were undervalued by $100,000 within the company's financial records. Any excess indicated by this acquisition is assigned to technical expertise to be amortized over a 10-year period.

Intercompany inventory transfers have been made between the two companies on a regular basis. Merchandise that is carried over from one year to the next is always sold in the subsequent period.

Year	Original Cost to Bub	Transfer Price to Fred	Ending Balance at Transfer Price
1997	$ 60,000	$ 72,000	$15,000
1998	70,000	84,000	25,000
1999	80,000	100,000	20,000
2000	100,000	125,000	40,000
2001	90,000	120,000	30,000

Half of the 2001 inventory transfers have not been paid for by Fred by the end of the year.

On January 1, 1998, Fred sold $15,000 in land to Bub for $22,000. Bub is still holding this land.

On January 1, 2001, Bub acquired $20,000 (face value) of Fred's bonds on the open market. These bonds had an 8 percent cash interest rate. On the date of repurchase, the liability was shown within Fred's records at $21,386, indicating an effective yield of 6 percent. Bub's acquisition price was $18,732 based on an effective interest rate of 10 percent.

Bub indicated earning a net income of $15,000 within its 2001 financial statements. The subsidiary also reported a beginning retained earnings balance of $300,000, dividends paid of $5,000, and common stock of $100,000. Bub has not issued any additional common stock since its takeover. The parent company has applied the equity method to record its investment in Bub.

Required:

a. Prepare consolidation entries for 2001.

b. Calculate the 2001 balance for the noncontrolling interest's share of consolidated net income. In addition, determine the ending 2001 balance for noncontrolling interest in the consolidated balance sheet.

c. Determine the consolidation entry needed in 2002 in connection with the intercompany bonds.

41. On January 1, 2001, Mona, Inc., purchased 80 percent of Lisa Company's common stock as well as 60 percent of its preferred shares. Mona paid $65,000 in cash for the preferred stock, which is considered a debt-type instrument (because no voting rights were granted and the stock has a call value of 110 percent of the $50 per share par value). Mona also paid $552,800 for the common stock, a price that recognized franchise contracts of $40,000. This intangible asset is being amortized over a 40-year period. Lisa pays all preferred stock dividends (a total of $8,000 per year) on an annual basis. During 2001, Lisa's book value increased by $50,000.

On January 2, 2001, Mona acquired one-half of Lisa's outstanding bonds payable to reduce the debt position of the business combination. Lisa's bonds had a face value of $100,000 and paid cash interest of 10 percent per year. These bonds had been issued to the public to yield 14 percent. Interest is paid each December 31. On January 2, 2001, these bonds payable had a total book value of $88,350. Mona paid $53,310, an amount indicating an effective interest rate of 8 percent.

On January 3, 2001, Mona sold fixed assets to Lisa. These assets had originally cost $100,000 but had accumulated depreciation of $60,000 when transferred. The transfer was made at a price of $120,000. These assets were estimated to have a remaining useful life of 10 years.

The individual financial statements for these two companies for the year ending December 31, 2002, are as follows:

	Mona, Inc.	Lisa Company
Sales and other revenues	$ 500,000	$ 200,000
Expenses	(220,000)	(120,000)
Dividend income—Lisa common stock	8,000	–0–
Dividend income—Lisa preferred stock	4,800	–0–
Net income	$ 292,800	$ 80,000
Retained earnings, 1/1/02	$ 700,000	$ 500,000
Net income (above)	292,800	80,000
Dividends paid—common stock	(92,800)	(10,000)
Dividends paid—preferred stock	–0–	(8,000)
Retained earnings, 12/31/02	$ 900,000	$ 562,000
Current assets	$ 130,419	$ 500,000
Investment in Lisa—common stock	552,800	–0–
Investment in Lisa—preferred stock	65,000	–0–
Investment in Lisa—bonds	51,781	–0–
Fixed assets	1,100,000	800,000
Accumulated depreciation	(300,000)	(200,000)
Total assets	$1,600,000	$1,100,000
Accounts payable	$ 400,000	$ 144,580
Bonds payable	–0–	100,000
Discount on bonds payable	–0–	(6,580)
Common stock	300,000	200,000
Preferred stock	–0–	100,000
Retained earnings, 12/31/02	900,000	562,000
Total liabilities and equities	$1,600,000	$1,100,000

Required:

a. What consolidation entry (or entries) would have been required as of January 1, 2001, to eliminate the subsidiary's common and preferred stocks?

b. What consolidation entry (or entries) would have been required as of December 31, 2001, to account for Mona's purchase of Lisa's bonds?

c. What consolidation entry (or entries) would have been required as of December 31, 2001, to account for the intercompany sale of fixed assets?

d. Assume that consolidated financial statements are being prepared for the year ending December 31, 2002. Calculate the consolidated balance for each of the following accounts:

> Franchises
> Fixed Assets
> Accumulated Depreciation
> Expenses
> Noncontrolling Interest in Lisa's Net Income
> Net Income

42. Rogers Company holds 80 percent of the common stock of Andrews, Inc., and 40 percent of this subsidiary's convertible bonds. The following consolidated financial statements are for 2001 and 2002:

Rogers Company and Consolidated Subsidiary

	2001	2002
Revenues	$ 760,000	$ 880,000
Cost of goods sold	(510,000)	(540,000)
Depreciation and amortization	(90,000)	(100,000)
Gain on sale of building	–0–	20,000
Interest expense	(30,000)	(30,000)
Noncontrolling interest	(9,000)	(11,000)
Net income	$ 121,000	$ 219,000
Retained earnings, 1/1	300,000	$ 371,000
Net income	121,000	219,000
Dividends paid	(50,000)	(100,000)
Retained earnings, 12/31	$ 371,000	$ 490,000
Cash	$ 80,000	$ 140,000
Accounts receivable	150,000	140,000
Inventory	200,000	340,000
Buildings and equipment (net)	640,000	690,000
Covenant contracts	150,000	145,000
Total assets	$1,220,000	$1,455,000
Accounts payable	140,000	100,000
Bonds payable	400,000	500,000
Noncontrolling interest in Andrews	32,000	41,000
Common stock	100,000	120,000
Additional paid-in capital	177,000	204,000
Retained earnings	371,000	490,000
Total liabilities and equities	$1,220,000	$1,455,000

Additional Information

- Bonds were issued during 2002 by the parent for cash.
- Amortization of covenants amounts to $5,000 per year.
- A building with a cost of $60,000 but a $30,000 book value was sold by the parent for cash on May 11, 2002.

- Equipment was purchased by the subsidiary on July 23, 2002, using cash.
- Late in November of 2002, the parent issued stock for cash.
- During 2002, the subsidiary paid dividends of $10,000.

Required:

Prepare a consolidated statement of cash flows for this business combination for the year ending December 31, 2002. Either the direct or the indirect approach may be used.

43. Following are separate income statements for Alexander, Inc., and Raleigh Corporation as well as a consolidated statement for the business combination as a whole.

	Alexander	**Raleigh**	**Consolidated**
Revenues	$ 700,000	$ 500,000	$1,000,000
Cost of goods sold	(400,000)	(300,000)	(495,000)
Operating expenses	(100,000)	(70,000)	(190,000)
Equity in earnings of Raleigh	104,000	–0–	–0–
Noncontrolling interest in Raleigh's income	–0–	–0–	(26,000)
Net income	$ 304,000	$ 130,000	$ 289,000

Additional Information

- Intercompany inventory transfers are all downstream.
- The parent applies the partial equity method to this investment.
- Alexander has 50,000 shares of common stock and 10,000 shares of preferred stock outstanding. Owners of the preferred are paid an annual dividend of $40,000, and each share can be exchanged for two shares of common stock.
- Raleigh has 30,000 shares of common stock outstanding. The company also has 5,000 stock warrants outstanding. For $10, each warrant can be converted into a share of Raleigh's common stock. Alexander holds half of these warrants. The price of Raleigh's common stock was $20 per share throughout the year.
- Raleigh also has convertible bonds, none of which is owned by Alexander. During the current year, total interest expense (net of taxes) was $22,000. These bonds can be exchanged for 10,000 shares of the subsidiary's common stock.

Required:

Determine basic and diluted earnings per share for this business combination.

44. On January 1, 2001, Paisley, Inc., paid $560,000 for all of the outstanding stock of Skyler Corporation. This cash payment was based on a price of $180 per share for Skyler's $100 par value preferred stock and $38 per share for the company's $20 par value common stock. The preferred shares are voting, cumulative, and fully participating; they have no set call value. At the date of purchase, the book values of Skyler's accounts equaled their market values. Any excess payment is assigned to an intangible asset and will be amortized over a 10-year period.

During 2001, Skyler sold inventory costing $60,000 to Paisley for $90,000. All but $18,000 (measured at transfer price) of this merchandise has been resold to outsiders by the end of the year. At the end of 2001, Paisley continues to owe Skyler for the last shipment of inventory priced at $28,000.

Also, on January 2, 2001, Paisley sold equipment to Skyler for $20,000 although it had a book value of only $12,000 (original cost of $30,000). Both companies depreciate such property according to the straight-line method with no salvage value. The remaining life at this date was four years.

The following financial statements are for each company for the year ending December 31, 2001. Determine consolidated financial totals for this business combination.

	Paisley, Inc.	Skyler Corporation
Sales	$ (800,000)	$(400,000)
Costs of goods sold	528,000	260,000
Expenses	180,000	130,000
Gain on sale of equipment	(8,000)	–0–
Net income	$ (100,000)	$ (10,000)
Retained earnings, 1/1/01	$ (400,000)	$(150,000)
Net income	(100,000)	(10,000)
Dividends paid	60,000	–0–
Retained earnings, 12/31/01	$ (440,000)	$(160,000)
Cash	$30,000	$40,000
Accounts receivable	300,000	100,000
Inventory	260,000	180,000
Investment in Skyler Corporation	560,000	–0–
Land, buildings, and equipment	680,000	500,000
Accumulated depreciation	(180,000)	(90,000)
Total assets	$ 1,650,000	$ 730,000
Accounts payable	$ (140,000)	$ (90,000)
Long-term liabilities	(240,000)	(180,000)
Preferred stock	–0–	(100,000)
Common stock	(620,000)	(200,000)
Additional paid-in capital	(210,000)	–0–
Retained earnings, 12/31/01	(440,000)	(160,000)
Total equities	$(1,650,000)	$(730,000)

Parentheses indicate a credit balance.

45. On June 30, 2001, Plaster, Inc., paid $916,000 for 80 percent of the outstanding stock of Stucco Company. At the date of acquisition, Stucco Company closed its books and reported the following assets and liabilities:

Cash	$ 60,000
Accounts receivable	127,000
Inventory	203,000
Land	65,000
Buildings	175,000
Equipment	300,000
Accounts payable	(35,000)

On June 30, Plaster allocated the excess of cost of book value of Stucco's net assets as follows:

Equipment (three-year life)	$ 75,000
Database (10-year life)	125,000

At the end of 2001, the following comparative (2000 and 2001) balance sheets and consolidated income statement were available:

	Plaster, Inc. December 31, 2000	Consolidated December 31, 2001
Cash	$ 43,000	$ 242,850
Accounts receivable (net)	362,000	485,400
Inventory	415,000	720,000
Land	300,000	365,000
Buildings (net)	245,000	370,000
Equipment (net)	1,800,000	2,037,500
Database		118,750
Total assets	$3,165,000	$4,339,500
Accounts payable	$ 80,000	$ 107,000
Long-term liabilities	400,000	1,200,000
Common stock	1,800,000	1,800,000
Noncontrolling interest		209,750
Retained earnings	885,000	1,022,750
Total liabilities and equities	$3,165,000	$4,339,500

PLASTER, INC., AND SUBSIDIARY STUCCO COMPANY
Consolidated Income Statement
For the Year Ended December 31, 2001

Revenues		$1,217,500
Cost of goods sold	$737,500	
Depreciation	187,500	
Database amortization	6,250	
Interest and other expenses	9,750	
Noncontrolling interest in Stucco's income	38,750	979,750
Net income		$ 237,750

Additional Information

- On December 1, 2001, Stucco paid a $40,000 dividend. During 2001, Plaster paid $100,000 in dividends.
- During 2001, Plaster issued $800,000 in long-term debt at par.
- Plaster reported no other asset purchases or dispositions during 2001 other than the acquisition of Stucco.

Required:

Prepare a 2001 consolidated statement of cash flows for Plaster and Stucco. Use the indirect method of reporting cash flows from operating activities.

7

Consolidated Financial Statements— Ownership Patterns and Income Taxes

QUESTIONS TO CONSIDER

- If a parent holds control over a subsidiary which, in turn, owns a majority of the voting stock of another company, the parent indirectly controls both of these subsidiaries. How does this type of ownership pattern affect the consolidation process for a business combination?

- If a subsidiary possesses stock of its parent company, what impact does the mutual ownership have on consolidated financial statements?

- How does a business combination qualify to file a consolidated income tax return? What advantages are gained by filing in this manner?

- Why does the filing of separate tax returns by the members of a business combination frequently create the need to recognize deferred income taxes?

Coverage of the accounting for business combinations is concluded here in Chapter 7 by analyzing two additional aspects of consolidated financial statements. First, the various patterns of ownership that can exist within a combination are presented. Indirect control of a subsidiary, connecting affiliations, and mutual ownership are all examined along with the consolidation procedures applicable to each of these organizational structures. The chapter then presents an overview of the income tax considerations relevant to the members of a business combination. Income tax accounting for both consolidated and separate corporate returns is discussed in light of current laws.

INDIRECT SUBSIDIARY CONTROL

Throughout previous chapters, only one type of relationship has been presented for every business combination. Specifically, a parent has always held a direct financial interest in a single subsidiary. This ownership pattern has been assumed to expedite the explanation of consolidation theories and techniques. In actual practice, though, much more elaborate corporate structures commonly exist. General Electric Company (GE), for example, controls literally scores of subsidiaries. However, GE owns voting stock in a relatively small number of these companies. Control is maintained often through indirect ownership; GE's subsidiaries hold the stock of many of the companies within this business combination. For example, GE, the parent company, owns the voting stock of NBC, Inc., which in turn has total ownership of CNBC and other companies. This type of corporate configuration is often referred to as a father-son-grandson relationship (or sometimes as a pyramid) because of the pattern created by the descending tiers.

Forming a business combination as a series of indirect ownerships is not an unusual practice. Many businesses organize their operations in this manner to group individual companies along product lines, geographic districts, or some other logical criteria. The philosophy behind this structuring is that clearer lines of communication and responsibility reporting can be developed by placing direct control in proximity to each subsidiary. However, other indirect ownership patterns are simply the result of years of acquisition and growth. As an example, in purchasing General Foods, Philip Morris Companies, Inc., actually gained control over a number of corporations (including Oscar Mayer Foods Corporation, Maxwell House Coffee Company, and Birds Eye, Inc.). This control was not achieved directly by Philip Morris but rather indirectly through the acquisition of their parent company.

The Consolidation Process When Indirect Control Is Present

Regardless of a company's reason for establishing indirect control over a subsidiary, a new accounting problem is encountered: The financial information generated by several connecting corporations must be consolidated into a single set of financial statements. Fortunately, indirect ownership does not introduce any new conceptual issues but affects only the mechanical elements of this process. For example, a purchase price allocation, as well as an annual amortization expense figure, must be computed and recognized for every investment. In addition, all of the worksheet entries previously demonstrated continue to apply. For business combinations involving indirect control, the entire consolidation process is basically repeated for each separate acquisition.

Calculation of Realized Income   Although most consolidation procedures are unchanged by the presence of an indirect ownership, the isolation of each subsidiary's realized income does pose an added degree of difficulty. Appropriate determination of this figure is essential because it serves as the basis for calculating (1) equity income accruals and (2) the noncontrolling interest's share of consolidated income.

In previous chapters, the subsidiary's realized income has been determined by adjusting reported earnings for the effects of any upstream intercompany transfers. *However, where indirect control is involved, at least one company within the business combination (and possibly many) holds both a parent and a subsidiary position.* Any company in that position must first give proper recognition to the equity income accruing from its subsidiaries before computing its own realized income total. This guideline is not a theoretical doctrine but merely a necessary arrangement for calculating income totals in a predetermined order. The process begins with the grandson, then moves to the son, and finishes with the father. Only by following this systematic approach can the correct amount of realized income be determined for each individual company.

Realized Income Computation Illustrated   For example, assume that three companies form a business combination: Top Company owns 70 percent of Midway Company, which, in turn, possesses 60 percent of Bottom Company. As can be seen from the following display, both subsidiaries are under the control of Top, although the parent's relationship with Bottom is only of an indirect nature.

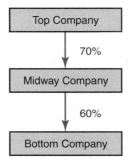

For illustration purposes, assume that the following information has been elicited from the 2001 individual financial records of the three companies making up this combination:

	Top Company	Midway Company	Bottom Company
Operating income	$600,000	$300,000	$100,000
Dividend income from investment in subsidiary (based on cost method)	80,000	50,000	
Reported net income	$680,000	$350,000	$100,000
Additional information:			
Net unrealized intercompany gains within current year income	$110,000	$ 80,000	$ 20,000
Amortization expense relating to purchase price of investment	20,000	15,000	–0–

Beginning, as specified, with the grandson of the organization, a calculation is made of each company's 2001 realized income. For example, from the perspective of the business combination, Bottom's income for the period would be only $80,000 after removing the $20,000 effect of the company's unrealized intercompany gains. Thus, $80,000 is the basis for the equity accrual by its parent as well as any noncontrolling interest recognition.

Once the grandson's income has been derived, this figure then can be used in computing the realized earnings of the son, Midway:

Operating income—Midway Company	$300,000
Equity income accruing from Bottom Company— 60% of *realized* income of $80,000	48,000
Recognition of amortization expense relating to purchase of Bottom Company (above)	(15,000)
Removal of Midway's unrealized intercompany gain (above)	(80,000)
Realized income of Midway Company	$253,000

The $253,000 realized income figure determined for Midway varies significantly from the company's reported profit of $350,000. This difference is not unusual and is merely the result of establishing an appropriate consolidation perspective in viewing both the investment in its subsidiary and the effects of intercompany transfers. The recognition of all transactions is being brought into line with the company's vantage point within this business combination.

Continuing with this systematic calculation of each company's earnings, Top's realized income now can be determined. Only after the appropriate figure is computed for the son can the father's earnings within the business combination be derived.

Operating income—Top Company	$ 600,000
Equity income accruing from Midway Company— 70% of *realized* income of $253,000	177,100
Recognition of amortization expense relating to purchase of Midway Company (above)	(20,000)
Removal of Top's unrealized intercompany gain (above)	(110,000)
Realized income of Top	$ 647,100

Having established realized income figures for each of these three companies, several aspects of this data should be noted:

1. Within the 2001 income statement reported for Top Company and its consolidated subsidiaries, a $107,900 balance would be disclosed as the "noncontrolling

interests' share of subsidiary income." This total is based on the realized income figures of the two subsidiaries and is computed as follows:

	Realized Income	Outside Ownership	Noncontrolling Interest in Income
Bottom Company	$ 80,000	40%	$ 32,000
Midway Company	253,000	30	75,900
Total			$107,900

2. Although the cost method was applied to both of the investments in this illustration, the parent's individual accounting is not a factor in determining realized income totals. The cost figures were omitted and replaced with equity accruals in preparation for consolidation. The selection of a particular method is only relevant for internal reporting purposes; computation of realized earnings, as shown here, is based entirely on the equity income accruing from each subsidiary.

3. As demonstrated previously, if appropriate equity accruals are recognized, the parent's realized income can serve as a "proof figure" for the consolidated total. Parent earnings calculated in this manner equal the net income for the entire business combination. Thus, if the consolidation process is carried out correctly, the earnings to be reported by this entire organization should equal $647,100, as indicated previously for Top.

4. Whenever indirect control is established, a discrepancy exists between the percentage of stock being held and the income contributed to the business combination by a subsidiary. In this illustration, Midway possesses 60 percent of Bottom's voting stock but, mathematically, only 42 percent of Bottom's income is attributed to Top's controlling interest (70 percent direct ownership of Midway × 60 percent indirect ownership of Bottom). The remaining income earned by this subsidiary is assigned to the owners outside of the combination.

The validity of this 42 percent accrual is one aspect of the consolidation that is not readily apparent. Therefore, an elementary example can be constructed to demonstrate the mathematical accuracy of this percentage. Assume that neither Top nor Midway reports any earnings during the year but that Bottom has $100 in realized income. If Bottom declares a $100 cash dividend, $60 goes to Midway with the remaining $40 distributed to Bottom's noncontrolling interest. Assuming then that Midway uses this $60 to pay its own dividend, $42 (70 percent) is transferred to Top with $18 going to the outside owners of Midway.

Thus, 58 percent of Bottom's income should be attributed to parties outside of the business combination. An initial 40 percent belongs to Bottom's own noncontrolling interest while an additional 18 percent is eventually accrued by the other shareholders of Midway. Consequently, only 42 percent of Bottom's original income is considered as having been earned by the combination. Consolidated financial statements reflect this allocation by including 100 percent of the subsidiary's revenues and expenses while simultaneously recognizing a reduction for the 58 percent of the subsidiary's net income that is attributed to noncontrolling interests.

Consolidation Process—Indirect Control

Having analyzed the calculation of realized income within a father-son-grandson configuration, a full-scale consolidation now can be produced. As is demonstrated, this type of ownership pattern does not significantly alter the worksheet process. In reality, most worksheet entries are simply made twice; first for the son's investment in the grandson and then for the father's ownership of the son. Although this sudden doubling of entries may initially seem overwhelming, close examination reveals that the individual procedures remain unaffected.

As an illustration, assume that on January 1, 1999, Big purchases 80 percent of the outstanding common stock of Middle for $640,000. On that date, Middle has a book value (total stockholders' equity) of $700,000, which indicates the parent paid $80,000 in excess of the subsidiary's underlying $560,000 book value ($700,000 × 80 percent). This $80,000 is assigned to franchises and amortized at the rate of $2,000 per year.

Following the acquisition, Middle's book value rises to $1,080,000 by the end of 2001, denoting a $380,000 increment during this three-year period ($1,080,000 − $700,000). Big applies the partial equity method; therefore, a $304,000 ($380,000 × 80%) increase in the investment account (to $944,000) is accrued by the parent over this same time span.

On January 1, 2000, Middle acquires 70 percent of Little for $461,000. Little's stockholders' equity accounts total $630,000, indicating that Middle has paid $20,000 more than the applicable book value of $441,000 ($630,000 × 70%). This entire $20,000 is allocated to franchises so that, over a 40-year assumed life, amortization expense of $500 is recognized each year by the business combination. During 2000–2001, Little's book value increases by $150,000, to a $780,000 total. Because Middle also applies the partial equity method, $105,000 ($150,000 × 70%) is added to the investment account to arrive at a $566,000 balance ($461,000 + $105,000).

To complete the introductory information for this illustration, assume that a number of intercompany upstream transfers have occurred over the past two years. The dollar volume of these transactions is chronicled here as well as the unrealized gain in each year's ending inventory.

	Little Company Transfers to Middle Company		Middle Company Transfers to Big Company	
Year	Transfer Price	Year-End Unrealized Gain	Transfer Price	Year-End Unrealized Gain
2000	$ 75,000	$20,000	$200,000	$30,000
2001	120,000	25,000	250,000	40,000

Exhibit 7–1 presents the worksheet to consolidate these three companies for the year ending December 31, 2001. The first three columns represent the individual statements for each of the organizations. This information is followed by the entries required to consolidate the various balances. To help identify the separate procedures, entries concerning the relationship between Big (father) and Middle (son) are marked with a "B," whereas an "L" denotes Middle's ownership of Little (grandson). The duplication of entries in this exhibit is done primarily to facilitate a clearer understanding of this consolidation. A number of these dual entries can be combined once a familiarity with the entire process is achieved.

To arrive at consolidated figures, Exhibit 7–1 incorporates the worksheet entries described next. By analyzing each of these adjustments and eliminations, the consolidation procedures necessitated by a father-son-grandson ownership pattern can be identified. Despite the presence of indirect control over Little, financial statements can be created for the business combination as a whole utilizing the process described in previous chapters.

Consolidation Entry *G   Entry *G defers the unrealized intercompany gains contained in the beginning financial figures. Within their separate accounting systems, two of the companies prematurely recorded income ($20,000 by Little and $30,000 by Middle) in 2000 at the time of transfer. For consolidation purposes, a worksheet entry must be included in 2001 to eliminate these unrealized gains from both beginning retained earnings as well as cost of goods sold (the present location of the beginning inventory). Consequently, gross profit is appropriately recognized on the consolidated income statement of the current period.

Exhibit 7–1

Consolidation: Purchase Method
Investment: Partial Equity Method

BIG COMPANY AND CONSOLIDATED SUBSIDIARIES
Consolidation Worksheet
For Year Ending December 31, 2001

Accounts	Big Company	Middle Company	Little Company	Consolidation Entries Debit	Consolidation Entries Credit	Noncontrolling Interest	Consolidated Totals
Income Statement							
Sales	(800,000)	(500,000)	(300,000)	(LTI) 120,000 (BTI) 250,000			(1,230,000)
Cost of goods sold	300,000	220,000	140,000	(LG) 25,000 (BG) 40,000	(L*G) 20,000 (LTI) 120,000 (B*G) 30,000 (BTI) 250,000		305,000
Expenses	200,000	80,000	60,000	(LE) 500 (BE) 2,000			342,500
Income of Little Company	–0–	(70,000)	–0–	(LI) 70,000			–0–
Income of Middle Company	(216,000)	–0–	–0–	(BI) 216,000			–0–
Noncontrolling interest in Little Company's net income	–0–	–0–	–0–			(28,500)	28,500
Noncontrolling interest in Middle Company's net income	–0–	–0–	–0–			(51,200)	51,200
Net income	(516,000)	(270,000)	(100,000)				(502,800)
Statement of Retained Earnings							
Retained earnings, 1/1/01:							
Big Company	(900,000)	–0–	–0–	(B*C) 39,600			(860,400)
Middle Company	–0–	(800,000)	–0–	(B*G) 30,000 (L*C) 14,500 (BS) 755,500			–0–
Little Company	–0–	–0–	(600,000)	(L*G) 20,000 (LS) 580,000			–0–
Net income (from above)	(516,000)	(270,000)	(100,000)				(502,800)
Dividends paid:							
Big Company	120,000	–0–	–0–				120,000
Middle Company	–0–	90,000	–0–		(BD) 72,000	18,000	–0–
Little Company	–0–	–0–	50,000		(LD) 35,000	15,000	–0–
Retained earnings, 12/31/01	(1,296,000)	(980,000)	(650,000)				(1,243,200)

Balance Sheet

	Big Company	Middle Company	Little Company	Consolidation Entries (Debit)	Consolidation Entries (Credit)	Noncontrolling Interest	Consolidated Totals
Cash and receivables	600,000	300,000	280,000				1,180,000
Investment in Middle Company	944,000	-0-	-0-	(BD) 72,000	(B*C) 39,600 (BS) 684,400 (BI) 216,000 (BA) 76,000		-0-
Investment in Little Company	-0-	566,000	-0-	(LD) 35,000	(L*C) 14,500 (LS) 497,000 (LI) 70,000 (LA) 19,500		-0-
Inventory	300,000	260,000	290,000		(LG) 25,000 (BG) 40,000		785,000
Land, building, equipment	192,000	154,000	510,000	(LA) 19,500 (BA) 76,000			856,000
Franchises	-0-	-0-	-0-		(LE) 500 (BE) 2,000		93,000
Total assets	2,036,000	1,280,000	1,080,000				2,914,000
Liabilities	(340,000)	(200,000)	(300,000)				(840,000)
Noncontrolling interest in Little Company, 1/1/01	-0-	-0-	-0-		(LS) 213,000	(213,000)	
Noncontrolling interest in Middle Company, 1/1/01	-0-	-0-	-0-		(BS) 171,100	(171,100)	
Total noncontrolling interest, 12/31/01	-0-	-0-	-0-		(430,800)	(430,800)	(430,800)
Common stock: Big Company	(400,000)	-0-	-0-				(400,000)
Middle Company	-0-	(100,000)	-0-	(BS) 100,000			-0-
Little Company	-0-	-0-	(130,000)	(LS) 130,000			-0-
Retained earnings (above)	(1,296,000)	(980,000)	(650,000)				(1,243,200)
Total liabilities and equities	(2,036,000)	(1,280,000)	(1,080,000)				(2,914,000)

Note: Parentheses indicate credit balance.

Consolidation entries: Entries labeled with a "B" refer to the investment relationship between Big and Middle. Entries with an "L" refer to Middle's ownership of Little.

(*G) Removal of unrealized gain from beginning inventory figures so that it can be recognized in current period.

(*C) Conversion of partial equity method to equity method. Amortization for prior years is recognized along with effects of beginning unrealized upstream gains.

(S) Elimination of subsidiaries' stockholders' equity accounts along with recognition of January 1, 2001, noncontrolling interests.

(A) Allocation to franchises, unamortized balance being recognized as of January 1, 2001.

(I) Elimination of intercompany income accrued during the period.

(D) Elimination of intercompany dividends.

(E) Recognition of amortization expense for the current period.

(TI) Elimination of intercompany sales/purchases balances created by the transfer of inventory.

(G) Removal of unrealized inventory gain from ending figures so that it can be recognized in subsequent period.

Consolidation Entry *C   Neither Big nor Middle has applied the full equity method to their investments; therefore, the figures recognized during the years prior to the current period (2001) must now be updated on the worksheet. This process begins with the son's ownership of the grandson. Hence, Middle must reduce its 2000 income (now closed into retained earnings) by $500 to reflect the amortization applicable to that year. This expense would not have been recorded by Middle in applying the partial equity method.

In addition, because $20,000 of Little's previously reported earnings have just been deferred (in preceding Entry *G), the effect of this reduction on Middle's ownership must also be recognized. The parent's original equity accrual for 2000 was based on reported rather than realized profit; thus, too much income was recorded. Little's deferral necessitates a parallel $14,000 decrease ($20,000 × 70%) by Middle. Consequently, Middle's retained earnings balance as of January 1, 2001, as well as the Investment in Little account are reduced on the worksheet by a total of $14,500:

Reduction in Middle's Beginning Retained Earnings

2000 amortization expense	$ 500
Income effect created by Little's deferral of 2000 unrealized gain (reduction of previous accrual) ($20,000 × 70%)	14,000
Required reduction to Middle's beginning retained earnings (Entry L*C)	$14,500

A similar equity adjustment also must be made in connection with Big's ownership of Middle. The calculation of the specific amount to be recorded follows the same procedural path identified earlier for Middle's investment in Little. Once again, amortization expense for all prior years (1999 and 2000, in this case) must be brought into the consolidation as well as the income reduction created by the deferral of Middle's $30,000 unrealized gain (Entry *G). *However, recognition also must be given to the effects associated with the $14,500 decrease in Middle's pre-2001 earnings described in the previous paragraph.* Although only recorded on the worksheet, this adjustment is a change in Middle's originally reported income. To reflect Big's ownership of Middle, the effect of this reduction must be included in arriving at the income balances actually accruing to the parent company. Thus, a decrease of $39,600 is needed in Big's beginning retained earnings to establish the proper accounting for its subsidiaries.

Reduction in Big's Beginning Retained Earnings

Amortization expense relating to acquisition of Middle Company—1999–2000 ($2,000 per year)	$ (4,000)
Income effect created by Middle Company's deferral of unrealized gain ($30,000 × 80%)	(24,000)
Income effect created by Middle Company's adjustment to its prior year's investment income ($14,500 × 80%) (above)	(11,600)
Required reduction to Big's beginning retained earnings (Entry B*C)	$(39,600)

Consolidation Entry S   The beginning stockholders' equity accounts of each subsidiary are eliminated here and noncontrolling interest balances as of the beginning of the year are recognized. As in previous chapters, the amounts involved in this entry have been directly affected by the preliminary adjustments described earlier. Because Entry *G removed a $20,000 beginning unrealized gain, Little's January 1, 2001, book value on the worksheet is $710,000 and not $730,000. This realized total serves as the basis for recording a $213,000 beginning noncontrolling interest (30 percent) as well as the $497,000 elimination (70 percent) from the parent's investment account.

In a similar vein, Middle's book value has already been decreased by $44,500 through Entries *G ($30,000) and *C ($14,500). Thus, the beginning stockholders' equity accounts for this company are now adjusted to a total of $855,500 ($900,000 − $44,500). This balance leads to a $171,100 initial noncontrolling interest valuation (20 percent) and a $684,400 (80 percent) offset against Big's Investment in Middle account.

Consolidation Entry A   The unamortized franchise balances remaining as of January 1, 2001, are removed from the two investment accounts so that this intangible asset can be identified separately on the consolidated balance sheet. Because amortization expense for the previous periods is already recognized in Entry *C, only beginning totals for the year of $19,500 ($20,000 − $500) and $76,000 ($80,000 − $4,000) still remain from the original amounts paid.

Consolidation Entry I   This entry eliminates the current intercompany income figures accrued by each of the parents through their application of the partial equity method.

Consolidation Entry D   Intercompany dividends distributed during the year are removed here from the consolidated financial totals.

Consolidation Entry E   The annual amortization expense relating to each of the franchise balances is recorded.

Consolidation Entry TI   The intercompany sales/purchases figures created by the transfer of inventory during 2001 are eliminated on the worksheet.

Consolidation Entry G   This final consolidation entry defers the intercompany inventory gains that remain unrealized as of December 31, 2001. The profit on these transfers is removed until the merchandise is subsequently sold to unrelated parties.

Noncontrolling Interests' Share of Consolidated Income   To complete the steps that constitute this consolidation worksheet, recognition must be given to the 2001 income accruing to owners outside of the business combination. This allocation is based on the realized earnings of the two subsidiaries, which, as previously discussed, is calculated beginning with the grandson (Little) followed by the son (Middle).

Little Company's Realized Income and Noncontrolling Interest

Reported operating income (from Exhibit 7–1)	$100,000
Realization of gains previously deferred from 2000 (Entry L*G)	20,000
Deferral of gains unrealized as of 12/31/01 (Entry LG)	(25,000)
Little Company's realized income, 2001	95,000
Outside ownership	30%
Noncontrolling interest in Little Company's income	$ 28,500

Middle Company's Realized Income and Noncontrolling Interest

Reported operating income (from Exhibit 7–1 after removing income of Little Company)	$200,000
Amortization expense relating to acquisition of Little Company, current year	(500)
Realization of gains previously deferred from 2000 (Entry B*G)	30,000
Deferral of gains unrealized as of 12/31/01 (Entry BG)	(40,000)
Equity income accruing from Little Company (70% of $95,000 realized income [above])	66,500
Middle Company's realized income, 2001	256,000
Outside ownership	20%
Noncontrolling interest in Middle Company's income	$ 51,200

Although computation of Big's realized earnings is not required here, as previously noted, this figure does provide a means of verifying the accuracy of the income total reported for the consolidated entity.

Big Company's Realized Income

Reported operating income (from Exhibit 7–1 after removing income of Middle Company)	$300,000
Amortization expense relating to acquisition of Middle Company, current year	(2,000)
Equity income accruing from Middle Company (80% of $256,000 realized income [above])	204,800
Big Company's realized income, 2001	$502,800

This $502,800 figure represents the income derived by the parent from its own operations plus the earnings accrued from the company's two subsidiaries (one directly owned and the other indirectly controlled). If calculated correctly, this balance equals the consolidated income of the business combination. As shown in Exhibit 7–1, the income reported by Big Company and consolidated subsidiaries does, indeed, net to this same total: $502,800. Although not completely conclusive, the agreement of these balances serves as strong evidence of the validity of the final figures on the consolidation worksheet.

INDIRECT SUBSIDIARY CONTROL—CONNECTING AFFILIATION

The father-son-grandson organization is hardly the only corporate ownership pattern that can be encountered. The number of possible configurations found in the modern world of business is almost limitless. To assist in illustrating the consolidation procedures necessitated by these alternative patterns, a second basic ownership structure referred to as a *connecting affiliation* is discussed briefly.

A connecting affiliation exists whenever two or more companies within a business combination own an interest in another member of that organization. The simplest form of this configuration is frequently drawn as a triangle:

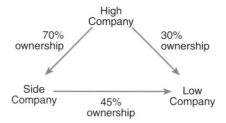

In this example, both High Company and Side Company maintain an ownership interest in Low Company, thus creating a connecting affiliation. Although neither of these individual companies possesses enough voting stock to establish direct control over Low's operations, a total of 75 percent of the outstanding shares is held by members of the combination. Consequently, control lies within the boundaries of the single economic entity, and the inclusion of Low's financial information as a part of consolidated statements is necessary.

Despite the potential for numerous variations in this basic ownership pattern, the process for consolidating a connecting affiliation is essentially unchanged from that demonstrated for a father-son-grandson organization. Perhaps the most noticeable alteration is that more than two investments are always going to be present. In this triangular business combination, High possesses an ownership interest in both Side and Low while Side also maintains an investment in Low. Thus, unless combined in some manner, three separate sets of consolidation entries would appear on the worksheet.

Although the added quantity of entries certainly provides a degree of mechanical complication, the basic concepts involved in the consolidation process remain the same regardless of the number of investments involved.

As with the father-son-grandson structure, one key aspect of the consolidation process warrants additional illustration: the determination of realized income figures for the individual companies. Therefore, assume that High, Side, and Low have separate operating incomes (without inclusion of any earnings from their subsidiaries) of $300,000, $200,000, and $100,000, respectively. Each company also retains a $30,000 net unrealized gain in their current year income figures. Assume further that annual amortization expense of $10,000 has been identified within the purchase price paid for each of the three investments.

In the same manner as a father-son-grandson organization, determination of realized earnings should begin with any companies that are solely in a subsidiary position (Low, in this case). Next, realized income is computed for companies that are both parents as well as subsidiaries (Side). Finally, this same calculation should be made for the one company (High) that has ultimate control over the entire combination. Realized income figures for the three companies in this combination would be derived as follows:

Low Company's Realized Income and Noncontrolling Interest

Reported operating income	$100,000
Deferral of Low Company's net unrealized gain	(30,000)
Low Company's realized income	70,000
Outside ownership	25%
Noncontrolling interest in Low Company's income	$ 17,500

Side Company's Realized Income and Noncontrolling Interest

Reported operating income	$200,000
Deferral of Side Company's net unrealized gain	(30,000)
Equity income accruing from Low Company (45% of $70,000 realized income)	31,500
Amortization expense relating to Side Company's acquisition of Low Company	(10,000)
Side Company's realized income	191,500
Outside ownership	30%
Noncontrolling interest in Side Company's income	$ 57,450

High Company's Realized Income

Reported operating income	$300,000
Deferral of High Company's net unrealized gain	(30,000)
Equity income accruing from Side Company (70% of $191,500 realized income)	134,050
Amortization expense relating to High Company's acquisition of Side Company	(10,000)
Equity income accruing from Low Company—direct ownership (30% of $70,000 realized income)	21,000
Amortization expense relating to High Company's acquisition of Low Company	(10,000)
High Company's realized income (and consolidated net income)	$405,050

Even though a connecting affiliation exists in this illustration, the basic tenets of the consolidation process remain the same:

- All effects from intercompany transfers are removed.
- The parents' beginning retained earnings figures are adjusted to recognize the equity income resulting from ownership of the subsidiaries in prior years. The

determination of realized earnings for this period is necessary to properly align the balances with the perspective of a single economic entity.

- The beginning stockholders' equity accounts of each subsidiary are eliminated and the noncontrolling interests' figures as of the first day of the year are recognized.
- All unamortized allocation balances created by the original purchase prices are entered onto the worksheet.
- Amortization expense for the current year is recorded.
- Intercompany income and dividends are removed.
- The noncontrolling interests' share of the subsidiaries' net income is computed (as just shown) and included in the financial statements of the business combination.

MUTUAL OWNERSHIP

One specific corporate structure that does require further analysis is a mutual ownership. This type of configuration exists whenever two companies within a business combination hold an equity interest in each other. This ownership pattern was sometimes created as a result of the financial battles that occurred during many of the takeover attempts prevalent during the 1980s. A defensive strategy (often referred to as the *Pac-Man Defense)* was occasionally adopted whereby the target company would attempt to avoid takeover by reversing roles and acquiring shares of its investor. Consequently the two parties came to hold shares of each other with one usually gaining control.

Two typical mutual ownership patterns follow. In situation A, the parent and the subsidiary possess a percentage of each other's voting shares; whereas in situation B, the mutual ownership exists between two subsidiary companies.

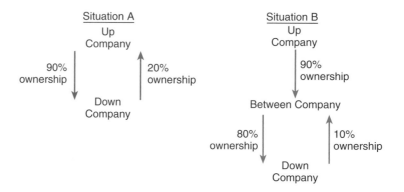

In accounting for a mutual ownership, unique conceptual issues are raised. These concerns center on the handling of any parent company stock owned by a subsidiary. *ARB 51* (par. 12) states that "shares of the parent held by a subsidiary should not be treated as outstanding stock in the consolidated balance sheet." The FASB's Exposure Draft (October 1995) agrees with this approach and recommends that "shares of a parent held by a subsidiary shall not be reported as outstanding stock in consolidated statements" (par. 21). This guidance is theoretically appropriate because the shares are not owned by parties outside of the business combination. Unfortunately, the actual reporting of such internally held stock can vary significantly, depending on the perspective taken as to the substance of the subsidiary's purchase. Until formal guidance is provided by standard setters, variations in practice will continue.

DISCUSSION QUESTION

Mutual Ownership: What Do Those Shares Represent?

During 2001, Pierpont Corporation began a plan to acquire control over Sandstone, Inc., a competing company of similar size. An offer of $27 per share (to be paid in a combination of cash and stock) was initially made for Sandstone's common stock. In an attempt to maintain its independence, Sandstone began a counterattack by purchasing the outstanding common stock of Pierpont on the open market. Pierpont increased its offer to $31 and, finally, to $38 per share before successfully winning control over Sandstone. Eventually, 80 percent of Sandstone's shares were obtained. However, during the takeover struggle, Sandstone managed to acquire 30 percent of Pierpont's stock (75,000 shares) at a total cost of $8 million.

Following the purchase, Sandstone remained a relatively autonomous organization. The president and administrative officers retained their positions with the company, and Sandstone's principal stockholder before the takeover is now on the board of directors of Pierpont.

Within Sandstone's separate accounting records, the investment in Pierpont's stock is reported using the equity method. Thus, at the end of 2002, the asset's balance has risen to $8.7 million. Accounting officials of Pierpont, who currently are preparing consolidated financial statements, are attempting to determine the proper accounting for these 75,000 shares. According to the controller, "these shares are our own stock and they are being held within the business combination. The acquisition is no more than the intercompany purchase of treasury shares. Reporting should be simple; we show $8 million as the cost of treasury stock and eliminate all other related figures."

The assistant vice president for finance does not agree. "If we just remove all the balances, we will be using an income for Sandstone that has not been correctly calculated. Sandstone owns this investment and it generates a profit; that profit must be assigned to Sandstone in some manner or we are understating the income that this subsidiary's assets are producing."

The controller is not convinced: "Sandstone has no earnings from this investment. The dividends that we pay them are just intercompany cash transfers and they should not even be recognizing equity income accruals. We control them; Sandstone certainly does not have significant influence over us."

In computing the noncontrolling interest in Sandstone's income, how should the ownership of these 75,000 shares affect the determination of the subsidiary's realized income?

Treasury Stock Approach

Interestingly, when parent shares are obtained by a subsidiary, both of the prevalent methods of accounting take the same perspective: Financial reporting should not vary based on the specific identity of the purchasing agent. For consolidation purposes, no legitimate accounting distinction can be drawn between an acquisition by the parent and the same transaction if it is made by a subsidiary. However, these two methods disagree as to the underlying nature of a subsidiary's purchase of the parent's stock: Should the shares be viewed as treasury stock or as an investment?

The *treasury stock approach* assumes that both parties should account for this transaction as the parent would record a purchase of its own stock. Conversely, according to the *conventional approach,* both the parent and the subsidiary must record all intercompany investments in the same manner. Because the parent recognizes income based on its ownership of the subsidiary, the subsidiary should recognize income from an investment in the parent. Although the distinction between these two approaches may seem subtle, the resulting financial figures can vary appreciably.

The treasury stock approach to mutual ownership focuses on the parent's control over the subsidiary. Even though the companies maintain separate legal incorporation, only a single economic entity actually exists, and it is under the dominance of the parent. Hence, according to proponents, stock or other items can be purchased by either company but all reporting for the business combination has to be from the parent's perspective. Although the subsidiary may serve as the purchasing agent, the acquisition of parent shares is still viewed as treasury stock in the consolidated statements. This perspective is firmly grounded in the parent company concept (discussed in Chapter 4), which accounts for all transactions from the vantage point of the parent's stockholders.

In present accounting practice, the treasury stock approach appears to predominate, although this popularity is undoubtedly based as much on the ease of application as on theoretical merit. *The cost of parent shares held by the subsidiary is merely reclassified on the worksheet into a treasury stock account.* Any dividend payments on this stock are considered intercompany cash transfers that must be eliminated. This reporting technique is simple and the shares are, indeed, no longer accounted for as if they were outstanding.

Conventional Approach

The conventional approach provides a different view of a subsidiary's ownership of parent shares. This alternative theory presumes that the acquisition of parent stock is no more than another equity purchase made in one of the affiliated companies within a business combination. Thus, the consolidation of a mutual ownership should parallel the process that has been demonstrated already for a connecting affiliation: Two investments are present rather than one. *In effect, this argument contends that accounting for the parent's investment and a subsidiary's investment by totally different methods is inconsistent.*

Proponents of the conventional approach believe that introducing a unique process, such as the treasury stock approach, simply because of the subsidiary's location within the corporate structure is not justified. To rectify this situation, the internally held shares of the parent company are consolidated in the same manner as an investment in a subsidiary. The conventional approach is aligned with the economic unit concept, which contends that each company should be accounted for as an individual component within the business combination.

Probably the most distinctive aspect of the conventional approach is the determination of realized income figures. Because of the mutual ownership, each company occupies both a parent and a subsidiary position within the combination. Immediately, a paradox is created by this relationship. The income of neither company can be computed first; each is partially dependent on the final balance of the other. Unlike the previous indirect ownership examples, no systematic calculation of earnings is possible. Rather, mutual income accruals can be derived only by solving two simultaneous equations.

Clearly, these two approaches represent alternative perceptions of the same event: the subsidiary's purchase of parent stock. However, the underlying question here concerns the theoretical concept that should provide the basis for consolidated statements. What is the purpose of a consolidation and for whom are the financial statements prepared? After these central issues have been resolved, the handling of mutual ownerships (as well as other theoretical concerns) should follow as logical extensions of the selected concept.

Mutual Ownership Illustrated

To illustrate both the treasury stock and the conventional approaches, assume that on January 1, 1999, Sun Company purchased 10 percent of Pop Company. Sun paid $120,000 for these shares, an amount that exactly equaled the proportionate book value of Pop. Many possible reasons could exist for this transaction. The acquisition may be simply an investment or possibly an attempt by Sun to forestall a takeover move by Pop. Regardless, Sun subsequently accounts for these shares according to *SFAS 115*. To simplify the illustration, it is assumed that Pop's shares are not traded actively and therefore continuous market values are unavailable. Under these circumstances, the investment in Pop is carried appropriately on Sun's books at original cost.

On January 1, 2000, Pop managed to gain control over Sun by acquiring a 70 percent ownership interest, thus creating a business combination. Details of Pop's purchase are as follows:

Purchase price of 70% interest, 1/1/00 . . . . $500,000
Sun Company's reported book value, 1/1/00   600,000
Excess cost over book value—assumed to be paid for franchise contracts . . . . .   40-year life
Investment is being accounted for internally by means of the cost method.

During the ensuing years, these two companies report the following balances and transactions:

	Sun Company			Pop Company		
Year	Reported Operating Income	Dividend Income (10 percent ownership)	Dividends Paid	Reported Operating Income	Dividend Income (70 percent ownership)	Dividends Paid
1999	$20,000	$3,000	$ 8,000	$ 90,000	–0–	$30,000
2000	30,000	5,000	10,000	130,000	$ 7,000	50,000
2001	40,000	7,000	15,000	160,000	10,500	70,000

Treasury Stock Approach Illustrated One possible consolidation of Pop and Sun for the year of 2001 is presented in Exhibit 7–2. This worksheet has been developed under the treasury stock approach to mutual ownerships so that Pop's investment in Sun is consolidated along routine lines. This process begins with the determination of the excess purchase price to be assigned to franchise contracts:

Purchase price . . . . $ 500,000
Proportionate interest in Sun's book value ($600,000 × 70%) . . . .   (420,000)

Franchises, January 1, 2000 . . . . $ 80,000

Annual amortization—40-year life . . . . $ 2,000

Unamortized balance, January 1, 2001 . . . . $ 78,000

Following the calculation of the franchise value and amortization, regular worksheet entries can be developed for Pop's investment. Because the cost method is applied, the $7,000 dividend income recognized in the prior years of ownership (only 2000, in this case) is converted to an equity accrual in Entry *C. The parent should recognize 70 percent of the subsidiary's $35,000 income for 2000, or $24,500.[1] However, inclusion of the $2,000 amortization expense (computed above) dictates that $22,500 is the appropriate equity accrual. Because $7,000 in dividend income has already been recognized by the parent, Entry *C records the necessary increase as $15,500 ($22,500 − $7,000).[2]

The remaining entries relating to Pop's investment are standard: The stockholders' equity accounts of the subsidiary are eliminated (Entry S), the franchises allocation is recognized (Entry A), and so on. Only two facets of Exhibit 7–2 are actually affected

---

[1]Although an intercompany transfer, the $5,000 dividend received from Pop is included here in measuring the subsidiary's previous income. Sun's book value was increased by this cash distribution; thus, some accounting must be made within the consolidation process. In addition, at the time of payment, the parent reduced its retained earnings. Hence, the intercompany portion of this dividend has to be reinstated or consolidated retained earnings will be too low.

[2]The necessary adjustment to beginning retained earnings also can be computed as follows:

Income of subsidiary—2000 . . . . $ 35,000
Dividends paid . . . .   (10,000)

Increase in book value . . . . $ 25,000
Ownership percentage 70%

Income accrual . . . . $ 17,500
Amortization—2000 . . . .   (2,000)

Increase in beginning retained earnings . . . . $ 15,500

Exhibit 7–2

| Investment: Cost Method Mutual Ownership: Treasury Stock Approach | POP AND CONSOLIDATED SUBSIDIARY Consolidation Worksheet For Year Ending December 31, 2001 | | | | | |

Accounts	Pop Company	Sun Company	Consolidation Entries		Noncontrolling Interest	Consolidated Totals
			Debit	Credit		
Income Statement						
Revenues	(900,000)	(400,000)				(1,300,000)
Expenses	740,000	360,000	(E) 2,000			1,102,000
Dividend income	(10,500)	(7,000)	(I) 17,500			–0–
Noncontrolling interest in Sun Company's income ($47,000 × 30%)	–0–	–0–			(14,100)	14,100
Net income	(170,500)	(47,000)				(183,900)
Statement of Retained Earnings						
Retained earnings, 1/1/01:						
Pop Company	(747,000)	–0–		(*C) 15,500		(762,500)
Sun Company	–0–	(425,000)	(S) 425,000			–0–
Net income (above)	(170,500)	(47,000)				(183,900)
Dividends paid:						
Pop Company	70,000	–0–		(I) 7,000		63,000
Sun Company	–0–	15,000		(I) 10,500	4,500	–0–
Retained earnings, 12/31/01	(847,500)	(457,000)				(883,400)
Balance Sheet						
Current assets	855,500	331,000				1,186,500
Investment in Sun Company	500,000	–0–	(*C) 15,500	(S) 437,500 (A) 78,000		–0–
Investment in Pop Company	–0–	120,000		(TS) 120,000		–0–
Land, building, equipment (net)	642,000	516,000				1,158,000
Franchises	–0–	–0–	(A) 78,000	(E) 2,000		76,000
Total assets	1,997,500	967,000				2,420,500
Liabilities	(550,000)	(310,000)				(860,000)
Noncontrolling interest in Sun Company, 1/1/01	–0–	–0–		(S) 187,500	(187,500)	
Noncontrolling interest in Pop Company, 12/31/01	–0–	–0–			(197,100)	(197,100)
Common stock	(600,000)	(200,000)	(S) 200,000			(600,000)
Retained earnings, 12/31/01 (above)	(847,500)	(457,000)				(883,400)
Treasury stock	–0–	–0–	(TS) 120,000			120,000
Total liabilities and equities	(1,997,500)	(967,000)				(2,420,000)

Note: Parentheses indicate a credit balance.

Consolidation entries:

(*C) Conversion of cost method to equity method. This entry recognizes 70 percent of the 2000 increase in Sun Company's book value ($25,000 × 70% = $17,500) less $2,000 amortization expense applicable to that year.

 (S) Elimination of subsidiary's stockholders' equity accounts along with recognition of January 1, 2001, noncontrolling interest.

(TS) Reclassification of Sun Company's ownership in Pop Company into a treasury stock account.

 (A) Allocation to franchises, unamortized balance being recorded as of January 1, 2001.

 (I) Elimination of intercompany dividend income for the period.

 (E) Recognition of amortization expense for the current year.

by the existence of the mutual ownership. First, the $120,000 payment made by Sun for the parent's shares is reclassified into a treasury stock account (through Entry TS). Second, the $7,000 intercompany dividend flowing from Pop to Sun during the current year of 2001 is eliminated within Entry I (Entry I is used because the collection was recorded as income). The simplicity of applying the treasury stock approach should be apparent from this one example.

Before leaving the treasury stock approach, a final comment needs to be made in connection with the computation of the noncontrolling interest's share of Sun's income. In Exhibit 7–2, this balance is recorded as $14,100, or 30 percent of the subsidiary's $47,000 net income figure. A question can be raised as to the validity of including the $7,000 dividend within this income total since that payment is eliminated within the consolidation.

These dividends, although intercompany in nature, do increase the book value of the subsidiary company (see footnote 1). Therefore, the increment must be reflected in some manner to indicate the change in the amount attributed to the outsider owners. For example, the increase could have been recognized through a direct adjustment of $2,100 (30 percent of $7,000) in the noncontrolling interest balance being reported. More often, as shown here, such cash transfers are considered to be income *when viewed from the perspective of these other unrelated parties.*

Conventional Approach Illustrated   Exhibit 7–3 presents the consolidation of this same business combination based on the conventional method of reporting mutual holdings. Although many aspects of the worksheet also are routine, several entries involve procedures unique to the conventional approach. These distinctive elements concern the investment income accruals recorded for both Pop and Sun. According to the conventional approach, these figures must be calculated by identical methods to avoid any inconsistency.

Because each of the stock purchases is maintained at cost, equity accruals (Entry *C) must be established to correct the recording of all pre-2001 investment earnings. This process should begin with the earliest acquisition: the purchase made by Sun. According to the schedule presented previously, Sun reported $23,000 in total earnings (operating income plus dividends) for 1999. However, based on the data given, Sun's *realized* income for that year was actually $29,000: its own $20,000 operating profit plus an accrual of 10 percent of Pop's earnings ($9,000, or 10 percent of $90,000). To record the appropriate investment income for this initial period, a $6,000 ($29,000 − $23,000) increase in Sun's beginning retained earnings must be included on the worksheet. No special difficulty is encountered in arriving at this first amount since the mutual ownership did not yet exist in 1999.

Before leaving this 1999 adjustment, an explanation is warranted concerning the validity of making an equity income accrual for a time period in which only 10 percent ownership was maintained. The business combination formed by these two companies did not come into existence until Pop's subsequent purchase on January 1, 2000.

Despite the limited level of ownership at the time, a $6,000 equity accrual is still required for 1999 to report the subsequently created combination. As discussed in Chapter 1, retroactive adjustment to the equity method is mandated when such changes occur in the relationship between two companies. Only by applying this approach consistently can comparable financial statements be produced from year to year. Consequently, this $6,000 income accrual is recorded within the 2001 consolidation as an increase in the subsidiary's beginning retained earnings. The amount is included as a component of Entry *C1 found on the worksheet.

Computation of equity income accruals becomes significantly more involved in 2000 upon the creation of the mutual ownership. Because neither company's realized earnings can be determined first, they must be solved simultaneously. The following set of equations provides the appropriate realized income figures for each company:

Exhibit 7-3

Investment: Cost Method
Mutual Ownership:
Conventional Approach

POP AND CONSOLIDATED SUBSIDIARY
Consolidation Worksheet
For Year Ending December 31, 2001

Accounts	Pop Company	Sun Company	Consolidation Entries Debit	Consolidation Entries Credit	Noncontrolling Interest	Consolidated Totals
Income Statement						
Revenues	(900,000)	(400,000)				(1,300,000)
Expenses	740,000	360,000	(E) 1,895 (I) 17,500			1,101,895
Dividend income	(10,500)	(7,000)				-0-
Noncontrolling interest in Sun Company's income	-0-	-0-			(18,003)	18,003
Net income	(170,500)	(47,000)			(18,003)	(180,102)
Statement of Retained Earnings						
Retained earnings, 1/1/01:						
Pop Company	(747,000)	-0-	(SS) 77,033	(*C2) 23,328		(693,295)
Sun Company	-0-	(425,000)	(S) 442,033	(*C1) 17,033		-0-
Net income (above)	(170,500)	(47,000)			(18,003)	(180,102)
Dividends paid:						
Pop Company	70,000	-0-		(I) 7,000		63,000
Sun Company	-0-	15,000		(I) 10,500	4,500	-0-
Retained earnings, 12/31/01	(847,500)	(457,000)				(810,397)

Balance Sheet

	Pop Company	Sun Company	Debit	Credit	Noncontrolling Interest	Consolidated
Current assets	855,500	331,000				1,186,500
Investment in Sun Company	500,000	-0-	(*C2) 23,328	(S) 449,423 / (A) 73,905		-0-
Investment in Pop Company	-0-	120,000	(*C1) 17,033	(SS) 137,033		-0-
Land, building, equipment (net)	642,000	516,000				1,158,000
Franchises	-0-	-0-	(A) 73,905	(E) 1,895		72,010
Total assets	1,997,500	967,000				2,416,510
Liabilities	(550,000)	(310,000)				(860,000)
Noncontrolling interest in Sun Company, 1/1/01	-0-	-0-		(S) 192,610	(192,610)	
Noncontrolling interest in Sun Company, 12/31/01					(206,113)	(206,113)
Common stock: Pop Company	(600,000)		(SS) 60,000			(540,000)
Common stock: Sun Company		(200,000)	(S) 200,000			-0-
Retained earnings, 12/31/01 (above)	(847,500)	(457,000)				(810,397)
Total liabilities and equities	1,997,500	(967,000)				(2,416,510)

Note: Parentheses indicate a credit balance.

Consolidation entries:

(*C1) Conversion of cost method to equity method for Sun's investment in Pop. This accrual for prior years (1999–2000) is computed by solving a set of simultaneous equations.

(*C2) Conversion of cost method to equity method for Pop's investment in Sun. This accrual for the prior year (2000) is computed by solving a set of simultaneous equations.

(S) Elimination of subsidiary's stockholders' equity accounts along with recognition of January 1, 2001, noncontrolling interest.

(SS) Elimination of 10 percent of Pop's stockholders' equity in recognition of intercompany holdings of Sun.

(A) Allocation to franchises, unamortized balance being recorded as of January 1, 2001.

(I) Elimination of intercompany dividend income for the period.

(E) Recognition of amortization expense for the current year.

Sun's realized income

> = Sun's operating income + 10% of Pop's realized income

and

Pop's realized income

> = Pop's operating income + 70% of Sun's realized income

Only two of the balances needed in these equations are available for 2000. Sun's operating income for this year already has been reported as $30,000 while Pop's profits amounted to $128,105. The total for Pop comes from the $130,000 figure indicated previously for 2000 less $1,895 in amortization expense relating to its investment in Sun. This expense differs from the annual $2,000 charge previously derived in producing Exhibit 7–2. The change is necessary because the $6,000 accrual attributed above to Sun for 1999 alters the realized book value of the subsidiary on the date of the parent's purchase to $606,000. This adjustment, based on application of the conventional approach, was not made in the treasury stock approach.

Purchase price—70% of Sun Company		$ 500,000
Proportionate interest in Sun Company's book value:		
Reported book value, 1/1/00	$600,000	
Adjustment to book value—1999 equity income accrual relating to investment	6,000	
Adjusted book value, 1/1/00	606,000	
Ownership interest	70%	(424,200)
Excess assumed to be paid for franchises		$ 75,800
Annual amortization—40-year life		$ 1,895

By inserting the two operating income figures, the simultaneous equations can be restated as follows. SRI and PRI are used here to indicate Sun's realized income and Pop's realized income, respectively.

> SRI = $30,000 + 10% of PRI
>
> and
>
> PRI = $128,105 + 70% of SRI

To arrive at a single equation containing only one unknown, the equivalency of PRI formulated in the second equation can be used as a replacement within the first. In addition, to facilitate making the necessary mathematical computations, all percentages are restated in their decimal equivalents. Through these two alterations, the first equation can be solved to derive Sun's realized income for 2000:

> SRI = $30,000 + .10 ($128,105 + .70 SRI)
> SRI = $30,000 + $12,810.50 + .07 SRI
> .93 SRI = $42,810.50
> SRI = $46,033 (rounded)

A quick comparison of Sun's 2000 realized income of $46,033 with the reported earnings of $35,000 (from operations and dividends) indicates a required increase in the subsidiary's retained earnings of $11,033. *This increment properly records the 2000 income of Sun derived from the investment in the parent company.* Thus, to consolidate the pre-2001 earnings of Sun, a total increase of $17,033 is recognized in Entry *C1 as of January 1, 2001, $6,000 in connection with 1999, and $11,033 for 2000.

Accrual of Sun's Equity Income for Years Prior to 2001

Year	Sun's Realized Income	Sun's Reported Income	Accrual
1999	$29,000	$23,000	$ 6,000
2000	46,033	35,000	11,033
Total increase in subsidiary's 2001 beginning retained earnings—Entry *C1			$17,033

A 2000 equity accrual for Pop's income also is required under the conventional approach because of the mutual ownership at that time. This adjustment must be determined in an identical manner. The second simultaneous equation is incorporated for this purpose along with the appropriate replacement from the first:

$$PRI = \$128,105 + .70\ (\$30,000 + .10\ PRI)$$
$$PRI = \$128,105 + \$21,000 + .07\ PRI$$
$$.93\ PRI = \$149,105$$
$$PRI = \$160,328\ \text{(rounded)}$$

Based on this calculated total of $160,328, Pop's originally reported income of $137,000 (operations plus dividends) must be updated on the worksheet by $23,328 (Entry *C2). Through this adjustment, the 2000 income earned from the investment in the subsidiary is correctly included in the consolidated retained earnings.

Having accounted for the pre-2001 operations of this business combination, the remaining consolidation entries utilized in Exhibit 7–3 are mostly routine. However, the elimination of Sun's Investment in Pop (Entry SS) merits further attention. The worksheet shows the parent with beginning stockholders' equity for 2001 of $1,370,328: common stock of $600,000 plus a January 1 retained earnings balance of $770,328 (after increasing the previously recorded income through Entry *C2). Because Sun's original purchase price was equal to Pop's proportionate book value, the newly adjusted investment balance of $137,033 necessarily equates to 10 percent of this same total. The investment was 10 percent of Pop's book value when acquired and Entry *C1 (based on the solution of the simultaneous equations) maintains this agreement.

Consequently, Sun's investment account can be eliminated on the worksheet (Entry SS) by a direct write-off against this portion of Pop's stockholders' equity; 10 percent of the company's common stock and 10 percent of its beginning retained earnings are eliminated. Although this process is more complicated than recording the cost of the intercompany purchase as treasury stock, the same goal is achieved: Parent shares held by the subsidiary are not reported as outstanding on the consolidated statements. However, income is assigned to the subsidiary in the same manner that Pop used in recognizing income on its investment.

One final aspect of the consolidation process presented in Exhibit 7–3 should be analyzed: the 2001 computation of the noncontrolling interest in Sun's income (shown on the worksheet as $18,003). As in all previous illustrations, this allocation is based on the realized income of the subsidiary. However, under the conventional approach, the figure must be determined by solving two simultaneous equations. For this computation, Pop's operating income for the period ($160,000) has, once again, been reduced by $1,895 in amortization.

$$SRI = \$40,000 + 10\%\ of\ PRI$$
$$\text{and}$$
$$PRI = \$158,105 + 70\%\ of\ SRI$$
$$\text{therefore}$$
$$SRI = \$40,000 + .10\ (\$158,105 + .70\ SRI)$$
$$SRI = \$40,000 + \$15,810.50 + .07\ SRI$$
$$.93\ SRI = \$55,810.50$$
$$SRI = \$60,011\ \text{(rounded)}$$

The subsidiary's realized income is $60,011. Because the noncontrolling interest possesses 30 percent of Sun's voting stock, $18,003 ($60,011 × 30%) of the consolidated income is assigned to these outside owners. This balance varies significantly from the $14,100 allocation that was calculated under the treasury stock approach and recognized in Exhibit 7–2. Indeed, several of the consolidated totals (retained earnings, net income, etc.) will differ depending on the method adopted. Under the conventional approach, a portion of the parent's income is being assigned to the subsidiary. Consequently, a higher realized earnings figure is normally calculated for the subsidiary each year, an increase that produces an impact on the consolidated income balances.

Although the discussion here focuses exclusively on mutual ownerships between a parent and a subsidiary, similar relationships can exist between two subsidiaries within a business combination. The consolidation principles applicable in this circumstance remain substantially unaltered. The only major difference created by this configuration is that the treasury stock approach is no longer a viable option because parent shares are not being held. Rather, the conventional approach must be utilized based, once again, on determining realized income figures through the solution of two simultaneous equations.

INCOME TAX ACCOUNTING FOR A BUSINESS COMBINATION

Up to this point, this textbook has not attempted to analyze the income tax implications involved in corporate mergers and acquisitions. Numerous complexities inherent in the tax laws in this area necessitate that only a comprehensive tax course can provide complete coverage. Furthermore, essential accounting issues may become overshadowed by intermingling an explanation of the financial reporting process with an in-depth study of related tax consequences.

Thus, coverage to this point of business combinations and consolidated financial statements has been designed solely to develop a basic understanding of the reporting that is required when one company gains control over another. The effort to isolate the examination of conceptual accounting matters is not intended to minimize the importance of the tax laws as they concern consolidated entities. In reality, one of the motives behind the creation of many business combinations is the reduction of tax liabilities.

Despite the desire to focus attention on basic accounting issues, income taxes can never be ignored. Certain elements of the tax laws have a direct impact on the financial reporting of any business combination. At a minimum, recognition of current income tax expense figures as well as deferred income taxes is required to present fairly the financial statements of the consolidated entity. Therefore, an introduction to the income taxation of a business combination is necessary for a complete understanding of the financial reporting process.

Affiliated Groups

A central issue in accounting for the income taxes of a business combination is the method by which the entity's tax returns are filed. For many combinations, only a single consolidated return is required whereas in other cases separate returns are prepared for some, or even all, of the component corporations. According to current tax laws, a business combination may elect to file a consolidated return encompassing all companies that comprise an *affiliated group* as defined by the Internal Revenue Code. All other corporations are automatically required to submit separate income tax returns. Consequently, a first step in working with the taxation process is the delineation of the boundaries of an affiliated group. Because of specific requirements outlined in the tax laws, this designation does not necessarily cover the same constituents as a business combination.

According to the Internal Revenue Code, the essential criterion for including a subsidiary within an affiliated group is the parent's ownership of at least 80 percent of the voting stock as well as at least 80 percent of each class of nonvoting stock. This ownership may be direct or indirect, although the parent must meet these requirements in connection with at least one directly owned subsidiary. As another condition, each company included in the affiliated group has to be a domestic (rather than a foreign) corporation. A company's options can be described as follows:

- Domestic subsidiary, 80 percent to 100 percent owned: May file as part of consolidated return or may file separately.
- Domestic subsidiary, less than 80 percent owned: Must file separately.
- Foreign subsidiary: Must file separately.

Clearly, a distinction can be drawn between business combinations (identified for financial reporting) and affiliated groups as defined for tax purposes. In Chapter 2, a business combination was described as containing all subsidiaries controlled by a parent company unless control was only temporary. Control is normally evidenced by the possession (either directly or indirectly) of a mere majority of voting stock. Conversely, the 80 percent rule established by the Internal Revenue Code creates a smaller circle of companies qualifying for inclusion in an affiliated group.

For the companies that compose an affiliated group, the filing of a consolidated tax return provides several distinct benefits:

- Intercompany profits are not taxed until realized, although in a similar manner, intercompany losses (which are rare) are not deducted until finally culminated.
- Intercompany dividends are nontaxable (this exclusion applies to all dividends between members of an affiliated group regardless of whether a consolidated return is filed).
- Losses incurred by one affiliated company can be used to reduce taxable income earned by other members of that group.

> Many companies can't resist the lure of consolidated tax returns. When corporate parent companies file such returns, they can offset profits with losses from any members of their affiliated groups.[3]

Deferred Income Taxes

Some of the deviations between generally accepted accounting principles and income tax laws create *temporary differences* whereby (1) a variation exists between an asset or liability's recorded book value and its tax basis and (2) this difference results in taxable or deductible amounts in future years. Whenever a temporary difference is present, the recognition of a deferred tax asset or liability is required for financial reporting purposes. The specific amount of this income tax deferral depends somewhat on whether consolidated or separate returns are being filed. Thus, the tax consequences of several common transactions are analyzed here as a means of demonstrating the recording of income tax expense by a business combination.

Intercompany Dividends For financial reporting, dividends between the members of a business combination always are eliminated; they represent intercompany transfers of cash. In tax accounting, dividends also are removed from income but only if at least 80 percent of the subsidiary's stock is held. Consequently, with this level of ownership, no difference exists between financial and tax reporting; all intercompany dividends are eliminated in both cases. Income tax expense is not recorded. Deferred tax recognition is also ignored because no temporary difference has been created.

However, if less than 80 percent of a subsidiary's stock is held, tax recognition becomes necessary. Any intercompany dividends are taxed partially because, at that level

---

[3]*Journal of Accountancy,* Tax Briefs, October 1993.

of ownership, 20 percent is taxable. The dividend-received deduction on the tax return (the nontaxable portion) is only 80 percent.[4] Thus, an income tax liability is immediately created for the recipient. *In addition, deferred income taxes are required for any of the subsidiary's income not paid currently as a dividend.* A temporary difference has been created because tax payments will be necessary in future years when the earnings of this investment eventually are distributed to the parent. Hence, a current tax liability is recorded based on the dividends collected and a deferred tax liability is recorded for the taxable portion of any income not paid to the parent during the year.

The Impact of Goodwill Historically, goodwill costs have not been deductible for tax purposes. However, the Revenue Reconciliation Act of 1993 allowed the amortization of goodwill and other purchased intangibles (referred to as Section 197 property) over a 15-year period. For financial reporting, goodwill is written off if it is impaired or if the related business is disposed of in some manner. Because the periods differ in which taxable income and financial income are reduced, the presence of goodwill creates a temporary difference that necessitates the recognition of deferred income taxes. The same is true for other purchased intangibles if a life other than 15 years is used for financial reporting.

Unrealized Intercompany Gains Taxes on the unrealized gains that can result from transfers made between the related companies within a business combination create a special accounting problem. On consolidated financial statements, the impact of all such transactions is deferred. The same handling is true for a consolidated tax return; the gains are removed until realized. No temporary difference is created.

If separate returns are filed, though, tax laws require the profits to be reported in the period of transfer even though unearned by the business combination. Thus, the income is taxed immediately, prior to being earned from a financial reporting perspective. This "prepayment" of the tax creates a deferred income tax asset.[5]

Consolidated Tax Returns—Illustration

As an illustration of the accounting effects created by the filing of a consolidated tax return, assume that Great Company possesses 90 percent of Small Company's voting and nonvoting stocks. Subsequent to the acquisition, the two companies continued normal operations, which included significant intercompany transactions. Each company's operational and dividend incomes for the current time period follow, as well as the effects of unrealized gains. No income tax accruals have been recognized within these totals.

	Great Company	Small Company (90% owned)
Operating income (excludes equity or dividend income from subsidiary)	$160,000	$40,000
Net unrealized gains in current year income (included in operating income above)	30,000	8,000
Dividend income (from Small)	9,000	–0–
Dividends paid	20,000	10,000

---

[4]If less than 20 percent of a company's stock is owned, the dividend-received deduction is only 70 percent. However, this level of ownership is not applicable to a subsidiary within a business combination.

[5]In *SFAS 109,* the FASB required deferral of the amount of taxes paid on the unrealized gain by the seller. This approach was taken rather than computing the deferral based on the future tax effect caused by the difference between the buyer's book value and tax basis, a procedure consistent with the rest of the pronouncement. According to paragraph 124, this decision was made to help "eliminate the need for complex cross-currency deferred tax computations" when the parties are in separate tax jurisdictions.

From the perspective of the single economic entity, Great's individual income for the period amounts to $130,000, $160,000 in operational earnings less $30,000 in unrealized gains. Using this same approach, Small's income is calculated as $32,000 after removing the effects of the intercompany transfers ($40,000 operating income less $8,000 in unrealized gains). Thus, the income to be reported in consolidated financial statements before the reduction for noncontrolling interest is $162,000 ($130,000 + $32,000). For financial reporting, both intercompany dividends and unrealized gains have been omitted in arriving at this total. Income prior to the noncontrolling interest has been computed here since any allocation to these other owners is not deductible for tax purposes.

Because the parent owns more than 80 percent of Small's stock, the dividends collected from the subsidiary are tax free. Likewise, the intercompany gains are not taxable presently since a consolidated return is being filed. Hence, *financial and tax accounting are the same for both items;* neither of these figures produces a temporary difference so that recognition of a deferred income tax is ignored.

The affiliated group pays taxes on $162,000. Assuming an effective rate of 30 percent, $48,600 ($162,000 × 30%) must be conveyed to the government this year. Because no temporary differences are present, deferred income tax recognition is not applicable. Consequently, $48,600 is the only expense reported in connection with current income. This amount should be recorded as the income tax expense for the consolidated entity by means of a worksheet entry or through an individual accrual recorded by each company.

Assigning Income Tax Expense—Consolidated Return

Whenever a consolidated tax return is filed, an allocation of the total expense between the two parties must be determined. This figure is especially important to the subsidiary if it has to produce separate financial statements for a loan or a future issuance of equity. The subsidiary's expense also is needed as a basis for calculating the noncontrolling interest's share of consolidated income.

Several techniques exist to accomplish this proration. For example, the expense charged to the subsidiary often is based on the percentage of the total taxable income that comes from each company (the percentage allocation method) or on the taxable income figures that would be appropriate if separate returns were filed (the separate return method).[6]

To illustrate, the figures from Great and Small in the previous example are again utilized. Great owned 90 percent of Small's outstanding stock. Based on filing a consolidated return, total income tax expense of $48,600 was recognized. How should this figure be allocated between these two companies?

Percentage Allocation Method   Total taxable income on this consolidated return was $162,000. Of this amount, $130,000 was applicable to the parent (operating income after deferral of unrealized gain) while $32,000 came from the subsidiary (computed in the same manner). Thus, 19.8 percent ($32,000/$162,000, rounded) of total expense should be assigned to the subsidiary, an amount that equals $9,622.80 (19.8 percent of $48,600).

Separate Return Method   On separate returns, intercompany gains are taxable. Therefore, the separate returns of these two companies would appear as follows:

---

[6]For other methods, see "How to Allocate a Consolidated Tax Liability among Members of the Affiliated Group," in the October 1986 issue of *The Practical Accountant;* or "Uncharted Territory: Subsidiary Financial Reporting," in the October 1989 issue of *Journal of Accountancy.*

	Great	Small	Total
Operating income	$160,000	$40,000	
Assumed tax rate	30%	30%	
Income tax expense—separate returns	$ 48,000	$12,000	$60,000

By filing a consolidated return, an expense of only $48,600 is recorded for the business combination. Because 20 percent of income tax expense on the separate returns ($12,000/$60,000) came from the subsidiary, $9,720 of the expense ($48,600 × 20%) should be assigned to Small.

Under this second approach, the noncontrolling interest's share of this subsidiary's income is computed as follows:

Small Company—reported income	$40,000
Less: Unrealized intercompany gains	(8,000)
Less: Assigned income tax expense	(9,720)
Small Company—realized income	22,280
Outside ownership	10%
Noncontrolling interest in Small Company's income	$ 2,228

Filing Separate Tax Returns

Despite the advantages of filing as an affiliated group, a single consolidated return cannot be used always to encompass every member of a business combination. Separate returns are mandatory for foreign subsidiaries as well as for domestic corporations not meeting the 80 percent ownership rule. However, even if the conditions for inclusion within an affiliated group are met, a company may still elect to file separately. If all companies in an affiliated group are profitable and few intercompany transactions occur, separate returns may be preferred. By filing in this manner, the various companies have more flexibility in their choice of accounting methods as well as fiscal tax years.[7] Tax laws, though, do not allow a company to switch back and forth between consolidated and separate returns. Once a company elects to file a consolidated tax return as part of an affiliated group, obtaining permission from the Internal Revenue Service to file separately can be difficult.

The filing of a separate tax return by a member of a business combination often creates temporary differences because of (1) the immediate taxation of unrealized gains (and losses) and (2) the possible future tax effect of any subsidiary income in excess of dividend payments. Since temporary differences can result, recognition of a deferred tax asset or liability may be necessary. For example, as mentioned previously, intercompany gains and losses must be included on a separate return at the time of transfer rather than when the earning process is culminated. These gains and losses appear on both sets of records but, if unrealized at year's end, in different time periods. The temporary difference produced between the transferred asset's book value and tax basis affects future tax computations; thus, deferred taxes must be reported.

For dividend payments, deferred taxes are not required if 80 percent or more of the subsidiary's stock is owned. The transfer is nontaxable even on a separate return; no expense recognition is required.

If the amount distributed by a subsidiary that is less than 80 percent owned is equal to current earnings, 20 percent of the collection is taxed immediately but no temporary difference is created because no future tax effect is produced. Hence, again, deferred income tax recognition is not appropriate.

---

[7]At one time, the filing of separate returns was especially popular as a means of taking advantage of reduced tax rates on lower income levels. However, in the early part of the 1970s, Congress eliminated the availability of this tax saving.

Conceptually, though, as discussed in Chapter 1, questions arise about the recognition of deferred taxes when a subsidiary less than 80 percent owned pays fewer dividends than its current income. If a subsidiary earns, for example, $100,000 but pays dividends of only $60,000, will the parent's share of the $40,000 remainder ever become taxable income? Do these undistributed earnings represent temporary differences? If so, immediate recognition of the associated tax effect is required even though payment of this $40,000 may not be anticipated for the foreseeable future.

In response to these concerns, *FASB Statement No. 109,* "Accounting for Income Taxes," February 1992 (par. 32) states that "a deferred tax liability shall be recognized for . . . an excess of the amount for financial reporting over the tax basis of an investment in a domestic subsidiary." Therefore, other than one exception noted later in this chapter, a temporary difference is created by any portion of the subsidiary's income not distributed in the form of dividends. These earnings would not be taxed until a later date; thus, a deferred tax liability is created. Because many companies retain a substantial portion of their income to finance growth, an expense is recognized here that might never be paid.

Deferred Tax on Undistributed Earnings—Illustrated   Accounting for the income tax effect created by undistributed earnings probably is demonstrated best through a practical example. Assume that Parent Company owns 70 percent of Child Company. Because ownership is less than 80 percent, the filing of separate tax returns for the two companies is mandatory. In the current year, Parent's operational earnings (excluding taxes and any income from this investment) amount to $200,000 while Child reports a pretax net income of $100,000. During the period, the subsidiary paid a total of $20,000 in cash dividends, $14,000 (70 percent) to Parent, with the remainder going to the other owners. To avoid complications in this initial example, the assumption is made that no unrealized intercompany gains and losses are present.

The reporting of Child's income taxes does not provide a significant difficulty because no temporary differences are involved. Using an assumed tax rate of 30 percent, the subsidiary accrues income tax expense of $30,000 ($100,000 × 30%), leaving an after-tax profit of $70,000. *Because only $20,000 in dividends were paid, undistributed earnings for the period amount to $50,000.*

For Parent, Child's undistributed earnings represent a temporary tax difference. The following schedules have been developed to calculate Parent's current tax liability and deferred tax liability:

Income Tax Currently Payable—Parent Company

Reported operating income—Parent Company		$200,000
Dividends received	$ 14,000	
Less: Dividend deduction (80%)	(11,200)	2,800
Taxable income—current year		202,800
Tax rate		30%
Income tax payable—current period (Parent)		$ 60,840

Deferred Income Tax Payable—Parent Company

Undistributed earnings of Child Company	$ 50,000
Parent Company's ownership	70%
Undistributed earnings accruing to Parent	35,000
Dividend deduction upon eventual distribution (80%)	(28,000)
Income to be taxed—subsequent dividend payments	7,000
Tax rate	30%
Deferred income tax payable	$ 2,100

These computations indicate a total income tax expense of $62,940: a current liability of $60,840 and a deferred liability of $2,100. The deferred balance results entirely from the undistributed earnings of Child. Although the subsidiary had an after-tax income of $70,000, only $20,000 was distributed in the form of dividends. According to *FASB Statement 109,* just quoted, the $50,000 being retained by Child represents a temporary tax difference to the stockholders. Thus, recognition of the deferred income tax associated with these undistributed earnings is required. The income is earned now; therefore, the liability must be recorded in the current period.

FASB Statement 109 is not completely inflexible on this matter; in connection with a subsidiary's undistributed income, one important exception to the recognition of deferred income taxes is provided. The pronouncement (par. 31) states that a deferred tax liability is not recognized for the excess of the amount for financial reporting over the tax basis of an investment in a *foreign* subsidiary unless the reversal of those temporary differences in the foreseeable future becomes apparent.

Thus, in the previous example, if the subsidiary is foreign and if the retention of these excess earnings seems to be permanent, the $2,100 deferred tax liability is omitted, reducing the total reported expense to $60,840.

Separate Tax Returns Illustrated   The full accounting impact created by the filing of separate tax returns is demonstrated best by a complete example. As a basis for this illustration, assume that Lion Corporation reported the following data with its 60 percent owned subsidiary, Cub Company (a domestic corporation), for the year 2001:

	Lion Corporation	Cub Company (60% owned by Lion)
Operating income	$500,000	$200,000
Unrealized intercompany inventory gains (included in operating income)	40,000	30,000
Dividend income from Cub Company	24,000	not applicable
Dividends paid	not applicable	40,000
Applicable tax rate	30%	30%

Subsidiary's Income Tax Expense   Because separate tax returns must be filed, the unrealized gains are not deferred but left within the operating incomes of both companies. Thus, Cub's taxable income for 2001 is $200,000, an amount that creates a current payable of $60,000 ($200,000 × 30%). The unrealized gain is a temporary difference for financial reporting purposes, creating a deferred income tax asset (payment of the tax comes before the income actually is earned) of $9,000 ($30,000 × 30%). Therefore, the appropriate expense to be recognized by the subsidiary for the period is only $51,000:

Income Tax Expense—Cub

Income currently taxable	$ 200,000	
Tax rate	30%	$60,000
Temporary difference (unrealized gain is taxed before being earned)	(30,000)	
Tax rate	30%	(9,000)
Income tax expense—Cub		$51,000

Consequently, Cub reports after-tax income of $119,000 ($200,000 operating income less $30,000 unrealized gain less $51,000 in income tax expense). This profit figure serves as the basis for recognizing $47,600 ($119,000 × 40% outside ownership) as the noncontrolling interest's share of consolidated income.

Parent's Income Tax Expense   On Lion's separate return, its own unrealized gains remain within income. The taxable portion of the dividends received from Cub also must be included. Hence, the parent's taxable earnings for 2001 would be $504,800, a balance that creates a $151,440 current tax liability for the company.

Income Tax Currently Payable—Lion

Operating income—Lion Corporation (includes $40,000 unrealized gains)		$500,000
Dividends received from Cub Company (60%)	$ 24,000	
Less: 80% dividend deduction	(19,200)	4,800
Taxable income		504,800
Tax rate		30%
Income tax payable—current (Lion)		$151,440

Although Lion's tax return information is presented here, the total tax expense to be reported for the period can be determined only by accounting for the impact of the two temporary differences: the parent's $40,000 in unrealized gains and the undistributed earnings of the subsidiary. The undistributed earnings amount to $47,400, computed as follows:

After-tax income of Cub (above)	$119,000
Dividends paid	(40,000)
Undistributed earnings	79,000
Lion's ownership	60%
Lion's portion of undistributed earnings	$ 47,400

The deferred income tax effects to be recorded by the parent now can be derived.

Deferred Income Taxes—Lion Company

Unrealized Gains

Amount taxable now prior to being earned	$ 40,000
Tax rate	30%
Deferred income tax asset	$ 12,000

Undistributed Earnings of Subsidiary

Undistributed earnings of Cub—to be taxed later (computed above)	$ 47,400
Dividend-received deduction upon distribution (80%)	(37,920)
Income eventually taxable	$ 9,480
Tax rate	30%
Deferred income tax liability	$ 2,844

The two temporary differences exert opposite effects on Lion's reported income taxes. Because separate returns are filed, the unrealized gains are taxable in the current period despite not actually having been earned. From an accounting perspective, paying the tax on these gains now creates a deferred income tax asset of $12,000 ($40,000 × 30%). In contrast, the undistributed earnings are recognized currently by the parent (through consolidation of the investment). However, this portion of the subsidiary's income is not yet taxable to the parent. Because the tax payment is not required until the dividends are received, a deferred income tax liability of $2,844 is necessary ($9,480 × 30%).

The deferred tax asset is reported as a current asset since it relates to inventory whereas the deferred tax liability is long-term because it was created by ownership of the investment. Lion's reported income tax expense results from the creation of these three accounts:

Lion's Financial Records

Deferred Income Tax Asset—Current	12,000	
Income Tax Expense....................................	142,284	
Deferred Income Tax Liability—Long-Term............		2,844
Income Tax Currently Payable.......................		151,440
To record current and deferred taxes of parent company.		

Temporary Differences Generated by Business Combinations

Based on the nature of the transaction, some purchase combinations are deemed tax free (to the seller) by the tax laws, whereas others are taxable. In most tax-free purchases and in a few taxable purchases, the resulting book values of the acquired company's assets and liabilities differ from their tax bases. Such differences result because the subsidiary's cost is retained for tax purposes (in tax-free exchanges) or because the allocations for tax purposes vary from those used for financial reporting (a situation found in some taxable transactions).

Thus, temporary differences may be created at the time that a business combination is formed. Any deferred income tax assets and liabilities previously recorded by the subsidiary are not at issue; these accounts are consolidated in the same manner as other assets and liabilities. The question addressed here concerns differences in book value and tax basis that stem from the takeover.

As an illustration, assume that Son Company owns a single asset, a building. This property has a tax basis of $150,000 (cost less accumulated depreciation) but it presently has a fair market value of $210,000. Pop Corporation conveys a total value of $300,000 to acquire this company. The exchange is structured to be tax free. After this transaction, the building continues to have a tax basis of only $150,000. However, its consolidated book value is $210,000, an amount $60,000 more than the figure applicable for tax purposes. How does this $60,000 difference affect the consolidated statements?

In 1992, the FASB issued *Statement of Financial Accounting Standards No. 109,* "Accounting for Income Taxes," which established guidelines for the reporting of deferred income tax assets and liabilities created in a business combination. According to paragraph 127:

> Values are assigned to identified assets and liabilities when a business combination is accounted for as a purchase. The assigned values frequently will be different from the tax bases of those assets and liabilities. The Board concluded that a liability or asset should be recognized for the deferred tax consequences of differences between the assigned values and the tax bases of the assets and liabilities (other than goodwill and leveraged leases) recognized in a purchase business combination.

Thus, according to this pronouncement, a deferred tax asset or liability is created by any temporary difference such as is found in Pop's purchase of Son. Because the tax basis of the asset is $150,000, but its recorded value within consolidated statements is $210,000, a temporary difference of $60,000 exists. Assuming that a 30 percent tax rate is appropriate, a deferred income tax liability of $18,000 ($60,000 × 30%) must be recognized by the newly formed business combination. Before *Statement 109,* this $18,000 would have been reported as a reduction in the consolidated value of the Buildings account. However, a liability is recorded now to reflect the future effect of recognizing lower depreciation for tax purposes (thus creating higher taxable income and additional payments). The FASB also apparently felt that this placement was more consistent with the asset and liability approach required by *Statement 109.*

Consequently, in a consolidated balance sheet prepared immediately after Pop obtains control over Son, the building would be recorded at fair market value of

$210,000. In addition, the new deferred tax liability of $18,000 computed earlier is recognized. Because the net value of these two accounts is $192,000, goodwill of $108,000 also is recorded as the figure remaining from the $300,000 purchase price.

This $18,000 liability systematically declines to zero over the life of the building. Depreciation for tax purposes must be computed on the $150,000 cost figure and would, therefore, be less each year than the expense shown for financial reporting purposes (based on $210,000). With less expense, taxable income would be more than book income for the remaining years of the asset's life. However, according to *Statement 109,* the extra payment that results is not charged to expense. Rather, the deferred tax liability (initially established at the date of purchase) is reduced by the additional amount.

To illustrate, assume that revenues of $40,000 per year are generated from this building. Assume also that it has a life of 10 years and that the straight-line method of depreciation is in use.

	Financial Reporting	Income Tax Reporting
Revenues	$40,000	$40,000
Depreciation expense:		
10% of $210,000	21,000	
10% of $150,000		$15,000
Income	$19,000	$25,000
Tax rate	30%	30%
Tax effect	$ 5,700	$ 7,500

Although $7,500 must be paid to the government, currently reported income would have caused only $5,700 of that amount. The other $1,800 ($6,000 reversal of temporary difference $\times$ 30%) resulted because of the use of the previous basis for tax purposes. Therefore, the following entry is made:

Income Tax Expense....................................	5,700	
Deferred Income Tax Liability (to remove part of balance		
created at date of purchase)	1,800	
Income Tax Currently Payable.......................		7,500
To accrue current income taxes as well as impact of temporary		
difference in asset of subsidiary.		

Business Combinations and Operating Loss Carryforwards

Tax laws in the United States provide a measure of relief for companies incurring net operating losses (NOLs) when filing current tax returns. Such losses may be carried back for two years and applied as a reduction to taxable income figures previously reported. This procedure generates a cash refund of income taxes paid by the company during these earlier periods.

If a loss still exists after the carryback (or if the taxpayer elects not to carry the loss back), a carryforward for the subsequent 20 years also is allowed.[8] Carrying the loss forward reduces subsequent taxable income levels until the NOL is eliminated entirely or the time period expires. *Thus, NOL carryforwards can benefit the company only if taxable income can be generated in the future.* The immediate recognition of NOL carryforwards has always been controversial because it requires the company to anticipate making profits. In 1992, *Statement 109* of the Financial Accounting Standards Board established reporting rules for the appropriate recognition of such carryforwards.

---

[8]If a taxpayer believes that tax rates will be higher in the future, choosing not to carry a loss back in favor of only a carryforward may be financially preferable.

Until recently, some business combinations were created, at least in part, to take advantage of tax carryforwards. If an acquired company had an unused NOL while the parent projected significant profitability, the carryforward was used on a consolidated return to reduce income taxes after the acquisition. However, U.S. laws have now been changed so that virtually all of an NOL carryforward can be used only by the company that reported the loss. Hence, the acquisition of companies with an NOL carryforward has ceased to be a popular business strategy. However, since the practice has not disappeared, reporting rules for a subsidiary's NOL carryforward are still needed.

Statement 109 requires the recording of a deferred income tax asset for any NOL carryforward. In addition, though, a valuation allowance also must be recognized

> if, based on the weight of available evidence, it is *more likely than not* (a likelihood of more than 50 percent) that some portion or all of the deferred tax assets will not be realized. The valuation allowance should be sufficient to reduce the deferred tax asset to the amount that is more likely than not to be realized. (par. 17e)

As an example, assume that a company has one asset (a building) worth $500,000. Because of recent losses, this company has an NOL carryforward of $200,000. The assumed tax rate is 30 percent so that a benefit of $60,000 ($200,000 × 30%) will be derived if future taxable profits are earned.

Assume that this company is purchased for $640,000. In accounting for the acquisition, the parent must anticipate the likelihood that some portion or all of the NOL carryforward will ever be utilized by the new subsidiary. If it is more likely than not that the benefit will be realized, goodwill of $80,000 results:

Purchase price		$640,000
Subsidiary assets:		
Building	$500,000	
Deferred income tax asset	60,000	560,000
Goodwill		$ 80,000

Conversely, if the chances that this subsidiary will use the NOL carryforward are only 50 percent or less, a valuation allowance must be recognized and consolidated goodwill is $140,000:

Purchase price			$640,000
Subsidiary assets:			
Building		$500,000	
Deferred income tax asset	$ 60,000		
Valuation allowance	(60,000)	–0–	500,000
Goodwill			$140,000

In this second case, a question arises if future taxes are successfully reduced by this carryforward: How should the valuation allowance be removed? *Statement 109* requires that these subsequent benefits be recorded as a reduction to goodwill. Only if this asset is decreased to zero should income tax expense be reduced.

SUMMARY

1. For consolidation purposes, a parent need not possess majority ownership of each of the component companies constituting a business combination. Often, control is of an indirect nature; a majority of one subsidiary's shares are held by another subsidiary. Although the parent might own stock in only one of these companies, control has been established over both. Such an arrangement often is referred to as a father-son-grandson or a pyramid configuration.

2. The consolidation of financial information for a father-son-grandson business combination does not differ conceptually from a consolidation involving only direct ownership. All intercompany, reciprocal balances are eliminated. Goodwill, other allocations, and amortization usually must be recognized if a purchase has taken place. Because more than one investment is involved, the quantity of worksheet entries increases, but that is more of a mechanical inconvenience than a conceptual concern.

3. One aspect of a father-son-grandson consolidation that does warrant attention is the determination of realized income figures for each of the subsidiaries. Any company within a business combination that holds both a parent and subsidiary position must determine the income accruing from ownership of its subsidiary before computing its own realized earnings. This procedure is important because realized income is the basis for each parent's equity accruals as well as noncontrolling interest allocations.

4. If a subsidiary possesses shares of its parent, a mutual affiliation exists. Although this investment is intercompany in nature and must be eliminated for consolidation purposes, the amount to be removed and the income allocated to the subsidiary can be computed in two different ways. The treasury stock approach simply reclassifies the cost of these shares as treasury stock with no equity accrual being recorded. In contrast, the conventional approach accounts for the shares as a regular investment in a related party. Under this second method, equity income accruals are attributed to the subsidiary in connection with ownership of the parent. Because the companies are both in parent and subsidiary positions, the amount of realized income cannot be directly derived by either party. These figures can be found only by solving two simultaneous equations.

5. Under present tax laws, a single consolidated income tax return can be filed by an affiliated group. Only domestic corporations are included and 80 percent of the voting stock as well as 80 percent of the nonvoting stock must be controlled (either directly or indirectly) by the parent. A consolidated return allows the companies to defer recognition of intercompany gains until realized. Furthermore, losses incurred by one member of the group reduce taxable income earned by the others. Intercompany dividends are also nontaxable on a consolidated return, although such distributions are never taxable when paid between companies within an affiliated group.

6. For some members of a business combination, separate tax returns are applicable. Foreign corporations, as an example, must report in this manner as well as any company not meeting the 80 percent ownership rule. In addition, a company might simply elect to file in this manner if no advantages are gained from a consolidated return. For financial reporting purposes, a separate return often necessitates recognition of deferred income taxes because temporary differences can result from unrealized transfer gains as well as intercompany dividends (if 80 percent ownership is not held).

7. When a purchase combination is created, the subsidiary's assets and liabilities sometimes have a tax basis that differs from their assigned values. In such cases, a deferred tax asset or liability must be recognized at the time of acquisition to reflect the tax impact of these differences.

COMPREHENSIVE ILLUSTRATION

Problem

(Estimated Time: 60 to 75 Minutes) On January 1, 2001, Gold Company purchased 90 percent of Silver Company for $570,000. Within the price, $30,000 was assigned to an intangible asset, a cost that is to be expensed over a 15-year period at the rate of $2,000 per year.

Subsequently, on January 1, 2002, Silver acquired 10 percent of Gold for $150,000. This price equaled the appropriately adjusted book value of Gold's underlying net assets. Consequently, no allocation was made to either goodwill or any specific accounts.

On January 1, 2003, Gold and Silver each purchased 30 percent of the outstanding shares of Bronze for $105,000 apiece. Bronze had a book value on that date of $300,000, so the underlying book value of each acquisition was $90,000 ($300,000 × 30%). The excess $15,000 in each investment is assigned to an intangible asset and is to be amortized over a 15-year period, necessitating an annual expense of $1,000 for Gold and Silver.

After the formation of this business combination, significant intercompany inventory sales were made from Silver to Gold. The volume of these transfers has been as follows:

Year	Transfer Price to Gold Company	Markup on Transfer Price	Inventory Retained at End of Year (at transfer price)
2001	$100,000	30%	$120,000
2002	160,000	25	90,000
2003	200,000	28	120,000

In addition, on July 1, 2003, Gold sold a tract of land to Bronze for $25,000. This property originally had cost $12,000 when acquired by the parent several years ago.

The cost method is used to account for all investments. Income from the investments is recognized by the individual firms when dividends are received. Because consolidated statements are prepared for the business combination, accounting for the investments affects internal reporting only. During 2001 and 2002, Gold and Silver individually reported the following information:

	Gold Company	Silver Company
2001:		
Operational income	$180,000	$120,000
Dividend income—Silver Company (90%)	36,000	–0–
Dividends paid	80,000	40,000
2002:		
Operational income	240,000	150,000
Dividend income—Gold Company (10%)	–0–	9,000
Dividend income—Silver Company (90%)	27,000	–0–
Dividends paid	90,000	30,000

The 2003 financial statements for each of the three companies composing this business combination are presented in Exhibit 7–4. Income tax effects have been ignored in deriving these figures.

Required:

a.   Prepare worksheet entries to consolidate the 2003 financial statements for this combination. Assume that the mutual ownership between Gold and Silver is accounted for by means of the conventional approach. Compute the noncontrolling interests in Bronze's income and in Silver's income.

b.   Assume that consolidated net income (before deducting any balance for the noncontrolling interests) amounts to $501,900. Assume further that the effective tax rate is 40 percent and that Gold and Silver file a consolidated tax return while Bronze files separately. Calculate the income tax expense to be recognized within the consolidated income statement for 2003.

Solution

a.   The 2003 consolidation entries for Gold, Silver, and Bronze follow.

Entry *G   The consolidation process begins with Entry *G that recognizes the intercompany gain (on transfers from Silver to Gold) created in the previous period. The unrealized gain within ending inventory is deferred from 2002 into the current period.

*Consolidation Entry *G*

Retained earnings, 1/1/03 (Silver Company)	22,500	
Cost of goods sold		22,500

To defer unrealized gains on intercompany sales made from
Silver to Gold during the preceding year (25% markup × $90,000).

Entry *C1   Gold's ownership of Silver has been recorded using the cost method. This worksheet entry converts that number to a balance appropriate for the equity method. According to

Exhibit 7–4
Individual Financial
Statements—2003

	Gold Company	Silver Company	Bronze Company
Sales	$ 800,000	$ 600,000	$ 300,000
Cost of goods sold	(380,000)	(300,000)	(120,000)
Operating expenses	(193,000)	(100,000)	(90,000)
Gain on sale of land	13,000	–0–	–0–
Dividend income from Gold Company	–0–	10,000	–0–
Dividend income from Silver Company	36,000	–0–	–0–
Dividend income from Bronze Company	6,000	6,000	–0–
Net income	$ 282,000	$ 216,000	$ 90,000
Retained earnings, 1/1/03	$ 923,200	$ 609,000	$ 200,000
Net income (above)	282,000	216,000	90,000
Dividends paid	(100,000)	(40,000)	(20,000)
Retained earnings, 12/31/03	$1,105,200	$ 785,000	$ 270,000
Cash and receivables	$ 295,000	$ 190,000	$ 130,000
Inventory	459,000	410,000	110,000
Investment in Silver Company	570,000	–0–	–0–
Investment in Gold Company	–0–	150,000	–0–
Investment in Bronze Company	105,000	105,000	–0–
Land, buildings, and equipment (net)	980,000	670,000	380,000
Total assets	$2,409,000	$1,525,000	$ 620,000
Liabilities	$ 603,800	$ 540,000	$ 250,000
Common stock	700,000	200,000	100,000
Retained earnings, 12/31/03	1,105,200	785,000	270,000
Total liabilities and equities	$2,409,000	$1,525,000	$ 620,000

the information provided, Gold has recognized dividend income on its 90 percent investment in Silver of $36,000 (2001) and $27,000 (2002). However, Silver's total operational income for these prior years, after adjustment for intercompany transfers, amounted to $102,000 and $145,500, respectively:

2001 reported operational income—Silver	$120,000
Less: Unrealized gains (30% markup × $60,000)	(18,000)
2001 operational income—Silver	$102,000
2002 reported operational income—Silver	$150,000
Add: 2001 gains actually realized in 2002 (from above)	18,000
Less: 2002 unrealized gains (25% markup × $90,000)	(22,500)
2002 operational income—Silver	$145,500

As the mutual relationship between these two companies did not exist in 2001, the solving of simultaneous equations is not applicable for this initial period. Gold's equity income can be computed directly: 90 percent of Silver's $102,000 in realized earnings ($91,800) less the $2,000 amortization expense associated with this acquisition. The resulting $89,800 balance indicates the need for an additional accrual of $53,800 on the worksheet to correct the $36,000 figure recognized by Gold.

In contrast, Gold's 2002 equity accrual should reflect the mutual relationship that has come into existence. As the conventional approach is to be applied, simultaneous equations will be incorporated. These equations include Silver's 2002 operational income of $145,500 (calculated above) and the $238,000 operational income of Gold (reported earnings for the year less the annual amortization expense).

Gold's 2002 realized income = $238,000 + 90% of Silver's realized income

and

Silver's 2002 realized income = $145,500 + 10% of Gold's realized income

therefore

$$GRI = \$238,000 + .9 \, (\$145,500 + .1 \, GRI)$$
$$GRI = \$238,000 + \$130,950 + .09 \, GRI$$
$$.91 \, GRI = \$368,950$$

Gold's realized income = $405,440 (rounded)

Gold recorded income in 2002 of only $267,000 ($240,000 from operations plus $27,000 in dividend income). Its realized income is computed to be $405,440 here; therefore, an additional accrual of $138,440 ($405,440 − $267,000) is required to reflect ownership in Silver during this period. Combined with the $53,800 accrual calculated previously for 2001, a total worksheet adjustment of $192,240 must be made for Gold (Entry *C1) to recognize the appropriate equity income for these two prior years.

Consolidation Entry *C1 (Gold)

Investment in Silver Company	192,240	
Retained Earnings, 1/1/02 (Gold Company)		192,240

    To convert Gold's investment income figures for the
two preceding years to equity income accruals.

Entry *C2 At the beginning of 2002, Silver obtained a 10 percent interest in Gold, an investment that also has been recorded using the cost method. To apply the conventional approach, Silver must solve the same simultaneous equations as Gold to determine the correct equity accrual. Using these equations, a realized income figure for Silver of $186,044 can be calculated for 2002.

$$SRI = \$145,500 + 10\% \text{ of } GRI$$

and

$$GRI = \$238,000 + 90\% \text{ of } SRI$$

therefore

$$SRI = \$145,500 + .1 \, (\$238,000 + .9 \, SRI)$$
$$SRI = \$145,500 + \$23,800 + .09 \, SRI$$
$$.91 \, SRI = \$169,300$$

Silver's 2002 realized income = $186,044 (rounded)

Consequently, total investment income of $40,544 ($186,044 realized earnings less $145,500 operating income) should be recognized by Silver for 2002. However, only the $9,000 received in the form of dividends actually was recorded during that period. Therefore, Entry *C2 is included on the worksheet to rectify the consolidated figures for this preceding year by recording $31,544 in additional earnings ($40,544 − $9,000).

Consolidation Entry *C2 (Silver)

Investment in Gold Company	31,544	
Retained Earnings, 1/1/03 (Silver Company)		31,544

    To convert Silver's investment income figures for
the prior year to equity income.

Remaining Consolidation Entries After the three previous entries have been recorded, the remainder of the worksheet entries to consolidate these companies are relatively uncomplicated.

Consolidation Entry S1

Common Stock (Silver Company)	200,000	
Retained Earnings, 1/1/03 (Silver Company) (as adjusted above)	618,044	
Investment in Silver Company (90%)		736,240
Noncontrolling Interest in Silver Company, 1/1/03 (10%) ...		81,804

    To eliminate the beginning stockholders' equity accounts of Silver and to
recognize a 10 percent noncontrolling interest in the subsidiary.
Retained earnings has been adjusted for Entry *G and Entry *C2.

Consolidation Entry S2

Common Stock (Gold Company) (10%)	70,000	
Retained Earnings (Gold Company) (10% of 1/1/03 balance as adjusted above)	111,544	
Investment in Gold Company (as adjusted above)		181,544

To eliminate the January 1, 2003, equity of Gold Company's shares being held by Silver Company. Retained earnings has been adjusted for Entry *C1.

Consolidation Entry S3

Common Stock (Bronze Company)	100,000	
Retained Earnings, 1/1/03 (Bronze Company)	200,000	
Investment in Bronze Company (60%)		180,000
Noncontrolling Interest in Bronze Company, 1/1/03 (40%)		120,000

To eliminate beginning stockholders' equity accounts of Bronze and to recognize outside ownership of the company's remaining shares. The investments of both Gold and Silver are accounted for concurrently through this one entry.

Consolidation Entry A

Intangible Asset	56,000	
Investment in Silver Company		26,000
Investment in Bronze Company		30,000

To recognize January 1, 2003, intangible asset balances. Although $30,000 was originally allocated within the purchase of Silver, the recognition of amortization for 2001 and 2002 has reduced that figure by $4,000 ($2,000 per year). Conversely, as of the beginning of 2003, no expense has been recorded yet on the $30,000 associated with the acquisitions of Bronze. Thus, a total allocation of $56,000 is appropriate as of January 1, 2003.

Consolidation Entry I

Dividend Income from Gold Company	10,000	
Dividend Income from Silver Company	36,000	
Dividend Income from Bronze Company	12,000	
Dividends Paid (Gold Company)		10,000
Dividends Paid (Silver Company)		36,000
Dividends Paid (Bronze Company)		12,000

To eliminate dividend payments made between the companies and recorded as income based on application of the cost method.

Consolidation Entry E

Amortization Expense	4,000	
Intangible Asset		4,000

To recognize the 2003 amortization expense for the various intangible asset balances. Amortization of $2,000 is recognized on the $30,000 allocation made in the acquisition of Silver while an additional $1,000 expense is associated with each of the two investments made in Bronze.

Consolidation Entry TI

Sales	200,000	
Cost of Goods Sold		200,000

To eliminate the intercompany transfer of inventory made in 2003 by Silver.

Consolidation Entry G

Cost of Goods Sold	33,600	
Inventory		33,600

To eliminate intercompany gains remaining in the December 31,
2003, inventory of Gold. The unrealized gain is 28 percent (the
markup for 2003) of the $120,000 ending inventory balance held
by the parent.

Consolidation Entry GL

Gain on Sale of Land	13,000	
Land		13,000

To eliminate gain on intercompany transfer of land made
from Gold Company to Bronze during the year.

Noncontrolling Interest in Bronze Company's Income   As in all past examples, the non-controlling interest's claim to a portion of consolidated income must be calculated based on the realized income of the subsidiary. In this illustration, the combination is a father-son-grandson configuration; therefore, computation of income must begin with Bronze. Because this subsidiary has neither unrealized intercompany gains nor amortization expense, the $90,000 income figure reported in Exhibit 7–4 is applicable. Thus, $36,000 ($90,000 × 40%) should be reported as the noncontrolling interest's share of Bronze's 2003 income.

Noncontrolling Interest in Silver Company's Income   Because of the mutual ownership with Gold, Silver's realized income for 2003 can be determined only by solving two simultaneous equations (since the conventional approach is being applied). Operational income figures for both parties are required as a prerequisite for this procedure.

Silver's Operational Income

Sales	$ 600,000
Cost of goods sold	(300,000)
Operating expenses	(100,000)
Amortization expense—purchase of Bronze	(1,000)
Equity in earnings of Bronze (30%)	27,000
2002 intercompany gains currently realized (Entry *G)	22,500
2003 intercompany unrealized gains being deferred (Entry G)	(33,600)
Operational income	$ 214,900

Gold's Operational Income

Sales	$ 800,000
Cost of goods sold	(380,000)
Operating expenses	(193,000)
Amortization expense—purchase of Silver	(2,000)
Amortization expense—purchase of Bronze	(1,000)
Equity in earnings of Bronze (30%)	27,000
Operational income	$ 251,000

Using these two income balances, the simultaneous equations can be constructed to determine Silver's realized income for the current year. This total serves as the basis for making the noncontrolling interest calculation.

$$SRI = \$214{,}900 + 10\% \text{ of GRI}$$

and

$$GRI = \$251{,}000 + 90\% \text{ of SRI}$$

therefore

$$SRI = \$214{,}900 + .1\ (\$251{,}000 + .9\ SRI)$$

$$SRI = \$214{,}900 + \$25{,}100 + .09\ SRI$$

$$.91\ SRI = \$240{,}000$$

Silver's realized income = $263,736

Noncontrolling interest in Silver's income (10%) = $26,374 (rounded)

b. For Bronze, no differences exist between book values and tax basis. No computation of deferred income taxes is required; thus this company's separate tax return is relatively straightforward. The $90,000 income figure being reported creates a current tax liability of $36,000 (based on the 40 percent tax rate).

   In contrast, the consolidated tax return filed for Gold and Silver must include the following financial information. Where applicable, figures reported in Exhibit 7–4 have been combined for the two companies.

Tax Return Information—Consolidated Return

Sales	$1,400,000	
Less: Intercompany sales (2003)	(200,000)	$1,200,000
Cost of goods sold	680,000	
Less: 2003 intercompany purchases	(200,000)	
Less: 2002 intercompany gains recognized in 2003 (90,000 × 25%)	(22,500)	
Add: 2003 unrealized intercompany gains (120,000 × 28%)	33,600	491,100
Gross profit		708,900
Operating expenses (including amortization)		297,000
Operating income		$ 411,900
Other income (since Bronze is not part of affiliated group):		
Gain on sale of land		13,000
Dividend income—Bronze Company	$ 12,000	
Less: 80% deduction	(9,600)	2,400
Taxable income		$ 427,300
Tax rate		40%
Income tax payable by Gold Company and Silver Company for 2003		$ 170,920

A total of $206,920 must be paid to the government in 2003 by the members of this business combination ($36,000 by Bronze and $170,920 in connection with the consolidated return of Gold and Silver). However, according to *FASB Statement 109,* accounting for deferred income tax assets and/or liabilities also is necessitated by any temporary differences that originate or reverse during the year. *In this illustration, only the dividend payments from Bronze and the unrealized gain on the sale of land to Bronze actually create such differences.* For example, amortization of the intangible asset would be the same for book and tax purposes. Other items encountered do not lead to deferred income taxes:

■ Because a consolidated return is being filed by Gold and Silver, the unrealized inventory gains are deferred for both tax purposes and financial reporting so that no difference is created.

■ The dividends paid from Silver to Gold are not subject to taxation because these distributions were made between members of an affiliated group.

However, recognition of a deferred tax liability is required because Bronze's realized income ($54,000 after income tax expense of $36,000) is greater than its $20,000 dividend distribution.

Gold and Silver own 60 percent of this subsidiary, indicating that $32,400 ($54,000 × 60%) of its income is included on the consolidated income statement. Because this figure is $20,400 larger than the amount of dividends paid to Gold and Silver ($12,000, or 60% of $20,000), a deferred tax liability is required. The temporary difference is actually $4,080 (20% of $20,400) because of the 80 percent dividend deduction. The future tax effect on this difference is $1,632 based on the 40 percent tax rate being applied.

A deferred tax asset also is needed in connection with the intercompany sale of land from Gold to Bronze. Separate returns are being filed by these companies. Thus, the gain is taxed immediately, although this $13,000 will not be realized for reporting purposes until a future resale occurs. From an accounting perspective, the tax of $5,200 ($13,000 × 40%) is being prepaid in 2003.

Recognition of the current payable as well as the two deferrals leads to an income tax expense of $203,352:

Income Tax Expense	203,352	
Deferred Income Tax—Asset	5,200	
Income Taxes Payable—Current		206,920
Deferred Income Tax—Liability		1,632

QUESTIONS

1. What is meant by a father-son-grandson relationship?

2. When an indirect ownership is present, why is a specific ordering necessary for determining the realized incomes of the component corporations?

3. Able Company owns 70 percent of the outstanding voting stock of Baker Company, which, in turn, holds 80 percent of Carter Company. Carter possesses 60 percent of the capital stock of Dexter Company. How much income actually accrues to the consolidated entity from each of these companies after giving consideration to the various noncontrolling interests?

4. How does the presence of an indirect ownership (such as a father-son-grandson relationship) affect the mechanical aspects of the consolidation process?

5. What is the difference between a connecting affiliation and a mutual ownership?

6. When a mutual ownership exists, two different views of this relationship can be adopted. What are these two views and how do they differ?

7. In accounting for mutual ownerships, why is the treasury stock approach more prevalent in practice than the conventional approach?

8. Alexander Company holds 80 percent of the outstanding common stock of Baxter Company. Baxter, in turn, owns 30 percent of the stock of Alexander. How is the realized income of these two companies computed if the conventional approach is being utilized?

9. For income tax purposes, how is an affiliated group defined?

10. What are the advantages to a business combination filing a consolidated tax return? Considering these advantages, why do some members of a business combination file separate tax returns?

11. Why is the allocation of the income tax expense figure between the members of a business combination important? By what methods can this allocation be made?

12. If separate income tax returns are filed by a parent and its subsidiary, why will the parent frequently have to recognize deferred income taxes? Why might the subsidiary have to recognize deferred income taxes?

13. In a recent acquisition, the consolidated value of a subsidiary's assets exceeded the basis appropriate for tax purposes. How does this difference affect the consolidated balance sheet?

14. Jones acquires Wilson, in part, because the new subsidiary has an unused net operating loss carryforward for tax purposes. How does this carryforward affect the consolidated figures at the date of acquisition?

15. A subsidiary is acquired that has a net operating loss carryforward. The related deferred income tax asset is $230,000. Because the parent believes that a portion of this carryforward likely will never be used, a valuation allowance of $150,000 also is

recognized. At the end of the first year of ownership, the parent reassesses the situation and determines that the valuation allowance should be reduced to $110,000. What effect does this change have on the reporting of the business combination?

INTERNET ASSIGNMENT

Internet sites are time and date sensitive. It is the purpose of these exercises to have you explore the Internet. You may need to refer to the text's Web site at http://www.mhhe.com/hoyle6e to find the most up-to-date links for the Web sites listed in the Internet Assignments.

1. Using the Web, access the current financial statements of Coca-Cola Company, www.coca-cola.com. Identify and discuss the following aspects of consolidated tax expense disclosed in the firm's financial statements:

   ■ Loss carryforwards and carrybacks.
   ■ Components of deferred tax assets and liabilities.
   ■ Deferred tax impacts of stock sales by equity investees.
   ■ Deferred tax impacts of sales of interests in investees.
   ■ Valuation allowances on deferred taxes.
   ■ Differences between statutory and effective tax rates.

LIBRARY ASSIGNMENTS

1. Locate PepsiCo, Inc., or General Electric Company, in the most recent edition of *Moody's Industrial Manual*. Find at least three examples of father-son-grandson ownership patterns. By reading the history of the company in the manual, determine, if possible, the method by which the parents gained control over the three grandson organizations.

   Locate at least one other company in *Moody's Industrial Manual* with a considerable number of subsidiaries. Are most of these subsidiaries controlled directly by the parent or indirectly?

2. Read "New Dawn for Japanese Holdings," *International Tax Review,* September 1999. Prepare a report that discusses some of the differences between the Japanese and U.S. tax treatments for consolidated entities. Do these differences affect the relative competitiveness of U.S. firms in comparison to Japanese firms?

3. Read some of the following articles and prepare a report on the qualifications and elections by entities that wish to prepare consolidated income tax returns.

   "Defining an Affiliated Group," *Journal of Accountancy,* November 1999.

   "New Elections Available in Wake of Final Consolidated Return Regulations," *The Tax Adviser,* June 1996.

   "Responding to the New Subsidiary Investment and Earnings and Profits Consolidated Return Regulations," *Tax Executive,* March 1995.

   "Consolidated Return Intercompany Transaction Regulations: Clearly Reflecting Income Is Clearly Not Simple," *Tax Executive,* September 1994.

PROBLEMS

1. In a father-son-grandson business combination, which of the following statements is true?
   a. The father company always must have its realized income computed first.
   b. The computation of a company's realized income has no effect on the realized income of other companies within a business combination.
   c. A father-son-grandson configuration does not require consolidation unless one company owns shares in all of the other companies.
   d. All companies that are solely in subsidiary positions must have their realized income computed first within the consolidation process.

2. A subsidiary owns shares of its parent company. Which of the following is true concerning the treasury stock approach?
   a. It is considered to be more difficult to apply than the conventional approach.
   b. The original cost of the subsidiary's investment is a reduction in consolidated stockholders' equity.
   c. The subsidiary accrues income on its investment by using the equity method.
   d. The treasury stock approach eliminates these shares entirely within the consolidation process.

3. On January 1, 2001, a subsidiary buys 10 percent of the outstanding shares of its parent company. Although the total book value and fair market value of the parent's net assets were $4 million, the purchase price for these shares was $420,000. An intangible asset is amortized in this business combination over a 40-year period. During 2001, the parent reported operational income (no investment income was included) of $510,000 while paying dividends of $140,000. How are these shares reported at December 31, 2001, if the treasury stock approach is used?
   a. The investment is recorded as $457,000 at the end of 2001 and then eliminated for consolidation purposes.
   b. Consolidated stockholders' equity is reduced by $457,000.
   c. The investment is recorded as $456,500 at the end of 2001 and then eliminated for consolidation purposes.
   d. Consolidated stockholders' equity is reduced by $420,000.

4. Which of the following is correct for two companies that want to file a consolidated tax return as an affiliated group?
   a. One company must hold at least 51 percent of the other company's voting stock.
   b. One company must hold at least 65 percent of the other company's voting stock.
   c. One company must hold at least 80 percent of the other company's voting stock.
   d. A consolidated tax return cannot be filed unless one company owns 100 percent of the voting stock of the other.

5. How does the amortization of goodwill affect the computation of income taxes on a consolidated tax return?
   a. It is a deductible expense but only if the parent owns 80 percent of the voting stock of the subsidiary.
   b. It is deductible only if it is impaired.
   c. It is a deductible item over a 15-year period.
   d. It is deductible for tax purposes but only if a consolidated tax return is being filed.

6. Which of the following is not a reason for two companies to file separate tax returns?
   a. The parent owns 68 percent of the subsidiary.
   b. They have no intercompany transactions.
   c. Intercompany dividends are tax free only on separate returns.
   d. Neither company historically has had an operating tax loss.

7. Bassett Company owns 80 percent of Crimson Corporation. Crimson Corporation owns 90 percent of Damson, Inc. Operational income totals for 2001 follow; these figures contain no investment income. Amortization expense was not required by any of these purchases. Included in Damson's income is a $40,000 unrealized gain on intercompany transfers to Crimson.

	Bassett	Crimson	Damson
Operational income	$300,000	$200,000	$200,000

What is Bassett's realized income for the year?
   a. $575,200
   b. $588,000
   c. $596,400
   d. $604,000

8. Gardner Corporation holds 80 percent of Healthstone, which, in turn, owns 80 percent of Icede. Operational income figures (without investment income) as well as unrealized upstream gains included in the income for the current year follow:

	Gardner	Healthstone	Icede
Operational income	$400,000	$300,000	$220,000
Unrealized gains	50,000	30,000	60,000

On a consolidated income statement for the year, what balance is reported for the noncontrolling interest in the subsidiaries' income?

a. $86,000
b. $100,000
c. $111,600
d. $120,800

9. Nesbitt Corporation owns 90 percent of Jones, Inc., while Jones owns 10 percent of the outstanding shares of Nesbitt. No goodwill or any other allocations were recognized in connection with either of these acquisitions. Nesbitt reports operational income of $190,000 for 2001 whereas Jones earned $70,000 during the same period. No investment income is included within either of these income totals. On a consolidated income statement, what is the noncontrolling interest in Jones's income if the conventional approach is being used?

a. $7,000
b. $7,740
c. $8,900
d. $9,780

10. Horton, Inc., owns 90 percent of the voting stock of Juvyn Corporation. The purchase price was in excess of book value and fair market value by $80,000. Juvyn holds 20 percent of the voting stock of Horton. That purchase price was in excess of book value and fair market value by $20,000. Any excess price is assigned to copyrights to be amortized over a 20-year period.

During the current year, Horton reported operational income of $160,000 and dividend income from Juvyn of $27,000. At the same time, Juvyn reported operational income of $50,000 and dividend income from Horton of $14,000.

If the treasury stock approach is utilized, what will be reported as the Noncontrolling Interest in Juvyn's Net Income?

a. $5,000
b. $5,400
c. $6,300
d. $6,400

11. What would be the answer to problem 10 if the conventional approach were being used?

a. $9,781
b. $9.964
c. $10,414
d. $11,864

12. Cremmins, Inc., owns 60 percent of Anderson. During the current year, Anderson reported net income of $200,000 but paid a total cash dividend of only $40,000. What deferred income tax liability must be recognized in the consolidated balance sheet? Assume the tax rate is 30 percent.

a. $5,760
b. $9,600
c. $12,840
d. $28,800

13. Prybylos, Inc., owns 90 percent of Station Corporation. Both companies have been profitable for many years. During the current year, the parent sold merchandise costing $70,000 to the subsidiary for $100,000. At the end of the year, 20 percent of this merchandise was still being held. Assume that the tax rate is 25 percent and that separate tax returns are filed. What deferred income tax asset is created?

a. –0–
b. $300
c. $1,500
d. $7,500

14. What would be the answer to problem 13 if a consolidated tax return were filed?
a. –0–
b. $300
c. $1,500
d. $7,500

15. Hastoon Company purchases all of Zedner Company for $420,000 in cash. On that date, the subsidiary has net assets with a $400,000 fair market value but a $300,000 book value and tax basis. The tax rate is 30 percent. Neither company has reported any deferred income tax assets or liabilities. What amount of goodwill should be recognized on the date of the acquisition?
a. $20,000
b. $36,000
c. $50,000
d. $120,000

16. On January 1, 2000, Tree Company purchased 70 percent of Limb Company's outstanding voting stock for $250,000. Limb had a $300,000 reported book value on that date. Subsequently, on January 1, 2001, Limb Company acquired 70 percent of Leaf Company for $90,000 when Leaf had a $100,000 book value. Any excess purchase price is to be assigned to an intangible asset with a 40-year life.

These companies report the following financial information. Investment income figures are not included.

	2000	**2001**	**2002**
Sales:			
Tree Company	$400,000	$500,000	$650,000
Limb Company	200,000	280,000	400,000
Leaf Company	Not available	160,000	210,000
Expenses:			
Tree Company	$310,000	$420,000	$510,000
Limb Company	160,000	220,000	335,000
Leaf Company	Not available	150,000	180,000
Dividends paid:			
Tree Company	$ 20,000	$ 40,000	$ 50,000
Limb Company	10,000	20,000	20,000
Leaf Company	Not available	2,000	10,000

Assume that the following questions are each independent:
a. If all companies use the equity method for internal reporting purposes, what is the December 31, 2001, balance in the Tree's Investment in Limb Company account?
b. If all companies use the cost method to account for their investments, what adjustments must Limb and Tree make to their beginning retained earnings balances on the 2002 consolidation worksheet?
c. What is the consolidated net income for this business combination for the year of 2002 prior to any reduction for the noncontrolling interests' share of the subsidiaries' net income?
d. What is the noncontrolling interests' share of the consolidated net income in 2002?
e. Assume that Limb made intercompany inventory transfers to Tree that have resulted in the following unrealized gains at the end of each year:

Date	Amount
12/31/00	$10,000
12/31/01	16,000
12/31/02	25,000

What is the realized income of Limb in 2001 and 2002, respectively?
f. Assuming the same unrealized gains as presented in part (*e*), what worksheet adjustment must be made to the January 1, 2002, Retained Earnings account of Tree if that company has applied the cost method to its investment?

17. On January 1, 2001, Uncle Company purchased 80 percent of Nephew Company's capital stock for $500,000 in cash and other assets. Nephew had a book value of $600,000 on that date.

   On January 1, 2000, Nephew acquired 30 percent of Uncle for $280,000. Uncle's appropriately adjusted book value as of that date was $900,000.

   Operational income figures (includes no investment income) for these two companies follow. In addition, Uncle pays $20,000 in dividends to shareholders each year while Nephew distributes $5,000 annually. Any purchase price allocations are amortized over a 10-year period.

Year	Uncle Company	Nephew Company
2001	$ 90,000	$30,000
2002	120,000	40,000
2003	140,000	50,000

   The following questions should be viewed as independent:
   a. Assume that the treasury stock approach is being utilized and that Uncle applies the equity method to account for this investment in Nephew. What is the Income of the Subsidiary being recognized by Uncle in 2003?
   b. If the treasury stock approach is applied, what is the noncontrolling interest's share of the subsidiary's 2003 income?
   c. Assume that the conventional approach is utilized and that Uncle applies the equity method to this investment in Nephew. What is the Income of the Subsidiary being recognized by Uncle in 2003?
   d. If the conventional approach is being applied, what is the noncontrolling interest's share of the subsidiary's 2003 net income?

18. Gaddy, Inc., obtained 60 percent of Mabry Corporation on January 1, 2001. Annual amortization of $25,000 is to be recorded on the allocations made in connection with this purchase. On January 1, 2002, Mabry acquired 90 percent of Tucson Company's voting stock. Amortization on this second purchase amounted to $2,000 per year.

   For the year of 2004, these three companies reported the following information as accumulated by their separate accounting systems. Operating income figures do not include any investment or dividend income.

	Operating Income	Dividends Paid
Gaddy	$220,000	$120,000
Mabry	160,000	50,000
Tucson	90,000	10,000

Required:
   a. On consolidated financial statements for 2004, what is the noncontrolling interests' share of the subsidiaries' income?
   b. What is consolidated net income for 2004?
   c. If Mabry's operating income figures for 2004 include a net unrealized gain of $12,000, what is consolidated net income for that year?

19. Fonseca owns 80 percent of the voting stock of Carson. The purchase price exceeded the underlying book value of Carson's assets and liabilities by $60,000. At the same time, Carson holds a 30 percent interest in the outstanding shares of Fonseca. This stock was bought at a price $10,000 in excess of underlying book value. All excess amounts are assigned to technical expertise with a 10-year life.

   Both of these companies use the cost method to record their investments for internal reporting purposes. During the current year, the following information was reported:

	Operating Income	Dividend Income	Total Reported Income
Fonseca	$80,000	$16,000 (all from Carson)	$96,000
Carson	30,000	15,000 (all from Fonseca)	45,000

Required:

    a. If the conventional approach is to be utilized, what reduction should be recorded in the consolidated income statement as the noncontrolling interest in Carson's net income?

    b. If the treasury stock approach is applied, what reduction should be recorded in the consolidated income statement as the noncontrolling interest in Carson's net income?

20. Baxter, Inc., owns 90 percent of Wisconsin, Inc., and 20 percent of the Cleveland Company. Wisconsin, in turn, holds 60 percent of the outstanding stock of Cleveland. Total annual amortization of $17,000 resulted from the purchases made by Baxter. During the current year, Cleveland sold a variety of inventory items to Wisconsin for $40,000 although the original cost had been $30,000. Of this total, $12,000 in inventory (at transfer price) was still held by Wisconsin at year's end.

    During this same period, Wisconsin sold merchandise to Baxter for $100,000 although the original cost had been only $70,000. At the end of the year, $40,000 of these goods (at the transfer price) was still on hand.

    The cost method is used to record each of these investments. No other investments are held by any of the companies.

    Using the following separate income statements, determine the figures that would appear on a consolidated income statement.

	Baxter	**Wisconsin**	**Cleveland**
Sales	$1,000,000	$450,000	$ 280,000
Cost of goods sold	(670,000)	(280,000)	(190,000)
Expenses	(110,000)	(60,000)	(30,000)
Dividend income:			
Wisconsin	36,000	–0–	–0–
Cleveland	4,000	12,000	–0–
Net income	$ 260,000	$122,000	$ 60,000

21. Alice Corporation bought 90 percent of the outstanding shares of Wonderland, Inc., several years ago for $610,000. Wonderland, in turn, acquired 10 percent of Alice for $111,000. Annual amortization expense of $12,000 resulted from Alice's purchase. The cost method is used to record each of these investments. No other investments are held by either company.

Required:

    a. Based on the following separate income statements, produce the figures that would appear on a consolidated income statement. Assume that the treasury approach is being used.

	Alice	**Wonderland**
Sales	$1,300,000	$ 500,000
Cost of goods sold	(750,000)	(270,000)
Expenses	(220,000)	(120,000)
Dividend income	45,000	16,000
Net income	$ 375,000	$ 126,000

    b. Assuming that the treasury stock approach is still in use, what are the consolidated totals for the following two accounts?

	Alice	**Wonderland**
Common stock	$880,000	$350,000
Treasury stock	–0–	–0–

22. The following figures are reported by Up and its 80 percent owned subsidiary (Down) for the year ending December 31, 2001. Down paid dividends of $30,000 during this period.

	Up	Down
Sales	$600,000	$300,000
Cost of goods sold	300,000	140,000
Operating expenses	174,000	60,000
Dividend income	24,000	–0–
Net income	$150,000	$100,000

In 2000, unrealized gains of $30,000 on upstream transfers of $90,000 were deferred into 2001. In 2001, unrealized gains of $40,000 on upstream transfers of $110,000 were deferred into 2002.

a. What figures appear in a consolidated income statement?

b. What income tax expense should be shown in the consolidated income statement if separate returns are filed? Assume that the tax rate is 30 percent.

23. Clarke has a controlling interest in the outstanding stock of Rogers. At the end of the current year, the following information has been accumulated for these two companies:

	Operating Income	Dividends Paid
Clarke	$500,000	$90,000
	(includes a $90,000 net unrealized gain on intercompany inventory transfers)	
Rogers	$240,000	$80,000

Clarke uses the cost method to account for the investment in Rogers. Neither dividend nor other investment income is included in the operating income figures just presented. The effective tax rate for both companies is 40 percent.

Required:

a. Assume that Clarke owns 100 percent of the voting stock of Rogers and that a consolidated tax return is being filed. What amount of income taxes would this affiliated group pay in connection with the current period?

b. Assume that Clarke owns 92 percent of the voting stock of Rogers and that a consolidated tax return is being filed. What amount of income taxes would this affiliated group pay in connection with the current period?

c. Assume that Clarke owns 80 percent of the voting stock of Rogers but the companies have elected to file separate tax returns. What is the total amount of income taxes that these two companies pay for the current period?

d. Assume that Clarke owns 70 percent of the voting stock of Rogers so that separate tax returns are required. What is the total amount of income tax expense to be recognized in the consolidated income statement for the current period?

e. Assume that Clarke owns 70 percent of the voting stock of Rogers so that separate tax returns are required. What amount of income taxes does Clarke have to pay in connection with the current year?

24. On January 1, 2001, Piranto acquires 90 percent of the outstanding shares of Slinton. Financial information for these two companies for the years of 2001 and 2002 are as follows:

	2001	2002
Piranto Company:		
Sales	$600,000	$800,000
Operational expenses	400,000	500,000
Unrealized gains as of end of year (included in above figures)	120,000	150,000
Dividend income—Slinton Company	18,000	36,000
Slinton Company:		
Sales	200,000	250,000
Operational expenses	120,000	150,000
Dividends paid	20,000	40,000

Assume that a tax rate of 40 percent is applicable to both companies.

Required:

    a. On consolidated financial statements for 2002, what would be the income tax expense and the income tax currently payable if Piranto and Slinton file a consolidated tax return as an affiliated group?

    b. On consolidated financial statements for 2002, what would be the income tax expense and income tax currently payable for each company if they choose to file separate returns?

25. Lake acquired a controlling interest in Boxwood several years ago. During the current fiscal period, these two companies have individually reported the following income figures (exclusive of any investment income):

Lake	$300,000
Boxwood	100,000

Lake paid a cash dividend of $90,000 during the current year while Boxwood distributed $10,000.

Boxwood sells inventory to Lake each period. Unrealized intercompany gains of $18,000 were present in Lake's beginning inventory for the current year while its ending inventory carried $32,000 in unrealized profits.

The following questions should be viewed as independent situations. The effective tax rate for both companies is 40 percent.

    a. If Lake owns a 60 percent interest in Boxwood, what total income tax expense must be reported on a consolidated income statement for this period?

    b. If Lake owns a 60 percent interest in Boxwood, what total amount of income taxes must be paid by these two companies for the current year?

    c. If Lake owns a 90 percent interest in Boxwood and a consolidated tax return is being filed, what amount of income tax expense would be reported on a consolidated income statement for the year?

    d. Assume that Lake owns a 90 percent interest in Boxwood while Boxwood possesses a 20 percent interest in Lake. Using the conventional approach to mutual ownership, determine the noncontrolling interest in Boxwood's income for the year. Ignore income taxes.

26. Garrison holds a controlling interest in the outstanding stock of Robertson. For the current year, the following information has been gathered about these two companies:

	Garrison	**Robertson**
Operating income	$300,000	$200,000
	(includes a $50,000 net unrealized gain on an intercompany transfer)	
Dividends paid	32,000	50,000
Tax rate	40%	40%

Garrison uses the cost method to account for the investment in Robertson. Dividend income for the current year is not included in Garrison's operating income figure.

Required:

    a. Assume that Garrison owns 80 percent of the voting stock of Robertson. On a consolidated tax return, what amount of income taxes would be paid?

    b. Assume that Garrison owns 80 percent of the voting stock of Robertson. On separate tax returns, what is the total amount of income taxes to be paid?

    c. Assume that Garrison owns 70 percent of the voting stock of Robertson. What is the total amount of income tax expense to be recognized on a consolidated income statement?

    d. Assume that Garrison holds 60 percent of the voting stock of Robertson. On a separate income tax return, what amount of income taxes would Garrison have to pay?

27. Leftwich recently purchased all of the stock of Kew Corporation and is now in the process of consolidating the financial data of this new subsidiary. Leftwich paid a total of $650,000 for the company, which has the following accounts:

	Fair Market Value	Tax Basis
Accounts receivable	$110,000	$110,000
Inventory	130,000	130,000
Land	100,000	100,000
Buildings	180,000	140,000
Equipment	200,000	150,000
Liabilities	220,000	220,000

Assume that the effective tax rate is 30 percent. On a consolidated balance sheet prepared immediately after this takeover, what impact would the acquisition of Kew have on the individual asset and liability accounts reported by the business combination?

28. House Corporation was created in 1950 and has been operating profitably since that time. At the beginning of 2000, House purchased a 70 percent ownership in Room Company. Room's financial accounts as of that date were as follows:

	Book Value	Fair Market Value
Cash and receivables	$300,000	$300,000
Inventory	380,000	380,000
Buildings (20-year life)	200,000	260,000
Equipment (4-year life)	160,000	140,000
Land	260,000	260,000
Liabilities	510,000	510,000

House paid $701,000 in cash for this investment. Any excess purchase price is attributed to franchise contracts to be amortized over a 40-year life.

During 2000 and 2001, Room earned net income totaling $160,000 while paying cash dividends of $50,000.

House has made regular acquisitions of inventory from Room at a markup of 25 percent more than cost. House's purchases during 2000 and 2001 as well as related ending inventory balances are as follows:

Year	Intercompany Purchases	Retained Intercompany Inventory—End of Year
2000	$120,000	$40,000
2001	150,000	60,000

On January 1, 2002, House and Room acted together as coacquirers of 80 percent of the outstanding common stock of Wall Company. The total price of these shares was $200,000, indicating that no goodwill or other specific valuation allocations were needed. Each company put up one-half of this purchase price.

During 2002, House acquired additional inventory at a price of $200,000 from Room. Of this merchandise, 45 percent is still being held at year's end.

Room loaned Wall $40,000 on a 10 percent note on October 1, 2002. Although interest has been properly recorded, no part of this debt has been repaid as of December 31, 2002.

Wall's preferred stock is owned entirely by outside parties. This stock pays an 8 percent annual cumulative dividend. The stock is neither participating nor voting, although it does have a call value of 106 percent of par value. No dividends are currently in arrears on these shares.

Following are the financial records for these three companies for 2002. Prepare a consolidation worksheet. The partial equity method based on *operational earnings* has been applied to each investment.

	House Corporation	Room Company	Wall Company
Sales and other revenues	$ 900,000	$ 700,000	$ 300,000
Cost of goods sold	(551,120)	(300,000)	(140,000)
Operating expenses	(218,400)	(268,400)	(90,000)
Income of Room Company	92,120	–0–	–0–
Income of Wall Company	26,400	26,400	–0–
Net income	$ 249,000	$ 158,000	$ 70,000
Retained earnings, 1/1/02	$ 820,000	$ 590,000	$ 153,000
Net income (above)	249,000	158,000	70,000
Dividends paid	(100,000)	(96,000)	(50,000)
Retained earnings, 12/31/02	$ 969,000	$ 652,000	$ 173,000
Cash and receivables	$ 244,880	$ 354,000	$ 70,000
Inventory	390,200	320,000	103,000
Investment in Room Company	802,920	–0–	–0–
Investment in Wall Company	108,000	108,000	–0–
Buildings	385,000	320,000	144,000
Equipment	310,000	130,000	88,000
Land	180,000	300,000	16,000
Liabilities	632,000	570,000	98,000
Preferred stock	–0–	–0–	50,000
Common stock	820,000	310,000	100,000
Retained earnings, 12/31/02	969,000	652,000	173,000

29. Mighty Company purchased a 60 percent interest in Lowly Company on January 1, 1998, for $400,000 in cash. Lowly's book value at that date was reported as $500,000. Any excess purchase price is assigned to trademarks to be amortized over 20 years. Subsequently, on January 1, 1999, Lowly acquired a 20 percent interest in Mighty. The price of $240,000 was equivalent to 20 percent of Mighty's book value.

Neither company has paid dividends since these acquisitions occurred. On January 1, 2004, Lowly's book value was $800,000, a figure which rises to $840,000 (common stock of $300,000 and retained earnings of $540,000) by the end of the year. Mighty's book value was $1.7 million at the beginning of 2004 and $1.8 million (common stock of $1 million and retained earnings of $800,000) at December 31, 2004. No intercompany transactions have occurred and no additional stock has been sold. Each company applies the cost method in accounting for the individual investments.

Required:

   a. What worksheet entries are required to consolidate these two companies for 2004? What is the noncontrolling interest in the subsidiary's net income for this year? Assume that the treasury stock approach is utilized.

   b. Answer the same questions as in requirement (*a*) but assume that the conventional approach is being applied to the mutual ownership.

   c. How do the answers in requirement (*b*) differ if, on January 1, 2002, Mighty sold equipment (costing $80,000) with a remaining life of 10 years and a $20,000 book value to Lowly for $50,000 in cash?

30. On January 1, 2001, Travers Company purchased 90 percent of the outstanding stock of Yarrow Company. On the same date, Yarrow acquired an 80 percent interest in Stookey Company. Although both of these investments are to be accounted for by applying the cost method, no dividends are distributed by either Yarrow or Stookey during 2001 or 2002. Travers follows a policy of paying out cash dividends each year equal to 40 percent of operational earnings. Reported income totals for 2001 are as follows:

Travers Company	$300,000
Yarrow Company	160,000
Stookey Company	120,000

Any excess payments are attributed to covenant contracts to be amortized over 15 years.

Following are the 2002 financial statements for these three companies. Stookey has made numerous transfers of inventory to Yarrow since the takeover: $80,000 (2001) and $100,000 (2002). These transactions include the same markup applicable to Stookey's outside sales. In each of these years, Yarrow has carried 20 percent of this inventory into the succeeding year before disposing of it.

An effective tax rate of 45 percent is applicable to all companies.

	Travers Company	Yarrow Company	Stookey Company
Sales	$ 900,000	$ 600,000	$ 500,000
Cost of goods sold	(480,000)	(320,000)	(260,000)
Operating expenses	(100,000)	(80,000)	(140,000)
Net income	$ 320,000	$ 200,000	$ 100,000
Retained earnings, 1/1/02	$ 700,000	$ 600,000	$ 300,000
Net income (above)	320,000	200,000	100,000
Dividends paid	(128,000)	–0–	–0–
Retained earnings, 12/31/02	$ 892,000	$ 800,000	$ 400,000
Current assets	$ 423,000	$ 375,000	$ 280,000
Investment in Yarrow Company	741,000	–0–	–0–
Investment in Stookey Company	–0–	349,000	–0–
Land, buildings, and			
equipment (net)	949,000	836,000	520,000
Total assets	$2,113,000	$1,560,000	$ 800,000
Liabilities	$ 721,000	$ 460,000	$ 200,000
Common stock	500,000	300,000	200,000
Retained earnings, 12/31/02	892,000	800,000	400,000
Total liabilities and equities	$2,113,000	$1,560,000	$ 800,000

Required:

a. Prepare the 2002 consolidation worksheet for this business combination. Ignore income tax effects.

b. Determine the amount of income taxes to be paid by Travers and Yarrow on a consolidated tax return for the year 2002.

c. Determine the amount of income taxes to be paid by Stookey on a separate tax return for the year 2002.

d. Based on the answers to requirements (b) and (c), what journal entry would be made by this combination to record 2002 income taxes?

31. Several years ago, Daniel Company purchased 90 percent of the outstanding voting stock of Murphy, Inc. At approximately the same time, Murphy acquired 10 percent of the common stock of Daniel. In both cases, the price paid was equal to the book value and fair market value of the underlying net assets. No allocations were made to either goodwill or specific asset or liability accounts.

Prior to the current year, the book value of Daniel has increased by $400,000 since the date of acquisition while Murphy's book value has risen by $150,000.

Both companies use the cost method to account for their investments.

Required:

Using the following information for the year 2001, prepare a consolidation worksheet based on the conventional approach to mutual holdings.

	Daniel	Murphy
Sales	$ 600,000	$ 220,000
Expenses	(400,000)	(126,000)
Dividend income	18,000	9,000
Net income	$ 218,000	$ 103,000
Retained earnings, 1/1/01	$ 850,000	$ 200,000
Net income	218,000	103,000
Dividends paid	(90,000)	(20,000)
Retained earnings, 12/31/01	$ 978,000	$ 283,000
Cash	$ 20,000	$ 40,000
Receivables	178,000	96,000
Inventory	125,000	108,000
Investment in Murphy	189,000	–0–
Investment in Daniel	–0–	50,000
Property, plant, and equipment (net)	651,000	361,000
Total assets	$1,163,000	$ 655,000
Liabilities	$ 135,000	$ 212,000
Common stock	50,000	160,000
Retained earnings, 12/31/01	978,000	283,000
Total liabilities and equities	$1,163,000	$ 655,000

32. Politan Company acquired an 80 percent interest in Soludan several years ago. Any portion of the purchase price in excess of the corresponding book value of Soludan Company was assigned to trademarks. This intangible asset has subsequently undergone annual amortization based on a 15-year life. In recent years, regular intercompany inventory sales have transpired between the two companies. No payment has yet been made on the latest transfer.

Following are the individual financial statements for the two companies as well as consolidated totals for the current year.

	Politan Company	Soludan Company	Consolidated Totals
Sales	$ 800,000	$ 600,000	$1,280,000
Cost of goods sold	(500,000)	(400,000)	(784,000)
Operating expenses	(100,000)	(100,000)	(202,000)
Income of Soludan	80,000	–0–	–0–
Noncontrolling interest in Soludan Company's income	–0–	–0–	(19,200)
Net income	$ 280,000	$ 100,000	$ 274,800
Retained earnings, 1/1	$ 620,000	$ 290,000	$ 607,600
Net income (above)	280,000	100,000	274,800
Dividends paid	(70,000)	(20,000)	(70,000)
Retained earnings, 12/31	$ 830,000	$ 370,000	$ 812,400
Cash and receivables	$ 290,000	$ 90,000	$ 360,000
Inventory	190,000	160,000	338,000
Investment in Soludan Company	390,000	–0–	–0–
Land, buildings, and equipment	380,000	260,000	640,000
Trademarks	–0–	–0–	22,000
Total assets	$1,250,000	$ 510,000	$1,360,000
Liabilities	$270,000	$ 60,000	$ 310,000
Noncontrolling interest in Soludan Company	–0–	–0–	87,600
Common stock	120,000	80,000	120,000
Additional paid-in capital	30,000	–0–	30,000
Retained earnings (above)	830,000	370,000	812,400
Total liabilities and equities	$1,250,000	$510,000	$1,360,000

Required:

a. By what method is Politan accounting for its investment in Soludan?

b. What is the balance of the unrealized inventory gain being deferred at the end of the current period?

  c. What figure was originally allocated to the trademarks?

  d. What was the amount of the current year intercompany inventory sales?

  e. Were the intercompany inventory sales made upstream or downstream?

  f. What was the balance of the intercompany liability at the end of the current year?

  g. What unrealized gain was deferred into the current year from the preceding period?

  h. The consolidated Retained Earnings account shows a balance of $607,600 rather than the $620,000 reported by the parent. What creates this difference?

  i. How was the ending Noncontrolling Interest in Soludan Company computed?

  j. Assuming a tax rate of 40 percent, what income tax journal entry is recorded if these two companies prepare a consolidated tax return?

  k. Assuming a tax rate of 40 percent, what income tax journal entry is recorded if these two companies prepare separate tax returns?

33. On January 1, 2001, Alpha acquired 80 percent of Delta. Of the total purchase price, $100,000 was allocated to copyrights. Subsequently, on January 1, 2002, Delta obtained 70 percent of the outstanding voting shares of Omega. In this second acquisition, $80,000 of the payment was assigned to copyrights. All copyright balances are being amortized over a 20-year life. Delta had a book value of $490,000 at January 1, 2001, whereas Omega reported a book value of $140,000 on January 1, 2002.

  Delta has made numerous inventory transfers to Alpha since the business combination was formed. Unrealized gains of $15,000 were present in Alpha's inventory as of January 1, 2006. During the year, $200,000 in additional intercompany sales were made with $22,000 in gains remaining unrealized at the end of the period.

  Both Alpha and Delta have utilized the partial equity method to account for their investment balances.

Required:

Following are the individual financial statements for these three companies for the year 2006, along with consolidated totals. Develop the worksheet entries necessary to derive these reported balances.

	Alpha Company	Delta Company	Omega Company	Consolidated Totals
Sales	$ 900,000	$ 500,000	$ 200,000	$1,400,000
Cost of goods sold	(500,000)	(240,000)	(80,000)	(627,000)
Operating expenses	(294,000)	(129,000)	(50,000)	(482,000)
Income of subsidiary	144,000	49,000	–0–	–0–
Noncontrolling interest in income of Delta Company	–0–	–0–	–0–	(33,800)
Noncontrolling interest in income of Omega Company	–0–	–0–	–0–	(21,000)
Net income	$ 250,000	$ 180,000	$ 70,000	$ 236,200
Retained earnings, 1/1/06	$ 600,000	$ 400,000	$ 100,000	$ 550,200
Net income (above)	250,000	180,000	70,000	236,200
Dividends paid	(50,000)	(40,000)	(50,000)	(50,000)
Retained earnings, 12/31/06	$ 800,000	$ 540,000	$ 120,000	$ 736,400
Cash and receivables	$ 262,000	$ 210,000	$ 70,000	$ 522,000
Inventory	290,000	310,000	160,000	738,000
Investment in Delta Company	628,000	–0–	–0–	–0–
Investment in Omega Company	–0–	234,000	–0–	–0–
Property, plant, and equipment	420,000	316,000	270,000	1,006,000
Copyrights	–0–	–0–	–0–	130,000
Total assets	$1,600,000	$1,070,000	$ 500,000	$2,396,000
Liabilities	$600,000	$ 410,000	$ 280,000	$1,270,000
Common stock	200,000	120,000	100,000	200,000
Retained earnings, 12/31/06	800,000	540,000	120,000	736,400
Noncontrolling interest in Delta Company	–0–	–0–	–0–	123,600
Noncontrolling interest in Omega Company	–0–	–0–	–0–	66,000
Total liabilities and equities	$1,600,000	$1,070,000	$ 500,000	$2,396,000

CHAPTER

Segment and Interim Reporting

8

QUESTIONS TO CONSIDER

■ The consolidation process brings together the many, varied components of a business combination to form a single set of financial statements. How can a reader of such statements evaluate the results and prospects of the individual segments that make up the organization?

■ How are the operating segments of a company identified, and how is the significance of each of these units determined?

■ What information must a company disclose in its financial statements about its various operating segments?

■ What information must a company disclose about its products and services, and about its operations in foreign countries?

■ What guidance has the FASB provided to reporting entities concerning disclosure of major customers?

■ What approach should a company take in preparing financial statements for time periods of less than one year?

■ What minimum information should a company disclose in its interim financial reports?

As one of the largest industrial firms in the United States, Philip Morris Companies, Inc., reported consolidated operating revenues of $74.4 billion in 1998.[1] Philip Morris is well-known as a cigarette manufacturer; it is less well-known as a maker of beer and food products. How much of the company's consolidated revenues was generated from these different lines of business? Knowing this could be very useful to potential investors as opportunities for future growth and profitability in these different industries could differ significantly.

To comply with U.S. GAAP, Philip Morris disaggregated its 1998 consolidated operating revenues and reported that the company's revenues were generated from these different ventures; approximately $42.7 billion came from tobacco, $27.3 billion from food, $4.1 billion from beer, and $275 million from financial services and real estate. Additional information disclosed by Philip Morris indicated that $41.4 billion of the 1998 consolidated operating revenues were generated in the United States, $25.2 billion in Europe, and $7.8 billion in other parts of the world.[2] Such information, describing the various components of Philip Morris' operations (both by line of business and by geographic area), often can be more useful to an analyst than the single sales figures reported in the consolidated income statement. "All investors like segment reporting—separate financials for each division—because it enables them to analyze how well each part of a corporation is doing."[3]

---

[1]Philip Morris Companies, Inc., 1998 Annual Report, p. 40.

[2]Philip Morris Companies, Inc., 1998 Annual Report, p. 50.

[3]Robert A. Parker, "How Do You Play the New Annual Report Game?" *Communication World,* September 1990, p. 26.

In its 1998 Annual Report, Philip Morris reported earnings of $5.4 billion for the year ended December 31, 1998. This information was not made available to the public until early in 1999 after the company had closed the books on 1998. To provide more timely information on which investors and could base their decisions about the company, Philip Morris published separate interim reports for each of the first three quarters of 1998. Earnings were $1.4 billion in the first quarter, $1.7 billion in the second quarter, and $2.0 billion in the third quarter, and then earnings dropped precipitously in the fourth quarter to $274 million. Information about the reports of operations for time intervals less than one year can be very useful to an analyst.

In the first part of this chapter, we examine the specific requirements for disaggregating financial statement information as required by the FASB. New rules for reporting segment information went into effect in 1998. Before examining those rules, we trace the history of segment reporting in the United States to better explain the importance of disaggregated information for financial analysts. In the second part of the chapter, we concentrate on the special rules that are required to be applied in the preparation of interim reports. All publicly traded companies in the United States are required to prepare interim reports on a quarterly basis.

SEGMENT REPORTING

To facilitate the analysis and evaluation of financial data, in the 1960s several groups began to push the accounting profession to require disclosure of segment information such as reported by Philip Morris. Not surprisingly, the timing of this movement corresponded with a period of significant corporate merger and acquisition activity. As business organizations expanded through ever-widening diversification, financial statement analysis became increasingly difficult. The broadening of an enterprise's activities into different products, industries, or geographic areas complicates the analysis of conditions, trends, and ratios and, therefore, the ability to predict. The various industry segments or geographic areas of operations of an enterprise may have different rates of profitability, degrees and types of risk, and opportunities for growth.

Because of the increasingly diverse activities of many organizations, disclosure of additional information was sought to help the readers of financial statements. The identity of the significant elements of an entity's operations was viewed as an important complement to consolidated totals. Thus, such organizations as the Financial Analysts Federation and the Financial Executives Institutes provided support for the inclusion of data describing the major components (or segments) of an enterprise as a means of enhancing the informational content of corporate financial statements.

As a result of the demand for disaggregated information, a number of official steps have been taken since the 1960s to encourage or mandate such presentation within financial statements. During this period, the Accounting Principles Board (APB) and the New York Stock Exchange both urged companies to present such data voluntarily. The Securities and Exchange Commission as well as the Federal Trade Commission required the reporting of certain line-of-business information within documents filed with those bodies.

Because of the cost to generate this data and the fear that confidential information would be disclosed to competitors, however, not all reporting corporations agreed with these requirements. "Segment reporting came into being after a vicious battle waged between the Federal Trade Commission and big corporations in the mid-1970s. The corporations fought the FTC's demands for income statements and balance sheets on each of their different lines of business all the way to the Supreme Court, and they lost."[4]

The move toward dissemination of disaggregated information culminated in December 1976 with the release by the FASB of *SFAS 14,* "Financial Reporting for Segments of a Business Enterprise." This pronouncement established guidelines for the presentation within corporate financial statements of information to describe the various segments that constitute each reporting entity.

FASB STATEMENT 14

Specifically, *Statement 14* required financial information to be presented portraying as many as four distinct aspects of a company's operations.

1. *Industry segments.* A company was required to disclose for each reportable industry segment:

    Revenues

    Operating profit or loss

    Identifiable assets

    Aggregate amount of depreciation, depletion, and amortization expense

    Capital expenditures

    Equity in the net income from an investment in the net assets of equity investees

2. *Domestic and foreign operations.* A company had to disclose for domestic operations as well as for operations in each significant foreign geographic area:

    Revenues

    Operating profit or loss

    Identifiable assets

3. *Export sales.* A company reported for domestic operations the amount of revenue derived from exporting products to unaffiliated customers in foreign countries.

4. *Major customers.* A company was required to disclose the amount of revenue derived from sales to each major customer.

Most companies made this information available within the notes to the financial statements. Companies also were allowed to report segment data in the body of the statements or as a separate schedule attached to the financial statements. In addition, some companies, such as the Colgate-Palmolive Company, provided this information in Management's Discussion and Analysis.

As an illustration of the industry segment disclosures required, a note to the 1996 financial statements of General Electric Company indicated that total consolidated revenues of $79.18 billion were generated by the following separately identifiable industry segments (in millions):

---

[4]Dana Wechsler and Katarzyna Wandycz, "'An Innate Fear of Disclosure,'" *Forbes,* February 5, 1990.

GE

Aircraft engines	$ 6,302
Appliances	6,375
Broadcasting	5,232
Industrial products and systems	10,412
Materials	6,509
Power generation	7,257
Technical products and services	4,692
All other	3,108
Corporate items and eliminations	(322)
Total GE	49,565

GECS

Financing	23,742
Specialty insurance	8,966
All other	5
Total GECS	32,713
Eliminations	(3,099)
Consolidated revenues	$79,179

The information reported by General Electric went on to give the operating profit, assets, depreciation and amortization, and the total amount of capital expenditures for each of these segments.

The 1996 annual report of the Hewlett-Packard Company disclosed the following information about its operations in several different geographic areas (in millions):

	Net Revenues	Earnings from Operations	Identifiable Assets
United States	$24,304	$2,470	$14,321
Europe	14,895	769	7,991
Japan, Other Asia Pacific, Canada, Latin America	13,597	1,173	7,200

Data describing industry segments and foreign operations was not the only disaggregated information to be disclosed based on the standards set by *SFAS 14*. As required by this same pronouncement, the financial statements of Caterpillar, Inc., reported that $5.13 billion of its 1995 sales came from exporting products to customers outside of the United States (the largest amount was $1.527 billion to the Asia/Pacific area). The toy manufacturer Hasbro, Inc., also complied with *Statement 14* by disclosing "sales to the Company's two largest customers, Toys R Us, Inc., and Wal-Mart Stores, Inc., amounted to 21 percent and 12 percent, respectively, of consolidated net revenues during each year of 1995 and 1994 and 20 percent and 11 percent, respectively, in 1993."

USEFULNESS OF SEGMENT INFORMATION

As can be seen from these illustrations, *SFAS 14* had a significant impact on the financial reporting process. The goal of reporting segment information is to enhance the usefulness of a corporation's financial statements. With disaggregation, the past and present operational success of each corporate component can be analyzed on an ongoing basis. Lockheed Martin, as an example, disclosed an overall decrease of $53 million in its revenues between 1994 and 1995. However, during that time, three of its five industry segments actually had an increase in revenues totaling more than $1,180 million. Although of significant interest to anyone evaluating the company, this information is not evident from the single revenue figure presented on the consolidated income statement.

Just as important, segment data can assist analysts in predicting the effects of future changes in an organization's environment. For example, if a recession is anticipated for textile manufacturing, the degree of a company's involvement in that industry is vital information to a present or potential investor. Similarly, data describing operations in a particular area of the world is of immediate interest if political turbulence becomes prevalent there.

In its 1993 position paper entitled *Financial Reporting in the 1990s and Beyond,* the Association for Investment Management and Research (formerly the Financial Analysts Federation) left no doubt as to the importance of segment reporting:

> It is vital, essential, fundamental, indispensable, and integral to the investment analysis process. Analysts need to know and understand how the various components of a multifaceted enterprise behave economically. One weak member of the group is analogous to a section of blight on a piece of fruit; it has the potential to spread rot over the entirety. Even in the absence of weakness, different segments will generate dissimilar streams of cash flows to which are attached disparate risks and which bring about unique values. Thus, without disaggregation, there is no sensible way to predict the overall amounts, timing, or risks of a complete enterprise's cash flows. There is little dispute over the analytic usefulness of disaggregated financial data (pages 59 and 60).

A substantial body of academic research has empirically investigated the usefulness of *SFAS 14* disclosures. Some of the major findings are

- Industry segment data improve analysts' accuracy in predicting consolidated sales and earnings; this is true for both large and small firms.
- The availability of industry segment data leads to greater consensus among analysts regarding their forecasts of sales and earnings.
- Segment *revenue* data (both industry and geographic) appear to be more useful than segment *earnings* data in making forecasts.
- The initial disclosure of geographic area data was used by stock market participants in assessing the riskiness of companies with foreign operations.[5]

When considered as a whole, the extant research clearly indicates that *SFAS 14* segment data have been useful to investors and creditors in evaluating the risk and return associated with investment or lending alternatives.

Notwithstanding the fact that in complying with *SFAS 14* companies provided information useful to external users of financial statements, financial analysts have consistently requested that information be disaggregated to a much greater degree than was done in practice. In its 1993 position paper referred to earlier, the AIMR indicated that "There is no disagreement among AIMR members that segment information is totally vital to their work. There also is general agreement among them that the current segment reporting standard, *Financial Accounting Standard No. 14,* is inadequate."[6] The AICPA's Special Committee on Financial Reporting echoed this sentiment by stating that "[users] believe that many companies define industry segments too broadly for business reporting and thus report on too few industry segments."[7]

One area of concern was the flexibility with which industry segments could be identified, especially when management determined that the company had a "dominant industry segment." *SFAS 14* provided that where a single segment made up more than 90 percent of a company's revenues, operating profit or loss, and identifiable assets,

---

[5]For an extensive review of the relevant literature, see Paul Pacter, *Reporting Disaggregated Information* (Stamford, CT: FASB, February 1993), pp. 131–202.

[6]Association for Investment Management and Research, *Financial Reporting in the 1990s and Beyond* (Charlottesville, VA: AIMR, 1993), page 5.

[7]American Institute of Certified Public Accountants, *Improving Business Reporting—A Customer Focus* (New York: AICPA, 1994). p. 69.

industry segment disclosures were not required. As an example, McDonald's Corporation, one of the largest corporations in the world, reported in its 1996 annual report that the company "operates exclusively in the food service industry," and thereby avoided providing industry segment information.[8]

Despite the apparent diversity of U.S. businesses, companies with dominant industry segments have been very common. In a survey of 600 companies, the AICPA's *Accounting Trends and Techniques* found that only 306 of these organizations reported industry segment revenues in their 1997 annual report.[9] The remainder must have viewed themselves as operating primarily in only one industry.

Both the AIMR and the AICPA's special committee recommended that segment reporting be aligned with internal reporting with segments defined on the basis of how an enterprise is organized and managed. Segments based on an enterprise's internal organization structure would have four advantages:

1. Knowledge of an enterprise's organization structure is valuable because it reflects the risks and opportunities believed to be important by management.

2. The ability to see the company the way it is viewed by management improves an analyst's ability to predict management actions that can significantly affect future cash flows.

3. Because segment information already is generated for management's use on the basis of the company's internal structure, the incremental cost of providing that information externally should be minimal.

4. Segments based on an existing internal structure should be less subjective than segments based on the term *industry*.[10]

Other recommendations for improving segment reporting made by the AIMR include:

■ Disclose segment information in interim financial statements.

■ Disclose revenues and profit by product or service line, even if the company is deemed to operate in only one industry.

■ Provide additional guidance as to how segments should be identified with the objectives to (1) disaggregate the company into more segments, (2) enhance the comparability of segments across companies, and (3) make segments consistent with the segmentation used by management in making decisions.

■ Disclose more information—such as cash flows, liabilities, net assets, cost of goods sold, and interest expense.

■ Disclose what is in segments designated as "other."

■ Provide more descriptive information about the segments.

In 1992, at the request of the AIMR, the AICPA Special Committee on Financial Reporting, and others, the FASB and the Accounting Standards Board (AcSB) in Canada decided to jointly reconsider segmental reporting with the objective of developing common standards that would apply in both the United States and Canada. After several years of study, in January 1996, the FASB issued an Exposure Draft for a Proposed Statement of Financial Accounting Standards entitled "Reporting Disaggregated Information about a Business Enterprise." The AcSB also issued an exposure draft identical in its applicable requirements to the FASB's proposed statement. In addition, the IASC issued an Exposure Draft on this topic which, while not identical, is similar to the FASB's. Members of both the FASB and the AcSB participated in IASC meetings on segment reporting to exchange views.

---

[8]McDonald's Corporation, 1996 Annual Report, p. 39.

[9]American Institute of Certified Public Accountants, *Accounting Trends and Techniques*—1997, 52nd ed. (New York: AICPA, 1998), p. 27.

[10]FASB, Proposed Statement of Financial Accounting Standards, "Reporting Disaggregated Information about a Business Enterprise," 1996, para. 66–67.

DISCUSSION QUESTION

Does IBM Really Have Only One Industry Segment?

Not all corporations have readily embraced segment reporting. All disclosure has a cost; gathering and monitoring information for each segment may not be cheap. In addition, some companies fear that such data could be useful to their competitors. One solution is to define the company as having only one segment so that disaggregation is not required. With the very flexible guidelines established in *SFAS 14* for identifying segments, many companies were able to avoid presenting segment information in this manner.

Consider IBM. As befits its size, the $63 billion (estimated 1989 sales) computer company is in several lines of business, including personal computers, mainframes, electronic mail systems and semiconductors (IBM's semiconductor facilities rank among the world's largest). How is each of these segments doing? That's hard to say. IBM reports figures for a grand total of one segment, called "information-processing systems, software, communications systems and other products and services." ... Does anybody care? They should. Says Eugene Glazer, technology analyst at Dean Witter Reynolds: "Investors need to know how a company is doing in each major business. Maybe one business is so dominant and earning such huge profits that it's masking errors in other businesses."[11]

To be fair, although under *SFAS 14* IBM indicated that a single segment "represents more than 90 percent of consolidated revenue, operating profit, and identifiable assets," it nevertheless voluntarily disaggregated revenues "by classes of similar products or services within the information technology segment." However, data on operating profit, assets, depreciation, and capital expenditures were not similarly disaggregated. Should the FASB tighten up its rules on defining segments to ensure that all companies present appropriately disaggregated information?

In June 1997, *FASB Statement 131,* "Disclosures about Segments of an Enterprise and Related Information," was approved. Effective for fiscal years beginning after December 15, 1997, this statement makes substantial changes to the segment disclosures required to be provided by U.S. companies. There is a significant change in *how reportable segments are determined,* as well as in the *amount and types of information* to be provided.

FASB STATEMENT 131

According to *SFAS 131,* the objective of segment reporting is to provide information about the different business activities in which an enterprise engages and the different economic environments in which it operates to help users of financial statements:

- Better understand the enterprise's performance.
- Better assess its prospects for future net cash flows.
- Make more informed judgments about the enterprise as a whole (para. 3).

The Management Approach

To achieve this objective, *SFAS 131* has adopted the so-called management approach for determining segments. The management approach is based on the way that management disaggregates the enterprise for making operating decisions. These disaggregated components are *operating segments,* which will be evident from the enterprise's organization structure. More specifically, an operating segment is a component of an enterprise:

- That engages in business activities from which it earns revenues and incurs expenses.

---

[11]Wechsler and Wandycz, "'An Innate Fear of Disclosure,'" p. 126.

- Whose operating results are regularly reviewed by the chief operating decision maker to assess performance and make resource allocation decisions.
- For which discrete financial information is available.

An organizational unit can be an operating segment even if all of its revenue or expense results from transactions with other segments as might be the case in a vertically integrated company. However, not all parts of a company will necessarily be included in an operating segment. For example, a research and development unit that incurs expenses but does not earn revenues would not be an operating segment. Similarly, corporate headquarters might not earn revenues or might earn revenues that are only incidental to the activities of the enterprise and therefore would not be considered an operating segment.

For many companies, only one set of organizational units qualifies as operating segments. In some companies, however, business activities are disaggregated in more than one way and multiple sets of reports are used by the chief operating decision maker. For example, a company might generate reports by geographic region *and* by product line. In those cases, two additional criteria must be considered to identify operating segments:

1. An operating segment has a segment manager who is directly accountable to the chief operating decision maker for its financial performance. If more than one set of organizational units exists, but there is only one set for which segment managers are held responsible, that set constitutes the operating segments.
2. If segment managers exist for two or more overlapping sets of organizational units (as in a matrix form of organization), the nature of the business activities must be considered, and the organizational units based on products and services constitute the operating segments. For example, if certain managers are responsible for different product lines and other managers are responsible for different geographic areas, the enterprise components based on products would constitute the operating segments.

DETERMINING REPORTABLE OPERATING SEGMENTS

After a company has identified its operating segments based on its internal reporting system, management must decide which of these segments should be reported separately. Generally, information must be reported separately for each operating segment that meets one or more quantitative thresholds established in *SFAS 131*. *However, if two or more operating segments have essentially the same business activities in essentially the same economic environments, information for those individual segments may be combined.* "For example, a retail chain may have 10 stores that individually meet the definition of an operating segment, but each store is essentially the same as the others."[12] In that case, the Board believes that the benefit to be derived from separately reporting each operating segment would not justify the cost of disclosure. In determining whether business activities and environments are similar, management must consider these aggregation criteria:

1. The nature of the products and services provided by each operating segment.
2. The nature of the production process.
3. The type or class of customer.
4. The distribution methods.
5. If applicable, the nature of the regulatory environment.

Segments must be similar in each and every one of these areas to be combined. However, aggregation of similar segments is not required.

---

[12]*FASB Statement 131,* "Disclosures about Segments of an Enterprise and Related Information," June 1997, para. 73.

Quantitative Thresholds

After determining whether any segments are to be aggregated, management next must determine which of its operating segments are significant enough to justify separate disclosure. In *Statement 131,* the FASB decided to retain the three tests introduced in *SFAS 14* for identifying operating segments for which separate disclosure is required:

■ A revenue test.
■ A profit or loss test.
■ An asset test.

An operating segment needs to satisfy only one of these tests to be considered of significant size to necessitate separate disclosure.

To apply these three tests, a segment's revenues, profit or loss, and assets must be determined. *SFAS 131* does not stipulate a specific measure of profit or loss, such as operating profit or income before taxes, to be used in applying these tests. Instead, the measure of profit used by the chief operating decision maker in evaluating operating segments is to be used. An operating segment is considered to be significant if it meets any one of the following tests:

1. *Revenue test.* Segment revenues, both external and intersegment, are 10 percent or more of the combined revenue, internal and external, of all reported operating segments.
2. *Profit or loss test.* Segment profit or loss is 10 percent or more of the greater (in absolute terms) of the combined reported profit of all profitable segments or the combined reported loss of all segments incurring a loss.
3. *Asset test.* Segment assets are 10 percent or more of the combined assets of all operating segments.

Application of the revenue and asset tests would seem to pose few problems. In contrast, the profit or loss test is more complicated and warrants illustration. For this purpose, assume that the Durham Company has five separate operating segments with the following profits or losses:

Durham Company Segments—Profits and Losses

Soft drinks	$1,700,000
Wine	(600,000)
Food products	240,000
Paper packaging	880,000
Recreation parks	(130,000)
Net operating profit	$2,090,000

Three of these industry segments (soft drinks, food products, and paper packaging) report profits that total $2,820,000. The two remaining segments have losses for the year in the amount of $730,000.

Profits		**Losses**	
Soft drinks	$1,700,000	Wine	$600,000
Food products	240,000	Recreation parks	130,000
Paper packaging	880,000		
Total	$2,820,000	Total	$730,000

Consequently, $2,820,000 serves as the basis for the profit or loss test because that figure is greater in absolute terms than $730,000. Based on the 10 percent threshold, any operating segment with either a profit *or loss* of more than $282,000 (10% × $2,820,000) is considered material and, thus, must be disclosed separately. According to this one test, the soft drink and paper packaging segments (with operating profits of

$1.7 million and $880,000, respectively) are both judged to be reportable as is the wine segment, despite having a loss of $600,000.

Operating segments that do not meet any of the quantitative thresholds may be combined to produce a reportable segment if they share a *majority* of the aggregation criteria listed earlier. For Durham Company, the food products and recreation parks operating segments would not meet any of the aggregation criteria. Operating segments that are not individually significant and that cannot be aggregated with other segments are combined and disclosed in an *all other* category. The sources of the revenues included in the All Other category must be disclosed.

TESTING PROCEDURES—COMPLETE ILLUSTRATION

To provide a comprehensive example of all three of these testing procedures, assume that the Atkinson Company is a large business combination comprised of six operating segments: automotive, furniture, textbook, motion picture, appliance, and finance. Complete information about each of these segments, as reported internally to the chief operating decision maker, appears in Exhibit 8–1.

The Revenue Test In applying the revenue test to the operating segments of the Atkinson Company, the combined revenue of all segments must be determined:

Operating Segment	Total Revenues
Automotive	$41.6
Furniture	9.0
Textbook	6.8
Motion picture	22.8
Appliance	5.3
Finance	12.3
Combined total	$97.8

Exhibit 8–1   Reportable Segment Testing

ATKINSON COMPANY						
	Automotive	Furniture	Textbook	Motion Picture	Appliance	Finance
Revenues:						
Sales to outsiders	$32.6*	$6.9	$6.6	$22.2	$3.1	–0–
Intersegment transfers	6.6	1.2	–0–	–0–	1.9	–0–
Interest revenue—outsiders	2.4	.9	.2	.6	.3	8.7
Interest revenue—intersegment loans	–0–	–0–	–0–	–0–	–0–	3.6
Total revenues	$41.6	$9.0	$6.8	$22.8	$5.3	$12.3
Expenses:						
Operating expenses—outsiders	$17.1	$3.6	$7.3	$24.0	$3.6	$ 2.3
Operating expenses—intersegment transfers	4.8	1.0	–0–	–0–	.8	.8
Interest expense	2.1	1.0	2.2	4.6	–0–	6.1
Income taxes	6.6	1.4	(1.5)	(3.1)	.4	.1
Total expenses	$30.6	$7.0	$8.0	$25.5	$4.8	$ 9.3
Assets:						
Tangible	$ 9.6	$1.1	$.8	$10.9	$.9	$ 9.2
Intangible	1.8	.2	.7	3.6	.1	–0–
Intersegment loans	–0–	–0–	–0–	–0–	–0–	5.4
Total assets	$11.4	$1.3	$1.5	$14.5	$1.0	$14.6

*All figures in millions.

Because these six segments have total revenues of $97.8 million, that figure is used in applying the revenue test. Based on the 10 percent significance level, any segment with revenues of more than $9.78 million qualifies for required disclosure. Accordingly, the automotive, the motion picture, and finance segments all have satisfied this particular criterion. Appropriate disaggregated information, therefore, must be presented within Atkinson's financial statements for each of these three operating segments.

The Profit or Loss Test   The profit or loss of each operating segment is determined by subtracting segment expenses from total segment revenues. *SFAS 131* does not require common costs to be allocated to individual segments to determine segment profit or loss if this is not normally done for internal purposes. For example, an enterprise that accounts for pension expense only on a consolidated basis is not required to allocate pension expense to each operating segment. Any allocations that are made must be done on a reasonable basis. Moreover, segment profit or loss does not have to be calculated in accordance with generally accepted accounting principles if the measure reported internally is calculated on another basis. To assist the readers of financial statements in understanding segment disclosures, *SFAS 131* does require disclosure of any differences in the basis of measurement between segment and consolidated amounts.

Each operating segment's profit or loss is calculated as follows:

Operating Segment	Total Revenues	Total Expenses	Profit	Loss
Automotive	$41.6*	$30.6	$11.0	–0–
Furniture	9.0	7.0	2.0	–0–
Textbook	6.8	8.0	–0–	$ 1.2
Motion picture	22.8	25.5	–0–	2.7
Appliance	5.3	4.8	.5	–0–
Finance	12.3	9.3	3.0	–0–
Totals	$97.8	$85.2	$16.5	$ 3.9

*All figures are in millions.

The $16.5 million total (the four profit figures) is greater in an absolute sense than the $3.9 million in losses. Therefore, this larger balance serves as the basis for the second quantitative test. Because the FASB has again established a 10 percent criterion, either a profit or loss of $1.65 million or more qualifies a segment for disaggregation. According to the income totals just calculated, the automotive, furniture, motion picture, and finance segments of the Atkinson Company are large enough to warrant separate disclosure.

The Asset Test   The final test designed by the FASB is based on the operating segments' combined total assets:

Operating Segment	Assets
Automotive	$11.4
Furniture	1.3
Textbook	1.5
Motion picture	14.5
Appliance	1.0
Finance	14.6
Combined total	$44.3

Because 10 percent of the combined total equals $4.43 million, any segment holding at least that amount of assets is viewed as a reportable segment. Consequently, according to this final significance test, the automotive, motion picture, and finance segments are each considered of sufficient size to require disaggregation. The three remaining segments do not have sufficient assets to pass this particular test.

Analysis of Test Results   A summary of all three significance tests as applied to the Atkinson Company is as follows:

Operating Segments	Revenue Test	Profit or Loss Test	Asset Test
Automotive	✔	✔	✔
Furniture		✔	
Textbook			
Motion picture	✔	✔	✔
Appliance			
Finance	✔	✔	✔

Four of this company's operating segments (automotive, furniture, motion picture, and finance) have been determined to be separately reportable. Because neither the appliance nor the textbook segments have met any of these three tests, disaggregated information describing their *individual* operations is not required. However, the financial data accumulated from these two nonsignificant segments still has to be presented. The figures can be combined and disclosed as aggregate amounts in an All Other category with appropriate disclosure of the source of revenues.

OTHER GUIDELINES

Several other FASB guidelines apply to the disclosure of operating segment information. These rules are designed to ensure that the disaggregated data is consistent from year to year and relevant to the needs of financial statement users. For example, any operating segment that has been reportable in the past and is judged by management to be of continuing significance should be disclosed separately in the current statements regardless of the outcome of the testing process. This degree of flexibility is included within the rules to assure the ongoing usefulness of the disaggregated information, especially for comparison purposes.

In a similar manner, if an operating segment newly qualifies for disclosure in the current year, prior period segment data presented for comparative purposes must be restated to reflect the newly reportable segment as a separate segment. Once again, the comparability of information has been given high priority in setting the standards for disclosure.

One final issue raised by *SFAS 131* concerns the number of operating segments that should be disclosed. To enhance the value of the disaggregated information, a substantial portion of a company's operations should be presented individually. Thus, the FASB has stated that a sufficient number of segments is presumed to be included only if their combined sales to unaffiliated customers is at least 75 percent of total company sales made to outsiders. If this lower limit is not achieved, additional segments must be disclosed separately despite their failure to satisfy even one of the three quantitative thresholds.

As an illustration, assume that the Brendan Corporation has identified seven industry segments that have generated revenues as follows (in millions):

Operating Segments	Sales to Unaffiliated Customers	Intersegment Transfers	Segment Revenues (and percent of total)	
Housewares	$ 5.5	$ 1.6	$ 7.1	(9.3%)
Toys	6.2	–0–	6.2	(8.1%)
Pottery	3.4	7.9	11.3	(14.8%) ✔
Lumber	6.6	10.4	17.0	(22.3%) ✔
Lawn mowers	7.2	–0–	7.2	(9.4%)
Appliances	2.1	6.2	8.3	(10.9%) ✔
Construction	19.2	–0–	19.2	(25.2%) ✔
Totals	$50.2	$26.1	$76.3	(100%)

Based on the 10 percent revenue test, four of these segments are reportable (because each has total revenues of more than $7.63 million): pottery, lumber, appliances, and construction. Assuming that none of the other segments qualify as significant in either of the two remaining tests, disclosure of disaggregated data is required only for these four segments. However, the FASB's 75 percent rule has not been met; the reportable segments generate just 62.4 percent of the company's total sales to unrelated parties (in millions):

Reportable Segments	Sales to Unaffiliated Customers
Pottery	$ 3.4
Lumber	6.6
Appliances	2.1
Construction	19.2
Total	$31.3

Information being disaggregated: $31.3 million/$50.2 million = 62.4%

To satisfy the 75 percent requirement, Brendan Corporation must also include the lawn mower segment within the disaggregated data being presented. With the addition of this nonsignificant segment, sales to outside parties of $38.5 million ($31.3 + $7.2) now are disclosed. This figure amounts to 76.7 percent of the company total ($38.5 million/$50.2 million). The two remaining segments—housewares and toys— could still be included separately within the disaggregated data; disclosure is not prohibited. However, information for these two segments would probably be combined and reported as aggregate figures.

One final aspect of these reporting requirements should be mentioned. Some companies might be organized in such a fashion that there exists a relatively large number of operating segments. The FASB suggests there may be a practical limit to the number of operating segments that should be reported separately. Beyond that limit, the information becomes too detailed to be of use. *SFAS 131* (para. 24) indicates that "Although no precise limit has been determined, as the number of segments that are reportable . . . increases above 10, the enterprise should consider whether a practical limit has been reached."

INFORMATION TO BE DISCLOSED BY OPERATING SEGMENT

Consistent with requests from the financial analyst community, *SFAS 131* has significantly expanded the amount of information to be disclosed for each operating segment:

1. *General information* about the operating segment:
   - Factors used to identify operating segments.
   - Types of products and services from which each operating segment derives its revenues.

2. *Segment profit or loss* and the following revenues and expenses included in segment profit or loss:
   - Revenues from external customers.
   - Revenues from transactions with other operating segments.
   - Interest revenue and interest expense (reported separately); net interest revenue may be reported for finance segments if this measure is used internally for evaluation.
   - Depreciation, depletion, and amortization expense.
   - Other significant noncash items included in segment profit or loss.
   - Unusual items (discontinued operations and extraordinary items).
   - Income tax expense or benefit.

3. *Total segment assets* and the following related items:

- Investment in equity method affiliates.
- Expenditures for additions to long-lived assets.

Although requested by the AIMR, the FASB does not specifically require cash flow information to be reported for each operating segment because this information often is not generated by segment for internal reporting purposes. The requirement to disclose noncash items other than depreciation is an attempt to provide information that might enhance users' ability to estimate cash flow from operations.

SFAS 131 need not be applied to immaterial items. For example, some segments do not have material amounts of interest revenue and expense, and therefore disclosure of these items of information would not be necessary. In addition, if an item of information is not generated by the internal financial reporting system on a segment basis, that item need not be disclosed. This is consistent with the FASB's desire that segment reporting creates as little additional cost to an enterprise as possible.

To demonstrate how the operating segment information might be disclosed, let us return to the Atkinson Company example referred to earlier in this chapter. Application of the quantitative threshold tests resulted in four separately reportable segments (automotive, furniture, motion picture, and finance). The nonsignificant operating segments (textbook and appliance) are combined in an All Other category. Exhibit 8–2 shows the operating segment disclosures included in the Atkinson Company's financial statements.

In addition to information provided in Exhibit 8–1, information on depreciation and amortization, other significant noncash items, and expenditures for long-lived segment assets has been gathered for each operating segment to comply with the disclosure requirements. Only the automotive segment has other significant noncash items, and none of the segments has equity method investments. Atkinson Company had no unusual items during the year.

To determine whether a sufficient number of segments is included, the ratio of combined sales to unaffiliated customers for the separately reported operating segments must be compared with total company sales made to outsiders. The combined amount

Exhibit 8–2   Operating Segment Disclosures

ATKINSON COMPANY					
	Operating Segment				
	Automotive	**Furniture**	**Motion Picture**	**Finance**	**All Other**
Revenues from external customers	$32.6*	$6.9	$22.2	$—	$ 9.7
Intersegment revenues	6.6	1.2	—	—	1.9
Segment profit (loss)	11.0	2.0	(2.7)	3.0	.1
Interest revenue	2.4	.9	—	—	.2
Interest expense	2.1	1.0	4.6	—	2.2
Net interest revenue	—	—	—	6.2	—
Depreciation and amortization	2.7	1.5	2.4	.9	.4
Other significant noncash items:					
Cost in excess of billings on long-term contracts	.8	—	—	—	—
Income tax expense (benefit)	6.6	1.4	(3.1)	.1	(1.1)
Segment assets	11.4	1.3	14.5	14.6	2.5
Expenditures for segment assets	3.5	.4	3.7	1.7	1.3

*All figures in millions.

of revenues from external customers disclosed for the automotive, furniture, motion picture, and finance segments is $61.7 million. Total revenues from external customers is $71.4 million:

$$\$61.7 \text{ million}/\$71.4 \text{ million} = 86.4\%.$$

Because 86.4 percent exceeds the lower limit of 75 percent imposed by the FASB, the level of disaggregation reported by Atkinson Company is adequate.

Reconciliations to Consolidated Totals

As noted earlier, *SFAS 131* does not require that disaggregated information be provided in accordance with generally accepted accounting principles. Instead, information is to be provided as it is prepared by the company's internal reporting system even if not based on GAAP. "Preparing segment information in accordance with the generally accepted accounting principles used at the consolidated level would be difficult because some generally accepted accounting principles are not intended to apply at a segment level" (*SFAS 131,* para 84). Examples are the accounting for inventory on a LIFO basis when inventory pools include items in more than one segment, accounting for companywide pension plans, and accounting for purchased goodwill. Accordingly, allocation of these items to individual operating segments is not required.

However, the total of the reportable segments' revenues must be reconciled to consolidated revenues and the total of reportable segments' profit or loss must be reconciled to income before tax for the company as a whole. Adjustments and eliminations that have been made to develop enterprise financial statements in compliance with generally accepted accounting principles must be identified. Examples would be the elimination of intersegment revenues and an adjustment for companywide pension expense. The same is true for reconciliation of total segments' assets to the enterprise's total assets.

In addition, in reconciling the total of segments' revenues, profit or loss, and assets to the enterprise totals, the aggregate amount of revenues, profit or loss, and assets from immaterial operating segments must be disclosed. The company also must disclose assets, revenues, expenses, gains, losses, interest expense, and depreciation, depletion, and amortization expense for components of the enterprise that are not operating segments. This would include, for example, assets and expenses associated with corporate headquarters. An example of how these reconciliations might be made by Atkinson Company is presented in Exhibit 8–3.

There are three adjustments that Atkinson Company must make in reconciling segment results with consolidated totals. The first adjustment is the elimination of intercompany revenues, profit or loss, and assets that are not included in consolidated totals. The elimination of intersegment revenues includes intersegment transfers amounting to $9.7 million plus $3.6 million of intersegment interest revenue generated by the finance segment. The second adjustment relates to corporate items that have not been allocated to the operating segments. These include purchased goodwill, a litigation settlement received by the company, and corporate headquarters expenses and assets. The third adjustment reconciles differences in segment accounting practices from accounting practices used in the consolidated financial statements. The only adjustment of this nature made by Atkinson Company is related to the accounting for pension expense. Individual operating segments measure pension expense based on cash payments made to the pension plan. Because GAAP requires pension expense to be measured on an accrual basis, an adjustment for the amount of pension expense to be recognized in the consolidated statements is necessary.

In addition to the operating segment disclosures and reconciliation of segment results to consolidated totals, companies also must provide an explanation of the measurement of segment profit or loss and segment assets. This explanation should include a description of any differences in measuring segment profit or loss and consolidated

Exhibit 8–3
Reconciliation of Segment
Results to Consolidated
Totals

ATKINSON COMPANY	
Revenues	
Total segment revenues	$ 97.8*
Elimination of intersegment revenues	(13.3)
Total consolidated revenues	$ 84.5
Profit or Loss	
Total segment profit or loss	$ 13.4
Total segment income taxes	3.9
Total segment profit before income taxes	$ 17.3
Elimination of intersegment profits	(2.3)
Unallocated amounts:	
Litigation settlement received	3.6
Other corporate expenses	(2.7)
Adjustment to pension expense in consolidation	(.8)
Consolidated income before income taxes	$ 15.1
Assets	
Total for reported segments	$ 44.3
Elimination of intersegment loans	(5.4)
Goodwill not allocated to segments	3.2
Other unallocated amounts	2.6
Total consolidated assets	$ 44.7

*All figures in millions.

income before tax, any differences in measuring segment assets and consolidated assets, and any differences in measuring segment profit or loss and segment assets. An example of this last item would be where depreciation expense is allocated to segments but the related depreciable assets are not. The basis of accounting for intersegment transactions also must be described.

EXAMPLES OF OPERATING SEGMENT DISCLOSURES

A majority of companies are organized along product and/or service lines. For example, we show operating segment disclosure for American Home Products Corporation in Exhibit 8–4. American Home Products does not disclose interest revenue and interest expense by operating segment as required by *SFAS 131*. As noted earlier, *SFAS 131* need not be applied to immaterial items and interest is likely to fit into this category. Income tax expense or benefit also is not reported by segment because the company evaluates the performance of its operating segments based on income before taxes. A study of 14 early adopters of *SFAS 131* found that half of the companies disclosed more segments under *SFAS 131* than they did under *SFAS 14,* six disclosed the same number, and one reported fewer segments.[13]

Some companies, like McDonald's, Coca-Cola, and Procter & Gamble are organized geographically and define operating segments as regions of the world. For example, Procter & Gamble states in its 1998 Annual Report that the company "is managed in four operating segments: North America, which includes the United States and Canada; Europe, Middle East and Africa; Asia; and Latin America."[14]

---

[13]Nancy Nichols and Donna Street, "Segment Information: What Early Adopters Reported," *Journal of Accountancy,* January 1999, pp. 37–41.

[14]Procter & Gamble Company, 1998 Annual Report, p. 32.

Exhibit 8–4
Operating Segment
Disclosures in American
Home Products
Corporation's 1998
Annual Report

11. Company Data by Operating and Geographic Segment

The Company has four reportable segments: Pharmaceuticals, Consumer Health Care, Agricultural Products, and Corporate and All Other . . .

The accounting policies of the segments described above are the same as those described in the summary of significant accounting policies. The Company evaluates performance based on income from operations before income taxes after goodwill amortization, special charges, gains on the sales of operating assets and certain other items. It does not include interest expense, net, gains on the sales of businesses, investments and other Corporate assets, certain litigation provisions and other miscellaneous items which are accumulated in Corporate.

The Company's reportable segments are strategic business units that offer different products and services. The reportable segments are managed separately because they manufacture, distribute and sell distinct products and services which require various technologies and marketing strategies.

Company Data by Operating Segment

(in millions)	Years Ended December 31		
	1998	1997	1996
Net Sales to Customers			
Pharmaceuticals	$ 8,901.8*	$ 8,669.1	$ 7,924.0
Consumer health care	2,174.7	2,091.3	2,054.6
Agricultural products	2,194.1	2,119.4	1,988.9
Corporate and all other	192.1	1,316.2	2,120.8
Consolidated total	$13,462.7	$14,196.0	$14,088.3
Income before Taxes			
Pharmaceuticals	$ 2,488.3	$ 2,169.6	$ 2,149.6
Consumer health care	509.7	505.1	426.1
Agricultural products	494.9	429.9	337.7
Corporate and all other	92.6	(289.9)	(157.9)
Consolidated total	$ 3,585.5	$ 2,814.7	$ 2,755.5
Depreciation and Amortization Expense			
Pharmaceuticals	$ 443.8	$ 416.0	$ 386.2
Consumer health care	52.3	40.0	31.3
Agricultural products	153.2	154.8	145.5
Corporate and all other	15.4	91.2	95.1
Consolidated total	$ 664.7	$ 702.0	$ 658.1
Total Assets			
Pharmaceuticals	$11,158.2	$10,758.8	$10,335.3
Consumer health care	1,809.6	1,319.2	1,232.2
Agricultural products	5,026.4	4,763.9	4,727.5
Corporate and all other	3,084.9	3,983.2	4,490.3
Consolidated total	$21,079.1	$20,825.1	$20,785.3
Expenditures for Long-Lived Assets			
Pharmaceuticals	$ 571.3	$ 568.4	$ 471.4
Consumer health care	100.3	95.8	26.0
Agricultural products	119.3	115.8	48.6
Corporate and all other	20.5	111.9	106.2
Consolidated total	$ 811.4	$ 891.9	$ 652.2

*Dollars in millions.

Some companies report a combination of product or services and international segments. Wal-Mart has three operating segments: Wal-Mart Stores, Sam's Club, and International. PepsiCo, Inc., has the following five reportable segments:

Pepsi-Cola	Frito-Lay	Tropicana
■ North America	■ North America	
■ International	■ International	

The nature of the segmentation of these companies provides considerable insight into the manner in which upper management views and evaluates the various parts that make up the consolidated enterprise.

ENTERPRISEWIDE DISCLOSURES

Information about Products and Services

The FASB recognizes that some enterprises are not organized along product or service lines. For example, some enterprises are organized by geographic areas. Moreover, some enterprises may have only one operating segment yet provide a range of different products and services. To provide some comparability between enterprises, *SFAS 131* requires *disclosure of revenues derived from transactions with external customers from each product or service* if operating segments have not been determined based on differences in products or services. An enterprise with only one operating segment also would have to disclose revenues from external customers on the basis of product or service. However, providing this information is not required if impracticable, that is, the information is not available and the cost to develop it would be excessive.

Lowes Companies, Inc., operates in only one segment, but nevertheless, reported "sales by product category" as required under *SFAS 131* in its 1998 annual report. That information is presented in Exhibit 8–5.

Information about Geographic Areas

In addition, the following two items of information must be reported *(1) for the domestic country, (2) for all foreign countries in which the enterprise derives revenues or holds assets, and (3) for each foreign country in which a material amount of revenues is derived or assets are held*:

- Revenues from external customers.
- Long-lived assets.

Geographic area information must be disclosed even if the company has only one operating segment and therefore does not otherwise provide segment information. The previous requirement under *SFAS 14* to disclose *profit or loss* by geographic area no longer exists.

Note that the FASB requires companies to disclose information for *each material country.* Requiring disclosure at the country level is a significant change from *SFAS 14.* The FASB believes reporting information about individual countries rather than larger areas has two benefits. First, it reduces the burden on preparers of financial statements as most operating segments are likely to have material operations in only a few countries. Second, the information is easier to interpret and therefore more useful because individual countries within a geographic area often experience very different rates of economic growth and economic conditions.

Although the FASB considered using a 10 percent rule for determining when a country is material, ultimately it decided to leave this determination to management's judgment. In determining materiality, management should apply the concept that an item is material if its omission could change a user's decision about the enterprise as a whole. The FASB does not provide more specific guidance on this issue.

Exhibit 8–5
Sales by Product Category
in Lowes Companies
1998 Annual Report

Product Category	1998	
	Total Sales	Percent
Fashion plumbing and electrical	$ 1,388*	11%
Tools	1,234	10
Building materials	1,207	10
Lumber	1,186	10
Outdoor hardlines	1,165	10
Major appliances/kitchens	1,115	9
Hardware	922	8
Millwork	908	8
Floors, windows, and walls	790	6
Rough plumbing and electrical	784	6
Paint and sundries	752	6
Nursery and gardening products	669	5
Electronics	125	1
Totals	$12,245	100%

*Dollars in millions.

The change in geographic area reporting under *SFAS 131* has resulted in some companies providing more information than under *SFAS 14* and other companies providing less information. Exhibit 8–6 presents the current year geographic area disclosures made by E.I. du Pont de Nemours and Company in the 1997 and 1998 annual reports. In complying with *SFAS 131,* DuPont has defined materiality at a very low amount; for example, less than 2 percent of total net sales are generated in Mexico. By reporting by individual country in 1998, DuPont clearly provides more detailed information than was provided previously. A limitation in the requirements of *SFAS 131,* however, is the fact that operating income is no longer required to be reported by geographic area.

Geographic area information reported by International Business Machines Corporation in its 1997 and 1998 annual reports is presented in Exhibit 8–7. The change from reporting by geographic segment under *SFAS 14* to reporting by material country under *SFAS 131* has resulted in less detail being provided by IBM with regard to the location of non-U.S. revenues. In 1998, the company disclosed the fact that 44 percent of its revenue is generated in the United States and 10 percent is generated in Japan, but there is no disclosure with regard to the location of the remaining 46 percent of revenues generated in other foreign countries.

Information about Major Customers

One final but important disclosure requirement originally established by *SFAS 14* has been retained in *Statement 131.* A reporting entity must indicate its reliance on any major customer. *Presentation of this information is required whenever 10 percent or more of a company's revenues are derived from a single customer.* The existence of all major customers must be disclosed along with the related amount of revenues and the identity of the operating segment earning the revenues. Interestingly enough, the company need not reveal the identity of the customer.

An example of how this information is disclosed can be found in the 1999 annual report for the Briggs & Stratton Corporation. Note 4 to the financial statements indicated that significant sales had been made to three "major engine customers that individually exceeded 10 percent of total Company net sales. The sales to these customers are summarized on the following page. (in thousands of dollars and percent of total Company sales:"

Exhibit 8–6

Comparison of DuPont's 1997 and 1998 Geographic Area Disclosures

E. I. DU PONT DE NEMOURS AND COMPANY
1997 Geographic Information

	United States	Europe	Other Regions	Consolidated
Sales to unaffiliated customers	$24,648*	$15,389	$5,042	$45,079
Transfers between geographic areas	3,108	625	832	–0–
Total	$27,756	$16,014	$5,874	$45,079
After-tax operating income	$1,346	$1,306	$126	$2,778
Identifiable assets at December 31	$20,015	$11,346	$5,242	$36,603

1998 Geographic Information

	Net Sales	Net Property
North America		
United States	$13,075	$8,454
Canada	881	459
Mexico	421	117
Other	93	135
Total	$14,470	$9,165
Europe, Middle East, and Africa		
Germany	$1,450	$388
United Kingdom	988	1,078
France	904	181
Italy	902	5
Other	2,108	1,188
Total	$6,352	$2,840
Asia Pacific		
Japan	$820	$159
Taiwan	591	707
China	398	208
Singapore	86	635
Other	947	244
Total	$2,842	$1,953
South America		
Brazil	$659	$83
Other	444	90
Total	$1,103	$173
Total	$24,767	$14,131

*Dollars in millions.

Customer	1999 Sales	1999 Percent	1998 Sales	1998 Percent	1997 Sales	1997 Percent
A	$250,755	17%	$235,552	18%	$282,428	21%
B	219,209	14	203,931	15	180,770	14
C	161,857	11	165,937	13	142,840	11
	$631,821	42%	$605,420	46%	$606,038	46%

Exhibit 8–7
Comparison of IBM's 1997
and 1998 Geographic Area
Disclosures

INTERNATIONAL BUSINESS MACHINES CORPORATION
1997 Geographic Information

United States
Revenue—Customers	$32,663*
Interarea transfers	9,426
Total	$42,089
Net earnings	2,354
Assets at December 31	41,633

Europe, Middle East, Africa
Revenue—Customers	$23,919
Interarea transfers	2,513
Total	$26,432
Net earnings	1,343
Assets at December 31	21,006

Asia Pacific
Revenue—Customers	$15,246
Interarea transfers	3,475
Total	$18,721
Net earnings	1,788
Assets at December 31	11,984

Americas
Revenue—Customers	$ 6,680
Interarea transfers	4,407
Total	$11,087
Net earnings	586
Assets at December 31	7,628

1998 Geographic Information

	Revenues	Long-lived Assets
United States	$35,303*	$18,450
Japan	8,567	4,310
Other non-U.S. countries	37,797	12,343
Total	$81,667	$35,103

*Dollars in millions.

Of 600 companies surveyed in *Accounting Trends and Techniques,* 111 indicated the existence of a major customer in their 1998 annual report.[15]

Statement 131 indicates that major customer disclosures are required even if a company operates only in one segment and therefore does not provide segment information (as is the case for Briggs and Stratton). Also, to avoid any confusion, "a group of entities under common control shall be considered as a single customer, and the federal government, a state government, a local government (for example, a county or municipality), or a foreign government shall each be considered as a single customer" (*SFAS 131,* para. 39).

In addition to requiring information about major customers, *SFAS 14* also required information about export sales. Providing information on export sales, however, is no longer necessary under *Statement 131.*

---

[15]AICPA, *Accounting Trends and Techniques—1998,* p. 23.

INTERIM REPORTING

To provide investors and creditors with more timely information than is provided by an annual report, companies provide financial information for periods of time less than one year. The U.S. Securities and Exchange Commission (SEC) requires publicly traded companies in the United States to provide financial statements on a quarterly basis. Unlike annual financial statements, financial statements included in quarterly reports filed with the SEC need not be audited. This allows companies to disseminate the information to investors and creditors as quickly as possible.

APB Opinion No. 28 was issued in 1973 to provide guidance to companies as to how to prepare interim statements. That opinion has stood the test of time with only two subsequent authoritative pronouncements related to interim reporting. *FASB Statement No. 3* amends *APB Opinion No. 28* with regard to the reporting of accounting changes in interim statements, and *FASB Interpretation No. 18* clarifies the application of *APB Opinion No. 28* with regard to income taxes.

Determining the results of operations for time periods less than one year has some inherent problems associated with it, especially with regard to expenses that do not occur evenly throughout the year. Two approaches can be followed in preparing interim reports: (1) treat the interim period as a **discrete** accounting period, standing on its own, or (2) treat it as an **integral** portion of a longer period. The distinction between these two approaches can be seen by considering the annual bonus paid by a company to key employees in December of each year. Under the *discrete* period approach, the entire bonus is recorded as an expense in December, reducing fourth quarter income only. Under the *integral* part of an annual period approach, a portion of the bonus to be paid in December is accrued as an expense in each of the first three quarters of the year. Obviously, application of the integral approach requires an estimate of the annual bonus to be made early in the year and a method for allocating the bonus to the four quarters of the year must be developed. The advantage of this approach is that there is less volatility in quarterly earnings as irregularly occurring costs are spread out over the entire year.

APB Opinion No. 28 requires companies to treat interim periods as integral parts of an annual period rather than as discrete accounting periods in their own right. Generally speaking, interim financial statements should be prepared following the same accounting principles and practices used in the preparation of annual statements. However, for several items, deviation from this general rule is necessary for the interim statements to better reflect the expected annual amounts. Special rules related to revenues, inventory and cost-of-goods-sold, other costs and expenses, extraordinary items, income taxes, accounting changes and seasonal items are discussed in turn below.

Revenues

Revenues should be recognized in interim periods in the same way as they are recognized on an annual basis. For example, revenue from long-term construction projects accounted for under the percentage of completion for annual purposes should also be recognized in interim statements on a percentage of completion basis. Moreover, projected losses on long-term contracts should be recognized to their full extent in the interim period in which it becomes apparent that a loss will arise.

Inventory and Cost of Goods Sold

Interim period accounting for inventory and cost of goods sold requires several modifications to procedures used on an annual basis. The modifications related to (1) a LIFO liquidation, (2) application of the lower-of-cost-or-market rule, and (3) standard costing.

1. *LIFO liquidation*—companies using the last-in, first-out (LIFO) cost flow assumption to value inventory experience a LIFO liquidation at the end of an interim

period when the number of units of inventory sold exceeds the number of units added to inventory during the period. When prices are rising, the matching of beginning inventory cost (carried at low LIFO amounts) against the current period's sales revenue results in an unusually high amount of gross profit. If, by year-end, the company expects to replace the units of beginning inventory sold, then on an annual basis, there will be no LIFO liquidation. In that case, gross profit for the interim period should not reflect the temporary LIFO liquidation and inventory reported on the interim balance sheet should include the expected cost to replace the beginning inventory sold.

To illustrate, assume that Liquid Products Company began the first quarter with 100 units of inventory that cost $10 per unit. During the first quarter, 200 units were purchased at a cost of $15 per unit, and sales of 240 units at $20 per unit were made. During the first quarter, the company experiences a liquidation of 40 units of beginning inventory. Gross profit would be calculated as follows:

Sales (240 units @ $20)		$4,800
Cost of goods sold		
200 units @ $15	$3,000	
40 units @ $10 (LIFO historical cost)	400	3,400
Gross profit		$1,400

However, during the second quarter, the company expects to replace the units of beginning inventory sold at a cost of $17 per unit, and inventory at year-end is expected to be at least 100 units. Therefore, gross profit for the first quarter is calculated as follows:

Sales (240 units @ $20)		$4,800
Cost of goods sold		
200 units @ $15	$3,000	
40 units @ $17 (replacement cost)	680	3,680
Gross profit		$1,120

The journal entry to record cost of goods sold in the first quarter is as follows:

Cost of goods sold	$3,680	
Inventory		$3,400
Excess of replacement cost over historical cost of LIFO liquidation		280

To record cost of goods sold with a historical cost of $3,400 and an excess of replacement cost over historical cost for beginning inventory liquidated of $280 [($17 − $10) × 40 units].

2. *Lower-of-cost-or-market*—if at the end of an interim period, the market value of inventory is less than its cost, inventory should be written down and a loss recognized so long as the decline in market value is deemed to be permanent. However, if the market value is expected to recover above the inventory's original cost by the end of the year, inventory should not be written down at the interim balance sheet date. Instead, inventory should continue to be carried at cost.

3. *Standard costing*—planned price, volume, or capacity variances arising from the use of a standard cost system that are expected to be absorbed by the end of the annual period should not be reflected in interim financial statements. Unplanned variances should be reported at the end of the interim period in the same fashion as they would be in the annual financial statements.

Other Costs and Expenses

Costs and expenses that are not directly matched with revenues should be charged to income in the interim period in which they occur unless they can be identified with activities or benefits of other interim periods. In that case, the cost should be allocated among interim periods on a reasonable basis through the use of accruals and deferrals. For example, assume that a company required to prepare quarterly financial statements pays annual property taxes of $100,000 on April 10. One-fourth of the estimated property tax should be accrued as expense in the first quarter of the year. When payment is made, one-fourth is applied against the accrued property tax payable from the previous quarter and one-fourth is charged to second-quarter income. One-half of the payment is deferred as a prepaid expense to be allocated to the third and fourth quarters of the year. The following journal entries demonstrate the procedures for ensuring that one-fourth of the annual payment is recognized as expense in each quarter of the year.

March 31

Property Tax Expense...............................	25,000	
Accrued Property Tax Payable......................		25,000
To accrue one-fourth of the estimated annual property tax as expense for the quarter ended March 31.		

April 10

Accrued Property Tax Payable.........................	25,000	
Property Tax Expense.................................	25,000	
Prepaid Property Tax (Current Asset).....................	50,000	
Cash		100,000
To record the payment of the annual property tax, recognize one-fourth as property tax expense for the quarter ending June 30, and defer one-half as a prepaid expense.		

September 30

Property Tax Expense...............................	25,000	
Prepaid Property Tax		25,000
To record property tax expense for the quarter ended September 30.		

December 31

Property Tax Expense...............................	25,000	
Prepaid Property Tax		50,000
To record property tax expense for the quarter ended December 31.		

Other items requiring similar treatment include annual major repairs and advertising. In addition, a number of adjustments normally made at year-end actually relate to the entire year such as bad debt expense, executive bonuses, and quantity discounts based on annual sales volume. To the extent that the annual amounts can be estimated, adjustments should be made at the end of each interim period so that the interim periods bear a reasonable portion of the expected annual amount.

Extraordinary Items

Extraordinary gains and losses should be reported separately and in full in the interim period in which they occur. Gains and losses are deemed extraordinary if they are: (1) unusual in nature, (2) infrequent in occurrence, and (3) material in amount. The materiality of extraordinary items should be determined by comparing the amount of the gain or loss to the expected income for the full year. Unusual and infrequent gains and losses that are material to the interim period but not to the year as a whole should be disclosed separately. Likewise gains and losses on the disposal of a segment of the business should be disclosed separately in the interim period in which the disposal takes place.

For example, assume that Charleston Company incurred a hurricane loss of $100,000 in the first quarter of 2001 that is deemed to be both unusual and infrequent. First-quarter income before subtracting the hurricane loss is $800,000, and annual income is expected to be $10 million. The loss is clearly material with respect to first-quarter income (12.5%) but is not considered material for the year as a whole (1%). Charleston Company should not label this loss as an extraordinary item on its first-quarter income statement, but it nevertheless should separately disclose the loss (either as a separate line item on the income statement or in the notes).

Contingencies should be disclosed in interim reports the same way as they are disclosed in annual reports. The contingency should continue to be reported in subsequent interim and annual reports until it is resolved or becomes immaterial. Materiality should be judged with respect to the year as a whole.

Income Taxes

Income tax related to ordinary income should be computed at an estimated *annual* effective tax rate. At the end of each interim period, a company makes its best estimate of the effective tax rate for the entire year. The effective tax rate reflects anticipated tax credits, foreign tax rates, and tax planning activities for the year. This rate is then applied to the pretax ordinary income earned to date during the year, resulting in the cumulative income tax expense to be recognized to date. The difference between the cumulative income tax recognized to date and income tax recognized in earlier interim periods is the amount of income tax expense recognized in the current interim period.

Assume that Viertel Company estimated its effective annual tax rate at 42 percent in the first quarter of 2001. Pretax income for the first quarter was $500,000. At the end of the second quarter of 2001, the company expects its effective annual tax rate will be only 40 percent because of the planned usage of foreign tax credits. Pretax income in the second quarter of 2001 is also $500,000. There are no items requiring net-of-tax presentation in either quarter. The income tax expense recognized in each of the first two quarters of 2001 is determined as follows:

First Quarter

Pretax income for first quarter of 2001	$ 500,000
Estimated annual income tax rate	42%
Income tax expense	$ 210,000

Second Quarter

Pretax income for first quarter of 2001	$500,000	
Pretax income for second quarter of 2001	500,000	
Year-to-date income statement		$1,000,000
Estimated annual income tax rate		40%
Year-to-date income tax expense		$ 400,000
Income tax expense recognized in first quarter		210,000
Income tax expense recognized in second quarter		$ 190,000

The same process is followed for the third and fourth quarters of the year.

Income tax related to those special items reported net-of-tax (extraordinary items, discontinued operations, and cumulative effect of a change in accounting principle) should be individually computed and recognized when the item occurs. *FASB Interpretation No. 18* explains that the income tax on an interim period special item is calculated at the margin as the difference between income tax on income including this item and income tax on income excluding this item.

Cumulative Effect Accounting Changes

The appropriate treatment in interim reports of the effects of a change in accounting principle is governed by *FASB Statement No. 3,* "Reporting Accounting Changes in Interim Financial Statements." Generally, a change in accounting principle requires a company to recalculate previous years' income based on the new accounting principle and include the cumulative effect in income in the year of change.[16] When a cumulative effect type accounting change occurs in the first interim period, the entire cumulative effect is included in income of the first interim period. If an accounting change is made in other than the first interim period, no cumulative effect is included in income for that period. Instead, income for the first interim period of the year is restated to include the cumulative effect of the accounting change. In addition, income must be restated for all prechange interim periods to reflect the change in accounting principle. For example, assume a company makes a change in its accounting policies in the third quarter of 2001. Income for the first quarter of 2001 must be restated (1) to include the estimated cumulative effect of having applied the new policy through the end of 2000 and (2) to recognize the effect of the accounting change on first quarter income. Second-quarter income also would be restated to reflect the effect of the accounting change.

Illustration of Cumulative Effect Change Made in First Interim Period   Assume that Wechsel Corporation adopts an accelerated method of depreciation for new equipment as well as for previously acquired equipment in the first quarter of 2001. In the past, the straight-line method was used. The effective income tax rate is 40 percent. Depreciation under the new and old methods is as follows:

	Straight-line Depreciation	Accelerated Depreciation	Difference	After-tax Difference
Prior to 2000	$80,000	$150,000	$70,000	$42,000
1st quarter 2000	20,000	36,000	16,000	9,600
2nd quarter 2000	20,000	32,000	12,000	7,200
3rd quarter 2000	20,000	28,000	8,000	4,800
4th quarter 2000	20,000	24,000	4,000	2,400
	$80,000	$120,000	$40,000	$24,000
1st quarter 2001	$20,000	$ 22,000	$ 2,000	$ 1,200

Income before the cumulative effect of accounting change is:

1st quarter 2000	$ 600,000
2nd quarter 2000	800,000
3rd quarter 2000	700,000
4th quarter 2000	760,000
....	$2,860,000
1st quarter 2001	$ 840,000*

*Calculated after deducting $22,000 based on the new depreciation method.

Wechsel has 100,000 shares of common stock outstanding. The cumulative effect of accounting change would be handled in the first quarter income statements for 2000 and 2001 in the following manner:

---

[16]In certain situations, such as a change in accounting for long-term construction contracts, a change in accounting principle is handled retroactively by restating previous periods' income; a cumulative effect is not reported. In addition, because it is impractical to calculate, a cumulative effect is not required for a change to the LIFO method.

	Three Months Ended March 31	
	2000	**2001**
Income before cumulative effect of accounting change	$600,000	$840,000
Cumulative effect of accounting change (net of income tax of $44,000)	–0–	(66,000)†
Net income	$600,000	$774,000
Per share amounts:		
Income before cumulative effect of accounting change	$ 6.00	$ 8.40
Cumulative effect of accounting change	–0–	(.66)
Net income	$ 6.00	$ 7.74
Pro forma amounts assuming the new depreciation method is applied retroactively:		
Net income	$576,000‡	$840,000
Net income per common share	$ 5.76	$ 8.40

†Calculated as the after-tax difference between straight-line and accelerated depreciation for the period prior to 2000 ($42,000) plus the difference in 1999 ($24,000).

‡Calculated as 2000 net income as originally reported ($600,000) less the after-tax difference between straight-line and accelerated depreciation for the year 2000 ($24,000).

Cumulative Effect Change Made in Other than First Interim Period   Assume the same facts as in the previous illustration except that the change in depreciation method takes place in the second quarter of 2001. Information for the second quarter of 2001 is as follows:

	Second Quarter
Income before the cumulative effect of an accounting change	$880,000
Straight-line depreciation	$ 20,000
Accelerated depreciation	21,000
Difference	$ 1,000
After-tax difference	$ 600

The manner in which the cumulative effect of accounting change would be reported in the second quarter of 2001, with year-to-date information, and comparative information for similar periods of 2000 is as follows:

	Three Months Ended June 30		Six Months Ended June 30	
	2000	**2001**	**2000**	**2001**
Income before cumulative effect of accounting change	$800,000	$880,000	$1,400,000	$1,720,000
Cumulative effect of accounting change (net of income tax of $44,000)	–0–	–0–	–0–	(66,000)
Net income	$800,000	$880,000	$1,400,000	$1,654,000
Per share amounts:				
Income before cumulative effect of accounting change	$ 8.00	$ 8.80	$ 14.00	$ 17.20
Cumulative effect of accounting change	–0–	–0–	–0–	(.66)
Net income	$ 8.00	$ 8.80	$ 14.00	$ 16.54

(continued)

	Three Months Ended June 30		Six Months Ended June 30	
	2000	**2001**	**2000**	**2001**
Pro forma amounts assuming the new depreciation method is applied retroactively:				
Net income	$790,400*	$880,000	$1,383,200†	$1,720,000
Net income per common share	$ 7.90	$ 8.80	$ 13.83	$ 17.20

*Calculated as $800,000 income for the second quarter 2000 less the $9,600 after-tax difference in depreciation for that quarter.

†Calculated as $1,400,000 ($600,000 + $800,000) income for the six months ended June 30, 2000 less the after-tax difference in depreciation of $16,800 ($9,600 + $7,200) for that period.

Net income as originally reported in the first quarter of 2001 must be restated to reflect: (1) the change in depreciation method adopted in the second quarter, and (2) the cumulative effect of the accounting change on net income of prior periods. The effect of the accounting change on the first quarter of 2001 income is as follows:

	Three Months Ended March 31, 2001
Net income as originally reported	$841,200‡
Effect of change in depreciation method	(1,200)
Income before cumulative effect of accounting change	$840,000
Cumulative effect on prior years of accounting change (net of income tax of $44,000)	(66,000)
Net income as restated	$774,000
Per share amounts:	
Net income as originally reported	$ 8.41
Effect of change in depreciation method	(.01)
Income before cumulative effect of accounting change	$ 8.40
Cumulative effect on prior years of accounting change	(.66)
Net income as restated	$ 7.74

‡First-quarter income was originally determined by subtracting $20,000 of straight-line depreciation; based on accelerated depreciation of $22,000, first-quarter income is reduced by $1,200 (the after-tax difference in depreciation).

Seasonal Items

Some companies experience significant seasonal variation in their sales volume. Manufacturers of summer sports equipment, for example, are likely to have a significant upward spike in sales during the second quarter of the year. To avoid the risk that investors and creditors are misled into believing that second-quarter earnings are indicative of earnings for the entire year, *APB Opinion No. 28* requires companies to disclose the seasonal nature of their business operations. In addition, such companies should supplement their interim reports with reports on the 12-month period ended at the interim date for both the current and preceding years.

MINIMUM DISCLOSURES IN INTERIM REPORTS

Many companies provide summary financial statements and notes in their interim reports that contain less information than is included in the annual financial statements. *APB Opinion No. 28* requires companies to provide the following minimum information in their interim reports:

a. Sales or gross revenues, provision for income taxes, extraordinary items, cumulative effect of change in accounting principles, and net income.

Quarterly Financial Data (Unaudited)				
	Quarters in 1998			
	Fourth	**Third**	**Second**	**First**
Sales and other operating revenues	$17,099*	$12,721	$13,389	$12,945
Earnings from operations	602	430	416	119
Net earnings	465	347	258	50
Basic earnings per share	.49	.36	.26	.05
Diluted earnings per share	.48	.36	.26	.05
Cash dividends per share	.14	.14	.14	.14
Market price:				
High	44.00	50.13	56.25	54.75
Low	29.50	30.38	42.13	42.81
Quarter end	32.63	34.31	44.56	52.13
*Dollars in millions except per share data.				

b. Earnings per share.

c. Seasonal revenues and expenses.

d. Significant changes in estimates or provisions for income taxes.

e. Disposal of a segment of a business and unusual or infrequently occurring items.

f. Contingent items.

g. Changes in accounting principles or estimates.

h. Significant changes in financial position.

APB Opinion No. 28 also encourages, but does not require, publication of balance sheet and cash flow information in interim reports. If this information is not included, significant changes since the last period in cash and cash equivalents, net working capital, long-term liabilities, and stockholders' equity must be disclosed.

Companies that provide interim reports on a quarterly basis are not required to publish a fourth-quarter report because this coincides with the end of the annual period. When separate fourth-quarter financial statements are not provided, special accounting items occurring in the fourth quarter should be disclosed in the notes to the annual financial statements. These items include extraordinary or unusual and infrequently occurring items, disposals of a segment of the business, the cumulative effect of a change in accounting principles, and the aggregate effect of year-end adjustments that are material to the results of the fourth quarter.

The SEC requires selected quarterly financial data to be included in a company's annual report to shareholders. Quarterly data provided by the Boeing Company in its 1998 Annual Report is shown in Exhibit 8–8.

SEGMENT INFORMATION IN INTERIM REPORTS

The management approach to determining operating segments should result in less costly disclosure because this information, by definition, already is collected by management. Since the information is readily available, *Statement 131* also requires segment disclosures to be made in interim reports. This was one of the major recommendations made by the AIMR for improving segment reporting. The following items of information are required to be included in interim reports for each operating segment:

■ Revenues from external customers.

■ Intersegment revenues.

- Segment profit or loss.
- Total assets, if there has been a material change from the last annual report.

In addition, total segments' profit or loss must be reconciled to the enterprise's total income before taxes, and any change from the last annual report in the basis on measurement of segment profit or loss must be disclosed. Requiring only a few items of information in interim reports is a compromise between the desire of users to have the same information as is provided in annual financial statements and the cost to preparers who must report the information.

The FASB does not require segment information to be provided in interim financial statements until the second year that a company applies *SFAS 131*. Without a full set of segment information in an annual report to compare with, the Board believes that segment information in interim reports would be less meaningful. There is no requirement to provide information about geographic areas or major customers in interim reports.

SUMMARY

1. The consolidation of information from many, varied companies into a set of consolidated financial statements tends to camouflage the characteristics of the individual components. Consequently, during the 1960s, several groups made a strong push to require that disaggregated information be included as an integral part of financial reporting to provide a means for analyzing the components of a business combination.

2. The move toward dissemination of disaggregated information culminated in 1976 with the release by the FASB of *Statement 14,* "Financial Reporting for Segments of a Business Enterprise." This pronouncement established guidelines for the required presentation of information describing the various segments that make up a reporting entity. *SFAS 14* required disclosure of information on as many as four distinct aspects of a company's operations: industry segments, geographic segments, export sales, and sales to major customers.

3. Over the years since *SFAS 14* was introduced, financial analysts consistently requested that financial statements be disaggregated to a much greater degree than was done in practice. In direct response to the criticisms and suggestions made by the financial analyst community, the FASB issued a new standard for segment reporting in 1997— *SFAS 131*.

4. *SFAS 131* adopts a so-called management approach in which operating segments are based on a company's organization structure and internal reporting system. The management approach should enhance the usefulness of segment information as it highlights the risks and opportunities that management believes are important and allows the analyst to see the company through the eyes of management. This approach also has the advantage of reducing the cost of providing segment information because that information already is being produced for internal use.

5. Once operating segments have been identified, a company must determine which of these segments is of significant magnitude to warrant separate disclosure. *SFAS 131* created three quantitative threshold tests to be applied to identify reportable segments: a revenue test, a profit or loss test, and an asset test. A segment need satisfy only one of these tests to be considered of sufficient size to necessitate disclosure. Each test is based on identifying segments that meet a 10 percent minimum of the related combined total. The profit and loss test has a 10 percent criterion based on the greater (in an absolute sense) of the total profit from all segments with profits or the total loss from all segments with losses.

6. For each reportable operating segment, several types of information must be reported: selected revenues, profit or loss, selected expenses, assets, capital expenditures, and equity method investment and income. Revenues from external customers must be reported separately from intersegment revenues. In addition, the types of products and services from which each segment derives its revenues must be disclosed.

7. *SFAS 131* establishes a set of parameters for the number of segments that should be reported by an enterprise. As a minimum, the separately disclosed units must generate at least 75 percent of the total sales made to unaffiliated parties. For an upper limit, the pronouncement suggests that the disclosure of more than 10 operating segments reduces the usefulness of the information.

8. Companies are required to reconcile the total of all segments' revenues, profit or loss, and assets to the consolidated totals. The major reconciliation adjustments relate to intercompany revenues, profit or loss, and assets eliminated in consolidation; revenues, profit or loss, and assets that have not been allocated to individual operating segments; and differences in accounting methods used by segments and in preparing consolidated financial statements.

9. *SFAS 131* requires several enterprisewide disclosures. If an enterprise does not define operating segments internally on a product line basis or has only one operating segment, disclosure of revenues derived from each product or service is required.

10. In addition, revenues from external customers and long-lived assets must be reported for the domestic country, for each foreign country in which a material amount of revenues is generated or assets are held, and for all foreign countries in total. *SFAS 131* does not provide any threshold tests for determining when operations in a foreign country are material.

11. Disclosure of one other type of information is required by *SFAS 131*. The reporting entity must indicate the existence of major customers whenever 10 percent or more of consolidated revenues are derived from a single unaffiliated party.

12. For interim reporting purposes, *APB Opinion No. 28* requires time intervals of less than one year to be treated as an integral part of the annual period.

13. Costs and expenses that are not directly matched with revenues should be charged to income in the interim period in which they occur unless they can be identified with activities or benefits of other interim periods. In that case, the cost should be allocated among interim periods on a reasonable basis through the use of accruals and deferrals. Items related to the whole year but only recorded as an adjustment at year-end should be estimated and accrued in each interim period of the year.

14. Extraordinary gains and losses should be reported separately and in full in the interim period in which they occur. The materiality of extraordinary items should be determined by comparing the amount of the gain or loss to the expected income for the full year. Unusual and infrequent gains and losses that are material to the interim period but not to the year as a whole should be disclosed separately.

15. Interim period income-tax expense is determined by applying the estimated annual effective income-tax rate to year-to-date pretax ordinary income, resulting in the cumulative income-tax expense to be recognized to date. The cumulative income tax to be recognized to date less income tax recognized in earlier interim periods is the amount of income-tax expense recognized in the current interim period.

16. When a cumulative effect type accounting change occurs in the first interim period, the entire cumulative effect is included in income of that period. If an accounting change is made in a subsequent interim period, no cumulative effect is included in income for that period. Instead, income for the first interim period of the year is restated to include the cumulative effect of the accounting change.

17. *APB Opinion No. 28* outlines the minimum information to be included in interim reports, including sales, income taxes, extraordinary items, net income, earnings per share, seasonal revenues and expenses, and significant changes in financial position. Publication of balance sheet and cash flow information in interim reports is not required. If this information is not included, significant changes since the last period in cash and cash equivalents, net working capital, long-term liabilities, and stockholders' equity must be disclosed.

18. At financial analysts' request, *SFAS 131* requires certain items of information to be disclosed in interim reports. Specifically, revenues from outside customers, intersegment revenues, and segment profit or loss must be disclosed in interim reports for each operating segment. In addition, total assets must be reported by segment if there has been a material change since the last annual report.

COMPREHENSIVE ILLUSTRATION

Problem

(*Estimated Time: 25 to 40 Minutes*) The Battey Corporation, an enterprise located in the United States, manufactures several different products: natural fibers, synthetic fibers, leather, plastics, and wood. The company is organized into five operating divisions based on these different products. The company has developed a number of subsidiaries that carry on operations throughout the world. At the end of 2001, as part of the internal reporting process the following revenues, profits, and assets (in millions) were reported to the chief operating decision maker:

Revenues by Operating Segment	United States	Canada	Mexico	France	Italy	Brazil
Natural fibers						
Sales to external customers . . .	$1,739	—	$342	$606	—	$1,171
Intersegment sales	—	—	—	—	—	146
Synthetic fibers						
Sales to external customers . . .	290	116	—	—	—	37
Intersegment sales	12	5	—	—	—	—
Leather						
Sales to external customers . . .	230	—	57	—	278	55
Intersegment sales	22	—	9	—	34	9
Plastics						
Sales to external customers . . .	748	286	—	83	92	528
Intersegment sales	21	12	—	—	—	72
Wood						
Sales to external customers . . .	116	22	—	—	—	149
Intersegment sales	17	3	—	—	—	28

Operating Profit or Loss by Operating Segment	United States	Canada	Mexico	France	Italy	Brazil
Natural fibers	$526	—	$92	$146	—	$404
Synthetic fibers	21	8	—	—	—	10
Leather	70	—	27	—	94	24
Plastics	182	74	—	18	24	68
Wood	18	5	—	—	—	37

Assets by Operating Segment	United States	Canada	Mexico	France	Italy	Brazil
Natural fibers	$1,005	—	$223	$296	—	$817
Synthetic fibers	163	50	—	—	—	74
Leather	146	—	41	—	150	38
Plastics	425	173	—	54	58	327
Wood	66	19	—	—	—	143

Required

a. Determine the operating segments that should be reported separately in Battey's 2001 financial statements using the criteria established in *SFAS 131*.

b. Determine the geographic areas for which revenues should be reported separately in Battey's 2001 financial statements. Assume that Battey has elected to define a material country as one in which sales to external customers are 10 percent or more of consolidated sales.

c. Determine the volume of revenues that has to be generated from a single customer to necessitate disclosure of a major customer under *SFAS 131*.

Solution

a. Battey Corporation determines its reportable operating segments by following the three-step process established in *SFAS 131*. First, operating segments are identified. Second, aggregation criteria are examined to determine whether any operating segments may be combined. Third, reportable operating segments are determined by applying the three quantitative threshold tests.

Identification of Operating Segments   Battey's internal reporting system provides information to the chief operating decision maker by operating division and by country. Either of these components conceivably could be identified as operating segments for segment reporting purposes. However, in this type of situation, *SFAS 131* stipulates that the components based on products and services constitute the operating segments. Thus, the five operating divisions are identified as Battey's operating segments.

Aggregation Criteria   The aggregation criteria included in *SFAS 131* are examined next to determine whether any operating segments can be combined. Management determines the economic characteristics of the Natural Fibers and Synthetic Fibers operating divisions to be very similar. In addition, there is considerable similarity with regard to the nature of the product, production process, customers, and distribution methods in these two divisions. Because each of *SFAS 131*'s aggregation criteria are met, Battey elects to combine these two segments into a single Fibers category.

Quantitative Threshold Tests   Determination of Battey's reportable operating segments is dependent on the three materiality tests described in this chapter. The revenue test can be performed directly from the information provided. Any operating segment with total revenues (including intersegment sales) equal to 10 percent or more of combined revenue (internal and external) must be reported separately:

Revenue Test (in millions)

Operating Segments	Total Revenues (including intersegment)	
Fibers	$4,464	60.8%
Leather	694	9.5
Plastics	1,842	25.1
Wood	335	4.6
Total combined revenues	$7,335	100.0%

Reportable segments—fibers and plastics.

The profit or loss test can be carried out next. Any operating segment with profit or loss equal to 10 percent or more of the greater, in absolute amount, of combined segment profit (for those segments with a profit) or combined segment loss (for those segments with a loss) must be reported separately. Because each of Battey's operating segments generated a profit in 2001, this test can be applied by determining the total combined profit:

Profit or Loss Test (in millions)

Operating Segments	Total Profit or Loss	
Fibers	$1,207	65.3%
Leather	215	11.6
Plastics	366	19.8
Wood	60	3.2
Total combined segment profit	$1,848	100.0%

Reportable segments—fibers, leather, and plastics.

Lastly, the asset test is performed:

Asset Test (in millions)

Operating Segments	Total Assets	
Fibers	$2,628	61.6%
Leather	375	8.8
Plastics	1,037	24.3
Wood	228	5.3
Total combined segment assets	$4,268	100.0%

Reportable segments—fibers and plastics.

Based on these three tests, information about the fibers, leather, and plastics operating segments must be reported separately. Information on the immaterial wood segment need not be reported. However, the revenues, profit, and assets of this segment would be included in reconciliations to consolidated totals.

b. Battey must report revenues from external customers for the United States, for all foreign countries, and for each foreign country in which the company generates a material amount of revenues. *SFAS 131* provides no quantitative tests for determining when a foreign country is material; this is left to management's judgment. Battey has decided to define materiality as sales to external customers equal to 10 percent or more of consolidated revenues. This was one of two criteria established in *SFAS 14* for determining significant geographic areas.

Revenue Test (in millions)

Country	Sales to External Customers	
United States	$3,123	45.0%
Canada	424	6.1
Mexico	399	5.8
France	689	9.9
Italy	370	5.3
Brazil	1,940	27.9
Total consolidated revenues	$6,945	100.0%

Using this criterion, Battey would report the United States and Brazil separately, and the remaining countries would be combined into an All Other category. Alternatively, if Battey had established a materiality threshold of 5 percent, each of the foreign countries in which the company generates revenues would be reported separately. Once again, determination of materiality is left to management's judgment.

c. The significance test for disclosure of a major customer is 10 percent of consolidated revenues. Under the guidelines of *SFAS 131*, Battey must report the existence of any major customer from which $694.5 million or more in revenues was generated during 1998.

QUESTIONS

1. How does the consolidation process tend to disguise information needed to analyze the financial operations of a diversified organization?
2. What is disaggregated financial information?
3. *SFAS 14* required many companies to present disaggregated information about several different aspects of current operations. What were the various types of segments that may have required disclosure?
4. What was *SFAS 14*'s dominant industry segment rule and what problem could this rule generate?
5. According to the FASB, what is the major objective of segment reporting?
6. *SFAS 131*'s management approach requires firms to define segments on the basis of the firm's internal organization structure. What are the advantages in defining segments on this basis?
7. What is an operating segment?
8. How are operating segments determined when business activities are disaggregated in more than one way and multiple sets of reports are used by the chief operating decision maker?
9. Describe the three tests for identifying reportable operating segments.
10. What information must an enterprise report for each of its material operating segments?
11. Under what conditions must an enterprise provide information about products and services?
12. Under what conditions must an enterprise provide information about geographic areas?

13.   What information must an enterprise report by geographic area?

14.   To satisfy *SFAS 131*'s geographic area disclosure requirements, what is the minimum and maximum number of countries for which information should be reported separately?

15.   Under what conditions should a company disclose the amount of sales from a major customer?

16.   Why are publicly traded companies in the United States required to prepare interim reports on a quarterly basis?

17.   What approach does *APB Opinion 28* require companies to follow in preparing interim financial statements?

18.   How should a LIFO liquidation be handled in an interim period when the liquidated inventory is expected to be replaced by year-end?

19.   How does a company determine the amount of income tax expense to be reported in an interim period?

20.   According to *SFAS 3*, what procedures must be followed to account for a cumulative effect-type accounting change made in other than the first interim period of the year?

21.   In accordance with *APB Opinion No. 28*, what minimum information must an enterprise provide in an interim report?

22.   According to *SFAS 131*, what type of segment information must be provided in interim financial statements?

INTERNET ASSIGNMENTS

Internet sites are time and date sensitive. It is the purpose of these exercises to have you explore the Internet. You may need to refer to the text's Web site at http://www.mhhe.com/hoyle6e to find the most up-to-date links for the Web sites listed in the Internet Exercises.

1.   Use the Internet to identify the reportable operating segments for each of the following companies:

   Abbott Laboratories (www.abbott.com)
   Anheuser-Busch (www.anheuser-busch.com)
   Cisco Systems (www.cisco.com)
   General Electric (www.ge.com)
   Lockheed Martin (www.lmco.com)

   For each company:

   a.   Determine the two most important segments in terms of percentage of total revenues.
   b.   Determine the two segments with the largest growth in revenues.
   c.   Determine the two most profitable segments in terms of profit margin.

   Assess each company's future prospects based on the operating segment information provided.

2.   Use the Internet to obtain geographic area information for each of the following companies in the pharmaceuticals industry:

   Abbott Laboratories (www.abbott.com)
   Bristol-Myers Squibb (www.bristolmyerssquibb.com)
   Eli Lilly (www.elililly.com)
   Merck (www.merck.com)
   Pfizer (www.pfizer.com)

   Prepare a report describing the comparability of geographic area information across these companies.

LIBRARY ASSIGNMENT

1.   Locate the latest annual reports for two companies generally considered to be competitors. Based solely on the segment information, write a report describing and evaluating the two companies. Possible companies include:

Chemical: DuPont, Dow Chemical, Monsanto, Union Carbide
Pharmaceutical: Merck, Schering-Plough, Pfizer, Eli Lilly
Computer: IBM, Hewlett-Packard, Apple Computer, Compaq, Dell
Food Products: Heinz, Quaker Oats, Sara Lee, Campbell Soup
Automobile: Ford, General Motors
Beverage: Coca-Cola, PepsiCo
Petroleum: Chevron, Texaco, Exxon Mobil

PROBLEMS

1. Which of the following is not considered by the FASB to be an objective of segment reporting?
   a. It helps users better understand the enterprise's performance.
   b. It helps users better assess the enterprise's prospects for future cash flows.
   c. It helps users make more informed judgments about the enterprise as a whole.
   d. It helps users make comparisons between a segment of one enterprise and a similar segment of another enterprise.

2. Under *SFAS* 131, which of the following items of information would Most Company not be required to disclose, even if it were material in amount?
   a. Revenues generated from sales of its Consumer Products line of goods.
   b. Revenues generated by its Japanese subsidiary.
   c. Revenues generated from export sales.
   d. Revenues generated from sales to Wal-Mart.

3. Which of the following operating segment disclosures is not required by *SFAS 131*?
   a. Liabilities.
   b. Interest expense.
   c. Intersegment sales.
   d. Unusual items (extraordinary items and discontinued operations).

4. In determining whether a particular operating segment is of significant size to warrant disclosure, which of the following statements is true?
   a. Three tests are applied and all three must be met.
   b. Four tests are applied and only one must be met.
   c. Three tests are applied and only one must be met.
   d. Four tests are applied and all four must be met.

5. Which of the following statements would not be true under *SFAS 131*?
   a. Operating segments can be determined by looking at a company's organization chart.
   b. Companies may combine individual foreign countries into geographic areas for purposes of complying with the geographic area disclosure requirements.
   c. If operating segments are defined by product lines, companies must provide revenue and asset information for the domestic country and each material foreign country.
   d. Companies must disclose total assets, investment in equity method affiliates, and total expenditures for long-lived assets by operating segment.

6. Which of the following is not necessarily true for an operating segment?
   a. An operating segment earns revenues and incurs expenses.
   b. An operating segment is regularly reviewed by the chief operating decision maker to assess performance and make resource allocation decisions.
   c. Discrete financial information generated by the internal accounting system is available for an operating segment.
   d. An operating segment regularly generates a profit from its normal, ongoing operations.

7. Which of the following is a criterion for determining whether an operating segment is separately reportable?
   a. Segment liabilities are 10 percent or more of consolidated liabilities.
   b. Segment profit or loss is 10 percent or more of consolidated net income.
   c. Segment assets are 10 percent or more of combined segment assets.

     d. Segment revenues from external sales are 5 percent or more of combined segment revenues from external sales.

8. Which of the following statements is true?
   - *a.* *SFAS 131* does not require segment information to be reported in accordance with generally accepted accounting principles.
   - *b.* *SFAS 131* does not require a reconciliation of segment assets to consolidated assets.
   - *c.* *SFAS 131* requires geographic area information to be disclosed in interim financial statements.
   - *d.* *SFAS 131* requires disclosure of the identity of a major customer.

9. The Plume Company has a paper products operating segment. Which of the following items does Plume not have to report for this segment?
   - *a.* Interest expense.
   - *b.* Research and development expense.
   - *c.* Depreciation and amortization expense.
   - *d.* Interest income.

10. Which of the following items is required to be disclosed by geographic area?
    - *a.* Total assets.
    - *b.* Revenues from external customers.
    - *c.* Profit or loss.
    - *d.* Capital expenditures.

11. According to *SFAS 131,* which of the following would be an acceptable grouping of countries for providing information by geographic area?
    - *a.* United States, Mexico, Japan, Spain, All Other Countries.
    - *b.* United States, Canada and Mexico, Germany, Italy.
    - *c.* United States, Taiwan, Japan, Europe.
    - *d.* Canada, Germany, France, All Other Countries.

12. What information should a company present about revenues by geographic area?
    - *a.* Disclose separately the amount of sales to unaffiliated customers and the amount of intracompany sales between geographic areas.
    - *b.* Disclose as a combined amount sales to unaffiliated customers and intracompany sales between geographic areas.
    - *c.* Disclose separately the amount of sales to unaffiliated customers but not the amount of intracompany sales between geographic areas.
    - *d.* No disclosure of revenues from foreign operations need be reported.

    (AICPA adapted)

13. Which of the following items of information must be disclosed with regard to a major customer?
    - *a.* The identity of the customer.
    - *b.* The percentage of total sales derived from the major customer.
    - *c.* The operating segment making the sale.
    - *d.* The geographic area from which the sale was made.

14. In considering interim financial reporting, how did the Accounting Principles Board conclude that such reporting should be viewed?
    - *a.* As a special type of reporting that need not follow generally accepted accounting principles.
    - *b.* As useful only if activity is evenly spread throughout the year so that estimates are unnecessary.
    - *c.* As reporting for a basic accounting period.
    - *d.* As reporting for an integral part of an annual period.

    (AICPA adapted)

15. How should material seasonal variations in revenue be reflected in interim financial statements?
    - *a.* The seasonal nature should be disclosed, and the interim report should be supplemented with a report on the 12-month period ended at the interim date for both the current and preceding years.
    - *b.* The seasonal nature should be disclosed, but no attempt should be made to reflect the effect of past seasonality on financial statements.

    c. The seasonal nature should be reflected by providing pro forma financial statements for the current interim period.

    d. There should be no attempt to reflect seasonality in interim financial statements.

16. For interim financial reporting, an extraordinary gain occurring in the second quarter should be

    a. Recognized ratably over the last three quarters.

    b. Recognized ratably over all four quarters, with the first quarter being restated.

    c. Recognized in the second quarter.

    d. Disclosed by footnote only in the second quarter.

    (AICPA adapted)

17. Which of the following items must be disclosed in interim reports?

    a. Total assets.

    b. Total liabilities.

    c. Cash flow from operating activities.

    d. Gross revenues.

18. Which of the following items is not required to be reported in interim financial statements for each material operating segment?

    a. Revenues from external customers.

    b. Intersegment revenues.

    c. Segment assets.

    d. Segment profit or loss.

19. The Estilo Company has three operating segments with the following information:

	Paper	Pencils	Hats
Sales to outsiders	$8,000	$4,000	$6,000
Intersegment transfers	600	1,000	1,400

In addition, revenues generated at corporate headquarters are $1,000.

    What is the minimum amount of revenue that each of these segments must have to be considered separately reportable?

    a. $1,800.

    b. $1,900.

    c. $2,000.

    d. $2,100.

20. The Carson Company has four separate operating segments:

	Apples	Oranges	Pears	Peaches
Sales to outsiders	$123,000	$81,000	$95,000	$77,000
Intersegment transfers	31,000	26,000	13,000	18,000

What amount of revenues must be generated from one customer before that party must be identified as a major customer?

    a. $37,600.

    b. $41,200.

    c. $46,400.

    d. $56,400.

21. The Jarvis Corporation has six different operating segments reporting the following operating profit and loss figures:

K	$ 80,000 loss	N	$440,000 profit
L	140,000 profit	O	90,000 profit
M	940,000 loss	P	100,000 profit

Which of the following statements is not true?

    a. K is not a reportable segment based on this one test.

    b. L is a reportable segment based on this test.

    c. O is not a reportable segment based on this one test.

    d. P is a reportable segment based on this test.

22. Quatro Corp. is engaged solely in manufacturing operations. The following data pertain to the operating segments for the year 2001.

Operating Segment	Total Revenues	Profit	Assets at 12/31/01
A	$10,000,000	$1,750,000	$20,000,000
B	8,000,000	1,400,000	17,500,000
C	6,000,000	1,200,000	12,500,000
D	3,000,000	550,000	7,500,000
E	4,250,000	675,000	7,000,000
F	1,500,000	225,000	3,000,000
....	$32,750,000	$5,800,000	$67,500,000

In its segment information for 2001, how many reportable segments does Quatro have?
   a. Three.
   b. Four.
   c. Five.
   d. Six.

(AICPA adapted)

23. What is the minimum number of operating segments that must be separately reported?
   a. Ten.
   b. Segments with at least 75 percent of revenues as measured by the revenue test.
   c. At least 75 percent of the segments must be separately reported.
   d. Segments with at least 75 percent of the revenues generated from outside parties.

24. The Medford Company has seven operating segments but only four (G, H, I, and J) are of significant size to warrant separate disclosure. Segments K, L, and M are not large enough. As a whole, these segments have revenues generated from outside parties of $710,000 ($520,000 + $190,000). In addition, the segments had $260,000 in intersegment transfers ($220,000 + $40,000).

	Outside Sales	Intersegment Sales
G	$120,000	$ 80,000
H	150,000	50,000
I	160,000	20,000
J	90,000	70,000
Totals	$520,000	$220,000

	Outside Sales	Intersegment Sales
K	$ 60,000	–0–
L	70,000	$20,000
M	60,000	20,000
Totals	$190,000	$40,000

Which of the following statements is true?
   a. A sufficient number of segments is being reported because those segments have $740,000 in revenues out of a total of $970,000 for the company as a whole.
   b. Not enough segments are being reported because those segments have $520,000 in outside sales out of a total of $710,000 for the company as a whole.
   c. Not enough segments are being reported because those segments have $740,000 in revenues out of a total of $970,000 for the company as a whole.
   d. A sufficient number of segments is being reported because those segments have $520,000 in outside sales out of a total of $710,000 for the company as a whole.

25. Philo Company has estimated that total depreciation expense for the year ending December 31 will amount to $60,000 and that year-end bonuses to employees will amount to $120,000. In Philo's quarterly income statement for the three months ended

June 30, what is the total amount of expense relating to these two items that should be reported?

a. $15,000.
b. $30,000.
c. $45,000.
d. $90,000.

26. Ming Company's $100,000 income for the quarter ended September 30 included the following after-tax items:

- $20,000 of a $40,000 extraordinary loss, realized on August 15; the other $20,000 was allocated to the fourth quarter of the year.

- A $16,000 cumulative effect loss resulting from a change in depreciation method recognized on September 1.

- $12,000 of the $48,000 annual property taxes paid on February 1.

For the quarter ended September 30, the correct amount of net income Ming should report is

a. $80,000.
b. $88,000.
c. $96,000.
d. $116,000.

27. In March 2000, Archibald Company estimated that its year-end bonus to executives would be $1,000,000. The bonus paid to executives in 1999 was $950,000. What amount of bonus expense, if any, should Archibald Company recognize in determining net income for the first quarter of 2000?

a. $0.
b. $237,500.
c. $250,000.
d. $1,000,000.

Use the following information for problems 28 and 29:
On March 15, 2000, Calloway, Inc., paid property taxes of $480,000 for the calendar year 2000.

28. How much of this expense should be reflected in Calloway's income statement for the quarter ending March 31, 2000?

a. $0.
b. $40,000.
c. $120,000.
d. $480,000.

29. The journal entry at March 15, 2000, to record the payment of property taxes would include which of the following?

a. A debit to Property Tax Expense of $480,000.
b. A credit to Cash of $120,000.
c. A debit to Prepaid Property Taxes of $360,000.
d. A credit to Prepaid Property Taxes of $40,000.

Use the following information for problems 30 and 31:
Lifetime Sports, Inc., uses the LIFO cost flow assumption to value inventory. The company began the year 2000 with 1,000 units of inventory carried at LIFO cost of $50 per unit. During the first quarter of 2000, 5,000 units were purchased at an average cost of $80 per unit, and sales of 5,300 units at $1,000 per unit were made.

30. The company does not expect to replace the units of beginning inventory sold; it plans to reduce inventory by year-end 2000 to 500 units. What is the amount of cost of goods sold to be recorded for the quarter ended March 31, 2000?

a. $415,000.
b. $424,000.
c. $424,600.
d. $434,600.

31. The company expects to replace the units of beginning inventory sold in April 2000 at a cost of $82 per unit, and inventory at year-end is expected to be between 1,500 and 2,000 units. What is the amount of cost of goods sold to be recorded for the quarter ended March 31, 2000?

a. $415,000.
b. $424,000.
c. $424,600.
d. $434,600.

32. The Fireside Corporation is organized into four operating segments. The following segment information was generated by the internal reporting system in 2001:

	Revenues from Outsiders	Intersegment Transfers	Operating Expenses
Cards	$1,200,000	$100,000	$ 900,000
Calendars	900,000	200,000	1,350,000
Clothing	1,000,000	—	700,000
Books	800,000	50,000	770,000

Additional operating expenses (of a general nature) incurred by the company amounted to $700,000.

What is the profit or loss of each of these segments? Carry out the profit or loss test to determine which of these segments is separately reportable.

33. The Ecru Company has identified five industry segments: plastics, metals, lumber, paper, and finance. Each of these segments has been consolidated appropriately by the company in producing its annual financial statements. Information describing each segment is presented here (in thousands):

	Plastics	Metals	Lumber	Paper	Finance
Sales to outside parties	$6,319	$2,144	$636	$347	–0–
Intersegment transfers	106	131	96	108	–0–
Interest income from outside parties	–0–	19	6	-0	$ 27
Interest income from intersegment loans	–0–	–0–	–0–	–0–	159
Operating expenses	3,914	1,612	916	579	16
Interest expense	61	16	51	31	87
Tangible assets	1,291	2,986	314	561	104
Intangible assets	72	361	–0–	48	–0–
Intersegment loans	–0–	–0–	–0–	–0–	664

In addition, Ecru has $1,250,000 in common expenses that are not allocated to the various segments.

Required

Perform the testing procedures designed by the FASB to determine the reportable operating segments of the Ecru Company.

34. Following is financial information describing the six operating segments that make up Fairfield, Inc., (in thousands):

	Segments					
	Red	Blue	Green	Pink	Black	White
Sales to outside parties	$1,811	$812	$514	$309	$121	$ 99
Intersegment revenues	16	91	109	–0–	16	302
Salary expense	614	379	402	312	317	62
Rent expense	139	166	81	92	42	31
Interest expense	65	59	82	49	14	5
Income tax expense (savings)	141	87	61	(86)	(64)	–0–

The following questions should be considered independently. Unless specified, none of the six segments has primarily a financial nature.

Required

a. What minimum amount of revenue must be generated by any one segment to be of significant size to require disaggregated disclosure?

b. If only Red, Blue, and Green are of sufficient size to necessitate separate disclosure, is Fairfield disclosing disaggregated data for enough segments?

c. What volume of revenues must be generated from a single client to necessitate disclosing the existence of a major customer?

d. If each of these six segments has a profit or loss (in thousands) as follows, which is of significant size to warrant separate disclosure?

Red	$1,074	Pink	$ (94)
Blue	449	Black	(222)
Green	140	White	308

35. The Mason Company has prepared consolidated financial statements for the current year and is now gathering information in connection with the following five operating segments it has identified.

Determine the reportable segments by carrying out each of the applicable tests. Also describe the procedure utilized to ensure that a sufficient number of segments is being separately disclosed. (Figures are in thousands.)

	Company Total	Books	Computers	Maps	Travel	Finance
Sales to outside parties	$1,547	$121	$696	$416	$314	–0–
Intersegment sales	421	24	240	39	188	–0–
Interest income—external	97	60	–0–	–0–	–0–	$37
Interest income— intersegment loans	147	–0–	–0–	–0–	–0–	147
Assets	3,398	206	1,378	248	326	1,240
Operating expenses	1,460	115	818	304	190	33
Expenses—intersegment sales	198	70	51	31	46	–0–
Interest expense—external	107	–0–	–0–	–0–	–0–	107
Interest expense— intersegment loans	177	21	71	38	47	–0–
Income tax expense (savings)	21	12	(41)	27	31	(8)
General corporate expenses	55					
Unallocated operating costs	80					

36. In the past, the Slatter Corporation has operated primarily in the United States. However, a few years ago, the company opened a plant in Spain to produce merchandise that is sold within that country. This foreign operation has been so successful that during the past 24 months, the company also started a manufacturing plant in Italy as well as another in Greece. Financial information for each of these facilities follows:

	Spain	Italy	Greece
Sales	$395,000	$272,000	$463,000
Intersegment transfers	–0–	–0–	62,000
Operating expenses	172,000	206,000	190,000
Interest expense	16,000	29,000	19,000
Income taxes	67,000	19,000	34,000
Long-lived assets	191,000	106,000	72,000

The company's domestic (U.S.) operations reported the following information for the current year:

Sales to unaffiliated customers	$4,610,000
Intersegment transfers	427,000
Operating expenses	2,410,000
Interest expense	136,000
Income taxes	819,000
Long-lived assets	1,894,000

Slatter has adopted the following criteria for determining the materiality of an individual foreign country: (1) sales to unaffiliated customers within a country are 10 percent or more of consolidated sales, or (2) long-lived assets within a country are 10 percent or more of consolidated long-lived assets.

Required

Apply the materiality tests adopted by Slatter to determine those countries to be reported separately.

37. Noventis Corporation prepared the following estimates for the four quarters of 2001:

	First Quarter	Second Quarter	Third Quarter	Fourth Quarter
Sales	$1,000,000	$1,200,000	$1,400,000	$1,600,000
Cost of goods sold	400,000	480,000	550,000	600,000
Administrative costs	250,000	155,000	160,000	170,000
Advertising costs	–0–	100,000	–0–	–0–
Executive bonuses	–0–	–0–	–0–	80,000
Provision for bad debts	–0–	–0–	–0–	52,000
Annual maintenance costs	60,000	–0–	–0–	–0–

Additional information:

First-quarter administrative costs include the annual insurance premium of $100,000.
Advertising costs paid in the second quarter relate to television advertisements that will be broadcast throughout the entire year.
There are no special items affecting income during the year.
Noventis estimates an effective income tax rate for the year of 40 percent.

Required

  a. Assuming that actual results do not vary from the estimates provided above, determine the amount of income to be reported each quarter of 2001.
  b. Assume that actual results do not vary from the estimates provided above except that in the third quarter, the estimated annual effective income tax rate is revised downward to 38 percent. Determine the amount of income to be reported each quarter of 2001.

38. In the quarter ending June 30, 2001, Mudar Company, Inc., adopted the straight-line method of depreciation for new machinery as well as for previously acquired machinery. In the past, an accelerated method of depreciation was used. Income before the cumulative effect of accounting change and depreciation under the new and old methods is as follows:

	Income before Cumulative Effect	Straight-line Depreciation	Accelerated Depreciation
Prior to 2000	n/a	$200,000	$320,000
First quarter 2000	$1,050,000	40,000	64,000
Second quarter 2000	1,200,000	40,000	58,000
Third quarter 2000	1,150,000	40,000	54,000
Fourth quarter 2000	1,300,000	40,000	50,000
	$4,700,000	$160,000	$226,000
First quarter 2001	$1,400,000	$ 40,000	$ 46,000
Second quarter 2001	$1,500,000	$ 40,000	$ 42,000

Accelerated depreciation was taken in calculating income through the first quarter 2001; straight-line depreciation was taken in calculating income in the second quarter 2001. The effective income tax rate is 40 percent.

Mudar Company, Inc., has 500,000 shares of common stock outstanding.

Required

    a. Prepare a schedule showing the calculation of net income and earnings per share to be reported by Mudar Company for the three-month period and the six-month period ended June 30, 2000, and 2001. Also, show pro forma amounts assuming the new depreciation method is applied retroactively.

    b. Prepare a schedule to restate net income and earnings per share for the three-month period ended March 31, 2001, to reflect the change in accounting principle.

39. The following information for Quadrado Corporation relates to the three-month period ending September 30, 2001.

	Units	Price per unit
Sales	110,000	$20
Beginning inventory	20,000	12
Purchases	100,000	14
Ending inventory	10,000	

Quadrado Corporation expects to purchase 150,000 units of inventory in the fourth quarter of 2001 at a cost of $15 per unit and 30,000 units of inventory are expected to be on hand at year-end. Quadrado uses the last-in, first-out (LIFO) method to account for inventory costs.

Required

Determine the amount of cost of goods sold and gross profit to be recorded for the three months ending September 30, 2001. Prepare journal entries to reflect these amounts.

40. The following information was extracted from Note 11 (Segment Reporting) in Philip Morris Companies, Inc., 1998 annual report:

Reportable segment data were as follows (In millions):

	December 31		
	1998	**1997**	**1996**
Operating revenues:			
Domestic tobacco	$15,310	$13,584	$12,462
International tobacco	27,390	26,240	24,087
North American food	17,312	16,838	16,447
International food	9,999	10,852	11,503
Beer	4,105	4,201	4,327
Financial services	275	340	378
Total operating revenues	$74,391	$72,055	$69,204
Operating companies income:			
Domestic tobacco	$1,489	$3,287	$4,206
International tobacco	5,029	4,572	4,078
North American food	3,055	2,873	2,628
International food	1,127	1,326	1,303
Beer	451	459	440
Financial services	183	297	193
Total operating companies income	11,334	12,814	12,848
General corporate expenses	(645)	(479)	(442)
Minority interest	(128)	(87)	(43)
Amortization of goodwill	(584)	(585)	(594)
Total operating income	9,977	11,663	11,769
Interest and other debt expense, net	(890)	(1,052)	(1,086)
Total earnings before income taxes	$ 9,087	$10,611	$10,683

In addition, Note 16 (Contingencies) to the consolidated financial statements consists of five pages of information on legal proceedings against the company, primarily class-action lawsuits filed in the United States related to disease allegedly caused by cigarette smoking.

Required

a. Calculate the following for each reportable segment:

Percentage of operating revenues; 1998.

Percentage growth in operating revenues; 1997 to 1998.

Percentage of total operating income; 1998.

Percentage growth in operating income; 1997 to 1998.

Operating income as a percentage of operating revenues (profit margin); 1998.

b. What do these ratios tell you about the importance of the various reportable segments to Philip Morris' overall profitability? How might Note 16 factor into an assessment of the company's future prospects?

41. In complying with the geographic area requirements of *SFAS 131* in its 1998 annual report, the Coca-Cola Company disclosed the following related to its reportable operating segments (in millions):

	North America	Africa	Greater Europe	Latin America	Middle & Far East	Corporate
1998						
Net operating revenues	$6,915	$603	$4,834	$2,244	$4,040	$ 177
Operating income	1,460	216	1,473	999	1,299	(480)
Interest income						219
Interest expense						277
Equity income	(1)	3	(40)	68	(70)	72
Identifiable operating assets	4,543	381	1,857	1,779	2,105	1,794
Investments	141	73	2,010	1,629	2,218	615
Capital expenditures	293	19	216	72	107	156
Depreciation and amortization	238	24	92	93	118	80
Income before income taxes	1,468	209	1,391	1,075	1,232	(177)
1997						
Net operating revenues	$6,443	$582	$5,395	$2,124	$4,110	$ 214
Operating income	1,311	165	1,479	957	1,377	(288)
Interest income						211
Interest expense						258
Equity income	(6)	2	(16)	96	22	57
Identifiable operating assets	4,406	418	2,410	1,593	1,625	1,535
Investments	138	48	1,041	1,461	2,006	200
Capital expenditures	261	17	327	78	196	214
Depreciation and amortization	195	22	123	99	106	81
Income before income taxes	1,308	158	1,461	1,060	1,380	688
1996						
Net operating revenues	$6,050	$482	$5,959	$2,050	$3,964	$ 178
Operating income	949	188	1,277	815	1,239	(483)
Interest income						238
Interest expense						286
Equity income	(16)	1	59	37	73	57
Identifiable operating assets	3,796	326	2,896	1,405	1,464	2,056
Investments	145	20	802	1,234	1,400	568
Capital expenditures	261	32	379	79	121	118
Depreciation and amortization	188	12	190	83	84	76
Income before income taxes	919	109	1,326	847	1,290	105

Required

a. Calculate the following ratios for each of Coca-Cola's operating segments:

Percentage of total net operating revenues (excluding Corporate); 1998.

Percentage growth in net operating revenues; 1997–1998.

Operating income as a percentage of operating revenues (profit margin); 1998.

b. Is there any particular area of the world in which you believe Coca-Cola should attempt to expand its operations to increase operating revenues and operating income?

c. Is there any additional information you would like to have in answering question *b?*

CHAPTER

9

Foreign Currency Transactions and Hedging Foreign Exchange Risk

QUESTIONS TO CONSIDER

■ How does a company that has transactions in a foreign currency determine the amounts to be reported in the financial statements?

■ Does a change in the value of a foreign currency asset or liability held by a company represent a gain or loss that should be reported in income?

■ What is foreign exchange risk? How does a company become exposed to foreign exchange risk?

■ What is the basic objective of hedging an exposure to foreign exchange risk?

■ What is a hedge of a foreign currency transaction? What is a hedge of a foreign currency commitment? How does the accounting for these two types of hedge differ?

■ How are foreign currency options used to hedge foreign exchange risk? How do firms account for foreign currency options?

■ What is the proper accounting for a foreign currency forward contract entered into for speculative reasons?

Today, international business transactions are a regular occurrence. In its 1998 annual report, Lockheed Martin Corporation reported export sales of $6.1 billion, representing 23 percent of sales made by its U.S. operations. Even small businesses are significantly involved in transactions occurring throughout the world as evidenced by this excerpt from Cirrus Logic, Inc.'s 1998 annual report: "Export sales include sales to overseas operations of domestic corporations and represented 53 percent, 62 percent and 56 percent of net sales in fiscal 1998, 1997 and 1996, respectively." Collections from export sales or payments for imported items may not be made in U.S. dollars but in pesos, pounds, yen, and the like depending on the negotiated terms of the transaction. As the foreign currency exchange rate fluctuates, so does the U.S. dollar value of these export sales and import purchases. Companies often find it necessary to engage in some form of hedging activity to reduce losses arising from fluctuating exchange rates. At the end of fiscal year 1998 as part of its foreign currency hedging activities, Alcoa, Inc., reported outstanding foreign currency forward contracts in the amount of $2.85 billion and foreign currency options totaling $79 million.

This chapter covers accounting issues related to foreign currency transactions and foreign currency hedging activities. To provide background for subsequent discussions of the accounting issues, the chapter begins with a description of foreign exchange markets. The accounting for import and export transactions is then discussed, followed by coverage of various hedging techniques. Because they are most popular, the discussion concentrates on forward contracts and options. Understanding how to account for these items is important for any company engaged in international transactions.

FOREIGN EXCHANGE MARKETS

Each country uses its own currency as the unit of value for the purchase and sale of goods and services. The currency used in the United States is the U.S. dollar, the currency used in Mexico is the Mexican peso, and so on. If a U.S. citizen travels to Mexico and wishes to purchase local goods, Mexican merchants require payment to be made in Mexican pesos. To make a purchase, a U.S. citizen has to purchase pesos using U.S. dollars. The price at which the foreign currency can be acquired is known as the foreign exchange rate. A variety of factors determine the exchange rate between two currencies; unfortunately for those engaged in international business, the exchange rate can fluctuate over time.[1]

Exchange Rate Mechanisms

Exchange rates have not always fluctuated. During the period 1945–1973, countries fixed the par value of their currency in terms of the U.S. dollar and the value of the U.S. dollar was fixed in terms of gold. Countries agreed to maintain the value of their currency within 1 percent of the par value. If the exchange rate for a particular currency began to move outside of this 1 percent range, the country's central bank was required to intervene by buying or selling its currency in the foreign exchange market. Due to the law of supply and demand, the purchase of currency by a central bank would cause the price of the currency to stop falling and the sale of currency would cause the price to stop rising.

The integrity of the system hinged on the U.S. dollar maintaining its value in gold and the ability of foreign countries to convert their U.S. dollar holdings into gold at the fixed rate of $35 per ounce. As the United States began to incur balance of payment deficits in the 1960s, a glut of U.S. dollars arose worldwide and foreign countries began converting their U.S. dollars into gold. This resulted in a decline in the U.S. government's gold reserve from a high of $24.6 billion in 1949 to a low of $10.2 billion in 1971. In that year, the United States suspended the convertibility of the U.S. dollar into gold signaling the beginning of the end for the fixed exchange rate system. In March 1973, most currencies were allowed to float in value.

Today, several different currency arrangements exist. Some of the more important ones and the countries affected are

1. Independent float—the value of the currency is allowed to fluctuate freely according to market forces with little or no intervention from the central bank (Canada, Japan, Sweden, Switzerland, United States).

2. Pegged to another currency—the value of the currency is fixed (pegged) in terms of a particular foreign currency and the central bank intervenes as necessary to maintain the fixed value. For example, 25 countries peg their currency to the U.S. dollar (including the Bahamas and Syria); 14 former African colonies peg to the French franc.

3. European Monetary System (euro)—in 1998, the countries comprising the European Monetary System adopted a common currency called the euro and a European Central Bank was established.[2] Until 2002, local currencies such as the German mark and French franc will continue to exist but will be fixed in value in terms of the euro. On January 1, 2002, local currencies will disappear and the euro will be used in day-to-day transactions. The value of the euro floats against other currencies such as the U.S. dollar.

---

[1]Several theories attempt to explain exchange rate fluctuations but with little success, at least in the short term. An understanding of the causes of exchange rate changes is not necessary to comprehend the concepts underlying the accounting for changes in exchange rates.

[2]Most members of the European Union (EU) are "euro zone" countries. The major exception is the United Kingdom which elected not to participate. Switzerland is another important European country not part of the euro zone because it is not a member of the EU.

Exhibit 9–1   The *Wall Street Journal* Foreign Exchange Quotes, February 9, 2000

CURRENCY TRADING

Wednesday, February 9, 2000
EXCHANGE RATES

The New York foreign exchange mid-range rates below apply to trading among banks in amounts of $1 million and more, as quoted at 4 p.m. Eastern time by Reuters and other sources. Retail transactions provide fewer units of foreign currency per dollar. Rates for the 11 Euro currency countries are derived from the latest dollar euro rate using the exchange ratios set 1/1/99.

Country	U.S. $ equiv. Wed	U.S. $ equiv. Tue	Currency per U.S. $ Wed	Currency per U.S. $ Tue
Argentina (Peso)	1.002	1.002	.9998	.9998
Australia (Dollar)	.6356	.6323	1.5734	1.5815
Austria (Schilling)	.07218	.07167	13.855	13.952
Bahrain (Dinar)	2.6525	2.6525	.3770	.3770
Belgium (Franc)	.0246	.0244	40.6161	40.9023
Brazil (Real)	.5656	.5666	1.7680	1.7650
Britain (Pound)	1.6170	1.6125	.6184	.6202
1-month forward	1.6167	1.6123	.6185	.6202
3-months forward	1.6167	1.6123	.6185	.6202
6-months forward	1.6172	1.6128	.6184	.6200
Canada (Dollar)	.6921	.6916	1.4448	1.4459
1-month forward	.6926	.6920	1.4439	1.4450
3-months forward	.6935	.6930	1.4419	1.4430
6-months forward	.6950	.6945	1.4389	1.4399
Chile (Peso) (d)	.001944	.001942	514.45	514.85
China (Renminbl)	.1208	.1208	8.2788	8.2788
Columbia (Peso)	.0005126	.0005122	1951.00	1952.50
Czech. Rep. (Koruna)				
Commercial rate	.02780	.02764	35.972	36.174
Denmark (Krone)	.1334	.1325	7.4963	7.5461
Ecuador (Sucre)				
Floating rate	.000040000	.000040000	24997.50	24997.50
Finland (Markka)	.1670	.1659	5.9864	6.0286
France (Franc)	.1514	.1504	6.6045	6.6510
1-month forward	.1518	.1507	6.5875	6.6375
3-months forward	.1525	.1513	6.5595	6.6087
6-months forward	.1535	.1523	6.5161	6.5649
Germany (Mark)	.5078	.5043	1.9692	1.9831
1-month forward	.5091	.5053	1.9642	1.9791
3-months forward	.5113	.5075	1.9558	1.9704
6-months forward	.5147	.5109	1.9429	1.9574
Greece (Drachma)	.002985	.002966	335.05	337.17
Hong Kong (Dollar)	.1285	.1285	7.7805	7.7805
Hungary (Forint)	.003885	.003859	257.40	259.15
India (Rupee)	.02294	.02294	43.585	43.590
Indonesia (Ruplah)	.0001378	.0001361	7255.00	7350.00
Ireland (Punt)	1.2610	1.2523	.7930	.7985

Country	U.S. $ equiv. Wed	U.S. $ equiv. Tue	Currency per U.S. $ Wed	Currency per U.S. $ Tue
Israel (Shekel)	.2460	.2458	4.0644	4.0677
Italy (Lira)	.0005129	.0005094	1949.53	1963.26
Japan (Yen)	.009169	.009136	109.06	109.46
1-month forward	.009212	.009178	108.55	108.95
3-months forward	.009307	.009272	107.44	107.85
6-months forward	.009457	.009422	105.75	106.14
Jordan (Dinar)	1.4085	1.4085	.7100	.7100
Kuwait (Dinar)	3.2690	3.2669	.3059	.3061
Lebanon (Pound)	.0006649	.0006649	1504.00	1504.00
Malaysia (Ringgit)	.2632	.2632	3.8001	3.8000
Malta (Lira)	2.4172	2.4067	.4137	.4155
Mexico (Peso)				
Floating rate	.1060	.1064	9.4300	9.4020
Netherland (Guilder)	.4507	.4475	2.2188	2.2344
New Zealand (Dollar)	.4944	.4922	2.0227	2.0317
Norway (Krone)	.1228	.1221	8.1425	8.1889
Pakistan (Rupee)	.01927	.01923	52.900	52.000
Peru (new Sol)	.2912	.2896	3.4345	3.4525
Phillippines (Peso)	.02469	.02468	40.500	40.520
Poland (Zloty)	.2416	.2416	4.1390	4.1385
Portugal (Escudo)	.004954	.004919	201.85	203.28
Russia (Ruble) (a)	.03486	.03479	28.685	28.745
Saudi Arabia (Riyal)	.2666	.2666	3.7505	3.7505
Singapore (Dollar)	.5910	.5894	1.6921	1.6965
Slovak Rep. (Koruna)	.02347	.02332	42.600	42.880
South Africa (Rand)	.1579	.1590	6.3313	6.2903
South Korea (Won)	.0008901	.0008855	1123.50	1129.25
Spain (Peseta)	.005969	.005927	167.53	168.71
Sweden (Krona)	.1171	.1164	8.5410	8.5893
Switzerland (Franc)	.6173	.6137	1.6199	1.6295
1-month forward	.6193	.6155	1.6148	1.6247
3-months forward	.6232	.6195	1.6047	1.6143
6-months forward	.6294	.6256	1.5888	1.5984
Taiwan (Dollar)	.03259	.03260	30.685	30.675
Thailand (Baht)	.02663	.02658	37.555	37.625
Turkey (Lira)	.00000179	.00000178	559495.00	560635.00
United Arab (Dirham)	.2722	.2723	3.6731	3.6729
Uruguay (New Peso)				
Financial	.08545	.08542	11.703	11.708
Venezuela (Bolivar)	.001520	.001522	657.75	657.01
SDR	1.3501	1.3464	.7407	.7427
Euro	.9932	.9863	1.0068	1.0139

Source: *Wall Street Journal,* February 10, 2000, page C–21. Republished with permission of Dow Jones, from *Wall Street Journal,* Thursday, February 10, 2000, page C–21; permission conveyed through Copyright Clearance Center, Inc.

Foreign Exchange Rates

Exchange rates between the U.S. dollar and most foreign currencies are published on a daily basis in *The Wall Street Journal* and major U.S. newspapers. To better illustrate exchange rates and the foreign currency market, next we examine the exchange rates published in *The Wall Street Journal* for Wednesday, February 9, 2000, as shown in Exhibit 9–1.

These exchange rates were quoted in New York at 4:00 P.M. Eastern time. The price for one Austrian schilling on Wednesday, February 9 at 4:00 P.M. in New York was .07218. The U.S. dollar price for a schilling at 4:01 P.M. Eastern time in New York was probably something different, as was the U.S. dollar price for a schilling in Vienna at 4:00 P.M. Eastern time. These exchange rates are for trades between banks in amounts of $1 million or more; that is, these are interbank or wholesale prices. Prices charged to retail customers, such as companies engaged in international business, are higher. These are selling rates, the rates at which banks in New York will sell currency to one another. The prices banks are willing to pay to buy foreign currency (buying rates) are somewhat less than the selling rates. The difference between the buying and selling rates is the spread through which the banks earn a profit on foreign exchange trades.

There are two columns of information for each day exchange rates are published. The first column, U.S. $ equiv., indicates the number of U.S. dollars needed to purchase one unit of foreign currency. These are known as direct quotes. The direct quote for the Swedish krona on February 9 was $.1171; in other words, one krona could be purchased with $.1171. The second column, Currency per U.S. $, indicates the number of foreign currency units that could be purchased with one U.S. dollar. These are called indirect quotes. Indirect quotes are simply the inverse of direct quotes. If one krona can be purchased with $.1171, then 8.541 kroner can be purchased with $1.00. (The arithmetic does not work out perfectly because the direct quotes for the Swedish krona published in *The Wall Street Journal* are carried out to only four decimal points.) To avoid confusion, direct quotes are used exclusively in this chapter.

For each currency, comparative exchange rates for two days are presented. In most cases, there has been a change in the exchange rate from Tuesday, February 8, 2000, to Wednesday, February 9, 2000. Some currencies, such as the British pound, increased in value or appreciated against the U.S. dollar (to $1.6170 from $1.6125). Other currencies, such as the Brazilian real, decreased in value or depreciated against the U.S. dollar (to $.5656 from $.5666).

Spot and Forward Rates

Foreign currency trades can be executed on a spot or forward basis. The *spot rate* is the price at which a foreign currency can be purchased or sold today. In contrast, the *forward rate* is the price today at which foreign currency can be purchased or sold sometime in the future. Because many international business transactions take some time to be completed, the ability to lock in a price today at which foreign currency can be purchased or sold at some future date has definite advantages.

Most of the quotes published in *The Wall Street Journal* are spot rates. In addition, it publishes forward rates quoted by New York banks for the major currencies (British pound, Canadian dollar, French franc, German mark, Japanese yen, and Swiss franc) on a daily basis. This is only a partial listing of possible forward contracts. A firm and its bank can tailor forward contracts in other currencies and for other time periods to meet the needs of the firm.

The forward rate can exceed the spot rate on a given date, in which case the foreign currency is said to be selling at a *premium* in the forward market, or the forward rate can be less than the spot rate, in which case it is selling at a *discount*. Currencies sell at a premium or a discount because of differences in interest rates between two countries. When the interest rate in the foreign country exceeds the interest rate domestically, the foreign currency sells at a discount in the forward market. Conversely, if the foreign interest rate is less than the domestic rate, the foreign currency sells at a premium.[3] Forward rates are said to be unbiased predictors of the future spot rate.

---

[3]This relationship is based on the theory of interest rate parity that indicates the difference in national interest rates should be equal to, but opposite in sign to, the forward rate discount or premium. This topic is covered in detail in international financial textbooks.

The spot rate for British pounds on February 9, 2000, indicates that one pound could have been purchased on that date for $1.6170. On the same day, the one-month forward rate was $1.6167. By entering into a forward contract on February 9, it was possible to guarantee that pounds could be purchased on March 9 at a price of $1.6167, regardless of what the spot rate turned out to be on March 9. Entering into the forward contract to purchase pounds would have been beneficial if the spot rate on March 9 were greater than $1.6167. On the other hand, such a forward contract would have been detrimental if the spot rate were less than $1.6167. In either case, the forward contract must be honored and pounds must be purchased on March 9 at $1.6167.

Option Contracts

To provide companies more flexibility than exists with a forward contract, a market for *foreign currency options* has developed. A foreign currency option gives the holder of the option *the right but not the obligation* to trade foreign currency in the future. A *put* option is for the sale of foreign currency by the holder of the option; a *call* is for the purchase of foreign currency by the holder of the option. The *strike price* is the exchange rate at which the option will be executed if the holder of the option decides to exercise the option. The strike price is similar to a forward rate. There are generally several strike prices to choose from at any particular time. Foreign currency options may be purchased either on the Philadelphia Stock Exchange or directly from a bank in the so-called over-the-counter market.

Unlike a forward contract, where banks earn their profit through the spread between buying and selling rates, options must actually be purchased by paying an *option premium*. The option premium is a function of two components: *intrinsic value* and *time value*. The *intrinsic value* of an option is equal to the gain that could be realized by exercising the option immediately. For example, if a spot rate for a foreign currency is $1.00, a *call* option (to purchase foreign currency) with a strike price of $.97 has an intrinsic value of $.03, whereas a *put* option with a strike price of $.97 has an intrinsic value of zero. An option with a positive intrinsic value is said to be "in the money." The *time value* of an option relates to the fact that the spot rate can change over time and cause the option to become in the money. Even though a 90-day call option with a strike price of $1.00 has zero intrinsic value when the spot rate is $1.00, it will still have a positive time value if there is a chance that the spot rate could increase over the next 90 days and bring the option into the money.

The value of a foreign currency option can be determined by applying an adaptation of the Black-Scholes option pricing formula. This formula is discussed in detail in international finance books. In very general terms, the value of an option is a function of the difference between the current spot rate and strike price, the difference between domestic and foreign interest rates, the length of time to expiration, and the potential volatility of changes in the spot rate. For purposes of this book, the premium originally paid for a foreign currency option and its subsequent fair value up to the date of expiration derived from applying the pricing formula will be given.

Option quotes reported in the *Wall Street Journal* on February 9, 2000, indicated that a March call option in euros with a strike price of $1.04 could have been purchased by paying a premium of $.0018 per euro. Thus, the right to purchase 10,000 euros in March 2000, at a price of $1.04 per euro could have been acquired by paying $18 ($.0018 × 10,000 euros). If the spot rate for euros in March is greater than $1.04, the option would have been exercised and euros purchased at the strike price of $1.04. If, on the other hand, the March spot rate is less than $1.04, the option would not be exercised; instead, euros would be purchased at the lower spot rate. The option contract establishes the maximum amount that would have to be paid for euros but does not lock in a disadvantageous price should the spot rate fall below the option strike price.

FOREIGN CURRENCY TRANSACTIONS

Export sales and import purchases are international transactions; they are components of what is called trade. When two parties from different countries enter into a transaction, they must decide which of the two countries' currencies to use to settle the transaction. For example, if a U.S. computer manufacturer sells to a customer in Japan, the parties must decide whether the transaction will be denominated (payment will be made) in U.S. dollars or Japanese yen.

Assume that a U.S. exporter (Amerco) sells goods to a German importer with payment to be made in German marks (deutschemarks or DM). In this situation, Amerco has entered into a foreign currency transaction. It must restate the German mark amount that actually will be received into U.S. dollars to account for this transaction. This is because Amerco keeps its books and prepares financial statements in U.S. dollars. Although the German importer has entered into an international transaction, it does not have a foreign currency transaction (payment will be made in its currency) and no restatement is necessary.

Assume that, as is customary in its industry, Amerco does not require immediate payment and allows its German customer 30 days to pay for its purchases. By doing this, Amerco runs the risk that the German mark might depreciate against the U.S. dollar between the sale date and the date of payment. Then, fewer U.S. dollars are generated from the sale than if the German mark had not decreased in value and the sale is less profitable because it was made on a credit basis. In this situation Amerco is said to have an *exposure to foreign exchange risk.* Specifically, Amerco has a transaction exposure that can be summarized as follows:

- *Export Sale*—a transaction exposure exists when the exporter allows the buyer to pay in a foreign currency and also allows the buyer to pay sometime after the sale has been made. The exporter is exposed to the risk that the foreign currency might depreciate (decrease in value) between the date of sale and the date of payment, thereby decreasing the U.S. dollars ultimately collected.

- *Import Purchase*—a transaction exposure exists when the importer is required to pay in foreign currency and is allowed to pay sometime after the purchase has been made. The importer is exposed to the risk that the foreign currency might appreciate (increase in price) between the date of purchase and the date of payment, thereby increasing the U.S. dollars that have to be paid for the imported goods.

Accounting Issue

The major issue in accounting for foreign currency transactions is how to deal with the change in U.S. dollar value of the sales revenue and account receivable resulting from the export when the foreign currency changes in value. (The corollary issue is how to deal with the change in the U.S. dollar value of the account payable and goods being acquired in an import purchase.) For example, assume that Amerco, a U.S. company, sells goods to a German customer at a price of 1 million German marks when the spot exchange rate is $.55 per mark. If payment were received at the date of sale, Amerco could have converted 1 million marks into $550,000 and this amount clearly would be the amount at which the sales revenue would be recognized. Instead, Amerco allows the German customer 30 days to pay for its purchase. At the end of 30 days, the German mark has depreciated to $.53 and Amerco is able to convert the 1 million marks received on that date into only $530,000. How should Amerco account for this $20,000 decrease in value?

Accounting Alternatives

Conceptually, the two methods of accounting for changes in the value of a foreign currency transaction are the one-transaction perspective and the two-transaction perspective. The *one-transaction perspective* assumes that an export sale is not complete until the foreign currency receivable has been collected and converted into U.S. dollars. Any change in the U.S. dollar value of the foreign currency is accounted for as an adjustment to Accounts Receivable and to Sales. Under this perspective, Amerco would ultimately report Sales at $530,000 and an increase in the Cash account of the same amount. This approach can be criticized because it hides the fact that the company could have received $550,000 if the German customer had been required to pay at the date of sale. The company incurs a $20,000 loss because of the depreciation in the DM, but that loss is buried in an adjustment to Sales. This approach is not acceptable under U.S. GAAP.

Instead, *FASB Statement No. 52* requires companies to use a *two-transaction perspective* in accounting for foreign currency transactions.[4] This perspective treats the export sale and the subsequent collection of cash as two separate transactions. Because management has made two decisions: (1) to make the export sale, and (2) to extend credit in foreign currency to the customer, the income effect from each of these decisions should be reported separately. The U.S. dollar value of the sale is recorded at the date the sale occurs. At that point the sale has been completed; there are no subsequent adjustments to the Sales account. Any difference between the number of U.S. dollars that could have been received at the date of sale and the number of U.S. dollars actually received at the date of payment due to fluctuations in the exchange rate is a result of the decision to extend foreign currency credit to the customer. This difference is treated as a Foreign Exchange Gain or Loss that is reported separately from Sales in the income statement. Using the two-transaction perspective to account for its export sale to Germany, Amerco would make the following journal entries:

Date of Purchase:	Accounts Receivable (DM).....................	550,000	
	Sales		550,000
	To record the sale and DM receivable at the spot rate of $.55.		
Date of Payment:	Foreign Exchange Loss.......................	20,000	
	Accounts Receivable (DM)		20,000
	To adjust the value of the DM receivable to the new spot rate of $.53 and record a foreign exchange loss resulting from the depreciation in the DM.		
	Cash	530,000	
	Accounts Receivable (DM)		530,000
	To record the receipt of DM 1 million and conversion at the spot rate of $.53.		

Sales are reported in income at the amount that would have been received if the customer had not been given 30 days to pay the 1 million marks, that is, $550,000. A separate Foreign Exchange Loss of $20,000 is reported in income to indicate that because of the decision to extend foreign currency credit to the German customer and because the DM decreased in value, fewer U.S. dollars are actually received.[5]

Note that Amerco keeps its Account Receivable (DM) account separate from its U.S. dollar receivables. Companies engaged in international trade need to keep separate payable and receivable accounts in each of the currencies in which they have transactions. Each foreign currency receivable and payable should have a separate account number in the company's chart of accounts.

---

[4]FASB, *Statement of Financial Accounting Standards No. 52,* "Foreign Currency Translation" Stamford, CT: FASB, December 1981).

[5]Note that the foreign exchange loss results because the customer is allowed to pay in German marks and is given 30 days to pay. If the transaction were denominated in U.S. dollars, no loss would result. Nor would there be a loss if the German marks had been received at the date the sale was made.

We can summarize the relationship between fluctuations in exchange rates and foreign exchange gains and losses as follows:

Transaction	Type of Exposure	Foreign Currency (FC)	
		Appreciates	**Depreciates**
Export sale	Asset	Gain	Loss
Import purchase	Liability	Loss	Gain

A foreign currency receivable arising from an export sale creates an *asset exposure* to foreign exchange risk. If the foreign currency appreciates, the foreign currency asset increases in U.S. dollar value and a foreign exchange gain arises; depreciation of the foreign currency causes a foreign exchange loss. A foreign currency payable arising from an import purchase creates a *liability exposure* to foreign exchange risk. If the foreign currency appreciates, the foreign currency liability increases in U.S. dollar value and a foreign exchange loss results; depreciation of the currency results in a foreign exchange gain.

Balance Sheet Date before Date of Payment

The question arises as to what accounting should be done if a balance sheet date falls between the date of sale and the date of payment. For example, assume that Amerco shipped goods to its German customer on December 10, 2001, with payment to be received on January 9, 2002. Assume that at December 10, the spot rate for DM is $.55, but by December 31, the DM has appreciated to $.56. Is any adjustment needed at December 31, 2001, when the books are closed to account for the fact that the foreign currency receivable has changed in U.S. dollar value since December 10?

The general consensus worldwide is that a foreign currency receivable or foreign currency payable should be revalued at the balance sheet date to account for the change in exchange rates. Under the two-transaction perspective, this means that a foreign exchange gain or loss arises at the balance sheet date. The next question then is what should be done with these foreign exchange gains and losses that have not yet been realized in cash. Should they be included in net income?

The two approaches to accounting for unrealized foreign exchange gains and losses are the deferral approach and the accrual approach. Under the *deferral approach,* unrealized foreign exchange gains and losses are deferred on the balance sheet until cash is actually paid or received. When cash is paid or received, a *realized* foreign exchange gain or loss would be included in income. This approach is not acceptable under U.S. GAAP.

SFAS 52 requires U.S. companies to use the *accrual approach* to account for unrealized foreign exchange gains and losses. Under this approach, a firm reports unrealized foreign exchange gains and losses in net income in the period in which the exchange rate changes. The statement says: "This is consistent with accrual accounting; it results in reporting the effect of a rate change that will have cash flow effects when the event causing the effect takes place."[6] Thus, any change in the exchange rate from the date of sale to the balance sheet date would result in a foreign exchange gain or loss to be reported in income in that period. Any change in the exchange rate from the balance sheet date to the date of payment would result

---

[6]*SFAS No. 52,* paragraph 124.

in a second foreign exchange gain or loss that would be reported in the second accounting period. The journal entries Amerco would make under the accrual approach would be:

12/10/01	Accounts Receivable (DM)........................	550,000	
	Sales		550,000
	To record the sale and DM receivable at the spot rate of $.55.		
12/31/01	Accounts Receivable (DM)........................	10,000	
	Foreign Exchange Gain........................		10,000
	To adjust the value of the DM receivable to the new spot rate of $.56 and record a foreign exchange gain resulting from the appreciation in the DM since December 10.		
1/9/02	Foreign Exchange Loss...........................	30,000	
	Accounts Receivable (DM).....................		30,000
	To adjust the value of the DM receivable to the new spot rate of $.53 and record a foreign exchange loss resulting from the depreciation in the DM since December 31.		
	Cash...	530,000	
	Accounts Receivable (DM).....................		530,000
	To record the receipt of DM 1 million and conversion at the spot rate of $.53.		

The net impact on income in 2001 is Sales of $550,000 and a Foreign Exchange Gain of $10,000; in 2002, a Foreign Exchange Loss of $30,000 is recorded. This results in a net increase in retained earnings of $530,000 that is balanced by an equal increase in Cash.

One criticism of the accrual approach is that it leads to a violation of conservatism when an unrealized foreign exchange gain arises at the balance sheet date. In fact, this is one of only two situations in U.S. GAAP where it is acceptable to recognize an unrealized gain in income. (The other situation relates to trading marketable securities reported at market value.) Germany, Austria, and several other countries more strictly adhere to the concept of conservatism than does the United States. In those countries, if at the balance sheet date the exchange rate has changed so that an unrealized gain arises, the change in exchange rate is ignored and the foreign currency account receivable or payable continues to be carried on the balance sheet at the exchange rate that existed at the date of the transaction. On the other hand, if the exchange rate had changed to cause a foreign exchange loss, the accounting receivable would be revalued and an unrealized loss would have been recorded and reported in income. This is a classic application of conservatism.

SFAS 52 requires restatement at the balance sheet date of all foreign currency assets and liabilities carried on a company's books. In addition to foreign currency payables and receivables arising from import and export transactions, companies might have dividends receivable from foreign subsidiaries, loans payable to foreign lenders, or lease payments receivable from foreign customers that are denominated in a foreign currency and therefore must be restated at the balance sheet date. Each of these foreign currency denominated assets and liabilities is exposed to foreign exchange risk; therefore, fluctuation in the exchange rate results in foreign exchange gains and losses.

Many U.S. companies report foreign exchange gains and losses on the income statement in a line item often titled "Other Income (Expense)." Other incidental gains and losses such as gains and losses on sales of assets would be included in this line item as well. *SFAS 52* requires companies to disclose the magnitude of foreign exchange gains and losses if material. For example, in the Notes to Financial Statements in its 1995 annual report, Merck indicated that the income statement item Other (Income) Expense, Net included a net exchange (gain) loss of $68.2 million, $26.2 million, and ($7.8) million in 1993, 1994, and 1995, respectively.

HEDGE OF A FOREIGN CURRENCY TRANSACTION

In the preceding example, Amerco has an asset exposure in German marks when it sells goods to the German customer and allows the customer 30 days to pay for its purchase. If the German mark depreciates over the next 30 days, Amerco incurs a foreign exchange loss. For many companies, the uncertainty of not knowing exactly how many U.S. dollars will be earned on this export sale is of great concern. To avoid this uncertainty, as soon as the sale is made, Amerco would like to lock in a price at which it can sell the 1 million marks that it will receive on January 9, 2002. Amerco can do this by entering into a 30-day forward contract to sell marks as soon as the goods are shipped to the German customer. There is no cost associated with obtaining the forward contract. *By entering into the forward contract, Amerco eliminates its exposure to foreign exchange risk; it knows with 100 percent certainty the number of U.S. dollars it will receive in 30 days.* The process of eliminating risk exposure is known as *hedging*.

Assume that on December 10, 2001, the 30-day forward rate for marks is $.535 and Amerco signs a contract with New Manhattan Bank to deliver 1 million marks in 30 days in exchange for $535,000. No cash changes hands on December 10, 2001. Given that the spot rate on December 10, 2001, is $.55, the mark is selling at a discount in the 30-day forward market (the forward rate is less than the spot rate). With the 30-day forward contract, Amerco locks in a U.S. dollar value for the 1 million marks that it will receive in 30 days. By entering into the forward contract, Amerco has hedged its German mark asset exposure. Amerco knows with 100 percent certainty the number of U.S. dollars it will receive from this export sale; management can sleep soundly at night without worrying about what is happening to the value of the German mark in the spot market.

Given that the future spot rate turns out to be only $.53, selling the marks at a forward rate of $.535 is obviously better than leaving the German mark receivable unhedged—Amerco will receive a $5,000 greater cash inflow as a result of the hedge. Because the mark is selling at a forward discount of $.015 per mark, Amerco receives $15,000 less than if the goods had been paid for at the time of delivery ($550,000 − $535,000). This $15,000 reduction in cash inflow is considered to be a loss; it is the cost of extending foreign currency credit to a foreign customer.[7] Conceptually, this loss is similar to the transaction loss that arises on the export sale. It exists only because the transaction is denominated in foreign currency. The major difference is that Amerco knows the exact amount of the loss at the date of sale, whereas, when left unhedged, Amerco does not know the size of the transaction loss until 30 days pass. (In fact, it is possible that the unhedged receivable could result in a transaction gain rather than a transaction loss.)

Accounting for a Hedge of a Foreign Currency Transaction

SFAS 133, *Accounting for Derivative Instruments and Hedging Activities,* issued in June 1998, governs the accounting for derivative instruments such as foreign currency forward contracts and options. *SFAS 133* requires forward contracts to be carried on the balance sheet at their fair value, measured by reference to the change in the forward rate. Changes in the fair value of the forward contract are recognized as gains and losses in income. Amerco must account for its foreign currency transaction and the related forward contract simultaneously but separately. The process can be better understood by referring to the steps involving the three parties—Amerco, the German customer, and New Manhattan Bank—shown in Exhibit 9–2.

---

[7]This should not be confused with the cost associated with normal credit risk; that is, the risk that the customer will not pay for its purchase. That is a separate issue unrelated to the currency in which the transaction is denominated.

Exhibit 9–2

Hedge of a Foreign Currency Account Receivable with a Forward Contract

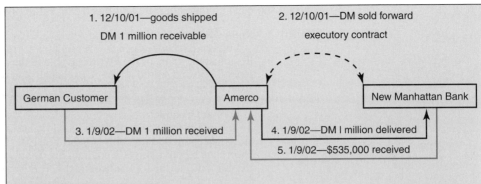

Steps on December 10, 2001

1. Amerco ships goods to the German customer thereby creating an Account Receivable of DM 1 million.
2. Amerco then sells DM 1 million 30-days forward to New Manhattan Bank creating an executory contract to pay DM 1 million and receive $535,000.

Steps on January 9, 2002

3. The German customer remits DM 1 million to Amerco—the DM Account Receivable has been received and Amerco has DM 1 million reflected in an account Foreign Currency (DM).
4. Amerco delivers DM 1 million to New Manhattan Bank.
5. New Manhattan Bank pays Amerco $535,000.

Amerco determines the fair value of the forward contract by referring to the change in the forward rate for a contract maturing on January 9, 2002. The relevant exchange rates, U.S. dollar value of the DM account receivable, and fair value of the forward contract are determined as follows:

| | | Account Receivable (DM) | | Forward | Forward Contract | |
Date	Spot Rate	U.S. Dollar Value	Change in U.S. Dollar Value	Rate to 1/9/02	Fair Value	Change in Fair Value
12/10/01	$.55	$550,000	—	$.535	$ 0	—
12/31/01	$.56	$560,000	+ 10,000	$.542	$(7,000)	− 7,000
1/9/02	$.53	$530,000	− 30,000	$.53	$5,000	+ 12,000

Amerco pays nothing to enter into the forward contract at December 10, 2001, and the forward contract has a fair value of zero on that date. At December 31, 2001, the forward rate for a contract to deliver DM on January 9, 2002 is $.542. At that rate, 1 million German marks could be sold forward for $542,000. Because Amerco is committed to sell DM 1 million for $535,000, the fair value of its forward contract is negative $7,000 (a liability). By locking in to sell DM 1 million for $535,000, Amerco has incurred a loss of $7,000. At January 9, 2002, the forward rate to sell DM on that date is the spot rate—$.53. At that rate, DM 1 million could be sold for $530,000. Because Amerco has a contract to sell DM 1 million for $535,000, the fair value of the forward contract on January 9, 2002, is $5,000. This represents an increase in fair value of $12,000 from December 31, 2001. Amerco would prepare the following journal entries to account for its foreign currency transaction and related forward contract:

2001 Journal Entries for Forward Contract Hedge of a Transaction

12/10/01	Accounts Receivable (DM)............................	550,000	
	Sales		550,000
	To record the sale and DM receivable at the spot rate of $.55 (Step 1 in Exhibit 9–2).		

There would be no formal journal entry for the forward contract as it is an executory contract (no cash changes hands) and has a fair value of zero (Step 2).

12/31/01	Accounts Receivable (DM).	10,000	
	Foreign Exchange Gain.		10,000
	To adjust the value of the DM receivable to the new spot rate of $.56 and record a foreign exchange gain resulting from the appreciation in the DM since December 10.		
	Loss on Forward Contract.	7,000	
	Forward Contract		7,000
	To record the forward contract at its fair value of negative $7,000 (reported as a liability on the 12/31/01 balance sheet) and record a forward contract loss for the change in the fair value of the forward contract.		

The net impact on the income statement for the year 2001 would be as follows:

Sales.		$550,000
Foreign exchange gain.	$10,000	
Loss on forward contract.	(7,000)	
Net gain (loss)		3,000
Net impact on income		$553,000

2002 Journal Entries for Forward Contract Hedge of a Transaction

1/9/02	Foreign Exchange Loss	30,000	
	Accounts Receivable (DM)		30,000
	To adjust the value of the DM receivable to the new spot rate of $.53 and record a foreign exchange loss resulting from the depreciation in the DM since December 31.		
	Forward Contract	12,000	
	Gain on Forward Contract		12,000
	To adjust the fair value of the forward contract to its current fair value and record a forward contract gain for the change in fair value since December 31.		
	Foreign Currency (DM)[8].	530,000	
	Accounts Receivable (DM)		530,000
	To record the receipt of DM 1 million from the German customer as an asset at the spot rate of $.53 (Step 3 in Exhibit 9–2).		
	Cash	535,000	
	Foreign Currency (DM)		530,000
	Forward Contract		5,000
	To record the remittance of DM 1 million to New Manhattan Bank and the receipt of $535,000 from New Manhattan Bank, and remove the forward contract from the books (Steps 4 and 5).		

The net impact on the income statement for the year 2002 would be:

Foreign exchange loss	$(30,000)
Gain on forward contract	12,000
Net impact on income	$(18,000)

Over the two accounting periods, the firm would report Sales of $550,000 and a net loss of $15,000 (a net gain of $3,000 in 2001 and a net loss of $18,000 in 2002). The increase in Retained Earnings of $535,000 is counterbalanced by an equal increase in Cash.

---

[8]The DM 1 million received represents an asset to the company. Amerco could use various account titles to record this asset including Foreign Currency (DM), Investment in DM, and Cash (DM).

The Essence of Hedging

Note that Amerco has hedged its DM receivable (asset) exposure by selling DM in the forward market. In selling DM forward, Amerco creates a DM payable (liability) exposure because the company must deliver 1 million marks to New Manhattan Bank. This liability is unrecorded because the forward contract is executory in nature. The DM payable offsets (hedges) the DM receivable such that the net exposure to foreign exchange risk is zero. *This is the essence of hedging—reducing exposure by offsetting foreign currency assets with foreign currency liabilities and vice versa.*

To see how a hedge works in an import purchase, assume Amerco also has a French franc (FF) payable from importing goods from a French supplier. Amerco needs to acquire FF to make payment 30 days in the future. The company can lock in a price at which it will acquire the FF by buying FF forward. By buying forward, Amerco creates an unrecorded FF receivable from the foreign currency broker that offsets its FF payable to the French supplier.

Discounts and Premiums

In the Amerco example, the German mark is selling at a discount in the 30-day forward market thus yielding an overall net loss on the account receivable and forward contract. What if the mark were selling at a premium? In that event, Amerco could lock in to sell its marks 30 days in the future at a higher price than it could obtain at the date of sale. The premium would generate a net gain on the account receivable and forward contract for Amerco over and above what was recognized as revenue from the sale.

Hedges of foreign currency payables give rise to a net gain when the forward rate is at a discount and a net loss when there is a premium. If the French franc is selling at a forward premium when Amerco enters into a contract to buy francs, then Amerco ends up spending more U.S. dollars than if it had purchased francs at the date the imported goods were received. In this case, the premium results in a net loss on the account payable and forward contract. If the French franc were selling at a discount, Amerco would spend fewer U.S. dollars than if it purchased francs at the date the goods were received; the discount results in a net gain. The relationship between forward contract discounts/premiums and gains/losses is as follows:

Nature of Foreign Currency Exposure	Type of Hedge	Forward Rate < Spot Rate Discount	Forward Rate > Spot Rate Premium
Asset	Sell FC forward	Net loss	Net gain
Liability	Buy FC forward	Net gain	Net loss

Regarding its export sale to Germany, Amerco has entered into a *perfect hedge* of its DM asset exposure. A perfect hedge exists when the hedging instrument (the forward contract) is denominated in the same currency, is of the same size, and has the same maturity as the hedged item (the DM receivable). With a perfect hedge, the net gain or loss reported in income is exactly equal to the forward rate discount or premium at the date the forward contract is entered into. If for some reason Amerco does not sell exactly 1 million marks forward, an imperfect hedge exists, and the mismatch gives rise to an additional gain or loss reported in net income. For example, if Amerco was able to sell only 800,000 marks forward on December 10, 2001, the overhang of 200,000 marks will be an unhedged asset exposure. Given that the German mark depreciated by $.02 over the period December 10, 2001, to January 9, 2002, the unhedged exposure will result in an additional loss of $4,000 [DM 200,000 × $.02] over and above the loss of $12,000 [DM 800,000 × ($.550 − $.535)] associated with the forward rate discount.

DISCUSSION QUESTION

Do We Have a Gain or What?

The Ahnuld Corporation, a health juice producer, recently has been expanding its sales through exports to foreign markets. Earlier this year, the company negotiated the sale of several thousand cases of turnip juice to a retailer in the country of Tcheckia. The customer is unwilling to assume the risk of having to make payment in U.S. dollars. Desperate to enter the Tcheckian market, the vice president for international sales agrees to denominate the sale in tchecks, the national currency of Tcheckia. The current exchange rate for tchecks is $2.00. In addition, the customer indicates that he cannot make payment until all of the juice has been sold. Payment is scheduled for six months from the date of sale.

Fearful that the tcheck might depreciate in value over the next six months, the head of the risk management department at Ahnuld Corporation enters into a forward contract to sell tchecks in six months at a forward rate of $1.80. Six months later, when payment is received from the Tcheckian customer, the exchange rate for the tcheck is $1.70. The corporate treasurer calls the head of the risk management department into her office.

> **Treasurer:** I see that your decision to hedge our foreign currency position on that sale to Tcheckia was a bad one.
> **Department Head:** What do you mean? We have a gain on that forward contract. We're $10,000 better off from having entered into that hedge.
> **Treasurer:** That's not what the books say. The accountants have recorded a net loss of $20,000 on that particular deal. I'm afraid I'm not going to be able to pay you a bonus this year. Another bad deal like this one and I'm going to have to demote you back to the interest rate swap department.
> **Department Head:** Those bean counters have messed up again. I told those guys in international sales that selling to customers in Tcheckia was risky, but at least by hedging our exposure, we managed to receive a reasonable amount of cash on that deal. In fact, we ended up with a gain of $10,000 on the hedge. Tell the accountants to check their debits and credits again. I'm sure they just put a debit in the wrong place or some accounting thing like that.

Have the accountants made a mistake? Does the company have a loss, a gain, or both from this forward contract?

FOREIGN CURRENCY OPTION AS HEDGE OF TRANSACTION

As an alternative to a forward contract, Amerco could hedge its exposure to foreign exchange risk arising from the German mark account receivable by purchasing a foreign currency *put* option. A put option would give Amerco the right but not the obligation to sell 1 million marks on January 9, 2002, at a predetermined strike price. Assume that on December 10, 2001, Amerco selects a strike price of $.54 when the spot rate is $.55 and pays a premium of $.009 per mark.[9] Thus, the purchase price for the option is $9,000 (DM 1,000,000 × $.009). Because the strike price is less than the spot rate, there is no intrinsic value associated with this option. The premium is based solely on time value; that is, it is possible that the DM will depreciate and the spot rate on January 9, 2002, will be less than $.54, in which case the option will be "in the money."

If the spot rate for German marks on January 9, 2002 is less than the strike price of $.54, Amerco will exercise its option and sell its 1 million German marks at the strike price of $.54. If the spot rate for marks in 30 days is greater than the strike price of $.54, Amerco will not exercise its option and instead will sell marks at the higher spot rate. By purchasing the option, Amerco is guaranteed a minimum cash flow of $531,000 ($540,000 from exercising the option less $9,000 to purchase the option). There is no limit to the maximum number of U.S. dollars that could be received.

---

[9]The price of the option (the premium) was determined by the seller of the option through the use of the Black-Scholes (or similar) option pricing formula.

Accounting for a Foreign Currency Option Used as a Hedge

As is true for other derivative financial instruments, *SFAS 133* requires foreign currency options to be reported on the balance sheet at fair value. Changes in the value of a foreign currency option must be recognized as gains and losses in net income in the period of change. The fair value of an option fluctuates over its life as a result of changes in its intrinsic value and time value. For example, as the spot rate for a foreign currency decreases over time, the intrinsic value of a put option in that currency increases. The ability to sell foreign currency at a fixed strike price has more value as the spot rate decreases. On the other hand, as the spot rate increases, the intrinsic value of a put option declines.

The fair value of a foreign currency option at the balance sheet date is determined by reference to the premium quoted by banks on that date for an option with a similar expiration date. Banks (and other sellers of options) determine the current premium by incorporating relevant variables at the balance sheet date into an option pricing formula such as Black-Scholes.

Returning to the Amerco illustration, the changes in value for the DM accounting receivable and DM put option are summarized as follows:

Date	Spot Rate	Account Receivable (DM)		Foreign Currency Option	
		U.S. Dollar Value	Change in U.S. Dollar Value	Fair Value	Change in Fair Value
12/10/01	$.55	$550,000	—	$9,000	—
12/31/01	$.56	$560,000	+10,000	$5,000	−4,000
1/9/02	$.53	$530,000	−30,000	$10,000	+5,000

The fair value of the option at December 10, 2001, is the premium paid of $9,000. Appreciation of the DM from December 10 to December 31 causes the fair value of the option to fall to $5,000 at December 31, 2001. The subsequent decrease in the DM spot rate from December 31 to January 9, 2002, results in an increase in the value of the foreign currency option. At January 9, 2002, the option's exercise date, the time value of the option is zero. Based on the strike price of $.54 and the spot rate of $.53, the intrinsic value of the option is $10,000 [DM 1 million × ($.54 − $.53)]. Thus, the option has a fair value of $10,000 ($0 + $10,000) at January 9.[10]

The entries to record the foreign currency transaction and related foreign currency option in 2001 are as follows:

2001 Journal Entries—Hedge of Transaction Using Foreign Currency Option

12/10/01	Accounts Receivable (DM)	550,000	
	Sales		550,000
	To record the sale and receivable (DM) at the spot rate of $.55.		
	Foreign Currency Options	9,000	
	Cash		9,000
	To record the purchase of the foreign currency option as an asset.		
12/31/01	Accounts Receivable (DM)	10,000	
	Foreign Exchange Gain		10,000
	To adjust the value of the DM receivable to the new spot rate of $.56 and record a foreign exchange gain resulting from the appreciation of the DM since December 10.		
	Loss on Foreign Currency Options.	4,000	
	Foreign Currency Options		4,000
	To adjust the fair value of the foreign currency option from $9,000 to $5,000 and record a loss on foreign currency options.		

---

[10]Although the fair value of the option at date of purchase and at the balance sheet date is determined using an option pricing formula, the option's fair value at the date of expiration is determined through a comparison of the option's strike price and the spot rate at expiration date.

As a result of these entries, Accounts Receivable (DM) will be reported as an asset on the balance sheet at $560,000 and Foreign Currency Options is reported as an asset at $5,000. The net impact on the income statement for the year 2001 is:

Sales		$550,000
Foreign exchange gain	$10,000	
Loss on foreign currency options	(4,000)	
Net gain (loss)		6,000
Net impact on income		$556,000

At January 9, 2002, the option has increased in value by $5,000 and the DM receivable has decreased in value by $30,000. A gain on foreign currency options and a foreign exchange loss will be recognized on that date. The accounting entries made in 2002 are as follows:

2002 Journal Entries—Hedge of Transaction Using Foreign Currency Option

1/9/02	Foreign Exchange Loss	30,000	
	Accounts Receivable (DM)		30,000
	To adjust the value of the DM receivable to the new spot rate of $.53 and record a foreign exchange loss resulting from the depreciation of the DM since December 31.		
	Foreign Currency Options	5,000	
	Gain on Foreign Currency Options		5,000
	To adjust the fair value of the foreign currency option from $5,000 to $10,000 and record a gain on foreign currency options.		
	Foreign Currency (DM)............................	530,000	
	Accounts Receivable (DM)		530,000
	To record the receipt of DM 1 million from the German customer as an asset at the spot rate of $.53 and close the DM account receivable.		
	Cash	540,000	
	Foreign Currency (DM)........................		530,000
	Foreign Currency Options		10,000
	To record the exercise of the option at the strike price of $.54 and close out the foreign currency options account.		

The option was exercised because the spot rate ($.53) on January 9, 2002, is less than the strike price of $.54. The impact on 2002 net income is:

Foreign exchange loss	$(30,000)
Gain on foreign currency options	5,000
Net impact on income	$(25,000)

Over the two accounting periods, Amerco would report Sales of $550,000 and a cumulative net loss of $19,000 ($6,000 net gain in 2001 and $25,000 net loss in 2002). The net impact on income over the two periods of $531,000 is equal to the net cash inflow arising from the export sale; $540,000 from exercising the option less $9,000 to purchase the option.

Spot Rate Exceeds Strike Price

If the spot rate at January 9, 2002, had been greater than the strike price of $.54, Amerco would allow its option to expire unexercised. Instead it would sell its Foreign Currency (DM) at the spot rate. The fair value of the foreign currency option on January 9, 2002, would be zero. The journal entries for 2001 to reflect this scenario would be the same as above. The option would be reported as an asset on the December 31,

2001, balance sheet at $5,000 and the DM receivable would have a carrying value of $560,000. The entries at January 9, 2002, assuming a spot rate on that date of $.57, would be as follows:

1/9/02	Accounts Receivable (DM)	10,000	
	Foreign Exchange Gain		10,000

To adjust the value of the DM receivable to the new spot rate of $.57 and record a foreign exchange gain resulting from the appreciation of the DM since December 31.

Loss on Foreign Currency Options	5,000	
Foreign Currency Options		5,000

To adjust the fair value of the foreign currency option from $5,000 to zero and record a loss on foreign currency options.

Foreign Currency (DM)	570,000	
Accounts Receivable (DM)		570,000

To record the receipt of DM 1 million from the German customer as an asset at the spot rate of $.57 and close the DM account receivable.

Cash	570,000	
Foreign Currency (DM)		570,000

To record the sales of DM 1 million at the spot rate of $.57.

The net impact on income over the two accounting periods is:

Sales—2001	$550,000
Net gain—2001	6,000
Net gain—2002	5,000
Net impact on income	$561,000

The net amount reflected in income equals the net cash inflow derived from the export sale ($570,000 from the sale of DM less $9,000 to purchase the option).

HEDGE OF A FUTURE FOREIGN CURRENCY COMMITMENT

In the examples thus far, Amerco does not enter into a hedge of its export sale until the sale is actually made. Quite often, however, companies engaged in foreign currency transactions will enter into hedging arrangements as soon as an order has been accepted. Assume now that Amerco receives and accepts an order in the amount of DM 1 million from the German customer on November 10, 2001, and that it will take Amerco 60 days to fill the order. Assume further that under the terms of the sales agreement Amerco will ship the goods to the German customer on January 9, 2002, and will receive immediate payment on delivery. In other words, Amerco will not allow the German customer time to pay. Although Amerco will not make the sale until January 9, 2002, it has a firm commitment to make the sale and receive 1 million marks in 60 days. This creates a German mark asset exposure to foreign exchange risk on November 10, 2001. On that date, Amerco wants to lock in a price at which it can sell 1 million marks in 60 days. It does this by entering into a 60-day forward contract at the date the goods are ordered.

This scenario differs from the previous hedge of a transaction in that Amerco enters into the forward contract hedge before the transaction actually takes place. This is known as a *fair value hedge of a foreign currency firm commitment. SFAS 133* requires the following procedures for fair value hedges of firm commitments:

- The hedging instrument (for example, forward contract) must be reported as an asset or liability on the balance sheet at fair value. Changes in the fair value of the hedging instrument are recognized currently as gains and losses in income.

- Although there is no transaction to account for, a gain or loss on the hedged firm commitment must be recognized and taken to income to offset a loss or gain on the hedging instrument. A firm commitment must be recognized as an asset or liability to counterbalance the gain or loss on firm commitment.

Recognizing a gain or loss on the underlying hedged item (the firm commitment) to exactly offset a loss or gain on the hedging instrument (the forward contract) is known as *hedge accounting.* According to *SFAS 133* (par. 20), hedge accounting is allowed only when:

1. At inception of the hedge, there is formal documentation of the hedging relationship.
2. The hedging relationship is expected to be highly effective.

If these two requirements are not met, changes in fair value of the hedging instrument (forward contract) are recognized in current income without any recognition of gains and losses on the foreign currency firm commitment. In other words, hedge accounting does not apply.

In fact, under *SFAS 133,* a nonderivative foreign-currency-denominated financial instrument, such as a foreign currency borrowing, can be designated as a hedge of a foreign currency commitment, as long as it is formally documented and highly effective as a hedge. For example, Amerco could have hedged its future receipt of German marks (an asset exposure) by taking out a German mark loan (a liability exposure) from a German bank.

Continuing with the Amerco example, assume the following exchange rates at November 10, 2001:

	$ per DM
Spot rate	$.555
60-day forward rate (to 1/1/02)	$.538

With a 60-day forward contract, Amerco locks in a price of $538,000 at which it will sell DM 1 million when received on January 9, 2002. The exposure to foreign exchange risk has been eliminated. Amerco knows with 100 percent certainty the number of U.S. dollars it will receive from this future export sale. The fair value of the forward contract is determined as follows:

Date	Forward Rate to 1/9/02	Forward Contract	
		Fair Value	Change in Fair Value
11/10/01	$.538	$ 0	—
12/31/01	$.542	$(4,000)	− 4,000
1/9/02	$.53	$ 8,000	+ 12,000

Amerco pays nothing to enter into the forward contract at November 10, 2001, and the forward contract has a fair value of zero on that date. At December 31, 2001, the forward rate for a contract to deliver DM on January 9, 2002 is $.542. At that rate, 1 million German marks could be sold forward for $542,000. Because Amerco is committed to sell DM 1 million for $538,000, the fair value of its forward contract is negative $4,000 (a liability). At January 9, 2002, the forward rate to sell DM on that date is the spot rate—$.53. At that rate, DM 1 million could be sold for $530,000. Because Amerco has a contract to sell DM 1 million for $538,000, the fair value of the forward contract on January 9, 2002, is $8,000. This represents an increase in fair value of $12,000 from December 31, 2001.

Amerco will assess hedge effectiveness by comparing the change in the fair value of the forward contract to changes in the fair value of the firm commitment. Because the firm commitment and forward contract are denominated in the same currency and have the same terms, the forward contract will be 100 percent effective in hedging the firm commitment. The journal entries to account for the hedge of a foreign currency sale commitment are as follows:

2001 Journal Entries—Hedge of Foreign Currency Firm Commitment

11/10/01	There is no entry to record either the sales agreement or the forward contract as both are executory contracts. A memorandum would be created documenting existence of the hedging relationship.		
12/31/01	Loss on Forward Contract	4,000	
	Forward Contract		4,000
	To record the forward contract at its fair value of negative $4,000 (reported as a liability on the 12/31/01 balance sheet) and a forward contract loss for the change in the fair value of the forward contract.		
	Firm Commitment	4,000	
	Gain on Firm Commitment.		4,000
	To record an offsetting gain on firm commitment (the firm commitment is reported as an asset on the 12/31/01 balance sheet).		

Consistent with the objective of hedge accounting, the gain on the firm commitment offsets the loss on the forward contract and the net impact on 2001 income is zero.

2002 Journal Entries—Hedge of Foreign Currency Firm Commitment

1/9/02	Forward Contract	12,000	
	Gain on Forward Contract		12,000
	To adjust the forward contract to its current fair value and record a forward contract gain for the change in fair value since December 31.		
	Loss on Firm Commitment.	12,000	
	Firm Commitment		12,000
	To record an offsetting loss on firm commitment.		
	Foreign Currency (DM)	530,000	
	Sales		530,000
	To record the sale and receipt of DM 1 million from the German customer at the spot rate of $.53.		
	Cash	538,000	
	Foreign Currency (DM)		530,000
	Forward Contract		8,000
	To record the remittance of DM 1 million to the foreign exchange broker, the receipt of $538,000 from the foreign exchange broker, and remove the forward contract from the books.		
	Firm Commitment	8,000	
	Sales		8,000
	To close the firm commitment account as an adjustment to sales.		

Once again, the gain on forward contract and the loss on firm commitment offset. As a result of the last entry, Amerco reports Sales in 2002 net income at $538,000, exactly the amount of cash received. This result is consistent with the one-transaction perspective to accounting for foreign currency transactions discussed earlier. The one-transaction perspective makes sense in this scenario because Amerco does not extend credit to the German customer.

OPTION USED AS HEDGE OF A COMMITMENT

Now assume that instead of entering into a forward contract to hedge its foreign currency commitment, Amerco purchases a DM 1 million put option on November 10,

2001, which matures on January 9, 2002. The strike price is $.548 and the premium is $.006 per DM. The option, which costs $6,000 (DM 1,000,000 × $.006), gives Amerco the right but not the obligation to sell 1 million marks on January 9, 2002, for $548,000. Amerco is sure to receive a minimum of $542,000 ($548,000 − $6,000) in cash from the sale to be made on January 9. Relevant exchange rates and the fair value of the foreign currency option are as follows:

| Date | Spot Rate | Foreign Currency Option | |
		Fair Value	Change in Fair Value
11/10/01	$.555	$ 6,000	—
12/31/01	$.56	$ 4,000	− 2,000
1/9/02	$.53	$18,000	+ 14,000

As of December 31, 2001, as a result of the appreciation of the DM from $.555 to $.56, the value of the foreign currency option (determined by applying the option pricing formula) decreases to $4,000. From December 31, 2001, to January 9, 2002, the DM depreciates to $.53. The fair value of the foreign currency option at January 9 is its intrinsic value of $18,000 [DM 1 million × ($.548 strike − $.53 spot)].

2001 Journal Entries—Hedge of Commitment Using Foreign Currency Option

11/10/01	Foreign Currency Options	6,000	
	Cash		6,000
	To record the purchase of the foreign currency option as an asset.		

There is no entry to record the sales agreement as it is an executory contract. A memorandum would be prepared documenting existence of the hedging relationship.

12/31/01	Loss on Foreign Currency Options	2,000	
	Foreign Currency Options		2,000
	To adjust the fair value of the foreign currency option from $6,000 to $4,000 and record a loss on foreign currency options.		
	Firm Commitment	2,000	
	Gain on Firm Commitment		2,000
	To record an offsetting gain on firm commitment.		

On the December 31, 2001, balance sheet, Foreign Currency Options and Firm Commitment will be reported as assets in the amounts of $4,000 and $2,000, respectively. These amounts will be offset by a decrease in Cash of $6,000. The net impact on 2001 income is zero.

2002 Journal Entries—Hedge of Commitment Using Foreign Currency Option

1/9/02	Foreign Currency Options	14,000	
	Gain on Foreign Currency Options		14,000
	To adjust the fair value of the foreign currency option from $4,000 to $18,000 and record a gain on foreign currency options.		
	Loss on Firm Commitment	14,000	
	Firm Commitment		14,000
	To record an offsetting loss on firm commitment.		
	Foreign Currency (DM)	530,000	
	Sales		530,000
	To record the sale and receipt of DM 1 million from the German customer at the spot rate of $.53.		

Cash...	548,000	
Foreign Currency (DM)........................		530,000
Foreign Currency Options		18,000
To record the exercise of the foreign currency option at a strike price of $.548 and close out the foreign currency options account.		
Firm Commitment...............................	12,000	
Sales.......................................		12,000
To close the firm commitment account as an adjustment to sales.		

The net impact on the income statement over the two years 2001 and 2002 would be:

Sales		$542,000
Net gain (loss) on options	$(12,000)	
Net gain (loss) on firm commitment ...	12,000	
Net gain (loss)		0
Net impact on income		$542,000

The net cash inflow realized from the export sale is $542,000; $548,000 from exercising the option less $6,000 to purchase the option. Consistent with a one-transaction perspective, Sales is reported at the amount of net cash inflow.

FORECASTED TRANSACTIONS

SFAS 133 also allows the use of hedge accounting for foreign currency forward contracts and options used to hedge forecasted foreign currency transactions (transactions which are expected to occur but for which a contractual agreement does not exist). A hedge of a forecasted transaction is referred to as a *cash flow hedge.* For hedge accounting to apply, the forecasted transaction must be probable (likely to occur), the hedging relationship must be appropriately documented, and the hedge must be highly effective in offsetting fluctuations in cash flows associated with foreign currency risk.

To demonstrate the nature of a cash flow hedge, assume that a U.S. company has purchased goods from a foreign supplier for several years. The company anticipates purchases from the foreign supplier in the coming year to be the same as last year. The expected timing and terms of the purchases can be identified, and the purchases are probable. In this case, hedge accounting would be allowed for a foreign currency option used to hedge against adverse fluctuations in the exchange rate.

The accounting for a hedge of a forecasted transaction (cash flow hedge) differs from the accounting for a hedge of a foreign currency firm commitment (fair value hedge) in two ways.

- Unlike the accounting for a firm commitment, there is no recognition of gains and losses on a forecasted transaction.
- The hedging instrument (forward contract or option) is reported at fair value, but because there is no gain or loss on the forecasted transaction to offset against, changes in the fair value of the hedging instrument are not reported as gains and losses in net income. Instead they are reported outside of net income in *other comprehensive income* (explained below). On the projected date of the forecasted transaction, the cumulative change in fair value is transferred from other comprehensive income to net income.

To demonstrate the accounting for a hedge of a forecasted transaction using a foreign currency option, assume the facts are the same as for the example of an option hedge of a firm commitment except that Amerco does not receive a sales order until January 2002. On November 10, 2001, Amerco purchases a DM 1 million put option to hedge a DM sale forecasted to occur on January 9, 2002. The option, which expires on January 9, 2002, has a strike price of $.548 and a premium of $.006 per DM. The fair value of the option at December 31, 2001, is $4,000. The accounting entries made in 2001 are as follows:

2001 Journal Entries—Hedge of Forecasted Transaction Using Foreign Currency Option

11/10/01	Foreign Currency Options......................	6,000	
	Cash..		6,000
	To record the purchase of the foreign currency option as an asset.		

There is no entry to record the forecasted sale. A memorandum would be prepared documenting existence of the hedging relationship.

12/31/01	Other Comprehensive Income....................	2,000	
	Foreign Currency Options....................		2,000
	To adjust the fair value of the foreign currency option from $6,000 to $4,000 and record an adjustment to other comprehensive income.		

On January 2, 2002, Amerco receives an order from its anticipated customer in Germany to deliver goods on January 9, 2002. Goods are shipped and payment is received on that date. The DM spot rate on January 9, 2002, is $.53. Accounting entries for the year 2002 are:

2002 Journal Entries—Hedge of Forecasted Transaction Using Foreign Currency Option

1/9/02	Foreign Currency Options......................	14,000	
	Other Comprehensive Income		14,000
	To adjust the fair value of the foreign currency option from $4,000 to $18,000 and record an adjustment to other comprehensive income.		
	Foreign Currency (DM)........................	530,000	
	Sales......................................		530,000
	To record the sale and receipt of DM 1 million from the German customer at the spot rate of $.53.		
	Cash..	548,000	
	Foreign Currency (DM)......................		530,000
	Foreign Currency Options...................		18,000
	To record the exercise of the foreign currency option at a strike price of $.548 and close out the foreign currency options account.		
	Other Comprehensive Income....................	12,000	
	Sales......................................		12,000
	To transfer other comprehensive income to sales.		

The net cash inflow realized from the export sale is $542,000; $548,000 from exercising the option less $6,000 to purchase the option. Consistent with a one-transaction perspective, Sales is reported at the amount of net cash inflow.

The reporting of comprehensive income was introduced by the FASB in 1997.[11] Comprehensive income is defined as all changes in equity from nonowner sources and consists of two components: *net income* and *other comprehensive income.* Other comprehensive income consists of income items that under previous FASB statements were required to be deferred in stockholders' equity such as gains and losses on available-for-sale marketable securities. Changes in the fair value of hedging instruments designated

---

[11]FASB Statement No. 130, *Reporting Comprehensive Income,* issued in June 1997.

as hedges of forecasted transactions would be reported in other comprehensive income as well. Other comprehensive income is reported as a separate line item in the stockholders' equity section of the balance sheet.

USE OF HEDGING INSTRUMENTS

There are probably as many different corporate strategies regarding hedging foreign exchange risk as there are companies exposed to that risk. Some companies simply require hedges of all foreign currency transactions. Others require the use of a forward contract hedge when the forward rate results in a greater cash inflow or smaller cash outflow than with the spot rate. Still other companies have proportional hedging policies that require hedging on some predetermined percentage (e.g., 50 percent, 60 percent, or 70 percent) of transaction exposure.

The notes to financial statements of multinational companies indicate the magnitude of foreign exchange risk and the importance of hedging contracts. The following has been extracted from the Coca-Cola Company's 1998 annual report.

Foreign Currency Management (in millions)

Forward contracts	
Assets	$ 809
Liabilities	1,325
Swap agreements	
Assets	344
Liabilities	704
Purchased options	
Assets	232
Other liabilities	243
	$3,657

Coca-Cola had $3.66 billion in foreign currency hedging instruments outstanding at December 31, 1998. To better appreciate the significance of this amount, consider that Coca-Cola had total sales of $18.8 billion and net income of $3.5 billion in 1998.

Coca-Cola uses a combination of foreign currency forward contracts, swaps, options, and foreign currency borrowings in its hedging strategy. In its 1998 annual report, Abbott Laboratories reported foreign exchange forward contracts of $1.6 billion and options of $406 million at December 31, 1998. Microsoft Corporation primarily uses options in its management of foreign exchange risk. Its 1998 annual report indicated options outstanding at fiscal year-end in the amount of $662 million.

As can be seen from the Coca-Cola illustration, a third popular means of hedging foreign exchange risk is through a *foreign currency swap*. A currency swap is a mechanism for converting a foreign currency receivable (or payable) into the domestic currency (U.S. dollar) prior to actual settlement. A discussion of the mechanics of foreign currency swaps is beyond the scope of this book. As is true for any derivative financial instrument, *SFAS 133* is applied in accounting for foreign currency swaps.

The Euro

The introduction of the euro as a common currency throughout much of Europe should reduce the need for hedging in that region of the world. For example, a German company purchasing goods from a Spanish supplier will no longer have an exposure to foreign exchange risk as both countries use a common currency. This will also be true for German subsidiaries of U.S. parent companies. However, any transactions denominated in euros between the U.S. parent and its German (or other euro zone) subsidiary will continue to be exposed to foreign exchange risk.

One advantage of the euro for U.S. companies is that a euro account receivable from sales to a customer in, say, the Netherlands, will act as a natural hedge of a euro account payable on purchases from, say, a supplier in Italy. Assuming similar amounts and time periods are involved, any foreign exchange loss (gain) arising from the euro payable will be offset by a foreign exchange gain (loss) on the euro receivable. There will be no need to hedge the euro account payable with a hedging instrument such as a foreign currency option.

FOREIGN CURRENCY BORROWING

In addition to the receivables and payables that arise from import and export activities, companies often must account for foreign currency borrowings, another type of foreign currency transaction. Companies borrow foreign currency from foreign lenders either to finance foreign operations or perhaps to take advantage of more favorable interest rates. Accounting for a foreign currency borrowing is complicated by the fact that both the principal and interest are denominated in foreign currency and both create an exposure to foreign exchange risk.

To demonstrate the accounting for foreign currency debt, assume that on July 1, 2001, Multicorp International borrowed 1 billion Japanese yen (¥) on a one-year note at a per annum interest rate of 5 percent. Interest is payable and the note comes due on July 1, 2002. The following exchange rates apply:

Date	U.S. Dollars per Japanese Yen Spot Rate
July 1, 2001	$.00921
December 31, 2001	$.00932
July 1, 2002	$.00937

On July 1, 2001, Multicorp borrows 1 billion yen and converts it into $9,210,000 in the spot market. Over the life of the note, Multicorp must record accrued interest expense at year-end and interest payments on the anniversary date of July 1. In addition, the firm must revalue the Japanese yen note payable at year-end, with foreign exchange gains and losses reported in income. These journal entries account for this foreign currency borrowing:

7/1/01	Cash	9,210,000	
	Note Payable (¥)		9,210,000
	To record the ¥ note payable at the spot rate of $.00921 and the conversion of ¥ 1 billion into U.S. dollars.		
12/31/01	Interest Expense	233,000	
	Accrued Interest Payable (¥)		233,000
	To accrue interest for the period July 1–December 31, 2001: ¥ 1 billion × 5% × 1/2 year = ¥ 25 million × $.00932 = $233,000.		
	Foreign Exchange Loss	110,000	
	Note Payable (¥)		110,000
	To revalue the ¥ note payable at the spot rate of $.00932 and record a foreign exchange loss of $110,000 [¥ 1 billion × ($.00932 − $.00921)].		
7/1/02	Interest Expense	234,250	
	Accrued Interest Payable (¥)	233,000	
	Foreign Exchange Loss	1,250	
	Cash		468,500
	To record the interest payment of ¥ 50 million acquired at the spot rate of $.00937 for $468,500; interest expense for the period of January 1–July 1, 2002: ¥ 25 million × $.00937; and a foreign exchange loss on the ¥ accrued interest payable—¥ 25 million × ($.00937 − $.00932).		

Foreign Exchange Loss	50,000	
Note Payable (¥)		50,000

To revalue the ¥ note payable at the spot rate of
$.00937 and record a foreign exchange loss of
$50,000 [¥ 1 billion × ($.00937 − $.00932)].

Note Payable ¥	9,370,000	
Cash		9,370,000

To record repayment of the ¥ 1 billion note through
purchase of ¥ at the spot rate of $.00937.

Foreign Currency Loan

At times companies might lend foreign currency to related parties, creating the opposite situation as with a foreign currency borrowing. The accounting involves keeping track of a note receivable and interest receivable both of which are denominated in foreign currency. Fluctuations in the U.S. dollar value of the principal and interest generally give rise to foreign exchange gains and losses that would be included in income. Under *SFAS 52,* an exception arises when the foreign currency loan is being made on a long-term basis to a foreign branch, subsidiary, or equity method affiliate. Foreign exchange gains and losses on "intercompany foreign currency transactions that are of a long-term investment nature (that is, settlement is not planned or anticipated in the foreseeable future)" are deferred in other comprehensive income until the loan is repaid.[12] Only the foreign exchange gains and losses related to the interest receivable are recorded currently in net income.

SPECULATIVE FOREIGN CURRENCY FORWARD CONTRACT

A forward exchange contract does not necessarily have to serve as a hedge. Companies also can acquire such contracts as investments for speculative purposes. If a fluctuation is anticipated in the value of a particular currency, a forward exchange contract can be negotiated in hopes of realizing a profit from the expected movement. *SFAS 133* requires a speculative forward contract to be reported at fair value with gains and losses recognized currently in income.

To demonstrate the procedures used in accounting for a speculative foreign currency forward contract, assume that on December 1, 2001, exchange rates between the Swiss franc (Sfr) and U.S. dollar are as follows:

	Spot	90-Day Forward
December 1, 2001	$.80	$.81

Mega Company believes that the Swiss franc will actually appreciate by more than $.01 against the U.S. dollar over the next 90 days. On December 1, 2001, the company therefore enters into a 90-day forward contract to buy 1 million Swiss francs at $.81 per franc, betting that it will be able to sell the francs at a higher spot rate on March 1, 2002. Mega Company has no business need for the Swiss francs. The company is not importing any goods from Switzerland—this is pure speculation.

Because the forward contract is an executory contract and has a fair value of zero at December 1, 2001, there are no accounting entries needed at that date.

At December 31, 2001, Mega Company must close its books and report the forward contract at its fair value. Fair value is determined by reference to the forward rate for a contract with a life remaining to the maturity date. On December 31, 2001, fair value of the forward contract maturing on March 1, 2002, is determined by reference to the 60-day forward rate. Relevant exchange rates are:

	Spot	60-Day Forward
December 31, 2001	$.805	$.817

---

[12]*SFAS 52,* para. 20(b).

Mega Company has contracted to purchase 1 million Swiss francs on March 1, 2002, for $810,000. The forward rate on December 31, 2001, indicates that the new price to purchase 1 million francs on March 1 is $817,000. As a result, the fair value of Mega Company's forward contract is $7,000. The following adjusting entry would be made:

12/31/01	Forward Contract	7,000	
	Gain on Forward Contract		7,000
	To record the forward contract at its fair value and		
	recognize the change in fair value as a gain.		

The forward contract is reported as an asset in the amount of $7,000 on the December 31, 2001, balance sheet, and the gain is reported in 2001 income.

On March 1, 2002, the spot rate is $.82. Mega Company purchases 1 million Swiss francs for $810,000 under the forward contract and then sells them at the spot rate for $820,000. Mega realizes a net gain of $10,000 through speculation; $7,000 was recognized in 2001 and the remaining $3,000 will be recognized in 2002 as follows:

3/1/02	Forward Contract	3,000	
	Gain on Forward Contract		3,000
	To adjust the fair value of the forward contract and		
	recognize the change in fair value as a gain.		
	Investment in Sfr	810,000	
	Cash		810,000
	To record the purchase of Sfr 1 million at the forward		
	rate of $.81.		
	Cash	820,000	
	Investment in Sfr		810,000
	Forward Contract		10,000
	To record the sale of the Sfr at the spot rate and		
	remove the forward contract from the books.		

The net impact on the balance sheet is an increase in Cash of $10,000, offset by an increase in Retained Earnings resulting from the $10,000 gain recognized over the two-year period.

SUMMARY

1. There are a variety of exchange rate mechanisms in use around the world. A majority of national currencies are allowed to fluctuate in value against other currencies over time.

2. Exposure to foreign exchange risk exists when a payment to be made or a payment to be received is denominated (stated) in terms of a foreign currency. Appreciation in a foreign currency will result in a foreign exchange gain on a foreign currency receivable and a foreign exchange loss on a foreign currency payable. Conversely, a decrease in the value of a foreign currency will result in a foreign exchange loss on a foreign currency receivable and a foreign exchange gain on a foreign currency payable.

3. Under *SFAS 52*, foreign exchange gains and losses on foreign currency balances are recorded in income in the period in which an exchange rate change occurs; this is a two-transaction perspective, accrual approach. Foreign currency balances must be revalued to their current U.S. dollar equivalent using current exchange rates whenever financial statements are prepared. This approach violates the conservatism principle when unrealized foreign exchange gains are recognized as income.

4. Exposure to foreign exchange risk can be eliminated through hedging. A foreign currency asset (receivable) exposure is hedged by creating a foreign currency liability (payable) of similar magnitude and maturity. A foreign currency liability exposure is hedged by creating an offsetting foreign currency asset.

5. One popular means of hedging is the forward exchange contract, an agreement to exchange currencies in the future at a predetermined rate. Under *SFAS 133*, a forward

contract is reported on the balance sheet (as either an asset or a liability) at its fair value. Foreign currency options are another popular tool for hedging foreign exchange risk. *SFAS 133* requires foreign currency options to be recorded as an asset when purchased, with changes in fair value recognized over time.

6. If a foreign currency firm commitment is being hedged (fair value hedge), gains and losses on the hedging instrument as well as on the underlying firm commitment should be recognized in net income. The firm commitment account created to offset the gain or loss on firm commitment is treated as an adjustment to the underlying transaction when it takes place.

7. If a forecasted transaction is being hedged (cash flow hedge), changes in the fair value of the hedging instrument are reported in other comprehensive income. The cumulative change in fair value reported in other comprehensive income is included in net income in the period in which the forecasted transaction was originally anticipated to take place.

COMPREHENSIVE ILLUSTRATION

Problem

(*Estimated Time: 55 to 65 Minutes*) The Zelm Company is a U.S. company that primarily imports and exports miscellaneous products. During the first quarter of 2001, the company engaged in the following foreign currency transactions.

Part A

On January 15, Zelm places an order to purchase 10,000 board feet of teakwood at a total price of 2 million baht (BT) from a lumber company in Thailand. Delivery will be made in 3 months on April 15. The spot rate at the date the order was placed was $.25 per baht. On that date, Zelm signed a 90-day forward contract to buy 2 million baht at a forward rate of $.242 per baht. The spot rate for baht is $.254 on March 31 and $.240 on April 15. The 15-day forward rate for baht is $.245 on March 31.

Part B

Zelm places an order to purchase footwear from a supplier in Brazil on February 15. Payment of 400,000 Brazilian reals (R$) will be made on March 15 when the footwear is received. On February 15, Zelm purchases a call option for R$400,000, paying a premium of $200. The strike price is $.90 per R$. At March 15, the spot rate is $.92 per R$.

Part C

Zelm sells 1,000 horse saddles to an Austrian customer on February 1 at a price of 500,000 euros, with payment to be received on March 1. The spot rate at the date of sale is $1.00 per euro. Zelm enters into a forward contract on the date of sale that will allow it to sell 500,000 euros on March 1 at a forward rate of $.99. The spot rate on March 1 is $1.01 per euro.

Part D

On March 1, to take advantage of lower interest rates in Switzerland, Zelm negotiates a two-year 100,000 Swiss franc (SFr) loan at 4 percent. Principal and interest are to be paid quarterly, with the first payments on June 1. The spot rate at the date of the loan is $.80 per franc. By March 31, the franc has depreciated to $.78, but recovers somewhat to $.786 by June 1.

Part E

Zelm completes the sale of computer printer ink cartridges to a Canadian computer parts store on March 10. The sales price of 100,000 Canadian dollars (C$) will be received in 30 days. On March 10, when the spot rate for the Canadian dollar is $.73, Zelm purchases a put option on 100,000 Canadian dollars at a strike price of $.73, paying a premium of $.005 per unit. The spot rate is $.727 on March 31 and $.723 on April 9. Due to the depreciation in the Canadian dollar, the foreign currency option has a fair value of $600 on March 31 and $700 on April 9.

Required

Prepare journal entries for each of these foreign currency activities in accordance with *SFAS 52* and *SFAS 133* and determine the amounts to be reported in income for the quarter ending March 31, 2001.

Solution

Part A. Forward Contract Hedge of a Foreign Currency Purchase Commitment

1/15/01	There are no journal entries related to the purchase agreement or forward contract. A memorandum would be prepared documenting the hedging relationship.		
3/31/01	Forward Contract	6,000	
	Gain on Forward Contract		6,000
	To record the forward contract at its fair value of $6,000 and a gain on forward contract for the change in the fair value since January 15.		

The fair value of the forward contract at March 31, 2001, is determined as the difference between the price at which Zelm is committed to purchase 2 million baht based on the January 15 90-day forward rate (BT 2 million × $.242 = $484,000) and the price at March 31 at which Zelm could lock in to purchase 2 million baht based on the 15-day forward rate (BT 2 million × $.245 = $490,000). The increase in the forward rate to purchase baht generates a fair value for the forward contract of $6,000 ($490,000 − $484,000). The fair value of the forward contract was zero at January 15, thus the gain on the forward contract is $6,000.

	Loss on Firm Commitment	6,000	
	Firm Commitment		6,000
	To record an offsetting loss on the firm commitment.		
4/15/01	Loss on Forward Contract	10,000	
	Forward Contract		10,000
	To adjust the forward contract to its current fair value and record a loss for the change in fair value since March 31.		

The fair value of the forward contract at April 15, 2001, is determined as the difference between the price at which Zelm is committed to purchase 2 million baht based on the January 15 90-day forward rate (BT 2 million × $.242 = $484,000) and the price at April 15 at which Zelm could purchase 2 million baht based on the spot rate (BT 2 million × $.24 = $480,000). The decrease in the spot rate to purchase baht results in a fair value for the forward contract of $(4,000) ($480,000 − $484,000). The fair value of the forward contract was $6,000 at March 31, thus the loss on forward contract at April 15 is $10,000.

	Firm Commitment	10,000	
	Gain on Firm Commitment		10,000
	To record an offsetting gain on the firm commitment.		
	Foreign Currency (BT)	480,000	
	Forward Contract	4,000	
	Cash		484,000
	To record the purchase of BT 2 million at the forward rate of $.242, record the BT 2 million received at the spot rate of $.24, and remove the forward contract from the books.		
	Inventory	480,000	
	Foreign Currency (BT)		480,000
	To record the purchase of inventory through the payment BT 2 million to the supplier.		
	Inventory	4,000	
	Firm Commitment		4,000
	To close the firm commitment account as an adjustment to the cost of inventory.		

Summary—Consistent with the one-transaction perspective, Inventory is carried at a cost of $484,000, the exact amount of cash paid. There is no impact on income.

Part B. Option Hedge of a Foreign Currency Purchase Commitment

2/15/01	Foreign Currency Options	200	
	Cash		200
	To record the purchase of the option as an asset.		

There is no journal entry to record the purchase order.

3/15/01	Foreign Currency Options	7,800	
	Gain on Foreign Currency Options		7,800
	To adjust the fair value of the option from $200 to $8,000 and record a gain on foreign currency options.		

The fair value of the option at March 15, 2001, is equal to the difference between the price that can be paid for R$400,000 by exercising the option ($360,000) and the price that would be paid at the spot rate (R$400,000 × $.92 = $368,000.

	Loss on Firm Commitment	7,800	
	Firm Commitment		7,800
	To record an offsetting loss on the firm commitment.		
	Foreign Currency (R$)	368,000	
	Cash		360,000
	Foreign Currency Options		8,000
	To record the purchase of R$ 400,000 at the option strike price of $.90, record the R$ 400,000 received at the spot rate of $.92, and remove the foreign currency options account from the books.		
	Inventory	368,000	
	Foreign Currency (R$)		368,000
	To record the purchase of inventory through the payment of R$ 400,000.		
	Firm Commitment	7,800	
	Inventory		7,800
	To close the firm commitment account as an adjustment to inventory.		

Summary—Inventory is recorded at a cost of $360,200, which is equal to the amount of cash outflow ($360,000 to exercise the option plus $200 to purchase the option). The first-quarter 2001 income statement will include a gain on option of $7,800 and an offsetting loss on firm commitment of $7,800.

Part C. Forward Contract Hedge of a Foreign Currency Sales Transaction

2/5/01	Accounts Receivable (euro)	500,000	
	Sales		500,000
	To record the sale and euro receivable at the spot rate of $1.00.		

There is no entry to record the forward contract as it is executory in nature and has a fair value of zero.

3/1/01	Accounts Receivable (euro)	5,000	
	Foreign Exchange Gain		5,000
	To adjust the value of the euro receivable to the new spot rate of $1.01 and record a foreign exchange gain resulting from the appreciation in the euro since February 1.		
	Loss on Forward Contract	10,000	
	Forward Contract		10,000
	To record the forward contract at its fair value of negative $10,000 and a loss for the change in the fair value of the forward contract since February 1.		

The fair value of the forward contract at March 1, 2001, is determined as the difference between the price at which Zelm is committed to sell 500,000 euros (500,000 euros × $.99 = $495,000) and the price at which Zelm could sell 500,000 euros if it had not entered into the forward contract (DM 500,000 × $1.01 = $505,000). The fair value of the forward contract was zero at February 1, and negative $10,000 at March 1, creating a loss of $10,000.

Foreign Currency (euro)............................	505,000	
Accounts Receivable (euro)......................		505,000
To record the receipt of 500,000 euros at the spot rate of $1.01.		
Cash	495,000	
Forward Contract	10,000	
Foreign Currency (DM)		505,000
To record delivery of 500,000 euros to the foreign currency broker, receipt of $495,000 from the foreign currency broker, and remove the forward contract from the books.		

Summary—the net impact on income in the first quarter 2001 would be:

Sales	$500,000	
Foreign exchange gain	$ 5,000	
Loss on forward contract	(10,000)	
Net gain (loss)		(5,000)
Net impact on income		$495,000

The net impact on income is equal to the net cash inflow of $495,000.

Part D. Foreign Currency Borrowing

3/1/01	Cash	80,000	
	Notes Payable (SFr)		80,000
	To record the SFr note payable at the spot rate of $.80 and the conversion of SFr 100,000 into U.S. dollars.		
3/31/01	Interest Expense	260	
	Accrued Interest Payable (SFr)		260
	To accrue interest for the month of March 2001: SFr 100,000 × 4% × 1/12 year = SFr 333.33 × $.78 = $260.		
	Notes Payable (SFr)	2,000	
	Foreign Exchange Gain		2,000
	To revalue the SFr note payable at the spot rate of $.78 and record a foreign exchange gain of $2,000 [SFr 100,000 × ($.78 − $.80)].		
6/1/01	Notes Payable (SFr)	9,750	
	Foreign Exchange Loss	75	
	Cash		9,825
	To record the first principal payment of SFr 12,500 acquired at the spot rate of $.786 ($9,825); remove one-eighth of the carrying value of the note payable ($9,750) from the books; and record a foreign exchange loss resulting from an appreciation in the SFr since March 31—SFr 12,500 × ($.786 − $.78).		
	Interest Expense	524	
	Accrued Interest Payable (SFr)	260	
	Foreign Exchange Loss	2	
	Cash		786
	To record the first interest payment of SFr 1,000 acquired at the spot rate of $.786; interest expense for the period March 31 to June 1: SFr 666.66 × $.786; and a foreign exchange loss on the SFr accrued interest payable—SFr 333.33 × ($.786 − $.78).		

Summary—the income statement for the quarter ended March 31, 2001, would include interest expense of $260 and a foreign exchange gain of $2,000.

Part E. Foreign Currency Option Hedge of Export Sale Transaction

3/10/01	Accounts Receivable (C$)	73,000	
	Sales		73,000

To record the sale and C$ receivable at the spot rate of $.73.

	Foreign Currency Options	500	
	Cash		500

To record the purchase of the option (C$100,000 × $.005) as an asset.

3/31/01	Foreign Exchange Loss	300	
	Accounts Receivable (C$)		300

To adjust the value of the C$ receivable to the new spot rate of $.727 and record a foreign exchange loss for the depreciation of the C$ since March 10.

	Foreign Currency Options	100	
	Gain on Foreign Currency Options		100

To adjust the fair value of the foreign currency option from $500 to $600 and record a gain on foreign currency options.

4/9/01	Foreign Exchange Loss	400	
	Accounts Receivable (C$)		400

To adjust the value of the C$ receivable to the new spot rate of $.723 and record a foreign exchange loss for the depreciation of the C$ since March 31.

	Foreign Currency Options	100	
	Gain on Foreign Currency Options		100

To adjust the fair value of the foreign currency option from $600 to $700 and record a gain on foreign currency options.

	Foreign Currency (C$)	72,300	
	Accounts Receivable (C$)		72,300

To record the receipt of C$100,000 from the Canadian customer at the spot rate of $.723 and close the C$ account receivable.

	Cash	73,000	
	Foreign Currency (C$)		72,300
	Foreign Currency Options		700

To record the exercise of the option at the strike price of $.73 and close the foreign currency options account.

The option was exercised because the spot rate on April 9, 2001, of $.723 is less than the strike price of $.73.

Summary—the impact on net income for the first quarter 2001 would be:

Sales		$73,000
Foreign exchange loss	$(300)	
Gain on foreign currency options	100	
Net gain (loss)		(200)
Net impact on income		$72,800

Overall, the first quarter 2001 income statement would include the following:

	A	B	C	D	E	Total
Sales			$500,000		$73,000	$573,000
Interest expense				$ (260)		(260)
Foreign exchange gain (loss)			5,000	2,000	(300)	6,700
Gain (loss) on forward contract . . .	$ 6,000		(10,000)			(4,000)
Gain (loss) on foreign currency options		$ 7,800			100	7,900
Gain (loss) on firm commitment	(6,000)	(7,800)				(13,800)
	$ 0	$ 0	$495,000	$1,740	$72,800	$569,540

QUESTIONS

1. What is the concept underlying the two-transaction perspective to accounting for foreign currency transactions?
2. Brown Company makes export sales denominated in several different foreign currencies. How are fluctuations in exchange rates handled under the two-transaction perspective, accrual approach?
3. What creates a foreign exchange gain and a foreign exchange loss, and where are these figures reported in a set of financial statements?
4. What does the term *hedging* mean, and why do companies elect to follow this strategy?
5. What is a forward exchange contract?
6. Why would a company enter into a forward exchange contract?
7. How are forward contracts reported on the balance sheet?
8. How is the fair value of a forward contract determined? What is the accounting treatment for changes in the fair value of a forward contract?
9. How is the economic benefit, that is, increase in cash flow, from the hedge of a foreign currency transaction accounted for?
10. What are the major differences in the accounting treatment of a hedge of a foreign currency transaction and a hedge of a foreign currency commitment?
11. Casper Corporation uses a forward contract to hedge a foreign currency commitment resulting from ordering machinery from a foreign manufacturer. How is the cost of the imported machinery determined?
12. How does the accounting for a forward exchange contract differ if the agreement is acquired for speculation rather than as a hedge?
13. What is a foreign currency put option?
14. How does a foreign currency option differ from a foreign currency forward contract?
15. Why might a company prefer to use an option rather than a forward contract? Why might a company prefer a forward contract over an option?
16. What is the proper accounting treatment for the premium paid for a foreign currency option?
17. What is hedge accounting?
18. How are changes in the fair value of a foreign currency option accounted for in a fair value hedge? In a cash flow hedge?
19. Why is the accounting for a foreign currency borrowing more complicated than the accounting for a foreign currency payable arising from an import purchase?

INTERNET ASSIGNMENTS

Internet sites are time and date sensitive. It is the purpose of these exercises to have you explore the Internet. You may need to refer to the text's Web site at http://www.mhhe.com/hoyle6e to find the most up-to-date links for the Web sites listed in the Internet Exercises.

1. Use the Internet to obtain the most recent annual report for each of the following U.S.-based multinational corporations:

   Federal-Mogul Corporation (www.federalmogul.com)
   Ford Motor Company (www.ford.com)
   General Motors Corporation (www.generalmotors.com)

   Locate the company's description of its foreign exchange risk management (hedging) activities. This usually is found in the "management discussion and analysis" and/or in the notes to the financial statements. Answer the following questions:
   a. What foreign currency hedging techniques does the company use?
   b. Does the company indicate using foreign currency contracts for speculative purposes?
   c. Does the company report a concentration of foreign exchange exposure in any particular currency or currencies?
   d. Does the company disclose the aggregate amount of foreign exchange gains/losses included in income? If yes, is this reported as a separate line item on the income statement?

2. Several Internet Web sites provide up-to-date foreign currency exchange rates. Examples include Xenon Laboratories universal currency converter at www.xe.net, Yahoo's currency exchange rates at finance.yahoo.com, and Bloomberg's currency calculator at www.bloomberg.com. Determine the spot exchange rate (U.S. $ per unit of foreign currency) for each of the following currencies:

   Argentine peso
   Brazilian real
   British pound
   French franc
   Euro
   Japanese yen
   Panama balboa
   Russian ruble
   Singapore dollar

   One week later, again determine the spot exchange rate (direct quote) for each of these currencies. Calculate the percentage change in the U.S. dollar value of each currency using the formula (Second Spot Rate − First Spot Rate)/First Spot Rate. Which currencies have strengthened against the U.S. dollar and which have weakened? For which of these currencies would an account receivable in that currency have generated a foreign exchange gain? a foreign exchange loss? Have any currencies not changed in value over time? Why do you think this might be the case?

LIBRARY ASSIGNMENTS

1. As the manager of international sales for Compex Global Corporation, you have made a major sale to a new customer in Great Britain. Payment of 500,000 British pounds will be received in 30 days. You must decide which of the following strategies to use: (a) leave the foreign currency exposure unhedged, (b) hedge the risk using a forward contract, or (c) hedge using a foreign currency option.

   To help make your decision, review current foreign exchange quotes published in the *Wall Street Journal* (or another major newspaper). Select one of the three strategies—a, b, or c. Prepare journal entries for all three strategies at the date of sale.

   At the end of 30 days, determine the current spot rate for British pounds. Prepare journal entries for all three strategies at the date that payment is received. Which strategy resulted in the greatest amount of cash inflow? Was your strategy the best?

2. Read the following as well as any other published articles on hedging and hedge accounting:

    "Perils of the Hedge Highwire," *Business Week,* October 26, 1998.
    "Indecent Exposure," *Institutional Investor,* September 1991.
    "Foreign Exchange Exposure Management," *CPA Journal* (Accounting for International Operations section), August 1988.
    "The Challenges of Hedge Accounting," *Journal of Accountancy,* November 1989.
    "(Dangerous) Fun and Games in the Foreign Exchange Market," *Forbes,* August 22, 1988.

    Write a report describing the various reasons for creating hedges and the methods by which hedges can be established.

PROBLEMS

1. Leickner Company ordered parts costing FC100,000 from a foreign supplier on May 12 when the spot rate was $.20 per FC. A one-month forward contract was signed on that date to purchase FC100,000 at a forward rate of $.21. On June 12, when the parts are received, the spot rate is $.23. At what amount should the parts be carried on Leickner's books?
    a. $20,000.
    b. $21,000.
    c. $22,000.
    d. $23,000.

2. Which of the following combinations correctly describes the relationship between foreign currency transactions, exchange rate changes, and foreign exchange gains and losses?

	Type of Transaction	Foreign Currency	Foreign Exchange Gain or Loss
a.	Export sale	Appreciates	Loss
b.	Import purchase	Appreciates	Gain
c.	Import purchase	Depreciates	Gain
d.	Export sale	Depreciates	Gain

3. A U.S. exporter has a French franc account receivable resulting from an export sale on April 1, 2001, to a French customer. The exporter signed a forward contract on April 1, 2001, to sell French francs. The spot rate was $.22 on that date and the forward rate was $.23. Which of the following would the U.S. exporter have reported in 2001 income?
    a. Net gain resulting from a forward rate discount.
    b. Net loss resulting from a forward rate premium.
    c. Net loss resulting from a forward rate discount.
    d. Net gain resulting from a forward rate premium.

4. In accounting for foreign currency transactions, which of the following approaches is used in the United States?
    a. One-transaction perspective; accrue foreign exchange gains and losses.
    b. One-transaction perspective; defer foreign exchange gains and losses.
    c. Two-transaction perspective; defer foreign exchange gains and losses.
    d. Two-transaction perspective; accrue foreign exchange gains and losses.

Use the following information for problems 5 and 6.

MNC Corp. (a U.S.-based company) sold parts to a Korean customer on December 16, 2001, with payment of 10 million Korean won to be received on January 15, 2002. The following exchange rates apply:

Date	Spot Rate	Forward Rate (to January 15, 2002)
December 16, 2001	$.0035	$.0034
December 31, 2001	.0033	.0032
January 15, 2002	.0038	

5. Assuming no forward contract was entered into, how much foreign exchange gain or loss should MNC report on its 2001 income statement with regard to this transaction?
   a. $5,000 gain.
   b. $3,000 gain.
   c. $2,000 loss.
   d. $1,000 loss.

6. Assuming a forward contract was entered into to hedge this foreign currency transaction, what would be the net impact on income in 2001 resulting from a fluctuation in the value of the won?
   a. No impact on income.
   b. $500 decrease in income.
   c. $1,000 decrease in income.
   d. $5,000 increase in income.

7. On October 1, 2001, Mud Co., a U.S. company, purchased parts from Terra, a Portuguese company, with payment due on December 1, 2001. If Mud's 2001 operating income included no foreign exchange gain or loss, the transaction could have
   a. Resulted in an extraordinary gain.
   b. Been denominated in U.S. dollars.
   c. Caused a foreign exchange gain to be reported as a deferred charge on the balance sheet.
   d. Caused a foreign exchange gain to be reported as a separate component of stockholders' equity.

   (AICPA adapted)

Use the following information for problems 8 through 10.

   On October 31, 2001, Jean-Louis Company received an order for a machine from a customer in Canada at a price of 100,000 Canadian dollars. The machine was shipped and payment was received on January 5, 2002. On October 31, 2001, Jean-Louis Company purchased a put option giving it the right to sell 100,000 Canadian dollars on January 5, 2002, at a price of $80,000. The option premium was $.015 per Canadian dollar. The option had a fair value of $1,700 on December 31, 2001. The following spot exchange rates apply:

Date	U.S. $ per Canadian $
October 31, 2001	$.80
December 31, 2001	.79
January 5, 2002	.77

8. What was the net impact on Jean-Louis's 2001 income as a result of this transaction and option hedge?
   a. $0.
   b. $200 increase in income.
   c. $200 decrease in income.
   d. $1,500 increase in income.

9. What was the net impact on Jean-Louis's 2002 income as a result of this transaction and option hedge?
   a. $0.
   b. $77,000 increase in income.
   c. $78,300 increase in income.
   d. $80,000 increase in income.

10. What was the net increase or decrease in cash flow from having purchased the foreign currency option to hedge this exposure to foreign exchange risk?
   a. $0.
   b. $1,500 increase in cash flow.
   c. $1,500 decrease in cash flow.
   d. $3,000 increase in cash flow.

11. Post, Inc., had a receivable from a foreign customer that is payable in the local currency of the customer. On December 31, 2001, this receivable for 200,000 local currency units (LCU) was correctly included in Post's balance sheet at $110,000. When the

receivable was collected on February 25, 2002, the U.S. dollar equivalent was $120,000. In Post's 2002 consolidated income statement, how much should be reported as a foreign exchange gain?

a. $0.
b. $10,000.
c. $30,000.
d. $40,000.

(AICPA adapted)

12. On July 1, 2001, Haywood Company borrowed 1,680,000 lire from a foreign lender, evidenced by an interest-bearing note due on July 1, 2002. The note is denominated in lire. The U.S. dollar equivalent of the note principal is as follows:

Date	Amount
July 1, 2001 (date borrowed)	$210,000
December 31, 2001 (Haywood's year-end)	$240,000
July 1, 2002 (date repaid)	$280,000

In its 2002 income statement, what amount should Haywood include as a foreign exchange gain or loss?

a. $0.
b. $70,000 gain.
c. $70,000 loss.
d. $40,000 gain.
e. $40,000 loss.

(AICPA adapted)

13. Slick Co. had a Japanese yen receivable resulting from exports to Japan and a Belgian franc payable resulting from imports from Belgium. Slick recorded foreign exchange gains related to both its yen receivable and franc payable. Did the foreign currencies increase or decrease in dollar value from the date of the transaction to the settlement date?

	Yen	Franc
a.	Increase	Increase
b.	Decrease	Decrease
c.	Decrease	Increase
d.	Increase	Decrease

(AICPA adapted)

14. Grete Corp. had the following foreign currency transactions during 2001:

■ Merchandise was purchased from a foreign supplier on January 20, 2001, for the U.S. dollar equivalent of $60,000. The invoice was paid on April 20, 2001, at the U.S. dollar equivalent of $68,000.

■ On September 1, 2001, Grete borrowed the U.S. dollar equivalent of $300,000 evidenced by a note that was payable in the lender's local currency on September 1, 2001. On December 31, 2001, the U.S. dollar equivalents of the principal amount and accrued interest were $320,000 and $12,000, respectively. Interest on the note is 10 percent per annum.

In Grete's 2001 income statement, what amount should be included as a foreign exchange loss?

a. $4,000.
b. $20,000.
c. $22,000.
d. $30,000.

15. The Pankow Corporation (a U.S. company) received an order to manufacture a special piece of equipment for a customer in Sweden. The machine is to be delivered in three months with payment of 1 million Swedish kronor on that date. On the date the order is accepted, the spot rate is $.15 per krona, and Pankow acquires a three-month option to sell 1 million Swedish kronor. The option strike price is $.15 and the premium is $.005 per unit. At the end of three months, Pankow delivers the equipment and receives

1 million kronor. The spot rate at that date is $.143 per krona. What is the amount that Pankow would report in income as a result of this transaction?

a. $140,000.
b. $143,000.
c. $145,000.
d. $150,000.

16. The Palmer Corporation operates as a U.S. corporation. Palmer recently entered into a forward exchange contract. The company promised to pay 200,000 ramda in six months in exchange for $31,000. This contract was entered into because the company has a firm commitment to sell merchandise to a customer in six months for 200,000 ramda. At the date of acquiring the forward contract, $.17 = 1 ramda. After two months, the spot rate is $.18 = 1 ramda and the rate on a forward contract maturing in four months is $.172 = 1 ramda. How does Palmer reflect the change in the value of the ramda at the end of two months?

a. Recognizes a $3,400 loss on forward contract only.
b. Recognizes a $3,400 gain on firm commitment only.
c. Recognizes a $3,400 loss on forward contract and a $3,400 gain on firm commitment.
d. Recognizes a $3,400 deferred foreign exchange loss.

17. Deveto Corporation acquired merchandise from a foreign supplier on November 12, 2001, for 60,000 LCU (local currency units). The debt was paid on January 19, 2002. The following currency rates are known:

November 12, 2001	$1 = .29 LCU
December 31, 2001	$1 = .33 LCU
January 19, 2002	$1 = .28 LCU

How is the 2001 income statement of Deveto affected by the fluctuations in currency values? How is the 2002 income statement of Deveto affected by the fluctuations in currency values?

18. On December 20, 2001, Butanta Company (a U.S. company headquartered in Miami, Florida) sold parts to a foreign customer at a price of 50,000 ostras. Payment is received on January 10, 2002. Currency exchange rates are as follows:

December 20, 2001	1 ostra = $1.05
December 31, 2001	1 ostra = $1.02
January 10, 2002	1 ostra = $.98

How is the 2001 income statement of Butanta affected by the fluctuations in currency values? How is the 2002 income statement of Butanta affected by the fluctuations in currency values?

19. New Colony Corporation (a U.S. company) made a sale to a foreign customer on September 15, 2001, for 100,000 foreign currency units (FCU). Payment was received on October 15, 2001. The following exchange rates apply:

September 15, 2001	FCU 1 = $.40
September 30, 2001	FCU 1 = $.42
October 15, 2001	FCU 1 = $.37

Required

Prepare all journal entries for New Colony in connection with this sale assuming that the company closes its books on September 30 to prepare interim financial statements.

20. On December 1, 2001, the Dresden Company (an American company in Albany, New York) purchases inventory from a foreign supplier for 60,000 local currency units (LCU). Payments will be made in 90 days after Dresden has sold this merchandise. Sales are made rather quickly and Dresden pays this entire obligation on January 28, 2002. Currency exchange rates are as follows:

December 1, 2001	$.88 = 1 LCU
December 31, 2001	$.82 = 1 LCU
January 28, 2002	$.90 = 1 LCU

Required

Prepare all journal entries for the Dresden Company in connection with the purchase and payment.

21. A U.S. company carries out a set of transactions in a foreign country during 2001. Prepare all journal entries in U.S. dollars along with an December 31, 2001, adjusting entries.

Currency exchange rates are as follows:

June 1, 2001	\$.52 = 1 ertu
August 1, 2001	\$.55 = 1 ertu
October 1, 2001	\$.60 = 1 ertu
November 1, 2001	\$.64 = 1 ertu
December 31, 2001	\$.65 = 1 ertu

June 1   Bought inventory of 20,000 ertus on credit.
Aug. 1   Sold all inventory for 30,000 ertus on credit.
Oct. 1   Paid 10,000 ertus on 6/1 purchase.
Nov. 1   Collected 10,000 ertus from 8/1 sale.

22. The Acme Corporation (a United States company in Sarasota, Florida) has the following import/export transactions in 2001:

Mar. 1   Bought inventory costing 50,000 pesos on credit.
May 1   Sold 60 percent of the inventory for 45,000 pesos on credit.
Aug. 1   Collected 40,000 pesos from customers.
Sept. 1   Paid 30,000 pesos to creditors.

Currency exchange rates are as follows:

March 1, 2001	\$.17 = 1 peso
May 1, 2001	\$.18 = 1 peso
August 1, 2001	\$.19 = 1 peso
September 1, 2001	\$.20 = 1 peso
December 31, 2001	\$.21 = 1 peso

For each of the following accounts, what will Acme report on its 2001 financial statements?

Inventory	Accounts Receivable
Cost of Goods Sold	Accounts Payable
Sales	Cash

23. The Brandlin Company of Anaheim, California, sells parts to a foreign customer on December 1, 2001, with payment of 20,000 korunas to be received on March 1, 2002. Brandlin enters into a forward contract on December 1, 2001, to sell 20,000 korunas on March 1, 2002.

Relevant exchange rates for the koruna (K) on various dates are as follows:

Date	Spot Rate	Forward Rate (to March 1, 2002)
December 1, 2001	\$2.00	\$2.08
December 31, 2001	\$2.10	\$2.20
March 1, 2002	\$2.25	

Required

Prepare journal entries for these transactions in U.S. dollars assuming that December 31 is Brandlin's year-end. What is the impact on 2001 income? What is the impact on 2002 income?

24. On November 10, 2001, the Ace Company sells inventory to a customer in a foreign country. Ace agrees to accept 80,000 matejkas (MJ) in full payment for this inventory. Payment is to be made on February 1, 2002. On December 1, 2001, Ace enters into a

forward exchange contract wherein 80,000 matejkas will be delivered to a currency broker in two months.

Relevant exchange rates for the matejka on various dates are as follows:

Date	Spot Rate	Forward Rate (to February 1, 2002)
November 10, 2001	$0.29	$0.30
December 1, 2001	$0.27	$0.29
December 31, 2001	$0.24	$0.27
February 1, 2002	$0.26	

Required

a. What is the 2001 income effect created by the company's dealings in their foreign currency?

b. What is the 2002 income effect created by the company's dealings in their foreign currency?

c. What would be the effect on net income in 2001 if the sale had originally occurred on December 1, 2001, the same date that the forward exchange contract was acquired?

d. Assume that the customer had made a firm commitment on December 1, 2001, to pay MJ 80,000 for the inventory when delivered on February 1, 2002. The forward exchange contract was acquired on that date to hedge this commitment. What would have been the effect on 2001 net income?

25. The Bartlett Company in Cincinnati, Ohio, has occasional transactions with companies in foreign countries. Prepare journal entries for the following transactions in U.S. dollars. Also prepare any necessary adjusting entries caused by fluctuations in the value of the foreign currencies. Assume that December 31 is Bartlett's year-end and that the company uses a perpetual inventory system.

2001

Feb. 1	Bought equipment for 40,000 lire on credit.
Apr. 1	Paid for the above equipment.
June 1	Bought inventory for 30,000 lire on credit.
Aug. 1	Sold 70 percent of above inventory for 40,000 lire on credit.
Oct. 1	Collected 30,000 lire from the sales made on August 1, 1999.
Nov. 1	Paid 20,000 lire on the debts incurred on June 1, 1999.

2002

Feb. 1	Collected remaining 10,000 lire from August 1, 1999 sales.
Mar. 1	Paid remaining 10,000 lire on the debts incurred on June 1, 1999.

Currency exchange rates are as follows:

February 1, 2001	$.44 = 1 lire
April 1, 2001	$.45 = 1 lire
June 1, 2001	$.47 = 1 lire
August 1, 2001	$.48 = 1 lire
October 1, 2001	$.49 = 1 lire
November 1, 2001	$.50 = 1 lire
December 31, 2001	$.52 = 1 lire
February 1, 2002	$.54 = 1 lire
March 1, 2002	$.55 = 1 lire

26. On June 1, 2001, Alexander Corporation sold goods to a customer in the country of Jungland at a price of 1,000,000 jungs (the local currency of Jungland—abbreviated JG). Payment will be received in three months on September 1, 2001. On June 1, 2001, Alexander enters into a contract to sell JG 1,000,000 in three months at a forward rate of $.049. The company must close its books and prepare its second-quarter financial statements on June 30.

Relevant exchange rates for the jung are as follows:

Date	Spot Rate	Forward Rate (to September 1, 2001)
June 1, 2001	$.045	$.049
June 30, 2001	$.048	$.051
September 1, 2001	$.044	

Required:

a. Determine the impact the change in the value of the JG has on Alexander's second-quarter 2001 income.

b. Determine the impact the change in the value of the JG has on Alexander's third-quarter 2001 income.

c. What is Alexander's net economic benefit (or loss) from hedging its foreign currency transaction? How is this benefit (or loss) recognized in the accounts?

27. On November 1, 2001, an American company buys inventory from a supplier in the country of Spagnola. The price of this inventory was 10,000 thads (the local currency of Spagnola—abbreviated TD) to be paid in three months on February 1, 2002.

Relevant exchange rates for the thad are as follows:

Date	Spot Rate	Forward Rate (to February 1, 2002)
November 1, 2001	$.21	$.24
December 1, 2001	$.24	$.26
December 31, 2001	$.28	$.30
February 1, 2002	$.25	

Required:

a. How is the American company's net income affected in 2001 by the changes in the relative value of the thad? How is the American company's net income affected in 2002?

b. Assume that on December 1, 2001, the American company enters into a two-month forward exchange contract whereby 10,000 thads will be received on February 1, 2002, in exchange for $2,600. How is the American company's net income affected in 2001 by the acquisition of the inventory and the forward exchange contract? How is the American company's net income affected in 2002?

28. On October 1, 2001, a forward exchange contract was acquired whereby the Hawkins Company was to pay 100,000 LCU in four months (on February 1, 2002) and receive $65,000 in U.S. dollars. Exchange rates for the LCU are as follows:

Date	Spot Rate	Forward Rate (to February 1, 2002)
October 1, 2001	$.69	$.65
December 31, 2001	$.71	$.74
February 1, 2002	$.72	

Required:

a. What journal entries are recorded if the forward exchange contract was entered into to hedge a LCU 100,000 receivable arising from a sale made on October 1, 2001? Include entries for both the sale and the forward contract.

b. What journal entries are made if the forward exchange contract was entered into to hedge a firm commitment related to a LCU 100,000 cash sale that will be made on February 1, 2002? Include entries for both the firm commitment and the forward contract.

29. On November 1, 2001, Tompson Company enters into a four-month forward exchange contract whereby the company will receive 20,000 LCUs (the currency of a foreign country) on March 1, 2002. In exchange, Tompson agrees to pay for these LCUs at the rate of 1 LCU = $.68. The actual spot rate on November 1, 2001, is 1 LCU = $.62 but rises to 1 LCU = $.64 by December 31, 2001, and 1 LCU = $.69 on March 1, 2002. On December 31, 2001, a two-month forward exchange contract has a rate of 1 LCU = $.72.

Required

a. Assume that Tompson entered into the four-month forward exchange contract to hedge the effects of a 20,000 LCU liability that was incurred on November 1, 2001, and will be paid on March 1, 2002. What amount of income should Tompson recognize in each of these two years?

b. Assume that Tompson entered into the four-month forward exchange contract to hedge the effects of a 20,000 LCU commitment that was made on November 1, 2001, to buy inventory on March 1, 2002. What amount of income should Tompson recognize in each of these two years? At what amount will the inventory be recorded on March 1, 2002?

c. Assume that Tompson entered into the four-month forward exchange contract for investment purposes and that the contract was sold on January 11, 2002, for $610 cash. What amount of income should Tompson recognize in each of these two years?

30. Benjamin, Inc., operates an export/import business. The company, located in Mobile, Alabama, has considerable dealings with companies in the country of Camerrand. All transactions with these companies are denominated in alaries (AL), the currency in use in Camerrand. During 2001, Benjamin acquires 20,000 widgets at a price of 8 alaries per widget with payment to be made when the items are sold. Currency exchange rates are as follows:

September 1, 2001	AL 1 = $.46
December 1, 2001	AL 1 = $.44
December 31, 2001	AL 1 = $.48
March 1, 2002	AL 1 = $.45

Required

a. Assume that Benjamin's acquisition took place on December 1, 2001, with payment being made on March 1, 2002. What is the effect of the rate fluctuations on reported income in 2001 and in 2002?

b. Assume that Benjamin's acquisition took place on September 1, 2001, with payment being made on December 1, 2001. What is the effect of the rate fluctuations on reported income in 2001?

c. Assume that Benjamin's acquisition took place on September 1, 2001, with payment being made on March 1, 2002. What is the effect of the rate fluctuations on reported income in 2001 and in 2002?

31. On November 1, 2001, the Derek Corporation of San Francisco acquires a six-month forward exchange contract. Under the terms of this agreement, Derek agrees to purchase 20,000 milazzos (MZ) at a forward rate of $.42 per MZ. The spot rate on that date is $.48 per MZ. Subsequent exchange rates are as follows:

December 31, 2001 (spot rate)	$.45 = 1 milazzo
December 31, 2001 (four-month forward rate)	$.40 = 1 milazzo
May 1, 2002 (spot rate)	$.50 = 1 milazzo

Required

a. Make all the journal entries for Derek if the contract was acquired for speculative purposes.

b. Make all the journal entries for Derek if the company had incurred a commitment on November 1, 2001, to acquire equipment on May 1, 2002, for 20,000 milazzos.

c. Make all the journal entries for Derek if the company acquired land on November 1, 2001, for 20,000 milazzos with payment to be made on May 1, 2002.

32. Eximco Corporation (based in Champaign, Illinois) has a number of transactions with companies in the country of Mongagua. On November 15, 2001, Eximco sold equipment at a price of 500,000 mongs to a Mongaguan customer with payment to be received on January 15, 2002. In addition, on November 15, 2001, Eximco purchased raw materials from a Mongaguan supplier at a price of 300,000 mongs; payment will be made on January 15, 2002. To hedge its net asset exposure in mongs, Eximco entered into a two-month forward contract on November 15, 2001, wherein Eximco will deliver 200,000 mongs to the foreign currency broker in exchange for $104,000. The following rates for the mong apply:

Date	Spot Rate	Forward Rate (to January 15, 2002)
November 15, 2001	$.53	$.52
December 31, 2001	$.50	$.48
January 15, 2002	$.49	

Required

Prepare all journal entries including December 31 adjusting entries to record these transactions. What is the net impact on net income in 2001? In 2002?

33. On September 30, 2001, the Ericson Company negotiated a two-year, 1,000,000 dudek loan from a foreign bank at an interest rate of 2 percent per annum. Interest payments are made annually on September 30 and the principal will be repaid on September 30, 2003. Ericson prepares U.S. dollar financial statements and has a December 31 year-end. Prepare all journal entries related to this foreign currency borrowing assuming the following exchange rates:

> September 30, 2001 . . . . 1 dudek = $.10
> December 31, 2001 . . . . 1 dudek = $.105
> September 30, 2002 . . . . 1 dudek = $.120
> December 31, 2002 . . . . 1 dudek = $.125
> September 30, 2003 . . . . 1 dudek = $.150

What is the effective cost of borrowing in dollars in each of the years 2001, 2002, and 2003?

34. The Big Arber Company ordered parts from a foreign supplier on May 25, 2001, at a price of 50,000 pijios when the spot rate was $.20 per pijio. Delivery and payment were scheduled for June 25, 2001. On May 25, 2001, Big Arber acquired a call option on 50,000 pijios at a strike price of $.19 and premium of $.008 per unit. The parts are delivered and paid for according to schedule.
   a. Assuming a spot rate of $.21 per pijio on June 25, 2001, at what amount will the parts be recorded when received?
   b. Assuming a spot rate of $.18 per pijio on June 25, 2001, at what amount will the parts be recorded when received?

35. On November 15, 2001, Anderson Company sold merchandise to a foreign customer for 100,000 LCU to be received on January 15, 2002. At the date of sale, when the spot rate was $1.10 per LCU, Anderson acquired a put option to sell 100,000 LCU in two months. Given a strike price of $1.12, the premium paid for the option was $.025 per LCU. The following information was gathered:

Date	Spot Rate	Fair Value of Option
December 31, 2001	$1.095	$2,750
January 15, 2002	$1.103	$1,700

Required

   a. Prepare all journal entries for the sale and option hedge assuming December 31 is Anderson's year-end. What is the impact on 2001 income? What is the impact on 2002 income?
   b. Assume the spot rate on January 15, 2002, is $1.123 and the option has a fair value of zero on that date. Prepare all journal entries for the sale and option hedge.

36. Based on past experience, the Leickner Company expects that it will need to purchase component parts from a foreign supplier at a cost of 1,000,000 marks on March 15, 2002. To hedge this forecasted transaction, a three-month call option to purchase 1,000,000 marks is acquired on December 15, 2001. Leickner selects a strike price of $.58 per mark, paying a premium of $.005 per unit, when the spot rate is $.57. The spot rate increases to $.58 at December 31, 2001, causing the fair value of the option to increase to $8,000. By March 15, 2002, when the parts are purchased, the spot rate has climbed to $.59 resulting in a fair value for the option of $10,000.

Required

Prepare all journal entries for the option hedge of a forecasted transaction and for the purchase of component parts assuming that December 31 is Leickner's year-end. What is the impact on 2001 income? What is the impact on 2002 income? What is the carrying value of the component parts inventory? What is the net cash outflow to acquire the component parts?

37. Vino Veritas Company, a U.S.-based importer of wines and spirits, placed an order with a French supplier for 1,000 cases of wine at a price of Fr 1,000 per case. The total purchase price is Fr 1 million. Relevant exchange rates are as follows:

Date	Spot Rate	Forward Rate (to October 15, 2002)
September 15, 2002	$.1695	$.1698
September 30, 2002	$.1700	$.1705
October 15, 2002	$.1703	

Vino Veritas Company closes the books and prepares financial statements at September 30.

Required

a. Assume the wine was received on September 15, 2002, and payment was made on October 15, 2002. There was no attempt to hedge the exposure to foreign exchange risk. Prepare journal entries to account for this import purchase.

b. Assume the wine was received on September 15, 2002, and payment was made on October 15, 2002. On September 15, Vino Veritas Corporation purchased Fr 1 million 30 days forward. Prepare journal entries to account for this import purchase and foreign currency forward contract.

c. The wine was ordered on September 15, 2002. It was received and paid for on October 15, 2002. On September 15, Vino Veritas Corporation purchased Fr 1 million 30 days forward. Prepare journal entries to account for this import purchase and foreign currency forward contract.

d. The wine was received on September 15, 2002, and payment was made on October 15, 2002. On September 15, Vino Veritas Corporation purchased a 30-day call option for Fr 1 million with a strike price of $.1695. The option premium was $.001 per Fr. The option had a fair value of $1,000 on September 15, $1,100 on September 30, and $800 on October 15. Prepare journal entries to account for this import purchase and foreign currency option.

e. The wine was ordered on September 15, 2002. It was received and paid for on October 15, 2002. On September 15, Vino Veritas Corporation purchased a 30-day call option for Fr 1 million with a strike price of $.1695 at a premium of $.001 per Fr. The option had a fair value of $1,000 on September 15, $1,100 on September 30, and $800 on October 15. Prepare journal entries to account for this import purchase and foreign currency option.

Translation of Foreign Currency Financial Statements

H.J. Heinz Company added to its roster of international affiliates with the opening of a factory in Russia, and the acquisition of an infant formula and dairy products company in the Czech Republic.[1]

During the year, Gillette augmented its thriving business in India, the world's largest blade market, with the acquisition of Wiltech India, Ltd.[2]

Under an agreement with the Israeli government announced in November, Intel will build a $1.6 billion plant in Kiryat Gat, thirty-five miles outside Jerusalem.[3]

Recent announcements like these have become more the norm than the exception in today's global economy. Companies establish operations in foreign countries for a variety of reasons including the development of new markets for their products, taking advantage of lower production costs, or gaining access to raw materials. Some multinational companies have reached a stage in their development in which domestic operations are no longer considered to be of higher priority than international operations. For example, U.S.-based International Flavors and Fragrances, Inc., has operations in 33 countries and has 64 percent of its assets outside of the United States. The Coca-Cola Company generates over 70 percent of its sales and almost 80 percent of its profits from foreign operations.

For the parent company foreign operations create numerous managerial problems that do not exist for domestic operations. Some of these problems arise from cultural differences between the home and foreign countries. Other problems exist because foreign operations

---

[1]H.J. Heinz, First Quarter 1996 Report, p. 1.
[2]The Gillette Company, 1995 Annual Report, p. 7.
[3]KPMG Peat Marwick, "Border Crossings," *World Business*, May–June 1996, p. 50.

generally are required to comply with the laws and regulations of the foreign country. For example, in most countries, companies are required to prepare financial statements in the local currency using local accounting rules.

To prepare worldwide consolidated financial statements, a U.S. parent company must (1) convert the foreign GAAP financial statements of its foreign operations into U.S. GAAP, and (2) translate the financial statements from the foreign currency into U.S. dollars. This conversion and translation process must be carried out regardless of whether the foreign operation is a branch, joint venture, majority owned subsidiary, or affiliate accounted for under the equity method. Differences in GAAP and problems associated with those differences are discussed in the next chapter. This chapter deals with the issue of translating foreign currency financial statements into the parent's reporting currency.

There are two major theoretical issues related to the translation process: (1) which **translation method** should be used and (2) where the resulting **translation adjustment** should be reported in the consolidated financial statements. In this chapter, these two issues are examined first from a conceptual perspective and second by the manner in which these issues have been resolved by the FASB in the United States.

EXCHANGE RATES USED IN TRANSLATION

Two types of exchange rates are used in translating financial statements:

1. **Historical exchange rate**—the exchange rate that exists when a transaction occurs.
2. **Current exchange rate**—the exchange rate that exists at the balance sheet date.

Translation methods differ as to which balance sheet and income statement accounts are translated at historical exchange rates and which are translated at current exchange rates.

Assume that the company described in the discussion question on the next page began operations in Gualos on December 31, 2001, when the exchange rate was $.20 per vilsek. When Southwestern Corporation prepared its consolidated balance sheet at December 31, 2001, it has no choice about the exchange rate it uses to translate the Land into U.S. dollars. Land carried on the foreign subsidiary's books at 150,000 vilseks is translated at an exchange rate of $.20; $.20 is both the *historical* and *current* exchange rate for Land at December 31, 2001.

Consolidated Balance Sheet: 12/31/01
Land (150,000 vilseks × $.20) $30,000

During the first quarter of 2002, the vilsek appreciates relative to the U.S. dollar by 15 percent; the exchange rate at March 31, 2002, is $.23 per vilsek. In preparing its balance sheet at the end of the first quarter of 2002, Southwestern now must decide whether Land carried on the subsidiary's balance sheet at 150,000 vilseks should be translated into dollars using the *historical exchange rate* of $.20 or the *current exchange rate* of $.23.

If the historical exchange rate is used at March 31, 2002, Land continues to be carried on the consolidated balance sheet at $30,000 with no change from December 31, 2001.

DISCUSSION QUESTION

How Do We Report This?

The Southwestern Corporation operates throughout Texas buying and selling widgets. In hopes of expanding into more profitable markets, the company recently decided to open a small subsidiary in the nearby country of Gualos. The currency in Gualos is the vilsek. For some time, the government of that country held the exchange rate constant: 1 vilsek equaled $.20 (or 5 vilseks equaled $1.00). Initially, Southwestern invested cash in this new operation; its $90,000 was converted into 450,000 vilseks ($90,000 × 5). One-third of this money (150,000 vilseks or $30,000) was used to purchase land to be held for the possible construction of a plant, one-third was invested in short-term marketable securities, and one-third was spent in acquiring inventory for future resale.

Shortly thereafter, the Gualos government officially revalued the currency so that 1 vilsek was worth $.23. Because of the strength of the local economy, the vilsek gained buying power in relation to the U.S. dollar. Now the vilsek was considered more valuable than in the past. The accountants for Southwestern realized that a change had occurred; each of the assets was now worth more in U.S. dollars than the original $30,000 investment: 150,000 vilseks × $.23 = $34,500. Two of the company's top officers met to determine the appropriate method for reporting this change in currency values.

Controller: Nothing has changed. Our cost is still $30,000 for each item. That's what we spent. Accounting uses historical cost wherever possible. Thus, we should do nothing.

Finance director: Yes, but the old rates are meaningless now. We would be foolish to report figures based on a rate that no longer exists. The cost is still 150,000 vilseks for each item. You are right, the cost has not changed. However, the vilsek is now worth $.23 so our reported value must change.

Controller: The new rate only affects us if we take money out of the country. We don't plan to do that for many years. The rate will probably change 20 more times before we remove money from Gualos. We've got to stick to our $30,000 historical cost. That's our cost and that's good, basic accounting.

Finance director: You mean that for the next 20 years we will be translating balances for external reporting purposes using an exchange rate that has not existed for years? That does not make sense. I have a real problem using an antiquated rate for the investments and inventory. They will be sold for cash when the new rate is in effect. These balances have no remaining relation to the original exchange rate.

Controller: You misunderstand the impact of an exchange rate fluctuation. Within Gualos, no impact occurs. One vilsek is still one vilsek. The effect is only realized when an actual conversion takes place into U.S. dollars at a new rate. At that point, we will properly measure and report the gain or loss. That is when realization takes place. Until then our cost has not changed.

Finance director: I simply see no value at all in producing financial information based entirely on an exchange rate that does not exist. I don't care when realization takes place.

Controller: You've got to stick with historical cost, believe me. The exchange rate today isn't important unless we actually convert vilseks to dollars.

How should Southwestern report each of these three assets on its current balance sheet? Does the company have a gain because the value of the vilsek has increased relative to the U.S. dollar?

Historical Rate—Consolidated Balance Sheet: 3/31/02

Land (150,000 vilseks × $.20) $30,000

If the current exchange rate is used, Land is carried on the consolidated balance sheet at $34,500, an increase of $4,500 from December 31, 2001.

Current Rate—Consolidated Balance Sheet: 3/31/02

Land (150,000 vilseks × $.23) $34,500

Translation Adjustments

To keep the accounting equation (A = L + OE) in balance, the increase of $4,500 on the asset (A) side of the consolidated balance sheet when the current exchange rate is used must be offset by an equal $4,500 *increase* in owners' equity (OE) on the other side of the balance sheet. The increase in owners' equity is called a **positive translation adjustment.** It has a *credit* balance.

The increase in dollar value of the Land due to appreciation of the vilsek creates a positive translation adjustment. This is true for any asset on the Gualos subsidiary's balance sheet that is translated at the *current* exchange rate. *Assets translated at the current exchange rate when the foreign currency has appreciated generate a positive (credit) translation adjustment.*

Liabilities on the Gualos subsidiary's balance sheet that are translated at the current exchange rate also increase in dollar value when the vilsek appreciates. For example, Notes Payable of 10,000 vilseks would be reported at $2,000 on the December 31, 2001, balance sheet and at $2,300 on the March 31, 2002, balance sheet. To keep the accounting equation in balance, the increase in liabilities (L) must be offset by a *decrease* in owners' equity (OE), giving rise to a **negative translation adjustment.** This has a *debit* balance. *Liabilities translated at the current exchange rate when the foreign currency has appreciated generate a negative (debit) translation adjustment.*

Balance Sheet Exposure

Balance sheet items (assets and liabilities) translated at the *current* exchange rate change in dollar value from balance sheet to balance sheet as a result of the change in exchange rate. These items are *exposed* to translation adjustment. Balance sheet items translated at *historical* exchange rates do not change in dollar value from one balance sheet to the next. These items are *not* exposed to translation adjustment. Exposure to translation adjustment is referred to as balance sheet, translation, or accounting exposure. **Balance sheet exposure** can be contrasted with the **transaction exposure** discussed in Chapter 9 that arises when a company has foreign currency receivables and payables in the following way: *Transaction exposure gives rise to foreign exchange gains and losses that are ultimately realized in cash; translation adjustments arising from balance sheet exposure do not directly result in cash inflows or outflows.*

Each item translated at the current exchange rate is exposed to translation adjustment. In effect, a separate translation adjustment exists for each of these exposed items. However, positive translation adjustments on assets when the foreign currency appreciates are offset by negative translation adjustments on liabilities. If total exposed assets are equal to total exposed liabilities throughout the year, the translation adjustments (although perhaps significant on an individual basis) net to a zero balance. The *net* translation adjustment needed to keep the consolidated balance sheet in balance is based solely on the *net asset* or *net liability* exposure.

A foreign operation has a **net asset balance sheet exposure** when assets translated at the current exchange rate are greater in amount than liabilities translated at the current exchange rate. A **net liability balance sheet exposure** exists when liabilities translated at the current exchange rate are greater than assets translated at the current exchange rate. The relationship between exchange rate fluctuations, balance sheet exposure, and translation adjustments is summarized as follows:

Balance Sheet Exposure	Foreign Currency (FC)	
	Appreciates	**Depreciates**
Net Asset	Positive Translation Adjustment	Negative Translation Adjustment
Net Liability	Negative Translation Adjustment	Positive Translation Adjustment

Exactly how the translation adjustment should be handled in the consolidated financial statements is a matter of some debate. The major question is whether the translation adjustments should be treated as a *translation gain or loss reported in net income* or whether the translation adjustment should be treated as a *direct adjustment to owners' equity without affecting net income.* We consider this issue in more detail later after examining methods of translation.

TRANSLATION METHODS

Two major methods of translation are currently used: (1) the current rate (or closing rate) method, and (2) the temporal method. We discuss these methods from the perspective of a U.S.-based multinational company translating foreign currency financial statements into U.S. dollars.

Current Rate Method

The basic assumption underlying the **current rate method** is that a company's *net investment* in a foreign operation is *exposed* to foreign exchange risk. In other words, a foreign operation represents a foreign currency net asset and if the foreign currency *decreases* in value against the U.S. dollar, then there is a *decrease in the U.S. dollar value of the foreign currency net asset*. This decrease in U.S. dollar value of the net investment will be reflected by reporting a *negative* (debit balance) translation adjustment in the consolidated financial statements. If the foreign currency *increases* in value, then there is an *increase in the U.S. dollar value of the net asset* which will be reflected through a *positive* (credit balance) translation adjustment.

To measure the net investment's exposure to foreign exchange risk, *all assets and all liabilities* of the foreign operation are translated at the *current* exchange rate. Stockholders' equity items are translated at historical rates. *The balance sheet exposure under the current rate method is equal to the foreign operation's net asset (total assets minus total liabilities) position.*[4]

$$\text{Total Assets} > \text{Total Liabilities} \rightarrow \text{Net Asset Exposure}$$

A positive translation adjustment arises when the foreign currency appreciates and a negative translation adjustment arises when the foreign currency depreciates.

As mentioned earlier, the major difference between the translation adjustment and a foreign exchange gain or loss is that the translation adjustment is not necessarily realized through inflows and outflows of cash. The translation adjustment arising when the current rate method is used is unrealized. It can become a realized gain or loss only if the foreign operation is sold (for its book value) and the foreign currency proceeds from the sale are converted into U.S. dollars.

Under the current rate method, all income statement items are translated at the exchange rate in effect at the date of accounting recognition. In most cases, an assumption can be made that the revenue or expense is incurred evenly throughout the accounting period and a weighted average-for-the-period exchange rate can be used for translation. However, when an income account, such as a gain or loss, occurs at a specific point in time, the exchange rate at that date should be used for translation.[5]

Temporal Method

The basic objective underlying the **temporal method** of translation is to produce a set of U.S. dollar translated financial statements as if the foreign subsidiary had actually used U.S. dollars in conducting its operations. Continuing with the Gualos subsidiary example presented earlier, Land should be reported on the consolidated balance sheet at the amount of U.S. dollars that would have been spent if the U.S. parent had sent dollars to the subsidiary to purchase Land. Since Land had a cost of 150,000 vilseks at a time when one vilsek could be acquired with $.20, the parent would have sent

---

[4]In rare cases, a foreign subsidiary might have liabilities greater than assets (negative stockholders' equity). In those cases, a net liability exposure exists under the current rate method.

[5]Alternatively, all income statement items may be translated at the current exchange rate. Later we demonstrate that translation at the current rate has a slight advantage over translation at the average-for-the-period rate.

$30,000 to the subsidiary to acquire the land—this is the land's historical cost *in U.S. dollar terms*. Consistent with the temporal method's underlying objective is the following rule:

1. Assets and liabilities carried on the foreign operation's balance sheet at *historical cost* are translated at *historical* exchange rates to yield an equivalent historical cost in U.S. dollars.

2. Conversely, assets and liabilities carried at a *current or future value* are translated at the *current* exchange rate to yield an equivalent current value in U.S. dollars.

Application of this rule maintains the underlying valuation method (current value or historical cost) used by the foreign subsidiary in accounting for its assets and liabilities. In addition, Stockholders' Equity accounts are translated at historical exchange rates.

Cash, marketable securities, receivables, and most liabilities are carried at current or future value and translated at the *current* exchange rate under the temporal method.[6] The temporal method generates either a net asset or a net liability balance sheet exposure depending on whether cash plus marketable securities plus receivables are greater than or less than liabilities.

Cash + Marketable Securities + Receivables > Liabilities → Net Asset Exposure

Cash + Marketable Securities + Receivables < Liabilities → Net Liability Exposure

Because liabilities (current plus long-term) usually are greater than assets translated at the current exchange rate, *a net liability exposure generally exists when the temporal method is used.*

One way of understanding the concept of exposure underlying the temporal method is to pretend that the foreign operation's cash, marketable securities, receivables, and payables are actually carried on the parent's balance sheet. For example, consider the Japanese subsidiary of a U.S. parent company. The Japanese yen receivables of the Japanese subsidiary which result from sales in Japan may be thought of as Japanese yen receivables of the U.S. parent which result from export sales to Japan. If the U.S. parent had yen receivables on its balance sheet, a decrease in the value of the yen would result in a *foreign exchange* loss. There also would be a foreign exchange loss on the Japanese yen held in cash by the U.S. parent and on the Japanese yen denominated marketable securities. These foreign exchange losses would be offset by a foreign exchange gain on the parent's Japanese yen payables resulting from foreign purchases. Whether a net gain or a net loss exists depends on the relative size of yen cash, marketable securities, and receivables versus yen payables. Under the temporal method, the translation adjustment measures the "net foreign exchange gain or loss" on the foreign operation's cash, marketable securities, receivables, and payables, *as if those items were actually carried on the books of the parent.*

Again, the major difference between the translation adjustment resulting from use of the temporal method and a foreign exchange gain or loss is that the translation adjustment is not necessarily realized through inflows or outflows of cash. The U.S. dollar translation adjustment in this case *could be realized* only if: (1) the parent sends U.S. dollars to the Japanese subsidiary to pay off all its yen liabilities, and (2) the Japanese subsidiary converts its yen receivables and marketable receivables into yen cash and then sends this amount plus the amount in its yen cash account to the parent in the U.S. where it is converted into U.S. dollars.

---

[6]Under *SFAS 105,* all marketable equity securities and marketable debt securities which are classified as "trading" or "available for sale" are carried at current market value. Marketable debt securities classified as "hold-to-maturity" are carried at cost. Throughout the remainder of this chapter it will be assumed that all marketable securities are reported at current value.

	Temporal Method Exchange Rate	Current Rate Method Exchange Rate
Assets		
Balance Sheet		
Cash and receivables	Current	Current
Marketable securities	Current*	Current
Inventory at market	Current	Current
Inventory at cost	Historical	Current
Prepaid expenses	Historical	Current
Property, plant, and equipment	Historical	Current
Intangible assets	Historical	Current
Liabilities		
Current liabilities	Current	Current
Deferred income	Historical	Current
Long-term debt	Current	Current
Stockholders' equity		
Capital stock	Historical	Historical
Additional paid-in capital	Historical	Historical
Retained earnings	Composite	Composite
Dividends	Historical	Historical
Income Statement		
Revenues	Average	Average
Most expenses	Average	Average
Cost of goods sold	Historical	Average
Depreciation of property, plant, and equipment	Historical	Average
Amortization of intangibles	Historical	Average

*Marketable debt securities classified as hold-to-maturity are carried at cost and translated at the historical exchange rate under the temporal method.

Under the temporal method, income statement items are translated at exchange rates that exist when the revenue is generated or the expense is incurred. For most items, an assumption can be made that the revenue or expense is incurred evenly throughout the accounting period and an average-for-the-period exchange rate can be used for translation. However, some expenses are related to assets carried at historical cost; for example, cost of goods sold, depreciation of fixed assets, and amortization of intangibles. Since the related assets are translated at historical exchange rates, these expenses must be translated at historical rates as well.

The current rate method and temporal method are the two methods currently used in the United States. They are also the predominant methods used worldwide. A summary of the appropriate exchange rate for selected financial statement items under these two methods is presented in Exhibit 10–1.

Translation of Retained Earnings

Stockholders' equity items are translated at historical exchange rates under both the temporal and current rate methods. This creates somewhat of a problem in translating retained earnings. This figure is actually a composite of many previous transactions: all revenues, expenses, gains, losses, and declared dividends occurring over the life of the company. At the end of the first year of operations, foreign currency (FC) retained earnings is translated as follows:

Net income in FC	[translated per method used to translate income statement items]	= Net income in $
− Dividends in FC	× historical exchange rate when declared	= − Dividends in $
Ending R/E in FC		Ending R/E in $

The ending dollar retained earnings in year one becomes the beginning dollar retained earnings for year two and the translated retained earnings in year two (and subsequent years) is then determined as follows:

Beginning R/E in FC	(from last year's translation)	= Beginning R/E in $
+ Net income in FC	[translated per method used to translate income statement items]	= + Net income in $
− Dividends in FC	× historical exchange rate when declared	= − Dividends in $
Ending R/E in FC		Ending R/E in $

The same approach translates retained earnings under both the current rate and the temporal methods. The only difference is that translation of the current period's net income is done differently under the two methods.

COMPLICATING ASPECTS OF THE TEMPORAL METHOD

Under the temporal method, it is necessary to keep a record of the exchange rates when inventory, prepaid expenses, fixed assets, and intangible assets are acquired because these assets, carried at historical cost, are translated at historical exchange rates. Keeping track of the historical rates for these assets is not necessary under the current rate method. Translating these assets at historical rates makes application of the temporal method more complicated than the current rate method.

Calculation of Cost of Goods Sold (COGS)

Under the *current rate method,* COGS in Foreign Currency (FC) is simply translated using the average-for-the-period exchange rate (ER):

$$COGS \text{ in } FC \times Average \text{ } ER = COGS \text{ in } \$$$

Under the *temporal method,* COGS must be decomposed into beginning inventory, purchases, and ending inventory and each component of COGS must then be translated at its appropriate historical rate. For example, if beginning inventory (FIFO basis) in the year 2001 was acquired evenly throughout the fourth quarter of 2000, then the average exchange rate in the fourth quarter of 2000 is used to translate beginning inventory. Likewise, the fourth quarter (4thQ) 2001 exchange rate is used to translate ending inventory. When purchases can be assumed to have been made evenly throughout 2001, then the average 2001 exchange rate is used to translate purchases:

Beginning inventory in FC	× Historical ER (4thQ 2000)	= Beginning inventory in $
+ Purchases in FC	× Average ER (2001)	= + Purchases in $
− Ending inventory in FC	× Historical ER (4thQ 2001)	= − Ending inventory in $
COGS in FC		COGS in $

No single exchange rate can be used to directly translate COGS in FC into COGS in $.

Application of the Lower-of-Cost-or-Market Rule

Under the *current rate method,* the ending inventory reported on the foreign currency balance sheet is translated at the current exchange rate regardless of whether it is carried at cost or a lower market value. Application of the *temporal method* requires the foreign currency cost and foreign currency market value of the inventory to be translated into U.S. dollars at appropriate exchange rates, and the *lower of the dollar cost and dollar market value* is reported on the consolidated balance sheet. As a result of this procedure, it is possible for inventory to be carried at cost on the foreign currency balance sheet and at market value on the U.S. dollar consolidated balance sheet, and vice versa.

Fixed Assets, Depreciation, Accumulated Depreciation

Under the *temporal method,* fixed assets acquired at different times must be translated at different (historical) exchange rates. The same is true for depreciation of fixed assets and accumulated depreciation related to fixed assets.

For example, assume a company purchases a piece of equipment on January 1, 2001, for FC 1,000 when the exchange rate is $1.00 per FC. Another item of equipment is purchased on January 1, 2002, for FC 5,000 when the exchange rate is $1.20 per FC. Both pieces of equipment have a five-year useful life. Under the temporal method, the amount at which Equipment would be reported on the consolidated balance sheet on December 31, 2003, when the exchange rate is $1.50 per FC, would be:

$$FC\ 1,000 \times \$1.00 = \$1,000$$
$$\underline{FC\ 5,000} \times \$1.20 = \underline{\$6,000}$$
$$\underline{\underline{FC\ 6,000}} \qquad \underline{\underline{\$7,000}}$$

Depreciation expense for 2003 under the temporal method would be calculated as:

$$FC\quad 200 \times \$1.00 = \$\quad 200$$
$$\underline{FC\ 1,000} \times \$1.20 = \underline{\$1,200}$$
$$\underline{\underline{FC\ 1,200}} \qquad \underline{\underline{\$1,400}}$$

Accumulated depreciation under the temporal method would be calculated as:

$$FC\quad 600 \times \$1.00 = \$\quad 600$$
$$\underline{FC\ 2,000} \times \$1.20 = \underline{\$2,400}$$
$$\underline{\underline{FC\ 2,600}} \qquad \underline{\underline{\$3,000}}$$

Similar procedures apply for intangible assets as well.

Under the *current rate method,* Equipment would be reported on the December 31, 2003, balance sheet at: FC 6,000 × $1.50 = $9,000. Depreciation expense would be: FC 1,200 × $1.40 = $1,680, and accumulated depreciation would be: FC 2,600 × $1.50 = $3,900.

In this example, the foreign subsidiary has only two fixed assets requiring translation. For subsidiaries that own hundreds and thousands of fixed assets, the temporal method can require substantial additional work as compared to the current rate method.

Gain or Loss on the Sale of an Asset

Assume that a foreign subsidiary sells land that cost FC 1,000 at a selling price of FC 1,200. A gain on the sale of land of FC 200 is reported in the subsidiary's income statement. The land was acquired when the exchange rate was $1.00 per FC; the sale was made when the exchange rate was $1.20 per FC; and the exchange rate at the balance sheet date is $1.50 per FC.

Under the *current rate method,* the gain on sale of land is translated at the exchange rate in effect at the date of sale:

$$FC\ 200 \times \$1.20 = \$240$$

Under the *temporal method*, the gain on sale of land cannot be translated directly. Instead, the cash received and the cost of the land sold are translated into U.S. dollars separately, with the difference being the U.S. dollar value of the gain. In accordance with the rules of the temporal method, Cash is translated at the current rate and Land is translated at the historical rate:

$$
\begin{array}{lll}
\text{Cash} & \text{FC } 1{,}200 \times \$1.50 = & \$1{,}800 \\
\text{Land} & \underline{\text{FC } 1{,}000} \times \$1.00 = & \underline{\$1{,}000} \\
\text{Gain} & \text{FC } \underline{\underline{\quad 200}} & \underline{\underline{\$ \quad 800}}
\end{array}
$$

DISPOSITION OF TRANSLATION ADJUSTMENT

The first issue related to the translation of foreign currency financial statements is selecting the appropriate method. The *second issue* in financial statement translation relates to deciding *where the resulting translation adjustment should be reported in the consolidated financial statements.* There are two prevailing schools of thought with regard to this issue:

1.   **Translation Gain or Loss**—Under this treatment, the translation adjustment is considered to be a gain or loss analogous to the gains and losses arising from foreign currency transactions and should be reported in net income in the period in which the fluctuation in the exchange rate occurs.

The first of two conceptual problems with treating translation adjustments as gains or losses in income is the gain or loss is unrealized; that is, there is no accompanying cash inflow or outflow. The second problem is the gain or loss may not be consistent with economic reality. For example, the depreciation of a foreign currency may have a *positive* impact on the foreign operation's export sales and income, but the particular translation method used gives rise to a translation *loss.*

2.   **Cumulative Translation Adjustment in Other Comprehensive Income**—The alternative to reporting the translation adjustment as a gain or loss in net income is to include it in other comprehensive income. In effect, this treatment defers the gain or loss in stockholders' equity until realized in some way. As a balance sheet account, the cumulative translation adjustment is not closed at the end of an accounting period and will fluctuate in amount over time.

The two major translation methods and the two possible treatments for the translation adjustment give rise to these four possible combinations:

Combination	Translation Method	Treatment of Translation Adjustment
A	Temporal	Gain or loss in net income
B	Temporal	Deferred in other comprehensive income
C	Current rate	Gain or loss in net income
D	Current rate	Deferred in other comprehensive income

U.S. RULES

Prior to 1975 the United States had no authoritative rules about which translation method to use or where the translation adjustment had to be reported in the consolidated financial statements. Different combinations were used by different companies. As an indication of the importance of this particular accounting issue, the first official pronouncement issued by the newly created FASB in 1974 was *SFAS No. 1,* "Disclosure of Foreign Currency Translation Information." *SFAS 1* did not express a preference for any particular combination, but simply required disclosure of the method used and the treatment of the translation adjustment.

The use of different combinations by different companies created a lack of comparability across companies. To eliminate this noncomparability, in 1975 the FASB issued *SFAS No. 8,* "Accounting for the Translation of Foreign Currency Transactions and Foreign Currency Financial Statements." *SFAS 8* mandated use of the *temporal method* with *translation gains or losses* reported in net income by all companies for all foreign operations (Combination A).

U.S. multinational companies (MNCs) were strongly opposed to *SFAS 8.* Specifically, they considered reporting translation gains and losses in income to be inappropriate given that they are unrealized. Moreover, as currency fluctuations often reversed themselves in subsequent quarters, artificial volatility in quarterly earnings resulted.

After releasing two exposure drafts proposing new translation rules, the FASB finally issued *SFAS No. 52,* "Foreign Currency Translation," in 1981. This resulted in a complete overhaul of U.S. GAAP with regard to foreign currency translation. *SFAS 52* was approved by a narrow four-to-three vote of the Board indicating how contentious the issue of foreign currency translation has been.

SFAS No. 52

Implicit in the **temporal method** is the assumption that foreign subsidiaries of U.S. MNCs have very close ties to their parent companies and would actually carry out their day-to-day operations and keep their books in the U.S. dollar if they could. To reflect the integrated nature of the foreign subsidiary with its U.S. parent, the translation process should create a set of U.S. dollar translated financial statements as if the dollar had actually been used by the foreign subsidiary. This is the **U.S. dollar perspective** to translation that was adopted in *SFAS* 8.

In *SFAS 52,* the FASB recognized two types of foreign entities. First, some foreign entities are so closely integrated with their parents that they do conduct much of their business in U.S. dollars. *Second, other foreign entities are relatively self-contained and integrated with the local economy; primarily, they use a foreign currency in their daily operations.* For the first type of entity, the FASB determined that the U.S. dollar perspective still applies and, therefore, *SFAS 8* rules are still relevant.

For the second relatively independent type of entity, a **local currency perspective** to translation is applicable. For this type of entity the FASB determined that a different translation methodology, namely the *current rate method,* should be used for translation and that translation adjustments should be reported as a *separate component in other comprehensive income* (Combination D on page 478). In addition, the FASB requires using the *average-for-the-period* exchange rate in translating income when the current rate method is used.

In rationalizing the placement of the translation adjustment in stockholders' equity rather than net income, *SFAS 52* (pars. 113, 114) offered two contrasting positions on the conceptual nature of the translation adjustment. One view is that the "change in the dollar equivalent of the net investment is an unrealized enhancement or reduction, having no effect on the functional currency net cash flow generated by the foreign entity which may be currently reinvested or distributed to the parent." Philosophically, this position holds that even though gains and losses are created by changes in the exchange rate, they are unrealized in nature and should, therefore, not be included within net income.

The alternative perspective put forth by the FASB "regards the translation adjustment as merely a mechanical by-product of the translation process." This second contention argues that no meaningful effect is created by exchange rate fluctuation; the resulting translation adjustment merely serves to keep the balance sheet in equilibrium.

Interestingly enough, the FASB chose not to express preference for either of these theoretical views. The Board felt no need to offer a hint of guidance as to the essential nature of the translation adjustment because both explanations point to its exclusion from net income. Thus, a balance sheet figure that can amount to millions of dollars is basically undefined.

Functional Currency   To determine whether a specific foreign operation is integrated with its parent or self-contained and integrated with the local economy, *SFAS 52* created the concept of the **functional currency.** The functional currency is the primary currency of the foreign entity's operating environment. It can be either the parent's currency (U.S.$) or a foreign currency (generally the local currency). *SFAS 52's* functional currency orientation results in the following rule:

Functional Currency	Translation Method	Translation Adjustment
U.S. dollar	Temporal method	Gain (loss) in net income
Foreign currency	Current rate method	Separate component of other comprehensive income (stockholders' equity)

In addition to introducing the concept of the *functional currency, SFAS 52* introduced some new terminology. The **reporting currency** is the currency in which the entity prepares its financial statements. For U.S.-based corporations, this is the U.S. dollar. If a foreign operation's functional currency is the U.S. dollar, foreign currency balances must be **remeasured** into U.S. dollars using the temporal method with translation adjustments reported as **remeasurement gains and losses** in income. When a foreign currency is the functional currency, foreign currency balances are **translated** using the current rate method and a **translation adjustment** is reported on the balance sheet.

The functional currency is essentially a matter of fact. However, *SFAS 52* (par. 8) states that for many cases "management's judgment will be required to determine the functional currency in which financial results and relationships are measured with the greatest degree of relevance and reliability." *SFAS 52* provides a list of indicators to guide parent company management in its determination of a foreign entity's functional currency (see Exhibit 10–2). *SFAS 52* provides no guidance as to how these indicators are to be weighted in determining the functional currency. Leaving the decision about identifying the functional currency up to management allows some leeway in this process. Different companies approach this selection in different ways:

> "For us it was intuitively obvious," versus "It was quite a process. We took the six criteria and developed a matrix. We then considered the dollar amount and the related percentages in developing a point scheme. Each of the separate criteria was given equal weight (in the analytical methods applied)."[7]

Research has shown that the weighting schemes used by U.S. multinationals for determining the functional currency might be biased toward selection of the *foreign currency* as the functional currency.[8] This would be rational behavior for multinationals given that, when the foreign currency is the functional currency, the translation adjustment is reported in stockholders' equity and does not affect net income.

Highly Inflationary Economies

For those foreign entities located in a **highly inflationary economy,** it is not necessary to determine the functional currency—*SFAS 52* mandates use of the *temporal method* with *remeasurement gains or losses reported in income.*

A country is defined has having a *highly inflationary economy* when its cumulative three-year inflation exceeds 100 percent. With compounding, this equates to an average of approximately 26 percent per year for three years in a row. Countries that have met this definition at some time since *SFAS 52* was implemented include Argentina, Brazil, Israel, Mexico, and Turkey. In any given year, a country may or may not be

---

[7] Jerry L. Arnold and William W. Holder, *Impact of Statement 52 on Decisions, Financial Reports and Attitudes* (Morristown, NJ: Financial Executives Research Foundation, 1986), p. 89.

[8] Timothy S. Doupnik and Thomas G. Evans, "Functional Currency as a Strategy to Smooth Income," *Advances in International Accounting,* 1988.

Exhibit 10–2
SFAS 52 Indicators for
Determining the
Functional Currency

| Indicator | Indication that Functional Currency Is the | |
	Foreign Currency	Parent's Currency
Cash flow	Primarily in FC and do not affect parent's cash flows	Directly impact parent's cash flows on a current basis
Sales price	Not affected on short-term basis by changes in exchange rate	Affected on short-term basis by changes in exchange rate
Sales market	Active local sales market	Sales market mostly in parent's country or sales denominated in parent's currency
Expenses	Primarily local costs	Primarily costs for components obtained from parent's country
Financing	Primarily denominated in foreign currency and FC cash flows adequate to service obligations	Primarily from parent or denominated in parent currency or FC cash flows not adequate to service obligations
Intercompany transactions	Low volume of intercompany transactions, not extensive interrelationship with parent's operations	High volume of intercompany transactions and extensive interrelationship with parent's operations

classified as highly inflationary depending on its most recent three-year experience with inflation.

One reason for this rule is to avoid a "disappearing plant problem" caused by using the current rate method in a country with high inflation. Remember that under the current rate method, all assets (including fixed assets) are translated at the current exchange rate. To see the problem this creates in a highly inflationary economy, consider the following hypothetical example.

The Brazilian subsidiary of a U.S. parent purchased Land at the end of 1984 for 10,000,000 cruzeiros (Cr$) when the exchange rate was $.001 per Cr$. Under the *current rate method,* the Land would be reported in the parent's Consolidated Balance Sheet at $10,000.

	Historical Cost		Current ER		Consolidated B.S.
1984	Cr$ 10,000,000	×	$ .001	=	$10,000

In 1985, Brazil experienced roughly 200 percent inflation. Accordingly, with the forces of purchasing power parity at work, the cruzeiro plummeted against the U.S. dollar to a value of $.00025 at the end of 1985. Under the current rate method, Land now would be reported in the parent's Consolidated Balance Sheet at $2,500, and a negative translation adjustment of $7,500 would result.

1985	Cr$ 10,000,000	×	$.00025	=	$ 2,500

Using the current rate method, Land has lost 75 percent of its U.S. dollar value in one year, and Land is not even a depreciable asset!

High rates of inflation continued in Brazil with the high point of roughly 1,800 percent reached in 1993. As a result of applying the current rate method, the Land originally reported on the 1984 Consolidated Balance Sheet at $10,000 was carried on the 1993 Balance Sheet at less than $1.00.

In the exposure draft leading to *SFAS 52,* the FASB proposed requiring companies with operations in highly inflationary countries to first **restate** the historical costs for inflation and then **translate** using the current rate method. For example, with 200 percent inflation in 1985, the Land would have been written up to Cr$ 40,000,000 and then translated at the current exchange rate of $.00025. This would have produced a translated amount of $10,000, the same as in 1984.

Companies objected to making inflation adjustments, however, because of a lack of reliable inflation indices in many countries. The FASB backed off from requiring the **restate/translate** approach; instead *SFAS 52* requires using the temporal method in high inflationary countries. In the previous example, under the *temporal method,* a firm would use the historical rate of $.001 to translate Land year after year. Land would be carried on the Consolidated Balance Sheet at $10,000 each year, thereby avoiding the disappearing plant problem.

THE PROCESS ILLUSTRATED

To provide a basis for demonstrating the translation and remeasurement procedures prescribed by *SFAS 52,* assume that USCO (a U.S.-based company) forms a wholly owned subsidiary in Germany (BERLINCO) on December 31, 2000. On that date, USCO invested $300,000 in exchange for all of the subsidiary's common stock. Given the exchange rate of DM 1 = $.60, the initial capital investment was DM 500,000, of which DM 150,000 was immediately invested in inventory and the remainder held in cash. Thus, BERLINCO begins operations on January 1, 2001, with stockholders' equity (net assets) of DM 500,000 and net monetary assets of DM 350,000.

BERLINCO
Opening Balance Sheet
January 1, 2001

Assets	DM	Liabilities and Equity	DM
Cash	DM 350,000	Common stock	DM 100,000
Inventory	150,000	Additional paid-in capital . . .	400,000
	DM 500,000		DM 500,000

During 2001, BERLINCO purchased property and equipment, acquired a patent, and made additional purchases of inventory, primarily on account. A five-year loan was negotiated to help finance the purchase of equipment. Sales were made, primarily on account, and expenses were incurred. Income after taxes of DM 470,000 was generated, with dividends of DM 150,000 declared on October 1, 2001.

As a company incorporated in Germany, BERLINCO must account for its activities using German accounting rules which differ from U.S. GAAP in many respects. As noted in the introduction to this chapter, to prepare consolidated financial statements USCO must first convert BERLINCO's financial statements to a U.S. GAAP basis.[9] BERLINCO's U.S. GAAP financial statements for the year 2001 in German marks appear in Exhibit 10–3.

To properly translate the DM financial statements into U.S. dollars, USCO must gather exchange rates between the DM and U.S. dollar at various points in time. Relevant exchange rates are as follows:

January 1, 2001	$.60
Rate when property and equipment were acquired and long-term debt was incurred, March 15, 2001	$.61
Rate when patent was acquired, April 10, 2001	$.62
Average 2001	$.65
Rate when dividends were declared, October 1, 2001	$.67
Average fourth quarter 2001	$.68
December 31, 2001	$.70

As can be seen, the DM steadily appreciated against the dollar during the year.

---

[9]Differences in accounting rules across countries are discussed in more detail in Chapter 11.

Exhibit 10–3
Foreign Currency Financial
Statements

BERLINCO
Income Statement
For Year Ending December 31, 2001

	DM
Sales	4,000,000
Cost of goods sold	3,000,000
Gross profit	1,000,000
Depreciation expense	100,000
Amortization expense	10,000
Other expenses	220,000
Income before income taxes	670,000
Income taxes	200,000
Net income	470,000

Statement of Retained Earnings
For Year Ending December 31, 2001

	DM
Retained earnings, 1/1/01	–0–
Net income, 2001	470,000
Less: Dividends, 10/1/01	150,000
Retained earnings, 12/31/01	320,000

Balance Sheet
December 31, 2001

Assets	DM	Liabilities and Equity	DM
Cash	130,000	Accounts payable	600,000
Accounts receivable	200,000	Total current liabilities	600,000
Inventory*	400,000	Long-term debt	250,000
Total current assets	730,000	Total current liabilities	850,000
Property and equipment	1,000,000	Common stock	100,000
Accumulated depreciation	(100,000)	Additional paid-in capital	400,000
Patents, net	40,000	Retained earnings	320,000
Total assets	1,670,000	Total equity	820,000
		Total liabilities and equity	1,670,000

*Inventory is valued at FIFO cost under the lower-of-cost-or-market-value rule; ending inventory was acquired evenly throughout the fourth quarter.

Statement of Cash Flows
For Year Ending December 31, 2001

	DM
Operating activities:	
Net income	470,000
Add: Depreciation expense	100,000
Amortization expense	10,000
Increase in accounts receivable	(200,000)
Increase in inventory	(250,000)
Increase in accounts payable	600,000
Net cash from operations	730,000
Investing activities:	
Purchase of property and equipment	(1,000,000)
Acquisition of patent	(50,000)
Net cash from investing activities	(1,050,000)
Financing activities:	
Proceeds from long-term debt	250,000
Payment of dividends	(150,000)
Net cash from financing activities	100,000
Decrease in cash	(220,000)
Cash at 12/31/00	350,000
Cash at 12/31/01	130,000

Exhibit 10–4
Translation of Income
Statement and Statement of
Retained Earnings—Current
Rate Method

Income Statement For Year Ending December 31, 2001			
	DM	**Translation Rate***	**US$**
Sales	DM 4,000,000	0.65 A	$ 2,600,000
Cost of goods sold	(3,000,000)	0.65 A	(1,950,000)
Gross profit	1,000,000		650,000
Depreciation expense	(100,000)	0.65 A	(65,000)
Amortization expense	(10,000)	0.65 A	(6,500)
Other expenses	(220,000)	0.65 A	(143,000)
Income before income taxes	670,000		435,500
Income taxes	(200,000)	0.65 A	(130,000)
Net income	DM 470,000		$ 305,500

*Indicates the exchange rate used and whether the rate is the current (C), average (A), or a historical (H) rate.

Statement of Retained Earnings For Year Ending December 31, 2001			
	DM	**Translation Rate***	**US$**
Retained earnings, 1/1/01	DM –0–		$ –0–
Net income, 2001	470,000	above	305,500
Less: Dividends, 10/1/01	(150,000)	0.67 H	(100,500)
Retained earnings, 12/31/01	DM 320,000		$ 205,000

TRANSLATION OF FINANCIAL STATEMENTS—CURRENT RATE METHOD

The first step in translating foreign currency financial statements is determining the functional currency. Assuming that the German mark is the functional currency, the income statement and statement of retained earnings would be translated into U.S. dollars using the current rate method as shown in Exhibit 10–4.

All revenues and expenses are translated at the exchange rate in effect at the date of accounting recognition. The weighted-average exchange rate for 2001 is utilized here because each revenue and expense in this illustration would have been recognized evenly throughout the year. However, when an income account, such as a gain or loss, occurs at a specific point in time, the exchange rate as of that date is applied. Depreciation and amortization expense also are translated at the average rate for the year. These expenses accrue evenly throughout the year even though the journal entry may have been delayed until year-end for convenience.

The translated amount of net income for 2001 is brought down from the income statement into the statement of retained earnings. Dividends are translated at the exchange rate on the date of declaration.

Translation of the Balance Sheet

Looking at BERLINCO's translated balance sheet in Exhibit 10–5, note that all assets and liabilities are translated at the current exchange rate. Common stock and additional paid-in capital are translated at the exchange rate on the day the common stock was originally sold. Retained earnings at December 31, 2001, is brought down from the statement of retained earnings. Application of these procedures results in total assets of

Exhibit 10–5
Translation of Balance
Sheet—Current Rate
Method

		Balance Sheet For Year Ending December 31, 2001		
		DM	**Translation Rate**	**US$**
Assets				
Cash	DM	130,000	0.70 C	$ 91,000
Accounts receivable		200,000	0.70 C	140,000
Inventory		400,000	0.70 C	280,000
Total current assets		730,000		511,000
Property and equipment		1,000,000	0.70 C	700,000
Less: Accumulated depreciation		(100,000)	0.70 C	(70,000)
Patents, net		40,000	0.70 C	28,000
Total assets	DM	1,670,000		$1,169,000
Liabilities and Equities				
Accounts payable	DM	600,000	0.70 C	$ 420,000
Total current liabilities		600,000		420,000
Long-term debt		250,000	0.70 C	175,000
Total liabilities		850,000		595,000
Common stock		100,000	0.60 H	60,000
Additional paid-in capital		400,000	0.60 H	240,000
Retained earnings		320,000	above	205,000
Cumulative translation adjustment			to balance	69,000
Total equity		820,000		574,000
Total liabilities and equity	DM	1,670,000		$1,169,000

$1,169,000, and total liabilities and equities of $1,100,000. The balance sheet is brought back into balance by creating a positive translation adjustment of $69,000 that is treated as an increase in stockholders' equity.

Note that the translation adjustment for 2001 is a *positive* $69,000 (credit balance). The sign of the translation adjustment (positive or negative) is a function of two factors: (1) the nature of the balance sheet exposure (asset or liability) and (2) the change in the exchange rate (appreciation or depreciation). In this illustration, BERLINCO has a *net asset exposure* (total assets translated at the current exchange rate are greater than total liabilities at the current exchange rate), and the DM has *appreciated* creating a *positive translation adjustment.*

The translation adjustment can be derived as the amount needed to bring the balance sheet back into balance. The translation adjustment also can be calculated by considering the impact of exchange rate changes on the beginning balance and subsequent changes in the net asset position:

1. The net asset balance of the subsidiary at the beginning of the year is translated at the exchange rate in effect on that date.

2. Individual increases and decreases in the net asset balance during the year are translated at the rates in effect when those increases and decreases occurred. Only a few events actually change net assets, such as net income, dividends, stock issuance, and the acquisition of treasury stock. Transactions such as the acquisition of equipment or the payment of a liability have no effect on total net assets.

3. The translated beginning net asset balance (*a*) and the translated value of the individual changes (*b*) are then combined to arrive at the relative value of the net assets being held prior to the impact of any exchange rate fluctuations.

4. The ending net asset balance is translated then at the current exchange rate to determine the reported value after all exchange rate changes have occurred.

5. The translated value of the net assets prior to any rate changes (*c*) is compared with the ending translated value (*d*). The difference is the result of exchange rate changes during the period. If (*c*) is greater than (*d*), then a negative (debit) translation adjustment arises. If (*d*) is greater than (*c*), a positive (credit) translation adjustment results.

Computation of Translation Adjustment   Based on the process just described, the translation adjustment for BERLINCO in this example is calculated as follows:

Net asset balance, 1/1/01	DM 500,000	× 0.60 =	$ 300,000
Change in net assets:			
Net income, 2001	470,000	× 0.65 =	$ 305,500
Dividends declared, 10/1/01	(150,000)	× 0.67 =	(100,500)
Net asset balance, 12/31/01	DM 820,000		$ 505,000
Net asset balance, 12/31/01 at current			
exchange rate	DM 820,000	× 0.70 =	(574,000)
Translation adjustment, 2001 (positive)			$ (69,000)

Since this subsidiary began operations at the beginning of the current year, the $69,000 translation adjustment is the only amount applicable for reporting purposes. If a balance already had been created by translations in previous years, that beginning balance would have been combined with the $69,000 to arrive at an appropriate year-end total to be presented as other comprehensive income within stockholders' equity.

The translation adjustment is reported in other comprehensive income only until the foreign operation is sold or liquidated. *SFAS 52* (para. 14) stipulates that, *in the period in which sale or liquidation occurs, the cumulative translation adjustment related to the particular entity must be removed from other comprehensive income and reported as part of the gain or loss on the sale of the investment.* In effect, the accumulated un-realized foreign exchange gain or loss that has been deferred in other comprehensive income becomes realized when the entity is disposed of.

Translation of the Statement of Cash Flows

Under the current rate method, all operating items in the statement of cash flows are translated at the average-for-the-period exchange rate (see Exhibit 10–6). This is the same rate used for translating income statement items. Although the ending balance in accounts receivable, inventory, and accounts payable on the balance sheet are trans-lated at the current exchange rate, the average rate is used for the *changes* in these ac-counts because those changes are caused by operating activities (such as sales and purchases) that are translated at the average rate.

Investing and financing activities are translated at the exchange rate on the day the activity took place. Although long-term debt is translated in the balance sheet at the current rate, in the statement of cash flows it is translated at the historical rate when the debt was incurred.

The $(4,500) "effect of exchange rate change on cash" is a part of the overall trans-lation adjustment of $69,000. It represents that part of the translation adjustment at-tributable to a decrease in cash and is derived as a plug figure.

Statement of Cash Flows For Year Ending December 31, 2001			
	DM	Translation Rate	US$
Operating activities:			
Net income	DM 470,000	0.65 A	$ 305,500
Add: Depreciation	100,000	0.65 A	$ 65,000
Amortization	10,000	0.65 A	$ 6,500
Increase in accounts receivable	(200,000)	0.65 A	(130,000)
Increase in inventory	(250,000)	0.65 A	(162,500)
Increase in accounts payable	600,000	0.65 A	390,000
Net cash from operations	730,000		474,500
Investing activities:			
Purchase of property and equipment	(1,000,000)	0.61 H	(610,000)
Acquisition of patent	(50,000)	0.62 H	(31,000)
Net cash from investing activities	(1,050,000)		(641,000)
Financing activities:			
Proceeds from long-term debt	250,000	0.61 H	152,500
Payment of dividends	(150,000)	0.67 H	(100,500)
Net cash from financing activities	100,000		52,000
Decrease in cash	(220,000)		(114,500)
Effect of exchange rate change on cash		to balance	(4,500)
Cash at December 31, 2000	DM 350,000	0.60 C	$ 210,000
Cash at December 31, 2001	DM 130,000	0.70 C	$ 91,000

REMEASUREMENT OF FINANCIAL STATEMENTS—TEMPORAL METHOD

Now assume that a careful examination of the functional currency indicators outlined in *SFAS 52* leads USCO's management to conclude that BERLINCO's functional currency is the U.S. dollar. In that case, the deutsche mark financial statements must be remeasured into U.S. dollars using the temporal method and the remeasurement gain or loss reported in income. To ensure that the remeasurement gain or loss is reported in income, it is easiest to remeasure the balance sheet first (as shown in Exhibit 10–7).

According to the procedures outlined in Exhibit 10–1, under the temporal method, cash, receivables, and liabilities are remeasured into U.S. dollars using the current exchange rate of $.70. Inventory (carried at FIFO cost), property and equipment, patents, and the contributed capital accounts (Common Stock and Additional Paid-In Capital) are remeasured at historical rates. These procedures result in total assets of $1,076,800, and liabilities and contributed capital of $895,000. To balance the balance sheet, retained earnings must be $181,800. The accuracy of this amount is verified later.

Remeasurement of the Income Statement

The remeasurement of BERLINCO's income statement and statement of retained earnings is demonstrated in Exhibit 10–8. Revenues and expenses incurred evenly throughout the year (sales, other expenses, and income taxes) are remeasured at the average exchange rate. Expenses related to assets remeasured at historical exchange rates (depreciation expense and amortization expense) are themselves remeasured at relevant historical rates.

Balance Sheet
December 31, 2001

		DM	Remeasurement Rate	US$
Assets				
Cash	DM	130,000	0.70 C	$ 91,000
Accounts receivable		200,000	0.70 C	140,000
Inventory		400,000	0.68 H	272,000
Total current assets		730,000		503,000
Property and equipment		1,000,000	0.61 H	610,000
Less: Accumulated depreciation		(100,000)	0.61 H	(61,000)
Patents		40,000	0.62 H	24,800
Total assets	DM	1,670,000		$1,076,800
Liabilities and Equities				
Accounts payable	DM	600,000	0.70 C	$ 420,000
Total current liabilities		600,000		420,000
Long-term debt		250,000	0.70 C	175,000
Total liabilities		850,000		595,000
Common stock		100,000	0.60 H	60,000
Additional paid-in capital		400,000	0.60 H	240,000
Retained earnings		320,000	to balance	181,800
Total equity		820,000		481,800
Total liabilities and equity	DM	1,670,000		$1,076,800

Income Statement
For Year Ending December 31, 2001

		DM	Remeasurement Rate	US$
Sales	DM	4,000,000	0.65 A	$ 2,600,000
Cost of goods sold		(3,000,000)	above	(1,930,500)
Gross profit		1,000,000		669,500
Depreciation expense		(100,000)	0.61 H	(61,000)
Amortization expense		(10,000)	0.62 H	(6,200)
Other expenses		(220,000)	0.65 A	(143,000)
Income before income taxes		670,000		459,300
Income taxes		(200,000)	0.65 A	(130,000)
Remeasurement Loss			to balance	(47,000)
Net income	DM	470,000		$ 282,300

Statement of Retained Earnings
For Year Ending December 31, 2001

		DM	Remeasurement Rate	US$
Retained earnings, 1/1/01	DM	–0–		$ –0–
Net income, 2001		470,000	above	282,300
Dividends		(150,000)	0.67 H	(100,500)
Retained earnings, 12/31/01	DM	320,000	to balance	$ 181,800

Cost of goods sold is remeasured at historical exchange rates using the following procedure. Beginning inventory acquired on January 1 is remeasured at the exchange rate from that date ($.60). Purchases made evenly throughout the year are remeasured at the average rate for the year ($.65). Ending inventory (at FIFO cost) purchased evenly throughout the fourth quarter of 2001 and the average exchange rate for the quarter ($.68) are used to remeasure that component of cost of goods sold. These procedures result in cost of goods sold of $1,930,500, calculated as follows:

Beginning inventory, 1/1/01	DM 150,000	× 0.60 =	$ 90,000
Plus: Purchases, 2001	3,250,000	× 0.65 =	2,112,500
Less: Ending inventory, 12/31/01	(400,000)	× 0.68 =	(272,000)
Cost of goods sold, 2001	DM 3,000,000		$1,930,500

The ending balance in retained earnings on the balance sheet and in the statement of retained earnings must reconcile with one another. Given that dividends are remeasured into a U.S. dollar equivalent of $100,500 and the ending balance in retained earnings on the balance sheet is $181,800, net income must be $282,300.

To reconcile the amount of income reported in the statement of retained earnings and in the income statement, a remeasurement loss of $47,000 is required in the calculation of income. Without this remeasurement loss, the income statement, statement of retained earnings, and balance sheet are not consistent with one another.

The remeasurement loss can be calculated by considering the impact of exchange rate changes on the subsidiary's balance sheet exposure. Under the temporal method, BERLINCO's balance sheet exposure is defined by its net monetary asset or net monetary liability position. BERLINCO began 2001 with net monetary assets (cash) of DM 350,000. During the year, however, expenditures of cash and the incurrence of liabilities caused monetary liabilities (accounts payable + long-term debt = DM 850,000) to exceed monetary assets (cash + accounts receivable = DM 330,000). A net monetary liability position of DM 520,000 exists at December 31, 2001. The remeasurement loss is computed by translating the beginning net monetary asset position and subsequent changes in monetary items at appropriate exchange rates and then comparing this with the dollar value of net monetary liabilities at year-end based on the current exchange rate.

Computation of Remeasurement Loss

Net monetary assets, 1/1/01	DM 350,000	× 0.60 =	$ 210,000
Increase in monetary items:			
Sales, 2001	4,000,000	× 0.65 =	2,600,000
Decreases in monetary items:			
Purchases, 2001	(3,250,000)	× 0.65 =	(2,112,500)
Other expenses, 2001	(220,000)	× 0.65 =	(143,000)
Income taxes, 2001	(200,000)	× 0.65 =	(130,000)
Purchase of property and equipment, 3/15/01 . .	(1,000,000)	× 0.61 =	(610,000)
Acquisition of patents, 4/10/01	(50,000)	× 0.62 =	(31,000)
Dividends, 10/1/01	(150,000)	× 0.67 =	(100,500)
Net monetary liabilities, 12/31/01	DM (520,000)		$ (317,000)
Net monetary liabilities, 12/31/01			
at the current exchange rate	DM (520,000)	× .070 =	(364,000)
Remeasurement loss			$ 47,000

If BERLINCO had maintained its net monetary asset position (cash) of DM 350,000 for the entire year, a remeasurement gain of $35,000 would have resulted. The DM held in cash was worth $210,000 (DM 350,000 × $.60) at the beginning of the year and $245,000 (DM 350,000 × $.70) at year-end. However, the net monetary asset

Statement of Cash Flows For Year Ending December 31, 2001		Remeasurement	
	DM	Rate	US$
Operating activities:			
Net income	DM 470,000	from I/S	$ 282,300
Add: Depreciation expense	100,000	0.61 H	61,000
Amortization expense	10,000	0.62 H	6,200
Remeasurement loss		from I/S	47,000
Increase in accounts receivable	(200,000)	0.65 A	(130,000)
Increase in inventory	(250,000)	*	(182,000)
Increase in accounts payable	600,000	0.65 A	390,000
Net cash from operations	(730,000)		474,500
Investing activities:			
Purchase of property and equipment	(1,000,000)	0.61 H	(610,000)
Acquisition of patent	(50,000)	0.62 H	(31,000)
Net cash from investing activities	(1,050,000)		(641,000)
Financing activities:			
Proceeds from long-term debt	250,000	0.61 H	152,500
Payment of dividends	(150,000)	0.67 H	(100,500)
Net cash from financing activities	100,000		52,000
Decrease in cash	(220,000)		(114,500)
Effect of exchange rate changes on cash			(4,500)
Cash at December 31, 2000	DM 350,000	0.6 C	$ 210,000
Cash at December 31, 2001	DM 130,000	0.7 C	$ 91,000

*In remeasuring cost of goods sold earlier, beginning inventory was remeasured as $90,000 and ending inventory was remeasured as $272,000; an increase of $182,000.

position is not maintained. Indeed, a net monetary liability position arises. The *appreciation* of the foreign currency coupled with an increase in *net monetary liabilities* generates a *remeasurement loss* for the year.

Remeasurement of the Statement of Cash Flows

In remeasuring the statement of cash flows (shown in Exhibit 10–9), the U.S. dollar value for net income is taken directly from the remeasured income statement. Depreciation and amortization are remeasured at the rates used in the income statement, and the remeasurement loss is added back to net income because it is a non-cash item. The increases in accounts receivable and accounts payable relate to sales and purchases and are therefore remeasured at the average rate. The U.S. dollar value for the increase in inventory is determined by referring to the remeasurement of the cost of goods sold.

The resulting U.S. dollar amount of "net cash from operations" ($474,500) is exactly the same as when the current rate method was used in translation. In addition, the investing and financing activities are translated in the same manner under both methods. This makes sense; the amount of cash inflows and outflows is a matter of fact and is not affected by the particular translation methodology employed.

Non-Local Currency Balances

One additional issue related to the translation of foreign currency financial statements needs to be considered. If any of the accounts of the German subsidiary are denominated in a currency other than the German mark, those balances would first have to be restated into marks in accordance with the rules discussed in Chapter 9. Both the foreign currency balance and any related foreign exchange gain or loss would then be translated (or remeasured) into U.S. dollars. For example, a note payable of 10,000 Belgian francs first would be remeasured into German marks before the translation process could commence.

COMPARISON OF THE RESULTS FROM APPLYING THE TWO DIFFERENT METHODS

The determination of the foreign subsidiary's functional currency (and the use of different translation methods) can have a significant impact on consolidated financial statements. The following chart shows differences for BERLINCO in several key items under the two different translation methods:

| | Translation Method | | |
Item	Current Rate	Temporal	Difference
Net income	$ 305,500	$ 282,300	+ 8.2%
Total assets	$1,169,000	$1,076,800	+ 8.6%
Total equity	$ 574,000	$ 481,000	+19.3%
Return on equity	53.2%	58.7%	− 9.4%

In this illustration if the German mark is determined to be BERLINCO's functional currency (and the current rate method is applied), net income reported in the consolidated income statement would be 8.2 percent greater than if the U.S. dollar is the functional currency (and the temporal method is applied). In addition, total assets would be 8.6 percent greater and total equity would be 19.3 percent higher using the current rate method. Because of the larger amount of equity, return on equity using the current rate method is 9.4 percent smaller.

Note that the current rate method does not always result in larger net income and a greater amount of equity than the temporal method. For example, if BERLINCO had maintained its net monetary asset position, a remeasurement gain would have been computed under the temporal method leading to higher income than under the current rate method. Moreover, if the deutsche mark had depreciated during 2001, the temporal method would have resulted in higher net income.

The important point is that the determination of the functional currency and resulting translation method can have a significant impact on the amounts reported by a parent company in its consolidated financial statements. The appropriate determination of the functional currency is an important issue.

> "Within rather broad parameters," says Peat, Marwick, Mitchell partner James Weir, choosing the functional currency is basically a management call. So much so, in fact, that Texaco, Occidental, and Unocal settled on the dollar as the functional currency for most of their foreign operations, whereas competitors Exxon, Mobil, and Amoco chose primarily the local currencies as the functional currencies for their foreign businesses.[10]

Different functional currencies selected by different companies in the same industry could have a significant impact on the comparability of financial statements within that industry. Indeed, one of the concerns raised by those FASB members dissenting on *SFAS 52* was that the functional currency rules might not result in similar accounting for similar situations.

In addition to differences in amounts reported in the consolidated financial statements, the results of the BERLINCO illustration demonstrate several conceptual differences between the two translation methods.

---

[10]John Heins, "Plenty of Opportunity to Fool Around," *Forbes*, June 2, 1986, p. 139.

Underlying Valuation Method

Using the temporal method, BERLINCO's property and equipment was remeasured as follows:

$$\text{Property and equipment DM } 1,000,000 \times \$0.61 \text{ H} = \$610,000$$

By multiplying the historical cost in DM by the historical exchange rate, $610,000 represents the U.S. dollar equivalent historical cost of this asset. It is the amount of U.S. dollars that the parent company would have had to pay to acquire assets having a cost of DM 1,000,000 when the exchange rate was $.61 per DM.

Property and equipment was translated under the current rate method as follows:

$$\text{Property and equipment DM } 1,000,000 \times \$0.70 \text{ C} = \$700,000$$

The $700,000 amount is not readily interpretable. It does not represent the U.S. dollar equivalent historical cost of the asset; that amount is $610,000. It also does not represent the U.S. dollar equivalent current cost of the asset because DM 1,000,000 is not the current cost of the asset in Germany. The $700,000 amount is simply the product of multiplying two numbers together!

Underlying Relationships

The following table reports the values for selected financial ratios calculated from the original foreign currency financial statements and from the U.S. dollar translated statements using the two different translation methods:

Ratio	DM	US$ Temporal	US$ Current Rate
Current ratio [current assets/current liabilities]	1.22	1.20	1.22
Debt/equity ratio [total liabilities/total equities]	1.04	1.24	1.04
Gross profit ratio [gross profit/sales]	25%	25.8%	25%
Return on equity [net income/total equity]	57.3%	58.7%	53.2%

The temporal method distorts all of the ratios as measured in the foreign currency. The subsidiary appears to be less liquid, more highly leveraged, and more profitable than it does in DM terms.

The current rate method maintains the first three ratios, but return on equity is distorted. The distortion occurs because income was translated at the average-for-the-period exchange rate whereas total equity was translated at the current exchange rate. In fact, any ratio combining balance sheet and income statement figures, such as turnover ratios, is distorted by the use of the average rate for income and the current rate for assets and liabilities.

Conceptually, when the current rate method is employed, income statement items can be translated at either the average or the current exchange rate. *SFAS 52* requires using the average exchange rate. In this illustration, if revenues and expenses had been translated at the current exchange rate, net income would have been $329,000 (DM 470,000 × $.70), and the return on equity would have been 57.3 percent ($329,000/$574,000), exactly the amount reflected in the DM financial statements. In several countries in which the current rate method is used, companies are allowed to choose between the average exchange rate and the current exchange rate in translating income. This is true, for example, in France and the United Kingdom.

HEDGING BALANCE SHEET EXPOSURE

When the U.S. dollar is the functional currency or when a foreign operation is located in a highly inflationary economy, remeasurement gains and losses are reported in the consolidated income statement. Management of U.S. multinational companies might wish to avoid reporting remeasurement losses in net income because of the perceived negative impact this has on the company's stock price. Likewise, when the foreign currency is the functional currency, management might wish to avoid negative translation adjustments because of the adverse impact on the debt to equity ratio.

> More and more corporations are hedging their translation exposure—the recorded value of international assets such as plant, equipment and inventory—to prevent gyrations in their quarterly accounts. Though technically only paper gains or losses, translation adjustments can play havoc with balance-sheet ratios and can spook analysts and creditors alike.[11]

Translation adjustments and remeasurement gains or losses are a function of two factors: (1) changes in the exchange rate and (2) balance sheet exposure. Although there is little if anything a company can do to influence exchange rates, parent companies can use several techniques to hedge the balance sheet exposures of their foreign operations.

Balance sheet exposure can be hedged through the use of a derivative financial instrument such as a forward contract or foreign currency option, or through the use of a nonderivative hedging instrument such as a foreign currency borrowing. To illustrate, assume that BERLINCO's functional currency is the German mark; this creates a net asset balance sheet exposure. USCO believes that the German mark will depreciate, thereby generating a negative translation adjustment that will reduce consolidated stockholders' equity. USCO could hedge this balance sheet exposure by borrowing German marks for a period of time, thus creating an offsetting German mark liability exposure. As the German mark depreciates, a foreign exchange gain will arise on the German mark liability that offsets the negative translation adjustment arising from the translation of BERLINCO's financial statements. As an alternative to the German mark borrowing, USCO might have acquired a German mark call option to hedge its balance sheet exposure. As the German mark depreciates, the fair value of the call option should increase resulting in a gain. *SFAS 133* provides that the gain or loss on a hedging instrument that is designated and effective as a *hedge of the net investment in a foreign operation* should be reported in the same manner as the translation adjustment being hedged. Thus, the foreign exchange gain on the German mark borrowing or the gain on the foreign currency option would be included in other comprehensive income along with the negative translation adjustment arising from the translation of BERLINCO's financial statements. In the event that the gain on the hedging instrument is greater than the translation adjustment being hedged, the excess is taken to net income.

The paradox of hedging a balance sheet exposure is that in the process of avoiding an unrealized translation adjustment, realized foreign exchange gains and losses can result. Consider USCO's foreign currency borrowing to hedge a German mark exposure. At initiation of the loan, USCO will convert the borrowed German marks into U.S. dollars at the spot exchange rate. When the liability matures, USCO will purchase German marks at the spot rate prevailing at that date to repay the loan. The change in exchange rate over the life of the loan will generate a realized gain or loss. If the German mark depreciates as expected, a realized foreign exchange gain will result which will offset the negative translation adjustment in other comprehensive income. Although the net effect on other comprehensive income is zero, there is a net increase in cash as a result of the hedge. If the German mark unexpectedly appreciates, a realized foreign exchange loss will occur. This will be offset by a positive translation adjustment in other comprehensive income, but a net decrease in cash will exist. While a hedge of a net investment in a foreign operation eliminates the possibility of reporting a negative translation adjustment in other comprehensive income, gains and losses realized in cash result.

---

[11]Ida Picker, "Indecent Exposure," *Institutional Investor*, September 1991, p. 82.

Exhibit 10–10

The Gillette Company and
Subsidiary Companies 1998
Annual Report

Foreign Currency Translation

Net exchange gains or losses resulting from the translation of assets and liabilities of foreign subsidiaries, except those in highly inflationary economies, are accumulated in a separate section of stockholders' equity. Also included are the effects of exchange rate changes on intercompany transactions of a long-term investment nature and transactions designated as hedges of net foreign investments.

An analysis of cumulative transaction adjustments follows:

(Millions of dollars)	1998	1997	1996
Balance at beginning of year	$(790)	$522)	$(500)
Translation adjustments, including the effect of hedging	(86)	(222)	18
Related income tax effect	50	(46)	(40)
Balance at end of year	$(826)	$(790)	$(522)

Included in Other charges in the Consolidated Statement of Income are net exchange losses of $23 million, $18 million, and $32 million for 1998, 1997, and 1996, respectively.

DISCLOSURES RELATED TO TRANSLATION

SFAS 52 (para. 31) requires firms to present an analysis of the change in the cumulative translation adjustment account in the financial statements or notes thereto. Many companies comply with this requirement by including an other comprehensive income column in their Statement of Stockholders' Equity. Other companies provide separate disclosure in the notes; see Exhibit 10–10 for an example of this disclosure for the Gillette Company.

An analysis of Gillette's cumulative translation adjustment account indicates a positive translation adjustment of $18 million in 1996, a negative translation adjustment of $222 million in 1997, and a negative translation adjustment of $86 million in 1998. From the signs of these adjustments one can infer that, in aggregate, the foreign currencies in which Gillette has operations appreciated against the U.S. dollar in 1996 and depreciated against the dollar in 1997 and 1998. On the whole, Gillette's management is probably pleased that the translation adjustment is not reflected in income. Before-tax income would have been 5 percent smaller in 1998 and 10 percent smaller in 1997 if translation adjustment had been included in net income.

Note that Gillette's cumulative translation adjustment account includes not only "net exchange gains and losses resulting from the translation of assets and liabilities of foreign subsidiaries" but also gains and losses on "intercompany transactions of a long-term investment nature" (as mentioned in Chapter 9) and on "transactions designated as hedges of net foreign investments." Gillette reports its remeasurement gains and losses in a line item titled "Other charges—net" on the income statement.

Although there is no specific requirement to do so, many companies include a description of their translation procedures in their "summary of significant accounting policies" in the notes to the financial statements. The following excerpt from International Business Machines Corporation's 1998 annual report illustrates this type of disclosure:

Translation of Non-U.S. Currency Amounts—Assets and liabilities of non-U.S. subsidiaries that operate in a local currency environment are translated to U.S. dollars at year-end exchange rates. Income and expense items are translated at average rates of exchange prevailing during the year. Translation adjustments are recorded in Accumulated gains and losses not affecting retained earnings within stockholders' equity.

Inventories and plant, rental machines and other non-monetary assets and liabilities of non-U.S. subsidiaries and branches that operate in U.S. dollars, or whose economic environment is highly inflationary, are translated at approximate exchange rates prevailing when acquired. All other assets and liabilities are translated at year-end exchange rates. Inventories charged to cost of sales and depreciation are translated at historical exchange rates. All other income and expense items are translated at average rates of exchange prevailing during the year. Gains and loses that result from translation are included in net income.

CONSOLIDATION OF A FOREIGN SUBSIDIARY

The final section of this chapter demonstrates the procedures used to consolidate the financial statements of a foreign subsidiary with those of its parent. Special attention should be paid to the treatment of the excess of cost over book value. As an item denominated in foreign currency, translation of the excess gives rise to a translation adjustment recorded on the consolidation worksheet.

On January 1, 2000, Altman, Inc., a U.S.-based manufacturing firm, purchased 100 percent of Bradford Ltd. in Great Britain. Altman paid £25,000,000 for its purchase. On January 1, 2000, Bradford had the following balance sheet:

Cash	£ 925,000	Accounts payable	£ 675,000
Accounts receivable	1,400,000	Long-term debt	4,000,000
Inventory	6,050,000	Common stock	20,000,000
Plant and equipment (net) . . .	19,000,000	Retained earnings	2,700,000
Total	£27,375,000	Total	£27,375,000

The excess of cost over book value of £2,300,000 was due to undervalued land (part of plant and equipment) and therefore is not subject to amortization. Altman uses the equity method to account for its investment in Bradford.

On December 31, 2001, two years after the date of acquisition, Bradford submitted the following trial balance for consolidation (credit balances are in parentheses):

Cash	£ 600,000
Accounts receivable	2,700,000
Inventory	9,000,000
Plant and equipment (net)	17,200,000
Accounts payable	(500,000)
Long-term debt	(2,000,000)
Common stock	(20,000,000)
Retained earnings, 1/1/01	(3,800,000)
Sales	(13,900,000)
Cost of goods sold	8,100,000
Depreciation expense	900,000
Other expenses	950,000
Dividends declared, 6/30/01	750,000
	£ –0–

Although Bradford generated net income of £1,100,000 in 2000, no dividends were declared or paid that year. Other than the payment of dividends in 2001, there were no intercompany transactions between the two affiliates. Altman has determined the British pound to be Bradford's functional currency.

Relevant exchange rates for the British pound were as follows:

	January 1	June 30	December 31	Average
2000	$1.51	—	$1.56	$1.54
2001	1.56	$1.58	1.53	1.55

Translation of Foreign Subsidiary Trial Balance

The initial step in consolidating the foreign subsidiary is to translate its trial balance from British pounds into U.S. dollars. Because the British pound has been determined to be the functional currency, this is carried out using the current rate method. The historical exchange rate for translating Bradford's common stock and January 1, 2000, retained earnings is the exchange rate that existed at the date of acquisition—$1.51.

	British Pounds	Rate	U.S. Dollars
Cash	£ 600,000	1.53 C	$ 918,000
Accounts receivable	2,700,000	1.53 C	4,131,000
Inventory	9,000,000	1.53 C	13,770,000
Property and plant (net)	17,200,000	1.53 C	26,316,000
Accounts payable	(500,000)	1.53 C	(765,000)
Long-term debt	(2,000,000)	1.53 C	(3,060,000)
Common stock	(20,000,000)	1.51 H	(30,200,000)
Retained earnings, 1/1/01	(3,800,000)	*	(5,771.000)
Sales	(13,900,000)	1.55 A	(21,545,000)
Cost of goods sold	8,100,000	1.55 A	12,555,000
Depreciation expense	900,000	1.55 A	1,395,000
Other expenses	950,000	1.55 A	1,472,500
Dividends declared, 6/30/01	750,000	1.58 H	1,185,000
Cumulative translation adjustment			(401,500)
	£ –0–		$ –0–
*Retained earnings, 1/1/00	£2,700,000	1.51 H	$4,077,000
Net income, 2000	1,100,000	1.54 A	1,694,000
Retained earnings, 12/31/00	£3,800,000		$5,771,000

A positive (credit balance) cumulative translation adjustment is required to make the trial balance actually balance. The cumulative translation adjustment is calculated as follows:

Net assets, 1/1/00	£22,700,000	1.51 H	$34,277,000
Change in net assets, 2000			
Net income, 2000	1,100,000	1.54 A	1,694,000
Net assets, 12/31/00	£23,800,000		$35,971,000
Net assets, 12/31/00 at current exchange rate	£23,800,000	1.56 C	37,128,000
Translation adjustment, 2000 (positive)			$(1,157,000)
Net assets, 1/1/01	£23,800,000	1.56 H	$37,128,000
Change in net assets, 2001			
Net income, 2001	3,950,000	1.55 A	6,122,500
Dividends 6/30/01	(750,000)	1.58 H	(1,185,000)
Net assets, 12/31/01	£27,000,000		$42,065,500
Net assets, 12/31/01 at current exchange rate	£27,000,000	1.53 C	41,310,000
Translation adjustment, 2001 (negative)			755,500
Cumulative translation adjustment, 12/31/01 (positive)			$ (401,500)

The translation adjustment in 2000 is positive because the British pound appreciated that year; the translation adjustment in 2001 is negative because of a depreciation in the British pound.

Determination of Balance in Investment Account—Equity Method

The original cost of the investment in Bradford, the net income earned by Bradford, and the dividends paid by Bradford are all denominated in British pounds. Relevant amounts must be translated from pounds into U.S. dollars so Altman can account for its investment in Bradford under the equity method. In addition, the translation adjustment calculated each year is included in the Investment account to update the foreign currency investment to its U.S. dollar equivalent. The counterpart is recorded as a translation adjustment on Altman's books:

12/31/00 Investment in Bradford $1,157,000		
Cumulative translation adjustment		$1,157,000
To record the positive translation adjustment related to the investment in a British subsidiary when the British pound appreciated.		
12/31/01 Cumulative translation adjustment .... $ 755,500		
Investment in Bradford		$ 755,500
To record the negative translation adjustment related to the investment in a British subsidiary when the British pound depreciated.		

The carrying value of the investment account in U.S. dollar terms at December 31, 2001, is determined as follows:

Investment in Bradford	British Pounds	Exchange Rate	U.S. Dollars
Original cost	£25,000,000	1.51 H	$37,750,000
Bradford net income, 2000	1,100,000	1.54 A	1,694,000
Translation adjustment, 2000			1,157,000
Balance, 12/31/00	£26,100,000		$40,601,000
Bradford net income, 2001	3,950,000	1.55 A	6,122,500
Bradford dividends, 6/30/01	(750,000)	1.58 H	(1,185,000)
Translation adjustment, 2001			(755,500)
Balance, 12/31/01	£29,300,000		$44,783,000

In addition to the investment in Bradford of $44,783,000, Altman also has equity income on its December 31, 2001, trial balance in the amount of $6,122,500.

Consolidation Worksheet

Once the subsidiary's trial balance has been translated into dollars and the carrying value of the investment is known, the consolidation worksheet at December 31, 2001, can be prepared. As is true in the consolidation of domestic subsidiaries, the investment account, the subsidiary's equity accounts, and the effects of intercompany transactions must be eliminated. The excess of cost over book value at the date of acquisition also must be allocated to the appropriate accounts (in this example, plant and equipment).

Unique to the consolidation of foreign subsidiaries is the fact that the excess of cost over book value, which is denominated in foreign currency, also must be translated into the parent's reporting currency. When the foreign currency is the functional currency, the excess is translated at the current exchange rate with a resulting translation adjustment. The excess is not carried on either the parent or the subsidiary's books but is recorded only in the consolidation worksheet. *The translation adjustment related to the excess has not yet been recognized by either the parent or the subsidiary and must be recorded in the consolidation worksheet.* Exhibit 10–11 presents the consolidation worksheet of Altman and Bradford at December 31, 2001.

Explanation of consolidation entries:

S—Eliminates the subsidiary's stockholders' equity accounts as of the beginning of the current year along with the equivalent book value component within the parent's purchase price in the Investment account.

Exhibit 10–11   Consolidation Worksheet—Parent and Foreign Subsidiary

ALTMAN, INC., AND BRADFORD LTD.
Consolidation Worksheet
For Year Ending December 31, 2001

Accounts	Altman	Bradford	Consolidation Entries Debits	Consolidation Entries Credits	Consolidated Totals
Income Statement					
Sales	$ (32,489,000)	$(21,545,000)			$ (54,034,000)
Cost of goods sold	16,000,000	12,555,000			28,555,000
Depreciation expense	9,700,000	1,395,000			11,095,000
Other expenses	2,900,000	1,472,500			4,372,500
Equity income	(6,122,500)		(I) 6,122,500		–0–
Net income	$ (10,011,500)	$ (6,122,500)			$ (10,011,500)
Statement of Retained Earnings					
Retained earnings, 1/1/01	$ (25,194,000)	$ (5,771,000)	(S) 5,771,000		$ (25,194,000)
Net income (above)	(10,011,500)	(6,122,500)			(10,011,500)
Dividends paid	1,500,000	1,185,000		(D) 1,185,000	1,500,000
Retained earnings, 12/31/01	$ (33,705,500)	$(10,708,500)			$ (33,705,500)
Balance Sheet					
Cash	$ 3,649,800	$ 918,000			$ 4,567,800
Accounts receivable	3,100,000	4,131,000			7,231,000
Inventory	11,410,000	13,770,000			25,180,000
Investment in Bradford	44,783,000			(S) 35,971,500	
				(A) 3,473,500	
			(D) 1,185,000	(I) 6,122,500	
				(T) 401,500	
Plant and equipment (net)	39,500,000	26,316,000	(A) 3,473,000		
			(E) 46,000		69,335,000
Total assets	$102,442,800	$ 45,135,000			$106,313,800
Accounts payable	$ (2,500,000)	$ (765,000)			$ (3,265,000)
Long-term debt	(22,728,800)	(3,060,000)			(25,788,800)
Common stock	(43,107,000)	(30,200,000)	(S) 30,200,000		(43,107,000)
Retained earnings, 12/31/01 (above)	(33,705,500)	(10,708,500)			(33,705,500)
Cumulative translation adjustment ...	(401,500)	(401,500)	(T) 401,500	(E) 46,000	(447,500)
Total liabilities and equities	$102,422,800	$ 45,135,000	$47,199,000	$47,199,000	$106,313,800

A—Allocates the excess of cost over book value at the date of acquisition to land (plant and equipment) and eliminates that amount within the parent's purchase price from the Investment account.

I—Eliminates the amount of equity income recognized by the parent in the current year and included in the Investment account under the equity method.

D—Eliminates the subsidiary's dividend payment that was a reduction in the Investment account under the equity method.

T—Eliminates the cumulative translation adjustment included in the Investment account under the equity method and eliminates the cumulative translation adjustment carried on the parent's books.

E—Revalues the excess of cost over book value for the change in exchange rate since the date of acquisition with the counterpart recognized as an increase in the consolidated cumulative translation adjustment. The revaluation is calculated as follows:

Excess of Cost over Book Value

U.S. dollar equivalent at 12/31/01	£2,300,000 × $1.53 = $3,519,000
U.S. dollar equivalent at 1/1/00	£2,300,000 × $1.51 = 3,473,000
Cumulative translation adjustment related to excess, 12/31/01	$ 46,000

SUMMARY

1. Because many companies have significant financial involvement in foreign countries, the process by which foreign currency financial statements are translated into U.S. dollars is of special accounting importance. The two major issues related to the translation process are (1) which method to use, and (2) where the resulting translation adjustment should be reported in the consolidated financial statements.

2. Translation methods differ on the basis of which accounts are translated at the current exchange rate and which are translated at historical rates. Accounts translated at the current exchange rate are exposed to translation adjustment. Different translation methods give rise to different concepts of balance sheet exposure and translation adjustments of differing signs and magnitude.

3. Under the temporal method, assets carried at current value (cash, marketable securities, receivables) and liabilities are translated at the current exchange rate. Assets carried at historical cost and stockholders' equity are translated at historical exchange rates. When liabilities are greater than the sum of cash, marketable securities, and receivables, a net liability balance sheet exposure exists. Appreciation in the foreign currency results in a negative translation adjustment (remeasurement loss). Depreciation in the foreign currency results in a positive translation adjustment (remeasurement gain). By translating assets carried at historical cost at historical exchange rates, the temporal method maintains the underlying valuation method used by the foreign operation, but relationships in the foreign currency financial statements are distorted.

4. Under the current rate method, all assets and liabilities are translated at the current exchange rate giving rise to a net asset balance sheet exposure. Appreciation in the foreign currency results in a positive translation adjustment. Depreciation in the foreign currency results in a negative translation adjustment. By translating assets carried at historical cost at the current exchange rate, the current rate method maintains relationships in the foreign currency financial statements but the underlying valuation method used by the foreign operation is distorted.

5. From 1975 through 1981, the temporal method—as prescribed by *Statement 8* of the Financial Accounting Standards Board—was used to translate the financial statements of foreign operations. Translation adjustments were reported as gains and losses in income. Because this approach came under increasing attack from the business community as well as from many accountants, the FASB eventually replaced it with *Statement 52*.

6. *Statement 52* creates two separate procedures for translating foreign currency financial statements into the parent's reporting currency. *Translation* through use of the current rate method is appropriate when the foreign operation's functional currency is a foreign currency. In this case, the translation adjustment is reported in other comprehensive income and reflected on the balance sheet as a separate component of stockholders' equity. *Remeasurement* through use of the temporal method is appropriate when the operation's functional currency is the U.S. dollar. Remeasurement also is applied when the operation is in a country with a highly inflationary economy. In these situations, the translation adjustment is treated as a remeasurement gain or loss in net income.

7. Some companies hedge their balance sheet exposures to avoid reporting remeasurement losses in net income and/or negative translation adjustments in other comprehensive income. Gains and losses on derivative or nonderivative instruments used to hedge net investments in foreign operations are reported in the same manner as the translation adjustment being hedged.

COMPREHENSIVE ILLUSTRATION

Problem

(Estimated Time: 55 to 65 Minutes) The Arlington Company is a U.S.-based organization with numerous foreign subsidiaries. As a preliminary step in preparing consolidated financial statements for 2001, the financial information from each of these foreign operations must be translated into the parent's reporting currency, the U.S. dollar.

Arlington owns a subsidiary in Sweden that has been in business for several years. On December 31, 2000, this entity's balance sheet was translated from Swedish kronor (SKr) (its functional currency) into U.S. dollars as prescribed by *SFAS 52.* Equity accounts at that date were as follows (all credit balances):

Common stock	SKr 110,000	=	$21,000
Retained earnings	194,800	=	36,100
Cumulative translation adjustment			3,860

At the end of 2001, the Swedish subsidiary produced the trial balance that follows. These figures include all of the entity's transactions for the year except for the results of several transactions related to sales made to a French customer. A separate ledger has been maintained for these transactions denominated in French francs. This ledger follows the company's trial balance.

Trial Balance—Swedish Subsidiary
December 31, 2001

	Debit	Credit
Cash	SKr 41,000	
Accounts receivable	126,000	
Inventory	128,000	
Land	160,000	
Fixed assets	228,000	
Accumulated depreciation		SKr 98,100
Accounts payable		39,000
Notes payable		56,000
Bonds payable		125,000
Common stock		110,000
Retained earnings, 1/1/01		194,800
Sales		350,000
Cost of goods sold	165,000	
Depreciation expense	10,900	
Salary expense	36,000	
Rent expense	12,000	
Other expenses	41,000	
Dividends paid, 7/1/01	25,000	
Totals	SKr 972,900	SKr 972,900

Ledger—Transactions in French Francs
December 31, 2001

	Debit	Credit
Cash	FF 10,000	
Accounts receivable	28,000	
Fixed assets	20,000	
Accumulated depreciation		FF 4,000
Notes payable		15,000
Sales		44,000
Depreciation expense	4,000	
Interest expense	1,000	
Totals	FF 63,000	FF 63,000

Additional Information:

- The Swedish subsidiary began selling to the French customer at the beginning of the current year. At that time, 20,000 francs were borrowed to acquire a truck for delivery purposes. One-fourth of that debt was paid before the end of the year. Sales to France were made evenly during the period.

- The U.S. dollar exchange rates for the Swedish krona are as follows:

January 1, 2001	$.200 = 1.00 krona
Weighted-average rate for 2001	$.192 = 1.00 krona
July 1, 2001	$.190 = 1.00 krona
December 31, 2001	$1.82 = 1.00 krona

- The exchange rates applicable for the remeasurement of the French franc transactions into Swedish kronor are as follows:

January 1, 2001	1.25 kronor = 1.00 franc
Weighted-average rate for 2001	1.16 kronor = 1.00 franc
December 1, 2001	1.10 kronor = 1.00 franc
December 31, 2001	1.04 kronor = 1.00 franc

- The Swedish subsidiary expended SKr 10,000 during the year for research and development. In accordance with Swedish accounting rules, this cost has been capitalized within the Fixed Assets account. This expenditure had no effect on the depreciation recognized for the year.

Required

Prepare financial statements for the year ending December 31, 2001, for the Swedish subsidiary. Translate these statements according to *SFAS 52* into U.S. dollars to facilitate the preparation of consolidated statements. The Swedish krona is the subsidiary's functional currency.

Solution

Remeasurement of Foreign Currency Balances. A portion of the Swedish subsidiary's operating results are presently stated in French francs. These balances must be remeasured into the functional currency, Swedish krona, before the translation process can begin. In remeasuring these accounts using the temporal method, the krona value of the monetary assets and liabilities are determined by using the current (C) exchange rate (1.04 kronor per franc) whereas all other accounts are remeasured at historical (H) or average (A) rates.

Remeasurement of Foreign Currency Balances

	Francs	Rate	Kronor
Sales	44,000	×1.16 A =	51,040
Interest expense	(1,000)	×1.16 A =	(1,160)
Depreciation expense	(4,000)	×1.25 H =	(5,000)
Income from franc transactions	39,000		44,880
Cash	10,000	×1.04 C =	10,400
Accounts receivable	28,000	×1.04 C =	29,120
Fixed assets	20,000	×1.25 H =	25,000
Accumulated depreciation	(4,000)	×1.25 H =	(5,000)
Total franc assets	54,000		59,520
Notes payable	15,000	×1.04 C =	15,600
Income from franc transactions	39,000	from above	44,880
	54,000		60,480
Remeasurement loss			(960)
Total			59,520

(continued)

Remeasurement Loss for 2001

	Francs	Rate	Kronor
Net monetary asset balance, 1/1/01	FF –0–		SKr –0–
Increases in net monetary items:			
Operations (sales less interest expense)	43,000	×1.16 =	49,880
Decreases in net monetary items:			
Purchased truck, 1/1/01	(20,000)	×1.25 =	(25,000)
Net monetary assets, 12/31/01	FF 23,000		SKr 24,880
Net monetary assets, 12/31/01 at current			
exchange rate	FF 23,000	×1.04 =	SKr 23,920
Remeasurement loss (gain)			SKr 960

The net monetary asset exposure (cash and accounts receivable > notes payable) and depreciation of the French franc create a remeasurement loss of SKr 960.

The remeasured figures from the French operation must be combined in some manner with the subsidiary's trial balance denominated in Swedish kronor. For example, the accounts may simply be added together on a worksheet. As an alternative, a year-end adjustment can be recorded in the accounting system of the Swedish subsidiary to add the remeasured balances for financial reporting purposes.

12/31/01 Adjustment	Debit	Credit
Cash	SKr 10,400	
Accounts receivable	29,120	
Fixed assets	25,000	
Depreciation expense	5,000	
Interest expense	1,160	
Remeasurement loss	960	
Accumulated depreciation		SKr 5,000
Notes Payable		15,600
Sales		51,040

To record foreign currency transactions originally denominated in francs.

One more adjustment is necessary before the Swedish krona financial statements of the subsidiary can be translated into the parent's reporting currency. The research and development costs incurred by the Swedish entity should be reclassified as an expense as required by *SFAS 2*, "Accounting for Research and Development Costs," December 1974. After this adjustment, the Swedish subsidiary's statements are in conformity with U.S. generally accepted accounting principles.

12/31/01 Adjustment	Debit	Credit
Other expenses	SKr 10,000	
Fixed assets		SKr 10,000

To adjust fixed assets and expenses to be in compliance with U.S. GAAP.

By combining all remeasured and adjusted balances with the Swedish subsidiary's trial balance, financial figures can be derived. For example, total sales for the subsidiary are SKr 401,040 (350,000 + 51,040) while cash is SKr 51,400 (41,000 + 10,400), and so on. Having established all account balances in the functional currency (Swedish krona), the subsidiary's statements now may be translated into U.S. dollars. Under the current rate method, the dollar values to be reported for income statement items are based on the average exchange rate for the current year. All assets and liabilities are based on the current exchange rate at the balance sheet date, and equity accounts are based on historical rates in effect at the date of accounting recognition.

SWEDISH SUBSIDIARY
Income Statement
For Year Ending December 31, 2001

Sales	SKr 401,040	× .192 A =	$ 77,000
Cost of goods sold	(165,000	× .192 A =	(31,680)
Gross profit	236,040		45,320
Depreciation expense	(15,900)	× .192 A =	(3,053)
Salary expense	(36,000)	× .192 A =	(6,912)
Rent expense	(12,000)	× .192 A =	(2,304)
Other expenses	(51,000)	× .192 A =	(9,792)
Interest expense	(1,160)	× .192 A =	(223)
Remeasurement loss	(960)	× .192 A =	(184)
Net income	SKr 119,020		$ 22,852

Statement of Retained Earnings
For Year Ending December 31, 2001

Retained earnings, 1/1/ 01	SKr 194,800	given	$36,100
Net income, 2001	199,020	above	22,852
Dividends paid, 7/1/01	(25,000)	× .192 H =	(4,750)
Retained earnings, 12/31/01	SKr 288,820		$54,202

Balance Sheet
December 31, 2001

Cash	SKr 51,400	× .182 C =	$ 9,355
Accounts receivable	155,120	× .182 C =	28,232
Inventory	128,000	× .182 C =	23,296
Land	160,000	× .182 C =	29,120
Fixed assets	243,000	× .182 C =	44,226
Accumulated depreciation	(103,100)	× .182 C =	(18,764)
Total	SKr 634,420		$115,465
Accounts payable	SKr 39,000	× .182 C =	$ 7,098
Notes payable	71,600	× .182 C =	13,031
Bonds payable	125,000	× .182 C =	22,750
Common stock	110,000	given	21,000
Retained earnings	288,820	above	54,202
Cumulative translation adjustment			(2,616)
Total	SKr 634,420		$115,465

The cumulative translation adjustment at 12/31/01 is comprised of the beginning balance (given) plus the translation adjustment for the current year.

Cumulative Translation Adjustment

Balance, 1/1/ 01	$ 3,861
Translation adjustment for 2001	(6,477)
Balance, 12/31/01	$(2,616)

The negative translation adjustment for 2001 of $6,477 is calculated by considering the effect of exchange rate changes on net assets:

Translation Adjustment for 2001

Net assets, 1/1/01	SKr 304,800*	× .200 =	$60,960
Increase in net assets:			
Net income, 2001	199,020	× .192 =	22,852
Decrease in net assets:			
Dividends, 7/1/01	(25,000)	× .190 =	(4,750)
Net assets, 12/31/01	SKr 398,820†		$79,062
Net assets, 12/31/01 at current exchange rate ...	SKr 398,820	× .182 =	72,585
Translation adjustment, 2001—negative			$ 6,477

*Indicated by January 1, 2001, stockholders' equity balances—Common stock, SKr 110,000; Retained earnings, SKr 194,800.

†Indicated by December 31, 2001, stockholders' equity balances—Common stock, SKr 110,000; Retained earnings, SKr 288,820.

QUESTIONS

1. What are the two major issues related to the translation of foreign currency financial statements?

2. What causes balance sheet (or translation) exposure to foreign exchange risk? How does balance sheet exposure compare with transaction exposure?

3. Why might a company want to hedge its balance sheet exposure? What is the paradox associated with hedging balance sheet exposure?

4. Under *SFAS 133,* how are gains and losses on financial instruments used to hedge the net investment in a foreign operation reported in the consolidated financial statements?

5. What is the concept underlying the temporal method of translation? What is the concept underlying the current rate method of translation? How does balance sheet exposure differ under these two methods?

6. In translating the financial statements of a foreign subsidiary, why is the value assigned to retained earnings considered especially difficult to determine? How is this problem normally resolved?

7. What are the major procedural differences in applying the current rate and temporal methods of translation?

8. Clarke Company has a subsidiary operating in a foreign country. In relation to this subsidiary, what is meant by the term *functional currency?* How is the functional currency determined?

9. A translation adjustment must be calculated and disclosed whenever financial statements of a foreign subsidiary are translated into the parent's reporting currency. How is this figure computed, and where is the amount reported in the financial statements?

10. The FASB put forth two theories about the underlying nature of a translation adjustment. What are these theories, and which one was considered correct by the FASB?

11. When is remeasurement rather than translation appropriate? How does remeasurement differ from translation?

12. Which translation method does FASB *SFAS 52* require for operations in highly inflationary countries? What is the rationale for mandating use of this method?

INTERNET ASSIGNMENT

Internet sites are time and date sensitive. It is the purpose of these exercises to have you explore the Internet. You may need to refer to the text's Web site at http://www.mhhe.com/hoyle6e to find the most up-to-date links for the Web sites listed in the Internet Exercises.

1. Use the Internet to obtain the most recent annual report for each of the following U.S.-based companies:

   Compaq Computer Corporation (www.compaq.com)

   Dell Computer Corporation (www.dell.com)

   Gateway (www.gateway.com)

   Answer the following questions for each company:
   a. What is the functional currency for the majority of foreign subsidiaries?
   b. What is the predominant translation method used by each company?
   c. What implication does this have for the comparability of consolidated financial statements across these three companies?
   d. Determine the amount of remeasurement gain or loss, if any, reported in income in each of the most recent three years. Are these amounts significant?
   e. Determine the amount of translation adjustment, if any, reported in other comprehensive income in each of the most recent three years. Are these amounts significant?
   f. Does the company hedge its foreign subsidiary balance sheet exposure to foreign exchange risk?

LIBRARY ASSIGNMENT

1. Read the following:

   "Plenty of Opportunity to Fool Around," *Forbes*, June 2, 1986.

   "Foreign Currency Translation," *Statement of Financial Accounting Standards No. 52,* FASB, paragraphs 5–10, 39–46, and 77–84.

   Write a short report addressing two questions: How could more guidance be given in the selection of a foreign subsidiary's functional currency? Should more official guidance be provided in connection with the selection of a foreign subsidiary's functional currency?

PROBLEMS

1. What is a subsidiary's functional currency?
   a. The parent's reporting currency.
   b. The currency in which transactions are denominated.
   c. The currency in which the entity primarily generates and expends cash.
   d. Always the currency of the country in which the company has its headquarters.

2. The translation process and the remeasurement process are being compared. Which of the following statements is true?
   a. The reported balance of inventory is normally the same under both methods.
   b. The reported balance of equipment is normally the same under both methods.
   c. The reported balance of sales is normally the same under both methods.
   d. The reported balance of depreciation expense is normally the same under both methods.

3. Which of the following statements is true for the translation process (as opposed to remeasurement)?
   a. A translation adjustment can affect consolidated net income.
   b. Equipment is translated at the historical exchange rate in effect at the date of its purchase.
   c. A translation adjustment is created by the change in the relative value of a subsidiary's net assets caused by currency rate fluctuations.

d.   A translation adjustment is created by the change in the relative value of a subsidiary's monetary assets and monetary liabilities caused by currency rate fluctuations.

4.   A subsidiary of Byner Corporation has one asset (inventory) and no liabilities. The functional currency for this subsidiary is the peso. The inventory was acquired for 100,000 pesos when the exchange rate was $.16 = 1 peso. Consolidated statements are to be produced and the current exchange rate is $.19 = 1 peso. Which of the following statements is true for the consolidated financial statements?
a.   A remeasurement gain must be reported.
b.   A positive translation adjustment must be reported.
c.   A negative translation adjustment must be reported.
d.   A remeasurement loss must be reported.

5.   At what rates should the following balance sheet accounts in foreign statements be translated into U.S. dollars?

	Accumulated Depreciation—Equipment	Equipment
a.	Current	Current
b.	Current	Average for year
c.	Historical	Current
d.	Historical	Historical

(AICPA adapted)

Questions 6 and 7 are based on the following information: Certain balance sheet accounts of a foreign subsidiary of the Rose Company have been stated in U.S. dollars as follows:

	Stated at	
	Current Rates	Historical Rates
Accounts receivable, current	$200,000	$220,000
Accounts receivable, long term	100,000	110,000
Prepaid insurance	50,000	55,000
Goodwill	80,000	85,000
	$430,000	$470,000

6.   A foreign currency is the functional currency of this subsidiary. What total should be included in Rose's balance sheet for the preceding items?
a. $430,000.
b. $435,000.
c. $440,000.
d. $450,000.

7.   The U.S. dollar is the functional currency of this subsidiary. What total should be included in Rose's balance sheet for the above items?
a. $430,000.
b. $435,000.
c. $440,000.
d. $450,000.

(AICPA adapted)

Questions 8 and 9 are based on the following information: A subsidiary of Salisbury, Inc., is located in a foreign country. The functional currency of this subsidiary is the schweikart (SWK). The subsidiary acquires inventory on credit on November 1, 2000, for SWK 100,000 that is sold on January 17, 2001, for SWK 130,000. The subsidiary pays for the inventory on January 31, 2001. Currency exchange rates between dollars and schweikart are as follows:

November 1, 2000	$.16 = 1 SWK
December 31, 2000	$.17 = 1 SWK
January 17, 2001	$.18 = 1 SWK
January 31, 2001	$.19 = 1 SWK
Average for 2001	$.20 = 1 SWK

8. What figure is reported for this inventory on Salisbury's consolidated balance sheet at December 31, 2000?
   a. $16,000.
   b. $17,000.
   c. $18,000.
   d. $19,000.

9. What figure is reported for cost of goods sold on Salisbury's consolidated income statement for the year ending December 31, 2001?
   a. $16,000.
   b. $17,000.
   c. $18,000.
   d. $19,000.

Questions 10 and 11 are based on the following information: A subsidiary of Clarke Corporation buys marketable equity securities and inventory on April 1, 2001, for 100,000 pesos each. Both these items are paid for on June 1, 2001 and are still on hand at year's end. Inventory is carried at cost under the lower-of-cost-or-market rule. Currency exchange rates are as follows:

January 1, 2001	$.15 = 1 peso
April 1, 2001	$.16 = 1 peso
June 1, 2001	$.17 = 1 peso
December 31, 2001	$.19 = 1 peso

10. Assume that the peso is the subsidiary's functional currency. On a consolidated balance sheet as of December 31, 2001, what balances are reported?
    a. Marketable equity securities = $16,000 and Inventory = $16,000.
    b. Marketable equity securities = $17,000 and Inventory = $17,000.
    c. Marketable equity securities = $19,000 and Inventory = $16,000.
    d. Marketable equity securities = $19,000 and Inventory = $19,000.

11. Assume that the U.S. dollar is the subsidiary's functional currency. On a consolidated balance sheet as of December 31, 2001, what balances are reported?
    a. Marketable equity securities = $16,000 and Inventory = $16,000.
    b. Marketable equity securities = $17,000 and Inventory = $17,000.
    c. Marketable equity securities = $19,000 and Inventory = $16,000.
    d. Marketable equity securities = $19,000 and Inventory = $19,000.

12. A U.S. company's foreign subsidiary had the following amounts in foreign currency units (FCU) in 2001:

Cost of goods sold	FCU 10 million
Ending inventory	FCU 500,000
Beginning inventory	FCU 200,000

The average exchange rate during 2001 was $.80 = FCU 1. The beginning inventory was acquired when the exchange rate was $1.00 = FCU 1. Ending inventory was acquired when the exchange rate was $.75 = FCU 1. The exchange rate at December 31, 2001, was $.70 = FCU 1. Assuming that the foreign country is highly inflationary, at what amount should the foreign subsidiary's cost of goods sold be reflected in the U.S. dollar income statement?
    a. $7,815,000.
    b. $8,040,000.
    c. $8,065,000.
    d. $8,090,000.

13. Ace Corporation starts a subsidiary in a foreign country; the subsidiary has the peso as its functional currency. On January 1, 2001, Ace buys all of the subsidiary's common stock for 20,000 pesos. On April 1, 2001, the subsidiary purchases inventory for 20,000 pesos with payment made on May 1, 2001. This inventory is sold on August 1, 2001, for 30,000 pesos, which is collected on October 1, 2001. Currency exchange rates are as follows:

January 1, 2001	$.15 = 1 peso
April 1, 2001	$.17 = 1 peso
May 1, 2001	$.18 = 1 peso
August 1, 2001	$.19 = 1 peso
October 1, 2001	$.20 = 1 peso
December 31, 2001	$.21 = 1 peso

In preparing consolidated financial statements, what translation adjustment will be reported at the end of 2001?
a. $400 positive (credit).
b. $600 positive (credit).
c. $1,400 positive (credit).
d. $1,800 positive (credit).

14. Which method of translation maintains, in the translated financial statements, the underlying valuation methods used in the foreign currency financial statements?
a.   Current rate method; income statement translated at average exchange rate for the year.
b.   Current rate method; income statement translated at exchange rate at the balance sheet date.
c.   Temporal method.
d.   Monetary/nonmonetary method.

15. The Houston Corporation operates a branch operation in a foreign country. Although this branch deals in pesos, the U.S. dollar is viewed as its functional currency. Thus, a remeasurement is necessary to produce financial information for external reporting purposes. The branch begins the year with 100,000 pesos in cash and no other assets or liabilities. However, the branch immediately uses 60,000 pesos to acquire equipment. On May 1, inventory costing 30,000 pesos is purchased for cash. This merchandise is sold on July 1 for 50,000 pesos cash. The branch transfers 10,000 pesos to the parent on October 1 and records depreciation on the equipment for the year of 6,000 pesos. Currency exchange rates are as follows:

January 1	$.16 = 1 peso
May 1	$.18 = 1 peso
July 1	$.20 = 1 peso
October 1	$.21 = 1 peso
December 31	$.22 = 1 peso
Average for the year	$.19 = 1 peso

What is the remeasurement gain to be recognized in the consolidated income statement?
a. $2,100.
b. $2,400.
c. $2,700.
d. $3,000.

16. Which of the following items is *not* remeasured using historical exchange rates under the temporal method?
a.   Accumulated depreciation on equipment.
b.   Cost of goods sold.
c.   Marketable equity securities.
d.   Retained earnings.

17. In accordance with U.S. generally accepted accounting principles, which translation combination would be appropriate for a foreign operation whose functional currency is the U.S. dollar?

	Method	Treatment of Translation Adjustment
a.	Temporal	Other comprehensive income
b.	Temporal	Gain or loss in net income
c.	Current rate	Other comprehensive income
d.	Current rate	Gain or loss in net income

18. A foreign subsidiary's functional currency is its local currency, which has not experienced significant inflation. The weighted-average exchange rate for the current year is the appropriate exchange rate for translating:

	Wages Expense	Wages Payable
a.	Yes	Yes
b.	Yes	No
c.	No	Yes
d.	No	No

19. The functional currency of DeZoort, Inc.'s British subsidiary is the British pound. DeZoort borrowed British pounds as a partial hedge of its investment in the subsidiary. In preparing consolidated financial statements, DeZoort's negative translation adjustment on its investment in the subsidiary exceeded its foreign exchange gain on the borrowing. How should the effects of the negative translation adjustment and foreign exchange gain be reported in DeZoort's consolidated financial statements?
    a. The translation adjustment is reported in other comprehensive income on the balance sheet and the foreign exchange gain is reported in the income statement.
    b. The translation adjustment is reported in the income statement and the foreign exchange gain is deferred in other comprehensive income on the balance sheet.
    c. The translation adjustment less the foreign exchange gain is reported in other comprehensive income on the balance sheet.
    d. The translation adjustment less the foreign exchange gain is reported in the income statement.

    (AICPA adapted)

20. Gains from remeasuring a foreign subsidiary's financial statements from the local currency, which is not the functional currency, into the parent's currency should be reported as a(n)
    a. Deferred foreign exchange gain.
    b. Translation adjustment in other comprehensive income.
    c. Extraordinary item, net of income taxes.
    d. Part of continuing operations.

    (AICPA adapted)

21. The foreign currency is the functional currency for a foreign subsidiary. At what exchange rate should each of the following accounts be translated:
    Rent Expense
    Dividends Paid
    Equipment
    Notes Payable
    Sales
    Depreciation Expense
    Cash
    Accumulated Depreciation
    Common Stock

22. On January 1, 2001, Dandu Corporation started a subsidiary in a foreign country. On April 1, 2001, the subsidiary purchased inventory at a cost of 120,000 local currency units (LCU). One-fourth of this inventory remained unsold at the end of 2001 while 40 percent of the liability from the purchase had not yet been paid. The exchange rates were

January 1, 2001	$1 = LCU 2.5
April 1, 2001	$1 = LCU 2.8
Average for 2001	$1 = LCU 2.7
December 31, 2001	$1 = LCU 3.0

What should be the December 31, 2001, inventory and accounts payable balances for this foreign subsidiary as translated into U.S. dollars?

23. The following series of accounts is denominated as of December 31, 2001, in pesos. For reporting purposes, these figures need to be stated in U.S. dollars. For each balance, indicate the exchange rate that would be used if a translation is made. Then, again for each account, provide the exchange rate that would be necessary if a remeasurement is being made. The company was started in 1980. The buildings were acquired in 1982 and the patents in 1983.

	Translation	**Remeasurement**
Accounts payable		
Accounts receivable		
Accumulated depreciation		
Advertising expense		
Amortization expense (patents)		
Buildings		
Cash		
Common stock		
Depreciation expense		
Dividends paid (10/1/01)		
Notes payable—due in 2003		
Patents (net)		
Salary expense		
Sales		

Exchange rates are as follows:

1980	1 peso = $.28
1982	1 peso = $.26
1983	1 peso = $.25
January 1, 2001	1 peso = $.24
April 1, 2001	1 peso = $.23
July 1, 2001	1 peso = $.22
October 1, 2001	1 peso = $.20
December 31, 2001	1 peso = $.16
Average for 2001	1 peso = $.19

24. On December 18, 2001, Stephanie Corporation acquired 100 percent of a Swiss company for Sfr 3.7 million. At the date of acquisition, the exchange rate was $.70 = Sfr 1. The acquisition price is attributable to the following assets and liabilities:

Cash	Sfr	500,000
Inventory		1,000,000
Fixed assets		3,000,000
Notes payable		(800,000)

Stephanie Corporation prepares consolidated financial statements on December 31, 2001. By that date, the Swiss franc has appreciated to $.75 = Sfr 1. Because of the year-end holidays, no transactions took place prior to consolidation.

Required

a. Determine the translation adjustment to be reported on Stephanie's December 31, 2001, consolidated balance sheet assuming that the Swiss franc is the Swiss subsidiary's functional currency. What is the economic relevance of this translation adjustment?

b. Determine the remeasurement gain or loss to be reported in Stephanie's 2001 consolidated net income assuming that the U.S. dollar is the functional currency. What is the economic relevance of this remeasurement gain or loss?

25. The Fenwicke Company began operating a subsidiary in a foreign country on January 1, 2001, by acquiring all of the common stock for LCU 40,000. This subsidiary immediately borrowed LCU 100,000 on a five-year note with 10 percent interest payable annually beginning on January 1, 2002. A building was then purchased for LCU 140,000. This property had a 10-year anticipated life and no salvage value and is to be

depreciated using the straight-line method. The building is rented for three years to a group of local doctors for LCU 5,000 per month. By year-end, payments totaling LCU 50,000 had been made. On October 1, LCU 4,000 was paid for a repair made on that date. A cash dividend of LCU 5,000 is transferred back to Fenwicke on December 31, 2001. The functional currency for the subsidiary is the LCU. Currency exchange rates are as follows:

January 1, 2001	$2.00 = LCU 1
October 1, 2001	$1.85 = LCU 1
Average for 2001	$1.90 = LCU 1
December 31, 2001	$1.80 = LCU 1

Required

Prepare an income statement, statement of retained earnings, and balance sheet for this subsidiary in LCU and then translate these amounts into U.S. dollars.

26. Refer to the information provided in problem 25. Prepare a statement of cash flows in LCU for Fenwicke's foreign subsidiary and then translate these amounts into U.S. dollars.

27. The Watson Company has a subsidiary in the country of Alonza where the local currency unit is the Kamel (KM). On December 31, 2000, the subsidiary has the following balance sheet:

Cash	KM 16,000	Notes payable (due 2002)	KM 19,000
Inventory	10,000	Common stock	20,000
Land	4,000	Retained earnings	10,000
Building	40,000		
Accumulated depreciation	(21,000)		
	KM 49,000		KM 49,000

This inventory was acquired on August 1, 2000; the land and buildings were acquired in 1984. The common stock was issued in 1978. During 2001, the following transactions took place:

2001	
Feb. 1	Paid 5,000 KM on the note payable.
May 1	Sold entire inventory for 15,000 KM on account.
June 1	Sold land for 5,000 KM cash.
Aug. 1	Collected all accounts receivable.
Sept. 1	Signed long-term note to receive 6,000 KM cash.
Oct. 1	Bought inventory for 12,000 KM cash.
Nov. 1	Bought land for 4,000 KM on account.
Dec. 1	Paid dividend to parent—3,000 KM cash.
Dec. 31	Recorded depreciation for the entire year of 2,000 KM.

The exchange rates are as follows:

1978	1 KM = $.24
1984	1 KM = $.21
August 1, 2000	1 KM = $.31
December 31, 2000	1 KM = $.32
February 1, 2001	1 KM = $.33
May 1, 2001	1 KM = $.34
June 1, 2001	1 KM = $.35
August 1, 2001	1 KM = $.37
September 1, 2001	1 KM = $.38
October 1, 2001	1 KM = $.39
November 1, 2001	1 KM = $.40
December 1, 2001	1 KM = $.41
December 31, 2001	1 KM = $.42
Average for 2001	1 KM = $.37

Required

    a. If this is a translation, what is the translation adjustment determined solely for 2001?

    b. If this is a remeasurement, what is the remeasurement gain or loss determined solely for 2001?

28. Aerkion Company starts the year of 2001 with two assets: cash of 22,000 LCU (local currency units) and land that originally cost 60,000 LCU when acquired on April 4, 1994. On May 1, 2001, the company rendered services to a customer for 30,000 LCU, an amount immediately paid in cash. On October 1, 2001, the company incurred an operating expense of 18,000 LCU that was immediately paid. No other transactions occurred during the year. Currency exchange rates were as follows:

April 4, 1994	1 LCU = $.23
January 1, 2001	1 LCU = $.24
May 1, 2001	1 LCU = $.25
October 1, 2001	1 LCU = $.26
Average for 2001	1 LCU = $.27
December 31, 2001	1 LCU = $.29

Required

    a. Assume that Aerkion is a foreign subsidiary of a U.S. multinational company that uses the U.S. dollar as its reporting currency. Assume also that the LCU is the functional currency of the subsidiary. What is the translation adjustment for this subsidiary for the year 2001?

    b. Assume that Aerkion is a foreign subsidiary of a U.S. multinational company that uses the U.S. dollar as its reporting currency. Assume also that the U.S. dollar is the functional currency of the subsidiary. What is the remeasurement gain or loss for 2001?

    c. Assume that Aerkion is a foreign subsidiary of a U.S. multinational company. On the December 31, 2001, balance sheet, what is the translated value of the Land account? On the December 31, 2001, balance sheet, what is the remeasured value of the Land account?

29. Lancer, Inc., starts a subsidiary in a foreign country on January 1, 2000. The following account balances are for the year ending December 31, 2001, and are stated in kanquo (KQ), the local currency.

Sales	KQ 200,000
Inventory (bought on 3/1/01)	100,000
Equipment (bought on 1/1/00)	80,000
Rent expense	10,000
Dividends (paid on 10/1/01)	20,000
Notes receivable (to be collected in 2004)	30,000
Accumulated depreciation—Equipment	24,000
Salary payable	5,000
Depreciation expense	8,000

The following exchange rates are applicable:

January 1, 2000	$1 = 13 KQ
January 1, 2001	$1 = 18 KQ
March 1, 2001	$1 = 19 KQ
October 1, 2001	$1 = 21 KQ
December 31, 2001	$1 = 22 KQ
Average for 2000	$1 = 14 KQ
Average for 2001	$1 = 20 KQ

Lancer is preparing account balances to produce consolidated financial statements.

    a. Assuming that the kanquo is the functional currency, what exchange rate would be used to report each of these accounts in U.S. dollar consolidated financial statements?

    b.   Assuming that the U.S. dollar is the functional currency, what exchange rate would be used to report each of these accounts in U.S. dollar consolidated financial statements?

30.   The Board Company has a foreign subsidiary that began operations at the start of 2001 with assets of 132,000 kites (the local currency unit) and liabilities of 54,000 kites. During this initial year of operation, the subsidiary reported a profit of 26,000 kites. Two dividends were distributed; each was for 5,000 kites with one dividend paid on March 1 and the other on October 1. Applicable exchange rates are as follows:

January 1, 2001 (start of business)	$0.80 = 1 kite
March 1, 2001	$0.78 = 1 kite
Weighted-average rate for 2001	$0.77 = 1 kite
October 1, 2001	$0.76 = 1 kite
December 31, 2001	$0.75 = 1 kite

Required:

    a.   Assume that the kite is the functional currency for this subsidiary. What translation adjustment would be reported by Board for the year 2001?

    b.   Assume that on October 1, 2001, Board entered into a forward exchange contract to hedge the net investment in this subsidiary. On that date, Board agreed to sell 200,000 kites in three months at a forward exchange rate of $0.76 = 1 kite. Prepare the journal entries required by this forward contract. In addition, compute the net translation adjustment to be reported in other comprehensive income by Board for the year 2001 under this second set of circumstances.

31.   Kingsfield starts a subsidiary operation in a foreign country on January 1, 2001. The currency in this country is the kumquat (KQ). To get this business started, Kingsfield invests 10,000 kumquats. Of this amount, 3,000 kumquats are expended immediately to acquire equipment. Later, on April 1, 2001, land also is purchased. All operational activities of the subsidiary occur at an even rate throughout the year. The currency exchange rates for this year are as follows:

January 1, 2001	KQ 1 = $1.71
April 1, 2001	KQ 1 = $1.59
June 1, 2001	KQ 1 = $1.66
Weighted average—2001	KQ 1 = $1.64
December 31, 2001	KQ 1 = $1.62

As of December 31, 2001, the subsidiary reports the following trial balance:

	Debits	Credits
Cash	KQ 8,000	
Accounts receivable	9,000	
Equipment	3,000	
Accumulated depreciation		KQ 600
Land	5,000	
Accounts payable		3,000
Notes payable (due 2003)		5,000
Common stock		10,000
Dividends paid (6/1/01)	4,000	
Sales		25,000
Salary expense	5,000	
Depreciation expense	600	
Miscellaneous expenses	9,000	
Totals	KQ 43,600	KQ 43,600

Kingsfield is a corporation based in East Lansing, Michigan, and, therefore, uses the U.S. dollar as its reporting currency.

Required

    a. Assume that the functional currency of the subsidiary is the kumquat. Prepare a trial balance for the subsidiary in U.S. dollars so that consolidated financial statements can be prepared.

    b. Assume that the subsidiary's functional currency is the U.S. dollar. Prepare a trial balance for the subsidiary in U.S. dollars so that consolidated financial statements can be prepared.

32. Livingston Company is a wholly owned subsidiary of Rose Corporation. Livingston operates in a foreign country with financial statements recorded in goghs (GH), the company's functional currency. Financial statements for the year of 2001 are as follows:

Income Statement
For Year Ending December 31, 2001

Sales	GH 270,000
Cost of goods sold	(155,000)
Gross profit	115,000
Less: Operating expenses	(54,000)
Gain on sale of equipment	10,000
Net income	GH 71,000

Statement of Retained Earnings
For Year Ending December 31, 2001

Retained earnings, 1/1/01	GH 216,000
Net income	71,000
Less: Dividends paid	(26,000)
Retained earnings, 12/31/01	GH 261,000

Balance Sheet
December 31, 2001
Assets

Cash	GH 44,000
Receivables	116,000
Inventory	58,000
Fixed assets (net)	339,000
Total assets	GH 557,000

Liabilities and Equities

Liabilities	GH 176,000
Common stock	120,000
Retained earnings, 12/31/01	261,000
Total liabilities and equities	GH 557,000

Additional Information:

■ The common stock was issued in 1989 when the exchange rate was $1.00 = .48 GH; fixed assets were acquired in 1990 when the rate was $1.00 = .50 GH.

■ As of January 1, 2001, the retained earnings balance was translated as $395,000.

■ The currency exchange rates for the current year are as follows:

January 1, 2001	$1.00 = .60 goghs
April 1, 2001	$1.00 = .62 goghs
September 1, 2001	$1.00 = .58 goghs
December 31, 2001	$1.00 = .65 goghs
Weighted-average rate for 2001	$1.00 = .63 goghs

- Inventory was acquired evenly throughout the year.
- A translation adjustment was reported on the December 31, 2000, balance sheet with a debit balance of $85,000.
- Dividends were paid on April 1, 2001, and a piece of equipment was sold on September 1, 2001.

Required

Translate the foreign currency statements into the parent's reporting currency, the U.S. dollar.

33. The following account balances are for the Agee Company as of January 1, 2001, and again as of December 31, 2001. All figures are denominated in kroner (Kr).

	1/1/01	**12/31/01**
Accounts payable	(18,000)	(24,000)
Accounts receivable	35,000	79,000
Accumulated depreciation—buildings	(20,000)	(25,000)
Accumulated depreciation—equipment	–0–	(5,000)
Bonds payable—due 2006	(50,000)	(50,000)
Buildings	118,000	97,000
Cash	35,000	8,000
Common stock	(70,000)	(80,000)
Depreciation expense	–0–	15,000
Dividends (10/1/01)	–0–	32,000
Equipment	–0–	30,000
Gain on sale of building	–0–	(6,000)
Rent expense	–0–	14,000
Retained earnings	(30,000)	(30,000)
Salary expense	–0–	20,000
Sales	–0–	(80,000)
Utilities expense	–0–	5,000

Additional Information:

- Additional shares of common stock were issued during the year on April 1, 2001. Common stock at January 1, 2001, also was sold at the start of operations in 1980.
- Buildings were purchased in 1982. One building with a book value of Kr 16,000 was sold on July 1 of the current year.
- Equipment was acquired on April 1, 2001.
- Retained earnings as of January 1, 2001, was reported as $62,319.

Relevant exchange rates were as follows:

1980	$2.40 = 1 Kr
1982	$2.20 = 1 Kr
January 1, 2001	$2.50 = 1 Kr
April 1, 2001	$2.60 = 1 Kr
July 1, 2001	$2.80 = 1 Kr
October 1, 2001	$2.90 = 1 Kr
December 31, 2001	$3.00 = 1 Kr
Average for 2001	$2.70 = 1 Kr

Required

a. If a remeasurement is being carried out, what would be the remeasurement gain or loss for 2001?

b. If a translation is being carried out, what would be the translation adjustment for 2001?

34. The Sendelbach Corporation is a U.S.-based organization with operations throughout the world. One of the company's subsidiaries is headquartered in Frankfurt. Although this wholly owned company operates primarily in Germany, some transactions are carried out through a branch in France. Therefore, the subsidiary maintains a ledger denominated in French francs (FF) as well as a general ledger in deutsche marks (DM).

As of December 31, 2001, the German subsidiary is preparing financial statements in anticipation of consolidation with the U.S. parent corporation. Both ledgers for the subsidiary are as follows:

Main Operation—Germany

	Debit	Credit
Accounts payable		DM 35,000
Accumulated depreciation		27,000
Buildings and equipment	DM 167,000	
Cash	26,000	
Common stock		50,000
Cost of goods sold	203,000	
Depreciation expense	8,000	
Dividends paid, 4/1/01	28,000	
Gain on sale of equipment, 6/1/01		5,000
Inventory	98,000	
Notes payable—due in 2003		76,000
Receivables	68,000	
Retained earnings, 1/1/01		135,530
Salary expense	26,000	
Sales		312,000
Utility expense	9,000	
Branch operation	7,530	
Totals	DM 640,530	DM 640,530

Branch Operation—France

	Debit	Credit
Accounts payable		FF 49,000
Accumulated depreciation		19,000
Building and equipment	FF 40,000	
Cash	59,000	
Depreciation expense	2,000	
Inventory (beginning—income statement)	23,000	
Inventory (ending—income statement)		28,000
Inventory (ending—balance sheet)	28,000	
Purchases	68,000	
Receivables	21,000	
Salary expense	9,000	
Sales		124,000
Main office		30,000
Totals	FF 250,000	FF 250,000

Additional Information:

- The functional currency for the German subsidiary is the deutsche mark while the reporting currency for Sendelbach is the U.S. dollar. The German and French operations are not viewed as separate accounting entities.
- The building and equipment used in the French operation were acquired in 1983 when the currency exchange rate was DM .25 = FF 1.
- Purchases should be assumed as having been made evenly throughout the fiscal year.
- Beginning inventory was acquired evenly throughout 2000; ending inventory was acquired evenly throughout 2001.

- The Main Office account found on the French records should be considered an equity account. This balance was remeasured into DM 7,530 on December 31, 2000, and no further transactions have occurred.
- Currency exchange rates applicable to the French operation are as follows:

Weighted average, 2000	DM .30 = FF 1
January 1, 2001	DM .32 = FF 1
Weighted-average rate for 2001	DM .34 = FF 1
December 31, 2001	DM .35 = FF 1

- On December 31, 2000, consolidated balance sheet, a cumulative translation adjustment was reported with a $36,950 credit (positive) balance.
- The subsidiary's common stock was issued in 1976 when the exchange rate was $.45 = DM 1.
- The December 31, 2000, balance of retained earnings for this subsidiary was DM 135,540, a figure that has been translated into $70,421.
- The applicable currency exchange rates for translation purposes are as follows:

January 1, 2001	$.70 = DM 1
April 1, 2001	$.69 = DM 1
June 1, 2001	$.68 = DM 1
Weighted-average rate for 2001	$.67 = DM 1
December 31, 2001	$.65 = DM 1

Required

a. Remeasure the French operational figures from francs into deutsche marks (Hint: Back into the beginning net monetary asset or liability position).
b. Prepare financial statements for this subsidiary in its functional currency.
c. Translate the functional currency financial statements into U.S. dollars so that Sendelbach can prepare consolidated financial statements.

35. On January 1, 2001, the Cayce Corporation purchased 100 percent of the Simbel Company at a cost of $126,000. Cayce is a U.S.-based company headquartered in Buffalo, New York, and Simbel is in Cairo, Egypt. Cayce accounts for its investment in Simbel under the cost method. Any excess of purchase price over book value is attributable to undervalued land on Simbel's books. Simbel had no retained earnings at the date of acquisition. Following are the 2002 financial statements for the two operations. Cayce's information is stated in U.S. dollars ($) while Simbel's statements are reported in Egyptian pounds (£E).

	Cayce Corporation	Simbel Company
Sales	$200,000	£E 800,000
Cost of goods sold	(93,800)	(420,000)
Salary expense	(19,000)	(74,000)
Rent expense	(7,000)	(46,000)
Other expenses	(21,000)	(59,000)
Dividend income—from Simbel	13,750	–0–
Gain on sale of fixed asset, 10/1/02	–0–	30,000
Net income	$ 72,950	£E 231,000
Retained earnings, 1/1/02	$318,000	£E 133,000
Net income	72,950	231,000
Dividends paid	(24,000)	(50,000)
Retained earnings, 12/31/02	$366,950	£E 314,000

(continued)

	Cayce Corporation	Simbel Company
Cash and receivables	$110,750	£E 146,000
Inventory	98,000	297,000
Prepaid expenses	30,000	–0–
Investment in Simbel (cost)	126,000	–0–
Fixed assets (net)	398,000	455,000
Total assets	$762,750	£E 898,000
Accounts payable	$ 60,800	£E 54,000
Notes payable—due in 2005	132,000	140,000
Common stock	120,000	240,000
Additional paid-in capital	83,000	150,000
Retained earnings, 12/31/02	366,950	314,000
Total liabilities and equities	$762,750	£E 898,000

Additional Information:

- During 2001, the first year of joint operation, Simbel reported income of 163,000 pounds earned evenly throughout the year. A dividend of 30,000 pounds was paid to Cayce on June 1 of that year. The 2002 dividend paid by Simbel also was made on June 1.

- On December 9, 2002, Simbel classified a 10,000 pound expenditures as a rent expense, although this payment related to prepayment of rent for the first few months of 2003.

- The exchange rates between the U.S. dollar and Egyptian pound are as follows:

January 1, 2001	$.300 = 1 pound
June 1, 2001	$.290 = 1 pound
Weighted-average rate for 2001	$.288 = 1 pound
December 31, 2001	$.280 = 1 pound
June 1, 2002	$.275 = 1 pound
October 1, 2002	$.273 = 1 pound
Weighted-average rate for 2002	$.274 = 1 pound
December 31, 2002	$.270 = 1 pound

Required

Prepare consolidated financial statements for Cayce Corporation and its consolidated subsidiary. Assume that the U.S. dollar is the reporting currency of the parent company whereas the Egyptian pound is the subsidiary's functional currency.

36. Diekmann Company, a U.S.-based company, acquired a 100 percent interest in Rakona A.S. in the Czech Republic on January 1, 2001, when the exchange rate for the Czech koruna (Kčs) was $.05. The financial statements of Rakona as of December 31, 2002, two years later, are as follows:

Balance Sheet
December 31, 2002

Assets

Cash	Kčs 2,000,000
Accounts receivable (net)	3,300,000
Inventory	8,500,000
Equipment	25,000,000
Less: accumulated depreciation	(8,500,000)
Building	72,000,000
Less: accumulated depreciation	(30,300,000)
Land	6,000,000
Total assets	Kčs 78,000,000

Liabilities and Stockholders' Equity

Accounts payable	Kčs 2,500,000
Long-term debt	50,000,000
Common stock	5,000,000
Additional paid-in capital	15,000,000
Retained earnings	5,500,000
Total liabilities and stockholders' equity	Kčs 78,000,000

Statement of Income and Retained Earnings
For the Year Ending December 31, 2002

Sales	Kčs 25,000,000
Cost of goods sold	(12,000,000)
Depreciation expense—equipment	(2,500,000)
Depreciation expense—building	(1,800,000)
Research and development expense	(1,200,000)
Other expenses (including taxes)	(1,000,000)
Net income	Kčs 6,500,000
Plus: Retained earnings, 1/1/02	500,000
Less: Dividends, 2002	(1,500,000)
Retained earnings, 12/31/02	Kčs 5,500,000

Additional Information:

- The January 1, 2002, beginning inventory of Kčs 6,000,000 was acquired on December 18, 2001, when the exchange rate was $.043. Purchases of inventory during 2002 were acquired uniformly throughout the year. The December 31, 2002, ending inventory of Kčs 8,500,000 was acquired in the latter part of 2002 when the exchange rate was $.032. All fixed assets were on the books when the subsidiary was acquired except for Kčs 5,000,000 of equipment acquired on January 3, 2002, when the exchange rate was $.036 and Kčs 12,000,000 in buildings acquired on March 5, 2002, when the exchange rate was $.034. Equipment is depreciated on a straight-line basis over 10 years. Buildings are depreciated on a straight-line basis over 40 years. A full year's depreciation is taken in the year of acquisition.

- Dividends were declared and paid on December 15, 2002, when the exchange rate was $.031.

- Other exchange rates are:

January 1, 2002	$.040
Average 2002	$.035
December 31, 2002	$.030

Required

Part I. Prepare U.S. dollar translated financial statements in accordance with FASB *Statement 52* at December 31, 2002, in the following three situations:

    a. The Czech koruna is the functional currency. The December 31, 2001, U.S. dollar translated balance sheet reported retained earnings of $22,500. The December 31, 2001, cumulative translation adjustment was negative $202,500 (debit balance).

    b. The U.S. dollar is the functional currency. The December 31, 2001, retained earnings in U.S. dollars (including a 2001 remeasurement gain) that appeared in Rakona's remeasured financial statements was $353,000.

    c. The U.S. dollar is the functional currency, but Rakona has no long-term debt. Instead, Rakona has common stock of Kčs 20,000,000 and additional paid-in capital of Kčs 50,000,000. The December 31, 2001, U.S. dollar translated balance sheet reported a negative balance in retained earnings of $147,000 (including a 2001 remeasurement loss).

Part II. Explain the positive or negative sign of the translation adjustment in Part I*a* and explain why there is a remeasurement gain or loss in Parts I*b* and I*c*.

37. On January 1, 2001, Parker, Inc., a U.S.-based firm, purchased 100 percent of Suffolk PLC located in Great Britain. Parker paid 52,000,000 British pounds (£) for its purchase. The excess of cost over book value is attributable to land (part of property, plant, and equipment) and is not subject to depreciation. Parker accounts for its investment in Suffolk at cost. On January 1, 2001, Suffolk reported the following balance sheet:

Cash	£ 2,000,000	Accounts payable	£ 1,000,000
Accounts receivable	3,000,000	Long-term debt	8,000,000
Inventory	14,000,000	Common stock	44,000,000
Property and equipment (net)	40,000,000	Retained earnings	6,000,000
	£59,000,000		£59,000,000

Suffolk's 2001 income was recorded at £2,000,000. No dividends were declared or paid by Suffolk in 2001.

On December 31, 2002, Suffolk submitted the following trial balance to Parker for consolidation.

Cash	£ 1,500,000
Accounts receivable	5,200,000
Inventory	18,000,000
Property, plant, and equipment	36,000,000
Accounts payable	(1,450,000)
Long-term debt	(5,000,000)
Common stock	(44,000,000)
Retained earnings (1/1/02)	(8,000,000)
Sales	(28,000,000)
Cost of goods sold	16,000,000
Depreciation	2,000,000
Other expenses	6,000,000
Dividends paid (1/30/02)	1,750,000
	£ –0–

Other than the payment of dividends, no intercompany transactions occurred between the two companies.

Relevant rates of exchange per British pound were as follows:

	January 1	January 30	Average	December 31
2001	$1.60	—	$1.62	$1.64
2002	$1.64	$1.65	$1.66	$1.68

Parker's December 31, 2002, financial statements (before consolidation with Suffolk) follow. Dividend income is the U.S. dollar amount of dividends received from Suffolk translated at the $1.65/£ exchange rate at January 30, 2002. The amounts listed for dividend income and all affected accounts, that is, net income, December 31 retained earnings, and cash reflect the $1.65/£ exchange rate at January 30, 2002. Credit balances are in parentheses.

	Parker
Sales	$ (70,000,000)
Cost of goods sold	34,000,000
Depreciation	20,000,000
Other expenses	6,000,000
Dividend income	(2,887,500)
Net income	$ (12,887,500)
Retained earnings, 1/1/02	$ (48,000,000)
Net income, 2002	(12,887,500)
Dividends, 1/30/02	4,500,000
Retained earnings, 12/31/02	$ (56,387,500)
Cash	$ 3,687,500
Accounts receivable	10,000,000
Inventory	30,000,000
Investment in Suffolk	83,200,000
Plant and equipment	105,000,000
Accounts payable	(25,500,000)
Long-term debt	(50,000,000)
Common stock	(100,000,000)
Retained earnings, 12/31/02	(56,387,500)
	$ –0–

Parker's chief financial officer wishes to determine the effect a change in the value of the British pound has on consolidated net income and consolidated stockholders' equity. To help assess the foreign currency exposure associated with the investment in Suffolk, he requests assistance in comparing consolidated results under actual exchange rate fluctuations with results that would have occurred if the dollar value of the pound had remained constant or declined during their first two years of ownership.

Required

Use an electronic spreadsheet to complete the following tasks.

Part I. Given the relevant exchange rates presented above:
- a. Translate Suffolk's December 31, 2002, trial balance from British pounds to U.S. dollars. The British pound is Suffolk's functional currency.
- b. Prepare a schedule that details the change in Suffolk's cumulative translation adjustment (i.e., beginning net assets, income, dividends, etc.) for 2001 and 2002.
- c. Prepare the December 31, 2002, consolidated worksheet for Parker and Suffolk.
- d. Prepare the 2002 consolidated income statement and the December 31, 2002, consolidated balance sheet.

Note: Worksheets should possess the following qualities:
- ■ Each spreadsheet should be programmed so that all relevant amounts adjust appropriately when different values of exchange rates (subsequent to January 1, 2001) are entered into the spreadsheet.
- ■ Be sure to program Parker's dividend income, cash, and retained earnings to reflect the dollar value of alternative January 30, 2002, exchange rates.

Part II. Repeat tasks *a., b., c.,* and *d.* above to determine consolidated net income and consolidated stockholders' equity if the exchange rate had remained at $1.60/£ over the period 2001–2002.

Part III. Repeat tasks *a., b., c.,* and *d.* on the previous page to determine consolidated net income and consolidated stockholders' equity if the following exchange rates had existed:

	January 1	January 30	Average	December 31
2001	$1.60	—	$1.58	$1.56
2002	$1.56	$1.55	$1.54	$1.52

Part IV. Prepare a report that provides Parker's CFO with the risk assessments he requests. Focus on profitability, cash flow from dividends, and the ratio of debt to equity.

C H A P T E R

11

Worldwide Accounting Diversity and International Standards

QUESTIONS TO CONSIDER

- Why do accounting and reporting principles differ throughout the world?

- What are the major classes of accounting systems worldwide?

- What benefits are gained from establishing international accounting standards? What obstacles stand in the way of international standards?

- What progress has the European Union achieved in establishing uniform accounting standards in that region of the world?

- What progress has the International Accounting Standards Committee achieved in establishing worldwide accounting standards? How does this group enforce its standards?

- How do the accounting principles differ between Japan, the United Kingdom, Germany, the United States, and other countries? What differences are found in the structure of the financial statements produced in these countries?

- By what methods are assets valued across countries? How are consolidated financial statements prepared in various countries?

Each country has its own unique set of accounting and financial reporting rules; no two countries are alike in this regard. Considerable differences exist across countries in the accounting treatment of many items. As shown in Chapter 3, for example, goodwill is an asset amortized to income in the United States; however, it may be a direct reduction of owners' equity in Germany. For the most part, U.S. companies are not allowed to report assets at amounts greater than historical cost. Mexican companies, on the other hand, must write up their assets on the balance sheet to inflation-adjusted amounts, and several Dutch companies report their assets on the balance sheet at current replacement cost. Research and development costs must be expensed as incurred in the United States, but development costs may be capitalized in Canada and France. Numerous other differences exist across countries. In its 1998 annual report, the Dutch electronics firm Philips described 4 significant differences between U.S. and Dutch accounting rules.[1] If Philips had used U.S. GAAP in 1998, its income from continuing operations would have been 97 percent larger than what the firm actually reported in conformity with Dutch GAAP. In its 1998 annual report, the British beverage company Cadbury Schweppes listed eight significant differences between U.S. and U.K. GAAP.[2] If Cadbury Schweppes had used U.S. accounting rules, its 1998 net income would have been 28 percent smaller than what

---

[1]The adjustments related to differences in accounting for pensions, restructuring charges, extraordinary items, and other unidentified items.

[2]The accounting differences requiring the greatest adjustments were related to goodwill and other intangibles, pensions, and deferred taxes.

the firm actually reported in accordance with U.K. GAAP, and its shareholders' equity would have been 56 percent larger.

This chapter is divided into two parts. Part one presents evidence of accounting diversity, explores the reasons for accounting diversity, describes international patterns or models of accounting, and discusses and evaluates accounting harmonization efforts. Regarding harmonization, we concentrate on the effort undertaken in the European Union and on the international accounting standards developed by the International Accounting Standards Committee.

Part two provides a description of accounting principles and the accounting profession in several major countries, and examines reporting principles utilized around the world in connection with specific accounting problems such as consolidations and the valuation of assets. This coverage provides a comparison of the similarities and differences between U.S. GAAP and principles used in other areas of the world.

EVIDENCE OF ACCOUNTING DIVERSITY

Exhibit 11–1 presents the 1998 balance sheet for the British company Imperial Chemical Industries PLC. A quick examination of this statement shows several differences in format and terminology between the United Kingdom and the United States. Noncurrent assets in general are called fixed assets in the United Kingdom, whereas plant, property, and equipment are referred to as tangible assets. Liabilities are called creditors, and accounts receivable are debtors. Unless one is fluent in the language of British accounting, stocks might be thought to be marketable securities, when in actuality stocks are inventories. Called up share capital is the par value and share premium account is the paid-in capital in excess of par on common stock. Retained earnings are not reported separately; instead they are included in the item labeled profit and loss account. Rather than being treated as an asset, goodwill is included in profit and loss account as a negative item. Goodwill written off to shareholders' equity exceeds the amount of retained earnings resulting in a negative balance in profit and loss account.

From the perspective of U.S. financial reporting, the U.K. balance sheet has an unusual structure. Rather than the U.S. norm of Assets = Liabilities + Shareholders' Equity, ICI's balance sheet is presented as Total Assets less Current Liabilities equals Long-term Liabilities plus Shareholders' Equity. Listed in reverse order of liquidity, assets start with tangible assets and move down to cash. Current liabilities follow current assets to arrive at net working capital.

All of these superficial differences would probably cause a financial analyst no problem in analyzing the company's financial statements. More important than the format and terminology differences are the differences in measurement rules employed to value assets and calculate income. Because ICI's common stock is listed on the New York Stock Exchange, the company is required to be registered and file financial statements with the U.S. Securities and Exchange Commission (SEC). For foreign registrants, the SEC requires income and stockholders' equity reported under foreign GAAP to be reconciled with U.S. GAAP. ICI's 1998 reconciliation to U.S. GAAP is in Exhibit 11–2. This reconciliation provides significant insight into the

Exhibit 11-1 Imperial Chemical Industries PLC U.K. Balance Sheet

Balance sheets at 31 December 1998		Group		Company	
		1998	**1997**	**1998**	**1997**
	Notes	**£m**	**£m**	**£m**	**£m**
Assets employed					
Fixed assets					
Intangible assets—goodwill	12	652			
Tangible assets	4, 13	3,816	3,956	320	431
Investments					
Subsidiary undertakings	14	—	—	10,025	10,093
Participating and other interests	15	170	254	24	68
		4,638	4,210	10,369	10,592
Current assets					
Stocks	16	1,213	1,319	62	75
Debtors	17	2,360	2,457	2,834	3,065
Investments and short-term deposits	18	455	935	—	1
Cash at bank	34	367	340	25	22
		4,395	5,051	2,921	3,163
Total assets		9,033	9,261	13,290	13,755
Creditors due within one year					
Short-term borrowings	19	(1,445)	(1,105)	—	(1)
Current installments on loans	21	(585)	(950)	(493)	(807)
Other creditors	20	(2,356)	(2,583)	(7,421)	(6,683)
		(4,386)	(4,638)	(7,914)	(7,491)
Net current assets (liabilities)		9	413	(4,993)	(4,328)
Total assets less current liabilities	4	4,647	4,623	5,376	6,264
Financed by					
Creditors due after more than one year					
Loans	21	2,954	2,975	360	694
Other creditors	20	55	67	2,784	3,262
		3,009	3,042	3,144	3,956
Provisions for liabilities and charges	22	1,429	1,342	210	218
Deferred income: Grants not yet credited to profit		11	14	—	—
Minority interests—equity		49	79		
Shareholders' fund—equity					
Called-up share capital	24	728	727	728	727
Reserves					
Share premium account		587	581	587	581
Associated undertakings' reserves		15	26		
Profit and loss account		(1,181	(1,188)	707	782
Total reserves	25	(579)	(581)	1,294	1,363
Total shareholders' funds		149	146	2,022	2,090
		4,647	4,623	5,376	6,264

major differences in accounting principles between the United States and the United Kingdom. Note that although only 11 items required adjustments, the aggregate effect on income and stockholders' equity was highly significant. Net income under U.S. GAAP was negative in 1998, but positive under British accounting rules. Stockholders' equity in 1998 under U.S. GAAP was 24 times larger than under U.K. GAAP. In 1997, return on total stockholders' equity is 177 percent under British GAAP, but only 4 percent under U.S. GAAP; this ratio is 49 times larger under British rules.

Magnitude of Accounting Diversity

Although it is generally assumed that accounting diversity results in significant differences in the measurement of income and equity across countries, until recently there was very little systematic empirical documentation of the effect these differences have on published financial statements. In 1993, the SEC published a survey that examines the U.S. GAAP reconciliations made by 444 foreign entities from 36 countries.[3] The results of that survey indicate that approximately two-thirds of the foreign companies showed material differences between net income and owners' equity reported on the basis of home GAAP and U.S. GAAP. Of those with material differences, net income would have been lower under U.S. GAAP for about two-thirds of the companies (higher using U.S. GAAP for about one-third). This indicates that, for the majority of foreign entities with stock listings in the United States, U.S. GAAP is more conservative than their home country GAAP. Similar results were found with regard to owners' equity. At the extremes, income was 29 times higher under U.S. GAAP for one foreign entity, and 178 times higher using British GAAP for another entity. In addition, the study found significant differences are spread relatively evenly across countries. In other words, material differences are as likely to exist for a British or Canadian company as for a company in South America, Asia, or Continental Europe.

Focusing on the U.S. GAAP reconciliations of British companies, a separate study found that all 39 companies examined reported material differences in income or equity. Over 90 percent reported lower income under U.S. GAAP and approximately 60 percent reported higher equity. The average difference in income, even after including those with higher U.S. GAAP income, was a 42 percent reduction in income when reconciling to U.S. GAAP.[4] It is clear that differences in accounting principles can have a material impact on amounts reported in financial statements.

REASONS FOR ACCOUNTING DIVERSITY

Why does each country have its own unique set of financial reporting practices? Accounting scholars have hypothesized numerous influences on a country's accounting system, including factors as varied as the nature of the political system, the stage of economic development, and the state of accounting education and research. A survey of the relevant literature identified the following five items as commonly accepted factors influencing a country's financial reporting practices: (1) legal system, (2) taxation, (3) providers of financing, (4) inflation, and (5) political and economic ties.[5]

---

[3]United States Securities and Exchange Commission, *Survey of Financial Statement Reconciliations by Foreign Registrants* (Washington, D.C., 1993).

[4]Vivian Periar, Ron Paterson, and Allister Wilson, *UK/US GAAP Comparison,* 2nd ed. (London: Kogan Page Limited, 1992), pp. 384–393.

[5]Gary K. Meek and Sharokh M. Saudagaran, "A Survey of Research on Financial Reporting in a Transnational Context," *Journal of Accounting Literature,* 1990, pp. 145–82.

Exhibit 11–2

Imperial Chemical Industries PLC Reconciliation to U.S. GAAP

	1998 £m	1997 £m	1996 £m
Net income after exceptional items—U.K. GAAP	193	259	275
Continuing operations	54	(331)	128
Discontinued operations	139	590	147
Adjustments to conform to U.S. GAAP			
Pension expense	(10)	(41)	(5)
Purchase accounting adjustments			
Amortisation of goodwill and intangibles	(134)	(83)	(25)
Disposals and other adjustments	31	112	5
Other disposal adjustments	(59)	(114)	—
Capitalisation of interest less amortisation			
and disposals	(24)	(113)	28
Restructuring costs	(81)	58	2
Foreign exchange	—	12	73
Discontinued operations	8	(8)	—
Deferred taxation			
Arising on U.K. GAAP results	(16)	(12)	(29)
Arising on other U.S. GAAP adjustments	45	54	10
Others	3	17	2
Total US GAAP adjustments	(237)	(118)	61
Net income—U.S. GAAP	(44)	141	336
Continuing operations	(82)	103	295
Discontinued operations	38	38	41

	Pence	Pence	Pence
Basic and diluted net earnings per Ordinary Share in accordance with U.S. GAAP	(6.1)	19.4	46.3
Continuing operations	11.3	14.2	40.7
Discontinued operations	5.2	5.2	5.6

	1998 £m	1997 £m
Shareholders' equity, as shown in the Group Balance sheets—U.K. GAAP	149	146
Adjustments to conform with U.S. GAAP		
Purchase accounting adjustments, including goodwill and intangibles	3,618	3,985
Disposal accounting adjustments	(25)	33
Capitalisation of interest less amortisation and disposals	128	152
Restructuring provision	56	105
Pension expense	(291)	(281)
Discontinued operations	—	(8)
Employee share trust agreements	(62)	—
Ordinary dividends	141	141
Deferred taxation	(147)	(156)
Other	(10)	(19)
Total U.S. GAAP adjustments	3,408	3,952
Shareholders' equity in accordance with U.S. GAAP . . .	3,557	4,098

Legal System

The two major types of legal systems used around the world are common law and codified Roman law. Common law began in England and is found primarily in the English-speaking countries of the world. Common law countries rely on a limited amount of statute law that is interpreted by the courts. Court decisions establish precedents thereby developing case law that supplements the statutes. A system of code law, followed in most non-English-speaking countries, originated in the Roman *jus civile* and was developed further in European universities during the Middle Ages. Code law countries tend to have relatively more statute or codified law governing a wider range of human activity.

What does a country's legal system have to do with accounting? Code law countries generally have a corporation law (sometimes called a commercial code or companies act) that establishes the basic legal parameters governing business enterprises. The corporation law often stipulates which financial statements must be published in accordance with a prescribed format. Additional accounting measurement and disclosure rules are included in an accounting law that has been debated and passed by the national legislature. The accounting profession tends to have little influence on the development of accounting standards. In countries with a tradition of common law, although a corporation law laying the basic framework for accounting might exist (such as in the United Kingdom), the profession or an independent, nongovernmental body representing a variety of constituencies establishes specific accounting rules. Thus, the type of legal system in a country determines whether the primary source of accounting rules is the government or the accounting profession.

In code law countries, the accounting law is rather general; it does not provide much detail regarding specific accounting practices and may provide no guidance at all in certain areas. Germany is a good example of a code law country. The current German accounting law passed in 1985 is only 47 pages in length and is silent with regard to issues such as leases, foreign currency translation, and a cash flows statement.[6] In those situations where no guidance is provided in the law, German companies must refer to other sources including tax law and opinions of the German auditing profession to decide how to do their accounting. Interestingly enough, an important source of accounting practice in Germany comes from textbooks and commentaries written by accounting academicians. Common law countries, where a nongovernment organization is likely to develop accounting standards, have much more detailed rules. The extreme case might be the FASB in the United States. The Board provides very specific detail in its Statements of Financial Accounting Standards about how to apply the rules and has been accused of producing a standards overload.

Taxation

In some countries, published financial statements form the basis for taxation, whereas in other countries, financial statements are adjusted for tax purposes and submitted to the government separately from the reports sent to stockholders. Continuing to focus on Germany, its so-called conformity principle (*Massgeblichkeitsprinzip*) requires that, in most cases, an expense also must be used in the calculation of financial statement income to be deductible for tax purposes. Well-managed German companies attempt to minimize income for tax purposes, for example, through the use of accelerated depreciation to reduce their tax liability. As a result of the conformity principle, accelerated depreciation also must be taken in the calculation of accounting income.

---

[6]Jermyn Paul Brooks and Dietz Mertin, *Neues Deutsches Bilanzrecht* (Düsseldorf: IDW-Verlag GmbH, 1986).

In the United States, on the other hand, conformity between the tax statement and financial statements is required only for the use of the LIFO inventory cost flow assumption. U.S. companies are allowed to use accelerated depreciation for tax purposes and straight-line depreciation in the financial statements. All else being equal, a U.S. company is likely to report higher income than its German counterpart.

Providers of Financing

The major providers of financing for business enterprises are family members, banks, governments, and shareholders. In those countries in which company financing is dominated by families, banks, or the state, there is less pressure for public accountability and information disclosure. Banks and the state often are represented on the board of directors and therefore are able to obtain information necessary for decision making from inside the company. As companies become more dependent on financing from the general populace through the public offering of shares of stock, the demand for more information made available outside the company becomes greater. It simply is not feasible for the company to allow the hundreds, thousands, or hundreds of thousands of shareholders access to internal accounting records. The information needs of those financial statement users can be satisfied only through extensive disclosures in accounting reports.

There also can be a difference in orientation, with stockholders more interested in profit (emphasis on the income statement) and banks more interested in solvency and liquidity (emphasis on the balance sheet). Bankers prefer companies to practice rather conservative accounting with regard to assets and liabilities.

Inflation

Countries with chronically high rates of inflation have been forced to adopt accounting rules that require the inflation adjustment of historical cost amounts. This has been especially true in South America, that as a region has had more inflation than any other part of the world. For example, prior to recent economic reform, Brazil regularly experienced annual inflation rates exceeding 100 percent. The high point was reached in 1993 when annual inflation was nearly 1,800 percent. Double- and triple-digit inflation rates render historical costs meaningless. This factor primarily distinguishes accounting in South America from the rest of the world.

Political and Economic Ties

Accounting is a technology that can be borrowed relatively easily from or imposed on another country. Through political and economic linkages, accounting rules have been conveyed from one country to another. For example, through previous colonialism, both England and France have transferred their accounting frameworks to a variety of countries around the world. British accounting systems can be found in countries as far flung as Australia and Zimbabwe. French accounting is prevalent in the former French colonies of western Africa. More recently, economic ties with the United States have had an impact on accounting in Canada, Mexico, and Israel.

Correlation of Factors

Whether by coincidence or not, there is a high degree of correlation between the legal system, tax conformity, and source of financing. Common law countries separate taxation from accounting and rely more heavily on the stock market as a source of capital. Code law countries link taxation to accounting statements and rely less on financing provided by shareholders.

PROBLEMS CAUSED BY DIVERSE ACCOUNTING PRACTICES

The diversity in accounting practice across countries causes problems that can be quite serious for some parties. One problem relates to the preparation of consolidated financial statements by companies with foreign operations. Consider Coca-Cola Company that has subsidiaries in more than 100 countries around the world. Each subsidiary incorporated in the country in which it is located is required to prepare financial statements in accordance with local regulations. These regulations usually require companies to keep books in the local currency and follow local accounting principles. Thus, Coca-Cola FEMSA S.A. prepares financial statements in Mexican pesos using Mexican accounting rules and Coca-Cola Amatil Ltd. prepares financial statements in Australian dollars using Australian standards. To prepare consolidated financial statements in the United States, in addition to translating the foreign currency financial statements into U.S. dollars, the parent company must also convert the financial statements of its foreign subsidiaries into U.S. GAAP. Each foreign subsidiary must either maintain two sets of books prepared in accordance with both local and U.S. GAAP or, as is more common, make reconciliations from local GAAP to U.S. GAAP at the balance sheet date. In either case, considerable effort and cost are involved; company personnel must develop an expertise in more than one country's accounting standards.

A second problem relates to companies gaining access to foreign capital markets. If a company desires to obtain capital by selling stock or borrowing money in a foreign country, it likely is required to present a set of financial statements prepared in accordance with the accounting standards in the country in which the capital is being obtained. Consider the case of the Swedish automaker Volvo. The equity market in Sweden is so small (there are fewer than 9 million Swedes) and Volvo's capital needs are so great that Volvo has found it necessary to have its common shares listed on stock exchanges in London, Frankfurt, Paris, Zurich, Brussels, Tokyo, and on NASDAQ in the United States. To have their stock traded in the United States, foreign companies must prepare financial statements using U.S. accounting standards. This can be quite costly. To prepare for a New York Stock Exchange (NYSE) listing in 1993, the German automaker Daimler-Benz estimated it spent $60 million to initially prepare U.S. GAAP financial statements; it planned to spend $15 to 20 million each year thereafter.[7]

A third problem relates to the lack of comparability of financial statements between companies from different countries. This can significantly affect the analysis of foreign financial statements for making investment and lending decisions. In 1998 alone, U.S. investors bought nearly $103 billion in debt and equity of foreign entities while foreign investors pumped approximately $218 billion into U.S. entities through similar acquisitions.[8] In recent years there has been an explosion in mutual funds that invest in the stock of foreign companies—from 123 in 1989 to 534 at the end of 1995.[9] T. Rowe Price's New Asia Fund, for example, invests exclusively in stocks and bonds of companies located in Asian countries other than Japan. The job of deciding which foreign company to invest in is complicated by the fact that foreign companies use different accounting rules from those used in the United States and those rules differ from country to country. It is very difficult, if not impossible, for a potential investor to directly compare the financial position and performance of a chemical company in Germany (BASF), the Netherlands (AKZO), and Great Britain (ICI) because these three

---

[7]Allan B. Afterman, *International Accounting, Financial Reporting, and Analysis* (New York: Warren, Gorham & Lamont, 1995), pp. C1–17 and C1–22.

[8]U.S. Department of Commerce, *Survey of Current Business,* December 1999, p. D–8.

[9]James L. Cochrane, James E. Shapiro, and Jean E. Tobin, "Foreign Equities and U.S. Investors: Breaking Down the Barriers Separating Supply and Demand," NYSE Working Paper 95–04, 1995.

countries have different financial accounting and reporting standards. According to Ralph E. Walters, former chairman of the steering committee of the International Accounting Standards Committee, "either international investors have to be extremely knowledgeable about multiple reporting methods or they have to be willing to take greater risk."[10]

A lack of comparability of financial statements also can have an adverse effect on corporations when making foreign acquisition decisions. As a case in point, consider the recent experience of foreign investors in Eastern Europe. After the fall of the Berlin Wall in 1989, officials invited Western companies to acquire newly privatized companies in Poland, Hungary, and other countries in the former communist bloc. The concept of profit and accounting for assets in those countries under communism was so much different from accounting practice in the West that most Western investors found financial statements useless in helping them determine the most attractive acquisition targets. Many investors asked the Big 5 public accounting firms to convert financial statements to a Western basis before acquisition of a company could be seriously considered.

Because of the problems associated with worldwide accounting diversity, attempts to reduce accounting differences across countries have been ongoing for more than three decades. This process is known as *harmonization*. The ultimate goal of harmonization is to have all companies around the world follow one set of international accounting standards.

ACCOUNTING CLUSTERS

Given the discussion regarding factors influencing accounting practice worldwide, it should not be surprising to learn that clusters of countries share common accounting practices. One classification scheme identifies four major accounting models: British-American, Continental, South American, and Mixed Economy.[11] **British-American** describes the approach used in the United Kingdom and United States where accounting is oriented toward the decision needs of large numbers of investors and creditors. Dutch accounting is quite similar. This model is used in most of the English-speaking countries, and other countries heavily influenced by the United Kingdom or United States. Most of these countries follow a common law legal system. The **Continental** model is used by most of continental Europe and Japan. Companies in this group usually are tied quite closely to banks that serve as the primary suppliers of financing. As these are code law countries, accounting is legalistic, designed to provide information for taxation or government planning purposes. The **South American** model resembles the Continental model in its legalistic, tax, and government planning orientation. This model distinguishes itself, however, through the extensive use of adjustments for inflation. The **Mixed Economy** model describes the approach recently developed in Eastern Europe and the former Soviet Union that combines elements of the former planned economic system and the recent market economy reforms.

Concentrating on the British-American and Continental model countries, Professor Chris Nobes has developed a more refined classification scheme that shows how the financial reporting systems in 14 developed countries relate to one another. An adaptation of Nobes's classification is in Exhibit 11–3.[12]

---

[10]Stephen H. Collins, "The Move to Globalization, *Journal of Accountancy,* March 1989, p. 82.

[11]Gerhard G. Mueller, Helen Gernon, and Gary Meek, *Accounting—An International Perspective,* 3rd ed. (Burr Ridge, Ill.: Richard D. Irwin, 1994), pp. 8–12.

[12]Source: C. W. Nobes, "A Judgemental International Classification of Financial Reporting Practices," *Journal of Business Finance and Accounting,* Spring 1983, p. 7.

Exhibit 11-3
A Hypothetical Classification
of Accounting Systems

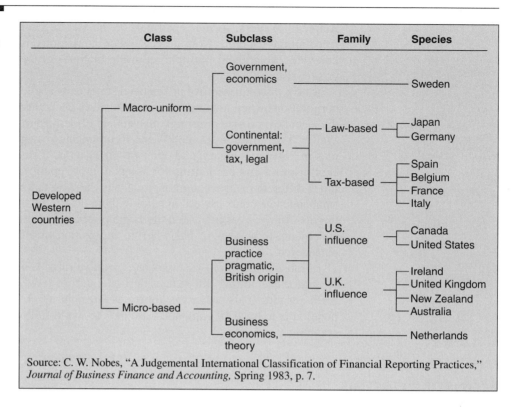

Source: C. W. Nobes, "A Judgemental International Classification of Financial Reporting Practices," *Journal of Business Finance and Accounting,* Spring 1983, p. 7.

A Hypothetical Model of Accounting Diversity

The terms *micro-based* and *macro-uniform* describe the British-American and Continental models, respectively. Each of these classes is divided into two subclasses that are further divided into families. Within the micro-based class of accounting system, there is a subclass heavily influenced by business economics and accounting theory. The Netherlands is the only country in this subclass. One manifestation of the influence of theory is that Dutch companies may use current replacement cost accounting in their primary financial statements. The other micro-based subclass is of British origin and is more pragmatic and oriented toward business practice, relying less on economic theory in the development of accounting rules. The British origin subclass can be split into two families; one dominated by the United States and one dominated by the United Kingdom. Nobes does not indicate how these two families differ from one another.

On the macro-uniform side of the model, a government, economics subclass has only one country, Sweden. Swedish accounting distinguishes itself from the other macro-uniform countries in its being closely aligned with national economic policies. For example, income smoothing is allowed to promote economic stability and social accounting has developed to meet macroeconomic concerns. The Continental government, tax, legal subclass contains Continental European countries divided into two families. Led by Germany, the law-based family includes Japan. The tax-based family consists of several Romance-language countries. The major difference between these families is that the accounting law is the primary determinant of accounting practice in Germany, whereas the tax law dominates in the Southern European countries.

The importance of this hierarchical model is that it shows the comparative distances between countries and could be used as a blueprint for determining where financial statement comparability is likely to be greater. For example, comparisons of financial statements between the United States and Canada (that are in the same family) are likely to be more valid than comparisons between the United States and the United Kingdom (that are not in the same family). However, the United States and the United

Exhibit 11–4

Results of Cluster Analysis on 100 Financial Reporting Practices

Micro Class		Macro Class		
Cluster 1	**Cluster 2**	**Cluster 3**	**Cluster 5**	**Cluster 7**
Australia	Bermuda	Costa Rica	Colombia	Finland
Botswana	Canada		Denmark	Sweden
Hong Kong	Israel	**Cluster 4**	France	
Ireland	United States	Argentina	Italy	**Cluster 8**
Jamaica		Brazil	Norway	Germany
Luxembourg		Chile	Portugal	
Malaysia		Mexico	Spain	**Cluster 9**
Namibia				Japan
Netherlands			**Cluster 6**	
Netherlands Antilles			Belgium	
Nigeria			Egypt	
New Zealand			Liberia	
Philippines			Panama	
Papua New Guinea			Saudi Arabia	
South Africa			Thailand	
Singapore			United Arab Emirates	
Sri Lanka				
Taiwan				
Trinidad and Tobago				
United Kingdom				
Zambia				
Zimbabwe				

Source: Timothy S. Doupnik and Stephen B. Salter, "An Empirical Test of a Judgemental International Classification of Financial Reporting Practices," *Journal of International Business Studies,* First Quarter 1993, p. 53.

Kingdom (which are in the same subclass) are more comparable than are the United States and the Netherlands (that are in different subclasses). Finally, comparisons between the United States and the Netherlands (that are in the same class) might be more meaningful than comparisons between the United States and any of the macro-uniform countries.

The hypothetical model in Exhibit 11–3 was empirically tested in 1993.[13] Data gathered on 100 financial reporting practices in 50 countries (including the 14 countries in Exhibit 11–3) were analyzed using the statistical procedure of hierarchical cluster analysis. The significant clusters arising from the analysis are in Exhibit 11–4.

The results clearly indicate two significantly different classes of accounting systems being used across these countries. The major deviations from Nobes' model are that the Netherlands is in the U.K. influence group rather than in a subclass by itself; Japanese accounting is not as similar to German accounting as hypothesized; and Belgium is not in the group with France, Spain, and Italy. Indeed, considerably less similarity appears among the macro countries (as evidence by the greater number of clusters) than among the countries comprising the micro class.

The large size of the U.K. influence cluster (Cluster 1) clearly shows the influence of British colonialism on accounting development. In contrast, Cluster 2, which includes the United States, is quite small. The emergence of Cluster 4, which includes several Latin American countries, is evidence of the importance of inflation as a factor affecting accounting practice.

---

[13]Timothy S. Doupnik and Stephen B. Salter, "An Empirical Test of a Judgemental International Classification of Financial Reporting Practices," *Journal of International Business Studies,* First Quarter 1993, pp. 41–60.

The two classes of accounting reflected in Exhibit 11–4 differ significantly on 66 of the 100 financial reporting practices examined.[14] Differences exist for 41 of the 56 disclosure practices studied. In all but one case, the micro class of countries provided a higher level of disclosure than the macro class of countries. There were also significant differences for 25 of the 44 practices examined affecting income measurement. Of particular importance is the item asking whether accounting practice adhered to tax requirements. The mean level of agreement with this statement among macro countries was 72 percent, whereas it was only 45 percent among micro countries. To summarize, companies in the micro-based countries provide more extensive disclosure than do companies in the macro-uniform countries, and companies in the macro countries are more heavily influenced by taxation than are companies in the micro countries. These results are consistent with the relative importance of equity finance and relatively weak link between accounting and taxation in the micro countries.

Major Deviations from U.S. GAAP

The discussion thus far has explained why accounting practices might differ across countries and how different countries' accounting systems relate to one another without specifically indicating where those differences exist. Before comparing specific accounting issues across selected countries in the second part of this chapter, we look at the major areas of difference. One way of looking at this is to consider the items most frequently requiring adjustment in foreign reconcilations to U.S. GAAP. In its 1993 study, the SEC found that the ten accounting issues most commonly requiring adjustments were

- Depreciation and amortization (137).
- Deferred or capitalized costs (117).
- Deferred taxes (114).
- Pension costs (including other post-retirement benefits) (66).
- Foreign currency translation (62).
- Gain/loss on disposal of assets (48).
- Business combinations (including goodwill) (37).
- Extraordinary items, discontinued operations, and accounting changes (37).
- Employee compensation (26).
- Investments in associated entities (equity method) (23).[15]

(The amounts in parentheses indicate the number of companies reporting the specific adjustment out of a total of 286 companies with reconciling items.)

INTERNATIONAL HARMONIZATION OF FINANCIAL REPORTING

The preceding sections make clear the significant, systematic differences in accounting practices across countries. As noted in the introduction, these differences cause complications for those preparing and using financial statements. Several organizations around the world are involved in an effort to harmonize financial reporting practices.

Harmonization is the process of reducing differences in financial reporting practices across countries, thereby increasing the comparability of financial statements.

---

[14]Doupnik and Salter, 1993, p. 56.

[15]United States Securities and Exchange Commission, *Survey of Financial Statement Reconciliations by Foreign Registrants* (Washington, D.C.: Government Printing Office, 1993), p. 10.

Ultimately, harmonization implies development of a set of international accounting standards that would be applied in all countries.

Arguments for Harmonization

Proponents of accounting harmonization argue that comparability of financial statement worldwide is necessary for the globalization of capital markets. Financial statement comparability would make it easier for investors to evaluate potential investments in foreign securities and thereby take advantage of the risk reduction possible through international diversification. It also would simplify the evaluation by multinational companies of possible foreign takeover targets. From the other side, with harmonization, companies could gain access to all capital markets in the world with one set of financial statements. This would allow companies to lower their cost of capital and would make it easier for foreign investors to acquire the company's stock.

One set of universally accepted accounting standards would reduce the cost of preparing worldwide consolidated financial statements, and the auditing of these statements also would be simplified. Multinational companies would find it easier to transfer accounting staff to other countries. This would be true for the international auditing firms as well.

Arguments against Harmonization

The greatest obstacle to harmonization is the magnitude of the current differences between countries and the fact that the political cost of eliminating those differences would be enormous. As stated by Dennis Beresford, former chairman of the FASB, "high on almost everybody's list of obstacles is nationalism. Whether out of deep-seated tradition, indifference born of economic power, or resistance to intrusion of foreign influence, some say that national entities will not bow to any international body."[16] Arriving at principles that satisfy all of the parties involved throughout the world seems an almost Herculean task.

Not only is harmonization difficult to achieve, the need for such standards is not universally accepted. As stated by Seagram's Richard Karl Goeltz: "Full harmonization of international accounting standards is probably neither practical nor truly valuable. . . . It is not clear whether significant benefits would be derived in fact. A well-developed global capital market exists already. It has evolved without uniform accounting standards."[17] Opponents of harmonization argue that it is unnecessary to force all companies worldwide to follow a common set of rules. The international capital market will force those companies that benefit from accessing the market to provide the required accounting information without harmonization.

Yet another argument against harmonization is that because of different environmental influences, differences in accounting across countries might be appropriate and necessary. For example, countries at different stages of economic development or that rely on different sources of financing perhaps should have differently oriented accounting systems.

Regardless of the arguments against harmonization, substantial effort to reduce differences in accounting practice have been ongoing for several decades. The question is no longer *whether* harmonization should be strived for, but *to what extent* can accounting practices be harmonized and *how fast*.

---

[16]Dennis R. Beresford, "Accounting for International Operations," *CPA Journal,* October 1988, pp. 79–80.

[17]Richard Karl Goeltz, "International Accounting Harmonization: The Impossible (and Unnecessary?) Dream," *Accounting Horizons,* March 1991, pp. 85–86.

MAJOR HARMONIZATION EFFORTS

While numerous organizations are involved in harmonization on either a regional or worldwide basis, the two most important players in this effort have been the European Union on a regional basis and the International Accounting Standards Committee on a global basis.

European Union

The major objectives embodied in the Treaty of Rome that created the European Economic Community in 1957 (now called the European Union) was the establishment of free movement of persons, goods and services, and capital across member countries. To achieve a common capital market, the European Union (EU) has attempted to harmonize financial reporting practices within the community. To do this, the EU issues directives that must be incorporated into the laws of member nations. Two directives have helped harmonize accounting: The Fourth Directive, issued in 1978, deals with valuation rules, disclosure requirements, and the format of financial statements. The Seventh Directive, issued in 1983, relates to the preparation of consolidated financial statements.

The Seventh Directive requires companies to prepare consolidated financial statements and outlines the procedures for their preparation. This directive has had a significant impact on European accounting as consolidations were previously uncommon on the Continent.

The Fourth Directive provides considerable flexibility with dozens of provisions beginning with the expression, "member states may require or permit companies to"; these allow countries to choose from among acceptable alternatives. One manifestation of this flexibility is that under Dutch and British law, companies may write up assets to higher market values, whereas in Germany this is strictly forbidden. Notwithstanding this flexibility, implementation of the directives into local law has caused extensive change in accounting practice in several countries. For example, some of the changes in German accounting practice brought about by the integration of EU Directives into local law are

1. Required inclusion of notes to the financial statements.
2. Preparation of consolidated financial statements on a worldwide basis, that is, foreign subsidiaries no longer can be excluded from consolidation.
3. Elimination of unrealized intercompany losses on consolidation.
4. Use of the equity method for investments in associated companies.
5. Disclosure of comparative figures in the balance sheet and income statement.
6. Disclosure of liabilities with a maturity of less than one year.
7. Accrual of deferred tax liabilities and pension obligations.[18]

Most of these innovations have been common practice in the United States for several decades.

Given that EU countries are in four of the nine clusters in Exhibit 11–4, the Fourth and Seventh Directives clearly have not created complete harmonization within the European Union. As an illustration of the effects of differing principles within the EU, the profits of one case study company were measured in European Currency Units using the accounting principles of various member states. The results are almost startling:

---

[18]Timothy S. Doupnik, "Recent Innovations in German Accounting Practice through the Integration of EC Directives," *Advances in International Accounting,* 1992, pp. 75–103.

Most Likely Profit—Case Study Company

Country	ECUs (millions)
Spain	131
Germany	133
Belgium	135
Netherlands	140
France	149
Italy	174
United Kingdom[19]	192

Part of the difference in profit across EU countries is the result of several important topics not covered in the directives including lease accounting, foreign currency translation, accounting changes, contingencies, income taxes, and long-term construction contracts. In 1990, the EU Commission indicated that there would be no further accounting directives. Instead, the Commission indicated in 1995 that it would associate the EU with efforts undertaken by the International Accounting Standards Committee toward a broader international harmonization of accounting standards.

Although the EU Directives have not led to complete comparability across member nations, they have not been a complete failure as differences in financial statements are not nearly as great as they once were. In addition, the EU Directives have served as a basic framework of accounting that has been adopted by other countries in search of an accounting model. With the economic reforms in Eastern Europe since 1989, several countries in that region have found it necessary to abandon the Soviet style accounting system previously used in favor of a Western, market-oriented system. Hungary, Poland, and the Czech and Slovak Republics have all written new accounting laws primarily based on the EU directives. Each of these countries appears to be looking ahead to the day when it will apply for EU membership. This is further evidence of the influence that economic ties among countries can have on accounting practice.

INTERNATIONAL ACCOUNTING STANDARDS COMMITTEE

In hopes of eliminating the diversity of principles used throughout the world, the International Accounting Standards Committee (IASC) was formed in June 1973 by accountancy bodies in Australia, Canada, France, Germany, Japan, Mexico, the Netherlands, the United Kingdom and Ireland, and the United States. Similar in some ways to the FASB and GASB, the IASC is a private organization based in London. Governments do not belong, only accounting organizations can be members. Since 1973, the initial group has grown to more than 140 accountancy bodies representing over 100 nations. From the United States, the American Institute of CPAs (AICPA) and the Institute of Management Accountants (IMA) are members.

The IASC Board consisting of representatives from 13 countries plus representatives from four other organizations produces IASC accounting pronouncements. In 2000, this board consisted of representatives from the eight founding nations plus India, Malaysia, Scandinavia, and South Africa. The board normally meets four times a year for three or four days. The board also holds meetings twice a year with its consultative group made up of a wide range of parties including a member of the FASB. For any official pronouncement to be issued, at least 11 of the 14 board members must agree.

---

[19]Anthony Carey, "Harmonization: Europe Moves Forward," *Accountancy,* March 1990, pp. 92–93.

The goals of the IASC are detailed in the body's constitution:

- To formulate and publish in the public interest accounting standards to be observed in the presentation of financial statements and to promote their worldwide acceptance and observance.

- To work generally for the improvement and harmonization of regulations, accounting standards and procedures relating to the presentation of financial statements.[20]

As of January 2000, the IASC had issued 39 International Accounting Standards, some of which have been subsequently revised (see Exhibit 11–5). A conceptual framework similar in scope to that developed by the U.S. FASB also has been created. International Accounting Standards (IASs) have addressed worldwide reporting concerns ranging from consolidated financial statements to accounting for income taxes and disclosure of related party transactions. Because the IASC is a private body, these pronouncements cannot be enforced. Instead, the IASC has attempted to gain acceptance in a number of ways. For example, countries that do not have extensive accounting principles are urged to adopt the IASC's guidelines, thus "guaranteeing a certain level of quality and compatibility for the particular standard."[21]

A growing number of countries requires companies to use IASs in preparing financial statements. The list includes 10 countries in which national standards consist of IASC standards or IASC standards supplemented with national standards for areas not covered by IASs:

Croatia	Malaysia	Pakistan
Cyprus	Malta	Papua New Guinea
Kuwait	Oman	Trinidad and Tobago
Latvia		

Another 14 countries use IASC standards with modifications for local conditions or circumstances:

Albania	Jordan	Thailand
Bangladesh	Kenya	Uruguay
Barbados	Poland	Zambia
Colombia	Sudan	Zimbabwe[22]
Jamaica	Swaziland	

Countries that already have a system of accounting standards in place are asked to eliminate any material differences with IASC pronouncements. "No enforcement mechanism exists to assure that the standards, once issued, are followed. Rather, the accounting professional body within each country has merely signed a pledge, representing that it will use its 'best efforts' to have the standard setters in their country move to accept the international standards."[23]

As a result of this best efforts pledge, the AICPA board of directors has formally stated that if significant variances exist between international standards and U.S. GAAP, "the AICPA will urge the FASB and/or GASB to give early consideration to such differences with a view to achieving harmonization of those areas in which a significant difference exists."[24]

---

[20]International Accounting Standards Committee Constitution, January 1983, para. 2.

[21]International Accounting Standards Committee, *Objectives and Procedures,* January 1983, para. 9.

[22]Financial Accounting Standards Board, *The IASC–U.S. Comparison Project: A Report on the Similarities and Differences between IASC Standards and U.S. GAAP,* 2nd ed., 1999, p. 11.

[23]Arthur R. Wyatt, "Seeking Credibility in a Global Economy," *New Accountant,* September 1992, p. 6.

[24]AICPA, *International Accounting and Auditing Standards,* October 1, 1988, page 11,002.

	Title	Issued
IAS 1	Presentation of Financial Statements	1975 (revised 1997)
IAS 2	Inventories	1975 (revised 1993)
IAS 3	(Superseded by IAS 27 and 28)	
IAS 4	Depreciation Accounting	1976
IAS 5	(Superseded by IAS 1 (revised)	1976
IAS 6	(Superseded by IAS 15)	
IAS 7	Cash Flow Statements	1977 (revised 1992)
IAS 8	Net Profit or Loss for the Period, Fundamental Errors and Changes in Accounting Policies	1978 (revised 1993)
IAS 9	Research and Development Costs	1978 (revised 1993)
IAS 10	Events after the Balance Sheet Date	1978 (revised 1999)
IAS 11	Construction Contracts	1979 (revised 1993)
IAS 12	Accounting for Taxes on Income	1979 (revised 1997)
IAS 13	Superseded by IAS 1 (revised)	1979
IAS 14	Segment Reporting	1981 (revised 1997)
IAS 15	Information Reflecting the Effects of Changing Prices	1981
IAS 16	Property, Plant and Equipment	1982 (revised 1998)
IAS 17	Leases	1982 (revised 1997)
IAS 18	Revenue	1982 (revised 1993)
IAS 19	Employee Benefits	1983 (revised 1997)
IAS 20	Accounting for Government Grants and Disclosure of Government Assistance	1983
IAS 21	The Effects of Changes in Foreign Exchange Rates	1983 (revised 1993)
IAS 22	Business Combinations	1983 (revised 1993)
IAS 23	Borrowing Costs	1984 (revised 1993)
IAS 24	Related Party Disclosures	1984
IAS 25	Accounting for Investments	1986
IAS 26	Accounting and Reporting by Retirement Benefit Plans	1987
IAS 27	Consolidated Financial Statements and Accounting for Investments in Subsidiaries	1989
IAS 28	Accounting for Investments in Associates	1989 (revised 1998)
IAS 29	Financial Reporting in Hyperinflationary Economies	1989
IAS 30	Disclosures in the Financial Statements of Banks and Similar Financial Institutions	1990
IAS 31	Financial Reporting of Interests in Joint Ventures	1990 (revised 1998)
IAS 32	Financial Instruments: Disclosure and Presentation	1995
IAS 33	Earnings per Share	1997
IAS 34	Interim Financial Reporting	1998
IAS 35	Discontinuing Operations	1998
IAS 36	Impairment of Assets	1998
IAS 37	Provisions, Contingent Liabilities and Contingent Assets	1998
IAS 38	Intangible Assets	1998
IAS 39	Financial Instruments: Recognition and Measurement	1998

One other method historically used by the IASC to gain support has been the acceptance of alternative accounting methods. To get at least 11 of the 14 board members to support a new standard, usually at least two methods (and often more) were allowed. For example, IAS 2, originally issued in 1975, allowed the use of specific identification, FIFO, LIFO, average cost, and the base stock method for valuing inventories, effectively sanctioning most of the alternative methods in worldwide use. For the same reason, both the U.S. treatment of expensing goodwill over a period of up to 40 years and the U.K. approach of writing off goodwill directly to stockholders' equity were allowed by the IASC. Although initially necessary from a political perspective perhaps, such compromise has brought the IASC under heavy criticism.

A study conducted by the IASC in 1988 found that all or most companies listed on the stock exchange in those countries in Exhibit 11–3 (except Italy and Germany) were in compliance with IASC standards.[25] Given that research has shown that these countries are following at least four significantly different models of accounting, it is obvious that IASC standards existing in 1988 introduced little if any comparability of financial statements across countries.

THE IOSCO AGREEMENT

In 1987, the International Organization of Securities Commissions (IOSCO) became a member of the IASC's Consultative Group. IOSCO's membership is comprised of the stock exchange regulators in almost 100 countries, including the U.S. SEC. As one of its objectives, IOSCO works to facilitate cross-border securities offerings and listings by multinational issuers. To this end, IOSCO has supported the IASC's efforts at developing International Accounting Standards that could be used by foreign issuers in lieu of local accounting standards when entering capital markets outside of their home country. "This could mean, for example, that if a French company has a simultaneous stock offering in the United States, Canada, and Japan, financial statements prepared in accordance with international standards could be used in all three nations."[26]

IOSCO supported the IASC's Comparability Project (begun in 1987), the purpose of which was "to eliminate most of the choices of accounting treatment currently permitted under International Accounting Standards."[27] As a result of the Comparability Project, 10 revised IASs were approved in 1993 becoming effective in 1995. In 1993, IOSCO and the IASC agreed upon a list of "core" standards for use in financial statements of companies involved in cross-border securities offerings and listings. The two organizations agreed upon a work program in 1995 for IASC to develop the "core" set of international standards, and upon their completion IOSCO agreed to evaluate the core standards for possible endorsement for cross-border listing purposes.

The IASC accelerated its pace of standards development issuing or revising 16 standards in the period 1997–1998. With the publication of IAS39 in December 1998, the IASC completed its work program to develop the core set of standards. IOSCO's Technical Committee began evaluation of the core standards in 1999 to determine whether they are of sufficient high quality to warrant permitting foreign issuers to use them to access a country's capital market as an alternative to using local standards. The Technical Committee consists of securities regulators representing the 14 largest and most developed capital markets including Australia, France, Germany, Japan, the United Kingdom, and the United States.

Support of Securities Exchange Regulators

To a great extent, the IASC's legitimacy as the international standard setter derives from its work being supported by IOSCO. In 1993, IOSCO endorsed IAS 7 "Cash Flows Statements" (revised in 1992), and in 1994 it indicated that another 14 standards

---

[25]International Accounting Standards Committee, *Survey of the Use and Application of International Accounting Standards,* 1988, p. 5.

[26]Stephen H. Collins, "The SEC on Full and Fair Disclosure," *Journal of Accountancy,* January 1989, p. 84.

[27]International Accounting Standards Committee, *International Accounting Standards 1990* (London: IASC, 1990), p. 13.

(including 8 of the 10 revised in the comparability project) needed no further improvement to be considered core standards.

Although IOSCO has not yet completely endorsed IASs, several stock exchanges around the world—including London and Amsterdam—have accepted IAS-based financial statements for cross-listings for several years. In 1998, the Frankfurt, Paris, Rome, and Vienna stock exchanges passed rules allowing foreign companies to use IASs.[28] The Tokyo stock exchange followed suit in 1999. Of the 14 countries represented on IOSCO's Technical Committee, only two do not allow foreign companies to use IASs—Canada and the United States.

As a member of IOSCO, the U.S. SEC also began its assessment of the IASC's core set of standards in 1999. In 1996, the SEC announced that to be acceptable for cross-listing purposes, IASs would have to meet three key criteria. The core set of standards would have to:

- Constitute a comprehensive, generally accepted basis of accounting.
- Be of high quality, resulting in comparability and transparency, and providing for full disclosure.
- Be rigorously interpreted and applied.

Partly in response to the third criterion, the IASC created a Standing Interpretations Committee (SIC) in 1997 to provide guidance on accounting issues where there is likely to be divergent or unacceptable treatment in the absence of specific guidance in an International Accounting Standard. As of January 1, 2000, the SIC had issued 18 Interpretations and 5 Draft Interpretations were outstanding. SIC Interpretations constitute authoritative pronouncements and must be followed to be in compliance with International Accounting Standards.

The U.S. SEC has given partial recognition to international standards. Since 1994, the SEC no longer requires reconciliation to U.S. GAAP if a foreign registrant uses the relevant IAS related to:

- Statement of cash flows.
- Amortization of goodwill.
- Translation of financial statements of subsidiaries in highly inflationary economies.
- Distinction between purchase and pooling of interests.

The FASB is sometimes criticized for not being interested in the IASC and its activities. However, there has actually been considerable cooperation between the two organizations over the years. The FASB is a member of IASC's consultative group, the only standard setter included in that group. The IASC and FASB worked together on an earnings per share project, and, these two bodies worked together with the Canadian Institute of Chartered Accountants to revise rules related to segmental reporting. The chairman of the FASB's parent organization, the Financial Accounting Foundation (FAF), has indicated that FAF will promote the development and acceptance of international standards.[29]

The FASB conducted a comparison of IASC standards with U.S. GAAP in 1996.[30] Although it is widely assumed that IAS and U.S. GAAP are generally consistent with one another, that study shows that considerable differences exist in the two sets of accounting principles.

---

[28]German, French, Italian, and Austrian law now allows *domestic* companies to use IASs in preparing *consolidated* financial statements; parent company financials still must be prepared using local GAAP.

[29]Glenn Cheney, "Cook Defends Independence, Pushes for Global Standards," *Accounting Today,* November 25–December 15, 1996, pp. 16 and 20.

[30]Financial Accounting Standards Board, *The IASC-U.S. Comparison Project: A Report on the Similarities and Differences between IASC Standards and U.S. GAAP,* ed. Carrie Bloomer (Norwalk, Conn.: FASB, 1996).

As some of the comparative analyses in this report show, some of the IASC standards and their U.S. GAAP counterparts do have a similar underlying approach to accounting in certain areas, and it may be possible to arrive at similar results under both standards. However, such similarity may be compromised by the existence of alternatives or the absence of implementation guidance within the standards. Either of those circumstances could lead to very different results in the financial statements.[31]

The FASB identified 218 items covered by both U.S. GAAP and IASC standards. The following table lists the degree of similarity across these items:

	Number	Percent
■ Similar approach and guidance	56	26%
■ Similar approach but different guidance	79	36
■ Different approach	56	26
■ Alternative approaches permitted	27	12
	218	100%

RESTRUCTURING OF IASC

Upon completion of its core set of standards, the IASC proposed a new structure that would allow the IASC and national standard setters to better work together toward global harmonization. After reviewing numerous and often highly critical comment letters, the proposal was significantly amended and approved in 2000.

Under the restructuring, the IASC Board consists of 14 members—12 full-time and 2 part-time. To ensure independence of the Board, all full-time members are required to sever their employment relationships with former employers and are not allowed to hold any position giving rise to perceived economic incentives that might call their independence into question. Seven of the full-time Board members have a formal liaison responsibility with one or more national standard setters; the other seven do not have such a responsibility. A minimum of five Board members must have a background as practicing auditors, three must have a background as preparers of financial statements, three as users of financial statements, and at least one member must come from academia. The Board has the responsibility of issuing International Accounting Standards and formally approving Interpretations drafted by the SIC. The most important criterion for selection as a Board member is technical competence.

The newly structured IASC is overseen by 19 Trustees drawn from diverse geographic and functional backgrounds. The Trustees select Board and SIC members, review strategic issues, and raise funds to finance the IASC's operations. U.S. SEC chairman Arthur Levitt chaired the Nominating Committee responsible for appointing the initial group of Trustees.

The FASB and SEC in the United States have expressed support for the restructuring of the IASC. With the creation of an independent IASC Board, it is more likely that the SEC will approve the use of IASs for cross-listing purposes in the U.S. securities market.

USE OF INTERNATIONAL ACCOUNTING STANDARDS

The IASC has identified over 800 companies and other organizations worldwide that refer to their use of IASs in their annual reports. More than 100 of these are Chinese companies that are listed on foreign stock exchanges. The accounting regulations in China *require* such companies to use IASs. In addition, more than 100 companies in Switzerland and a similar number in Germany refer to their *voluntary* use of IASs.

---

[31]Ibid., p. 15.

Swiss-listed companies must follow standards issued by the Swiss Foundation for Accounting and Reporting. Compliance with IASs ensures compliance with the Foundation's standards. The Swiss food products company Nestlé S.A. indicates the following in its 1998 summary of significant accounting policies:

> The Group accounts comply with International Accounting Standards (IAS) issued by the International Accounting Standards Committee (IASC) and with the Standing Interpretations issued by the Standing Interpretations Committee of the IASC (SIC).

Nestlé also indicates that all disclosures required by the Fourth and Seventh EU directives are provided even though Switzerland is not a member of the European Union.

In its 1998 Annual Report, the German pharmaceutical company Schering AG indicated that:

> The Consolidated Financial Statements of Schering AG are prepared in accordance with the German Commercial Code (HGB). The Standards of the International Accounting Standards Committee which apply for 1998 are also observed where they do not conflict with the accounting and valuation principles of the German Commercial Code.

Schering's approach to the use of IASs demonstrates the importance of IAS 1 (revised 1997), "Presentation of Financial Statements," which stipulates that companies can claim to be in compliance with IASs only if they comply with all IASs and SIC interpretations. Former IASC Secretary-General David Cairns has identified numerous cases where a company claims to follow IASs but a careful reading of the financial statements reveals that it does not.[32]

In 1998, the German parliament passed a law freeing German companies from the requirement to follow the German Commercial Code in preparing *consolidated* financial statements. German companies like Schering now are able use IASs in their consolidated statements without following the Commercial Code so long as the EU's Seventh Directive is not violated. Parent company statements still must be prepared in accordance with the German Commercial Code. Similar laws allowing consolidated statements to be prepared using IASs have been passed in Belgium, France, and Italy.

In its accounting policies note to its 1998 financial statements, the French firm Thomson-CSF stated that:

> In a February 1998 recommendation, the C.O.B. (the French Securities Regulator) observed that for operating periods starting as from July 1,1998, a company could no longer state that it complied with the International Accounting Standards Committee (I.A.S.C.) reference system, if it did not apply all I.A.S.C. standards currently in force. Consequently, as from the 1998 operating period, the consolidated financial statements of Thomson-CSF, prepared in accordance with accounting principles applicable in France, as also the provisions of the Seventh European Directive, no longer refer to the I.A.S.C. standards. (p. 82)

Prior to 1998, Thomson-CSF claimed to follow IASs when it apparently did not. From the excerpt above, it appears that Thomson-CSF has elected not to fully comply with IASs and no longer claims to do so as required by the French Securities Regulator. Because the IASC itself does not have the power to do so, the enforcement of IAS 1 must be carried out by securities regulators and auditors.

International Accounting Standards largely have been ignored by U.S. companies primarily because IASs are not acceptable in the United States. The IASC has identified only two U.S. companies that refer to IASs in their annual reports: Microsoft and FMC Corporation. However, these companies do not claim strict compliance with IASs as reflected in this excerpt from FMC Corporation's 1998 Annual Report:

---

[32]David Cairns, "Compliance Must be Enforced," *Accountancy International,* September 1998, pp. 64–65.

The statements have been prepared in conformity with accounting principles generally accepted in the United States and are *generally* consistent with standards issued by the International Accounting Standards Committee (emphasis added).

Although Microsoft referred to IASs in previous years' annual reports, it no longer continues to do so.

ACCOUNTING PRINCIPLES AROUND THE WORLD

Just like food dishes and native dress, accounting principles vary from country to country. To understand each unique set of reporting standards that has evolved, one must examine the structure and development of the accounting profession in these areas. To aid your understanding of the techniques in use, the remainder of this chapter analyzes national accounting principles by presenting two types of information:

1. A discussion of the accounting profession as it is structured in several key countries, along with an introduction to the financial statements currently produced by these countries.

2. A study of several specific accounting problems and the method by which these issues have been resolved in different countries.

THE ACCOUNTING PROFESSION AND FINANCIAL STATEMENT PRESENTATION

United Kingdom

"The United Kingdom has the oldest accounting profession in the world today, and its reputation is second to none."[33] As this quotation indicates, no discussion of world accounting principles would be complete without a study of the United Kingdom, a world leader in commerce and accounting. The legal foundation for accounting is provided by the Companies Acts, a series of legislation culminating in the Companies Act of 1989. The Companies Acts are basic commercial legislation designed to provide legal rules for U.K. corporations concerning issues dealing with management, administration, and dissolution. However, these laws also cover the issuance and content of financial statements. Prior to the 1980s, the law provided little more than a framework within which the accounting profession could set more detailed principles.[34] In 1981, the Companies Act was amended to incorporate the European Union's Fourth Directive and in 1989 it was amended to implement the Seventh Directive thereby increasing the importance of legislation in determining GAAP. Although the law prescribes some specific accounting procedures consistent with the EU directives, the law also requires companies to present a "true and fair view" of their results and financial position. This principle overrides the detailed requirements of the law. That is, if strict compliance with legislated accounting rules (or professional accounting standards) would not allow for a true and fair view to be presented, British companies should deviate from the rules. A survey of some 450 British companies in 1993 found that 10 percent used the true and fair view override.[35] The concept of true and fair view has been adopted by the EU in its accounting directives.

---

[33]Geoffrey Alan Lee, "Accounting in the United Kingdom," *International Accounting* (New York: Harper & Row, 1984), p. 261.

[34]Lee H. Radebaugh and Sidney J. Gray, *International Accounting and Multinational Enterprises,* 3rd ed. (New York: John Wiley and Sons, 1993), p. 83.

[35]J. M. Samuels, R. E. Brayshaw, and J. M. Cramer, *Financial Statement Analysis in Europe* (London: Chapman and Hall, 1995), p. 361.

In the United Kingdom, professional accounting organizations are quite important—membership now nears 200,000. A person may be a chartered accountant only through membership in the Institutes of Chartered Accountants in England and Wales, of Scotland, or in Ireland. Normally, once required exams have been passed, a license to practice is available to members after two years of approved experience.

In total, six different professional groups exist with the largest being the Institute of Chartered Accountants in England and Wales. Until recently, these organizations collectively controlled the accounting standard-setting process. Together, they formally created a Consultative Committee of Accountancy Bodies. A subcommittee of this group, the Accounting Standards Committee (ASC), produced 25 Statements of Standard Accounting Practice (SSAPs) between 1971 and 1990.

The ASC was originally created "to reduce and regularize the range of permissable accounting treatments applicable to comparable transactions and situations."[36] Over the years, the ASC gradually branched into a standard-setting role. However, the committee experienced difficulty because its pronouncements had to be accepted by each of the six professional organizations before being issued. Thus, the creation of accounting standards was agonizingly slow at times.

Consequently, the Accounting Standards Board (ASB) was formed on August 1, 1990, to replace the ASC as the standard-setting organization in the United Kingdom. The ASB is an independent body styled somewhat along the lines of the FASB in the United States. The ASB issues Financial Reporting Standards (FRSs) on its own authority. The ASB has sanctioned all of the SSAPs and has issued several FRSs including one that requires cash flow information. Any deviation from the ASB's standards must be explained and the financial effects disclosed.

A second body, the Review Panel, was created along with the ASB. The Review Panel monitors compliance with the accounting standards. This panel has the authority to seek a court order against companies producing financial statements that fail to provide a true and fair view.

Financial statements must be submitted to the shareholders at the annual meeting. A directors' report is included describing the directors' activities for the period, post balance sheet events, the business year in general, research and development activities, and a host of other information. The financial statements themselves are normally the balance sheet, the profit and loss account, and a cash flows statement. In addition, a statement of total recognized gains and losses often is presented that among other things reports the amount of translation adjustments included in stockholders' equity but not in income. In contrast to the United States, parent company financial statements also are provided along with the consolidated statements.

For the balance sheet and profit and loss account, two different formats (allowed under the EU's Fourth Directive) are available—a vertical or a horizontal presentation. Most British companies provide a vertical balance sheet; an example is that of Imperial Chemical Industries PLC in Exhibit 11–1. An example of a British profit and loss account is in Exhibit 11–6.

In the United Kingdom, the group profit and loss account is the equivalent of a consolidated income statement. The statement begins with *turnover* (the British term for net sales) followed by operating expenses, interest, and then taxes. Exceptional items related to continuing operations and discontinued operations appear in separate columns. Exceptional items primarily consist of restructuring costs (operating costs) and gains on closure of operations. Similar to the United States, British companies must report earnings per share at the bottom of the profit and loss account. Also as in the United States, reported figures tend to be highly condensed with much of the information provided in the notes to the statements. On the face of the financial statements, specific references relate the notes to particular line items.

---

[36]Emile Woolf, "The ASC at the Crossroads," *Accountancy,* September 1988, p. 72.

Exhibit 11–6   United Kingdom Income Statement

IMPERIAL CHEMICAL INDUSTRIES PLC
Group profit and loss account
for the year ended 31 December 1998

	Notes	**Continuing operations** Before exceptional items £m	Exceptional items £m	Discontinued operations £m	Total £m
Turnover	4, 5	9,095		191	9,286
Operating costs	3, 5	(8,591)	(164)	(161)	(8,916)
Other operating income	5	86	—	7	93
Trading profit (loss)	3, 4, 5	590	(164)	37	463
After deducting goodwill amortisation		*(23)*			*(23)*
Share of profits less losses of associated undertakings	7	3			3
		593	(164)	37	466
Profits less losses on sale or closure of operations	3		11	179	190
Profits less losses on disposals of fixed assets	3		3		3
Amounts written off investments	3		(34)		(34)
Profit (loss) on ordinary activities before interest	4	593	(184)	216	625
Net interest payable	3, 8	(332)			(332)
Profit (loss) on ordinary activities before taxation		261	(184)	216	293
Tax on profit (loss) on ordinary activities	9	(69)	34	(77)	(112)
Profit (loss) on ordinary activities after taxation		192	(150)	139	181
Attributable to minorities		8	4		12
Net profit (loss) for the financial year		200	(146)	139	193
Dividends	10				(232)
Profit (loss) retained for the year	25				(39)
Earnings (loss) per £1 Ordinary Share	11				
Basic		27.6p	(20.1)p	19.2p	26.7p
Diluted		27.5p	(20.1)p	19.1p	26.5p

Germany

Accounting principles in Germany are set by the national legislature. Currently, these mandatory principles are outlined in detail in the Third Book of the Commercial Code. Tax laws have had a significant influence on the reporting principles established by the code. In addition, as the code is silent with regard to many accounting issues, German companies refer to tax law, professional pronouncements, academic commentaries, and international accounting standards to fill in the gaps. Actual changes in the accounting laws are rare because they must be passed by the legislature. As noted earlier in this chapter, the most recent accounting law was passed in December 1985 to bring German accounting principles in line with the directives of the European Union. Although this law introduced the notion of a true and fair view into German accounting practice, application of this principle differs from that in the United Kingdom. Günter Seckler found, "It still seems to be the dominant opinion in Germany that compliance with legal requirements ensures a true and fair presentation."[37] Financial statements must be prepared in accordance with the code. If this does not result in a true and fair view, additional information must be presented in the notes to the financial statements.

As in many countries where legislated accounting rules exist. German accounting is considered quite conservative. This is true for two major reasons: One is the so-called tax conformity principle that is almost unknown in other countries. In Germany, commercial financial statements are the basis for taxation. Thus, for an item to be deducted for tax purposes, it must be recorded as an expense in calculating income in the financial statements. Companies interested in taking advantage of provisions in the tax law to reduce taxable income are required to report lower financial income as well. Two, German accounting "is greatly influenced by the German banks, because they provide the major investment and mandate the reporting requirements for many industries in Germany. . . . When individuals in other countries analyze the financial statements, they generally write up the figures because of the extreme conservatism of German policies and procedures."[38] In fact, the German Association of Financial Analysts (DVFA) has developed a standardized procedure for adjusting reported earnings to assess the real profitability of German companies. The adjustments include adding back to income special depreciation allowed for tax purposes and excess amounts transferred to provisions.

The accounting profession in Germany is well established. The *Wirtschaftsprüfer* is the equivalent of a Certified Public Accountant. A person can use this designation only after passing a series of difficult examinations and gaining six years of relevant experience. Only college graduates with degrees in economics, law, or a related subject may sit for the exams. "Because of the comprehensive requirements for entry to the profession, it is almost impossible to fulfill all of them before the age of 30, and most are 35 before they are admitted."[39] The profession's self-governing body is the *Wirtschaftsprüferkammer* that enforces strict rules on independence and ethics.

In Germany, companies must produce a balance sheet each year as well as an income statement and notes to the financial statements. Also required is a management report to discuss issues such as current business position, significant subsequent events, future prospects, and research and development activities. Many companies fulfill a disclosure requirement regarding changes in fixed assets by providing a statement of fixed assets in addition to the balance sheet and income statement. A law passed in 1998 requires publicly traded companies to prepare a statement of cash flows.

The income statement must be produced according to one of two formats. The cost of sales approach, which has grown in popularity in recent years with Germany's larger multinationals, is similar to the structure of the income statement typically found in the United States. In contrast, the type-of-cost statement is more traditional in Germany. The consolidated statement of income for Brau und Brunnen AG for the year ending December 31, 1998, is an example of this format (see Exhibit 11–7).

In the traditional cost of sales format used in the United States, manufacturing costs (materials, labor, overhead) are included in the cost of sales line item in the income statement and administrative costs are reported in a separate line. Under this approach, the total wages and salaries paid by a company are disaggregated into two parts— manufacturing wages are reported in cost of sales and administrative wages are reported in administrative expense. The same is true for depreciation and other operating expenses. Using the type-of-cost approach, Brau und Brennen reports total wages and

[37]Günter Seckler, "Germany," in *European Accounting Guide,* 3rd ed., ed. David Alexander and Simon Archer (New York: Harcourt Brace & Company, 1998), p. 361.

[38]Roger K. Doost and Karen M. Ligon, "How U.S. and European Accounting Practices Differ," *Management Accounting,* October 1986, p. 40.

[39]Thomas G. Evans, Martin E. Taylor, and Robert J. Rolfe, *International Accounting and Reporting,* 3rd ed. (Houston, Texas: Dame Publications, 1999), p. 38.

BRAU UND BRUNNEN AG
Consolidated Profit and Loss Account
For the Year Ended December 31, 1998

	Note No.	1998 (DM)
Sales revenue	11	1,540,528,362.81
Decrease in work-in-process and finished goods		−2,724,164.38
		1,537,804,198.43
Other manufacturing costs capitalised		7,044.15
Other operating income	12	125,428,367.37
		1,663,239,609.95
Cost of materials	13	
Expenses for raw materials, supplies and merchandise purchased		316,311,498.05
Expenses for services purchased		16,469,159.51
		332,780,657.56
Staff expenses	14	
Wages and salaries		275,046,079.32
Social security levies and cost of pension schemes and related benefits		118,805,399.69
of which for pension schemes DM 65,546,178.50		
		393,851,479.01
Depreciation and amortisation	16	
Depreciation and amortisation on intangible fixed assets and on tangible assets		159,832,677.66
Other operating expenses	17	612,794,494.13
		163,980,301.59
Income from profit transfer agreements		721,907.14
Income from equity interests		2,376,547.80
of which from affiliated companies DM 2,374,404.94		
Income from other securities and from loans forming part of the financial assets		6,082,660.26
Other interest and similar income		4,066,435.48
of which from affiliated companies DM 433,542.86		
		177,227,852.27
Depreciation on financial assets and on securities held as current assets	18	24,051,725.20
Expenses from the assumption of losses		5,878,661.68
Interest and similar expenses	19	27,008,667.58
of which for affiliated companies DM 13,631,551.59		
Results from ordinary activities		120,288,797.81
Taxes on income and profit	20	1,004,577.74
Other taxes	20	132,818,048.71
NET LOSS/PROFIT FOR THE YEAR		−13,533,828.64

salaries (manufacturing and administrative) in a single line. Similarly, total depreciation and amortization is reported in one line, as is total other operating expenses. The materials component of cost of sales is reported by Brau und Brunnen in two parts—purchases are reported as an expense in cost of materials, and the difference between beginning and ending work-in-process and finished goods inventory is treated as an adjustment to sales. Although quite unique in appearance when compared to a U.S. income statement, the type-of-cost approach results in the same calculation of earnings as the cost of sales approach. One analytical limitation of this approach, however, is that it is not possible to calculate the cost of sales; therefore, gross profit cannot be determined.

Note the 1999 consolidated balance sheet for the equipment manufacturer MAN AG in Exhibit 11–8. Similar to the financial reporting in the United Kingdom, the German balance sheet begins with noncurrent assets followed by current assets. Prepaid expenses are not classified as either current or noncurrent. Stockholders' equity usually appears next before the reporting of any liabilities. Capital reserves is paid-in capital in excess of par value and unappropriated profit reflects the amount earmarked for dividends, unlike in the United States, minority interest is specifically included in stockholders' equity.

German companies do not classify obligations on the balance sheet as current and noncurrent. Instead, they classify obligations as either accruals or liabilities. The major distinction between the two is that accruals are generally estimated whereas liabilities are of a fixed, contractual nature. German companies have traditionally considered liabilities due within the next five years as short term. However, the 1985 accounting law requires companies to disclose in the notes the amount of liabilities due within one year; many companies also continue to indicate those liabilities due in more than five years.

MAN's accruals include estimates for such items as pensions, taxes, warranties, and other identifiable risks. In addition to being extremely conservative, German companies are notorious for their use of provisions to conceal profits and create hidden reserves. In profitable years, provisions are created for items such as deferred repairs, that is, repairs the company plans to make sometime in the future, or for undetermined obligations resulting from general business risks that might occur in the future. The counterpart to the balance sheet accrual is an expense or loss reported in income. In years in which profits are below expectations, provisions are released with an offsetting increase to income. This income smoothing is an acceptable practice, done within the law, and very much a part of German business culture.

One of the most dramatic examples of the use of hidden reserves was carried out by Daimler-Benz AG in 1989. In 1988, the company reported income of 1.7 billion deutschemarks (DM). Because 1989 was a bad year for automobile sales, analysts expected Daimler-Benz's 1989 income to be somewhat lower than the year before. It created quite a stir in the German business community when the company reported 1989 income as DM6.8 billion, a fourfold increase over the prior year. The notes to the 1989 financial statements provide the following explanation:

> Provisions for old-age pensions and similar obligations are actuarially computed in accordance with the tax regulation of Section 6a of the Income Tax Act, at an interest rate of 6 percent per annum. Previously, a rate of 3.5 percent was used. Using the higher interest rate resulted in higher income of about DM4.9 billion and is shown in the income statement under "Other Operating Income."

Through the selection of a low (and therefore more conservative) discount rate from a range accepted by tax law, Daimler-Benz was able to report higher expenses in years prior to 1989 and thus establish hidden reserves. The release of those reserves in 1989 through a change in the discount rate significantly affected net income. Without the change, income would have been only DM 1.9 billion.

In 1992, Daimler-Benz reported net income of DM 1.45 billion after creating provisions for loss contingencies of DM 774 million. Otherwise, 1992 profit would have been D M2.22 billion. In 1993, reported income was DM 615 million, but included the release of previous provisions of DM 4.26 billion, thus masking a loss of some DM 3.65 billion.

Exhibit 11-8
German Balance Sheet

MAN AKTIENGESELLSCHAFT Consolidated Balance Sheet June 30, 1999	Note No.	DM million
Assets		
Intangible assets		65
Tangible fixed assets		4,954
Financial assets		330
Fixed assets	(8)	**5,349**
Inventories......................................	(9)	6,906
Prepayments		(3,621)
Trade receivables	(10)	5,522
Other receivables and current assets	(11)	1,591
Securities......................................	(12)	1,638
Cash and cash equivalents	(12)	981
Current assets		**13,017**
Prepaid expenses		75
		18,441
Liabilities and shareholders' equity		
Share capital		771
Capital reserves		1,322
Retained earnings		2,282
Unappropriated profit		278
Equity of the shareholders of MAN AG		**4,653**
Minority interest		477
Shareholders' equity	(13)	**5,130**
Pension accruals	(14)	3,224
Other accruals	(15)	4,211
Total accruals		**7,435**
Financial liabilities		1,176
Trade payables		2,930
Other payables..................................		1,657
Liabilities	(16)	**5,763**
Deferred income		**113**
		18,441

Perhaps the ultimate in income smoothing was done by the electrical equipment manufacturer AEG that reported net income of exactly zero in each of the three years—1985, 1986, and 1987. The odds of a company generating net income of zero in any given year, let alone three years in a row, without the help of income smoothing are extremely small.

There is considerable evidence that German accounting is in the process of change. As noted earlier in this chapter, German law was amended in 1998 to allow German companies to use IASs in their consolidated financial statements. In fact, German companies may choose to use U.S. GAAP, U.K. GAAP, or any other internationally accepted standards in lieu of German law in preparing consolidated statements. The German stock market recently created a new exchange known as the "Neuer Markt" for the trading of primarily small- to medium-sized high tech companies. Companies listing on the Neuer Markt are *required* to prepare their financial statements in accordance with either International Accounting Standards or U.S. GAAP and in both the German and English languages.

Japan

Japan is an increasingly dominant industrial and financial power; we will need to come to terms with that country's accounting policies. Japanese accounting in the 1990s is a product of a native medieval double entry bookkeeping system, a borrowing from German (and French) commercial legal codes in the late 19th century, and U.S.-inspired securities legislation of the postwar period.[40]

In Japan and most other code law countries, basic accounting principles are set primarily by the government. The Japanese Commercial Code requires annual audited financial statements of joint stock corporations (known as *Kabushiki Kaisha* or KK) that have stated capital of at least 500 million yen or total liabilities of 20 billion yen or more. The Securities and Exchange Law imposes a similar reporting requirement on companies listed on Japanese stock exchanges as well as companies issuing stocks and bonds in the amount of 100 million yen or more. Consequently, many Japanese companies must produce two sets of financial statements: one to fulfill the requirements of the Commercial Code and the other based on securities laws. The two sets of statements are very similar except that the securities laws require more disclosure and its requirements are more precisely defined.

The Commercial Code prescribes a few basic accounting principles (valuation of assets and liabilities, recording of deferred assets, and the like). These rules are supplemented by the *Financial Accounting Standards for Business Enterprises* developed by the Business Accounting Deliberation Council (BADC). The BADC is, therefore, the single most important source of accounting principles in Japan. The BADC is made up of individuals drawn from the government, business, education, and the accounting profession. Membership in this council is by appointment of the Ministry of Finance which, therefore, allows government control.

Financial reporting in Japan is quite heavily influenced by tax laws. Companies usually follow the tax guidelines in producing their statements unless absolutely prohibited. Fortunately, the tax laws are written so that actual differences with official accounting pronouncements are few.

The adjustment of book income to taxable income on the tax return is not allowed in principle. Therefore, the so-called two sets of books problem prevalent in the United States is rarely mentioned in Japan. When a discrepancy exists between the income tax code and other financial accounting regulations, the corporation inevitably follows the procedures endorsed by the income tax code.[41]

The Japanese Institute of Certified Public Accountants (JICPA) has not become a powerful force in establishing accounting principles. The Audit Committee of the JICPA, though, does issue papers describing preferable accounting practices.

To become a certified public accountant in Japan, applicants must pass three examinations: the first (from which college graduates are exempted) consists of mathematics, the Japanese language, and a thesis. The second is comprised of accounting, cost accounting, auditing, management, economics, and commercial law. Passing this second test qualifies one as a Junior CPA. Then, after three years of experience, a third examination is required to become a CPA. This final test is made up of accounting practice, auditing practice, and financial analysis.

---

[40]Christopher Nobes and Sadayoshi Maeda, "Japanese Accounts: Interpreters Needed," *Accountancy,* September 1990, p. 82.

[41]Toshio Iino and Ryoji Inouye, "Financial Accounting and Reporting in Japan," in *International Accounting,* ed. H. Peter Holzer (New York: Harper & Row, 1984), p. 377.

Historically, accounting has not had the importance in Japan that is found in other developed nations.

> Not only do officials of Japanese companies generally ignore the stock market, they don't use complex financial information much themselves either. "Cost accounting doesn't exist," [says Daniel Maher, partner of Chuo/Coopers & Lybrand Consulting in Tokyo]. "There are more accountants in Missouri than in all of Japan." In fact, there are only about 11,000 certified public accountants in Japan, compared with some 300,000 in the United States. Instead of corporate accounting departments or professional accountants, most Japanese companies have small accounting groups attached to projects and staffed by generalists who rotated through accounting between assignments to, say, personnel and sales.[42]

Financial statements required by the Japanese Commercial Code consist of the following:

- Balance sheet.
- Income statement.
- Proposal of appropriation of profit or disposition of loss.
- Business report.

Although a statement of cash flows is not specifically required, companies must provide extensive cash flow information in supplementary information filed with the Ministry of Finance. It is not uncommon for companies to voluntarily provide a cash flows statement in their annual reports.

The Japanese balance sheet is similar in appearance to that used in the United States. Assets usually are either current or long-term, and liabilities are divided between current and noncurrent. Long-term assets usually are categorized as investments; property, plant, and equipment; and deferred charges. Differences in presentation primarily relate to differences in accounting principles. For example, as allowed by Japanese accounting principles, Nippon Light Metal Company, Ltd. reported translation adjustments arising from consolidation of foreign operations as an asset on its March 31, 1999, balance sheet, and Kobe Steel Ltd. reported research and development expense as a deferred asset on its March 31, 1995, balance sheet. Retained earnings may show amounts that have been voluntarily reserved by corporate officials.

In addition, the stockholders' equity section reports a legal reserve required to be established. As an example, Mitsubishi Heavy Industries, Ltd. reported a legal reserve of 61,079 million yen ($540 million) on its March 31, 1998 balance sheet. A note explained this balance as follows:

> The Japanese Commercial Code provides that an amount equivalent to not less than 10 percent of cash dividends and bonuses to directors and statutory auditors paid be appropriated as a legal reserve until such reserve equals 25 percent of stated capital. The legal reserve may be used to reduce a deficit or may be transferred to stated capital, but it is not available for distribution as dividends.

The Japanese income statement is divided into two sections to arrive at income before income taxes: ordinary income and extraordinary (or special) items. The income statement of Nippon Light Metal Company, Ltd., in Exhibit 11–9 is an example of this structure. The first part of this statement includes operating revenues and expenses as well as nonoperating items such as interest and equity method income. The definition of an extraordinary (or special) item is not as restrictive in Japan as it is in the United States. Moreover, extraordinary items appear on a gross basis before taxes rather than net of tax as required in the United States. Japanese companies are required to report

---

[42]Paula Doe, "What's Buried Inside Japanese Annual Reports?" *Electronic Business,* February 10, 1992, p. 28.

Exhibit 11–9
Japanese Income Statement

NIPPON LIGHT METAL COMPANY, LTD.
Consolidated Statement of Operations
For the Year Ended March 31, 1999

	Millions of Yen 1999	Thousands of U.S. Dollars (Note 2) 1999
Net sales	¥569,036	$4,720,332
Cost of sales (Note 7)	466,369	3,868,677
Gross profit	102,667	851,655
Selling, general and administrative expenses (Note 5)	106,820	886,105
Operating loss	4,153	34,450
Nonoperating income:		
Interest income	397	3,293
Gains on sale of marketable securities	642	5,325
Other	3,613	29,971
Total nonoperating income	4,652	38,589
Nonoperating expenses:		
Interest expense	8,392	69,614
Equity in earnings of affiliated companies (Note 1)	660	5,475
Other	4,893	40,589
Total nonoperating expenses	13,945	115,678
Ordinary loss	13,446	111,539
Special losses:		
Additional retirement allowance to early retirement program	8,365	69,390
Loss on devaluation of marketable securities	659	5,467
Pension premiums for prior service cost, net of reversal of related allowance for severance indemnities	549	4,554
Suspension expenses	417	3,459
Loss on devaluation of investment securities	235	1,949
Total special losses	10,225	84,819
Loss before income taxes and others	23,671	196,358
Income taxes (Note 5)	1,834	15,214
Minority interest	(6,257)	(51,904)
Net loss	¥ 19,248	$ 159,668

Per share of common stock:	Yen	U.S. dollars
Net loss	¥ 40.98	$ 0.34
Cash dividends	¥ 2.00	$ 0.02

earnings per share calculated as net income divided by the weighted average number of shares outstanding during the period. There is no requirement to present earnings per share on a fully diluted basis.

It is very common for large Japanese companies to prepare an English language version of their annual report—these are known as convenience translations. (The same is true for the larger European companies.) In their English language convenience translations, Japanese companies usually translate yen amounts into U.S. dollars for the benefit of foreign readers. Note 2 to Nippon Light Metal's financial statements indicates how this is carried out.

> The U.S. dollar amounts are included solely for convenience. These translations should not be construed as representations that the yen amounts actually represent, or have been or could be converted into, U.S. dollars. The amounts shown in U.S. dollars are not intended to be computed in accordance with generally accepted translation procedures.
>
> The rate of ¥120.55=U.S.$1, the approximate current rate prevailing at March 31, 1998, has been used for the purpose of presentation of the U.S. dollar amounts in the accompanying consolidated financial statements.

Because each financial statement item is translated using the same rate, no translation adjustment arises.

Differences in business environments and accounting principles can have a significant impact on the comparability of financial ratios across countries. Consider the following ratios calculated in 1983:[43]

Average Japanese and U.S. Financial Ratios for Manufacturing Companies

Country	Current Ratio	Debt Ratio	Average Collection Period	Profit Margin	Return on Assets
Japan	1.15	.84	86 days	1.3%	1.2%
United States	1.94	.47	43 days	5.4%	7.4%

Based on these ratios, it appears that the average Japanese company is less liquid, less solvent, less efficient, and less profitable than the average U.S. company. From a U.S. perspective, the average Japanese firm appears to be an unattractive potential investment teetering on the brink of bankruptcy. However, a direct comparison of these ratios can be misleading. One should consider the differences in U.S. and Japanese business environments as well as differences in accounting principles when comparing financial data from companies in these two countries.

Japan's lower current ratio arises through the extensive use of short-term debt, rolled over when it comes due, to finance fixed assets. This is preferred by both banks and borrowers as interest rates are lower than on long-term debt but can be more frequently adjusted by the banks. The higher debt ratio in Japan is evidence of the importance of banks as providers of capital. After World War II, little equity capital existed and the major source of funds for rebuilding the country was government-supported bank loans. Close relationships between banks and companies have evolved to the point where banks seldom impose penalties for late interest payments or call delinquent loans, instead they postpone interest and principal payments. The longer accounts receivable collection period is due to the Japanese tradition of life-time employment and the willingness of companies to help one another out when times are tough. Customers receive extensions on paying their accounts so they are not put in a financial bind where they might have to reduce the workforce. The survival and stability of the customer in turn allows the supplier to maintain a stable level of production and employment. The smaller profit margin and return on assets results from both the environment and conservative accounting practices. Gross margins are smaller because of the highly competitive export markets in which Japanese companies tend to operate. Japanese managers are not as concerned with short-term profits, partly because of greater job security, and prefer to focus their attention on sales growth and

---

[43]Frederick D. S. Choi, Hisaaki Hino, Sang Kee Min, Sang Oh Nam, Junichi Ujiie, and Arthur I. Stonehill, "Analyzing Foreign Financial Statements: The Use and Misuse of International Ratio Analysis," *Journal of International Business Studies,* Spring–Summer 1983, p. 116.

market share rather than net income. The negative impact these environmental factors have on profitability is exacerbated by conservative accounting partly due to the linkage with taxation.

THE HANDLING OF SPECIFIC ACCOUNTING PROBLEMS AROUND THE WORLD

The final section of this chapter examines several specific financial reporting issues from the perspective of individual countries as well as the current international accounting standards. We make no attempt to describe the accounting principles of every nation. Instead, we present a cross-section of countries to indicate the range of possible treatments that have developed throughout the world. These countries are the United Kingdom, France, and Germany in Europe; Japan and Korea in Asia; and Canada, Mexico, and Brazil in the Americas. Each of these countries is a major location of direct foreign investment by U.S. corporations.

Reported Value of Assets

United Kingdom　In the United Kingdom, companies are free to choose the method by which they value assets. Although historical cost can serve as the basis, they may report some (or all) accounts at a current value. The method of current valuation depends on the type of asset. They can state intangible assets, tangible fixed assets, inventory, and short-term investments at their current cost. Current cost is the lower of replacement cost or net realizable value. Market value is used for long-term investments and serves as an allowed alternative for tangible fixed assets. If revaluation occurs, any accumulated depreciation is usually eliminated with the reported balance then being adjusted to the new basis. The change in the asset's value creates a "revaluation reserve" that is reported in the capital and reserves section of the balance sheet. Subsequent depreciation is based on the revalued figures. If assets are revalued, companies must indicate what the historical cost profit would have been. Bass PLC's calculation of historical cost profit for the year ended September 30, 1999, is as follows:

	£m
Reported profit on ordinary activities before taxation	572
Realisation of revaluation gains of previous periods	3
Difference between historical cost depreciation charge and actual depreciation charge	1
Historical cost profit on ordinary activities before taxation	576

France　Although historical cost is the basis for reporting, revaluing property, plant, and equipment as well as inventory to current value has been permitted in France since 1984. If revaluation occurs, it must apply to all applicable assets. To record the change, a separate reserve balance must be established within stockholders' equity. Revaluation tends to be infrequent because increases in value are taxed (although the extra depreciation is subsequently allowed as a tax deduction). The revaluation of intangibles is not permitted. Occasional tax-free revaluations are allowed or required by the government when inflation rates are high. Such revaluations occurred in 1945, 1959, and 1976.

Germany　Accountants use historical cost as the basis for reporting assets. Following a conservative approach, upward revaluations of assets are not allowed but provisions for extraordinary depreciation are required if a permanent impairment of value is anticipated.

Japan   The Japanese approach to reporting assets resembles the procedures used in the United States. Current assets appear at cost unless market value is significantly less and recovery is not expected. Unlike the United States, marketable securities are not allowed to be written up in value. The reporting of fixed assets is based on historical cost unless a permanent impairment of value has occurred.

Korea   Korean companies utilize historical cost. Revaluation to market value is allowed if the Bank of Korea wholesale price index has risen 25 percent or more since the date of an asset's acquisition or previous revaluation. Such adjustments are optional but can be made only on the first day of the business year. A company that records a revaluation through an increase in a capital reserve pays a 3 percent tax.

Canada   Historical cost is capitalized and amortized over the useful life of the asset. Prior to 1990, Canadian companies could write assets up to an appraised value above cost. The procedure was rarely used and now has been eliminated.

Mexico   Inventories and fixed assets are reported initially at historical cost and then restated to current values at the balance sheet date. Public companies must restate these assets to current replacement cost and use that figure for calculating cost of sales and depreciation. Nonpublic companies may restate using replacement cost or a consumer price index.

Brazil   Publicly traded companies are allowed but not required to prepare financial statements in units of constant purchasing power. If they choose to do so, companies adjust inventories, investments, and fixed assets upward for inflation on each balance sheet date and discount receivables to their present value. They then would base cost of goods sold and depreciation on the inflation-adjusted values of assets.

International Accounting Standards   Under IAS 16, the benchmark treatment for property, plant, and equipment is to report it at historical cost less accumulated depreciation. The allowed alternative treatment is to revalue property, plant, and equipment at its fair value. If assets are revalued, an entire class must be adjusted or some systematic approach must be applied; assets cannot be revalued selectively. Any reduction in value is recorded as a decrease in net income, whereas an increase creates a revaluation surplus to be shown within the shareholders' equity section of the balance sheet.

Business Combinations and Consolidation Accounting

United Kingdom   All subsidiaries are consolidated unless (1) control is only temporary, (2) restrictions hinder the parent's ability to exercise its rights, or (3) the subsidiary's activities are so dissimilar that consolidation would be misleading. Rules for pooling of interests or merger accounting are more lenient in the United Kingdom than in the United States. A company that makes an offer for all outstanding shares and obtains at least 90 percent can use pooling of interests accounting. Otherwise, the combination is a purchase or acquisition.

France   Consolidation of financial statements has been required only since 1986, although voluntary preparation has been common for some time. Purchase accounting in France is similar to that used in the United States; however, control is assumed if 40 percent or more of a company's voting stock is held and no other stockholder owns more. The pooling of interests method is not considered acceptable. A subsidiary need not be consolidated if restrictions hinder the parent's control, the shares are held for resale, or the subsidiary's operations are so dissimilar to those of the parent that consolidated statements would be misleading. In addition, subsidiaries not significant in relation to the group as a whole and subsidiaries whose financial statements are not produced in time for inclusion in the consolidated accounts are accounted for by the cost method.

Germany   Historically, large companies (defined by size of assets, sales, and employees) had to consolidate all domestic subsidiaries but could omit foreign ones. Beginning in 1990, the size limit was reduced significantly for preparing consolidated statements. In addition, after that date, all foreign subsidiaries had to be included in the consolidated figures. The purchase method predominates, but the pooling of interests method may be used if 90 percent of a subsidiary's voting stock is exchanged for new shares of the parent. However, income figures are not consolidated retroactively when this method is applied. Reasons for excluding a subsidiary from consolidation are similar to those in France.

Japan   Acquistions and mergers are so rare in Japan that consolidation accounting has not been well developed. As a result, until 1992, firms produced parent company statements rather than consolidated statements. Mergers are accomplished through an exchange of stocks and are usually recorded by the pooling of interests method. However, if one company is clearly in a subsidiary position, purchase accounting is used. For a pooling, income statement figures are not combined retroactively as is the practice in the United States.

Korea   Unaudited consolidated statements are supplements to the parent company statements. On its own statements, the parent records all subsidiaries using the cost method. In preparing consolidated statements, companies use the purchase method unless any relevant regulation requires the pooling of interests method.

Canada   Use of the pooling of interests method is very rare in Canada; it is only considered appropriate if the acquiring party cannot be identified. The purchase method applies to all other business combinations. Consolidation is required unless control of a subsidiary is seriously impaired, control is temporary, or the activities of the subsidiary are considered to be dissimilar to that of the remainder of the combination.

Mexico   All subsidiaries that are more than 50 percent controlled must be consolidated unless the subsidiary is bankrupt or, for foreign subsidiaries, foreign exchange controls limit the payment of dividends to the parent. In addition, a company that is 50 percent or less owned can be considered a subsidiary if the parent exercises control. Only the purchase method is appropriate.

Brazil   Companies must prepare consolidated financial statements if their subsidiaries make up more than 30 percent of total equity. Controlled subsidiaries must be consolidated unless control is temporary, the subsidiary is bankrupt, or the subsidiary's operations are dissimilar to those of the parent. Control is assumed to exist when more than 50 percent of voting shares are owned, either directly or indirectly.

International Accounting Standards   IAS 22 requires use of the purchase method for a business combination except in the rare case of a uniting of interests when an acquirer cannot be identified. In that situation, the pooling of interests method is appropriate. According to IAS 27, all subsidiaries, both foreign and domestic, should be consolidated unless control is temporary because the subsidiary is to be disposed of in the near future or severe long-term restrictions impair control.

Accounting for Goodwill

United Kingdom   Certainly one of the most controversial accounting rules in the United Kingdom has been the handling of purchased goodwill. Although the amount is computed in the same manner as in the United States, goodwill traditionally has been written off immediately against an equity reserve. This can have a significant impact on the amount of stockholders' equity reported in the balance sheet as demonstrated in Exhibit 11–1 where Imperial Chemical Industries, a company with total reported assets of £9,033 million, reports shareholders' funds of only £149 million. U.K. accounting rules were changed in 1997 and now require a company to record goodwill as an asset and then amortize the cost over up to 20 years, unless it can be shown that the asset has an economic life longer than 20 years. In that case, amortization will be over the longer (perhaps indefinite) period, with an annual impairment test conducted to determine whether the longer period is still justified.

France Firms capitalize goodwill and amortize it as an expense generally over 5 to 20 years although French law does not specify a maximum amortization period.

Germany Goodwill may be capitalized as an asset and amortized over five years (including the year of acquisition) or the period expected to be benefited. For tax purposes, a life of 15 years is used. Alternatively, goodwill may be written off immediately to an equity account.

Japan Computation of goodwill is similar to that in the United States. Accountants charge the amount of goodwill directly to income if the amount is not considered significant. If capitalized, goodwill is amortized over up to five years unless some other period of time can be justified.

Korea Reported on the balance sheet as an intangible asset, goodwill is amortized to income over a five-year period. To the extent that the excess of purchase price over fair market value of acquired net assets does not represent goodwill it should be recorded as an expense immediately.

Canada The treatment of positive goodwill is similar to that used in the United States, but negative goodwill is not recognized.

Mexico Goodwill is recognized as an asset and amortized over a reasonable period not exceeding 20 years. Similar to Korea, any excess of purchase price that cannot be considered to be goodwill should be expensed immediately.

Brazil The excess of cost over fair market value of net assets is recognized as an asset—goodwill. Unlike other countries, in Brazil the cost of goodwill must be divided into that portion attributable to unrecorded intangible assets, such as customer lists, and that portion attributable to future profitability. Firms account for and amortize the two components of goodwill separately over appropriate time periods. They amortize that portion attributable to future profitability over the time horizon used in making future profit projections and the portion attributable to intangible assets over the expected period of use.

International Accounting Standards The recent revision to IAS 22 now requires that goodwill be recognized as an asset and amortized on a straight-line basis over its useful life. There is a rebuttable presumption that useful life does not exceed 20 years. The previous option of an immediate write off to equity is no longer acceptable.

Translation of Foreign Currency Financial Statements

United Kingdom Companies normally use the current rate method with translation adjustments taken to reserves. Income items may be translated using either the average rate of the current rate at the balance sheet date. If the business activities of the foreign operation are closely aligned with those of the parent, the temporal method is used with a translation gain or loss reported in income. Although the concept of a functional currency is not formally used, British translation rules are very similar to those in the United States. The major difference is the optional use of the current rate for translating income when using the current rate method. Another deviation is the recommendation that financial statements of subsidiaries in hyperinflationary countries be restated for inflation and then translated using the current rate method.

France   French accounting rules specify no particular translation method. Majority practice is to use the current rate method, using the average exchange rate to translate income items, with translation adjustments taken to equity.

Germany   As in France, the Commercial Code specifies no method. Moreover, there appears to be no prevalent practice. Accountants use a variety of methods and deal with translation adjustments in different ways. One conservative variation is to report negative translation adjustments in income and positive translation adjustments in stockholders' equity.

Japan   Japanese translation rules are much different from those in the United States. These rules stipulate assets carried at historical cost, noncurrent liabilities, and equity accounts must be translated at historical rates. Assets carried at current value and current liabilities are translated at current rates. Revenues and expenses are translated at average rates except for expenses related to assets carried at historical cost that are translated at historical rates. Translation adjustments are reported as assets (negative) or liabilities (positive) in the consolidated balance sheet. Actual compliance with these rules is limited.

Korea   Firms use the current rate method to translate the financial statements of foreign subsidiaries. They use average exchange rates to translate income.

Canada   Translation rules in Canada are very similar to those in the United States. The major difference is that when the temporal method is used, the translation adjustment related to long-term monetary items may be deferred and amortized to income over the life of the item.

Mexico   No regulations pertain to the translation of foreign currency financial statements. Many companies follow the U.S. rule, *SFAS 52;* where this rule is not followed, practice varies considerably.

Brazil   Firms use the current rate method and recognize translation gains and losses in the income statement.

International Accounting Standards   Foreign subsidiaries fall into two classes: those that are an integral part of the parent's operations (foreign operations) and those that are self-sustaining (foreign entities). Whether a subsidiary is a foreign operation or a foreign entity is determined by the currency in which the subsidiary makes sales, incurs expenses, and obtains finance, as well as whether the subsidiary is relatively autonomous or has few transactions with the parent. Foreign entities should use the current rate method with income statement items translated at the actual or average exchange rate. Firms should adjust the financial statements of foreign entities in hyperinflationary environments for inflation prior to translation, and use the current rate for translating the income statement. For foreign operations, they should use the temporal method with translation gains and losses reported in income.

Inventory Valuation

United Kingdom   Inventory is carried at the lower of cost or net realizable value. FIFO, average cost, or any similar cost flow assumption may be used. LIFO is not acceptable for tax purposes, and therefore, its application is rare.

France   Inventory is carried at the lower of cost or either realizable value or replacement cost. FIFO and averaging are the only methods allowed for statutory reporting purposes. LIFO is allowed for consolidated financial statements.

Germany   Inventory is carried at the lower of cost or market, where market is replacement cost for materials and net realizable value for work in process and finished goods. Specific identification is preferred; however, if not possible, the moving average method is recommended. FIFO and LIFO also are allowed.

Japan   Inventory is reported at the lower of cost or market. Market value is usually the repurchase price. FIFO, LIFO, average cost, specific identification, and latest purchase price are all acceptable costing methods.

Korea   Firms value inventories at the lower of cost or market. Specific identification, FIFO, LIFO, average cost, or a retail pricing method are all acceptable for determining cost. Market value is based on a price survey index published by a reputable price survey institute, or net realizable value if an index is not available.

Canada   Inventory is carried at the lower of cost or market. Market value can be determined by any appropriate method. FIFO, LIFO, and averaging are all acceptable by Canadian accounting standards. The reporting entity selects the method that provides the fairest matching of costs. As in the United Kingdom, LIFO is not accepted for tax purposes so its use is limited.

Mexico   Inventory is reported on the balance sheet at the lower of restated value and realizable value. LIFO, FIFO, average cost, specific identification, and last purchase price are all acceptable methods.

Brazil   FIFO, LIFO, average cost, and specific identification are all acceptable cost flow assumptions. Because it is not acceptable for tax purposes, LIFO is rarely used. Inventories are reported at the lower of cost or market (lower of inflation-adjusted cost or market for public companies). Market is defined differently for various types of inventory—replacement cost for materials and net realizable value for work in process and finished goods.

International Accounting Standards   IAS 2 (as revised in 1993) recommends that inventories be carried at the lower of cost or net realizable value. Specific identification should be used for items that are not ordinarily interchangeable. For other items, the benchmark treatment is either FIFO or weighted average cost. However, LIFO is also sanctioned as an allowed alternative treatment.

Reporting Accounting Changes

United Kingdom   Changes are permitted only if the new method can be justified as preferable; these changes are handled retroactively. Thus, no cumulative effect of an accounting change is included in the current year's figures. Instead, firms adjust past balances to reflect the impact of the change in method.

France   Generally, a company recognizes the cumulative effect of a change in current income as an exceptional item. When the accounting change is mandated by a change in statutory requirements, however, it treats the effect as a prior period adjustment with adjustments being made to opening balances.

Germany   Changes in general measurement and valuation principles are allowed only in justifiable, exceptional situations. An exception to this is an accounting change made to realize income tax savings; to qualify for tax purposes, the change also must be reflected in the financial statements. The cumulative effect of an accounting change is reported in current income. Retroactive restatement is not allowed. The extent to which income was affected by accounting changes made solely for tax savings also must be disclosed.

Japan   In Japan, accounting changes are not made except for good reason and tend to be rare. When made, a retroactive restatement is not allowed and the cumulative effect is not recognized. The effect of the change is limited to the change in the current year's income from applying the new principle.

Korea   Changes in accounting principles are applied prospectively so that neither a retroactive restatement nor a cumulative effect adjustment is needed. Such changes can be made only if they make the statements more reliable or if they are mandated by a new accounting principle.

Canada   Accounting for a change in method is retroactive and, thus, similar to the approach used in the United Kingdom. Current recognition is appropriate, though, if necessary data cannot be gathered for restatement purposes. In contrast to the United Kingdom, a new method does not have to be preferable; changes are allowed as long as the method being adopted is a generally accepted accounting principle.

Mexico   Similar to Japan and Korea, the effect of an accounting change is recognized prospectively beginning with the current year's income.

Brazil   Accounting changes are allowed and need not be justified as being preferable to the previous principle used. The cumulative effect of an accounting change is handled as a prior period adjustment by adjusting the opening balance in retained earnings.

International Accounting Standards   IAS 8 (as revised in 1993) indicates that accounting changes should be made only if required by law or by an accounting standard setting body or if the change would result in a more appropriate presentation of financial information. Firms should apply the change retrospectively with the cumulative effect of the change treated as an adjustment to the opening balance in retained earnings. As an allowed alternative, they may include the cumulative effect in the calculation of the current period's income. Comparative information should be restated unless this is impracticable. If the amount of the adjustment to the beginning balance in retained earnings cannot be reasonably determined, firms should apply the accounting change prospectively.

Other Accounting Issues

Lease Capitalization   There is no consensus among the eight countries regarding the capitalization of leases. The United Kingdom, Korea, Canada, and Mexico require capitalization when specified criteria are met. This is also the treatment required in IAS 17. In contrast, all leases are accounted for as operating leases in Japan and Brazil. In France, only operating lease accounting is allowed in the statutory accounts; lease capitalization is optional for consolidated financial statements. Lease accounting in Germany depends on complex tax rules.

DISCUSSION QUESTION

Which Accounting Method Really Is Appropriate?

In this era of rapidly changing technology, research and development expenditures are one of the most important factors in the future success of many companies. Organizations that spend too little on R&D risk being left behind by the competition. Conversely, companies that spend too much may waste money or not be able to make efficient use of the results.

In the United States, all research and development expenditures are expensed as incurred. Germany and Mexico use this same treatment. However, expensing all research and development costs is not an approach used in much of the world. Firms in the United Kingdom can capitalize development costs if a clearly defined project exists, the expenditure is separately identifiable, future revenues are expected to be greater than the capitalized cost, the company has the ability to complete the project, and the outcome has been assessed with reasonable certainty. Similarly, Canadian companies must capitalize development costs when certain criteria are met. Japanese accounting allows both research and development costs to be capitalized if the research is directed toward new goods or techniques, development of markets, or exploitation of resources. Korean businesses capitalize their research and development costs when they are incurred in relation to a specific product or technology, when costs can be separately identified, and when the recovery of costs is reasonably expected. France and Brazil also allow research and development costs to be capitalized under certain conditions.

Should any portion of research and development costs be capitalized? Is the expensing of all research and development expenditures the best method of reporting these vital costs? Is the U.S. system necessarily the best approach? Which approach provides the best representation of the company's activities?

Long-Term Contracts   IAS 11 (revised in 1993) requires use of the percentage of completion method for long-term construction contracts when certain criteria are met. Similar procedures are followed in the United Kingdom, Canada, Mexico, and Brazil. In France, Japan, and Korea, firms may use the percentage of completion method when criteria are met, but the method is not required. Although not specifically disallowed, the percentage of completion method is almost never used in Germany.

Interest Capitalization   The benchmark treatment recognized in IAS 23 is that all interest should be expensed immediately. Capitalization of interest directly attributable to the acquisition, construction, or production of a qualifying asset is an allowed alternative treatment. Brazil and Japan follow the benchmark treatment, requiring all interest to be expensed. The other countries allow for interest capitalization with the method and conditions under which interest may be capitalized varying from country to country.

Income Taxes   The international standard (IAS 12) requires use of the liability method in accounting for differences between accounting and taxable income (deferred income taxes). Companies in France may choose between the deferred or liability method. The deferred method is preferred in Canada, whereas the liability method is used in the United Kingdom, Germany, Mexico, and Brazil. Deferred taxes are not recognized in Japan or Korea.

Investment in Associates   IAS 28 requires the use of the equity method for accounting for investments in associated companies. An associate is an enterprise in which the investor has significant influence. Significant influence is presumed when the investor holds, directly or indirectly, 20 percent or more of the voting power of the investee. Similar rules exist in each of the eight countries under examination. The only exceptions are that, in Mexico, significant influence is presumed on 10 percent ownership and, in Brazil, the equity method must be used with only 10 percent ownership if administrative influence exists.

SUMMARY

1. The world is rapidly developing a global economy with numerous multinational corporations. U.S. companies are expanding into other countries while foreign investors are acquiring businesses in the United States. Thus, a knowledge of the accounting principles applied throughout the world is necessary to be an efficient decision maker, especially when dealing with international capital markets. The wide diversity of these accounting principles can make the understanding of reported financial information as well as the comparison of companies a difficult task.

2. Accounting rules differ significantly across countries partially because of environmental factors such as the type of legal system followed in the country, the importance of equity as a source of capital, and the extent to which accounting statements serve as the basis for taxation. The two major classes of accounting systems in the world are the macro-uniform and the micro-based classes. Each class is comprised of several families, the largest of which is heavily influenced by accounting development in the United Kingdom.

3. The International Accounting Standards Committee was formed in 1973 to develop a set of accounting principles universally applicable in all countries. The IASC includes more than 100 member organizations from around the world and had produced 39 International Accounting Standards by January 2000. As a private organization, the IASC cannot legally enforce these pronouncements. Instead, member organizations pledge to work toward adoption of these standards in their respective countries. The IASC recently completed its set of core standards for possible IOSCO endorsement. Most major stock exchanges allow foreign companies to use IASs, and many major multinational companies have adopted IASs in preparing their financial statements.

4. The accounting standards in Japan, Germany, and other macro-uniform countries are based on government regulation and are quite conservative. Financial institutions and tax authorities are considered the primary users of published financial data. In the United Kingdom, a micro-based country, individual investors are the main users of statements. Accounting standards are set by the accounting profession and measurement rules are less conservative. The financial statements of each of these countries exhibit a number of unique characteristics when viewed from the perspective of a U.S. company. For example, the profit and loss statement in Japan labels a wide variety of transactions as extraordinary (or special). In both Germany and the United Kingdom, the balance sheet begins with fixed assets.

5. Accounting principles throughout the world often differ from those applied in the United States. For example, although the recording of assets such as inventory, land, buildings, and equipment is based on historical cost in the United States, some countries allow companies to adjust these balances to higher values. This procedure can be carried out using inflation indices (as in Brazil) or by determining current values (as in the United Kingdom). In addition, goodwill resulting from the purchase of another company may be charged to stockholders' equity (as in Germany) or written off over a period as short as 5 years (France) or as long as 20 years (the United Kingdom). Other areas in which significant differences exist include use of the pooling of interests method, translation of foreign currency financial statements, accounting changes, lease accounting, interest capitalization, and accounting for investments in associates.

COMPREHENSIVE ILLUSTRATION

Problem

(Estimated Time: 20 to 30 minutes)

Part A

A company is preparing financial statements for the year ending December 31, 2000. To arrive at final figures, the company must account for goodwill of $1 million resulting from the acquisition of a subsidiary on January 1. The company wants to report the minimum amount of expense each year and can justify an almost unlimited life for the intangible benefits of the business combination from which the goodwill was derived.

What expense should be reported if the company is preparing statements under the accounting rules and principles of each of the following?

United Kingdom

France

Germany

Japan

Canada

United States

International Accounting Standards Committee

Part B

A company plans to switch from one accounting principle to another at the beginning of 2001 and can justify this decision. Application of the new method would have increased net income in past years by $300,000 while raising net income in 2001 by $100,000.

What is the impact on current net income if the company is preparing statements under the accounting rules and principles of each of the following?

United Kingdom

France

Korea

Canada

Mexico

United States

International Accounting Standards Committee

Part C

A company owns a piece of land that cost $400,000 when acquired in 1990. At the end of 2000, the land has a fair market value of $760,000, and during the period 1990–2000 prices have increased in general due to inflation by 150 percent.

What figure should be reported for this asset if the company is preparing statements under the accounting rules and principles of each of the following?

United Kingdom

France

Germany

Japan

Korea

Canada

Brazil

United States

International Accounting Standards Committee

Solution

Part A

United Kingdom   Since 1998, British firms have been required to capitalize goodwill as an asset and amortize it to expense over a period not to exceed 20 years, unless a longer life can be justified. With an almost unlimited life, no expense would be required in 2000. An annual impairment test will be conducted to determine whether the goodwill has decreased in value.

France   Firms use a 5- to 20-year period as the life for goodwill. Since the minimum expense is desired, a 20-year period would be chosen to arrive at an expense of $50,000 each year.

Germany   Goodwill may be written off directly to stockholders' equity with no impact on income. If this option is elected, no expense would be reported in 2000 or subsequent years.

Japan   A five-year period is the normal amortization when this intangible asset is encountered. Thus, an expense of $200,000 is appropriate for 2000. A longer life may be used but only if that period of time can be justified.

Canada A period of up to 40 years can be used for amortization purposes so that the minimum expense for 2000 is $25,000.

United States Goodwill is tested for impairment. Assuming no impairment in 2000, the expense to be recognized would be zero.

International Accounting Standards The IASC requires an amortization period not to exceed 20 years, unless a longer period can be justified. Assuming a 20-year life cannot be rebutted, the minimum amount of amortization expense would be $50,000.

Part B

United Kingdom In reporting this change in accounting principle, previous years' income and the beginning balance in retained earnings would be increased by $300,000 while current income would rise by $100,000. Retroactive adjustment is utilized in the United Kingdom for accounting changes.

France In addition to the increase in 2001 income of $100,000, an exceptional gain of $300,000 also would be reported in 2001, the total impact would be $400,000.

Korea The effect on the prior years would be left as is. Proper accounting would be limited to the effect on the current year; this change would increase 2001 net income by $100,000.

Canada As with the United Kingdom, the impact on past years would not affect the 2001 income. A $300,000 retroactive restatement is made to adjust all historical figures to the newly selected method. For 2001, only the $100,000 increase in net income is recognized.

Mexico The entire $400,000 impact is recorded within the current period. For legal reasons, a retroactive change in the reported figures for the past years is not allowed.

United States For most accounting changes, firms would adjust the affected income account (or accounts) for the $100,000 so that no special treatment is required in the current operating figures. However, the $300,000 increase in past years' income is shown, net of taxes, at the bottom of the current income statement as a cumulative effect of an accounting change. Thus, similar to France and Mexico, the entire $400,000 is reported in current income. A few changes, such as a switch from LIFO, are handled through retroactive restatement rather than by the calculation and reporting of a cumulative effect.

International Accounting Standards Accounting changes are allowed if required by official or legal accounting pronouncements or to achieve a more appropriate presentation. The effect on the current year ($100,000) and on past years ($300,000) must be calculated and disclosed. The preferred treatment is to adjust the beginning balance of retained earnings by $300,000; alternatively, reporting the $300,000 retroactive adjustment in current income also is allowed.

Part C

United Kingdom The reporting entity has the option of using either the $400,000 historical cost to report the land or adjusting this asset to its $760,000 market value.

France The $400,000 historical cost would be the basis for reporting; however, the company is allowed to adjust the value upward to $760,000 if all applicable assets are revalued. Since this increment is taxable, companies rarely avail themselves of the opportunity for such increases. When inflation is severe, the government also may allow (or mandate) a tax-free write-up to fair market value.

Germany In the conservative German system, the $400,000 historical cost would be retained.

Japan In Japan, the historical cost of $400,000 would be utilized unless a permanent impairment of value had occurred.

Korea Historical cost is used unless the effects of inflation have been extreme. If the inflation rate since acquisition (as measured by the Bank of Korea wholesale price index) has been 25 percent or more, an adjustment to fair market value is allowed, although not required.

Canada   Historical cost figures of $400,000 are retained.

Brazil   The historical cost of $400,000 could be restated using a government inflation index. Assuming 150 percent inflation, the new figures would be $600,000.

United States   The historical cost of $400,000 is appropriate for U.S. companies. Any permanent impairment of value requires a downward adjustment.

International Accounting Standards   The benchmark treatment is historical cost of $400,000. As an alternative, the asset may be written up to the fair value of $760,000. The increase in value would be reflected in a reserve account in stockholders' equity.

QUESTIONS

1. Why would the knowledge of accounting principles used throughout the world be important to a businessperson in the United States?
2. Since a multitude of different sets of accounting principles exist in the world, which sets of principles are applicable to a particular company?
3. Why have international accounting standards been developed?
4. Why has the ability to make comparisons between companies in different countries become important in recent years?
5. What factors contribute to the diversity of accounting principles worldwide?
6. What are the major classes of accounting systems used throughout the world? What are the major influences on these different accounting systems?
7. What major accounting families comprise the macro-uniform class of accounting system? What families make up the micro-based class?
8. What arguments can be made in favor of international harmonization? What arguments can be made against it?
9. What are the Fourth and Seventh Directives?
10. What groups compose the membership of the International Accounting Standards Committee?
11. What are the goals of the IASC?
12. Why is the IASC not able to enforce the accounting standards that it issues?
13. Over the years, how has the IASC attempted to gain acceptance of the international standards that it has produced?
14. What problems has the IASC encountered in trying to gain acceptance for the international standards that have been issued?
15. How do the work of the IASC and the harmonization efforts of the European Union differ?
16. Why were several of the original standards issued by the IASC revised in 1993?
17. Why has interest in international accounting standards increased in recent years?
18. What impact would the acceptance of international accounting standards by the regulators of the global capital markets have?
19. What is the basis for the accounting principles used in the United Kingdom, Japan, and Germany?
20. How does a balance sheet prepared for a U.K. company differ from that produced by a U.S. company?
21. Why is the net income figure computed by a German company often assumed to be understated?
22. How does an income statement produced by a Japanese company differ from that produced by a U.S. company?
23. In the United States, historical cost is the basis for valuing assets, especially inventory, land, buildings, and equipment. What other valuation methods are utilized in countries around the world?

24. How do some companies in Germany account for goodwill? Why is this approach considered controversial?

25. How are the financial statements of foreign subsidiaries translated in different countries around the world?

26. How are research and development costs recorded around the world?

INTERNET ASSIGNMENTS

Internet sites are time and date sensitive. It is the purpose of these exercises to have you explore the Internet. You may need to refer to the text's Web site at http://www.mhhe.com/hoyle6e to find the most up-to-date links for the Web sites listed in the Internet Exercises.

1. Refer to the International Accounting Standards Committee's Web site at www.iasc.org.uk to complete this assignment. Click on "About IASC"

  a. Determine which (if any) of the following countries is not represented among the IASC's member bodies:

Czech Republic	Slovenia
Iran	Uganda
Pakistan	Vietnam

  b. Identify five countries in the world that are not represented among the IASC's member bodies.

  c. Determine the number of companies from each of the following countries that refer to the use of IASs in their annual reports:

Australia	Japan
Austria	Mexico
Brazil	Russia
Croatia	United Kingdom
Finland	United States

  d. Determine the way in which IASs are allowed to be used by the stock exchanges in each of the following countries:

Brazil	Spain
Korea	Switzerland
Mexico	Thailand
Netherlands	

  Click on "Interpretations"
  a. Identify the most recent final interpretation issued by the Standing Interpretations Committee (SIC).
  b. Briefly summarize the requirements of that interpretation.

  Click on "Projects"
  a. Determine the number of active projects underway at the IASC.
  b. List two of the accounting issues being considered in active projects.

2. Electrolux AB is a Swedish manufacturer of household appliances. Refer to Electrolux's Web site at www.electrolux.com, and click on "Media and Investor Information." Find the company's most recent annual report under "Latest Financial Reports." List five major differences between Electrolux's consolidated balance sheet and the balance sheet of a typical U.S. corporation.

3. Bass PLC is a British company that primarily operates in the hotels and resorts industry. Refer to Bass's Web site at www.bass.com, and click on "Our Performance" to download the company's most recent annual report. List five major differences between Bass's consolidated profit and loss account and the income statement of a typical U.S. corporation.

4. Shanghai Petrochemicals Company (SPC) is a major Chinese company operating in the petrochemicals industry. Refer to SPC's Web site at www.spc.com.cn, and click on "Annual Report." Answer the following questions based on the most recent annual report provided:

    a. How many sets of financial statements does SPC prepare? What are the accounting standards used in preparing them? Are the financial statements audited? If so, by whom?

    b. What is included in "Supplementary Information for North American Shareholders?" What are the major areas of difference between IASs and U.S. GAAP for SPC?

LIBRARY ASSIGNMENTS

1. Obtain the financial statements for a foreign company such as Volkswagen (Germany), Michelin (France), Vodafone–Airtouch (UK), Nestlé (Switzerland), Toyota (Japan), Electrolux (Sweden), or The News Corporation (Australia). List five major differences between the statements of a foreign company and the statements of a U.S. corporation.

2. Read the following articles and any other published information concerning international accounting standards and the IASC:

    "IASC Accepts Proposal for Worldwide Standard Setting," *Accounting Today,* January 24–February 6, 2000.

    "International Accounting Standards: The World's Standards by 2002," *CPA Journal,* July 1998.

    "International Accounting Standards: Are They Coming to America?" *CPA Journal,* October 1992.

    "The International Harmonization of Accounting: In Search of Influence," *International Journal of Accounting* 27, no. 3, 1992.

    "The Growing Importance of International Accounting Standards," *Journal of Accountancy,* September 1991.

    "Is GAAP the Gap to International Markets?" *Management Accounting,* August 1990.

    "Commentary—Internationalization of Accounting Standards," *Accounting Horizons,* March 1990.

    Write a report describing the activities of the International Accounting Standards Committee to date and discussing this group's chance of future success, especially in the United States.

PROBLEMS

1. Which of the following is not a reason for establishing international accounting standards?

    a. Some countries do not have the resources to develop accounting standards on their own.

    b. Comparability is needed between companies operating in different areas of the world.

    c. Some of the accounting principles allowed in various countries report markedly different results for similar transactions.

    d. Demand in the United States is heavy for an alternative to U.S. generally accepted accounting principles.

2. The International Accounting Standards Committee (IASC) was formed by representatives of several different

    a. Government agencies.

    b. Accountancy bodies.

    c. Legislative organizations.

    d. Academic organizations.

3. The goal of the IASC is to
   a. Formulate and publish accounting standards as well as harmonize accounting standards.
   b. Establish a quality review process for all international financial statements.
   c. Promote adequate reporting disclosure so that unique accounting standards can continue to be employed around the world.
   d. Require that all financial standards be consistent with the standards used in the United States because of its central role in the capital markets of the world.

4. Why does the IASC currently have only limited powers?
   a. The IASC is a private organization and, thus, cannot enforce the use of its official pronouncements.
   b. The IASC has always refused to mandate that its pronouncements must be followed.
   c. International capital markets establish and use their own accounting principles that must be followed in all cases.
   d. The IASC is a new organization that has not yet had time to exert significant influence in the world of accounting.

5. How does the macro-uniform class differ from the micro-based class of accounting system?
   a. The micro-based class is more heavily influenced by taxation.
   b. In the macro-uniform class, accounting rules tend to be set by the government.
   c. The macro-uniform class consists primarily of countries in the U.S.-influence and U.K.-influence accounting families.
   d. The micro-based class provides lower levels of disclosure in financial statements than the macro-uniform class.

6. The IASC
   a. Held its first meeting in 1911.
   b. Is composed of representatives of various governmental accounting bodies.
   c. Began with 84 member organizations.
   d. Was formed in 1973.

7. Which of the following countries is not in the micro-based class of accounting systems?
   a. Hong Kong.
   b. Spain.
   c. Australia.
   d. Canada.

8. According to critics, what is the major problem with the original standards produced by the IASC?
   a. Too many popular methods have been eliminated.
   b. Too many optional methods have remained.
   c. The IASC has failed to examine and report on key accounting issues.
   d. The pronouncements tend to be too similar to U.S. GAAP.

9. Why would some German companies probably prefer to follow the accounting standards of the IASC?
   a. German accounting principles are extremely complicated so that appropriate financial statements can be difficult to produce.
   b. The Germans have tended to follow U.S. generally accepted accounting principles rather than develop their own accounting principles.
   c. The use of IASC standards allows German companies to be more fairly compared with companies from other countries.
   d. The Germans have virtually no accounting principles so that comparison between companies within the country is virtually impossible.

10. Why have international accounting principles become a topic of special interest in recent times?
    a. The development of international capital markets and the continued consolidation of the European Community have created a need for comparable information from companies located around the world.
    b. The Financial Accounting Standards Board recently has asked the IASC to develop solutions to several specific accounting issues, including earnings per share.

    c. Most multinational companies have switched to international accounting standards rather than continuing to use national standards.

    d. A number of IASC pronouncements have forced the FASB to change several significant American accounting principles.

11. What attempt has been made by the IASC to gain greater acceptance of international accounting standards?

    a. Rules are being mandated now for individual countries.

    b. An attempt is being made to provide more flexibility within the international standards.

    c. The IASC is developing a new system of accounting principles to be applied according to the size of the organization.

    d. Optional methods have been eliminated.

12. Japanese accounting principles are

    a. Promulgated by the Japanese Institute of Certified Public Accountants.

    b. Established by the government.

    c. Quite liberal in nature.

    d. Similar in most respects to international accounting standards.

13. In Japan, extraordinary (or special) items are

    a. Never reported.

    b. More limited than in the United States.

    c. Items not necessarily considered extraordinary in the United States.

    d. Unusual and infrequent.

14. In the United Kingdom, a balance sheet

    a. Begins with fixed assets and then reports current assets less current liabilities.

    b. Is not required except for companies of a specific size.

    c. Begins with stockholders' equity.

    d. Is similar to a balance sheet that would be produced by a U.S. company.

15. In the United Kingdom, one encounters Stocks and Debtors accounts. What do these balances represent?

	Stocks	**Debtors**
a.	Investments	Minority interest
b.	Treasury stock	Notes payable
c.	Capital stock	Notes receivable
d.	Inventory	Receivables

16. In the financial reporting utilized in the United Kingdom, to what does the term *turnover* refer?

    a. Net sales.

    b. Age of inventory.

    c. Length of time needed to collect accounts receivable.

    d. Profit as a percentage of net assets.

17. In German accounting, hidden reserves are

    a. Assets invested for specified future use.

    b. Created to be able to smooth income from one period to the next.

    c. Equity balances used to record adjustments not included in computing net income.

    d. Annual adjustments to net income caused by the effects of inflation.

18. Which of the following does *not* help to explain why Japanese profitability ratios are lower than in the United States?

    a. Japanese companies are not as concerned about generating profit.

    b. Japanese accounting rules are more conservative.

    c. Japanese companies tend to borrow short term to finance asset acquisitions.

    d. Japanese companies rely more heavily on debt than on equity financing.

19. How do Japanese and United Kingdom accounting principles differ in the valuation of assets?

    a. In the United Kingdom, all assets are based on historical cost, while in Japan market value is always used.

    b. Both countries revalue assets. In the United Kingdom, current cost is required, while in Japan market value is appropriate.

c. In the United Kingdom, revaluation is permitted but in Japan historical cost is appropriate unless a permanent impairment of value has occurred.

d. In the United Kingdom, assets always are recorded at net present value, whereas in Japan current cost must be used.

20. Which of the following is a major influence on German financial reporting?
    a. Financial analysts and investors in equity securities.
    b. The Securities Transactions Committee.
    c. German banks because they provide a major portion of the financial capital.
    d. The International Accounting Standards Committee.

21. Which of the following is true for the German type-of-cost format income statement?
    a. All income items other than revenues from the sale of inventory are labeled as extraordinary gains and losses.
    b. Changes in inventory levels are reported as adjustments to sales.
    c. Cost of goods sold is shown prior to revenues.
    d. Income taxes are not viewed as expenses.

22. Why is the revaluation of assets rare in France?
    a. Inflation is low.
    b. Revaluation gains are taxed by the government.
    c. Revaluations can be made only with specific types of objective proof.
    d. Accounting principles are extremely conservative in France.

23. What basis is used for valuing assets in Germany?
    a. Historical cost.
    b. Lower of cost or market.
    c. Current market value.
    d. Historical cost adjusted for general inflation.

24. In Mexico, business combinations usually are reported through
    a. Consolidated statements including only domestic companies.
    b. Consolidated statements including subsidiaries in which more than 50 percent of the voting stock is held.
    c. Consolidated statements using the pooling of interests method only.
    d. Parent company statements only.

25. Goodwill
    a. Can be amortized over a 50-year period in France.
    b. Can be written off directly to stockholders' equity in Germany.
    c. Is accounted for in the same manner in Japan as in the United States.
    d. Is expensed immediately in Canada.

26. LIFO
    a. Is a preferred method according to international accounting standards.
    b. Is required in Japan.
    c. Is an allowed method in Canada.
    d. Is the predominant method used in the United Kingdom because of the rate of inflation.

27. In reporting research and development costs:
    a. Most countries capitalize research costs but expense development costs when incurred.
    b. Some countries capitalize some portion of development costs.
    c. Usually only one approach is found throughout the world.
    d. Most countries record all research and development costs as expenses when incurred.

28. Answer the following questions about the IASC:
    a. What factors have tended to prevent the acceptance of the IASC's international accounting standards?
    b. What is the present composition of the IASC?
    c. What are the goals of the IASC?
    d. What was the IASC's comparability project? What was its objective? What was the outcome of the project?
    e. What evidence is there that IASC standards are becoming acceptable around the world?

29. A multinational company is planning to raise a significant amount of capital funds by issuing stocks and bonds in the United States, the United Kingdom, Japan, and Canada. What impact might the IASC's international accounting standards have on the reporting of this company?

30. A financial advisor is investigating two companies as possible investment recommendations. One of the companies is headquartered in Japan while the other operates in the United Kingdom. In comparing the financial statements of these two organizations, what aspects of the national accounting principles (and business practices) should the investor consider?

31. A German company reports a net income figure that is to be compared with that of a counterpart company in the United States. What factors should be considered in making this evaluation?

32. Chapter 11, as well as several previous chapters, describes a number of techniques used to account for goodwill. List the possible methods for reporting and amortizing this intangible asset. Which method actually provides the fairest presentation of the consolidated company's financial operations and position?

33. In what situations do the countries of the world allow some portion of research and development expenditures to be capitalized?

34. Compare and contrast a balance sheet produced by a German company with a balance sheet developed by a British company.

35. Compare and contrast an income statement prepared by a German company with an income statement prepared by a Japanese company.

Financial Reporting and the Securities and Exchange Commission

---

QUESTIONS TO CONSIDER

- How does the U.S. government ensure that adequate reliable information is available to encourage investors to buy and sell securities so that sufficient capital can be raised by businesses for financing purposes?

- What companies are subject to the rules and regulations of the Securities and Exchange Commission?

- How does the SEC influence the development of accounting principles in the United States?

- What is the purpose of the registration statements filed with the SEC? What various periodic filings must also be made?

- What steps usually occur in the registration process?

- Which types of securities are exempt from registration with the SEC?

The Securities and Exchange Commission was born on June 6, 1934—a time of despair in the markets. Americans were still suffering from the 1929 market crash after a roaring 1920s when they bought about $50 billion in new securities—half of which turned out to be worthless. Their confidence also was eroded by the 1932 indictment (later acquittal) of Samuel Insull for alleged wrongs in the collapse of his utility "empire," and by the 1933–34 Senate hearings on improper market activity.[1]

The financing of the American industrial complex is very much dependent on raising vast amounts of monetary capital. During every business day in the United States, billions of dollars of stocks, bonds, and other securities are sold to thousands of individuals, corporations, trust funds, pension plans, mutual funds, and other institutions. Such investors cannot be expected to venture their money without forethought. They have to be able to assess the risks involved: the possibility of either a profit or loss being returned to them as well as the expected amount.

Consequently, disclosure of sufficient, accurate information is absolutely necessary to stimulate the inflow of large quantities of capital. Enough data must be available to encourage investors to consider buying and selling securities in hopes of generating profits. *Without adequate information on which to base these decisions, investing becomes no more than gambling.*

THE WORK OF THE SECURITIES AND EXCHANGE COMMISSION

In the United States, the responsibility for ensuring that complete and reliable information is available to investors lies with the Securities and Exchange Commission

---

[1] "D-Day for the Securities Industry, 1934," *The Wall Street Journal*, May 9, 1989, p. B1.

(SEC), an independent agency of the federal government created by the Securities Exchange Act of 1934. Although the SEC's authority applies mainly to publicly held companies, the commissions' guidelines and requirements surely have been a major influence in the United States on the development of all generally accepted accounting principles.

> The primary mission of the U.S. Securities and Exchange Commission (SEC) is to protect investors and maintain the integrity of the securities markets. As more and more first-time investors turn to the markets to help secure their futures, pay for homes and send children to college, these goals are more compelling than ever. The world of investing is fascinating, complex, and can be very fruitful. But unlike the banking world, where deposits are guaranteed by the federal government, stocks, bonds and other securities can lose value. There are no guarantees. That's why investing should not be a spectator sport; indeed, the principal way for investors to protect the money they put into the securities markets is to do research and ask questions. The laws and rules that govern the securities industry in the United States derive from a simple and straightforward concept: all investors, whether large institutions or private individuals, should have access to certain basic facts about an investment prior to buying it. To achieve this, the SEC requires public companies to disclose meaningful financial and other information to the public, which provides a common pool of knowledge for all investors to use to judge for themselves if a company's securities are a good investment. Only through the steady flow of timely, comprehensive and accurate information can people make sound investment decisions.[2]

The SEC is headed by five commissioners appointed by the president of the United States (with the consent of the Senate) to serve five-year staggered terms. To ensure the bipartisan nature of this group, no more than three of these individuals can belong to the same political party. The chairman is from the same political party as the president. The commissioners provide leadership for an agency that has grown over the years into a large organization with approximately 3,000 employees. The SEC is composed of four divisions and 18 offices including the following:

- The *Division of Corporation Finance* has responsibility for ensuring that disclosure requirements are met by publicly held companies. This division reviews registration statements as well as tender offers and proxy solicitations.
- The *Division of Market Regulation* oversees the securities markets in this country and is responsible for registering and regulating brokerage firms.
- The *Division of Enforcement* helps to ensure compliance with federal securities laws. This division investigates possible violations of securities laws and recommends appropriate remedies.
- The *Division of Investment Management* oversees the $15 trillion investment management industry and administers the securities laws affecting investment companies including mutual funds and investment advisers.
- The *Office of Information Technology* supports the SEC and its staff in all aspects of information technology. This office operates the Electronic Data Gathering Analysis and Retrieval (EDGAR) system, which electronically receives, processes, and disseminates more than 500,000 financial statements every year.
- The *Office of Compliance Inspections and Examinations* determines whether brokers, dealers, and investment companies and advisors are in compliance with federal securities laws.
- The *Office of the Chief Accountant* is the principal adviser to the commission on accounting and auditing matters that arise in connection with the securities laws. The office also works closely with private-sector bodies such as the FASB and the AICPA that set standards.

---

[2]The U.S. Securities and Exchange Commission, SEC Web Site, July, 2000. Available from http://www.SEC.gov; INTERNET.

The SEC's budget for 1996 was nearly $350 million. A breakdown of this appropriation gives some indication of the work of the organization:

Major Programs—Percentage of Overall Budget

Prevention and suppression of fraud	30 percent
Investment management regulation	22 percent
Full disclosure	19 percent
Supervision and regulation of securities markets	13 percent
Program direction	10 percent
Legal and economic services	6 percent

This chapter provides an overview of the workings of the Securities and Exchange Commission along with the agency's relationship to the accounting profession. Unfortunately, a complete examination of the organization is beyond the scope of this textbook. Therefore, only a portion of the SEC's functions are discussed here. This coverage provides an introduction to the role the agency currently plays in the world of American business.

Purpose of the Federal Securities Laws

Before examining the SEC and its various functions in more detail, a historical perspective should be established. The development of laws regulating companies involved in interstate commerce were discussed as early as 1885. In fact, the Industrial Commission created by Congress suggested in 1902 that all publicly held companies should be required to disclose material information including annual financial reports. However, only the crisis following the stock market crash of 1929 and the subsequently discovered fraud prompted Congress to act in hopes of reestablishing the trust and stability needed for capital markets.

> Before the Great Crash of 1929, there was little support for federal regulation of the securities markets. This was particularly true during the post-World War I surge of securities activity. Proposals that the federal government require financial disclosure and prevent the fraudulent sale of stock were never seriously pursued. Tempted by promises of "rags to riches" transformations and easy credit, most investors gave little thought to the dangers inherent in uncontrolled market operation. During the 1920s, approximately 20 million large and small shareholders took advantage of post-war prosperity and set out to make their fortunes in the stock market. It is estimated that of the $50 billion in new securities offered during this period, half became worthless. When the stock market crashed in October 1929, the fortunes of countless investors were lost. . . . With the Crash and ensuing depression, public confidence in the markets plummeted. There was a consensus that for the economy to recover, the public's faith in the capital markets needed to be restored.[3]

As a result, Congress enacted two primary pieces of securities legislation destined to restore investor confidence in the capital markets by providing more structure and government oversight.

- The Securities Act of 1933 regulates the initial offering of securities by a company or underwriter.
- The Securities Exchange Act of 1934 regulates the subsequent trading of securities through brokers and exchanges.

These laws put an end to the legality of many abuses that previously had been common practices such as the manipulation of stock market prices and the misuse of

---

[3]The U.S. Securities and Exchange Commission, SEC Web Site, July, 2000. Available from http://www.SEC.gov; INTERNET.

corporate information by officials and directors (often referred to as *inside parties*[4]) for their own personal gain. Just as important, these two legislative actions were designed to help rebuild public confidence in the capital market system. Because of the large losses suffered during the market crash and subsequent depression, many investors had begun to avoid buying stocks and bonds. This reduction in the pool of available capital dramatically compounded the economic problems of the day.

The creation of federal securities laws did not end with the 1933 Act and the 1934 Act. During the decades since the first commissioners were appointed, the SEC has administered rules and regulations created by a number of different congressional actions. Despite the passage of subsequent legislation, the major objectives of this organization have remained relatively constant. Over the years, the SEC has attempted to achieve several interconnected goals that include:

- Ensuring that full and fair information is disclosed to all investors before the securities of a company are allowed to be bought and sold.
- Prohibiting the dissemination of materially misstated information.
- Preventing the misuse of information especially by inside parties.
- Regulating the operation of securities markets such as the New York Stock Exchange and American Stock Exchange.

As judged by the dollar amounts exchanged each day in the trading of securities, the capital market system in the United States is flourishing. Corporations registered approximately $2.5 trillion of securities with the SEC in 1998 alone, an increase of 77 percent over the prior year. At least part of the responsibility for this success lies with the SEC and the agency's ability to attain the preceding goals. Today, most investors apparently believe in the overall integrity of the market system as well as the sufficiency and fair presentation of the data that they receive. Thus, any introduction to the SEC must examine the methods used to maintain public confidence as it regulates the honest distribution of both financial and nonfinancial information.

Full and Fair Disclosure

Probably no responsibility of the SEC is more vital than the task of ensuring that sufficient, reliable information is disclosed by a company before its stocks, bonds, or other securities can be publicly traded. Unless specifically exempted, all publicly held companies (frequently referred to as *registrants*) must file detailed reports with the SEC periodically. These filings are required and regulated by the Securities and Exchange Commission as a result of a number of laws passed by Congress over the years:

1. Securities Act of 1933: Requires the registration of new securities offered for public sale so that potential investors can have adequate information. The act is also intended to prevent deceit and misrepresentation in connection with the sale of securities.[5]
2. Securities Exchange Act of 1934: Requires continuous reporting by publicly owned companies and registration of securities, security exchanges, and certain

---

[4]Inside parties usually are identified as the officers of a company as well as its directors and any owners of more than 10 percent of any class of equity security. An individual's level of ownership is measured by a person's own holdings of equity securities as well as ownership by a spouse, minor children, relatives living in the same house as the person in question, and a trust in which the person is the beneficiary.

[5]Interestingly, one of the provisions originally suggested for this act would have created a federal corps of auditors. The defeat of this proposal (after some debate) has allowed for the rise of the independent auditing profession as it is currently structured in the United States. For more information, see "The SEC and the Profession, 1934–1984: The Realities of Self-Regulation," by Mark Moran and Gary John Previts, *Journal of Accountancy,* July 1984.

brokers and dealers. This act prohibits fraudulent and unfair behavior such as sales practice abuses and insider trading.

3. **Public Utility Holding Company Act of 1935:** Requires registration of interstate holding companies of public utilities covered by this law. This act was passed because of abuses in the 1920s where huge, complex utility empires were created to minimize the need for equity financing.

4. **Trust Indenture Act of 1939:** Requires registration of trust indenture documents and supporting data in connection with the public sale of bonds, debentures, notes, and other debt securities.

5. **Investment Company Act of 1940:** Requires registration of investment companies that engage in investing and trading in securities.

6. **Investment Advisers Act of 1940 and Securities Investor Protection Act of 1970:** Require registration of investment advisers. Also require them to follow certain standards created to protect investors.

7. **Foreign Corrupt Practices Act of 1977:** Affects registration only indirectly through amendment to the Securities Exchange Act of 1934. This act requires the maintenance of accounting records and adequate internal accounting controls.

8. **Insider Trading Sanctions Act of 1984 and Insider Trading and Securities Fraud Enforcement Act of 1988:** Also affect registration only indirectly. Increase the penalties against persons who profit from illegal use of inside information and who are associated with market manipulation and securities fraud.

SEC Requirements As is obvious from the previous list of laws, the filing requirements administered by the SEC are extensive. Thus, accountants who specialize in working with the federal securities laws must develop a broad knowledge of a great many reporting rules and regulations. The SEC specifies most of these disclosure requirements in two basic documents, *Regulation S–K* and *Regulation S–X,* which are supplemented by periodic releases and staff bulletins.

Regulation S–K establishes requirements for all nonfinancial information contained in filings with the SEC. A description of the registrant's business as well as its securities are just two items covered by these regulations. A partial list of other nonfinancial data to be disclosed includes specified data about the company's directors and management, a discussion and analysis by the management of the current financial condition and the results of operations, and descriptions of both legal proceedings and the company's properties.

Regulation S–X prescribes the form and content of the financial statements (as well as the accompanying notes and related schedules) included in the various reports filed with the SEC. Thus, before being accepted, all financial information must meet a number of clearly specified requirements.

The SEC's Impact on Financial Reporting to Stockholders The SEC's disclosure and accounting requirements are not limited to the filings made directly with that body. *Rule 14c–3* of the 1934 Act states that the annual reports of publicly held companies should include financial statements that have been audited. This information (referred to as *proxy information* because it accompanies the management's request to cast votes for the stockholders at the annual meeting) must present balance sheets as of the end of the two most recent fiscal years along with income statements and cash flow statements for the three most recent years. *Rule 14c–3* also states that additional information, as specified in *Regulation S–K,* should be included in this annual report.

In recent years, the SEC has moved toward an *integrated disclosure system.* Under this approach, much of the same reported information that is required by the SEC must also go to the shareholders. Thus, the reporting process is simplified because only a single set of information must be generated in most cases. The integrated disclosure system is also intended as a way of improving the quality of the disclosures received directly by the shareholders.

Information required in proxy statements includes the following:

1. Five-year summary of operations including sales, total assets, income from continuing operations, and cash dividends per share.
2. Description of the business activities including principal products and sources and availability of raw materials.
3. Three-year summary of industry segments, export sales, and foreign and domestic operations.
4. Listing of company directors and executive officers.
5. Market price of the company's common stock for each quarterly period within the two most recent fiscal years.
6. Any restrictions on the company's ability to continue paying dividends.
7. Management's discussion and analysis of financial condition, changes in financial condition, and results of operations. Discussion should include liquidity, trends and significant events, causes of material changes in the financial statements, and the impact on the company of inflation.

In addition, the SEC has required certain disclosures in proxy statements describing the services provided by the registrant's independent external auditor. This information is intended as a means of helping to ensure that true independence is not endangered. Such disclosure must include:

1. All nonaudit services provided by the independent auditing firm.
2. A statement as to whether the board of directors (or its audit committee) approved all nonaudit services after considering the possibility that such services might impair the external auditor's independence.
3. The percentage of nonaudit fees to the total annual audit fee. This disclosure helps indicate the importance of the audit work to the firm versus the reward from any other services provided to the registrant.
4. Individual nonaudit fees that are larger than 3 percent of the annual audit fee.

The SEC's Authority over Generally Accepted Accounting Principles

Since financial reporting standards can be changed merely by amending *Regulation S–X,* the SEC holds the ultimate legal authority for establishing accounting principles for most publicly held companies in this country. In the past, the SEC has usually restricted the application of this power to disclosure issues while looking to the private sector (with the SEC's oversight) to formulate accounting principles. For this reason, the Financial Accounting Standards Board rather than the SEC is generally viewed today as the main standards-setting body for financial accounting in the United States. "Under federal law, the SEC has the mandate to determine accounting principles for publicly traded companies. But it has generally ceded that authority to private-sector accounting bodies such as the Financial Accounting Standards Board."[6]

However, the Securities and Exchange Commission does retain the ability to exercise its power with regard to the continuing evolution of accounting principles. The chief accountant of the SEC is responsible for providing the commissioners and the commission staff with advice on all current accounting and auditing matters and also helps to draft rules for the form and content of financial statement disclosure and other reporting requirements. "Perhaps the most powerful accounting position in the United

---

[6]Kevin G. Salwen and Robin Goldwyn Blumenthal, "Tackling Accounting, SEC Pushes Changes with Broad Impact," *The Wall Street Journal,* September 27, 1990, p. A1.

States is that of Chief Accountant of the SEC."[7] The work of the chief accountant can lead to amendments being passed by the SEC as needed to alter various aspects of *Regulation S–X.*

Financial Reporting Releases (FRRs) are issued currently by the SEC as needed to supplement *Regulation S–X* and *Regulation S–K.* They explain desired changes in the reporting requirements. By the end of 1998, 50 FRRs had been issued.[8] In addition, the staff of the SEC publishes a series of *Staff Accounting Bulletins* (SABs) as a means of informing the financial community of its views on current matters relating to accounting and disclosure practices.[9] For example, *SAB 101* was released late in 1999 to provide guidance in connection with the recognition of revenue. The bulletin first stated that any transaction that fell within the scope of specific authoritative literature (a FASB Statement, for example) should be reported based on that pronouncement. *SAB 101* then went on to establish guidelines for revenue recognition situations where authoritative standards were not available. In such cases, revenue should be recognized by a reporting entity when realized (or realizable) and earned. However, *SAB 101* then went further to establish four criteria for revenue recognition: evidence of an arrangement exists, delivery has occurred or services have been rendered, the price is fixed or can be determined, and collectibility is reasonably assured. To help apply these criteria in actual practice, *SAB 101* included nine examples to show how revenue recognition would be judged in such cases as the receipt of money in layaway programs and annual membership fees received by discount retailers.

Additional Disclosure Requirements Historically, the SEC has tended to restrict use of its authority (as can be seen in *SAB 101* above) to the gray areas of accounting where official guidance is not available. New reporting problems arise each year while many other accounting issues, even after years of discussion, have never been completely addressed by any authoritative body. As another response to such problems, the SEC will often require the disclosure of additional data if current rules are viewed as insufficient.

> It was in the 1970s that the SEC seemed to single out disclosure as the area in which it would take the standard-setting lead, leaving measurement issues to the FASB. This was when the SEC was expanding the coverage of Management's Discussion & Analysis (MD&A), an extensive narrative disclosure that is required to be appended to the financial statements.[10]

For example, in the early part of 1997, while the FASB worked on a project concerning the accounting for derivatives, the SEC approved rules so that more information would be available immediately. Footnote disclosure had to include more information about accounting policies in use. In addition, information was required about the risk of loss from market rate or price changes inherent in derivatives and other financial instruments. By means of these disclosures, the SEC enabled investors to have data about the potential consequences of the company's financial position.

Moratorium on Specific Accounting Practices The commission also can exert its power by declaring a moratorium on the use of specified accounting practices. When

---

[7]Skousen, An Introduction to the SEC, p. 16.

[8]From 1937 until 1982, more than 300 *Accounting Series Releases* (ASRs) were issued by the SEC to (1) amend *Regulation S–X,* (2) express interpretations regarding specific accounting and auditing issues, and (3) report disciplinary actions against public accountants. The ASRs that dealt with financial reporting matters of continuing interest were codified by the SEC in 1982 and issued as *Financial Reporting Release No. 1.*

[9]The SEC also releases *Accounting and Auditing Enforcement Releases* (AAER) when SEC enforcement activities are involved.

[10]Stephen A. Zeff, "A Perspective on the U.S. Public/Private-Sector Approach to the Regulation of Financial Reporting," *Accounting Horizons,* March 1995, pp. 58–59.

authoritative guidance is not present, the SEC can simply prohibit a particular method from being applied. As an example, in the 1980s, companies were utilizing a variety of procedures to account for internal computer software costs because no official pronouncement had yet been issued. Hence, the SEC

> imposed a moratorium that will prohibit companies that plan to go public from capitalizing the internal costs of developing computer software for sale or lease or marketed to customers in other ways. . . . The decision doesn't prevent companies currently capitalizing internal software expenses from continuing, but the companies must disclose the effect of not expensing such costs as incurred. The moratorium continues until the Financial Accounting Standards Board issues a standard on the issue.[11]

When the FASB eventually arrived at a resolution of this question by issuing *Statement 86,* "Accounting for the Costs of Computer Software to Be Sold, Leased, or Otherwise Marketed," the SEC dropped the moratorium. Hence, the FASB was allowed to set the accounting rule, but the SEC ensured appropriate reporting until that time.

Challenging Individual Statements   As described above, officially requiring additional disclosure and prohibiting the application of certain accounting practices are two methods used by the SEC to control the financial reporting process. Forcing a specific registrant to change its filed statements is another, less formal approach that can create the same effect. For example:

> Advanced Micro Devices, Inc., agreed to settle an investigation by the Securities and Exchange Commission of the semiconductor company's public disclosures. The SEC found AMD "made inaccurate and misleading statements" concerning development of its 486 microprocessor. In 1992 and 1993, AMD "led the public to believe that it was independently designing the microcode for its 486 microprocessor without access" to the code of its rival chipmaker, Intel Corp., the SEC said, "when, in fact, AMD had provided its engineers . . . with Intel's copyright 386 microcode to accelerate the company's development efforts." Without admitting or denying the commission's findings, AMD, based in Sunnyvale, California, consented to an order barring it from committing future violations of SEC rules. No fines were imposed.[12]

Following the action taken by the SEC, any company involved in a similar event would certainly be well advised to provide the suggested disclosure.

Overruling the FASB   The SEC's actions are not necessarily limited, however, to the gray areas of accounting. Although the commission has allowed the FASB (and previous authoritative groups) to establish accounting principles, the SEC retains the authority to override or negate any pronouncements produced in the private sector. This power was dramatically demonstrated in 1977 when the FASB issued *SFAS 19* "Financial Accounting and Reporting by Oil and Gas Producing Companies." After an extended debate over the merits of alternative methods, this statement was issued requiring oil and gas producing companies to apply the successful-efforts method when accounting for unsuccessful exploration and drilling costs.

In response, the SEC almost immediately invoked a moratorium on the use of this practice until an alternative approach could be evaluated. Thus, companies filing with the SEC were not allowed to follow the method established by the FASB (after years of formal study and deliberation by that body). Although the commission's reaction toward the accounting profession was a unique instance, the handling of this one issue clearly demonstrates the veto power that the SEC maintains over the work of the FASB.[13]

---

[11]"SEC Imposes 'Software Costs' Moratorium," *Journal of Accountancy,* September 1983, p. 3.

[12]"SEC Inquiry on Disclosure to Public Is Being Settled," *The Wall Street Journal,* October 1, 1996, p. B4.

[13]For a detailed account of the activities surrounding the SEC's rejection of *SFAS 19,* see "The SEC Decision Not to Support SFAS 19: A Case Study of the Effect of Lobbying on Standard Setting," by Donald Gorton in *Accounting Horizons,* March 1991.

Filings with the SEC

Because of legal regulations, registrants may be required to make a number of different filings with the SEC. The SEC actually receives hundreds of thousands of filings per year. However, for the overview being presented here, the reporting process is divided into two broad categories:

■ Registration statements.
■ Periodic filings.

Registration statements ensure the disclosure of sufficient, relevant financial data before a security can be *initially offered* to the public by either a company or its underwriters. The dissemination of such information is mandated by the Securities Act of 1933. Registration is necessary except in certain situations described at a later point in this chapter. The SEC charges a registration fee that was decreased in 1999 to an amount equal to $264 for each $1 million in value of the securities offered. In that year, the SEC collected about $1.7 billion in fees, an amount that was approximately five times its cost of operations. Not surprisingly, Congress has made known its intent that the SEC collect only enough fees to cover the government's cost. A nine-year program is underway to reduce certain fees and remove others to eliminate the surplus generated by the SEC.

After initial registration, periodic filings with the SEC are required of registrants by a number of federal laws, the most important of which is the Securities Exchange Act of 1934. This legislation has resulted in the *continual reporting of specified data* by all companies that have securities publicly traded on either a national securities exchange or an over-the-counter market.[14]

For registration statements as well as periodic filings, the SEC has established forms that provide the format and content to be followed in providing required information. "These forms contain no blanks to be filled in as do tax forms. Instead, they are narrative in character, giving general instructions about the items of information to be furnished. Detailed information must be assembled by the companies using the form designed for the type of security being offered as well as the type of company making the offer."[15]

Registration Statements   As indicated, a registration statement must be filed with and made effective by the Securities and Exchange Commission before a company can offer a security publicly. A security is broadly identified to include items such as a note, stock, treasury stock, bond, debenture, investment contract, evidence of indebtedness, or transferable share.

The SEC's role is not to evaluate the quality of the investment. Rather, the SEC seeks to ensure that the content and disclosure of the filing complies with all applicable regulations. The responsibility for the information always rests with the corporate officials. The SEC is charged with ensuring full and fair disclosure of relevant financial information. The registrant has the responsibility to provide such data, but the decision to invest must remain with the public.

A number of different forms are available for this purpose, depending on the specific circumstances. Some of the most commonly encountered registration statement forms are:

■ S–1   Used when no other form is prescribed. Usually used by new registrants or by companies that have been filing reports with the SEC for less than 36 months.

■ S–2   Used by companies that have filed with the SEC for 36 months or longer but are not large enough to file a Form S–3.

---

[14]A company that has securities traded on an over-the-counter market does not have to file under the 1934 Act unless it has at least $10 million in assets and 500 shareholders.

[15]Skousen, *An Introduction to the SEC,* p. 47.

- **S–3**   Used by companies that are large in size and already have a significant following in the stock market (at least $75 million of its voting stock is held by nonaffiliates). Disclosure is reduced for these organizations because the public is assumed to already have access to a considerable amount of information. Form F–3 is used if registration is by a foreign issuer.

- **S–4**   Used for securities issued in connection with business combination transactions.

- **S–8**   Used as a registration statement for employee stock plans.

- **S–11**   Used for the registration of securities by certain real estate companies.

- **SB–1**   Used by small business issuers to register up to $10 million of securities but only if the company has not registered more than $10 million of securities offerings during the previous 12 months. A small business issuer has annual revenues of less than $25 million and less than $25 million of voting securities held by nonaffiliates.

- **SB–2**   Used by small business issuers to register securities to be sold for cash.

The use of several of these forms, especially Form S–3, offer a distinct advantage to established companies that are issuing securities. Rather than duplicate voluminous information already disclosed in other filings with the SEC—frequently the annual report to shareholders—the registrant can simply indicate the location of the data in these other documents, a process referred to as *incorporation by reference.*

Registration Procedures   The actual registration process is comprised of a series of events leading up to the permission to "go effective" by the SEC. Since the registrant is seeking to obtain significant financial resources through the issuance of new securities in public markets, each of these procedures is of vital importance.

After selecting the appropriate form, information is accumulated by the company according to the requirements of *Regulation S–K* and *Regulation S–X*. If problems or questions are anticipated, a prefiling conference with the SEC staff may be requested by the company to seek guidance prior to beginning the registration. For example, if uncertainty exists concerning the handling or disclosure of an unusual transaction, a prefiling conference can save all parties considerable time and effort.

> The Commission has a long-established policy of holding its staff available for conferences with prospective registrants or their representatives in advance of filing a registration statement. These conferences may be held for the purpose of discussing generally the problems confronting a registrant in effecting registration or to resolve specific problems of an unusual nature which are sometimes presented by involved or complicated financial transactions.[16]

When received by the SEC, the registration statement is reviewed by the Division of Corporation Finance.[17] An analyst makes a determination as to whether all nonfinancial information complies with the SEC's disclosure requirements in *Regulation S–K*. At the same time, an accountant verifies that the financial statement data included in the filing meet the standards of *Regulation S–X* and have been prepared according to generally accepted accounting principles. *Since a formal audit is not conducted by the SEC, the report of the company's independent CPA is essential to this particular evaluation.* In addition, an SEC lawyer also reviews the registration statement to verify the legal aspects of the document.

---

[16]Stanley Weinstein, Daniel Schechtman, and Michael A. Walker, *SEC Compliance,* vol. 4 (Englewood Cliffs, NJ: Prentice-Hall, 1999), para. 30,641.

[17]All registration statements filed by issuers offering securities to the public for the first time are carefully reviewed. Subsequent registration statements and periodic filings are only reviewed on a selective basis.

The Division of Corporation Finance will almost invariably request clarifications, changes, or additional information, especially for those filings involving an initial registration. A *letter of comments* (also known as a *deficiency letter*) is issued to the company to communicate these findings. In most cases, the registrant attempts to provide the necessary data or changes to expedite the process. However, in controversial areas, the issuer may begin discussions directly with the SEC staff in hopes of resolving the problem without making the requested adjustments or disclosure or, at least, with limited inconvenience.

When the Division of Corporate Finance is eventually satisfied that all SEC regulations have been fulfilled, the registration statement is made effective and the securities can be sold. *Effectiveness does not, however, indicate an endorsement of the securities by the SEC.* With most offerings, the stock is actually sold by the company using one or more underwriters (stock brokerage firms) that market the shares to their clients to earn commissions.

For convenience and to save time and money, large companies are allowed to use a process known as *shelf registration.* They file once with the SEC and are then allowed to offer those securities at any time over the subsequent two years without having to go back to the SEC. For example, "Enterprise Products Partners L. P. announced today that it has filed an $800 million universal shelf registration statement with the Securities and Exchange Commission for the proposed sale of debt and equity securities over the next two years."[18]

In a similar manner, in recent years the SEC has considered moving more toward a system of registering companies rather than registering individual transactions to ease the burden of extensive reporting requirements. A company could possibly register on a periodic basis to cover all issuances during a set time.

The registration statement is physically composed of two parts. Part I, referred to as a *prospectus,* contains extensive information that includes:

1. Financial statements for the issuing company audited by an independent CPA along with appropriate supplementary data.
2. An explanation of the intended use of the proceeds to be generated by the sale of the new securities.
3. A description of the risks associated with the securities.
4. A description of the business and the properties owned by the company.

The registrant must furnish every potential buyer of the securities with a copy of this prospectus, thus ensuring the adequate availability of information for their investment analysis.

One interesting change in recent years has been the proposal that each prospectus be written in "plain English" to promote the investor's ability to understand the information. In the early part of 1997, the SEC proposed that the cover page of the prospectus as well as the summary and risk factors sections be written using six principles of clear writing: active voice, short sentences, everyday language, tabular presentation of complex material, no legal jargon, and no multiple negatives. For example,

Before Plain English: "The proxies solicited hereby for the Heartland Meeting may be revoked, subject to the procedures described herein, at any time up to and including the date of the Heartland Meeting."

In Plain English: "You may revoke your proxy at any time up to and including the day of the meeting by following the directions on page 18."[19]

---

[18]"Enterprise Files $800 Million Universal Shelf Registration with SEC," *Business Wire,* December 27, 1999.

[19]"SEC Proposes Mandating Plain English," *Journal of Accountancy,* April 1997, p. 10.

The use of plain English has been a popular initiative for the SEC. "The plain-language movement is enjoying a resurgence, and this time it could have staying power. Disdaining jargon and celebrating short, conversational sentences with active verbs, the latest effort began two years ago when the Securities and Exchange Commission ordered mutual funds to rewrite their prospectuses by December 1, 1999."[20] The SEC has even gone so far as to place a plain English handbook on its Web site (www.sec.gov/consumer/plaine.htm) with its preface written by famed investor Warren Buffett.[21]

Part II of the registration statement is primarily for the informational needs of the SEC staff. Additional data should be disclosed about the company and the securities being issued such as marketing arrangements, expenses of issuance, sales to special parties, and the like. The registrant is not required to provide this information to prospective buyers, although the entire registration statement is available to the public through the SEC.

Securities Exempt from Registration　　According to the 1933 Act, not all securities issued by companies and their underwriters require registration. For example, securities sold to the residents of the state in which the issuing company is chartered and principally doing business are exempted. However, these offerings are still regulated by the securities laws of the individual states (commonly known as *blue sky laws*) which vary significantly across the country.[22]

Other exempt offerings include but are not limited to the following:

- Securities issued by governments, banks, and savings and loan associations.
- Securities issued that are restricted to a company's own existing stockholders where no commission is paid to solicit the exchange.
- Securities issued by nonprofit organizations such as religious, educational, or charitable groups.
- Small offerings of no more than $5 million within a 12-month period. In most cases, though, a Regulation A offering circular must still be filed with the SEC and given to prospective buyers. However, much less information is required of a company in an offering circular than in a registration statement.
- Offerings of no more than $1 million made to any number of investors within a 12-month period. No specific disclosure of information is required. General solicitations are allowed. The issuer must give notice of the offering to the SEC within 15 days of the first sale.
- Offerings of no more than $5 million made to 35 or fewer purchasers in a 12-month period. No general solicitation is allowed for securities issued in this manner. Accredited investors (such as banks, insurance companies, and individuals with net worth of more than $1 million) are not included in the restriction on the number of buyers. Unaccredited investors must still be furnished with an audited balance sheet and other specified information. Parties making purchases have to hold the securities for at least two years or the filing exemption is lost.
- The private placement of securities to no more than 35 sophisticated investors (having knowledge and experience in financial matters) who already have sufficient information available to them about the issuing company. Again, the

---

[20]David Leonhardt, "In Language You Can Understand; SEC Edict Revives Push to Keep Documents Simple," *New York Times,* December 8, 1999, p. C–1.

[21]For further guidance in the use of plain English, consult "Securities Disclosure in Plain English" written by Byran A. Garner and published in 1999 by CCH Incorporated of Chicago, Illinois.

[22]"These early laws became known as 'blue sky' laws after a judicial decision characterized some transactions as 'speculative schemes which have no more basis than so many feet of blue sky.'" (Skousen, *An Introduction to the SEC,* p. 3.)

number of accredited investors is unlimited and general solicitation is not permitted. These private placement rules have become quite important in recent years. Private placements in the United States rose from $16 billion in 1980 to more than $200 billion in 1996. For example, "Digene Corporation today announced that it and certain of its stockholders completed a private placement of an aggregate of 1,500,000 shares of its common stock to selected institutions and other accredited investors on December 23, 1999."[23]

Periodic Filings with the SEC   Once a company has issued securities that are publicly traded on a securities exchange or an over-the-counter market, information must be continually filed with the SEC so that adequate disclosure is available. As with registration statements, several different forms are utilized for this purpose. However, for most companies with actively traded securities, three of these are common: Form 10–K (an annual report), Form 10–Q (a quarterly report), and Form 8–K (disclosure of significant events). Smaller businesses use Form 10–KSB for annual reports and Form 10–QSB for quarterly reports.

In addition, as mentioned previously, proxy statements must be filed with the SEC. These statements are issued to a company's owners by the management or another interested party in hopes of securing voting rights to be used at stockholders' meetings.

Form 10–K   A 10–K form is an annual report filed with the SEC to provide information and disclosures required by *Regulation S–K* and *Regulation S–X*. Fortunately, because of the integrated disclosure system, the annual report that is distributed by companies to their stockholders now includes most of the basic financial disclosures required by the SEC in Form 10–K. Thus, many companies simply attach the stockholders' annual report to the Form 10–K each year and use the incorporation by reference procedure to meet most of the SEC's filing requirements. This process is sometimes known as a *wrap around filing*.

Form 10–K, as with the various other SEC filings, is constantly undergoing assessment to determine if investor needs are being met. Thus, the SEC's reporting requirements are evolutionary and change over time.

> The Securities and Exchange Commission issued guidelines aimed at making public companies provide a more detailed look at the trends and business changes that management expects in the future. . . . In the main part of yesterday's interpretation, the commissioners said that in the 10–K reports, companies must discuss "trends, demands, commitments or events" that it knows are "reasonably likely" to occur and have a material effect on financial condition or results.[24]

As indicated by this quote, the SEC is especially interested in the quality of the information provided by the Management's Discussion and Analysis (MD&A) section of a registrant's filings. Basically, the management should describe verbally the company's past, present, and future. This information can furnish investors with a feel for the prospects of the company; it is a candid narrative to provide statement readers with a sense of management's priorities, accomplishments, and concerns. The MD&A is a feature carefully reviewed by the SEC staff. "If the management of a company knows something that could have a material impact on earnings in the future, officials have an obligation to share that information with shareholders."[25]

---

[23]"Digene Corporation Announces Completion of $19.5 Million Private Placement of Common Shares," *PR Newswire,* December 28, 1999.

[24]Paul Duke, Jr., "SEC Issues Guidelines for 10–K Filings Seeking More Details on Trends, Changes," *Wall Street Journal,* May 19, 1989, p. A2.

[25]Kevin G. Salwen, "SEC Charges Caterpillar Failed to Warn Holders of Earnings Risk Posed by Unit," *Wall Street Journal,* April 2, 1992, p. A3.

Form 10–Q   A 10–Q form contains condensed interim financial statements for the registrant and must be filed with the SEC shortly after the end of each quarter. However, no Form 10–Q is required following the fourth quarter of the year since a Form 10–K is forthcoming shortly thereafter. A Form 10–Q does not have to be audited by an independent CPA.

Information to be contained in each Form 10–Q includes the following:

- Income statements must be included for the most recent quarter and for the year to date as well as for the comparative periods in the previous year.
- A statement of cash flows is also necessary, but only for the year to date as well as for the corresponding period in the preceding year.
- Two balance sheets are reported: one as of the end of the most recent quarter with the second showing the company's financial position at the end of the previous fiscal year.
- Each Form 10–Q should also include any needed disclosures pertaining to the current period including the management's discussion and analysis of the financial condition of the company and results of operations.

Form 8–K   An 8–K form is used to disclose a unique or significant happening. Consequently, the 8–K is not filed at regular time intervals but rather within 15 calendar days of the event (or within 5 business days in certain specified instances). During 1996, the SEC received more than 20,000 8–K reports. According to the SEC's guidelines, Form 8–K may be filed to report any action that company officials believe is of importance to security holders. However, several events are designated for required disclosure in this manner; this list includes the following:

- Resignation of a director.
- Changes in control of the registrant.
- Acquisition or dispositions of assets.
- Changes in the registrant's certified accountants.
- Bankruptcy or receivership.

Proxy Statements   As was mentioned in a previous section, most of the significant actions undertaken by a company first must be approved at stockholders' meetings. For example, the members of the board of directors are elected in this manner to oversee the operations of the company. Although such votes are essential to the operations of a business, few major companies could possibly assemble enough shareholders at any one time and place for a voting quorum. The geographic distances are simply too great. Hence, before each of the periodic meetings, the management (or any other interested party) usually requests signed proxies from shareholders granting the legal authority to cast votes for the owners in connection with the various actions to be taken.[26]

Because of the power conveyed by a proxy, any such solicitation sent to shareholders (by any party) must include specific information as required by the SEC in its *Regulation 14A*. This proxy statement has to be filed with the SEC at least 10 days before being distributed. A number of the disclosed items were described previously. Other data that must be reported to the owners include:

- The proxy statement needs to indicate on whose behalf the solicitation is being made.
- The proxy statement must disclose fully all matters that are to be voted on at the meeting.
- In most cases, the proxy statement has to be accompanied (or preceded) by an annual report to the shareholders.

---

[26]Any person who owns at least 5 percent of the company's stock or has been an owner for six months or longer has the right to look at a list of shareholders to make a proxy solicitation.

DISCUSSION QUESTION

Is the Disclosure Worth the Cost?

Filing with the SEC requires a very significant amount of time and effort on the part of the registrant. Companies frequently resist attempts by the commission to increase the levels of disclosure. Usually, the argument is made that additional information will not necessarily be useful to a great majority of investors. Regardless of the issue, critics claim that the cost of the extra data will far outweigh any benefits that might be derived from this disclosure.

Such contentions are not necessarily made just to avoid disclosing information. One survey estimated the cost of SEC disclosures to be more than $400 million in 1975 alone. "The table reports an estimated $213,500,000 for the fully variable costs of 10–K, 10–Q and 8–K disclosures in 1975. To this should be added the separate estimate (not shown) of $191,900,000 for disclosure related to new issues in 1975, for a total estimate of about $400,000,000 for SEC disclosure costs in 1975. These estimates are biased downward because they do not include various fixed costs."[27] Such costs are either passed along to the consumer in the form of higher prices or serve to retard the growth of the reporting company.

The author of one survey (that has been widely discussed and debated over the years) held that federal securities laws are not actually helpful to investors.

> I found that there was little evidence of fraud related to financial statements in the period prior to the enactment of the Securities Acts. Nor was there a widespread lack of disclosure.... Hence, I conclude that there was little justification for the accounting disclosure required by the Acts.... These findings indicate that the data required by the SEC do not seem to be useful to investors.[28]

The SEC was created, in part, to ensure that the public has fair and full disclosure about companies that have their securities publicly traded. However, the commission must be mindful of the cost of such disclosures. How can the SEC determine whether the cost of a proposed disclosure is more or less than the benefits that will be derived by the public?

As with all areas of disclosure, the SEC's regulation of proxy statements has greatly enhanced the information available to investors. Historically, shareholders have not always been able to get adequate information.

> Thus was the president of one company able to respond cavalierly to a shareholder's request for information, "I can assure you that the company is in a good financial position. I trust that you will sign and mail your proxy at an early date." Quaint. But that was nothing. One unlisted company printed its proxy on the back of the dividend check—so when you endorsed the check you voted for management.[29]

> From a 1902 annual report to shareholders: "The settled plan has been to withhold all information from stockholders and others that is not called for by the stockholders in a body. So far no request for information has been made in the manner prescribed by the directors."[30]

Electronic Data Gathering, Analysis, and Retrieval System (Edgar)

During recent years, the SEC has become almost overwhelmed by the sheer mountains of documents that it receives, reviews, and makes available to the public. Filings with the SEC are estimated to contain 5 million pieces of paper each year.

In 1984, the SEC began to develop an electronic data gathering, analysis, and retrieval system nicknamed EDGAR. As originally envisioned, all filings would arrive

[27]J. Richard Zecher, "An Economic Perspective of SEC Corporate Disclosure," *The SEC and Accounting: The First 50 Years,* ed. Robert H. Mundheim and Noyes E. Leech (Amsterdam: North-Holland, 1985), pp. 75–76.

[28]George J. Benston, "The Value of the SEC's Accounting Disclosure Requirements," *The Accounting Review,* July 1969, p. 351.

[29]Laura Jereski, "You've Come a Long Way, Shareholder," *Forbes,* July 13, 1987, p. 282.

[30]Skousen, *An Introduction to the SEC,* p. 75.

at the SEC on disks or through some other electronic transmission. Each filing could be reviewed, analyzed, and stored by SEC personnel on a computer so they would no longer constantly have to shift through stacks of paper. Perhaps more importantly, investors would have the ability to access this data through the Internet. Thus, investors throughout the world could have information available for their decisions literally minutes after the documents are made effective by the SEC.

Because of the ambitious nature of the EDGAR project, approximately a decade was required to get the system effectively operational. For years, EDGAR was the object of much scorn; "one member of the House Energy and Commerce Committee suggested renaming the project Mr. Ed, 'since the SEC has a much better chance of finding a talking horse than it does of achieving an efficient computer filing system'."[31] However, the beginning of the explosive use of the Internet in the mid-1990s corresponded with the widescale availability of information on EDGAR. Not surprisingly, EDGAR's popularity grew rapidly.

> If you're suspicious about a certain stock, then go to the Securities and Exchange Commission's EDGAR database—chockablock with annual reports, prospectuses and all the other paperwork demanded of public companies.[32]

> For a thorough financial history of a company or mutual fund, or to view a prospectus, there's no more complete source than EDGAR, a Web site established by the SEC. Quarterly 10–Q and annual 10–K financial reports and other mandatory filings from public companies are posted on EDGAR within 24 hours after they are submitted to the SEC, as are prospectuses issued by public companies and mutual funds.[33]

This system is designed to benefit the registrant as well as the investor. The SEC hopes to make the entire filing system simpler for all parties.

> General Motors Acceptance Corporation, which has been filing on the EDGAR pilot program for several years, reports that EDGAR has substantially reduced the amount of time it takes to get SEC approval for GMAC deals. . . . Mr. Folbigg, of GMAC, agrees that small companies should be able to convert from paper to electronic filing without much trouble. "The key to the EDGAR system is a good secretary who can follow instructions," he says. GMAC does its filings via personal computer.[34]

SUMMARY

1. In the United States, the Securities and Exchange Commission (SEC) has been entrusted with the responsibility for ensuring that complete and reliable information is available to investors who buy and sell securities in public capital markets. Since being created in 1934, this agency has administered numerous reporting rules and regulations created by congressional actions starting with the Securities Act of 1933 and the Securities Exchange Act of 1934.

2. Before a company's securities (such as either equity or debt) can be publicly traded, appropriate filings must be made with the SEC to ensure that sufficient data is made available to potential investors. Disclosure requirement for this process are outlined in two documents: *Regulation S–K* (for nonfinancial information) and *Regulation S–X* (describing the form and content of all included financial statements).

---

[31]Block, "SEC Gets Closer to Electronic Filing," p. C1.

[32]The address for EDGAR is www.SEC.gov/edgarhp.htm. This site provides useful preliminary information about searching the EDGAR database. Joseph R. Garber, "Click Before You Leap," *Forbes*, February 24, 1997, p. 162.

[33]Randy Myers, "The Wired World of Investment Information," *Nation's Business*, March 1997, pp. 58–59.

[34]Block, "SEC Gets Closer to Electronic Filing," pp. C1 and C5.

3. The ability to require the reporting of special information gives the SEC enormous legal power over the accounting profession in the United States. Traditionally, this authority has been wielded only to increase disclosure requirements and to provide guidance where none was otherwise available. However, in a significant demonstration of its authority, the SEC overruled the FASB's decision in 1977 as to the appropriate method to account for unsuccessful exploration and drilling costs incurred by oil and gas producing companies.

4. Filings with the SEC are divided generally into two broad categories: registration statements and periodic filings. Registration statements are designed to provide information about a company prior to its issuance of a security to the public. Depending on the circumstances, several different registration forms are available for this purpose. After the statement is produced by the registrant and initially reviewed by the SEC, a letter of comments is furnished describing desired explanations or changes. These concerns must be resolved before the security can be sold.

5. Not all securities issued in the United States require registration with the SEC. As an example, formal registration is not necessary for securities sold by either government units or banks. Certain issues for relatively small amounts are also exempt although some amount of disclosure is normally required. Securities sold solely within the state in which the business operates are not subject to federal securities laws but must comply with state laws frequently referred to as *blue sky laws.*

6. Companies that have their stocks or bonds publicly traded on a securities exchange must also submit periodic filings to the SEC to ensure that adequate disclosure is constantly maintained. Among the most common of these filings are Form 10–K (an annual report) and Form 10–Q (condensed interim financial information). Form 8–K also is required to report any significant events that occur. In addition, proxy statements (documents that are used to solicit votes at stockholders' meetings) also come under the filing requirements monitored by the SEC.

7. The SEC has created the EDGAR database to allow companies an easier method of filing with the Commission. More importantly, EDGAR allows any person with access to the Internet to review these documents in a timely fashion. Thus, access to financial and other information about filing entities has become much more widely available.

QUESTIONS

1. Why were federal securities laws originally passed by Congress?
2. What is covered by *Regulation S–K*?
3. What is covered by *Regulation S–X*?
4. What are some of the major divisions within the SEC?
5. What is covered by the Securities Act of 1933?
6. What is covered by the Securities Exchange Act of 1934?
7. What are the goals of the SEC?
8. What information is required in a proxy statement?
9. Why is the content of a proxy statement considered to be so important?
10. How does the SEC affect the development of generally accepted accounting principles in the United States?
11. What is the purpose of Financial Reporting Releases and Staff Accounting Bulletins?
12. What was the SEC's response to the FASB's handling of accounting for oil and gas producing companies, and why was this action considered so significant?
13. What is the purpose of a registration statement? Under what law is a registration statement filed?
14. What are the two parts of a registration statement? What is contained in each part?
15. How does the SEC generate revenues?
16. Three forms commonly used in the registration process are Form S–1, Form S–3, and Form SB–2. Which registrants should use each of these forms?
17. What is incorporation by reference?

18. What is a prefiling conference, and why might it be helpful to a registrant?

19. What is a letter of comments? By what other name is a letter of comments often referred?

20. What is a prospectus? What is contained in a prospectus?

21. What is a shelf registration?

22. Under what circumstances is a company exempt from filing a registration statement with the SEC prior to the issuance of securities?

23. What is a private placement of securities?

24. What are blue sky laws?

25. What is a wrap around filing?

26. When is a Form 8–K issued by a company? What specific information does a Form 8–K convey?

27. What is the purpose of the Management's Discussion and Analysis?

28. What is the difference in a Form 10–K and a Form 10–Q?

29. What was the purpose of creating the EDGAR system?

INTERNET ASSIGNMENT

Internet sites are time and date sensitive. It is the purpose of these exercises to have you explore the Internet. You may need to refer to the text's Web site at http://www.mhhe.com/hoyle6e to find the most up-to-date links for the Web sites listed in the Internet Exercises.

1. Open the following Web site: www.SEC.gov/EDGARHP.HTM

   This site is the Search page for the EDGAR database maintained by the SEC. Enter the name of a well-known company such as PepsiCo or Xerox. You should receive a listing of available official documents. Answer the following questions:

   ■ How many documents has the company filed with the SEC during the most recent 12 months?

   ■ Has the company filed an 8–K during this period? If so, open the document and determine the reason that the form was filed with the SEC.

   ■ Has the company filed a 10–K during this period? If so, open the document and determine total assets and net income for the latest set of financial statements.

   ■ Has the company filed a 14A (a proxy statement) during this period? If so, open the document and determine what issues were to be voted on in the annual meeting.

LIBRARY ASSIGNMENTS

1. Locate a recent annual report of a publicly traded company such as Ford Motor Company or IBM. Read the Management's Discussion and Analysis for the most recent years. Write a report to answer the following questions:

   ■ What information is provided in the MD&A that is not found in the financial statements?

   ■ What were the most important pieces of information in the MD&A?

   ■ Was anything included in the MD&A that was purely speculation on the part of the management?

   ■ Was anything omitted from the MD&A that would have been helpful information?

2. Read the following as well as any other published information on the work of the SEC:

   "Tackling Accounting, SEC Pushes Changes with Broad Impact," *The Wall Street Journal,* September 27, 1990, p. A1.

   "Annual Reports: The SEC Cracks the Whip," *Business Week,* April 10, 1989.

   "A Perspective on the U.S. Public/Private-Sector Approach to the Regulation of Financial Reporting," *Accounting Horizons,* March 1995.

"The SEC and the Profession, 1934–84: The Realities of Self-Regulation," *Journal of Accountancy,* July 1984.

"Arthur Young Professors' Roundtable: The SEC—Past, Present, Future," *Journal of Accountancy* (News Feature Section), March 1985.

Write a report discussing the work of the SEC. Give a historical perspective as well as information on its current activities.

PROBLEMS

1. Which of the following statements is true?
    a. The Securities Exchange Act of 1934 regulates intrastate stock offerings made by a company.
    b. The Securities Act of 1933 regulates the subsequent public trading of securities through brokers and markets.
    c. The Securities Exchange Act of 1934 is commonly referred to as blue sky legislation.
    d. The Securities Act of 1933 regulates the initial offering of securities by a company.

2. What is the purpose of *Regulation S–K*?
    a. Defines generally accepted accounting principles in the United States.
    b. Establishes required disclosure of nonfinancial information with the SEC.
    c. Outlines enforcement procedures carried out by the SEC.
    d. Indicates which companies must file with the SEC on an annual basis.

3. What is the difference between *Regulation S–K* and *Regulation S–X*?
    a. *Regulation S–K* establishes reporting requirements for companies in their initial issuance of securities whereas *Regulation S–X* is directed toward the subsequent issuance of securities.
    b. *Regulation S–K* establishes reporting requirements for companies smaller than a certain size whereas *Regulation S–X* is directed toward companies larger than that size.
    c. *Regulation S–K* establishes regulations for nonfinancial information filed with the SEC whereas *S–X* prescribes the form and content of financial statements included in SEC filings.
    d. *Regulation S–K* establishes reporting requirements for publicly held companies whereas *S–X* is directed toward private companies.

4. The Securities Exchange Act of 1934:
    a. Regulates the public trading of previously issued securities through brokers and exchanges.
    b. Prohibits blue sky laws.
    c. Regulates the initial offering of securities by a company.
    d. Requires the registration of investment advisors.

5. What is a registration statement?
    a. A statement that must be filed with the SEC before a company can begin an initial offering of securities to the public.
    b. A required filing with the SEC before a large quantity of stock can be obtained by an inside party.
    c. An annual filing made with the New York Stock Exchange.
    d. A filing made by a company with the SEC to indicate that a significant change has occurred.

6. Which of the following is a registration statement used by large companies that already have a significant following in the stock market?
    a. Form 8–K.
    b. Form 10–K.
    c. Form S–1.
    d. Form S–3.

7. What was the significance of the controversy in 1977 over the appropriate accounting principles to be used by oil and gas producing companies?
   a. Several major lawsuits resulted.
   b. Companies refused to follow the dictates of the SEC.
   c. Partners of a major accounting firm were indicted on criminal charges.
   d. The SEC overruled the FASB on the handling of this matter.

8. Which of the following must be provided to every potential buyer of a new security?
   a. A letter of comments.
   b. A deficiency letter.
   c. A prospectus.
   d. Form S–16.

9. What is meant by the term *incorporation by reference*?
   a. The legal incorporation of a company in more than one state.
   b. Filing information with the SEC by indicating that the information is already available in another document.
   c. A reference guide indicating informational requirements specified in *Regulation S–X*.
   d. Incorporating a company in a state outside of its base of operations.

10. What is a letter of comments?
    a. A letter sent to a company by the SEC indicating needed changes or clarifications in a registration statement.
    b. A questionnaire supplied to the SEC by a company suggesting changes in *Regulation S–X*.
    c. A letter included in a Form 10–K to indicate the management's assessment of the company's financial position.
    d. A letter composed by a company asking for information or clarification prior to the filing of a registration statement.

11. What is a prospectus?
    a. A document attached to a Form 8–K.
    b. A potential stockholder as defined by *Regulation S–K*.
    c. A document filed with the SEC prior to the filing of a registration statement.
    d. The first part of a registration statement that must be furnished by a company to all potential buyers of a new security.

12. Which of the following is not exempt from registration with the SEC under the Securities Act of 1933?
    a. Securities issued by a nonprofit religious organization.
    b. Securities issued by a government unit.
    c. A public offering of no more than $5.9 million.
    d. An offering made to only 26 sophisticated investors.

13. Which of the following is usually not filed with the SEC on a regular periodic basis?
    a. Form 10–Q.
    b. A prospectus.
    c. A proxy statement.
    d. Form 10–K.

14. What is a shelf registration?
    a. A registration statement that is formally rejected by the SEC.
    b. A registration statement that is rejected by the SEC due to the lapse of a specified period of time.
    c. A registration process for large companies that allows them to offer securities over a period of time without seeking additional approval by the SEC.
    d. A registration form that is withdrawn by the registrant without any action having been taken.

15. What is EDGAR?
    a. A system used by the SEC to reject registration statements that do not contain adequate information.
    b. The enforcement arm of the SEC.
    c. A system designed by the SEC to allow electronic filings.
    d. A branch of the government that oversees the work of the SEC.

16. Identify each of the following as they pertain to the SEC.
    - Blue sky laws.
    - S–1 Statement.
    - Letter of deficiencies.
    - Prospectus.

17. Discuss the objectives of the Securities Act of 1933 and the Securities Exchange Act of 1934. How are these objectives accomplished?

18. What are the steps involved in filing a registration statement with the SEC?

19. Discuss the methods by which the SEC can influence the development of generally accepted accounting principles in the United States.

20. Which forms do most companies file with the SEC on a periodic basis? Explain the purpose of each form and its primary contents.

21. Which forms do most companies file with the SEC in connection with the offering of securities to the public?

22. What is the importance of a Form 8-K? What is the importance of a proxy statement?

23. Discuss each of the following items:
    - Financial reporting relases.
    - Wrap around filing.
    - Incorporation by reference.
    - Division of corporation finance.
    - Integrated disclosure system.
    - Management's discussion and analysis.
    - Chief accountant of the SEC.

24. Which organizations are normally exempted from the registration requirements imposed by the SEC?

13

Accounting for Legal Reorganizations and Liquidations

QUESTIONS TO CONSIDER

- What is the difference between a voluntary and an involuntary bankruptcy petition?

- How does the liquidation of an insolvent company (a Chapter 7 bankruptcy) differ from a reorganization (a Chapter 11 bankruptcy)?

- Why would the creditors of an insolvent company allow it to reorganize rather than attempt to force a liquidation of its assets?

- What assistance can be provided to an insolvent company by an accountant?

- What provisions are frequently found in a bankruptcy reorganization plan?

- What financial reporting is made for a company while it is going through reorganization?

- What financial reporting is made for a company that successfully leaves bankruptcy reorganization?

- If an insolvent company is liquidated, what distribution is made of the assets that result? How is a fair and equitable settlement produced?

- In bankruptcy cases, what is meant by terms such as *debtor in possession,* *cram down,* and *order for relief?*

One common thread that runs through a significant portion of this textbook is the accounting for an organization when viewed as a whole.[1] Several chapters, for example, examine the consolidation of financial information generated by two or more companies that have been united in a business combination. Although the handling of specific accounts was included in that coverage, the primary emphasis was placed on reporting these companies as a single economic entity.

Likewise, the analysis of foreign currency translation demonstrated the procedures to be used in consolidating the financial position and operating results of a subsidiary doing business anywhere in the world. The various reporting requirements for disaggregated information have been presented as another means of disclosing complete information to describe an entity. Once again, in both cases, the accounting goal was to convey data about the entire operation.

Continuing with this theme, subsequent chapters present the specialized accounting procedures utilized by partnerships, state and local government units, not-for-profit organizations, estates, and trusts.

The method by which financial data should be accumulated and disclosed to describe an organization is not a rigid structure. Accounting is adaptable; its development in specific circumstances is influenced by several factors: the purpose of the information, the nature of the organization, the environment in which the entity operates, and so on. Thus, in reporting the operations and financial position of a business combination, a foreign subsidiary, an industry

---

[1] Intermediate accounting, in contrast, tends to examine the reporting of specific assets and liabilities such as leases, pensions, deferred income taxes, and bonds.

segment, a partnership, a government unit, an estate, or a not-for-profit organization, accountants must develop unique reporting techniques that address particular needs and problems.

The current chapter extends this coverage by presenting the accounting procedures required in bankruptcy cases. A financially troubled company as well as its owners and creditors all face the prospect of incurring significant losses. Thus, the accountant must adapt financial reporting to meet many and varied informational needs. The large number of failed businesses in recent years has made this accounting process especially important.

ACCOUNTING FOR LEGAL REORGANIZATIONS AND LIQUIDATIONS

> Centuries ago in Italy the bankrupt merchant would be forced into an odd form of pillory. He would have the table he did business at in the town square broken. At least one source says the word *bankruptcy* derives from the Italian words for this practice, which translate to *broken bench.*[2]

A basic assumption of accounting is that a business is considered a *going concern* unless evidence to the contrary is discovered. As a result, assets such as inventory, land, buildings, and equipment are reported based on historical cost rather than net realizable value. Unfortunately, not all companies prove to be going concerns. In 1999 alone, 37,884 businesses failed in the United States.[3] That number has actually been falling in recent years because of the strong national economy.

A list of organizations beginning bankruptcy proceedings during recent years contains some of the best-known corporate names in America:

Boston Chicken	Long John Silver's Restaurants
Crown Books	Dow Corning
Grand Union	Kiwi International Air Lines
Presidential Airlines	Service Merchandise
L. A. Gear	Geneva Steel
Montgomery Ward	This End Up
Phar-Mor	Zenith Electronics
Tultex	Iridium[4]
Kaiser Steel	

What happens to these businesses after they fail? Who gets the assets? Are the creditors protected? How does the accountant reflect the economic plight of the company?

Virtually all businesses undergo financial difficulties at various times. Economic downturns, poor product performance, or litigation losses can create cash flow difficulties for even the best-managed organizations. Most companies take remedial actions and work to return their operations to normal profitability. However, as the preceding list indicates, not all companies are able to solve their monetary difficulties. If problems persist, a company can eventually become *insolvent,* unable to pay debts as the obligations come due. When creditors are not paid, they obviously attempt to protect

---

[2]"In Pursuit of a Balanced Bankruptcy Law," *ABA Banking Journal,* May 1993, p. 50.

[3]Patricia Manson, "Bankruptcy Filings Drop 8.5% Nationally, Report Shows," *Chicago Daily Law Bulletin,* March 6, 2000, p. 1.

[4]The author (JH) is personally aware of the trauma associated with bankruptcy because he owned several hundred shares of Presidential Airlines, Tultex, and Kaiser Steel at the time each company filed for bankruptcy. The demise of these companies may be taken as an indication of the author's astute investment expertise.

their financial interests in hopes of reducing the possibility of loss. They may seek recovery from the distressed company in several ways: repossession of assets, the filing of lawsuits, foreclosure on loans, and so on. An insolvent company can literally become besieged by its creditors.

If left unchecked, pandemonium would be the possible outcome of a company's insolvency. As a result, some of the creditors and stockholders as well as the company itself could find themselves treated unfairly. One party might be able to collect in full while another is left with a total loss. *Thus, bankruptcy laws have been established in the United States to structure this process, provide protection for all parties, and ensure fair and equitable treatment.*

Although a complete coverage of bankruptcy statutes is more appropriate for a business law textbook, significant aspects of this process directly involve accountants. "In many small business situations, the company accountant is the sole outside financial advisor and the first to recognize that the deteriorating financial picture mandates consideration of bankruptcy in one form or another. In many such situations, the accountant's role in convincing management that a timely reorganization under the bankruptcy law is the sole means of salvaging any part of the business may be critical."[5]

Bankruptcy Reform Act of 1978

Over the ages debtors who found themselves unable to meet obligations were dealt with harshly. Not only were all their assets taken from them, but they were given little or no relief through legal forgiveness of debts. Many of them ended up in debtors' prisons with all means of rehabilitation removed. A large number of the early settlers in this country left their homelands to escape such a fate.[6]

Based on an original provision of the U.S. Constitution, all bankruptcy laws in this country must be created by Congress. However, virtually no federal bankruptcy laws were actually passed until the Bankruptcy Act of 1898 (which was subsequently revised in 1938 by the Chandler Act). Later, following a decade of study and debate by Congress, these laws were replaced with the Bankruptcy Reform Act of 1978. Congress subsequently revised and updated that act by passing the Bankruptcy Reform Act of 1994. In 2001, the U.S. House of Representatives and Senate both passed legislation to revise the bankruptcy laws. To date, reconciliation of these two bills has progressed slowly. Most of the proposed changes deal with personal bankruptcy because of the tremendous growth in such cases recently. Little push seems evident at this time for sweeping changes in bankruptcy laws that apply to businesses.

Currently, the Bankruptcy Reform Act of 1978 as amended continues to provide the legal structure for most bankruptcy proceedings.[7] *To this end, it strives to achieve two goals in connection with insolvency cases: (1) the fair distribution of assets to creditors and (2) the discharge of an honest debtor from debt.*

Voluntary and Involuntary Petitions   When insolvency occurs, any interested party has the right to seek protection under the Bankruptcy Reform Act.[8] Thus, the company itself can file a petition with the court to begin bankruptcy proceedings. If the company

---

[5]John K. Pearson, "The Role of the Accountant in Business Bankruptcies," *The National Public Accountant,* November 1982, p. 22.

[6]Homer A. Bonhiver, *The Expanded Role of the Accountant under the 1978 Bankruptcy Code* (New York: Deloitte Haskins & Sells, 1980), p. 7.

[7]The Bankruptcy Reform Act applies to corporations, partnerships, and individuals. However, certain types of companies are excluded from portions or even all of its provisions because other laws are applicable. Such organizations include insurance companies, banks, railroads, and stockbrokers.

[8]As is discussed later in this chapter, insolvency (not being able to pay debts as they come due) is not necessary for the filing of a bankruptcy petition. Such companies as the Manville Corporation, Texaco, and A. H. Robins have filed for protection under the Bankruptcy Reform Act in hopes of settling massive litigation claims.

is the instigator, the process is referred to as a *voluntary* bankruptcy. In such cases, the company's petition has to be accompanied by exhibits listing all debts as well as assets (reported at fair market value). Company officials also must respond to questions concerning various aspects of the business's affairs. Such questions include:

- When did the business commence?
- In whose possession are the books of account and records?
- When was the last inventory of property taken?

Creditors also may seek to force a debtor into bankruptcy (known as an *involuntary* bankruptcy) in hopes of reducing their potential losses. To avoid nuisance actions, bankruptcy laws regulate the filing of involuntary petitions. Where a company has 12 or more unsecured creditors, at least 3 have to sign the petition. In addition, under current rules, the creditors that sign must have unsecured debts of at least $10,775. If fewer than 12 unsecured creditors exist, only a single signer is required but the $10,775 minimum debt limit remains. "L. L. Knickerbocker Co., of Lake Forest, California, said three Asian creditors filed an involuntary bankruptcy petition seeking to force the company to liquidate its assets. Knickerbocker didn't identify the creditors further, but said 'the company is currently evaluating its options,' including opposing the petition."[9]

Neither a voluntary nor an involuntary petition automatically creates a bankruptcy case. Voluntary petitions are rejected by the court if the action is considered detrimental to the creditors. Involuntary petitions also can be rejected unless evidence exists to indicate that the debtor is not actually able to meet obligations as they come due. Merely being slow to pay is not sufficient. The debtor may well fight an involuntary petition fearing that it will taint its reputation in the business community.

If the petition is accepted by the court, an *order for relief* is granted. This order halts all actions against the debtor, thus providing time for the various parties involved to develop a course of action. In addition, the company comes under the authority of the bankruptcy court so that any distributions must be made in a fair manner. "To prevent creditors from seizing whatever is handy once the bankruptcy is filed, the Bankruptcy Code provides for an automatic stay or injunction that prohibits actions by creditors to collect debts from the debtor or the debtor's property without the court's permission. The automatic stay bars any creditor (including governmental creditors such as the Internal Revenue Service) from taking any action against the debtor or the debtor's property."[10]

Classification of Creditors   Following the issuance of an order for relief, each creditor's view of a bankruptcy case is obviously influenced by the possible risk of loss. However, many creditors may have already obtained some measure of security for themselves. At the time a debt is created, the parties can agree that a mortgage lien or security interest will be attached to specified assets (known as *collateral*) owned by the debtor. Such action is most likely when the amounts involved are great or the debtor is experiencing financial difficulty. In the event that the liability is not paid when due, the creditor has the right to force the sale (or, in some cases, the return) of the pledged property with the proceeds being used to satisfy all or part of the obligation. Thus, in bankruptcy proceedings, a secured creditor is in a much less vulnerable position than an unsecured creditor.

Because of the possible presence of liens, all loans and other liabilities are reported to the court according to their degree of protection against loss. Hence, some debts are identified as *fully secured* to indicate that the net realizable value of the collateral exceeds the amount of the obligation. Despite the debtor's insolvency, these creditors will

[9]"Three Creditors Petition to Liquidate the Company," *Wall Street Journal,* August 26, 1999, p. C15.
[10]Pearson, "The Role of the Accountant," p. 24.

not suffer loss; they are completely protected by the pledged property. Any money received from the asset that is in excess of the balance of the debt is used to pay unsecured creditors.

Conversely, if a liability is labeled as *partially secured,* the value of the collateral covers only a portion of the obligation. The remainder is considered unsecured so that the creditor risks losing some or all of this additional amount. As an example, a bank might have a $90,000 loan due from an insolvent party protected by a lien attached to land valued at $64,000. This debt is only partially secured; $26,000 of the balance would not be satisfied by the asset so that this portion must be reported to the court as unsecured.

All other liabilities are unsecured; these creditors have no legal right to any specific assets of the debtor. They are only entitled to share in any funds that remain after all secured claims have been settled. Obviously, unsecured creditors are in a precarious position. Unless a debtor's assets greatly exceed secured liabilities (which is unlikely in most insolvency cases), significant losses can be expected if liquidation is necessary. Hence, one of the most important aspects of the bankruptcy laws is the ranking of unsecured claims. Only in this manner is a systematic distribution of any remaining assets possible.

The Bankruptcy Reform Act does identify several types of unsecured liabilities that have priority and must be paid before other unsecured debts are settled. *These obligations are ranked with each level having to be satisfied in full before any payment is made to the next.*

Unsecured Liabilities Having Priority[11]

1. Claims for administrative expenses such as the costs of preserving and liquidating the estate. All trustee expenses are included in this category as well as the costs of outside attorneys, accountants, or other consultants. Without this high-priority ranking, insolvent companies would have extreme problems convincing qualified individuals to serve in these essential positions. However, in recent years, the amounts assessed for such services have come under fire from many critics: "The 26 firms involved in the Eastern Air Lines Inc. bankruptcy in 1989 charged close to $86 million in fees."[12] "After six years in Chapter 11 bankruptcy-court proceedings, the documents show, the trustee of (Finley Kumble's) estate collected $60 million in cash for the creditors. But some $48 million, or 80 percent, has been spent just on operating and administering the bankruptcy case."[13]

2. Obligations arising between the date that a petition is filed with the bankruptcy court and the appointment of a trustee or the issuance of an order for relief. In voluntary cases, such claims are quite rare since an order for relief is usually entered at the time the petition is filed. This provision is important, however, in helping the debtor to continue operations if an involuntary petition is presented but no legal action is immediately taken. Without this ranking, suppliers would stop supplying merchandise to the debtor until the matter was resolved. The debtor can continue to buy goods and stay in business while resisting an involuntary petition.

3. Employee claims for wages earned during the 90 days preceding the filing of a petition. The amount of this priority is limited, though, to $4,300 per

---

[11]Only the most significant unsecured liabilities that are given priority are included here. For a complete list, please check a current business law textbook.

[12]Ronald Glover, Kathleen Kerwin, and Lisa Driscoll, "There's Plenty for All at the Bankruptcy Banquet," *Business Week,* November 4, 1991, p. 124.

[13]Amy Stevens, "Finley Kumble's Creditors Left Wanting but Bankruptcy Pros Collect Their Fees," *Wall Street Journal,* April 8, 1994, p. B1.

DISCUSSION QUESTION

What Do We Do Now?

The Toledo Shirt Company manufactures men's shirts sold to department stores and other outlets throughout Ohio, Illinois, and Indiana. For the past 14 years, one of the Toledo's major customers has been Abraham and Sons, a chain of nine stores selling men's clothing, Unfortunately, 18 months ago, Mr. Abraham retired and his two sons took complete control of the organization. Since that time, they have invested enormous sums of money in an attempt to expand each store by selling women's clothing. Success in this new market has been difficult; Abraham and Sons is not known for selling women's clothing and no one in the company has much expertise in the area.

Approximately seven months ago, James Thurber, the chief financial officer of the Toledo Shirt Company, began to notice that it was taking longer than usual to collect payments from Abraham and Sons. Instead of the normal 30 days, the retailer was taking at least 45 days—and frequently longer—to pay each invoice. Because of the amount of money involved, Thurber began to monitor the balance each day. When the age of the receivable ($71,000) hit 65 days, he placed a call to Abraham and Sons. The treasurer assured him that the company was merely having seasonal cash flow problems but that payments would soon be back on a normal schedule.

Thurber was still concerned and shortly thereafter placed Abraham and Sons on a "cash and carry" basis; no sales were to be made unless cash was collected in advance. The company's treasurer immediately called Thurber to complain bitterly. "We have been one of your best customers for well over a decade but now that we have gotten into a bit of trouble you stab us in the back. When we straighten things out here, we will remember this. We can get our shirts from someone else. Our expansions are now complete; we have hired an expert to help us market women's clothing. We can see the light at the end of the tunnel. Abraham and Sons will soon be more profitable than ever." In hopes of appeasing the customer while still protecting his own position, Thurber agreed to sell merchandise to Abraham and Sons on a very limited credit basis.

A few days later, Thurber received a disturbing phone call from a vice president with another clothing manufacturer. "We've got to force Abraham and Sons into bankruptcy immediately to protect ourselves. Those guys are running the company straight into the ground. They owe me $38,000 and I can only hope to collect a small portion of it now. I need two other creditors to sign the petition and I want Toledo Shirt to be one of them. Abraham and Sons has already mortgaged all of its buildings and equipment so we can't get anything from those assets. Inventory stocks are dwindling and sales have disappeared since they've tried to change the image of their stores. We can still get some of our money but if we wait much longer nothing will be left but the bones."

Should the Toledo Shirt Company be loyal to a good customer or start the bankruptcy process to protect itself? What actions should Thurber take?

individual.[14] This priority ranking does not include officers' salaries. It is designed to prevent employees from being penalized by the company's problems and also encourages them to continue working until the bankruptcy issue is settled. In addition, employees are not company creditors in the traditional sense of that term. They did not enter employment to serve as lenders to the corporation.

4. Employee claims for contributions to benefit plans earned during the 180 days preceding the filing of a petition. Once again, a limit of $4,300 per individual (reduced by certain specified payments) is enforced.

5. Claims for the return of deposits made by customers to acquire property or services which were never delivered or provided by the debtor. The priority figure, in this case, is limited to $1,950. These claimants did not intend to be creditors; they were merely trying to make a purchase.

6. Government claims for unpaid taxes.

---

[14]Throughout the bankruptcy laws, a number of monetary standards such as this exist. For example, as indicated earlier, creditors must hold a minimum debt of $10,775 to force a company into bankruptcy. Such dollar amounts were last adjusted for inflation on April 1, 1998. These balances are to be adjusted every three years based on the Consumer Price Index for All Urban Consumers.

All other obligations of an insolvent company are classified as general unsecured claims that can be repaid only after the creditors with priority have been satisfied. *If the funds that remain for the general unsecured debts are not sufficient to settle all claims, the available money must be divided proportionally.*

Liquidation versus Reorganization   The most important decision in any bankruptcy filing (either voluntary or involuntary) is the method by which the debtor will be discharged from its obligations. One obvious option is to liquidate the company's assets with the proceeds being distributed to creditors based on their secured positions and the priority ranking system just outlined. However, a very important alternative to liquidation does exist. The debtor company may survive insolvency and continue operations if a proposal for reorganization is accepted by the parties involved.

> There are many reasons why a business gets sick, but they don't necessarily mean it should be destroyed. Hundreds of thousands of businesses that at one time or another had financial difficulties survive today as the result of Chapter 11 proceedings. They continue to contribute to employment, to tax revenues, to overall growth. It's counterproductive to destroy the business value of an asset by liquidating it and paying it out in a Chapter 7 if that company shows signs of being able to recover in a reorganization.[15]

Under most reorganization plans, the creditors agree to absorb a partial loss rather than force the insolvent company to liquidate. Before accepting such an arrangement, the creditors (as well as the bankruptcy court) must be convinced that a greater return will be achieved by helping to rehabilitate the debtor. Often, as an example, payment of a specified percentage of the debt is promised to the creditors but usually only at some future date. One benefit associated with reorganizations is that the creditor may be able to retain the insolvent company as a customer. In many cases, continuation of this relationship is an important concern if the debtor historically has been a good client. Furthermore, the priority ranking system often leaves the general unsecured creditors with very little to lose in trying to avoid a liquidation.

Legal guidelines for the liquidation of a debtor are contained in Chapter 7 of Title I of the Bankruptcy Reform Act while Chapter 11 describes the reorganization process. Consequently, the proceedings have come to be referred to as a "Chapter 7 bankruptcy" (liquidation) or a "Chapter 11 bankruptcy" (reorganization). Accountants face two entirely different reporting situations depending on the type of bankruptcy encountered. However, in both cases, sufficient data must be obtained and reported to keep all parties adequately informed about the events as they occur.

Statement of Financial Affairs

Normally, at the start of bankruptcy proceedings, a statement of financial affairs is prepared for the debtor.[16] This schedule provides information about the current financial position of the company and helps all of the parties as they consider what actions to take. This statement is especially important in assisting the unsecured creditors as they decide whether to push for reorganization or liquidation. The debtor's assets and liabilities are reported according to the classifications relevant to a liquidation.

Consequently, assets are labeled as:

1. Pledged with fully secured creditors.

2. Pledged with partially secured creditors.

---

[15]James A. Goodman as interviewed by Robert A. Mamis, "Why Bankruptcy Works," *Inc.,* October 1996, p. 39.

[16]The questionnaire completed by the insolvent company at the beginning of the bankruptcy proceedings is referred to as a statement of affairs. Although the titles are similar, the schedule of assets and liabilities discussed here is quite different from the legal questionnaire.

How Much Is That Building Really Worth?

Viron, Inc., was created in 1996 to recycle plastic products and manufacture a variety of new items. The actual production process was quite complex in that the old plastic had to be divided into categories and then reclaimed based on the composition. New products were made based on the type of plastic available and the market demand.

In December 1998, the company spent $2.3 million to construct a building for manufacturing purposes. The facility was designed specifically to meet the needs of Viron. The building was constructed near Gaffney, South Carolina, to take advantage of a large labor force available because of high unemployment in the area.

Unfortunately, the company was not able to generate revenues quickly enough to reach a break-even point and was forced to file for bankruptcy. An accountant has been hired to produce a statement of financial affairs to aid the parties in deciding whether to liquidate or reorganize.

In producing the statement of financial affairs, the accountant needed to establish a liquidation value for the building that was the company's largest asset. A real estate appraiser was brought in who made the following comments about the building: "The building is well made and practically new. It is clearly worth over $2 million. However, I doubt that anyone is going to pay that much for it. We don't get a lot of new industry in this area, so not many companies need to buy large buildings. Even if a company did buy the building, it would have to spend a significant amount of money for conversion purposes. Unless a company just wanted to recycle plastics, the building would have to be completely adapted to any other purpose. To tell you the truth, I am not sure it can be sold at any price. Of course, if someone wants to recycle plastics, it just might bring $2 million."

In producing the statement of financial affairs, how should the accountant report this building?

3. Available for priority liabilities and unsecured creditors (often referred to as *free assets*).

The debts of the company are then listed in a parallel fashion as:

1. Liabilities with priority.
2. Fully secured creditors.
3. Partially secured creditors.
4. Unsecured creditors.

Stockholders are included in this final group.

The statement of financial affairs is produced under the assumption that liquidation will occur. Thus, historical cost figures are not relevant. The various parties to the bankruptcy desire information that reflects (1) the net realizable value of the debtor's assets and (2) the ultimate application of these proceeds to specific liabilities. Based on this data, both creditors and stockholders are able to estimate the monetary resources that will be available after all secured claims and priority liabilities have been settled. By comparing this total with the amount of unsecured liabilities, any member of these groups can approximate the potential loss that is being faced.

The information found in a statement of financial affairs can affect the outcome of the bankruptcy. If, for example, the statement indicates that unsecured creditors are destined to suffer a material loss in a liquidation, this group will probably favor reorganizing the company in hopes of averting such a consequence. Conversely, if the statement shows that all creditors will be paid in full and that a distribution to the stockholders is also possible, liquidation becomes a much more viable option. Thus, all parties involved with an insolvent company should consult a statement of financial affairs before deciding on the fate of the operation.

Statement of Financial Affairs Illustrated

To demonstrate the preparation of this statement, assume that the Chaplin Company has experienced severe financial difficulties in recent times and is currently insolvent. A voluntary bankruptcy petition will soon be filed and company officials are trying to

Exhibit 13–1
Financial Position Prior to
Bankruptcy Petition

CHAPLIN COMPANY
Balance Sheet
June 30, 2001
Assets

Current assets:

Cash	$ 2,000	
Investment (equity method)	15,000	
Accounts receivable (net)	23,000	
Inventory	41,000	
Prepaid expenses	3,000	$ 84,000

Land, building, equipment, and other assets:

Land	100,000	
Building (net)	110,000	
Equipment (net)	80,000	
Intangible assets	15,000	305,000
Total assets		$389,000

Liabilities and Stockholders' Equity

Current liabilities:

Notes payable (secured by inventory)	$ 75,000	
Accounts payable	60,000	
Accrued expenses	18,000	$153,000

Long-term liabilities:

Notes payable (secured by lien on land and buildings)		200,000

Stockholders' equity:

Common stock	100,000	
Retained earnings (deficit)	(64,000)	36,000
Total liabilities and stockholders' equity		$389,000

decide whether to seek liquidation or reorganization. Consequently, they have asked their accountant to produce a statement of financial affairs to assist them in formulating an appropriate strategy. A current balance sheet for Chaplin, prepared as if the company were a going concern, is presented in Exhibit 13–1.

Prior to the creation of a statement of financial affairs, additional data must be ascertained concerning the insolvent company and its assets and liabilities. Hence, in this illustration, the following information has been accumulated about the Chaplin Company:

- The investment reported on the balance sheet has appreciated in value since being acquired and is now worth $20,000. Dividends of $500 are currently due from this investment, although the revenue has not yet been recognized by Chaplin.

- Officials estimate that $12,000 of the company's accounts receivable can still be collected despite the bankruptcy proceedings.

- By spending $5,000 for repairs and marketing, the inventory currently held by Chaplin can be sold for $50,000.

- A refund of $1,000 will be received from the various prepaid expenses but the company's intangible assets have no resale value.

- The land and building are in an excellent location and can be sold for a figure 10 percent more than book value. However, the equipment was specially designed for Chaplin. Company officials anticipate having trouble finding a buyer unless the price is reduced considerably. Hence, they expect to receive only 40 percent of current book value for these assets.

■ Administrative costs of $21,500 are projected if liquidation of the company does occur.

■ Accrued expenses include salaries of $13,000. Of this figure, one person is owed a total of $5,300 but that individual is the only employee due an amount in excess of $4,300. Payroll taxes withheld from wages but not yet paid to the government total $3,000. However, company records currently show only a $1,000 portion of this liability.

■ Interest of $5,000 on the company's long-term liabilities has not been accrued for the first six months of 2001.

From this information, the statement of financial affairs presented in Exhibit 13–2 for the Chaplin Company can be prepared. Several aspects of this statement should be specifically noted:

1. The current and long-term distinctions usually applied to assets and liabilities are omitted. Because the company is on the verge of going out of business, such classifications are meaningless. Instead, the statement is designed to separate the secured and unsecured balances.

2. Book values are included on the left side of the schedule but only for informational purposes. These figures are not relevant in a bankruptcy. *All assets are reported at estimated net realizable value, whereas liabilities are shown at the amount required for settlement.*

3. The dividend receivable and the interest payable are both included in Exhibit 13–2, although neither has been recorded on the balance sheet. The payroll tax liability also is reported at the amount presently owed by the company. Since these balances represent future cash flows, currently updated figures must be disclosed within the statement of financial affairs.

4. Liabilities having priority are individually identified within the liability section (point A). Because these claims will be paid before other unsecured creditors, the $36,500 total also is subtracted directly from the free assets (point B). Although not yet incurred, estimated administrative costs are included in this category since such expenses will be necessary for a liquidation. Salaries payable are also considered priority liabilities. However, the $1,000 owed to an employee in excess of the individual $4,300 limit is separated as an unsecured claim (point C).

5. According to this statement, if liquidation occurs, Chaplin expects to have $57,000 in free assets remaining after settling all liabilities with priority (point D). Unfortunately, the liability section shows unsecured claims with a total of $95,000. These creditors, therefore, face a $38,000 loss ($95,000 − $57,000) if the company is liquidated (point E). This final distribution is often stated in a percentage form:

$$\frac{\text{Free assets}}{\text{Unsecured claims}} = \frac{\$57,000}{\$95,000} = 60\%$$

Thus, unsecured creditors can anticipate receiving only 60 percent of their claims. An individual, for example, who is owed $400 by this company should anticipate collecting only $240 ($400 × 60%) following liquidation.

6. If the statement of financial affairs had shown the company with more free assets (after subtracting liabilities with priority) than unsecured claims, all creditors could expect to be paid in full with any excess money going to Chaplin's stockholders.

Exhibit 13–2

		CHAPLIN COMPANY	
		Statement of Financial Affairs	
		June 30, 2001	
Book Values			**Available for Unsecured Creditors**
	Assets		
	Pledged with fully secured creditors:		
$210,000	Land and building	$231,000	
	Less: Notes payable (long term)	(200,000)	
	Interest payable	(5,000)	$ 26,000
	Pledged with partially secured creditors:		
41,000	Inventory	$ 45,000	
	Less: Notes payable (current)	(75,000)	–0–
	Free assets:		
2,000	Cash		2,000
15,000	Investment in marketable securities		20,000
–0–	Dividends receivable		500
23,000	Accounts receivable		12,000
3,000	Prepaid expenses		1,000
80,000	Equipment		32,000
15,000	Intangible assets		–0–
	Total available to pay liabilities with priority and unsecured creditors		93,500
	Less: Liabilities with priority (see Ⓐ)		(36,500) Ⓑ
	Available for unsecured creditors		57,000 Ⓓ
	Estimated deficiency		38,000 Ⓔ
$389,000			$ 95,000
Book Values			**Unsecured— Nonpriority Liabilities**
	Liabilities and Stockholders' Equity		
	Liabilities with priority:		
–0–	Administrative expenses (estimated)	$ 21,500	
$ 13,000	Salaries payable (accrued expenses)	12,000	$ 1,000 Ⓒ
1,000	Payroll taxes payable (accrued expenses) ...	3,000	
	Total	$ 36,500 Ⓐ	
	Fully secured creditors:		
200,000	Notes payable	200,000	
–0–	Interest payable	5,000	
	Less: Land and building.	(231,000)	–0–
	Partially secured creditors:		
75,000	Notes payable	75,000	
	Less: Inventory	(45,000)	30,000
	Unsecured creditors:		
60,000	Accounts payable		60,000
4,000	Accrued expenses (other than salaries and payroll taxes)		4,000
36,000	Stockholders' equity		
$389,000			$ 95,000

LIQUIDATION—A CHAPTER 7 BANKRUPTCY

When an insolvent company is to be liquidated, the process is regulated by the provisions found in Chapter 7 of the Bankruptcy Reform Act. This set of laws was written to provide an orderly and equitable structure for the selling of assets and payment of debts. To this end, several events occur after an order for relief has been entered by the court in either a voluntary or involuntary liquidation case.

First, an interim trustee is appointed by the court to oversee the company and its liquidation. This individual is charged with preserving the assets and preventing loss of the estate. Thus, creditors are protected from any detrimental actions that might be undertaken by the management, the ownership, or any of the other creditors. The interim trustee (as well as the permanent trustee if one is subsequently selected by the creditors) must carry out a number of tasks shortly after being appointed. These functions would include (but not be limited to) the following:

- Changing locks and moving all assets and records to locations controlled by the trustee.
- Posting notices that all assets of the business are now in the possession of the U.S. trustee and that tampering with or removing any contents is a violation of federal laws.
- Notifying the post office that all mail for the company is to be sent to the trustee.
- Opening a new bank account in the name of the trustee, and notifying banks that no withdrawals of the company's money are allowed except by the trustee.
- Compiling all financial records and placing them in the custody of the trustee's own accountant.
- Obtaining possession of any corporate records including minute books and other official documents.[17]

The court then calls for a meeting of all creditors who have appropriately filed a proof of claim against the debtor. This group may choose to elect a permanent trustee to replace the person temporarily appointed by the court. A majority (in number as well as in dollars due from the company) of the unsecured, nonpriority creditors must agree to this new trustee. If a decision cannot be reached by the creditors, the interim trustee is retained.

As a further action taken to ensure fairness, a committee of between 3 and 11 unsecured creditors is selected to help protect the group's interests. This committee of creditors:

- Consults with the trustee regarding the administration of the estate.
- Makes recommendations to the trustee regarding the performance of the trustee's duties.
- Submits to the court any questions affecting the administration of the estate.[18]

Role of the Trustee

In the liquidation of any company, the trustee is a central figure. This individual must recover all property belonging to the insolvent company, preserve the estate from any further deterioration, liquidate noncash assets, and make distributions to the proper claimants. Additionally, the trustee may even need to continue operating the company to complete business activities that were in progress when the order for relief was entered. To accomplish such a multitude of objectives, this individual holds wide-

---

[17]Bonhiver, *The Expanded Role of the Accountant,* pp. 50–51.
[18]Ibid., p. 26.

ranging authority in bankruptcy matters. For example, the trustee has the right to appoint attorneys, accountants, consultants, and other outside professionals as needed to provide assistance.

The trustee can also void any transfer of property (known as a *preference)* made by the debtor within 90 days *prior* to the filing of the bankruptcy petition if the company was already insolvent at the time. These payments must then be returned by the recipient and be included within the debtor's free assets.[19] For example,

> Drexel Burnham Lambert Group Inc. made more than $600 million in payments that may be recoverable under bankruptcy law because the transactions occurred during the three months immediately prior to the company's bankruptcy-court filing. The payments were disclosed in the company's statement of financial affairs, . . . such payments, with certain exceptions, can be recovered if it is shown that a company gave preference to some creditors and if the debtor was insolvent at the time.[20]

This rule is intended to prevent one party from gaining advantage over another in the sometimes hectic period just before a bankruptcy petition is filed. Return of the asset is not necessary, however, if the transfer was for no more than would have been paid to this party in a liquidation.

Not surprisingly, the trustee must make a proper recording of all activities and report them periodically to the court and other interested parties. For this purpose, the trustee can either establish a separate set of financial records or simply use the accounting system of the insolvent company. To reflect the stewardship responsibility being accepted, trustees frequently prefer to start their own independent recordkeeping system, especially in cases where liquidation is to occur.

Interestingly, the actual reporting rules created by the Bankruptcy Reform Act are quite general: "Each trustee, examiner, and debtor-in-possession is required to file 'such reports as are necessary or as the court orders.' . . . In the past there have been no specific guidelines or forms used in the preparation of these reports."[21] Consequently, a wide variety of statements and reports may be encountered in liquidations. However, *a statement of realization and liquidation* is commonly used by the trustee to report the major aspects of the liquidation process. This statement is designed to convey the following information:

- The account balances reported by the company at the date on which the order for relief was filed.
- The cash receipts generated by the sale of the debtor's property.
- The cash disbursements made by the trustee to wind up the affairs of the business and to pay the secured creditors.
- Any other transactions of the company such as the write off of assets and the recognition of unrecorded liabilities.

Any cash that remains after this series of events is paid to the unsecured creditors with the priority claims being settled first.

---

[19]The 90-day limit is extended to one year if the transfer is made to an inside party such as an officer or a director or an affiliated company. The one-year limit also applies to any transfer made by the debtor with the intent to defraud another party.

[20]Wade Lambert, "Drexel Payments of Over $600 Million Before Chapter 11 May Be Recoverable," *Wall Street Journal,* May 7, 1990, p. A3.

[21]In a reorganization, the ownership usually remains in possession of the company. This group is allowed to continue operating the business and is referred to as a debtor in possession. To monitor the debtor in possession's activities, the court has the right to appoint an examiner. This individual investigates the business so that reports and recommendations can be made to the courts. (See, for example, "The CPA's Role as Bankruptcy Examiner," *CPA Journal,* September 1991, pp. 42–50.) Quote from Bonhiver, *The Expanded Role of the Accountant, p.* 69.

Statement of Realization and Liquidation Illustrated

To demonstrate the production of a statement of realization and liquidation, the information previously presented for the Chaplin Company is once again utilized. Assume that company officials have decided to liquidate the business, a procedure regulated by Chapter 7 of the Bankruptcy Reform Act. An interim trustee is appointed by the court and then confirmed by the creditors to oversee the liquidation of assets and distribution of cash. A creditors' committee is also formed to ensure a fair and impartial distribution.

The dollar amounts resulting from this liquidation do not necessarily agree with the balances used in creating the statement of financial affairs in Exhibit 13–2. The previous statement was based on projected sales and other estimations, whereas a statement of realization and liquidation reports the actual transactions and other events as they occur. Consequently, discrepancies should be expected. The following transactions occur in liquidating this company:

Liquidation of Chaplin Company

2001

July 1 — The accounting records shown in Exhibit 13–1 are adjusted to correct balances as of June 30, 2001, the date on which the order for relief was entered. Hence, the dividends receivable, interest payable, and additional payroll tax liability are recognized.

July 23 — The trustee expends $7,000 to dispose of the company's inventory at a negotiated price of $51,000. The net cash results are applied to the notes payable for which the inventory served as partial security.

July 29 — Collection is made of the $500 cash dividend accrued as of June 30. The related investments (being reported at $15,000) are then sold for $19,600.

Aug. 17 — Accounts receivable of $16,000 are collected. The remaining balances are written off as bad debts.

Aug. 30 — The trustee determines that no refund is available from any of the company's prepaid expenses. The intangible assets also are removed from the financial records because they have no cash value.

Sept. 25 — The land and building are sold for $208,000 with $205,000 of this money being immediately used by the trustee to pay off the secured creditors.

Oct. 9 — After an extended search for a buyer, the equipment is sold for $42,000 in cash.

Nov. 1 — An invoice of $24,900 is received for various administrative expenses incurred in liquidating the company. The trustee also reclassifies the remaining partially secured liabilities as unsecured.

Nov. 9 — Since the noncash assets have now been converted into cash and all secured claims settled, the trustee begins to plan for the distribution of any remaining funds. The liabilities with priority are to be paid first. The excess will then be applied to the claims of unsecured nonpriority creditors.

The actual structure used in producing a statement of realization and liquidation can vary significantly. One popular form presents the various account groups on a horizontal plane with the liquidating transactions shown vertically. In this manner, accountants are able to record the events as they occur as well as the effect on each account classification. Exhibit 13–3 has been constructed in this style to display the liquidation of the Chaplin Company.

As can be seen from this exhibit, many aspects of the statement of realization and liquidation are no more than mechanical bookkeeping procedures used to record the

Exhibit 13–3   Final Statement

CHAPLIN COMPANY
Statement of Realization and Liquidation
June 30, 2001 to November 9, 2001

Date		Cash	Noncash Assets	Liabilities with Priority	Fully Secured Creditors	Partially Secured Creditors	Unsecured— Nonpriority Liabilities	Stockholders' Equity (Deficit)
6/30/01	Book balances	$ 2,000	$ 387,000	$13,000*	$ 200,000	$ 75,000	$65,000†	$ 36,000
7/1/01	Adjustments for dividends, interest, and payroll taxes		500	2,000	5,000			(6,500)
7/1/01	Adjusted book balances	2,000	387,500	15,000	205,000	75,000	65,000	29,500
7/23/01	Inventory sold—recorded net of disposal costs	44,000	(41,000)					3,000
7/23/01	Proceeds from inventory paid to secured creditors	(44,000)				(44,000)		
7/29/01	Investments sold and dividends received	20,100	(15,500)					4,600
8/17/01	Receivables collected with remainder written off	16,000	(23,000)					(7,000)
8/30/01	Intangible assets and prepaid expenses written off		(18,000)					(18,000)
9/25/01	Land and building sold	208,000	(210,000)					(2,000)
9/25/01	Proceeds from land and building paid to secured creditors	(205,000)			(205,000)			
10/9/01	Equipment sold	42,000	(80,000)					(38,000)
11/1/01	Administrative expenses accrued			24,900				(24,900)
11/1/01	Excess of partially secured liabilities reclassified as an unsecured claim					(31,000)	31,000	
11/9/01	Final balances remaining for unsecured creditors	$ 83,100	–0–	$39,900	–0–	–0–	$96,000	$(52,800)

*Includes salary payable of $12,000 (amount due employees but limited to $4,300 per individual) and $1,000 in payroll taxes owed to the government.
†Accounts payable plus accrued expenses other than salary payable (within $4,300 per person limitation) and payroll tax liability.

liquidating transactions: Inventory is sold at a profit, creditors are paid, receivables and dividends are collected, and so forth. Probably the most significant information presented in this statement is the measurement and classification of the insolvent company's liabilities. In the same manner as the statement of financial affairs, both fully and partially secured claims are reported separately from liabilities with priority and unsecured nonpriority claims.

For the Chaplin Company, Exhibit 13–3 discloses that $135,900 in debts remain as of November 9 ($39,900 in priority claims and $96,000 in unsecured nonpriority liabilities). Unfortunately, after satisfying all of the secured liabilities, only $83,100 in cash is retained by the company. The trustee must first use this money to pay the three liabilities with priority according to the following ranking:

Administrative expenses	$24,900
Salaries payable (within the $4,300 per person limitation)	12,000
Payroll taxes payable	3,000
Total	$39,900

These disbursements leave the company with $43,200 ($83,100 − $39,900) in cash but $96,000 in unsecured liabilities. Consequently, the remaining creditors are able to collect only 45 percent of their claims against the Chaplin Company:

$$\frac{\$43,200}{\$96,000} = 45 \text{ percent}$$

Because all liabilities have not been paid in full, the stockholders receive nothing from the liquidation process.

Interestingly, the unsecured nonpriority creditors are receiving a smaller percentage of their claims than the 60 percent figure projected in the statement of financial affairs (produced in Exhibit 13–2). Although this earlier statement plays an important role in bankruptcy proceedings, its accuracy is limited by the preparer's ability to foretell future events.

REORGANIZATION—A CHAPTER 11 BANKRUPTCY

Reorganization under the federal Bankruptcy Code is a way to salvage a company, not liquidate it. Although the original owners of a company rescued in this way are often left without anything, others whose livelihoods depend on the company's fortunes may come out with their interests intact. The company's creditors, for example, may take over as the new owners. Its suppliers might be able to maintain the company as a customer. Its customers still may count on the company as a supplier. And perhaps most important, many of its employees may be able to keep the jobs that otherwise would have been sacrificed in a liquidation.[22]

For the year ending March 1999, over 8,000 petitions (both voluntary and involuntary) were filed in the United States to reorganize insolvent corporations based on Chapter 11 of the Bankruptcy Reform Act.[23] "While the overall number of bankruptcy filings by all businesses in the United States has fallen 30 percent since 1997—a by-product of the booming economy—the number of public companies seeking shelter under Chapter 11 has surged 75 percent in the past two years."[24] In such cases, an attempt is being made to salvage the company so that operations can continue. Although this legal procedure offers the company some hope of survival, reorganization is

---

[22]John Robbins, Al Goll, and Paul Rosenfield, "Accounting for Companies in Chapter 11 Reorganization," *Journal of Accountancy,* January 1991, p. 75.

[23]Josh Goldberg, "Bankruptcy Filings Drop a Bit Nationally," *Chicago Daily Law Bulletin,* May 24, 1999, p. 1.

[24]Dean Foust, "Chapter 11 Never Looked So Good," *Business Week,* March 20, 2000, p. 44.

certainly not a guarantee of future prosperity. Most companies that attempt to reorganize eventually are liquidated. In practice, though, reorganization appears to be biased in favor of large organizations. One expert estimates that 90 percent of big corporations that attempt to reorganize emerge as functioning entities while fewer than 20 percent of smaller companies survive.[25]

Many reorganizations may actually fail because the debtor struggles too long before filing a petition:

> Seeking bankruptcy because disaster looms—not after it has arrived—helps (gives the corporation time and provides equality of treatment). . . . Once a company files under the bankruptcy laws, suppliers are likely to demand cash on delivery. So management that moves before liquid assets are depleted has a better chance of making a go of reorganization.[26]

Obviously, the activities and events surrounding a reorganization differ significantly from a liquidation. One important distinction is that control over the company is normally retained by the ownership (referred to as a *debtor in possession*). However, if fraud or gross mismanagement can be proven, the court has the authority to appoint an independent trustee to assume control. For example, a trustee was brought in to take over Eastern Airlines after the bankruptcy judge found the management of Eastern and its parent to be "unfit" to operate the airline.[27] Unless replaced, the debtor in possession continues to operate the company and has the primary responsibility for developing an acceptable plan of reorganization.

While a reorganization is in process, the owners and managers are legally required to preserve the company's estate as of the date that the order for relief is entered. In this way, the bankruptcy regulations seek to reduce the losses that may have to be absorbed by creditors and stockholders when either reorganization or liquidation eventually occurs. For this reason, a newsletter distributed by the A. H. Robins Company to employees a few days after the corporation filed for Chapter 11 protection specified that "the company cannot pay any creditor or supplier for goods delivered or services rendered before August 21, 1985. The company is prohibited from making such payments unless there is a special court order. Monthly bills will have to be prorated to assure all creditors are treated the same."[28]

The Plan for Reorganization

> The plan is the heart of every Chapter 11 reorganization. The provisions of the plan specify the treatment of all creditors and equity holders upon its approval by the Bankruptcy Court. Moreover, the plan shapes the financial structure of the entity that emerges.[29]

The most intriguing aspect of a Chapter 11 bankruptcy is the plan developed to rescue the company from insolvency. Initially, proposals can be filed with the court only by the debtor in possession. However, if a plan for reorganization is not put forth within 120 days of the order for relief or accepted within 180 days (unless an extension is granted by the court), any interested party has the right to prepare and file a proposal. Creditors of Revco D. S., Inc., had the interesting quandary of choosing between three

[25]Michael Selz, "For Many Small Businesses, Chapter 11 Closes the Book," *Wall Street Journal,* November 4, 1992, p. B2.

[26]Daniel B. Moskowitz and Mark Ivey, "You Don't Have to Be Broke to Need Chapter 11," *Business Week,* April 27, 1987, p. 108.

[27]Carolyn Phillips, "Marty Shugrue Has Background Needed to Save Eastern Air," *Wall Street Journal,* April 20, 1990, p. A6.

[28]Thomas R. Morris, "Some Questions Went Unasked," *Richmond Times-Dispatch,* May 18, 1986, p. B1.

[29]AICPA Statement of Position 90–7, *Financial Reporting by Entities in Reorganization Under the Bankruptcy Code,* November 19, 1990, par. 3.

different reorganization plans: one backed by the company's management, one proposed by Rite Aid Corporation, and one submitted by Jack Eckerd Corporation.[30]

A reorganization plan may contain an unlimited number of provisions: proposed changes in the company, additional financing arrangements, alterations in the debt structure, and the like.[31] Regardless of the specific contents, the intent of all such plans is to provide a feasible long-term solution to the company's monetary difficulties. However, to gain acceptance by the parties involved, convincing evidence must be presented that the plan will enable the business to emerge from bankruptcy as a viable going concern. Although a definitive list of elements that could be included in a reorganization proposal is not possible, some of the most common are

1.   *Plans proposing changes in the company's operations.* In hopes of improving liquidity, officials may decide to introduce new product lines or sell off unprofitable assets or even entire businesses. The closing of failing operations is especially common. A debtor in possession bears the burden of proving that the problems that led to insolvency can be eliminated and then avoided in the future. As an example, before emerging from Chapter 11 reorganization, House of Fabrics, Inc., made a number of significant business changes:

> Since it opted to reorganize under bankruptcy court protection, the company, among other things, has closed more than 200 stores, reduced debt, secured a new three-year $60 million credit facility and disposed of surplus real estate. Earlier this week, the retail fabric and craft store operator announced the addition of three new board members.[32]

2.   *Plans for generating additional monetary resources.* Companies faced with insolvency must develop new sources of cash, often in a short time period. Loans and the sale of both common and preferred stocks are frequently negotiated during reorganization to provide funding for the continuation of the business. For example, as part of the initial reorganization plan put forth by Orion Pictures, its majority owner, Metromedia Company, agreed to invest $15 million in cash. Without the willingness of the owners to back the company, creditors would probably be hesitant about agreeing to a reorganization.

3.   *Plans for changes in the management of the company.* Frequently, a financial crisis is blamed on poor management. In that situation, proposing to reorganize a company with the management team intact is probably not a practical suggestion. Therefore, many plans include the hiring of new individuals to implement the reorganization and run important aspects of the company. These changes may even affect the board of directors elected by the stockholders to oversee the company and its operations: "Manville Corporation agreed to let creditors have the final say in any board appointments, eliminating the last major obstacle in gaining approval of its 3 1/2 year bankruptcy-law reorganization."[33]

4.   *Plans to settle the debts of the company that existed when the order for relief was entered.* No element of a reorganization plan is more important than the proposal for satisfying the various creditors of the company. In most cases, their agreement is necessary before the court will confirm any plan of reorganization. The actual proposal to settle these debts may take one of several forms:

---

[30]Gabriella Stern, "Timing of Revco Status Change Stays Uncertain," *Wall Street Journal,* January 6, 1992, p. A3.

[31]See, for example, "When Will Somebody—Anybody—Rescue Battered Allegheny?" *Wall Street Journal,* April 19, 1990, p. A1.

[32]"Bankruptcy Period Ends; Stock to Resume Trading," *Wall Street Journal,* August 1, 1996, p. B4.

[33]Cynthia F. Mitchell, "Manville Is Said to Have Agreed to Let Creditors Decide Board Appointments," *Wall Street Journal,* April 25, 1986, p. 5.

- Assets can be transferred to creditors who accept this payment in exchange for extinguishing a specified amount of debt. The book value of the liability being canceled is usually greater than the fair market value of the assets rendered. "Dow Corning Corp. made public a $4.4 billion bankruptcy-reorganization plan, its third attempt to forge a solution for exiting from bankruptcy court and hammering out a way to resolve thousands of claims that silicone breast implants cause diseases and injuries. The company, which for years was the leading maker of silicone implants in the United States, offered $3 billion of that total to resolve an estimated 200,000 existing silicone claims."[34]

- An equity interest (such as common stock, preferred stock, or stock rights) can be conveyed to creditors to settle an outstanding debt. "Previously, plaintiffs put forth a proposal that would have called for silicone claimants to wind up with as much as 95 percent of the stock in Dow Corning, depending on how several trials wound up."[35]

- The terms of the outstanding liabilities can be modified: maturity dates extended, interest rates lowered, face values reduced, accrued interest forgiven, and so on.

One recent development that appears to be growing in popularity is the use of "prepackaged bankruptcies." In such cases, the company and its debtors agree upon the terms of the reorganization plan before a bankruptcy petition is signed. Thus, the parties go into the bankruptcy with a detailed agreement to present to the court. In this manner, extensive legal fees can be avoided by all parties. Furthermore, the parties have more protection because the Bankruptcy Court is likely to accept the plan without requiring extensive changes or revisions.

Acceptance and Confirmation of Reorganization Plan

The creation of a plan for reorganization does not guarantee its implementation. The Bankruptcy Reform Act specifies that a plan must be voted on by both the company's creditors and stockholders before being confirmed by the court. *To be accepted, each class of creditors must vote for the plan.* Acceptance requires the approval of two-thirds in dollar amount and more than one-half in the number of claims that cast votes. A separate vote is also required of each class of shareholders. For approval, at least two-thirds (measured by the number of shares held) of the owners who vote must agree to the proposed reorganization. Convincing all parties to support any specific plan is not an easy task since agreement often means the acceptance of a significant loss. However, any class of creditors that is not damaged by a reorganization is assumed to have accepted the plan without the necessity of a vote.

Although creditor and stockholder approval may be gained, confirmation by the court is still required. The court reviews the proposal and can reject the reorganization plan if a claimant (who did not vote for acceptance) would receive more through liquidation. The court also has the authority to confirm a reorganization plan that was not accepted by a particular class of creditors or stockholders. This provision is referred to as a *cram down;* it occurs when the court determines that the plan is fair and equitable. As an alternative, the court may convert a Chapter 11 reorganization into a Chapter 7 liquidation at any time if the development of an acceptable plan does not appear to be possible. That threat often encourages the parties to work together to achieve a workable resolution.

---

[34]Thomas M. Burton, "Dow Corning Has $4.4 Billion Plan on Chapter 11 and Implant Claims," *Wall Street Journal*, February 18, 1998, p. B2.

[35]Ibid.

Financial Reporting during Reorganization

Developing and gaining approval for a reorganization plan can take years. During that period, the company continues operating under the assumption that it is eventually going to emerge from the bankruptcy proceedings. In the past, official accounting literature has provided virtually no guidance for the financial statements to be prepared by a company while in reorganization. However, the increased volume of companies (especially larger organizations) going through reorganization during the 1980s emphasized the need for some type of guidelines to be established.

Finally, in 1990, the AICPA Task Force on Financial Reporting by Entities in Reorganization Under the Bankruptcy Code issued Statement of Position 90–7 *(Financial Reporting by Entities in Reorganization Under the Bankruptcy Code)* (referred to as SOP 90–7). This pronouncement provides standards for the preparation of financial statements at two times:

1. During the period when a company is going through reorganization.
2. At the point that the company emerges from reorganization.

While going through reorganization, the company faces several specific accounting questions:

- Should the income effects resulting from operating activities be differentiated from transactions connected solely with the reorganization process?
- How should liabilities be reported? Since some of the debts may not be paid for years and then may require payment of an amount considerably less than face value, how should this information be conveyed?
- Does reorganization necessitate a change in the reporting basis of the company's assets?

The Income Statement during Reorganization   According to SOP 90–7, any gains, losses, revenues, and expenses resulting from the reorganization of the business should be reported separately. Such items are placed on the income statement before any income tax expense or benefits.[36]

Reorganization items would include any gains and losses on the sale of assets necessitated by the reorganization. In addition, as mentioned previously, enormous amounts of professional fees may be incurred. Historically, these items could be handled by any one of several different methods. SOP 90–7 requires that these costs be expensed as incurred.

> What's the proper way to account for lawyers' and investment bankers' fees that can run to millions monthly for large cases like LTV? It makes sense to expense them along the way—and that's what the new rules call for. In the past, some clever companies capitalized the fees on the theory that part of the work would benefit the company as a going concern.[37]

Interest expense and interest revenue were also discussed in SOP 90-7. During reorganization, interest expense usually does not accrue on debts owed at the date on which the order for relief is granted. The amount of liability on that date is frozen. Thus, recognition of interest is only necessary if payment will be made during the proceeding (for example, on debts incurred during the bankruptcy) or if the interest will probably be an allowed claim (for example, if the amount was owed but unrecorded prior to the granting of the order for relief). Any interest expense that is recognized is

---

[36]In a similar manner, the statement of cash flows should be constructed so that reorganization items are shown separately within the operating, investing, and financing categories.

[37]Laura Jereski, "Starting Fresh," *Forbes,* April 15, 1991, p. 105.

not really a result of the reorganization process and should not be separately reported as a reorganization item.

In contrast, interest revenue can increase to a quite substantial amount during reorganization. Because the company is not forced to pay the debts incurred prior to the date of the order for relief, cash reserves tend to grow and the resulting interest can become a significant source of income. *Any interest revenue that would not have been earned except for the proceeding is reported separately as a reorganization item.*

For example, the 1997 financial statements for Discover Zone disclosed that "reorganization items of $11.6 million (increase to income) and $21.3 million (decrease to income) were incurred by the Company during its reorganization under Chapter 11 for the years ended December 31, 1997, and 1996, respectively, including $6.2 million and $7.1 million incurred for professional fees in the 1997 and 1996 periods, respectively."

To illustrate, assume that the Crawford Corporation files a voluntary bankruptcy petition and is granted an order for relief on January 1, 2001. Thereafter, the ownership and management of the company begins to (1) work on a reorganization plan and (2) rehabilitate the company. Several branch operations are closed and accountants, lawyers, and other professionals are hired to assist in the reorganization. At the end of 2001, the bankruptcy is still in progress. The company prepares the income statement shown in Exhibit 13–4 which is structured so that the reader can distinguish the results of operating activities from the reorganization items.

The Balance Sheet during Reorganization   A new entity is not created when a company moves into reorganization. Therefore, traditional generally accepted accounting principles continue to apply. Assets, for example, should still be reported at their book values. However, many of the liabilities are likely to be reduced as part of the final reorganization plan. In addition, because of the order for relief, the current/noncurrent classification system is no longer applicable; payments may be delayed for years.

Exhibit 13–4
Income Statement during Reorganization

CRAWFORD CORPORATION (Debtor-in-Possession) Income Statement For Year Ended December 31, 2001		
Revenues:		
Sales		$ 650,000
Cost and expenses:		
Cost of goods sold	$346,000	
General and administrative expenses	165,000	
Selling expenses	86,000	
Interest expense	4,000	601,000
Earnings before reorganization items and tax effects		49,000
Reorganization items:		
Loss on closing of branches	(86,000)	
Professional fees	(75,000)	
Interest revenue	26,000	(135,000)
Loss before income tax benefit		(86,000)
Income tax benefit		18,800
Net loss		(67,200)
Loss per common share		$ (.56)

Thus, in reporting the liabilities of a company being reorganized, debts subject to compromise (reduction by the court through acceptance of a reorganization plan) must be disclosed separately. Unsecured and partially secured obligations existing as of the granting of the order for relief fall into this category. Fully secured liabilities and all debts incurred since that date are not subject to compromise and must be reported in a normal manner as either a current or noncurrent liability.

According to SOP 90–7 (par. 24), liabilities subject to compromise "should be reported on the basis of the expected amount of the allowed claims . . . as opposed to the amounts for which those allowed claims may be settled." Thus, the company does not attempt to anticipate the payment required by a final plan but simply discloses the amount of these claims. The November 1998 balance sheet of Bonneville Pacific Corp. showed liabilities that were not subject to compromise of $12.5 million whereas the liabilities that were subject to compromise amounted to $215.3 million.

The liability section of a company during this reorganization period would appear as follows:

Liabilities Not Subject to Compromise
Current liabilities:

Short-term notes payable	$ 62,000	
Accounts payable	86,000	
Accrued expenses and other liabilities	13,000	$161,000
Long-term liabilities: notes payable		40,000
Liabilities not subject to compromise		$201,000

Liabilities Subject to Compromise

Prior tax claims	$ 77,000	
Notes payable	100,000	
Trade and other miscellaneous claims	133,000	310,000
Total liabilities		$511,000

Financial Reporting for Companies Emerging from Reorganization

Is a company that successfully leaves Chapter 11 status considered a new entity so that current values should be assigned to its asset and liability accounts (referred to as fresh start reporting)? Or, is the company simply a continuation of the organization that entered bankruptcy so that historical figures are still applicable? SOP 90–7 holds that these accounts should be adjusted to current value if two criteria are met (par. 36):

■ The reorganization (or market) value of the assets of the emerging company is less than the total of the allowed claims as of the date of the order for relief plus the liabilities incurred subsequently.

■ The original owners of the voting stock are left with less than 50 percent of the voting stock of the company when it emerges from bankruptcy.

Meeting the first criterion shows that the old company could not have continued in business as a going concern. The second criterion indicates that control of the company has changed.

These two criteria are met in many, if not most, Chapter 11 bankruptcies. Consequently, the entity is reported as if it were a brand new business. For example, Golden Books Entertainment reported that "on January 27, 2000, the Company formally emerged from protection under the Bankruptcy Code upon the consummation of the Amended Joint Plan of Reorganization. The Company has applied the reorganization and fresh-start reporting adjustments as required by SOP 90–7 to the consolidated balance sheet as of December 25, 1999 . . . Under fresh start accounting, a new reporting entity is deemed to be created and the recorded amounts of assets and liabilities are adjusted to reflect their estimated fair values."

In applying fresh start accounting, the reorganization value of the entity that emerges from bankruptcy must first be determined. According to paragraph 9 of SOP 90–7, "reorganization value generally approximates fair value of the entity before considering liabilities and approximates the amount a willing buyer would pay for the assets of the entity immediately after the restructuring . . . generally it is determined by discounting future cash flows for the reconstituted business that will emerge." This total value is then assigned to the specific tangible and intangible assets of the company in the same way as in a purchase combination.

If the reorganization value for the company is greater than the amounts assigned to these specific assets, an account akin to goodwill is recognized. For example, because of its reorganization, the 1998 balance sheet of Trans World Airlines reported a reorganization value in excess of amounts allocable to identifiable assets of over $699 million. This one asset balance made up over 27 percent of the company's total reported assets of $2.55 billion. This balance can be amortized to expense over a period of up to 40 years. However, to avoid the extended write offs that have been common with goodwill, SOP 90–7 (par. 38) does state that factors usually indicate "a useful life of substantially less than forty years."

To illustrate, assume that a company has a reorganization value of $280,000 but only two specific assets. Land (with a book value of $90,000) is worth $150,000 and a building (with a book value of $78,000) is valued at $100,000. If the criteria for fresh start accounting are met, this company will emerge from bankruptcy with these assets recorded at their market values of $150,000 and $100,000 rather than the historical book values. In addition, the excess $30,000 ($280,000 − $250,000) should be assigned to this new intangible asset account.

The reporting of liabilities following a reorganization also creates a concern because many of these balances will be reduced and the payment period extended. SOP 90–7 requires that all liabilities (except for deferred income taxes which should be accounted for according to the provisions of FASB *Statement 109)* must be reported at the present value of the future cash payments.

To make the necessary asset adjustments to fresh start accounting, additional paid-in capital is normally increased or decreased. However, any write-down of a liability creates a recognized gain. Finally, because the company is viewed as a new entity, it must leave reorganization with a zero balance reported for retained earnings.

Fresh Start Accounting Illustrated

Assume that a company has the following trial balance just prior to emerging from bankruptcy:

	Debit	Credit
Current assets	$ 50,000	
Land	100,000	
Buildings	400,000	
Equipment	250,000	
Accounts payable (incurred since the order for relief was granted)		$ 100,000
Liabilities when the order for relief was granted:		
Accounts payable		60,000
Accrued expenses		50,000
Notes payable (due in 3 years)		300,000
Bonds payable (due in 5 years)		600,000
Common stock (50,000 shares with a $1 par value)		50,000
Additional paid-in capital		40,000
Retained earnings (deficit)	400,000	
Totals	$1,200,000	$1,200,000

Other Information

- *Assets.* The company's land has a market value of $120,000; the building is worth $500,000. Other assets are worth their book values. The reorganization value of the company's assets is assumed to be $1,000,000 based on discounted future cash flows.

- *Liabilities.* The $100,000 of accounts payable incurred since the order for relief was granted must be paid in full as the individual balances come due. The accounts payable and accrued expenses that were owed when the order for relief was granted will be converted into one-year notes payable of $70,000, paying interest of 10 percent. The $300,000 note payable on the trial balance will be converted into a 10-year, 8 percent note of $100,000. These creditors also get 20,000 shares of stock that is to be turned in to the company by the common stockholders. Finally, the $600,000 bonds payable will be converted into eight-year, 9 percent notes totaling $430,000. The bondholders also get 15,000 shares of common stock turned in by the current owners.

- *Stockholders' Equity.* The owners of the common stock will return 70 percent of their stock (35,000 shares) to the company to be issued as specified above. The reorganization value of the assets is $1,000,000 and the debts of the company after the proceeding total $700,000 ($100,000 + $70,000 + $100,000 + $430,000). Thus, stockholders' equity must be the $300,000 difference. Since shares with a $50,000 par value would still be outstanding, additional paid-in capital is adjusted to $250,000.

In accounting for this reorganization, the initial question to be resolved is whether fresh start accounting is appropriate. The first criterion is met since the reorganization value of the assets ($1,000,000) is less than the sum of all postpetition liabilities ($100,000 in accounts payable) and allowed claims (the $1,010,000 total of liabilities remaining from the date of the order for relief before any write-down). The second criterion is also met since the original stockholders receive less than 50 percent of the shares after the plan takes effect. At that point, they will hold only 15,000 of the 50,000 outstanding shares.

Because fresh start accounting is appropriate, the assets must be adjusted to market value. In addition, an intangible asset is recognized for the $80,000 reorganization value of the company in excess of the value assigned to specific assets. The reorganization value is $1 million, but the market value of the assets is only $920,000 (current assets $50,000, land $120,000 [adjusted], buildings $500,000 [adjusted], and equipment $250,000). Since the accounts are already recorded at book value, adjustment is only necessary when market value differs from this book value:

Land	20,000	
Buildings.	100,000	
Reorganization Value in Excess of Amount Allocable		
to Identifiable Assets	80,000	
Additional Paid-In Capital		200,000

    To adjust asset accounts to fresh start accounting and to recognize
    excess value as an intangible asset subject to amortization.

Next, the 35,000 shares of common stock returned to the company by the original owners should be recorded:

Common Stock.	35,000	
Additional Paid-In Capital		35,000

    To record shares of common stock returned to the company
    by owners as part of the reorganization agreement.

The liability accounts on the records at the date of the order for relief must now be adjusted for the provisions of the bankruptcy reorganization plan. Because all of the new debts bear a reasonable interest rate, present value computations are not necessary. The first entry is a straight conversion with a gain recorded for the difference between the old debt and the new.

Accounts Payable	60,000	
Accrued Expenses	50,000	
Notes Payable (1 year)		70,000
Gain on Debt Discharge		40,000
To convert liabilities to a one-year note as per reorganization plan.		

The other two debt entries require a computation for the amount to be assigned to additional paid-in capital. The assumed total APIC for the company as computed earlier is $250,000. Since the holders of the notes receive 20,000 shares of stock (or 40 percent of the 50,000 share total), this stock is assigned additional paid-in capital of $100,000 (40 percent). The holders of the bonds are to get 15,000 shares (30 percent of the company total). Hence, additional paid-in capital of $75,000 (30 percent) is recorded.

Notes Payable (3 years)	300,000	
Notes Payable (10 years)		100,000
Common Stock (par value of 20,000 shares)		20,000
Additional Paid-In Capital (40 percent of company total)		100,000
Gain on Debt Discharge		80,000
To record exchange with gain recorded for difference between book value of old note and the amount recorded for new note and shares of stock.		

Bonds Payable	600,000	
Notes Payable (8 years)		430,000
Common Stock (par value of 15,000 shares)		15,000
Additional Paid-In Capital (30 percent of company total)		75,000
Gain on Debt Discharge		80,000
To record exchange with gain recorded for difference between book value of old bonds and the amount recorded for new notes and shares of stock.		

Additional Paid-In Capital now has a balance of $450,000 ($40,000 beginning balance plus $200,000 for adjusting assets plus $35,000 for shares returned by owners plus $100,000 because of shares issued for note and $75,000 because of shares issued for bonds). Therefore, this balance is $200,000 more than the amount to be reported as established through the provisions of the reorganization agreement. In addition, the Gain on Debt Discharge account has a balance of $200,000 ($40,000 + $80,000 + $80,000), a figure that must be closed out. Adjusting and closing these accounts eliminates the deficit in retained earnings so that the emerging company has no balance in this equity account.

Additional Paid-In Capital	200,000	
Gain on Debt Discharge	200,000	
Retained Earnings (Deficit)		400,000
To adjust Additional Paid-In Capital balance to correct amount, close out Gain account, and eliminate deficit balance.		

After posting these entries, this company emerges from bankruptcy with

1. Its assets reported at fair market value along with a reorganization asset.
2. Its debts equal to the present value of the future cash payments (except for any deferred income taxes).
3. No deficit balance.

Is This the Real Purpose of the Bankruptcy Laws?

Insolvency is not a necessary condition for bankruptcy. Moreover a firm may petition the court for protection under Chapter 11 even though it is not insolvent. If the business can demonstrate real financial trouble, the court will generally not dismiss the petition. In recent years, Chapter 11 has been looked upon as a safe harbor for gaining time to restructure the business and to head off more serious financial problems. *For example, when Johns Manville filed a petition under Chapter 11, it was a profitable, financially sound company. Yet, it faced numerous lawsuits for damages resulting from asbestos products it sold. Reorganization helped Johns Manville deal with its financial problems (emphasis added).*[38]

During recent years, the filing of a voluntary Chapter 11 bankruptcy petition has become a tool sometimes used by companies to settle significant financial problems. Just as Johns Manville reorganized to settle the claims of asbestos victims, A. H. Robins followed a similar path to resolve thousands of lawsuits stemming from injuries resulting from the Dalkon Shield intrauterine device. The Wilson Foods Corporation managed to reduce union wages by filing under Chapter 11 as did Continental Airlines Corporation.

Not surprisingly, seeking protection under Chapter 11 to force a bargained resolution of a financial difficulty is a controversial legal maneuver. Creditors and claimants often argue that this procedure is used to avoid responsibility while the companies counter that bankruptcy can become the only realistic means of achieving any settlement.

Should companies be allowed to use the provisions of Chapter 11 in this manner?

	Debit	Credit
Current assets	$ 50,000	
Land	120,000	
Buildings	500,000	
Equipment	250,000	
Reorganization value in excess of amounts allocable to identifiable assets	80,000	
Accounts payable		$ 100,000
Note payable (due in 1 year)		70,000
Note payable (due in 10 years)		100,000
Notes payable (due in 8 years)		430,000
Common stock (50,000 shares with a $1 par value)		50,000
Additional paid-in capital		250,000
Retained earnings	–0–	–0–
Totals	$1,000,000	$1,000,000

SUMMARY

1. Every year a significant number of businesses in the United States become insolvent, unable to pay debts as they come due. Since creditors as well as owners hold financial interests in each failed company, bankruptcy laws have been written to provide protection for all parties. The Bankruptcy Reform Act of 1978 (as amended) currently serves as the primary structure for these legal proceedings. This act was designed to ensure a fair distribution of all remaining properties while discharging the obligations of an honest debtor.

2. Bankruptcy proceedings can be instigated voluntarily by the insolvent debtor or involuntarily by a group of creditors. In either case, an order for relief is usually granted by the court to halt all actions against the debtor. Some creditors may have already gained protection for themselves by having a mortgage lien or security interest attached to specific assets. A creditor is considered fully secured if the value of any collateral

---

[38]Paul J. Corr and Donald D. Bourque, "Managing in a Reorganization," *Management Accounting,* January 1988, p. 34.

exceeds the related debt balance but is only partially secured if the obligation is larger. All other liabilities are unsecured; these creditors have legal rights but not to any specific assets of the debtor. The Bankruptcy Reform Act does list several types of unsecured liabilities (including administrative expenses and government claims for unpaid taxes) that have priority and must be paid before other unsecured debts are settled.

3. The parties involved in a bankruptcy want, and need, to be informed of the possible outcome, especially if liquidation is being considered. Thus, a Statement of Financial Affairs can be prepared for an insolvent company. This document lists the net realizable value of all remaining assets along with an indication of any property pledged to specific creditors. In addition, the liabilities of the business are segregated and disclosed within four classifications: fully secured, partially secured, unsecured with priority, and unsecured. Prior to the filing of a bankruptcy petition, this information can help the parties in deciding whether either liquidation or reorganization is the best course of action. However, this statement should be viewed as a projection since many of the reported values are merely estimations.

4. If the assets of the insolvent company will be liquidated to satisfy obligations (a Chapter 7 bankruptcy), a trustee is appointed to oversee the process. This individual must recover all property belonging to the company, liquidate noncash assets, possibly continue running operations to complete any business in progress, and make appropriate payments. To convey information about these events and transactions, a Statement of Realization and Liquidation is commonly prepared by the trustee. This statement provides a current report of all account balances as well as transactions to date.

5. Liquidation is not the only alternative available to an insolvent business. The company may seek to survive by developing a reorganization plan (a Chapter 11 bankruptcy). Reorganization is possible only if the plan is accepted by creditors, shareholders, and the court. While a reorganization is in process, the owners and management must preserve the company's estate as of the date on which the order of relief was entered. Although the ownership has the initial opportunity for creating a proposal for action, any interested party has the right to file a reorganization plan after a period of time.

6. Reorganization plans usually contain a number of provisions for modifying operations, generating new financing by equity or debt, and settling the liabilities existing when the order for relief was entered. To be accepted, each class of creditors and shareholders has to support the agreement. Thereafter, the reorganization plan must be confirmed by the court.

7. During reorganization, a company reports its liabilities as being subject to compromise or not subject to compromise. The first category includes all unsecured and partially secured debts that existed on the day the order for relief was granted. The balance to be reported is the expected amount of allowed claims rather than the estimated amount of settlement. Liabilities not subject to compromise are those debts fully secured or incurred following the granting of the order for relief.

8. An income statement prepared during the period of reorganization should disclose operating activities separately from reorganization items. Professional fees associated with the reorganization such as lawyers' charges are reorganization items that are expensed as incurred. Any interest revenue earned during this period because of an increase in the company's cash reserves should also be reported as a reorganization item.

9. Many companies that emerge from reorganization proceedings must apply fresh start accounting. Assets are recorded at fair market value and an intangible asset, "reorganization value in excess of amounts allocable to identifiable assets," might also be necessary. Liabilities (except for deferred income taxes) are reported at the present value of required cash flows. Retained earnings (or a deficit) is eliminated. Additional paid-in capital is adjusted to keep the balance sheet in equilibrium.

COMPREHENSIVE ILLUSTRATION

Problem *(Estimated Time: 50 to 65 Minutes)* The Roth Company is insolvent and in the process of filing for relief under the provisions of the Bankruptcy Reform Act of 1978. Roth has no cash and the company's balance sheet currently shows accounts payable of $48,000. An additional $8,000 is owed in connection with various expenses but these amounts have not yet been recorded. The company's assets with an indication of both book value and anticipated net realizable value follow:

	Book Value	Expected Net Realizable Value
Accounts receivable	$ 31,000	$ 9,000
Inventory	48,000	36,000
Investments	10,000	18,000
Land	80,000	75,000
Buildings	90,000	60,000
Accumulated depreciation	(38,000)	
Equipment	110,000	20,000
Accumulated depreciation	(61,000)	
Other assets	5,000	–0–
Totals	$275,000	$218,000

Roth has three notes payable, each with a different maturity date:

- Note one due in 5 years—$120,000, secured by a mortgage lien on Roth's land and buildings.
- Note two due in 8 years—$30,000, secured by Roth's investments.
- Note three due in 10 years—$35,000, unsecured.

Of the accounts payable owed by Roth, $10,000 represents salaries to employees, However, no individual is entitled to receive more than $1,300. An additional $3,000 is included in this liability figure that is due to the U.S. government in connection with taxes.

The stockholders' equity balance reported by the company at the current date is $42,000: common stock of $140,000 and a deficit of $98,000. If the company is liquidated, administrative expenses of approximately $20,000 will be incurred.

Required

a. Prepare a statement of financial affairs for Roth to indicate the expected availability of funds if the company is liquidated.

b. Assume that Roth owes Philip, Inc., a total of $2,000. This liability is unsecured. If Roth is liquidated, what amount of money can Philip expect to receive?

c. What amount will be paid on note two if Roth is liquidated?

d. Assume that Roth is immediately reorganized. The company has a reorganization value of $230,000, and the net realizable value is to be the assigned value for each asset. The accounts payable and accrued expenses are reduced to $20,000. Note one is reduced to a $30,000 note due in four years with a 7 percent annual interest rate. This creditor also receives half of the outstanding stock of the company from the owners. Note two is reduced to a $12,000 note due in five years with an 8 percent annual interest rate. This creditor also receives 10 percent of the outstanding stock of the company from the owners. Note three is reduced to $5,000 due in three years with a 9 percent annual interest rate. Prepare a trial balance for this company after it emerges from bankruptcy.

Solution

a. To develop a statement of financial affairs for this company, the following preliminary actions must be taken:

- The $8,000 in unrecorded accounts payable must be entered into the company's accounting records. Since these debts were incurred in connection with expenses, the deficit is increased by a corresponding amount.

■ The unsecured liabilities that have priority are identified:

Administrative costs (estimated)	$20,000
Salary payable	10,000
Amount due to government for taxes	3,000
Total liabilities with priority	$33,000

■ The secured claims should be appropriately classified:

Note one is fully secured because Roth's land and buildings can be sold for an amount in excess of the $120,000 balance.

Note two is only partially secured because Roth's investments are worth less than $30,000.

With this information, the statement of financial affairs in, Exhibit 13–5 can be produced.

b.   Based on the information provided by the statement of financial affairs, Philip, Inc., should receive 52.2 percent of its $2,000 unsecured claim or $1,044. Roth anticipates having $47,000 in free assets remaining at the end of the liquidation. This amount must be distributed to unsecured creditors with total claims of $90,000. Therefore, only 52.2 percent of each obligation can be paid:

$$\frac{\$47,000}{\$90,000} = 52.2 \text{ percent (rounded)}$$

c.   The $30,000 note payable is partially secured by Roth's investments, an asset having a net realizable value of only $18,000. The remaining $12,000 is an unsecured claim which (as computed in requirement *b.*) will be paid 52.2 percent of face value. Thus, the holder of this note can expect to receive $24,264:

Net realizable value of investments	$18,000
Payment on $12,000 unsecured claim (52.2 percent)	6,264
Amount to be received	$24,264

d.   Fresh start accounting is appropriate. The reorganization value of $230,000 is less than the $241,000 total amount of claims (no liabilities after the issuance of the order for relief are indicated).

Accounts payable	$ 48,000
Accrued expenses	8,000
Note one	120,000
Note two	30,000
Note three	35,000
Total claims	$241,000

In addition, the original owners of the stock retain only 40 percent of the shares after the company leaves the bankruptcy proceeding.

The company's assets are assigned values equal to their net realizable value based on the information provided. Since the reorganization value of $230,000 is $12,000 in excess of the total net realizable value of $218,000, an intangible asset is recognized for that amount.

The liabilities are each adjusted to the newly agreed-on amounts: Present value computations are not required because a reasonable interest rate is included in each case. These debts now total $67,000 ($20,000 + $30,000 + $12,000 + $5,000).

Because the reorganization value is $230,000, stockholders' equity must be $163,000 ($230,000 − $67,000). The number of outstanding shares of common stock has not changed so

Exhibit 13–5

ROTH COMPANY
Statement of Financial Affairs

Book Values	Assets		Available for Unsecured Creditors
	Pledged with fully secured creditors:		
$132,000	Land and buildings	$ 135,000	
	Less: Note payable	(120,000)	$ 15,000
	Pledged with partially secured creditors:		
10,000	Investments	18,000	
	Less: Note payable	(30,000)	–0–
	Free assets:		
31,000	Accounts receivable		9,000
48,000	Inventory		36,000
49,000	Equipment		20,000
5,000	Intangible assets		–0–
	Total available for liabilities with priority and unsecured creditors		80,000
	Less: Liabilities with priority (listed below)		(33,000)
	Available for unsecured creditors		47,000
	Estimated deficiency		43,000
$275,000			$ 90,000

Book Values	Liabilities and Stockholders' Equity		Available for Nonpriority Liabilities
	Liabilities with priority:		
–0–	Administrative expenses (estimated)	$ 20,000	
	Accounts payable:		
$ 10,000	Salaries payable	10,000	
3,000	Taxes payable	3,000	
	Total	$ 33,000	
	Fully secured creditors:		
120,000	Note payable	120,000	
	Less: Land and buildings	(135,000)	–0–
	Partially secured creditors:		
30,000	Note payable	30,000	
	Less: investments	(18,000)	$12,000
	Unsecured creditors:		
35,000	Note payable		35,000
43,000	Accounts payable (other than salaries and taxes, plus unrecorded liabilities have been included)		43,000
34,000	Stockholders' equity (adjusted for unrecorded liabilities)		–0–
$275,000			$90,000

that account retains its balance of $140,000. The other $23,000 of stockholders' equity is recorded as additional paid-in capital.

	Debit	Credit
Accounts receivable	$ 9,000	
Inventory	36,000	
Investments	18,000	
Land	75,000	
Buildings	60,000	
Equipment	20,000	
Reorganization value in excess of amounts allocable to identifiable assets	12,000	
Accounts payable and accrued expenses		$ 20,000
Note payable one		30,000
Note payable two		12,000
Note payable three		5,000
Common stock		140,000
Additional paid-in capital		23,000
Totals	$230,000	$230,000

QUESTIONS

1. What is meant by the term *insolvent?*
2. At present, what federal legislation governs most bankruptcy proceedings?
3. What are the primary objectives of a bankruptcy proceeding?
4. A bankruptcy case may begin with either a voluntary or an involuntary petition. What is the difference? What are the requirements for an involuntary petition?
5. An order for relief is entered by a bankruptcy court. How does this action affect an insolvent company and its creditors?
6. What is the difference in fully secured liabilities, partially secured liabilities, and unsecured liabilities?
7. In a bankruptcy proceeding, what is the significance of a liability with priority? What are the general categories of liabilities that have priority in a liquidation?
8. Why are the administrative expenses incurred during a liquidation classified as liabilities having priority?
9. What is the difference between a Chapter 7 bankruptcy and a Chapter 11 bankruptcy?
10. Why might unsecured creditors favor reorganizing an insolvent company rather than forcing it into liquidation?
11. What is the purpose of a statement of financial affairs? Why might this statement be prepared before a bankruptcy petition is filed?
12. In the liquidation of a company, what actions are performed by the trustee?
13. A trustee for a company that is being liquidated voids a preference transfer. What has happened, and why was this action taken by the trustee?
14. A statement of realization and liquidation is prepared for a company that is being liquidated. What information can be ascertained from this statement?
15. What is meant by the term *debtor in possession?*
16. Who can develop reorganization plans in a Chapter 11 bankruptcy?
17. What types of proposals might be found in a reorganization plan?
18. Under normal conditions, how does a reorganization plan become effective?
19. In a bankruptcy proceeding, what is a *cram down?*
20. While a company goes through reorganization, how should its liabilities be reported?
21. During reorganization, how should a company's income statement be structured?

22. What accounting is made of the professional fees incurred during a reorganization?

23. What is meant by *fresh start accounting?*

24. Under what conditions is fresh start accounting used by a company emerging from a bankruptcy reorganization?

25. When fresh start accounting is utilized, how are a company's assets reported? How are its liabilities reported?

26. How is a "reorganization value in excess of amounts allocable to identifiable assets" account computed? Where is this balance reported? What happens to the balance?

INTERNET ASSIGNMENT

Internet sites are time and date sensitive. It is the purpose of these exercises to have you explore the Internet. You may need to refer to the text's Web site at http://www.mhhe.com/hoyle6e to find the most up-to-date links for the Web sites listed in the Internet Assignments.

1. On the Internet go to the following Web site: www.10kwizard.com

   Under "Word Search" enter "fresh start" or "reorganization items" or "bankruptcy."

   Under "Form Group" enter "Annual Reports."

   Under "Form" enter "10–K."

   Click on "Search."

A list of companies should appear. Click on the name of a company and see what information is being reported by that company about the topic that you entered. Click on highlighted term to expand coverage. Write a report to indicate the information that you have discovered about this company and this word search.

LIBRARY ASSIGNMENTS

1. Locate the *Wall Street Journal General Index* for a recent year. Under the heading, "Bankruptcies" identify one company that has recently completed bankruptcy proceedings. Then, in the *Wall Street Journal Corporate Index,* under the name of this company, locate articles that describe the various stages of the process from beginning through resolution. Write a report to answer the following questions:
   - Was the bankruptcy voluntary or involuntary?
   - What events led up to the filing of the bankruptcy petition?
   - What actions did the company take to bring the matter to a final resolution?
   - Did the bankruptcy end in liquidation or reorganization?
   - What were the significant provisions of the liquidation or the reorganization plan?
   - What losses, if any, were the creditors forced to suffer?

2. Read the following as well as any other published articles describing the work of the accountant in bankruptcy cases:

   "Managing in a Reorganization," *Management Accounting,* January 1988.

   "What to Do When Chapter 11 Threatens," *Journal of Accountancy,* May 1993.

   "A New Chapter in Bankruptcy Reform," *Journal of Accountancy,* February 1999.

   "When Your Customer Goes Belly-Up," *Journal of Accountancy,* April 1999.

   "The Rewards of Insolvency," *The Practical Accountant,* August 1998.

   "Management Accounting—How a Workout Specialist Operates," *Journal of Accountancy,* January 1992.

   "What a CPA Should Know Before a Business Fails," *Journal of Accountancy,* June 1991.

   "The CPA's Role as Bankruptcy Examiner," *CPA Journal,* September 1991.

   "What Accountants Need to Know About the Bankruptcy Valuation Process," *Ohio CPA Journal,* June 1992.

Write a report describing the services that can be performed by an accountant during a corporate bankruptcy. Include activities to be carried out prior to the filing of a petition as well as any functions thereafter.

3. Read the following as well as any other published articles concerning possible changes in the bankruptcy laws pertaining to Chapter 11 reorganizations:

"The Untenable Case for Chapter 11," *Yale Law Journal,* March 1992.

"Bankruptcy Lawyers Dispute Call for Scrapping Chapter 11 Process," *Wall Street Journal,* March 19, 1992, p. B5.

"The Bankruptcy Game," *Time,* May 18, 1992.

"As Bankruptcies Surge, Creditors Lobby Hard to Get Tougher Laws," *Wall Street Journal,* June 17, 1998, p. A1.

"House Approves Bankruptcy Overhaul Amid Criticism Bill May Be Too Tough," *Wall Street Journal,* May 6, 1999, p. A28.

"Blimey! CPAs!" *Forbes,* March 15, 1992.

"For Many Small Businesses, Chapter 11 Closes the Book," *Wall Street Journal,* November 4, 1992, p. B2.

Write a report describing possible problems with the current laws and changes in these laws that might be justified.

PROBLEMS

1. What are the objectives of the bankruptcy laws in the United States?
   a. Provide relief for the court system in this country and ensure that all debtors are treated the same.
   b. Distribute assets fairly and discharge honest debtors from their obligations.
   c. Protect the economy and stimulate growth.
   d. Prevent insolvency and protect shareholders.

2. In a bankruptcy, which of the following statements is true?
   a. An order for relief only results from a voluntary petition.
   b. Creditors entering an involuntary petition must have debts totaling at least $20,000.
   c. Secured notes payable are considered liabilities with priority on a statement of affairs.
   d. A liquidation is referred to as a Chapter 7 bankruptcy, whereas a reorganization is a Chapter 11 bankruptcy.

3. In the reporting of a liquidation, assets are shown at:
   a. Present value calculated using an appropriate effective rate.
   b. Net realizable value.
   c. Historical cost.
   d. Book value.

4. An involuntary bankruptcy petition must be filed by:
   a. The insolvent company's attorney.
   b. The holders of the insolvent company's debenture bonds.
   c. Unsecured creditors with total debts of at least $10,775.
   d. The management of the company.

5. An order for relief:
   a. Prohibits creditors from taking action to collect from an insolvent company without court approval.
   b. Calls for the immediate distribution of free assets to unsecured creditors.
   c. Can only be entered in an involuntary bankruptcy proceeding.
   d. Gives an insolvent company time to file a voluntary bankruptcy petition.

6. Which of the following is not a liability that has priority in a liquidation?
   a. Administrative expenses incurred in the liquidation.
   b. Salary payable of $800 per person owed to 26 employees.
   c. Payroll taxes due to the federal government.
   d. Advertising expense incurred before the company became insolvent.

7. Which of the following is the minimum limitation necessary for the filing of an involuntary bankruptcy petition?
   a. The signature of 12 creditors to whom the debtor owes at least $4,300 in unsecured debt.
   b. The signature of six creditors to whom the debtor owes at least $20,000 in unsecured debt.
   c. The signature of three creditors to whom the debtor owes at least $10,775 in unsecured debt.
   d. The signature of nine creditors to whom the debtor owes at least $25,000 in unsecured debt.

8. On a statement of financial affairs, how are liabilities classified?
   a. Current and noncurrent.
   b. Secured and unsecured.
   c. Monetary and nonmonetary.
   d. Historic and futuristic.

9. What is a debtor in possession?
   a. The holder of a note receivable issued by an insolvent company prior to the granting of an order for relief.
   b. A fully secured creditor.
   c. The ownership of an insolvent company that continues in control of the organization during a bankruptcy reorganization.
   d. The stockholders in a Chapter 7 bankruptcy.

10. How are anticipated administrative expenses reported on a statement of financial affairs?
    a. As a footnote until actually incurred.
    b. As a liability with priority.
    c. As a partially secured liability.
    d. As an unsecured liability.

11. Prior to filing a voluntary Chapter 7 bankruptcy petition, Haynes Company pays a supplier $1,000 to satisfy an unsecured claim. Haynes was insolvent at the time. Subsequently, the trustee appointed to oversee this liquidation forces the return of this $1,000. Which of the following is correct?
    a. A preference transfer has been voided.
    b. All transactions just prior to a voluntary bankruptcy proceeding must be nullified.
    c. The supplier should sue for the return of this money.
    d. The $1,000 claim becomes a liability with priority.

12. Which of the following is not an expected function of a bankruptcy trustee?
    a. The filing of a plan of reorganization.
    b. Recovery of all property belonging to a company.
    c. Liquidation of noncash assets.
    d. The distribution of assets to the proper claimants.

13. What is an inherent limitation of the statement of financial affairs?
    a. Many of the amounts reported are only estimations that might prove to be inaccurate.
    b. The statement is only applicable to a Chapter 11 bankruptcy.
    c. The statement covers only a short time, whereas a bankruptcy may last much longer.
    d. The figures on the statement vary between a voluntary and an involuntary bankruptcy.

14. What is a cram down?
    a. An agreement about the total amount of money to be reserved to pay creditors who have priority.
    b. The confirmation by the bankruptcy court of a reorganization even though it was not accepted by a class of creditors or stockholders.
    c. The filing of an involuntary bankruptcy petition, especially by the holders of partially secured debts.
    d. The decision made by the court as to whether a particular creditor has priority.

15. On a balance sheet prepared for a company during its reorganization, how are liabilities reported?
    a. As current and long term.
    b. As monetary and nonmonetary.
    c. As subject to compromise and not subject to compromise.
    d. As equity related and debt related.

16. On a balance sheet prepared for a company during its reorganization, at what balance are liabilities reported?
    a. At the expected amount of the allowed claims.
    b. At the present value of the expected future cash flows.
    c. At the expected amount of the settlement.
    d. At the amount of the anticipated final payment.

17. Which of the following is not a reorganization item for purposes of reporting a company's income statement during a Chapter 11 bankruptcy?
    a. Professional fees.
    b. Interest income.
    c. Interest expense.
    d. Gains and losses on closing facilities.

18. What accounting is made for professional fees incurred during a bankruptcy reorganization?
    a. They must be expensed immediately.
    b. They must be capitalized and written off over 40 years or less.
    c. They must be capitalized until the company emerges from the reorganization.
    d. They are either expensed or capitalized depending on the nature of the expenditure.

19. Which of the following is necessary for a company to use fresh start accounting?
    a. The original owners must hold at least 50 percent of the stock of the company when it emerges from bankruptcy.
    b. The reorganization value of the company must exceed the value of all assets.
    c. The reorganization value of the company must exceed the value of all liabilities.
    d. The original owners must hold less than 50 percent of the stock of the company when it emerges from bankruptcy.

20. If the reorganization value of a company emerging from bankruptcy is larger than the values that can be assigned to specific assets, what accounting is made of the difference?
    a. Because of conservatism, the difference is simply ignored.
    b. The difference is expensed immediately.
    c. The difference is capitalized as an intangible asset.
    d. The difference is recorded as a professional fee.

21. For a company emerging from bankruptcy, how are its liabilities (other than deferred income taxes) reported?
    a. At their historical value.
    b. At zero because of fresh start accounting.
    c. At the present value of the future cash flows.
    d. At the negotiated value less all professional fees incurred in the reorganization.

22. A company is to be liquidated and has the following liabilities:

Income taxes	$ 8,000
Notes payable (secured by land)	120,000
Accounts payable	85,000
Salary payable (evenly divided between two employees)	6,000
Bonds payable	70,000
Administrative expenses for liquidation	20,000

The company has the following assets:

	Book Value	Fair Market Value
Current assets	$ 80,000	$ 35,000
Land	100,000	90,000
Buildings and equipment	100,000	110,000

How much money will the holders of the notes payable collect following the liquidation?

23. The Xavier Company is going through a Chapter 7 bankruptcy. All assets have been liquidated and the company retains only $12,000 in free cash. The following debts, totaling $27,600, remain:

Government claims to unpaid taxes	$5,000
Salary during last month owed to Mr. Key (not an officer)	7,300
Administrative expenses	3,000
Salary during last month owed to Ms. Rankin (not an officer)	5,300
Unsecured accounts payable	7,000

For each of these debts, indicate how much money will be paid to the creditor.

24. Ataway Company has had severe financial difficulties and is considering the possibility of filing a bankruptcy petition. At this time, the company has the following assets (stated at net realizable value) and liabilities.

Assets (pledged against debts of $70,000)	$116,000
Assets (pledged against debts of $130,000)	50,000
Other assets	80,000
Liabilities with priority	42,000
Unsecured creditors	200,000

In a liquidation, how much money would be paid on the partially secured debt?

25. The Chesterfield Company has cash of $50,000, inventory worth $90,000, and a building worth $130,000. Unfortunately, the company also has accounts payable of $180,000, a note payable of $80,000 (secured by the inventory), liabilities with priority of $20,000, a bond payable of $150,000 (secured by the building). In a Chapter 7 bankruptcy, how much money will the holders of the bond expect to receive?

26. The Mondesto Company has the following:

Unsecured creditors	$230,000
Liabilities with priority	110,000
Secured liabilities:	
Debt one, $210,000; value of pledged asset	180,000
Debt two, $170,000; value of pledged asset	100,000
Debt three, $120,000; value of pledged asset	140,000

The company also has a number of other assets that are not pledged in any way. The creditors holding debt two want to receive at least $142,000. For how much do these free assets have to be sold so that debt two would receive exactly $142,000?

27. A statement of financial affairs created for an insolvent corporation that is beginning the process of liquidation discloses the following data (assets are shown at net realizable values):

Assets pledged with fully secured creditors	$200,000
Fully secured liabilities	150,000
Assets pledged with partially secured creditors	380,000
Partially secured liabilities	490,000
Assets not pledged	300,000
Unsecured liabilities with priority	160,000
Accounts payable (unsecured)	390,000

Required

a. This company owes $3,000 to an unsecured creditor (without priority). How much money can this creditor expect to collect?

b. This company owes $100,000 to a bank on a note payable that is secured by a security interest attached to property with an estimated net realizable value of $80,000. How much money can this bank expect to collect?

28. A company preparing for a Chapter 7 liquidation has the following.

Liabilities:
- Note payable A of $90,000 secured by land having a book value of $50,000 and a fair market value of $70,000.
- Note payable B of $120,000 secured by a building having a book value of $60,000 and a fair market value of $40,000.
- Note payable C of $60,000, unsecured.
- Administrative expenses payable of $20,000.
- Accounts payable of $120,000.
- Income taxes payable of $30,000.

Other assets:
- Cash $10,000.
- Inventory $100,000, but with fair market value of $60,000.
- Equipment $90,000, but with fair market value of $50,000.

How much will each of the company's liabilities be paid after liquidation?

29. The Olds Company declares Chapter 7 bankruptcy. Here are the accounts at that time; administrative expenses are estimated to be $12,000.

Cash	$ 24,000	
Accounts receivable	60,000	(worth $28,000)
Inventory	70,000	(worth $56,000)
Land (secures note A)	200,000	(worth $160,000)
Building (secures bonds)	400,000	(worth $320,000)
Equipment	120,000	(worth unknown)
Accounts payable	180,000	
Taxes payable to government	20,000	
Note payable A	170,000	
Note payable B	250,000	
Bonds payable	300,000	

The holders of note payable B want to collect at least $125,000. To achieve that goal, how much does the company have to receive in the liquidation of its equipment?

30. A company is going through a Chapter 7 bankruptcy and has the following account balances:

Cash	$ 30,000
Receivables (30 percent collectible)	50,000
Inventory (worth $39,000)	90,000
Land (worth $120,000) (secures note payable)	100,000
Buildings (worth $180,000) (secures bonds payable)	200,000
Salary payable (seven workers owed equal amounts for last two weeks)	10,000
Accounts payable	90,000
Note payable (secured by land)	110,000
Bonds payable (secured by building)	300,000
Common stock	100,000
Retained earnings	(140,000)

How much will be paid on each of the following:

Salary payable

Accounts payable

Note payable

Bonds payable

31. The Pumpkin Company is going through bankruptcy reorganization. It has a note payable for $200,000 that was incurred prior to the order for relief. The company

believes that the note will be settled for $60,000 in cash. It is also possible that the creditor will take a piece of land instead that cost the company $50,000 but is worth $72,000. On a balance sheet during the reorganization period, how will this debt be reported?

32. A company is coming out of reorganization with the following accounts:

	Book Value	Fair Market Value
Receivables	$ 80,000	$ 90,000
Inventory	200,000	210,000
Buildings	300,000	400,000
Liabilities	300,000	300,000
Common Stock	330,000	
Additional paid-in capital	20,000	
Retained earnings (Deficit)	(70,000)	

The company's assets have a reorganization value of $760,000. The owners of the company before the reorganization have transferred 80 percent of the outstanding stock to the creditors.

Required

Prepare the journal entry that is necessary to adjust the company's records to fresh start accounting.

33. The Addison Corporation is currently going through a Chapter 11 bankruptcy. The company has the following account balances. Prepare an income statement for this organization. The effective tax rate is 20 percent (realization of any tax benefits is anticipated).

	Debit	Credit
Advertising expense	$ 24,000	
Cost of goods sold	211,000	
Depreciation expense	22,000	
Interest expense	4,000	
Interest revenue		$ 32,000
Loss on closing of branch	109,000	
Professional fees	71,000	
Rent expense	16,000	
Revenues		467,000
Salary expense	70,000	

34. The Kansas City Corporation holds three assets when it comes out of Chapter 11 bankruptcy:

	Book Value	Market Value
Inventory	$ 86,000	$ 50,000
Land and buildings	250,000	400,000
Equipment	123,000	110,000

The company has a reorganization value of $600.000.

Required

a. Describe the rules to determine whether to apply fresh start accounting to the Kansas City Corporation.
b. If fresh start accounting is appropriate, how will the assets of this company be reported?
c. If a "reorganization value in excess of amounts allocable to identifiable assets" account is recognized, where should it be reported? What happens to this balance?

35. The Jaez Corporation is in the process of going through a reorganization. As of December 31, 2001, the company's accountant has determined the following

information although the company is still several months away from emerging from the bankruptcy proceeding. Prepare a balance sheet in appropriate form.

	Book Value	Market Value
Assets		
Cash	$ 23,000	$ 23,000
Inventory	45,000	47,000
Land	140,000	210,000
Buildings	220,000	260,000
Equipment	154,000	157,000

	Allowed Claims	Expected Settlement
Liabilities as of the date of the order for relief		
Accounts payable	$ 123,000	$ 20,000
Accrued expenses	30,000	4,000
Income taxes payable	22,000	18,000
Note payable (due 2004, secured by land)	100,000	100,000
Note payable (due 2006)	170,000	80,000
Liabilities since the date of the order for relief		
Accounts payable	$60,000	
Note payable (due 2003)	110,000	
Stockholders' equity		
Common stock	$ 200,000	
Deficit	(233,000)	

36. The Ristoni Company is in the process of emerging from a Chapter 11 bankruptcy. The company will apply fresh start accounting as of December 31, 2001. The company currently has 30,000 shares of common stock outstanding with a $240,000 par value. As part of the reorganization, the owners will contribute 18,000 shares of this stock back to the company. A deficit balance of $330,000 also is being reported.

The company has the following asset accounts:

	Book Value	Market Value
Accounts receivable	$100,000	$ 80,000
Inventory	112,000	90,000
Land and buildings	420,000	500,000
Equipment	78,000	65,000

The company's liabilities will be settled as follows. Assume that all notes will be issued at reasonable interest rates.

- Accounts payable of $80,000 will be settled with a note for $5,000. These creditors will also get 1,000 shares of the stock contributed by the owners.
- Accrued expenses of $35,000 will be settled with a note for $4,000.
- Note payable (due 2005) of $100,000 was fully secured and has not been renegotiated.
- Note payable (due 2004) of $200,000 will be settled with a note for $50,000 and 10,000 shares of the stock contributed by the owners.
- Note payable (due 2002) of $185,000 will be settled with a note for $71,000 and 7,000 shares of the stock contributed by the owners.
- Note payable (due 2003) of $200,000 will be settled with a note for $110,000.

The company has a reorganization value of $780,000.

Required

Prepare all of the journal entries for Ristoni so that the company can emerge from the bankruptcy proceeding.

37. The Smith Corporation has gone through bankruptcy and is ready to emerge as a reorganized entity on December 31, 2001. On this date, the company has the following assets (market value is based on the discounted future cash flows that are anticipated):

	Book Value	Market Value
Accounts receivable	$ 20,000	$ 18,000
Inventory	143,000	111,000
Land and buildings	250,000	278,000
Machinery	144,000	121,000
Patents	100,000	125,000

The company has a reorganization value of $800,000.

The company has 50,000 shares of $10 par value common stock outstanding. A deficit retained earnings balance of $670,000 also is reported. The owners will distribute 30,000 shares of this stock as part of the reorganization plan.

The company's liabilities will be settled as follows:

- Accounts payable (existing at the date on which the order for relief was granted) of $180,000 will be settled with an 8 percent, two-year note for $35,000.
- Accounts payable (incurred since the date on which the order for relief was granted) of $97,000 will be paid in the regular course of business.
- Note payable—First Metropolitan Bank of $200,000 will be settled with an 8 percent, five-year note for $50,000 and 15,000 shares of the stock contributed by the owners.
- Note payable—Northwestern Bank of Tulsa of $350,000 will be settled with a 7 percent, eight-year note for $100,000 and 15,000 shares of the stock contributed by the owners.

Required

a. How does the accountant for Smith Corporation know that fresh start accounting must be utilized?

b. Prepare a balance sheet for the Smith Corporation upon its emergence from reorganization.

38. Ambrose Corporation reports the following information:

	Book Value	Liquidation Value
Assets pledged with fully secured creditors	$220,000	$245,000
Assets pledged with partially secured creditors . . .	111,000	103,000
Other assets	140,000	81,000
Liabilities with priority	36,000	
Fully secured liabilities	200,000	
Partially secured liabilities	180,000	
Accounts payable (unsecured)	283,000	

In liquidation, what amount of cash should each class of the liabilities expect to collect?

39. The following balance sheet has been prepared by the accountant for the Limestone Company as of June 3, 2001, the date on which the company is to file a voluntary petition of bankruptcy.

LIMESTONE COMPANY
Balance Sheet
June 3, 2001

Assets

Cash	$ 3,000
Accounts receivable (net)	65,000
Inventory	88,000
Land	100,000
Buildings (net)	300,000
Equipment (net)	180,000
Total assets	$736,000

Liabilities and Equities

Accounts payable	$ 98,000
Notes payable—current (secured by equipment)	250,000
Notes payable—long term (secured by land and buildings)	190,000
Common stock	120,000
Retained earnings	78,000
Total liabilities and equities	$736,000

Additional Information

- If the company is liquidated, administrative expenses estimated at $18,000 are expected to be incurred.
- The accounts payable figure includes $10,000 in wages earned by the company's 12 employees during May. No one earned more than $1,300.
- Taxes of $14,000 owed to the U.S. government have not been included in the liabilities.
- Company officials estimate that 40 percent of the accounts receivable will be collected in a liquidation and that the inventory can be disposed of for $80,000. The land and buildings are to be sold together for approximately $310,000; the equipment should bring $130,000 at auction.

Required

Prepare a statement of financial affairs for the Limestone Company as of June 3, 2001.

40. Creditors of Jones Corporation are considering petitioning the courts to force the company into Chapter 7 bankruptcy. The following information has been determined. Administrative expenses in connection with the liquidation are estimated to be $22,000. Indicate the amount of money that each class of creditors can anticipate receiving.

	Book Value	Net Realizable Value
Cash	$ 6,000	$ 6,000
Accounts receivable	32,000	18,000
Inventory	45,000	31,000
Supplies	3,000	–0–
Investments	2,000	8,000
Land	60,000	72,000
Buildings	90,000	68,000
Equipment	50,000	35,000
Notes payable (secured by land)	65,000	
Notes payable (secured by buildings)	78,000	
Bonds payable (secured by equipment)	115,000	
Accounts payable	70,000	
Salary payable (two weeks' salary for the four employees)	6,000	
Taxes payable	10,000	

41. The Anteium Company owes $80,000 on a note payable that is currently due. The note is held by a local bank and is secured by a mortgage lien attached to three acres of land worth $48,000. The land originally cost Anteium $31,000 when acquired several years ago. The only other account balances for this company are investments of $20,000 (but worth $25,000), accounts payable of $20,000, common stock of $40,000, and a deficit of $89,000. Anteium is insolvent and attempting to arrange a reorganization so that the business can continue to operate. The reorganization value of the company is $82,000.

Each of the following should be viewed as independent situations:

a. On a statement of financial affairs, how would this note be reported? How would the land be shown?

b. Assume that Anteium develops an acceptable reorganization plan. Sixty percent of the common stock is transferred to the bank to settle that particular obligation. A 7 percent, three-year note payable for $5,000 is used to settle the accounts payable. How would Anteium record the reorganization?

c. Assume that Anteium is liquidated. The land and investments are sold for $50,000 and $26,000, respectively. Administrative expenses amount to $11,000. How much will the various parties collect?

42. The following balance sheet has been produced for the Litz Corporation as of August 8, 2001, the date on which the company is to begin selling assets as part of a corporate liquidation.

LITZ CORPORATION
Balance Sheet
August 8, 2001

Assets

Cash	$ 16,000
Accounts receivable (net)	82,000
Investments	32,000
Inventory (net realizable value is expected	
to approximate cost)	69,000
Land	30,000
Buildings (net)	340,000
Equipment (net)	210,000
Total assets	$779,000

Liabilities and Equities

Accounts payable	$150,000
Notes payable—current (secured by inventory)	132,000
Notes payable—long term (secured by land	
and buildings [valued at $300,000])	259,000
Common stock	135,000
Retained earnings	103,000
Total liabilities and equities	$779,000

The following events occur during the liquidation process:

■ The investments are sold for $39,000.

■ The inventory is sold at auction for $48,000.

■ The money derived from the inventory is applied against the short-term notes payable.

■ Administrative expenses of $15,000 are incurred in connection with the liquidation.

■ The land and buildings are sold for $315,000. The long-term notes payable are paid.

■ The accountant determines that $34,000 of the accounts payable are liabilities with priority.

■ The company's equipment is sold for $84,000.

■ Accounts receivable of $34,000 are collected. The remainder of the receivables are considered uncollectible.

■ The administrative expenses are paid.

Required

    a. Prepare a statement of realization and liquidation for the period just described.

    b. What percentage of their claims should the unsecured creditors receive?

43. The following balance sheet has been prepared by the accountant of the Becket Corporation as of November 10, 2001, the date on which the company is to release a plan for reorganizing operations under Chapter 11 of the Bankruptcy Reform Act.

BECKET CORPORATION
Balance Sheet
November 10, 2001
Assets

Cash	$ 12,000
Accounts receivable (net)	61,000
Investments	26,000
Inventory (net realizable value is expected to approximate 80% of cost)	80,000
Land	57,000
Buildings (net)	248,000
Equipment (net)	117,000
Total assets	$601,000

Liabilities and Equities

Accounts payable	$129,000
Notes payable—current (secured by equipment)	220,000
Notes payable—(due in 2004) (secured by land and buildings)	325,000
Common stock ($10 par value)	60,000
Retained earnings (deficit)	(133,000)
Total liabilities and equities	$601,000

The company presented the following proposal:

1. The reorganization value of the company's assets just prior to emerging from bankruptcy is set at $650,000.

2. Accounts receivable of $20,000 are written off as uncollectible. Investments are worth $40,000, land is worth $80,000, the buildings are worth $300,000, and the equipment is worth $86,000.

3. An outside investor has been found who will buy 7,000 shares of common stock at $11 per share.

4. The company's investments are to be sold for $40,000 in cash with the proceeds going to the holders of the current note payable. The remainder of these short-term notes will be converted into $130,000 of notes due in 2005 and paying 10 percent annual cash interest.

5. All accounts payable will be exchanged for $40,000 in notes payable due in 2002 and paying 8 percent annual interest.

6. Title to land costing $20,000 but worth $50,000 will be transferred to the holders of the note payable due in 2004. In addition, these creditors will receive $180,000 in notes payable (paying 10 percent annual interest) coming due in 2008. These creditors also are issued 3,000 shares of previously unissued common stock.

Required

Prepare journal entries for Becket to record the transactions as put forth in this reorganization plan.

44. The Oregon Corporation has filed a voluntary petition to reorganize the company under Chapter 11 of the Bankruptcy Reform Act. The creditors are considering an attempt to force liquidation. The company currently holds cash of $6,000 and accounts receivable of $25,000. In addition, the company owns four pieces of land. The first two (labeled A and B) cost $8,000 each. Plots C and D cost the company $20,000 and $25,000,

respectively. A mortgage lien is attached to each parcel of land as security for four different notes payable of $15,000 apiece. Presently, the land can be sold for:

Plot A	$16,000
Plot B	$11,000
Plot C	$14,000
Plot D	$27,000

Another $25,000 note payable is unsecured. Accounts payable at this time total $32,000. Of this amount, $12,000 is salary owed to the company's workers. No employee is due more than $1,800.

The company expects to collect $12,000 from the accounts receivable if liquidation becomes necessary. Administrative expenses required for liquidation are anticipated to be $16,000.

Required

    a. Prepare a statement of financial affairs for the Oregon Corporation.

    b. If the company is liquidated, how much cash would be paid on the note payable secured by plot B?

    c. If the company is liquidated, how much cash would be paid on the note payable that is unsecured?

    d. If the company is liquidated and plot D is sold for $30,000, how much cash would be paid on the note payable secured by plot B?

45. Lynch, Inc., is a hardware store operating in Boulder, Colorado. Management has recently made some poor inventory acquisitions that have loaded the store with unsalable merchandise. Because of the drop in revenues, the company is now insolvent. The entire inventory can be sold for only $33,000. Following is a trial balance as of March 14, 2001, the day the company files for a Chapter 7 liquidation.

	Debit	Credit
Accounts payable		$ 33,000
Accounts receivable	$ 25,000	
Accumulated depreciation, building		50,000
Accumulated depreciation, equipment		16,000
Additional paid-in capital		8,000
Advertising payable		4,000
Building	80,000	
Cash	1,000	
Common stock		50,000
Equipment	30,000	
Inventory	100,000	
Investments	15,000	
Land	10,000	
Note payable—Colorado Savings and Loan (secured by lien on land and building)		70,000
Note payable—First National Bank (secured by equipment)		150,000
Payroll taxes payable		1,000
Retained earnings (deficit)	126,000	
Salary payable (owed equally to two employees)		5,000
Totals	$387,000	$387,000

Company officials believe that 60 percent of the accounts receivable can be collected if the company is liquidated. The building and land have a market value of $75,000, while the equipment is worth $19,000. The investments represent shares of a nationally traded company that can be sold at the current time for $21,000. Administrative expenses necessary to carry out a liquidation would approximate $16,000.

Required

Prepare a statement of financial affairs for Lynch, Inc., as of March 14, 2001.

46. Use the trial balance presented for Lynch, Inc., in problem 45. Assume that the company will be liquidated and the following transactions occur:

- Accounts receivable of $18,000 are collected with remainder written off.
- All of the company's inventory is sold for $40,000.
- Additional accounts payable of $10,000 incurred for various expenses such as utilities and maintenance are discovered.
- The land and building are sold for $71,000.
- The note payable due to the Colorado Savings and Loan is paid.
- The equipment is sold at auction for only $11,000 with the proceeds applied to the note owed to the First National Bank.
- The investments are sold for $21,000.
- Administrative expenses total $20,000 as of July 23, 2001, but no payment has yet been made.

Required

a. Prepare a statement of realization and liquidation for the period from March 14, 2001, through July 23, 2001.
b. How much cash would be paid to an unsecured, nonpriority creditor who is owed a total of $1,000 by Lynch, Inc.?

47. The Holmes Corporation has filed a voluntary petition with the bankruptcy court in hopes of reorganizing the company. A statement of financial affairs has been prepared for Holmes showing the following debts:

Liabilities with priority:	
Salary payable	$ 18,000
Fully secured creditors:	
Notes payable (secured by land and buildings valued at $84,000)	70,000
Partially secured creditors:	
Notes payable (secured by inventory valued at $30,000)	140,000
Unsecured creditors:	
Notes payable	50,000
Accounts payable	10,000
Accrued expenses	4,000

The company has 10,000 shares of common stock outstanding with a par value of $5 per share. In addition, the company is currently reporting a deficit balance of $132,000. Company officials have proposed the following reorganization plan:

- The company's assets have a total book value of $210,000, an amount considered to be equal to fair market value. The reorganization value of the assets as a whole, though, is set at $225,000.
- Employees will receive a one-year note in lieu of all salaries owed. Interest will be 10 percent, a normal rate for this type of liability.
- The fully secured note will have all future interest dropped from a 15 percent rate, which is now unrealistic, to a 10 percent rate.
- The partially secured note payable will be satisfied by the signing of a new six-year $30,000 note paying 10 percent annual interest. In addition, this creditor will receive 5,000 new shares of Holmes' common stock.
- An outside investor has been enlisted to buy 6,000 new shares of common stock at $6 per share.
- The unsecured creditors will be offered 20 cents on the dollar to settle the remaining liabilities.

If this plan of reorganization is accepted and becomes effective, what journal entries would be recorded by the Holmes Corporation?

C H A P T E R

Partnerships: Formation and Operation

QUESTIONS TO CONSIDER

- Why are some businesses legally organized as partnerships rather than as corporations?

- Why do the equity accounts of a partnership differ from those of a corporation?

- If a partner brings an intangible attribute (such as a business expertise or an established clientele) to a partnership, how is this contribution valued and recorded?

- How is the annual net income that is earned by a partnership allocated among the individual capital accounts maintained for each partner?

- If a partner withdraws from a partnership and receives more cash than the amount recorded in the appropriate capital account, what accounting does the business make of the excess payment?

A reader of college accounting textbooks might well come to the conclusion that business activity is carried out exclusively by corporations. Because most large companies are legally incorporated, a vast majority of textbook references and illustrations concern corporate organizations. Contrary to the perception being relayed, partnerships (as well as sole proprietorships) make up a vital element of the business community. Based on the filing of income tax returns, nearly 1.6 million partnerships were in the United States in 1995 (as compared to nearly 4.5 million corporations). One author makes a very important assessment of the significance of partnerships to the economy: "One-quarter of all start-ups begin as partnerships."[1]

The partnership form is found in a wide range of business activities, from small local operations to worldwide enterprises. Examples found in the American economy include:

- Individual proprietors often join together in the formation of a partnership as a means of reducing expenses, expanding services, and adding increased expertise. Partnerships also provide important tax benefits.

- Partnerships are a common means by which friends and relatives can easily create and organize a business endeavor.

- Historically doctors, lawyers, and other professionals have formed partnerships because of legal prohibitions against the incorporation of their practices. Although most states now permit alternative forms for such organizations, operating as a partnership or sole proprietorship is still necessary in many areas.

---

[1]Nick Kochan, "Two Is Company," *Director,* August 1996, p. 42.

Over the years, some partnerships have grown to enormous sizes. Connell Limited Partnership, for example, recycles and manufactures metal products; in 1996 it had revenues of $1.26 billion.[2] An announcement of the merger of Deloitte Haskins & Sells and Touche Ross stated that the combined organization would have 5,470 partners. "The new international firm will have 1989 worldwide revenue in excess of $4 billion, will employ 65,000 people and will be one of the world's largest accounting and consulting firms, with a leading position in substantially all major U.S. and international markets."[3] In 1999, Ernst & Young International had 97,800 employees and nearly $13.0 billion in revenues.

Certainly some of the most successful organizations in business today are partnerships. "Winning teams include Hanson's James Hanson and Gordon White, the Body Shop's Anita and Gordon Roddick, the partners of the U.S. investment bank Goldman Sachs, and in a different way, the partners of the country's largest law and accounting firms."[4]

PARTNERSHIPS—ADVANTAGES AND DISADVANTAGES

The popularity of the partnership format is based on several advantages inherent to this type of organization. An analysis of these attributes explains why nearly 1.6 million enterprises in the United States are partnerships rather than corporations.

One of the most common motives is the ease of formation. Only an oral agreement is necessary to create a legally binding partnership. In contrast, depending on specific state laws, incorporation requires the filing of a formal application along with the completion of various other forms and documents. Operators of small businesses may find the convenience involved in creating a partnership to be an especially appealing characteristic.

Other justifications for structuring a business as a partnership can be discovered within the tax laws.

> The partnership form of business has become increasingly popular in the United States, and it may account for a significant portion of new business formation in the future. One reason for the burgeoning of partnerships is that this form of business offers many of the risk-sharing opportunities of the corporate form without the burden of corporate income taxation.[5]

Although a detailed investigation of taxation rules and regulations goes beyond the scope of this textbook, a few aspects are quite relevant to the current discussion. One area of the law warrants particular attention: the method by which partnerships are taxed. Although an informational tax return must be filed on an annual basis, *the partnership itself pays no income taxes.* For taxation purposes, the government does not view a partnership as an entity apart from its owners.

---

[2]Steve Kichen, Tina Russo McCarthy, and Peter Newcomb, "The Private 500," *Forbes,* December 2, 1996, p. 166.

[3]*DH & S Review,* July 17, 1989, pp. 1–2.

[4]Kochan, p. 42.

[5]Harry Watson, "An Analysis of the Formation and Behavior of Partnerships," *Public Finance Quarterly,* July 1989, p. 281.

Partnership revenue and expense items (as defined by the tax laws) must be assigned directly to the individual partners with the income taxes being paid by them. By passing income balances through to the partners in this manner, double-taxation of the profits that are earned by a business and then distributed to its owners is avoided. In a corporation, income is taxed twice: when earned and again when conveyed as a dividend. A partnership's income is only taxed at the time that it is initially earned by the business.

As an illustration, assume that a business earns $100. After paying any income taxes, the remainder is immediately conveyed to its owners. A tax rate of 30 percent is assumed for both individuals and corporations. As the following table shows, if this business is a partnership rather than a corporation, the owners are left with $21 more expendable income, which is 21 percent of the business income. This difference, though, does narrow as tax rates are lowered.

	Partnership	Corporation
Income before income taxes	$100	$100
Income taxes paid by business (30%)	–0–	(30)
Income distributed to owners	$100	$ 70
Income taxes paid by owners (30%)	(30)	(21)
Expendable income	$ 70	$ 49

The advantage of single taxation has led some larger companies in recent years to convert to the partnership form: The Boston Celtics and Motel 6 are just two examples of corporations that converted to partnerships to maximize after-tax returns to investors.[6]

Historically, a second tax advantage has long been associated with partnerships. Because income is taxable to the partners as it is earned by the business, any operating losses can be used to reduce their personal taxable income directly. In contrast, a corporation is viewed as separate from its owners so losses cannot be passed through to them. A corporation does have the ability to carry back any net operating losses and reduce previously taxed income (usually for the two prior years) and carry forward remaining losses to decrease future taxable income (for up to 20 years). However, if a corporation is newly formed or has not been profitable, operating losses provide no immediate benefit to a corporation and its owners as losses do for a partnership.

The tax advantage of deducting partnership losses has been reduced somewhat in recent years by changes in the tax laws. Because of the chance to pass through losses and reduce personal taxes, partnerships were often structured as tax shelters to report immediate losses (and, hence, tax deductions) with profits deferred into the future. Now, ownership of a partnership is labeled as a passive activity unless the partner materially participates in the actual business activities. For tax purposes, passive activity losses only serve to offset other passive activity profits. In most cases, these partnership losses can no longer be used to reduce earned income such as salaries. Thus, unless a taxpayer has significant passive activity income (from rents, for example), little or no tax advantage is created by losses reported by a partnership unless the partner materially participates in the actual business activity.

The partnership form of business also has certain significant disadvantages. Perhaps the most severe problem is the unlimited liability automatically incurred by each partner. Partnership law specifies that any partner can be held personally liable for *all* debts of the business. The potential risk is especially significant when coupled with the concept of *mutual agency*. This legal term refers to the right that each partner has to incur

---

[6]Keith Wishon and Robert P. Roche, "Making the Switch: Corporation to Partnership," *Journal of Accountancy,* March 1987, p. 90.

liabilities in the name of the partnership. Consequently, partners acting within the normal scope of the business have the power to obligate the company for any amount. If the partnership fails to pay these debts, creditors can seek satisfactory remuneration from any partner that they choose.

> Partners are jointly and severally liable for the firm's obligations. As an example, if a bank had made a $10 million loan to the partnership that it could not pay, and the bank obtained a judgment against the partnership, the bank could attempt to attach the assets of any particular partner in the firm. The bank could pick and choose the partners it wished to proceed against in order to satisfy the judgment. If a partner ended up paying more than his or her share, he or she would have a right to recover from the other partners.[7]

This problem is more than just a theoretical concern. As noted in the *Wall Street Journal,*

> At least 10 partners of Laventhol & Horwath, a major accounting firm that collapsed two years ago, have filed for personal bankruptcy. They are trying to protect their savings and their homes because partners and principals of the now-defunct firm owe creditors $47.3 million.[8]

Such legal concepts as unlimited liability and mutual agency describe partnership characteristics that have been defined and interpreted over a great number of years. To provide consistent application across state lines in regard to these terms as well as many other legal aspects of a partnership, the Uniform Partnership Act (UPA) was created. This act, which was first proposed in 1914 (and revised in 1994) now has been adopted by all states in some form. It establishes uniform standards in such areas as the nature of a partnership, the relationship of the partners to outside parties, and the dissolution of the partnership. For example, the most common legal definition of a partnership is provided by Section 6 of the act: "an association of two or more persons to carry on a business as co-owners for profit."

ALTERNATIVE LEGAL FORMS

Because of the possible liability, partnerships often experience difficulty in attracting large amounts of capital. Potential partners frequently prefer to avoid the risk that is a basic characteristic of a partnership. However, the tax benefits of avoiding double taxation still provide a strong pull toward the partnership form. Hence in recent years, a number of alternative types of organizations have been developed. The availability of these legal forms depends on state laws as well as applicable tax laws. In each case, though, the purpose is to limit the owners' personal liability while providing the tax benefits of a partnership.[9]

Subchapter S Corporation   A Subchapter S Corporation (often referred to as an S Corporation) is created as a corporation and, therefore, has all of the legal characteristics of that form.[10] According to the U.S. tax laws, if certain regulations are met, the corporation will be taxed in virtually the same way as a partnership. Thus, the Subchapter S Corporation pays no income taxes although its income (and losses) pass

---

[7]An interview with Leslie D. Corwin, Esq., "What's a Partner to Do?" *The CPA Journal,* April 1991, p. 22.

[8]Lee Berton and Joann S. Lublin, "Partnership Structure Is Called in Question as Liability Risk Rises," *Wall Street Journal,* June 10, 1992, p. A9.

[9]Many factors should be considered in choosing a specific legal form for an organization. The information shown here is merely an overview. For more information, consult a tax guide or a business law textbook.

[10]Unless a corporation qualifies as a Subchapter S Corporation or some other legal variation, it is referred to as a Subchapter C Corporation. Therefore, a vast majority of all businesses are C Corporations.

through to the taxable income of the individual owners. Double taxation is avoided but the owners do not face unlimited liability. The business can have only one class of stock and is limited to only 75 stockholders. All owners must be individuals, estates, certain tax-exempt entities, or certain types of trusts. The most significant problem associated with this business form is that its growth potential is limited because of the restriction on the number and type of owners.

Limited Partnership (LPs)　A limited partnership is a type of investment designed primarily for individuals who want the tax benefits of a partnership but who do not wish to work in a partnership. In such organizations, a number of limited partners invest money as owners but are not allowed to participate in the management of the company. These partners can still incur a loss on their investment, but the amount is restricted to that which has been contributed. To protect the creditors of a limited partnership, one or more general partners must be designated to assume responsibility for all obligations created in the name of the business.

Buckeye Partners, L.P. (with annual revenues of over $180 million) is an example of a limited partnership that trades on the New York Stock Exchange. According to Buckeye's December 31, 1999, balance sheet, capital of $2.5 million is reported for the company's general partners whereas the same account shows a total of $314.4 million for its limited partners.

Many limited partnerships were originally formed as tax shelters to create immediate losses (to reduce the taxable income of the partners) with profits spread out into the future. As mentioned earlier, changes in the tax laws to limit the deduction of passive activity losses have significantly reduced the number of limited partnerships being formed.

Limited Liability Partnerships (LLPs)　The limited liability partnership has most of the same characteristics of a general partnership except that the liability of the partners is significantly reduced. Partners may lose their investment in the business and are also responsible for the contractual debts of the business. The advantage is created in connection with any liability resulting from damages. In such cases, the partners are only responsible for their own acts or omissions plus the acts and omissions of individuals under their supervision. Thus, a partner in the Houston office of a public accounting firm would probably not be held liable for a poor audit performed by that firm's San Francisco office. Not surprisingly, limited liability partnerships have become very popular with professional service organizations that have multiple offices. In 1994, for example, all of the Big Five accounting firms became LLPs.

Limited Liability Companies (LLCs)　The limited liability company is a relatively new type of organization in the United States although long used in Europe and other areas of the world. It is classified as a partnership for tax purposes. However, depending on state laws, the owners are only risking their own investments. In contrast to a Subchapter S Corporation, the number of owners is not usually restricted so that growth is easier to accomplish.

PARTNERSHIP ACCOUNTING—CAPITAL ACCOUNTS

Despite legal distinctions, questions should be raised as to the need for an entirely separate study of partnership accounting.

- Does an association of two or more persons require accounting procedures significantly different from those of a corporation?
- Is proper accounting dependent on the legal form of an organization?

The answer to these questions is both yes and no. Accounting procedures are normally standardized for assets, liabilities, revenues, and expenses regardless of the legal form of a business. *Partnership accounting, though, does exhibit unique aspects that warrant study, but they lie primarily in the handling of the partners' capital accounts.*

The stockholders' equity accounts of a corporation do not correspond directly with the capital balances found in a partnership's financial records. The various equity accounts reported by an incorporated enterprise display a greater degree of structuring: They are more precisely defined. These characteristics reflect the wide variety of equity transactions that can occur in a corporation as well as the influence of state and federal laws. Government regulation has had an effect on the accounting for corporate equity transactions in that extensive disclosure is required to protect stockholders and other outside parties such as potential investors.

To provide adequate information as well as to meet legal requirements, corporate accounting must provide details about numerous possible equity transactions and account balances. For example, the amount of a corporation's paid-in capital is shown separately from earned capital; the par value of each class of stock is disclosed; treasury stock, stock options, stock dividends, and other capital transactions are reported based on prescribed accounting principles.

In comparison, partnerships provide only a limited amount of equity disclosure primarily in the form of individual capital accounts that are accumulated for every partner or every class of partners. These balances measure each partner or group's interest in the book value of the net assets of the business. Thus, the equity section of a partnership balance sheet is comprised solely of capital accounts that can be affected by many different events: contributions from partners as well as distributions to them, earnings, and any other equity transactions.

However, no differentiation is drawn in the reporting of a partnership between the various sources of ownership capital. Disclosing the composition of the capital balances has not been judged necessary because partnerships have historically tended to be small with equity transactions that were rarely complex. Additionally, absentee ownership is not common, a factor that minimizes both the need for government regulation as well as the outside interest in detailed information about the capital balances.

Articles of Partnership

Because the demand for information about capital balances is limited, accounting principles specific to partnerships are based primarily on traditional approaches that have evolved over the years rather than on official pronouncements. These procedures attempt to mirror the relationship between the partners and their business especially as defined by the partnership agreement. This legal covenant, which may be either oral or written, is often referred to as the Articles of Partnership and forms the central governance for the operation of a partnership. The financial arrangements spelled out in this contract establish guidelines for the various capital transactions. Therefore, the Articles of Partnership, rather than laws or official rules, provide much of the underlying basis for partnership accounting.

Since the Articles of Partnership is a negotiated agreement created by the partners, an unlimited number of variations can be encountered in practice. Partners' rights and responsibilities frequently differ from business to business. Consequently, accountants often are hired in an advisory capacity to participate in the creation of this document to assure the equitable treatment of all parties. Although the Articles of Partnership may contain a number of provisions, an explicit understanding should always be reached in regard to the following:

- Name and address of each partner.
- Business location.
- Description of the nature of the business.
- Rights and responsibilities of each partner.

- Initial contribution to be made by each partner along with the method to be used for valuation.
- Specific method by which profits and losses are to be allocated.
- Periodic withdrawal of assets by each partner.
- Procedure for admitting new partners.
- Method for arbitrating partnership disputes.
- Life insurance provisions enabling remaining partners to acquire the interest of any deceased partner.
- Method for settling a partner's share in the business upon withdrawal, retirement, or death.[11]

Despite the importance of the Articles of Partnership, an unusual number of partnerships fail to produce this needed document.

"You'd be surprised at the number of American law firms that operate without partnership agreements or [use] agreements that are out of date," says Ward Bower of Altman & Weil, a consulting firm that specializes in law-firm management. "Lawyers," he adds, "will sign agreements they'd never let their clients sign."[12]

But despite 20 years of advice on the value of partnership agreements, the reality is that, in the majority of cases, well-structured agreements are the exception, rather than the rule, in practice units.[13]

Accounting for Capital Contributions

Several types of capital transactions occur in a partnership: allocation of profits and losses, retirement of a current partner, admission of a new partner, and so on. The initial transaction, however, is the contribution made by the partners to begin the business. In the simplest situation, the partners invest only cash amounts. For example, assume that Carter and Green form a business to be operated as a partnership. Carter contributes $50,000 in cash whereas Green invests $20,000. The initial journal entry to record the creation of this partnership is as follows:

Cash	70,000	
Carter, Capital		50,000
Green, Capital		20,000
To record cash contributed to start new partnership.		

Complications have been avoided in this first illustration by the assumption that only cash was invested. Often, though, one or more of the partners transfers noncash assets such as inventory, land, equipment, or a building to the business. Although fair market value is used to record these assets, a case could be developed for initially valuing any contributed asset at the partner's current book value. According to the concept of unlimited liability (as well as present tax laws), a partnership does not exist as an entity apart from its owners. A logical extension of the idea is that the investment of an asset is not a transaction occurring between two independent parties such as would warrant revaluation. This contention holds that the semblance of an arm's-length transaction is necessary to justify a change in the book value of any account.

---

[11] A complete discussion of the provisions to be included in a partnership agreement can be found in "Get It in Writing," in the August 1996 issue of *C A Magazine* and "The Importance of Partnership Agreements," in the January 1994 issue of the *Journal of Accountancy*.

[12] Christi Harlan, "Lawyers Find It Difficult to Break Up Partnerships," *Wall Street Journal,* October 6, 1988, p. B1.

[13] Herman J. Lowe, "Partnership Agreements: Realities into Formalities," *Journal of Accountancy,* September 1986, p. 158.

DISCUSSION QUESTION

What Kind of Business Is This?

After graduating from college, Shelley Williams held several different jobs but found that she did not enjoy working for other people. Finally, she and Yvonne Hargrove, her college roommate, decided to start a business of their own. They rented a small building and opened a florist shop selling cut flowers such as roses and chrysanthemums that they bought from a local greenhouse.

Williams and Hargrove agreed to share profits and losses equally, although they also decided to take no money from the operation for at least four months. No other arrangements were made but the business did reasonably well and, after the first four months had passed, each began to draw out $500 in cash every week.

At year's end, they took their financial records to a local accountant so that they could get their income tax returns completed. He informed them that they had been operating as a partnership and that they should draw up a formal Articles of Partnership or consider incorporation or some other legal form of organization. They confessed that they had never really considered the issue and asked for his advice on the matter.

What advice should the accountant give to his clients?

Although retaining the recorded value for assets contributed to a partnership may seem reasonable, this method of valuation proves to be inequitable to any partner investing appreciated property. A $50,000 capital balance always results from a cash investment of that amount but the recording of other assets would be entirely dependent on the partner's original book value.

Should a partner, for example, who contributes a building having a recorded value of $18,000 but a fair market value of $50,000 be credited with only an $18,000 interest in the partnership? Since $50,000 in cash and $50,000 in appreciated property are equivalent contributions, a $32,000 difference in the partners' capital balances cannot be justified. To prevent such inequities, each item transferred to a partnership is initially recorded for external reporting purposes at current value.[14]

Requiring revaluation of contributed assets can, however, be advocated for reasons other than just the fair treatment of all partners. Despite some evidence to the contrary, a partnership can be viewed legitimately as an entity standing apart from its owners. As an example, a partnership maintains legal ownership of its assets and (depending on state law) can instigate lawsuits. For this reason, accounting practice has traditionally held that the contribution of assets (and liabilities) to a partnership is an exchange between two separately identifiable parties that should be recorded based on fair market values.

The determination of an appropriate valuation for each capital balance is more than just an accounting exercise. Over the life of a partnership, these figures serve in a number of important capacities:

1. The totals in the individual accounts often influence the assignment of profits and losses to the partners.
2. The capital account balance is usually a factor in determining the final distribution that will be received by a partner at the time of withdrawal or retirement.
3. Ending capital balances indicate the allocation to be made of any assets that remain following the liquidation of a partnership.

To demonstrate the accounting for these capital balances, assume that Carter invests $50,000 in cash to begin the previously discussed partnership while Green contributes the following assets:

---

[14]For federal income tax purposes, the $18,000 book value is retained as the basis for this building, even after transfer to the partnership. Within the tax laws, no difference is seen between partners and their partnership.

	Book Value to Green	Fair Market Value
Inventory	$ 9,000	$10,000
Land	14,000	11,000
Building	32,000	46,000
Totals	$55,000	$67,000

As an added factor, Green's building is encumbered by a $23,600 mortgage that the partnership has agreed to assume.

Based on the applicable values of these accounts, Green's net investment is equal to $43,400 ($67,000 less $23,600). The following journal entry records the formation of the partnership created by these contributions:

Cash	50,000	
Inventory......................................	10,000	
Land	11,000	
Building	46,000	
Mortgage Payable..................................		23,600
Carter, Capital...................................		50,000
Green, Capital....................................		43,400
To record properties contributed to start partnership. Assets and liabilities are recorded at fair market value.		

One further point should be made before leaving this illustration. Although Green has contributed inventory, land, and a building, this partner holds no further right to these individual assets; they now belong to the partnership. The $43,400 capital balance represents an ownership interest in the business as a whole but does not constitute a specific claim. Having transferred title to the partnership, Green has no more right to these assets than does Carter.

Intangible Contributions   In forming a partnership, the contributions made by one or more of the partners may go beyond assets and liabilities. A doctor, for example, can bring a particular line of expertise to a partnership while a practicing dentist might have already developed an established clientele. These attributes, as well as many others, are frequently as valuable to a partnership as cash and fixed assets. *Hence, formal accounting recognition of such special contributions may be appropriately included as a provision of any partnership agreement.*

To illustrate, assume that James and Joyce plan to open an advertising agency and decide to organize the endeavor as a partnership. James contributes cash of $70,000 whereas Joyce invests only $10,000. Joyce, however, is an accomplished graphic artist, a skill that is considered especially valuable to this business. Therefore, in producing the Articles of Partnership, the partners agree to start the business with equal capital balances. Often such decisions result only after long, and sometimes heated, negotiations. Because the value assigned to an intangible contribution such as artistic talent is arbitrary at best, proper reporting depends on the ability of the partners to arrive at an equitable arrangement.

In recording this agreement, James and Joyce have two options available: (1) the bonus method and (2) the goodwill method. Each of these approaches achieves the desired result of establishing equal capital account balances. Recorded figures, however, can vary significantly depending on the procedure selected. Thus, the partners should reach an understanding prior to beginning business operations as to the method to be used. The accountant can help avoid conflicts in this area by assisting the partners in evaluating the impact created by each of these two alternatives.

The Bonus Method   The bonus method assumes that a specialization such as Joyce's artistic abilities does *not* constitute a recordable partnership asset with a measurable cost. Hence, this approach recognizes only the assets that are physically transferred to the business (such as cash, patents, inventory, etc.). Although total partnership capital is determined by these contributions, the establishment of specific capital balances is viewed as an independent process based solely on the agreement of the partners. Since the initial equity figures are the result of negotiation, they do not need to correspond directly with the individual investments.

James and Joyce have contributed a total of $80,000 in identifiable assets to their partnership and have decided on equal capital balances. According to the bonus method, this agreement is fulfilled simply by splitting the $80,000 capital figure evenly between the two partners. The following entry records the formation of this partnership under this assumption:

Cash	80,000	
James, Capital....................................		40,000
Joyce, Capital....................................		40,000
To record cash contributions with bonus to Joyce because of artistic abilities.		

Joyce received a capital bonus here of $30,000 (the recorded capital balance in excess of the $10,000 cash contribution) from James in recognition of the artistic abilities she brought into the business.

The Goodwill Method   The goodwill method is based on the assumption that an implied value can be calculated mathematically and recorded for any intangible contribution. In the present illustration, Joyce invested $60,000 less cash than James but receives an equal amount of capital according to the partnership agreement. Proponents of the goodwill method argue that Joyce's artistic talent has an apparent value of $60,000, a figure that should be included as part of this partner's capital investment. If not recorded, Joyce's primary contribution to the business is completely ignored within the accounting records.

Cash	80,000	
Goodwill...	60,000	
James, Capital....................................		70,000
Joyce, Capital....................................		70,000
To record cash contributions with goodwill attributed to Joyce in recognition of artistic abilities.		

Comparison of Methods   Both of these approaches achieve the intent of the partnership agreement: Equal capital balances are recorded despite a difference in the partners' cash contributions. The bonus method allocates the $80,000 invested capital according to the percentages designated by the partners, whereas the goodwill method capitalizes the implied value of Joyce's intangible contribution.

Although nothing prohibits the use of either technique, the recognition of goodwill poses definite theoretical problems. In previous discussions of both the equity method (Chapter 1) and purchase consolidations (Chapter 2), goodwill was recorded but only as a result of an acquisition made by the reporting entity. Consequently, this asset had a historical cost in the traditional accounting sense. Partnership goodwill has no such cost; the business recognizes an asset even though no funds have been spent.

The partnership of James and Joyce, for example, is able to record $60,000 in goodwill without any expenditure. Furthermore, the value attributed to this asset is based solely on a negotiated agreement between the partners; the $60,000 balance has no objectively verifiable basis. Thus, although partnership goodwill is sometimes encountered in actual practice, this "asset" should be viewed with a strong degree of professional skepticism.

Additional Capital Contributions and Withdrawals

Subsequent to the formation of a partnership, the owners may choose to contribute additional capital amounts. These investments can be made to stimulate expansion or to assist the business in overcoming working capital shortages or other problems. Regardless of the reason, the contribution is again recorded as an increment in the partner's capital account based on fair market value. For example, in the previous illustration, assume that James decides to invest another $5,000 cash in the partnership to help finance the purchase of new office furnishings. The partner's capital account balance is immediately increased by this amount to reflect the transfer being made to the partnership.

The partners also may reverse this process by withdrawing assets from the business for their own personal use. For example, one partnership, Andersons, reported recently in its financial statements partner withdrawals for the year of $1,759,072 as well as increases in invested capital of $733,675. To protect the interests of the other partners, the amount and timing of such withdrawals should be clearly specified in the Articles of Partnership.

In many instances, withdrawals are allowed on a regular periodic basis as a reward for ownership or as compensation for work done in the business. Often such distributions are recorded initially in a separate drawing account that is closed into the individual partner's capital account at year's end. Assume, for illustration purposes, that James and Joyce take out $1,200 and $1,500, respectively, from their business. The journal entry to record these payments is as follows:

James, Drawing	1,200	
Joyce, Drawing	1,500	
Cash		2,700
To record withdrawal of cash by partners.		

Larger amounts might also be withdrawn from a partnership on occasion. A partner may have a special need for money or just desire to reduce the basic investment that has been made in the business. Such transactions are usually sporadic occurrences and in amounts significantly greater than the partner's periodic drawing. Prior approval by the other partners may be required by the Articles of Partnership.

Allocation of Income

At the end of each fiscal period, partnership revenues and expenses are closed out with the resulting net income or loss being reclassified to the partners' capital accounts. Since a separate equity balance is maintained for each partner, a method must be devised for this assignment of annual income. Because of the importance of the process, the procedure established by the partners should always be stipulated in the Articles of Partnership. If no arrangement has been specified, state partnership law normally holds that all partners share equally in any income or loss earned by the business. If an agreement has been set forth specifying only the allocation of profits, any subsequent losses must be divided in that same manner.

Actual procedures for allocating profits and losses can range from the simple to the elaborate.[15] Partnerships can avoid all complications by assigning net income on an equal basis among all partners. Other organizations attempt to devise plans that reward such factors as the expertise of the individuals or the amount of time that each works. Some agreements also consider the capital invested in the business as an element that should be recognized within the allocation process.

---

[15]See, for example, "Profit Allocation in CPA Firm Partnership Agreements," in the March 1986 issue of the *Journal of Accountancy,* pp. 91–95; "Paying Partners: A Challenge for the 1990s," in the June 1989 issue of the *Journal of Accountancy,* pp. 117–22; or "Selecting the Best Partner Compensation Method," in the December 1991 issue of the *Journal of Accountancy,* pp. 40–44.

DISCUSSION QUESTION

**How Will the
Profits Be Split?**

James J. Dewars has been the sole owner of a small CPA firm for the past 20 years. Now 52 years old, Dewars is concerned about the continuation of his practice after he retires. He would like to begin taking more time off now although he wants to remain active in the firm for at least another 8 to 10 years. He has worked hard over the decades to build up the practice so that he presently makes a profit of $160,000 annually.

Lewis Huffman has been working for Dewars for the past four years. He now earns a salary of $58,000 per year. He is a very dedicated employee who generally works 44–60 hours per week. In the past, Dewars has been in charge of the bigger, more profitable audit clients whereas Huffman, with less experience, worked with the smaller clients. Both Dewars and Huffman do some tax work although that segment of the business has never been emphasized.

Sally Scriba has been working for the past seven years with another CPA firm as a tax specialist. She has no auditing experience but has a great reputation in tax planning and preparation. She currently has an annual salary of $70,000.

Dewars, Huffman, and Scriba are negotiating the creation of a new CPA firm as a partnership. Dewars plans to reduce his time in this firm although he will continue to work with many of the clients that he has served for the past two decades. Huffman will begin to take over some of the major audit jobs. Scriba will start and develop an extensive tax practice for the firm.

Because of the changes in the firm, the three potential partners anticipate earning a total net income in the first year of operations of between $130,000 and $220,000. Thereafter, they hope that profits will increase at the rate of 10 to 20 percent annually for the next five years or so.

How should this new partnership allocate its future net income to the partners?

To serve as an initial illustration, assume that Tinker, Evers, and Chance form a partnership by investing cash of $120,000, $90,000, and $75,000, respectively. The Articles of Partnership are drawn up to specify that Evers will be allotted 40 percent of all profits and losses because of previous business experience while Tinker and Chance are to divide the remaining 60 percent equally. This agreement also stipulates that each partner is allowed to withdraw $10,000 in cash annually from the business. The amount of this withdrawal is not directly dependent on the method utilized for income allocation. *From an accounting perspective, the assignment of income and the setting of withdrawal limits are two separate decisions.*

At the end of the first year of operations, the partnership reports net income of $60,000. To reflect the changes made in the partners' capital balances, the closing process consists of the following two journal entries. The assumption is made here that each partner has taken the allowed amount of drawing during the year. In addition, all revenues and expenses already have been closed into an Income Summary account.

Tinker, Capital	10,000	
Evers, Capital	10,000	
Chance, Capital	10,000	
Tinker, Drawing		10,000
Evers, Drawing		10,000
Chance, Drawing		10,000
To close out drawing accounts of the three partners.		

Income Summary	60,000	
Tinker, Capital (30%)		18,000
Evers, Capital (40%)		24,000
Chance, Capital (30%)		18,000
To allocate net income based on partnership agreement.		

Statement of Partners' Capital   Since no Retained Earnings balance is separately disclosed by a partnership, the statement of retained earnings usually reported by a corporation is replaced by a statement of partners' capital. The following financial statement is based on the data presented for the partnership of Tinker, Evers, and Chance. The changes made during the year in the individual capital accounts are outlined along with totals representing the partnership as a whole.

TINKER, EVERS, AND CHANCE
Statement of Partners' Capital
For Year Ending December 31, Year 1

	Tinker, Capital	Evers, Capital	Chance, Capital	Totals
Capital balances beginning of year ...	$120,000	$ 90,000	$ 75,000	$285,000
Allocation of net income	18,000	24,000	18,000	60,000
Drawings	(10,000)	(10,000)	(10,000)	(30,000)
Capital balances end of year	$128,000	$104,000	$ 83,000	$315,000

Alternative Allocation Techniques—Example One   Assigning net income based on a ratio may be simple, but this approach is not necessarily equitable to all partners. For example, assume that Tinker does not participate in the operations of the partnership but is the contributor of the largest amount of capital. Evers and Chance both work full time in the business, but Evers has considerably more experience in this line of work.

Under these circumstances, no single ratio would properly reflect the various contributions being made by each of the partners. Indeed, an unlimited number of alternative allocation plans could be devised in hopes of achieving fair treatment for all parties. For example, because of the different levels of capital being invested, consideration should be given to the inclusion of interest within the allocation process. A compensation allowance is also a possibility, usually in an amount corresponding to the number of hours worked or the level of a partner's business expertise.

To demonstrate one possible option, assume that Tinker, Evers, and Chance begin their partnership based on the facts presented originally except that they arrive at a more detailed method of allocating profits and losses. After considerable negotiations, an Articles of Partnership agreement is drawn up that credits each partner annually for interest in an amount equal to 10 percent of the beginning capital balance for the year. Evers and Chance also will be allotted $15,000 apiece as a compensation allowance in recognition of their participation in daily operations. Any remaining profit or loss will be split 4:3:3, with the largest share going to Evers because of the work experience that this partner brings to the business. As with any appropriate allocation, this pattern is an attempt to be fair to all three of the partners.

Under this arrangement, the $60,000 net income earned by the partnership in the first year of operation would be prorated as follows. The sequential alignment of the various provisions is irrelevant except that the ratio, which is used to divide the remaining profit or loss, must be calculated last.

	Tinker	Evers	Chance	Totals
Interest (10% of beginning capital)	$12,000	$ 9,000	$ 7,500	$28,500
Compensation allowance	–0–	15,000	15,000	30,000
Remaining income:				
$60,000				
(28,500)				
(30,000)				
$ 1,500	450 (30%)	600 (40%)	450 (30%)	1,500
Totals	$12,450	$24,600	$22,950	$60,000

For the partnership of Tinker, Evers, and Chance, the allocations just calculated lead to the following closing entry:

Income Summary	60,000	
Tinker, Capital		12,450
Evers, Capital		24,600
Chance, Capital		22,950

To allocate income for the year to the individual partners based on partnership agreement.

Alternative Allocation Techniques—Example Two   As indicated by the preceding illustration, the assignment process is no more than a series of mechanical steps reflecting the change in each partner's capital balance resulting from the provisions of the partnership agreement. The number of different allocation procedures that could be employed is limited solely by the imagination of the partners. Although interest, compensation allowances, and various ratios are the predominant factors encountered in practice, other possibilities do exist. Therefore, another approach to the allocation process is presented to further illustrate some of the variations that can be utilized. A two-person partnership is used here to simplify the computations.

Assume that Webber and Rice formed a partnership in 1990 to operate a bookstore. Webber contributed the initial capital while Rice managed the business. With the assistance of their accountant, they wrote an Articles of Partnership agreement that contains the following provisions:

1. Each partner is allowed to draw $1,000 in cash from the business every month. Any withdrawal in excess of that figure will be accounted for as a direct reduction to the partner's capital balance.
2. Partnership profits and losses will be allocated each year according to the following plan:
    a. Interest of 15 percent will be accrued by each partner based on the monthly average capital balance for the year (calculated without regard for normal drawings or current income).
    b. As a reward for operating the business, Rice is to receive credit for a bonus equal to 20 percent of the year's net income. However, no bonus is earned if the partnership reports a net loss.
    c. Any remaining profit or loss will be divided equally between the two partners.

Assume that Webber and Rice subsequently begin the year of 2001 with capital balances of $150,000 and $30,000, respectively. On April 1 of that year, Webber invests an additional $8,000 cash in the business, while on July 1, Rice withdraws $6,000 in excess of the specified drawing allowance. Assume further that the partnership reports income of $30,000 for 2001.

Because the interest factor established in this allocation plan is based on a monthly average figure, the amount to be credited to each partner has to be determined by means of a preliminary calculation:

Webber—Interest Allocation

Beginning balance:	$150,000 × 3 months =	$ 450,000
Balance, 4/1/01:	$158,000 × 9 months =	1,422,000
		1,872,000
		× $\frac{1}{12}$
Monthly average capital balance		156,000
Interest rate		× 15%
Interest credited to Webber		$ 23,400

Rice—Interest Allocation

Beginning balance:	$30,000 × 6 months =	$180,000
Balance, 7/1/01:	$24,000 × 6 months =	144,000
		324,000
		× ¹⁄₁₂
Monthly average capital balance		27,000
Interest rate		× 15%
Interest credited to Rice		$ 4,050

Following this initial computation, the actual assignment of income can proceed according to the provisions specified in the partnership agreement. The stipulations drawn up by Webber and Rice must be followed exactly, even though the business's $30,000 profit in 2001 is not sufficient to cover both the interest and the bonus. Income allocation is a mechanical process that should always be carried out as stated in the Articles of Partnership without regard for the specific level of income or loss.

Based on the plan that was created, Webber's capital increases by $21,675 during 2001 while Rice is assigned only $8,325:

	Webber	Rice	Totals
Interest (above)	$23,400	$ 4,050	$27,450
Bonus (20% × $30,000)	–0–	6,000	6,000
Remaining income (loss):			
$ 30,000			
(27,450)			
(6,000)			
$ (3,450)	(1,725) (50%)	(1,725) (50%)	(3,450)
Totals	$21,675	$ 8,325	$30,000

ACCOUNTING FOR PARTNERSHIP DISSOLUTION

In many partnerships, capital transactions are limited almost exclusively to contributions, drawings, and profit and loss allocations. Normally, though, over any extended period, changes occur in the members who make up a partnership. Employees may be promoted into the partnership or new owners brought in from outside the organization to add capital or expertise to the business. Current partners eventually retire, die, or simply elect to leave the partnership. Large operations may even experience such changes on a routine basis. One international accounting firm has estimated that 50 to 70 partners leave the organization each year for a variety of reasons. That, apparently, is not an isolated situation; "major accounting firms have gotten rid of between 5 percent and 14 percent of their partners over the past 18 months."[16]

Regardless of the nature or the frequency of the event, any alteration in the specific individuals composing a partnership automatically leads to legal dissolution. In many instances, the breakup is merely a prerequisite to the formation of a new partnership. For example, if Abernethy and Chapman decide to allow Miller to become a partner in their business, the legally recognized partnership of Abernethy and Chapman has to be dissolved first. The business property as well as the right to future profits can then be conveyed to the newly formed partnership of Abernethy, Chapman, and Miller. The change is a legal change. Actual operations of the business would probably continue unimpeded by this alteration in ownership.

---

[16]Berton and Lublin, p. A9.

Conversely, should the partners so choose, dissolution can be a preliminary step in the termination and liquidation of the business. The death of a partner, lack of sufficient profits, or internal management differences may lead the partners to the breakup of the partnership business. Under this circumstance, partnership properties are sold, debts paid, and any remaining assets distributed to the individual partners. Thus, in liquidations (which are analyzed in detail in the next chapter) both the partnership and the business cease to exist.

Dissolution—Admission of a New Partner

One of the most prevalent changes in the makeup of a partnership is the addition of a new partner. An employee may have worked for years to gain this opportunity or a prospective partner might offer new investment capital or business experience necessary for future business success. An individual can gain admittance to a partnership in one of two ways: (1) by purchasing an ownership interest from a current partner or (2) by contributing assets directly to the business.

In recording either type of transaction, the accountant has the option, once again, of retaining the book value of all partnership assets and liabilities (as exemplified by the bonus method) or revaluing these accounts to their present market values (the goodwill method). Although both are acceptable, the decision as to a theoretical preference between the bonus and goodwill methods hinges on one single question: *Should the dissolved partnership and the newly formed partnership be viewed as two separate reporting entities?*

If the new partnership is merely an extension of the old, no basis exists for restatement. The transfer of ownership is only a change in a legal sense and has no direct impact on business assets and liabilities. However, if the continuation of the business represents a legitimate transfer of property from one partnership to another, revaluation of all accounts and recognition of goodwill can be justified.

Because both approaches are encountered in practice, each is presented in this textbook. However, the concerns previously discussed in connection with partnership goodwill still exist: Recognition is not based on historical cost and no objective verification can be made of the amount being capitalized. One alternative revaluation approach has been devised that attempts to circumvent the problems involved with partnership goodwill. This hybrid method revalues all partnership assets and liabilities to fair market value without any corresponding recognition being made of goodwill.

Admission through Purchase of a Current Interest   As mentioned, one method of gaining admittance to a partnership is by the purchase of a current interest. One or more partners may choose to sell their portion of the business to an outside party. This type transaction is most common in operations that rely primarily on monetary capital rather than on the business expertise of the partners.

In making a transfer of ownership, a partner can actually convey only three rights:

1. *The right of co-ownership in the business property.* This right justifies the partner's periodic drawings from the business as well as the distribution settlement paid at liquidation or at the time of a partner's withdrawal.
2. *The right to share in profits and losses as specified in the Articles of Partnership.*
3. *The right to participate in the management of the business.*

Unless restricted by the Articles of Partnership, every partner has the power to sell or assign the first two of these partnership rights at any time. Their transfer poses no threat of financial harm to the remaining partners. In contrast, partnership law states that the right to participate in the management of the business can only be conveyed with the consent of all partners. This particular right is considered essential to the future earning power of the enterprise as well as the maintenance of business assets. Therefore, current partners are protected from the intrusion of parties who might be considered detrimental to the management of the company.

As an illustration, assume that Scott, Thompson, and York formed a partnership several years ago. Subsequently, York decides to leave the partnership and offers to sell his interest to Morgan. Although York may transfer the right of property ownership as well as the specified share of future profits and losses, Morgan is not automatically admitted into the partnership. York legally remains a partner until such time as both Scott and Thompson agree to allow Morgan to participate in the management of the business.

To demonstrate the accounting procedures applicable to the transfer of a partnership interest, assume that the following information is available relating to the partnership of Scott, Thompson, and York:

Partner	Capital Balance	Profit and Loss Ratio
Scott	$ 50,000	20%
Thompson	30,000	50
York	20,000	30
Total capital	$100,000	

In this example, the relationship of the capital accounts to one another does not correspond with the partners' profit and loss ratio. Capital balances are historical cost figures. They result from contributions and withdrawals made throughout the life of the business as well as from the allocation of partnership income. Therefore, any correlation between a partner's recorded capital at a particular point in time and the profit and loss percentage would probably be coincidental. Scott, for example, has 50 percent of the current partnership capital ($50,000/$100,000), although entitled to only a 20 percent allocation of income.

Instead of York selling his interest to Morgan, assume that each of these three partners elects to transfer a 20 percent interest to Morgan for a total payment of $30,000. According to the sales contract, *the money is to be paid directly to the owners.* One approach to the recording of this transaction is that, since Morgan's purchase is carried out between the individual parties, the acquisition has no impact on the assets and liabilities held by the partnership. Because the business is not involved, the transfer of ownership requires a simple capital reclassification without any accompanying revaluation. Book value is retained. This approach is similar to the bonus method; only a legal change in ownership is occurring so that neither revaluation of assets or liabilities nor goodwill is appropriate.

Book Value Approach

Scott, Capital (20% of capital balance)	10,000	
Thompson, Capital (20%)...............................	6,000	
York, Capital (20%)	4,000	
Morgan, Capital (20% of total)......................		20,000
Reclassification of capital to reflect Morgan's acquisition.		
Money is paid directly to partners.		

An alternative for recording this acquisition by Morgan relies on a different perspective of the new partner's admission. Legally, the partnership of Scott, Thompson, and York is transferring all assets and liabilities to the partnership of Scott, Thompson, York, and Morgan. Therefore, according to the logic underlying the goodwill method, a transaction is occurring between two separate reporting entities, an event that necessitates the complete revaluation of all assets and liabilities.

Since Morgan is paying $30,000 for a 20 percent interest in the partnership, the implied value of the business as a whole is $150,000 ($30,000/20%). However, the book value is only $100,000; thus, a $50,000 upward revaluation is indicated. This adjustment is reflected by restating specific partnership asset and liability accounts to market value with any remaining balance being recorded as goodwill. After the implied value of the partnership is established, the reclassification can be recorded based on the new capital balances.

Goodwill (Revaluation) Approach		
Goodwill (or specific accounts)	50,000	
Scott, Capital (20% of goodwill)		10,000
Thompson, Capital (50%)		25,000
York, Capital (30%)		15,000
Recognition of goodwill based on size of Morgan's purchase price.		
Scott, Capital (20% of new capital balance)	12,000	
Thompson, Capital (20%)	11,000	
York, Capital (20%)	7,000	
Morgan, Capital (20% of new total)		30,000
Reclassification of capital to reflect Morgan's acquisition.		
Money is paid directly to partners.		

As can be seen here, the $50,000 revaluation is credited to the original partners based on the profit and loss ratio rather than on their percentages of capital. Recognition of goodwill (or an increase in the book value of specific accounts) indicates that unrecorded gains have accrued to the business during the previous years of operation. Therefore, the equitable treatment is to allocate this increment among the partners according to their profit and loss percentages.

Admission by a Contribution Made to the Partnership   Entrance into a partnership is not obtained solely by the purchase of a current partner's interest. An outsider may be admitted to the ownership by contributing cash or other assets directly to the business rather than to the partners. For example, assume that King and Wilson maintain a partnership and presently report capital balances of $80,000 and $20,000, respectively. According to the Articles of Partnership, King is entitled to 60 percent of all profits and losses with the remaining 40 percent credited to Wilson. By agreement of the partners, Simpson is being allowed to enter the partnership for a payment of $20,000 *with this money going into the business.* Based on negotiations that preceded the acquisition, all parties have agreed that Simpson receives an initial 10 percent interest in partnership property.

Bonus Credited to Original Partners   The bonus (or no revaluation) method maintains the same recorded value for all partnership assets and liabilities despite Simpson's admittance. The capital balance for this new partner is simply set at the appropriate 10 percent level based on the book value of the partnership taken as a whole (after the payment is recorded). Since $20,000 is being invested, total reported capital increases to $120,000. Thus, Simpson's 10 percent interest is computed as $12,000. *The $8,000 difference between the amount contributed and this allotted capital balance is viewed as a bonus.* Because Simpson is willing to accept a capital balance that is less than the investment being made, this bonus is attributed to the original partners (based on their profit and loss ratio). Because of the nature of the transaction, no need is perceived for recognizing goodwill or revaluing any of the assets or liabilities.

Cash	20,000	
Simpson, Capital (10% of total capital)		12,000
King, Capital (60% of bonus)		4,800
Wilson, Capital (40% of bonus)		3,200
To record Simpson's entrance into partnership with $8,000		
extra payment recorded as bonus to original partners.		

Goodwill Credited to Original Partners   The goodwill method views Simpson's payment as evidence that the partnership as a whole possesses an actual value of

$200,000 ($20,000/10 percent). Since, even with the new partner's investment, only $120,000 in net assets is being reported, a valuation adjustment of $80,000 is implied.[17] Over the previous years, unrecorded gains have apparently accrued to the business. This $80,000 figure might reflect the need to revalue specific accounts such as inventory or equipment, although the entire amount, or some portion, may simply be recorded as goodwill.

Goodwill (or specific accounts)	80,000	
King, Capital (60% of goodwill)		48,000
Wilson, Capital (40%)		32,000
To recognize goodwill based on Simpson's purchase price.		
Cash	20,000	
Simpson, Capital.		20,000
To record Simpson's admission into partnership.		

Comparison of Bonus Method and Goodwill Method   Completely different capital balances (as well as asset and liability figures) result from these two approaches. In both cases, though, the new partner is properly credited with 10 percent of total partnership capital.

	Bonus Method	**Goodwill Method**
Assets less liabilities (as reported)	$100,000	$100,000
Simpson's contribution	20,000	20,000
Goodwill	–0–	80,000
Total	$120,000	$200,000
Simpson's capital	$ 12,000	$ 20,000

Because Simpson contributed an amount greater than 10 percent of the resulting book value of the partnership, this business is perceived as being worth more than the recorded accounts presently indicate. Therefore, the bonus in the first instance and the goodwill in the second were both assumed as accruing to the two original partners. Such a presumption is not unusual in an established business, especially if profitable operations have been developed over a number of years.

Hybrid Method of Recording Admission of New Partner   One other approach to the admission of Simpson can be devised. Assume that the assets and liabilities of the King and Wilson partnership have a book value of $100,000 as stated earlier. Also assume that a piece of land held by the business is actually worth $30,000 more than its currently recorded book value. Thus, the identifiable assets of the partnership are worth $130,000. Simpson pays $20,000 for a 10 percent interest.

In this approach, the identifiable assets (such as land) are revalued but no goodwill is recognized.

Land	30,000	
King, Capital (60% of revaluation)		18,000
Wilson, Capital (40%)		12,000
To record current market value of land in preparation for		
admission of new partner.		

The admission of Simpson and the payment of $20,000 brings the total capital balance to $150,000. Because Simpson is acquiring a 10 percent interest, a capital balance of $15,000 is recorded. The extra $5,000 payment ($20,000 − $15,000) is attributed as a bonus to the original partners.

---

[17]Because the $20,000 is being put into the business in this example, total capital to be used in the goodwill computation has increased to $120,000. If, as in the previous illustration, payment had been made directly to the partners, the original capital of $100,000 is retained in determining goodwill.

Cash	20,000	
Simpson, Capital (10% of total capital)		15,000
King, Capital (60% of bonus).		3,000
Wilson, Capital (40% of bonus)		2,000

To record entrance of Simpson into partnership and bonus assigned to original partners.

Bonus or Goodwill Credited to New Partner   As previously discussed, Simpson also may be contributing some attribute other than tangible assets to this partnership. Therefore, the Articles of Partnership may be written to credit the new partner rather than the original partners, with either a bonus or goodwill. Because of an excellent professional reputation, valuable business contacts, or myriad other possible factors, Simpson might be able to negotiate a beginning capital balance in excess of the $20,000 cash contribution. This same circumstance may also result if the business is desperate for new capital and is willing to offer favorable terms as an enticement to the potential partner.

To illustrate, assume that Simpson receives a 20 percent interest in the preceding partnership (rather than the originally stated 10 percent) in exchange for the $20,000 cash investment. The specific rationale for the higher ownership percentage need not be identified.

The bonus method sets Simpson's initial capital at $24,000 (20 percent of the $120,000 book value). To achieve this balance, a capital bonus of $4,000 must be credited to Simpson by the present partners:

Cash	20,000	
King, Capital (60% of bonus).	2,400	
Wilson, Capital (40% of bonus)	1,600	
Simpson, Capital.		24,000

To record Simpson's entrance into partnership with reduced payment reported as a bonus from original partners.

If goodwill rather than a bonus is attributed to the *entering partner,* a mathematical problem arises in determining the implicit value of the business as a whole. In the current illustration, Simpson paid $20,000 for a 20 percent interest. Therefore, the value of the company is calculated as only $100,000 ($20,000/20 percent), a figure that is less than the $120,000 in net assets being reported after the new contribution. Negative goodwill appears to exist. One possibility is that individual partnership assets are overvalued and require reduction. As an alternative, the cash contribution might not be an accurate representation of the new partner's investment. Simpson could be bringing an intangible contribution (goodwill) to the business along with the $20,000. This additional amount can be determined only algebraically:

$$\text{Simpson's capital} = 20 \text{ percent of partnership capital}$$

Therefore

$$\$20,000 + \text{Goodwill} = .20\ (\$100,000 + \$20,000 + \text{Goodwill})$$
$$\$20,000 + \text{Goodwill} = \$20,000 + \$4,000 + .20\ \text{Goodwill}$$
$$.80\ \text{Goodwill} = \$4,000$$
$$\text{Goodwill} = \$5,000$$

If the partners determine that Simpson is, indeed, making an intangible contribution (a particular skill, for example, or a developed clientele), Simpson should be credited with a $25,000 capital investment: $20,000 cash and $5,000 goodwill. When added to the original $100,000 in net assets reported by the partnership, this contribution raises the total capital for the business to $125,000. As specified by the purchase agreement, Simpson's interest now represents a 20 percent share of the partnership ($25,000/$125,000).

Recognizing $5,000 in goodwill has established the proper relationship between the new partner and the partnership. Therefore, the following journal entry should be recorded to reflect this transaction:

Cash	20,000	
Goodwill	5,000	
Simpson, Capital		25,000
To record Simpson's entrance into partnership with goodwill attributed to this new partner.		

Dissolution—Withdrawal by a Partner

Admission of a new partner is not the only method by which a partnership can undergo a change in composition. Over the life of the business, partners occasionally leave the organization. Death or retirement can occur, or a partner may simply elect to withdraw from the partnership. The Articles of Partnership also can allow for the expulsion of a partner under certain conditions.

Once again, any change in membership legally dissolves the partnership, although the business's operations usually continue uninterrupted under the ownership of the remaining partners. Regardless of the reason for dissolution, some method of establishing an equitable settlement of the withdrawing partner's interest in the business is necessary. Often, the partner (or the partner's estate) may simply sell the interest to an outside party, with approval, or to one or more of the remaining partners. As an alternative, cash or other assets can be distributed from the business as a means of settling a partner's right of co-ownership. Consequently, life insurance policies are held by many partnerships solely to provide adequate cash to liquidate a partner's interest upon death.

Whether withdrawal is caused by death or some other reason, a final distribution will not necessarily equal the book value of the partner's capital account. A capital balance is only a recording of historical transactions and rarely represents the true value inherent in a business. Instead, payment is frequently based on the value of the partner's interest as ascertained by either negotiation or appraisal. Since the determination of a settlement can be derived in many ways, the Articles of Partnership should contain exact provisions regulating this procedure.

The withdrawal of an individual partner and the resulting distribution of partnership property can, again, be accounted for by either the bonus (no revaluation) method or the goodwill (revaluation) method. However, once again, a hybrid option is available.

As in earlier illustrations, if a bonus is recorded, the amount can be attributed to either of the parties involved: the withdrawing partner or the remaining partners. Conversely, any revaluation of partnership property (as well as the establishment of a goodwill balance) is allocated among all partners in recognition of possible unrecorded gains. As before, the hybrid approach restates assets and liabilities to fair market value but makes no recording of goodwill. In this last alternative, the legal change in ownership is reflected but the theoretical problems associated with partnership goodwill are avoided.

Accounting for the Withdrawal of a Partner—Illustration To demonstrate the various approaches that can be taken to account for a partner's withdrawal, assume that the partnership of Duncan, Smith, and Windsor has been in existence for a number of years. At the present time, the partners have the following capital balances as well as the indicated profit and loss percentages:

Partner	Capital Balance	Profit and Loss Ratio
Duncan	$ 70,000	50%
Smith	20,000	30
Windsor	10,000	20
Total capital	$100,000	

Windsor decides to withdraw from the partnership but Duncan and Smith plan to continue operating the business. As per the original partnership agreement, a final settlement distribution for Windsor is computed based on the following specified provisions:

1. An appraisal will be made by an independent expert to determine the estimated fair market value of the business.

2. Any individual who leaves the partnership is to receive cash or other assets equal to that partner's current capital balance after recording an appropriate share of any adjustment indicated by the previous valuation. The allocation of unrecorded gains and losses is based on the normal profit and loss ratio.

Following Windsor's decision to withdraw from the partnership, an immediate appraisal is made of the business and its property. Total fair market value is estimated at $180,000, a figure $80,000 in excess of book value. According to this valuation, land held by the partnership is currently worth $50,000 more than its original cost. In addition, $30,000 in goodwill is attributed to the partnership based on the value of the business as a going concern. *Therefore, Windsor is paid $26,000 on leaving the partnership: the original $10,000 capital balance plus a 20 percent share of this $80,000 increment.* The amount of payment is not in dispute, only the method of recording the withdrawal is in question.

Bonus Method Applied   If the bonus method is used by the partnership to record this transaction, the extra $16,000 paid to Windsor is simply recorded as a decrease in the remaining partners' capital accounts. Historically, Duncan and Smith have been credited with 50 percent and 30 percent of all profits and losses, respectively. This same relative ratio is used now to allocate the reduction between these two remaining partners on a ⅝ and ⅜ basis:

Bonus Method

Windsor, Capital (to remove account balance)	10,000	
Duncan, Capital (⅝ of excess distribution)	10,000	
Smith, Capital (⅜ of excess distribution)	6,000	
Cash		26,000
To record Windsor's withdrawal with $16,000 excess distribution taken from remaining partners.		

Goodwill Method Applied   This same transaction can also be accounted for by means of the goodwill (or revaluation) approach. The appraisal indicates that land is undervalued on the partnership's records by $50,000 and that goodwill of $30,000 has apparently accrued to the business over the years. The first of the following entries recognizes these valuations. This adjustment properly equates Windsor's capital balance with the $26,000 cash distribution. Windsor's equity balance is merely removed in the second entry at the time of payment.

Goodwill Method

Land	50,000	
Goodwill	30,000	
Duncan, Capital (50%)		40,000
Smith, Capital (30%)		24,000
Windsor, Capital (20%)		16,000
Recognition of land value and goodwill as a preliminary step to Windsor's withdrawal.		
Windsor, Capital (to remove account balance)	26,000	
Cash		26,000
Cash distribution made to Windsor in settlement of partnership interest.		

The implied value of a partnership as a whole cannot be determined directly from the amount distributed to a withdrawing partner. For example, paying Windsor $26,000 did not indicate that total capital should be $130,000 ($26,000/20%). This computation is appropriate only when (1) a new partner is admitted or (2) the percentage of capital is the same as the profit and loss ratio. Here, the valuation indicated that the company was worth $80,000 more than book value. As a 20 percent owner, Windsor was entitled to $16,000 of that amount, raising the appropriate capital account from $10,000 to $26,000, the amount of the final payment to that partner.

Hybrid Method Applied   As indicated previously, a hybrid approach also can be adopted to record a partner's withdrawal. Asset and liability revaluations are still recognized but goodwill is ignored. A bonus must be recorded to reconcile the partner's adjusted capital balance with the final distribution.

In the current illustration, for example, no goodwill is recorded. However, the book value of the land is increased by $50,000 in recognition of present worth. This adjustment increases Windsor's capital balance to $20,000, a figure that is still less than the $26,000 distribution. The $6,000 difference is recorded as a bonus taken from the remaining two partners according to their relative profit and loss ratio.

Hybrid Method

Land	50,000	
Duncan, Capital (50%)		25,000
Smith, Capital (30%)		15,000
Windsor, Capital (20%)		10,000
To adjust land account to fair market value as a preliminary step in Windsor's withdrawal.		
Windsor, Capital (to remove account balances)	20,000	
Duncan, Capital (⅗ of bonus)	3,750	
Smith, Capital (⅖ of bonus)	2,250	
Cash		26,000
Final distribution made to Windsor with $6,000 bonus taken from remaining partners.		

SUMMARY

1. A partnership is defined as "an association of two or more persons to carry on a business as co-owners for profit." This form of business organization exists throughout the American economy ranging in size from small, part-time operations to international enterprises. The partnership format is popular for many reasons, including the ease of creation and the avoidance of the double taxation that is inherent in corporate ownership. However, the unlimited liability incurred by each general partner normally restricts the growth potential of most partnerships. Thus, although the quantity of partnerships in the United States is great, their size tends to be small.

2. Over the years, a number of different types of organizations have been developed to take advantage of the single taxation of partnerships and the limited liability afforded to corporate stockholders. Such legal forms include S Corporations, Limited Partnerships, Limited Liability Partnerships, and Limited Liability Companies.

3. The unique elements of partnership accounting are found primarily in the capital accounts that are accumulated for each partner. The basis for recording these balances is the Articles of Partnership, a document that should be established as a prerequisite to the formation of any partnership. One of the principal provisions of this agreement is the initial investment to be made by each partner. Noncash contributions such as inventory or land are entered into the partnership's accounting records at fair market value.

4. In forming a partnership, the contributions made by the partners need not be limited to tangible assets. A particular line of expertise possessed by a partner or an established clientele are attributes that can have a significant value to a partnership. Two methods of recording this type of investment are found in practice. Under the bonus method, only

identifiable assets are recognized. The capital accounts are then aligned to indicate the balances negotiated by the partners. According to the goodwill approach, all contributions (even those of a nebulous nature such as an expertise) are valued and recorded, often as goodwill.

5. Another accounting issue to be resolved in forming a partnership is the allocation of annual net income. In closing out the revenue and expense accounts at the end of each period, some assignment must be made to the individual capital balances. Although an equal division can be used to allocate the profit or loss, partners frequently devise unique plans in an attempt to be equitable. Such factors as time worked, expertise, and invested capital should be considered in creating an allocation procedure.

6. Over time, changes occur in the makeup of a partnership because of the death or retirement of the individuals or the admission of new partners. Such changes dissolve the existing partnership, although the business frequently continues uninterrupted through a newly formed partnership. If, for example, a new partner is admitted by the acquisition of a present interest, the capital balances can simply be reclassified to reflect the change in ownership. As an alternative, the purchase price may be viewed as evidence of the underlying value of the organization as a whole. Based on this calculation, asset and liability balances are adjusted to market value, and any residual goodwill is recognized.

7. Admission into an existing partnership also can be achieved by a direct capital contribution to the business. Because of negotiations between the parties, the amount invested will not always agree with the beginning capital balance attributed to the new partner. The bonus method resolves this conflict by simply reclassifying the various capital accounts to align the balances with specified totals and percentages. Revaluation of assets and liabilities is not carried out under this approach. Conversely, according to the goodwill method, all accounts are adjusted first to fair market value. The price paid by the new partner is used to compute an implied value for the partnership, and any excess over market value is recorded as goodwill.

8. The composition of a partnership also can undergo changes because of the death or retirement of a partner. Individuals may decide to simply withdraw. Such changes legally dissolve the partnership, although business operations frequently continue under the ownership of the remaining partners. In compensating the departing partner, the final asset distribution may differ from the ending capital balance. This disparity can, once again, be accounted for by means of the bonus method, which adjusts the remaining capital accounts to absorb the bonus being paid. The goodwill approach also can be applied wherein all assets and liabilities are restated to fair market value with any goodwill being recognized. Finally, a hybrid method revalues the assets and liabilities but ignores goodwill. Under this last approach, any amount paid to the departing partner in excess of the newly adjusted capital balance is accounted for by means of the bonus method.

COMPREHENSIVE ILLUSTRATION

Problem

(Estimated Time: 30 to 55 Minutes) Heyman and Mullins begin a partnership on January 1, 2001. Heyman invests $40,000 cash as well as inventory costing $15,000 but with a current appraised value of only $12,000. Mullins contributes a building with a $40,000 book value and a $48,000 fair market value. The partnership also accepts responsibility for a $10,000 note payable owed in connection with this building.

The partners agree to begin operations with equal capital balances. The Articles of Partnership also provide that at the end of each year profits and losses are allocated as follows:

1. For managing the business, Heyman is credited with a bonus of 10 percent of partnership income after subtracting the bonus. No bonus is accrued if the partnership records a loss.

2. Both partners are entitled to interest equal to 10 percent of the average monthly capital balance for the year without regard for the income or drawings of that year.

3. Any remaining profit or loss is divided 60 percent to Heyman and 40 percent to Mullins.

4. Each partner is allowed to withdraw $800 per month in cash from the business.

On October 1, 2001, Heyman invests an additional $12,000 cash in the business. For 2001, the partnership reports income of $33,000.

Lewis, an employee, is allowed to join the partnership on January 1, 2002. The new partner invests $66,000 directly into the business for a one-third interest in the partnership property. The revised partnership agreement still allows for both the bonus to Heyman as well as the 10 percent interest, but all remaining profits and losses are now split 40 percent each to Heyman and Lewis with the remaining 20 percent to Mullins. Lewis is also entitled to $800 per month in drawings.

Mullins chooses to withdraw from the partnership a few years later. After negotiations, all parties agree that Mullins should be paid a $90,000 settlement. The capital balances on that date were as follows:

Heyman, capital	$88,000
Mullins, capital	78,000
Lewis, capital	72,000

Required

a. Assuming that the bonus method is used exclusively by this partnership, make all necessary journal entries. Entries for the monthly drawings of the partners are not required.

b. Assuming that the goodwill method is used exclusively by this partnership, make all necessary journal entries. Again, entries for the monthly drawings are not required.

Solution

a. **Bonus Method**

2001

Jan. 1   All contributed property is recorded at fair market value. Under the bonus method, total capital is then divided as specified between the partners.

Cash	40,000	
Inventory	12,000	
Building	48,000	
Note Payable		10,000
Heyman, Capital (50%)		45,000
Mullins, Capital (50%)		45,000
To record initial contributions to partnership along with equal capital balances.		

Oct. 1

Cash	12,000	
Heyman, Capital		12,000
To record additional investment by partner.		

Dec. 31   Both the bonus assigned to Heyman and the interest accrual must be computed as preliminary steps in the income allocation process. Since the bonus is based on income after subtracting the bonus, the amount must be calculated algebraically:

$$\text{Bonus} = .10 (\$33,000 - \text{Bonus})$$
$$\text{Bonus} = \$3,300 - .10 \text{ Bonus}$$
$$1.10 \text{ Bonus} = \$3,300$$
$$\text{Bonus} = \$3,000$$

According to the partnership agreement, the interest allocation is based on a monthly average figure. Mullins's capital balance of $45,000 did not change during the year; therefore $4,500 (10 percent) is the appropriate interest accrual for that partner. However, because of the October 1, 2001, contribution, Heyman's interest must be determined as follows:

Beginning balance:	$45,000 × 9 months =	$405,000
New balance:	$57,000 × 3 months =	171,000
		576,000
		× 1/12
Monthly average—capital balance		48,000
Interest rate		× 10%
Interest credited to Heyman		$ 4,800

Following the bonus and interest computations, the $33,000 income earned by the business in 2001 can be allocated according to the previously specified arrangement:

	Heyman	Mullins	Totals
Bonus (on page 665)	$ 3,000	–0–	$ 3,000
Interest (on page 665)	4,800	$4,500	9,300
Remaining income:			
$33,000			
(3,000)			
(9,300)			
$20,700	12,420 (60%)	8,280 (40%)	20,700
Income allocation	$20,220	$12,780	$33,000

Thus, the partnership's closing entries for the year of 2001 would be recorded as follows:

Heyman, Capital	9,600	
Mullins, Capital	9,600	
Heyman, Drawing		9,600
Mullins, Drawing		9,600
To close out $800 per month drawing accounts for the year of 2001.		
Income Summary	33,000	
Heyman, Capital		20,220
Mullins, Capital		12,780
To close out profit for year to capital accounts as computed above.		

At the end of this initial year of operation, the partners' capital accounts hold the following balances:

	Heyman	Mullins	Totals
Beginning balance	$45,000	$45,000	$ 90,000
Additional investment	12,000	–0–	12,000
Drawing	(9,600)	(9,600)	(19,200)
Net income (above)	20,220	12,780	33,000
Total capital	$67,620	$48,180	$115,800

2002

Jan. 1

Lewis contributed $66,000 to the business for a one-third interest in the partnership property. Combined with the $115,800 balance computed above, the partnership now has total capital of $181,800. Since no revaluation is recorded under the bonus approach, a one-third interest in the partnership equals $60,600 ($181,800 × ⅓). Lewis has invested $5,400 in excess of this amount, a balance viewed as a bonus accruing to the original partners:

Cash	66,000	
Lewis, Capital		60,600
Heyman, Capital (60% of bonus)		3,240
Mullins, Capital (40% of bonus)		2,160
To record Lewis's entrance into partnership with bonus to original partners.		

Several years later

The final event in this illustration is Mullins's withdrawal from the partnership. Although a capital balance of only $78,000 is reported for this partner, the final distribution is set at $90,000. The extra $12,000 payment represents a bonus assigned to Mullins, an amount that decreases the capital of the remaining two partners. Since Heyman and Lewis have previously accrued equal 40 percent shares of all profits and losses, the reduction is split evenly between the two.

Mullins, Capital	78,000	
Heyman, Capital (½ of bonus payment)	6,000	
Lewis, Capital (½ of bonus payment)	6,000	
Cash		90,000

Withdrawal of Mullins with bonus taken from remaining partners.

b. **Goodwill Method**

2001

Jan. 1   The fair market value of Heyman's contribution is $52,000, whereas Mullins is investing only a net $38,000 (the value of the building less the accompanying debt). Because the capital accounts are initially to be equal, Mullins is presumed to be contributing goodwill of $14,000.

Cash	40,000	
Inventory	12,000	
Building	48,000	
Goodwill	14,000	
Note payable		10,000
Heyman, Capital		52,000
Mullins, Capital		52,000

Creation of partnership with goodwill attributed to Mullins.

Oct. 1

| Cash .... | 12,000 | |
| Heyman, Capital .... | | 12,000 |

To record additional contribution by partner.

Dec. 31   Although Heyman's bonus is still $3,000 as derived in requirement *a.,* the interest accruals must be recalculated because the capital balances are different. Mullins's capital for the entire year was $52,000; thus, interest of $5,200 (10 percent) is appropriate. However, Heyman's balance changed during the year so that a monthly average must be determined as a basis for computing interest:

Beginning balance:	$52,000 × 9 months = $468,000
New balance:	$64,000 × 3 months = 192,000
	660,000
	× ⅟₁₂
Monthly average—capital balance	55,000
Interest rate	× 10%
Interest credited to Heyman	$ 5,500

Consequently, the $33,000 partnership income reported for 2001 is allocated as follows:

	Heyman	**Mullins**	**Totals**
Bonus (above)	$ 3,000	–0–	$ 3,000
Interest (above)	5,500	$ 5,200	10,700
Remaining income:			
$33,000			
(3,000)			
(10,700)			
$19,300	11,580 (60%)	7,720 (40%)	19,300
Income allocation	$20,080	$12,920	$33,000

The 2001 closing entries made under the goodwill approach would be as follows:

Heyman, Capital	9,600	
Mullins, Capital	9,600	
Heyman, Drawing		9,600
Mullins, Drawing		9,600
To close out drawing accounts for the year.		
Income Summary	33,000	
Heyman, Capital		20,080
Mullins, Capital		12,920
To assign 2001 profits per allocation		
determined above.		

After the closing process, the capital balances are composed of the following items:

	Heyman	**Mullins**	**Totals**
Beginning balance	$52,000	$52,000	$104,000
Additional investment	12,000	–0–	12,000
Drawing	(9,600)	(9,600)	(19,200)
Net income	20,080	12,920	33,000
Total capital	$74,480	$55,320	$129,800

2002

Jan. 1   Lewis's investment of $66,000 for a one-third interest in the partnership property implies that the business as a whole is worth $198,000 ($66,000 divided by ⅓). After adding Lewis's contribution to the present capital balance of $129,800, the business reports total net assets of only $195,800. Thus, a $2,200 gain in value ($198,000 − $195,800) is indicated and will be recognized at this time. Assuming that all partnership assets and liabilities are appropriately valued, this entire balance is attributed to goodwill.

Goodwill	2,200	
Heyman, Capital (60%)		1,320
Mullins, Capital (40%)		880
To recognize goodwill based on Lewis's		
acquisition price.		
Cash	66,000	
Lewis, Capital		66,000
Admission of Lewis to the partnership.		

Several years later   To conclude this illustration, Mullins's withdrawal must be recorded. This partner is to receive a distribution that is $12,000 greater than the corresponding capital balance of $78,000. Since Mullins is entitled to a 20 percent share of profits and losses, the additional $12,000 payment indicates that the partnership as a whole is undervalued by $60,000 ($12,000/20%). Only in that circumstance would the extra payment to Mullins be justified. Therefore, once again, goodwill is recognized with the final distribution then being made.

Goodwill	60,000	
Heyman, Capital (40%)		24,000
Mullins, Capital (20%)		12,000
Lewis, Capital (40%)		24,000
Recognition of goodwill based on withdrawal		
amount paid to Mullins.		
Mullins, Capital	90,000	
Cash		90,000
Money distributed to partner.		

QUESTIONS

1. What are the advantages of operating a business as a partnership rather than as a corporation? What are the disadvantages?

2. How does partnership accounting differ from corporate accounting?

3. What information is conveyed by the capital accounts found in partnership accounting?

4. Describe the differences between a Subchapter S Corporation and a Subchapter C Corporation.

5. A company is being created and the owners are trying to decide whether to form a general partnership, a limited liability partnership, or a limited liability company. What are the advantages and disadvantages of each of these legal forms?

6. What is an Articles of Partnership agreement, and what information should this document contain?

7. What valuation should be recorded for noncash assets transferred to a partnership by one of the partners?

8. If a partner is contributing attributes to a partnership such as an established clientele or a particular expertise, what two methods can be applied to record the contribution? Describe each of these methods.

9. What is the purpose of a drawing account in a partnership's financial records?

10. At what point in the accounting process does the allocation of partnership income become significant?

11. What provisions can be used in a partnership agreement to establish an equitable allocation of income among all partners?

12. If no agreement exists in a partnership as to the allocation of income, what method is appropriate?

13. What is a partnership dissolution? Does dissolution automatically necessitate the cessation of business and the liquidation of partnership assets?

14. By what methods can a new partner gain admittance into a partnership?

15. When a partner sells an ownership interest in a partnership, what rights are conveyed to the new owner?

16. A new partner enters a partnership and goodwill is calculated and credited to the original partners. How is the specific amount of goodwill assigned to these partners?

17. Under what circumstance might goodwill be allocated to a new partner entering a partnership?

18. When a partner withdraws from a partnership, why is the final distribution often based on the appraised value of the business rather than on the book value of the capital account balance?

INTERNET ASSIGNMENT

Internet sites are time and date sensitive. It is the purpose of these exercises to have you explore the Internet. You may need to refer to the text's Web site at http://www.mhhe.com/hoyle6e to find the most up-to-date links for the Web sites listed in the Internet Assignments.

1. Go to the following Web site: www.10kwizard.com.

   When the site is open, enter "BPL" in the "Ticker" box.

   Make sure the dates covered are for the most recent year.

   In the "Form Group" box, click on "Annual Reports."

   In the "Form" box, click on 10–K

   Click on Search.

   A listing of the most recent 10–K form for Buckeye Partners LP should come up.

   Click on the name of the company and information about the 10–K should come up.

A window will appear with "Item 1" listed in it.

Click on the down arrow for that window until you locate "Organization." Click on "Organization" and read the related footnote. Write a description of the information that is provided.

Click on down arrow again and find "Consolidated Balance Sheet." Click on that item. Write a description of the Partners' Capital section.

LIBRARY ASSIGNMENTS

1. Read the following as well as any other published materials describing the creation of a partnership:

   "Understanding the Appropriate Business Form," *National Public Accountant*, December 1997.

   "A New Breed Of Company," *Financial Executive*, January–February 1996.

   "What Form of Ownership Is Best?" *The CPA Journal*, August 1998.

   "Should Your Firm Operate as a LLC?" *Business Forum*, Summer–Fall 1996.

   "Should You Convert Your Practice to a Limited Liability Company?" *Law Practice Management,* September 1996.

   "Choosing a Business Entity in the 1990s," *Pennsylvania CPA Journal*, August 1995.

   "Selecting a Form of Business," *The CPA Journal,* April 1997.

   Write a report discussing the issues to be considered in deciding whether a partnership or some other legal form is preferable.

2. Read the following as well as any other published materials discussing the legal liability faced by partners:

   "Partnership Structure Is Called in Question as Liability Risk Rises," *Wall Street Journal,* June 10, 1992.

   "What's a Partner to Do?" *The CPA Journal,* April 1991.

   "Big 6 Firms Consider Incorporation," *World Accounting Report,* August 1994.

   "Goldman Chooses Limited Liability for New Structure," *Wall Street Journal,* May 22, 1996.

   Write a report discussing whether the potential liability of partners should be limited in some manner.

PROBLEMS

1. Which of the following is not a reason for the popularity of partnerships as a legal form for businesses?
   a. Partnerships need only be formed by an oral agreement.
   b. Partnerships can more easily generate significant amounts of capital.
   c. Partnerships avoid the double-taxation of income that is found in corporations.
   d. In some cases, losses may be used to offset gains for tax purposes.

2. How does partnership accounting differ from corporate accounting?
   a. The matching principle is not considered appropriate for partnership accounting.
   b. Revenues are recognized at a different time by a partnership than is appropriate for a corporation.
   c. Individual capital accounts replace the contributed capital and retained earnings balances found in corporate accounting.
   d. All assets are reported by partnerships at fair market value as of the latest balance sheet date.

3. Pat, Jean Lou, and Diane are partners with capital balances of $50,000, $30,000, and $20,000, respectively. These three partners share profits and losses equally. For an

investment of $50,000 cash (being paid to the business), MaryAnn is to be admitted as a partner with a one-fourth interest in capital and profits. Based on this information, the amount of MaryAnn's investment can best be justified by which of the following?

a. MaryAnn will receive a bonus from the other partners upon her admission to the partnership.

b. Assets of the partnership were overvalued immediately prior to MaryAnn's investment.

c. The book value of the partnership's net assets was less than the fair value immediately prior to MaryAnn's investment.

d. MaryAnn is apparently bringing goodwill into the partnership, and her capital account will be credited for the appropriate amount.

(AICPA adapted)

4. A partnership has the following capital balances:

Albert (50% of gains and losses)	$ 80,000
Barrymore (20%)	60,000
Candroth (30%)	140,000

Danville is going to invest $70,000 into the business to acquire a 30 percent ownership interest. Goodwill is to be recorded. What will be Danville's beginning capital balance?

a. $70,000.
b. $90,000.
c. $105,000.
d. $120,000.

5. A partnership has the following capital balances:

Elgin (40% of gains and losses)	$100,000
Jethro (30%)	200,000
Foy (30%)	300,000

Oscar is going to pay a total of $200,000 to these three partners to acquire a 25 percent ownership interest from each. Goodwill is to be recorded. What will be Jethro's capital balance after the transaction?

a. $150,000.
b. $175,000.
c. $195,000.
d. $200,000.

6. Bolcar has a capital balance of $110,000 with Neary having a $40,000 balance. These two partners share profits and losses 70 percent (Bolcar) and 30 percent (Neary). Kansas invests $50,000 in cash into the partnership for a 30 percent ownership. The bonus method will be used. What is Neary's capital balance after Kansas's investment?

a. $35,000.
b. $37,000.
c. $40,000.
d. $43,000.

7. Bishop has a capital balance in a local partnership of $120,000 with Cotton having a $90,000 balance. These two partners share profits and losses by a ratio of 60 percent to Bishop and 40 percent to Cotton. Lovett invests $60,000 in cash into the partnership for a 20 percent ownership. The goodwill method will be used. What is Cotton's capital balance after this new investment?

a. $99,600.
b. $102,000.
c. $112,000.
d. $126,000.

8. Messalina has a capital balance of $210,000 with Romulus having a $140,000 balance. These two partners share profits and losses 60 percent (Messalina) and 40 percent (Romulus). Claudius invests $100,000 in cash into the partnership for a 20 percent ownership. The bonus method will be used. What are the capital balances for Messalina, Romulus, and Claudius after this investment is recorded?

a. $216,000, $144,000, $90,000.
b. $218,000, $142,000, $88,000.
c. $222,000, $148,000, $80,000.
d. $240,000, $160,000, $100,000.

9. A partnership begins 2001 with the following capital balances:

Arthur, Capital	$ 60,000
Baxter, Capital	80,000
Cartwright, Capital	100,000

The Articles of Partnership stipulate that profits and losses be assigned in the following manner:

■   Each partner is allocated interest equal to 10 percent of the beginning capital balance.

■   Baxter is allocated compensation of $20,000 per year.

■   Any remaining profits and losses are allocated on a 3:3:4 basis, respectively.

■   Each partner is allowed to withdraw up to $5,000 cash per year.

Assuming that the net income for 2001 is $50,000 and that each partner withdraws the maximum amount allowed, what is the balance in Cartwright's Capital account at the end of that year?

a. $105,800.
b. $106,200.
c. $106,900.
d. $107,400.

10. A partnership begins its first year of operations with the following capital balances:

Winston, Capital	$110,000
Durham, Capital	80,000
Salem, Capital	110,000

According to the Articles of Partnership, all profits will be assigned as follows:

■   Winston will be awarded an annual salary of $20,000 with $10,000 assigned to Salem.

■   The partners will be attributed with interest equal to 10 percent of the capital balance as of the first day of the year.

■   The remainder will be assigned on a 5:2:3 basis, respectively.

■   Each partner is allowed to withdraw up to $10,000 per year.

Assume that the net loss for the first year of operations is $20,000 with net income of $40,000 in the subsequent year. Assume further that each partner withdraws the maximum amount from the business each period. What is the balance in Winston's Capital account at the end of the second year?

a. $102,600.
b. $104,400.
c. $108,600.
d. $109,200.

11. A partnership has the following capital balances:

Allen, Capital	$60,000
Burns, Capital	30,000
Costello, Capital	90,000

Profits and losses are split as follows: Allen (20%), Burns (30%), and Costello (50%). Costello wants to leave the partnership and is paid $100,000 from the business based on provisions in the Articles of Partnership. If the partnership uses the bonus method, what is the balance of Burns's Capital account after Costello withdraws?

a. $24,000.
b. $27,000.
c. $33,000.
d. $36,000.

12. As of December 31, 2001, the Cisco partnership has the following capital balances:

Montana, Capital	$130,000
Rice, Capital	110,000
Craig, Capital	80,000
Taylor, Capital	70,000

Profits and losses are split on a 3:3:2:2 basis, respectively. Craig decides to leave the partnership and is paid $90,000 from the business based on the original contractual agreement. If the goodwill method is to be applied, what is the balance of Montana's Capital account after Craig withdraws?

  a. $133,000.
  b. $137,500.
  c. $140,000.
  d. $145,000.

Problems 13 and 14 are independent problems based on the following capital account balances:

William (40% of gains and losses)	$220,000
Jennings (40%)	160,000
Bryan (20%)	110,000

13. Darrow invests $270,000 in cash for a 30 percent ownership interest. The money goes to the original partners. Goodwill is to be recorded. How much goodwill should be recognized, and what is Darrow's beginning capital balance?

  a. $410,000 and $270,000.
  b. $140,000 and $270,000.
  c. $140,000 and $189,000.
  d. $410,000 and $189,000.

14. Darrow invests $250,000 in cash for a 30 percent ownership interest. The money goes to the business. No goodwill or other revaluation is to be recorded. After the transaction, what is Jennings's capital balance?

  a. $160,000.
  b. $168,000.
  c. $170,200.
  d. $171,200.

15. Lear is to become a partner in the WS partnership by paying $80,000 in cash to the business. At present, Hamlet has a capital balance of $70,000 while MacBeth reports a total of only $40,000. Hamlet and MacBeth share profits on a 7:3 basis. Lear is acquiring 40 percent of the new partnership.

  a. If the goodwill method is applied, what will the three capital balances be following the payment by Lear?
  b. If the bonus method is applied, what will the three capital balances be following the payment by Lear?

16. The AKS partnership has the following capital balances at the beginning of the current year:

Arond (40% of profits and losses)	$80,000
Kant (40%)	70,000
Selvin (20%)	60,000

Required

  a. If Tronsty invests $60,000 in cash into the business for a 20 percent interest, what journal entry is recorded? Assume the bonus method is in use.
  b. If Tronsty invests $50,000 in cash into the business for a 20 percent interest, what journal entry is recorded? Assume the bonus method is in use.
  c. If Tronsty invests $55,000 in cash into the business for a 20 percent interest, what journal entry is recorded? Assume the goodwill method is in use.

17. A partnership has the following account balances: Cash $50,000; Other Assets $600,000; Liabilities $240,000; Nixon, Capital (50% of profits and losses) $200,000;

Hoover, Capital (20%) $120,000; Polk, Capital (30%) $90,000. Each of the following questions should be viewed as an independent situation:

a. Grant invests $80,000 into the partnership for an 18 percent capital interest. Goodwill is to be recognized. What are the capital accounts thereafter?

b. Grant invests $100,000 into the partnership to get a 20 percent capital balance. Goodwill is not to be recorded. What are the capital accounts thereafter?

18. The C-P partnership has the following capital account balances on January 1, 2001:

> Com, Capital $150,000
> Pack, Capital 110,000

Com is allocated 60 percent of all profits and losses with the remaining 40 percent assigned to Pack after interest of 10 percent is given to each partner based on beginning capital balances.

On January 2, 2001, Hal invests $76,000 cash for a 20 percent interest in the partnership. This transaction is recorded by the goodwill method. After this transaction, 10 percent interest is still to go to each partner. Profits and losses will then be split as follows: Com (50%), Pack (30%), and Hal (20%). In 2001, the partnership reports a net income of $36,000.

Required

a. Prepare the journal entry to record Hal's entrance into the partnership on January 2, 2001.

b. Determine the allocation of income at the end of 2001.

19. The partnership agreement of Jones, King, and Lane provides for the annual allocation of the business's profit or loss in the following sequence:

- Jones, the managing partner, receives a bonus equal to 20 percent of the business's profit.
- Each partner receives 15 percent interest on average capital investment.
- Any residual profit or loss is divided equally.

The average capital investments for 2001 were

> Jones $100,000
> King 200,000
> Lane 300,000

How much of the $90,000 partnership profit for 2001 should be assigned to each partner?

(AICPA adapted)

20. Purkerson, Smith, and Traynor have operated a bookstore for a number of years as a partnership. At the beginning of 2001, capital balances were as follows:

> Purkerson $60,000
> Smith 40,000
> Traynor 20,000

Because of a cash shortage, Purkerson invests an additional $8,000 in the business on April 1, 2001.

Each partner is allowed to withdraw $1,000 cash each month.

The partners have used the same method of allocating profits and losses since the business's inception:

- Each partner is given the following compensation allowance for work done in the business: Purkerson, $18,000; Smith, $25,000; and Traynor, $8,000.
- Each partner is credited with interest equal to 10 percent of the average monthly capital balance for the year without regard for normal drawings.
- Any remaining profit or loss is allocated 4:2:4 to Purkerson, Smith, and Traynor, respectively.

The net income for 2001 is $23,600. Each partner withdraws the allotted amount each month. What are the ending capital balances for 2001?

21. On January 1, 2001, the dental partnership of Left, Center, and Right was formed when the partners contributed $20,000, $60,000, and $50,000, respectively. Over the next three years, the business reported net income and (loss) as follows:

2001	($30,000)
2002	$20,000
2003	$40,000

During this period, each partner withdrew cash of $10,000 per year. Right invested an additional $12,000 in cash on February 9, 2002.

At the time that the partnership was created, the three partners agreed to allocate all profits and losses according to a specified plan written as follows:

■ Each partner is entitled to interest computed at the rate of 12 percent per year based on the individual capital balances at the beginning of that year.

■ Because of prior work experience, Left is entitled to an annual salary allowance of $12,000 while Center is credited with $8,000 per year.

■ Any remaining profit will be split as follows: Left, 20 percent; Center, 40 percent; and Right, 40 percent. If a loss remains, the balance will be allocated: Left, 30 percent; Center, 50 percent; and Right, 20 percent.

Required

Determine the ending capital balance for each partner as of the end of each of these three years.

22. The HELP partnership has the following capital balances as of December 31, 2001:

Lennon	$230,000
McCartney	190,000
Harrison	160,000
Starr	140,000
Total capital	$720,000

Answer each of the following independent questions:
a. Assume the partners share profits and losses 3:3:2:2, respectively. Harrison retires and is paid $190,000 based on the terms of the original partnership agreement. If the goodwill method is in use, what is the capital balance of the remaining three partners?
b. Assume the partners share profits and losses 4:3:2:1, respectively. Lennon retires and is paid $280,000 based on the terms of the original partnership agreement. If the bonus method is in use, what is the capital balance of the remaining three partners?

23. In the early part of 2002, the partners of Page, Childers, and Smith went to a local accountant seeking assistance. They had begun a new business in 2001 but had never previously used the services of an accountant.

Page and Childers began the partnership by contributing $80,000 and $30,000 in cash, respectively. Page was to work occasionally at the business whereas Childers would be employed full time. They decided that year-end profits and losses should be assigned as follows:

■ Each partner was to be allocated 10 percent interest computed on the beginning capital balances for the period.

■ A compensation allowance of $5,000 was to go to Page with a $20,000 amount assigned to Childers.

■ Any remaining income would be split on a 4:6 basis to Page and Childers, respectively.

In 2001, revenues totaled $90,000 with expenses reported as $64,000 (not including the compensation allowance assigned to the partners). Page withdrew cash of $8,000 during the year while Childers took out $11,000. In addition, $5,000 for repairs made to Page's home was paid by the business and charged to repair expense.

On January 1, 2002, a 20 percent interest in the partnership was sold to Smith for $43,000 cash. This money was contributed to the business with the bonus method used for accounting purposes.

Answer the following questions:

a. Why was the original profit and loss allocation, as just outlined, designed by the partners?

b. Why did the drawings for 2001 not agree with the compensation allowances provided for in the partnership agreement?

c. What journal entries should have been recorded by the partnership on December 31, 2001?

d. What journal entry should have been recorded by the partnership on January 1, 2002?

24. Following is the current balance sheet for a local partnership of doctors:

Cash and current		Liabilities	$ 40,000
assets	$ 30,000	A, capital	20,000
Land	180,000	B, capital	40,000
Building and		C, capital	90,000
equipment (net)	100,000	D, capital	120,000
Totals	$310,000		$310,000

The following questions represent independent situations:

a. E is going to invest enough money into this partnership to receive a 25 percent interest. No goodwill or bonus is to be recorded. How much should E invest?

b. E contributes $36,000 in cash to the business to receive a 10 percent interest in the partnership. Goodwill is to be recorded. Profits and losses have previously been split according to the following percentages: A, 30%; B, 10%; C, 40%; and D, 20%. After E makes this investment, what are the individual capital balances?

c. E contributes $42,000 in cash to the business to receive a 20 percent interest in the partnership. Goodwill is to be recorded. The four original partners share all profits and losses equally. After E makes this investment, what are the individual capital balances?

d. E contributes $55,000 in cash to the business to receive a 20 percent interest in the partnership. No goodwill or other asset revaluation is to be recorded. Profits and losses have previously been split according to the following percentages: A, 10%; B, 30%; C, 20%; and D, 40%. After E makes this investment, what are the individual capital balances?

e. C retires from the partnership and, as per the original partnership agreement, is to receive cash equal to 125 percent of her final capital balance. No goodwill or other asset revaluation is to be recognized. All partners share profits and losses equally. After the withdrawal, what are the individual capital balances of the remaining partners?

25. Partnership agreements usually specify a profit and loss ratio. They may also provide such additional features as salaries, bonuses, and interest allowances on invested capital.

Required

a. What is the objective of profit and loss sharing arrangements? Why may other features be needed in addition to a profit and loss ratio?

b. Discuss the arguments for recording salary and bonus allowances to partners as expenses of the business.

c. Discuss the arguments against treating partnership salary and bonus allowances as expenses.

d. In addition to other profit and loss sharing features, a partnership agreement might state that "interest is to be allowed on invested capital." List the additional provisions that should be included in the partnership agreement so that "interest to be allowed on invested capital" can be computed.

(AICPA adapted)

26. Boswell and Johnson form a partnership on May 1, 2001. Boswell contributes cash of $50,000; Johnson conveys title to the following properties to the partnership:

	Book Value	Fair Market Value
Land	$15,000	$28,000
Building and equipment	35,000	36,000

The partners agree to start their partnership with equal capital balances. No goodwill is to be recognized.

According to the Articles of Partnership written by the partners, profits and losses are allocated based on the following formula:

■ Boswell receives a compensation allowance of $1,000 per month.
■ All remaining profits and losses are split 60:40 to Johnson and Boswell, respectively.
■ Annual cash drawings of $5,000 can be made by each partner beginning in 2002.

Net income of $11,000 is earned by the business during 2001.

Walpole is invited to join the partnership on January 1, 2002. Because of Walpole's business reputation and financial expertise, she is given a 40 percent interest for $54,000 cash. The bonus approach is used to record this investment, made directly to the business. The Articles of Partnership are amended to give Walpole a $2,000 compensation allowance per month and an annual cash drawing of $10,000. Remaining profits are now allocated:

Johnson 48%
Boswell 12%
Walpole 40%

All drawings are taken by the partners during 2002. At the end of that year, the partnership reports an earned net income of $28,000.

On January 1, 2003, Pope (previously a partnership employee) is admitted into the partnership. Each partner transfers 10 percent to Pope. Pope makes the following payments directly to the partners:

To Johnson $5,672
To Boswell 7,880
To Pope 8,688

Once again, the Articles of Partnership must be amended to allow for the entrance of the new partner. This change entitles Pope to a compensation allowance of $800 per month and an annual drawing of $4,000. Profits and losses are now assigned.

Johnson 40.5%
Boswell 13.5%
Walpole 36.0%
Pope 10.0%

For the year of 2003, the partnership earned a profit of $46,000, and each partner withdrew the allowed amount of cash.

Required

Determine the capital balances for the individual partners as of the end of each year: 2001 through 2003.

27. Gray, Stone, and Lawson open an accounting practice on January 1, 2001, in San Diego, California. The business is to be operated as a partnership with Gray and Stone serving as the senior partners because of their years of experience. To establish the business, Gray, Stone, and Lawson contribute cash and other properties valued at $210,000, $180,000, and $90,000, respectively. A partnership agreement is drawn up that carries the following stipulations:

■ Personal drawings are allowed annually up to an amount equal to 10 percent of the beginning capital balance for the year.
■ Profits and losses are allocated according to the following plan:

(1) A salary allowance is credited to each partner in an amount equal to $8 per billable hour worked by that individual during the year.

(2) Interest is credited to the partners' capital accounts at the rate of 12 percent of the average monthly balance for the year (computed without regard for current income or drawings).

(3) An annual bonus is to be credited to Gray and Stone. Each bonus is to be 10 percent of net income after subtracting the bonus, the salary allowance, and the interest. Also included in the agreement is the provision that the bonus cannot be a negative amount.

(4) Any remaining partnership profit or loss is to be divided evenly among all partners.

Because of monetary problems encountered in getting the business started, Gray invests an additional $9,100 on May 1, 2001. On January 1, 2002, the partners allow Monet to buy into the partnership. Monet contributes cash directly to the business in an amount equal to a 25 percent interest in the book value of the partnership property subsequent to this contribution. The partnership agreement as to splitting profits and losses is not altered at the time of Monet's entrance into the firm; the general provisions continue to be applicable.

The billable hours for the partners during the first three years of operation are as follows:

	2001	2002	2003
Gray	1,710	1,800	1,880
Stone	1,440	1,500	1,620
Lawson	1,300	1,380	1,310
Monet	–0–	1,190	1,580

The partnership reports net income for 2001 through 2003 as follows:

2001	$ 65,000
2002	(20,400)
2003	152,800

Each partner withdraws the maximum allowable amount each year.

Required

a. Determine the allocation of income for each of these three years (to the nearest dollar).

b. Prepare in appropriate form a statement of partners' capital for the year ending December 31, 2001.

28. A partnership of attorneys in the St. Louis, Missouri, area has the following balance sheet accounts as of January 1, 2002:

Assets	$320,000	Liabilities	$120,000
		Athos, capital	80,000
		Porthos, capital	70,000
		Aramis, capital	50,000

According to the Articles of Partnership, Athos is to receive an allocation of 50 percent of all partnership profits and losses while Porthos gets 30 percent and Aramis 20 percent. The book value of each asset and liability should be considered an accurate representation of fair market value.

Required

For each of the following *independent* situations, prepare the journal entry or entries to be recorded by the partnership. (Round to nearest dollar.)

a. Porthos, with permission of the other partners, decides to sell half of his partnership interest to D'Artagnan for $50,000 in cash. No asset revaluation or goodwill is to be recorded by the partnership.

b. All three of the present partners agree to sell 10 percent of each partnership interest to D'Artagnan for a total cash payment of $25,000. Each partner receives a negotiated portion of this amount. Goodwill is being recorded as a result of the transaction.

    c.   D'Artagnan is allowed to become a partner with a 10 percent ownership interest by contributing $30,000 in cash directly into the business. The bonus method is used to record this admission.

    d.   Use the same facts as in requirement *c,* except that the entrance into the partnership is recorded by the goodwill method.

    e.   D'Artagnan is allowed to become a partner with a 10 percent ownership interest by contributing $12,222 in cash directly to the business. The goodwill method is used to record this transaction.

    f.   Aramis decides to retire and leave the partnership. An independent appraisal of the business and its assets indicates a current fair market value of $280,000. Goodwill is to be recorded. Aramis will then be given the exact amount of cash that will close out his capital account.

29.   Steve Reese is a well-known interior designer in Fort Worth, Texas. He wants to start his own business and convinces Rob O'Donnell, a local merchant, to contribute the capital to form a partnership. On January 1, 2001, O'Donnell invests a building worth $52,000 and equipment valued at $16,000 as well as $12,000 in cash. Although Reese makes no tangible contribution to the partnership, he will operate the business and be an equal partner in the beginning capital balances.

    To entice O'Donnell to join this partnership, Reese draws up the following agreement:

■ O'Donnell will be credited annually with interest equal to 20 percent of the beginning capital balance for the year.

■ O'Donnell will also have added to his capital account 15 percent of partnership income each year (without regard for the preceding interest figure) or $4,000, whichever is greater. All remaining income is credited to Reese.

■ Neither partner is allowed to withdraw funds from the partnership during 2001. Thereafter, they can each draw out $5,000 annually or 20 percent of the beginning capital balance for the year, whichever is greater.

    A net loss of $10,000 is reported by the partnership during the first year of its operation. On January 1, 2002, Terri Dunn becomes a third partner in this business by contributing $15,000 cash to the partnership. Dunn receives a 20 percent share of the business's capital. The profit and loss agreement is altered as follows:

■ O'Donnell is still entitled to (1) interest on his beginning capital balance as well as (2) the share of partnership income just specified.

■ Any remaining profit or loss will be split on a 6:4 basis between Reese and Dunn, respectively.

    Partnership income for 2002 is reported as $44,000. Each partner withdraws the full amount that is allowed.

    On January 1, 2003, Dunn falls ill and sells her interest in the partnership (with the consent of the other two partners) to Judy Postner. Postner pays $46,000 directly to Dunn. Net income for 2003 is $61,000 with the partners again taking their full drawing allowance.

    On January 1, 2004, Postner elects to withdraw from the business for personal reasons. The Articles of Partnership contain a provision stating that any partner may leave the partnership at any time and is entitled to receive cash in an amount equal to the recorded capital balance at that time plus 10 percent.

Required

    a.   Prepare journal entries to record the preceding transactions on the assumption that the bonus (or no revaluation) method is used. Drawings need not be recorded, although the balances should be included in the closing entries.

    b.   Prepare journal entries to record the previous transactions on the assumption that the goodwill (or revaluation) method is used. Drawings need not be recorded, although the balances should be included in the closing entries.

    (Round all amounts off to the nearest dollar)

C H A P T E R

15

Partnerships: Termination and Liquidation

QUESTIONS TO CONSIDER

- Under what conditions would a partnership be liquidated?

- What information should an accountant report to reflect the liquidation of a partnership?

- In a partnership liquidation, what happens if one or more partners reports a deficit capital balance?

- How are any remaining assets distributed if a partnership or one of its partners becomes insolvent?

- What are safe capital balances and how are they determined?

- How does the accountant determine which partners receive cash during a partnership liquidation?

Termination of business activities followed by the liquidation of partnership property can take place for a variety of reasons, both legal and personal.

I'm spending a great deal of time helping physician clients patch up partnership disputes and pull together. That is until I run up against a group where personalities, philosophies, or work styles are truly irreconcilable. In these cases, the best solution is a split. . . . Once the doctors know they want to split, they can meet to discuss their problems. While these sessions are often stormy, in the end the doctors usually find themselves agreeing for once. Their consensus? They'll each benefit more from going their separate ways than enduring a situation that's not working. Still, there's no denying that severing any partnership is emotionally wrenching.[1]

These sentiments, expressed by a financial consultant in the medical management field, indicate the potential frailty of a partnership. Although a business organized in this manner can exist indefinitely through periodic changes within the ownership, the actual cessation of operations is not an uncommon occurrence. As indicated by the preceding quotation, the partners may simply be incompatible and choose to cease operations. The same outcome might result if profit figures fail to reach projected levels. "In the best of times, partnerships are fragile. But in the current recession, the breakup rate has worsened as cost-cutting and other pressures heighten tensions between partners."[2]

The death of a partner is another event that dissolves a partnership and frequently leads to the termination of business operations. Rather than continuing under a new partnership arrangement, the remaining owners may discover that liquidation is necessary to settle the

---

[1]Leif C. Beck, "When a Group Is Better Off Splitting Up," *Medical Economics,* March 5, 1984, p. 183.
[2]Sue Shellenbarger, "Cutting Losses When Partners Face a Breakup," *Wall Street Journal,* May 21, 1991, p. B1.

681

claims of the deceased partner's estate. A similar action may be required if one or more of the partners elects to change careers or retire. Under that circumstance, liquidation is often the most convenient method for winding up the financial affairs of the business.

As a final possibility, a partnership can be legally forced into selling its noncash assets by the bankruptcy of the business or even that of an individual partner. Laventhol & Horwath, the seventh largest public accounting firm in the United States, filed for bankruptcy protection after the firm came under intense financial pressure from numerous lawsuits. "Laventhol said that at least 100 lawsuits are pending in state and federal courts. Bankruptcy court protection 'is absolutely necessary in order to protect the debtor and its creditors from the devastating results a destructive race for assets will cause' the firm said."[3]

The bankruptcy of Laventhol & Horwath was not an isolated incident.

> Law firms are going out of business at a steady clip, and a few major accounting firms have collapsed in recent years. "At least a dozen [major law] firms have failed in the past three or four years," figures Bradford W. Hildebrandt, chairman of a legal consulting firm in Somerville, N.J. "In the next year or two, there could be another half-dozen."[4]

TERMINATION AND LIQUIDATION—PROTECTING THE INTERESTS OF ALL PARTIES

As discussed in the chapter on bankruptcy, accounting for the termination and liquidation of a business can prove to be a delicate task. Losses are commonly incurred. For example, "former partners in Keck, Mahin and Cate have pledged to pay slightly over $3 million to general unsecured creditors to settle the bankrupt firm's debts . . . this figure represents about 36 percent of the money owed."[5] Here, both the partners and the debtors suffered heavy losses.

Consequently, throughout any liquidation, both creditors and owners demand continuous accounting information that enables them to monitor and assess their financial risks. In generating this data for a partnership, the accountant must record:

- The conversion of partnership assets into cash.
- The allocation of the resulting gains and losses.
- The payment of liabilities and expenses.
- Any remaining unpaid debts to be settled or the distribution of any remaining assets to the partners based on their final capital balances.

Beyond the goal of merely reporting these transactions, the accountant must work to ensure the equitable treatment of all parties involved in the liquidation. The accounting records, for example, serve as the basis for allocating available assets to creditors as well as to the individual partners. If assets are limited, the accountant also may have to make recommendations as to the appropriate method for distributing any remaining funds. Protecting the interests of partnership creditors is an especially significant duty since the Uniform Partnership Act specifies that they have first priority to

---

[3]Peter Pae, "Laventhol Bankruptcy Filing Indicates Liabilities May Be as Much as $2 Billion," *Wall Street Journal,* November 23, 1990, p. A4.

[4]Lee Berton and Joann S. Lublin, "Partnership Structure Is Called in Question as Liability Risk Rises," *Wall Street Journal,* June 10, 1992, p. A9.

[5]*Chicago Daily Law Bulletin,* August 13, 1999, p. 3.

the assets held by the business at the time of dissolution. The accountant's desire for an equitable settlement is enhanced, no doubt, in that any party to a liquidation who is not treated fairly can seek legal recovery from the responsible party.

Not only the creditors but also the partners themselves have a great interest in the financial data produced during the period of liquidation. They must be concerned, as indicated above, about the possibility of incurring substantial monetary losses. The potential for loss is especially significant because of the unlimited liability to which the partners are exposed.

As long as a partnership can meet all obligations, a partner's risk is normally no greater than that of a corporate stockholder. However, should the partnership become insolvent, each partner faces the possibility of having to satisfy *all* remaining obligations personally. Although any partner suffering more than a proportionate share of these losses can seek legal retribution from the remaining owners, this process is not always an effective remedy. The other partners may themselves be insolvent, or anticipated legal costs might discourage the damaged party from seeking recovery. Therefore, each partner usually has a keen interest in monitoring the progress of a liquidation as it transpires.

Termination and Liquidation Procedures Illustrated

The procedures involved in terminating and liquidating a partnership are basically mechanical. Partnership assets are converted into cash that is used to pay business obligations as well as liquidation expenses. *Any remaining assets are then distributed to the individual partners based on their final capital balances.* As no further ledger accounts exist, the partnership's books are permanently closed. If each partner has a large enough capital balance to absorb all liquidation losses, the accountant should experience little difficulty in recording this series of transactions.

To illustrate the typical process, assume that Morgan and Houseman have been operating an art gallery as a partnership for a number of years. On May 1, 2001, the partners decide to terminate business activities, liquidate all noncash assets, and dissolve their partnership. Although a specific explanation for this action is not given, any number of reasons might exist. The partners, for example, could have come to a disagreement so that they no longer believe they can work together. As an alternative possibility, business profits may have been inadequate to warrant the continuing investment of their time and capital.

Following is a balance sheet for the partnership of Morgan and Houseman as of the termination date. The revenue, expense, and drawing accounts have been closed out as a preliminary step in terminating the business. A separate reporting will subsequently be made of the gains and losses that occur during the final winding-down process.

MORGAN AND HOUSEMAN
Balance Sheet
May 1, 2001

Assets		Liabilities and Capital	
Cash	$ 45,000	Liabilities	$ 32,000
Accounts receivable	12,000	Morgan, capital	50,000
Inventory	22,000	Houseman, capital	38,000
Land, building, and equipment (net)	41,000		
		Total liabilities and	
Total assets	$120,000	capital	$120,000

The assumption is made here that the liquidation of Morgan and Houseman proceeds in an orderly fashion through the following events:

2001

June 1	The inventory is sold at auction for $15,000. Morgan and Houseman allocate all profits and losses on a 6:4 basis, respectively.
July 15	Of the total accounts receivable, $9,000 is collected with the remainder being written off as bad debts.
Aug. 20	The fixed assets are sold for a total of $29,000.
Aug. 25	All partnership liabilities are paid.
Sept. 10	A total of $3,000 in liquidation expenses is paid to cover costs such as accounting and legal fees as well as the commissions incurred in disposing of partnership property.
Oct. 15	All remaining cash is distributed to the owners based on their final capital account balances.

As can be seen, the partnership of Morgan and Houseman incurs a number of losses in liquidating this property. Such losses are almost anticipated because the need for immediate sale is usually held as a high priority in a liquidation. Furthermore, a portion of the assets used by any business, such as equipment and buildings, may have a utility that is strictly limited to a particular type of operation. If the property is not easily adaptable, disposal at any reasonable price often proves to be a problem.

To record the liquidation of Morgan and Houseman, the following journal entries would be made. Rather than report specific income and expense balances, gains and losses are traditionally recorded directly to the partners' capital accounts. Since operations have ceased, determination of a separate net income figure for this period would provide little informational value. *Instead, a primary concern of the parties involved in any liquidation is the continuing changes in each partner's capital balance.*

6/1/01	Cash	15,000	
	Morgan, Capital (60% of loss)	4,200	
	Houseman, Capital (40% of loss)	2,800	
	Inventory		22,000
	To record sale of partnership inventory at a $7,000 loss.		
7/15/01	Cash	9,000	
	Morgan, Capital	1,800	
	Houseman, Capital	1,200	
	Accounts Receivable		12,000
	To record collection of accounts receivable with write off of remaining $3,000 in accounts as bad debts.		
8/20/01	Cash	29,000	
	Morgan, Capital	7,200	
	Houseman, Capital	4,800	
	Land, Building, and Equipment (net)		41,000
	To record sale of fixed assets and allocation of $12,000 loss.		
8/25/01	Liabilities	32,000	
	Cash		32,000
	Payment made to settle the liabilities of the partnership.		
9/10/01	Morgan, Capital	1,800	
	Houseman, Capital	1,200	
	Cash		3,000
	To pay liquidation expenses with the amounts recorded as direct reductions to the partners' capital accounts.		

After liquidating the partnership assets and paying off all obligations, the cash that remains can be divided between Morgan and Houseman personally. The following schedule is utilized to determine the partners' ending capital account balances and, thus, the appropriate distribution for this final payment.

Cash and Capital Account Balances*

	Cash	Morgan, Capital	Houseman, Capital
Beginning balances	$ 45,000	$50,000	$38,000
Sold inventory	15,000	(4,200)	(2,800)
Collected accounts receivable	9,000	(1,800)	(1,200)
Sold fixed assets	29,000	(7,200)	(4,800)
Paid liabilities	(32,000)	–0–	–0–
Paid liquidation expenses	(3,000)	(1,800)	(1,200)
Final totals	$ 63,000	$35,000	$28,000

*Because of the presence of other assets as well as liabilities, the Cash and Capital accounts will not be in agreement until the end of the liquidation process.

After the ending capital balances have been calculated, the remaining cash can be distributed to the partners to close out the financial records of the partnership:

10/15/01	Morgan, Capital	35,000	
	Houseman, Capital	28,000	
	Cash		63,000
	To distribute cash to partners in accordance with final capital balances.		

Schedule of Liquidation

Liquidation may take a considerable length of time to complete. Because the various parties involved seek continually updated financial information, the accountant should produce frequent reports summarizing the transactions as they occur. Consequently, a statement (often referred to as the schedule of liquidation) can be prepared at periodic intervals to disclose:

- Transactions to date.
- Property still being held by the partnership.
- Liabilities remaining to be paid.
- Current cash and capital balances.

Although the preceding Morgan and Houseman example has been condensed into a few events occurring during a relatively brief period of time, partnership liquidations usually require numerous transactions that transpire over months and, perhaps, even years. By receiving frequent schedules of liquidation, both the creditors and the partners are able to stay apprised of the results of this lengthy process.

Exhibit 15–1 presents the final schedule of liquidation for the partnership of Morgan and Houseman. Previous statements should have been distributed by the accountant at each important juncture of this liquidation to meet the informational needs of the parties involved. The example produced here demonstrates the stair-step approach incorporated in preparing a schedule of liquidation. The effects of each transaction (or group of transactions) are outlined in a horizontal fashion so that current account balances as well as all prior transactions are evident. This structuring also facilitates the preparation of future statements: A new layer summarizing recent events can simply be added to the bottom each time that a new schedule is to be produced.

Exhibit 15–1

MORGAN AND HOUSEMAN
Schedule of Partnership Liquidation
Final Balances

	Cash	Noncash Assets	Liabilities	Morgan, Capital (60%)	Houseman, Capital (40%)
Beginning balances, 5/1/01	$ 45,000	$ 75,000	$ 32,000	$ 50,000	$ 38,000
Sold inventory, 6/1/01	15,000	(22,000)		(4,200)	(2,800)
Updated balances	60,000	53,000	32,000	45,800	35,200
Collected receivables, 7/15/01	9,000	(12,000)		(1,800)	(1,200)
Updated balances	69,000	41,000	32,000	44,000	34,000
Sold fixed assets, 8/20/01	29,000	(41,000)		(7,200)	(4,800)
Updated balances	98,000	–0–	32,000	36,800	29,200
Paid liabilities, 8/25/01	(32,000)		(32,000)		
Updated balances	66,000	–0–	–0–	36,800	29,200
Paid liquidation expenses, 9/10/01	(3,000)			(1,800)	(1,200)
Updated balances	63,000	–0–	–0–	35,000	28,000
Distributed remaining cash, 10/15/01	(63,000)			(35,000)	(28,000)
Closing balances	–0–	–0–	–0–	–0–	–0–

Deficit Capital Balance—Contribution Made by Partner

In Exhibit 15–1, the liquidation process ended with all partners continuing to report positive capital balances. Thus, Morgan and Houseman were both able to share in the $63,000 cash that remained. Unfortunately, such an outcome is not always assured. At the end of a liquidation, one or more partners may be reporting a negative capital account. Or, the partnership may not even be able to generate enough cash to satisfy all of the claims of its creditors. Such deficits are most likely to occur when the partnership is already insolvent at the start of the liquidation or when the disposal of noncash assets results in material losses. Under these circumstances, the accounting procedures to be applied depend on legal regulations as well as the individual actions of the partners.

As an example, assume that the partnership of Holland, Dozier, and Ross was dissolved at the beginning of the current year. Business activities were terminated and all noncash assets were subsequently converted into cash. During the liquidation process, the partnership incurred a number of large losses that have been allocated to the partners' capital accounts on a 4:4:2 basis, respectively. A portion of the resulting cash is then used to pay all partnership liabilities and liquidation expenses.

Following these transactions, only the following four account balances remain open within the partnership's records:

Cash	$20,000	Holland, Capital	$ (6,000)
		Dozier, Capital	15,000
		Ross, Capital	11,000
		Total	$20,000

Holland is now reporting a negative capital balance of $6,000; the assigned share of partnership losses has exceeded this partner's net contribution. In such cases, the Uniform Partnership Act (Section 18[a]) stipulates that the partner "must contribute toward the losses, whether of capital or otherwise, sustained by the partnership according to his share in the profits." Therefore, Holland is legally required to convey an additional $6,000 to the partnership at this time to eliminate the deficit balance. This contribution raises the cash balance to $26,000 so that a complete distribution can be made to Dozier ($15,000) and Ross ($11,000) in line with their capital accounts. The journal entry for this final payment closes out the partnership records.

Cash..	6,000	
Holland, Capital..................................		6,000
To record contribution made by Holland to extinguish negative capital balance.		

Dozier, Capital....................................	15,000	
Ross, Capital	11,000	
Cash...		26,000
To distribute remaining cash to partners in accordance with their ending capital balances.		

Deficit Capital Balance—Loss to Remaining Partners

An alternative scenario can easily be conceived for the previous partnership liquidation. Although Holland's capital account shows a $6,000 deficit balance, this partner may resist any attempt to force an additional investment, especially since the business is in the process of being terminated. The possibility of such recalcitrance is enhanced if the individual is having personal financial difficulties. Thus, the remaining partners may eventually have to resort to formal litigation to gain Holland's contribution. Until that legal action is concluded, the partnership records remain open, although inactive.

Distribution of Safe Payments   While awaiting the final resolution of this matter, no compelling reason exists for the partnership to continue holding $20,000 in cash. These funds will eventually be paid to Dozier and Ross regardless of any action taken by Holland. Thus, an immediate transfer should be made to these two partners to allow them the use of their money. However, since Dozier has a $15,000 capital account balance while Ross currently reports $11,000, a complete distribution is not possible. A method must be devised, therefore, to allow for a fair allocation of the available $20,000.

To ensure the equitable treatment of all parties, this initial distribution is based on the assumption that the $6,000 capital deficit will prove to be a total loss to the partnership. Holland may, for example, be completely insolvent so that no further payment will ever be forthcoming. By making this conservative presumption, the accountant is able to calculate the lowest possible amounts (or safe balances) that Dozier and Ross must retain in their capital accounts to be able to absorb all future losses.

Should Holland's $6,000 deficit (or any portion of it) prove uncollectible, the loss will be written off against the capital accounts of Dozier and Ross. Allocation of this amount is based on the relative profit and loss ratio specified in the Articles of Partnership. According to the information provided in this illustration, Dozier and Ross are credited with 40 percent and 20 percent of all partnership income, respectively. This 40:20 ratio equates to a 2:1 relationship (or $\frac{2}{3}$:$\frac{1}{3}$) between the two. Thus, if no part of the $6,000 deficit balance is ever recovered from Holland, $4,000 (two-thirds) of the loss will be assigned to Dozier and $2,000 (one-third) to Ross.

Allocation of Potential $6,000 Loss

Dozier	$\frac{2}{3}$ of $(6,000) = $(4,000)
Ross	$\frac{1}{3}$ of $(6,000) = $(2,000)

These amounts represent the maximum potential reductions that might still be incurred by the two remaining partners. Depending on Holland's actions, Dozier could be forced to absorb an additional loss of $4,000 while Ross's capital account may decrease by as much as $2,000. These balances must, therefore, remain in the respective capital accounts until the issue is resolved. Hence, Dozier is entitled to receive $11,000 at the present time; this distribution reduces that partner's capital account from $15,000 to the minimum $4,000 level. Likewise, a $9,000 payment to Ross decreases the $11,000 capital balance to the $2,000 limit. These $11,000 and $9,000 figures represent safe payments that can be distributed to the partners without fear of new deficits being created subsequently.

Dozier, Capital	11,000	
Ross, Capital	9,000	
Cash		20,000

To distribute cash to Dozier and Ross based on safe capital balances, using the assumption that Holland will not contribute further to the partnership.

After this $20,000 in cash has been distributed, only a few other events can possibly occur during the remaining life of the partnership. Holland, either voluntarily or through legal persuasion, may contribute the entire $6,000 needed to eradicate the capital deficit. In that situation, the money should be immediately turned over to Dozier ($4,000) and Ross ($2,000) based on their remaining capital balances. The partnership records are effectively closed by this final distribution.

A second possibility is that Dozier and Ross may be unable to recover any part of the deficit from Holland. These two remaining partners must then absorb the $6,000 loss themselves. Since safe capital balances have been maintained, recording a complete default by Holland serves to close out the partnership books.

Dozier, Capital (⅔ of loss)	4,000	
Ross, Capital (⅓ of loss)	2,000	
Holland, Capital		6,000

To allocate deficit capital balance of insolvent partner.

Deficit Is Partly Collectible   One other ending to this partnership liquidation is conceivable. A portion of the $6,000 may be recovered from Holland although the remainder proves to be uncollectible. This partner may become bankrupt or the other partners might simply give up trying to collect. The partners could also negotiate this settlement to avoid protracted legal actions.

To illustrate, assume that Holland manages to contribute $3,600 to the partnership but subsequently files for relief under the provisions of the bankruptcy laws. In a later legal arrangement, $1,000 additional cash goes to the partnership, but the final $1,400 will never be collected. This series of events creates the following effects within the liquidation process:

1.   The initial $3,600 contribution is distributed to Dozier and Ross based on a new computation of their safe capital balances.
2.   The $1,400 default is charged against the two positive capital balances in accordance with the relative profit and loss ratio.
3.   The final $1,000 contribution is then paid to Dozier and Ross in amounts equal to their ending capital accounts, a transaction that closes the partnership's financial records.

The distribution of the first $3,600 depends on a recalculation of the minimum capital balances that Dozier and Ross must maintain to absorb all potential losses. Each of these computations is produced because of a basic realization: Holland's remaining deficit balance ($2,400 at this time) could prove to be a total loss. This approach guarantees that the other two partners will continue to report adequate capital until the liquidation is ultimately resolved.

	Current Capital	Allocation of Potential Loss	Safe Capital Payments
Dozier	$4,000	⅔ of $(2,400) = $(1,600)	$2,400
Ross	2,000	⅓ of $(2,400) = $ (800)	1,200

Thus, the $3,600 in cash that is now available is distributed immediately to Dozier and Ross based on their safe balances.

Cash	3,600	
Holland, Capital		3,600

Dozier, Capital	2,400	
Ross, Capital...	1,200	
Cash		3,600

To record capital contribution by Holland and subsequent distribution of funds to Dozier and Ross based on safe capital balances.

After recording this $3,600 contribution from Holland and the subsequent disbursement, the capital accounts for the partnership stay open, registering the following individual balances:

Holland, Capital (deficit)	$(2,400)
Dozier, Capital (safe balance)	1,600
Ross, Capital (safe balance)	800

These accounts continue to remain on the partnership books until the final resolution of Holland's obligation.

In this illustration, the $1,000 legal settlement and the remaining $1,400 loss ultimately allow the parties to close out the records:

Cash	1,000	
Dozier, Capital (⅔ of loss)	933	
Ross, Capital (⅓ of loss).................................	467	
Holland, Capital		2,400

To record final $1,000 cash settlement of Holland's interest and resulting $1,400 loss.

Dozier, Capital	667	
Ross, Capital...	333	
Cash		1,000

To distribute final cash balance based upon remaining capital account totals.

Marshaling of Assets

In the previous example, one partner (Holland) became insolvent during the liquidation process. Personal bankruptcy is not uncommon and raises questions as to the legal right that damaged partners have to proceed against an insolvent partner. *More specifically, is a deficit capital balance the legal equivalent of any other personal liability? Do partners who must absorb additional losses have the same rights against their partners as other creditors?*

Addressing this issue, the Uniform Partnership Act (Section 40[i]) stipulates that:

Where a partner has become bankrupt or his estate is insolvent the claims against his separate property shall rank in the following order:
(I) Those owing to separate creditors,
(II) Those owing to partnership creditors,
(III) Those owing to partners by way of contribution.

This ranking of the claims against an individual is normally referred to as the marshaling of assets and allows for an orderly distribution of property in bankruptcy cases. It clearly shows that partners rank last in collecting from a bankrupt partner.

To demonstrate the effects created by this legal doctrine, assume that Stone is a partner in a business that is undergoing final liquidation. The partnership is insolvent: All assets have been expended but liabilities of $15,000 still remain. Stone is also personally insolvent. The assets currently held by this individual cannot satisfy all obligations:

Personal assets	$50,000
Personal liabilities	40,000
Deficit capital balance—partnership	19,000

Under these circumstances, the ranking established by the Uniform Partnership Act becomes extremely important. Stone does hold $50,000 in assets. However, since these assets are limited, recovery by the various parties is dependent on the pattern of distribution. According to the marshaling of assets doctrine, Stone's own creditors have first priority. After these claims have been satisfied, the $10,000 in remaining assets should be used to remunerate any partnership creditors who have sought recovery directly from Stone.

As indicated, remaining partnership debts are $15,000 and these creditors may seek to collect from Stone (or any other general partner). Only then, after personal creditors as well as partnership creditors are paid, can the other partners lay claim to the residual portion of Stone's assets. Obviously, because of this individual's financial condition, the chances are not good that these partners will be able to recover all or even a significant portion of the $19,000 deficit capital balance. By ranking last on this priority list, partners are forced to accept whatever assets remain.

To analyze and understand the possible effects created by the marshaling of assets concept, a variety of other situations should be considered. Assume, as an alternative to the previous example, that Stone failed to have sufficient property to satisfy even personal creditors: Stone holds $50,000 in assets but $80,000 in personal liabilities. Because of the volume of these debts, neither the partnership creditors nor the other partners will be able to recoup any money from this partner. All of the personal assets must be used to pay Stone's own obligations. Even with preferential treatment, the personal creditors still face a $30,000 shortfall because of the limited quantity of available assets. This potential loss raises another legal question: Can Stone's personal creditors seek recovery of the $30,000 remaining debt directly from the partnership?

In response to this issue, the marshaling of assets doctrine specifies that personal creditors can, indeed, claim a partner's share of partnership assets. However, recovery of all, or even a portion, of the $30,000 is only possible if two specific criteria are met:

1. Payment of all partnership debts must be assured.
2. The insolvent partner has to have a positive capital balance.

Even if both of these conditions are met, personal creditors have no right to receive more than the total of that partner's capital balance nor more than the amount of the debt.

This priority ranking of claims provides legal guidance in insolvency cases. For a more complete demonstration of the marshaling of assets principle, three additional examples follow. Each presents the legal and accounting responses to a specific partnership liquidation problem. In the first two illustrations, one or more of the partners is personally insolvent. The third analyzes the marshaling of assets in connection with an insolvent partnership.

Insolvency—Example One   The following balance sheet has been produced for the Able, Baker, Cannon, and Duke partnership. Profit and loss percentages are also included.

Cash	$ 30,000	Liabilities	$ 80,000
Noncash assets	150,000	Able, capital (40%)	15,000
		Baker, capital (30%)	40,000
		Cannon, capital (20%)	30,000
		Duke, capital (10%)	15,000
		Total liabilities and	
Total assets	$180,000	capital	$180,000

Baker is insolvent, and personal creditors have filed a $30,000 claim against this partner's share of partnership property. The litigation has forced the partnership to begin liquidation to settle Baker's interest. As shown in the balance sheet, the partnership has $30,000 in cash and Baker has a capital balance of $40,000.

Assume, in this example, that the noncash assets (with a book value of $150,000) subsequently are sold for $100,000 with the partnership's liabilities ($80,000) then being paid. These two actions increase the cash balance by $20,000 to a $50,000 figure. No other assets or liabilities exist. The adjusted capital accounts for each partner follow. Other than Baker, all partners are personally solvent.

	Able, Capital	Baker, Capital	Cannon, Capital	Duke, Capital
Beginning balances	$ 15,000	$ 40,000	$ 30,000	$15,000
$50,000 loss on liquidating of assets	(20,000) (40%)	(15,000) (30%)	(10,000) (20%)	(5,000) (10%)
Capital balances	$ (5,000)	$ 25,000	$ 20,000	$10,000

An additional contribution of $5,000 should be forthcoming from Able to eradicate the single negative capital balance. This investment raises the partnership's cash to $55,000 and permits a final distribution to Cannon ($20,000), Duke ($10,000), and *Baker's creditors* ($25,000). The liquidation losses have reduced Baker's capital account below the $30,000 level; therefore, this partner's personal creditors will be unable to recover the entire amount of their claims. Despite the remaining $5,000 debt, they have no further legal recourse here; no right of recovery exists against the other partners once the capital account has been depleted.

Baker will receive nothing from this liquidation settlement because the personal obligations have not been completely satisfied. In contrast, if the final capital balance had been in excess of $30,000, Baker would have been entitled to any residual amount after all of the personal liabilities were extinguished.

Insolvency—Example Two   The following balance sheet for the partnership of Morris, Newton, Olsen, and Prince also contains the applicable profit and loss percentages. Both Morris and Prince are personally insolvent. Morris's creditors have brought an $8,000 claim against the partnership's assets while $15,000 is being sought by Prince's creditors. These claims have forced the partnership to terminate operations so that the business property can be liquidated. The question is again raised as to which partner is entitled to any cash balance that remains.

Cash	$ 10,000	Liabilities	$ 70,000
Noncash assets	140,000	Morris, capital (40%)	15,000
		Newton, capital (20%)	10,000
		Olsen, capital (20%)	23,000
		Prince, capital (20%)	32,000
		Total liabilities and	
Total assets	$150,000	capital	$150,000

The noncash assets are sold for a total of $80,000 and all liabilities paid. The partnership's accounting system records these two events as follows:

Cash...	80,000	
Morris, Capital (40% of loss)............................	24,000	
Newton, Capital (20% of loss)............................	12,000	
Olsen, Capital (20% of loss)............................	12,000	
Prince, Capital (20% of loss)............................	12,000	
Noncash Assets (or specific accounts).................		140,000
To record sale of noncash assets and allocation of resulting $60,000 loss.		
Liabilities......................................	70,000	
Cash...		70,000
To extinguish partnership obligations.		

Because of these two transactions, the partnership's cash has risen from $10,000 to $20,000.

After the allocation of this loss, the capital accounts for Morris and Newton report deficit balances of $9,000 ($15,000 − $24,000) and $2,000 ($10,000 − $12,000), respectively. Although Newton is solvent and would be expected to compensate the partnership, Morris's personal financial condition does not allow for any further contribution. The $9,000 deficit must, therefore, be absorbed by Newton, Olsen, and Prince. Because these three partners have historically shared profits evenly (20:20:20), they continue to do so in recording this additional capital loss.

Newton, Capital (⅓ of loss).............................	3,000	
Olsen, Capital (⅓ of loss).............................	3,000	
Prince, Capital (⅓ of loss).............................	3,000	
Morris, Capital....................................		9,000
To write off deficit capital balance of insolvent partner.		

This last allocation increases Newton's deficit to a $5,000 balance ($2,000 + $3,000), an amount which the partner should now contribute in accordance with partnership law.

Cash...	5,000	
Newton, Capital....................................		5,000
To record contribution necessitated by negative capital balance.		

Following this series of transactions, only the cash balance (now $25,000) as well as the capital accounts of Olsen and Prince remain open within the partnership records:

	Cash	Morris, Capital	Newton, Capital	Olsen, Capital	Prince, Capital
Beginning balances.........	$ 10,000	$ 15,000	$ 10,000	$ 23,000	$ 32,000
Sold assets...............	80,000	(24,000)	(12,000)	(12,000)	(12,000)
Paid liabilities.............	(70,000)	–0–	–0–	–0–	–0–
Default by Morris..........	–0–	9,000	(3,000)	(3,000)	(3,000)
Contribution by Newton.....	5,000	–0–	5,000	–0–	–0–
Current balances...........	$ 25,000	–0–	–0–	$ 8,000	$ 17,000

Although $8,000 of the partnership's remaining cash goes directly to Olsen, the $17,000 attributed to Prince is first subjected to the claims of the partner's personal creditors. Because of their claims, $15,000 of this amount must be used to satisfy these obligations, with only the final $2,000 being paid to Prince.

Insolvency—Example Three The two previous illustrations have analyzed liquidations in which one or more of the partners has been personally insolvent. Another possibility is that the partnership itself may come to meet this same fate. In an active partnership, insolvency can occur if losses, drawings, or litigation deplete the working capital of the operation. A bankruptcy petition may follow if debts cannot be met as they come due. Liquidation of business assets might be necessary unless additional capital is quickly generated. Even a financially sound partnership may become insolvent if material losses are incurred during a voluntary liquidation.

To serve as a basis for examining the accounting and legal ramifications of an insolvent partnership, assume that the law firm of Keller, Lewis, Monroe, and Norris is in the final stages of liquidation. All noncash assets have been sold, and available cash has been used to pay a portion of the business's liabilities. Following these transactions, the following account balances remain open within the partnership's records. The four partners in this endeavor share profits and losses equally.

Liabilities.	$ 20,000
Keller, capital.	(30,000)
Lewis, capital.	(5,000)
Monroe, capital	5,000
Norris, capital	10,000

Note: Parentheses indicate deficit.

This partnership is insolvent; it continues to owe creditors $20,000, even after liquidation and distribution of all assets. However, additional money should be forthcoming from two of the partners. Because of their deficit capital accounts, Keller and Lewis are legally required to contribute an additional $30,000 and $5,000, respectively, to the business. With these newly available funds, the partnership will be able to pay all $20,000 of its remaining liabilities as well as make cash distributions to Monroe ($5,000) and Norris ($10,000) in accordance with their capital account balances. The partnership books would be closed by this final payment.

Once again, the possibility exists that a partner who is reporting a negative capital balance will not step forward to make a further investment. Assume, for example, that Keller is personally insolvent and cannot contribute, whereas Lewis simply refuses to supply additional funds in hopes of avoiding the obligation. *At this point, the remaining creditors may instigate legal recovery proceedings against any or all of the partners regardless of their capital balances.* Any action, however, against the insolvent partner may prove to be a futile effort because of the marshaling of assets principle.

Predicting the exact outcome of litigation is rarely possible. Thus, the assumption is made that Norris is forced to contribute $20,000 cash to settle the remaining liabilities. The following journal entries would then be required for this partnership:

Cash	20,000	
Norris, Capital		20,000
Liabilities	20,000	
Cash		20,000

To record capital contribution by Norris made to pay remaining partnership creditors.

After all liabilities have been extinguished, the partners who still maintain positive capital accounts can demand remuneration from any partner with a negative balance. Despite this legal obligation, the chances of a significant recovery from the insolvent Keller, especially under the marshaling of assets doctrine, is not likely. Thus, the partners may choose to write off this deficit to move toward closing the partnership's financial records. Legal recovery proceedings can still continue against Keller regardless of the accounting treatment. As equal partners, the $30,000 loss is absorbed evenly by Lewis, Monroe, and Norris.

Lewis, Capital (⅓ of loss)	10,000	
Monroe, Capital (⅓ of loss)	10,000	
Norris, Capital (⅓ of loss)	10,000	
Keller, Capital		30,000

To write off deficit capital balance of insolvent partner.

DISCUSSION QUESTION

What Happens if a Partner Becomes Insolvent?

In 1990, three dentists—Ben Rogers, Judy Wilkinson, and Henry Walker—formed a partnership to open a practice in Toledo, Ohio. The primary purpose of the partnership was to reduce expenses since the partners could share building and equipment costs, supplies, and the services of a clerical staff. They each contributed $50,000 in cash and, with the help of a bank loan, constructed a building and acquired furniture, fixtures, and equipment. Because the partners maintained their own separate clients, annual net income has been allocated as follows: Each partner receives the specific amount of revenues that he or she generated during the period less one-third of all expenses. From the beginning, the partners did not anticipate expansion of the practice; consequently, they could withdraw cash each year up to 90 percent of their share of income for the period.

The partnership had been profitable for a number of years. Over the years, Rogers used much of his income to speculate in real estate in the Toledo area. By 2001, he was spending less time with the dental practice so that he could concentrate on his investments. Unfortunately, a number of these deals proved to be bad decisions and he incurred significant losses. On November 8, 2001, while Rogers was out of town, a $97,000 claim was filed by his personal creditors against the partnership assets. Unbeknownst to Wilkinson and Walker, Rogers had become insolvent.

Wilkinson and Walker hurriedly held a meeting to discuss the problem since Rogers could not be located. Rogers's capital account was currently at $105,000, but the partnership had only $19,000 in cash and liquid assets. The partners knew that Rogers's equipment had been used for a number of years and could be sold for relatively little. In contrast, the building has appreciated in value and the claim could be satisfied by selling the property. However, this action would have a tremendously adverse impact on the dental practice of the remaining two partners.

What alternatives are available to Wilkinson and Walker, and what are the advantages and disadvantages of each?

The partners' capital accounts now hold the following balances:

	Keller, Capital	Lewis, Capital	Monroe, Capital	Norris, Capital
Beginning balances	$(30,000)	$ (5,000)	$ 5,000	$ 10,000
Capital contribution	–0–	–0–	–0–	20,000
Write off of deficit balance	30,000	(10,000)	(10,000)	(10,000)
Current balances	–0–	$(15,000)	$ (5,000)	$ 20,000

Both Lewis and Monroe now have a legal obligation to reimburse the partnership to offset their deficit capital balances. Upon their payment of $15,000 and $5,000, respectively, the entire $20,000 will be distributed to Norris (the only partner with a positive balance) and the partnership's books will be closed. Should either Lewis or Monroe fail to make the appropriate contribution, the additional loss must be allocated between the two remaining partners.

Preliminary Distribution of Partnership Assets

In all of the illustrations analyzed in this chapter, distributions have been made to the partners only after all assets were sold and all liabilities paid. As previously mentioned, a liquidation may take an extended time to complete. During this lengthy process, the partnership need not retain those assets that will eventually be disbursed to the partners. If the business is safely solvent, waiting until all affairs have been settled before transferring property to the owners is not warranted. The partners should be allowed to make use of their own funds at the earliest possible time.

The objective in making any type of preliminary distribution is to assure that enough capital is maintained by the partnership to absorb all future losses. Any capital in excess of this maximum requirement is a safe balance, an amount that can be immediately conveyed to the partner. To determine safe capital balances at any time, the accountant simply assumes that all subsequent events will result in maximum losses: No cash will be received in liquidating remaining noncash assets and each partner is personally insolvent. Any positive capital balance that would remain even after inclusion of all potential losses should be paid to the partner without delay. Although the assumption that no further funds will be generated may be unrealistic, it does ensure that negative capital balances are not created by premature payments being made to any of the partners.

Preliminary Distribution Illustrated To demonstrate the computation of safe capital distributions, assume that a liquidating partnership reports the following balance sheet:

Cash	$ 60,000	Liabilities	$ 40,000
Noncash assets	140,000	Mason, loan	20,000
		Mason, capital (50%)	60,000
		Lee, capital (30%)	30,000
		Dixon, capital (20%)	50,000
		Total liabilities and	
Total assets	$200,000	capital	$200,000

Assume further that the partners estimate that $6,000 will be the maximum expense incurred in carrying out this liquidation. Consequently, the partnership needs only $46,000 to meet all obligations: $40,000 to satisfy partnership liabilities and $6,000 for these final expenses. Since $60,000 in cash is being held, the partnership can transfer the extra $14,000 to the partners immediately without fear of injuring any of the participants in the liquidation. However, the appropriate allocation of this money is not readily apparent; therefore, safe capital balances must be computed to guide the actual distribution.

Before the allocation of this $14,000 is demonstrated, the appropriate handling of a partner's loan balance should be examined. According to the balance sheet, Mason has conveyed $20,000 to the business at some point in the past, an amount that was considered a loan rather than additional capital. Perhaps the partnership was in desperate need of funds and could only generate new financing by accepting a high interest rate loan. Regardless of the reason, the question remains as to the status of this account: Is the $20,000 to be viewed as a liability to the partner or as a capital balance? The answer becomes especially significant during the liquidation process since available funds often are limited. In this regard, the Uniform Partnership Act (UPA) (Section 40[b]) stipulates that loans to partners rank behind obligations to outside creditors in order of payment but ahead of the partners' capital balances.

Although this legal provision indicates that the debt to Mason must be repaid entirely before any distribution of capital can be made to the other partners, actual accounting practice seems to have taken a different view. "In preparing predistribution schedules, accountants typically offset partners' loans with the partners' capital accounts and then distribute funds accordingly."[6] In other words, the loan is merged in with the partner's capital account balance at the beginning of liquidation. Thus, practice and the UPA seem to differ on the handling of a loan from a partner.

To illustrate the potential problem with this conflict, assume that a partnership has $20,000 in cash left after liquidation. Partner A has a positive capital balance of $20,000 whereas Partner B has a negative capital of $20,000. In addition, Partner B has previously loaned the partnership $20,000. If Partner B is insolvent, a distribution

[6]Robert E. Whitis and Jeffrey R. Pittman, "Inconsistencies Between Accounting Practices and Statutory Law in Partnership Liquidations," *Accounting Educators' Journal,* Fall 1996, p. 99.

problem arises.[7] If the provisions of the UPA are followed literally, the $20,000 cash should be given to Partner B (probably to the creditors of Partner B) to repay the loan. Because Partner B is insolvent, no more assets can be expected from this individual. Thus, Partner A has to absorb the entire $20,000 deficit capital balance and will get no portion of the $20,000 in cash that is held by the business.

However, despite the UPA, common practice appears to be that the loan from Partner B will be used to offset that partner's negative capital balance. Using that approach, Partner B is left with a zero capital balance so that the entire $20,000 goes to Partner A; the creditors of Partner B get nothing. Thus, when a loan comes from a partner who later becomes insolvent and also reports a negative capital balance, the handling of the loan becomes significant. Unfortunately, further legal guidance does not exist at this time because "no reported state or federal opinion has directly ruled on the right of offset of potential capital deficits."[8]

In this textbook, in order to follow common practice, a loan from a partner will always be accounted for in liquidation as if the balance were a component of the partner's capital. By this offset, the accountant can reduce the amount accumulated as a negative capital balance for any insolvent partner. Any such loan can be transferred into the corresponding capital account at the start of the liquidation process. Similarly, any loans due from a partner should be shown as a reduction in the appropriate capital balance.

Proposed Schedule of Liquidation   Returning to the current illustration, the accountant needs to determine an equitable distribution for the $14,000 cash presently available. To structure this computation, a proposed schedule of liquidation is developed *based on the underlying assumption that all future events will result in total losses.* In Exhibit 15–2, this statement is presented for the Mason, Lee, and Dixon partnership. To expedite coverage, the $20,000 loan has already been transferred into Mason's capital account. Thus, regardless of whether this partner arrives at a deficit or a safe capital balance, the loan figure already will have been included.

In producing Exhibit 15–2, complete losses ($140,000) are forecast in connection with the disposition of all noncash assets, and liquidation expenses are anticipated at maximum amounts ($6,000). Following the projected payment of liabilities, any partner reporting a negative capital account is assumed to be personally insolvent. These potential deficit balances are written off with the losses being assigned to the remaining solvent partners based on their relative profit and loss ratio. Lee, with a negative $13,800, is eliminated first. This allocation creates a deficit of $2,857 for Mason, an amount that must be absorbed solely by Dixon. After this series of maximum losses has been simulated, any positive capital balance that still remains is considered safe; a cash distribution of that amount can be made to the specific partners.

Exhibit 15–2 indicates that only Dixon has a large enough capital balance at the present time to absorb all possible future losses. Thus, the entire $14,000 can be distributed to this partner with no fear that the capital account will ever report a deficit. Based on current practice, Mason, despite having made a $20,000 loan to the partnership, is entitled to no part of this initial distribution. The loan is of insufficient size to prevent potential deficits from occurring in Mason's capital account.

One series of computations found in this proposed schedule of liquidation merits additional attention. The simulated losses initially create a $13,800 negative balance in Lee's capital account while the other two partners continue to report positive figures. Lee's projected deficit must then be absorbed by Mason and Dixon according to their relative profit and loss percentages. Previously, Mason has been allocated 50 percent

---

[7]The same problem should not exist if the partner is solvent. The partner is legally required to contribute enough funds to delete any capital deficit. Thus, in this case, Partner B would be entitled to the $20,000 loan repayment but then has to contribute $20,000 because of the negative capital balance. That cash amount would go to Partner A because of that partner's positive capital balance.

[8]Whitis and Pittman, "Inconsistencies Between Accounting Practices," p. 93.

Exhibit 15–2

MASON, LEE, AND DIXON
Proposed Schedule of Liquidation—Initial Safe Capital Balances

	Cash	Noncash Assets	Liabilities	Mason, Capital (50%)	Lee, Capital (30%)	Dixon, Capital (20%)
Beginning balances	$ 60,000	$ 140,000	$ 40,000	$ 80,000	$ 30,000	$ 50,000
Maximum loss on noncash assets	–0–	(140,000)	–0–	(70,000)	(42,000)	(28,000)
Maximum liquidation expenses	(6,000)	–0–	–0–	(3,000)	(1,800)	(1,200)
Payment of liabilities	(40,000)	–0–	(40,000)	–0–	–0–	–0–
Potential balances	14,000	–0–	–0–	7,000	(13,800)	20,800
Assume Lee to be insolvent	–0–	–0–	–0–	(9,857) (5/7)	13,800	(3,943) (2/7)
Potential balances	14,000	–0–	–0–	(2,857)	–0–	16,857
Assume Mason to be insolvent	–0–	–0–	–0–	2,857	–0–	(2,857)
Safe balances	$ 14,000	–0–	–0–	–0–	–0–	$ 14,000

of net income with 20 percent recorded to Dixon. These figures equate to a 50/70:20/70 or a 5/7:2/7 ratio. Based on this realigned relationship, the $13,800 potential deficit is allocated between Mason (5/7 or $9,857) and Dixon (2/7 or $3,943), reducing Mason's own capital account to a negative balance as shown in Exhibit 15–2.

Continuing with the assumption that maximum losses occur in all cases, Mason's $2,857 deficit is accounted for as if that partner were also personally insolvent. Therefore, the entire negative balance is assigned to Dixon, the only partner still retaining a positive capital account. Since all potential losses have been recognized at this point, the remaining $14,000 capital is a safe balance that should be paid to this partner. Even after the money is distributed, Dixon's capital account will still be large enough to absorb all future losses.

Liquidation in Installments In practice, maximum liquidation losses are not likely to occur to any business. Thus, at various points during this process, additional cash amounts usually become available as partnership property is sold. If the assets are disposed of in a piecemeal fashion, cash may actually flow into the company on a regular basis for an extended period of time. As needed, updated safe capital schedules have to be developed to dictate the recipients of newly available funds. Because numerous capital distributions may be required, this process is often referred to as a *liquidation made in installments.*

To illustrate, assume that the partnership of Mason, Lee, and Dixon actually undergoes the following events in connection with its liquidation:

- As indicated by the proposed schedule of liquidation in Exhibit 15–2, Dixon receives $14,000 in cash as a preliminary capital distribution.
- Noncash assets with a book value of $50,000 are sold for $20,000.
- All $40,000 in liabilities are settled.
- Liquidation expenses of $2,000 are paid; the partners now believe that only a maximum of $3,000 more will be expended in this manner. The original estimation of $6,000 was apparently too high.

As a result of these transactions, the partnership has an additional $21,000 in cash that is now available for distribution to the partners: $20,000 received from the sale of noncash assets and another $1,000 because of the reduced estimation of liquidation expenses. Once again, the accountant must assume maximum future losses as a means

Exhibit 15–3   Liquidation for Installments

	Cash	Noncash Assets	Liabilities	Mason, Capital (50%)	Lee, Capital (30%)	Dixon, Capital (20%)

MASON, LEE, AND DIXON
Proposed Schedule of Liquidation—Subsequent
Safe Capital Balances

	Cash	Noncash Assets	Liabilities	Mason, Capital (50%)	Lee, Capital (30%)	Dixon, Capital (20%)
Beginning balances.............	$ 60,000	$ 140,000	$ 40,000	$ 80,000	$ 30,000	$ 50,000
Capital distribution—safe balances ..	(14,000)	–0–	–0–	–0–	–0–	(14,000)
Disposal of noncash assets.........	20,000	(50,000)	–0–	(15,000)	(9,000)	(6,000)
Liabilities paid	(40,000)	–0–	(40,000)	–0–	–0–	–0–
Liquidation expenses	(2,000)	–0–	–0–	(1,000)	(600)	(400)
Current balances.............	24,000	90,000	–0–	64,000	20,400	29,600
Maximum loss on remaining noncash assets................	–0–	(90,000)	–0–	(45,000)	(27,000)	(18,000)
Maximum liquidation expenses	(3,000)	–0–	–0–	(1,500)	(900)	(600)
Potential balances............	21,000	–0–	–0–	17,500	(7,500)	11,000
Assume Lee to be insolvent........	–0–	–0–	–0–	(5,357) (⅗)	7,500	(2,143) (⅖)
Safe balances—current............	$ 21,000	–0–	–0–	$ 12,143	–0–	$ 8,857

of determining the appropriate distribution of these funds. A second proposed schedule of liquidation is produced in Exhibit 15–3, indicating that $12,143 of this amount should go to Mason with the remaining $8,857 to Dixon. To facilitate a better visual understanding, actual transactions are recorded first on this schedule, followed by the assumed losses. *A dotted line separates the real from the potential occurrences.*

Predistribution Plan

The liquidation of a partnership can require numerous transactions occurring over a lengthy time. The continual production of proposed schedules of liquidation may become a burdensome chore. Two separate statements already have been required in the previous illustration, and the partnership still possesses $90,000 in noncash assets awaiting conversion. *Therefore, at the start of a liquidation, most accountants produce a single predistribution plan to serve as a guideline for all future payments.* Thereafter, whenever cash becomes available, this plan indicates the appropriate recipients without the necessity of drawing up ever-changing proposed schedules of liquidation.

A predistribution plan is developed by simulating a series of losses that are each just large enough to eliminate, one at a time, all of the partners' claims to cash. This approach recognizes that the individual capital accounts exhibit differing degrees of sensitivity to losses. These accounts possess varying balances and may be charged with losses at different rates. Consequently, a predistribution plan is based on calculating the losses (the "maximum loss allowable") that would eliminate each of these capital balances in a sequential pattern. This series of absorbed losses then forms the basis for the predistribution plan.

To demonstrate the creation of a predistribution plan, assume that the following partnership is to be liquidated:

Cash	–0–	Liabilities	$100,000
Noncash assets	$221,000	Rubens, capital (50%)	30,000
		Smith, capital (20%)	40,000
		Trice, capital (30%)	51,000
Total assets	$221,000	Total liabilities and capital	$221,000

The partnership capital reported by this organization totals $121,000. However, the individual balances for the partners range from $30,000 to $51,000 while profits and losses are assigned according to three different percentages. Thus, each partner's current capital balance would be reduced to zero by differing losses. *As a prerequisite to developing a predistribution plan, the sensitivity to losses exhibited by each of these capital accounts must be measured.*

Partner	Capital Balance/ Loss Allocation	Maximum Loss that Can Be Absorbed
Rubens..........	$30,000/50%	$ 60,000 ✔
Smith..........	40,000/20%	200,000
Trice..........	51,000/30%	170,000

Rubens is the partner in the most vulnerable position at the present time. Based on a 50 percent share of income, a loss of only $60,000 is needed to reduce this partner's capital account to a zero balance. If the partnership does incur a loss of this amount, Rubens can no longer hope to recover any funds from the liquidation process. Thus, the potential effects of this loss (referred to as a Step 1 loss) is simulated through the following schedule:

	Rubens, Capital	Smith, Capital	Trice, Capital
Beginning balances	$ 30,000	$ 40,000	$ 51,000
Assumed $60,000 loss..........	(30,000) (50%)	(12,000) (20%)	(18,000) (30%)
Step 1 balances	–0–	$ 28,000	$ 33,000

As previously discussed, the predistribution plan is based on describing the series of losses that would eliminate each partner's capital in turn and, thus, all claims to cash. In the previous Step 1 schedule, the $60,000 loss did reduce Rubens's capital account to zero. Assuming, as a precautionary step, that Rubens is personally insolvent, all further losses would have to be allocated between Smith and Trice. Since these two partners have previously shared partnership profits and losses on a 20 percent and 30 percent basis, a $^{20}\!/_{50}$:$^{30}\!/_{50}$ relationship exists between them (or 40%:60%). Therefore, these realigned percentages must now be utilized in calculating a Step 2 loss, the amount just large enough to exclude one of these two remaining partners from sharing in any future cash distributions.

Partner	Capital Balance/ Loss Allocation	Maximum Loss that Can Be Absorbed
Smith..........	$28,000/40%	$ 70,000
Trice..........	33,000/60%	55,000 ✔

Since Rubens's capital balance already has been eliminated, Trice is now in the most vulnerable position: only a $55,000 Step 2 loss is required to reduce this partner's capital account to a zero balance.

	Rubens, Capital	Smith, Capital	Trice, Capital
Beginning balances	$ 30,000	$ 40,000	$ 51,000
Assumed $60,000 loss..........	(30,000) (50%)	(12,000) (20%)	(18,000) (30%)
Step 1 balances	–0–	$ 28,000	$ 33,000
Assumed $55,000 loss..........	–0–	(22,000) (40%)	(33,000) (60%)
Step 2 balances	–0–	$ 6,000	–0–

According to this second schedule, a total loss of $115,000 ($60,000 from Step 1 plus $55,000 from Step 2) would leave capital of only $6,000, a balance attributed entirely to Smith. At this final point in the simulation, an additional loss of this amount also ends Smith's right to receive any funds from the liquidation process. Having the sole positive capital account remaining, this partner would have to absorb the entire amount of the final loss.

	Rubens, Capital	Smith, Capital	Trice, Capital
Beginning balances	$ 30,000	$ 40,000	$ 51,000
Assumed $60,000 loss	(30,000) (50%)	(12,000) (20%)	(18,000) (30%)
Step 1 balances	–0–	$ 28,000	$ 33,000
Assumed $55,000 loss	–0–	(22,000) (40%)	(33,000) (60%)
Step 2 balances	–0–	6,000	–0–
Assumed $6,000 loss	–0–	(6,000) (100%)	–0–
Final balances	–0–	–0–	–0–

Once each partner's capital account has been reduced to zero through this series of simulated losses, a predistribution plan for the liquidation can be devised. *This procedure requires working backward through the final schedule above, determining the effects that will result if the assumed losses do not occur.* Without these losses, cash becomes available for the partners; therefore, a direct relationship exists between the volume of losses and the distribution pattern. The last $6,000 loss, for example, is to be absorbed entirely by Smith. Should that loss fail to materialize, Smith is left with a positive safe capital balance of this amount. Thus, as cash becomes available, the first $6,000 received (in excess of partnership obligations and anticipated liquidation expenses) should be distributed solely to Smith.

In a similar manner, the preceding $55,000 Step 2 loss was divided between Smith and Trice on a 4:6 basis. Again, if such losses do not occur, these balances need not be retained to protect the partnership against capital deficits. Therefore, after Smith has received the initial $6,000, any further cash that becomes available (up to an additional $55,000) will be split between Smith (40 percent) and Trice (60 percent). For example, if exactly $61,000 in cash is held by the partnership in excess of liabilities and possible liquidation expenses, the following distribution should be made:

	Rubens	Smith	Trice
First $6,000	–0–	$ 6,000	–0–
Next $55,000	–0–	22,000 (40%)	$33,000 (60%)
Cash distribution	–0–	$28,000	$33,000

The predistribution plan can be completed by including the Step 1 loss, an amount that was to be absorbed by the partners on a 5:2:3 basis. Thus, all money that becomes available to the partners after the initial $61,000 is to be distributed according to the original profit and loss ratio. At this point in the liquidation, enough cash would have been generated to ensure that each partner has a safe capital balance: No possibility exists that a future deficit can occur. Any further increases in the projected capital balances will be allocated by the 5:2:3 allocation pattern. *For this reason, once all partners begin to receive a portion of the cash disbursements, any remaining funds are divided based on the original profit and loss percentages.*

To inform all parties of the order by which available cash will be disbursed, the predistribution plan should be formally prepared in a schedule format prior to beginning liquidation. Following is the predistribution plan for the partnership of Rubens, Smith, and Trice. To complete this illustration, liquidation expenses of $12,000 have been estimated. Since these expenses have the same effect on the capital accounts as losses, they do not change the sequential pattern by which assets eventually will be distributed.

RUBENS, SMITH, AND TRICE
Predistribution Plan

Available Cash		Recipient
First	$112,000	Creditors ($100,000) and liquidation expenses (estimated at $12,000)
Next.	6,000	Smith
Next.	55,000	Smith (40%) and Trice (60%)
All further cash balances		Rubens (50%), Smith (20%), and Trice (30%)

SUMMARY

1. Although a partnership can exist indefinitely through the periodic admission of new partners, termination of business activities and liquidation of property may take place for a number of reasons. A partner's death or retirement can trigger this process as well as the insolvency of a partner or even the partnership itself. Because of the risk that large losses will be incurred during liquidation, all parties usually seek frequent and timely information describing ongoing developments. The accountant is expected to furnish this data while also working to ensure the equitable treatment of all parties.

2. The liquidation process entails (a) converting partnership property into cash, (b) paying off liabilities and liquidation expenses, and (c) conveying any remaining property to the partners based on their final capital balances. As a means of reporting these transactions, a schedule of liquidation should be produced at periodic intervals. This statement discloses all recent transactions, the assets and liabilities still being held, and the current capital balances. Distribution of this schedule on a regular basis allows the various parties involved in the liquidation to monitor the progress being made.

3. During a liquidation, negative capital balances can arise for one or more of the partners, especially if material losses are incurred in disposing of partnership property. In such cases, the specific partner or partners should contribute enough additional assets to eliminate their deficits. If payment is slow in coming, any cash still held by the partnership can be immediately divided among the partners that have safe capital balances. A safe balance is the amount of capital that would remain even if maximum future losses occur: Noncash assets are lost in total and all partners with deficits fail to fulfill their legal obligations. In making these computations, negative capital balances are absorbed by the remaining partners based on their relative profit and loss ratio.

4. To enable an orderly and fair distribution during liquidation, the Uniform Partnership Act establishes a priority listing for all claims, a ranking referred to as the *marshaling of assets*. This principle states that partners with positive capital balances can recover losses from a partner reporting a deficit but only after adequate protection has been ensured for that individual's creditors as well as the partnership's creditors. The act also specifies that a partner's personal creditors can seek recovery of losses from the partnership to the extent of that person's capital balance after protection of partnership creditors is assured.

5. The actual liquidation of a partnership can take an extended period to complete. Oftentimes, cash is generated during the early stages of this process in excess of the amount needed to cover liabilities and liquidation expenses. The accountant should propose a fair and immediate distribution of these available funds. A proposed schedule of liquidation can be created as a guide for such cash distributions. This statement is based on a *simulated* series of transactions: sale of all noncash assets, payment of liquidation expenses, and so on. At every point, maximum losses are assumed: Noncash assets have no resale value, liquidation expenses are set at the maximum level, and all partners are personally insolvent. Any safe capital balance that would remain after incurring such losses represents a distribution that can be made at the present time. Even after this payment, the capital account will still be large enough to absorb all potential losses.

6. The liquidation of a partnership can require numerous transactions occurring over a lengthy time. Thus, the accountant may discover that the continual production of

proposed schedules of liquidation becomes a burdensome chore. For this reason, a single predistribution plan is usually produced at the start of the liquidation process. This plan serves as a definitive guideline for all payments to be made to the partners. To create this plan, a series of losses is simulated with each one, in turn, exactly eliminating the capital balance of a partner. After all capital accounts have been reduced to zero through these assumed losses, the predistribution plan is devised by working backward through the series. In effect, the accountant is measuring the cash that will become available if such losses do not occur.

COMPREHENSIVE ILLUSTRATION

Problem

(Estimated Time: 30 to 40 Minutes) For the past several years, the partnership of Andrews, Caso, Quinn, and Sheridan has operated a local department store. Based on the provisions of the original Articles of Partnership, all profits and losses have been allocated on a 4:3:2:1 ratio, respectively. Recently, both Caso and Quinn have undergone personal financial problems, and as a result, each of these individuals is now insolvent. Caso's creditors have filed a $20,000 claim against the partnership's assets while $22,000 is being sought to repay Quinn's personal debts. To satisfy these legal obligations, the partnership property must be liquidated. The partners estimate that they will incur $12,000 in expenses in disposing of all noncash assets.

At the time that active operations cease and the liquidation is begun, the following balance sheet is produced for this partnership. All measurement accounts have been closed out to arrive at the current capital balances.

Cash	$ 20,000	Liabilities	$140,000
Noncash assets	280,000	Caso, loan	10,000
		Andrews, capital (40%)	76,000
		Caso, capital (30%)	14,000
		Quinn, capital (20%)	51,000
		Sheridan, capital (10%)	9,000
Total assets	$300,000	Total liabilities and capital	$300,000

During the lengthy liquidation process, the following transactions take place:

- Noncash assets with a book value of $190,000 are sold for $140,000 cash.
- Liquidation expenses of $14,000 are paid. No further expenses are expected.
- Safe capital distributions are made to the partners.
- Payment is made of all business liabilities.
- The remaining noncash assets are sold for $10,000.
- Deficit capital balances for any insolvent partners are deemed to be uncollectible.
- Appropriate cash contributions are received from any solvent partner who is reporting a negative capital balance.
- Final cash distributions are made.

Required

a.   Using the information that is available prior to the start of the liquidation process, develop a predistribution plan for this partnership.
b.   Prepare journal entries to record the actual liquidation transactions.

Solution

a.   This partnership begins the liquidation process with capital amounting to $160,000. This total includes the $10,000 loan from Caso since the liability must be retained as a possible offset against any eventual deficit capital balance. Therefore, the predistribution plan is based on the assumption that $160,000 in losses will be incurred, entirely eliminating all partnership capital. As discussed in this chapter, these simulated losses are arranged in a series so that each capital account is sequentially reduced to a zero balance.

At the start of the liquidation, Caso's capital position is the most vulnerable.

Partner	Capital Balance/ Loss Allocation	Maximum Loss that Can Be Absorbed
Andrews	$76,000/40%	$190,000
Caso	24,000/30%	80,000 ✔
Quinn	51,000/20%	255,000
Sheridan	9,000/10%	90,000

As indicated by this schedule, an $80,000 loss would eradicate both Caso's $14,000 capital balance and the $10,000 loan. Therefore, to start the development of a predistribution plan, this loss is assumed to have occurred.

	Andrews, Capital	Caso, Loan and Capital	Quinn, Capital	Sheridan, Capital
Beginning balances	$ 76,000	$ 24,000	$ 51,000	$ 9,000
Assumed $80,000 loss	(32,000) (40%)	(24,000) (30%)	(16,000) (20%)	(8,000) (10%)
Step 1 balances	$ 44,000	–0–	$ 35,000	$ 1,000

With Caso's capital account eliminated, further losses are to be split among the remaining partners in the ratio of 4:2:1 (or ⁴⁄₇:²⁄₇:¹⁄₇). As only an additional $7,000 loss (the $1,000 capital above divided by ¹⁄₇) is now needed to reduce Sheridan's account to zero, this partner is in the second most vulnerable position.

	Andrews	Caso	Quinn	Sheridan
Step 1 balances (above)	$44,000	–0–	$35,000	$ 1,000
Assumed $7,000 loss	(4,000) (⁴⁄₇)	–0–	(2,000) (²⁄₇)	(1,000) (¹⁄₇)
Step 2 balances	$40,000	–0–	$33,000	–0–

Following these two simulated losses, only Andrews and Quinn continue to report positive capital balances. Thus, they divide further losses on a 4:2 basis or 66⅔%:33⅓%. Based on these realigned percentages, Andrews's position has become the most vulnerable. A further loss of $60,000 ($40,000/66⅔%) reduces this partner's remaining capital to zero whereas a $99,000 loss ($33,000/33⅓%) is required to eliminate Quinn's balance.

	Andrews	Caso	Quinn	Sheridan
Step 2 balances (above)	$ 40,000	–0–	$ 33,000	–0–
Assumed $60,000 loss	(40,000) (66⅔%)	–0–	(20,000) (33⅓%)	–0–
Step 3 balances	–0–	–0–	$ 13,000	–0–

The final $13,000 capital balance belongs to Quinn; an additional loss of this amount is necessary to remove the last element of partnership capital.

Based on the results of this series of simulated losses, a predistribution plan can be created. However, the $140,000 in liabilities owed by the partnership still have first priority to available cash. Additionally, $12,000 must be retained to cover the anticipated liquidation expenses.

ANDREWS, CASO, QUINN, AND SHERIDAN
Predistribution Plan

Available Cash		Recipient
First	$152,000	Creditors and anticipated liquidation expenses
Next	13,000	Quinn
Next	60,000	Andrews (66⅔%) and Quinn (33⅓%)
Next	7,000	Andrews (⁴⁄₇), Quinn (²⁄₇), and Sheridan (¹⁄₇)
All further cash		Andrews (40%), Caso (30%), Quinn (20%), and Sheridan (10%)

Because of their insolvency, initial payments to Caso ($20,000) and Quinn ($22,000) may actually go to their personal creditors.

b. Journal entries for the liquidation:

Caso, Loan	10,000	
Caso, Capital		10,000
To offset loan against capital balance in anticipation of liquidation.		

Cash	140,000	
Andrews, Capital (40% of loss)	20,000	
Caso, Capital (30% of loss)	15,000	
Quinn, Capital (20% of loss)	10,000	
Sheridan, Capital (10% of loss)	5,000	
Noncash Assets		190,000
To record sale of noncash assets and allocation of $50,000 loss.		

Andrews, Capital (40%)	5,600	
Caso, Capital (30%)	4,200	
Quinn, Capital (20%)	2,800	
Sheridan, Capital (10%)	1,400	
Cash		14,000
Payment of liquidation expenses.		

- The partnership is now holding $146,000 in cash, $6,000 more than is needed to satisfy all liabilities and estimated expenses. According to the predistribution plan drawn up in requirement *a,* this entire amount can be safely distributed to Quinn (or to Quinn's creditors).

Quinn, Capital	6,000	
Cash		6,000
To distribute available cash based on safe capital balance.		

Liabilities	140,000	
Cash		140,000
To extinguish all partnership debts.		

Cash	10,000	
Andrews, Capital (40% of loss)	32,000	
Caso, Capital (30% of loss)	24,000	
Quinn, Capital (20% of loss)	16,000	
Sheridan, Capital (10% of loss)	8,000	
Noncash Assets		90,000
To record sale of remaining noncash assets and allocation of $80,000 loss.		

- At this point in the liquidation, only the cash and the capital accounts remain open on the partnership books.

	Cash	Andrews, Capital	Caso, Capital	Quinn, Capital	Sheridan, Capital
Beginning balances	$ 20,000	$ 76,000	$ 14,000	$ 51,000	$ 9,000
Loan offset	–0–	–0–	10,000	–0–	–0–
Sale of noncash assets	140,000	(20,000)	(15,000)	(10,000)	(5,000)
Liquidation. expenses	(14,000)	(5,600)	(4,200)	(2,800)	(1,400)
Cash distribution	(6,000)	–0–	–0–	(6,000)	–0–
Payment of liabilities	(140,000)	–0–	–0–	–0–	–0–
Sale of noncash assets	10,000	(32,000)	(24,000)	(16,000)	(8,000)
Current balances	$ 10,000	$ 18,400	$(19,200)	$ 16,200	$(5,400)

Because Caso is personally insolvent, the $19,200 deficit balance will not be repaid and must be absorbed by the remaining three partners on a 4:2:1 basis.

Andrews, Capital (⅔ of loss)	10,971	
Quinn, Capital (⅓ of loss)	5,486	
Sheridan, Capital (⅙ of loss)	2,743	
Caso, Capital		19,200

To write off deficit capital balance of insolvent partner.

■ This last allocation decreases Sheridan's capital account to a $8,143 negative total. Since this partner is personally solvent, that amount should be contributed to the partnership in accordance with regulations of the Uniform Partnership Act.

Cash	8,143	
Sheridan, Capital		8,143

To record contribution made to eliminate deficit
capital balance.

■ Sheridan's contribution brings the final cash total for the partnership to $18,143. This amount is distributed to the two partners who continue to maintain positive capital balances: Andrews and Quinn (or Quinn's creditors).

	Andrews, Capital	Quinn, Capital
Balances above	$ 18,400	$16,200
Caso deficit	(10,971)	(5,486)
Final balances	$ 7,429	$10,714

Andrews, Capital	7,429	
Quinn, Capital	10,714	
Cash		18,143

To distribute remaining cash according to final
capital balances.

QUESTIONS

1. What is the difference between the dissolution of a partnership and the liquidation of partnership property?
2. Why would the members of a partnership elect to terminate business operations and liquidate all noncash assets?
3. Why are liquidation gains and losses usually recorded as direct adjustments to the partners' capital accounts?
4. After liquidating all property and paying partnership obligations, on what basis is the remaining cash allocated among the partners?
5. What is the purpose of a schedule of liquidation? What information does this statement convey to its readers?
6. According to the Uniform Partnership Act, what events should occur if a partner incurs a negative capital balance during the liquidation process?
7. How are safe capital balances computed when preliminary distributions of cash are to be made during a partnership liquidation?
8. What is the purpose of the marshaling of assets doctrine? What does this doctrine specifically state?
9. A partner is personally insolvent. Can this partner's creditors lay claim to partnership assets?
10. How do loans from partners affect the distribution of assets in a partnership liquidation? What alternatives can affect the handling of such loans?
11. What is the purpose of a proposed schedule of liquidation, and how is it developed?
12. How is a predistribution plan created for a partnership liquidation?

LIBRARY ASSIGNMENTS

1. Read the following as well as any other published articles on partnership liquidation:

    "Partnerships: If There's a Beginning . . . There's an End," *National Public Accountant,* April 1992.

    "Breaking Up Is Hard to Do," *Nation's Business,* July 1988.

    "Reconcilable Differences," *Inc.,* April 1991.

    "Cutting Losses When Partners Face a Breakup," *Wall Street Journal,* May 21, 1991, p. B1.

    "When a Group Is Better Off Splitting Up," *Medical Economics,* March 5, 1984.

    Write a short report describing various situations that lead to the dissolution of a partnership.

2. Read the following as well as any other published articles on the bankruptcy of the partnership of Laventhol & Horwath:

    "Laventhol Says It Plans to File for Chapter 11," *Wall Street Journal,* November 20, 1990, p. A3.

    "Laventhol Partners Face Long Process that Could End in Personal Bankruptcy," *Wall Street Journal,* November 20, 1990, p. B5.

    "Laventhol Bankruptcy Filing Indicates Liabilities May Be as Much as $2 Billion," *Wall Street Journal,* November 23, 1990, p. A4.

    Write a report describing the potential liabilities incurred by the members of a partnership.

PROBLEMS

1. If a partnership is liquidated, how is the final allocation of business assets made to the partners?
    a. Equally.
    b. According to the profit and loss ratio.
    c. According to the final capital account balances.
    d. According to the initial investment made by each of the partners.

2. Which of the following statements is true concerning the accounting that is made for a partnership going through liquidation?
    a. Gains and losses are reported directly as increases and decreases in the appropriate capital account.
    b. A separate income statement is created just to measure the profit or loss generated during liquidation.
    c. Since gains and losses rarely occur during liquidation, no special accounting treatment is warranted.
    d. Within a liquidation, all gains and losses are divided equally among the partners.

3. During a liquidation, a partner's capital account balance drops below zero. What *should* happen?
    a. The other partners should file a legal suit against the partner with the deficit balance.
    b. The partner with the highest capital balance should contribute sufficient assets to eliminate the deficit.
    c. The deficit balance should be removed from the accounting records with only the remaining partners sharing in future gains and losses.
    d. The partner with a deficit should contribute enough assets to offset the deficit balance.

4. What is the marshaling of assets?
    a. A listing of all partnership assets that is prepared whenever a formal accounting is to be made.
    b. A ranking of claims to be paid when a partner has become insolvent.
    c. The method by which a retiring partner's share of partnership is determined.

    d. The gathering of partnership assets just prior to the commencement of the liquidation process.

5. A local partnership is in the process of liquidating and is currently reporting the following capital balances:

Angela, capital (50% share of all profits and losses)	$ 19,000
Woodrow, capital (30%)	18,000
Cassidy, capital (20%)	(12,000)

Cassidy has indicated that the $12,000 deficit will be covered by a forthcoming contribution. However, the two remaining partners have asked to receive the $25,000 in cash that is presently available. How much of this money should each partner be given?
    a. Angela, $13,000; Woodrow, $12,000.
    b. Angela, $11,500; Woodrow, $13,500.
    c. Angela, $12,000; Woodrow, $13,000.
    d. Angela, $12,500; Woodrow, $12,500.

6. A local partnership is considering the possibility of liquidation because one of the partners (Bell) is insolvent. Capital balances at the current time are as follows. Profits and losses are divided on a 4:3:2:1 basis, respectively.

Bell, capital	$50,000
Hardy, capital	56,000
Dennard, capital	14,000
Suddath, capital	80,000

Bell's creditors have filed a $21,000 claim against the partnership's assets. The partnership currently holds assets reported at $300,000 and liabilities of $100,000. If the assets can be sold for $190,000, what is the minimum amount that Bell's creditors would receive?
    a. –0–
    b. $2,000.
    c. $2,800.
    d. $6,000.

7. What is a predistribution plan?
    a. A guideline for the cash distributions made to partners during a liquidation.
    b. A list of the procedures to be performed during a liquidation.
    c. A determination of the final cash distribution to be made to the partners on the settlement date.
    d. A detailed list of the transactions that will transpire in the reorganization of a partnership.

8. A partnership has the following balance sheet just before final liquidation is to begin:

Cash	$ 26,000	Liabilities	$ 50,000
Inventory	31,000	Art, capital (40% of	
Other assets	62,000	profits and losses)	18,000
		Raymond, capital (30%) . . .	25,000
		Darby, capital (30%)	26,000
Total	$119,000	Total	$119,000

Liquidation expenses are estimated to be $12,000. The other assets are sold for $40,000. What distribution can be made to the partners?
    a. –0– to Art, $1,500 to Raymond, $2,500 to Darby.
    b. $1,333 to Art, $1,333 to Raymond, $1,334 to Darby.
    c. –0– to Art, $1,200 to Raymond, $2,800 to Darby.
    d. $600 to Art, $1,200 to Raymond, $2,200 to Darby.

9. A partnership has the following capital balances: A (20% of profits and losses) = $100,000; B (30% of profits and losses) = $120,000; C (50% of profits and losses) = $180,000. If the partnership is to be liquidated and $30,000 becomes immediately available, who gets that money?

    a. $6,000 to A, $9,000 to B, $15,000 to C.

    b. $22,000 to A, $3,000 to B, $5,000 to C.

    c. $22,000 to A, $8,000 to B, –0– to C.

    d. $24,000 to A, $6,000 to B, –0– to C.

10. A partnership is currently holding $400,000 in assets and $234,000 in liabilities. The partnership is to be liquidated and $20,000 is the best estimation of the expenses that will be incurred during this process. The four partners share profits and losses on a 4:3:1:2 basis, respectively. Capital balances at the start of the liquidation are as follows:

Kevin, capital	$59,000
Michael, capital	39,000
Brendan, capital	34,000
Jonathan, capital	34,000

The partners realize that Brendan will be the first partner to start receiving cash. How much cash will Brendan receive before any of the other partners collect any cash?

    a. $12,250.

    b. $14,750.

    c. $17,000.

    d. $19,500.

11. Carney, Pierce, Menton, and Hoehn are partners who share profits and losses on a 4:3:2:1 basis, respectively. They are presently beginning to liquidate the business. At the start of this process, capital balances are as follows:

Carney, capital	$60,000
Pierce, capital	27,000
Menton, capital	43,000
Hoehn, capital	20,000

Which of the following statements is true?

    a. The first available $2,000 will go to Hoehn.

    b. Carney will be the last partner to receive any available cash.

    c. The first available $3,000 will go to Menton.

    d. Carney will collect a portion of any available cash prior to Hoehn receiving money.

12. A partnership has gone through liquidation and now reports the following account balances:

Cash	$16,000
Loan from Jones	3,000
Wayman, capital	(2,000) (deficit)
Jones, capital	(5,000) (deficit)
Fuller, capital	13,000
Rogers, capital	7,000

Profits and losses are allocated on the following basis: Wayman, 30 percent; Jones, 20 percent; Fuller, 30 percent; and Rogers, 20 percent. Which of the following events should occur now?

    a. Jones should receive $3,000 cash because of the loan balance.

    b. Fuller should receive $11,800 and Rogers $6,200.

    c. Fuller should receive $10,600 and Rogers $5,400.

    d. Jones should receive $3,000, Fuller $8,800, and Rogers $4,200.

13. A partnership has the following account balances: Cash, $70,000; Other Assets, $540,000; Liabilities, $260,000; Nixon (50% of profits and losses), $170,000; Cleveland (30%), $110,000; Pierce (20%), $70,000. The company liquidates and $8,000 becomes available to the partners. Who gets the $8,000?

14. A local partnership has only two assets (cash of $10,000 and land with a cost of $35,000). All liabilities have been paid and the following capital balances are currently being recorded. The partners share profits and losses on a 4:3:3 basis, respectively. All partners are insolvent.

Brown, capital	$25,000
Fish, capital	15,000
Stone, capital	5,000

Required

a. If the land is sold for $25,000, how much cash does each of the partners receive in a final settlement?

b. If the land is sold for $15,000, how much cash does each of the partners receive in a final settlement?

c. If the land is sold for $5,000, how much cash does each of the partners receive in a final settlement?

15. A local dental partnership has been liquidated and the final capital balances are as follows:

Atkinson, capital (40% of all profits and losses)	$ 60,000
Kaporale, capital (30%)	20,000
Dennsmore, capital (20%)	(30,000)
Rasputin, capital (10%)	(50,000)

If Rasputin contributes additional cash to partnership of $20,000, what should happen to that money?

16. A partnership currently holds three assets: cash, $10,000; land, $35,000; and a building, $50,000. The partners anticipate that expenses required to liquidate their partnership will amount to $5,000. Capital balances are as follows:

Ace, capital	$25,000
Ball, capital	28,000
Eaton, capital	20,000
Lake, capital	22,000

The partners share profits and losses as follows: Ace (30%), Ball (30%), Eaton (20%), and Lake (20%). If a preliminary distribution of cash is to be made, how much will each of these partners receive?

17. The following condensed balance sheet is for the partnership of Hardwick, Saunders, and Ferris, who share profits and losses in the ratio of 4:3:3 respectively:

Cash	$ 90,000	Accounts payable	$210,000
Other assets	820,000	Ferris, loan	40,000
Hardwick, loan	30,000	Hardwick, capital	300,000
		Saunders, capital	200,000
		Ferris, capital	190,000
		Total liabilities and	
Total assets	$940,000	capital	$940,000

The partners decide to liquidate the partnership. Forty percent of the other assets are sold for $200,000. Prepare a proposed schedule of liquidation.

18. The following condensed balance sheet is for the partnership of Miller, Tyson, and Watson, who share profits and losses in the ratio of 6:2:2 respectively:

Cash	$ 40,000	Liabilities	$ 70,000
Other assets	140,000	Miller, capital	50,000
		Tyson, capital	50,000
		Watson, capital	10,000
		Total liabilities and	
Total assets	$180,000	capital	$180,000

For how much money do the other assets have to be sold so that each partner receives some amount of cash in a liquidation?

19. A partnership's balance sheet is as follows:

Cash	$ 60,000	Liabilities	$ 50,000
Noncash assets	120,000	Babb, capital	60,000
		Whitaker, capital	20,000
		Edwards, capital	50,000
		Total liabilities and	
Total assets	$180,000	capital	$180,000

Babb, Whitaker, and Edwards share profits and losses in the ratio of 4:2:4, respectively. This business is to be terminated and the partners estimate that $8,000 in liquidation expenses will be incurred. How should the $2,000 in safe cash that is presently held be disbursed?

20. A partnership has liquidated all assets but still reports the following account balances:

Loan from White	$ 6,000
Black, capital	3,000
White, capital	(9,000) (deficit)
Green, capital	(3,000) (deficit)
Brown, capital	15,000
Blue, capital	(12,000) (deficit)

The partners split profits and losses as follows: Black, 30 percent; White, 30 percent; Green, 10 percent; Brown, 20 percent; and Blue, 10 percent.

Assuming that all partners are personally insolvent except for Green and Brown, how much cash must Green now contribute to this partnership?

21. The following balance sheet is for a local partnership in which the partners have become very unhappy with each other. To avoid further conflict, they have decided to cease operations and sell all assets. Using this information, answer the following questions. Each question should be viewed as an independent situation.

Cash	$ 40,000	Liabilities	$ 30,000
Land	130,000	Adams, capital	80,000
Building	120,000	Baker, capital	30,000
		Carvil, capital	60,000
		Dobbs, capital	90,000
		Total liabilities and	
Total assets	$290,000	capital	$290,000

Required

a. The partnership is to be liquidated and the $10,000 cash that exceeds the partnership liabilities is to be disbursed immediately. If profits and losses are allocated on a 2:3:3:2 basis, respectively, how will the $10,000 be divided?

b. The partnership is to be liquidated and the $10,000 cash that exceeds the partnership liabilities is to be disbursed immediately. If profits and losses are allocated on a 2:2:3:3 basis, respectively, how will the $10,000 be divided?

c. The partnership is to be liquidated. The building is immediately sold for $70,000 to give total cash of $110,000. The liabilities are then paid leaving a cash balance of $80,000. This cash is to be distributed to the partners. How much of this money will each partner get if profits and losses are allocated on a 1:3:3:3 basis, respectively?

d. The partnership is to be liquidated. Assume that profits and losses are allocated on a 1:3:4:2 basis, respectively. How much money must be received from selling the land and building to assure that Carvil receives a portion?

22. The partnership of Larson, Norris, Spencer, and Harrison has decided to terminate operations and liquidate all business property. During this process, the partners expect to incur $8,000 in liquidation expenses. All of the partners are currently solvent.

The balance sheet reported by this partnership at the time that the liquidation commenced follows. The percentages indicate the allocation of profits and losses to each of the four partners.

Cash	$ 28,250	Liabilities	$ 47,000
Accounts receivable	44,000	Larson, capital (20%)	15,000
Inventory	39,000	Norris, capital (30%)	60,000
Land and buildings	23,000	Spencer, capital (20%)	75,000
Equipment	104,000	Harrison, capital (30%) . . .	41,250
		Total liabilities and	
Total assets	$238,250	capital	$238,250

Required

Based on the information that has been provided, prepare a predistribution plan for the liquidation of this partnership.

23. The following partnership is being liquidated beginning on July 13, 2001:

Cash	$ 36,000	Liabilities	$50,000
Noncash assets	174,000	Able, loan	10,000
		Able, capital (20%)	40,000
		Moon, capital (30%)	60,000
		Yerkl, capital (50%)	50,000

Required

a. Liquidation expenses are estimated to be $12,000. Prepare a predistribution schedule to guide the distribution of cash.

b. Assume assets costing $28,000 are sold for $40,000. How is the available cash to be divided?

24. A local partnership is to be liquidated. Commissions and other liquidation expenses are expected to total $19,000. The business's balance sheet prior to the commencement of liquidation is as follows:

Cash	$ 27,000	Liabilities	$ 40,000
Noncash assets	254,000	Simpson, capital (20%) . . .	18,000
		Hart, capital (40%)	40,000
		Bobb, capital (20%)	48,000
		Reidl, capital (20%)	135,000
		Total liabilities and	
Total assets	$281,000	capital	$281,000

Prepare a predistribution schedule for this partnership.

25. The following information concerns two different partnerships. These problems should be viewed as independent situations.

Part A

The partnership of Ross, Milburn, and Thomas has the following account balances:

Cash	$ 36,000	Liabilities	$17,000
Noncash assets	100,000	Ross, capital	69,000
		Milburn, capital	(8,000) (deficit)
		Thomas, capital	58,000

This partnership is in the process of being liquidated. Ross and Milburn are each entitled to 40 percent of all profits and losses with the remaining 20 percent to Thomas.

a. What is the maximum amount that Milburn might have to contribute to this partnership because of the deficit capital balance?

b. How should the $19,000 cash that is presently available in excess of liabilities be distributed?

c. If the noncash assets are sold for a total of $41,000, what is the minimum amount of cash that could be received by Thomas?

Part B

The partnership of Sampson, Klingon, Carton, and Romulan is being liquidated and currently holds cash of $9,000 but no other assets. Liabilities amount to $24,000. The capital balances are as follows:

Sampson	$ 9,000
Klingon	(17,000)
Carton	5,000
Romulan	(12,000)

Profits and losses are allocated on the following basis: Sampson, 40 percent, Klingon, 20 percent, Carton, 30 percent, and Romulan, 10 percent.

    a. If both Klingon and Romulan are personally insolvent, how much money does Carton have to contribute to this partnership?

    b. If only Romulan is personally insolvent, how much money does Klingon have to contribute? How will these funds be disbursed?

    c. If only Klingon is personally insolvent, how much money should Sampson receive from the liquidation?

26. March, April, and May have been in partnership for a number of years. Recently, the partners have each become personally insolvent and, thus, have decided to liquidate the business in hopes of remedying their personal financial problems. The partners allocate all profits and losses on a 2:3:1 basis, respectively. As of September 1, 2001, the partnership balance sheet is as follows:

Cash	$ 11,000	Liabilities		$ 61,000
Accounts receivable	84,000	March, capital		25,000
Inventory	74,000	April, capital		75,000
Land, building, and equipment		May, capital		46,000
(net)	38,000			
		Total liabilities and		
Total assets	$207,000	capital		$207,000

Prepare journal entries for the following transactions:

- Sold all of the inventory for $56,000 cash.
- Paid $7,500 in liquidation expenses.
- Paid $40,000 of the partnership's liabilities.
- Collected $45,000 of the accounts receivable.
- Safe cash balances are distributed; no further liquidation expenses are anticipated by the partners.
- The remaining accounts receivable are sold for 30 percent of face value.
- The land, building, and equipment are sold for $17,000.
- All remaining liabilities of the partnership are paid.
- The cash held by the business is distributed to the partners.

27. The partnership of W, X, Y, and Z has the following balance sheet:

Cash	$ 30,000	Liabilities	$42,000
Other assets	220,000	W, capital (50% of profits	
		and losses)	60,000
		X, capital (30%)	78,000
		Y, capital (10%)	40,000
		Z, capital (10%)	30,000

    Z is personally insolvent and one of his creditors is considering suing the partnership for the $5,000 that is currently due. The creditor realizes that liquidation may result from this litigation and does not wish to force such an extreme action unless reasonably assured of getting the money that is due. If the other assets are sold, how much money must be received by the partnership to ensure that $5,000 would become available from Z's portion of the business? Liquidation expenses are expected to be $15,000.

28. On January 1, 2001, the partners of Van, Bakel, and Cox (who share profits and losses in the ratio of 5:3:2, respectively) decide to liquidate their partnership. The trial balance at this date is as follows:

	Debit	Credit
Cash	$ 18,000	
Accounts receivable	66,000	
Inventory	52,000	
Machinery and equipment, net	189,000	
Van, loan	30,000	
Accounts payable		$ 53,000
Bakel, loan		20,000
Van, capital		118,000
Bakel, capital		90,000
Cox, capital		74,000
Totals	$355,000	$355,000

The partners plan a program of piecemeal conversion of the business's assets to minimize liquidation losses. All available cash, less an amount retained to provide for future expenses, is to be distributed to the partners at the end of each month. A summary of the liquidation transactions is as follows:

2001

January $51,000 is collected on the accounts receivable; the balance is deemed uncollectible.

$38,000 is received for the entire inventory.

$2,000 in liquidation expenses is paid.

$50,000 is paid to the outside creditors, after offsetting a $3,000 credit memorandum received by the partnership on January 11, 2001.

$10,000 cash is retained in the business at the end of January to cover any unrecorded liabilities and anticipated expenses. The remainder is distributed to the partners.

February $3,000 in liquidation expenses is paid.

$6,000 cash is retained in the business at the end of the month to cover unrecorded liabilities and anticipated expenses.

March $146,000 is received on the sale of all machinery and equipment.

$5,000 in final liquidation expenses is paid.

No cash is retained in the business.

Required

Prepare a schedule to compute the safe installment payments made to the partners at the end of each of these three months.

(AICPA adapted)

29. Following is a series of independent cases. In each situation, indicate the cash distribution to be made at the end of the liquidation process. *Unless otherwise stated, assume that all solvent partners will reimburse the partnership for their deficit capital balances.*

Part A

The following accounts are presently being reported by the Simon, Haynes, and Jackson partnership:

Cash	$ 30,000
Liabilities	22,000
Haynes, loan	10,000
Simon, capital (40%)	16,000
Haynes, capital (20%)	(6,000)
Jackson, capital (40%)	(12,000)

Jackson is personally insolvent and can contribute only an additional $3,000 to the partnership. Simon is also insolvent and has no available funds.

Part B

Hough, Luck, and Cummings operate a local accounting firm as a partnership. After working together for several years, they have decided to liquidate the partnership's property. The partners have prepared the following balance sheet:

Cash	$ 20,000	Liabilities	$ 40,000
Hough, loan	8,000	Luck, loan	10,000
Noncash assets	162,000	Hough, capital (50%)	90,000
		Luck, capital (40%)	30,000
		Cummings, capital (10%) . .	20,000
		Total liabilities and	
Total assets	$190,000	capital	$190,000

The noncash assets are sold for $80,000, with $21,000 of this amount being used to pay liquidation expenses. All three of these partners are personally insolvent.

Part C

Use the same information as in part B, except assume that the profits and losses are split 2:4:4 to Hough, Luck, and Cummings, respectively, and that liquidation expenses are only $6,000.

Part D

Following the liquidation of all noncash assets, the partnership of Redmond, Ledbetter, Watson, and Sandridge has the following account balances:

Liabilities	$ 28,000
Redmond, loan	5,000
Redmond, capital (20%)	(21,000)
Ledbetter, capital (10%)	(30,000)
Watson, capital (30%)	3,000
Sandridge, capital (40%)	15,000

Redmond is personally insolvent.

30. The partnership of Frick, Wilson, and Clarke has elected to cease all operations and liquidate its business property. A balance sheet drawn up at this time shows the following account balances:

Cash	$ 48,000	Liabilities	$ 35,000
Noncash assets	177,000	Frick, capital (60%)	101,000
		Wilson, capital (20%)	28,000
		Clarke, capital (20%)	61,000
		Total liabilities and	
Total assets	$225,000	capital	$225,000

The following transactions occur in liquidating this business:

- Safe capital balances are immediately distributed to the partners. Liquidation expenses of $9,000 are estimated as a basis for this computation.
- Noncash assets with a book value of $80,000 are sold for $48,000.
- All liabilities are paid.
- Safe capital balances are again distributed.
- Remaining noncash assets are sold for $44,000.
- Liquidation expenses of $7,000 are paid.
- Remaining cash is distributed to the partners and the financial records of the business permanently closed.

Required

Produce a final schedule of liquidation for this partnership.

31. **Part A**

The partnership of Wingler, Norris, Rodgers, and Guthrie was formed several years ago as a local architectural firm. Several of the partners have recently undergone personal financial problems and decided to terminate operations and liquidate the business. The following balance sheet is drawn up as a guideline for this process:

Cash	$ 15,000	Liabilities	$ 74,000
Accounts receivable	82,000	Rodgers, loan	35,000
Inventory	101,000	Wingler, capital (30%)	120,000
Land	85,000	Norris, capital (10%)	88,000
Building and equipment (net)	168,000	Rodgers, capital (20%)	74,000
		Guthrie, capital (40%)	60,000
		Total liabilities and	
Total assets	$451,000	capital	$451,000

At the time the liquidation commences, expenses of $16,000 are anticipated as being necessary to dispose of all property.

Required

Prepare a predistribution plan for this partnership.

Part B

The following transactions transpire during the liquidation of the Wingler, Norris, Rodgers, and Guthrie partnership:

- Of the total accounts receivable, 80 percent are collected with the rest judged as uncollectible.
- The land, building, and equipment are sold for $150,000.
- Safe capital distributions are made.
- Guthrie becomes personally insolvent. No further contributions will be forthcoming from this partner.
- All liabilities are paid.
- All inventory is sold for $71,000.
- Safe capital distributions are again made.
- Liquidation expenses of $11,000 are paid.
- Final cash disbursements are made to the partners based on the assumption that all partners other than Guthrie are personally solvent.

Required

Prepare journal entries to record these liquidation transactions.

CHAPTER

16

Accounting for State and Local Governments (Part One)

QUESTIONS TO CONSIDER

- Why did the GASB believe that radical changes were needed in the reporting of state and local governments?

- How has *GASB Statement No. 34* affected the financial reporting of state and local governments?

- Who are the users of the financial data produced by state and local government units, and why is such a wide variety of informational needs encountered?

- What is fund accounting, and why is it utilized by state and local governments?

- Why is budgetary control considered so important in a government? In what ways is budgetary control established in the accounting system?

- How do government-wide financial statements differ from fund-based financial statements and why are two sets of financial statements necessary?

- What measurement focus and basis of accounting is utilized in the various financial statements produced for a state or local government?

- Why are encumbrances recorded by a government?

- When are revenues, expenses, and expenditures recognized by a government?

robably no pronouncement in the history of accounting has had more impact on an area of financial reporting than *Statement No. 34* of the Governmental Accounting Standards Board (GASB) entitled "Basic Financial Statements—and Management's Discussion and Analysis—for State and Local Governments." This 400-page document issued in June 1999 affected virtually every area of financial reporting by state and local government units. Major changes were made in the way that these governments had traditionally reported their operations and financial position. More important, an entirely new method of reporting was devised and added to the financial statements being externally distributed.

Consequently, with just this one official statement, fund accounting which had served as the basis of reporting by state and local governments for decades was modified significantly and a second group of financial statements was created based on a completely different approach to financial reporting. When *GASB 34* becomes effective, state and local government units will have to produce and report two sets of financial statements with widely differing information. Not surprisingly, reaction to *GASB 34* has been quite vocal:

"With *GASB Statement 34*, the board has taken a bold step forward in the evolution and refinement of government financial reporting."[1]

"*GASB 34* changes the notion of accountability, elevating the importance of full cost, giving prominence to long-term debt and assets, assessing

---

[1]Robert J. Freeman and Craig D. Shoulders, "A Bold Step Forward," *The Government Accountants Journal,* Spring 2000, p. 15.

year-to-year financial improvements for the government as a whole, and in general, making greater use of business criteria."[2]

"The Governmental Accounting Standards Board (GASB) describes *Statement 34* as 'the most comprehensive governmental accounting rule ever developed.' Unfortunately, the statement has serious defects, but they can be remedied."[3]

Because of the magnitude of these changes, application of *GASB Statement 34* is being phased in over several years. Governments with total annual revenues of $100 million or more need not follow the provisions of this pronouncement until fiscal periods beginning after June 15, 2001. If total annual revenues are $10 million or more but less than $100 million, *GASB Number 34* must be utilized for financial statements created for periods beginning after June 15, 2002. Smaller governments with less than $10 million in total revenues are not required to apply these new rules until periods beginning after June 15, 2003. Therefore, most larger government units will probably first adopt these new requirements in their financial statements for the year ending June 30, 2002. Until that time, traditional government financial statements will continue to be allowed although early adoption of the new rules is permitted.

Accounting for state and local governments is obviously in a period of great transition. The traditional rules can be used for a short time longer but all such governments are gearing up for a massive change in the way financial information is reported. Once applied, governments will still have to report information through fund-based financial statements that are similar to the traditional method of reporting that has been used for decades. In addition, the same events must be reported in a very different manner through government-wide financial statements. To help understand both approaches, this chapter focuses on the handling of typical transactions. Where necessary, two different methods of accounting are shown. Only in that way can the distinctions between fund-based accounting and government-wide accounting be highlighted. The next chapter demonstrates how all of the resulting information is actually reported within the various financial statements that must be produced.

INTRODUCTION TO THE ACCOUNTING FOR STATE AND LOCAL GOVERNMENTS

In this country, literally thousands of state and local government reporting entities touch the lives of the citizenry on a daily basis. In 1997, nearly 90,000 local government units existed just in the United States.[4] Income and sales taxes are collected, property taxes are assessed, schools are operated, fire departments are maintained,

---

[2]John Sacco, "Part of Changing Political and Global Market Pressures," *The Government Accountants Journal,* Spring 2000, p. 20.

[3]Robert N. Anthony and Susan M. Newberry, "GASB 34 Should Be Revised," *The Government Accountants Journal,* Spring 2000, p. 36.

[4]U.S. Department of Commerce, Bureau of the Census, 1997 Census of Governments, vol. 1, no. 1 (Washington, DC: U. S. Government Printing Office), p. v.

garbage is collected, and roads are paved. Actions of one or more governments affect every individual. Accounting for a government is not merely a matching of expenses with revenues so that net income can be determined. For many governments, deficit spending has become a troubling practice. The allocation of resources between such worthy causes as education, police, welfare, and the environment creates heated debates throughout the nation. To keep the public informed so that proper decisions can be made, government reporting has historically identified the source of financial resources and what use is made of them, which activities are financed and which are not. Indeed, this approach is appropriate for the short-term decisions necessitated by gathering and allocating limited financial resources. For the longer term, though, information is needed to reflect the overall financial stability of the government, one primary goal of the changes mandated by *GASB Statement Number 34.*

Over the years, a slow evolution has transpired in the generally accepted accounting principles used by state and local governments. The American Institute of Certified Public Accountants (AICPA) and the National Council on Governmental Accounting (NCGA) made significant strides during previous decades in establishing sound accounting principles.[5] In June of 1984, the Governmental Accounting Standards Board (GASB) became the public sector counterpart of the Financial Accounting Standards Board. The GASB holds the primary responsibility in the United States for setting authoritative accounting standards for state and local government units.

In the same manner as the Financial Accounting Standards Board, the GASB is an independent body functioning under the oversight of the Financial Accounting Foundation. Thus, a formal mechanism is in place to continue the development of governmental accounting. Since its creation, the GASB has produced a number of governmental accounting standards as well as technical bulletins, interpretations, and a concepts statement. In 1997, GASB produced a codification of authoritative pronouncements as a guideline for reporting purposes.

Governmental Accounting—User Needs

The unique aspects of governmental accounting are a direct result of the perceived needs of financial statement users. Identification of these informational requirements is, therefore, a logical first step in the study of the accounting principles applied by state and local governments. Specific procedures utilized in the reporting process can be understood best as an outgrowth of these needs. Often, though, user expectations are complex and even contradictory. The taxpayer, the government employee, the bondholder, and the public official may each be seeking distinctly different types of financial information about a governmental unit.

> My own reflection on the subject leads me to the conviction that appropriate and adequate accounting for state and local governmental units involves a far more complex set of interrelationships, to be reported to a more diverse set of users with a greater variety of interests and needs, than exists in business accounting and reporting.[6]

---

[5]The NCGA was a quasi-independent agency of the Government Finance Officers Association. The NCGA held authority for state and local government accounting from 1973 through 1984. The National Committee on Municipal Accounting had this responsibility from 1934 until 1941 while the National Committee on Governmental Accounting established government accounting principles from 1949 through 1954 and again from 1967 until 1973. During several periods, no group held responsibility for the development of governmental accounting. For an overview of the history of governmental accounting standards and the creation of the GASB, see "The Evolution of Governmental Accounting Standard Setting," by David R. Bean published in the December 1984 issue of *Governmental Finance.* Another coverage of the history in this area can be found in "The Governmental Accounting Standards Board: Factors Influencing Its Operation and Initial Technical Agenda," by Martin Ives published in the Spring 2000 issue of *The Government Accountants Journal.*

[6]Robert K. Mautz, "Financial Reporting: Should Government Emulate Business?" *Journal of Accountancy,* August 1981, p. 53.

In its *Concepts Statement No. 1,* "Objectives of Financial Reporting," the GASB recognized this same problem by identifying three groups of primary users of external state and local governmental financial reports: the citizenry, legislative and oversight bodies, and creditors and investors. The needs and interests of each of these groups were then described:

Citizenry—Want to evaluate the likelihood of tax or service fee increases, to determine the sources and uses of resources, to forecast revenues in order to influence spending decisions, to ensure that resources were used in accordance with appropriations, to assess financial condition, and to compare budgeted to actual results.

Legislative and oversight bodies—Want to assess the overall financial condition when developing budgets and program recommendations, to monitor operating results to assure compliance with mandates, to determine the reasonableness of fees and the need for tax changes, and to ascertain the ability to finance new programs and capital needs.

Investors and creditors—Want to know the amount of available and likely future financial resources, to measure the debt position and the ability to service that debt, and to review operating results and cash flow data.[7]

Thus, a significant obstacle is encountered in the quest for fair governmental reporting: User needs are so broad that no one set of financial statements or accounting principles can possibly satisfy all expectations. How can voters, bondholders, city officials, and the other users of the financial statements provided by state and local governments all receive the information that is needed? The question of satisfying a wide variety of user needs is a constant theme in discussions of state and local government accounting.

Eventually, the desire to produce financial statements that would satisfy such diverse demands for information led the GASB to require in *Statement Number 34* the production of two distinct sets of statements.

Fund-based financial statements have been designed "to show restrictions on the planned use of resources or to measure, *in the short term,* the revenues and expenditures arising from certain activities."[8]

Government-wide financial statements will have a longer-term focus because they will report "*all* revenues and *all* costs of providing services each year, not just those received or paid in the current year or soon after year-end."[9]

Thus, fund-based financial statements focus on specific activities and the amount of financial resources given to those activities during the period as well as the use made of those resources. For example, these fund-based financial statements should tell the amount spent this year on such services as public safety, education, health and sanitation, and the construction of a new road. The primary measurement focus in these statements is on the flow and amount of current financial resources while the basis of accounting in most cases is a system known as modified accrual accounting. Modified accrual accounting recognizes revenues when the current financial resources are measurable and available and expenditures when they cause a reduction in current financial resources.

In contrast, government-wide financial statements report a government's activities and financial position as a whole. This approach helps users make long-term evaluations of the finances of the government by allowing them to:

■ Assess the finances of the government in its entirety, including the year's operating results.

---

[7]*GASB Concepts Statement No. 1,* "Objectives of Financial Reporting," May 1987, para. 33–37.

[8]*Governmental Accounting Standards Board Statement No. 34,* "Basic Financial Statements—and Management's Discussion and Analysis—for State and Local Governments," June 1999, preface p. 1.

[9]Ibid., p. 2.

- Determine whether the government's overall financial position improved or deteriorated.
- Evaluate whether the government's current-year revenues were sufficient to pay for current-year services.
- See the cost of providing services to its citizenry.
- See how the government finances its programs—through user fees and other program revenues versus general tax revenues.
- Understand the extent to which the government has invested in capital assets, including roads, bridges, and other infrastructure assets.
- Make better comparisons between governments.[10]

To achieve these goals, the government-wide financial statements measurement focus is on all economic resources (and not just current financial resources) and it utilizes accrual accounting much like any for-profit entity. All assets and liabilities are reported and all revenues and expenses are recognized in a way comparable to business-type accounting.

Accountability and Governmental Accounting

Despite the variety of users, one aspect of governmental reporting has remained constant over the years: the goal of making the government accountable to the public. Because of the essential role of democracy within American society, governmental accounting principles have attempted to provide a vehicle for evaluating the actions of the government. Citizens should be aware of the means used by officials to raise money and the allocations made of these scarce resources. Voters must evaluate the wisdom, as well as the honesty, of the members of government. Since most voters are also taxpayers, they naturally exhibit special interest in the results obtained from their involuntary contributions, such as taxes. *Because elected and appointed officials hold authority over the public's money, governmental reporting has traditionally stressed this stewardship responsibility.*

> Accountability is the cornerstone of all financial reporting in government. . . . Accountability requires governments to answer to the citizenry—to justify the raising of public resources and the purposes for which they are used. Governmental accountability is based on the belief that the citizenry has a "right to know," a right to receive openly declared facts that may lead to public debate by the citizens and their elected representatives.[11]

For this reason, accounting emphasis has traditionally been directed toward measuring and identifying the public funds generated and expended by each of a government's diverse activities. *GASB Statement 34* is not an attempt to overturn this reporting philosophy. Instead, this new pronouncement actually seeks to refine the reporting of individual government activities and then go beyond that to provide information about the government as a whole.

In general, the fund-based financial statements are used to answer three questions:

- Where did the government's current financial resources come from?
- Where did those financial resources go?
- What amount of those financial resources is presently held?

The term *current financial resources* normally encompasses monetary assets that are available to be spent by officials to meet the government's needs. Thus, when measuring current financial resources, a government is primarily monitoring cash, investments, and receivables. Since officials are accountable for generating and using

---

[10]Ibid., p. 3.

[11]*GASB Concepts Statement No. 1*, para. 56.

cash (along with other assets that can be readily turned into cash), the traditional government accounting system has focused on these financial resources as well as current claims against them. For this reason, little reporting emphasis has been placed on accounts such as buildings, equipment, and long-term debts that have no direct impact on current financial resources.

Obviously, stressing government accountability in using current financial resources is an approach to accounting that by itself is not capable of meeting all user needs; thus, many conventional reporting objectives long have been ignored. Not surprisingly, investors and creditors have frequently been sharp critics of governmental accounting. "When cities get into financial trouble, few citizens know about it until the day the interest can't be met or the teachers paid. . . . Had the books been kept like any decent corporation's that could never have happened."[12]

Although accountability is a central concern, other user needs must be addressed. Consequently, government-wide financial statements have now been created by *GASB Statement Number 34* to provide an additional dimension for government reporting. These statements do not focus solely on current financial resources but rather seek to report all of the assets at the disposal of government officials as well as all liabilities that must eventually be paid. Likewise, all revenues and expenses are recognized according to accrual accounting to provide a completely different level of financial information.

Control of Public Funds

Over the decades, the desire to stress accountability has led to a system of procedures that convey information to the public about current financial resources while helping to establish control over these public funds. This process is especially important since public officials often hold authority over sums of money that can be staggering in size. The city of Anaheim, California, for example, reported revenues of more than $700 million for the year ending June 30, 1999. Such funds are accumulated through charges and taxes. Although laws require the appropriate utilization of such monies, compliance is not always easy for the average citizen to ascertain.

Stressing accountability and the stewardship role played by government officials is in diametric contrast to a profit-oriented business where stockholders contribute capital voluntarily and then elect a board of directors to monitor operating and financial activities. Board members along with stockholders and other interested parties have access to accounting data, such as net income, earnings per share, and return on investment, which allows an assessment to be made of management's utilization of the resources provided. In a government, though, oversight and computed measures of success are more difficult to achieve. For example, neither net income nor earnings per share can measure the performance of a fire department.

Because of the citizens' desire to monitor elected officials, governmental accounting has developed its own specialized control procedures. Budgets, for example, must be legally adopted by a government's legislative body to indicate anticipated revenues and approved expenditures. To highlight these projections, many of the budget figures are physically entered into the government's accounting records and then presented within required supplemental information attached to the annual financial statements. In this manner, comparisons can be drawn between the expected activity for each specific function and actual revenue and expenditure figures.

Additional control over government spending is achieved by recording purchase commitments (commonly referred to as *encumbrances*). The acquisition of a fax machine, for example, is formally journalized as an encumbrance at the time the item is

---

[12]Richard Greene, "You Can't Fight City Hall—If You Can't Understand It," *Forbes,* March 3, 1980, p. 92.

ordered rather than when the title transfers. By measuring both expended as well as committed funds, the entity is less likely to overspend available resources. Through the creation of separate government-wide financial statements, the GASB obviously wants to retain the control features traditionally found in government accounting while adding another layer of information to report the overall finances of the state or locality.

Reporting Diverse Governmental Activities—Fund Accounting

Beyond the goal of establishing accountability and fiscal control, the accountant also faces the challenge of reporting the diverse array of activities within most government units. Because no common profit motive exists to tie all of these functions and services together, consolidated balances have historically been omitted. Combining operating results from the city zoo, the fire department, the motor pool, the water system, and the like would provide figures of questionable utility if accountability and control over the usage of current financial resources is the primary goal. For this reason, an underlying assumption of government accounting has been that most statement users prefer information segregated by function so that each activity can be assessed individually. Hence, the accounting process has evolved over the years to accumulate separate data to describe the financial affairs of every activity (library, school system, police department, road construction, etc.). Then revenues, expenditures, financial resources, and the like can be reported for each specific function. *GASB Statement 34* continues to retain much of this focus on individual activities while also mandating government-wide financial statements to provide a broader view of the government as a whole.

The diversity inherent in most state or local government units mandates that a single set of accounting records simply is not sufficient to monitor all activities. Therefore, financial transactions and adjustments are recorded in quasi-independent bookkeeping systems referred to as funds. *Each fund is a self-balancing set of accounts used to record data generated by an identifiable government function. All of these funds taken together make up the government's financial reporting system.*

> The diverse nature of governmental operations and the necessity of assuring legal compliance preclude recording and summarizing all governmental financial transactions and balances in a single accounting entity. Unlike a private business, which is accounted for as a single entity, a governmental unit is accounted for through several separate fund and account group entities, each accounting for designated assets, liabilities, and equity or other balances.[13]

Although a single list of separately reportable functions of a state or local government is not possible, the following commonly are encountered:

Public safety	Judicial system
Highway maintenance	Debt repayment
Sanitation	Bridge construction
Health	Water and sewer system
Welfare	Municipal swimming pool
Culture and recreation	Data processing center
Education	Endowment funds
Parks	Employee pensions

For external control purposes, the actual number of funds in use depends on the extent of services being offered by the government and the grouping of related activities.

---

[13]*Codification of Governmental Accounting and Financial Reporting Standards* (Norwalk, Conn.: Governmental Accounting Standards Board, 1997), sec. 1300.101.

As an example, separate funds may be set up for a high school and its athletic programs or these activities may be combined into a single fund.

> The general rule is to establish the minimum number of separate funds consistent with legal specifications and operational requirements. . . . Using too many funds causes inflexibility and undue complexity . . . and is best avoided in the interest of efficient and economical financial administrations.[14]

If a government only had to account for service activities such as police and fire protection, reporting problems could be minimized. Although establishing separate funds would still be necessary for the individual functions, accounting procedures could be similar in each case, if not identical. Within these various funds, the emphasis would be placed on control and accountability through the reporting of revenues and expenditures relating to the specified service.

However, many government operations (such as municipal golf courses, toll roads, convention centers, and airports) attempt to generate revenues rather than simply serve the populace. Because this goal parallels that held by business-type enterprises, traditional government accounting procedures are not appropriate to these functions. In effect, a municipality cannot fully report the activities of a police department and a golf course by using the same accounting principles; the objectives are simply too diverse.

To add to the accountant's difficulty, a third distinct type of government function (beyond governmental activities and business-type activities) also can be identified. State and local governments frequently serve in a trustee capacity, holding money or other assets to be used for a particular purpose. Employee pension funds, for example, often are maintained so that government workers can receive benefits after their retirement. Thus, all funds can be categorized into one of three distinct groups:

- Governmental activities—functions designed primarily to serve the public.
- Business-type activities—functions where a user charge is assessed.
- Fiduciary activities—functions where money or other assets are held for use outside of the government.

As shown below, this classification system has been formally incorporated into the structure of government accounting systems.

Fund Accounting Classifications

Because of the large number of activities carried out by many government units, designing distinct internal accounting procedures for each fund is neither feasible nor desirable. Instead, to facilitate the bookkeeping process, a grouping system has been devised with all funds being placed into one of three broad classifications:

- *Governmental funds*—account for activities of a government that are carried out primarily to provide services to citizens and that are financed primarily through taxes. A police department would be reported within the governmental funds.
- *Proprietary funds*—account for a government's ongoing organizations and activities that are similar to those operated by for-profit organizations. This fund type normally encompasses operations where a user charge is assessed so that determining operating income or cost recovery is important. A toll road would be reported within the proprietary funds.
- *Fiduciary funds*—account for monies held by the government in a trustee capacity. *GASB Statement 34* modified the definition of fiduciary funds a bit by requiring that such assets must be held for others and cannot be used by the

---

[14]GASB Cod. Sec. 1100.108.

government for its own programs. Assets held for a pension plan would be reported within the fiduciary funds.

Governmental Funds   In most state or municipal accounting systems, the governmental funds tend to dominate because a service orientation usually prevails. For reporting purposes, individual records are maintained for every distinct function: public safety, libraries, construction of a town hall, and so on. In each of these governmental funds, financial resources are accumulated and expended to achieve one or more desired public goals.

To provide better reported information and control as well as to allow for the development of more precise accounting principles, the governmental funds are subdivided into five categories: the General Fund, Special Revenue Funds, Capital Projects Funds, Debt Service Fund, and Permanent Funds. Although the basic accounting objectives are the same for each of these fund types, actual procedures may vary depending on the nature of the service. Thus, this classification system allows specific accounting guidelines to be directed toward each fund type while providing an overall structure for financial reporting purposes.

The General Fund   The GASB's definition of the General Fund appears to be somewhat understated: "to account for all financial resources except those required to be accounted for in another fund."[15] This description seems to imply that the General Fund records only miscellaneous revenues and expenditures when, in actuality, this fund type accounts for many of a government's most important services. Whereas the other governmental funds report specific events or projects, the General Fund records a broad range of ongoing activities. For example, the financial statements for the city of Des Moines, Iowa, disclose six major areas of current expenditures within its General Fund: community protection, leisure-time opportunities, physical environment, social and economic well-being, transportation, and general administration and support. Expenditures reported for these categories of the General Fund made up more than 58 percent of the total for all of the city's governmental funds for the year ended June 30, 1998.

Special Revenue Funds   Special revenue funds account for revenues that have been legally restricted as to expenditure. These financial resources must be spent in a specified fashion. Saint Paul, Minnesota, for example, reported approximately $80 million of revenues within special revenue funds during the 1998 fiscal year. This money was generated from sources as diverse as cable television franchising fees, rent received from the use of Municipal Stadium, administration fees for charitable gambling, money received from recycling programs, and the sale of zoo animals. The Special Revenue Funds category accounts for these monies because *legal restrictions had been attached to the revenue to require that expenditure be limited to specific purposes.* As an example, the city council of Saint Paul had specified that any money collected from the sale of zoo animals had to be spent to acquire new animals. Thus, any resources received from this source are monitored by inclusion in the special revenue funds until properly expended.

The Special Revenue Fund classification also is appropriate if a gift is made to the government whereby the principal and any subsequent income must be spent for a purpose designated by the donor. For example, the 1998 financial statements for Fort Wayne, Indiana, show that money has been contributed to the city for public park purposes while other funds have been given for animal care needs. Prior to *GASB Statement 34,* such donations were reported within the fiduciary funds as Expendable Trust Funds.

---

[15]GASB Cod. sec. 1300.104.

Capital Projects Funds   As the title implies, this fund type accounts for costs incurred in acquiring or constructing major government facilities such as bridges, high schools, roads, or municipal office complexes. Funding for these projects is normally derived from grants, the sale of bonds, or is transferred from general revenues. The actual asset being obtained is not recorded here but merely the money to finance the purchase or construction. For example, the city of Fort Lauderdale, Florida, reported as of September 30, 1998, that it was holding more than $60 million in financial resources in its capital projects funds to be used in such projects as a radio communications system, a post office, and other major facilities.

Debt Service Funds   These funds record monies accumulated to pay long-term liabilities and interest as they come due.[16] However, this fund type does not account for a government's long-term debt. Rather, debt service funds monitor the financial resources currently available to satisfy long-term liabilities and also record the eventual payment. Thus, on June 30, 1998, the city of Charlotte, North Carolina, reported nearly $80 million of cash and investments in its debt service funds, money being held to pay long-term debt and interest. For the year then ended, over $34 million in principal payments had been made from this fund along with another $28 million in interest payments.

Permanent Funds   The Permanent Funds category is a new fund type within the governmental funds. It accounts for assets contributed to the government by an external donor with the stipulation that the principal cannot be spent but any income can be used within the government, often for a designated purpose. Such gifts are frequently referred to as endowments and prior to *GASB Statement 34* were reported as Nonexpendable Trust Funds within the fiduciary funds. However, since the income can be used to support government programs, this new category was placed within the governmental funds.

Proprietary Funds   The proprietary funds account for ongoing activities similar to those found in the business world. To facilitate financial reporting, the proprietary funds are broken down into two major divisions:

Enterprise Funds   Any government operation that is financed, at least in part, by outside user charges may be classified as an Enterprise Fund. A municipality, for example, may generate revenues from the use of a public swimming pool, golf course, airport, water and sewage service, and the like. As an illustration, the city of Charlotte, North Carolina, reports the operation of its airport as an Enterprise Fund.

A question arises, though, as to how much revenue an activity must generate before it is viewed as an Enterprise Fund. For example, if a city wants to promote mass transit and only charges a nickel to ride on its bus line, should that activity be viewed as part of an Enterprise Fund (a business-type activity) or within the General Fund (a governmental activity)? According to *GASB Statement 34,* any activity that charges a user fee to the public can be classified as an Enterprise Fund. However, this designation is required if the activity meets any one of the following criteria:

- Net revenues generated by the activity provide the sole security for the debts of the activity.
- Laws or regulations require the activity's costs (including depreciation and debt service) to be recovered through fees or charges.
- Fees and charges are set at prices intended to recover costs including depreciation and debt service.

---

[16]Some state and local governments choose to maintain assets for debt service within the General Fund rather than in a separate category. This approach is acceptable, especially if the amounts are relatively small.

Because customers are assessed direct fees, Enterprise Fund activities resemble businesses. Not surprisingly, the accounting process parallels that found in for-profit reporting. The funds use accrual basis accounting with a focus on economic, not just current financial, resources.

Internal Service Funds   This second proprietary fund accounts for any operation that provides services to another department or agency within the government on a cost-reimbursement basis. As with Enterprise Funds, fees are charged but the service is performed for the primary benefit of the government rather than for outside users. The city of Lincoln, Nebraska, for example, lists eight operations in its 1999 financial statements that are accounted for as separate internal service funds:

Information services fund—to account for the cost of operating a central data processing facility.

Engineering revolving fund—to account for the cost of operating a central engineering pool.

Insurance revolving fund—to account for the cost of providing several types of self-insurance programs.

Fleet services fund—to account for the operations of a centralized maintenance facility for equipment.

Police garage fund—to account for the operation of a maintenance facility for police and other government vehicles.

Communication services fund—to account for the costs of providing graphic arts and telecommunications services.

Copy services fund—to account for the cost of providing copy services.

Warehouse revolving fund—to account for the operation of a centralized supply facility.

Fiduciary Funds   The final classification, the fiduciary funds account for assets that are held in a trustee capacity for external parties so that the money cannot be used to support the government's own programs. Like proprietary funds, all fiduciary funds use the economic resources measurement focus and accrual accounting for the timing of revenues and expenses. Because these assets are not used for the government, fiduciary funds are not included in government-wide financial statements but have separate statements within the fund-based financial statements.

Four distinct types of fiduciary funds can exist:

Investment Trust Funds   The first fund type accounts for the outside portion of investment pools where the reporting government has accepted funds from other governments to have more money to invest and, hopefully, earn a higher return.

Private-Purpose Trust Funds   The second fund type accounts for any monies held in a trustee capacity where principal and interest are for the benefit of external parties outside of the government such as individuals, private organizations, or other governments.

Pension Trust Funds   The third type accounts for an employee retirement system. Because of the need to provide adequate benefits for government workers, this fund type can grow to be quite large. The state of Alaska, as an example, reported assets of more than $9.8 billion in its pension trust fund at the end of 1996.

Agency Funds   The fourth type records any resources held by a government as an agent for individuals, private organizations, or other government units. Taxes and tolls, for example, are occasionally collected by one body on behalf of another. To ensure safety and control, this money should be separately maintained in an Agency Fund until transferred to the proper authority.

Coverage of Fund Accounting Procedures   The formal classification system just described is extremely useful in the financial reporting of a state or local government. However, a basic understanding of appropriate accounting procedures can best be achieved by setting up a matrix:

	Fund-based Financial Statements	**Government-wide Financial Statements**
Governmental funds	Use the current financial resources measurement focus and modified accrual accounting for the timing of revenue and expenditure recognition.	Use the economic resources measurement focus and accrual accounting for the timing of revenue and expense recognition.
Proprietary funds	Use the economic resources measurement focus and accrual accounting for the timing of revenue and expense recognition.	Use the economic resources measurement focus and accrual accounting for the timing of revenue and expense recognition.
Fiduciary funds	Use the economic resources measurement focus and accrual accounting for the timing of revenue and expense recognition.	Not applicable

The reporting process utilized by the governmental funds is examined in this chapter, both for the fund-based financial statements and government-wide financial statements. In the following chapter, accounting by the proprietary funds and the fiduciary funds will be analyzed along with the actual structure of both sets of financial statements.

OVERVIEW OF STATE AND LOCAL GOVERNMENT FINANCIAL STATEMENTS

Although we present a complete review of the financial statements of a state or local government in the following chapter, an overview of four basic financial statements is helpful here to illustrate how certain events are reported. These outlines are not complete but simply show how various accounts are presented.

Government-wide Financial Statements   Only two financial statements make up the governmental-wide financial statements: *the statement of net assets* and *the statement of activities.* Exhibit 16–1 shows the basic outline of a statement of net assets. Under the economic resources measurement focus used in the government-wide financial statements, all assets and liabilities are reported.

The final section of this statement, the Net Assets category, indicates (1) the amount of capital assets less related debt, (2) restrictions on any net assets, and (3) the total amount of unrestricted net assets. Note as mentioned earlier that, even in these government-wide financial statements, the assets of any fiduciary funds are not reported but are shown in a separate fund-based financial statement. The statements here only present the governmental activities (all governmental funds and most Internal Service Funds) and the business-type activities (any Enterprise Funds and remaining Internal Service Funds).

In Exhibit 16–2, the statement of activities shows the revenues and expenses, once again separated into governmental activities and business-type activities. Here, program revenues are amounts generated from the specific activity and are shown in more detail on the actual statement (as demonstrated in the subsequent chapter). Thus, the net profit or loss generated by each function can be seen horizontally while total expenses and total revenues can be determined vertically. General revenues not applicable to a particular function are reported at the bottom of the statement.

Fund-based Financial Statements   A number of fund-based financial statements are produced by a state or local government. However, at this introductory stage, only the

Exhibit 16–1
Statement of Net Assets—
Government-wide Financial
Statements

	Governmental Activities	Business-type Activities	Total
Assets			
Cash	$ 100	$ 130	$ 230
Investments	900	40	940
Receivables	600	400	1,000
Internal balances	50	(50)	–0–
Supplies and materials	30	40	70
Capital assets (net of depreciation)	2,950	2,750	5,700
Total assets	$4,630	$3,310	$7,940
Liabilities			
Accounts payable	$ 750	$ 230	$ 980
Noncurrent liabilities			
Due within one year	400	180	580
Due in more than one year	1,800	700	2,500
Total liabilities	$2,950	$1,110	$4,060
Net Assets			
Invested in capital assets, net of related debt	$1,410	$2,110	$3,520
Restricted for:			
Capital projects	50	–0–	50
Debt service	140	60	200
Unrestricted	80	30	110
Total net assets	$1,680	$2,200	$3,880

Exhibit 16–2   Statement of Activities—Government-wide Financial Statements

			Net (Expense) Revenue		
Function	Expenses	Program Revenues	Governmental Activities	Business-type Activities	Total
Governmental activities					
General government	$ 3,200	$ 1,400	$ (1,800)		$ (1,800)
Public safety	9,700	880	(8,820)		(8,820)
Public works	2,600	600	(2,000)		(2,000)
Education	8,400	300	(8,100)		(8,100)
Total governmental activities	$23,900	$ 3,180	$(20,720)		$(20,720)
Business-type activities					
Water	$ 3,600	$ 4,030		$ 430	$ 430
Sewer	4,920	5,610		690	690
Airport	2,300	3,120		820	820
Total business-type activities	$10,820	$12,760		$1,940	$ 1,940
Total government	$34,720	$15,940	$(20,720)	$1,940	$(18,780)
General revenues:					
Property taxes			$ 20,400		$ 20,400
Investment earnings			420	70	490
Transfers			600	(600)	0
Total general revenues and transfers			$ 21,420	$ (530)	$ 20,890
Change in net assets			$700	$1,410	$ 2,110
Beginning net assets			980	790	1,770
Ending net assets			$ 1,680	$2,200	$ 3,880

Exhibit 16-3   Balance Sheet—Governmental Funds
                       Fund-based Financial Statements

	General Fund	Library Program	Other Governmental Funds	Total Governmental Funds
Assets				
Cash	$ 40	$ 10	$ 50	$ 100
Investments	580	120	200	900
Receivables	120	200	210	530
Supplies and materials	10	10	10	30
Total assets	$750	$340	$470	$1,560
Liabilities				
Accounts payable	$230	$170	$110	$ 510
Notes payable	300	–0–	100	400
Total liabilities	$530	$170	$210	$ 910
Fund Balances				
Reserved for:				
Supplies	$ 10	$ 10	$ 10	$ 30
Encumbrances	120	30	40	190
Debt service	–0–	–0–	110	110
Unreserved:				
General fund	90	–0–	–0–	90
Special revenue fund	–0–	130	20	150
Capital projects fund	–0–	–0–	80	80
Total fund balances	$220	$170	$260	$ 650
Total liabilities and fund balances	$750	$340	$470	$1,560

two fundamental statements are presented that parallel the two government-wide statements just produced. First, in Exhibit 16–3, *a balance sheet* is shown for the governmental funds and then, in Exhibit 16–4, *a statement of revenues, expenditures, and changes in fund balances* is produced for the same governmental funds. Note that the figures here will not be the same as those presented for the governmental activities in the government-wide statement of net assets (Exhibit 16–1) and statement of activities (Exhibit 16–2) for three reasons:

1. Internal service funds are not included in these statements but in separate fund-based financial statements.
2. The current financial resources measurement basis is used instead of the economic resources measurement basis.
3. Modified accrual accounting is used to time revenues and expenditures rather than accrual accounting.

Because of these differences, a reconciliation should be reported between the governmental totals presented in Exhibits 16–1 and 16–3 as well as between Exhibits 16–2 and 16–4. Those reconciliations are shown in the following chapter.

For these fund-based financial statements, a separate column is required for the General Fund and every individual governmental fund that qualifies as major. Assume that the Library Program is the only fund within the Special Revenue Funds considered to be major.

Exhibit 16–4   Statement of Revenues, Expenditures, and Changes in Fund Balances—Governmental Funds
Fund-based Financial Statements

	General Fund	Library Program	Other Governmental Funds	Total Governmental Funds
Revenues				
Property taxes	$ 17,200	$ 900	$ 2,300	$20,400
Investment earnings	100	200	180	480
Program revenues	500	100	2,500	3,100
Total revenues	$ 17,800	$1,200	$ 4,980	$23,980
Expenditures				
Current:				
General government	$ 3,400	–0–	$ 100	$ 3,500
Public safety	5,100	–0–	400	5,500
Education	6,700	800	–0–	7,500
Debt service:				
Principal	–0–	–0–	1,000	1,000
Interest	–0–	–0–	600	600
Capital outlay	1,100	300	3,300	4,700
Total expenditures	$ 16,300	$1,100	$ 5,400	$22,800
Excess (deficiency) of revenues over expenditures	$ 1,500	$ 100	$ (420)	$ 1,180
Other Financing Sources (Uses)				
Bond proceeds	–0–	–0–	$ 1,000	$ 1,000
Transfers in	–0–	$ 20	580	600
Transfers out	$ (1,300)	–0–	$ (1,000)	(2,300)
Total other financing sources and uses	$ (1,300)	$ 20	$ 580	$ (700)
Change in fund balances	$200	$ 120	$ 160	$ 480
Fund balances—beginning	20	50	100	170
Fund balances—ending	$ 220	$ 170	$ 260	$ 650

The final fund-based financial statement shown here is found in Exhibit 16–4. The statement of revenues, expenditures, and changes in fund balances discloses the inflow and outflow of current financial resources into the governmental funds. Once again, a difference is seen here from the statement of activities in Exhibit 16–2 because only current financial resources are being measured, the modified accrual method is used to guide the timing of recognition, and no internal service funds are included.

ACCOUNTING FOR GOVERNMENTAL FUNDS

The remainder of this chapter presents many of the unique aspects of the accounting process utilized within the governmental funds: the General Fund, Special Revenue Funds, Capital Projects Funds, Debt Service Funds, and Permanent Funds. Because of the dual nature of the reporting required by *GASB Statement Number 34,* much of this accounting must be demonstrated twice. For the traditional fund-based financial statements, the current financial resources measurement focus requires events to be viewed in one particular manner. However, in creating government-wide financial statements that utilize the economic resources measurement focus, most recording procedures are different to correspond to the financial accounting utilized by for-profit enterprises.

For organizational purposes, coverage of the accounting appropriate for governmental funds includes the following discussions, events, and transactions:

- The importance of budgets and the recording of budgetary entries.
- The purpose of, and accounting for, encumbrances.
- The recognition of expenditures and expenses.
- The recognition of revenues.
- The issuance of bonds and other debts.
- The accounting for special assessment projects.
- The recording of interfund transactions.

Each of these elements is an important aspect of the accounting process for the governmental funds of a state or local government. Knowledge of the reporting of each of these elements is an essential beginning step in understanding governmental accounting.

The Importance of Budgets and the Recording of Budgetary Entries

"Financing is an important part of the governmental environment, particularly for governmental type activities. For those activities, the budget is the primary method of directing and controlling the financial process."[17] In a chronological sense, the first significant accounting procedure encountered in a state or locality is the recording of budgetary entries. To enhance accountability, government officials normally are required to adopt an annual budget for each separate activity to anticipate the inflow of financial resources and establish approved expenditure levels. In its "Objectives of Financial Reporting," the GASB indicates that the budget serves several important purposes:

1. Expresses public policy. If, for example, more money is budgeted for child care and less for the environment, the citizens are made aware of the decision that has been made to allocate limited government resources.
2. Serves as an expression of financial intent for the upcoming fiscal year. The budget presents the financial plan for the government for the period.
3. Provides control because authorized spending limitations are established.
4. Offers a means of evaluating performance by allowing a comparison between actual results and the levels of funding found in the budget.

The GASB even states that "many believe the budget is the most significant financial document produced by a government unit."[18]

Once a budget has been produced and enacted into law, formal accounting recognition is frequently required as a means of enhancing the benefits just described. In this way, the public is given the opportunity to learn of the expected amounts to be received and the expenditures to be made with these financial resources. Reporting revenue projections as well as compliance with spending limitations is considered essential for government accountability. Therefore, the approved budget figures are entered into the accounting records formally at the start of each fiscal year. Citizens can then draw comparisons between actual and budgeted figures at any interim point during the period.

To enhance the importance of the information conveyed by budget figures, each government must report comparisons between the original budget, the final budget, and actual figures for the period as required supplemental information presented after the notes to its financial statements. This budget information must be presented for the General Fund and each major fund within the Special Revenue Funds. As an alterna-

[17]*GASB Statement No. 11*, para. 9.

[18]*GASB Concepts Statement No. 1*, para. 19.

tive, the information can be shown as a separate statement within the government's fund-based financial statements which was the method employed prior to *GASB Statement Number 34*. This official pronouncement defines a "major" fund as:

> The reporting government's main operating fund (the general fund or its equivalent) should always be reported as a major fund. Other individual governmental and enterprise funds should be reported in separate columns as major funds based on these criteria:
>
> a. Total assets, liabilities, revenues, or expenditures/expenses of that individual governmental or enterprise fund are at least 10 percent of the corresponding total (assets, liabilities, and so forth) for all funds of that category or type (that is, total governmental or total enterprise funds), *and*
>
> b. Total assets, liabilities, revenues, or expenditures/expenses of the individual governmental fund or enterprise fund are at least 5 percent of the corresponding total for all governmental and enterprise funds combined.
>
> In addition to funds that meet the major fund criteria, any other governmental or enterprise fund that the government's officials believe is particularly important to financial statement users (for example, because of public interest or consistency) may be reported as a major fund.[19]

As an illustration, assume that a city enacts a motel excise tax to promote tourism and conventions. Because the funding is legally restricted for this specified purpose, a separate Special Revenue Fund is established. Assume further that for the 2001 fiscal year an estimation is made that $490,000 in revenues will be generated by the tax. Based on this projection, the city council authorizes the expenditure of $400,000 (referred to as an *appropriation*) for programs during the current year. Of this amount, $200,000 is designated for salaries, $30,000 for utilities, $80,000 for advertising, and $90,000 for supplies. The $90,000 difference between the anticipated inflow and this appropriation is a budgeted surplus accumulated by the government in case the levy proves to be too small or for future use. To highlight the council's action, the following journal entry is included in the accounting records of this fund. Because this information falls outside of both the fund-based financial statements and the government-wide financial statements, it is made using the budgetary basis applied by the reporting entity.

Special Revenue Fund—Tourism and Convention Promotions

Estimated Revenues—Tax Levy	490,000	
Appropriations—Salaries		200,000
Appropriations—Utilities		30,000
Appropriations—Advertising		80,000
Appropriations—Supplies		90,000
Fund Balance		90,000

To record annual budget for tourism and convention promotions.

This entry indicates the source of the funding (the tax revenue) as well as the approved amount of expenditures. The Fund Balance account indicates the presence of an anticipated surplus (or, in some cases, a shortage) projected for the period. Here, the size of the fund is expected to increase by $90,000 during the year.

Each of these figures remains within the records of this Special Revenue Fund for the entire year to allow for planning and control. Citizens can see how much is to be spent for these programs and the source of this funding.

Use of budgetary entries is also one method by which readers can be made aware of interperiod equity. This concept is designed to measure whether spending and revenues are in alignment for a period or whether money has to be borrowed to fund current expenditures, debt that will be paid back by future citizens. If revenues are projected as $10 million but expenditures are budgeted at $11 million, the extra million must be paid for in some manner, usually by debt to be repaid in the future. "Financial reporting

---

[19]*GASB Statement No. 34*, para. 76.

should help users assess whether current-year revenues are sufficient to pay for services provided that year and whether future taxpayers will be required to assume burdens for services previously provided.[20]

The original budget is not always the final appropriations budget for the year. For example, extra money may become available and government officials may vote to increase appropriations. Assume, to illustrate, that officials in charge of tourism for this city make an appeal during the year for an additional $50,000 to create a special advertising campaign. If properly approved, the original budgetary entry must be adjusted:

Special Revenue Fund—Tourism and Convention Promotions

Fund Balance	50,000	
Appropriations—Advertising		50,000
To record additional appropriation for advertising.		

If this activity meets the criteria for a major fund, budgetary data for the year is included as required supplemental information with the financial statements of this city. Assume that $488,000 was actually received during the year and $437,000 spent as follows:

Salaries	$196,000
Utilities	29,000
Advertising	125,000
Supplies	87,000

This information should be reported as follows. The variance column is recommended but not required:

Tourism and Convention Promotions
Year ended December 31, 2001
Budget Comparison Schedule

	Budgeted Amounts		Actual Amounts (Budgetary Basis)	Variance with Final Budget—Positive (Negative)
	Original	Final		
Resources (Inflows):				
Tax levy	$490,000	$490,000	$488,000	$ (2,000)
Charges to appropriations (Outflows):				
Salaries	$200,000	$200,000	$196,000	$ 4,000
Utilities	30,000	30,000	29,000	1,000
Advertising	80,000	130,000	125,000	5,000
Supplies	90,000	90,000	87,000	3,000
Total charges	$400,000	$450,000	$437,000	$ 13,000
Change in fund balance	$ 90,000	$ 40,000	$ 51,000	$ 11,000

Because of the numerous activities encompassed by the General Fund (or any other fund), the accounting system is often designed to utilize subsidiary ledgers so that each balance can be identified separately by specific function. For example, the overall budget for the General Fund could include revenue projections and approved spending limitations for scores of diverse activities such as the school system, garbage collection, and the fire department. To facilitate the recording process, control accounts can be maintained in the general ledger with balances that are explained elsewhere in the system using individual subsidiary ledgers.

---

[20]*GASB Concepts Statement No. 1*, para. 61.

As an illustration, assume that a city estimates all General Fund revenues for the current year will equal $1,640,000 while spending levels of $1,180,000 have been set by the city council. Transfers to other funds (referred to as an other financing use since the money does not leave the government) totaling $400,000 have also been approved. These budgeted totals are entered into the General Fund. Simultaneously, separate subsidiary ledgers record detailed information to list the actual source of anticipated revenues (such as property taxes, income taxes, sales taxes, tolls, licenses, and the like) and the individual appropriations and approved transfers. The accounting system is accumulating information both in total and by separate functions.

General Fund (beginning of year)

Estimated Revenues Control	1,640,000	
Appropriations Control............................		1,180,000
Estimated Other Financing Uses—Operating Transfers Out		400,000
Fund Balance		60,000

To record legally adopted operating budget for the General Fund with separate subsidiary ledger accounts used by the government to explain individual revenues and appropriations.

The budget figures remain in the accounting records for informational purposes throughout the period. They are ultimately removed at the end of the fiscal year through a simple reversal of the amended entry. In this manner, budgetary entries create no permanent impact on the accounting system but still serve in a control capacity throughout the year.

In some governmental funds, budgets need not be recorded if oversight can be established by alternative means. Formal budgetary entries, for example, are normally omitted from Debt Service Funds. All activities of this particular fund type (accumulation of financial resources and payment of long-term debts and interest) are governed by contractual provision. Budget entries would provide little additional control or other informational value; thus, accounting recognition is not warranted. Likewise, in Permanent Funds, a budget is not normally necessary because spending is legally restricted by the person or organization conveying the funds to the government.

Conversely, the recording of a budget is optional in reporting Capital Projects Funds. This fund type accounts for the construction and acquisition of projects that in some instances consist of no more than a simple contractual arrangement. A city, as an example, might hire an independent contractor to construct a sidewalk. In such cases, a signed contract usually sets the legal level of expenditure; thus, a budgetary entry is not necessary. However, if the government unit is building a major facility (such as a fire station) or if a number of contractors are involved in a single project, the inclusion of budgetary entries may be helpful to accentuate planning and control.

Encumbrances

One additional budgetary procedure that plays a central role in this system is the recording of financial commitments referred to as *encumbrances. In diametric contrast to for-profit accounting, purchase commitments and contracts are recorded in the governmental funds prior to becoming legal liabilities.* Encumbrance accounting is appropriate in any governmental fund. Maintaining a record of these encumbrances provides an additional means of controlling fund spending. At any point during the fiscal year, information on both expended and committed funds is available. "An encumbrance accounting system acts as an early warning device. By controlling expenditure commitments, the government significantly reduces the opportunity to overexpend an appropriation."[21]

---

[21]Government Finance Officers Association, *Governmental Accounting, Auditing, and Financial Reporting* (Chicago: 1988), p. 17.

To illustrate, assume that the police department of a city orders $18,000 in supplies. As an ongoing service activity, the police department is accounted for within the General Fund. Since only an order has been made and no transaction has occurred, a for-profit business would make no entry at this point. However, this amount of the government's financial resources has been committed even though no formal liability exists until the supplies are received. To control against spending more than has been appropriated, this commitment is physically recorded through the following journal entry whenever a purchase order, contract, or other formal commitment is made by one of the governmental funds.

Fund-based Financial Statements

General Fund—Police Department

Encumbrances Control	18,000	
Fund Balance—Reserved for Encumbrances		18,000
To record an order that was placed for supplies.		

The Encumbrances account records the commitment that has been incurred while the Fund Balance account is an equity-type balance indicating the amount of the city's assets required to fulfill future obligations.

Although this commitment to use current financial resources appears on the fund-based financial statements, it does not appear in the government-wide statements. Because no liability has been incurred by the government, no entry is made for this second set of financial statements.

When the preceding items are received, the commitment is replaced by a legal liability. Hence, the encumbrance is removed from the accounting records and an Inventory of Supplies account (or an Expenditure account if the purchases method rather than the consumption method is in use) is recognized. (We describe these methods later in this chapter.) Often, because of sales taxes, freight costs, or other price adjustments, the actual invoice total differs from the estimated figure recorded at the time the order was processed. For this reason, the expenditure does not necessarily agree with the corresponding encumbrance. Assume, for illustration purposes, that the supplies received here are accompanied by an invoice for $18,160.

Fund-based Financial Statements

General Fund

Fund Balance—Reserved for Encumbrances	18,000	
Encumbrances Control		18,000
To remove encumbrance for supplies that have now been received.		
Inventory of Supplies (or Expenditures—Supplies)	18,160	
Vouchers Payable		18,160
To record the receipt of supplies and the accompanying liability.		

In producing government-wide financial statements, the only entry created by this ordering and receiving of supplies would be an increase in the asset and the liability when legal title is received.

A problem arises for any encumbrances that are not filled by the end of the year. In such cases, the commitment simply lapses and the entry creating the encumbrance is reversed off the financial records. However, in many cases, a government chooses to honor these commitments even though the financial resources must come from a subsequent period. From an accounting perspective, a government can reflect this type of commitment in several ways. Assume, for example, that the above supplies are not received in the year of order but rather in the subsequent period. One approach would be to take the following steps:

■   At the end of the first year, the Encumbrance entry is reversed to remove the commitment from the financial records.

- On the year-end balance sheet, $18,000 of the ending fund balance is presented as "reserved for encumbrances" rather than as "unrestricted." In this manner, the reader can see that this amount of financial resources needs to be held to fulfill a commitment that has been made.

- At the start of the subsequent year, the Encumbrance entry is returned to the records to monitor the committed resources.

- When an Expenditure is recorded for these supplies, the $18,000 balance can be shown as a Year One balance while the additional amount paid is a Year Two Expenditure.

Recognition of Expenditures for Operations and Capital Additions

Although budgetary entries are unique, their impact on the accounting process is somewhat limited because they do not directly affect a fund's financial results for the period. Conversely, the method by which a state or locality records the receipt and disbursement of resources can significantly alter the entire complexion of the reported data. For example, because a primary emphasis in the governmental funds is on the measurement of changes in current financial resources, *neither expenses nor capital assets are recorded.*

Instead, an Expenditures account reflects any outflow or reduction of net financial resources from the acquisition of a good or service (or some other utility). A subsidiary ledger (or a system of separate accounts) normally identifies the exact reason for each change, but the actual decrease is recorded as an expenditure whether it is for rent, a fire truck, salaries, or a computer. As shown in Exhibit 16–4, this method of recording allows the reader to see the utilization of an activity's current financial resources. Spending $1,000 for electricity for the past three months is an expenditure of a fund's financial resources in exactly the same way that buying a $70,000 ambulance is.

Fund-based Financial Statements

Expenditures—Electricity	1,000	
Vouchers (or Accounts) Payable.....................		1,000
To record charges covering the past three months.		
Expenditures—Ambulance.............................	70,000	
Vouchers (or Accounts) Payable.....................		70,000
To record acquisition of new ambulance.		

Within the governmental funds, expenditures (and revenues) are recognized on the *modified accrual basis* of accounting. For expenditures, modified accrual accounting requires recognition to be made when a claim against current financial resources is created. "The measurement focus of governmental fund accounting is on *expenditures*—decreases in net financial resources—rather than expenses. Most expenditures and transfers out are measurable and should be recorded when the related liability is incurred."[22]

The recording of expenditures rather than expenses and capital assets is one of the most distinctive characteristics of traditional governmental accounting. A for-profit business enterprise that purchases a building or a machine capitalizes all related costs and then recognizes depreciation expense during each year of the asset's useful life. This depreciation is a factor in the computation of the organization's annual net income.

In contrast, a governmental fund records the entire cost of all buildings, machines, and other capital assets as expenditures. The outflow of current financial resources is important and is reflected in the statement of revenues, expenditures, and changes in fund balance (Exhibit 16–4) of the fund-based financial statements. No income figure

---

[22]GASB Cod. Sec. 1600.117.

is computed for these funds; thus, the computation and recording of subsequent depreciation is not relevant to the reporting process and is omitted entirely.

For the government-wide financial statement, all economic resources are being measured and accrual accounting is utilized. Consequently, the previous two journal entries would be changed to:

Government-wide Financial Statements

Utilities Expense......................................	1,000	
Voucher (or Accounts) Payable		1,000
To record electricity charges for the past three months.		
Ambulance	70,000	
Voucher (or Accounts) Payable		70,000
To record acquisition of new ambulance.		

Capital Assets and Fund-based Financial Statements   One interesting result of measuring and reporting only expenditures within the governmental funds is that virtually no assets are recorded other than financial resources such as cash, receivables, and investments. All capital assets such as buildings, equipment, vehicles, and the like have been recorded as expenditures at the time of purchase and then closed out at the end of the fiscal period.

With the creation of *GASB Statement Number 34,* a record of all capital assets can be found in the statement of net assets (see Exhibit 16–1) within the government-wide financial statements. Thus, recording only Expenditures in the fund-based financial statements does not leave a gap in the information being presented. However, prior to *Statement 34,* a record of the capital assets could not be found within the governmental funds. At that time, to disclose information, a separate account group was maintained for such assets (as well as for the long-term liabilities of the governmental funds). These two account groups (the General Fixed Assets Account Group and the General Long-term Debt Account Group) were no more than a listing of the individual accounts, balances not otherwise recorded or presented by the traditional accounting model. *Statement Number 34* eliminated the need for these two account groups since fixed assets and long-term liabilities are reported in the government-wide statements.

In conversion to the production of government-wide financial statements, officials can simply take the cost of fixed assets found in the General Fixed Assets Account Group (or fair market value for donated items) to determine the initial asset balances to be reported. One problem, though, is the initial reporting of "infrastructure" assets. These assets include roads, sidewalks, bridges, and the like that are normally stationary and can be preserved for a significant period of time. A bridge, for example, might last for more than 100 years. Traditionally, the recording of infrastructure assets within the General Fixed Assets Account Group was optional. To save time and energy, many governments simply did not record such assets after the initial expenditure was recorded. Thus, in creating government-wide financial statements, records may well be unavailable for some or all of the infrastructure assets that have been bought or constructed over the years.

Because of the problem of establishing initial balances for infrastructure assets, the GASB made an exception in the reporting of government-wide financial statements. After adopting *Statement 34,* infrastructure assets bought or built must be capitalized. However, an additional four years beyond the date when *Statement 34* becomes effective is allowed to establish the capitalization of previous infrastructure assets. In this manner, government officials are given additional time to arrive at cost figures for miles of highways, curbing, sidewalks, and the like. If accurate information is not available within the accounting system, the GASB does suggest methods by which these costs may be approximated for reporting purposes. For example, current costs for such projects can be determined and then adjusted for inflation and usage since the assets were originally obtained.

DISCUSSION QUESTION

Is It an Asset or a Liability?

In the August 1989 issue of the *Journal of Accountancy*, R. K. Mautz discusses the unique reporting needs of governments and not-for-profit organizations (such as charities) in "Not-For-Profit Financial Reporting: Another View." As an illustration of their accounting problems, Mautz examines the method by which a city should record a newly constructed high school building. Conventional business wisdom would say that such a property represents an asset of the government. Thus, the cost should be capitalized and then depreciated over an estimated useful life. However, in paragraph 26 of FASB *Concepts Statements No. 6*, an essential characteristic of an asset is "a probable future benefit . . . to contribute directly or indirectly to future cash inflows."

Mautz reasons that the school building cannot be considered an asset since it provides no net contribution to cash inflows. In truth, a high school requires the government to make significant cash outflows for maintenance, repairs, utilities, salaries, and the like. Public educational facilities (as well as most of the other properties of a government such as a fire station or municipal building) are acquired with the understanding that net cash outflows will result.

Consequently, Mautz considers whether the construction of a high school is not actually the incurrence of a liability since the government is taking on an obligation that will necessitate future cash payments. This idea also is rejected, once again based on the guidance of *Concepts Statement No. 6* (paragraph 36), because the cash outflow is not required at a "specified or determinable date, on occurrence of a specified event, or on demand."

Is a high schools building an asset or is it a liability? If it is neither, how should the cost be recorded? Prior to adoption of *GASB Statement Number 34*, how would a government have reported a high school building? After adoption of *Statement 34*, how would a government report a high school building? Which of these two approaches provides the best portrayal of the decision to acquire or construct this building? Can a government be accounted for in the same manner as a for-profit enterprise?

In fund-based financial statements, depreciation expense has never been needed in connection with governmental funds for two reasons:

1. These funds recorded expenditures rather than expenses and the entire cost of the asset was reported as an expenditure at the time of the original claim against current financial resources. Thus, the impact of the acquisition was recorded when obtained so that reporting a Depreciation Expense account would measure the impact twice—once when acquired and once when depreciated.

2. These funds traditionally do not record expenses. Thus, the reporting of depreciation expense (rather than an expenditure) is not consistent with measuring the change in current financial resources.

However, the government-wide financial statements list assets rather than expenditures so that depreciation is appropriate. Consequently, on these new financial statements, depreciation on all long-lived assets other than land should be calculated and reported each period.

Supplies and Prepaid Items   In gathering information for government-wide financial statements, the acquisition of items such as supplies and prepaid costs like rent or insurance is not particularly complicated. An asset is recorded at the time of acquisition and then subsequently reclassified to an expense account as the utility of the asset is consumed. However, in the fund-based financial statements, handling is not so clear. Such assets are neither current financial resources that can be expended nor are they capital assets to be reported immediately as expenditures. Supplies and prepaid items are not current financial resources but they do impact day-to-day operations. Thus, neither method of recording utilized for fund-based statements seems to apply exactly.

Traditionally, supplies and prepaid items have been recorded as expenditures at the point in time that a liability is created. No asset is initially recorded because neither supplies nor prepaid items (such as rent or insurance) can be expended. For reporting purposes, though, materials or prepayments that remain at year's end must be entered into the accounting records as assets prior to production of financial statements. This adjustment is created by utilizing an equity balance with a title such as Fund Balance Reserved for Inventory of Supplies (or Prepaid Items). This account indicates that an asset is being reported but it is not available for spending purposes.

This traditional approach, referred to as the *purchases method,* is based on the modified accrual method of accounting. The expenditure is recorded when the claim to current financial resources is first incurred. However, many governments choose to measure supplies expenditures on an alternative method, the *consumption method.*

The consumption method parallels the process that would be applied by a for-profit business. Any supplies or prepayments are recorded as assets when acquired. Subsequently, as the items are consumed by usage or over time, the cost is reclassified into an Expenditures account. Therefore, under this approach, the expenditure is matched with the period of specific usage. Because an account reported in the asset section cannot be spent for government programs or other needs, a portion of the Fund Balance account should be reclassified as Reserved for Inventory of Supplies as is shown in Exhibit 16–3.

As an illustration, assume that $20,000 in supplies is purchased by a municipality for various General Fund activities. During the remainder of the period, $18,000 of this amount is used so that only $2,000 remains at year's end. These events could be recorded through either of the following sets of entries:

Fund-based Financial Statements

Purchases Method

Expenditures—Supplies	20,000	
Vouchers Payable		20,000
To record purchase of supplies for various ongoing activities.		
Inventory of Supplies	2,000	
Fund Balance—Reserved for Inventory of Supplies		2,000
To record supplies remaining at year's end.		

Consumption Method

Inventory of Supplies	20,000	
Vouchers Payable		20,000
To record purchase of supplies for various ongoing activities.		
Expenditures—Control.	18,000	
Inventory of Supplies		18,000
To record consumption of supplies during period.		

Because a $2,000 asset remains that cannot be spent, that portion of the Fund Balance should be reclassified as being Reserved for Inventory of Supplies.

Recognition of Revenues—Overview

The recognition of revenues has always posed a problem for state and local government units. For most revenues, such as property taxes, income taxes, and grants, no earning process exists in the same manner as is encountered in a for-profit business. Property taxes are not "earned" and neither are income taxes nor many other sources of government funds. Taxes, fines, and the like are assessed or imposed on the citizens to support the operations of the government.

For decades, state and local government units have used a modified accrual system to determine the proper timing of revenue recognition. Under this approach to reporting, such revenues were recognized at the point in time when they were both measurable and available. The term *measurable* meant subject to a reasonable estimation whereas *available* indicated that the resulting financial resources would be received within the fiscal period or soon enough thereafter to pay current claims. In practice, these two criteria meant that revenues were rarely recognized prior to being received because most revenues were either not measurable or available until collected. Consequently, modified accrual accounting frequently resembled a cash accounting system. One major exception was property taxes which were normally accrued when levied based on an estimation of the amounts to be collected using historical data. For this reason, modified accrual accounting required most revenue recognition to occur when cash was collected while property taxes were accrued when levied.

In December 1998 the GASB released its *Statement Number 33,* "Accounting and Financial Reporting for Nonexchange Transactions," to provide a comprehensive system for recognizing the wide array of revenues applicable to state and local government units. This statement did not apply to true revenues such as interest or rents where an earning process exists. Instead, the GASB concentrated on "nonexchange transactions," a classification that would encompass most taxes, fines, grants, and the like because the government does not have to provide a direct and equal benefit for the amount received.

> In a nonexchange transaction, a government (including the federal government, as a provider) either gives value (benefit) to another party without directly receiving equal value in exchange or receives value (benefit) from another party without directly giving equal value in exchange.[23]

For organizational purposes, the GASB classified all such nonexchange transactions into four distinct classifications, each with its own rules as to proper recognition:

- *Derived tax revenues.* Income taxes and sales taxes are the best example of this type of revenue. In a derived tax revenue transaction, a tax assessment is imposed because an underlying exchange takes place. A sale occurs and a tax is imposed, or income is earned and an income tax is assessed.

- *Imposed nonexchange revenues.* Property taxes and fines and penalties are viewed as imposed nonexchange revenues because the government imposes an assessment but no underlying transaction exists. Real estate or other property is owned and a property tax is levied each period. Ownership is being taxed by the government and not a specific transaction.

- *Government-mandated nonexchange transactions.* This category is used for monies such as grants that are conveyed from one government to another to help pay for the costs of required programs. For example, if a state specifies that a city must create a homeless shelter and then provides a grant of $400,000 to help defray the cost, that money should be recorded using these prescribed rules because the final goal for the money has been mandated by the state. City officials have no choice; the state government has required the shelter to be constructed and provided part or all of the funding.

- *Voluntary nonexchange transactions.* In this final classification, money has been conveyed willingly to the state or local government by an individual, another government, or an organization usually for a particular purpose. For example, assume that a state grants a city $300,000 to help improve reading programs in its schools. Unless the state has mandated an improvement in these reading programs, this grant would be accounted for as a voluntary nonexchange transaction. The decision has been made that use of the money will provide an important benefit but no government requirement exists led to the conveyance.

---

[23]*GASB Statement No. 33,* "Accounting and Financial Reporting for Nonexchange Transactions," December 1998, para. 7.

Derived Tax Revenues Such as Income Taxes and Sales Taxes

Accounting for derived tax revenues is relatively straightforward. According to *GASB Statement Number 33,* these revenues are normally recognized in government-wide financial statements when the underlying transaction has occurred. Thus, when income is earned by a taxpayer, the government should record the income tax revenue. Likewise, when a sale is made, the government should recognize the resulting sales tax revenue. Obviously, a government cannot make an entry every time that income is earned or a sale made. For convenience, recognition of such revenues is normally made when information becomes available.

Assume, for example, that sales within a government amount to $10 million for 2001 and a sales tax of 4 percent is assessed. In the period in which the sales are made, the following entry is required. The amounts should be reported net of any estimated refunds or uncollectible balances.

Government-wide Financial Statements

Receivable—Sales Taxes	400,000	
Revenue—Sales Taxes		400,000

To recognize amount of sales tax that will be collected in
connection with sales for the current period.

In the above entry, if—because of the nature of the tax or assessment—cash is received prior to the occurrence of the underlying exchange, a deferred revenue (liability) is recognized initially. Later, when the underlying exchange occurs, this liability is reclassified as a revenue.

For fund-based financial statements, the above rules are also used except for one additional requirement that the resources must be available before the revenue can be recognized. In that way, the essence of modified accrual accounting is still being utilized at the fund level of reporting.

A separate issue is raised with any tax revenue if government officials have specified that a certain use must be made of the resources. For example, in the above entry, assume that the city government has stated that 25 percent of the tax must be used for park beautification. Thus, $100,000 will have to be spent in this designated fashion. According to *Statement Number 33,* such purpose restrictions are only disclosed in the financial statements by reclassifying an appropriate amount of the fund balance or equity to disclose the intended usage. As indicated here, revenue recognition is not altered:

> Purpose restrictions do not affect the timing of recognition for any class of nonexchange transactions. Rather, recipients of resources with purpose restrictions should report resulting net assets (or equity or fund balance, as appropriate) as restricted until the resources are used for the specified purpose or for as long as the provider requires the resources to be maintained intact (for example, endowment principal.)"[24]

Consequently, in the statement of net assets for the government-wide financial statements (as shown in Exhibit 16–1), $100 000 should be reported in the net assets section as restricted for park beautification. A similar treatment is proper for the balance sheet created according to the fund-based financial statements (as shown in Exhibit 16–3) except that the amount is shown as a separate fund balance figure reserved for park beautification.

If a revenue is recognized and a purpose restriction is not fulfilled, the money will probably have to be returned based on the requirements. In such a situation, if the return is made in a subsequent period, the government should recognize an expense rather than a revenue reduction.

---

[24]*GASB Statement No. 33,* "Accounting and Financial Reporting for Nonexchange Transactions," para. 14.

Imposed Nonexchange Revenues Such as Property Taxes and Fines

Accounting for imposed nonexchange revenues is a bit more complicated than derived tax revenues because no underlying transaction is present to guide the timing of the revenue recognition. Thus, the GASB held that the *asset* should be recorded when the government first had an enforceable legal claim (or when the cash is received if a prepayment is being made). For the *revenue* side of the transaction, according to paragraph 103, recognition should be made in the time "period when resources are required to be used or the first period that use is permitted."

Because the government imposes such taxes, the period for which the proceeds are to be used is normally specified. That period of use identifies the period of revenue recognition. If a tax is assessed and usage is not allowed for five years, a deferred revenue is recognized until the time restriction passes.

For property taxes, which are the largest source of income for many governments, revenue recognition is for the period for which the taxes are levied. Assume, for example, that a city assesses $900,000 in property taxes on the first day of the year and expects to collect $830,000. The initial entry for either set of financial statements would be as follows:

Property Tax Receivable..............................	900,000	
Allowance for Uncollectible Taxes		70,000
Revenues—Property Taxes..........................		830,000
To record assessment of property taxes for the current year.		

Government-mandated Nonexchange Transactions and Voluntary Nonexchange Transactions

Although these two sources of revenues are identified separately, the timing of accounting recognition is the same so that they are frequently discussed together. These grants and other revenue sources are recognized by the government when all eligibility requirements have been met. Until eligibility has been established, some degree of uncertainty exists that precludes recognition. Thus, in government-wide financial statements, revenue recognition occurs at the time of eligibility even if the money is actually received earlier. For fund-based financial statements, the amounts must also be available for revenue recognition, once again in the same manner as modified accrual accounting.

GASB Statement Number 33 divides all eligibility requirements into the following four general classifications. All applicable requirements must be met before revenues can be recorded from either government-mandated nonexchange transactions or voluntary nonexchange transactions.

1. *Required characteristics of the recipients.* In many programs, the unit receiving funds is provided with standards that have to be met in advance. For example, assume that a state grant has been awarded to a city to help teach all kindergarten children in its school system to read. However, as part of this program, state law has been changed to mandate that all kindergarten teachers must become properly accredited. Hence, the grant will not be conveyed to the city until all kindergarten teachers have achieved accreditation. The city must conform to state law first. Because of this requirement by the state, revenue recognition should be delayed until the final teacher has qualified.

2. *Time requirements.* Programs can specify when money is to be used. To illustrate, assume that in April, a state provides a grant to a city so that milk can be bought for each child during the subsequent school year starting in September. When should the grant be recognized as revenue? Recognition should be in the period of use or in the period when use of the funds is first permitted.

3. *Reimbursement.* Many grants and other programs are designed to reimburse a designated government for amounts appropriately spent. These arrangements are often called "expenditure-driven" programs. For example, assume that the state informs a locality that it will reimburse the city government for money paid to provide milk to school children who could not otherwise afford it. In such cases, no revenue is recognized until the money is spent. Thus, the expense should equal the amount of revenue recognized.

4. *Contingencies.* In voluntary nonexchange transactions (but not in government-mandated nonexchange transactions), revenue may be withheld until a specified action is taken. A grant might be given to buy park equipment, for example, but only after an appropriate piece of land has been acquired for the park. Until the lot is obtained, a contingency exists and the revenue should not be recognized.

To aid in understanding the appropriate timing of revenue recognition, page 48 of *GASB Statement Number 33* provides the chart in Exhibit 16–5 to outline the criteria for each classification of revenue.

Exhibit 16–5   Classes and Timing of Recognition of Nonexchange Transactions

Class	Recognition
Derived tax revenues Examples: sales taxes, personal and corporate income taxes, motor fuel taxes, and similar taxes on earnings or consumption	**Assets*** Period when *underlying exchange has occurred* or when resources are received, whichever is first. **Revenues** Period when *underlying exchange has occurred.* (Report advance receipts as deferred revenues.) When modified accrual accounting is used, resources *also* should be "available."
Imposed nonexchange revenues Examples: property taxes, most fines and forfeitures	**Assets*** Period when an *enforceable legal claim has arisen* or when resources are received, whichever is first. **Revenues** Period when *resources are required to be used* or first period that use is permitted (for example, for property taxes, the *period for which levied*). When modified accrual accounting is used, resources also should be "available." (For property taxes, apply NCGA Interpretation 3, as amended.)
Government-mandated nonexchange transactions Examples: federal government mandates on state and local governments **Voluntary nonexchange transactions** Examples: certain grants and entitlements, most donations	**Assets* and liabilities** Period when *all eligibility requirements have been met* or (for asset recognition) when resources are received, whichever is first. **Revenues and expenses or expenditures** Period when *all eligibility requirements have been met.* (Report advance receipts or payments for use in the following period as deferred revenues or advances, respectively. However, when a provider precludes the sale, disbursement, or consumption of resources for a specified number of years, until a specified event has occurred, or permanently[for example, permanent and term endowments], report revenues and expenses or expenditures when the resources are, respectively, received or paid and report resulting net assets, equity, or fund balance as restricted.) When modified accrual accounting is used for revenue recognition, resources also should be "available."

*If there are purpose restrictions, report restricted net assets (or equity or fund balance) or, for governmental funds, a reservation of fund balance.

Issuance of Bonds

Although not a revenue, the issuance of bonds serves as a major source of funding for many state and local governments. Proceeds from such sales may be used for many purposes, including general financing and a wide variety of construction projects. As of June 30,1998, the city of Des Moines, Iowa, had approximately $400 million of long-term debts outstanding. Of that amount, $233.2 million was general long-term debts whereas $165.7 million was for various proprietary funds. At December 31,1998, the city of Saint Paul, Minnesota, had over $356.7 million in bonds payable outstanding.

Because the proceeds of a bond have to be repaid, no revenues are recognized under either method of financial reporting. In the government-wide financial statements, the reporting is quite easy: The cash and the debt are both increased to reflect the issuance. Conversely, in the fund-based financial statements, recording is not so simple since the debt is not a claim on current financial resources. Thus, the inflow is neither a revenue nor a debt to be reported.

Assume, for example, that the town of Ruark sells $5 million in general obligation bonds to finance the construction of a new school building. Because of the purpose of this action, a Capital Projects Fund is designated to receive the cash. To emphasize that this money is not derived from a revenue, a special designation, *Other Financing Sources,* is utilized. Note in Exhibit 16–4, the placement of Other Financing Sources (Uses) at the bottom of statement of revenues, expenditures, and changes in fund balance to indicate changes in the amount of financial resources that were created through transactions other than revenues and expenditures.

Thus, the following journal entry would be needed to reflect the sale of these bonds:

Fund-based Financial Statements

Capital Projects Funds—School Building

Cash	5,000,000	
Other Financing Sources—Bond Proceeds		5,000,000
To record issuance of bonds to finance construction project.		

Although an inflow of cash into this fund has taken place, no revenue has been generated. However, in the same manner as a revenue, Other Financing Sources is a measurement account that is closed out at the end of the year. As shown in the above entry, the $5 million liability is completely omitted from the Capital Projects Funds. Since the governmental funds stress accountability for the inflows and outflows of financial resources, recognition of long-term debts in these funds has traditionally been considered inappropriate. For example, a look at the balance sheet in Exhibit 16–3 shows no long-term liabilities at all for the governmental funds, only claims to current financial resources.

GASB Statement Number 34 now provides information about such long-term debts as can be seen in the statement of net assets found in Exhibit 16–1. Prior to this pronouncement, though, a method had to be devised to report the long-term liabilities incurred by the governmental funds. A separate account group, termed the General Long-Term Debt Account Group, maintained and reported a list of these debts. As with the General Fixed-Assets Account Group, this system was devised to report balances that did not impact current financial resources. Because of the change in reporting, both of these account groups will no longer be necessary.

Payment of Long-Term Liabilities   The payment of long-term liabilities once again brings up the huge differences between the government-wide financial statements and the fund-based financial statements. For the government-wide financial statements, payment of principal and interest is the same as would be encountered in a for-profit organization. Conversely, for the fund-based statements, an Expenditure account is recognized for the debt and related interest (usually in the Debt Service Funds) but only when the amounts come due so that they are a claim on the current financial resources. This approach was developed so that the expenditure is reported in the same time period as the appropriation for the expenditure. In that way, the budgeting of financial resources is properly handled.

Assume, as an illustration, that a government has a $500,000 bond payment coming up in October along with three months of interest that amounts to $10,000. This example assumes that cash has been set aside previously in the Debt Service Fund to satisfy this payment. The needed entries would be as follows:

Fund-based Financial Statements

Debt Service Funds

Expenditure—Bond Principal	500,000	
Expenditure—Interest.	10,000	
Cash		510,000
To record payment of bond and related interest.		

Government-wide Financial Statements

Bond Payable	500,000	
Interest Expense	10,000	
Cash		510,000
To record payment of bond and related interest.		

Tax Anticipation Notes   One type of formal debt is recorded in the same manner for government-wide and fund-based financial statements. State and local governments often issue short-term debts to provide financing until revenue sources have been collected. For example, if property tax payments are expected at a particular point in time, the government may need to borrow money for operations until that date. These short-term liabilities are often referred to as tax anticipation notes because they are being issued until a sufficient amount of taxes can be collected. As short-term liabilities, these debts are a claim on current financial resources. Thus, for the fund-based financial statements, the issuance is not recorded as an other financing source but rather as a liability in the same manner as the government-wide financial statements. Amounts paid for interest, though, would be recorded as an expenditure in producing the fund-based statements and as an expense on the government-wide financial statements.

To illustrate, assume that a city borrows $300,000 on a 60-day note on January 1 and pays back $305,000 on March 1. The debt will be repaid with the receipts from property taxes. For both sets of financial statements, the following entry would be made on January 1:

Cash	300,000	
Tax Anticipation Note Payable.		300,000
To record issuance of short-term debt to be repaid using money collected from property taxes.		

At repayment, though, two different entries are used because the fund-based statement is measuring current financial resources while the government-wide statement measures all economic resources.

Fund-based Financial Statement

Tax Anticipation Note Payable.	300,000	
Expenditure—Interest	5,000	
Cash		305,000
To record payment of short-term debt and interest for two months.		

Government-wide Financial Statements

Tax Anticipation Note Payable...........................	300,000	
Interest Expense	5,000	
Cash		305,000
To record payment of short-term debt and interest for two months.		

Special Assessments

Governments frequently provide improvements or services that directly benefit a particular property and assess the costs (in whole or part) to the owner. In many cases, the owners actually petition the government to initiate such projects because of the enhancement of property values. Paving streets, laying water and sewage lines, and the construction of curbing and sidewalks are typical examples. To finance the work being done, the government usually issues debt while concurrently placing a lien on the property to ensure reimbursement. Payment by the owners often is made in installments, sometimes stretching over several years. If public property also is benefited or if the governing body so chooses, a portion of the cost may be absorbed by the state or locality.

In the government-wide financial statements, the debt and subsequent construction are handled as they would be in a for-profit enterprise. The asset is recorded at cost and taxes are assessed and collected. These receipts are then used to settle the debt. For example, assume that a sidewalk is to be added to a neighborhood by a city at a cost of $20,000. A two-year bond of this amount is to be sold to finance the construction with repayment being made using funds collected from the owners of the property benefited. Total interest to be paid is $2,000. Of that amount, $1,300 occurred during construction and is considered a capitalized cost. The assessment is made at $22,000 to cover all costs.

Government-wide Financial Statements

Cash	20,000	
Bond Payable—Special Assessment		20,000
Debt is issued to finance sidewalk construction.		
Infrastructure Asset—Sidewalk	20,000	
Cash		20,000
Contractor is paid the cost of building new sidewalk.		
Taxes Receivable—Special Assessment....................	22,000	
Revenue—Special Assessment.......................		22,000
Citizens are charged for special assessment project.		
Cash	22,000	
Taxes Receivable—Special Assessment................		22,000
Money is collected from assessment of citizens for sidewalk construction.		
Bond Payable—Special Assessment	20,000	
Interest Expense	700	
Infrastructure Asset—Sidewalk	1,300	
Cash		22,000
Debt is paid off on special assessment bond. Interest incurred during construction is capitalized.		

In the fund-based financial statements, this series of transactions would have a completely different appearance. Neither the infrastructure nor the long-term debt would be recorded since the current financial resources measurement basis is being used. Because of the handling of the interest, the tax assessment and the bond payment entries are allocated between two different funds. In practice, a single transaction would have occurred with amounts being allocated to the appropriate fund for recording purposes.

The entries here have been numbered so that the recording in the Capital Projects Fund corresponds with the parallel entry in the Debt Service Fund.

Fund-based Financial Statements

Capital Projects Fund—Special Assessment Project

1.	Cash	20,000	
	Other Financing Sources—Bond Proceeds		20,000
	To record issuance of bonds to finance sidewalk construction with payment to be made from a special assessment levy.		
2.	Expenditures—Special Assessment	20,000	
	Cash		20,000
	To record payment to contractor for the cost of constructing sidewalk.		
3.	Tax Receivable—Special Assessment	1,300	
	Revenue—Special Assessment		1,300
	To record portion of assessment that will be used to pay interest incurred during construction.		
4.	Cash	1,300	
	Tax Receivable—Special Assessment		1,300
	To record collection of portion of assessment for interest incurred during construction of sidewalk.		
5.	Expenditure—Special Assessment.	1,300	
	Cash		1,300
	To record payment of portion of interest incurred during construction of sidewalk.		

Another set of entries will appear in the Debt Service Fund. The numbering of these entries enables the reader to match the entries above and those made in this fund.

Debt Service Fund—Special Assessment Project

3.	Tax Receivable—Special Assessment	20,700	
	Revenue—Special Assessment		20,700
	To record portion of assessment that will be used to pay bond principal and related interest incurred after construction.		
4.	Cash	20,700	
	Tax Receivable—Special Assessment		20,700
	To record collection of portion of assessment paid by citizens to extinguish bond and interest incurred after construction of sidewalk.		
5.	Expenditure—Special Assessment Bond.	20,000	
	Expenditure—Interest	700	
	Cash		20,700
	To record payment of bonds payable and portion of interest incurred after construction of sidewalk.		

Once again, the two different approaches to reporting government transactions can be seen here.

- In the government-wide financial statements, an asset is reported for $21,300 along with a debt (until paid off) of $20,000 and interest expense of $700.
- With the fund-based financial statements, expenditures of $21,300 and $700 are reported but no capital asset or debt ever appears.

One other aspect of special assessment projects should be mentioned. In some cases, the government may facilitate a project but accepts no legal obligation for it. The government's role will be limited to conveying funds from one party to another but assumes no liability (either primary or secondary) for the debt. Normally, the money goes from the citizens to the government and then directly to the contractors. If the government has no liability for defaults, overruns, or other problems, the recording of special assessment assets, liabilities, revenues, expenses, other financing sources, and expenditures is not really relevant. In that situation, all transactions are recorded in an Agency Fund as increases and decreases in accounts such as cash, amount due from citizens, and amount due to contractors. No reportable impact appears within the government-wide or the fund-based financial statements.

Interfund Transactions

Interfund transactions are commonly used within most government units as a means of directing sufficient resources to all activities and functions. Monetary transfers made from the General Fund are especially prevalent since many government revenues are initially accumulated in this fund. Such transactions should be recorded in both funds simultaneously at the time of authorization.

However, within the government-wide financial statements, many such transfers are not reported at all because they occur solely within either the governmental activities or the business-type activities. A transfer from the General Fund to the Debt Service Fund would be reported on fund-based financial statements but creates no impact within the governmental activities found in the government-wide financial statements.

Thus, for government-wide financial reporting, the following distinctions are drawn between transfers:

- *Intra-activity transactions* occur between governmental funds (totals reported for governmental activities are not affected), between enterprise funds (totals reported for business-type activities are not affected), and frequently between governmental funds and internal service funds. Transfers between governmental funds and internal service funds are included in this classification because, as discussed in Chapter 17, internal service funds are usually reported as governmental activities in government-wide statements despite being proprietary funds. Intra-activity transactions are not reported on government-wide financial statements.

- *Inter-activity transactions* occur between governmental funds and enterprise funds. In these cases, the totals reported for both governmental activities and business-type activities are impacted. Inter-activity transactions are reported on government-wide financial statements. In Exhibit 16–1, for example, within the asset section of the statement of net assets, internal balances are reported and then eliminated to arrive at a total figure. Likewise in Exhibit 16–2, transfers are shown at the very bottom of the general revenues section. Again, individual totals are shown and then offset so that no total figure is reported.

Consequently, in discussing interfund transactions, the reporting for government-wide statements is shown only when an inter-activity transaction is involved.

Interfund Transfers   The most common interfund transactions are transfers that are used primarily within the government funds to ensure adequate financing of budgeted expenditures. A county might transfer unrestricted funds, for example, to debt service to ensure that future obligations can be paid. A city council could vote to transfer $800,000 from the General Fund to the Capital Projects Funds to cover a portion of the cost of a new school building. In this second scenario, the following entries would be recorded:

Fund-based Financial Statements

General Fund

Other Financing Uses—Transfers Out—		
Capital Projects Fund	800,000	
Due to Capital Projects Fund		800,000
Transfer is authorized for school construction.		

Capital Projects Funds

Due from General Fund	800,000	
Other Financing Source—Transfers In—		
General Fund		800,000
Transfer is to be received for school construction.		

The *Other Financing Uses/Sources* designations are appropriate here; financial resources are being moved into and out of these funds although neither revenues nor expenditures have been earned or incurred. As shown in Exhibit 16–4, these balances are eventually reported by the funds in the Statement of Revenues, Expenditures, and Changes in Fund Balances. Both accounts are then closed out at the end of the current year. The *Due to/Due from* accounts are the equivalent of interfund payable and receivable balances.

When the actual transfer occurs, the following entries result:

Fund-based Financial Statements

General Fund

Due to Capital Projects Fund	800,000	
Cash		800,000
To transfer cash to Capital Projects Fund.		

Capital Projects Funds

Cash	800,000	
Due from General Fund		800,000
Receipt of transfer from General Fund.		

Because they are intra-activity transactions, none of the above entries would be made within the government-wide financial statements. Financial resources are simply being shifted around within the governmental activities.

Not all monetary transfers are for normal operating purposes; nonrecurring or nonroutine transfers may also take place. For example, money might be transferred from the General Fund to create or expand an Enterprise Fund such as a subway system. Prior to *GASB Statement 34,* this type of transaction was known as a "residual equity transfer" and was accounted for in a method different from other transfers.

Assume that a city does set aside $1 million of unrestricted money to help finance a new subway system that will be open to the public. Under the new rules, the entries will be unchanged because of the nature of the transfer.

Fund-based Financial Statements

General Fund

Other Financing Uses—Transfers Out—Subway System	1,000,000	
Cash		1,000,000
To record transfer to help finance subway system.		

Enterprise Fund

Cash	1,000,000	
Other Financing Sources—Transfers In—General Fund . . .		1,000,000
To record receipt of transfer from unrestricted funds.		

Because this transfer is an interactivity transaction, virtually the same entry will be made for the government-wide financial statements. In this case, the assets of the governmental activities are being reduced while the assets in the business-type activities go up.

Government-wide Financial Statements

Governmental Activities

Transfers Out—Subway System	1,000,000	
Cash		1,000,000
To record transfer to help finance subway system.		

Business-type Activities

Cash 1,000,000
    Transfers In—General Fund....................... 1,000,000
    To record receipt of transfer from unrestricted funds.

Internal Exchange Transactions Some transfers made within a government actually replace revenues and expenditures. For example, a payment made by a city to its own print shop (or any other Internal Service Fund or Enterprise Fund) for services or materials is treated as the equivalent of a transaction with an outside party. To avoid confusion in reporting, such transfers are recorded as revenues and expenditures or expenses just as if the transaction had occurred with an unrelated party. No differentiation is made. Because an earning process exists that would be the same as dealing with an outside party, the accounting mirrors that reality.

All internal exchange transactions are recorded by the fund-based financial statements. However, since internal service funds are usually reported as governmental activities in the government-wide statements, any such exchanges between governmental funds and an internal service fund has no net impact on overall figures being reported and should be omitted.

To illustrate, assume that a government pays its print shop (an internal service fund) $8,000 for work done for the fire department. In addition, another $1,000 is paid to a toll road operated by the government as an enterprise fund. The payment is made to allow government vehicles to ride on the highway without individual payments having to be made. Both of these transfers are made for services being rendered.

Fund-based Financial Statements

General Fund

Expenditures—Printing 8,000
Expenditures—Toll Road Privileges 1,000
    Cash 9,000
    To pay for printing supplies for fire department and for use of
    toll road.

Internal Service Fund—Print Shop

Cash 8,000
    Revenues...................................... 8,000
    To record collection of money paid by the fire department for
    printing supplies.

Enterprise Fund—Toll Road

Cash 1,000
    Revenues...................................... 1,000
    To record money collected from government for vehicular use
    of toll roads.

On government-wide financial statements, the $8,000 transaction with the print shop would not be reflected. An internal service fund is usually reported as a government activity rather than a business-type activity so that this transfer is viewed as an intra-activity transaction. The payment made to the enterprise fund, though, is with a business-type activity and is recorded because it is an inter-activity transaction.

Government-wide Financial Statements

Governmental Activities

Expenses—Toll Road Privileges 1,000
    Cash 1,000
    To pay for use of toll road by government's vehicles.

Business-type Activities

Cash 1,000
    Revenues...................................... 1,000
    To record money collected from government for vehicular use
    of toll roads.

SUMMARY

1. Traditional government accounting was radically changed in 1999 when the Governmental Accounting Standards Board issued *Statement Number 34,* "Basic Financial Statements—and Management's Discussion and Analysis—for State and Local Governments." This pronouncement made numerous changes in traditional government accounting procedures as well as adding a second set of financial statements to reflect government-wide activities.

2. The readers of government financial statements have a wide variety of informational needs. No one set of financial statements seems capable of meeting all user needs, a factor that influenced the actions taken by the GASB in its *Statement 34.* Accountability of government officials and control over public spending have always been essential elements of government accounting. In *Statement 34,* the GASB has attempted to keep those priorities in place while broadening the scope of the financial statements being produced.

3. Fund-based financial statements are produced by a state or local government unit utilizing fund accounting. In this system, activities are classified into three broad categories (governmental, proprietary, and fiduciary). Governmental funds account for service activities; proprietary funds account for activities where a user charge is assessed; and fiduciary funds account for assets held by the government for an external party.

4. Governmental funds are composed of several fund types: the General Fund, Special Revenue Funds, Capital Projects Funds, Debt Service Funds, and Permanent Funds. Proprietary funds are made up of Enterprise Funds and Internal Service Funds. Fiduciary Funds encompass Pension Trust Funds, Investment Trust Funds, Private-purpose Funds, and Agency Funds.

5. Government-wide financial statements present a statement of net assets and a statement of activities which are divided between governmental activities (the governmental funds and usually the internal service funds) and business-type activities (enterprise funds and occasionally an internal service fund). These statements measure all economic resources with timing of recognition guided by accrual accounting.

6. Fund-based financial statements include a number of financial statements. This chapter focused on the balance sheet and the statement of revenues, expenditures, and changes in fund balances for the governmental funds. In these statements, the General Fund and any other major fund must be shown separately. These statements measure current financial resources with timing of recognition guided by modified accrual accounting.

7. To aid in control over financial resources, most of the governmental funds will record their approved budgets each year. This initial budget as well as any final amended budget and actual figures for the period are then reported as required supplemental information to the financial statements.

8. Commitments for purchase orders and contracts are actually recorded in the individual governmental funds through the recognition of encumbrances. These balances are recorded when the commitment is made and removed when replaced by an actual claim to current financial resources.

9. The fund-based financial statements recognize expenditures for capital outlay, long-term debt payment, and expense-type costs at the time that a claim to current financial resources comes into existence. Government-wide financial statements capitalize capital outlay, reduce liabilities for debt payments, and record expenses in Expense accounts.

10. Revenue recognition by governments is based on a classification system. Recognition depends on whether the revenue is a derived tax revenue, imposed nonexchange revenue, government-mandated nonexchange transaction, or voluntary nonexchange transaction.

11. The issuance of long-term bonds is recorded as an "other financing source" by the governmental funds but as a long-term liability in the proprietary funds and in the government-wide financial statements.

12. Transfers between funds are normally reported as an "other financing source" and "other financing use" within the fund-based financial statements. Such transactions are usually not reported in the government-wide statements because they do not create an

impact in overall government activities or business-type activities. For internal exchange transactions where payment is being made for a good or service, a revenue is recognized along with an expenditure in the fund-based statements. The government-wide financial statements do not reflect such transfers unless between an enterprise fund and a governmental fund. In that case, a revenue is increased along with an expense.

COMPREHENSIVE ILLUSTRATION

Problem

(Estimated Time: 50 Minutes). The town of Drexel has the following financial transactions. The government has formally adopted *GASB Statement Number 34*. First, prepare journal entries for the town based on the production of fund-based financial statements. Then, prepare journal entries in anticipation of preparing government-wide financial statements.

1. The town council adopts an annual budget for the General Fund estimating general revenues of $1.7 million, approved expenditures of $1.5 million, and approved transfers out of $120,000.
2. Property taxes of $1.3 million are levied. The town expects to collect all but 3 percent of these taxes during the year.
3. Two new police cars are ordered at an approximate cost of $150,000.
4. A transfer of $50,000 is made from the General Fund to the Debt Service Fund.
5. A bond payable of $40,000 is paid along with $10,000 of interest.
6. A $2 million bond is issued at face value to acquire a building to be converted into a high school.
7. The two police cars are received with an invoice price of $152,000. The voucher has been approved for this amount but not yet paid.
8. The building for the high school is acquired for $2 million in cash. Renovation is immediately begun.
9. Depreciation on the new police cars is computed as $30,000 for the period.
10. The town borrows $100,000 on a 90-day tax anticipation note.
11. A special assessment curbing project is begun. The government sells $80,000 in bonds at face value to finance this project. If the debt is not paid by the assessments collected, the town has pledged to guarantee the debt.
12. A contractor completes the curbing project and is paid $80,000.
13. Citizens are assessed $85,000 for the curbing project that has been completed.
14. The special assessments of $85,000 are collected in full. The debt is repaid plus $5,000 in interest.
15. The town receives a $10,000 grant to beautify a park. The grant will be paid to reimburse specific costs incurred by the town.
16. The town spends $4,000 to beautify the above park.

Solution

Fund-based Financial Statements

1.	General Fund		
Estimated Revenues Control		1,700,000	
Appropriations Control			1,500,000
Estimated Other Financing Uses Control			120,000
Fund Balance			80,000

2.	General Fund		
Property Tax Receivable		1,300,000	
Allowance for Uncollectible Taxes			39,000
Revenues—Property Taxes			1,261,000

3.   **General Fund**

Encumbrances Control	150,000	
Fund Balance—Reserved for Encumbrances		150,000

4.   **General Fund**

Other Financing Uses—Transfers Out	50,000	
Cash		50,000

Debt Service Fund

Cash	50,000	
Other Financing Sources—Transfers In		50,000

5.   **Debt Service Fund**

Expenditures—Principal	40,000	
Expenditures—Interest	10,000	
Cash		50,000

6.   **Capital Projects Funds**

Cash	2,000,000	
Other Financing Sources—Bond Proceeds		2,000,000

7.   **General Fund**

Fund Balance—Reserved for Encumbrances	150,000	
Encumbrances Control		150,000
Expenditures Control	152,000	
Vouchers Payable		152,000

8.   **Capital Projects Funds**

Expenditures—Building	2,000,000	
Cash		2,000,000

9. No entry is recorded. Expenditures rather than expenses are recorded by the governmental funds.

10.   **General Fund**

Cash	100,000	
Tax Anticipation Note Payable		100,000

11.   **Capital Projects Funds**

Cash	80,000	
Other Financing Sources—Special Assessments Note		80,000

12.   **Capital Projects Funds**

Expenditures—Curbing	80,000	
Cash		80,000

13.   **Debt Service Funds**

Taxes Receivable—Special Assessment	85,000	
Revenues—Special Assessment		85,000

14.   **Debt Service Funds**

Cash	85,000	
Taxes Receivable—Special Assessment		85,000
Expenditures—Principal	80,000	
Expenditures—Interest	5,000	
Cash		85,000

15.   **Special Revenue Funds**

Cash	10,000	
Deferred Revenues		10,000

16.   **Special Revenue Funds**

Expenditures—Park Beautification	4,000	
Cash		4,000
Deferred Revenues	4,000	
Revenues—Grants		4,000

Government-wide Financial Statements

1. Budgetary entries are not reported within the government-wide financial statements. They are recorded in the individual funds and then shown in required supplementary information.

2.   **Governmental Activities**

Property Tax Receivable	300,000	
Allowance for Uncollectible Taxes		39,000
Revenues—Property Taxes		1,261,000

3. Commitments are not reported in the government-wide financial statements.

4. This transfer was within the governmental funds and would, therefore, have had no net effect on the governmental activities. No journal entry is needed.

5.   **Governmental Activities**

Bonds Payable	40,000	
Interest Expense	10,000	
Cash		50,000

6.   **Governmental Activities**

Cash	2,000,000	
Bonds Payable		2,000,000

7.   **Governmental Activities**

Police Cars (or Vehicles)	152,000	
Vouchers Payable		152,000

8.   **Governmental Activities**

Building	2,000,000	
Cash		2,000,000

9.   **Governmental Activities**

Depreciation Expense	30,000	
Accumulated Depreciation		30,000

10.   **Governmental Activities**

Cash	100,000	
Tax Anticipation Note Payable		100,000

11.   **Governmental Activities**

Cash	80,000	
Special Assessment Notes Payable		80,000

12.   **Governmental Activities**

Infrastructure Assets—Curbing	80,000	
Cash		80,000

13.   **Governmental Activities**

Taxes Receivable—Special Assessment	85,000	
Revenues—Special Assessment		85,000

14.   **Governmental Activities**

Cash	85,000	
Taxes Receivable—Special Assessment		85,000
Special Assessment Notes Payable	80,000	
Interest Expense	5,000	
Cash		85,000

15.   **Governmental Activities**

Cash	10,000	
Deferred Revenues		10,000

16.   **Governmental Activities**

Expenses—Park Beautification	4,000	
Cash		4,000
Deferred Revenues	4,000	
Revenues—Grants		4,000

QUESTIONS

1. How have users' needs impacted the development of accounting principles for state and local government units?

2. Why have accountability and control been so important in the traditional accounting for state and local government units?

3. In general, how has *GASB Statement Number 34* impacted the financial reporting of state and local governments?

4. What are the basic financial statements now produced by a state or local government?

5. In fund-based financial statements, what measurement basis is used and what system is applied to determine the timing of revenue and expenditure recognition?

6. In government-wide financial statements, what measurement basis is used and what system is applied to determine the timing of revenue and expense recognition?

7. What accounts are included in current financial resources?

8. In applying the current financial resources measurement basis, when are liabilities recognized?

9. What are the three classifications of funds? What types of funds are included in each of these three?

10. What are the five fund types within the governmental funds? For each of these five, what types of events are reported?

11. What are the two fund types within the proprietary funds? For each of these two, what types of events are reported?

12. What are the four fund types within the fiduciary funds? For each of these four, what types of events are reported?

13. In government-wide financial statements, what are the two major divisions that are reported? What funds are not reported in these financial statements?

14. In fund-based financial statements, separate columns are reported for each activity. Which activities are reported in this manner?

15. Why are budgetary entries reported in the individual funds of a state or local government?

16. How are budget results shown in the financial reporting of a state or local government?

17. When is an encumbrance recorded? What happens to this balance? How are encumbrances reported in government-wide financial statements?

18. An encumbrance is still outstanding at the end of the fiscal year. The government anticipates that it will honor this encumbrance in the next year. What reporting is made of this encumbrance?

19. What costs lead a governmental fund to report an expenditure?

20. At what point in time does a governmental fund report an expenditure?

21. How do governmental funds report capital outlay? How are capital expenditures reported in the government-wide financial statements?

22. On fund-based financial statements, what are the two different ways that supplies and prepaid items can be recorded?

23. What are the four classifications of revenues that a state or local government can recognize? In each case, when are revenues normally recognized?

24. On fund-based financial statements, how is the issuance of a long-term bond reported? On government-wide financial statements, how is the issuance of a long-term bond reported?

25. What is a special assessment project? How are special assessment projects reported?

26. In fund-based financial statements, how are interfund transfers reported?

27. In government-wide financial statements, what is the difference in an intra-activity transaction and an inter-activity transaction? How is each reported?

28. What is an internal exchange transaction and how is it reported?

INTERNET ASSIGNMENT

Internet sites are time and date sensitive. It is the purpose of these exercises to have you explore the Internet. You may need to refer to the text's Web site at www.mhhe.com/hoyle6e to find the most up-to-date links for the Web sites listed in the Internet Assignment.

1. Go to the following Web site for the Governmental Accounting Standards Board:

   http://www.rutgers.edu/Accounting/raw/gasb/st/stpg.html

   Scroll down until you find information about *GASB Statement Number 34.*

   Click on "preface and summary."
   Read the information provided about this pronouncement.
   Write a short report giving the major points provided about *GASB Statement Number 34.*

LIBRARY ASSIGNMENTS

1. Read the following articles and any other published information discussing the changes required by *GASB Statement Number 34:*

   "Government Reporting Faces an Overhaul," *Journal of Accountancy,* January 2000.

   "A Bold Step Forward," *The Government Accountants Journal,* Spring 2000.

   "GASB Statement No. 34: Dawn of a New Governmental Financial Reporting Model," *The CPA Journal,* December 1999.

   "New Look for Government Statements," *Practical Accountant,* August 1999.

   "GASB's Brave New World of Government Accounting," *Accounting Today,* June 21, 1999.

   "GASB Statement 34—Part of Changing Political and Global Market Pressures," *The Government Accountants Journal,* Spring 2000.

   Write a report on the major changes created by the issuance of this pronouncement.

2. Obtain a copy of the latest comprehensive annual financial report of a state or local government. If one is not available in the library, request a copy, either by telephone or mail, from the director of finance of the governmental unit. Write a report to answer the following questions:

   ■ Has the government adopted the requirements of *GASB Statement Number 34?*

   ■ If the government has not adopted *GASB Statement Number 34,* is information provided about the timing of recognition and the impact?

   ■ What is the total revenue reported by the General Fund?

   ■ What is the total amount of expenditures reported by the General Fund?

   ■ What was the total amount of revenues budgeted for the General Fund?

   ■ What amount of fixed assets (or capital assets) is reported by the government and where was this information found?

   ■ What specific activities are listed within the Special Revenue Funds?

   ■ Does the government show any amount reserved for encumbrances?

   ■ What assets are reported by the General Fund?

PROBLEMS

1. Which of the following is not a Governmental Fund?
    a. Special Revenue Fund.
    b. Internal Service Fund.
    c. Capital Projects Fund.
    d. Debt Service Fund.

2. What is the purpose of a Special Revenue Fund?
    a. To account for revenues legally restricted as to expenditure.
    b. To account for ongoing activities.
    c. To account for gifts where only subsequently earned income can be expended.
    d. To account for the cost of long-lived assets bought with designated funds.

3. What is the purpose of Enterprise Funds?
    a. To account for operations that provide services to other departments within a government.
    b. To account for asset transfers.
    c. To account for ongoing activities such as the police and fire departments.
    d. To account for operations financed in whole or in part by outside user charges.

4. Which of the following statements is true?
    a. There are three different types of Proprietary Funds.
    b. There are three different types of Fiduciary Funds.
    c. There are five different types of Fiduciary Funds.
    d. There are five different types of Governmental Funds.

5. A government expects to receive revenues of $400,000 but has approved expenditures of $430,000. The anticipated shortage will have an impact on which of the following terms?
    a. Interperiod equity.
    b. Modified accrual accounting.
    c. Consumption accounting.
    d. Account groups.

6. A citizen of the city of Townsend gives the city a gift of $22,000 in investments. The citizen requires that the investments be held but any resulting income must be used to help maintain the city's cemetery. In which fund should this asset be maintained?
    a. Special Revenue Funds.
    b. Capital Projects Funds.
    c. Permanent Funds.
    d. General Fund.

7. Which of the following statements is correct?
    a. Fund-based financial statements measure economic resources.
    b. Government-wide financial statements measure only current financial resources.
    c. Fund-based financial statements measure both economic resources and current financial resources.
    d. Government-wide financial statements measure economic resources.

8. Which of the following statements is correct?
    a. Fund-based financial statements measure revenues and expenditures based on modified accrual accounting.
    b. Government-wide financial statements measure revenues and expenses based on modified accrual accounting.
    c. Fund-based financial statements measure revenues and expenses based on accrual accounting.
    d. Government-wide financial statements measure revenues and expenditures based on accrual accounting.

9. Which financial statements match up properly with which level of reporting?

	Fund-based Financial Statements	Government-wide Financial Statements
a.	Statement of net assets	Balance sheet
b.	Statement of net assets	Statement of net assets
c.	Balance sheet	Statement of net assets
d.	Balance sheet	Balance sheet

10. Which of the following statements is true concerning the recording of a budget?
    a. At the beginning of the year, Appropriations is debited.
    b. A debit to the Budgetary Fund Balance account indicates an expected surplus.
    c. At the beginning of the year, Estimated Revenues is debited.
    d. At the end of the year, Appropriations is credited.

11. Rent for two months is paid by the General Fund. Which of the following is not correct?
    a. In the government-wide financial statements, rent expense should be reported.
    b. In the General Fund, rent expense should be reported.
    c. In the fund-based financial statements, an expenditure should be reported.
    d. If one month of rent is in one year with the other month in the next year, either the purchases method or the consumption method can be used.

12. In the General Fund, a purchase order for $3,000 is recorded for the purchase of a new computer. The computer is received at an actual cost of $3,020. Which of the following is correct?
    a. Machinery is increased in the General Fund by $3,020.
    b. An Encumbrance account is reduced by $3,020.
    c. An Expenditure is increased by $3,020.
    d. An Expenditure is recorded for the additional $20.

13. At the end of the current year, a government reports a fund balance reserved for encumbrances of $9,000. What information is being conveyed?
    a. The government has been given $9,000 by a donor that must be used in a specified fashion.
    b. The government has made $9,000 in commitments in one year that will be honored in the subsequent year.
    c. Encumbrances exceeded expenditures by $9,000 during the current year.
    d. The government spent $9,000 less than was appropriated.

14. A government buys equipment for its police department at a cost of $54,000. Which of the following is not true?
    a. In the government-wide financial statements, equipment will increase by $54,000.
    b. Depreciation in connection with this equipment will be reported in the fund-based financial statements.
    c. In the fund-based financial statements, the equipment will not appear within the reported assets.
    d. In the fund-based financial statements, an expenditure for $54,000 will be reported.

15. A city acquires supplies and is using the consumption method of accounting. Which of the following statements is true for the fund-based statements?
    a. An Expenditures account was debited at the time of receipt.
    b. An expense is recorded as the supplies are consumed.
    c. An Inventory account is debited at the time of the acquisition.
    d. The supplies are recorded within the General Fixed Assets Account Group.

16. An income tax is an example of which of the following:
    a. Derived tax revenue.
    b. Imposed nonexchange revenue.
    c. Government-mandated nonexchange revenue.
    d. Voluntary nonexchange transaction.

17. The state government passes a law requiring localities to upgrade their water treatment facilities. The state awards a grant of $500,000 to the town of Midlothian to help pay for this cost. What type of revenue is this grant?
    a. Derived tax revenue.
    b. Imposed nonexchange revenue.
    c. Government-mandated nonexchange revenue.
    d. Voluntary nonexchange transaction.

18. The state awards a grant to the town of Glenville of $50,000. The grant money will be paid to the town as a reimbursement for money spent on road repair. At the beginning, $8,000 is paid in advance. During the first year of this program, the town spent $14,000 and applied for reimbursement. What amount of revenue should be recognized?
    a. $0.
    b. $8,000.

    c. $14,000.

    d. $50,000.

19. A city issues a 60-day tax anticipation note to fund operations. What recording should be made?

    a. In the government-wide financial statements, the liability should be reported whereas in the fund-based financial statements, an other financing source should be shown.

    b. In the government-wide financial statements and in the fund-based financial statements, a liability should be reported.

    c. In the government-wide financial statements and in the fund-based financial statements, an other financing source should be shown.

    d. In the government-wide financial statements, an other financing source should be shown whereas in the fund-based financial statements, a liability is reported.

20. A city issues a five-year bonds payable to finance construction of a new school. What recording should be made?

    a. In the government-wide financial statements, the liability should be reported whereas in the fund based financial statements, an other financing source should be shown.

    b. In the government-wide financial statements and in the fund-based financial statements, a liability should be reported.

    c. In the government-wide financial statements and in the fund-based financial statements, an other financing source should be shown.

    d. In the government-wide financial statements, an other financing source should be shown whereas in the fund-based financial statements, a liability is reported.

21. A $110,000 payment is made on a long-term liability. Of this amount, $10,000 represents interest. Which of the following is not true?

    a. In the government-wide financial statements, liabilities are reduced by $100,000.

    b. In the fund-based financial statements, an expenditure is recorded for $110,000.

    c. In the fund-based financial statements, liabilities are reduced by $100,000.

    d. In the government-wide financial statements, interest expense of $10,000 is recognized.

22. A city constructs a special assessment project (a sidewalk) for which it is secondarily liable. Bonds of $90,000 are issued. Another $10,000 is authorized and transferred out of the General Fund. The sidewalk is built for $100,000. The citizens are billed for $90,000. They pay this amount and the debt is paid off. Where is the $100,000 expenditure recorded?

    a. No recording is made by the city.

    b. Agency Fund.

    c. General Fund.

    d. Capital Projects Fund.

23. Work is done by a city as a special assessment. Curbing is constructed in a new neighborhood. Under what condition should this activity be recorded in an Agency Fund?

    a. Never; the work is reported in the Capital Projects Funds.

    b. Only if the city is secondarily liable for any debt incurred to finance construction costs.

    c. Only if the city is in no way liable for the costs of the construction.

    d. In all cases.

24. Which of the following is an example of an inter-activity transaction?

    a. Money is transferred from the General Fund to a Debt Service Fund.

    b. Money is transferred from a Capital Projects Fund to the General Fund.

    c. Money is transferred from a Special Revenue Fund to the Debt Service Fund.

    d. Money is transferred from the General Fund to an Enterprise Fund.

25. Cash of $60,000 is transferred from the General Fund to a Debt Service Fund. On the government-wide financial statements, what is reported?

    a. No reporting is made.

    b. Other Financing Sources increase by $60,000 while Other Financing Uses increase by $60,000.

    c.   Revenues increase by $60,000 while Expenditures increase by $60,000.

    d.   Revenues increase by $60,000 while Expenses increase by $60,000.

26.   Cash of $60,000 is transferred from the General Fund to a Debt Service Fund. On the fund-based financial statements, what is reported?

    a.   No reporting is made.

    b.   Other Financing Sources increase by $60,000 while Other Financing Uses increase by $60,000.

    c.   Revenues increase by $60,000 while Expenditures increase by $60,000.

    d.   Revenues increase by $60,000 while Expenses increase by $60,000.

27.   Cash of $20,000 is transferred from the General Fund to an Enterprise Fund to pay for work that was done. On the government-wide financial statements, what is reported?

    a.   No reporting is made.

    b.   Other Financing Sources increase by $20,000 while Other Financing Uses increase by $20,000.

    c.   Revenues increase by $20,000 while Expenditures increase by $20,000.

    d.   Revenues increase by $20,000 while Expenses increase by $20,000.

28.   Cash of $20,000 is transferred from the General Fund to an Enterprise Fund to pay for work that was done. On the fund-based financial statements, what is reported?

    a.   No reporting is made.

    b.   Other Financing Sources increase by $20,000 while Other Financing Uses increase by $20,000.

    c.   Revenues increase by $20,000 while Expenditures increase by $20,000.

    d.   Revenues increase by $20,000 while Expenses increase by $20,000.

29.   The board of commissioners of the city of Hartmoore adopted a General Fund budget for the year ending June 30, 2001, which indicated revenues of $1,000,000, bond proceeds of $400,000, appropriations of $900,000, and operating transfers out of $300,000. If this budget is formally integrated into the accounting records, what is the required journal entry at the beginning of the year? What later entry is required?

30.   A city orders a new computer at an anticipated cost of $88,000. It is received with an actual cost of $89,400. Payment is subsequently made. Give all of the required journal entries and identify the type of fund or account group in which each entry is recorded. What information would be presented in the government-wide financial statements? What information would be presented in the fund-based financial statements?

31.   Cash of $90,000 is transferred from a city's general fund to start construction on a police station. A bond of $830,000 is issued at face value. The police station is built for $920,000. Prepare all necessary journal entries for these transactions and identify the type of fund or account group in which each entry is recorded. Assume that the commitment is not recorded by the city. What information would be presented in the government-wide financial statements? What information would be presented in the fund-based financial statements?

32.   A local government incurs the following transactions during the current fiscal period. Prepare journal entries without dollar amounts. Prepare the entries the first time for fund-based financial statements. Then, prepare them again for government-wide financial statements.

    a.   Budget is passed for the police department, ambulance service, and other ongoing activities. Funding is from property taxes, transfers, and bond proceeds. All monetary outflows will be for expenses and fixed assets. A deficit is projected.

    b.   A bond is issued at face value to fund the construction of a new municipal building.

    c.   A computer is ordered to be used by the tax department.

    d.   The computer is received.

    e.   The invoice for the computer is paid.

    f.   City council agrees to transfer money from General Fund as partial payment for a special assessments project. This money has not yet been transferred. The city will be secondarily liable for any money borrowed for this work.

    g.   City council creates a motor pool to service all government vehicles. Money is transferred from General Fund to provide permanent financing for this facility.

    h.   Property taxes are levied. Although officials believe that most of these taxes should be collected during the current period, a small percentage is estimated to be uncollectible.

    i.   Grant money is collected from the state to be spent as a supplement to the salaries of the police force. No entry has previously been recorded.

    j.   A portion of the grant money in (*i*) is properly spent.

33. Make journal entries for the governmental funds of the city of Pudding to record the following transactions. Prepare the entries the first time for fund-based financial statements. Then, prepare them again for government-wide financial statements.

    a.   Ordered a new truck for the sanitation department at a cost of $94,000.

    b.   The city print shop did work for the school system (but has not yet been paid). The printing was charged out at $1,200.

    c.   A $700,000 bond was issued to build a new road.

    d.   Cash of $20,000 is transferred from the General Fund to provide permanent financing for a municipal swimming pool that will be viewed as an Enterprise Fund.

    e.   The truck ordered in (*a*) is received at an actual cost of $96,000. Payment is not made at this time.

    f.   Cash of $32,000 is transferred from the General Fund to a Capital Projects Fund.

    g.   A state grant of $30,000 is received that must be spent to promote recycling.

    h.   The first $5,000 of the state grant received in (*g*) is appropriately expended.

34. Prepare journal entries for a local government to record the following transactions. Prepare the entries the first time for fund-based financial statements. Then, prepare them again for government-wide financial statements.

    a.   A $300,000 bond is sold at face value by the government to finance construction of a warehouse.

    b.   A $400,000 contract is signed for construction of the warehouse.

    c.   A $20,000 transfer of unrestricted funds was made for the eventual payment of the debt in (*a*).

    d.   Equipment for the fire department is received with a cost of $12,000. When ordered, an anticipated cost of $11,800 had been recorded.

    e.   Supplies to be used in the schools are bought for $2,000 cash. The consumption method is being used.

    f.   A state grant of $5,000 is awarded to supplement police salaries. The money will be paid to reimburse the government after the supplements have been paid to the police officers.

    g.   Property tax assessments are mailed to citizens of the government. The total assessment is $600,000 although officials anticipate that 4 percent will never be collected.

35. The following trial balances are for the governmental funds of the city of Copeland prepared from the current accounting records:

General Fund

	Debit	Credit
Cash	$ 19,000	
Taxes receivable	112,000	
Allowance for uncollectible taxes		$ 2,000
Vouchers payable		24,000
Due to debt service fund		10,000
Deferred revenues		16,000
Budgetary fund balance—Reserved for encumbrances		9,000
Fund balance—Unreserved, undesignated		103,000
Revenues control		176,000
Expenditures control	110,000	
Other financing uses control	90,000	
Encumbrances control	9,000	
Estimated revenues control	190,000	
Appropriations control		171,000
Budgetary fund balance		19,000
Totals	$530,000	$530,000

Debt Service Fund

	Debit	Credit
Cash	$ 8,000	
Investments	51,000	
Taxes receivable	11,000	
Due from general fund	10,000	
Fund balance—Designated for debt service		$ 45,000
Revenues control		20,000
Other financing sources—Operating transfers in		90,000
Expenditures control	75,000	
Totals	$155,000	$155,000

Capital Projects Fund

	Debit	Credit
Cash	$ 70,000	
Special assessments receivable	90,000	
Contracts payable		$ 50,000
Deferred revenues		90,000
Budgetary fund balance—Reserved for encumbrances		16,000
Fund balance—Unreserved, undesignated		–0–
Other financing sources		150,000
Expenditures control	130,000	
Encumbrances	16,000	
Estimated other financing sources	150,000	
Appropriations		150,000
Totals	$456,000	$456,000

Special Revenue Fund

	Debit	Credit
Cash	$ 14,000	
Taxes receivable	41,000	
Inventory of supplies	4,000	
Vouchers payable		$ 25,000
Deferred revenues		3,000
Fund balance—Reserved for inventory of supplies		4,000
Budgetary fund balance—Reserved for encumbrances		3,000
Fund balance—Unreserved, undesignated		19,000
Revenues control		56,000
Expenditures control	48,000	
Encumbrances	3,000	
Estimated revenues	75,000	
Appropriations		60,000
Budgetary fund balance		15,000
Totals	$185,000	$185,000

Required

Based on the information presented for each of these governmental funds, answer the following questions:

a. How much more money can be expended or committed by the General Fund during the remainder of the current year?

b. Why does the Capital Projects Fund have no construction or capital asset accounts?

c. What does the $150,000 Appropriations balance found in the Capital Projects Fund represent?

d. Several of the funds have balances for Encumbrances and Budgetary Fund Balance—Reserved for Encumbrance. How will these amounts be accounted for at the end of the fiscal year?

e. Why does the Fund Balance—Unreserved, Undesignated account in the Capital Projects Fund have a zero balance?

f. What are possible explanations for the $150,000 Other Financing Sources balance found in the Capital Projects Fund?

g. What does the $75,000 balance in the Expenditures Control account of the Debt Service Fund represent?

h. What is the purpose of the Special Assessments Receivable found in the Capital Projects Fund?

i. In the Special Revenue Fund, what is the purpose of the Fund Balance—Reserved for Inventory of Supplies account?

j. Why does the Debt Service Fund not have budgetary account balances?

36. Following are descriptions of transactions and other financial events for the city of Tetris for the year ending December 2001. Not all transactions have been included here. Only the General Fund formally records a budget. No encumbrances were carried over from 2000.

Paid salary for police officers	$ 21,000
Government grant is received to pay ambulance drivers	40,000
Estimated revenues	232,000
Invoices were received for rent on equipment used by fire department during last four months of the year	3,000
Paid for newly constructed city hall	1,044,000
Commitment made to acquire new ambulance	111,000
Cash received from bonds sold for construction purposes	300,000
Order placed for new sanitation truck	69,000
Paid salary of ambulance drivers—money derived from state government grant given for that purpose	24,000
Paid for supplies for school system	16,000
Transfer made by General Fund to eventually pay off a long-term debt	33,000
Received but did not pay for new ambulance	120,000
Property tax receivables were levied. City anticipates that 95 percent will be collected and 5 percent will be bad	200,000
Acquired and paid for new school bus	40,000
Cash received from business taxes and parking meters (not previously accrued)	14,000
Appropriations	225,000

The following questions are independent although each is based on the preceding information. Assume the government is preparing information for its fund-based financial statements.

a. What is the balance in the Fund Balance account for the budget for the year and is it a debit or credit?

b. Assume that 60 percent of the school supplies are used during the year so that 40 percent remain. If the consumption method is being applied, how is the recording handled?

c. The sanitation truck that was ordered was not received prior to the end of the year. The commitment will be honored in the subsequent year when the truck arrives. What journal entries are needed at the end of 2001?

d. Assume the ambulance was received on December 31, 2001. Provide all necessary journal entries on that date.

e. Give all journal entries that should have been made when the $33,000 transfer was made to eventually pay off a long-term debt.

f. What amount of revenue would be recognized for the period? Explain the makeup of this total.

g. What are the total expenditures? Explain the makeup of this total.

h. What journal entry or entries were prepared when the bonds were issued?

37. Chesterfield County incurred the following list of transactions. Prepare the entries the first time for fund-based financial statements. Then, prepare them again for government-wide financial statements.

    a. A budget is passed for all ongoing activities. Revenue is anticipated to be $834,000 with approved spending of $540,000 and operating transfers out of $242,000.

    b. A contract is signed with a construction company to build a new central office building for the government at a cost of $8 million. A budget for this project has previously been recorded.

    c. Bonds are sold for $8 million (face value) to finance construction of the new office building.

    d. The new building is completed. An invoice is received and paid.

    e. Previously unrestricted cash of $1 million is set aside to begin paying the bonds issued in (c).

    f. A portion of the bonds comes due and $1 million is paid. Of this total, $100,000 represents interest. The interest had not been previously accrued.

    g. Property tax levies are assessed to the citizens. Total billing for this tax is $800,000. Ninety percent is assumed to be collectible in this period with receipt of an additional 6 percent during subsequent periods, but in time to be available to pay current period liabilities. The remainder is expected to be uncollectible.

    h. Cash of $120,000 is received from a toll road. This money has to be spent on highway maintenance.

    i. Investments valued at $300,000 are received by the county as a donation from a grateful citizen. Income from these investments must be used to beautify local parks.

38. The following trial balance is taken from the General Fund of the city of Jennings for the year ending December 31, 2001. Prepare a condensed statement of revenues, expenditures, and changes in fund balance and also prepare a condensed balance sheet.

	Debit	Credit
Budgetary fund balance—Reserved for encumbrances ...		$ 90,000
Cash	$ 30,000	
Contracts payable		90,000
Deferred revenues		40,000
Due from capital projects funds	60,000	
Due to debt service funds		40,000
Encumbrances	90,000	
Expenditures	420,000	
Fund balance—Unreserved, undesignated		170,000
Investments	410,000	
Revenues		740,000
Other financing sources—Bond proceeds		300,000
Other financing sources—Transfers in		50,000
Other financing uses—Transfers out	470,000	
Taxes receivable	220,000	
Vouchers payable		180,000
Totals	$1,700,000	$1,700,000

17

Accounting for State and Local Governments (Part Two)

QUESTIONS TO CONSIDER

- How does the accounting for capital leases utilized for fund-based financial statements differ from the procedures used in producing government-wide financial statements?

- What liability does a government have for closure and cleanup costs of a solid waste landfill and how are these costs reported?

- How does a state or local government record artworks or historical treasures that are bought or obtained through donation?

- What is meant by using the modified approach in connection with the depreciation of infrastructure assets?

- What is included in the management's discussion and analysis (MD&A) and why is this now required of state and local governments?

- What is a component unit and how is it reported by a state or local government?

- What is the difference in the statement of net assets in the government-wide financial statements and the balance sheet presented by the governmental funds?

- How does governmental accounting apply to public colleges and universities?

The previous chapter of this book served as an introduction to the unique aspects of accounting applicable to state and local governments. Fund accounting, budgetary entries, encumbrances, expenditures, revenue recognition, and the like were all analyzed in light of traditional government accounting procedures as well as the massive changes brought on by the issuance of *GASB Statement Number 34*, "Basic Financial Statements—and Management's Discussion and Analysis—for State and Local Governments" in June 1999. That initial coverage was designed to present the basic essentials underlying the accounting required of these government entities, especially in light of the dual nature of financial reporting which can best be seen by comparing fund-based financial statements with government-wide financial statements.

The current chapter carries this coverage further by delving into more complex financial situations. Obviously, many state and local government units are quite large with transactions as complicated as any encountered by a for-profit business. In this chapter, issues such as the handling of solid waste landfills, donated artworks, and the depreciation of infrastructure assets are examined to broaden the scope of understanding of state and local government accounting. Next, the overall financial reporting model is studied. As indicated, *GASB Statement 34* has radically altered this structure by requiring both fund-based financial statements and government-wide financial statements. Many of the transactions that affect a government must now be reported in two different ways: first to measure current financial resources according to modified accrual accounting and second to measure all economic resources using accrual accounting.

After looking at both these additional transactions of a government and the financial reporting model, the chapter closes by examining the reporting for public colleges and universities such as the University of Virginia or the University of Colorado. The subsequent chapter includes coverage of private not-for-profit schools such as Notre Dame and Duke. A tremendous difference exists between the accounting for public schools in comparison to the requirements applicable to private institutions.

CAPITAL LEASES

The notes to the 1999 financial statements of the city of Sioux City, Iowa, describe one of its capital leases by indicating that "the City entered into a lease agreement with the Sioux City Chamber Foundation as lessee for the construction of the Sioux City Convention Center." Likewise, the city of Greensboro, North Carolina, notes in 1998 that "the City has entered into lease-purchase and other financing agreements for certain equipment and land that bear interest rates from 3.6 percent to 6.7 percent and redevelopment projects that bear interest at graduated rates from 7.7 percent to 8.2 percent."

Obviously, state and local governments (in the same manner as a for-profit business) sometimes obtain use of property by lease rather than by direct purchase. Leasing may provide lower interest rates or reduce the risk of obsolescence and damage. Leasing is simply a way that many organizations (private or governmental) can acquire needed equipment, machinery, buildings, or other assets. For reporting purposes, such leases must be recorded as either capital leases or operating leases. The initial issue is to separate one type from another. In that regard, the GASB has accepted the method applied in *FASB Statement Number 13,* "Accounting for Leases," as the method of differentiation. That pronouncement established the following four criteria; a lease that meets any one of these is held to be a capital lease:

1. The lease transfers ownership of the property to the lessee by the end of the lease term.
2. The lease contains an option to purchase the leased property at a bargain price.
3. The lease term is equal to or greater than 75 percent of the estimated economic life of the leased property.
4. The present value of rental or other minimum lease payments equals or exceeds 90 percent of the fair value of the leased property less any investment tax credit retained by the lessor.

Thus, for example, assume that a city leases a truck which has a 10-year life and a fair market value of $50,000. Here are four sample situations where the city is required to account for the property as a capital lease:

- The lease is for six years but the city automatically receives title to the truck at the end of that term (so that criterion one is met).
- The lease is for five years but the city can buy the truck for $3,000 at the end of that time, an amount that is viewed as significantly less than the expected fair value of $11,000 (so that criterion two is met).
- The lease is for eight years after which the truck will be returned to the lessor (so that criterion three is met).
- The lease is for seven years but the present value of minimum lease payments is over $45,000 (so that criterion four is met). In this last example, the lessee is viewed as paying the equivalent of the purchase price to obtain use of the asset.

Government-wide Financial Statements

In reporting a capital lease within the government-wide financial statements, the accounting is the same as that appropriate for a for-profit enterprise. Both an asset and a liability are reported initially at the present value of the minimum lease payments in the same manner as a debt-financed acquisition. Assume, for example, that either a police department (recorded in the General Fund) or a bus system (recorded as an Enterprise Fund) signs an 8-year lease for a truck with a 10-year life. Because the third criterion above is met, this transaction must be recorded as a capital lease. Assume further that the lease calls for annual payments of $10,000 per year with the first payment made at the signing of the lease and that a 10 percent interest rate is appropriate for the city.

The present value of the minimum lease payments applying a 10 percent interest rate to an annuity due for eight years is $58,680 (rounded). In either the governmental activities (if obtained by the police department) or the business-type activities (if obtained by the bus system), the following journal entry is required. In the government-wide financial statements, both the governmental activities and the business-type activities utilize accrual accounting and the economic resources measurement basis so that no distinction is necessary.

Truck—Capital Lease.	58,680	
Cash		10,000
Capital Lease Obligation		48,680
To record capital lease and first payment.		

Assuming that the straight-line method is being used, depreciation expense of $7,335 should be recognized ($58,680/8 years) at the end of this first year. However, if title to the asset is to transfer to the city or if a bargain purchase option exists, the full 10-year life should be used for depreciation purposes because the lessee will expect to get full use of the asset.

At the end of the first year, when the next payment is made, part of that $10,000 will be attributed to interest with the remainder viewed as a reduction in the liability principal. Because the obligation is being reported at $48,680 and the interest rate is 10 percent, the interest recorded for the first year will be $4,868. The remaining $5,132 ($10,000 less $4,868) decreases the debt to $43,548.

Interest Expense	4,868	
Capital Lease Obligation	5,132	
Cash		10,000
To record payment on capital lease at end of first year.		

Fund-based Financial Statements

Assume that the same lease is being recorded in the fund-based financial statements. If a proprietary fund is involved, the handling is the same as above. A difference only appears for the governmental funds.

For example, the recording of this same lease by the General Fund may actually appear to double count expenditures. However, this required approach seeks to mirror the reporting that would have resulted if the city had performed a series of events: (1) borrowed money on a long-term liability, (2) used that money to acquire the asset in question, and (3) subsequently paid off this long-term liability. If that series of events had occurred, the recording would have been as follows in the fund-based statements:

1. When the money was borrowed on a long-term liability, the city would have reported an other financing source because the inflow of financial resources did not come from a revenue.

2. When the money was spent to acquire this asset, an expenditure would be recorded in keeping with the goal of measuring the amount of current financial resources.

3. When the debt and interest were subsequently paid, an Expenditure amount would have been recorded for both payments.

Thus, an acquisition would have led to an other financing source at the time money was borrowed, an expenditure when the asset was acquired, and *an additional second expenditure when the debt and interest were paid.* In fund-based financial statements, identical results are mirrored for a capital lease. Using the same eight-year lease in connection with the above truck for $10,000 per year, an amount with a present value of $58,680, the General Fund (or whichever governmental fund was gaining use of the asset) records the following entry:

Fund-based Financial Statements

General Fund

Expenditures—Leased Asset	58,680	
Other Financing Sources—Capital Lease		58,680
To record signing of an eight-year lease for a truck that meets the requirements of a capital lease.		

Note that neither the asset nor the long-term liability are reported because they do not fall within the definition of current financial resources. Prior to *GASB Statement Number 34,* an asset account would have appeared in the General Fixed Assets Account Group with the related liability in the General Long-Term Debt Account Group. However, those balances now are reported in the government-wide financial statements so that the account groups are no longer needed for this purpose.

At the end of this initial year, when the next payment is made, $4,868 (10 percent of the obligation after the first payment) is considered interest while the rest reduces the principal.

Fund-based Financial Statements

General Fund

Expenditures—Interest................................	4,868	
Expenditures—Principal..............................	5,132	
Cash		10,000
To record payment at the end of first year on leased truck being recorded as a capital lease.		

Once again, the radical differences between these two different methods of reporting are quite striking. At the end of this first year, the resulting figures are not comparable in any way. Because the capital lease is being recorded within the governmental funds, the distinctions are quickly apparent:

	Fund-based Financial Statements	Government-wide Financial Statements
Asset	Not applicable	$58,680
Accumulated depreciation	Not applicable	7,335
Liability	Not applicable	43,548
Expenditures:		
Asset	$58,680	Not applicable
Debt principal	5,132	Not applicable
Interest	4,868	Not applicable
Other financing sources	58,680	Not applicable
Depreciation expense	Not applicable	7,335
Interest expense	Not applicable	4,868

SOLID WASTE LANDFILL

The following information is disclosed in the notes to the financial statements of the city of Colonial Heights, Virginia, as of June 30, 1999. The requirements of *GASB 34* had not yet been applied at the time of these statements so that long-term liabilities were being reported in a separate account group.

> The City is currently in the process of closing the former City landfill. The North End has been closed and approved by the Virginia Division of Waste Management. The South End closure plan has been submitted to the Virginia Division of Waste Management and the City expects final approval during fiscal year 2000. As of June 30, 1999, $800,000 has been estimated and reported as a landfill closure care liability in the General Long-Term Debt Account Group. The postclosure costs for both the North and South Ends of the former City landfill are currently projected to be approximately $451,000 based on a minimum ten years of testing. These costs were recorded in the General Long-Term Debt Account Group at June 30, 1999. . . . Actual costs may be higher due to inflation, changes in technology, or changes in regulations.

A great many state and local governments operate solid waste landfills to provide a place for citizens and local companies to dispose of trash and other forms of garbage and refuse. Landfill operations are frequently reported within the Enterprise Funds because many of these facilities require a user fee. However, some landfills are open to the public so that reporting within the General Fund is more appropriate.

Regardless of the type of fund utilized, solid waste landfills can be sources of huge liabilities for governments. The U.S. Environmental Protection Agency has strict rules on closure requirements as well as groundwater monitoring and other postclosure activities. Following such requirements can be quite costly. Thus, the operation of a landfill eventually necessitates large payments to ensure that the facility is properly closed and then monitored and maintained for an extended period. Theoretically, the question has always been how to report closure costs while the landfill was still in operation.

To illustrate, assume that a city opens a landfill in Year One that is expected to take 10 years to fill. Currently, the city expects that a total of $1 million in closure costs will be necessary as well as an additional $400,000 in postclosure costs. During Year One, the city makes an initial $30,000 payment of the closure costs. At the end of the year, the city estimates that 16 percent of the space has been filled.

Government-wide Financial Statements

Regardless of whether this solid waste landfill is reported as a governmental activity (within the General Fund) or as a business-type activity (within an Enterprise Fund), recognition in the government-wide statements is based on accrual accounting and the economic resources measurement basis. Because the government anticipates total costs of $1.4 million and the landfill is 16 percent filled, $224,000 should be accrued in this first year ($1.4 million × 16%).

Year One

Expense—Landfill Closure	224,000	
Landfill Closure Liability...........................		224,000
To recognize Year One portion of cost for eventual closing of landfill.		

An initial payment was made during the year of a part of this cost. This payment simply reduces the liability being reported.

Landfill Closure Liability...............................	30,000	
Cash		30,000
To record first payment of costs necessitated by eventual closure of the landfill.		

To extend this example, assume that the landfill is judged to be 27 percent filled at the end of Year Two and another $30,000 payment has been made. However, because of inflation and newly anticipated changes in technology, the city now believes that closure costs will total $1.1 million and postclosure costs will amount to $500,000.

Using this new and revised information, the city should recognize total costs of $432,000 at the end of Year Two ($1.6 million × 27%). Because $224,000 has already been recorded in Year One, an additional $208,000 is accrued for Year Two ($432,000 less $224,000).

Year Two

Expense—Landfill Closure	208,000	
Landfill Closure Liability...........................		208,000
To recognize Year Two portion of cost for eventual closing of landfill.		
Landfill Closure Liability..............................	30,000	
Cash		30,000
To record second payment of costs necessitated by eventual closure of the landfill.		

Consequently, in the Year Two government-wide financial statements, the city reports:

Expense—Landfill Closure	$208,000
Landfill Closure Liability	
($224,000 + $208,000 − $30,000 − $30,000)	$372,000

Fund-based Financial Statements

If a solid waste landfill is being recorded as an Enterprise Fund, the reporting will be the same in the fund-based financial statements as is shown above. All economic resources are still being measured based on accrual accounting.

However, if the landfill is recorded in the General Fund, only the change in current financial resources is reported. Despite the huge eventual liability, the change in financial resources has been limited to the annual payment of $30,000. Thus, the only entry required each year for the fund-based financial statements is as follows.

Year One and Year Two

General Fund

Expenditures—Closure Costs..........................	30,000	
Cash		30,000
To record annual payment toward the eventual closure costs of the city's solid waste landfill.		

As with capital leases, before the adoption of *GASB Statement Number 34,* the long-term obligation ($372,000 in this case, at the end of Year Two) is reported to the public through the use of a General Long-term Debt Account Group. This method of reporting will no longer be necessary after government-wide financial statements are published.

COMPENSATED ABSENCES

State and local governments have numerous employees: police officers, school teachers, maintenance workers, and the like. As of June 30, 1998, the city of Charlotte, North Carolina, reported having 5,011 employees.[1] In the same manner as the employees of a for-profit organization, government employees earn vacation days, sick leave days, or holidays that can amount to a fairly significant amount of money. At the

---

[1] Statistical information listed at the end of the comprehensive annual financial report provides a wide array of information about the reporting government. For example, in 1998, Charlotte had 54,051 street lights, 1,922 miles of streets, 32 fire stations, 2,764 miles of sanitary sewer lines, 8,900 fire hydrants, 83 elementary schools, and 13 hospitals.

end of the fiscal period, any liability for such compensated absences should be reported. For example, footnotes to the financial statements for the city of Charlotte spell out this issue:

> Employees earn vacation leave at the rate of 10 to 20 days per year and can accrue a maximum of 20 to 40 days, depending on length of service. Unused vacation days are payable upon termination, resignation, retirement or death. Employees accumulate sick leave at the rate of one day per month and can accrue an unlimited number of days. Sick leave can be taken for personal illness or illness of a member of the immediate family. Sick leave is lost upon termination or resignation. However, 20 percent of outstanding sick leave, with a maximum of two months, is payable upon retirement or death.

Clearly, a city such as Charlotte has a liability for any compensated absences that have been earned by government employees. In many ways, accounting for such liabilities is the same as was demonstrated above for capital leases and solid waste landfills because each is based on a particular measurement basis and a method to guide time recognition. For example, assume that a city reaches the end of Year One and owes its employees $40,000 because of compensated absences to be taken in the future for vacation days, holidays, and sick leave which were earned but not yet taken. However, $5,000 of these absences is expected early enough in Year Two to require current financial resources. Perhaps a number of employees are expected to take their vacations in the first month of the subsequent period.

Consequently, a liability of $40,000 exists at the end of Year One but only $5,000 of that amount will be a claim on the government's current financial resources:

Government-wide Financial Statements

Expenses—Compensated Absences.....................	40,000	
Liability—Compensated Absences		40,000
To accrue amount owed to employees for vacations, sick leave, and holidays.		

In contrast, when reporting the governmental funds in the fund-based financial statements, only the changes in current financial resources are reflected. Thus, as shown below, only the $5,000 that will be paid early in the next year is included if the employees are being reported within the governmental funds. The remainder of the debt is not reported, although the reader can determine the total amount from the government-wide statements. Once again, though, if the employees work in an area reported as a proprietary fund, the accounting is the same as above in the government-wide statements.

Fund-based Financial Statements

Year One

General Fund

Expenditures—Compensated Absences..................	5,000	
Liability—Compensated Absences		5,000
To accrue amount of compensated absences that will be taken early in Year Two so that it requires the use of Year One financial resources.		

WORKS OF ART AND HISTORICAL TREASURES

As we cover in the following chapter, private not-for-profit organizations have long debated the proper reporting of artworks and other museum pieces such as paintings that are given to them. This same issue is faced in governmental accounting. Should the donation or purchase of artworks, museum artifacts, and other historical treasures be reported and, if so, what is the proper method of inclusion within the financial statements? *GASB Statements Number 33* and *Number 34* provide authoritative guidance to resolve these reporting questions.

Assume, for example, that a city maintains a small museum in the basement of its main city office building. The museum was created to display documents, maps, and paintings that depict the history of the city and the surrounding area. Several of these items were bought by the city government but a number were donated by local citizens. Many of these purchased and donated pieces are quite valuable.

GASB Number 34 is quite clear on the handling of the items acquired for this city museum. Except in certain specified cases, paragraph 27 states "governments should capitalize works of art, historical treasures, and similar assets at their historical cost or fair value at date of donation." Thus, the government-wide statement of net assets reports an antique map bought for $5,000 as an asset at cost. In the same manner, a map received as a gift should be recorded as a $5,000 asset owned by the city.

When a map is bought by the city for cash, the appropriate journal entry is:

Government-wide Financial Statements

Museum Piece—Map.................................	5,000	
Cash		5,000
To record acquisition of map for the city's museum.		

Because cash was paid for the map, a decrease occurs in current financial resources so that an entry also is needed in the fund-based financial statements if the museum is accounted for within the General Fund. However, if the museum has a user charge and is reported in an Enterprise Fund, the entry above is also made in accounting for the proprietary funds.

Fund-based Financial Statements

General Fund

Expenditure—Museum Piece...........................	5,000	
Cash		5,000
To record acquisition of map for the city's museum which is being reported within the General Fund.		

Conversely, if this map had been donated to the city, capitalization of the asset for government-wide financial statements should still be reported based on its fair market value at the date of the gift. *GASB Statement Number 33* classifies such a gift as a voluntary nonexchange transaction so that a revenue is properly recognized when all eligibility requirements have been met. Assuming the map was given without such requirements, the following entry is made when the gift is received. No parallel entry is made in the fund-based financial statements for the governmental funds because no change is occurring here in the amount of available current financial resources.

Government-wide Financial Statements

Museum Piece—Map.................................	5,000	
Revenue—Donation...............................		5,000
To record gift of map for the city's museum.		

A theoretical problem arises in the recognition of this asset for government-wide financial reporting regardless of whether it was obtained by purchase or by gift. Unless a user charge is assessed, a map displayed for the public to see does not generate cash flows or any other direct economic benefit. Therefore, does the map actually qualify as an asset to be reported?

In *Statement Number 34,* the GASB "encouraged" the recognition of all such artworks and historical treasures. However, if three criteria are all met, recording of the item as an asset is optional. Those criteria apply to a collection if it is:

1. Held for public exhibition, education, or research in furtherance of public service, rather than financial gain.
2. Protected, kept unencumbered, cared for, and preserved.

3. Subject to an organizational policy that requires the proceeds from sales of collection items to be used to acquire other items for collections.[2]

The GASB's handling of this issue closely parallels rules established by the FASB in its *Statement Number 116,* "Accounting for Contributions Received and Contributions Made," issued in June 1993 and utilized by private not-for-profit organizations. However, if a government chooses not to record a qualifying asset in its government-wide financial statements as shown on the previous page, an expense must be reported in place of the asset regardless of whether the item was obtained by purchase or gift.

If a work of art or other historical treasure is capitalized, an additional theoretical question arises, this time about depreciation. Does the map on display in the museum actually depreciate in value over time? In connection with this type of asset, *GASB Statement 34* only requires depreciation if the asset is "exhaustible," in other words, its utility will be used up by display, education, or research. Depreciation is not required, though, if the artwork or historical treasure is viewed as being inexhaustible. For example, a bronze statue seems to be an inexhaustible asset according to these guidelines so that depreciation would be allowed but not necessary.

INFRASTRUCTURE ASSETS AND DEPRECIATION

Infrastructure assets are defined in paragraph 19 of *GASB Statement Number 34* as "long-lived capital assets that normally are stationary in nature and normally can be preserved for a significantly greater number of years than most capital assets." Examples include roads, bridges, tunnels, lighting systems, curbing, and sidewalks. As discussed in the previous chapter, recording of infrastructure items as assets within a city's General Fixed Asset Account Group was an optional practice prior to the issuance of *GASB Statement 34.* However, this pronouncement (once adopted by a government) mandates that infrastructure costs be recorded as assets on the government-wide statement of net assets. In contrast, for the governmental funds such costs are recorded only as expenditures in the fund-based statements because they do not represent current financial resources.

Beyond simply recording new infrastructure items as assets, a state or local government also has to capitalize major general infrastructure assets previously acquired. A major road system constructed in 1988, for example, must be shown as an asset in the government-wide statements. Because cost figures on these earlier acquisitions and constructions may not be available, estimations often are necessary. To allow sufficient time for governments to develop these figures, application of the retroactive reporting of these major infrastructure assets is one area of *GASB Statement Number 34* where required implementation has been delayed.

- For governments with revenues of $100 million or more, this particular reporting is not required until fiscal years beginning after June 15, 2005, (although all other aspects of *Statement 34* are mandated for years beginning after June 15, 2001).

- For governments with revenues of $10 million or more but less than $100 million, retroactive reporting of major infrastructure assets is required for years beginning after June 15, 2006, with other changes necessary in years beginning after June 15, 2002.

- For governments with revenues of less than $10 million, capitalization of previous infrastructure items is encouraged but not required. All other requirements of *Statement 34* must be in place for years beginning after June 15, 2003.

---

[2]*GASB Statement Number 34,* para. 27.

As has been discussed previously, *GASB Statement 34* requires depreciation of all capital assets appearing in the government-wide financial statements except for land and artworks and historical treasures that are inexhaustible. A similar issue was debated in connection with infrastructure items: Is depreciation appropriate for this type of asset? For example, construction of the Brooklyn Bridge was finished in 1883 at a cost of about $15 million. That particular piece of infrastructure has been operating for approximately 120 years and, with proper maintenance, might well be able to continue to carry traffic for another 120 years. Much the same can be said of some roads, sidewalks, and the like. With appropriate repair and maintenance care, such assets could have lives that are almost indefinite. What life should New York City use to depreciate the initial cost incurred in constructing Fifth Avenue?

Consequently, *GASB Statement Number 34* provides an alternative to depreciating eligible infrastructure assets such as the Brooklyn Bridge or Fifth Avenue. This method is known as the "modified approach" and eliminates the need for depreciation for qualifying infrastructure. If specified guidelines are met, the government can expense all maintenance costs each year in lieu of recording depreciation. Additions and improvements still must be capitalized but the cost of maintaining the infrastructure in proper working condition is expensed. Thus, the amount spent by New York City on repair and other maintenance of Fifth Avenue can be expensed directly so that depreciation of the street's capitalized cost is not recorded.

Use of the modified approach requires the government to accumulate information about particular infrastructure assets within either a network or a subsystem of a network. For example, all roads could be deemed a network while state roads, rural roads, and interstate highways might make up three subsystems of that network.

- For these eligible assets, the government must establish a minimum acceptable condition level for the network or subsystem of the network and then maintain documentation that this minimum condition level is being met.

- The government has to have an asset management system in place to monitor the particular network or subsystem of a network in question. This system should maintain records of these infrastructure assets. It must also assess the ongoing condition of the eligible assets to ensure that they are, indeed, able to operate at the predetermined level. Finally, the government must be able to make an annual estimation of the cost of maintaining and preserving the infrastructure to meet the condition level requirements that have been established.

For example, a city might view its entire water system as an infrastructure network. The city could then state that it wants to maintain this network so that water stoppages occur less than two days per year on the average. To achieve this level of performance, the city believes that it will have to spend at least $5 million per year in repair and other maintenance costs. To apply the modified approach, the city has to establish an asset management system to (1) keep an up-to-date inventory of the water system, (2) assess the system to determine if it is operating at (or above) the condition level established, and (3) document the level of operations achieved. As a result, no depreciation would be reported in connection with the capitalized cost of the water system. All costs to maintain the water system should be expensed as incurred although additions and actual improvements still must be capitalized. For example, if the water system is extended into a new neighborhood, that is a capitalized cost and not a maintenance expense.

GASB Statement Number 34 provides an example of the type of disclosure that is necessary to explain the use of the modified approach:

> The City manages its streets using the XYZ pavement management system. The City's policy is to maintain 85 percent of its streets at a pavement condition index of at least 70 (on a 100-point scale) and no more than 10 percent of its streets at a pavement condition index below 50. The most recent assessment found that the City's streets were within the

prescribed parameters with 87 percent having a pavement condition index of 70 or better and only 2 percent of the streets having a pavement condition index below 50.[3]

MANAGEMENT'S DISCUSSION AND ANALYSIS

As described in an earlier chapter of this textbook on the Securities and Exchange Commission, inclusion of a verbal explanation of a for-profit company's operations and financial position to accompany its financial statements has long been advocated by the SEC. This memorandum, known generally as the management's discussion and analysis (MD&A), provides a wealth of vital information for the reader of the financial statements. Thus, in evaluating such organizations, outside decision makers are quite used to having a "plain English" explanation of the figures and other critical information disclosed within the statements. For example, the 1999 financial statements of the General Electric Company contained

- 9 pages of explanation entitled "Management's Discussion of Operations."
- 4 pages of explanation entitled "Management's Discussion of Financial Resources and Liquidity."
- 2 pages of explanation entitled "Management's Discussion of Selected Financial Data."
- Half a page of explanation entitled "Management's Discussion of Financial Responsibility."

Consequently, a stockholder, creditor, potential investor, or other interested party is provided with extensive details to describe and supplement the facts and figures presented within the company's financial statements.

One of the most important changes created by *GASB Statement Number 34* was the requirement that a similar MD&A be required of state and local governments. This authoritative pronouncement actually divided the general purpose external financial statements of a state or local government into three distinct sections:

1. Management's discussion and analysis.
2. Financial statements:
   a. Government-wide financial statements.
   b. Fund-based financial statements.
   c. Notes to the financial statements.
3. Required supplementary information (other than the MD&A). For example, comparison of budgetary figures to actual figures is now shown in this final section although a separate statement within the financial statements can also be used.

In *Statement Number 34,* the GASB explains its justification for requiring officials to provide readers of the government's financial statements with an MD&A:

The basic financial statements should be preceded by MD&A, which is required supplementary information (RSI). MD&A should provide an objective and easily readable analysis of the government's financial activities based on currently known facts, decisions, or conditions. The financial managers of governments are knowledgeable about the transactions, events, and conditions that are reflected in the government's financial report and of the fiscal policies that govern its operations. MD&A provides financial managers with the opportunity to present both a short- and a long-term analysis of the government's activities. MD&A should discuss current-year results in comparison with the prior year, with emphasis on the current year. This fact-based analysis should discuss the positive

---

[3]*GASB Statement Number 34,* p. 181.

and negative aspects of the comparison with the prior year. The use of charts, graphs, and tables is encouraged to enhance the understandability of the information.[4]

As further guidance for the government officials who will have to write this MD&A, *GASB Statement 34* provides an extensive sample of the type of information and format that should be included. Reproduction of GASB's complete MD&A illustration is beyond the scope of this textbook. However, the following small sample provided in *Statement Number 34* facilitates an understanding of the intended purpose of the MD&A. This particular portion of the illustration explains operating changes that occurred during the year in connection with the government's business-type activities:

> Revenues of the City's business-type activities increased by 5.6 percent ($15 million in 2002 compared to $14.2 million in 2001) and expenses decreased by 1.7 percent. The factors driving these results include:
>
> ■ The City water and sewer system, benefiting from growth in hook-ups by residential customers who are converting from septic systems, saw its operating revenues climb 10 percent to $11.3 million, but operating expenses rose only 4 percent, to $6.9 million. High maintenance costs—caused by the harsh winter months in 2001—did not occur this year.
>
> ■ The City parking facilities, however, continue to operate at a deficit (by $1.4 million this year versus $1.3 million in 2001). In both years, this decrease is attributable primarily to the largest of the three City-owned parking garages, located on State Street. This year, the garage had to be closed for two extended periods due to ruptured gas lines beneath nearby streets, which now have been repaired, and the State Street Mall fire. These closings stopped revenues from being generated by the garage for two months, while only slightly reducing expenses.[5]

As can be seen from this one short example, the MD&A is intended to provide a clear description of events to highlight and explain financial results for the period. The MD&A goes well beyond just numerical totals to convey background information so that the causes of the various figures and the changes encountered are more understandable.

GASB Statement Number 34 provides minimum requirements for the types of disclosures that must be included in the MD&A although a government is not prohibited from providing additional information and explanations. The MD&A presented by a government must have all of the following according to paragraph 11:

1. A brief discussion of the basic financial statements. This discussion should describe the relationship of the statements to each other and the significant differences in information provided. Analysis should also be included to help explain why measurements and results reported in the fund-based statements reinforce or provide additional information to the government-wide financial statements.

2. Condensed financial information derived from government-wide financial statements comparing the current year to the prior year. At a minimum, governments should include:
   a. Total assets, distinguishing between capital and other assets.
   b. Total liabilities, divided between long-term and other liabilities.
   c. Total net assets, distinguishing among amounts invested in capital assets, net of related debt; restricted amounts; and unrestricted amounts.
   d. Program revenues, by major source.
   e. General revenues, by major source.
   f. Total revenues.
   g. Program expenses, at a minimum by function.
   h. Total expenses.

---

[4]*GASB Statement Number 34,* para. 8 and 9.

[5]*GASB Statement Number 34,* p. 191.

    i. Excess or deficiency before contributions to term and permanent endowments or permanent fund principal, special and extraordinary items, and transfers.

    j. Contributions.

    k. Special and extraordinary items.

    l. Transfers.

    m. Change in net assets.

    n. Ending net assets.

3. An analysis of overall financial position and results of operations to aid assessment of whether financial position has improved or deteriorated as a result of the year's operations.

4. An analysis of balances and transactions of individual funds explaining the reasons for significant changes in fund balances or net assets as well as any significant restrictions.

5. An analysis of significant variations between original and final budget amounts along with variations between final budget amounts and actual results for the General Fund.

6. A description of significant capital asset and long-term debt activity during the year.

7. If the modified approach is used for some or all infrastructure assets, information should be provided about its application.

8. A description of currently known facts, decisions, or conditions that are expected to have a significant effect on financial position or results of operations.

As can be seen, the MD&A is intended to provide a broad range of information to help decision makers evaluate the operations and financial position of the government unit.

The general purpose external financial statements outlined previously are normally presented to the public as part of a comprehensive annual financial report (often referred to as a CAFR). Even prior to *GASB Statement Number 34,* the CAFR has included extensive information about the reporting government. For example, the 1998 CAFR for the city of Saint Paul, Minnesota, with total revenues of about $320 million was 250 pages long. In comparison, the 1999 annual report for the General Electric Company with $111 billion in revenues was only 77 pages.

GASB Statement 34 stipulates that the CAFR of a state or local government will include three broad sections:

1. *Introductory Section*—includes a letter of transmittal from appropriate government officials, an organization chart, and a list of principal officers.

2. *Financial Section*—presents the general purpose external financial statements. In addition, the auditor's report is reproduced. The government also usually prepares additional supplementary information such as combining statements to present financial information for funds that do not qualify as major.

3. *Statistical Section*—presents a wide range of data about the government. For example, the 1998 CAFR for Boise City, Idaho, included the following within its statistical section as well as a considerable amount of other information:

    10-year recap of general government expenditures.

    10-year recap of property tax levies and collections.

    10-year recap of property tax rates.

    Principal taxpayers for the current year.

    10-year recap of special assessment debt and collections.

    Schedule of long-term debts.

    Top 10 employers during the current year.

Business indicators for the current year.

Salaries for city officials.

THE PRIMARY GOVERNMENT AND COMPONENT UNITS

Although gathering and maintaining financial information is a vital step in government accounting, the actual reporting of this data to the public is equally important.

> Governmental accountability is based on the belief that the citizenry has a "right to know," a right to receive openly declared facts that may lead to public debate by the citizens and their elected representatives. Financial reporting plays a major role in fulfilling government's duty to be publicly accountable in a democratic society.[6]

In producing financial statements, a state or locality often encounters a unique problem—determining the specific activities to be included. Except in rare cases, a business enterprise such as IBM or Ford Motor Company simply consolidates all corporations over which control has been achieved. A state or locality, however, may interact with numerous departments, agencies, boards, institutes, commissions, and the like that have various relationships with these governments. Should all of these functions be included as either governmental activities or business-type activities within the CAFR of the government? If not, what reporting is appropriate?

An almost unlimited number of activities create problems for government officials attempting to outline the parameters of the entity being reported. Separate organizations such as turnpike commissions, port authorities, public housing boards, and downtown development commissions have become commonplace in recent years. Many of these are created by the government but remain legally separate from it. Such entities are designed to focus attention on specific issues or problems and can possibly offer better efficiency because of their corporate-style structure.

In the introductory section of its 1998 CAFR, the city of Fort Lauderdale, Florida, discusses various organizations that are related to the government including:

■ Fort Lauderdale Community Redevelopment Agency.

■ Downtown Development Authority.

■ Housing Authority of the City of Fort Lauderdale.

Likewise, the 1998 CAFR for the city of Greensboro, North Carolina, identifies several legally separate activities that are still reported within the city's financial statements:

■ Redevelopment Commission of Greensboro.

■ Greensboro Transit Authority.

■ Greensboro ABC Board.

Because of the extremely wide variety of possible activities and functions, determining which components actually comprise a state or locality is not always an easy task. According to paragraphs 2 and 8 of *GASB Statement Number 14*, "The Financial Reporting Entity," the major criterion for inclusion in a government's comprehensive annual financial report is financial accountability:

> Financial reporting based on accountability should enable the financial statement reader to focus on the body of organizations that are related by a common thread of accountability to the constituent citizenry. . . . Elected officials are accountable to those citizens for their public policy decisions, regardless of whether these decisions are carried out directly by the elected officials through the operations of the primary government or *by their designees through the operations of specially created organizations* (emphasis added).

_____

[6]*GASB Cod.* sec. 100.156.

In defining the overall reporting entity, the primary government must be identified. The primary government includes and must report all funds, activities, organizations, agencies, offices, and departments that are not legally separate from it. A primary government is any state government or general-purpose local government such as a city or county. However, a special-purpose local government such as a school system also may be deemed a primary government if it meets three criteria:

1. It has a separately elected governing body.
2. It is legally independent which can be demonstrated by having corporate powers such as the right to sue and be sued in its own name as well as the right to buy, sell, and lease property in its own name.
3. It is fiscally independent of other state and local governments.

The term *fiscally independent* requires some clarification. Fiscal independence is normally demonstrated by an activity if its leadership can determine its own budget without having to seek approval from an outside party, levy taxes or set rates without having to seek outside approval, and issue bonded debt without having to seek outside approval.

Thus, a city is clearly a primary government but its police department and fire department are not. However, if a school system is a legally separate entity according to the laws of its state and has a publicly elected board which sets its own budget, levies its own tax, and issues its own bonds, it is a primary government that would issue its own CAFR. In contrast, a school system which must have its annual budget and tax levies set or approved by the local city council is not a primary government.

Some activities can be legally separate from a primary government but still be so closely connected that omission from the statements of the primary government cannot be justified. The elected officials of the primary government are still financially accountable for these separate organizations known as component units of the primary government.

Because component units are included within the financial statements of the primary government, identification of such activities can be quite important. Two sets of criteria have been established for this purpose. If either set of criteria is met, the activity in question is a component unit to be reported within the CAFR of the primary government.

Criterion One   The separate organization is fiscally dependent on the primary organization regardless of the extent of other relationships. As defined above, fiscal dependency means that the organization cannot do one or more of the following without approval of the primary government: adopt its own budget, levy taxes or set rates, or issue bonded debt. For example, if the budget of a legally separate museum board must be approved by the city government, this board is classified as a component unit.

Criterion Two   First, the officials of the primary government must appoint a voting majority of the governing board of the separate organization. And second, either the primary government must be able to impose its will on the board of the separate organization, or the separate organization must provide a financial benefit or impose a financial burden on the primary government.

For example, a commission to oversee off-track betting might be legally established as a separate entity. However, if the state (the primary government) appoints a voting majority of the board membership and the benefits from revenues generated by the commission accrue to the state, the commission will be considered a component unit of the state for reporting purposes.

Several aspects of this second criterion should be explained further to allow for proper application in actual practice:

DISCUSSION QUESTION

Is It Part of the County?

Harland County is in a financially distressed portion of Missouri. In hopes of enticing business to this area, the state legislature appropriated $3 million to start an industrial development commission. The federal government provided an additional $1 million. The state appointed 15 individuals to a board to oversee the operations of this commission while county officials named 5 members. The commission began operations by raising funds from local citizens and businesses. It received an extra $700,000 in donations and pledges. The county provided clerical assistance and allowed the commission to use one floor of the county office building for its headquarters. The commission's budget must be approved by the county government.

During the current period, the commission spent $2.4 million and produced financial statements. Notable success was achieved as several large manufacturing companies have begun to explore the possibility of opening plants in the county.

Harland County is presently beginning the process of producing its own comprehensive annual financial report. Should the revenues, expenditures, assets, and liabilities of the industrial development commission be included? Is it part of the county's primary government, a component unit, or a related organization?

Is the industrial development commission a component unit of the state of Missouri? How should its activities be presented in the state's comprehensive annual financial report?

Voting Majority of the Governing Board   The authority to elect a voting majority must be substantive. If, for example, the primary government simply confirms the choices made by other parties, financial accountability is not created. In the same way, financial accountability does not result when the primary government is allowed to select the governing board from only a limited slate of candidates (such as three individuals from an approved list of five). Thus, the primary government must have the actual responsibility of appointing a voting majority of the board before the organization qualifies as a component unit.

Imposition of the Primary Government's Will on the Governing Board   Such power is indicated if the government can significantly influence the programs, projects, activities, or the level of services provided by the organization. This degree of influence is present if the primary government can remove an appointed board member at will, modify or approve budgets, override decisions of the board, modify or approve rate or fee changes, and hire or dismiss the individuals responsible for day-to-day operations.

Financial Benefit or Financial Burden on the Primary Government   A financial connection exists between the organization and the government if the government is entitled to the organization's resources, the government is legally obligated to finance any deficits or provide support, or the government is responsible for the debts of the organization.

As shown in the next section on general purpose external financial statements, component units normally are reported in one of two ways: Many component units are discretely presented to the far right side of the statement. For example, the 1998 CAFR for the city of Fort Wayne, Indiana, shows that the primary government had total revenues of more than $118 million while the discretely presented component units shown just to the right of the primary government had revenues of $4 million.

As an alternative placement, certain component units can be included by a primary government as if they were part of the government (a process referred to as *blending*). Although the organization is legally separate, it is so intertwined with the primary government that inclusion is necessary for the appropriate presentation of the financial information. In discussing the accounting for the Housing and Redevelopment Authority of the city of Saint Paul, the notes to the 1998 financial statements explain that the "following component unit has been presented as a blended component unit because the component unit's governing body is substantively the same as the governing body of the City."

One other aspect of the reporting process should be noted—the possible existence of related organizations. In such cases, the primary government is accountable because it appoints a voting majority of the governing board. However, financial accountability does not exist. Fiscal dependency as defined above is not present and the primary government cannot impose its will on the board or gather financial benefits or burdens from the relationship. Without financial accountability, the organization does not qualify as a component unit to be included in the government's financial reporting. Instead, because of the ability to appoint a voting majority of the board, the primary government must disclose the nature of the accountability. For example, the 1998 CAFR for the city of Charlotte, North Carolina, indicates "the Charlotte Housing Authority (Housing Authority), which is excluded from the City's financial statements, is considered a related organization. The City Council appoints the Housing Authority's governing board; however, the City is not financially accountable for the Housing Authority."

GENERAL PURPOSE EXTERNAL FINANCIAL STATEMENTS

As described in the previous chapter, a central element of the reporting requirements created by *GASB Statement Number 34* was the development of new general purpose external financial statements for governments. The first two of these statements are deemed to be government-wide financial statements because they present all of the governmental funds and the proprietary funds. These statements measure economic resources and utilize accrual accounting to time the recognition of revenues and expenses.

A number of other financial statements also have been designed to present information describing individual funds. These fund-based statements are much more like the financial statements traditionally reported by state and local government units. At the fund level, the method of accounting depends on the fund in question. For governmental funds, the current financial resources measurement basis is used along with modified accrual accounting. However, both proprietary funds and fiduciary funds use accrual accounting to measure economic resources.

In the previous chapter, four of these statements were outlined briefly to give direction to the initial coverage. However, now that a deeper understanding of government accounting has been established, these same statements as well as several others can be studied in more detail. Having an appreciation for the end result of the accounting process helps to show how the many elements of government accounting fit together into a complete reporting package.

Statement of Net Assets—Government-wide Financial Statements

In Exhibit 17–1, we present a sample statement of net assets. As a government-wide financial statement, it is designed to present the economic resources of the government as a whole except for the fiduciary funds. Fiduciary funds are not included here because those assets must be used for a purpose outside of the primary government. These funds are only shown in the fund-based statements.

Several aspects of the statement of net assets should be noted specifically:

- All assets including capital assets are reported because the measurement basis is the economic resources controlled by the government. Long-term liabilities are included for the same reason.
- Capital assets are reported net of accumulated depreciation because depreciation is required to be reported on the government-wide statements. Newly acquired infrastructure assets are included as capital assets. Eventually, the reporting of major infrastructure assets previously obtained will be required.

Exhibit 17–1   Government-wide Financial Statements

	SAMPLE CITY **Statement of Net Assets** **December 31, 2002**			
	Primary Government			
	Governmental Activities	**Business-type Activities**	**Total**	**Component Units**
Assets				
Cash and cash equivalents	$ 13,597,899	$ 10,279,143	$ 23,877,042	$ 303,935
Investments	27,365,221	—	27,365,221	7,428,952
Receivables (net)	12,833,132	3,609,615	16,442,747	4,042,290
Internal balances	175,000	(175,000)	—	—
Inventories	322,149	126,674	448,823	83,697
Capital assets, net	170,022,760	151,388,751	321,411,511	37,744,786
Total assets	224,316,161	165,229,183	389,545,344	49,603,660
Liabilities				
Accounts payable	6,783,310	751,430	7,534,740	1,803,332
Deferred revenue	1,435,599	—	1,435,599	38,911
Noncurrent liabilities				
Due within one year	9,236,000	4,426,286	13,662,286	1,426,639
Due in more than one year	83,302,378	74,482,273	157,784,651	27,106,151
Total liabilities	100,757,287	79,659,989	180,417,276	30,375,033
Net Assets				
Invested in capital assets, net of related debt	103,711,386	73,088,574	176,799,960	15,906,392
Restricted for:				
Capital projects	11,705,864	—	11,705,864	492,445
Debt service	3,020,708	1,451,996	4,472,704	—
Community development projects	4,811,043	—	4,811,043	—
Other purposes..........................	3,214,302	—	3,214,302	—
Unrestricted (deficit)	(2,904,429)	11,028,624	8,124,195	2,829,790
Total net assets	$123,558,874	$ 85,569,194	$209,128,068	$19,228,627

- The primary government is divided into governmental activities and business-type activities. At the government-wide level, both of these columns are based on accrual accounting. Governmental funds are all in the governmental activities whereas enterprise funds comprise the business-type activities. Even though recorded within the proprietary funds, internal service funds are normally included within the governmental activities because those services are rendered primarily to benefit activities within the governmental funds. However, if a particular internal service fund predominately serves an enterprise fund, that internal service fund should be included as a business-type activity.

- The internal balances shown in the asset section come from inter-activity transactions between the governmental activities and the business-type activities. Intra-activity transactions occur solely within a category and should not be reported here because the liability and receivable cancel out. The internal balances reported on this statement offset each other so that no impact affects the total for the primary government.

- Investments are reported at fair market value rather than historical cost.

- Discretely presented component units are shown to the far right side of the statement so that the reported amounts do not affect the primary government figures. However, if any blended component units exist, those balances are included, as appropriate, within either the governmental activities or the business-type activities.

- Since this is a statement of net assets, the format is not structured to stress that assets are equal to liabilities plus equities as is found in a typical balance sheet. Rather, the assets ($389 million for the primary government) less liabilities of $180 million leaves net assets of $209 million.

- As seen in the final section, several amounts within the net assets being held have been restricted for capital projects, debt service, and the like. Restrictions are shown in this manner only if assets have been restricted either externally by creditors, grantors, or the like, or because of laws passed through constitutional provisions or enabling legislation.

- Although not restricted, the amount of net assets tied up in capital assets less any related debt is reported as a separate figure within the net assets.

Statement of Activities—Government-wide Financial Statements

The statement of activities is one of the most important governmental financial statements because of the wide array of information that it presents. As can be seen in Exhibit 17–2, the same general classification system of governmental activities, business-type activities, and component units used in Exhibit 17–1 provides the basis for reporting revenues and expenses. However, the format is much more complex and requires close analysis.

- Expenses are not presented according to individual causes such as salaries, rent, depreciation, or insurance. Instead, all expenses are shown by function: general government, public safety, public works, and the like. For example, the salary of police officers is a part of the total expenses incurred for public safety as is the depreciation of the police cars. As stated in paragraph 41 of *GASB Statement Number 14,* "as a minimum, governments should report direct expenses for each function. Direct expenses are those that are specifically associated with a service, program, or department and, thus, are clearly identifiable to a particular function." Many indirect expenses are simply assigned to a relatively generic function such as general government; however, as an alternative, indirect expenses can be allocated in some appropriate manner to the various operating functions.

- Interest expense on general long-term debt is normally an indirect expense because it benefits many government operations; because of its size and informational value, this expense frequently is shown as in Exhibit 17–2 as a separate "function."

- After expenses have been determined for each function (governmental activities, business-type activities, and component units), related program revenues should be reported. Program revenues are those revenues derived from the program itself or from outsiders seeking to reduce the cost of the function. As can be seen in Exhibit 17–2, program revenues are divided into three columns:

  1. Charges rendered for services. For example, a monthly charge might be assessed for garbage collection; therefore, the health and sanitation category shows more than $5 million in program revenues.

  2. Operating grants and contributions. This column reports revenues from grants and similar sources that were designated for some type of operating purpose. For example, the $2.45 million in operating grants and contributions shown for culture and recreation could have been state funds provided to supplement the salaries of summer recreation workers.

Exhibit 17–2   Government-wide Financial Statements

SAMPLE CITY
Statement of Activities
For the Year Ended December 31, 2002

Functions/Programs	Expenses	Program Revenues		
		Charges for Services	Operating Grants and Contributions	Capital Grants and Contributions
Primary government:				
Governmental activities:				
General government	$ 9,571,410	$ 3,146,915	$ 843,617	$ —
Public safety	34,844,749	1,198,855	1,307,693	62,300
Public works	10,128,538	850,000	—	2,252,615
Engineering services	1,299,645	704,793	—	—
Health and sanitation	6,738,672	5,612,267	575,000	—
Cemetery	735,866	212,496	—	—
Culture and recreation	11,532,350	3,995,199	2,450,000	—
Community development	2,994,389	—	—	2,580,000
Education (payment to school district)	21,893,273	—	—	—
Interest on long-term debt	6,068,121	—	—	—
Total governmental activities	105,807,013	15,720,525	5,176,310	4,894,915
Business-type activities:				
Water	3,595,733	4,159,350	—	1,159,909
Sewer	4,912,853	7,170,533	—	486,010
Parking facilities	2,796,283	1,344,087	—	—
Total business-type activities	11,304,869	12,673,970	—	1,645,919
Total primary government	$117,111,882	$28,394,495	$5,176,310	$6,540,834
Component units:				
Landfill	$ 3,382,157	$ 3,857,858	$ —	$ 11,397
Public school system	31,186,498	705,765	3,937,083	—
Total component units	$ 34,568,655	$ 4,563,623	$3,937,083	$ 11,397

General revenues:
 Taxes:
  Property taxes, levied for general purposes . . . .
  Property taxes, levied for debt service . . . .
  Franchise taxes . . . .
  Public service taxes . . . .
 Payment from Sample City . . . .
 Grants and contributions not restricted to specific programs . . . .
 Investment earnings . . . .
 Miscellaneous . . . .
 Special item—Gain on sale of park land . . . .
 Transfers . . . .
  Total general revenues, special items, and transfers . . . .
   Change in net assets . . . .
 Net assets—beginning . . . .
 Net assets—ending . . . .

SAMPLE CITY
Statement of Activities
For the Year Ended December 31, 2002

	Net (Expense) Revenue and Changes in Net Assets			
	Primary Government			
	Governmental Activities	Business-type Activities	Total	Component Units
	$ (5,580,878)	$ —	$ (5,580,878)	$ —
	(32,275,901)	—	(32,275,901)	—
	(7,025,923)	—	(7,025,923)	—
	(594,852)	—	(594,852)	—
	(551,405)	—	(551,405)	—
	(523,370)	—	(523,370)	—
	(5,087,151)	—	(5,087,151)	—
	(414,389)	—	(414,389)	—
	(21,893,273)	—	(21,893,273)	—
	(6,068,121)	—	(6,068,121)	—
	(80,015,263)	—	(80,015,263)	—
	—	1,723,526	1,723,526	—
	—	2,743,690	2,743,690	—
	—	(1,452,196)	(1,452,196)	—
	—	3,015,020	3,015,020	—
	(80,015,263)	3,015,020	(77,000,243)	—
	—	—	—	487,098
	—	—	—	(26,543,650)
	—	—	—	(26,056,552)
	51,693,573	—	51,693,573	—
	4,726,244	—	4,726,244	—
	4,055,505	—	4,055,505	—
	8,969,887	—	8,969,887	—
	—	—	—	21,893,273
	1,457,820	—	1,457,820	6,461,708
	1,958,144	601,349	2,559,493	881,763
	884,907	104,925	989,832	22,464
	2,653,488	—	2,653,488	—
	501,409	(501,409)	—	—
	76,900,977	204,865	77,105,842	29,259,208
	(3,114,286)	3,219,885	105,599	3,202,656
	126,673,160	82,349,309	209,022,469	16,025,971
	$123,558,874	$85,569,194	$209,128,068	$ 19,228,627

3. Capital grants and contributions. This column shows revenues from grants and similar sources designated for capital asset additions.

- After expenses have been assigned to each function as well as related program revenues, a net (expense) or revenue figure can be determined for each function. This net figure provides a measure of the cost of the various operations of the government. As explained in paragraph 38 of *GASB Statement Number 14,* "an objective of using the net (expense) revenue format is to report the relative financial burden of each of the reporting government's functions on its taxpayers." For example, in Exhibit 17–2, the cemetery incurred $735,866 in expenses while only $212,496 in related charges were generated. Thus, taxpayers had to bear the burden of the other $523,370 in cemetery costs for that year. In contrast, the water system reported expenses of about $3.6 million whereas charges were over $4.1 million and capital grants provided another $1.2 million so that the net revenues resulting from this business-type activity was a positive $1.7 million.

- Net expenses and revenues can be determined in total for each category of the government. In this example, all of the governmental activities combined for net expenses of over $80 million while the business-type activities generated net revenues of approximately $3 million. The component units reported net expenses of just over $26 million.

- Once again, the internal service funds have been combined with the governmental activities (or with the business-type activities if that is more appropriate). The revenues and expenses should be assigned to the appropriate functions. For example, the cost of work done by an internal service fund for engineering services should be assigned to that function. However, in allocating such amounts, any intra-activity figures must be eliminated to avoid double counting. For example, assume an internal service fund buys supplies that it sells to the General Fund. If the General Fund then uses these supplies, both funds are recording an expense for the supplies and the internal service fund reports an intra-activity revenue for the sale. Such balances must be removed.

- General revenues are reported at the bottom of the statement as additions to either the governmental activities, business-type activities, or component units. All taxes are general revenues because they do not reflect a charge for services; they are obtained from the population as a whole. In addition, such transactions as unrestricted grants and investment income fall under this same category.

- Note the "special item" shown under the general revenues in Exhibit 17–2. Paragraph 56 of *GASB Statement Number 34* explains "significant transactions or other events within the control of management that are either unusual in nature or infrequent in occurrence are special items. Special items should also be reported separately in the statement of activities, before extraordinary items, if any."

- Transfers made between governmental activities and business-type activities are also shown under the general revenues but they are offset so that no impact is created on the total that is reported for the primary government.

Balance Sheet—Governmental Funds

Exhibit 17–3 presents a balance sheet for the governmental funds. This statement measures only current financial resources and uses modified accrual accounting for timing purposes. No proprietary funds, component units, or fiduciary funds are included; the statement reflects just the governmental funds. Several parts of this statement should be noted:

- *GASB Statement Number 34* requires that a separate column be shown here for the General Fund and any other major fund monitored within the governmental

Exhibit 17–3   Fund-based Financial Statements

SAMPLE CITY
Balance Sheet
Governmental Funds
December 31, 2002

	General	HUD Programs	Community Redevelopment	Route 7 Construction	Other Governmental Funds	Total Governmental Funds
Assets						
Cash and cash equivalents	$3,418,485	$1,236,523	$ —	$ —	$ 5,606,792	$ 10,261,800
Investments	—	—	13,262,695	10,467,037	3,485,252	27,214,984
Receivables, net	3,644,561	2,953,438	353,340	11,000	10,221	6,972,560
Due from other funds	1,370,757	—	—	—	—	1,370,757
Receivables from other governments	—	119,059	—	—	1,596,038	1,715,097
Liens receivable	791,926	3,195,745	—	—	—	3,987,671
Inventories	182,821	—	—	—	—	182,821
Total assets	$9,408,550	$7,504,765	$13,616,035	$10,478,037	$10,698,303	$ 51,705,690
Liabilities and Fund Balances						
Liabilities:						
Accounts payable	$3,408,680	$ 129,975	$ 190,548	$ 1,104,632	$ 1,074,831	$ 5,908,666
Due to other funds	—	25,369	—	—	—	25,369
Payable to other governments	94,074	—	—	—	—	94,074
Deferred revenue	4,250,430	6,273,045	250,000	11,000	—	10,784,475
Total liabilities	7,753,184	6,428,389	440,548	1,115,632	1,074,831	16,812,584
Fund balances:						
Reserved for:						
Inventories	182,821	—	—	—	—	182,821
Liens receivable	791,926	—	—	—	—	791,926
Encumbrances	40,292	41,034	119,314	5,792,587	1,814,122	7,807,349
Debt service	—	—	—	—	3,832,062	3,832,062
Other purposes	—	—	—	—	1,405,300	1,405,300
Unreserved, reported in:						
General fund	640,327	—	—	—	—	640,327
Special revenue funds	—	1,035,342	—	—	1,330,718	2,366,060
Capital projects funds	—	—	13,056,173	3,569,818	1,241,270	17,867,261
Total fund balances	1,655,366	1,076,376	13,175,487	9,362,405	9,623,472	34,893,106
Total liabilities and fund balances	$9,408,550	$7,504,765	$13,616,035	$10,478,037	$10,698,303	

Amounts reported for *governmental activities* in the statement of net assets are different because:

Capital assets used in governmental activities are not financial resources and therefore are not reported in the funds.	161,082,708
Other long-term assets are not available to pay for current-period expenditures and therefore are deferred in the funds.	9,348,876
Internal service funds are used by management to charge the costs of certain activities, such as insurance and telecommunications, to individual funds. The assets and liabilities of the internal service funds are included in governmental activities in the statement of net assets.	2,994,691
Long-term liabilities, including bonds payable, are not due and payable in the current period and therefore are not reported in the funds.	(84,760,507)
Net assets of governmental activities (See Exhibit 17–1)	$123,558,874

funds. In this example, HUD programs, community redevelopment, and Route 7 construction have been identified by the reporting entity as major. The government can classify any fund as major if officials believe it is particularly important to statement users. However, as mentioned in the previous chapter, a fund is considered major and reported separately if it meets two criteria:

1. Total assets, liabilities, revenues, or expenses/expenditures of the fund are at least 10 percent of the corresponding total for all such funds.

2. Total assets, liabilities, revenues, or expenses/expenditures of the fund are at least 5 percent of the corresponding total for all governmental funds and enterprise funds combined.

- All funds that are not considered to be major are combined and reported as "other governmental funds."

- No capital assets or long-term debts are being reported on this balance sheet because only current financial resources are being measured.

- Totals for the governmental funds appear in the final column. However, internal balances such as "due from other funds" (a receivable) and "due to other funds" (a liability) have not been offset. Thus, these totals are just mathematical summations.

- The Fund Balances Reserved figures show amounts of the reported financial resources that are not available for spending because of inventories, encumbrances, and the like.

- The final total fund balances figure for the governmental funds of approximately $34.9 million is significantly different from the $123.6 million in total net assets reported for governmental activities as a whole in the statement of net assets (Exhibit 17–1). To help understand that large discrepancy, a reconciliation is included at the bottom of the balance sheet. This reconciliation shows that four amounts were left off of the balance sheet here: capital assets, other long-term assets, internal service fund accounts, and long-term debt. Those items made up the difference in the two totals.

Statement of Revenues, Expenditures, and Changes in Fund Balances—Governmental Funds

As shown in Exhibit 17–4, a statement of revenues, expenditures, and changes in fund balances should be shown for the governmental funds. Once again, the General Fund is detailed in a separate column along with each of the other major funds previously identified in the balance sheet in Exhibit 17–3. All remaining nonmajor funds are then accumulated and shown together.

- Revenues are not separately identified as either program revenues or general revenues as was the case in Exhibit 17–2. For that reason, program revenues are not assigned to a specific function and no net revenue or expense figure is determined for each of the functions such as general government or public safety.

- Because the current financial resources measurement basis is being utilized, expenditures rather than expenses are being reported. For example, "capital outlay" is presented here but would not have been appropriate on the statement of activities. In the same way, "debt service—principal" is reported on the statement in Exhibit 17–4.

- Since the modified accrual method of accounting is being used for timing purposes, reported amounts will be different than reported previously. For example, total expenditures for interest and other charges are listed on Exhibit 17–4 as $5,215,151 whereas interest on long-term debt disclosed in Exhibit 17–2 is $6,068,121. The difference results in part because the first figure measures expenditures during the period using modified accrual accounting while the second figure is the amount of expense recognized according to accrual accounting.

■ Other financing sources and uses are presented in this statement to reflect the proceeds from bond sales and transfers made between the funds. Because these statements are designed to present fund activities rather than government-wide figures, no elimination of the transfers is made.

■ The "special item" reported at the bottom of Exhibit 17–2 is also displayed in Exhibit 17–4. However, in Exhibit 17–2, the gain was reported to indicate the increase in economic resources, the amount received in excess of cost. In Exhibit 17–4, the entire amount received is reported because that was the increase created in current financial resources.

■ A reconciliation should be shown between the ending change in fund balances (a negative $106,657) in Exhibit 17–4 and the ending change in net assets for governmental activities in Exhibit 17–2 (a negative $3,114,286). Because of space considerations, that reconciliation is not being presented here although it would need to be included in the general purpose external financial statements.

Statement of Net Assets—Proprietary Funds

The assets and liabilities of the proprietary funds are presented in Exhibit 17–5. Information about the two individual enterprise funds is shown separately here along with a total for these business-type activities. In this way, specific information is available about the water and sewer system as well as the parking facilities and for the enterprise funds in total.

■ The internal service funds also are exhibited in this statement because they are proprietary funds. However, in the government-wide financial statements, these same internal service funds were combined with the governmental activities.

■ Assets and liabilities are classified as either current or noncurrent to provide additional information.

■ Because the proprietary funds utilize accrual accounting to measure economic resources, most of the totals for the business-type activities here in Exhibit 17–5 will agree with the total figures found in Exhibit 17–1. The amount of detail, though, is more extensive in Exhibit 17–5. For example, four different figures are reported under Capital Assets rather than just one.

■ The Internal Balance figure of $175,000, which was reported in Exhibit 17–1 within the assets so that it could be eliminated, is reported as a Due to Other Funds liability in Exhibit 17–5 and is not eliminated. Thus, total business-type activity assets in Exhibit 17–1 of $165,229,183 will show a $175,000 difference from total assets of $165,404,183 in Exhibit 17–5.

■ Restricted cash and cash equivalents of $1,493,322 is listed under noncurrent assets. This amount must have been designated in some manner by an external source or by specific laws.

Statement of Revenues, Expenses, and Changes in Fund Net Assets— Proprietary Funds

Just as the previous statement of net assets provides individual information about specific enterprise funds (as well as the internal service funds), the statement of revenues, expenses, and changes in fund net assets shown in Exhibit 17–6 gives the revenues and expenses for the water and sewer system, the parking facilities, and the internal service funds. In Exhibit 17–2, expenses of the water and sewer system amounted to $8,508,586 ($3,595,733 plus $4,912,853). That figure is more completely delineated

Exhibit 17–4   Fund-based Financial Statements

SAMPLE CITY
Statement of Revenues, Expenditures, and Changes in Fund Balances
Governmental Funds
For the Year Ended December 31, 2002

	General	HUD Programs	Community Redevelopment	Route 7 Construction	Other Governmental Funds	Total Governmental Funds
Revenues						
Property taxes	$51,173,436	$ —	$ —	$ —	$ 4,680,192	$ 55,853,628
Franchise taxes	4,055,505	—	—	—	—	4,055,505
Public service taxes	8,969,887	—	—	—	—	8,969,887
Fees and fines	606,946	—	—	—	—	606,946
Licenses and permits	2,287,794	—	—	—	—	2,287,794
Intergovernmental	6,119,938	2,578,191	—	—	2,830,916	11,529,045
Charges for services	11,374,460	—	—	—	30,708	11,405,168
Investment earnings	552,325	87,106	549,489	270,161	364,330	1,823,411
Miscellaneous	881,874	66,176	—	2,939	94	951,083
Total revenues	86,022,165	2,731,473	549,489	273,100	7,906,240	97,482,467
Expenditures						
Current:						
General government	8,630,835	—	417,814	16,700	121,052	9,186,401
Public safety	33,729,623	—	—	—	—	33,729,623
Public works	4,975,775	—	—	—	3,721,542	8,697,317
Engineering services	1,299,645	—	—	—	—	1,299,645
Health and sanitation	6,070,032	—	—	—	—	6,070,032
Cemetery	706,305	—	—	—	—	706,305
Culture and recreation	11,411,685	—	—	—	—	11,411,685
Community development	—	2,954,389	—	—	—	2,954,389
Education—payment to school district	21,893,273	—	—	—	—	21,893,273
Debt service:						
Principal	—	—	—	—	3,450,000	3,450,000
Interest and other charges	—	—	—	—	5,215,151	5,215,151
Capital outlay	—	—	2,246,671	11,281,769	3,190,209	16,718,649
Total expenditures	88,717,173	2,954,389	2,664,485	11,298,469	15,697,954	121,332,470
Excess (deficiency) of revenues over expenditures	(2,695,008)	(222,916)	(2,114,996)	(11,025,369)	(7,791,714)	(23,850,003)
Other Financing Sources (Uses)						
Proceeds of refunding bonds	—	—	—	—	38,045,000	38,045,000
Proceeds of long-term capital-related debt	—	—	17,529,560	—	1,300,000	18,829,560
Payment to bond refunding escrow agent	—	—	—	—	(37,284,144)	(37,284,144)
Transfers in	129,323	—	—	—	5,551,187	5,680,510
Transfers out	(2,163,759)	(348,046)	(2,273,187)	—	(219,076)	(5,004,068)
Total other financing sources and uses	(2,034,436)	(348,046)	15,256,373	—	7,392,967	20,266,858
Special Item						
Proceeds from sale of park land	3,476,488	—	—	—	—	3,476,488
Net change in fund balances	(1,252,956)	(570,962)	13,141,377	(11,025,369)	(398,747)	(106,657)
Fund balances—beginning	2,908,322	1,647,338	34,110	20,387,774	10,022,219	34,999,763
Fund balances—ending	$ 1,655,366	$1,076,376	$13,175,487	$ 9,362,405	$ 9,623,472	$ 34,893,106

Exhibit 17-5   Fund-based Financial Statements

SAMPLE CITY
Statement of Net Assets
Proprietary Funds
December 31, 2002

	Business-type Activities—Enterprise Funds			Governmental Activities—Internal Service Funds
	Water and Sewer	Parking Facilities	Totals	
Assets				
Current assets:				
Cash and cash equivalents	$ 8,416,653	$ 369,168	$ 8,785,821	$ 3,336,099
Investments	—	—	—	150,237
Receivables, net	3,564,586	3,535	3,568,121	157,804
Due from other governments	41,494	—	41,494	—
Inventories	126,674	—	126,674	139,328
Total current assets	12,149,407	372,703	12,522,110	3,783,468
Noncurrent assets:				
Restricted cash and cash equivalents	—	1,493,322	1,493,322	—
Capital assets:				
Land	813,513	3,021,637	3,835,150	—
Distribution and collection systems	39,504,183	—	39,504,183	—
Buildings and equipment	106,135,666	23,029,166	129,164,832	14,721,786
Less accumulated depreciation	(15,328,911)	(5,786,503)	(21,115,414)	(5,781,734)
Total noncurrent assets	131,124,451	21,757,622	152,882,073	8,940,052
Total assets	143,273,858	22,130,325	165,404,183	12,723,520
Liabilities				
Current liabilities:				
Accounts payable	447,427	304,003	751,430	780,570
Due to other funds	175,000	—	175,000	1,170,388
Compensated absences	112,850	8,827	121,677	237,690
Claims and judgments	—	—	—	1,687,975
Bonds, notes, and loans payable	3,944,609	360,000	4,304,609	249,306
Total current liabilities	4,679,886	672,830	5,352,716	4,125,929
Noncurrent liabilities:				
Compensated absences	451,399	35,306	486,705	—
Claims and judgments	—	—	—	5,602,900
Bonds, notes, and loans payable	54,451,549	19,544,019	73,995,568	—
Total noncurrent liabilities	54,902,948	19,579,325	74,482,273	5,602,900
Total liabilities	59,582,834	20,252,155	79,834,989	9,728,829
Net Assets				
Invested in capital assets, net of related debt	72,728,293	360,281	73,088,574	8,690,746
Restricted for debt service	—	1,451,996	1,451,996	—
Unrestricted	10,962,731	65,893	11,028,624	(5,696,055)
Total net assets	$ 83,691,024	$ 1,878,170	$ 85,569,194	$ 2,994,691

Exhibit 17–6   Fund-based Financial Statements

SAMPLE CITY
Statement of Revenues, Expenses, and Changes in Fund Net Assets
Proprietary Funds
For the Year Ended December 31, 2002

	Business-type Activities—Enterprise Funds			Governmental Activities—Internal Service Funds
	Water and Sewer	**Parking Facilities**	**Totals**	
Operating revenues:				
Charges for services	$11,329,883	$ 1,340,261	$12,670,144	$15,256,164
Miscellaneous	—	3,826	3,826	1,066,761
Total operating revenues	11,329,883	1,344,087	12,673,970	16,322,925
Operating expenses:				
Personal services	3,400,559	762,348	4,162,907	4,157,156
Contractual services	344,422	96,032	440,454	584,396
Utilities	754,107	100,726	854,833	214,812
Repairs and maintenance	747,315	64,617	811,932	1,960,490
Other supplies and expenses	498,213	17,119	515,332	234,445
Insurance claims and expenses	—	—	—	8,004,286
Depreciation	1,163,140	542,049	1,705,189	1,707,872
Total operating expenses	6,907,756	1,582,891	8,490,647	16,863,457
Operating income (loss)	4,422,127	(238,804)	4,183,323	(540,532)
Nonoperating revenues (expenses):				
Interest and investment revenue	454,793	146,556	601,349	134,733
Miscellaneous revenue	—	104,925	104,925	20,855
Interest expense	(1,600,830)	(1,166,546)	(2,767,376)	(41,616)
Miscellaneous expense	—	(46,846)	(46,846)	(176,003)
Total nonoperating revenue (expenses)	(1,146,037)	(961,911)	(2,107,948)	(62,031)
Income (loss) before contributions and transfers	3,276,090	(1,200,715)	2,075,375	(602,563)
Capital contributions	1,645,919	—	1,645,919	18,788
Transfers out	(290,000)	(211,409)	(501,409)	(175,033)
Change in net assets	4,632,009	(1,412,124)	3,219,885	(758,808)
Total net assets—beginning	79,059,015	3,290,294	82,349,309	3,753,499
Total net assets—ending	$83,691,024	$ 1,878,170	$85,569,194	$ 2,994,691

in Exhibit 17–6 within several categories: personal services ($3,400,559), depreciation ($1,163,140), interest ($1,600,830), and so forth. Because this statement measures all changes in net assets, both capital contributions and transfers are reported.

Statement of Cash Flows—Proprietary Funds

One of the most interesting of the fund-based financial statements is the statement of cash flows for the proprietary funds, as demonstrated in Exhibit 17–7. Because the proprietary funds operate in a manner similar to for-profit businesses, conveying information about cash flows is considered vital just as it is for Xerox or CocaCola. In addition, this information is not already available in a condensed form within the government-wide financial statements.

Exhibit 17–7   Fund-based Financial Statements

SAMPLE CITY
Statement of Cash Flows
Proprietary Funds
For the Year Ended December 31, 2002

| | Business-type Activities—Enterprise Funds | | | Governmental Activities— |
	Water and Sewer	Parking Facilities	Totals	Internal Service Funds
Cash Flows from Operating Activities				
Receipts from customers	$11,400,200	$ 1,345,292	$ 12,745,492	$15,326,343
Payments to suppliers	(2,725,349)	(365,137)	(3,090,486)	(2,812,238)
Payments to employees	(3,360,055)	(750,828)	(4,110,883)	(4,209,688)
Internal activity—payments to other funds	(1,296,768)	—	(1,296,768)	—
Claims paid	—	—	—	(8,482,451)
Other receipts (payments)	(2,325,483)	—	(2,325,483)	1,061,118
Net cash provided by operating activities	1,692,545	229,327	1,921,872	883,084
Cash Flows from Noncapital Financing Activities				
Operating subsidies and transfers to other funds	(290,000)	(211,409)	(501,409)	(175,033)
Cash Flows from Capital and Related Financing Activities				
Proceeds from capital debt	4,041,322	8,660,778	12,702,100	—
Capital contributions	1,645,919	—	1,645,919	—
Purchases of capital assets	(4,194,035)	(144,716)	(4,338,751)	(400,086)
Principal paid on capital debt	(2,178,491)	(8,895,000)	(11,073,491)	(954,137)
Interest paid on capital debt	(1,479,708)	(1,166,546)	(2,646,254)	(41,616)
Other receipts (payments)	—	19,174	19,174	131,416
Net cash (used) by capital and related financing activities	(2,164,993)	(1,526,310)	(3,691,303)	(1,264,423)
Cash Flows from Investing Activities				
Proceeds from sales and maturities of investments	—	—	—	15,684
Interest and dividends	454,793	143,747	598,540	129,550
Net cash provided by investing activities	454,793	143,747	598,540	145,234
Net (decrease) in cash and cash equivalents	(307,655)	(1,364,645)	(1,672,300)	(411,138)
Balances—beginning of the year	8,724,308	3,227,135	11,951,443	3,747,237
Balances—end of the year	$ 8,416,653	$ 1,862,490	$ 10,279,143	$ 3,336,099
Reconciliation of operating income (loss) to net cash provided (used) by operating activities:				
Operating income (loss)	$ 4,422,127	$ (238,804)	$ 4,183,323	$ (540,532)
Adjustments to reconcile operating income to net cash provided (used) by operating activities:				
Depreciation expense	1,163,140	542,049	1,705,189	1,707,872
Change in assets and liabilities:				
Receivables, net	653,264	1,205	654,469	31,941
Inventories	2,829	—	2,829	39,790
Accounts and other payables	(297,446)	(86,643)	(384,089)	475,212
Accrued expenses	(4,251,369)	11,520	(4,239,849)	(831,199)
Net cash provided by operating activities	$ 1,692,545	$ 229,327	$ 1,921,872	$ 883,084

As compared to a for-profit business, the statement of cash flows shown here has four sections rather than just three:

1. Cash flows from operating activities.
2. Cash flows from noncapital financing activities.
3. Cash flows from capital and related financing activities.
4. Cash flows from investing activities.

- The presentation of cash flows from operating activities is very similar to that which would be prepared by a for-profit business. However, in *GASB Statement Number 34,* the direct method of reporting operating activities has been required. In for-profit accounting, the direct method is recommended but not required so that the indirect method often is used where adjustments and eliminations are made to net income to arrive at cash from operating activities.

- Because the direct approach to reporting cash flows from operating activities is required here, the proprietary funds must also provide a reconciliation of operating income to net cash from operating activities. This reconciliation is illustrated at the bottom of Exhibit 17–7.

- Cash flows from noncapital financing activities should include (1) proceeds and payments on debt not attributable to the acquisition or construction of capital assets and (2) grants and subsidies not restricted for capital purposes or operating activities.

- Cash flows from capital and related financing activities focuses on the amounts spent on capital assets and the source of that funding. Exhibit 17–7 shows typical examples: proceeds from capital debt, capital contributions (from the governmental funds), purchases of capital assets, principal paid on capital debt, and the like.

- Cash flows from investing activities discloses amounts paid and received from investments.

Financial Statements—Fiduciary Funds

Fiduciary funds monitor assets being held for the benefit of an individual, group, or government outside of the reporting entity. The government cannot use these funds for its own programs and obtains no benefit from holding the assets. As such, information about the fiduciary funds is not included in the government-wide financial statements. Therefore, any financial data about these funds must be obtained by examining their separate statements within the general purpose external financial statements or their independently released statements (if those are prepared). The statement of fiduciary net assets is shown in Exhibit 17–8 and the statement of changes in fiduciary net assets appears in Exhibit 17–9. According to *GASB Statement Number 34,* these two statements should appear within the general purpose external financial statements produced by a state or locality. As indicated in the previous chapter, a government can have as many as four separate fiduciary fund types:

1. *Pension trust funds as well as other employee benefit trust funds.* These funds are used to report resources that are held for the members and beneficiaries of defined benefit pension plans, defined contribution plans, other postemployment benefit plans, or other employee benefit plans. As shown in Exhibit 17–8, such trust funds tend to hold large amounts of investments that are expected to grow and provide anticipated benefits for employees and their families. In Exhibit 17–9, the changes occurring in the pension trust fund (employment retirement fund) are reported. Additions are divided between contributions made to the plan by members and by employers and actual investment income such as dividends and interest. Because any investments being held are reported at fair market

Exhibit 17–8
Fund-based Financial
Statements

	Employee Retirement Plan	Private-purpose Trusts	Agency Funds
SAMPLE CITY **Statement of Fiduciary Net Assets** **Fiduciary Funds** **December 31, 2002**			
Assets			
Cash and cash equivalents	$ 1,973	$ 1,250	$ 44,889
Receivables:			
Interest and dividends	508,475	760	—
Other receivables	6,826	—	183,161
Total receivables	515,301	760	183,161
Investments, at fair value:			
U.S. government obligations	13,056,037	80,000	—
Municipal bonds	6,528,019	—	—
Corporate bonds	16,320,047	—	—
Corporate stocks	26,112,075	—	—
Other investments	3,264,009	—	—
Total investments	65,280,187	80,000	—
Total assets	65,797,461	82,010	$228,050
Liabilities			
Accounts payable	—	1,234	—
Refunds payable and others	1,358	—	228,050
Total liabilities	1,358	1,234	$228,050
Net Assets			
Held in trust for pension benefits and other purposes	$65,796,103	$80,776	

value, the change in value during the period is also reflected in this statement. Deductions from a pension trust fund include benefits paid to employees and other beneficiaries, contribution refunds, and administrative expenses.

The city of Lincoln, Nebraska, provides the following information in the notes to its 1999 financial statements: "The employees of the City are covered by several retirement plans. The Police and Fire Department Plan is administered by the city and is included in the Fiduciary Fund type. All other plans are administered by outside trustees and are not included in the City's combined financial statements." The notes go on to say that 886 current and former employees are covered by the Police and Fire Department Plan and the statements show that over $121 million of net assets is held in the pension trust fund.

2. *Investment trust funds.* This fund category reports the external portion of any investments that are being held by the entity for other governments. Such investment pools may be created in hopes of generating higher returns. Many governments do not hold investments for external parties so that this fiduciary fund is not included in the statement examples.

3. *Private-purpose trust funds.* This trust fund reports assets held for the benefit of outside parties. Governments can be required to hold assets in a fiduciary capacity for a score of reasons. For example, if a person dies without a will and without heirs, the person's property will be maintained in this trust fund until

Exhibit 17–9
Fund-based Financial
Statements

SAMPLE CITY Statement of Changes in Fiduciary Net Assets Fiduciary Funds For the Year Ended December 31, 2002	Employee Retirement Plan	Private-purpose Trusts
Additions		
Contributions:		
Employer	$ 2,721,341	$ —
Plan members	1,421,233	—
Total contributions	4,142,574	—
Investment earnings:		
Net (decrease) in fair value of investments	(272,522)	—
Interest	2,460,871	4,560
Dividends	1,445,273	—
Total investment earnings	3,633,622	4,560
Less investment expense	216,428	—
Net investment earnings	3,417,194	4,560
Total additions	7,559,768	4,560
Deductions		
Benefits	2,453,047	3,800
Refunds of contributions	464,691	—
Administrative expenses	87,532	678
Total deductions	3,005,270	4,478
Change in net assets	4,554,498	82
Net assets—beginning of the year	61,241,605	80,694
Net assets—end of the year	$65,796,103	$80,776

properly distributed according to state law. Likewise, cash abandoned in a savings or checking account is often turned over to the government to dispose of based on the proper legal regulations.

4. *Agency funds.* A government will often hold money temporarily that has to be transferred to some outside party. A city, for example, might have to share a portion of the collections from a toll road with the local county government. As stated in the notes to the 1998 financial statements of the city of Boise City, Idaho, "Agency Funds are custodial in nature (assets equal liabilities) and do not involve measurement of results of operations." Until transferred, these funds should be managed within the agency funds. As can be seen in Exhibit 17–8, only assets and liabilities are reported in the agency funds. An asset is received that must be turned over to an external individual, organization, or government; no accounting beyond the asset and related liability is needed.

REPORTING PUBLIC COLLEGES AND UNIVERSITIES

During the last decade, public colleges and universities such as Ohio State and the University of Kansas have been in a somewhat awkward position in terms of financial accounting. Private schools like Harvard, Duke, and Stanford must follow the pronouncements of the FASB, especially those created for private not-for-profit organizations. Recent FASB statements issued on contributions and the form of financial statements have provided a significant amount of official guidance for the financial information reported by these private institutions. As will be discussed extensively in the following chapter, the reporting standards developed for not-for-profit organizations have progressed greatly over the last few years.

In contrast, the GASB has retained primary authority over the financial reporting of public colleges and universities. Much of the GASB's work, though, has been directed at improving the accounting standards utilized by state and local government units. Consequently, the evolution of financial statements for public schools has lagged behind other types of reporting.

For example, the June 30, 1999, balance sheet of the University of Kentucky resembles a not-for-profit organization from an earlier period of time. Separate columns are reported for Current Funds, Loan Funds, Endowment and Similar Funds, and Plant Funds. In the statement of changes in fund balances, revenues and expenditures (not expenses) are reported individually for each of these four types of funds along with both mandatory and nonmandatory transfers. The 1999 statements for James Madison University are similar to those of the University of Kentucky except that changes reported in fund balances were spread over eight columns with no total column provided for the school as a whole. Literally, eight different figures are shown for "total revenues and other additions." Furthermore, these statements indicate that "no provision is made in the accounts for depreciation of plant assets." Clearly, such financial statements do not resemble either those shown in the government financial statements outlined earlier in this chapter (Exhibits 17–1 through 17–9) or the private not-for-profit statements covered in the following chapter.

Generally, public colleges and universities do differ in at least two important ways from private schools: First, the state or local government directly provides a significant amount of funding (at least for qualifying students) so that reliance on tuition charges tends to be reduced. For example, information provided with the 1999 financial statements of Utah State University disclosed that the state of Utah had contributed $112.1 million in current funds during the year while revenues from tuition and fees totaled only $49.3 million.

Second, because of the ability to generate funds each year from the government, the amount of endowment funds raised and accumulated is often smaller. Private schools usually try to build up a large endowment to ensure financial security; this often is not necessary at a public school backed by the state or another government. The University of Iowa reported endowment and similar funds at June 30, 1999, of about $112 million while the University of Southern California held permanently restricted net assets on the same date of $688 million.

The question can then be raised if such differences warrant unique financial statements for public colleges and universities. In many ways, public and private schools are very much alike: They both educate students and charge tuition and other fees, conduct scholarly research, maintain a library and sports teams, operate cafeterias and museums, and the like. What measurement basis should be applied and what should be the form of the financial statements reported by a public college or university? These questions are especially relevant because of the frustration that has grown up about the utilization of current statements: "The Board has found that few resource providers—especially citizens and legislators—or others with an interest in the financial activities of public colleges and universities read the institutions' external financial reports."[7]

Four basic ideas have been put forth as to the proper construction of the financial statements that should be prepared and distributed by public colleges and universities:

---

[7]*GASB Statement Number 35,* "Basic Financial Statements—and Management's Discussion and Analysis—for Public Colleges and Universities," para. 25.

1. Simply adopt the requirements of the FASB for private not-for-profit organizations so that all colleges and universities (public and private) would prepare financial statements that were comparable. As shown in the next chapter, the private reporting model is now relatively well developed. This suggestion holds some problems, though, because the unique aspects of public schools could possibly be misunderstood by the FASB, a group that has not had to deal with the intricacies found in governmental entities. The wants and needs of public schools might simply be ignored. In addition, this loss of authority would appear to weaken the GASB somewhat. Politically, reducing the power of this board might not be pleasing to those organizations that provide much of the support and financing of the GASB.

2. Leave the financial statements as they are currently being prepared using a fund basis for reporting. However, as indicated above, the current statements seem to have few readers so that some change appears to be warranted. Private not-for-profit organizations and governments (at least in part) have abandoned the reporting of individual funds so that continuing to utilize this approach for a public school seems to be outdated.

3. Create an entirely new set of financial statements designed to meet the unique needs of a public college or university. If the pronouncements of the FASB are not going to be followed, then some fundamental differences between the two types of schools must be present. If those differences can be identified, new statements could be developed to satisfy the informational needs of users and mirror the significant events and transactions of these public institutions. Unfortunately, though, creation of a new set of financial statements would require an enormous amount of work by the GASB. Would the benefit gained from tailor-made financial statements outweigh the cost of producing new standards for reporting?

4. Adopt the same reporting model that has recently been created for states and local governments. In many cases, public schools are component units of a primary government or can even be viewed as a special-purpose government unit. Since a large amount of funding comes directly from the government after oversight by the appropriate legislative body, the same financial statements utilized by a city or county could be applied.

In *GASB Statement Number 35*, "Basic Financial Statements—and Management's Discussion and Analysis—for Public Colleges and Universities," issued in November 1999, this last option was officially selected. According to paragraph 25, "the objective of this Statement is to amend Statement 34 to include public colleges and universities in the financial reporting model established by that Statement."

With just these few words, all of the requirements of the previous chapter and the first part of the current chapter have been applied to public colleges and universities:

■ A Management's Discussion and Analysis (MD&A) must be written to provide oral explanations for the numerical information being provided.

■ A government-wide statement of net assets (Exhibit 17–1) and statement of activities (Exhibit 17–2) must be produced if both governmental activities and business-type activities are carried out by the school. A slightly different version is produced if the school has only governmental activities or business-type activities.

■ For these government-wide statements, the economic resource measurement basis is applied based on using accrual accounting for timing purposes.

■ If governmental activities are carried out, statements must also be produced at the fund level for the General Fund and other major governmental funds (Exhibits 17–3 and 17–4).

- Business-type activities such as food services, the bookstore, and industrial training are monitored within proprietary funds and reported at the fund level through various statements as shown previously (Exhibits 17–5, 17–6, and 17–7).

GASB Statement 35 will become effective on the same staggered schedule as Statement 34. Thus, over the next several years, public colleges and universities will be adapting their financial statements to meet these new requirements. Consequently, their financial statements will closely parallel those of state and local governments but will demonstrate a number of distinct differences from the statements prepared and distributed by private colleges and universities. Whether this severe change in the reporting process will improve the use made by potential readers of these financial statements can only be determined over time. However, when this statement was issued, reactions were certainly mixed. "A few schools have said the changes will cost them time and resources for no reason. Some will have to buy new systems for their capital assets so that they can report their depreciation. Those with older systems will have a harder time adjusting. . . . Jeffrey West, associate controller at the University of Arizona, said he expects the new rules to be more beneficial to public schools than harmful."[8]

SUMMARY

1. State and local governments sometimes obtain assets through lease arrangements. The same criteria used by a for-profit organization for identifying a capital lease are applied in government accounting. For government-wide financial statements, both the resulting asset and liability are reported initially at the present value of the minimum lease payments. This asset is depreciated over the time that the government will make use of it. Interest expense is recognized on the reported liability each period. For fund-based financial statements, an expenditure as well as an other financing source are recognized at present value when the contract is initiated. Subsequent payments on the debt and interest also are recognized as expenditures.

2. Solid waste landfills create large potential debts for a government because of closure and postclosure costs. In the government-wide statements, this liability is accrued each period based on the latest estimations and the portion of the property that has been filled. For fund-based financial statements, no expenditures are reported until a claim to current financial resources comes into existence.

3. Government employees often have the right to future compensated absences because of holidays, vacations, sick leave, and the like. For government-wide statements, the debt for these days must be estimated and recognized when earned by the employees. In the fund-based statements, no liability is recognized until current financial resources are expected to be used.

4. When a state or local government obtains an artwork or historical treasure, it normally must be recorded as a capital asset on the government-wide financial statements. However, if specified guidelines are met, recognition of the asset is optional. In contrast, no capital assets are reported in the fund-based financial statements. If an artwork or historical treasure is received through donation, revenue must be recognized according to the rules established for voluntary nonexchange transactions.

5. Depreciation must be recorded each period for artworks and historical treasures that are capitalized unless they are viewed as inexhaustible.

6. Infrastructure assets must now be capitalized and depreciated on the government-wide financial statements. However, depreciation is not recorded if the modified approach is applied. Under this method, if a system is created to ensure that a network of infrastructure is maintained yearly at a predetermined condition, the cost of this care is expensed in lieu of recording depreciation.

---

[8]Sonja Ryst, "Accounting Standards: Public Colleges Must Report Depreciation Under GASB Rule," *The Bond Buyer*, December 13, 1999, p. 6.

7. A state or local government must now include a Management's Discussion and Analysis (MD&A) as part of its general purpose external financial reporting. This MD&A is designed to provide a verbal explanation for the operations and financial position of the government. Extensive requirements have been established by the GASB for the contents of the MD&A.

8. A primary government must produce a comprehensive annual financial report (CAFR). Both state and local governments are viewed as primary governments as well as any special purpose government that meets certain provisions. In addition, a component unit is any function that is legally separate from the primary government but where financial accountability still exists. Component units can be discretely presented to the right of the primary government or can be blended within the actual funds of the primary government.

9. A statement of net assets and a statement of activities are produced as government-wide financial statements based on the economic resources measurement basis and accrual accounting. These statements separate governmental activities from business-type activities. Internal service funds are usually included within the governmental activities. The statement of activities reports expenses by function along with related program revenues to determine the net expenses or revenues resulting from each function.

10. Fund-based financial statements report the governmental funds by showing separately the General Fund and any other major fund. When reporting the governmental funds, the statements are based on measuring current financial resources using modified accrual accounting. Additional statements are presented for proprietary funds and fiduciary funds.

11. The financial statements to be produced by public colleges and universities must now follow the same guidelines as those created in GASB 34 for state and local government units. Those statements differ from those produced by private schools which follow the pronouncements of the FASB but will be basically the same as a state or local government.

COMPREHENSIVE ILLUSTRATION

Problem

(Estimated Time: 40 minutes) Presented below are a series of transactions for a city. For each transaction, indicate how the event should be reported on the government-wide financial statements and then on the fund-based financial statements. Assume that this city has adopted the requirements of *GASB Statement Number 34.*

1. Money is borrowed by issuing a 20-year bond for $3 million, its face value. This money is to be used to construct a highway around the city.

2. Cash of $100,000 is transferred from the General Fund to the Debt Service Funds to make the first payment of principal and interest on the above bonds.

3. The above cash is paid on the bond. Of this total, $70,000 is recorded as interest with the remainder reducing the principal of the bond payable.

4. Construction of the highway is completed and the entire $3 million is paid.

5. The above highway is expected to last for 30 years. However, the government qualifies to use the modified approach which it has adopted for this system. A cost of $35,000 is incurred during the year to maintain the highway at an appropriate, predetermined condition. Of this amount, $29,000 was paid currently but the other $6,000 will not be paid until the sixth month of the subsequent year.

6. A local business donates lights for the new highway. The lights are valued at $200,000 and should last for 20 years. The modified approach is not used for this network of infrastructure but rather straight-line depreciation is applied.

7. A truck is leased by the city to maintain the new highway. The lease qualifies as a capital lease. The present value of the minimum payments is $70,000. Depreciation for this year is $10,000 and interest is $6,000. A single payment of $11,000 in cash is made.

8. The local subway system takes in cash revenues of $2 million and records salary expenses for its employees of $300,000.

9. At the beginning of the year, a solid waste landfill is opened that will take 20 years to fill completely. This year an estimated 4 percent of the capacity is filled. The city anticipates total closure and postclosure costs of $2 million although no costs have been incurred to date.

Solution

1. *Government-wide financial statements.* On the statement of net assets, under the governmental activities column, cash and noncurrent liabilities will both be increased by $3 million.

    Fund-based financial statements. The cash balance will increase on the balance sheet whereas other financing sources will increase on the statement of revenues, expenditures, and changes in fund balances. These amounts will be shown in the column for other governmental funds unless this particular capital projects fund is judged to be major so that a separate column is presented.

2. *Government-wide financial statements.* No recording is shown of this transfer since the amount was an intra-activity transaction entirely carried out within the governmental activities.

    Fund-based financial statements. On the balance sheet, the cash balance for the General Fund will go down while the cash listed for other governmental funds (or debt service) will rise. On the statement of revenues, expenditures, and other changes in fund balances, the General Fund will show an other financing use whereas the other governmental funds will report an other financing source. These balances will not be offset.

3. *Government-wide financial statements.* On the statement of net assets, for the governmental activities, cash will go down by $100,000 while the noncurrent liabilities will drop by $30,000 because of the principal payment. The statement of activities should report $70,000 to interest expense as a governmental activity.

    Fund-based financial statements. First, cash will be reduced by $100,000 on the balance sheet under the other governmental funds (or debt service) column. Second, on the statement of revenues, expenditures, and changes in fund balances, a $30,000 principal expenditure is reported and a $70,000 interest expenditure. These figures are shown within the other governmental funds under debt service.

4. *Government-wide financial statements.* Under the governmental activities listed on the statement of net assets, cash will decrease by the $3 million amount and capital assets will go up by the same figure. All new infrastructure costs must be capitalized according to *GASB Statement Number 34.*

    Fund-based financial statements. On the balance sheet, cash reported for other governmental funds will decrease. Once again, though, if this particular capital projects fund qualifies as major, the effects will be shown in a separate column rather than in the "other" column. Within the statement of revenues, expenditures, and changes in fund balances, a $3 million expenditure will be reported as a capital outlay.

5. *Government-wide financial statements.* Under governmental activities on the statement of net assets, cash will decrease by $29,000 and a current liability of $6,000 will be reported. On the statement of activities, the $35,000 expense will be included within an appropriate function such as "public works." Since the modified approach is being applied, depreciation expense is not recorded; the maintenance expense is recognized instead.

    Fund-based financial statements. Because the $6,000 liability will not require the use of current financial resources, it will not be recorded at this time at the fund level. Thus, only a $29,000 drop in cash is reported in the balance sheet, probably under the General Fund. On the statement of revenues, expenditures, and changes in fund balances, a $29,000 expenditure will be recorded for public works.

6. *Government-wide financial statements.* The lights do not qualify as artworks or historical treasures and must, therefore, be reported as capital assets on the statement of net assets at the $200,000 market value. Based on a 20-year life, accumulated depreciation of $10,000 must be recognized to reduce the reported net asset to $190,000. For the statement of activities, a revenue of $200,000 is appropriate unless eligibility requirements for the donation have not yet been fulfilled. This revenue should be shown as a program revenue ("capital grants and contributions") to offset the expenses reported for public works. Depreciation of $10,000 should also be included as an expense for public works.

Fund-based financial statements. If the organization had donated $200,000 in cash for these lights and then the money had been properly spent, the city would have recognized both a revenue and an expenditure. Therefore, the city will make the same reporting if the lights are received directly. Within the statement of revenues, expenditures, and changes in fund balances, a revenue of $200,000 should be reported along with a $200,000 expenditure for a capital outlay. The amounts will probably be shown for the General Fund. The capital asset is not recorded by the funds because it not a current financial resource.

7. *Government-wide financial statements.* On the statement of net assets, under the governmental activities, the leased truck and the lease liability will both be reported at $70,000. The truck will then be reduced by $10,000 in accumulated depreciation while the liability is reduced by $5,000, the amount of the $11,000 payment less $6,000 attributed to interest. Next, on the statement of activities, interest of $6,000 and depreciation of $10,000 are both reported as expenses directly related to the public works function.

   Fund-based financial statements. On the balance sheet, probably under the General Fund, an $11,000 reduction in cash is reported. In the statement of revenues, expenditures, and changes in fund balances, a $70,000 expenditure should be recorded as a capital outlay. Also, an other financing source of the same amount is recognized. Finally, another $11,000 in expenditures should be shown: $6,000 as interest and $5,000 for debt reduction.

8. *Government-wide financial statements.* For the statement of net assets, cash is increased under the business-type activities by $1.7 million. On the statement of activities, expenses for the subway system are reported as $300,000 while the related program revenues for charges for services rendered would go up by $2 million so that the net revenue resulting from this proprietary fund is $1.7 million.

   Fund-based financial statements. On the statement of net assets for the proprietary funds (see Exhibit 17–5), a separate column for the subway system should be set up under the business-type activities. Cash in this column increases by $1.7 million. Likewise, on the statement of revenues, expenses, and changes in fund net assets for the proprietary funds (see Exhibit 17–6), operating revenues of $2 million are reported for the subway system. In addition, personal services of $300,000 should be recognized under the list of operating expenses. Both the inflow and outflow of cash are also reported on the statement of cash flows (see Exhibit 17–7) under cash flows from operating activities.

9. *Government-wide financial statements.* Because the landfill is 4 percent filled, that portion of the overall $2 million cost must be recognized (or $80,000). On the statement of net assets, this amount is shown as a noncurrent liability. The balance could be presented as either a governmental activity or a business-type activity depending on the internal classification of the landfill. Likewise, on the statement of activities, the same $80,000 expense figure is reported.

   Fund-based financial statements. This liability does not require the use of current financial resources and would not be reported if the landfill is considered a governmental fund. However, if the liability is viewed as an enterprise fund, the $80,000 expense and liability is shown on the separate statements prepared for the proprietary funds (see Exhibits 17–5 and 17–6).

QUESTIONS

1. What criteria are applied by a state or local government to determine whether a lease should be capitalized?

2. On January 1, 2001, a city signs a capital lease for new equipment for the police department. How is this transaction reported on the government-wide financial statements? How is this transaction reported on the fund-based financial statements?

3. On December 31, 2001, the city indicated in question (2) makes its first annual lease payment. How is the payment reported on the government-wide financial statements? How is the payment reported on the fund-based financial statements?

4. Why does the operation of a solid waste landfill create reporting concerns for a local government?

5. A landfill is scheduled to be filled to capacity over a 10-year period. However, at the end of the first year, the landfill is only 7 percent filled. How much liability should be recognized on the government-wide financial statements? How much liability should be recognized on the fund-based financial statements assuming that the landfill is recorded in an enterprise fund? How much liability should be recognized on the fund-based financial statements assuming that the landfill is recorded in the General Fund?

6. A city operates a solid waste landfill. This facility is 11 percent filled after the first year and 24 percent filled after the second. For government-wide financial statements, how much expense should be recognized in the second year? Assuming the landfill is reported in the General Fund, how much of an expenditure should be recognized in the second year on the fund-based financial statements?

7. A teacher in the city of Lights earns vacation pay of $2,000 during 2001. However, the vacation will not be taken until the end of 2002. In the government-wide financial statements for 2001, how is this compensated absence reported? In the fund-based financial statements for 2001, how is this compensated absence reported?

8. In question (7), assume the teacher takes the vacation late in 2002 and is paid the entire $2,000. What journal entry is reported for each of the two methods of reporting?

9. The city of Salem is given a painting by Picasso to be displayed in its city hall. Under what condition will the city not report this painting as a capital asset on its government-wide financial statements? If the painting is reported as a capital asset, must depreciation be reported?

10. In question (9), assume that the painting is not reported on the government-wide financial statements as a capital asset, does the city have to report a revenue for the gift?

11. Under what condition is the modified approach applied?

12. If the modified approach is being utilized, what impact does that have on the reporting within the government-wide financial statements?

13. What is normally included in the Management's Discussion and Analysis (MD&A)? Where is this information presented by a state or local government?

14. What is included in a comprehensive annual financial report (known as the CAFR)?

15. How does a reporting entity qualify as a primary government?

16. How does a reporting entity qualify as a component unit?

17. What is the difference between a blended component unit and a discretely presented component unit?

18. What are the two government-wide financial statements? What is normally presented on each?

19. What are the two fund-based financial statements for governmental funds? What is normally presented on each?

20. What is the difference in program revenues and general revenues and why is that distinction important?

21. Why does a government determine the net expenses or revenues for each of the functions within its governmental activities?

22. How are internal service funds reported on government-wide financial statements?

23. How are fiduciary funds reported on government-wide financial statements?

24. What are some of the differences that exist between private colleges and universities and public colleges and universities?

25. What is the appropriate form for the financial statements of public colleges and universities?

INTERNET ASSIGNMENT

Internet sites are time and date sensitive. It is the purpose of these exercises to have you explore the Internet. You may need to refer to the text's Web site at http://www.mhhe.com/hoyle6e to find the most up-to-date links for the Web sites listed in the Internet Assignment.

1. Go to the Web site of the Governmental Accounting Standards Board at http://www.rutgers.edu/Accounting/raw/gasb.main.htm Scroll down to "performance measurement for government" and click on that.

Scroll down to "what you can find" and click on that.

Scroll down to "related links" and click on that.

Scroll down to "current research efforts" and click on that.

Write a short report on current research efforts regarding performance measurement for governments.

LIBRARY ASSIGNMENTS

1. Read the following articles and any other published information describing the history of governmental accounting:

    "Capital Accounts of a Municipality," *The Journal of Accountancy*, October 1918.

    "Governmental Sinking Funds, Serial Bonds and Depreciation Reserves," *The Journal of Accountancy*, October 1918.

    "25 Years of State and Local Governmental Financial Reporting—An Accounting Standards Perspective," *The Government Accountants Journal*, Fall 1992.

    "The Governmental Accounting Standards Board: Factors Influencing Its Operation and Initial Technical Agenda," *The Government Accountants Journal*, Spring 2000.

    Write a short paper discussing the changes in governmental accounting that have occurred over the past 100 years.

2. Obtain a copy of the latest comprehensive annual financial report (CAFR) of a state or local government. If one is not available in the library, request a copy, either by telephone or mail, from the director of finance of the government unit. Use this CAFR, especially the notes to the financial statements as well as the letter of transmittal, to answer the following questions:

    ■ What information does the government provide about the effects of adopting *GASB Statement Number 34*?

    ■ Does the government operate a solid waste landfill? If so, what information is presented in the notes to describe the operations of this landfill and any potential liability?

    ■ Is the government reporting any liability for compensated absences? If so, what information is provided?

    ■ How are the parameters of the primary government defined?

    ■ Does the government have any component units? If so, are they discretely presented or blended?

    ■ Does the government operate any internal service funds? If so, how many can be identified?

    ■ Does the government operate any enterprise funds? If so, what information is disclosed?

    ■ Did the government issue any bonds during the year and, if so, how much money was received?

    ■ Looking at the statistical section at the back of the CAFR, what individuals or companies paid the most in property taxes during the last year?

PROBLEMS

1. A city government has obtained an asset through a capital lease. For the government-wide financial statements, which of the following is true?

    a. The accounting parallels that which is appropriate in for-profit accounting.

    b. The city must report an other financing source.

    c. The city must report an expenditure.

    d. Recognition of depreciation is optional.

2. A city government has a six-year capital lease for property being used within the General Fund. Minimum lease payments total $70,000 starting next year but have a

current present value of $49,000. For the fund-based financial statements, what is the total amount of expenditures to be recognized over the six-year period?
   a. $0.
   b. $49,000.
   c. $70,000.
   d. $119,000.

3. A city government has a six-year capital lease for property being used within the General Fund. Minimum lease payments total $70,000 starting next year but have a current present value of $49,000. For the fund-based financial statements, what is the total amount of other financing sources to be recognized over the six-year period?
   a. $0.
   b. $49,000.
   c. $70,000.
   d. $119,000.

4. A city government has a nine-year capital lease for property being used within the General Fund. The lease was signed on January 1, 2001. Minimum lease payments total $90,000 starting at the end of the first year but have a current present value of $69,000. Annual payments are $10,000 and the interest rate being applied is 10 percent. When the first payment is made on December 31, 2001, which of the following recordings is made?

		Government-wide statements	Fund-based statements
a.		Interest Expense $0.	Interest Expense $0.
b.		Interest Expense $6,900.	Expenditures $6,900.
c.		Expenditures $10,000.	Expenditures $10,000.
d.		Interest Expense $6,900.	Expenditures $10,000.

5. A city government has a nine-year capital lease for property being used within the General Fund. The lease was signed on January 1, 2001. Minimum lease payments total $90,000 starting at the end of the first year but have a current present value of $69,000. Annual payments are $10,000 and the interest rate being applied is 10 percent. On the fund-based financial statements, what liability is reported as of December 31, 2001, after the first payment is made?
   a. $0.
   b. $59,000.
   c. $65,900.
   d. $80,000.

6. A city creates a solid waste landfill. Every person or company that uses the landfill is assessed a charge based on the amount of materials. The landfill will probably be recorded in which of the following?
   a. General Fund.
   b. Special Revenues Funds.
   c. Internal Service Funds.
   d. Enterprise Funds.

7. A city starts a solid waste landfill that it expects to fill to capacity evenly over a 10-year period. At the end of the first year, it is 8 percent filled. At the end of the second year, it is 19 percent filled. Closure and postclosure costs are estimated at $1 million. None of this amount will be paid until the landfill has reached its capacity. On government-wide financial statements, which of the following is true for the Year Two statements?
   a. Expense will be zero and liability will be zero.
   b. Expense will be $110,000 and liability will be $110,000.
   c. Expense will be $110,000 and liability will be $190,000.
   d. Expense will be $100,000 and liability will be $200,000.

8. Use the same information as in question (7). If this landfill is judged to be a proprietary fund, what liability will be reported at the end of the second year on fund-based financial statements?
   a. $0.
   b. $110,000.
   c. $190,000.
   d. $200,000.

9. Use the same information as in question (7). If this landfill is judged to be a governmental fund, what liability will be reported at the end of the second year on fund-based financial statements?

   a. $0.
   b. $110,000.
   c. $190,000.
   d. $200,000.

10. The employees of the city of Jones earn vacation time that totals to $1,000 per week during the year. Of this amount, $12,000 is actually taken in Year One and the remainder is taken in Year Two. On government-wide financial statements, what liability should be reported at the end of Year One?

    a. It depends on whether the employees work at governmental activities or business-type activities.
    b. $0.
    c. $40,000.
    d. $52,000.

11. The employees of the city of Jones will earn vacation time equal to $1,000 per week during the year. Of this total, $12,000 is taken in Year One with the remainder to be taken in Year Two. On fund-based financial statements, what amount of liability should be recognized at the end of Year One? *Assume all vacations will be taken in July.*

    a. It depends on whether the employees work at governmental activities or business-type activities.
    b. $0.
    c. $40,000.
    d. $52,000.

12. The city of Wilson receives a large piece of sculpture as a gift to be placed in front of the municipal building. This artwork is valued at $240,000. Which of the following is true for the government-wide financial statements?

    a. A capital asset of $240,000 must be reported.
    b. No capital asset will be reported.
    c. If conditions are met, recording of the artwork as a capital asset is optional.
    d. The artwork will be recorded but only for the amount paid by the city.

13. In question (12), which of the following statements is true about the reporting of a revenue?

    a. Unless eligibility requirements have not been met for this gift, a revenue should be reported.
    b. Revenue is reported but only if the asset is reported.
    c. If the asset is not capitalized, no revenue should be recognized.
    d. As a gift, no revenue would ever be reported.

14. In question (12), assume the work is reported as a capital asset. Which of the following is true?

    a. Depreciation is not recorded because the city has no cost.
    b. Depreciation is not required if the asset is held to be inexhaustible.
    c. Depreciation must be recognized because the asset is capitalized.
    d. Because the property was received as a gift, recognition of depreciation is optional.

15. A city builds sidewalks throughout its various neighborhoods at a cost of $200,000. Which of the following is not true?

    a. Because the sidewalks qualify as infrastructure, the asset is viewed as the same as land so that depreciation is not recorded.
    b. Depreciation is required unless the modified approach is utilized.
    c. The modified approach recognizes maintenance expense in lieu of depreciation expense for qualifying infrastructure assets.
    d. The modified approach is only allowed if the city maintains the network of sidewalks at least at a predetermined condition.

16. Which of the following is true about use of the modified approach?

    a. The modified approach can be applied to all capital assets of a state or local government.
    b. The modified approach is used to adjust depreciation expense either up or down based on conditions for the period.

    c.   The modified approach is required for infrastructure assets.

    d.   For qualified assets, the modified approach eliminates the recording of depreciation.

17.   Which of the following is true about the Management's Discussion and Analysis (MD&A)?

    a.   It is an optional addition to the comprehensive annual financial report but inclusion is encouraged by the GASB.

    b.   It adds a verbal explanation for the numbers and trends presented in the financial statements.

    c.   It appears at the very end of a government's comprehensive annual financial report.

    d.   It replaces a portion of the fund-based financial statements traditionally produced by a state or local government.

18.   Which of the following is not necessary for a special-purpose local government to be viewed as a primary government for reporting purposes?

    a.   It must have a separately elected governing body.

    b.   It must have specifically defined geographic boundaries.

    c.   It must be fiscally independent.

    d.   It must have corporate powers to prove that it is legally independent.

19.   An accountant is trying to determine if the school system of the city of Abraham is fiscally independent. Which of the following is not a requirement for being deemed fiscally independent?

    a.   It can hold property in its own name.

    b.   It can issue bonded debt without outside approval.

    c.   It can pass its own budget without outside approval.

    d.   It can set taxes or rates without outside approval.

20.   An employment agency for the handicapped works closely with the city of Hanover. The employment agency is legally separate from the city but is still fiscally dependent on it. How should Hanover report the employment agency in its CAFR?

    a.   No reporting is needed because the agency is legally separate.

    b.   As a part of the General Fund.

    c.   As a component unit.

    d.   As a related organization.

21.   Which of the following statements are reported within the government-wide financial statements?

    a.   Statement of net assets and statement of cash flows.

    b.   Balance sheet and statement of net assets.

    c.   Statement of activities and statement of changes in fund balances.

    d.   Statement of net assets and statement of activities.

22.   For component units, what is the difference in discrete presentation and blending?

    a.   A blended component unit is shown to the left of the statements while a discretely presented component unit is shown to the right.

    b.   A blended component unit is shown at the bottom of the statements while a discretely presented component unit is shown within the statements like a fund.

    c.   A blended component unit is shown within the statements like a fund while a discretely presented component unit is shown to the right.

    d.   A blended component unit is shown to the right of the statements while a discretely presented component unit is shown in completely separate statements.

23.   A government reports that its public safety function had expenses last year of $900,000 and program revenues of $200,000 so that its net expenses were $700,000. On which financial statement is this information presented?

    a.   Statement of activities.

    b.   Statement of cash flows.

    c.   Statement of revenues and expenditures.

    d.   Statement of net assets.

24.   On government-wide financial statements, a difference is drawn between program revenues and general revenues. How is that difference shown?

    a.   Program revenues are offset against the expenses of a specific function while general revenues are assigned to governmental activities and business-type activities in general.

  b. General revenues are shown at the top of the statement of revenues and expenditures while program revenues are shown at the bottom.

  c. General revenues are labeled as operating revenues while program revenues are shown as miscellaneous income.

  d. General revenues are broken down by type while program revenues are reported as a single figure.

25. Which of the following is true about the statement of cash flows for the proprietary funds of a state or local government?

  a. The indirect method of reporting cash flows from operating activities is allowed although the direct method is recommended.

  b. The structure of the statement is virtually identical to that of a for-profit business.

  c. The statement is divided into four separate sections of cash flows.

  d. Amounts spent on capital assets are reported in a separate section from amounts raised to finance those capital assets.

26. Which of the following is true about the financial reporting of a public college or university?

  a. It will soon resemble the financial reporting of private colleges and universities.

  b. It will continue to use its own unique style of financial reporting.

  c. It will soon resemble the financial reporting of state and local governments.

  d. The GASB is scheduled to create a financial statement format unique to the needs of public colleges and universities.

27. On January 1, 2001, a city government leased the following pieces of equipment. Each lease qualifies as a capital lease. Initial payments are on December 31, 2001. An interest rate of 10 percent is viewed as appropriate. No bargain purchase options exist.

Fund	Annual Payments	Total Payments	Present Value of Total Payments
General	$8,000	$40,000	$33,350
Enterprise	$6,000	$36,000	$28,750

  a. On government-wide financial statements for December 31, 2001, and the year then ended, what balances should be reported?

  b. On fund-based financial statements for December 31, 2001, and the year then ended, what balances should be reported?

28. On January 1, 2001, a city government leased the following pieces of equipment. Each lease qualifies as a capital lease. Initial payments are on December 31, 2001. An interest rate of 12 percent is viewed as appropriate. No bargain purchase options exist.

Fund	Annual Payments	Total Payments	Present Value of Total Payments
General	$3,000	$30,000	$19,000
Enterprise	$9,000	$36,000	$30,600

  a. Prepare journal entries for the year of 2001 for both of these leases for government-wide financial statements.

  b. Prepare journal entries for the year of 2001 for both of these leases for fund-based financial statements.

29. On January 1, 2001, the city of Verga leased a large truck for five years and made the initial annual payment of $22,000 immediately. The present value of these payments based on an 8 percent interest rate is assumed to be $87,800. The truck has an expected useful life of five years.

  a. Assuming that the truck will be used by the fire department of the city, what journal entries should be made for 2001 and 2002 for the government-wide financial statements?

  b. Assuming that the truck will be used by the fire department of the city, what journal entries should be made for 2001 and 2002 for the fund-based financial statements?

  c. Assuming that the truck will be used by the airport (an Enterprise Fund) operated by the city, what journal entries should be made for 2001 and 2002 for the fund-based financial statements?

30. On January 1, 2001, the city of Hastings created a solid waste landfill that it expects to reach capacity gradually over the next 20 years. The city anticipates that closure costs will be $1.2 million and postclosure costs will be an additional $700,000. Of these totals, $50,000 must be paid on December 31 of each year for preliminary closure work. At the end of 2001, the landfill has reached 3 percent of capacity. At the end of 2002, the landfill has reached 9 percent of capacity. Also, at the end of 2002, a reassessment is made and total closure costs are determined to be $1.4 million rather than $1.2 million.

    a. Assuming that the landfill is viewed as an Enterprise Fund, what journal entries are made in 2001 and 2002 for the government-wide financial statements?

    b. Assuming that the landfill is viewed as a General Fund, what journal entries are made in 2001 and 2002 for the government-wide financial statements?

    c. Assuming that the landfill is viewed as an Enterprise Fund, what journal entries are made in 2001 and 2002 for fund-based financial statements?

    d. Assuming that the landfill is viewed as a General Fund, what journal entries are made in 2001 and 2002 for fund-based financial statements?

31. The city of Lawrence operates a solid waste landfill that is at 54 percent of capacity on January 1, 2001. The city had anticipated closure costs of $2 million but later that year decides that closure costs should actually be $2.4 million. None of these costs will be incurred until 2009 when the landfill is scheduled to be closed.

    a. What will appear on the government-wide financial statements for this landfill for December 31, 2001, and the year then ended?

    b. Assuming that the landfill is recorded within the General Fund, what will appear on the fund-based financial statements for this landfill for December 31, 2001, and the year then ended?

32. Mary T. Lincoln works for the city of Columbus. She volunteered to work over the 2001 Christmas break so that she could earn a short vacation during the first week of January 2002. She earns three vacation days because of working on the holiday and will be paid $400 per day. She takes her vacation in January and is paid for those days.

    a. For government-wide financial statements, prepare journal entries for 2001 and 2002 because of these events.

    b. Assuming that Lincoln works in an activity reported within the General Fund, prepare journal entries for 2001 and 2002 for the fund-based financial statements because of these events.

    c. Assume that Lincoln works in an activity reported within the General Fund. However, assume that she does not plan to take her three vacation days until near the end of 2002. For the fund-based financial statements, what journal entries should be made in 2001 and 2002?

33. On January 1, 2001, a rich citizen of the town of Ristoni donates an artwork valued at $300,000 to be displayed to the public in a government building. This artwork meets the qualifications for not being capitalized. However, town officials choose to record the asset. There are no eligibility requirements for the gift. The asset is judged to be inexhaustible so that depreciation will not be reported.

    a. On government-wide financial statements for December 31, 2001, and the year then ended, what will be reported in connection with this gift?

    b. How does the answer to question (a) change if the government had decided to depreciate this asset over a 10-year period using straight-line depreciation?

    c. How does the answer to question (a) change if the government had decided not to capitalize the asset?

34. On January 1, 2001, a city pays $60,000 for artwork. The city will put the artwork on display in the local library and will take appropriate measures to protect and preserve the piece. However, if the work is ever sold the money received will go into unrestricted funds. The work is viewed as inexhaustible but the city has opted to depreciate the cost over 20 years (using the straight-line method).

    a. How will this artwork be reported in the government-wide financial statements for December 31, 2001, and the year then ended?

    b. How will this artwork be reported in the fund-based financial statements for December 31, 2001, and the year then ended?

35. A city government adds street lights within its boundaries at a total cost of $100,000. The lights should last for at least 10 years but can last significantly longer if maintained

properly. The city sets up a system to monitor these lights with the goal that 97 percent will be working at any one time. During the year, the city spends $6,300 to clean and repair the lights so that they are working according to the specified conditions. However, another $9,000 is spent to construct lights for several new streets within the city.

For government-wide reporting purposes, describe the various ways by which these costs could be reported.

36. The city of Francois, Texas, has begun the process of producing its comprehensive annual financial report (CAFR). Within the city, several organizations operate that are related in some way to the primary government. The city's accountant is attempting to determine how these organizations should be included in the reporting process.

   a. What is the major criterion for inclusion in a government's CAFR?
   b. How is a primary government unit identified?
   c. How is the legal separation of a government unit evaluated?
   d. How is the fiscal independence of a government unit evaluated?
   e. What is a component unit and how is a component unit normally reported on the government-wide financial statements?
   f. How does a primary government prove that it can impose its will on a component unit?
   g. What is meant by the blending of a component unit?
   h. What is a related organization and how does a primary government report a related organization?

37. The county of Maxnell decides to create a sanitation department and offer its services to the public for a fee. As a result, county officials plan to account for this activity with the enterprise funds. Make journal entries for this operation for the following transactions as well as necessary adjusting entries at the end of the year. Only entries for the sanitation department are required here.

   January 1, 2001—Unrestricted funds of $90,000 are received as a transfer from the General Fund as permanent financing.

   February 1, 2001—An additional $130,000 is borrowed from a local bank at a 12 percent annual interest rate.

   March 1, 2001—A truck is ordered at an expected cost of $108,000.

   April 1, 2001—The truck is received and payment is made. The actual costs amount to $110,000. The truck has a 10-year life and no salvage value. Straight-line depreciation is to be used.

   May 1, 2001—The city receives a cash grant of $20,000 from the state to help supplement the pay of the sanitation workers.

   June 1, 2001—A garage for the truck is rented at a cost of $1,000 per month with 12 months of rent being paid in advance.

   July 1, 2001—Citizens were charged $13,000 for services. Of this amount, $11,000 has been collected.

   August 1, 2001—A $10,000 cash payment is made on the 12 percent note above. This payment covers both interest and principal.

   September 1, 2001—Salaries of $18,000 are paid using the grant received above.

   October 1, 2001—Maintenance costs of $1,000 are paid on the truck.

   November 1, 2001—Additional salaries of $10,000 are paid, partially using the rest of the grant money received earlier.

   December 31, 2001—Invoices are sent to customers for services over the past six months that total $19,000. Cash of $3,000 is collected immediately.

38. The following information pertains to the city of Williamson for 2001, its first year of legal existence. For convenience, assume that all transactions are for the General Fund which carries out three separate functions: general government, public safety, and health and sanitation.

Receipts:

Property taxes	$320,000
Franchise taxes	42,000
Charges for general government services	5,000
Charges for public safety services	3,000
Charges for health and sanitation services	42,000
Issued long-term note payable	200,000

Receivables at end of year:

Property taxes (90 percent estimated to be collected)	$ 90,000

Payments:

Salary:

General government	$ 66,000
Public safety	39,000
Health and sanitation	22,000

Rent:

General government	$ 11,000
Public safety	18,000
Health and sanitation	3,000

Maintenance:

General government	$ 21,000
Public safety	5,000
Health and sanitation	9,000

Insurance:

General government	$ 8,000
Public safety ($2,000 still prepaid at end of year)	11,000
Health and sanitation	12,000
Interest on debt	16,000
Principal payment on debt	4,000
Building	120,000
Equipment	80,000
Supplies (20 percent still held) (public safety)	15,000
Investments	90,000

Ordered but not received:

Equipment	$ 12,000

Due at end of year:

Salaries:

General government	$ 4,000
Public safety	7,000
Health and sanitation	8,000

Compensated absences for general government workers at the end of the year amount to $13,000. These amounts will not be taken until late in the year 2002.

The city received artwork this year valued at $14,000 that is being used for general government purposes. There are no eligibility requirements. The city chose not to capitalize this property.

The building is used for the general government and is being depreciated over 10 years using the straight-line method and no salvage value. The equipment is used for health and sanitation and is depreciated using the straight-line method over five years with no salvage value.

The investments are valued at $103,000 at the end of the year.

a. Prepare a statement of activities and a statement of net assets for governmental activities for December 31, 2001, and the year then ended.

b. Prepare a statement of revenues, expenditures, and changes in fund balances and a balance sheet for the General Fund as of December 31, 2001, and the year then ended. Assume that the consumption method is being applied.

39. The city of Bernard starts the year of 2001 with the following unrestricted amounts in its General Fund: cash of $20,000 and investments of $70,000. In addition, it holds a building bought on January 1, 2000, for general government purposes for $300,000 and related long-term debt of $240,000. The building is being depreciated on the straight-line method over 10 years. The interest rate is 10 percent. The General Fund carries out four separate functions: general government, public safety, public works, and health and sanitation.

Receipts:

Property taxes	$510,000
Sales taxes	99,000
Dividend income	20,000
Charges for general government services	15,000
Charges for public safety services	8,000
Charges for public works	4,000
Charges for health and sanitation services	31,000
Charges for landfill	8,000
Grant to be used for salaries for health workers (no eligibility requirements)	25,000
Issued long-term note payable	200,000
Sold above investments	84,000

Receivables at end of year:

Property taxes ($10,000 is expected to be uncollectible)	$130,000

Payments:

Salary:

General government	$ 90,000
Public safety	94,000
Public works	69,000
Health and sanitation (all from grant)	22,000

Utilities:

General government	$ 9,000
Public safety	16,000
Public works	13,000
Health and sanitation	4,000

Insurance:

General government	$ 25,000
Public safety	12,000
Public works (all prepaid as of the end of the year)	6,000
Health and sanitation	4,000

Miscellaneous:

General government	$ 12,000
Public safety	10,000
Public works	9,000
Health and sanitation	7,000
Interest on previous debt	24,000
Principal payment on previous debt	10,000
Interest on new debt	18,000
Building (public works)	210,000

Equipment (public safety)	90,000
Public works supplies (30 percent still held)	20,000
Investments	111,000

Ordered but not received:

| Equipment | $ 24,000 |
| Supplies | 7,000 |

Due at end of year:

Salaries:

General government	$ 14,000
Public safety	17,000
Public works	5,000

A truck was leased on the last day of the year. The first payment will be at the end of the next year. Total payments amount to $90,000 but have a present value of $64,000.

The city started a landfill within its General Fund this year. It is included as a public works function. Closure costs are expected to be $260,000 in about nine years. No costs have been incurred to date although the landfill is now 15 percent filled.

The new building is being depreciated over 20 years using the straight-line method and no salvage value whereas the equipment is similar except that the life is only 10 years.

The investments are valued at $116,000 at the end of the year.

a. Prepare a statement of activities and a statement of net assets for governmental activities for December 31, 2001, and the year then ended.

b. Prepare a statement of revenues, expenditures, and changes in fund balances and a balance sheet for the General Fund as of December 31, 2001, and the year then ended. Assume that the purchases method is being applied.

C H A P T E R

18

Accounting and Reporting for Private Not-for-Profit Organizations

QUESTIONS TO CONSIDER

■ Individuals, foundations, and businesses contribute large amounts of resources to not-for-profit organizations. What financial information do contributors want regarding the not-for-profit organization?

■ How can a contributor to a charity determine the utilization being made of the resources contributed?

■ How should a not-for-profit organization recognize pledges of support?

■ Should a not-for-profit organization record donations of services?

■ What accounting is made of donations to a not-for-profit organization that must be conveyed to a different beneficiary?

The Governmental Accounting Standards Board was established to set accounting standards for state and local governments as well as organizations controlled by state and local governments, such as state universities. In contrast, the Financial Accounting Standards Board (FASB) has authority for establishing accounting standards for business organizations and *private not-for-profit* organizations. The term *private* indicates that the organization is not owned by a government, while the term *not-for-profit* denotes the absence of a profit objective. Private not-for-profits include churches, charities, voluntary health and welfare organizations, many hospitals, and private colleges and universities.

Until recently, even though the FASB had standard-setting authority, specific accounting standards for private not-for-profits were established by industry audit guides issued by the American Institute of Certified Public Accountants (AICPA). The accounting standards set by these industry audit guides differed somewhat among the various types of not-for-profits. In 1993 the FASB standardized the reporting of private not-for-profit organizations with the issuance of two standards. *FASB Statement No. 116,* "Accounting for Contributions Received and Contributions Made," established guidelines for determining when and how these not-for-profit organizations should recognize and report contributions. *FASB Statement No. 117,* "Financial Statements of Not-for-Profit Organizations," specified the required financial statements and financial statement format for private not-for-profit organizations.[1]

As a result of these two standards, the financial statements of private colleges and universities are very similar to those of voluntary health and welfare organizations, civic

---

[1]The AICPA now issues an annual audit and accounting guide, *Not for-Profit Organizations,* to provide guidelines for preparing and auditing financial statements prepared by these organizations.

organizations, labor unions, and political parties. However, because government-owned colleges and universities continue to follow accounting standards established by the GASB, the financial statements of public universities differ greatly from those of private schools.

FINANCIAL REPORTING

Many private not-for-profit organizations operate throughout the world. The purpose of each is to achieve one or more stated objectives such as the cure of a particular disease or the cleanup of the environment. Many individuals (especially current and potential contributors) are interested in how the organization spends the money it receives. They want to know:

- Which of these organizations should receive money and how much?
- Is contributing to a particular charity a wise allocation of resources?
- Will donated funds be used effectively by an organization to accomplish its specified purpose or will the money be wasted?

Such questions are faced by every not-for-profit entity relying on voluntary contributions from the general public, (i.e., *public support*). Future gifts and grants are based, at least in part, on the organization's ability to convince donors that resources are being used wisely to accomplish stated goals. The financial statements are vital to this objective since they report the resources generated and the spending decisions that have been made.

Several basic goals form the framework for the FASB's standards for private not-for-profit organizations. These include:

1. The financial statements should focus on the entity as a whole.
2. Reporting requirements for private not-for-profit organizations should be similar to business entities unless there are critical differences in the information needs of financial statement users.

The first goal is important because the organization's financial statements should not be centered around the funds that many not-for-profit organizations use for internal record-keeping. Historically, the reporting of not-for-profit organizations has been patterned after government accounting with a heavy emphasis on separate fund types. The FASB eliminated this approach in order to focus on the operations and financial position of the entire entity. The second goal is significant because it allows the utilization of many of the same accrual basis techniques used by business entities for recording and reporting most transactions. Consequently, existing FASB standards for capital leases, pensions, contingent liabilities, and many other issues do not have to be rewritten for not-for-profit organizations.

Although not-for-profit organizations have much in common with business entities, such as accrual based measurement of assets and liabilities, the FASB identified three critical differences. First, the contributions not-for-profit organizations receive create transactions that have no counterparts in commercial accounting. Second, contributions often have donor-imposed restrictions. Third, no single indicator can describe performance as effectively as net income does for commercial entities, thus other indicators are necessary. These differences suggest the need for a different basic set of financial statements for not-for-profit organizations.

As a result, *FASB Statement 117,* "Financial Statements of Not-for-Profit Organizations," requires three financial statements:

1. The *statement of financial position* reports the assets, liabilities, and net assets of private not-for-profits. The final category, net assets, is used in place of owners' equity or fund balance. The amount of net assets held by the organization must be classified as unrestricted, temporarily restricted, or permanently restricted.

2. The *statement of activities and changes in net assets* reports revenues, expenses, gains, and losses for the period. Revenues and expenses are determined using the accrual basis of accounting, including depreciation of fixed assets. The statement presents the *change in each category of net assets* for the period and reconciles to net assets appearing on the statement of financial position.

3. The *statement of cash flows* uses the standard FASB classifications of cash flows from operations, investing activities, and financing activities. Cash flows from operating activities may be prepared on either the direct or indirect basis. Because this statement follows the traditional format, it will not be discussed in this coverage.

In addition to these statements, voluntary health and welfare organizations are required to prepare a *Statement of Functional Expense* (see Exhibit 18–3). Voluntary health and welfare organizations are entities which promote humanitarian activities, such as public health clinics, homeless shelters, the American Diabetes Association, and the Christian Children's Fund. These organizations typically receive some revenues from their activities, but rely on support from gifts made by individuals and foundations, government grants, United Way allocations, and similar sources to support their activities. The statement of functional expense provides a detailed schedule of expenses by function (such as various programs and administrative activities) and by object (salaries, supplies, depreciation, etc.). This statement is considered especially important because many charities are evaluated based on the percentage of their expenses incurred in connection with program services rather than supporting services such as general and administrative and fund-raising.

Statement of Financial Position

Exhibit 18–1 presents the statement of financial position for Christian Children's Fund, Inc. The asset and liability sections resemble those of business enterprises. Unlike business enterprises, individuals and organizations provide resources to not-for-profit organizations without the expectation of earning a return on their investment. As a result, the concept of owners' equity does not apply to not-for-profit organizations. In the place of paid-in-capital and retained earnings, the final section of the statement presents net assets, the excess of assets over liabilities.

Net assets are presented in three categories created by the FASB: unrestricted, temporarily restricted, and permanently restricted. Restrictions must be imposed by donors from outside the organization before an asset is classified as restricted. Board designated or internally restricted assets are classified as unrestricted for financial statement purposes.

Temporarily restricted assets are restricted for a particular purpose or for use in a future time period. For example, a private college might receive a grant for drug research. The amounts received from the grant are temporarily restricted for that particular use. Alternatively, the college might receive a grant supporting education programs over the next three years. The amounts received or promised for future periods also are restricted temporarily. Temporarily restricted assets represent resources that are expected to be released from restriction on performance of some act or the passage of time. The statement of financial position for the University of Notre Dame as of June 30, 1999, indicates temporarily restricted net assets of over $831 million, including $52 million that was contributed specifically for the acquisition of buildings and equipment.

In contrast, permanently restricted assets are expected to remain restricted for as long as the organization exists. The most common form of permanently restricted assets are endowments in which the principal must remain intact. For example, a

Exhibit 18–1

CHRISTIAN CHILDREN'S FUND, INC.
Statement of Financial Position
June 30, 1999

Assets

Cash and cash equivalents	$11,005,618
Investments	26,311,770
Accounts receivable and other assets	5,258,671
Land, buildings, and equipment, net	11,290,926
Total Assets	$53,866,985

Liabilities and Net Assets

Liabilities:

Accounts payable and accrued expenses	$ 5,568,481
Bonds payable	1,555,000
Total Liabilities	7,123,481

Net Assets:

Unrestricted	26,938,141
Temporarily restricted	16,431,762
Permanently restricted	3,373,601
Total Net Assets	46,743,504
Total Liabilities and Net Assets	$53,866,985

footnote to the financial statements of the Christian Children's Fund indicates that "permanently restricted net assets were $3,373,601 and $2,988,924 at June 30, 1999, and 1998, respectively. The principal of these net assets must be invested in perpetuity; however, the income is expendable to support a subsidy for children and other restricted program activities." Additionally, land and works of art are classified as permanently restricted if they are donated with stipulations that they be used for a specified purpose and not sold.

Statement of Activities and Changes in Net Assets

Exhibit 18–2 presents the statement of activities for Christian Children's Fund. Note the use of separate columns for the three categories of net assets: unrestricted, temporarily restricted, and permanently restricted. The bottom line agrees with the net asset balances presented on the statement of financial position. Measured on the accrual basis, recognition of revenues and expenses follow the same standards applicable to business enterprises. A unique feature of not-for-profit organizations is that they receive significant resources through contributions. *FASB Statement No. 116* requires not-for-profit organizations to recognize contributions as revenue in the period the contribution is made. According to Exhibit 18–2, the Christian Children's Fund received total public support for sponsorships of nearly $98.8 million and additional contributions of over $18.0 million. Private not-for-profit organizations recognize unconditional promises to give (including pledges) as both a receivable and a revenue in the period promised. For example, as of June 30, 1999, Wake Forest University reported contributions receivable (net) of over $28 million. In an accompanying footnote, the school explained "contributions, including unconditional promises to give, are recognized as revenues in the period received. Conditional promises to give are not recognized until they become unconditional, that is, when the conditions on which they depend are substantially met."

Exhibit 18–2

CHRISTIAN CHILDREN'S FUND, INC.
Statement of Activities
For the fiscal year ended June 30, 1999

	Unrestricted	Temporarily Restricted	Permanently Restricted	Total
Public Support:				
Sponsorships				
U.S. sponsors	$ —	$ 67,652,388	—	$ 67,652,388
International sponsors	—	20,809,014	—	20,809,014
Special gifts from sponsors for children	—	10,315,615	—	10,315,615
Total sponsorships	—	98,777,017	—	98,777,017
Contributions				
General contributions	6,739,964	6,391,385	$ 323,554	13,454,903
Major gifts and bequests	2,858,371	1,767,744	—	4,626,115
Gifts-in-kind	—	—	—	—
Total contributions	9,598,335	8,159,129	323,554	18,081,018
Grants				
Grants and contracts	2,615,768	—	—	2,615,768
Total Public Support	12,214,103	106,936,146	323,554	119,473,803
Revenue:				
Investment and currency transactions	1,215,584	3,432	—	1,219,016
Service fees and other	2,211,312	—	—	2,211,312
Total Revenue	3,426,896	3,432		3,430,328
NET ASSETS RELEASED FROM RESTRICTIONS:				
Satisfaction of program restrictions	105,442,225	(105,442,225)	—	—
Total Public Support and Revenue	121,083,224	1,497,353	323,554	122,904,131
Expenses:				
Program				
Health	42,257,734	—	—	42,257,734
Education	55,200,141	—	—	55,200,141
Total Program	97,457,875	—	—	97,457,875
Fund-raising	12,159,774	—	—	12,159,774
Management and general	10,416,146	—	—	10,416,146
Total Expenses from Operations	120,033,795	—	—	120,033,795
Change in net assets from operations	1,049,429	1,497,353	323,554	2,870,336
Non-operating Revenue (Expenses):				
Realized gain (loss) on sale of investments	(210,522)	—	—	(210,522)
Unrealized gain (loss) on investments	797,091	—	—	797,091
Systems redesign project (management and general)	(1,823,113)	—	—	(1,823,113)
Total Non-operating Expenses	(1,236,544)	—	—	(1,236,544)
Change in net assets	(187,115)	1,497,353	323,554	1,633,792
Net assets at beginning of year	27,182,000	14,938,788	2,988,924	45,109,712
Cash transfers	(56,744)	(4,379)	61,123	—
Net assets at end of year	$ 26,938,141	$ 16,431,762	$3,373,601	$ 46,743,504

Expenses are reported only in the unrestricted column of the statement of activities. Usually, a portion of the expenses relates to activities funded through restricted contributions or grants. In such cases, the expense is still reflected as a reduction in unrestricted net assets. To the extent any of these expenses meet stipulations established by external donors, net assets are released from temporary restriction. As shown in Exhibit 18–2, this reclassification is reflected in the statement of activities in a section following the Revenue section. For the Christian Children's Fund, over $105 million is shown being reclassified as "net assets released from restrictions." Thus, that amount of temporarily restricted net assets was (1) appropriately expended for an expense as designated by the donor, (2) appropriately expended for an asset as designated by the donor, or (3) a donor restriction based on time was satisfied.

Assume that a not-for-profit organization receives three cash gifts in Year One of $10,000 each. The donor has specified that the first gift is for employee salaries, the second gift is for equipment, and the third gift must be held for one year before being expended. In Year One, all three gifts would be shown in the statement of activities as increases in Temporarily Restricted Net Assets.

Assume that this example is extended into Year Two when the first two gifts are properly spent and the time restriction on the third gift is satisfied. For the first gift, cash is decreased and a salary expense is recorded. In addition, $10,000 is reclassified on the statement of activities from the Temporarily Restricted column to the Unrestricted column. With the second gift, equipment (an asset) is increased and cash is decreased but the same reclassification is made to indicate that the restriction has been met. A reclassification of $10,000 must also be made for the third gift even though it has not been spent because it was restricted only as to time.

An alternative does exist for the handling of the equipment bought with the restricted gift. The donor may specify how long the asset must be held. If that is the case, no immediate reclassification is made. Instead, a gradual reclassification is made equal to the depreciation of the asset. The same approach is used if the organization adopted a policy of time restriction on the use of such assets.

Information about the expenses incurred by a not-for-profit organization are considered of importance to contributors. The primary concern of contributors is determining the extent to which the not-for-profit is using the resources provided to fulfill the organizational mission. Expenses are presented in two broad categories, *program services* and *supporting services*. Program services are activities relating to the social services, research, or other objectives of the organization. Within this category, organizations may report several programs or only one. Christian Children's Fund reports just two program categories: health and education. Supporting service costs consist of administrative costs (management and general costs) and fund-raising expenses. These activities generally are regarded as not directly related to one of the organization's stated missions. Frequently analysts use the ratio of program service expenses to total expenses to rank not-for-profits. The Better Business Bureau suggests that ratio values of less than 60 percent are not desirable. Christian Children's Fund reports a ratio of 81.2 percent ($97.457 million/$120.033 million) for the year ended June 30, 1999.

Below expenses, the Christian Children's Fund reports "Non-operating Revenue (Expenses)." *FASB Statement 124*, "Accounting for Certain Investments Held by Not-for-profit Organizations" requires that investments in equity securities with readily determinable market values and all debt investments be reported at fair market value.[2] The resulting unrealized gains and losses are reported in the statement of activities. Gains and losses on investments, along with dividend and interest income, are reported as increases or decreases in unrestricted net assets, unless the income is ex-

---

[2] The system of classifying marketable securities into portfolios such as "trading securities" and "available for sale" that must be utilized by business entities does not apply to not-for-profit organizations.

plicitly restricted by the donor or by a law that extends a donor's restrictions to them. Christian Children's Fund reports a realized loss on the sale of investments of $210,522, along with an unrealized gain on adjusting investments to fair market value of $797,091.

Statement of Functional Expense

Exhibit 18–3 presents the statement of functional expense for the Christian Children's Fund. Because contributors are concerned with how their gifts are used, this statement provides a detailed analysis of expenses by both function and object. The columns represent functions and include two programs as well as the supporting services of management and general fund-raising. These are the same categories reported on the statement of activities, and column totals agree with operating expenses reported on the statement of activities. The rows list expenses according to their nature; for example, salaries, professional services, travel, and depreciation.

Because of the scrutiny placed on the amount that a not-for-profit organization spends on fund-raising, the allocation of costs is quite important. Until recently, joint costs expended for fund-raising appeals that also contained educational literature were routinely divided between fund-raising and program services. Thus, most direct mail appeals for contributions were accompanied by informational pamphlets and the like so that some portion of the cost of the mailing could be reflected as a program service expense. To bring control to this area, in 1998 the American Institute of Certified Public Accountants issued its Statement of Position (SOP) 98–2, *Accounting for Costs of Activities of Not for-Profit Organizations and State and Local Governmental Entities That Include Fund-Raising.* A full description of SOP 98–2 is beyond the scope of this textbook; however, a portion of such fund-raising campaigns can still be assigned to program service costs but only if several identified criteria are met.[3] Within the literature that is mailed or otherwise distributed, there must be a specific call for action that would have been the same even without the fund-raising appeal. This appeal cannot be directed purely at potential contributors and the requested action must be specific and help accomplish the entity's overall mission. If all of these criteria are met, some or all of the costs associated with this call to action should be reported under program services rather than fund-raising.

Evolution of Standard-setting Authority

Hospitals as well as colleges and universities can function as either private not-for-profit organizations or be part of a government. A municipal hospital, for example, may be in direct competition with a not-for-profit hospital.[4] After the creation of the Governmental Accounting Standards Board (GASB), questions of standard setting in such areas were raised:

- Should two sets of accounting principles be developed or just one?
- If just one set of principles was to be applied to all hospitals and colleges and universities, which body should create these principles?

A crisis finally arose in connection with the recording of depreciation expense by not-for-profit organizations that eventually led to a solution as to the division of authority for standard setting.

---

[3]For more information on SOP 98–2, see "How to Report a Joint Activity" in the August 1998 issue of the *Journal of Accountancy.*

[4]As discussed later in this chapter, hospitals (and schools) also can operate as not-for-profit organizations. However, no question exists as to authority for accounting principles in such cases—the FASB holds that responsibility.

Exhibit 18–3

CHRISTIAN CHILDREN'S FUND, INC.
Statement of Functional Expenses
For the fiscal year ended June 30, 1999

	Program Services		
	Health	**Education**	**Total**
Subsidy for children	$33,527,102	$43,795,550	$77,322,652
Program grants	3,964,856	5,179,185	9,144,041
Supplies	122,059	159,442	281,501
Occupancy	234,994	306,967	541,961
Professional services	19,938	26,044	45,982
Contract services	335,878	438,749	774,627
Travel	406,836	531,440	938,276
Conferences and meetings	42,319	55,280	97,599
Automobile and truck expense	130,182	170,053	300,235
Advertising and public education	14,461	18,891	33,352
Equipment purchases and rentals	114,753	149,899	264,652
Telephone and cables	115,604	151,010	266,614
Postage and freight	282,495	369,016	651,511
Staff training	105,064	137,242	242,306
Miscellaneous expenses	161,536	211,009	372,545
Total Expenses Before Personnel Costs and Other Expenses	39,578,077	51,699,777	91,277,854
Salaries	1,981,664	2,588,595	4,570,259
Employee benefits	318,685	416,289	734,974
Payroll taxes	155,116	202,623	357,739
Total Personnel Costs	2,455,465	3,207,507	5,662,972
Interest	—	—	—
Depreciation	224,192	292,857	517,049
Total Other Expenses	224,192	292,857	517,049
Total Expenses	42,257,734	55,200,141	97,457,875
Less: Non-operational systems redesign project	—	—	—
Total Non-operating Expenses	—	—	—
Total Expenses from Operations	$42,257,734	$55,200,141	$97,457,875

Exhibit 18-3—concluded

CHRISTIAN CHILDREN'S FUND, INC.
Statement of Functional Expenses
For the fiscal year ended June 30, 1999

	Supporting Services			
Fund-raising	Management and General	Total	1999 Total Program and Supporting Services
—	—	—	$ 77,322,652
—	—	—	9,144, 041
$ 48,999	$ 108,153	$ 157,152	438,653
4,746	616,647	621,393	1,163,354
4,280	351,185	355,465	401,447
179,377	2,751,948	2,931,325	3,705,952
7,908	86,641	94,549	1,032,825
5,770	28,189	33,959	131,558
1,993	3,495	5,488	305,723
11,111,182	491,108	11,602,290	11,635,642
12,016	740,561	752,577	1,017,229
9,797	154,916	164,713	431,327
37,603	1,010,368	1,047,971	1,699,482
5,649	60,094	65,743	308,049
74,337	892,832	967,169	1,339,714
11,503,657	7,296,137	18,799,794	110,077,648
555,665	3,536,951	4,092,616	8,662,875
41,320	531,004	572,324	1,307,298
39,367	257,104	296,471	654,210
636,352	4,325,059	4,961,411	10,624,383
—	132,787	132,787	132,787
19,765	485,276	505,041	1,022,090
19,765	618,063	637,828	1,154,877
12,159,774	12,239,259	24,399,033	121,856,908
—	(1,823,113)	(1,823,113)	(1,823,113
—	(1,823,113)	(1,823,113)	(1,823,113)
$12,159,774	$10,416,146	$22,575,920	$120,033,795

Traditionally, not-for-profit organizations, especially colleges and universities, have been permitted but not required to report depreciation expense. Not surprisingly, because of the impact on current balances (and the work necessary to compute amounts), few institutions chose to include annual depreciation figures. In discussing depreciation, the argument was frequently made that profitability is not a goal of these organizations so that the calculation and recording of this expense is inappropriate. College officials usually contended that new acquisitions are commonly financed by fundraising campaigns (rather than from operations) so that ensuring the availability of adequate resources through the recognition of depreciation was not considered necessary.

However, in August 1987, the FASB issued *Statement No. 93,* "Recognition of Depreciation by Not-for-Profit Organizations." This pronouncement required the recognition of depreciation by all not-for-profit organizations (other than state and local governments). The rule pertained to both purchased assets and properties acquired by donation and was aimed at colleges and universities as well as religious institutions and other not-for-profit organizations. The FASB justified this action by stating in paragraph 20:

> Using up assets acquired involves a cost to the organization because the economic benefits (or service potential) used up are no longer available to the organization. That is as true for assets acquired without cost as it is for assets acquired at a cost.

At that time, several types of public not-for-profit organizations (governmental colleges and universities, public benefit corporations and authorities, public employee retirement systems, governmental utilities, and governmental hospitals and other health care providers) had been directed to follow the pronouncements of the GASB. However, if the accounting treatment of a transaction or event was not explicitly specified by a GASB pronouncement, applicable FASB pronouncements had to be utilized. Thus, the GASB found itself in the position of having to respond to each statement of the FASB unless it wanted the provisions to apply automatically to this list of governmental not-for-profit organizations.

Consequently, in January of 1988, the GASB countered with a pronouncement of its own, *Statement 8,* "Applicability of FASB Statement No. 93, *Recognition of Depreciation by Not-for-Profit Organizations,* to Certain State and Local Governmental Entities.*" This standard exempted public colleges and universities (as well as the other governmental not-for-profit institutions) from the necessity of recording depreciation. According to paragraph 4,

> Some governmental entities that engage in activities similar to private, not-for-profit organizations covered by *FASB Statement 93* follow governmental fund accounting and reporting principles. Those governmental entities follow GASB standards for depreciation and are therefore not affected by *FASB Statement 93.*

Suddenly, colleges and other organizations found themselves being guided by two different bodies. Public schools, such as Ohio State University and the University of Texas, were to follow GASB so that the recording of depreciation was voluntary. In contrast, private institutions such as Harvard and Duke came under the auspices of the FASB and had to report depreciation expense. A power struggle quickly resulted with the reporting organizations caught in the middle. "I see the two groups as somewhat entrenched in their positions," said Carl Hanes, the vice president for administration at the State University of New York at Stonybrook. "I see it as a real mess. We have two credible, professional organizations with different voices, and the imposition of their views on the different types of institutions could generate financial information that's not comparable."[5]

---

[5]John B. Thomas, "Higher Education Is the Victim in FASB-GASB Dispute," *Business Officer,* January 1988, p. 20.

Officials reacted with dismay at the dual set of rules that had been established. Debates arose as to whether depreciation was truly applicable to these types of not-for-profit organizations. Many administrators (but certainly not all) seemed to prefer the traditional view that the cost of generating depreciation data would outweigh any possible benefits.

> "Depreciating the university's 160 buildings and equipment worth over $1 billion could cost us up to $200,000 for new computer software to do the figuring each year," estimates William J. Hogan, comptroller of the University of Chicago, a private institution. "It really isn't worth it."[6]

versus

> Depreciation accounting not only ought to be adopted, but it should be adopted in the operating statement and funded by mandatory transfer to the plant funds. Only in this way will financial statements show the true impact and cost of depreciation, providing users of such statements with more accurate information.[7]

Just before *Statement No. 93* was scheduled to take effect, the FASB postponed the effective date to allow time for a compromise to be developed. No one at that time appeared to want the establishment of two sets of rules. The Financial Accounting Foundation (FAF), which oversees and funds both the FASB and the GASB, stepped in to help mediate a solution to the territorial argument. Numerous compromises were proposed. On October 30, 1989, the FAF voted to give the FASB jurisdiction over both public and private not-for-profit organizations. Thus, only one set of accounting standards would apply to such entities.

However, that ruling did not stop the controversy. Ten different government groups immediately threatened to stop supporting the GASB unless all public entities (such as state universities) remained under its jurisdiction.[8] Faced with a problem having no end in sight, the FAF reversed itself and gave the GASB authority over governmental not-for-profit organizations. Thus, for a number of years, a significant difference in reporting existed. The FASB required the reporting of depreciation by private colleges and universities (and other private not-for-profit organizations) whereas public groups following the GASB had the option of recording depreciation. For this reason, the University of Southern California (a private school) reported depreciation expense for the year ending June 30, 1999, of $60.6 million. Conversely, the University of Kentucky (a public institution) indicated at the same time that its "land, land improvements, buildings, equipment and library books are stated at cost at date of acquisition or, in the case of gifts, at fair market value at date of gift." Apparently, no depreciation has been recorded.

This part of the debate seems to have been settled finally in November 1999 when the GASB issued its *Statement Number 35,* "Basic Financial Statements—and Management's Discussion and Analysis—for Public Colleges and Universities," which applied the reporting standards established by GASB *Statement Number 34* to public schools. As indicated in the previous chapter, once adopted these new rules require the recognition of depreciation in the government-wide financial statements so that both private and public schools will now be comparable as to the recording of depreciation. Other vast differences, though, still remain.

The GAAP Hierarchy

At some point, the relationship between governmental not-for-profit organizations and FASB pronouncements almost had to be redefined. The GASB could not stop its

---

[6]Lee Berton, "Several Private Colleges May Ignore New Accounting Rule on Depreciation," *Wall Street Journal,* February 4, 1988.

[7]Phillip Jones, Sr.; Clarence Jung, Jr.; and Herbert Peterson, "Why Not Depreciate and Why Not in Operations?" *Business Officer,* April 1989, p. 33.

[8]See, for more information, "The Great GASB," *Forbes,* December 11, 1989, p. 60.

ongoing work every time an FASB statement was issued to evaluate whether the new standard should be voided for governmental not-for-profit organizations. Apparently, an adequate resolution was crafted by the AICPA Auditing Standards Board in its *Statement on Auditing Standards 69,* "The Meaning of 'Presents Fairly in Conformity with Generally Accepted Accounting Principles' in the Independent Auditor's Report" issued in 1991. This standard creates a hierarchy for determining whether an accounting treatment should be judged as being in compliance with generally accepted accounting principles (GAAP). For both nongovernmental entities as well as state and local governments, accounting pronouncements and other potential guidelines are grouped into five layers. The higher levels are more authoritative than the lower levels.

The GAAP hierarchy created by *SAS 69* is presented in Exhibit 18–4. For state and local governments, GASB statements and interpretations are placed at the highest level. This same ranking is appropriate for AICPA and FASB pronouncements *but only if they are made applicable to state and local governments by a GASB Statement or Interpretation.* Thus, even though a GASB statement may not provide specific guidance in a particular area of financial reporting, FASB statements no longer become automatically appropriate for governmental not-for-profit organizations. Instead, the GASB can study and evaluate each new pronouncement and act if it believes that the guidelines should be followed.

ACCOUNTING FOR CONTRIBUTIONS

Contributions are obviously a major source of support for most private not-for-profits. *FASB Statement 116* defines contributions as unconditional transfers of cash or other resources to an entity in a voluntary nonreciprocal transaction. According to *Statement 116,* contributions are recognized as revenue in the period received at their fair market value. Conditional promises to give are not recognized as revenue until the conditions are met. Conditions, however, are different from restrictions. Conditional promises require some future action on the part of the not-for-profit organization before the asset will be transferred and are not recognized as revenue until the condition is met. Restricted contributions specify how the contributions are expected to be used and are recognized as permanently or temporarily restricted revenue when the promise is received.

Pledges and other unconditional promises to give are recognized as a receivable and revenue in the period pledged. Consequently, the University of Southern California reports pledges receivable of over $101 million as of June 30, 1999. Before recording, these pledges have to reflect an unconditional promise to give rather than just the donor's intention to make a gift. For that reason, pledge statements that allow donors to change their minds are viewed as intentions to give and should not be recorded until the promise becomes unconditional or the gift is actually received.

Because contribution revenue is recognized at fair market value, the estimated uncollectible portion of pledged amounts should be deducted from contribution revenue and an allowance account established to present the receivable at its expected net realizable value. Furthermore, promises that are not expected to be collected within a year are discounted to present value using an appropriate interest rate, such as the organization's incremental borrowing rate or the rate of return on its investment portfolio. The University of Southern California has reduced its pledges receivable balance being reported by an allowance for doubtful accounts of approximately $3.6 million. In addition, because many of the pledges will not be received until well into the future, an additional reduction of approximately $42.8 million has been made to state the figure at present value.

Cash is not the only type of support received by not-for-profits. Many organizations receive donations of materials intended either to be used by the charity itself (such as vehicles, office furniture, and computers) or distributed to needy groups or individuals (food, clothing, and toys). For organizations such as the Salvation Army and Goodwill

Exhibit 18–4
GAAP Hierarchy Summary

Nongovernmental Entities	State and Local Governments
Established Accounting Principles	
FASB Statements and Interpretations, APB Opinions, and AICPA Accounting Research Bulletins	GASB Statements and Interpretations, plus AICPA and FASB pronouncements if made applicable to state and local governments by a GASB Statement or Interpretation
FASB Technical Bulletins and (if cleared by the FASB) AICPA Industry Audit and Accounting Guides and AICPA Statements of Position	GASB Technical Bulletins, and the following pronouncements if specifically made applicable to state and local governments by the GASB: AICPA Industry Audit and Accounting Guides and AICPA Statements of Position
Consensus positions of the FASB Emerging Issues Task Force and (if cleared by the FASB) AICPA Practice Bulletins	Consensus positions of the GASB Emerging Issues Task Force and AICPA Practice Bulletins if specifically made applicable to state and local governments by the GASB
AICPA accounting interpretations, "Qs and As" published by the FASB staff, as well as industry practices widely recognized and prevalent	"Qs and As" published by the GASB staff, as well as industry practices widely recognized and prevalent
Other Accounting Literature*	
Other accounting literature, including FASB Concepts Statements; APB Statements; AICPA Issues Papers; International Accounting Standards Committee Statements; GASB Statements, Interpretations, and Technical Bulletins; pronouncements of other professional associations or regulatory agencies; AICPA Technical Practice Aids; and accounting textbooks, handbooks, and articles.	Other accounting literature, including GASB Concepts Statements; pronouncements in the first four categories of the hierarchy for nongovernmental entities when not specifically made applicable to state and local governments; APB Statements; FASB Concepts Statements; AICPA Issues Papers; International Accounting Standards Committee Statements; pronouncements of other professional associations or regulatory agencies; AICPA Technical Practice Aids; and accounting textbooks, handbooks, and articles

*In the absence of established accounting principles, the auditor may consider other accounting literature, depending on its relevance in the circumstances.

Industries, these donations provide a central resource essential to the charity's ongoing operations.

Because donated supplies and other materials provide resources for the organization, these contributions should be reported as support unless they cannot be used or sold by the organization. Although a value is sometimes apparent (for example, if a new vehicle is given), donations such as used clothing, furniture, and toys can be difficult to assess. In such cases, the guide allows the use of estimates and averages, provided they reasonably approximate the results of detailed measurements.

Assume, as an illustration, that a local voluntary health and welfare organization begins a drive to gather furniture and clothing for needy families living in the area. The following items are received:

Bed	$200 fair market value
Tables and chairs	130 fair market value
New clothing	500 fair market value
Used clothing	75 estimated resale value
Total	$905

In addition, one merchant donates a new desk (with an established sales price of $400) for use in the organization's office. Assume that the furniture and clothing are distributed to needy individuals as soon as they are received. The following journal entries would be recorded by the not-for-profit organization:

Inventory of Donated Material	905	
Unrestricted Net Assets—Contributions		905
Gifts made to organization to be distributed to needy individuals.		

Community Service Expenses—Assistance to Needy	905	
Inventory of Donated Materials		905
Distribution of furniture and clothing to needy individuals.		

Furniture—Office	400	
Unrestricted Net Assets—Contributions		400
Organization received donated office furniture; the asset will be depreciated over estimated useful life. The credit here could also be recorded as an increase in Temporarily Restricted Net Assets. In that case, a reclassification would be made to Unrestricted Net Assets as the asset is depreciated.		

Donations of Works of Art and Historical Treasures

In 1990, the FASB issued an exposure draft that would have required all contributions, including artworks and museum pieces, to be recorded as assets with a corresponding increase in revenues. Perhaps no accounting proposal ever put forth created such adverse public reaction. The FASB was deluged with more than 1,000 letters, virtually all of them in opposition. The argument against recognizing *additions to collections* is that the contribution does not provide the same kinds of benefits as contributions of cash or investments. Items held for research or public exhibit create little or no direct increase in cash flows. In fact, most such items will actually require continual outflows of cash for insurance, maintenance, and the like. Thus, they are not assets in the traditional sense. Opponents of the exposure draft argued that recognizing donations as revenues would mislead potential donors who were evaluating the operating results of the organization.

The opposition apparently influenced the Board, because *Statement No. 116* exempted gifts of artworks, historical treasures, and similar assets. Recognition of these contributions is not required if (1) they are added to a collection for public exhibition, education, or research; (2) they are protected and preserved; and (3) they are ever sold, any receipts will be used to acquire other collection items. For this reason, a note to the financial statements of Georgetown University explains that the school "has elected not to capitalize the cost or value of its collection of works of art, historical treasures, and similar assets."

Holding Contributions for Others

Some not-for-profit organizations, such as the United Way, raise donations that will be distributed to other designated charities. Or they accept gifts that must be conveyed to other specified beneficiaries. A community group might solicit donations by allowing the donor to identify the charity to be benefited. Such conveyances raise questions as to the recording that is appropriate for the donor, the initial recipient, and the specified beneficiary.

In 1999, the FASB issued *Statement No. 136,* "Transfers of Assets to a Not-for-Profit Organization or Charitable Trust That Raises or Holds Contributions for Others" to provide authoritative guidance for such donations. For example, assume that Donor A gives $10,000 in cash to Charity M that must be conveyed to Beneficiary Z. Several reporting questions are raised by this contribution:

- Does Donor A always record an expense when the cash is conveyed to the charity or must there be an actual transfer to the eventual beneficiary?
- Does Charity M report a contribution revenue of $10,000 or only a liability to Z?
- At what point should Beneficiary Z recognize a contribution revenue in connection with this gift?

For a conveyance of this type of gift, the donor normally records an expense at the time that the property is conveyed to the not-for-profit organization (Charity M) because control over the asset has been lost. In the above case, Donor A would probably make the following entry:

Donor A
_____

Expense—Charitable Contribution	10,000	
Cash		10,000

However, if the donor retains the right to redirect the use of the gift or if the donation can be revoked, Donor A continues to have power over the asset and should not record an expense until conveyance is actually made. Until that time, Donor A should make the following entry instead of the one above:

Donor A
_____

Refundable Advance to Charity M	10,000	
Cash		10,000

For such gifts, the not-for-profit organization will usually record a liability to the beneficiary (rather than a contribution revenue). Thus, for the example above, the charity will most likely make the following journal entry for the money received:

Charity M

Cash..	10,000	
Liability to Beneficiary Z		10,000

If the donor retains the right to revoke or redirect the gift, the charity will not be certain as to whether the money will actually go to the named beneficiary. Thus, if such rights are retained by the donor, the charity's entry above is adjusted to the following:

Charity M

Cash..	10,000	
Refundable Advance from Donor A		10,000

In this kind of arrangement, the charitable organization will record neither a contribution revenue nor a contribution expense except in one situation. If the donor has not held on to the right to revoke or redirect the gift and also has given the charity variance powers to change the beneficiary, then the charity is in control of the asset and should record the following entry rather than either of the two entries above. Then an expense is recorded when the $10,000 goes to the beneficiary.

Charity M

Cash..	10,000	
Temporarily Restricted Net Assets—Contributions		10,000

In this situation where the donor has granted the not-for-profit organization variance powers, the donor should record its expense immediately at the time of the gift to the charity.

The beneficiary of such a gift also has to record its own contribution revenue. In such cases, if the donor has retained the right to revoke or redirect the gift or if the charitable organization is given variance powers to change the beneficiary, the named beneficiary makes no entry at all until the gift is received. That party really has no power to control the movement of the property until it is in possession. However, if the donor has not kept the right to revoke or redirect the gift and the charity has not received variance powers, the beneficiary should record the donation as soon as the gift is made to the not-for-profit organization:

Beneficiary Z

Contribution Receivable	10,000	
Contribution Revenue		10,000

If Beneficiary Z is a not-for-profit organization, this final entry would need to indicate whether the donation was unrestricted, temporarily restricted, or permanently restricted.

Contributed Services

Donated services are an especially significant means of support for many not-for-profits. The number of volunteers working in some organizations can reach into the thousands. Charities rely heavily on these individuals to fill administrative positions as well as to service fund-raising and program activities.

Contributed services are recognized as revenue but only if the service (1) creates or enhances a nonfinancial asset, or (2) requires a specialized skill possessed by the contributor and would have had to be purchased if not donated. Examples of the first type include donated labor by carpenters, electricians, and masons. The fair value of the services received would be recognized as an increase in both fixed assets and contribution revenue. Examples of the second type include contributed legal or accounting services and would be recognized as both an expense and revenue when contributed. Contributed services (such as volunteer servers at a soup kitchen) that fail to meet these criteria are not recognized as revenue. This is not because the services have no value, but because of the difficulty in measuring their fair value.

To illustrate, assume that a certified public accountant provides accounting services that would have cost a local charity $2,000 if not donated. Further, assume that a carpenter donated materials ($4,000) and labor ($3,500) to construct an addition to the charity's facilities. The following journal entries would be recorded by the not-for-profit organization:

General and Administrative Expenses—Accounting Services	2,000	
Unrestiuted Net Assets—Contributed Services		2,000
Contribution of professional services.		
Buildings and Improvements	7,500	
Unrestricted Net Assets—Contributed Services		3,500
Unrestricted Net Assets—Contributed Materials		4,000
Contribution of professional services and materials.		

Exchange Transactions

Exchange transactions are *reciprocal* transfers where both parties give and receive something of value. All or a portion of membership dues are frequently reciprocal transfers; the member typically receives benefits in the form of newsletters, journals, and use of organization facilities and services. Because these transactions do not meet the definition of a contribution, they follow normal accrual basis accounting and are recognized as revenue when earned. In contrast to contributions, reciprocal transfers received in advance are recorded as unearned revenue, a liability, rather than as revenue.[9] For example, assume a not-for-profit association received $5,000 in dues for the next fiscal year and that these membership dues are deemed to be a reciprocal transaction because members receive a journal and other organization publications of value. The journal entry to record the receipt would be as follows:

Cash	5,000	
Unearned Revenue—Membership Dues		5,000
Collection of dues for the next fiscal year.		

In the next year, the following journal entry would be made:

Unearned Revenue—Membership Dues	5,000	
Unrestricted Net Assets—Membership Dues		5,000
Recognition of dues earned in the current period, but collected in		
the previous year.		

TRANSACTIONS ILLUSTRATED

The following transactions demonstrate some typical journal entries for a private not-for-profit. Since *FASB Statement 117* does not require using a fund basis, it is not necessary to record transactions in separate funds. However, many not-for-profits choose to use a fund format for internal management purposes and frequently design their general ledger using separate funds. *FASB Statement 117* permits reporting by funds as supplemental information, provided all interfund transactions are eliminated.

Assume Shenandoah Seminary, a private college, began the year 2001 with unrestricted net assets of $1,250,000 and a permanent endowment of $700,000. During 2001 the seminary received the following contributions from alumni and friends:

---

[9]Guidance for determining how much of a member's dues are contributions is provided in the AICPA accounting and audit guide, *Not-for-Profit Organizations*. For example, membership dues have characteristics of an exchange transaction if nonmembers can obtain similar benefits for a fee.

Unrestricted pledges due within 12 months $130,000

Cash contributions to the endowment   50,000

Because the pledges should be collected within 12 months, no present value computation and recording is necessary. The seminary estimated that it will collect 85 percent of the unrestricted pledges and made the following entry:

1. Cash	50,000	
Pledges Receivable	130,000	
Allowance for Uncollectible Pledges		19,500
Unrestricted Net Assets—Contributions		110,500
Permanently Restricted Net Assets—Contributions		50,000
To record contributions received.		

Before the end of the fiscal period, the seminary collected $100,000 of the amount pledged and $5,000 of the pledges were written off, as reflected in this journal entry:

2. Cash	100,000	
Allowance for Uncollectible Pledges	5,000	
Pledges Receivable		105,000
To record pledges collected and written off.		

In addition, the seminary charged tuition of $800,000 and collects an additional $20,000 restricted by an outside donor to be used to support a series of lectures by visiting scholars. Because of the high costs involved in obtaining a college education, many schools must award a significant amount of financial aid to students. At one time, such financial aid was reported as an expense. Now, however, it is normally shown as a direct reduction to revenues. Consequently, the University of Notre Dame, as an example, reported within its revenues for the year ended June 30, 1999, tuition and fees of over $202 million less tuition scholarships and fellowships of nearly $51 million. Based on these figures, students paid on the average only 75 percent of the tuition and fees charged by the school. Thus, assume in this example, that financial aid of $200,000 is awarded. The seminary would make the following journal entries:

3. Tuition Receivable	800,000	
Cash	20,000	
Unrestricted Net Assets—Tuition Revenue		800,000
Temporarily Restricted Net Assets—Contributions		20,000
Financial Aid	200,000	
Tuition Receivable		200,000
To record tuition and restricted contributions as well as		
discount in tuition for financial aid awards.		

The seminary incurred liabilities of $640,000 ($575,000 for operating expenses and $65,000 for equipment). Of this, $625,000 was paid before year-end. The seminary would make the following journal entries:

4. Instruction Expenses	265,000	
Student Services Expenses	120,000	
Maintenance Expense	75,000	
Administrative Expenses	115,000	
Accounts Payable		575,000
To record expenses for the year.		
5. Equipment	65,000	
Accounts Payable		65,000
To record purchases of equipment.		
6. Accounts Payable	625,000	
Cash		625,000
To record partial payment of outstanding accounts payable.		

Depreciation on buildings and equipment amounted to $135,000 for the year, as shown in the following journal entry:

7. Depreciation Expense—Instruction.	80,000	
Depreciation Expense—Student Services.	20,000	
Depreciation Expense—Adminstration.	35,000	
Accumulated Depreciation, Buildings, and Equipment		135,000
To record depreciation on fixed assets.		

Reporting Transactions on Statement of Activities

The year-end reporting must reflect the changes in net assets within the three categories of net assets. In preparing the statement of activities, not-for-profits must report any temporarily restricted resources that may have been released from restriction through performance of some activity or the passage of time. Assume here that the instructional expenses include $15,500 of expenses relating to the series of lectures by visiting scholars. The following table summarizes changes in unrestricted, temporarily restricted, and permanently restricted net assets for the year:

Calculation of Change in Net Assets

Journal Entry	Unrestricted Net Assets	Temporarily Restricted Net Assets	Permanently Restricted Net Assets
1	$ 110,500		$50,000
3	800,000	$ 20,000	
	(200,000)		
4	(575,000)		
7	(135,000)		
Net assets released from restriction	15,500	(15,500)	
Increase (decrease) in net assets	$ 16,000	$ 4,500	$50,000

Because all expenses are reflected as a decrease in unrestricted net assets, the $15,500 decrease in temporarily restricted net assets is added to unrestricted net assets. Journal entries 2, 5, and 6 are not reflected in the preceding table because they did not change the seminary's net assets.

ACCOUNTING FOR HEALTH CARE ORGANIZATIONS

Each type of not-for-profit organization tends to retain some unique elements of financial reporting that have evolved over the years. Voluntary health and welfare organizations, for example, must report a statement of functional expenses whereas other not-for-profits do not. Probably the most distinctive accounting belongs to health care organizations. From a quantitative perspective, the providers of health care services are quite prevalent throughout the United States with many thousands of institutions in operation; virtually every city and town has hospitals, nursing homes, and medical clinics. The large number of enterprises is not surprising; health care expenditures now make up more than 13 percent of the gross national product in this country.[10]

One major factor influencing the financial reporting of health care organizations is the presence of third-party payors such as insurance companies, Medicare, Medicaid, and Blue Cross/Blue Shield. These organizations, rather than the individual patient, pay all or some of the cost of medical services received. For example, third-party payors may be responsible for more than 90 percent of the fees from hospital care. Because of the significant monetary amounts involved, third-party payors have historically sought reliable financial data, especially concerning the costs of patient care.

---

[10]John H. Engstrom and Leon E. Hay, *Essentials of Accounting for Governmental and Not-for-Profit Organizations,* 5th ed. (New York: Irwin McGraw-Hill: 1999), p. 282.

Financial Reporting by Health Care Organizations

Because of the unique nature of the health care industry, specialized reporting standards have been developed. The AICPA audit and accounting guide, *Health Care Organizations,* provides guidance for hospitals, HMOs, nursing homes, laboratories, and group or individual medical practices. Not limited to not-for-profit organizations, this guide provides accounting standards for these three classes of health care providers:

1. *Investor-owned health care enterprises.* Owned by investors or medical practitioners, these businesses provide goods or services to make a profit. Like other business enterprises, the financial reporting for these entities follows FASB statements other than those statements relating exclusively to not-for-profits.

2. *Not-for-profit organizations.* Not owned by investors or by governments these organizations receive some contributions, but for the most part they are self-sustaining from the fees charged for goods and services. Like other not-for-profit entities, their financial reporting follows *FASB Statements 116* and *117* and other applicable FASB statements.

3. *Governmental health care organizations.* These organizations are either controlled by governments or meet the definition of a governmental entity. Like other governmental organizations, they follow GASB reporting standards. Because these entities are typically treated as enterprise funds, they use accrual basis measurement and reporting. Although *FASB Statements 116* and *117* do not apply, the financial reports of government-owned health care organizations are similar to those of private not-for-profits.

Identifying the type of health care organization is necessary because various types use different accounting standards. For example, *FASB Statement 95* and *GASB Statement 9* establish standards for the statement of cash flows. Hospitals operated by state or local governments would prepare cash flow statements with the four category format of *GASB Statement 9.* Meanwhile, private not-for-profit hospitals and for-profit hospitals would prepare cash flow statements with the three category format of *FASB Statement 95.*

Despite the differences in the ownership and purpose of various types of health care organizations, all three types use accrual accounting in recording both revenues and expenses. In addition, they calculate and recognize depreciation expense each year for all buildings, equipment, and other long-lived assets (other than land). Because of these procedures, the reporting process used by health care organizations resembles that of commercial enterprises.

The most apparent difference between the three types of organizations is in the equity section of the statement of financial position. The equities of investor-owned health care enterprises include common stock and retained earnings. The difference between total assets and total liabilities of private not-for-profit enterprises is reflected in unrestricted, temporarily restricted, and permanently restricted net assets. The equity section of government-owned health care organizations includes unrestricted and restricted fund balances.

Regardless of the type of health care organization, the AICPA audit and accounting guide requires these four basic financial statements:

- Balance sheet (or statement of financial position).
- Statement of operations.
- Statement of changes in equity (or net assets/fund balance).
- Statement of cash flows.

The statement of operations for private not-for-profit organizations follows *FASB Statement 117* requirements for reporting changes in unrestricted net assets. Changes in temporarily restricted and permanently restricted net assets are included on the statement of changes in net assets.

Generally the accounting for not-for-profit health care organizations resembles that of charities and other private not-for-profit organizations. However, health care organizations have particular requirements for the display of items within the statement of operations. Many of these requirements resulting from the unique nature of health care organizations are described in the following sections.

Accounting for Patient Service Revenues

The largest source of revenues normally comes from patient services. These include fees for surgery, nursing services, medicine, laboratory work, X rays, blood, housing, food, and so forth.

Patient (or Resident) Service Revenues and Reductions   For a variety of reasons, health care entities (especially hospitals) often receive less than the total payment normally charged for patient services. Bad debts as well as other fee reductions can be significant. *However, to provide complete financial data about the operations of the organization, revenues are still recorded at standard rates if the intention of full collection is present.* A footnote in the financial statements for Georgetown University explains "patient service revenues of the Hospital and Medical Center clinical practice plans are accounted for at established rates when the service is provided. Appropriate allowances to recognize third-party prospective payments, cost reimbursement arrangements and charity care are also reported in the period when the service is provided."

Assume, for example, that patient charges for the current month at a local hospital total $750,000. Of this amount, $170,000 is due from patients with the remaining $580,000 billed to third-party payors: Medicare, Medicaid, Blue Cross/Blue Shield, and various insurance companies. Regardless of expected receipts, the hospital should record revenues through the following journal entry:

Accounts Receivable—Third-Party Payors	580,000	
Accounts Receivable—Patients	170,000	
Patient Service Revenues		750,000
To accrue patient charges for current month.		

The entire $750,000 is reported initially as patient service revenue by this hospital although complete collection is doubtful. This approach is considered the best method of allowing the hospital to monitor activities during the period.

To continue with this illustration. assume that $20,000 of patient receivables are estimated to be uncollectible. Furthermore, not-for-profit hospitals and other similar entities often make no serious attempt to collect amounts owed by indigent patients. In many cases, these facilities were originally created to serve the poor. Assume, therefore, that $18,000 of the accounts receivable will never be collected because several patients earn incomes at or below the poverty level. Thus, to mirror these anticipated revenue reductions, the hospital records two additional entries. Of the $170,000 due from patients, collection of $38,000 is not expected.

As shown here, the handling of the two reductions is not the same. The bad debts create an expense but the revenue and receivable for the charity care are removed.

Bad Debt Expense	20,000	
Allowance for Uncollectible and Reduced Accounts		20,000
To record estimation of receivables that will prove to be uncollectible.		

Patient Service Revenues (or Charity Care)	18,000	
Accounts Receivable—Third Party Payors		18,000
To remove accounts that will not be collected because patients' earned income is at the poverty level.		

Contractual Agreements with Third-party Payors   The adjustments just recorded reflect amounts that will not be collected from patients. An additional reduction is usually encountered but only in connection with receivables due from third-party payors. Organizations such as Medicare and Blue Cross/Blue Shield often establish contractual arrangements with health care providers stipulating that set rates are to be paid for specific services. The entity agrees, in effect, to accept as *payment in full* an amount computed by the third-party payor as reasonable (based frequently on the average cost within the locality for the service rendered). Thus, although a patient is charged $3,000, for example, the health care entity might collect only $2,700 (or some other total) from a third-party payor if the lower figure is determined to be an appropriate cost. The remaining $300 must be written off by the hospital and is commonly referred to as a *contractual adjustment.*

An alternative method of determining the amount to be paid is known as a prospective payment plan. Under this system, reimbursement is not based on the cost of the health services being provided but on the diagnosis of the patient's illness or injury. Thus, if a patient has a broken leg, as an example, the hospital would be entitled to a set reimbursement regardless of the actual expense incurred. Such plans were developed in an attempt to encourage a reduction in medical costs since no additional charge is collected if a patient remains in a hospital longer than necessary.

In many cases, the health care entity is not certain of the amount to be collected under these reimbursement plans. The AICPA audit and accounting guide requires that this amount be estimated and any reductions recognized in the same period as the patient service revenue. In the example just presented, the hospital probably does not anticipate collecting the entire $580,000 billed to third-party payors. Assume, for illustration purposes, that this hospital projects only $520,000 of the $580,000 charge will actually be received. To establish a proper value for the hospital's revenues, another $60,000 adjustment must be recorded.

Contractual Adjustments	60,000	
Allowance for Uncollectible and Reduced Accounts.		60,000
To recognize estimated reduction in patient billings because		
of contractual arrangements made with third-party payors.		

To determine the exact amount to be paid (especially under cost-reimbursement plans), the health care entity's costs are usually subject to audit by the third-party payors. Although payment is normally made currently, adjustments may be made later based on this examination. Thus, a facility might receive additional payments at a later date or be required to make reimbursements based on subsequent cost calculations made by the third-party payor.

Under that circumstance, a question must be addressed: Should any differences that arise between the expected collection and the final total be carried back to the period of accrual to correct the originally recorded contractual adjustment? If the hospital in the previous example recognizes a $60,000 contractual adjustment because it expects to collect $520,000, what accounting is made if the correct amount is ultimately determined to be only $509,000?

As no error has occurred in an accounting sense, GAAP is followed; any change needed to alter the initial estimation is recorded in the subsequent year. A prior period adjustment would not be considered appropriate.

Assume that in the previous illustration $520,000 is collected as anticipated. However, in the subsequent year, an audit of the hospital's costs by a third-party payor indicates that only $509,000 was appropriate. Thus, an $11,000 reimbursement from the hospital would now be required. Although this change relates to the first time period, no retroactive restatement is permitted.

DISCUSSION QUESTION

Is This Really an Asset?

Mercy Hospital is located near Springfield, Missouri. The not-for-profit hospital was created over 70 years ago by a religious organization to meet the needs of area residents who could not otherwise afford adequate health care. Although the hospital is open to the public in general, its primary mission has always been to provide medical services for the poor.

On December 23, 2001, a gentleman told the hospital's chief administrative officer the following story: "My mother has been in your hospital since October 30. The doctors have just told me that she will soon be well and can go home. I cannot tell you how relieved I am. The doctors, the nurses, and your entire staff have been just wonderful; my mother could not have gotten better care. She owes her life to your hospital.

"I am from Idaho. Now that my mother is on the road to recovery, I must return immediately to my business. I am in the process of attempting to sell an enormous tract of land in Idaho. When this acreage is sold, I will receive $15 million in cash. Because of the services that Mercy Hospital has provided for my mother, I want to make a donation of $5 million of this money." The gentlemen proceeded to write this promise on a piece of stationery that he dated and signed.

Obviously, all of the hospital's officials were overwhelmed by the gentleman's generosity. This $5 million gift was 50 times larger than the biggest gift ever received. However, the controller was a bit concerned about preparing the financial statements for 2001. "I have a lot of problems with recording this type of donation as an asset. At present, we are having serious cash flow problems; but if we show $5 million in this manner, our normal donors are going to think we have become rich and don't need their support."

What problems are involved in accounting for the $5 million pledge and how should the amount be reported by Mercy Hospital?

Initial Period

Cash	520,000	
Allowance for Uncollectible and Reduced Accounts..........	60,000	
Accounts Receivable—Third-Party Payor.............		580,000
To record collection from third party based on initial analysis of costs.		

Subsequent Period

Allowance for Uncollectible and Reduced Accounts (or Contractual Adjustments).....................................	11,000	
Cash		11,000
To record reimbursement paid to third-party payor based on audit indicating that costs were too high.		

Reductions—Financial Statement Presentation   As indicated, the AICPA audit and accounting guide requires that bad debts be shown as expenses rather than as reductions to patient service revenues. Furthermore, revenues and related charity care deductions are not recorded at all if the health care entity has no intention of collecting. Finally, contractual adjustments reduce patient service revenues but are not shown explicitly on the financial statements. Rather, patient service revenues are shown as a net figure after removing all such reductions. Since the entity has little chance of collecting the entire balance, reporting total revenues could mislead readers.

SUMMARY

1. *FASB Statement No. 117* establishes reporting requirements for private not-for-profit organizations. The intent is to provide financial statement users, including contributors, an overall view of the organization's financial position and results of operations.

2. The required financial statements for not-for-profit organizations include: statement of financial position, statement of cash flows, and statement of activity and changes in net assets. Voluntary health and welfare organizations also are required to issue statements of functional expense.

3. The statements must distinguish between assets, liabilities, revenues, and expenses that are permanently restricted, temporarily restricted, and unrestricted. Such restrictions are donor-imposed. Temporarily restricted assets are expected to be released from restriction due to the passage of time or the performance of some act by the not-for-profit. Permanently restricted net assets are expected to be restricted for as long as the organization exists.

4. Expenses should be reported by their functional classification such as major classes of program services and supporting services. Program services are goods or services provided to beneficiaries or customers that fulfill the purpose or mission of the organization. Supporting services are general administration and fund-raising.

5. Because of a conflict over the recording of depreciation expense, a GAAP hierarchy was created to identify the applicability of GASB and FASB pronouncements and other authoritative sources to businesses and nonbusiness entities.

6. *FASB Statement 116* establishes accounting and reporting requirements for contributions. Contributions are unconditional transfers of cash or other resources to an entity in a voluntary nonreciprocal transaction.

7. Contributions received by not-for-profit organizations, including unconditional written or oral promises to give, are recognized as revenues or support in the period received at fair-market value. Contributions made to not-for-profit organizations (generally by for-profit organizations) including unconditional promises to give, are recognized as expenses in the period made at their fair market value.

8. Not-for-profit organizations must distinguish between contributions that are permanently restricted, temporarily restricted, and unrestricted. Such restrictions are donor-imposed.

9. Contributed services are recognized as revenues or support if they either create or enhance nonfinancial assets or require a specialized skill (e.g., accountant, architect, nurse) and would have to be purchased if not provided by donation.

10. Not-for-profit organizations can sometimes receive donations that must be passed along to a different beneficiary. While the gift is being held by the charity, it is normally recorded as an asset along with an accompanying liability. However, if the organization is given variance powers to change the beneficiary, the not-for-profit records a revenue rather than a liability. In contrast, the beneficiary records a revenue unless the original donor has the right to revoke or redirect the gift or the charity has variance powers that allow a change in the beneficiary.

11. Health care organizations fall into three types: first, investor-owned health care enterprises that follow FASB accounting and reporting standards other than those standards relating exclusively to not-for-profits, second, private, not-for-profit health care organizations that follow *FASB Statements 116* and *117* for not-for-profits and other applicable FASB statements and third, governmental health care organizations that follow GASB reporting standards.

12. Health care organizations frequently receive less than the full amount of patient charges. Contractual adjustments with third-party payors are shown as a deduction from revenue in reporting *net patient service revenue*. Bad debts are estimated and reported as an expense. Charity care charges are not recorded as revenue.

COMPREHENSIVE ILLUSTRATION

Problem

(Estimated time: 30 to 45 minutes) Augusta Regional Hospital is a private not-for-profit hospital offering medical care to a variety of patients, including some with no ability to pay for the services received. In addition, the hospital sponsors a consortium on childhood diseases with the financial support of a private foundation. The hospital holds an endowment, the principal of which must be maintained, but the earnings are available to provide charity care. During 2001, the hospital has the following financial transactions:

1. The hospital rendered $900,000 in services to patients, of which $700,000 is charged to third-party payors. The administration estimates that only $750,000 will be collected. Of the $150,000 difference, $85,000 is estimated contractual allowances with insurance and Medicare providers, $20,000 is charity care, and $45,000 is estimated bad debts.

2. A local business donated linens with a fair value $3,000.

3. Cafeteria sales to nonpatients and gift shop receipts totaled $76,000.

4. The hospital incurred expenses of $12,000 in connection with the childhood disease consortium. Funding for this consortium had been received in 2000.

5. The hospital received unrestricted, unconditional pledges of $12,500. The administration expects only 80 percent of these to be collected. In addition, securities with a market value of $8,000 were received and designated for the endowment by the donor.

6. A computer consultant donated services to upgrade several of the hospital's computer systems. The value of these services was $3,000 and would have been acquired if not donated.

7. The hospital incurred the following liabilities:
   $102,000 for purchase of supplies
   $699,000 for salaries
   $50,000 for purchase of equipment

8. End of year adjustment included supplies expense of $99,000 and depreciation expense of $72,000.

Required

  a. Prepare the journal entries for these transactions.
  b. Prepare a schedule showing the change in unrestricted, temporarily restricted, and permanently restricted net assets.

Solution

1. Accounts Receivable—Patients	200,000	
Accounts Receivable—Third-Party Payors	700,000	
Patient Service Revenues (Unrestricted)		900,000
To accrue billings for the current period.		

Contractual Adjustments	85,000	
Allowance for Contractual Adjustment		85,000
To recognize estimated amounts not expected to be collected from third-party payors.		

Patient Service Revenue (Unrestricted)	20,000	
Accounts Receivable—Patients		20,000
To remove amount for charity care where no intention exists to collect.		

Bad Debt Expense	45,000	
Allowance for Uncollectible Accounts		45,000
To recognize estimated amounts not expected to be collected from patients.		

2. Inventory of Supplies	3,000	
Unrestricted Net Assets—Contribution of Materials		3,000
To recognize fair value of donated items.		

3. Cash	76,000	
Unrestricted Net Assets—Revenues—Cafeteria and Shops		76,000
To record cafeteria and gift shop revenue.		

4. Consortium Expenses	12,000	
Cash		12,000
To record expenses in connection with the childhood disease consortium.		

5. Pledges Receivable 12,500
Investments 8,000
  Allowance for Uncollectible Pledges 2,500
  Permanently Restricted Net Assets—Contributions . . 8,000
  Unrestricted Net Assets—Contributions 10,000
To record pledges and investments received at estimated
fair value.

6. Expenses for Professional Services 3,000
  Unrestricted Net Assets—Contributed Services 3,000
To record donated services.

7. Supplies Inventory 102,000
Equipment 50,000
  Accounts Payable 152,000
To record goods received.

Salaries Expense 699,000
  Accrued Salaries Payable 699,000
To record salaries payable.

8. Supplies Expense 99,000
  Supplies Inventory 99,000
To record supplies expense for the period.

Depreciation Expense 72,000
  Accumulated Depreciation 72,000
To record depreciation expense for the period.

Calculation of Change in Net Assets

Journal Entry	Unrestricted Net Assets	Temporarily Restricted Net Assets	Permanently Restricted Net Assets
1	$ 900,000		
	(85,000)		
	(20,000)		
	(45,000)		
2	3,000		
3	76,000		
4	(12,000)		
5	10,000		$8,000
6	(3,000)		
	3,000		
7	(699,000)		
8	(99,000)		
	(72,000)		
Net assets released from restriction— childhood disease consortium . . .	12,000	$(12,000)	
Increase (decrease) in net assets . . .	$ (31,000)	$(12,000)	$8,000

APPENDIX

Financial Statements for Private Not-for-profit Colleges or Universities

Following are examples of the financial statements for private colleges and universities (and other private not-for-profit organizations) required by the FASB in its *Statement No. 117*, "Financial Statements of Not-for-profit Organizations." The notes to these financial statements have not been included.

VILLANOVA UNIVERSITY
Statement of Financial Position
May 31, 1999, and 1998
(in thousands)

	1999	1998
Assets		
Cash and cash equivalents	$ 21,556	$ 18,765
Short-term investments	963	5,756
Accounts receivable, net	4.824	3,277
Inventories	1,206	1,299
Other assets	6,120	6,313
Deposits with bond trustees	59,834	82,278
Pledges receivable, net	9,266	10,250
Student loans receivable, net	10,165	9,978
Investments	159,631	138,599
Land, buildings, and equipment, net	184,553	156,705
Total assets	$458,118	$433,220
Liabilities		
Accounts payable	$ 5,731	$ 4,815
Accrued expenses	18,964	16,538
Deposits	2,671	2,359
Deferred revenues	6,386	8,145
Accrued postretirement benefits	7,980	7,628
Refundable government loan funds	4,416	4,366
Long-term debt	196,944	198,132
Total liabilities	$243,092	$241,983
Net Assets		
Unrestricted	$125,559	$114,438
Temporarily restricted	37,324	31,836
Permanently restricted	52,143	44,963
Total net assets	215,026	191,237
Total liabilities and net assets	$458,118	$433,220

VILLANOVA UNIVERSITY
Statement of Activities
Year Ended May 31, 1999
(in thousands)

	Unrestricted	Temporarily Restricted	Permanently Restricted	Total
Operating Revenue				
Student related revenue:				
Student tuition and fees, net of $29,505 in student financial aid	$124,074			$124,074
Sales and services of auxiliary enterprises, net of $1,466 in student financial aid	37,899			37,899
	161,973			161,973
Private gifts and grants	6,294	$ 650		6,944
Government grants	3,647			3,647
Endowment resources	3,916	505		4,421
Investment income	5,538			5,538
Other sources	9,888			9,888
Net assets released from restrictions	1,563	(2,563)	$ 1,000	—
Total operating revenue	192,819	(1,408)	1,000	192,411
Operating Expense				
Instruction	76,886			76,886
Research	2,568			2,568
Academic support	22,922			22,922
Student services	22,712			22,712
Institutional support	21,252			21,252
Auxiliary enterprises	42,168			42,168
Total operating expense	188,508	—	—	188,508
Change in net assets from operating activities	4,311	(1,408)	1,000	3,903
Non-operating				
Net realized and unrealized gains on investments	8,141	6,896	—	15,037
Endowment and other gifts	—	—	6,180	6,180
Change in net assets from non-operating activities	8,141	6,896	6,180	21,217
	12,452	5,488	7,180	25,120
Extraordinary Item				
Loss from bond defeasance	(1,331)	—	—	(1,331)
Change in net assets	11,121	5,488	7,180	23,789
Net assets at beginning of year	114,438	31,836	44,963	191,237
Net assets at end of year	$125,559	$37,324	$52,143	$215,026

VILLANOVA UNIVERSITY
Statement of Cash Flows
Years Ended May 31, 1999, and 1998
(in thousands)

	1999	1998
Cash Flow from Operating Activities		
Increase in net assets	$25,120	$27,177
Adjustments to reconcile change in net assets to net cash provided by operating activities:		
Loss from bond defeasance	(1,331)	—
Depreciation	9,493	9,004
Contributions restricted for long-term investment	(6,180)	(4,001)
Change in market value of investments	(15,037)	(17,141)
Changes in operating assets and liabilities:		
Accounts receivable	(1,547)	339
Pledges receivable	984	(1,115)
Accounts payable and accrued expenses	3,342	5,719
Accrued postretirement benefits	352	(22)
Other changes	(1,161)	(506)
Net cash provided by operating activities	14,035	19,454
Cash Flow from Investing Activities		
Proceeds from sales of investments	47,049	29,492
Purchases of investments	(53,044)	(37,910)
Student loans receivable	(187)	(414)
Purchase of land, buildings, and equipment	(37,341)	(33,885)
Short-term investments, net	4,793	6
New deposits with bond trustees	(18,089)	(77,091)
Use of deposits with bond trustees	40,456	24,043
Net cash used by investing activities	(16,363)	(95,759)
Cash Flow from Financing Activities		
Contributions restricted for endowments	6,180	4,001
Borrowing of new debt	16,673	77,962
Repayment of debt	(17,861)	(2,718)
Government loan funds	50	203
Bond settlement cost	77	144
Net cash provided by financing activities	5,119	79,592
Net increase in cash and cash equivalents	2,791	3,287
Cash and cash equivalents at beginning of year	18,765	15,478
Cash and cash equivalents at end of year	$21,556	$18,765

QUESTIONS

1. Which organization is responsible for issuing reporting standards for private not-for-profit colleges and universities?

2. What information do financial statement users want to know about a not-for-profit organization?

3. What are the required financial statements for private not-for-profit colleges and universities?

4. What are temporarily restricted assets?

5. What are permanently restricted assets?

6. What are the two general types of expenses reported by not-for-profit organizations?

7. What ratio is frequently used to assess not-for-profit organizations?

8. Why is a statement of functional expense prepared for a voluntary health and welfare organization?

9. What controversy was created by the question of whether not-for-profit organizations should record depreciation expense? How was this issue resolved?

10. What is the GAAP hierarchy? What purpose does it serve and why was it developed?

11. If a donor gives a charity a gift that must be conveyed to a separate beneficiary, what is the normal method of reporting for each of these parties?

12. If a donor gives a charity a gift that must be conveyed to a separate beneficiary, what is the method of reporting for each of these parties if the donor retains the right to revoke or redirect use of the gift?

13. If a donor gives a charity a gift that must be conveyed to a separate beneficiary, what is the method of reporting for each of these parties if the charity is given variance powers enabling it to change the identity of the beneficiary?

14. When are donated services recorded by a not-for-profit organization?

15. A not-for-profit organization sends out a direct mail solicitation for donations. However, the charity also includes other information with the mailing. Under what conditions can the organization report part of the cost of this mailing as a program service cost rather than as a fund-raising cost?

16. A not-for-profit organization receives numerous pledges of financial support to be conveyed at various times over the next few years. Under what condition should these pledges be recognized as receivables and contribution revenues? At what amount should these pledges be reported?

17. What is the difference between an unconditional promise to give and an intention to give?

18. When should membership dues be considered revenue rather than contributions?

19. What is a third-party payor, and how does the presence of third-party payors affect the financial accounting of a health care organization?

20. What is a contractual adjustment? How is a contractual adjustment accounted for by a health care organization?

INTERNET ASSIGNMENTS

Internet sites are time and date sensitive. It is the purpose of these exercises to have you explore the Internet. You may need to refer to the text's Web site at http://www.mhhe.com/hoyle6e to find the most up-to-date links for the Web sites listed in the Internet Assignments.

1. Go to the following Web site: www.nonprofits.org. Click on "Nonprofit Library." Scroll down the page and click on "How to Read Non-profit Financial Statements." Write a short report describing the advice given about understanding the financial reporting of a not-for-profit organization.

2. Go to the following Web site: www.rutgers.edu/Accounting/raw/fasb/st/stpg.html. Click to read a summary of *Statement 136* of the FASB. Scroll down to *Statement 136* of the FASB and click on summary. Read the summary provided of this pronouncement and write a short report to explain the most significant points of this statement.

LIBRARY ASSIGNMENTS

1. Locate an annual report for a voluntary health and welfare organization. If one cannot be found in the school library, obtain a copy by calling the local office of an organization such as the American Lung Association, American Cancer Society, or National Multiple Sclerosis Society.

   Using the annual report obtained, answer the following questions about the voluntary health and welfare organization:

   How many different program services are being offered?

   What percentage of total expenses went to supporting services?

   Did the organization have a program service entitled public or professional education?

   Do the notes to the financial statements indicate that any contributed services are recognized within the financial statements?

   What dollar amount was spent on fund-raising?

   How much public support was received and how much revenue was earned?

   What is the largest expense category?

   What amount of depreciation was recognized for the period?

2. Locate an annual report for a private college or university (such as Duke University) and one for a public college or university (such as the University of North Carolina). If one cannot be found in the school library, obtain a copy by writing directly to the Vice President—Financial Operations of the university. Compare the two sets of financial statements and write a report identifying as many differences as possible.

PROBLEMS

1. A hospital has the following account balances:

Revenue from newsstand	$ 50,000
Amounts charged to patients	800,000
Interest income	30,000
Salary expense—nurses	100,000
Bad debts	10,000
Undesignated gifts	80,000
Contractual adjustments	110,000

   What is the hospital's net patient service revenue?

   a. $880,000.
   b. $800,000.
   c. $690,000.
   d. $680,000.

2. A large not-for-profit organization's statement of activities should report the net change for net assets that are

	Unrestricted	Permanently Restricted
a.	Yes	Yes
b.	Yes	No
c.	No	No
d.	No	Yes

   (AICPA adapted)

3. Which of the following statements is true?

   I. Private not-for-profit universities must report depreciation expense.

   II. Public universities must report depreciation expense.

   a. Neither I nor II is true.
   b. Both I and II are true.
   c. Only I is true.
   d. Only II is true.

4. A private not-for-profit organization receives three donations:

    One gift of $70,000 is unrestricted.

    One gift of $90,000 is restricted to pay for the salary of the organization's workers.

    One gift of $120,000 is restricted forever with the income to be used to provide food for needy families.

    Which of the following statements is not true?

    a. Temporarily restricted net assets have increased by $90,000.
    b. Permanently restricted net assets have increased by $210,000.
    c. When the money is spent for salaries, unrestricted net assets increase and decrease by the same amount.
    d. When the money is spent for salaries, temporarily restricted net assets decrease.

5. A donor gives Charity One $50,000 in cash that must be conveyed to Charity Two. However, the donor can revoke the gift at any time prior to its conveyance to Charity Two. Which of the following statements is true?

    a. Charity One should report a contribution revenue.
    b. The donor continues to report an asset even after it is given to Charity One.
    c. As soon as the gift is made to Charity One, Charity Two should recognize a contribution revenue.
    d. As soon as the gift is made to Charity One, Charity Two should recognize an asset.

6. A private not-for-profit university charges its students tuition of $1 million. However, financial aid grants total $220,000. In addition, the school receives a $100,000 grant that is restricted for faculty salaries. Of this amount, $30,000 is spent appropriately this year. On the statement of activities, the school reports three categories: (1) revenues and support, (2) net assets reclassified, and (3) expenses. Which of the following is not true?

    a. In the unrestricted net assets, an increase of $30,000 should be shown for net assets reclassified.
    b. In the unrestricted net assets, the revenues and support should total $1 million.
    c. In the unrestricted net assets, expenses of $30,000 should be recognized.
    d. In the unrestricted net assets, the $220,000 is shown as a direct reduction to the tuition revenue balance.

7. A private not-for-profit organization has the following activities performed by volunteers. In which case should no amount of contribution be reported?

    a. A carpenter builds a porch on the back of one building for free so that patients can sit outside.
    b. An accountant does the organization's financial reporting for free.
    c. A local librarian comes each day to read to the patients for free.
    d. A computer expert repairs the organization's computer for free.

8. A private not-for-profit organization spends $100,000 to send out a mailing. The mailing solicits donations but it also provides educational and other information about the charity. Which of the following is true?

    a. No part of the $100,000 can be reported as a program service expense.
    b. Some part of the $100,000 must be reported as a program service expense.
    c. No authoritative guidance exists so the organization can allocate the cost as it believes best.
    d. Under certain specified circumstances, a portion of the $100,000 should be allocated to program service expenses.

9. *FASB Statement No. 117*, "Financial Statements of Not-for-Profit Organizations," focuses on

    a. Basic information for the organization as a whole.
    b. Standardization of funds nomenclature.
    c. Inherent differences of not-for-profit organizations that impact reporting presentations.
    d. Distinctions between current fund and noncurrent fund presentations.

    (AICPA adapted)

10. On December 30, 2001, Leigh Museum, a not-for-profit organization, received a $7,000,000 donation of Day Co. shares with donor stipulated requirements as follows:

    Shares valued at $5,000,000 are to be sold with the proceeds used to erect a public viewing building.

Shares valued at $2,000,000 are to be retained with the dividends used to support current operations.

As a consequence of the receipt of the Day shares, how much should Leigh report as temporarily restricted net assets on its 2001 statement of financial position?

a. $0
b. $2,000,000
c. $5,000,000
d. $7,000,000

(AICPA adapted)

11. The Jones family lost its home in a fire. On December 25, 2001, a philanthropist sent money to the Amer Benevolent Society, a not-for-profit organization, to purchase furniture for the Jones family. During January 2002, Amer purchased this furniture for the Jones family. How should Amer report the receipt of the money in its 2001 financial statements?

a. As an unrestricted contribution.
b. As a temporarily restricted contribution.
c. As a permanently restricted contribution.
d. As a liability.

(AICPA adapted)

12. Pel Museum is a not-for-profit organization. If Pel received a contribution of historical artifacts, it need not recognize the contribution if the artifacts are to be sold and the proceeds used to

a. Support general museum activities.
b. Acquire other items for collections.
c. Repair existing collections.
d. Purchase buildings to house collections.

(AICPA adapted)

13. What is the significance of the GAAP hierarchy?

a. It tells which accounting body has more overall authority.
b. When two sources of accounting guidance are in conflict, it tells which has priority.
c. It describes the development of new accounting principles.
d. It lists the various FASB and GASB statements.

14. A not-for-profit organization receives two gifts. One is $80,000 and is restricted for use in paying salaries of teachers who will teach children to read. The other is $110,000 which is restricted for the purchase of playground equipment. Both amounts are properly spent at the end of this year. No depreciation is recorded this period and the organization has elected to view the equipment as having a time restriction. On the statement of activities, what is reported for unrestricted net assets?

a. An increase of $80,000 and a decrease of $80,000.
b. An increase of $190,000 and a decrease of $190,000.
c. An increase of $190,000 and a decrease of $80,000.
d. An increase of $80,000 and no decrease.

15. In the accounting for health care providers, what are third-party payors?

a. Doctors who reduce fees for indigent patients.
b. Charities who supply medicines to hospitals and other health care providers.
c. Friends and relatives who pay the medical costs of a patient.
d. Insurance companies and other groups who pay a significant portion of the medical fees in the United States.

16. Mercy for America, a not-for-profit health care facility located in Durham, North Carolina, charged a patient $8,600 for services. This amount was actually billed to a third-party payor. The third-party payor submitted a check for $7,900 with a note stating that "the reasonable amount is paid in full." Which of the following statements is true?

a. The patient was responsible for paying the remaining $700.
b. The health care facility will rebill the third-party payor for the remaining $700.
c. The health care facility recorded the $700 as a contractual adjustment that will not be collected.
d. The $700 was retained by the third-party payor and will be conveyed to the health care facility at the start of the next fiscal period.

17. What is a contractual adjustment?
    a. An increase in a patient's charges caused by revisions in the billing process utilized by a health care entity.
    b. A year-end journal entry to recognize all of a health care entity's remaining receivables.
    c. A reduction in patient service revenues caused by agreements with third-party payors that allows them to pay a health care entity based on their determination of reasonable costs.
    d. The results of a cost allocation system that allows a health care entity to determine a patient's cost by department.

18. A not-for-profit hospital provides its patients with services that would normally be charged at $1 million. However, a $200,000 reduction is estimated because of contractual adjustments. Another $100,000 reduction is expected because of bad debts. Finally, $400,000 will not be collected because the amounts are deemed to be charity care. Which of the following is correct?
    a. Patient service revenues = $1 million; net patient service revenues = $300,000.
    b. Patient service revenues = $1 million; net patient service revenues = $400,000.
    c. Patient service revenues = $600,000; net patient service revenues = $300,000.
    d. Patient service revenues = $600,000, net patient service revenues = $400,000.

19. A local citizen gives a not-for-profit organization a donation that is restricted for research activities. The money should be recorded in:
    a. Unrestricted Net Assets.
    b. Temporarily Restricted Net Assets.
    c. Permanently Restricted Net Assets.
    d. Deferred Revenue.

20. Theresa Johnson does voluntary work for a local not-for-profit organization as a community service. She replaces without charge an administrator who would have otherwise been paid $31,000. Which of the following statements is true?
    a. A restricted gain of $31,000 should be recognized.
    b. Public support of $31,000 should be recognized as an increase in unrestricted net assets.
    c. An expense reduction of $31,000 should be recognized.
    d. No entry should be made.

21. In 2001, Wells Hospital received an unrestricted bequest of common stock with a fair market value of $50,000. The testator had paid $20,000 for the stock in 1995. Wells should record the bequest to
    a. Increase temporarily restricted net assets by $50,000.
    b. Increase temporarily restricted net assets by $20,000.
    c. Increase unrestricted net assets by $50,000.
    d. Increase unrestricted net assets by $20,000.

22. An organization of high school seniors performs services for the patients at a nearby nursing home. These students volunteer to perform services that the nursing home would not otherwise provide, such as wheeling patients in the park and reading to them. At the minimum wage rate, these services would amount to $21,320, while the actual market value of these services is estimated to be $27,400. In the nursing home's statement of revenues and expenses, what amount should be reported as public support?
    a. $27,400.
    b. $21,320.
    c. $6,080.
    d. $0.

23. A voluntary health and welfare organization receives a gift of new furniture having a fair market value of $2,100. The group gives the furniture to needy families following a flood. How should the receipt and distribution of this donation be recorded by the organization?
    a. No entry should be made.
    b. Public support of $2,100 should be recorded along with community assistance expense of $2,100.
    c. Recognize revenue of $2,100.
    d. Recognize revenue of $2,100 and community expenditures of $2,100.

24. George H. Ruth takes a leave of absence from his job to work full-time for a voluntary health and welfare organization for six months. Ruth fills the position of finance director, a position that normally pays $38,000 per year. Ruth accepts no remuneration for his work. How should these donated services be recorded?
    a. As public support of $19,000 and an expense of $19,000.
    b. As public support of $19,000.
    c. As an expense of $19,000.
    d. No entry should be recorded.

25. A voluntary health and welfare organization produces a statement of functional expenses. What is the purpose of this statement?
    a. Separates current unrestricted and current restricted funds.
    b. Separates program service expenses from supporting service expenses.
    c. Separates cash expenses from noncash expenses.
    d. Separates fixed expenses from variable expenses.

26. A voluntary health and welfare organization has the following expenditures:

Research to cure disease	$60,000
Fund-raising costs	70,000
Work to help disabled	40,000
Administrative salaries	90,000

    How should these be reported by the organization?
    a. Program service expenses of $100,000 and supporting service expenses of $160,000.
    b. Program service expenses of $160,000 and supporting service expenses of $100,000.
    c. Program service expenses of $170,000 and supporting service expenses of $90,000.
    d. Program service expenses of $190,000 and supporting service expenses of $70,000.

27. A voluntary health and welfare organization sends out a mailing to all of its members including those who have donated in the past and others who have not donated. The mailing has a cost of $22,000. The mailing asks for monetary contributions to help achieve the organization's mission. In addition, 80 percent of the material included in the mailing is educational in nature, providing data about the organization's goals. Which of the following is true?
    a. Some part of the $22,000 should be reported as a program service cost because of the educational materials that were included.
    b. No part of the $22,000 should be reported as a program service cost because there is no specific call to action.
    c. No part of the $22,000 should be reported as a program service cost because the mailing was sent to both previous donors and individuals who have not made donations.
    d. Some part of the $22,000 should be reported as program service cost because over 50 percent of the material was educational in nature.

28. A voluntary health and welfare organization receives $32,000 in cash from solicitations made in the local community. The organization receives an additional $1,500 from members in payment of annual dues. How should this money be recorded?
    a. Revenues of $33,500.
    b. Public support of $33,500.
    c. Public support of $32,000 and a $1,500 increase in the fund balance.
    d. Public support of $32,000 and revenue of $1,500.

29. During the year ended December 31, 2001, the Anderson Hospital (operated by a not-for-profit organization) received and incurred the following:

Fair market value of donated medicines	$ 54,000
Fair market value of donated services (replaced salaried workers)	38,000
Fair market value of additional donated services (did not replace salaried workers)	11,000
Interest income on board-designated funds	23,000
Regular charges to patients	176,000
Charity care	210,000
Bad debts	66,000

    How should this hospital report these various items?

30. The following questions concern the appropriate accounting for a not-for-profit health care entity. Write complete answers for each question.
- *a.* What is a third-party payor and how have third-party payors affected the development of accounting principles for health care entities?
- *b.* What is a contractual adjustment and how is this figure recorded in accounting for a health care entity?
- *c.* How are donated materials and services accounted for by a not-for-profit health care entity?

31. Under Lennon Hospital's rate structure, the hospital earned patient service revenue of $9 million for the year ended December 31, 2001. However, Lennon did not expect to collect this amount because $1.4 million was deemed to be charity care and contractual adjustments were estimated to be $800,000.

During 2001, Lennon purchased bandages and other supplies from Harrison Medical Supply Company at a cost of $4,000. Harrison notified Lennon that the supplies were being donated to the hospital.

At the end of 2001, Lennon had board-designated assets consisting of cash of $60,000 and investments of $800,000.

How much should Lennon record as patient service revenue and how much as net patient service revenue? How should Lennon record the donation of the bandages? How are the board-designated assets shown on the balance sheet?

32. The Wilson Center is a voluntary health and welfare organization. During 2001, unrestricted pledges of $600,000 were received by the center, 60 percent of which were payable in 2001, with the remainder payable in 2002 (for use in 2002). Officials estimate that 15 percent of these pledges will be uncollectible.

How much should the Wilson Center report as revenue for 2001?

In addition, a local social worker, earning $9 per hour working for the state government, contributed 600 hours of time to the Wilson Center at no charge. Except for these donated services, an additional staff person would have been hired by the organization.

How should the Wilson Center record the contributed service?

33. A private not-for-profit organization is working to create a cure for a deadly disease. The organization starts the year with cash of $700,000. Of this amount, unrestricted net assets total $400,000, temporarily restricted net assets total $200,000, and permanently restricted net assets total $100,000. Within the temporarily restricted net assets, 80 percent must be used for equipment and the rest is restricted for salaries. No implied time restriction has been designated for the equipment when purchased. For the permanently restricted net assets, 70 percent of income must be used to cover the purchase of advertising for fund-raising purposes and the rest is unrestricted.

During the year of 2001, the organization has the following transactions:
- Unrestricted cash gifts of $210,000 are received.
- Salaries of $80,000 are paid with $20,000 of that amount coming from restricted funds. Of the total salaries, 40 percent is for administrative personnel with the remainder evenly divided between individuals working on research to cure the designated disease and individuals employed for fund-raising purposes.
- Equipment is bought for $300,000 with a long-term note signed for $250,000 and restricted funds being used for the remainder. Of this amount, 80 percent is used in research with 10 percent used in administration and the remainder in fund-raising.
- Membership dues of $30,000 are collected. The members do receive certain rights in exchange for these dues including a monthly newsletter describing research activities.
- A donor gives $10,000 to the charity that must be conveyed to another organization doing work on a related disease.
- Investment income of $13,000 is generated by the permanently restricted net assets.
- Advertising of $2,000 is paid using restricted funds.

- An unrestricted pledge of $100,000 is received that will be collected in three years. The organization expects to collect the entire amount. Present value of the pledge is $78,000. Interest of $3,000 is then recognized in the year.
- Depreciation on the equipment acquired as listed on page 852 is computed as $20,000.
- The organization spends $93,000 on research supplies that are utilized during the year.
- Salaries of $5,000 are owed at the end of the year. Half of this amount is for individuals doing fund-raising and half for individuals doing research.
- A painting that qualifies as a museum piece was donated to the organization. It has a value of $800,000. Officials do not want to record this gift, if possible.

Required

   a. Prepare a statement of activities for this organization for this year.
   b. Prepare a statement of financial position for this organization for this year.

34. A local not-for-profit health care entity incurred the following transactions during 2001. Record each of these transactions in appropriate journal entry form. Prepare a schedule calculating the change in unrestricted, permanently restricted, and temporarily restricted net assets.

   a. The governing board of the organization announced that $160,000 in previously unrestricted cash will be used in the future for the acquisition of equipment. The funds are invested until the purchase eventually occurs.
   b. A donation of $80,000 was made to the entity with the stipulation that all income derived from this money be used to supplement nursing salaries.
   c. The health care entity expended $25,000 for medicines. The money was received the previous year as a restricted gift for this purpose.
   d. The organization charged its patients $600,000. Of this amount, 80 percent is expected to be covered by third-party payors.
   e. Depreciation expense is $38,000.
   f. Interest income of $15,000 was received on the investments acquired by the board in the first transaction.
   g. The health care entity estimated that $20,000 of current accounts receivable from patients will not be collected and amounts owed by third-party payors will be reduced by $30,000 because of contractual adjustments.
   h. The medicines acquired in (*c*) were consumed.
   i. The investments acquired in (*a*) were sold for $172,000. All restricted cash and $25,000 that had been previously given to the organization (with the stipulation that the money be used to acquire plant assets) are spent for new equipment.
   j. This health care entity receives pledges for $126,000 in unrestricted donations. Ten percent of the pledges are paid immediately with the remainder to be received and used in future years. Officials estimate that $9,000 of this money will never be collected. Present value of the receivable is $98,000.

35. Prepare the following journal entries for Ames Hospital, a not-for-profit hospital:
   a. Patients were charged $300,000 for work done. Of this amount, $50,000 was actually charged to the patients although hospital officials anticipate that $12,000 will be bad accounts. The remaining $250,000 was billed to insurance companies and other third-party payors. Officials believe that these companies will only pay $220,000 after determining reasonable costs for the procedures performed.
   b. Insurance companies and other third-party payors paid $187,000 to cover 80 percent of the charges in (*a*). The remaining invoices are under investigation.
   c. An unrestricted pledge for $40,000 was received from a wealthy individual but the money cannot be spent for several years.
   d. Interest income of $1,000 was received.
   e. The administration decided to set aside $100,000. Investments were acquired for that amount with this money to be held to cover part of the cost of building a new wing to the hospital.
   f. A local volunteer contributes services to the hospital to replace a retired worker. The value of these services is $9,000.

36. The following questions concern the accounting principles and procedures applicable to a voluntary health and welfare organization. Write out answers to each of these questions.

    a. What is the difference in revenue and public support?
    b. What is the significance of the statement of functional expenses?
    c. What accounting process is used in connection with donated materials?
    d. What is the difference in the two types of restricted net assets found in the financial records of a voluntary health and welfare organization?
    e. Under what conditions should donated services be recorded?
    f. What controversy has arisen as to the handling of costs associated with direct mail and other solicitations for money that also contain educational materials?
    g. A not-for-profit organization receives a painting. Under what conditions would this painting be judged as an artwork? If it meets the criteria for an artwork, how is the financial reporting of the organization affected?

37. The following adjusted trial balances are for the Community Association for Handicapped Children, a voluntary health and welfare organization, at June 30, 2001. For internal purposes the association maintains its books on a fund basis.

Required

    a. Prepare a statement of activity for the year ended June 30, 2001.
    b. Prepare a statement of financial position as of June 30, 2001.

    (AICPA adapted)

COMMUNITY ASSOCIATION FOR HANDICAPPED CHILDREN
Adjusted Current Funds Trial Balances
June 30, 2001

	Unrestricted		Restricted	
	Dr.	Cr.	Dr.	Cr.
Cash	$ 40,000		$ 9,000	
Bequest receivable			5,000	
Contributions receivable	12,000			
Accrued interest receivable	1,000			
Investments (at cost, which approximate market value)	100,000			
Accounts payable and accrued expense		$ 50,000		$ 1,000
Deferred revenue		2,000		
Allowances for uncollectible pledges		3,000		
Fund balances, July 1, 2000				
Temporarily restricted		12,000		
Unrestricted		26,000		
Permanently restricted				3,000
Transfers of endowment fund income		20,000		
Contributions		300,000		15,000
Membership dues		25,000		
Program service fees		30,000		
Investment income		10,000		
Deaf children's program	120,000			
Blind children's program	150,000			
Management and general services	45,000		4,000	
Fund-raising services	8,000		1,000	
Provision for uncollectible pledges	2,000			
	$478,000	$478,000	$19,000	$19,000

38. Children's Agency, a voluntary health and welfare organization, began operations on July 1, 2000. It conducts two programs: a medical services program and a community information services program. This charity had the following transactions during the year ended June 30, 2001:

   a. Received the following contributions:

Unrestricted pledges	$800,000
Restricted cash	95,000
Building fund pledges	50,000
Endowment fund cash	1,000

   b. Collected the following pledges:

Unrestricted	450,000
Building fund	20,000

   c. Received the following unrestricted cash revenues:

From theater party (net of direct costs)	12,000
Bequests	10,000
Membership dues	8,000
Interest and dividends	5,000

   d. Program expenses incurred (vouchers created for these amounts):

Medical services	60,000
Community information services	15,000

   e. Service expenses incurred (vouchers created for these amounts):

General administration	150,000
Fund-raising	200,000

   f. Fixed assets purchased with unrestricted cash ... 18,000

   g. Depreciation of all buildings and equipment in the Land, Buildings, and Equipment Fund was allocated as follows:

Medical services program	4,000
Community information services program	3,000
General administration	6,000
Fund-raising	2,000

   h. Paid vouchers payable ... 330,000

   Required

   a. Prepare journal entries for these transactions.
   b. Calculate the balances in
      - Unrestricted Net Assets.
      - Temporarily Restricted Net Assets.
      - Permanently Restricted Net Assets.

39. The Watson not-for-profit organization starts the year with cash of $100,000, pledges receivable (net) of $200,000 and investments of $300,000 and land, buildings, and equipment of $200,000. In addition, unrestricted net assets were $400,000, temporarily restricted net assets of $100,000, and permanently restricted net assets of $300,000. Of the temporarily restricted net assets, 50 percent must be used for a new building and the rest is restricted for salaries. No implied time restriction has been designated for the building when purchased. For the permanently restricted net assets, all income is unrestricted.

   During the year of 2001, the organization has the following transactions:
   - Interest of $20,000 is computed on the pledge receivable.

- Cash of $100,000 is received on the pledges while another $4,000 is written off as uncollectible.
- Unrestricted cash gifts of $180,000 are received.
- Salaries of $90,000 are paid with $15,000 of that amount coming from restricted funds.
- A cash gift of $12,000 is received that must be conveyed to another not-for-profit organization. However, Watson has the right to give the money to a different organization if it so chooses.
- A building is bought for $500,000 with a long-term note signed for $450,000 and restricted funds being used for the remainder.
- Membership dues of $30,000 are collected. Individuals receive substantial benefits from the memberships.
- Income of $30,000 is generated by the permanently restricted net assets.
- The charity pays rent of $12,000, advertising of $15,000, and utilities of $16,000.
- An unrestricted pledge of $200,000 is received that will be collected in five years. The organization expects to collect the entire amount. Present value is $149,000. Interest of $6,000 is then recognized in the year.
- Depreciation is computed as $40,000.
- The organization pays $15,000 in interest on the note signed to acquire the building.

Required

a. Prepare a statement of activities for this organization for this year.
b. Prepare a statement of financial position for this organization for this year.

Accounting for Estates and Trusts

QUESTIONS TO CONSIDER

- If a person dies without having written a valid will, how are the estate's assets managed and distributed?

- If the assets held by an estate are insufficient to satisfy all claims against the estate as well as all bequests made by the decedent, what distributions are made?

- How can an individual or a couple limit the federal estate taxes that must be paid so that the amount of assets being conveyed to beneficiaries is maximized?

- In accounting for an estate or trust, why is the distinction between principal and income often considered to be especially significant?

- What are the most common types of trust funds? What is each type of trust designed to accomplish?

Individuals labor throughout their lives in part to accumulate property that eventually can be conveyed for the benefit of spouses, children, relatives, friends, charities, and the like. After amassing such funds, human nature usually seeks to achieve two goals:

- To minimize the amount of these assets that must be surrendered to the government.

- To ensure that the ultimate disposition of all property is consistent with the person's own wishes.

Over the next decade or so, some $10 trillion is going to pass from one generation to another. It is a sum equal to the recent value of all the companies listed on the stock exchange.[1]

Therefore, accountants (as well as attorneys and financial planners) often assist individuals who are developing estate plans or creating trust funds. At a later date, the accountant may serve in the actual administration of the estate or trust. In either estate or trust planning, the person's intentions must be spelled out in clear detail so that no misunderstanding can ever arise. All available techniques also should be considered to limit the impact of taxes. To carry out all of these varied responsibilities properly, a knowledge of the legal and reporting aspects of estates and trusts is of paramount importance.

Although many of the complex legal rules and regulations in these areas are beyond the scope of an accounting textbook, an overview of both estates and trusts can serve as an introduction to the issues frequently encountered by members of the accounting profession.

---

[1]Gregory Bresiger, "Prudence Redefined," *Financial Planning,* October 1, 1999, p. 165.

ACCOUNTING FOR AN ESTATE

> While none of us want to contemplate our death, or that of our spouse, we all need an estate plan. If you need motivation to reach this decision, remember that every dollar you keep from the folks in Washington goes to someone you like a heck of a lot better—such as your kids, your younger sister, or your alma mater.[2]

The term *estate* simply refers to the property owned by an individual. However, in this chapter, an estate is more specifically defined as a separate legal entity holding title to the assets of a deceased person. *Thus, estate accounting refers to the recording and reporting of financial events from the time of a person's death until the ultimate distribution of all property.* To ensure that this disposition is as intended and to avoid disputes, each individual should prepare a will, "a legal declaration of a person's wishes as to the disposition of his or her property after death."[3] If an individual dies *testate* (having written a valid will), this document serves as the blueprint for settling the estate and disbursing all remaining assets.

Whenever a person dies *intestate* (without a legal will), state inheritance laws must be followed. Although these legal rules vary from state to state, they are normally designed to correspond with the most common patterns of distribution. When inheritance laws rather than a will are applicable, real property is conveyed based on the *laws of descent* whereas personal property transfers are made according to the *laws of distribution.*

Laws governing wills and estates are established by each individual state and are known as *probate laws.* A *Uniform Probate Code* has been developed by the National Conference of Commissioners on Uniform State Laws in hopes of creating consistent treatment in this area. To date, approximately half of the states have officially adopted the Uniform Probate Code. In many of the other states, the rules and regulations applied are somewhat similar to the Uniform Probate Code. In practice, though, an accountant should become familiar with the specific laws of the state having jurisdiction over an estate.

Administration of the Estate

Regardless of the locale, probate laws generally are designed to achieve three goals:

1. Gather and preserve all of the decedent's property.
2. Carry out an orderly and fair settlement of all debts.
3. Discover the decedent's intent for the remaining property held at death and then follow those wishes.

This process usually begins with the filing of a will with the probate court or an indication that no will has been discovered. If a will is presented, the probate court must rule on the document's validity. A will must meet specific legal requirements to be accepted. For example, would the following signed and dated statement constitute a valid will?

> "I want my children to have my money."

Since the writer is dead, the intention of this statement cannot be verified. Was this an idle wish made without thought or did the decedent truly intend for this one sentence to constitute a will conveying all money to these specified individuals upon death? Did the decedent mean for all noncash assets to be liquidated with the proceeds being split among the children? Or, did the writer strictly mean that just the cash on hand at the time of death should be transferred to these individuals? Obviously, in some cases, the validity (and the intention) of a will are not easily proven.

---

[2]Ellen P. Gunn, "How to Leave the Tax Man Nothing," *Fortune,* March 18, 1996, p. 94.

[3]Stuart Berg Flexner, Editor-in-Chief, *The Random House Dictionary of the English Language,* 2nd ed. (New York: Random House, 1987), p. 2175.

If deemed to be both authentic and valid, a will is admitted to probate and the decedent's specific intentions will be carried to conclusion. Whether a will is present or not, an estate administrator must be chosen to serve in a stewardship capacity. All property of the decedent must be located, debts paid, and distributions appropriately conveyed. This individual serves in a fiduciary position and is responsible for (1) satisfying all applicable laws and (2) making certain that the decedent's wishes are achieved (if known and if possible).

If a specific person is named in the will to hold this position, the individual is referred to as the *executor of the estate.* If the will does not designate an executor or if the named person is unwilling to serve in this capacity (or if the decedent dies without a will), the courts must select a personal representative. A court-appointed individual is known legally as the *administrator of the estate.* An executor/administrator is not forced to serve in this role for free; that person is legally entitled to reasonable compensation for all services rendered.[4]

The executor is normally responsible for fulfilling several tasks:

- Taking possession of all the decedent's assets and completing an inventory of this property.
- Discovering all of the claims against the decedent and settling these obligations.
- Filing estate income tax returns, federal estate tax returns, and state inheritance or estate tax returns.
- Distributing property according to the provisions of the will, or according to state laws if a valid will is not available.
- Making a full accounting to the probate court to demonstrate that the executor has properly fulfilled the fiduciary responsibility.

Property Included in the Estate

The basis for all estate accounting is the property held by the decedent at death. These assets are used to settle claims and pay taxes. Any property that remains is distributed according to the decedent's will (or applicable state laws). For reporting purposes, all items are shown at fair market value; the historical cost originally paid by the deceased individual is no longer relevant. Fair market value is especially important because the sale of some or all properties may be required to obtain enough cash to satisfy claims against the estate. If valuation problems arise, hiring an appraiser might become necessary.

Normally, an estate includes assets such as

- Cash.
- Investments in stocks and bonds.
- Interest accrued to the date of death.
- Dividends declared prior to death.
- Investments in businesses.
- Unpaid wages.
- Accrued rents and royalties.
- Valuables such as paintings and jewelry.

At the time of death, certain assets are legally owned by the decedent. The executor is merely trying to locate and value each item belonging to the estate as of that date.

Some states specify that real property such as land and buildings (and possibly certain types of personal property) are conveyed directly to the beneficiary at the time of death. Therefore, in these states, these assets are not included in the inventory of estate

---

[4]To avoid having to use convoluted terminology, the term *executor is* generally used throughout this textbook to indicate both executors and administrators.

property that is developed by the executor for probate purposes. However, in the filing of estate and inheritance tax returns, such items must still be listed because a legal transfer has occurred.

Discovery of Claims against the Decedent

An adequate opportunity should be given to the decedent's creditors to allow them to file claims against the estate. Usually, the printing of a public notice in an appropriate newspaper is required one time per week for three weeks. In many states, all claims have to be presented within four months of the first of these notices. The validity of these claims must be verified by the executor and placed in order of priority. If insufficient funds are available, this ordering becomes quite important in establishing which parties receive payment. Consequently, claims in category 4 of the following list have the greatest chance of going unpaid.

Order of Priority

1. Expenses of administering the estate. Without this preferential treatment, the appointment of an acceptable executor and the hiring of lawyers, accountants, and/or appraisers could become a difficult task in estates with limited funds.
2. Funeral expenses and the medical expenses of any last illness.
3. Debts and taxes given preference under federal and state laws.
4. All other claims.

As indicated, the Uniform Probate Code has been adopted by a number of states. However, many states have passed a wide variety of individual probate laws that vary in many distinct ways. Thus, no absolute rules about probate laws can be listed. Normally, though, some amount of protection is provided for a surviving spouse and/or the decedent's minor and dependent children. Small monetary allowances are conveyed to these parties prior to the payment of legal claims. For example, a homestead allowance is provided to a surviving spouse and/or minor and dependent children. Even an estate heavily in debt would still furnish some amount of financial relief for the members of the decedent's immediate family.

In addition, a small family allowance is frequently given to these same individuals during a limited period of time while the estate is being administered. Family members are also entitled to a limited amount of exempt property such as automobiles, furniture, and jewelry. All other property is included in the estate to pay claims and be distributed as per the decedent's will or state inheritance laws.

Estate Distributions

If a will has been located and probated, property remaining after all claims are settled is conveyed according to that document's specifications.[5] A gift of real property such as land or a building is referred to as a *devise* whereas a gift of personal property such as stocks or furniture is a *legacy* or a *bequest*. A devise is frequently specific: "I leave three acres of land in Henrico County to my son," or "I leave the apartment building on Monument Avenue to my niece." Unless the estate is unable to pay all claims, a devise is simply conveyed to the intended party. However, if claims cannot be otherwise satisfied, the executor may be forced to sell the property despite the will's intention.

In contrast, a legacy may take one of several forms. The identification of the type of legacy becomes especially important if the estate has insufficient resources to meet the specifications of the will.

---

[5]Property legally held in joint tenancy with one or more individuals will pass to the surviving joint tenants at death and not be subject to the provisions of a will or intestate distribution.

A *specific legacy* is a gift of personal property that is directly identified. "I leave my collection of pocket watches to my son" is an example of a specific legacy because the property is named.

A *demonstrative legacy* is a cash gift made from a particular source. The statement "I leave $10,000 from my savings account in the First National Bank to my sister" is a demonstrative legacy because the source is identified. If the savings account does not hold $10,000 at the time of death, the beneficiary will receive the amount available. In addition, the decedent may specify alternative sources if sufficient funds are not available. Ultimately, any shortfall usually is considered a general legacy.

A *general legacy* is a cash gift with the source being undesignated. "I leave $8,000 in cash to my nephew" is a gift viewed as a general legacy.

A *residual legacy* is a gift of any remaining estate property. Thus, assets left after all claims, taxes, and other distributions are conveyed according to the residual provisions of the will. ("The balance of my estate is to be divided evenly between my two brothers.")

An obvious problem arises if an estate does not hold enough funds to satisfy all of the legacies specified in the will. The necessary reduction of the various gifts is referred to as the *process of abatement*. For illustration purposes, assume that a will lists the following provisions:

I leave 1,000 shares of AT&T to my brother (a specific legacy).

I leave my savings account of $20,000 to my sister (a demonstrative legacy).

I leave $40,000 cash to my son (a general legacy).

I leave all remaining property to my daughter (a residual legacy).

Example One   *Assume that the estate holds the shares of AT&T stock, the $20,000 savings account, and $46,000 in other cash.* The first three parties (the brother, sister, and son) get the specific assets stated in the will, while the residual legacy (to the daughter) would be the $6,000 cash balance left after the $40,000 general legacy is paid.

Example Two   *Assume that the estate holds the shares of AT&T stock, the savings account, but only $35,000 in other cash.* The first two individuals (the brother and sister) get the specified assets but the son can claim only the remaining $35,000 cash rather than the promised $40,000. Based on the process of abatement, the daughter receives nothing; no amount is left after the other legacies have been distributed.

Example Three   *Assume that the estate holds the shares of AT&T stock but the savings account has a balance of only $12,000 rather than the promised $20,000. Other cash held by the estate totals $51,000.* The stock is distributed to the brother, but the sister gets just the $12,000 cash in the savings account. In most cases, the courts would hold that the remaining $8,000 is a general legacy. Consequently, the sister gets the additional $8,000 in this manner and the son receives the specified $40,000. The daughter is then left with only the $3,000 in cash that remains.

Example Four   *Assume that the shares of AT&T stock were sold by the decedent before death and that the savings account holds $22,000. Other cash amounts to $30,000.* The brother receives nothing from the estate since the specific legacy did not exist at death.[6] The sister collects the promised $20,000 from the savings account with the remaining $2,000 being added to the general legacy. Therefore, the son receives a total of $32,000 from the two cash sources. Since the general legacy was not fulfilled, no remainder exists as a residual legacy; thus, the daughter collects nothing from the estate.

---

[6]The legal term *ademption* refers to a situation where a specific bequest or devise fails because the property is not available for distribution. As a different possibility, a bequest or devise is said to lapse if the beneficiary cannot be located or dies before the decedent. This property then becomes part of the residuary estate.

Insufficient Funds   The debts and expenses of the administration are paid first in settling an estate. If the estate has insufficient available resources to satisfy these claims, the process of abatement is again utilized. Each of the following categories is exhausted completely to pay all debts and expenses before money is taken from the next:

> Residual legacies.
> General legacies.
> Demonstrative legacies.
> Specific legacies and devises.

Estate and Inheritance Taxes

Taxes incurred after death can be quite costly. For example, Helen Walton received $5.1 billion in stock at the death of her husband Sam Walton (founder of Wal-Mart Stores). At this value, these shares could eventually cost her heirs as much as *$2.8 billion* in taxes at her death: $2.2 billion to the United States government and $640 million to the state of Arkansas.[7]

Historically, estate taxes have been used as a method for redistributing wealth and raising revenues. The budget surpluses that appeared in the latter part of the 1990s began to cast doubts on the continued need for a federal estate tax. Many arguments can be made both for this tax (to some there is a perceived limit to the amount that a beneficiary should receive without work or effort) and against it (income that has been taxed once when earned should not be taxed again when the resulting assets are conveyed at death).

In 1999 (and again in 2000), the U.S. Congress voted a phased-in repeal of the estate tax, a measure that was vetoed by then President Bill Clinton as too costly. However, on May 26, 2001, Congress passed the Economic Growth and Tax Relief Reconciliation Act of 2001, which included provisions to abolish this tax by 2010. The measure was signed into law by President George Bush. The estate tax reappears in 2011 unless Congress moves to make the repeal permanent in the interim.

The eventual abolition of this tax will have a major impact on estate planning. Prior to passage of this legislation, the tax was as high as 55 percent, with an added 5 percent surcharge on large estates. Consequently, most individuals who were subject to the tax were willing to spend significant amounts to reduce the eventual burden. However, for the next few years, during the phase-out period, estates of a substantial size will still be subject to a federal estate tax although at a lower rate. Estate planning will undoubtedly continue as an important issue at least during this period.

The new law has no impact on state inheritance taxes.[8] In the past, the federal government allowed a limited credit for such taxes assessed by the state. Within certain parameters, amounts paid to a state could be used to reduce assessments that were due to the federal government. For 2002 through 2004, however, the ability to utilize this credit has been repealed by the new law. After that time, Congress must decide whether further legislation will be passed to revive or eliminate the credit.

Federal Estate Taxes   The federal estate tax is an excise tax assessed on the right to convey property. The computation begins by determining the fair market value of all property held at death. Therefore, even if real property is transferred immediately to the beneficiary and is not subject to probate, the value must still be included for federal estate tax purposes.[9] In establishing fair market value, the executor may choose an alternative valuation date if that decision will reduce the amount of estate taxes. This

---

[7]Warren Midgett, "Mrs. Walton's Options," *Forbes,* October 19, 1992, pp. 22–23.

[8]Coverage of the many and varied state inheritance and estate tax laws is beyond the scope of this textbook. An overview is provided by "How to Minimize State Death Tax Liabilities," by Paul J. Lochray in the July 1990 issue of the *Journal of Financial Planning,* pp. 120–23.

[9]Life insurance policies with named beneficiaries are included in the value of the estate as long as the decedent had the right to change the beneficiary.

date is six months after death (or the date of disposition for any property disposed of within six months after death). Thus, the federal estate tax process starts by determining all asset values at death or this alternative date. Note that a piecemeal valuation cannot be made; one of these two must be used for all properties.

The gross estate figure is then reduced by several items to arrive at the taxable value of the estate:

- Funeral expenses.
- Estate administration expenses.
- Liabilities.
- Casualties and thefts during the administration of estate.
- Charitable bequests.
- Marital deduction for property conveyed to spouse.

Individuals are allowed to deduct a specified amount from the value of the estate in arriving at the federal estate tax. Historically, for many years, any estate of $600,000 or less was tax free. In 1997, a gradual rise in that tax-free amount was mandated by Congress so that it was equal to $675,000 for 2001. The new tax legislation has escalated the portion of an estate that is exempted. Any remaining figure is taxed at graduated rates based upon the year of death.

Date of Death	Estate Tax Exemption at Death	Highest Estate Tax Rate
2002	$1 million	50%
2003	1 million	49
2004	1.5 million	48
2005	1.5 million	47
2006	2 million	46
2007	2 million	45
2008	2 million	45
2009	3.5 million	45
2010	Tax is repealed	
2011	Estate tax returns unless repealed in the interim	

As mentioned earlier, state inheritance taxes have served as another credit (to the upper limit allowed) in arriving at the amount to be paid to the federal government. This credit has now been repealed but only for the years 2002 through 2004. There is no way to anticipate what Congress will choose to do for those estates created beginning in 2005.

In the past, individuals often sought to avoid estate taxes by making gifts during their lifetimes. Therefore, several years ago the gift tax rules were joined to the estate tax rules to create standard laws. A single unified transfer credit was allowed for both taxable gifts and estates to establish an overall amount that could be conveyed without incurring a tax.

Even beyond the unified credit, annual gifts of $10,000 per person could be made tax free. While the gift tax is not being eliminated by the new tax act, it will change to a $1 million lifetime exclusion. Furthermore, instead of having a separate tax rate schedule as in the past, the maximum gift tax rate eventually will be the same as the maximum individual income tax rate.

What is the impact of these changes?

> The death of the estate tax is at best premature, and any planner thinking of abandoning an estate planning practice is missing a large opportunity. In fact, the estate planning provisions within the Economic Growth and Tax Relief Reconciliation Act of 2001 should be a boon for most planners, not a death toll.[10]

---

[10]Thomas J. Brzezenski, "New Era for Estate Planning," *Financial Planning,* July 1, 2001.

Federal Estate Taxes—Example One   The determination of the taxable estate is obviously an important step in calculating estate taxes. Assume for illustration purposes that a person dies holding assets valued at $3 million. Assume further that no taxable gifts were made during the individual's lifetime. Total debts of $400,000 were owed at death. Funeral expenses had a cost of $20,000, and estate administration expenses amounted to $10,000. In this person's will, $300,000 has been left to charitable organizations, with the remaining $2,270,000 (after debts and expenses) given to the surviving spouse.[11] Under this set of circumstances, no taxable estate exists:

Gross estate (fair market value)		$ 3,000,000
Funeral expenses	$ 20,000	
Administration expenses	10,000	
Debts	400,000	
Charity bequests	300,000	
Marital deduction	2,270,000	(3,000,000)
Taxable estate		–0–
Estate tax		–0–

Federal Estate Taxes—Example Two   Because of the current exemptions, a limited amount of estate property ($675,000 in 2001 and $1 million in 2002 and 2003) can be conveyed tax free to a beneficiary other than a spouse. The ability to shelter this amount of assets from tax has an important impact on estate planning. For example, in the preceding case, if the couple has already identified the recipient of the estate at the eventual death of the second spouse (their children, for example), a conveyance of the tax-free exclusion amount at the time of the first death is usually advantageous. The second estate will then be smaller for subsequent taxation purposes. Frequently, a trust fund is established for this purpose as a means of protecting the money and ensuring its proper distribution.

To illustrate, assume that the first spouse dies in 2001. Assume further that the will that is written is identical except that only $1,595,000 is conveyed to the surviving spouse with $675,000 being placed in a trust fund for the couple's children (a nondeductible amount for estate tax purposes). The estate tax return must now be adjusted to appear as follows:

Gross estate		$ 3,000,000
Funeral expenses	$ 20,000	
Administration expenses	10,000	
Debts	400,000	
Charity bequests	300,000	
Marital deduction	1,595,000	(2,325,000)
Taxable estate (conveyed to trust)		$ 675,000
Estate tax on $675,000 value in 2001		$ 220,500
Tax-free amount (first $675,000)		(220,500)
Taxes to be paid		–0–

Once again, no taxes are paid by the estate, but only $1,595,000 is added to the surviving spouse's taxable estate rather than $2,270,000, as in the previous example. Thus, an eventual decrease in the couple's *total* estate taxes of $220,500 has been established.

---

[11]Although not applicable in this case, surviving spouses do have the right in many states to denounce the provisions of a will and take an established percentage (normally one-third) of the decedent's estate. Such laws protect surviving spouses from being disinherited.

However, for couples, this strategy may not work unless the title to their assets is properly designated. This illustrates a situation where the success of estate planning can hinge on a proper understanding of how the laws function.

> The trick is to divide the first $1.2 million[12] of your assets between you so that you and your spouse have separate estates that can each receive the tax credit. The standard individual credit is $192,800, essentially the tax that would be due on an estate of $600,000. If everything is jointly owned, you'd get that deduction only once because the tax man considers jointly held assets to constitute a single estate that isn't taxed until the second death.[13]

Legally, if a couple holds property as joint tenants or tenants by the entirety, the property passes automatically to the survivor at the death of the other party. Thus, if all property were held in one of these ways, the decedent would have no estate and would not be able to get the benefit of the tax-free amount. However, if property is held by the couple as tenants in common, the portion owned by the decedent is included in that person's estate and, up to the set limit, can be conveyed tax free.

Other Approaches to Reducing Estate Taxes   Previously, one technique used by families with large fortunes to reduce estate taxes was the transfer of assets to grandchildren or even great-grandchildren. In this manner, the number of separate conveyances (each of which would have been subject to taxation at a top rate of 55 percent) from parent to child to grandchild was reduced. However, the government effectively eliminated the appeal of this option several years ago by establishing a generation-skipping transfer tax. Under this law, after an exemption, a flat tax of 55 percent was assessed on transfers by gift, bequest, or trust distribution to individuals two or more generations younger than the donors or decedents. (However, the exemption was unlimited for a transfer to a grandchild where the grandchild's parent was deceased and was a lineal descendent of the transferor.)

More recently, with its passage of the Economic Growth and Tax Relief Reconciliation Act of 2001, Congress has begun to phase out the generation-skipping transfer tax. Without an estate tax, no justification exists for a generation-skipping tax. The exemptions and the highest tax rates will follow the same changes shown earlier for the federal estate tax so that complete repeal will occur in 2010. Of course, in the interim, individuals can take advantage of the $1 million lifetime exemption for gifts. Even under the prior rules, gifts were used to avoid estate taxes. "You can also give away your money in $10,000 chunks as run-of-the-mill gifts, of course. Tidy sums on their own, they soon add up to small fortunes for your beneficiaries."[14]

State Inheritance Taxes   State inheritance taxes are assessed on the right to receive property, with the levy and all other regulations varying, as discussed earlier, based on state laws. However, the actual impact on the individual beneficiaries is determined by the specifications of the will. Many wills dictate that all inheritance tax payments are to be made out of any residual amounts held by the estate. Consequently, any individuals receiving residual legacies are forced to bear the entire burden of this tax.

If the will makes no provisions for state inheritance taxes (or if the decedent dies intestate), the amounts conveyed to each party must be reduced proportionately based on the fair market value received. Thus, the recipient of land valued at $200,000 would have to contribute twice the inheritance tax of a beneficiary collecting cash of $100,000. Decreasing a cash legacy to cover the cost of inheritance taxes creates little problem for the executor. However, a direct reduction of an estate asset such as land, buildings, or corporate stocks might be virtually impossible. Normally, the beneficiary

---

[12]The exemption amount has now increased because of changes in the tax laws.

[13]Gunn, "Leave the Tax Man Nothing," p. 94.

[14]Gunn, "Leave the Tax Man Nothing," p. 95.

in such cases is required to pay enough cash to satisfy the applicable inheritance tax. Often, life insurance policies are established in the estate planning process to provide cash for such payments.

Estate Income Taxes   Although all estates require time to be settled, the period can become quite lengthy if complex matters arise. From the date of death until ultimate resolution, the estate is viewed legally as a taxable entity and must file and pay income taxes to the federal government if gross income is $600 or more. The return is due by the 15th day of the fourth month following the close of the estate's taxable year. The calendar year may be adopted for this purpose or any other fiscal year may be chosen as the taxable year.

Applicable income tax rules are generally the same as those utilized by individual taxpayers. Therefore, dividend, rental, interest, and other income earned by the estate in the period following death are taxable to the estate unless of a type that is specifically nontaxable (such as municipal bond interest).

A personal exemption of $600 is provided as a decrease to the taxable balance. In addition, a reduction is allowed for (1) any taxable income donated to charity as well as (2) any taxable income for the year distributed to a beneficiary. In 1999, federal tax rates were 15 percent on the first $1,750 of taxable income per year with various rates levied on any excess income earned up to $8,450. At a taxable income level more than $8,450, a 39.6 percent rate is incurred.

As an illustration, assume that an estate earns net rental income during the current year of $30,000 and dividend income of $8,000. The dividend income is distributed immediately to a beneficiary and is taxable income for that individual, while $6,000 of the rental income is given to charity. Estate income taxes for the year would be computed as follows:

Rental income	$ 30,000
Dividend income	8,000
Total revenue	$ 38,000
Personal exemption	(600)
Gift to charity	(6,000)
Distributed to beneficiary	(8,000)
Taxable income	$ 23,400
Income tax:	
15% of first $1,750	$ 262.50
28% of next $2,300 ($4,050 − $1,750)	644.00
31% of next $2,150 ($6,200 − $4,050)	666.50
36% of next $2,250 ($8,450 − $6,200)	810.00
39.6% on remaining $14,950 ($23,400 − $8,450)	5,920.20
Income tax payable	$8,303.20[15]

The Distinction between Income and Principal

In many estates, the executor is faced with the problem of differentiating between income and principal transactions. For example, a will might state "all income earned on my estate for five years after death is to go to my sister, with the estate then being con-

---

[15]As fiduciary entities, estates and trusts are taxed at the same income tax rates. Note that their top rate of 39.6 percent becomes applicable at a taxable income level of only $8,450. In comparison, for 1999, this same top income tax rate of 39.6 percent is not assessed for a single taxpayer, head of household, or joint return until taxable income hits $283,151. Historically, fiduciary entities have had lower income tax rates so that taxpayers would move income-producing property into trusts to lower the taxes to be paid. As can be seen, Congress has changed the rate schedules so that it is now advantageous to keep income-producing property out of trusts.

veyed to my children." The recipient of the income is known as an *income beneficiary* whereas the party that ultimately receives the principal (also known as the *corpus*) is called a *remainderman.* As the fiduciary for the estate, the executor must ensure that all parties are treated fairly. Thus, if amounts are distributed incorrectly, the executor can be held legally liable by the court.

The definitional difference between principal and income appears to pose little problem. The estate principal encompasses all assets of the decedent at death; income is the earnings on these assets after death. However, many transactions are not easily categorized as either principal or income. As examples,

- Are funeral expenses charged to principal or income?
- Is the executor's fee charged to principal or income?
- Are dividends that are declared before death but received after death viewed as principal or income?
- If stocks are sold for a gain, is this gain viewed as income or an increase in principal?
- Are repairs to rental property considered a reduction of principal or of income?

Clearly, the distinction between principal and interest is not always obvious. For this reason, in writing a will, an individual may choose to spell out the procedure by which principal and income are to be calculated. If defined in this manner, the executor merely has to follow these instructions.

In many cases, no guidance is provided by the decedent as to the method by which transactions are to be classified. State laws must then be applied by the executor to determine these two figures. The *Revised Uniform Principal and Income Act* has been adopted as a standard by many states for this purpose. However, some states have created their own distinct laws while still others have adopted modified versions of the *Revised Uniform Principal and Income Act.* Generally accepted accounting principles are not applicable; the distinction between principal and income is defined solely by the decedent's intentions or by state laws.

Although differences exist because of unique state laws or the provisions of a will, the following transactions are normally viewed as adjustments (either increases or decreases) to the *principal of the estate:*

- Life insurance proceeds if the estate is named as the beneficiary.
- Dividends declared prior to death and any other income earned prior to death.
- Liquidating dividends even if declared after death.
- Debts incurred prior to death.
- Gains and losses on the sale of corporate securities or rental property.
- Major repairs (improvements) to rental property.
- Investment commissions and other costs.
- Funeral expenses.
- Homestead and family allowances.

The *income of the estate* includes all revenues and expenses recognized after the date of death. Within this calculation, the following items are included as reductions to income:

- Recurring taxes such as property taxes.
- Ordinary repair expenses.
- Water and other utility expenses.
- Insurance expenses.
- Other ordinary expenses necessary for the management and preservation of the estate.

Several costs such as the executor's fee, court costs, and attorney's and accountant's charges must be apportioned between principal and interest in some fair manner.

Recording the Transactions of an Estate

The accounting process used by the executor of an estate is quite unique. *Since this individual has been given responsibility by the probate court over the assets of the estate, the accounting system is designed to demonstrate the proper distribution of these properties.* Thus, several features of estate accounting should be noted:

- All estate assets are recorded at fair market value to indicate the amount of the executor's accountability. Any assets that are subsequently discovered are disclosed separately so that these adjustments to the original estate value can be noted when reporting to the probate court. The ultimate disposition of all properties must then be recorded to provide evidence that the fiduciary responsibility has been fulfilled.

- Debts, taxes, or other obligations are only recorded at the date of payment. In effect, the system is designed to monitor the disposition of assets. Thus, claims are relevant to the accounting process only at the time that the assets are disbursed. Likewise, distributions of legacies are not entered into the records until actually conveyed. As mentioned earlier, devises of real property are often transferred at death so that no accounting is necessary.

- Because of the importance in many estates of separately identifying income and principal transactions, the accounting system must always note whether income or principal is being affected. Quite frequently, two cash balances are maintained to assist in this process.

To illustrate, assume that James T. Wilson dies on April 1, 2001. The following valid will has been discovered:

> I name Bob King as executor of my estate.
> I leave my house, furnishings, and artwork to my aunt, Ann Wilson.
> I leave my investments in stocks to my uncle, Jack E. Wilson.
> I leave my automobile and personal effects to my grandmother, Nancy Wilson.
> I leave $38,000 in cash to my brother, Brian Wilson.
> I leave any income earned on my estate to my niece, Karen Wilson.
> All remaining property is to be placed in trust for my children.

The executor will have to (1) make a search to discover all estate assets and (2) allow an adequate opportunity for every possible claim to be filed. The assets should be recorded immediately at fair market value along with the creation of an Estate Principal account. This total represents the amount of assets for which the executor is accountable. The following journal entry establishes the values for the assets owned by James T. Wilson at his death that have been found to date:

Cash—Principal	11,000	
Interest Receivable on Bonds	3,000	
Dividends Receivable on Stocks	4,000	
Life Insurance—Payable to Estate	40,000	
Residence	90,000	
Household Furnishings and Artwork	24,000	
Automobile	4,000	
Personal Effects	2,000	
Investment in Bonds	240,000	
Investment in Stocks	50,000	
Estate Principal		468,000

Following is a list of subsequent transactions incurred by this estate along with each appropriate journal entry. Since estate income is to be conveyed to one party but the remaining principal is to be placed in trust, careful distinction between these two elements is necessary.

Transaction 1   Funeral expenses of $4,000 are paid by the executor.

Funeral and Administrative Expenses	4,000	
Cash—Principal		4,000

Transaction 2   The life insurance policy payable to the estate (shown in the initial entry) is collected.

Cash—Principal	40,000	
Life Insurance—Payable to Estate		40,000

Transaction 3   The title to four acres of land is discovered in a safe deposit box. This asset was not included in the original inventory of estate property. An appraiser sets the value of the land at $22,000.

Land	22,000	
Assets Subsequently Discovered		22,000

Transaction 4   The executor receives claims totaling $24,000 for debts incurred by the decedent prior to death. This figure includes medical expenses covering the decedent's last illness ($11,000), property taxes ($4,000), utilities ($1,000), personal income taxes ($5,000), and other miscellaneous expenses ($3,000). The executor pays all of these claims.

Debts of the Decedent	24,000	
Cash—Principal		24,000

Transaction 5   Interest of $8,000 is collected on the bonds held by the estate. Of this amount, $3,000 was earned prior to the decedent's death and was included as a receivable in the initial recording of the estate assets.

Cash—Principal	3,000	
Cash—Income	5,000	
Interest Receivable on Bonds		3,000
Estate Income		5,000

Transaction 6   Dividends of $6,000 are collected from the stocks held by the estate. Of this amount, $4,000 was declared prior to the decedent's death and was included as a receivable in the initial recording of the estate assets.

Cash—Principal	4,000	
Cash—Income	2,000	
Dividends Receivable on Stocks		4,000
Estate Income		2,000

Transaction 7   The executor now has a problem. The Cash—Principal balance is currently $30,000:

Beginning balance	$ 11,000
Funeral expenses	(4,000)
Life insurance	40,000
Payment of debts	(24,000)
Interest income	3,000
Dividends	4,000
Current balance	$ 30,000

Is This Really an Asset?

Robert Sweingart died during December 1997 at the age of 96. Sweingart had outlived many of his relatives, including the person named in his will as executor of his estate. Thus, the decedent's nephew Timothy J. Lee was selected by the probate court as administrator. Lee promptly began his duties including the reading of the will and the taking of an inventory of Sweingart's properties. Although the will had been written in 1966, Lee could see that most of the provisions would be easy to follow. Sweingart had made a number of specific and demonstrative legacies that could simply be conveyed to the beneficiaries. Also included in the will was a $20,000 general legacy to a local church with a residual legacy to a well-known charity. Unfortunately, after all other legacies were distributed, the estate would have only about $14,000 cash.

One item in the will concerned the administrator. Sweingart had made the following specific legacy: "I leave my collection of my grandfather's letters which are priceless to me to my cousin, William." Lee discovered the letters in a wall safe in Sweingart's home. About 40 letters existed, all in excellent condition. They were written by Sweingart's grandfather during the Civil War and described in vivid detail the Second Battle of Bull Run and the Battle of Gettysburg, Unfortunately, Lee could find no trace of a cousin named William. He apparently had died or vanished during the period since the will was written.

Lee took the letters to two different antique dealers. One stated: "A museum that maintains a Civil War collection would love to have these. They do a wonderful job of explaining history. But a museum would not pay for them. They have no real value since many letters written during this period still exist. I would recommend donating them to a museum."

The second dealer took a different position: "I think if you can find individuals who specialize in collecting Civil War memorabilia they might be willing to pay a handsome price especially if these letters help to fill out their collections. A lot of people in this country are fascinated by the Civil War. The number seems to grow each day. The letters are in great condition. It would take some investigation on your part but they could be worth a small fortune."

Lee now has to prepare an inventory of his uncle's property for probate purposes. How should these letters be reported? What should Lee do next with the letters?

However, the decedent's brother has been bequeathed $38,000 in cash. This general legacy cannot be fulfilled without the sale of some property. Most of the assets have been promised as specific legacies and cannot, therefore, be used to satisfy a general legacy. Two assets, though, are residual: the investment in bonds and the land that was discovered. The executor must sell enough of these properties to generate the remaining funding needed for the $38,000 conveyance. In this illustration, assume that the executor chooses to dispose of the land and negotiates a price of $24,000. Because a principal asset is being sold, the extra $2,000 received above the recorded value is considered an adjustment to principal rather than an increase in income.

Cash—Principal	24,000	
Land		22,000
Gain on Realization		2,000

Transaction 8   Fees of $1,000 charged for administering the affairs of the estate are paid. Of this amount, $200 is considered to be applicable to estate income.

Funeral and Administrative Expenses	800	
Expenses—Income	200	
Cash—Principal		800
Cash—Income		200

Transaction 9   On October 13, 2001, the house, furnishings, and artwork are given to the decedent's aunt (Ann), the stocks are transferred to the uncle (Jack), and the grandmother (Nancy) receives the decedent's automobile and personal effects.

Legacy—Ann Wilson (residence, furnishings, and artwork)....	114,000	
Legacy—Jack E. Wilson (stocks)........................	50,000	
Legacy—Nancy Wilson (automobile and personal effects).....	6,000	
Residence		90,000
Household Furnishings and Artwork		24,000
Investment in Stocks................................		50,000
Automobile.......................................		4,000
Personal Effects		2,000

Charge and Discharge Statement

As necessary, the executor files periodic reports with the probate court to disclose the progress being made in settling the estate. This report is referred to as a *charge and discharge statement*. If income and principal must be accounted for separately, the statement is prepared in two parts. For both principal and income, the statement should indicate:

1. The assets under the control of the executor.
2. Disbursements made to date.
3. Any property still remaining.

Thus, Exhibit 19–1 can be produced by the executor of James T. Wilson's estate immediately after Transaction 9. (Transaction numbers are included in parentheses for clarification purposes.)

At this point in the illustration, only three transactions remain: distribution to the decedent's brother of the $38,000 cash, conveyance to the niece of the $6,800 cash generated as income since death, and establishment of the trust fund with the remaining principal. The trust fund will receive the $240,000 in bonds and the $15,200 in cash that is left in principal ($53,200 total less $38,000 paid to the brother).

Legacy—Brian Wilson...............................	38,000	
Cash—Principal		38,000
Distribution to Income Beneficiary—Karen Wilson	6,800	
Cash—Income		6,800
Principal Assets Transferred to Trustee	255,200	
Cash—Principal		15,200
Investment in Bonds................................		240,000

A final charge and discharge statement would then be prepared by the executor followed by closing entries to signal the conclusion of the estate as a reporting entity.

ACCOUNTING FOR A TRUST

A trust is created by the conveyance of assets to a fiduciary (or trustee) who manages the assets and ultimately disposes of them to one or more beneficiaries. The trustee may be an individual or an organization such as a bank. Over the years, trust funds have become quite popular in this country for a number of reasons. Often they are established to reduce the size of a person's estate and, thus, the amount of estate taxes that must eventually be paid. As one financial advisor has stated: "Who needs to establish a trust? You do, and so does your spouse. There may be several good reasons, but start with this: If you don't set up trusts, your heirs may pay hundreds of thousands of dollars in unnecessary estate taxes."[16]

Estate taxes are not the only reason for establishing a trust. People form trust funds as a means of protecting assets and ensuring that eventual use of these assets is as intended. Trusts can also result from the provisions of a will, specified by the decedent as a means of guiding the distribution of estate property. In legal terms, an *inter vivos*

---

[16]Jeff Burger, "Which Trust Is Best for Your Family?" *Medical Economics,* August 1, 1988, p. 141.

E x h i b i t   1 9 – 1   Executor's Charge and Discharge Statement

---

Estate of James T. Wilson
Charge and Discharge Statement
April 1, 2001–October 13, 2001
Bob King, Executor

As to Principal

I charge myself with:

Assets per original inventory		$468,000
Assets subsequently discovered: land (Trans. 3)		22,000
Gain on sale of land (Trans. 7)		2,000
Total charges		$492,000

I credit myself with:

Debts of decedent (Trans. 4):

Medical expenses	$ 11,000		
Property taxes	4,000		
Utilities	1,000		
Personal income taxes	5,000		
Others	3,000	$ 24,000	
Funeral and administrative expenses (Trans. 1 and 8)		4,800	

Legacies distributed (Trans. 9):

Ann Wilson (house, furnishings, and artwork)	114,000		
Jack E. Wilson (stocks)	50,000		
Nancy Wilson (automobile and personal effects)	6,000	170,000	
Total credits			198,800
Estate principal			$293,200

Estate principal:

Cash		$ 53,200
Investment in bonds		240,000
Estate principal		$293,200

As to Income

I charge myself with:

Interest income (Trans. 5)		$ 5,000
Dividend income (Trans. 6)		2,000
Total charges		7,000

I credit myself with:

Administrative expenses charged to income (Trans. 8)		200
Balance as to income		$ 6,800

Balance as to income:

Cash		$ 6,800

---

trust is one started by a living individual, whereas a *testamentary trust is* created by a will.

Frequently, the *trustor* (the person who funds the trust) will believe that a chosen trustee is simply better suited to manage complicated investments than is the beneficiary. A young child, for example, would not be capable of directing the use of a large sum of money. The trustor may have the same opinion of an individual who possesses little business expertise. Likewise, the creation of a trust for the benefit of a person with a mental or severe physical handicap might be considered a wise decision.

During recent years, one specific type of trust fund, a revocable living trust, has become especially popular as well as controversial. The trustor usually manages the fund and receives most, if not all, of the income until death. After that time, future income and possibly principal payments are made to one or more previously named beneficiaries. Because the trust is revocable, the trustor can change these beneficiaries or other terms of the fund at any time.

> You want to leave knowing your loved ones have the best financial breaks possible. That's why the idea of a revocable living trust may sound so promising. During your lifetime, you turn over all assets to a trust. But you act as your own trustee, so you determine how the assets will be managed and distributed. Then, happy in the knowledge that you can change the trust at any time, you have the joy of knowing you're setting up a financial plan for your life and after death.[17]

Revocable living trusts offer several advantages that appeal to certain individuals. First, this type of trust avoids the delay and expense of probate. At the death of the trustor, the trust continues with future payments being made as defined in the trust agreement. In some states, this advantage can be quite important, but in others the cost of establishing the trust may be more expensive than the potential probate costs.

Second, conveyance of assets through a trust can be made without publicity whereas a will is a public document. Thus, anyone who values privacy may want to consider the revocable living trust. The entertainer Bing Crosby, for example, set up such a trust so that no outsider would know how his estate was distributed.[18]

Although the number of other types of trust funds is quite large, several of the more common include:

- *Credit Shelter Trust* (also known as a Bypass Trust or Family Trust). A credit shelter trust is designed for couples. Each spouse agrees to transfer at death an amount of up to the tax-free exclusion ($675,000 in 2001) to a trust fund for the benefit of the other. Thus, the income generated by these funds goes to the surviving spouse, but at the time of this second individual's subsequent death, the principal is conveyed to a different beneficiary. As discussed in the previous section, this arrangement can be used to reduce the estate of the surviving spouse and, therefore, the amount of estate taxes paid by the couple.

- *Qualified Terminable Interest Property Trust* (known as a QTIP Trust). A QTIP trust is frequently created to serve as a credit shelter trust. Property is conveyed to the trust with the income, and possibly a portion of the principal, being paid to the surviving spouse (or other beneficiary). At a specified time, the remainder is conveyed to a designated party. Such trusts are popular because the spouse is provided with a steady income, but the principal can be guarded by the trustee and then conveyed at a later date to the individual's children or other designated parties.

- *Charitable Remainder Trust.* All income is paid to one or more beneficiaries identified by the trustor. After a period of time (or at the death of the beneficiaries), the principal is given to a stated charity. Thus, the trustor is guaranteeing a steady income to the intended parties while still making a gift to a charitable organization. These trusts are especially popular if a taxpayer holds property that has appreciated greatly (such as real estate or stocks) that is to be liquidated. By conveying it to the trust prior to liquidation, the sale is viewed as that of the charity and is, hence, nontaxable. Thus, tax on the gain is avoided and

---

[17]Estelle Jackson, "Living Trust May Sound Promising," *Richmond Times–Dispatch,* October 13, 1991, p. C1.

[18]Ibid., p. C5.

significantly more money remains available to generate future income for the beneficiaries (possibly the original donor). "This trust lets you leave assets to your favored charity, get a tax break, but retain income for life."[19]

■ *Charitable Lead Trust.* This trust is the reverse of a charitable remainder trust. Income from the trust fund goes to benefit a charity for a specified time with the remaining principal then being given to a different beneficiary. For example, a charity might receive the income from trust assets until the donor's children reach their 21st birthdays. "Jacqueline Kennedy Onassis used this technique and ended up sheltering roughly 90 percent of the trust assets from estate taxes. Setup and operating costs, however, preclude the use of this type of trust unless the assets involved are substantial. As such this is a vehicle for the very wealthy, allowing them to keep an asset in the family but greatly reducing the cost of passing it on."[20]

■ *Grantor Retained Annuity Trusts* (known as GRATs). The trustor maintains the right to collect fixed payments from the trust fund with the principal being given to a beneficiary after a stated time or at the death of the trustor. For example, the trustor might retain the right to receive an amount equal to 7 percent of the initial investment annually with any remaining balance of the trust fund to go to his or her children at death. Because the beneficiary will not receive the residual amount for years, a current value is computed for gift tax purposes. Depending on (1) the length of time before final distribution to the beneficiary, (2) the assumed rate of income, and (3) the amounts to be distributed periodically to the trustor, this value is often quite small so that the gift tax is reduced or eliminated entirely. However, certain risks are present with GRATs. "When setting up a GRAT, remember that the annuity you establish at its outset could drain the trust if the expected growth doesn't materialize. Then you will have paid taxes and legal costs . . . and will have left little to your heirs. Equally important, the grantor must outlive the trust. If you die before the GRAT ends, the assets will revert to your estate."[21]

■ *Minor's Section 2503(c) Trust.* Established for a minor, this trust fund usually is designed to receive a tax-free gift of up to $10,000 each year ($20,000 if the transfer is made by a couple). Over a period of time, especially if enough beneficiaries are available, a significant amount of assets can be removed from a person's estate. The change in the gift tax laws and the gradual repeal of the estate tax will impact this type of trust.

■ *Spendthrift Trust.* This trust is established so that the beneficiary cannot transfer or assign any unreceived payments. Such trusts are usually established in hopes of preventing the beneficiary from squandering the assets being held by the fund.

■ *Irrevocable Life Insurance Trust.* Money is contributed to the trust to buy life insurance on the donor. If a couple is creating the trust, usually the life insurance policy is designed so that proceeds are paid only after the second spouse dies. The proceeds are not part of the estate and the beneficiary can use the cash to pay estate and inheritance taxes.

■ *Qualified Personal Resident Trust (QPRT).* The donor's home is given to the trust but the donor retains the right to live in the house for a period of time rent free. This removes what is often an individual's most valuable asset from the estate. This type of trust has characteristics similar to a GRAT.

---

[19]Lynn Asinof, "Estate-Planning Techniques for the Rich," *Wall Street Journal,* January 11, 1995, p. C1.

[20]Ibid., p. C15.

[21]Pam Black, "A GRAT Can Be Great for Saving Your Kids a Bundle," *Business Week,* March 1, 1999, p. 116.

The term of the trust can be as short or as long as desired. The longer the term the lower the value of the gift. If the grantor dies before the term of the trust expires, however, the property will revert back to the estate of the deceased and be subject to estate taxes at its current value. Therefore, a term should be picked that the grantor believes he or she will outlive for the benefits of the QPRT to be effective.[22]

As can be seen from these examples, many trust funds generate income for one or more beneficiaries (known as *life tenants* if the income is to be conveyed until the person dies). At death or at the end of a specified period, the remaining principal is transferred to a different beneficiary (a *remainderman*). Therefore, as with estates, differentiating between principal and income is ultimately important in accounting for trust funds. This distinction is especially significant because trusts frequently exist for decades and can control and generate enormous amounts of assets.

The reporting function is also important because of the legal responsibilities of the trustee. This fiduciary is charged with carrying out the wise use of all funds and may be sued by the beneficiaries if actions are considered to be unnecessarily risky or in contradiction to the terms of the trust arrangement. To avoid potential legal problems, the trustee is normally called on to exercise reasonable and prudent care in managing the assets of the fund.

Record-Keeping for a Trust Fund

Trust accounting is quite similar to the procedures that were demonstrated previously for an estate. However, because of the many different types of trusts that can be created as well as the extended time period that might be involved, the accounting process may become more complex than for an estate. As an example, an apartment house or a significant portion of a business could be placed in a trust for 20 years or longer. Thus, the possible range of transactions to be recorded becomes quite broad. In such cases, the fiduciary might choose to establish two separate sets of accounts: one for principal and one for income. As an alternative, a single set of records could be utilized with the individual accounts identified as to income or principal.

In the same manner as an estate, the trust agreement should specify the distinction between transactions to be recorded as income and those to be recorded as principal. If the agreement is silent or if a transaction is incurred that is not covered by the agreement, state laws are applicable. Generally accepted accounting principles usually are not considered appropriate. For example, the cash method rather than accrual accounting is utilized by trusts in recording most transactions. Although a definitive set of rules is not possible, the following list indicates the typical division of principal and income transactions.

Adjustments to the Trust's Principal:

Investing costs and commissions.
Income taxes on gains added to the principal.
Costs of preparing property for rent or sale.
Extraordinary repairs (improvements).

Adjustments to the Trust's Income:

Rent expense.
Lease cancellation fees.
Interest expense.
Insurance expense.

[22]Michael Mingione, "Trust Your House," *The CPA Journal,* September 1996, p. 40.

Income taxes on trust income.

Property taxes.

Trustee fees and the cost of periodic reporting must be allocated evenly between trust income and principal.

Accounting for the Activities of a Trust

For an *inter vivos* trust, reporting on an annual basis (or perhaps more frequently) is made to all of the income and principal beneficiaries. However, testamentary trusts come under the jurisdiction of the courts so that additional reporting becomes necessary. Normally, a statement resembling the charge and discharge statement of an estate is adequate for these purposes. Two accounts, Trust Principal and Trust Income, are established to monitor changes that occur. For a testamentary trust, the opening principal balance is the fair market value used by the executor for estate tax purposes.

To illustrate, assume that the following events occur in connection with the creation of a charitable remainder trust. In the will of Samuel Statler, a trust is created with the income earned each year to go to his niece for 10 years with the principal then being conveyed to a local university.

1. Cash of $80,000 and stocks (that originally cost $39,000 but are now worth $47,000) are transferred from the estate to the First National Bank of Michigan because this organization has agreed to serve as trustee for these funds.

2. Cash of $76,000 is invested by the trustee in bonds paying 11 percent annual cash interest.

3. Dividends of $6,000 are collected on the stocks, and interest of $7,000 is received on the bonds. No receivables had been included in the estate for these amounts.

4. At the end of the year, an additional $3,000 in interest is due on the bonds.

5. As trustee, the bank charges $2,000 for services rendered for the year.

6. The niece is paid the appropriate amount of money from the trust fund.

As the trustee, the bank should record these transactions as follows:

1.	Cash—Principal	80,000	
	Investment in Stocks	47,000	
	Trust Principal		127,000
	To record trust assets at the fair market value figure used for estate tax purposes.		
2.	Investment in Bonds	76,000	
	Cash—Principal		76,000
	To record acquisition of bonds using cash in trust fund.		
3.	Cash—Income	13,000	
	Trust—Income		13,000
	To record dividends and interest collected.		

4. No entry is recorded. These earnings cannot be paid to the income beneficiary until collected so that accrual provides no benefit. Therefore, a cash system rather than accrual accounting is used by the trustee.

5.	Expenses—Income	1,000	
	Expenses—Principal	1,000	
	Cash—Income		1,000
	Cash—Principal		1,000
	To allocate the trustee's fees evenly between principal and income.		

6. Equity in Income: Beneficiary 12,000
        Cash—Income   12,000
        To record yearly payment made to income beneficiary.
        Amount is computed as the dividends and interest of
        $13,000 less expenses of $1,000.

SUMMARY

1. An estate is the legal entity that holds title to a decedent's property until a final settlement and distribution can be made. State laws, known as probate laws, govern this process. These laws become particularly significant if the decedent has died intestate (without a will).

2. An executor to oversee the estate should be named in the decedent's will. If not, the probate court selects an administrator. The executor takes possession of all properties, settles valid claims, files tax returns, pays taxes due, and distributes any remaining assets according to the provisions of the decedent's will or state inheritance laws. The executor must issue a public notice so that all creditors have adequate opportunity to file a claim against the estate. Prior to paying these claims, a homestead allowance and a family allowance are provided to the members of the decedent's immediate family. Claims are then ranked in order of priority to indicate the payment schedule if existing funds prove to be insufficient. For example, administrative expenses and funeral expenses are at the top of this priority listing.

3. Devises are gifts of real property; legacies (or bequests) are gifts of personal property. Legacies can be classified legally as specific, demonstrative, general, or residual depending on the type of property and the identity of the source. If insufficient funds are available to fulfill all legacies, the process of abatement is applied to determine the loss allocations. After residual legacies are reduced to zero, general legacies are decreased if necessary. Demonstrative legacies are reduced next, followed by specific legacies.

4. Federal estate taxes are assessed on the value of estate property. Reductions in the total value of an estate are allowed for funeral and administrative expenses as well as for liabilities, charitable gifts, and all property conveyed to a spouse. The Economic Growth and Tax Relief Reconciliation Act of 2001 will eventually lead to the complete elimination of the federal estate tax but not until the year 2010. In the interim period of time, a tax-free exemption amount is allowed that grows from $1 million in 2002 to $3.5 million in 2009. The same gradual elimination is made to the generation-skipping tax. Gift taxes will remain, but individuals now will be allowed a $1 million lifetime exclusion.

5. In both estates and trusts, the distinction between income and principal is frequently an important issue. Income may be assigned to one party with the principal eventually going to a different beneficiary. Such arrangements are especially common in trust funds such as charitable remainder trusts. The decedent (for an estate) or the trustor (for a trust) should have identified the method of classification to be used for complicated transactions. If no guidance is provided, state laws become applicable. For example, major repairs and investment costs usually are considered reductions in principal, whereas expenses such as property taxes and ordinary repairs are charged to income. The bookkeeping procedures for estates and trusts are designed to separate and then reflect the transactions affecting principal and income.

6. To provide evidence of the fiduciary's proper handling of an estate or trust, a charge and discharge statement is produced. This statement reports the assets over which the individual has been given responsibility. The statement also indicates all disbursements of assets as well as the property remaining at the current time. Separate reports are prepared for income and principal.

COMPREHENSIVE ILLUSTRATION

Problem   *(Estimated Time: 30 to 40 Minutes)*

Part A
The will of James Daily contains the following provisions:

> *I leave my house, my personal effects, and my investments in corporate stocks to my wife, Nora.*
> *I leave the balance in my savings account up to a total of $26,000 to my son, George.*
> *I leave $6,000 in cash to my niece, Susan.*
> *I direct that all remaining assets, including my rental properties, be placed in trust. The income from this trust will go to my wife. At her death, the principal of this trust fund will be conveyed to the First United Church of Burlington, Alabama.*

The executor of this estate has now paid all claims and the following properties remain (fair market value is indicated):

House and personal effects	$320,000
Savings account	23,000
Cash	9,000
Investment in bonds	35,000

All rental property as well as corporate stocks were sold by Daily prior to his death.

Required:

a. Identify the following:
- Trustor.
- Life tenant.
- Remainderman.
- General legacy.
- Demonstrative legacy.

b. Answer the following questions:
- Is this trust an *inter vivos* trust or a testamentary trust?
- What specific type of trust has been created?
- To whom will the properties be distributed?

Part B
The will of Susan York contains the following provisions:

> *I leave my house and personal effects to James J. York.*
> *I leave $9,000 in cash to M. J. York.*
> *I leave all my investments to Bishop University.*
> *Any income earned on my investments prior to distribution I leave to the Freedom Church of Lubbock, Texas.*
> *I leave the remainder of my estate to Cindy Ruark.*

The executor, Brendan Jaminson, takes an inventory and discovers the following assets. An appraisal is made of every item to determine its fair market value at the time of York's death.

Cash	$ 46,000
House and personal effects	310,000
Investments:	
Stocks	21,000
Bonds	44,000
Land (rental property)	65,000
Collection of antiques	19,000
Dividends receivable	1,000
Interest receivable	2,000
Rent receivable	4,000
Total	$512,000

The following valid claims are made against the estate and paid by the executor:

Funeral expenses	$17,000
Executor charges	9,000
Medical expenses	11,000
Debts	5,000

The following cash collections are received by the estate:

Dividends	$ 2,000
Interest	3,000
Rent	7,000
Sold antique collection	21,000

Prior to June 25, 2001, the current date, the executor made complete distributions to both James J. York and M. J. York.

Required:

Prepare a charge and discharge statement for this estate. The date of death was January 23, 2001.

Solution

Part A

a.

- James Daily established the trust fund and would, therefore, be legally referred to as the trustor.
- James Daily's wife, Nora, will receive the benefits of the trust fund until her death. She is a life tenant.
- The First United Church of Burlington, Alabama, has been designated to receive the principal of the trust fund after the death of Nora Daily. Thus, the church is termed the remainderman of the fund.
- Since the $6,000 gift to Daily's niece Susan does not come from a designated source, it is known as a general legacy.
- The cash gift to Daily's son is to be taken from a savings account. A conveyance that is to be derived from a specified source is known as a demonstrative legacy.

b.

- This trust fund is a testamentary trust because it was created by the provisions of the decedent's will.
- This trust is an example of a charitable remainder trust. For a stated time, the earnings generated by the trust are to be conveyed to an income beneficiary. After that date (the death of Nora Daily, in this case), the principal is transferred to a charitable organization.
- The following distributions should be made by the executor of this estate:

    House and personal effects are given to Nora Daily. Since investments in corporate stocks are no longer held by the estate, this portion of the will cannot be fulfilled.

    The $23,000 cash found in the savings account is conveyed to George Daily. Although a maximum of $26,000 was promised, the account is not large enough to reach the upper limit specified by the will. However, because the provisions as written have been fulfilled, the remaining $3,000 is not a general legacy.

    Cash of $6,000 is given to Daily's niece.

    The remaining property (the investment in bonds and the $3,000 cash) is placed in the trust.

Part B

Estate of Susan York
Charge and Discharge Statement
January 23, 2001–June 25, 2001
Brendan Jaminson, Executor

As to Principal

I charge myself with:

Assets per original inventory		$512,000
Gain on sale of antiques		2,000
Total charges		$514,000

I credit myself with:

Debts of decedent:

Medical expenses	$ 11,000		
Other debts	5,000	$ 16,000	
Funeral and administrative expenses ($17,000 + $9,000)		26,000	
Legacies distributed:			
James J. York (house and personal effects)	$310,000		
M. J. York (cash)	9,000	319,000	
Total credits			$361,000
Estate principal			$153,000

Estate principal:

Cash (see below)	$ 23,000
Investments:	
Stocks	21,000
Bonds	44,000
Land	65,000
Estate principal	$153,000

Cash balance:

Beginning balance	$ 46,000
Sale of antique collection	21,000
Collection of receivables (dividends $1,000, interest $2,000, and rent $4,000)	7,000
Payment of debts and expenses (funeral expenses $17,000, executor charges $9,000, medical expenses $11,000, and debts $5,000)	(42,000)
Legacy distribution (M. J. York)	(9,000)
Cash balance	$ 23,000

As to Income

I charge myself with:

Dividend income ($2,000 collection less $1,000 receivable at death)	$ 1,000
Interest income ($3,000 less $2,000)	1,000
Rent income ($7,000 less $4,000)	3,000
Balance as to income	$ 5,000

Balance as to income:

Cash	$ 5,000

QUESTIONS

1. What is the meaning of the terms *testate* and *intestate?*
2. If a person dies without having written a will, how is the distribution of property regulated?
3. What are probate laws? What are their objectives?

4. What responsibilities are given to the executor of an estate?

5. At what value are the assets within an estate reported?

6. How are the claims against an estate discovered by an executor?

7. What claims against an estate have priority?

8. What are homestead and family allowances?

9. What is the difference between a devise and a legacy?

10. Describe and give examples of the four types of legacies.

11. What is the purpose of the process of abatement? How is this process utilized by the executor of an estate?

12. How is the federal estate tax computed?

13. What was the impact of the Economic Growth and Tax Relief Reconciliation Act of 2001 on the conveyance of property?

14. What is a taxable gift?

15. For couples, why is the establishment of a credit shelter trust fund considered a good estate planning technique?

16. What deductions are allowed in computing estate income taxes?

17. In accounting for an estate or trust, how is the distinction between principal and income determined?

18. What transactions are normally viewed as changes in the principal of an estate? What transactions are normally viewed as changes in the income of an estate?

19. What is the alternative date for valuing the assets of an estate? When should this alternative date be used?

20. In the initial accounting for an estate, why does the executor only record the assets?

21. What is the purpose of the charge and discharge statement that is issued by the executor of an estate?

22. What is a trust fund? Why have trust funds become especially popular in recent years?

23. What is an *inter vivos* trust? What is a testamentary trust?

24. What are QTIP trusts, GRATs, and charitable remainder trusts?

25. Why is the distinction between principal and income so important in accounting for most trusts?

LIBRARY ASSIGNMENT

1. Read the following and any other published materials on estate planning:

"Advantages of Planned Giving," *The CPA Journal,* September 1992.

"Charitable Remainder and Wealth Replacement Trusts: Too Good to Be True?" *Journal of Accountancy* (Personal Financial Planning Section), April 1992.

"A Primer on Trusts," *Journal of Accountancy,* May 1993.

"Get Your Estate in Shape," *Money,* May 1997.

"Estate-Planning Techniques for the Rich," *Wall Street Journal,* January 11, 1995.

"How to Leave the Tax Man Nothing," *Fortune,* March 18, 1996.

"Who Will Inherit Your Wealth?" *Fortune,* December 16, 1994.

"Caveat Testator," *Forbes,* June 16, 1997.

"Gifts with Strings Attached," *Business Week,* September 27, 1999.

"Till Death Do Us Part," *Forbes,* June 14, 1999.

"A GRAT Can Be Great for Saving Your Kids a Bundle," *Business Week,* March 1, 1999.

"Tarot Card Estate Planning," *Forbes,* October 4, 1999.

Write a report describing the various techniques used in estate planning to both reduce estate taxes and ensure that a decedent's assets are utilized as intended.

PROBLEMS

1. Which of the following is not a true statement?

   a. *Testate* refers to a person having a valid will.

   b. Personal property is conveyed by the laws of descent if an individual dies without a valid will.

    c.   *Intestate* refers to a person having no valid will.

    d.   A specific legacy is a gift of personal property that is specifically identified.

2.   Why might real estate be omitted from an inventory of estate property?

    a.   Real estate is subject to a separate inheritance tax.

    b.   State laws prohibit real property from being conveyed by an estate.

    c.   State laws require a separate listing of all real estate.

    d.   In some states, real estate is considered to be conveyed directly to a beneficiary at the time of death.

3.   What is the purpose of the laws of distribution?

    a.   They guide the distribution of personal property when an individual dies without a will.

    b.   They are used to verify the legality of a will, especially an oral will.

    c.   They guide the distribution of real property when an individual dies without a will.

    d.   They outline the functions of the executor of an estate.

4.   A bond was owned by a deceased individual. Which of the following amounts is included in the estate principal?

    a.   All interest collected prior to distributing the bonds to a beneficiary is considered part of the estate principal.

    b.   Only the first cash payment after death is included in the estate principal.

    c.   Interest that was not collected prior to death is excluded from the estate principal.

    d.   Interest earned prior to death is considered part of the estate principal even if received after death.

5.   Which of the following is not a goal of probate laws?

    a.   To gather and preserve all of the decedent's property.

    b.   To ensure that each individual produces a valid will.

    c.   To discover the decedent's intent for property held at death and then to follow those wishes.

    d.   To carry out an orderly and fair settlement of all debts and distribution of property.

6.   How are claims against a decedent's estate discovered by an executor?

    a.   Public notice must be printed in an appropriate newspaper to alert all possible claimants.

    b.   The executor waits for nine months until all possible bills have been received.

    c.   All companies that the decedent did business with are contacted directly by the executor.

    d.   Claims to be paid by the estate are limited to all of the bills received, but not paid, prior to the date of death.

7.   Why are claims against an estate put into an order of priority?

    a.   To help the executor determine the due date for each claim.

    b.   To determine which claims are to be paid if funds are insufficient to pay all claims.

    c.   To assist in determining which specific assets are to be used to satisfy these claims.

    d.   To list the claims in order of age so that the oldest can be paid first.

8.   Which of the following claims against an estate does not have priority?

    a.   Funeral expenses, since the amounts incurred are usually at the discretion of family members.

    b.   Medical expenses associated with the decedent's last illness.

    c.   The costs of administering the estate.

    d.   Unpaid rent on the decedent's home if not paid for the three months immediately prior to death.

9.   How does a devise differ from a legacy?

    a.   A devise is a gift of money and a legacy is a nonmonetary gift.

    b.   A devise is a gift to an individual and a legacy is a gift to a charity or other organization.

    c.   A devise is a gift of real property and a legacy is a gift of personal property.

    d.   A devise is a gift made prior to death and a legacy is a gift made at death.

10.   What is the homestead allowance?

    a.   A reduction of $20,000 that is made in estate assets prior to computing the amount of federal estate taxes.

    b.   The amount of property conveyed in a will to a surviving spouse.

c. An allotment of cash made from an estate to a surviving spouse and/or minor and dependent children before any claims are paid.

d. A decrease made in the value of property on which state inheritance taxes are assessed. The reduction is equal to the value of property conveyed to a surviving spouse.

11. Which of the following is a specific legacy?
a. The gift of all remaining estate property to a charity.
b. The gift of $44,000 cash from a specified source.
c. The gift of $44,000 cash.
d. The gift of 1,000 shares of stock in IBM.

12. A will has the following statement: "I leave $20,000 cash from my savings account in the Central Fidelity Bank to my sister, Angela." This gift is an example of:
a. A residual legacy.
b. A general legacy.
c. A demonstrative legacy.
d. A specific legacy.

13. What is the objective of the process of abatement?
a. To give legal structure to the reductions that must be made if an estate has insufficient assets to satisfy all legacies.
b. To ensure that all property distributions take place in a timely manner.
c. To provide adequate compensation for the estate executor and any appraisers or other experts that must be hired.
d. To ensure that all legacies are distributed to the appropriate party as specified by the decedent's will or state laws.

14. For estate tax purposes, what date is used for valuation purposes?
a. Property is always valued at the date of death.
b. Property is always valued at the date of distribution.
c. Property is valued at the date of death unless the alternative date is selected which is the date of distribution or six months after death, whichever comes first.
d. Property is valued at the date of death although a reduction is allowed if the value declines within one year of death.

15. Which of the following is true concerning the Economic Growth and Reconciliation Act of 2001?
a. This tax law leads to the immediate elimination of the federal estate tax.
b. This tax law leads to the immediate elimination of the federal gift tax.
c. This tax law provides for a $1 million tax-free exemption for estates created in 2002.
d. This tax law leads to the immediate elimination of the generation-skipping tax.

16. In computing federal estate taxes, deductions from the value of the estate are allowed for all of the following except
a. Charitable bequests.
b. Losses on the disposal of investments.
c. Funeral expenses.
d. Debts of the decedent.

17. The following individuals all died in 2001: The estate of John Lexington has a taxable value of $550,000. The estate of Dorothy Alexander has a taxable value of $710,000. The estate of Scotty Fitzgerald has a taxable value of $850,000. None of these individuals made any taxable gifts during their lifetimes. Which of the following statements is true?
a. Only Fitzgerald's estate will have to pay federal estate taxes.
b. All three of the estates will have to pay federal estate taxes.
c. None of these estates is large enough to necessitate the payment of estate taxes.
d. Only the estates of Alexander and Fitzgerald are large enough to necessitate the payment of estate taxes.

18. Sally Anne Williams dies on January 1, 2001. All of her property is conveyed to several relatives on April 1, 2001. For federal estate tax purposes, the executor chooses the alternative valuation date. On what date is the value of the property determined?
a. January 1, 2001.
b. April 1, 2001.

    c.   July 1, 2001.

    d.   December 31, 2001.

19.   M. Wilson Waltman dies on January 1, 2001. All of his property is conveyed to beneficiaries on October 1, 2001. For federal estate tax purposes, the executor chooses the alternative valuation date. On what date is the value of the property determined?

    a.   January 1, 2001.

    b.   July 1, 2001.

    c.   October 1, 2001.

    d.   December 31, 2001.

20.   Which of the following is not true concerning gift taxes?

    a.   Gift taxes will not be abolished but a lifetime exclusion of $1 million is created.

    b.   The Economic Growth and Tax Relief Reconciliation Act of 2001 eventually eliminates the federal gift tax.

    c.   Historically, gift taxes and estate taxes have been linked through a unified transfer credit.

    d.   Gift taxes are different from generation-skipping taxes.

21.   A couple has written a will that leaves part of their money to a trust fund. The income from this trust will benefit the surviving spouse until death, with the principal then going to their children. Why was the trust fund created?

    a.   To reduce the estate of the surviving spouse and, thus, decrease the total amount of estate taxes to be paid by the couple.

    b.   To make certain that the surviving spouse is protected from lawsuits filed by the children of the couple.

    c.   To give the surviving spouse discretion over the ultimate use of these funds.

    d.   Trust funds generate more income than other investments so that the earning potential of the money is maximized.

22.   The executor of an estate is filing an income tax return for the current period. Revenues of $12,000 have been earned. Which of the following is not a deduction allowed in computing taxable income?

    a.   Income distributed to a beneficiary.

    b.   Funeral expenses.

    c.   A personal exemption.

    d.   Charitable donations.

23.   What is a remainderman?

    a.   A beneficiary that receives the principal left in an estate or trust after a specified time.

    b.   The beneficiary of the decedent's life insurance policy.

    c.   An executor or administrator after an estate has been completely settled.

    d.   If a legacy is given to a group of people, the remainderman is the last of the individuals to die.

24.   In an estate, which of the following is charged to income rather than to principal?

    a.   Funeral expenses.

    b.   Investment costs.

    c.   Property taxes.

    d.   Losses on the sale of investments.

25.   In recording the transactions of an estate, when are liabilities recorded?

    a.   When incurred.

    b.   At the date of death.

    c.   When the executor takes responsibility for the estate.

    d.   When paid.

26.   What is the difference between an *inter vivos* trust and a testamentary trust?

    a.   A testamentary trust conveys money to a charity, while an *inter vivos* trust conveys money to individuals.

    b.   A testamentary trust is created by a will, while an *inter vivos* trust is created by a living individual.

    c.   A testamentary trust conveys income to one party and the principal to another, while an *inter vivos* trust conveys all monies to the same party.

    d.   A testamentary trust ceases after a specified period of time, while an *inter vivos* trust is assumed to be permanent.

27. Which of the following is a charitable lead trust?
    a. The income of the trust fund goes to an individual until death with the principal then being conveyed to a charitable organization.
    b. Charitable gifts are placed into the trust until a certain dollar amount is achieved that is then transferred to a specified charitable organization.
    c. The income of a trust fund goes to a charitable organization for a specified time with the principal then being conveyed to a different beneficiary.
    d. A charity conveys money to a trust that generates income for use by the charity in its various projects.

28. The estate of Nancy Hanks reports the following information:

Value of estate assets	$1,400,000
Conveyed to spouse	700,000
Conveyed to children	100,000
Conveyed to charities	420,000
Funeral expenses	50,000
Administrative expenses	20,000
Debts	110,000

   What is the taxable estate value?
    a. $70,000
    b. $100,000
    c. $180,000
    d. $420,000

29. An estate has the following income:

Rental income	$5,000
Interest income	3,000
Dividend income	1,000

   The interest income was immediately conveyed to the appropriate beneficiary. The dividends were given to charity as per the decedent's will. What is the taxable income of the estate?
    a. $4,400
    b. $5,000
    c. $8,000
    d. $8,400

30. Define each of the following terms:
    - Will.
    - Estate.
    - Intestate.
    - Probate laws.
    - Trust.
    - *Inter vivos* trust.
    - Charitable remainder trust.
    - Remainderman.
    - Executor.
    - Homestead allowance.

31. Answer each of the following questions:
    - What are the objectives of probate laws?
    - What tasks are performed by the executor of an estate?
    - What assets are normally included as estate properties?
    - What claims have priority to the distributions made by an estate?

32. The will of Victor Laslo has the following stipulations:
    Antique collection goes to Ilsa Lunn.
    All money in the First Savings Bank goes to Richard Blaine.

Cash of $9,000 goes to Nelson Tucker.

All remaining assets are put into a trust fund with the income going to Lucy Van Jones. At her death, the principal is to be conveyed to Howard Amadeus.

Identify the following:

a. Remainderman.
b. Trustor.
c. Demonstrative legacy.
d. General legacy.
e. Specific legacy.
f. Life tenant.

33. The will of Carson M. Newman has the following provisions:

"I leave the cash balance deposited in the First National Bank (up to a total of $50,000) to Jack Abrams. I leave $18,000 cash to Suzanne Benton. I leave 1,000 shares of Coca-Cola Company stock to Cindy Cheng. I leave my house to Dennis Davis. I leave all of my other assets and properties to Wilbur N. Ed."

a. Assume that the estate has the following assets: $41,000 cash in the First National Bank, $16,000 cash in the New Hampshire Savings and Loan, 800 shares of Coca-Cola stock, 1,100 shares of Xerox stock, a house, and other property valued at $13,000. What distributions will be made from this estate?

b. Assume that the estate has the following assets: $55,000 cash in the First National Bank, $6,000 cash in the New Hampshire Savings and Loan, 1,200 shares of Coca-Cola stock, 600 shares of Xerox stock, and other property valued at $22,000. What distributions will be made from this estate?

34. The estate of Jeb Stewart reports the following information:

Value of estate assets	$2,300,000
Conveyed to spouse	1,000,000
Conveyed to children	230,000
Conveyed to trust fund for benefit of spouse	500,000
Conveyed to charities	260,000
Funeral expenses	23,000
Administrative expenses	41,000
Debts	246,000

What is the taxable estate value?

35. An estate has the following assets (all figures approximate market value):

Investments in stocks and bonds	$900,000
House	260,000
Cash	70,000
Investment land	60,000
Automobiles (three)	51,000
Other assets	100,000

The house, cash, and other assets are left to the decedent's spouse. The investment land is contributed to a charitable organization. The automobiles are to be given to the decedent's brother. The investments in stocks and bonds are to be put into a trust fund. The income generated by this trust will go to the decedent's spouse annually until all of the couple's children have reached the age of 25. At that time, the trust will be divided evenly among the children.

The following amounts are paid prior to distribution and settlement of the estate: funeral expenses of $20,000 and estate administration expenses of $10,000.

a. What is the value to be reported as the taxable estate for federal estate tax purposes?

b. How does the year in which an individual dies affect the estate tax computation? For example, what is the impact of dying on December 30, 2008, versus January 2, 2009?

36. During the current year, an estate generates income of $20,000:

Rental income	$9,000
Interest income	6,000
Dividend income	5,000

The interest income is conveyed immediately to the beneficiary stated in the decedent's will. Dividends of $1,200 are given to the decedent's church.

What amount of federal income tax must be paid by this estate?

37. The executor of the estate of Wilbur Stone has listed the following properties (at fair market value):

Cash	$300,000
Life insurance receivable	200,000
Investments in stocks and bonds	100,000
Rental property	90,000
Personal property	130,000

The following transactions occur in the months following the decedent's death:

- Claims of $80,000 are made against the estate for various debts incurred before the decedent's death.
- Interest of $12,000 is received from bonds held by the estate. Of this amount, $5,000 had been earned prior to death.
- Ordinary repairs costing $6,000 are made to the rental property.
- All debts ($80,000) are paid.
- Stocks recorded in the estate at $16,000 are sold for $19,000 cash.
- Rental income of $14,000 is collected. Of this amount, $2,000 had been earned prior to the decedent's death.
- Cash of $6,000 is distributed to Jim Arness, an income beneficiary.
- The proceeds from the life insurance policy are collected with the money being immediately distributed to Amanda Blake as specified in the decedent's will.
- Funeral expenses of $10,000 are paid.

Required:

a. Prepare journal entries to record each of the preceding transactions.

b. Prepare in proper form a charge and discharge statement.

38. The executor of the estate of James Cooper has recorded the following information:

Assets discovered at death (at fair market value):

Cash	$600,000
Life insurance receivable	200,000
Investments:	
Walt Disney Company	11,000
Polaroid Corporation	27,000
Ford Motor Company	34,000
Compaq Computer Corporation	32,000
Rental property	300,000

Cash outflows:

Funeral expenses	$ 21,000
Executor fees	12,000
Ordinary repairs of rental property	2,000
Debts	81,000
Distribution of income to income beneficiary	4,000
Distribution to charitable remainder trust	300,000

Cash inflows:

Sale of Polaroid stock	$ 30,000
Rental income ($4,000 earned prior to death)	11,000
Dividend income ($2,000 declared prior to death)	12,000
Life insurance proceeds	200,000

Debts of $17,000 still remain to be paid. The shares of Compaq have been conveyed to the appropriate beneficiary.

Required:

Prepare a charge and discharge statement for this estate.

39. The will of Jane T. Simmons has the following provisions:
    - $150,000 in cash goes to Thomas Thorne.
    - All shares of Coca-Cola go to Cindy Phillips.
    - Residence goes to Kevin Simmons.
    - All other estate assets are to be liquidated with the resulting cash going to the First Church of Freedom, Missouri.

    Prepare journal entries for the following transactions:
    a. The executor of this estate has discovered the following assets (at fair market value):

Cash	$ 80,000
Interest receivable	6,000
Life insurance policy	300,000
Residence	200,000
Shares of Coca-Cola Company	50,000
Shares of Polaroid Corporation	110,000
Shares of Ford	140,000

    b. Interest of $7,000 is collected.
    c. Funeral expenses of $20,000 are paid.
    d. Debts of $40,000 are discovered.
    e. An additional savings account of $12,000 is located by the executor.
    f. Title to the residence is conveyed to Kevin Simmons.
    g. Life insurance policy is collected.
    h. Additional debts of $60,000 are discovered. Debts totaling $100,000 are paid.
    i. Cash of $150,000 is conveyed to appropriate beneficiary.
    j. The shares of Polaroid are sold for $112,000.
    k. Administrative expenses of $10,000 are paid.

40. After the death of Lawrence Pope, his will was read. It contained the following provisions:
    - $110,000 in cash goes to decedent's brother, Ned Pope.
    - Residence and other personal property go to his sister, Sue Pope.
    - Proceeds from the sale of Ford stock go to uncle, Harwood Pope.
    - $300,000 goes into a charitable remainder trust.
    - All other estate assets are to be liquidated with the cash going to Victoria Jones.

    The following transactions subsequently occur:
    a. The executor of this estate discovers the following assets (at fair market value):

Cash	$ 19,000
Certificates of deposit	90,000
Dividends receivable	3,000
Life insurance policy	450,000
Residence and personal effects	470,000
Shares of Ford Motor Company	72,000
Shares of Xerox Corporation	97,000

    b. Life insurance policy is collected.
    c. Dividends of $4,000 are collected.
    d. Debts of $71,000 are discovered.
    e. Title to the residence is conveyed to Sue Pope along with the decedent's personal effects.
    f. Title to land valued at $15,000 is discovered by the executor.
    g. Additional debts of $37,000 are discovered. All of the debts, totaling $108,000, are paid.
    h. Funeral expenses of $31,000 are paid.

    i.   Cash of $110,000 is conveyed to Ned Pope.

    j.   The shares of Ford are sold for $81,000.

    k.   Administrative expenses of $16,000 are paid.

    l.   The appropriate payment is made to Harwood Pope.

Required:

    a.   Prepare journal entries for the preceding transactions.

    b.   Prepare a charge and discharge statement.

41. James Albemarle creates a trust fund at the beginning of 2001. The income from this fund will go to his son, Edward. When Edward reaches the age of 25, the principal of the fund will be conveyed to United Charities of Cleveland.

    Prepare all necessary journal entries for the trust to record the following transactions:

    a.   Cash of $300,000, stocks worth $200,000, and rental property valued at $150,000 are transferred by James Albemarle to the trustee of this fund.

    b.   Cash of $260,000 is immediately invested in bonds issued by the U.S. government. Commissions of $3,000 are paid on this transaction.

    c.   Permanent repairs of $7,000 are incurred so that the property can be rented. Payment is made immediately.

    d.   Dividends of $4,000 are received. Of this amount, $1,000 had been declared prior to the creation of the trust fund.

    e.   Insurance expense of $2,000 is paid on the rental property.

    f.   Rental income of $8,000 is received.

    g.   The trustee collects $4,000 from the fund for services rendered.

    h.   Cash of $5,000 is conveyed to Edward Albemarle.

42. An *inter vivos* trust fund is created by Henry O'Donnell. O'Donnell owns a large department store in Higgins, Utah. Adjacent to the store, he also owns a tract of land used as an extra parking lot when the store is having a sale or during the Christmas season. O'Donnell expects the land to appreciate in value and eventually be sold for an office complex or additional stores.

    O'Donnell places this land into a charitable lead trust which will hold the land for 10 years until O'Donnell's son is 21. At that time, title will be transferred to the son. The store will pay rent to use the land during the interim. The income generated each year from this usage will be given to a local church. The land is currently valued at $320,000.

    During the first year of this arrangement, the trustee records the following cash transactions:

Cash inflows:

Rental income	$60,000

Cash outflows:

Insurance	$ 4,000
Property taxes	6,000
Paving (considered an extraordinary repair)	4,000
Maintenance	8,000
Distribution to income beneficiary	30,000

Prepare all journal entries for this trust fund including the entry to create the trust.

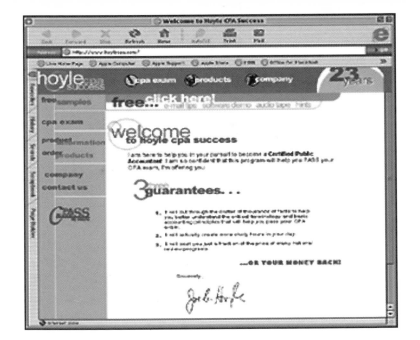

RECEIVE $50 OFF

the hoyle cpa success cpa
exam review course
at any time that you
are ready to take
the CPA exam.

For more details about the
**hoyle cpa success cpa exam
review course**, please visit
the website at
http://www.hoylecpa.com

the hoyle cpa success cpa exam review course offers you:

- A 90 day daily study planner
- A 200 page study guide
- A 3,000 question computer software package
- A 2,600 question problems book
- 25.5 hours of audio retention tapes
- 15 weeks of e-mail lessons

to order the self-study program, please see the back of this card.

hoyle cpa success, inc.

R.C. BOX 0065
28 WESTHAMPTON WAY
UNIVERSITY OF RICHMOND
RICHMOND, VA 23173

ORDER FORM

SAVE $50

when you purchase the
hoyle cpa success study program.

<u>special code</u> = mhi

PURCHASER'S NAME: _____

ADDRESS: _____

CITY, STATE, ZIP: _____

WORK PHONE: _____   **HOME PHONE:** _____

E-MAIL: _____

ITEM	QTY.	Description	Price	Amount
		HOYLE CPA SUCCESS COMPREHENSIVE SELF-STUDY PROGRAM BOTH 90 DAY AND 60 DAY PROGRAMS INCLUDE DAILY STUDY PLANNER, COMPLETE AUDIO TAPES, SOFTWARE PROGRAM, STUDY GUIDE, WILEY PROBLEMS AND *FREE* E-MAIL LESSONS		
1		**90 DAYS TO SUCCESS COMPREHENSIVE SELF-STUDY PROGRAM**	$499.00	
2		**60 DAYS TO SUCCESS COMPREHENSIVE SELF-STUDY PROGRAM**	$499.00	

SUBTOTAL

SALES TAX (Add 4.5% Sales Tax if Virginia Resident)

SHIPPING & HANDLING

UPS Ground (7-10 Business Days - See Table Below)

UPS Air (2-3 Business Days- See Table Below)

TOTAL ORDER AMOUNT

METHOD OF PAYMENT:

☐ **Check or Money Order Enclosed**

Make payable to:
hoyle cpa success, inc.

Charge to: ☐ **VISA** ☐ **MASTERCARD**

CARD NUMBER

EXP.

SIGNATURE _____

UPS Shipping within U.S.	7-10 Business Days	2-3 Business Days
Up To $100	$8	$15
$101-250	$12	$28
$251-500	$16	$35
INTERNATIONAL ORDERS CONTACT *hoylecpa@hoylecpa.com* FOR S&H		

Seal Here